W9-ARY-351

International Perspective

Inside the Legal Environment

Landmark in the Legal Environment

The Legal and E-Commerce Environment Today

Business in Its Ethical, Regulatory, and International Setting

Third Edition

Roger LeRoy Miller

Institute for University Studies
Arlington, Texas

Frank B. Cross

Associate Director,
Center for Legal and Regulatory Studies
University of Texas at Austin

WEST

™

THOMSON LEARNING

Australia · Canada · Mexico · Singapore · Spain · United Kingdom · United States

The Legal and E-Commerce Environment Today:
Business in Its Ethical, Regulatory, and International Setting, Third Edition
Roger Leroy Miller and Frank B. Cross

Publisher/Team Director: Jack Calhoun
Acquisitions Editors: Rob Dewey
Senior Developmental Editor: Jan Lamar
Marketing Manager: Nicole Moore
Senior Production Editor: Ann Borman
Manufacturing Coordinator: Charlene Taylor
Internal Design: Ann Borman
Cover Design: Grannan Graphic Design, Cincinnati
Cover Images: ©PhotoDisc, Inc., ©EyeWire, Inc., and ©CORBIS
Copy Editor: Suzie DeFazio
Proofreader: Heather Jones
Indexer: Bob Marsh
Compositor: Parkwood Composition
Printer: Quebecor World, Taunton, MA

Printed in the United States of America

2 3 4 04 03 02 01

For more information contact West Legal Studies in Business, South-Western, 5101 Madison Road, Cincinnati, Ohio, 45227 or find us on the Internet at http://www.westbuslaw.com

For permission to use material from this text or product contact us by
• telephone: 1-800-730-2214
• fax: 1-800-730-2215
• web: http://www.thomsonrights.com

Library of Congress Cataloging-in-Publication Data
Miller, Roger LeRoy.
   The legal and e-commerce environment today: business in its ethical, regulatory, and international setting/Roger LeRoy Miller, Frank B. Cross.—3rd ed.
      p. cm.
   Rev. ed. of: Legal environment today. 2nd ed. c1999.
   Includes bibliographical references and index.
   ISBN 0-324-06188-9
      1. Business law—United States. 2. Electronic commerce—Law and legislation—United States. I. Cross, Frank B. II. Miller, Roger LeRoy. Legal environment today. III. Title.

KF889 .M536 2001
346.7307—dc21   00-068552

Photo credits appear on p. xxxiv.

The Legal and E-Commerce Environment Today, 3e

Today's Most Current Law...
In Print and Online

Dear Student:

The 21st Century brings a changing legal environment—driven by the latest technology. The key to your success in today's business world is understanding not only how this technology has affected the law... but how the law has affected technology.

This text has been written to address both issues—exploring important developments in law for e-commerce while maintaining extensive coverage of the traditional legal environment. You can count on this proven text for its:

Currency. With a focus on the latest e-commerce and cyberlaw developments, our case coverage is more timely and relevant than ever.

Student-Friendly Style. A variety of high-interest, reality-based features make learning about the law compelling.

Advanced Learning Technology. From interactive quizzes to important legal links to video and audio segments, our technology options will engage you.

We hope you will find that this edition of *The Legal and E-Commerce Environment Today* connects law with today's business and e-commerce world in an exciting way.

Sincerely,

Roger Miller

Roger Miller

Frank Cross

Frank Cross

Expanded E-Commerce Coverage

Extensive coverage of e-commerce and cyberlaw offers expert insight into a changing legal environment—including new ways of resolving disputes, the latest legislation affecting e-contracts, and more.

page 128

chapter
5

E-Commerce and Dispute Resolution

contents

Jurisdiction in Cyberspace

E-Commerce Disputes
• Common Disputes
• Online Dispute Resolution

Online Resolution of Domain Name

A completely new chapter 5 examines how the electronic environment has affected jurisdictional concepts, and a new chapter 14 looks at new legislation designed to facilitate the formation and enforcement of e-contracts.

page 402

The Uniform Computer Information Transactions Act

Among the proposed new laws that go beyond the existing law is the Uniform Computer Information Transactions Act (UCITA). The UCITA is a draft of legislation suggested to the states by the National Conference of Commissioners on Uniform State Laws (NCCUSL) and the American Law Institute (ALI). These organizations have initiated many of the most significant laws that apply to traditional commerce, including the Uniform Commercial Code (UCC).

The UCITA's History

In the early 1990s, with the continued development of the software industry, it became apparent that Article 2 of the Uniform Commercial Code (UCC), which deals with the sale of goods (tangible property), could not be applied to most transactions involving software.

There are two basic reasons for this. First, software is not a "good" (tangible property)—it is electronic information (intangible property). Second, the "sale" of software generally involves a license (right to use) rather than a sale (passage of title from the seller to the purchaser). The producer of the software either directly contracted with the licensee (user) or employed a distribution system—for example, authorizing retailers to distribute (sell) copies of its software to customers (end users). Because neither transaction involved the sale of goods, new rules needed to be established.

In addition to extensive discussion of The Uniform Computer Information Transaction Act in the text, this edition now includes in the appendix excerpts from the UCITA as well as from other new documents such as The Electronic Signatures in Global and National Commerce Act.

page 409

Ethical Issue 14.1

Does the UCITA favor the software industry over consumers?

Some consumer groups argue that the UCITA favors the software industry and will have harsh effects for consumers. One of the initial concerns of these groups was the licensor's right of electronic self-help under the act. As already mentioned, this concern was addressed by the August 2000 amendments, which prohibited the use electronic self-help with respect to mass-market transactions. Notwithstanding these amendments, a number of consumer advocates continue to oppose the UCITA. Among other things, they object to the automatic enforceability of licensing agreements, including shrink-wrap or click-on agreements, which can easily go unread by consumers. To be sure, consumers often do not take the time to read the "fine print" even in printed documents. Consumer groups who object to the enforceability of licensing agreements claim that this problem is even more prevalent with shrink-wrap and click-on agreements. (Consumers also face other problems in the e-commerce environment—for a discussion of some of these problems, see the *Legal E-nvironment* feature in Chapter 20.)

There is not always a clear answer in the law or in the new e-commerce environment. This text highlights some of those questions for students to consider in "Ethical Issues."

page 18

Legal *e*-nvironment

The Internet, MP3.com, File-Sharing, and the Law

The intersection of the law and cyberspace, and the dramatic tension arising therefrom, is nowhere more evident than in the music world. Owners of intellectual property (see Chapter 11), such as songwriters, record labels, musicians, and the like, have long been protected by copyright legislation. That is to say, if a band creates a set of songs and a record label publishes the album, both are protected by copyright law. Anyone attempting to produce ments with four of the five major record labels for a reported $20 million payoff to each. In exchange, the company received licenses to allow users to download songs from well-known artists. Universal Music Group (UMG) refused to settle, however, so the suit against UMG went forward. The U.S. District Court of New York ruled in favor of Universal.[a] The judge's initial order was a $25,000 penalty for each CD that MP3.com copied and then distributed through its MyMP3.com site.

On the one hand, online music dissemination should slow down because of the *MP3.com* decision. On the other hand, a relatively new way to share files on a much more personal basis, called peer-to-peer (P2P) networking, is causing file-sharing via the Internet to explode.

Enter Napster, Gnutella,

The "Legal E-nvironment" feature brings to light several recent technology developments (like file sharing through MP3) and their relevance to the law.

page 7

Landmark in the Legal Environment

Internet Corporation for Assigned Names and Numbers (ICANN)

In 1997, the U.S. government directed the secretary of the Department of Commerce to privatize the domain name system in a manner that increased competition and facilitated international participation in its management. The end result of the Commerce Department's efforts was the creation, in October 1998, of the Internet Corporation for Assigned Names and Numbers (ICANN), a private, nonprofit organization, to act as a technical coordination body for the Internet.

DOMAIN NAME REGISTRATION

Part of the impetus behind ICANN's creation was to remove domain name registration oversight from the U.S. government to a private organization that could work to serve the broader interests of the international community. Previously, because the Internet developed from a U.S. military and research network, domain name registration had been under the direction of U.S. government organizations. From 1993 to 1998, Network Solutions, Inc. (NSI), under contract with the U.S. government, exclusively controlled the allocation of domain names.

"Landmark in the Legal Environment" presents cases, statutes, or other laws that have become landmarks in the legal environment of business, including areas newly affected by the Internet.

Proven Student-Friendly Features

To keep the reader engaged and eager to read more, our key features offer practical examples of how the law applies to real-world situations.

page 393

Case 14.2 ● Klocek v. Gateway, Inc.

United States District Court,
District of Kansas, 2000.
104 F.Supp.2d 1332.

Background and Facts Whenever it sells a computer, Gateway, Inc., includes a copy of its "Standard Terms and Conditions Agreement" in the box that contains the computer battery power cables and instruction manuals. At the top of the first page, in a printed box and in emphasized type, is the following: "NOTE TO THE CUSTOMER: * * * By keeping your Gateway 2000 computer system beyond five (5) days after the date of delivery, you accept these Terms and Conditions." This document is four pages long and contains sixteen numbered paragraphs. Paragraph 10 states, "dispute resolution. Any dispute or controversy arising out of or relating to this Agreement or its interpretation shall be settled exclusively and finally by arbitration." William Klocek bought a Gateway computer. Dissatisfied when it proved to be incompatible with his other computer equipment, he filed a suit in a federal district court against Gateway and others, alleging in part breach of contract. Gateway filed a motion to dismiss, asserting that Klocek was required to submit his claims to arbitration under Gateway's "Standard Terms." Klocek argued that these terms were not part of the contract for the purchase of the computer.

> New cases have been selected to interest students with relevant connections to business while also illustrating key legal points.

page 260

Inside the Legal Environment

How Far Should Foreseeability Extend?

Foreseeability is an important element in tort law because it establishes an outer case, the defendant's duty of care is usually held to extend only to those who might foreseeably be harmed or placed at risk by the defendant's action. If a defendant could not reasonably forsee that his or her actions would place the plaintiff at risk, then it would be unfair to hold the defendant liable for the plaintiff's injury.

Deciding whether a given risk is reasonably foreseeable is not easy, and it is difficult to predict how the courts might hold in particular cases. Consider an example. On the evening of March 28, 1990, Tonya Brown was using a pay telephone located on the corner of a busy intersection in the city of Flint, Michigan. Tonya

> "Inside the Legal Environment" explores real-life situations and legal challenges facing businesspeople and consumers.

page 53

International Perspective

ADR in Japan and China

INTERNATIONAL STANDARDS FOR SOCIAL ACCOUNTABILITY

The International Standards Organization (ISO) has created standards for environmental auditing that have been widely adopted by corporate managers around the world. When such standards are issued or revised, they are given a numbers, such as ISO14001. Recently, the Council on Economics Priorities Accreditation Agency (CEPAA) used the ISO's model for its new human rights standards, called Social Accountability 8000 (SA8000). These standards call on corporate leaders to restrict child labor and forced labor, limit workweeks to forty-eight hours, respect workers' rights to form unions, provide safe working conditions, any pay wages that meet basic needs. By adopting these standards and agreeing to "Social Accountability audits," firms can demonstrate their commitment to international human rights and help to dispel stories that they make profits by using "sweat-shop labor."

> "International Perspectives" give students an awareness of the global legal environment by indicating how international laws or the laws of other nations deal with specific legal topics.

page 449

 A Question of Ethics and Social Responsibility

15–10.   McQuade was the manager of the New York Giants baseball team. McQuade and John McGraw purchased shares in the National Exhibition Co., the corporation that owned the Giants, from Charles Stoneham, who owned a majority of National Exhibition's stock. As part of the transaction, each of the three agreed to use his best efforts to ensure that the others continued as directors and officers of the organization. Stoneham and McGraw, however, subsequently failed to use their best efforts to ensure that McQuade continued as the treasurer and a director of the

 Case Treatment

Examine Case A.1. (Rodriguez de Quijas v. Shearson/American Express, Inc., 490 U.S. 477, 109 S.Ct. 1917, 104 L.Ed.2D 379 (1989) in Appendix A. The case has been excerpted there in great detail. Review and then brief the case, making sure that your brief answers the following questions.

1. What is the legislative policy "embodied in the Arbitration Act"?
2. How did the Court reconcile the protections afforded Investors under the Securities Act and the legislative policy advanced by the Arbitration Act? Did the Court believes that by submitting to arbitration investors forgo

As in past editions of this book, there is a range of chapter-end materials, including ethics problems and case analysis.

page 353

 Interacting with the Internet

■ For updated links to resources available on the Web, as well as a variety of other materials, visit this text's Web site at http://leet.westbuslaw.com. The 'Lectric Law Library provides information on contract law, including a definition of contract, the elements required for a contract, and so on. Go to:

http://www.lectlaw.com

■ Then go to Laypeople's Law Lounge, and scroll down to Contracts. You can find articles and information on various area of law - including contracts - a the Law Office's Web site. Go to

http://lawoffice.com

■ Select the topic of Business and Commerical Law from the Law Knowledgabase list on the right-hand side of the home page.
To find recent cases on contract law decided by the United States Supreme Court and the federal appellate courts, access Cornell University School of Law site at http://www.law.cornell.edu/topics/contracts.html

Students can expand their knowledge of the chapter's contents by exploring related sites on the Internet, which include information on the most recent developments in e-commerce and cyberlaw.

page 415

 Online Legal Research Exercises

Go to http://leet. westbuslaw.com, the Web site that accompanies this text. Select "Interactive Study Center," and then click on "Chapter 14." There you will find the following Internet research exercise that you can perform to learn more about electronic contracts:

Activity 14–1: E-Contracts

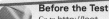 **Before the Test**

Go to http://leet. westbuslaw.com, the Web site that accompanies this text. Select "Interactive Quizzes." You will find interactive questions relating to this chapter.

For more in-depth exploration of Internet resources, go to the "Online Legal Research Exercises" on the book's web site at **http://leet.westbuslaw.com**

The Latest Technology Advancements

Cutting-edge technology tools promote interactivity with text topics. The only legal environment text to include a CD-ROM edition, The Legal and E-Commerce Environment Today *also offers a comprehensive Web site—featuring online quizzes, research activities, legal links, and more.*

The web site for *The Legal and E-Commerce Environment Today* provides dedicated textbook support for instructors and students. In addition to quizzes, the site features online exercises, court case summaries organized by topic, and supplements. Visit **http://leet.westbuslaw.com**.

WebTutor (on WebCT or Blackboard) features chat, discussion groups, testing, student progress tracking, and legal environment course materials. For more information, see **http://webtutor.swcollege.com**.

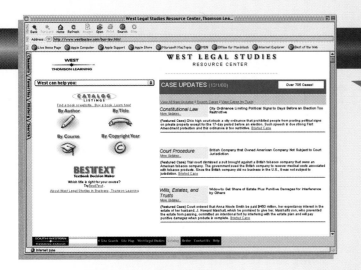

The West Legal Studies Resource Center provides publisher service, book information, and monthly court case updates. See more at **http://www.westbuslaw.com**.

Review a chapter or dive in-depth into a topic. *The Legal and E-Commerce Environment Today Interactive CD-ROM* includes the full textbook, the study guide, quizzes, video clips, reference materials, full Westlaw cases, and links to resources on the Web.

With more and more technology choices for the legal environment course, BESTech makes it easy to find out how to integrate various levels of technology into your course. Learn more at **http://bestech.westbuslaw.com**.

Contents in Brief

Contents

unit two

The Public Environment   151

unit three

The Private Environment 237

unit four

The Employment Environment   491

unit five

The Regulatory Environment   579

unit six

The International Environment 717

Preface

I t is no exaggeration to say that today's legal environment is changing at a pace never before experienced. In many instances, technology is both driving and facilitating this change. The expanded use of the Internet during the 1990s for both business and personal transactions has led to new ways of doing business, and, consequently, to a changing legal environment for the twenty-first century. In the midst of this changing environment, however, one thing remains certain: for those entering the business world, an awareness of the legal and regulatory environment of business is critical.

The Third Edition of *The Legal and E-Commerce Environment Today: Business in Its Ethical, Regulatory, and International Setting* is designed to bring this awareness to your students. They will learn not only about the traditional legal environment but also about some of the most significant recent developments in the e-commerce environment. They will also be motivated to learn more through our use of high-interest pedagogical features, such as *Inside the Legal Environment*, that explore real-life situations and legal challenges facing businesspersons and consumers. We believe that teaching the legal environment can be enjoyable and so, too, can learning about it.

Emphasis on E-Commerce and Cyberlaw

We have spent considerable time and effort to make sure that the Third Edition of *The Legal and E-Commerce Environment Today* reflects the most significant developments in e-commerce and cyberlaw. In a completely new chapter, Chapter 5, we examine how the electronic environment has affected traditional jurisdictional concepts and has offered new ways of resolving disputes. In another entirely new chapter, Chapter 14, we look at e-contracts and new legislation and uniform laws designed to facilitate the formation and enforcement of electronic contracts.

Perhaps one of the most challenging legal issues confronting businesses and government bodies today is how to protect intellectual property rights in cyberspace. In Chapter 11, we look closely at this issue and at some of the steps being taken by lawmakers and industry groups to resolve it. Additionally, we have included in every chapter in this book a special feature, entitled *Legal E-nvironment*, to inform your students of how technological developments are affecting other areas of law and the legal environment.

This is not all. Each chapter concludes with a special section, entitled *Interacting with the Internet*, that provides Internet addresses, or URLs. Students can access these URLs online to find legal resources, including some that cover the most recent developments in e-commerce and cyberlaw. Each of these sections concludes with one or more online legal research exercises that students can perform to acquaint them with various legal resources available online.

A Comprehensive Web Site

When you visit our Web site at http://leet.westbuslaw.com, you will find a broad array of teaching/learning resources, including the following:

- **Interactive quizzes** for every chapter in this text.
- **Internet activities** for each chapter.
- **Case updates** from various legal publications, all linked to this text.
- **Hot links to other important legal resources** available for free on the Web.
- A **"Talk to the Authors"** feature that allows you to e-mail your questions about *The Legal and E-Commerce Environment Today*, Third Edition, to the authors.

An Interactive CD-ROM Edition

For this edition of *The Legal and E-Commerce Environment Today*, we have expanded the supplements package to include a CD-ROM Edition of the text. Instead of just placing the entire text on the CD-ROM, however, we have gone several steps further. The CD-ROM not only includes video segments, audio segments, and the like but also organizes the information in a very appropriate, pedagogically sound manner. Your students will find sections on *Content*, *Chapters*, and *Applications*. No other legal environment text offers such advanced learning capacity.

Special Features

We have already discussed one of the key features included in the Third Edition of *The Legal and E-Commerce Environment Today*—the cyberlaw feature entitled *Legal E-nvironment*. In addition, every chapter in this text has one or more of the special features described below. Most of these features conclude with a *For Critical Analysis* question that invites the student to reflect on some aspect or implication of the topic discussed in the feature. These questions can also be used to stimulate classroom discussions.

- **Landmark in the Legal Environment**—A special feature that presents cases, statutes, or other laws that have become landmarks in the legal environment of business.
- **Inside the Legal Environment**—This feature offers practical and instructive examples of how the law applies to real-world situations.
- **Ethical Issues**—Each of these features, which are closely integrated with the text, opens with a question addressing an ethical dimension of the topic under discussion. The *Ethical Issues* are numbered so that they can be easily located for review or discussion.
- **International Perspectives**—These features give students an awareness of the global legal environment by indicating how international laws or the laws of other nations deal with specific legal topics being discussed in the text.
- **Highlighted, numbered examples**—Throughout each chapter, we have included numbered examples, highlighted in color, to illustrate important points of law.

A Special Case Format

In each chapter, we present cases that have been selected to illustrate principles of law discussed in the text. The cases are numbered sequentially for easy referencing in class discussions, homework assignments, and examinations. In selecting the cases to be included in this edition, our goal has been to choose cases that reflect the most current law or that represent a significant precedent in case law.

Each case is presented in a special format, which begins with the case title and citation (including parallel citations). Whenever possible, we also include a URL, just below the case citation, that can be used to access the case online. Whenever a URL is presented, a footnote to the URL explains how students can navigate the site accessed to find the specific case. Following the citations for the case, we present sections giving the background and facts of the case, excerpts from the court opinion showing the court's reasoning on the issue, and the decision and remedy in the case.

In addition, many of the cases are preceded by a *Company Profile,* which provides background information on a party to the case, or a *Historical and Social [or other] Setting.* These settings, along with case-concluding *For Critical Analysis* questions, address the AACSB's curriculum requirements by focusing on how particular aspects of the dispute or the court's decision relate to ethical, international, technological, cultural, or other types of issues.

Other Special Pedagogical Devices

The Legal and E-Commerce Environment Today, Third Edition, offers a number of additional pedagogical devices, including those listed below.

Pedagogical Devices in the Text

- **Chapter objectives.**
- **Contents.**
- **Margin definitions.**
- **Margin reminders or instructional notes.**
- **Quotations.**
- **Exhibits and forms.**
- **Photographs** (with critical thinking questions).

Chapter-Ending Pedagogy

- **Key Terms** (with appropriate page references).
- **Chapter Summary** (in graphic format with page references).
- **For Review** (a series of brief review questions).
- **Questions and Case Problems** (including hypotheticals as well as problems based on actual cases).
- **A Question of Ethics and Social Responsibility.**
- **Case Briefing Assignment** (instructing students to brief selected cases contained in Appendix A of this book, in selected chapters only).
- **For Critical Analysis.**
- **Interacting with the Internet** (including online legal research exercises).
- **Before the Test** (referring students to interactive quizzes on the text's Web site).

Unit-Ending Cumulative Questions

At the end of the final chapter in each unit, we present a *Cumulative Hypothetical Problem*. The problem introduces a hypothetical business firm and then asks a series of questions about how the law applies to various actions taken by the firm. To answer the questions, the student must apply the laws discussed throughout the unit. Suggested answers to these questions are included in the *Answers Manual*.

Appendices

To help students learn how to find published primary sources of law, including those cited in footnotes throughout this text, we have included a special appendix at the end of Chapter 1. There your students will find information, including an exhibit, on how to read citations to cases, statutes, and agency regulations.

Because the majority of students keep their legal environment texts as a reference source, we have also included at the end of the book a full set of appendices. Since the last edition of this text was published, several new statutes, uniform laws, and policies have been created to regulate certain aspects of e-commerce. Because of their significance in the legal environment, excerpts from the following documents are included in the appendices:

- **The Digital Millennium Copyright Act of 1998** (Appendix K).
- **The Electronic Signatures in Global and National Commerce Act of 2000** (Appendix L).
- **The Uniform Electronic Transactions Act** (Appendix M).
- **The Uniform Computer Information Transactions Act** (Appendix N).
- **ICANN's Uniform Domain Name Dispute Resolution Policy** (Appendix O).

Supplements

The Legal and E-Commerce Environment Today, Third Edition, is accompanied by an expansive number of teaching and learning supplements, including those listed below. For further information on the elements contained in the teaching/learning package, contact your local West sales representative or go to the Web site that accompanies this text at **http://leet.westbuslaw.com**.

Printed Supplements

- *Online Legal Research* (free with every new copy of the text).
- *Instructor's Course Planning Guide and Media Handbook.*
- *Instructor's Manual.*
- *Study Guide.*
- A comprehensive *Test Bank.*
- *Answers to Questions and Case Problems.*
- *Case Printouts.*
- *Handbook of Landmark Cases and Statutes in Business Law and the Legal Environment.*
- *Guide to Personal Law.*

- *Handbook on Critical Thinking and Writing in Business Law and the Legal Environment.*
- *Instructor's Manual* for the *Drama of the Law* video series.
- Transparency Acetates.

Multimedia Supplements

- *The Legal and E-Commerce Environment Today Interactive CD-ROM Edition.*
- *Quicken Business Law Partner®* CD-ROM.
- *Instructor's Manual* on CD-ROM.
- *Answers Manual* on CD-ROM.
- Web Tutor on WebCT.
- ExamView—Computerized Testing Software (allows instructors to tailor their exams using software compatible with Microsoft Windows, as well as administer tests online via the Internet or wide-area or local-area networks).
- PowerPoint slides.
- Case-Problem Cases on CD-ROM.
- Westlaw®.
- Videocassettes, including those discussed next.

CNN Legal Issues Update Video

You can update your coverage of legal issues and cyberlaw, as well as spark a lively classroom discussion and foster a deeper understanding of business law, by using the *CNN Legal Issues* update video. This video is produced by Turner Learning, Inc., using the resources of CNN, the world's first twenty-four-hour, all-news network.

Additional Videos

South-Western's *Business Law* video series, a set of situational videos, covers a range of topics for the full legal environment course, including the Uniform Commercial Code and employment law.

The New York Times Guide to Legal Studies in Business

The New York Times Guide to Legal Studies in Business, by Marianne Jennings and Jamie Murphy, is more than just a printed collection of articles. The guide gives you access, via password, to an online collection of the most current and relevant *New York Times* articles that are continually posted as news breaks. Also included are articles from *CyberTimes,* the online technology section of the *New York Times* on the Web. Correlation guides for all South-Western legal studies in business texts are available on the South-Western *New York Times* Web site at **http://nytimes.swcollege.com**. Ask your West sales representative about this great new supplement for your students.

For Users of the Second Edition

We thought that those of you who have been using the Second Edition of this book would like to know some of the major changes that have been made for the Third Edition. This new edition continues the coverage of the essential legal environment topics covered in the previous edition, but we think that we have improved it greatly, thanks in part to the many letters, telephone calls, and reviews that we have received.

Two New Cyberlaw Chapters

- **Chapter 5 (E-Commerce and Dispute Resolution)**—Covers jurisdiction in cyberspace, new policies and organizations facilitating the resolution of domain name disputes, and emerging online dispute-resolution forums.
- **Chapter 14 (E-Contracts)**—Examines a number of important developments in the e-commerce arena, including shrink-wrap and click-on agreements, e-signatures, e-agents, the Uniform Computer Information Transactions Act, and the Uniform Electronic Transactions Act.

Significantly Revised Chapters

- **Chapter 1 (The Legal and International Foundations)**—Now contains an expanded discussion of the distinction between civil law and criminal law, as well as an exhibit showing the most significant differences in these two bodies of law.
- **Chapter 2 (Ethics and Social Responsibility)**—Has been significantly revised and now includes a discussion of the principle of rights and a new section on ethical decision making.
- **Chapter 9 (Torts)**—Now incorporates the coverage of basic business torts that appeared as a separate chapter in the previous edition.
- **Chapter 10 (Strict Liability and Product Liability)**—Contains a new section on the *Restatement (Third) of Torts* and incorporates provisions from this *Restatement* in the discussion of strict product liability. Additionally, the discussion of strict liability, which appeared in the previous edition in the torts chapter, has been moved to this chapter for this edition.
- **Chapter 11 (Intellectual Property and Cyberlaw)**—The section on cyberlaw has been thoroughly updated and now includes a discussion of the Digital Millennium Copyright Act of 1988.
- **Chapter 12 (Contract Formation)** and **Chapter 13 (Contract Defenses, Discharge, and Remedies)**—The presentation of contract law has been reorganized so that the discussion of this topic progresses more smoothly and logically. Chapter 12 now includes first-level sections on the law governing contracts (including sales contracts), the function of contracts, types of contracts, the requirements of a contract, and third party rights in contracts. Chapter 13 covers defenses to contract enforceability, contract discharge, damages, equitable remedies, election of remedies, remedies for breach of a sales contract, provisions limiting remedies, and contracts for the international sale of goods. Additionally, a discussion of the parol evidence rule has been added to Chapter 13.
- **Chapter 15 (Creditors' Rights and Bankruptcy)**—Reflects recent adjustments to the dollar amounts for exempted property and distribution under the Bankruptcy Code.
- **Chapter 16 (Business Organizations)**—Now includes an expanded discussion of limited liability companies and limited liability partnerships, plus a two-page exhibit comparing these relatively new types of business organizations with the major traditional forms with respect to how they are formed, the liability of owners, and other characteristics.

- **Chapter 18 (Equal Employment Opportunities)**—Has been extensively revised to include recent decisions by the courts, including the United States Supreme Court, on employment discrimination issues and an expanded discussion of workplace harassment.
- **Chapter 21 (Protecting the Environment)**—The section on air pollution has been largely rewritten, and the discussion of Superfund has been updated and revised.

What Else Is New?

In addition to the changes noted above, you will find a number of other new items or features in *The Legal and E-Commerce Environment Today*, Third Edition, as listed below.

- *Legal E-nvironment* features.
- Numbered *Ethical Issues* closely integrated with the text.
- Highlighted and numbered examples.
- Online Legal Research Exercises.
- *Before the Test* sections.
- New cases and case problems (many from 1999 and 2000).
- New exhibits.
- New appendices (see the list of new appendices earlier in this preface).

New Supplements

- *The Legal and E-Commerce Environment Today Interactive CD-ROM Edition.*
- *Online Legal Research.*
- Web Tutor on WebCT.
- ExamView Testing Software.
- *The New York Times Guide to Legal Studies in Business.*
- Internet Activities.
- Interactive Quizzes.

Acknowledgments

We owe a debt of extreme gratitude to the numerous individuals at West who worked on this project. We especially wish to thank Rob Dewey and Jan Lamar for their helpful advice and guidance during all of the stages of this new edition. Jan Lamar also assisted us in making sure that we addressed all reviewers' criticisms and suggestions, and she was instrumental in ensuring that the supplements came out on time. Kurt Gerdenich and Vicky True deserve a special note of appreciation for their incredibly masterful work on the Web site, the CD-ROM Edition, and just about everything else relating to technology for this text. Our long-time production editor at West, Bill Stryker, made sure that we came out with an error-free edition on time. We will always be in his debt. We also give special thanks to Ann Borman, also at West, for her assistance and particularly for designing an attractive, visually striking edition.

We also extend our thanks to a number of other people who worked directly with us on this project. We wish to thank Lavina Leed Miller for her management of the project, as well as for the application of her superb research, editorial, and proofreading skills. We must especially thank William Eric Hollowell, co-author of the *Instructor's Manual, Study Guide, Test Bank*, and *Instructor's Course Planning Guide and Media Handbook,* for his excellent research and writing efforts. Our appreciation also goes to Suzie DeFazio, whose copyediting skills will not go unnoticed. We also thank Roxanna Lee for her proofreading services and many other contributions, and Suzanne Jasin for her many special efforts on the project.

Finally, numerous careful and conscientious users of previous editions have been kind enough to offer us their comments and suggestions on how to improve this text. We are particularly indebted to these reviewers, whom we list below. With their help, we have been able to make this book even more useful for professors and students alike.

Acknowledgments for Previous Editions

Jane Bennett
Orange Coast College

Tom Moore
Georgia College and State University

Mark Phelps
University of Oregon

Martha Sartoris
North Hennepin Community College

Gwen Seaquist
Ithaca College

Acknowledgments for the Third Edition

Jane Bennett
Orange Coast College

Penelope L. Herickhoff
Mankato State University

Susan Key
University of Alabama at Birmingham

Mark Phelps
University of Oregon

Gary Sambol
Rutgers, the State University of
New Jersey, Camden Campus

We know that we are not perfect. If you or your students find something that you don't like or want us to change, write or e-mail us your thoughts. That is how we can make *The Legal and E-Commerce Environment Today,* Third Edition, an even better book in the future.

Roger LeRoy Miller
Frank B. Cross

Dedication

To Kim and Bill Hunter.
May the future be even brighter than the present.
Congratulations!
R.L.M.

To my parents and sisters.
F.B.C.

Photo Credits

All chapter and unit openers are comprised of PhotoDisc images.

5 From the painting by Benjamin Ferrers in National Portrait Gallery, Photo: Corbis-Bettmann; 10 © Michael Evans, Sygma; 11 © Spencer Grant, PhotoEdit; 32 © PhotoDisc; 40 © Ted Horowitz, The Stock Market; 46 © Vincent De Witt, Stock Boston; 55 (left) © Steven Starr, Stock Boston; 55 (right) courtesy Corporate Watch; 63 © Bettmann; 75 © Richard Strauss, Smithsonian Institution, Collection of the Supreme Court of the United States; 79 © Aaron Haupt, Stock Boston; 95 © Jeff Greenberg, PhotoEdit; 97 © PhotoDisc; 102 © Tom McCathy, PhotoEdit; 158 © Matthew McVay, Tony Stone Images; 163 © Chris Brown, Stock Boston; 165 © Amy C. Etra, PhotoEdit; 168 © A. Ramey, PhotoEdit; 217 © PhotoDisc; 226 © Michael Newman, PhotoEdit; 251 © Frederick D. Bodlin, Stock Boston; 253 Drawing by Maslin, © 1990 The New Yorker Magazine, Inc; 263 Courtesy Jane Borman; 273 © Mark Richards, PhotoEdit; 277 © Steve Leonard, Black Star; 294 © Mike Mazzaschi, Stock Boston; 320 © Al Cook, Stock Boston; 321 © Ron Chapple, FPG; 325 © Billy E. Barnes, PhotoEdit; 329 © PhotoDisc; 337 © Michael Newman, PhotoEdit; 340 © M. Borchi, Photo Researchers; 372 © PhotoDisc; 379 © Elizabeth Simpson, FPG; 382 © PhotoDisc; 417 © Myrleen Ferguson, PhotoEdit; 423 © Tony Freeman, PhotoEdit; 428 © Tony Freeman, PhotoEdit; 452 © Jim Erickson, The Stock Market; 454 © PhotoDisc; 471 © McIntyre, Photo Researchers; 475 © PhotoDisc; 497 © Comstock; 500 © Amy C. Etra, PhotoEdit; 503 © Michael Newman, PhotoEdit; 505 © The Library of Congress; 534 © PhotoDisc; 539 © John Boykin, PhotoEdit; 549 © Deborah Davis, PhotoEdit; 564 © Jonathan Nourok, PhotoEdit; 581 © Tony Freeman, PhotoEdit; 614 © PhotoDisc; 617 © Michael Rosenfeld, Tony Stone Images; 623 © Jack Dermid, Photo Researchers, Inc; 633 © Jonathan Nourok, PhotoEdit; 641 © Vic Bider, PhotoEdit; 655 © PhotoDisc; 670 © John Coletti, Stock Boston; 691 © David Young-Wolff, PhotoEdit

The Foundations

The Legal and International Foundations

contents

chapter objectives

After reading this chapter, you should be able to:

1. Explain what is generally meant by the term *law.*

2. Describe the origins and importance of the common law tradition.

3. Identify the four major sources of American law.

4. List some important classifications of law.

5. Distinguish between national law and international law.

L ord Balfour's assertion in the quotation alongside emphasizes the underlying theme of every page in this book—that law is of interest to all persons, not just to lawyers. Those entering the world of business will find themselves subject to numerous laws and government regulations. A basic knowledge of these laws and regulations is beneficial—if not essential—to anyone contemplating a successful career in the business world of today.

In this introductory chapter, we first look at the nature of law and at some concepts that have significantly influenced how jurists and scholars view the nature and function of law. We then examine the common law tradition of the United States, as well as some of the major sources and classifications of American law. The chapter concludes with a discussion of the global legal environment, which frames many of today's business transactions.

> "The law is of as much interest to the layman as it is to the lawyer."
>
> Lord Balfour, 1848–1930
> (British prime minister, 1902–1905)

The Nature of Law

There have been and will continue to be different definitions of law. The Greek philosopher Aristotle (384–322 B.C.E.) saw law as a "pledge that citizens of a state will do justice to one another." Aristotle's mentor, Plato (427–347 B.C.E.), believed that law was a form of social control. The Roman orator and politician Cicero (106–43 B.C.E.) contended that law was the agreement of reason and nature, the distinction between the just and the unjust. The British jurist Sir William Blackstone (1723–1780) described law as "a rule of civil conduct prescribed by the supreme power in a state, commanding what is right, and prohibiting what is wrong." In America, the eminent jurist Oliver Wendell Holmes, Jr. (1841–1935), contended that law was a set of rules that allowed one to predict how a court would resolve a particular dispute—"the prophecies of what the courts will do in fact, and nothing more pretentious, are what I mean by the law."

Although these definitions vary in their particulars, they all are based on the following general observation: **law** consists of enforceable rules governing relationships among individuals and between individuals and their society. In the study of law, often referred to as **jurisprudence,** this very broad statement concerning the nature of law is the point of departure for all legal scholars and philosophers. We look here at three of the most influential schools of legal thought, or philosophies of law: the natural law tradition, legal positivism, and legal realism.

Law A body of enforceable rules governing relationships among individuals and between individuals and their society.

Jurisprudence The science or philosophy of law.

The Natural Law Tradition

The oldest and one of the most significant schools of jurisprudence is the natural law tradition, which dates back to ancient Greece and Rome. **Natural law** denotes a system of moral and ethical principles that are inherent in human nature and that can be discovered by humans through the use of their natural intelligence, or reason. The Greek philosopher Aristotle distinguished between natural law (which applies universally to all humankind) and **positive law** (the conventional, or written, law of a particular society at a particular point in time). In essence, the natural law tradition presupposes that the legitimacy of positive, or conventional, law derives from natural law. Whenever positive law conflicts with natural law, positive law loses its legitimacy and should be changed.

Natural Law The belief that government and the legal system should reflect universal moral and ethical principles that are inherent in human nature. The natural law school is the oldest and one of the most significant schools of legal thought.

Positive Law The body of conventional, or written, law of a particular society at a particular point in time.

> **"There is in fact a true law—namely, right reason—which is in accordance with nature [and] applies to all men and is unchangeable and eternal."**
>
> Cicero, 106–43 B.C.E.
> (Roman statesman and orator)

Legal Positivism A school of legal thought centered on the assumption that there is no law higher than the laws created by the government. Laws must be obeyed, even if they are unjust, to prevent anarchy.

Legal Realism A school of legal thought of the 1920s and 1930s that generally advocated a less abstract and more realistic approach to the law, an approach that takes into account customary practices and the circumstances in which transactions take place. The school left a lasting imprint on American jurisprudence.

● **Example 1.1** A law prohibiting murder reflects not only the values accepted by a particular society at a particular time (positive law) but also a universally accepted precept that murder is wrong (natural law). To murder someone is thus a violation of natural law. If a law allowed persons to murder each other, that law would be wrong, because it did not accord with natural law. In a sense, the natural law tradition encourages individuals to disobey conventional, or written, laws if those individuals believe that the laws are in conflict with natural law. ●

Legal Positivism

Another school of legal thought is known as **legal positivism.** Legal positivists believe that there can be no higher law than a nation's positive laws—the laws created by a particular society at a particular point in time. Essentially, from the positivist perspective, the law is the law and must be obeyed on pain of punishment. Whether a particular law is bad or good is irrelevant. The merits or demerits of a given law can be discussed, and laws can be changed in an orderly manner through a legitimate lawmaking process. As long as a law exists, however, that law must be obeyed. If people felt justified in disobeying particular laws just because they did not feel the laws were just, anarchy would ensue.

Legal Realism

Legal realism, which became a popular school of legal thought in the 1920s and 1930s, left a strong imprint on American jurisprudence. Contrary to the dominant legal thinking of their time, the legal realists believed that the law could not—and should not—be an abstract body of rules applied uniformly to cases with similar circumstances. According to the legal realists, impartial and uniform application of the law is not possible. After all, judges are human beings with unique personalities, value systems, and intellects. Given this obvious fact, it would be impossible for any two judges to engage in an identical reasoning process when evaluating the same case.

The legal realists argued that each case also involves a unique set of circumstances—no two cases, no matter how similar, are ever exactly the same. Therefore, judges should take into account the specific circumstances of each case, rather than rely on some abstract rule that might not relate to those particular circumstances. When making decisions, judges should also consider extra-legal sources, such as economic and sociological data, to the extent that such sources could illuminate the circumstances and issues involved in specific cases. In other words, the law should take social and economic realities into account.

United States Supreme Court Justice Oliver Wendell Holmes, Jr. (1841–1935), and Karl Llewellyn (1893–1962) were both influential proponents of legal realism. Llewellyn is best known for his dominant role in drafting the Uniform Commercial Code (UCC), a set of rules for commercial transactions that will be discussed later in this chapter. The UCC reflects the influence of legal realism in its emphasis on practicality, flexibility, reasonability, and customary trade practices.

The Common Law Tradition

How jurists view the law is particularly important in a legal system in which judges play a paramount role, as they do in the American legal system. Because of our colonial heritage, much of American law is based on the English legal system. A knowledge of this tradition is necessary to an understanding of the nature of our legal system today.

Early English Courts of Law

In medieval England, courts developed the **common law** rules from the principles underlying judges' decisions in actual legal controversies. Judges attempted to be consistent, and whenever possible, they based their decisions on the principles suggested by earlier cases. They sought to decide similar cases in a similar way and considered new cases with care, because they knew that their decisions would make new law. Each interpretation became part of the law on the subject and served as a legal **precedent**—that is, a decision that furnished an example or authority for deciding subsequent cases involving similar legal principles or facts.

In the early years of the common law, there was no single place or publication in which court opinions, or written decisions, could be found. In the late thirteenth and early fourteenth centuries, however, portions of significant decisions of each year were gathered together and recorded in *Year Books*. The *Year Books* were useful references for lawyers and judges. In the sixteenth century, the *Year Books* were discontinued, and other reports of cases became available. (See the appendix to this chapter for a discussion of how cases are reported, or published, in the United States today.)

Stare Decisis

The practice of deciding new cases with reference to former decisions, or precedents, eventually became a cornerstone of the English and American judicial systems. The practice forms a doctrine called ***stare decisis***[1] ("to stand on decided cases"). The doctrine means that once a court has set forth a principle of law as being applicable to a certain set of facts, that court and courts of lower rank will adhere to that principle and apply it in future cases involving similar fact patterns.

• **Example 1.2** Suppose that the lower state courts in California have reached conflicting conclusions on whether drivers are liable for accidents they cause while merging into freeway traffic, even though the drivers looked and did not see any oncoming traffic and even though witnesses (passengers in their cars) testified to that effect. To settle the law on this issue, the California Supreme Court decides to review a case involving this fact pattern. The court rules that in such a situation, the driver who is merging into traffic is liable for any accidents caused by the driver's failure to yield to freeway traffic—regardless of whether the driver looked carefully and did not see an approaching vehicle. The California Supreme Court's decision on the matter will influence the outcome of all future cases on this issue brought before the California state courts.•

Similarly, a decision on a given issue by the United States Supreme Court (the nation's highest court) is binding on all inferior courts. Controlling precedents are referred to as **binding authorities,** as are statutes or other laws that must be followed.

Common Law That body of law developed from custom or judicial decisions in English and U.S. courts, not attributable to a legislature.

Precedent A court decision that furnishes an example or authority for deciding subsequent cases involving identical or similar facts.

Stare Decisis A common law doctrine under which judges are obligated to follow the precedents established in prior decisions.

Binding Authority Any source of law that a court must follow when deciding a case. Binding authorities include constitutions, statutes, and regulations that govern the issue being decided, as well as court decisions that are controlling precedents.

The court of chancery in the reign of George I. Early English court decisions formed the basis of what type of law?

---

1. Pronounced *ster*-ay dih-*si*-ses.

The doctrine of *stare decisis* helps the courts to be efficient, because if other courts have carefully reasoned through a similar case, their legal reasoning and opinions can serve as guides. *Stare decisis* also helps make the law stable and predictable. If the law on a given subject is well settled, someone bringing a case to court can usually rely on the court to make a decision based on what the law has been.

DEPARTURES FROM PRECEDENT   Sometimes a court will depart from the rule of precedent if it decides that a given precedent should no longer be followed. If a court decides that a precedent is simply incorrect or that technological or social changes have rendered the precedent inapplicable, the court might rule contrary to the precedent. Cases that overturn precedent often receive a great deal of publicity.

• **Example 1.3** In *Brown v. Board of Education of Topeka,*[2] the United States Supreme Court expressly overturned precedent when it concluded that separate educational facilities for whites and blacks, which had been upheld as constitutional in numerous previous cases,[3] were inherently unequal. The Supreme Court's departure from precedent in *Brown* received a tremendous amount of publicity as people began to realize the ramifications of this change in the law.•

WHEN THERE IS NO PRECEDENT   Sometimes there is no precedent within a jurisdiction on which to base a decision, or there are conflicting precedents. A court then may look to precedents set in other jurisdictions for guidance. Such precedents, because they are not binding on the court, are referred to as

---

2. 347 U.S. 483, 74 S.Ct. 686, 98 L.Ed. 873 (1954). (See the appendix at the end of this chapter for an explanation of how to read legal citations.)
3. See *Plessy v. Ferguson,* 163 U.S. 537, 16 S.Ct. 1138, 41 L.Ed. 256 (1896).

International Perspective

The "Americanization" of Israeli Law

In the past, all Israeli courts generally adhered to the doctrine of *stare decisis* and only rarely departed from precedent. Recently, however, the Israeli parliament released the supreme court in Israel (but not the lower courts) from this obligation. The parliament concluded that, given the nation's cultural diversity and the security threats it faces in the Middle East, the high court should be given more flexibility to adapt the law to changing circumstances. Since then, the Israeli supreme court has turned for guidance to other nations' laws, including U.S. laws and court decisions. For example, in a recent case the court held that Israel's all-male air force academy could not deny admission to a female applicant—a position that was strikingly similar to that taken by U.S. courts on similar issues.

Many Israelis believe that the supreme court's application of American legal principles threatens their culture by, among other things, giving the rights of the individual more weight on the scales of justice than the rights of the community. Traditionally, Israel placed significant restrictions on speech, including prohibitions against "hate speech," in the interest of protecting the welfare and security of its society. In contrast, courts in the United States have been reluctant to impose any restrictions on the right to freely express opinions, even if they qualify as "hate speech."

For Critical Analysis: *Would the United States be better or worse off if the United States Supreme Court, like Israel's highest court, could look to other nations' laws for guidance?*

persuasive authorities. A court may also consider a number of factors, including legal principles and policies underlying previous court decisions or existing statutes, fairness, social values and customs, public policy, and data and concepts drawn from the social sciences.

Equitable Remedies and Courts of Equity

In law, a **remedy** is the means given to a party to enforce a right or to compensate for the violation of a right. • **Example 1.4** Suppose that Shem is injured because of Rowan's wrongdoing. A court may order Rowan to compensate Shem for the harm by paying Shem a certain amount of money.•

In the early king's courts of England, the kinds of remedies that could be granted were severely restricted. If one person wronged another, the king's courts could award as compensation either money or property, including land. These courts became known as *courts of law,* and the remedies were called *remedies at law.* Even though this system introduced uniformity in the settling of disputes, when plaintiffs wanted a remedy other than economic compensation, the courts of law could do nothing, so "no remedy, no right."

REMEDIES IN EQUITY   Equity is that branch of unwritten law, founded in justice and fair dealing, that seeks to supply a fairer and more adequate remedy than any remedy available at law. In medieval England, when individuals could not obtain an adequate remedy in a court of law, they petitioned the king for relief. Most of these petitions were decided by an adviser to the king called the *chancellor.* The chancellor was said to be the "keeper of the king's conscience." When the chancellor thought that the claim was a fair one, new and unique remedies were granted. In this way, a new body of rules and remedies came into being, and eventually formal *chancery courts,* or *courts of equity,* were established. The remedies granted by these courts were called *remedies in equity.* Thus, two distinct court systems were created, each having a different set of judges and a different set of remedies.

Plaintiffs (those bringing lawsuits) had to specify whether they were bringing an "action at law" or an "action in equity," and they chose their courts accordingly. • **Example 1.5** A plaintiff might ask a court of equity to order a **defendant** (a person against whom a lawsuit is brought) to perform within the terms of a contract. A court of law could not issue such an order, because its remedies were limited to payment of money or property as compensation for damages. A court of equity, however, could issue a decree for *specific performance*—an order to perform what was promised. A court of equity could also issue an *injunction,* directing a party to do or refrain from doing a particular act. In certain cases, a court of equity could allow for the *rescission* (cancellation) of the contract so that the parties would be returned to the positions that they held prior to the contract's formation.• Equitable remedies will be discussed in greater detail in Chapter 13.

THE MERGING OF LAW AND EQUITY   Today, in most states, the courts of law and equity are merged, and thus the distinction between the two courts has largely disappeared. A plaintiff may now request both legal and equitable remedies in the same action, and the trial court judge may grant either form— or both forms—of relief. The merging of law and equity, however, does not diminish the importance of distinguishing legal remedies from equitable remedies. To request the proper remedy, one must know what remedies are

Persuasive Authority Any legal authority or source of law that a court may look to for guidance but on which it need not rely in making its decision. Persuasive authorities include cases from other jurisdictions and secondary sources of law.

Remedy The relief given to an innocent party to enforce a right or compensate for the violation of a right.

Plaintiff One who initiates a lawsuit.

Defendant One against whom a lawsuit is brought; the accused person in a criminal proceeding.

Remember Even though, in most states, courts of law and equity have merged, the principles of equity still apply.

Exhibit 1–1   **Procedural Differences between an Action at Law and an Action in Equity**

PROCEDURE	ACTION AT LAW	ACTION IN EQUITY
Initiation of lawsuit	By filing a complaint	By filing a petition
Decision	By jury or judge	By judge (no jury)
Result	Judgment	Decree
Remedy	Monetary damages	Injunction, specific performance, or rescission

Equitable Principles and Maxims General propositions or principles of law that have to do with fairness (equity).

Statute of Limitations A federal or state statute setting the maximum time period during which a certain action can be brought or certain rights enforced.

available for the specific kinds of harms suffered. Today, as a rule, courts will grant an equitable remedy only when the remedy at law (money damages) is inadequate. Exhibit 1–1 summarizes the procedural differences (applicable in most states) between an action at law and an action in equity.

EQUITABLE PRINCIPLES AND MAXIMS   Over time, a number of **equitable principles and maxims** evolved that have since guided the courts in deciding whether plaintiffs should be granted equitable relief. Because of their importance, both historically and in our judicial system today, these principles and maxims are set forth in the following *Landmark in the Legal Environment*.

Landmark in the Legal Environment

Equitable Principles and Maxims

In medieval England, courts of equity had the responsibility of using discretion in supplementing the common law. Even today, when the same court can award both legal and equitable remedies, such discretion is exercised. Courts often invoke equitable principles and maxims when making their decisions. Here are some of the more significant equitable principles and maxims:

1. *Whoever seeks equity must do equity.* (Anyone who wishes to be treated fairly must treat others fairly.)
2. *Where there is equal equity, the law must prevail.* (The law will determine the outcome of a controversy in which the merits of both sides are equal.)
3. *One seeking the aid of an equity court must come to the court with clean hands.* (Plaintiffs must have acted fairly and honestly.)
4. *Equity will not suffer a wrong to be without a remedy.* (Equitable relief will be awarded when

there is a right to relief and there is no adequate remedy at law.)
5. *Equity regards substance rather than form.* (Equity is more concerned with fairness and justice than with legal technicalities.)
6. *Equity aids the vigilant, not those who rest on their rights.* (Equity will not help those who neglect their rights for an unreasonable period of time.)

The last maxim has become known as the *equitable doctrine of laches.* The doctrine arose to encourage people to bring lawsuits while the evidence was fresh; if they failed to do so, they would not be allowed to bring a lawsuit. What constitutes a reasonable time, of course, varies according to the circumstances of the case. Time periods for different types of cases are now usually fixed by **statutes of limitations.** After the time allowed under a statute of limitations has expired, no action can be brought, no matter how strong the case was originally.

For Critical Analysis: *Do you think that the government should establish, through statutes of limitations, the time limits within which different types of lawsuits can be brought?*

Sources of American Law

There are numerous sources of American law. **Primary sources of law,** or sources that establish the law, include the following:

1. The U.S. Constitution and the constitutions of the various states.
2. Statutes, or laws, passed by Congress and by state legislatures.
3. Regulations created by administrative agencies, such as the federal Food and Drug Administration.
4. Case law (court decisions).

We describe each of these important primary sources of law in the following pages.

Secondary sources of law are books and articles that summarize and clarify the primary sources of law. Legal encyclopedias, compilations (such as *Restatements of the Law*—to be discussed later in this chapter), official comments to statutes, treatises, articles in law reviews published by law schools, and articles in other legal journals are examples of secondary sources of law. Courts often refer to secondary sources of law for guidance in interpreting and applying the primary sources of law discussed here.

Constitutional Law

The federal government and the states have separate written constitutions that set forth the general organization, powers, and limits of their respective governments. **Constitutional law** is the law as expressed in these constitutions.

The U.S. Constitution is the supreme law of the land. As such, it is the basis of all law in the United States. A law in violation of the Constitution, no matter what its source, will be declared unconstitutional and will not be enforced. Because of its paramount importance in the American legal system, we discuss the Constitution at length in Chapter 6 and present the complete text of the U.S. Constitution in Appendix B.

The Tenth Amendment to the U.S. Constitution, which defines the powers and limitations of the federal government, reserves all powers not granted to the federal government to the states. Each state in the union has its own constitution. Unless they conflict with the U.S. Constitution or a federal law, state constitutions are supreme within their respective borders.

Statutory Law

Statutes enacted by legislative bodies at any level of government make up another source of law, which is generally referred to as **statutory law.**

FEDERAL STATUTES   Federal statutes are laws that are enacted by the U.S. Congress. As mentioned, any law—including a federal statute—that violates the U.S. Constitution will be held unconstitutional.

Federal statutes that affect business operations include laws regulating the purchase and sale of securities (corporate stocks and bonds—discussed in Chapter 24), consumer protection statutes (discussed in Chapter 20), and statutes prohibiting employment discrimination (discussed in Chapter 18). Whenever a particular statute is mentioned in this text, we usually provide a footnote showing its **citation** (a reference to a publication in which a legal authority—such as a statute or a court decision—or other source can be found). In the appendix following this chapter, we explain how you can use these citations to find statutory law.

Primary Source of Law A document that establishes the law on a particular issue, such as a constitution, a statute, an administrative rule, or a court decision.

Secondary Source of Law A publication that summarizes or interprets the law, such as a legal encyclopedia, a legal treatise, or an article in a law review.

Constitutional Law Law based on the U.S. Constitution and the constitutions of the various states.

Statutory Law The body of law enacted by legislative bodies (as opposed to constitutional law, administrative law, or case law).

Citation A reference to a publication in which a legal authority—such as a statute or a court decision—or other source can be found.

Young students view the U.S. Constitution on display in Washington, D.C. Can a law be in violation of the Constitution and still be enforced? Why or why not?

STATE AND LOCAL STATUTES AND ORDINANCES   State statutes are laws enacted by state legislatures. Any state law that is found to conflict with the U.S. Constitution, with federal laws enacted by Congress, or with the state's constitution will be deemed unconstitutional. Statutory law also includes the ordinances passed by cities and counties, none of which can violate the U.S. Constitution, the relevant state constitution, or federal or state laws.

State statutes include state criminal statutes (discussed in Chapter 8), state corporation statutes (discussed in Chapter 16), state deceptive trade practices acts (referred to in Chapter 20), and state versions of the Uniform Commercial Code (to be discussed shortly). Local ordinances include zoning ordinances and local laws regulating housing construction and such things as the overall appearance of a community.

A federal statute, of course, applies to all states. A state statute, in contrast, applies only within the state's borders. State laws thus vary from state to state.

UNIFORM LAWS   The differences among state laws were particularly notable in the 1800s, when conflicting state statutes frequently made the rapidly developing trade and commerce among the states very difficult. To counter these problems, a group of legal scholars and lawyers formed the National Conference of Commissioners (NCCUSL) on Uniform State Laws in 1892 to

A housing development is under construction. What types of law govern the way houses are constructed?

draft uniform ("model") statutes for adoption by the states. The NCCUSL still exists today and continues to issue uniform statutes.

Adoption of a uniform law is a state matter, and a state may reject all or part of the statute or rewrite it as the state legislature wishes. Hence, even when a uniform law is said to have been adopted in many states, those states' laws may not be entirely "uniform." Once adopted by a state legislature, a uniform act becomes a part of the statutory law of that state.

Be Careful Even though uniform laws are intended to be adopted without changes, states often modify them to suit their particular needs.

The earliest uniform law, the Uniform Negotiable Instruments Law, was completed by 1896 and was adopted in every state by the early 1920s (although not all states used exactly the same wording). Over the following decades, other acts were drawn up in a similar manner. In all, over two hundred uniform acts have been issued by the NCCUSL since its inception. The most ambitious uniform act of all, however, was the Uniform Commercial Code.

THE UNIFORM COMMERCIAL CODE (UCC)   The Uniform Commercial Code (UCC), which was created through the joint efforts of the NCCUSL and the American Law Institute,[4] was first issued in 1952. The UCC has been adopted in all fifty states,[5] the District of Columbia, and the Virgin Islands. The UCC facilitates commerce among the states by providing a uniform, yet flexible, set of rules governing commercial transactions. The UCC assures businesspersons that their contracts, if validly entered into, normally will be enforced.

Because of its importance in the area of commercial law, we cite the UCC frequently in this text. We also present excerpts from the latest version of the UCC in Appendix D. (For a discussion of the creation of the UCC, see the *Landmark in the Legal Environment* in Chapter 12.)

---

4. This institute was formed in the 1920s and consists of practicing attorneys, legal scholars, and judges.
5. Louisiana has adopted only Articles 1, 3, 4, 5, 7, 8, and 9.

Administrative Law

Administrative Law The body of law created by administrative agencies (in the form of rules, regulations, orders, and decisions) in order to carry out their duties and responsibilities.

An important source of American law consists of **administrative law**—the rules, orders, and decisions of administrative agencies. An **administrative agency** is a federal, state, or local government agency established to perform a specific function. Rules issued by various administrative agencies now affect virtually every aspect of a business's operation, including the firm's capital structure and financing, its hiring and firing procedures, its relations with employees and unions, and the way it manufactures and markets its products.

Administrative Agency A federal or state government agency established to perform a specific function. Administrative agencies are authorized by legislative acts to make and implement rules to administer and enforce the acts.

At the national level, numerous **executive agencies** exist within the cabinet departments of the executive branch. For example, the Food and Drug Administration is within the Department of Health and Human Services. Executive agencies are subject to the authority of the president, who has the power to appoint and remove officers of federal agencies. There are also major **independent regulatory agencies** at the federal level, including the Federal Trade Commission, the Securities and Exchange Commission, and the Federal Communications Commission. The president's power is less pronounced in regard to independent agencies, the officers of which serve for fixed terms and cannot be removed without just cause.

Executive Agency An administrative agency within the executive branch of government. At the federal level, executive agencies are those within the cabinet departments.

There are administrative agencies at the state and local levels as well. Commonly, a state agency (such as a state pollution-control agency) is created as a parallel to a federal agency (such as the Environmental Protection Agency). Just as federal statutes take precedence over conflicting state statutes, so do federal agency regulations take precedence over conflicting state regulations. Because the rules of state and local agencies vary widely, we focus here exclusively on federal administrative law.

Independent Regulatory Agency An administrative agency that is not considered part of the government's executive branch and is not subject to the authority of the president. Independent agency officials cannot be removed without cause.

AGENCY CREATION   Because Congress cannot possibly oversee the actual implementation of all the laws it enacts, it must delegate such tasks to others, particularly when the issues relate to highly technical areas, such as air and water pollution. Congress creates an administrative agency by enacting **enabling legislation,** which specifies the name, composition, purpose, and powers of the agency being created.

Enabling Legislation A statute enacted by Congress that authorizes the creation of an administrative agency and specifies the name, composition, purpose, and powers of the agency being created.

● **Example 1.6** The Federal Trade Commission (FTC) was created in 1914 by the Federal Trade Commission Act.[6] This act prohibits unfair and deceptive trade practices. It also describes the procedures the agency must follow to charge persons or organizations with violations of the act, and it provides for judicial review (review by the courts) of agency orders. Other portions of the act grant the agency powers to "make rules and regulations for the purpose of carrying out the Act," to conduct investigations of business practices, to obtain reports from interstate corporations concerning their business practices, to investigate possible violations of the act, to publish findings of its investigations, and to recommend new legislation. The act also empowers the FTC to hold trial-like hearings and to **adjudicate** (resolve judicially) certain kinds of trade disputes that involve FTC regulations.●

Adjudicate To render a judicial decision. In the administrative process, the proceeding in which an administrative law judge hears and decides on issues that arise when an administrative agency charges a person or a firm with violating a law or regulation enforced by the agency.

Note that the FTC's grant of power incorporates functions associated with the legislative branch of government (rulemaking), the executive branch (investigation and enforcement), and the judicial branch (adjudication). Taken together, these functions constitute what has been termed **administrative process,** which is the administration of law by administrative agencies.

Administrative Process The procedure used by administrative agencies in the administration of law.

---

6. 15 U.S.C. Sections 45–58.

RULEMAKING   One of the major functions of an administrative agency is **rulemaking**—creating or modifying rules, or regulations, pursuant to its enabling legislation. The Administrative Procedure Act of 1946[7] imposes strict procedural requirements that agencies must follow in their rulemaking and other functions.

The most common rulemaking procedure involves three steps. First, the agency must give public notice of the proposed rulemaking proceedings, where and when the proceedings will be held, the agency's legal authority for the proceedings, and the terms or subject matter of the proposed rule. The notice must be published in the *Federal Register,* a daily publication of the U.S. government. Second, following this notice, the agency must allow ample time for interested parties to comment in writing on the proposed rule. After the comments have been received and reviewed, the agency takes them into consideration when drafting the final version of the regulation. The third and final step is the drafting of the final version and the publication of the rule in the *Federal Register.* (See the appendix at the end of this chapter for an explanation of how to find agency regulations.)

INVESTIGATION AND ENFORCEMENT   Agencies have both investigatory and prosecutorial powers. An agency can request individuals or organizations to hand over specified books, papers, records, or other documents. In addition, agencies may conduct on-site inspections, although a search warrant is normally required for such inspections. Sometimes the search of a home, an office, or a factory is the only means of obtaining evidence needed to prove a regulatory violation. Agencies investigate a wide range of activities, including coal mining, automobile manufacturing, and the industrial discharge of pollutants into the environment.

Rulemaking The process undertaken by an administrative agency when formally adopting a new regulation or amending an old one. Rulemaking involves notifying the public of a proposed rule or change and receiving and considering the public's comments.

---

7. 5 U.S.C. Sections 551–706.

Ethical Issue 1.1

Do administrative agencies exercise too much authority?

Administrative agencies, such as the FTC, combine functions normally divided among the three branches of government into a single governmental entity. The broad range of authority that agencies exercise sometimes engenders questions of fairness. After all, agencies create rules that are as legally binding as the laws passed by Congress—the only federal government institution authorized by the Constitution to make laws.

To be sure, arbitrary rulemaking by agencies is checked by the procedural requirements set forth in the Administrative Procedure Act (APA), as well as by the courts, to which agency decisions may be appealed. Yet some people claim that these checks are not enough.

Consider that in addition to *legislative rules,* which are subject to the procedural requirements of the APA, agencies also create *interpretive rules*—rules that specify how the agency will interpret and apply its regulations. The APA does not apply to interpretive rulemaking. Additionally, although a firm that challenges an agency's rule may be able to appeal the agency's decision in the matter to a court, the policy of the courts is generally to defer to agency rules, including interpretative rules, and to agency decisions.

Administrative Law Judge (ALJ) One who presides over an administrative agency hearing and who has the power to administer oaths, take testimony, rule on questions of evidence, and make determinations of fact.

ADJUDICATION   After conducting its own investigation of a suspected rule violation, an agency may decide to take action against a specific party. The action may involve a trial-like hearing before an **administrative law judge (ALJ)**. The ALJ may compel the charged party to pay fines or may forbid the party to carry on some specified activity. Either side may appeal the ALJ's decision to the commission or board that governs the agency. If the party fails to get relief there, appeal can be made to a federal court.

Case Law and Common Law Doctrines

The body of law that was first developed in England and that is still used today in the United States consists of the rules of law announced in court decisions. These rules of law include interpretations of constitutional provisions, of statutes enacted by legislatures, and of regulations created by administrative agencies. Today, this body of law is referred to variously as the common law, judge-made law, or **case law.**

Case Law The rules of law announced in court decisions. Case law includes the aggregate of reported cases that interpret judicial precedents, statutes, regulations, and constitutional provisions.

The common law—the doctrines and principles embodied in case law—governs all areas not covered by statutory law (or agency regulations issued to implement various statutes). • **Example 1.7** In disputes concerning contracts for the sale of goods, the Uniform Commercial Code (statutory law) applies when one of its provisions supersedes the common law of contracts. Similarly, in a dispute concerning a particular employment practice, if a statute regulates that practice, the statute will apply rather than the common law doctrine governing employment relationships that applied prior to the enactment of the statute.•

THE RELATIONSHIP BETWEEN THE COMMON LAW AND STATUTORY LAW   The body of statutory law has expanded greatly since this nation began, and this expansion has resulted in a proportionate reduction in the applicability of common law doctrines. Nonetheless, there is a significant overlap between statutory law and the common law, and thus common law doctrines remain a significant source of legal authority.

Many statutes essentially codify existing common law rules, and therefore the courts, in interpreting the statutes, often rely on the common law as a guide to what the legislators intended. Additionally, how the courts interpret a particular statute determines how that statute will be applied. • **Example 1.8** If you wanted to learn about the coverage and applicability of a particular statute, for example, you would, of course, need to locate the statute and study it. You would also need to see how the courts in your jurisdiction have interpreted the statute—in other words, what precedents have been established in regard to that statute. Often, the applicability of a newly enacted statute does not become clear until a body of case law develops to clarify how, when, and to whom the statute applies.•

RESTATEMENTS OF THE LAW   The American Law Institute (ALI) drafted and published compilations of the common law called *Restatements of the Law,* which generally summarize the common law rules followed by most states. There are *Restatements of the Law* in many areas of the law, including contracts, torts, agency, trusts, property, restitution, security, judgments, and conflict of laws. The *Restatements,* like other secondary sources of law, do not in themselves have the force of law but are an important source of legal analysis and opinion on which judges often rely in making their decisions.

Be Aware *Restatements of the Law* are authoritative sources, but they do not have the force of law.

The ALI periodically revises the *Restatements,* and many of the *Restatements* are now in their second or third editions. For instance, as you will read in Chapter 10, the ALI has recently published the first volume of the third edition of the *Restatement of the Law of Torts.*

We refer to the *Restatements* frequently in subsequent chapters of this text, indicating in parentheses the edition to which we are referring. For example, we refer to the second edition of the *Restatement of the Law of Contracts* simply as the *Restatement (Second) of Contracts.*

Classifications of Law

The huge body of the law may be broken down according to several classification systems. For example, one classification system divides law into **substantive law** (all laws that define, describe, regulate, and create legal rights and obligations) and **procedural law** (all laws that establish the methods of enforcing the rights established by substantive law). Other classification systems divide law into federal law and state law, private law (dealing with relationships between persons) and public law (addressing the relationship between persons and their government), and so on.

We look below at two broad classifications. One divides the law into criminal and civil law; the other divides the law into national law and international law. Following that, we mention an emerging body of law regulating transactions in cyberspace, informally characterized as "cyberlaw."

Civil Law and Criminal Law

Civil law spells out the rights and duties that exist between persons and between persons and their governments, and the relief available when a person's rights are violated. Typically, in a civil case, a private party sues another private party (although the government can also sue a party for a civil law violation) to make that other party comply with a duty or pay for the damage caused by the failure to comply with a duty. • **Example 1.9** If a seller fails to perform a contract with a buyer, the buyer may bring a lawsuit against the seller. The purpose of the lawsuit will be either to compel the seller to perform as promised or, more commonly, to obtain money damages for the seller's failure to perform.• Much of the law that we discuss in this text is civil law. Contract law, for example, which we discuss in Chapters 12 and 13, is civil law. The whole body of tort law (see Chapters 9 and 10), is civil law.

Criminal law has to do with a wrong committed against society for which society demands redress (see Chapter 8). Criminal acts are proscribed by local, state, or federal government statutes. Criminal defendants are thus prosecuted by public officials, such as a district attorney (D.A.), on behalf of the state, not by their victims or other private parties. Whereas in a civil case the object is to obtain remedies (such as money damages) to compensate the injured party, in a criminal case the object is to punish the wrongdoer in an attempt to deter others from similar actions. Penalties for violations of criminal statutes consist of fines and/or imprisonment—and, in some cases, death. Exhibit 1–2 on the next page summarizes the key differences between civil and criminal law.

Substantive Law Law that defines, describes, regulates, and creates legal rights and obligations.

Procedural Law Law that establishes the methods of enforcing the rights established by substantive law.

Civil Law The branch of law dealing with the definition and enforcement of all private or public rights, as opposed to criminal matters.

Criminal Law Law that defines and governs actions that constitute crimes. Generally, criminal law has to do with wrongful actions committed against society for which society demands redress.

Exhibit 1–2
Civil and Criminal Law Compared

ISSUE	CIVIL LAW	CRIMINAL LAW
Area of concern	Rights and duties between individuals	Offenses against society as a whole
Wrongful act	Harm to a person	Violation of a statute that prohibits some type of activity
Party who brings suit	Person who suffered harm	The state
Standard of proof	Preponderance of the evidence	Beyond a reasonable doubt
Remedy	Damages to compensate for the harm, or a decree to achieve an equitable result	Punishment (fine, removal from public office, imprisonment, or death)

National and International Law

Although the focus of this book is U.S. business law, increasingly businesspersons in this country engage in transactions that extend beyond our national borders. In these situations, the laws of other nations or the laws governing relationships among nations may come into play. For this reason, those who pursue a career in business today should have an understanding of the global legal environment.

National Law Law that pertains to a particular nation (as opposed to international law).

NATIONAL LAW   The law of a particular nation, such as the United States or Sweden, is **national law.** National law, of course, varies from country to country, because each country's law reflects the interests, customs, activities, and values that are unique to that nation's culture. You will learn about some of the differences among national laws in the *International Perspectives* that appear throughout this text. Even though the laws and legal systems of various countries differ substantially, broad similarities do exist.

Basically, there are two legal systems in today's world. One of these is the common law system of England and the United States, which we have already discussed. The other system is based on Roman civil law, or "code law." The term *civil law,* as used here, refers not to civil as opposed to criminal law but to codified law—an ordered grouping of legal principles enacted into law by a legislature or governing body. In a **civil law system,** the primary source of law is a statutory code, and case precedents are not judicially binding, as they normally are in a common law system. Although judges in a civil law system commonly refer to previous decisions as sources of legal guidance, they are not bound by precedent; in other words, the doctrine of *stare decisis* does not apply.

Civil Law System A system of law derived from that of the Roman Empire and based on a code rather than case law; the predominant system of law in the nations of continental Europe and the nations that were once their colonies. In the United States, Louisiana, because of its historical ties to France, has in part a civil law system.

Exhibit 1–3 lists the countries that today follow either the common law system or the civil law system. Generally, those countries that were once colonies of Great Britain retained their English common law heritage after they achieved their independence. Similarly, the civil law system, which is followed in most of the continental European countries, was retained in the Latin American, African, and Asian countries that were once colonies of the conti-

CIVIL LAW		COMMON LAW	
Argentina	Indonesia	Australia	Nigeria
Austria	Iran	Bangladesh	Singapore
Brazil	Italy	Canada	United Kingdom
Chile	Japan	Ghana	United States
China	Mexico	India	Zambia
Egypt	Poland	Israel	
Finland	South Korea	Jamaica	
France	Sweden	Kenya	
Germany	Tunisia	Malaysia	
Greece	Venezuela	New Zealand	

Exhibit 1–3
The Legal Systems of Nations

nental European nations. Japan and South Africa also have civil law systems, and ingredients of the civil law system are found in the Islamic courts of predominantly Muslim countries. In the United States, the state of Louisiana, because of its historical ties to France, has in part a civil law system. The legal systems of Puerto Rico, Québec, and Scotland are similarly characterized as having elements of the civil law system.

INTERNATIONAL LAW   In contrast to national law, international law applies to more than one nation. **International law** can be defined as a body of written and unwritten laws observed by independent nations and governing the acts of individuals as well as governments. International law is an intermingling of rules and constraints derived from a variety of sources, including the laws of individual nations, the customs that have evolved among nations in their relations with one another, and treaties and international organizations. In essence, international law is the result of centuries-old attempts to reconcile the traditional need of each nation to be the final authority over its own affairs with the desire of nations to benefit economically from trade and harmonious relations with one another.

International Law The law that governs relations among nations. National laws, customs, treaties, and international conferences and organizations are generally considered to be the most important sources of international law.

The key difference between national law and international law is the fact that national law can be enforced by government authorities. If a nation violates an international law, however, the most that other countries or international organizations can do (if persuasive tactics fail) is resort to coercive actions against the violating nation. Coercive actions range from severance of diplomatic relations and boycotts to, at the last resort, war. We examine the laws governing international business transactions in Chapter 2.

Cyberlaw

Increasingly, traditional laws are being adapted and applied to new legal issues stemming from the use of a new medium—the Internet—to conduct business transactions. Additionally, new laws are being created to deal specifically with such issues. Frequently, people use the term **cyberlaw** to designate the emerging body of law (consisting of court decisions, newly enacted or amended statutes, and so on) that governs cyberspace transactions. Note that cyberlaw is not really a classification of law; rather, it is an informal term used to describe how traditional classifications of law, such as civil law and criminal law, are being applied to online activities.

Cyberlaw An informal term used to refer to all laws governing electronic communications and transactions, particularly those conducted via the Internet.

Anyone preparing to enter today's business world will find it useful to know how old and new laws are being applied to activities conducted online, such as advertising, contracting, banking, filing documents with the courts or government agencies, employment relations, and a variety of other transactions. For that reason, Chapters 5 and 14 of this text are devoted entirely to this topic. Sections in other chapters and special features throughout the text also focus on how technology, particularly the use of the Internet, is transforming the business world. (One business group that is being dramatically affected by new technology is the music recording industry—see this chapter's *Legal E-nvironment* for a discussion of this issue and its implications.)

Legal *e*-nvironment

The Internet, MP3.com, File-Sharing, and the Law

The intersection of the law and cyberspace, and the dramatic tension arising therefrom, is nowhere more evident than in the music world. Owners of intellectual property (see Chapter 11), such as songwriters, record labels, musicians, and the like, have long been protected by copyright legislation. That is to say, if a band creates a set of songs and a record label publishes the album, both are protected by copyright law. Anyone attempting to produce copies of copyrighted materials can be sued, unless such usage is considered personal. Enter the expanding use of the Internet and file-compression technology.

MP3.com versus the Record Labels

After the Internet became popular, it was not long before a few enterprising programmers decided to create software to compress large data files, particularly those associated with music. The reduced size of such files allows for the feasibility of transmitting music over the Internet. The compression system most in use is called MP3. A heavily trafficked site, **http://www.mp3.com**, compresses files for free, downloading tens of thousands of well-known music tracks. With the advent of small portable MP3 players, the digital copying music revolution went into full swing. It received an increased boost with the marketing of sophisticated portable players, with 6- to 10-gigabyte hard drives, that are capable of downloading, categorizing, and playing 1,500 or more songs.

Of course, music artists and recording companies were not pleased. Five recording companies sued MP3.com, Inc., a company based in San Diego. Over the course of the lawsuit, the company reached agreements with four of the five major record labels for a reported $20 million payoff to each. In exchange, the company received licenses to allow users to download songs from well-known artists. Universal Music Group (UMG) refused to settle, however, so UMG's suit went forward. The U.S. District Court of New York ruled in favor of Universal.[a] The judge's initial order was a $25,000 penalty for each CD that MP3.com copied and then distributed through its MyMP3.com site.

On the one hand, online music dissemination should slow down because of the *MP3.com* decision. On the other hand, a relatively new way to share files on a much more personal basis, called peer-to-peer (P2P) networking, is causing file-sharing via the Internet to explode.

Enter Napster, Gnutella, and Other File-Sharing Systems

By now, most college students have heard of Napster's Web site (at **http://www.napster.com**), which uses a file-sharing system invented by New Jersey teenager Shawn Fanning. Although the concept is simple, the software developed is complex. No large servers or mainframe computers are involved. Rather, individuals who have downloaded the Napster program (over forty million according to Napster) can share files, particularly music files, with anybody else that has downloaded the program. Those who share their existing files of music with others must, of course, leave their computers on. The reason this is called peer-to-peer file-sharing is that all of the participants are individuals simply using personal PCs.

The recording industry quickly sued Napster.[b] The district court judge hearing the case had no problem issuing an injunction. Judge Marilyn Hall Patel said,

---

a. *UMG Recording, Inc. v. MP3.com*, 2000 WL 1262568 (S.D.N.Y.), Sept. 6, 2000.
b. *A&M Records, Inc. v. Napster*, 114 F.Supp.2d 896 (N.D.Cal. 2000).

Legal *e*-nvironment

"Given the vast scale of Napster use among anonymous individuals, the court finds that downloading and uploading MP3 music files with the assistance of Napster are not private uses. Moreover, the fact that Napster users get for free something they would ordinarily have to buy suggests that they reap economic advantages from Napster use."

In spite of the injunction, Napster use quadrupled during the several months before the court issued its conclusion. On appeal, Napster's attorneys argued that the same logic behind the Supreme Court's decision to allow the videotaping of television programs by individuals[c] should be applied to the Napster case. In the meantime, Napster and one of the plaintiff companies reached a settlement.

Soon after the initial Napster decision, peer-to-peer networking received a boost from chip-making giant Intel. While not officially commenting on Napster and other music file-sharing services, Intel argued that peer-to-peer networking should receive wide adoption by Internet service providers and consumers. Intel created a working group of eighteen companies, including IBM and Hewlett-Packard, to develop standards in this area. Intel envisions consumers and companies

alike creating self-organizing Web communities. These could consist of employees at a single company, family members, or any group with common interests.

Super Audio Compact Discs (SACDs) to the Rescue?

Perhaps the introduction of SACDs may reduce (but never eliminate) the copyright infringement issue with respect to works of music shared on the Internet. This new CD format not only offers a higher quality of reproduction; it cannot be copied. It uses pit signal processing (PSP), which allows for recording on the surface of each CD a group of microscopic chips that constitute an invisible marking detectable by CD players. Pirated discs would generate no sound. This relatively new format, however, must be widely adopted by consumers if it is to have an impact on the transmission of music files over the Internet.

For Critical Analysis: *Many new bands claim that they have benefited from MP3 and Napster, arguing that they could not have become well known otherwise. Is there a way to reconcile the copyright-protection concerns of the major music labels with the desires of struggling musicians to seek to improve their popularity?*

---

c. *Sony Corp. v. Universal City Studios,* 464 U.S. 417, 104 S.Ct. 774, 78 L.Ed.2d 574 (1984).

Key Terms

Chapter Summary • The Legal and International Foundations

The Nature of Law
(See pages 3–4.)

Law can be defined as a body of rules of conduct with legal force and effect, prescribed by the controlling authority (the government) of a society. Three important schools of legal thought, or legal philosophies, are the following:

1. **Natural law tradition**—One of the oldest and most significant schools of legal thought. Those who believe in natural law hold that there is a universal law applicable to all human beings and that this law is of a higher order than positive, or conventional, law.

2. **Legal positivism**—A school of legal thought centered on the assumption that there is no law higher than the laws created by the government. Laws must be obeyed, even if they are unjust, to prevent anarchy.

3. **Legal realism**—A popular school of legal thought during the 1920s and 1930s that left a lasting imprint on American jurisprudence. Legal realists generally advocated a less abstract and more realistic approach to the law, an approach that would take into account customary practices and the circumstances in which transactions take place.

The Common Law Tradition
(See pages 4–8.)

1. **Common law**—Law that originated in medieval England with the development of a body of rules that were common to (or applied throughout) the land.

2. *Stare decisis*—A doctrine under which judges "stand on decided cases"—or follow the rule of precedent—in deciding cases. *Stare decisis* is the cornerstone of the common law tradition.

3. **Remedies**—

   a. **Remedies at law**—Money or something else of value.

   b. **Remedies in equity**—Remedies that are granted when the remedies at law are unavailable or inadequate. Equitable remedies include specific performance, an injunction, and contract rescission (cancellation).

Sources of American Law
(See pages 9–15.)

1. **Constitutional law**—The law as expressed in the U.S. Constitution and the various state constitutions. The U.S. Constitution is the supreme law of the land. State constitutions are supreme within state borders to the extent that they do not violate the U.S. Constitution or a federal law.

2. **Statutory law**—Laws or ordinances created by federal, state, and local legislatures and governing bodies. None of these laws can violate the U.S. Constitution or the relevant state constitutions. Uniform laws, when adopted by a state legislature, become statutory law in that state.

3. **Administrative law**—The rules, orders, and decisions of federal or state government administrative agencies. Federal administrative agencies are created by enabling legislation enacted by the U.S. Congress. Agency functions include rulemaking, investigation and enforcement, and adjudication.

4. **Case law and common law doctrines**—Judge-made law, including interpretations of constitutional provisions, of statutes enacted by legislatures, and of regulations created by administrative agencies. The common law—the doctrines and principles embodied in case law—governs all areas not covered by statutory law (or agency regulations issued to implement various statutes).

Chapter Summary • The Legal and International Foundations

Classifications of Law (See pages 15–19.)	The law may be broken down according to several classification systems, such as substantive or procedural law, federal or state law, and private or public law. Two broad classifications are civil and criminal law, and national and international law. Cyberlaw is not really a classification of law but a term that is applied to the growing body of case law and statutory law that applies to Internet transactions.

For Review

1. What is the common law tradition?
2. What is a precedent? When might a court depart from precedent?
3. What is the difference between remedies at law and remedies in equity?
4. What is the Uniform Commercial Code?
5. What are some important differences between civil law and criminal law?

Questions and Case Problems

1–1. Philosophy of Law. After World War II, which ended in 1945, an international tribunal of judges convened at Nuremberg, Germany. The judges convicted several Nazi war criminals of "crimes against humanity." Assuming that the Nazis who were convicted had not disobeyed any law of their country and had merely been following their government's (Hitler's) orders, what law had they violated? Explain.

1–2. Legal Systems. What are the key differences between a common law system and a civil law system? Why do some countries have common law systems and others have civil law systems?

1–3. Reading Citations. First read the appendix to this chapter. Assume that you want to read the entire court opinion in the case of *Millennium Enterprises, Inc. v. Millennium Music, LP,* 33 F.Supp.2d 907 (D.Or. 1999). The case considers whether a South Carolina business firm could be sued in Oregon based on the circumstance that its Web site could be accessed in Oregon. Explain specifically where you would find the court's opinion.

1–4. Sources of American Law. This chapter discussed a number of sources of American law. Which source of law takes priority in the following situations, and why?

(a) A federal statute conflicts with the U.S. Constitution.
(b) A federal statute conflicts with a state constitution.
(c) A state statute conflicts with the common law of that state.

(d) A state constitutional amendment conflicts with the U.S. Constitution.
(e) A federal administrative regulation conflicts with a state constitution.

1–5. *Stare Decisis.* In the text of this chapter, we stated that the doctrine of *stare decisis* "became a cornerstone of the English and American judicial systems." What does *stare decisis* mean, and why has this doctrine been so fundamental to the development of our legal tradition?

1–6. Court Opinions. Read through the section entitled "Case Titles and Terminology" in the appendix following this chapter. What is the difference between a concurring opinion and a majority opinion? Between a concurring opinion and a dissenting opinion? Why do judges and justices write concurring and dissenting opinions, given the fact that these opinions will not affect the outcome of the case at hand, which has already been decided by majority vote?

1–7. Statute of Limitations. The equitable principle "Equity aids the vigilant, not those who rest on their rights" means that courts will not aid those who do not pursue a cause of action while the evidence is fresh and while the true facts surrounding the issue can be discovered. State statutes of limitations are based on this principle. Under Article 2 of the Uniform Commercial Code, which has been adopted by virtually all of the states, the statute of limitations governing sales contracts says that parties must bring an action for the breach of a sales contract within four years, although the parties (the seller and the buyer) can reduce this period by agreement to only one year. Which party (the seller or the buyer) would benefit more by a one-year period, and which would benefit more by a four-year period? Discuss.

1–8. Binding versus Persuasive Authority. A county court in Illinois is deciding a case involving an issue that has never been addressed before in that state's courts. The Iowa Supreme Court, however, recently decided a case involving a very similar fact pattern. Is the Illinois court obligated to follow the Iowa Supreme Court's decision on the issue? If the United States Supreme Court had decided a similar case, would that decision be binding on the Illinois court? Explain.

A Question of Ethics and Social Responsibility

1–9. On July 5, 1884, Dudley, Stephens, and Brooks—"all able-bodied English seamen"—and an English teen-age boy were cast adrift in a lifeboat following a storm at sea. They had no water with them in the boat, and all they had for sustenance were two one-pound tins of turnips. On July 24, Dudley proposed that one of the four in the lifeboat be sacrificed to save the others. Stephens agreed with Dudley, but Brooks refused to consent—and the boy was never asked for his opinion. On July 25, Dudley killed the boy, and the three men then fed

on the boy's body and blood. Four days later, the men were rescued by a passing vessel. They were taken to England and tried for the murder of the boy. If the men had not fed on the boy's body, they would probably have died of starvation within the four-day period. The boy, who was in a much weaker condition, would likely have died before the rest. [*Regina v. Dudley and Stephens*, 14 Q.B.D. (Queen's Bench Division, England) 273 (1884)]

1. The basic question in this case is whether the survivors should be subject to penalties under English criminal law, given the men's unusual circumstances. You be the judge, and decide the issue. Give the reasons for your decisions.
2. Should judges ever have the power to look beyond the written "letter of the law" in making their decisions? Why or why not?

For Critical Analysis

1–10. Courts of equity tend to follow general rules or maxims rather than common law precedents, as courts of law do. Some of these maxims were listed in this chapter's *Landmark in the Legal Environment*. Why would equity courts give credence to such general maxims rather than to a hard-and-fast body of law?

Interacting with the Internet

◾ Today, business law professors and students can go online to access information on virtually every topic covered in this text. A good point of departure for online legal research is the Web site for *The Legal and E-Commerce Environment Today,* Third Edition, at **http://leet.westbuslaw.com.** There you will find numerous materials relevant to this text and to the legal environment of business generally, including links to various legal resources on the Web. Additionally, every chapter in this text ends with an *Interacting with the Internet* feature that contains selected Web addresses.

You can access many of the sources of law discussed in Chapter 1 at the FindLaw Web site, which is probably the most comprehensive source of free legal information on the Internet. Go to

http://www.findlaw.com

◾ The Legal Information Institute (LII) at Cornell Law School, which offers extensive information about U.S. law, is also a good starting point for legal research. The URL for this site is

http://www.law.cornell.edu

◾ The Library of Congress offers numerous links to state and federal government resources at

http://www.loc.gov

◾ The Virtual Law Library Index, created and maintained by the Indiana University School of Law, provides an index of legal sources categorized by subject at

http://www.law.indiana.edu

Online Legal Research Exercises

The text's Web site also offers online research exercises. These exercises will help you find and analyze particular types of legal information available at specific Web sites. To access these exercises, go to this book's Web site at **http://leet.westbuslaw.com** and click on "Interactive Study Center." When that page opens, select the relevant chapter to find the exercise or exercises relating to topics in that chapter. The following activity will direct you to some of the important sources of law discussed in Chapter 1:

Activity 1–1: Internet Sources of Law

Before the Test

Go to **http://leet.westbuslaw. com**, the Web site that accompanies this text. Select "Interactive Quizzes." You will find a number of interactive questions relating to this chapter.

chapter

1

Appendix

Finding and Analyzing the Law

The statutes, agency regulations, and case law referred to in this text establish the rights and duties of businesspersons engaged in various types of activities. The cases presented within the following chapters provide you with concise, real-life illustrations of how the courts interpret and apply these laws. Because of the importance of knowing how to find statutory, administrative, and case law, this appendix offers a brief introduction to how these laws are published and to the legal "shorthand" employed in referencing these legal sources.

Finding Statutory and Administrative Law

When Congress passes laws, they are collected in a publication titled *United States Statutes at Large.* When state legislatures pass laws, they are collected in similar state publications. Most frequently, however, laws are referred to in their codified form—that is, the form in which they appear in the federal and state codes.

In these codes, laws are compiled by subject. The *United States Code* (U.S.C.) arranges all existing federal laws of a public and permanent nature by subject. Each of the fifty subjects into which the U.S.C. arranges the laws is given a title and a title number. For example, laws relating to commerce and trade are collected in Title 15, which is titled "Commerce and Trade." Titles are subdivided by sections. A citation to the U.S.C. includes title and section numbers. Thus, a reference to "15 U.S.C. Section 1" means that the statute can be found in Section 1 of Title 15. ("Section" may also be designated by the symbol §, and "Sections" by §§.)

Sometimes a citation includes the abbreviation *et seq.*—as in "15 U.S.C. Sections 1 *et seq.*" The term is an abbreviated form of *et sequitur,* which in Latin means "and the following"; when used in a citation, it refers to sections that concern the same subject as the numbered section and follow it in sequence.

State codes follow the U.S.C. pattern of arranging law by subject. The state codes may be called codes, revisions, compilations, consolidations, general statutes, or statutes, depending on the preference of the states. In some codes, subjects are designated by number. In others, they are designated by name. For example, "13 Pennsylvania Consolidated Statutes Section 1101" means the statute can be found in Title 13, Section 1101, of the Pennsylvania code. "California Commercial Code Section 1101" means the statute can be found under the subject heading "Commercial Code" of the California code in Section 1101. Abbreviations may be used. For example, "13 Pennsylvania Consolidated Statutes Section 1101" may be abbreviated "13 Pa. C.S. § 1101," and "California Commercial Code Section 1101" may be abbreviated "Cal. Com. Code § 1101."

Rules and regulations adopted by federal administrative agencies are compiled in the *Code of Federal Regulations* (C.F.R.). Like the U.S.C., the C.F.R. is divided into fifty titles. Rules within each title are assigned section numbers. A full citation to the C.F.R. includes title and section numbers. For example, a reference to "17 C.F.R. Section 230.504" means that the rule can be found in Section 230.504 of Title 17.

Commercial publications of these laws and regulations are available and are widely used. For example, West Group publishes the *United States Code Annotated* (U.S.C.A.). The U.S.C.A. contains the complete text of laws included in the U.S.C., as well as notes of court decisions that interpret and apply specific sections of the statutes, plus the text of presidential proclamations and executive orders. The U.S.C.A. also includes research aids, such as cross-references to related statutes, historical notes, and library references. A citation to the U.S.C.A. is similar to a citation to the U.S.C.: "15 U.S.C.A. Section 1."

Finding Case Law

Before discussing the case reporting system, we need to look briefly at the court system (which will be discussed in detail in Chapter 3). There are two types of courts in the United States, federal courts and state courts. Both the federal and state court systems consist of several levels, or tiers, of courts. *Trial courts,* in which evidence is presented and testimony given, are on the bottom tier (which also includes lower courts handling specialized issues). Decisions from a trial court can be appealed to a higher court, which commonly would be an intermediate *court of appeals,* or an *appellate court.* Decisions from these intermediate courts of appeals may be appealed to an even higher court, such as a state supreme court or the United States Supreme Court.

State Court Decisions

Most state trial court decisions are not published. Except in New York and a few other states that publish selected opinions of their trial courts, decisions from the state trial courts are merely filed in the office of the clerk of the court, where the decisions are available for public inspection. Written decisions of the appellate, or reviewing, courts, however, are published and distributed. The reported appellate decisions are published in volumes called *reports* or *reporters,* which are numbered consecutively. State appellate court decisions are found in the state reporters of that particular state.

Additionally, state court opinions appear in regional units of the *National Reporter System,* published by West Group. Most lawyers and libraries have the West reporters because they report cases more quickly and are distributed more widely than the state-published reports. In fact, many states have eliminated their own reporters in favor of West's National Reporter System. The National Reporter System divides the states into the following geographical areas: *Atlantic* (A. or A.2d), *South Eastern* (S.E. or S.E.2d), *South Western* (S.W. or S.W.2d), *North Western* (N.W. or N.W.2d), *North Eastern* (N.E. or N.E.2d), *Southern* (So. or So.2d), and *Pacific* (P. or P.2d). (The *2d* in the abbreviations refers to *Second Series.* In the near future, the designation *3d,* for *Third Series,* will be used for some of the regional reporters.) The states included in each of these regional divisions are indicated in Exhibit 1A–1 on the next page, which illustrates West's National Reporter System.

Exhibit 1A-1   West's National Reporter System—Regional/Federal

Regional Reporters	Coverage Beginning	Coverage
Atlantic Reporter (A. or A.2d)	1885	Connecticut, Delaware, Maine, Maryland, New Hampshire, New Jersey, Pennsylvania, Rhode Island, Vermont, and District of Columbia.
North Eastern Reporter (N.E. or N.E.2d)	1885	Illinois, Indiana, Massachusetts, New York, and Ohio.
North Western Reporter (N.W. or N.W.2d)	1879	Iowa, Michigan, Minnesota, Nebraska, North Dakota, South Dakota, and Wisconsin.
Pacific Reporter (P. or P.2d)	1883	Alaska, Arizona, California, Colorado, Hawaii, Idaho, Kansas, Montana, Nevada, New Mexico, Oklahoma, Oregon, Utah, Washington, and Wyoming.
South Eastern Reporter (S.E. or S.E.2d)	1887	Georgia, North Carolina, South Carolina, Virginia, and West Virginia.
South Western Reporter (S.W. or S.W.2d)	1886	Arkansas, Kentucky, Missouri, Tennessee, and Texas.
Southern Reporter (So. or So.2d)	1887	Alabama, Florida, Louisiana, and Mississippi.

Federal Reporters		
Federal Reporter (F., F.2d, or F.3d)	1880	U.S. Circuit Court from 1880 to 1912; U.S. Commerce Court from 1911 to 1913; U.S. District Courts from 1880 to 1932; U.S. Court of Claims (now called U.S. Court of Federal Claims) from 1929 to 1932 and since 1960; U.S. Court of Appeals since 1891; U.S. Court of Customs and Patent Appeals since 1929; and U.S. Emergency Court of Appeals since 1943.
Federal Supplement (F.Supp.)	1932	U.S. Court of Claims from 1932 to 1960; U.S. District Courts since 1932; and U.S. Customs Court since 1956.
Federal Rules Decisions (F.R.D.)	1939	U.S. District Courts involving the Federal Rules of Civil Procedure since 1939 and Federal Rules of Criminal Procedure since 1946.
Supreme Court Reporter (S.Ct.)	1882	U.S. Supreme Court since the October term of 1882.
Bankruptcy Reporter (Bankr.)	1980	Bankruptcy decisions of U.S. Bankruptcy Courts, U.S. District Courts, U.S. Courts of Appeals, and U.S. Supreme Court.
Military Justice Reporter (M.J.)	1978	U.S. Court of Military Appeals and Courts of Military Review for the Army, Navy, Air Force, and Coast Guard.

NATIONAL REPORTER SYSTEM MAP

After appellate decisions have been published, they are normally referred to (cited) by the name of the case; the volume, name, and page number of the state's official reporter (if different from West's National Reporter System); the volume, unit, and page number of the *National Reporter;* and the volume, name, and page number of any other selected reporter. This information is included in the *citation.* (Citing a reporter by volume number, name, and page number, in that order, is common to all citations.) When more than one reporter is cited for the same case, each reference is called a *parallel citation.* For example, consider the following case: *State v. Ollens,* 89 Wash.App. 437, 949 P.2d 407 (1998). We see that the opinion in this case may be found in Volume 89 of the official *Washington Appellate Reports,* on page 437. The parallel citation is to Volume 949 of the *Pacific Reporter, Second Series,* page 407. In presenting appellate opinions in this text, in addition to the reporter, we give the name of the court hearing the case and the year of the court's decision.

A few of the states—including those with intermediate appellate courts, such as California, Illinois, and New York—have more than one reporter for opinions given by courts within their states. Sample citations from these courts, as well as others, are listed and explained in Exhibit 1A–2 on page 28.

Federal Court Decisions

Federal district court decisions are published unofficially in West's *Federal Supplement* (F.Supp.), and opinions from the circuit courts of appeals (federal reviewing courts) are reported unofficially in West's *Federal Reporter* (F., F.2d, or F.3d). Cases concerning federal bankruptcy law are published unofficially in West's *Bankruptcy Reporter* (Bankr.). The official edition of United States Supreme Court decisions is the *United States Reports* (U.S.), which is published by the federal government. Unofficial editions of Supreme Court cases include West's *Supreme Court Reporter* (S.Ct.) and the *Lawyers' Edition of the Supreme Court Reports* (L.Ed. or L.Ed.2d). Sample citations for federal court decisions are also listed and explained in Exhibit 1A–2.

Old Case Law

On a few occasions, this text cites opinions from old, classic cases dating to the nineteenth century or earlier; some of these are from the English courts. The citations to these cases appear not to conform to the descriptions given above, because the reporters in which they were published have since been replaced.

Reading and Understanding Case Law

The cases in this text have been condensed from the full text of the courts' opinions and paraphrased by the authors. For those wishing to review court cases for future research projects or to gain additional legal information, the following sections will provide useful insights into how to read and understand case law.

Case Titles and Terminology

The title of a case, such as *Adams v. Jones,* indicates the names of the parties to the lawsuit. The *v.* in the case title stands for *versus,* which means "against." In the trial court, Adams was the plaintiff—the person who filed the suit.

Exhibit 1A-2 **How to Read Citations**

State Courts

256 Neb. 170, 589 N.W.2d 318 (1999)[a]

N.W. is the abbreviation for West's publication of state court decisions rendered in the *North Western Reporter* of the National Reporter System. *2d* indicates that this case was included in the *Second Series* of that reporter. The number 589 refers to the volume number of the reporter; the number 318 refers to the first page in that volume on which this case can be found.

Neb. is an abbreviation for *Nebraska Reports,* Nebraska's official reports of the decisions of its highest court, the Nebraska Supreme Court.

75 Cal.App.4th 500, 89 Cal.Rptr.2d 146 (1999)

Cal.Rptr. is the abbreviation for West's unofficial reports, titled *California Reporter*, of the decisions of California courts.

85 N.Y.2d 549, 650 N.E.2d 829, 626 N.Y.S.2d 982 (1995)

N.Y.S. is the abbreviation for West's unofficial reports, titled *New York Supplement*, of the decisions of New York courts.

N.Y. is the abbreviation for *New York Reports,* New York's official reports of the decisions of its court of appeals. The New York Court of Appeals is the state's highest court, analogous to other states' supreme courts. In New York, a supreme court is a trial court.

236 Ga.App. 582, 512 S.E.2d 27 (1999)

Ga.App. is the abbreviation for *Georgia Appeals Reports,* Georgia's official reports of the decisions of its court of appeals.

Federal Courts

___ U.S. ___, 119 S.Ct. 1961, 144 L.Ed.2d 319 (1999)

L.Ed. is an abbreviation for *Lawyers' Edition of the Supreme Court Reports,* an unofficial edition of decisions of the United States Supreme Court.

S.Ct. is the abbreviation for West's unofficial reports, titled *Supreme Court Reporter*, of decisions of the United States Supreme Court.

U.S. is the abbreviation for *United States Reports,* the official edition of the decisions of the United States Supreme Court. Volume and page numbers are not included in this citation because they have not yet been assigned.

a. The case names have been deleted from these citations to emphasize the publications. It should be kept in mind, however, that the name of a case is as important as the specific numbers of the volumes in which it is found. If a citation is incorrect, the correct citation may be found in a publication's index of case names. The date of a case is also important because, in addition to providing a check on errors in citations, the value of a recent case as an authority is likely to be greater than that of an earlier case.

Exhibit 1A–2 How to Read Citations (Continued)

Federal Courts (continued)

177 F.3d 114 (2d Cir. 1999)

> *2d Cir.* is an abbreviation denoting that this case was decided in the United States Court of Appeals for the Second Circuit.

38 F.Supp.2d 1233 (D.Colo. 1999)

> *D.Colo.* is an abbreviation indicating that the United States District Court for the District of Colorado decided this case.

English Courts

9 Exch. 341, 156 Eng.Rep. 145 (1854)

> *Eng.Rep.* is an abbreviation for *English Reports, Full Reprint,* a series of reports containing selected decisions made in English courts between 1378 and 1865.

> *Exch.* is an abbreviation for *English Exchequer Reports,* which includes the original reports of cases decided in England's Court of Exchequer.

Statutory and Other Citations

18 U.S.C. Section 1961(1)(A)

> *U.S.C.* denotes *United States Code,* the codification of *United States Statutes at Large.* The number 18 refers to the statute's U.S.C. title number and 1961 to its section number within that title. The number 1 refers to a subsection within the section and the letter A to a subdivision within the subsection.

UCC 2–206(1)(b)

> *UCC* is an abbreviation for *Uniform Commercial Code.* The first number 2 is a reference to an article of the UCC and 206 to a section within that article. The number 1 refers to a subsection within the section and the letter b to a subdivision within the subsection.

Restatement (Second) of Contracts, Section 162

> *Restatement (Second) of Contracts* refers to the second edition of the American Law Institute's *Restatement of the Law of Contracts.* The number 162 refers to a specific section.

17 C.F.R. Section 230.505

> *C.F.R.* is an abbreviation for *Code of Federal Regulations,* a compilation of federal administrative regulations. The number 17 designates the regulation's title number, and 230.505 designates a specific section within that title.

Exhibit 1A–2 How to Read Citations (Continued)

Westlaw® Citations

2001 WL 12345

WL is an abbreviation for Westlaw®. The number 2001 is the year of the document that can be found with this citation in the Westlaw® database. The number 12345 is a number assigned to a specific document. A higher number indicates that a document was added to the Westlaw® database later in the year.

Uniform Resource Locators[b]

www.westlaw.com

The suffix *com* is the top-level domain (TLD) for this Web site. The TLD *com* is an abbreviation for "commercial," which means that a for-profit entity hosts (maintains or supports) this Web site.

westlaw is the host name—the part of the domain name selected by the organization that registered the name. In this case, West Group registered the name. This Internet site is the Westlaw database on the Web.

www is an abbreviation for "World Wide Web." The Web is a system of Internet servers[c] that support documents formatted in *HTML* (hypertext markup language). HTML supports links to text, graphics, and audio and video files.

www.uscourts.gov

This is the "Federal Judiciary Home Page." The host is the Administrative Office of the U.S. Courts. The TLD *gov* is an abbreviation for "government." This Web site includes information and links from, and about, the federal courts.

www.law.cornell.edu/index.html

This part of a URL points to a Web page or file at a specific location within the host's domain. This page, at this Web site, is a menu with links to documents within the domain and to other Internet resources.

This is the host name for a Web site that contains the Internet publications of the Legal Information Institute (LII), which is a part of Cornell Law School. The LII site includes a variety of legal materials and links to other legal resources on the Internet. The TLD *edu* is an abbreviation for "educational institution" (a school or a university).

www.ipl.org.ref./RR

RR is an abbreviation for this Web site's "Ready Reference Collection," which contains links to a variety of Internet resources.

ref is an abbreviation for "Internet Public Library Reference Center," which is a map of the topics into which the links at this Web site have been categorized.

ipl is an abbreviation for Internet Public Library, which is an online service that provides reference resources and links to other information services on the Web. The IPL is supported chiefly by the School of Information at the University of Michigan. The TLD *org* is an abbreviation for "organization (nonprofit)."

b. The basic form for a URL is "service://hostname/path." The Internet service for all of the URLs in this text is *http* (hypertext transfer protocol). Most Web browsers will add this prefix automatically when a user enters a host name or a hostname/path.

c. A *server* is hardware that manages the resources on a network. For example, a network server is a computer that manages the traffic on the network, and a print server is a computer that manages one or more printers.

Jones was the defendant. If the case is appealed, however, the appellate court will sometimes place the name of the party appealing the decision first, so that the case may be called *Jones v. Adams*. Because some reviewing courts retain the trial court order of names, it is often impossible to distinguish the plaintiff from the defendant in the title of a reported appellate court decision. You must carefully read the facts of each case to identify each party.

The following terms and phrases are frequently encountered in court opinions and legal publications. Because it is important to understand what is meant by these terms and phrases, we define and discuss them here.

PLAINTIFFS AND DEFENDANTS   As mentioned in Chapter 1, the plaintiff in a lawsuit is the party that initiates the action. The defendant is the party against which a lawsuit is brought. Lawsuits frequently involve more than one plaintiff and/or defendant.

APPELLANTS AND APPELLEES   The *appellant* is the party that appeals a case to another court or jurisdiction from the court or jurisdiction in which the case was originally brought. Sometimes, an appellant that appeals a judgment is referred to as the *petitioner.* The *appellee* is the party against which the appeal is taken. Sometimes, the appellee is referred to as the *respondent.*

JUDGES AND JUSTICES   The terms *judge* and *justice* are usually synonymous and represent two designations given to judges in various courts. All members of the United States Supreme Court, for example, are referred to as justices. And justice is the formal title usually given to judges of appellate courts, although this is not always the case. In New York, a justice is a judge of the trial court (which is called the Supreme Court), and a member of the Court of Appeals (the state's highest court) is called a judge. The term *justice* is commonly abbreviated to J., and *justices* to JJ. A Supreme Court case might refer to Justice O'Connor as O'Connor, J., or to Chief Justice Rehnquist as Rehnquist, C.J.

DECISIONS AND OPINIONS   Most decisions reached by reviewing, or appellate, courts are explained in written *opinions.* The opinion contains the court's reasons for its decision, the rules of law that apply, and the judgment. When all judges or justices unanimously agree on an opinion, the opinion is written for the entire court and can be deemed a *unanimous opinion.* When there is not a unanimous opinion, a *majority opinion* is written, outlining the views of the majority of the judges or justices deciding the case.

Often, a judge or justice who feels strongly about making or emphasizing a point that was not made or emphasized in the unanimous or majority opinion will write a *concurring opinion.* That means the judge or justice agrees (concurs) with the judgment given in the unanimous or majority opinion but for different reasons. In other than unanimous opinions, a *dissenting opinion* is usually written by a judge or justice who does not agree with the majority. The dissenting opinion is important because it may form the basis of the arguments used years later in overruling the precedential majority opinion. Occasionally, a court issues a *per curiam* (Latin for "of the court") opinion, and there is no indication of which judge or justice authored the opinion.

A Sample Court Case

To illustrate the various elements contained in a court opinion, we present in Exhibit 1A–3 an annotated court opinion. The opinion is from an actual case that the U.S. Court of Appeals for the Second Circuit decided in 2000. Federal Express Corporation initiated the lawsuit against Federal Espresso, Inc., and others, claiming in part that the name "Federal Espresso" infringed on the Federal Express trademark. The court denied the plaintiff's request for a *preliminary injunction* (an injunction granted at the beginning of a suit to restrain the defendant from doing some act, the right to which is in dispute). Thus, the issue before the appellate court was whether the trial court erred in refusing to grant the injunction.

You will note that triple asterisks (* * *) and quadruple asterisks (* * * *) frequently appear in the opinion. The triple asterisks indicate that we have deleted a few words or sentences from the opinion for the sake of readability or brevity. Quadruple asterisks mean that an entire paragraph (or more) has been omitted. Additionally, when the opinion cites another case or legal source, the citation to the case or other source has been omitted to save space and to improve the flow of the text. These editorial practices are continued in the other court opinions presented in this text. In addition, whenever we present a court opinion that includes a term or phrase that may not be readily understandable, a bracketed definition or paraphrase has been added.

Knowing how to read and understand court opinions and the legal reasoning used by the courts is an essential step in undertaking accurate legal research. Yet a further step is "briefing," or summarizing, the case. Legal researchers routinely brief cases by reducing the texts of the opinions to their essential elements. Instructions on how to brief a case are given in Appendix A, which also includes a briefed version of the sample court case presented in Exhibit 1A–3.

The Supreme Court building in Washington, D.C.

Exhibit 1A–3 A Sample Court Case

FEDERAL EXPRESS CORP. v.
FEDERAL ESPRESSO, INC.
United States Court of Appeals, Second Circuit, 2000.
201 F.3d 168.

This line gives the name of the judge who authored the opinion of the court.	KEARSE, Circuit Judge.

* * * *

I. BACKGROUND

The court divides the opinion into three parts, headed by roman numerals. The first part of the opinion summarizes the factual background of the case.	* * * Federal Express, incorporated in 1972, invented the overnight shipping business. It has used the name "Federal Express" since 1973. * * * Federal Express currently has 140,000 employees, ships 2.9 million packages per day, and has annual revenues of more than \$11 billion.

Federal Express provides service in at least 210 countries * * * .

* * * *

In March 1994, defendants Anna Dobbs ("Dobbs") and David J. Ruston, her brother, formed a business called New York Espresso in Syracuse, New York, for the wholesale distribution of commercial espresso machines. In April 1994, Dobbs, her husband defendant John Dobbs, and Ruston decided to change the name of the business from New York Espresso to "Federal Espresso." * * *

* * * [I]n November 1995, Dobbs opened a coffee shop, called "Federal Espresso," [in] Syracuse * * * .

* * * *

The unauthorized use or imitation of another's trademark.	Defendants opened a second store * * * in August 1997. * * *
	* * * Federal Express commenced the present action in August 1997. It principally asserted claims of * * * **trademark infringement**
A doctrine that protects a trademark from infringement by another party even when there is no competition or likelihood of confusion, such as when products are dissimilar.	* * * and claims of **dilution** of the distinctive quality of its famous mark * * * ; and it moved for a preliminary injunction.
A federal trial court in which a lawsuit is initiated.	* * * [T]he **district court denied the motion** * * * .

* * * *

II. DISCUSSION

The decision of the trial court, from which the appeal was taken.	* * * [A] party seeking a preliminary injunction must demonstrate (1) the likelihood of **irreparable injury** in the absence of such an injunction, and (2) * * * likelihood of success on the **merits** * * * .
The second major section of the opinion analyzes the issue before the court.	

* * * *

A wrong of a repeated and continuing nature for which damages are difficult to estimate.	* * * The hallmark of [trademark] infringement * * * is **likelihood of confusion.**
The substance, elements, or grounds of a cause of action.	
Likelihood of confusion occurs when a substantial number of ordinarily prudent purchasers are likely to be misled or confused as to the source of a product.	

Exhibit 1A–3   **A Sample Court Case (Continued)**

A *presumption* is an assumption of fact that the law requires to be made from another fact.

To make apparent or clear, by evidence; to prove.

To justify or call for; to deserve.

Impending; near at hand; on the point of happening.

The final section of the opinion, in which the court gives its order.

* * * [P]roof of a likelihood of confusion would create a **presumption** of irreparable harm, and thus a plaintiff would not need to prove such harm independently. By the same token, however, if the plaintiff does not **show** likelihood of success on the merits, it cannot obtain a preliminary injunction without making an independent showing of likely irreparable harm.

As to Federal Express's claims of trademark infringement, we have no difficulty with the district court's ruling that Federal Express did not show likelihood of confusion and hence did not show that it was likely to succeed on the merits of those claims. * * * Accordingly, since Federal Express did not make any independent showing of likelihood of irreparable harm, the trademark infringement claims did not **warrant** the granting of a preliminary injunction.

* * * *

The type of dilution pertinent to the present case is "blurring," a process that may occur where the defendant uses or modifies the plaintiff's trademark to identify the defendant's goods and services, raising the possibility that the mark will lose its ability to serve as a unique identifier of the plaintiff's product. * * *

* * * *

* * * Here, * * * the principal products—coffee and overnight delivery service—are dissimilar; there would seem to be little likelihood of confusion; and while Federal Express is a vast organization, operating in 210 countries, employing 140,000 persons, and grossing more than \$11 billion annually, defendants are three individuals with two stores in Syracuse. * * * The court was entitled to conclude, given these facts and the tiny extent of the overlap among customers of Federal Express and Federal Espresso, that dilution was not **imminent** and that a preliminary injunction was not needed.

* * * *

III. CONCLUSION

* * * The order of the district court denying a preliminary injunction is affirmed.

Ethics and Social Responsibility

chapter objectives

After reading this chapter, you should be able to:

1. Define business ethics and its relationship to personal ethics.

2. Explain the relationship between the law and ethics.

3. Compare and contrast duty-based ethics and utilitarian ethics.

4. Discuss the questions that are typically considered in the ethical decision-making process.

5. Identify the various groups to whom corporations are perceived to owe duties.

Business owners and managers traditionally have had to ensure that their profit-making activities do not exceed the ethical boundaries established by society. In the past, though, these boundaries were often regarded as being coterminous with the law—that is, if something was legal, it was ethical. Shady business dealings were regarded as "just business" more often than not.

In the last few decades, however, the ethical boundaries within which business firms must operate have narrowed significantly. As indicated in the quotation alongside, "New occasions teach new duties," and in today's rights-conscious world a business firm that decides it has no duties other than those prescribed by law may find it difficult to survive. If a firm's behavior is perceived as unethical—even though it may be legal—that firm may suffer negative publicity, boycotts, and lost profits.

In preparing for a career in business, you will find that a background in business ethics and a commitment to ethical behavior is just as important as a knowledge of the specific laws that you will read about in this text. In this chapter, we first examine the nature of business ethics and some of the sources of ethical standards that have guided others in their business decision making. We then look at some of the obstacles to ethical behavior faced by businesspersons. In the remaining pages of the chapter, which deal with corporate social responsibility, we explore the following question: How can businesspersons act in an ethically responsible manner and at the same time make profits for their firms or their firms' owners?

The Nature of Business Ethics

To understand the nature of business ethics, we need to define what is meant by ethics generally. **Ethics** can be defined as the study of what constitutes right or wrong behavior. It is the branch of philosophy that focuses on morality and the way in which moral principles are applied to daily life. Ethics has to do with questions relating to the fairness, justness, rightness, or wrongness of an action. What is fair? What is just? What is the right thing to do in this situation?—these are essentially ethical questions.

Ethics Moral principles and values applied to social behavior.

Often, moral principles serve as the guiding force in an individual's personal ethical system. Although the terms *ethical* and *moral* are often used interchangeably, the terms refer to slightly different concepts. Whereas ethics has to do with the philosophical, rational basis for morality, morals are often defined as universal rules or guidelines (such as those rooted in religious precepts) that determine our actions and character.

Defining Business Ethics

Business Ethics Ethics in a business context; a consensus of what constitutes right or wrong behavior in the world of business and the application of moral principles to situations that arise in a business setting.

Business ethics focuses on what constitutes ethical behavior in the world of business. Personal ethical standards, of course, play an important role in determining what is or is not ethical, or appropriate, business behavior. Business activities are just one part of the human enterprise, and the ethical standards that guide our behavior as, say, mothers, fathers, or students apply equally well to our activities as businesspersons. Businesspersons, though, often must address more complex ethical issues and conflicts in the workplace than they do in their personal lives—as you will learn in this chapter and throughout this book.

Business Ethics and the Law

Because the law reflects and codifies a society's ethical values, many of our ethical decisions are made for us—by our laws. Nevertheless, simply obeying the law does not fulfill all ethical obligations. In the interest of preserving personal freedom, as well as for practical reasons, the law does not—and cannot—codify all ethical requirements. No law says, for example, that it is *illegal* to lie to one's family, but it may be *unethical* to do so.

Likewise, in the business world, numerous actions might be unethical but not necessarily illegal. Even though it may be convenient for businesspersons to satisfy themselves by mere compliance with the law, such an approach may not always yield ethical outcomes. For example, a pharmaceutical company may be banned from marketing a particular drug in the United States because of the drug's adverse side effects. Yet no law prohibits the company from selling the drug in foreign markets—even though some consumers in those markets may suffer serious health problems as a result of using the drug. At issue here is not whether it would be legal to market the drug in other countries but whether it would *ethical* to do so.

In short, the law has its limits—it cannot make all our ethical decisions for us. When it does not, ethical standards must guide the decision-making process.

Sources of Ethical Standards

Religious and philosophical inquiry into the nature of "the good" is an age-old pursuit. Broadly speaking, though, ethical reasoning relating to business traditionally has been characterized by two fundamental approaches. One approach defines ethical behavior in terms of *duty*. The other approach determines what is ethical in terms of the *consequences*, or outcome, of any given action. We examine each of these approaches here.

Duty-Based Ethics

Is it wrong to cheat on an examination, if nobody will ever know that you cheated and if it helps you get into law school so that you can eventually volunteer your legal services to the poor and needy? Is it wrong to lie to your parents if the lie harms nobody but helps to keep family relations congenial? These kinds of ethical questions implicitly weigh the "end" of an action against the "means" used to attain that end. If you believe that you have an ethical *duty* not to lie or cheat, however, then lying and cheating can never be justified by the consequences, no matter how benevolent or desirable those consequences may be. Duty-based ethics may be rooted in religious precepts or philosophical reasoning.

RELIGION   Duty-based ethical standards are often derived from moral principles rooted in religious sources. For example, in the Judeo-Christian tradition, the Ten Commandments of the Old Testament establish rules for moral action. Other religions have their own sources of revealed truth; for example, the Koran in the Muslim world. Within the confines of their influence, moral principles are universal and *absolute*—they are not to be questioned.
● **Example 2.1** Consider one of the Ten Commandments: "Thou shalt not steal." This is an absolute mandate. Even a benevolent motive for stealing

(such as Robin Hood's) cannot justify the act, because the act itself is inherently immoral and thus wrong. When an act is prohibited by religious teachings that serve as the foundation of a person's moral or ethical standards, the act is unethical for that person and should not be undertaken, regardless of its consequences.●

Ethical standards based on religious teachings also may involve an element of compassion. Therefore, even though it might be profitable for a firm to lay off a less productive employee, if that employee were to find it difficult to find employment elsewhere and his or her family were to suffer as a result, this potential suffering would be given substantial weight by the decision makers. Compassionate treatment of others is also mandated—to a certain extent, at least—by the Golden Rule of the ancients ("Do unto others as you would have them do unto you"), which has been adopted by most religions.

KANTIAN PHILOSOPHY   Ethical standards based on a concept of duty may also be derived solely from philosophical principles. Immanuel Kant (1724–1804), for example, identified some general guiding principles for moral behavior based on what he believed to be the fundamental nature of human beings. Kant held that it is rational to assume that human beings are qualitatively different from other physical objects occupying space. Persons are endowed with moral integrity and the capacity to reason and conduct their affairs rationally. Therefore, their thoughts and actions should be respected. When human beings are treated merely as a means to an end, they are being regarded as the equivalent of objects and are being denied their basic humanity.

A central postulate in Kantian ethics is that individuals should evaluate their actions in light of the consequences that would follow if everyone in society acted in the same way. This **categorical imperative** can be applied to any action. For example, say that you are deciding whether to cheat on an examination. If you have adopted Kant's categorical imperative, you will decide not to cheat, because if everyone cheated, the examination would be meaningless.

THE PRINCIPLE OF RIGHTS   Duty-based ethical standards imply that human beings have basic rights, because a duty cannot exist without a corresponding right. For example, the commandment "Thou shalt not kill" implies that individuals have a right to live. Additionally, religious ethics may involve a rights component because of the belief—characteristic of many religions—that an individual is "made in the image of God" or "Allah." This belief confers on the individual great dignity as a person. For one who holds this belief, not to respect that dignity—and the rights and status that flow from it—would be morally wrong. Kantian ethics also implies fundamental rights based on the personal dignity of each individual. Just as individuals have a duty not to treat others as means to an end, so individuals have a right to have their status and moral integrity as human beings treated with respect.

The principle that human beings have certain fundamental rights (to life, freedom, and the pursuit of happiness, for example) is deeply embedded in Western culture. As discussed in Chapter 1, the natural law tradition embraces the concept that certain actions (such as killing another person) are morally wrong because they are contrary to nature (the natural desire to continue living). Those who adhere to this **principle of rights,** or "rights theory," believe that a key factor in determining whether a business decision is ethical is how

Categorical Imperative
A concept developed by the philosopher Immanuel Kant as an ethical guideline for behavior. In deciding whether an action is right or wrong, or desirable or undesirable, a person should evaluate the action in terms of what would happen if everybody else in the same situation, or category, acted the same way.

Principle of Rights The principle that human beings have certain fundamental rights (to life, freedom, and the pursuit of happiness, for example). Those who adhere to this "rights theory" believe that a key factor in determining whether a business decision is ethical is how that decision affects the rights of others. These others include the firm's owners, its employees, the consumers of its products or services, it suppliers, the community in which it does business, and society as a whole.

that decision affects the rights of others. These others include the firm's owners, its employees, the consumers of its products or services, its suppliers, the community in which it does business, and society as a whole.

Outcome-Based Ethics

"Thou shalt act so as to generate the greatest good for the greatest number." This is a paraphrase of the major premise of the utilitarian approach to ethics. **Utilitarianism** is a philosophical theory first developed by Jeremy Bentham (1748–1832) and then advanced, with some modifications, by John Stuart Mill (1806–1873)—both British philosophers. In contrast to duty-based ethics, utilitarianism is outcome oriented. It focuses on the consequences of an action, not on the nature of the action itself or on any set of preestablished moral values or religious beliefs.

Under a utilitarian model of ethics, an action is morally correct, or "right," when, among the people it affects, it produces the greatest amount of good for the greatest number. When an action affects the majority adversely, it is morally wrong. Applying the utilitarian theory thus requires (1) a determination of which individuals will be affected by the action in question; (2) a **cost-benefit analysis**—an assessment of the negative and positive effects of alternative actions on these individuals; and (3) a choice among alternative actions that will produce maximum societal utility (the greatest positive benefits for the greatest number of individuals).

The utilitarian approach to decision making commonly is employed by businesses, as well as by individuals. Weighing the consequences of a decision in terms of its costs and benefits for everyone affected by it is a useful analytical tool in the decision-making process. At the same time, utilitarianism is often criticized because it tends to focus on society as a whole rather than on individual human rights. For example, from a utilitarian standpoint, it might be ethically acceptable to test drugs or medicines on human beings because presumably a majority of the population would benefit from the experiments. If, however, one accepts the principle that each individual has basic human rights (to life, freedom, and the pursuit of happiness), then an action that deprives an individual or group of individuals of these rights—even for the greater good of society—is ethically unacceptable. No amount of cost-benefit analysis can justify the action.

Ethical Decision Making

Most major companies today ask three questions about any action before it is undertaken: Is the action profitable? Is it legal? Is it ethical? The first prong of this test for business decision making—determining whether a given course of action will be profitable—is foremost. After all, for-profit firms remain in business only if they make a profit. If the action would not be profitable, it probably will not be undertaken. If the action would be profitable, then the decision makers need to evaluate whether it also would be legal and ethical.

Is the Contemplated Action Legal?

In today's business world, legal compliance usually is regarded as the *moral minimum*. In other words, the minimal acceptable standard for ethical business behavior is compliance with the law.

Utilitarianism An approach to ethical reasoning in which ethically correct behavior is not related to any absolute ethical or moral values but to an evaluation of the consequences of a given action on those who will be affected by it. In utilitarian reasoning, a "good" decision is one that results in the greatest good for the greatest number of people affected by the decision.

Cost-Benefit Analysis A decision-making technique that involves weighing the costs of a given action against the benefits of the action.

Be Careful Ethical concepts about what is right and what is wrong can change.

A lab worker conducts research for the development of a drug. If the drug proves beneficial to most people but adverse to a few, would it, under a utilitarian model of ethics, be marketed?

It may seem that answering a question concerning the legality of a given action should be simple. Either something is legal or it is not. In fact, one of the major challenges businesspersons face is that the legality of a particular action is not always clear. In part, this is because there are so many laws regulating business that it is possible to violate one of them without realizing it. There are also numerous "gray areas" in the law, making it difficult to predict with certainty how a court may apply a given law to a particular action.

LAWS REGULATING BUSINESS   Today's business firms are subject to extensive government regulation. Virtually every action a firm undertakes—from the initial act of going into business to hiring and firing personnel to selling products in the marketplace—is subject to statutory law and to numerous rules and regulations issued by administrative agencies. Furthermore, these rules and regulations are changed or supplemented frequently.

Note A business that examines its conduct, and the conduct of its managers and employees, can prevent unethical and illegal acts.

Determining whether a planned action is legal thus requires the decision makers to keep abreast of the law. Normally, large business firms have attorneys on their staffs to assist them in making key decisions. Small firms must also seek legal advice before making important business decisions—because the consequences of just one violation of a regulatory rule may be costly.

Ignorance of the law will not excuse a business owner or manager from liability for violating a statute or regulation. ● **Example 2.2** In one typical case, the court imposed criminal fines, as well as imprisonment, on a company's supervisory employee for violating a federal environmental act—even though the employee was totally unaware of what was required under the provisions of that act.[1] ●

---

1. *United States v. Hanousek*, 176 F.3d 1116 (9th Cir. 1999).

"GRAY AREAS" IN THE LAW   In many situations, business firms can predict with a fair amount of certainty whether a given action would be legal. For example, firing an employee solely because of that person's race or gender would clearly violate federal laws prohibiting employment discrimination. In some situations, though, the legality of a particular action may be less clear.

   • **Example 2.3** Suppose that a firm decides to launch a new advertising campaign. How far can the firm go in making claims for its product or services? Federal and state laws prohibit firms from engaging in "deceptive advertising." At the federal level, the test for deceptive advertising normally used by the Federal Trade Commission is whether an advertising claim would deceive a "reasonable consumer."[2] At what point, though, would a reasonable consumer be deceived by a particular ad?• Another gray area in the law has to do with product misuse, as will be discussed later in this chapter.

   In short, whether a given action will be deemed legal or illegal often depends on how an administrative agency or a court in a particular jurisdiction decides to interpret and apply the law to the facts and issues of a particular case. Business decision makers thus need to proceed with caution and evaluate the action and its consequences from an ethical perspective. Generally, if a company can demonstrate that it acted in good faith and responsibly in the circumstances, it has a better chance of successfully defending its action in court or before an administrative law judge.

Is the Contemplated Action Ethical?

Usually, in deciding whether a given action would be ethical, a firm's decision makers are guided not only by their own ethical principles and reasoning processes but also by their company's ethical policies and code of conduct. Virtually all large corporations today have established ethical policies or codes of conduct to help guide their executives and managers (and all company personnel) in making decisions. Typically, an ethical code, or code of conduct, will indicate the company's commitment to legal compliance, as well as to the welfare of its employees, suppliers, consumers, and others who may be affected by the company's decisions and practices. • **Example 2.4** Look at the fold-out exhibit in this chapter showing Costco's Code of Ethics. This code clearly indicates Costco's commitment to legal compliance, as well as to the welfare of its members (those who belong to its clubs and purchase its products), its employees, and its vendors (suppliers).•

   In a large corporation, an ethical code usually is just one part of a comprehensive corporate compliance program. Other components of such a program may include a corporate ethics committee, ethical training programs, and internal audits (to monitor compliance with applicable laws and the company's standards of conduct). Some companies also have a special office to which employees can report—in person or perhaps anonymously via an 800 number—suspected improper conduct, including any legal, ethical, or policy violations that may occur.

   By making ethical and legal conduct a top priority, ethical codes and compliance programs help business managers to conduct their firms' affairs responsibly. Still, questions often arise for which there are no clear-cut answers, particularly when they involve conflicting goals. • **Example 2.5** Suppose that

---

2. See Chapter 24 for a discussion of the Federal Trade Commission's role in regulating deceptive trade practices, including misleading advertising.

a company's employees are pressuring management for a wage increase. If the company agrees to increase employees' wages, this will cut into the firm's profits and thus adversely affect the shareholder-owners' interests. The decision to be made here involves not a choice between an ethical and an unethical action but rather a choice between two conflicting goals.•

Public Opinion and Business Decision Making

In the last two decades, and particularly since the advent of the Internet, the actions of business firms have been much more closely scrutinized by the media and various interest groups (groups supporting human rights, animal rights, the environment, consumers, employees, and so on) than they ever were in the past. What this means is that if a corporation undertakes or continues an action deemed to be unethical by one or more of these groups, the firm's "unethical" behavior will probably become widely known. In the interests of preserving their good reputations, business firms thus pay attention to public opinion when making decisions.

•**Example 2.6** As a manager, you might personally be convinced that there is nothing unethical about a certain business action. If a highly vocal interest group believes otherwise, though, you might want to reassess your decision with a view toward preserving the firm's goodwill and reputation in the community. If you decide to pursue the action regardless of public opinion, you may violate your ethical (and legal) duty to act in the firm's best interests.•

Corporate Social Responsibility

We now turn to the concept of **corporate social responsibility**—the idea that corporations can and should act ethically and be accountable to society for their actions. No one contests the claim that corporations have duties to their shareholders, employers, and product users (consumers). Many of these duties are written into law—that is, they are legal duties. The question of corporate social responsibility concerns the extent to which a corporation has ethical duties to various groups in society that go beyond its legally prescribed duties.

To understand the debate over corporate social responsibility, consider a hypothetical firm: the Farris Company. This firm markets its products, primarily paints and glues, throughout the world. The company is facing a financial crisis and must find a way to increase its profits if it is to survive. In so doing, however, Farris will need to take into account the ethical ramifications of any decisions it makes. In the following pages, we examine some of the problematic aspects of a corporation's responsibilities in regard to shareholders, employees, consumers, the community, and society. As you will see, corporations such as the Farris Company face difficult choices in trying to be ethically responsible.

Duty to Shareholders

Corporate directors and officers have a duty to act in the shareholders' interest. Because of the nature of the relationship between corporate directors and officers and the shareholder-owners, the law holds directors and officers to a high standard of care in business decision making (see Chapter 16).

Traditionally, it was perceived that this duty to shareholders took precedence over all other corporate duties and that the primary goal of corporations

---

> **"Next to doing the right thing, the most important thing is to let people know you are doing the right thing."**
>
> John D. Rockefeller, 1839–1897
> (Industrialist and philanthropist)

Corporate Social Responsibility The concept that corporations can and should act ethically and be accountable to society for their actions.

should be profit maximization. Those who support the profit-maximization view of social responsibility contend that the duty to maximize profits must outweigh any other duty when duties conflict—to the extent, of course, that in maximizing shareholders' profits a firm does not violate the "basic rules of society." The question here is, what are these basic rules?

• **Example 2.7** Suppose that our hypothetical firm, the Farris Company, has suffered a setback because the U.S. government banned the sale of one of its paint thinners. The paint thinner, if allowed to touch the skin of some users, can cause severe irritation, and many consumers have complained of such problems. The product is not banned in foreign markets, though, and thus Farris faces an ethical question: Should it continue marketing the product in other countries? Certainly, it would benefit the shareholders to do so, but would such an action violate society's basic rules and ethical customs? Even if the action violated the ethical rules of even a small minority of Americans, that small minority, through activism and publicity, could harm Farris's reputation as an ethically responsible corporation.•

Duty to Employees

As you will read in Chapters 17, 18, and 19, by law employers are required to provide a safe workplace, to pay a minimum wage, and to provide equal employment opportunities for all potential and existing employees. As mentioned earlier, however, there are many "gray areas" in the law, and it is not always clear to employers just how the law will apply to a certain set of circumstances.

• **Example 2.8** Under federal laws employers must "reasonably accommodate" the religious needs of their employees and the needs of employees or job applicants with disabilities—unless to do so creates an "undue hardship" for the employer. No law, however, spells out exactly what "reasonable accommodation" means or the point at which an employer experiences "undue hardship." Generally, the courts decide these issues on a case-by-case basis.•

When facing legal uncertainties such as these, business decision makers need to proceed with caution and evaluate the action and its consequences from an ethical perspective. Generally, if a company can demonstrate that it acted responsibly and in good faith in the circumstances, it has a better chance of defending its action successfully in court or before an administrative law judge.

We look next at some employment decisions facing employers in which ethical considerations often come into play. (You will read about other ethical issues that arise in the employment context in Chapters 17, 18, and 19.)

SEXUAL HARASSMENT IN THE WORKPLACE   An ongoing problem for employers is how to prevent sexual harassment from occurring in the workplace. This is particularly true with respect to "hostile-environment harassment," which occurs when an employee is subjected to sexual conduct or comments that he or she perceives as offensive. Generally, employers are expected to take immediate and appropriate corrective action in response to employees' complaints of sexual harassment or abuse. If they do not, they may face costly damages in a subsequent lawsuit. Yet taking immediate corrective action—such as firing an employee for harassing behavior—may lead to other problems.

• **Example 2.9** Suppose that an employee complains to her supervisor that a co-worker is sexually harassing her—physically touching her in objectionable ways, making lewd comments to her, and so on. The company immediately investigates the claim, and on finding that it is somewhat substantiated, promptly fires the harassing employee. In taking this action, the company assumes that it is acting responsibly. The fired employee, however, then sues the firm for *wrongful discharge* (firing an employee without good cause or for discriminatory reasons—see Chapter 17). Will the fired employee win the lawsuit? Perhaps. Under some state laws and employment agreements, employers are prohibited from firing employees without "just cause," and particular incidents of sexual harassment may or may not constitute just cause for firing the purported harasser. •

In an attempt to protect their employees from harassment—and shield themselves from liability—most large companies today, as well as many smaller ones, have implemented harassment policies. These policies typically establish procedures that employees can follow if they feel they are being harassed by supervisors or co-workers. The policies also instruct management and supervisory personnel on the proper corrective actions to take in response to employees' complaints. For most situations, corrective actions involve a series of steps. Initially, the harassing employee is informed of the problem and asked to cease the offensive behavior. If the behavior continues, then the employee may be placed on probation. Finally, if the problem recurs, the employee will be fired. A company that can demonstrate that it established and followed such procedures may be able to avoid liability for either sexual harassment or wrongful discharge.

The following case illustrates what can result when an employer maintains and distributes a sexual-harassment policy and reporting procedures, and a harassed employee delays in using them.

Case 2.1 ● Montero v. AGCO Corp.

United States District Court,
Eastern District of California, 1998.
19 F.Supp.2d 1143.

Historical and Social Setting
Title VII of the Civil Rights Act of 1964 prohibits employment discrimination on the basis of "sex," or gender. This discrimination includes acts or comments that create a hostile working environment, which is a situation that a reasonable person would find offensive. Courts have often been asked to determine whether particular acts or comments are extreme enough to create a hostile environment. What has been rarely at issue is what defense employers might use to avoid liability for the wrongful behavior of their employees. (It was long ago held that an employer is not "automatically" liable.[a]) In 1998, the United States Supreme Court set out two elements of such a defense. The Court indicated that an employer might avoid liability if it has established a harassment policy and complaint

procedures and employees alleging harassment failed to follow those procedures.[b]

Background and Facts AGCO Corporation's employee policies include provisions against sexual harassment and procedures for reporting and handling allegations of harassment. Shortly after being hired by AGCO, Carrie Ann Montero was subjected to sexual harassment by Glenn Carpenter, a warehouse manager, and Russ Newman, a warehouse supervisor. Although Montero knew of AGCO's harassment policies, she did not report the sexual harassment for nearly two years. When she did report it, AGCO immediately began an investigation. Carpenter was discharged, and Newman was disciplined. Montero took a short leave of absence, after which she did not return to work, despite encouragement from AGCO executives. Montero filed a suit in a federal district court against AGCO and others, alleging, in part, violations of Title VII. AGCO filed a motion for summary judgment on the Title VII charge.

a. *Meritor Savings Bank, FSB v. Vinson*, 477 U.S. 57, 106 S.Ct. 2399, 91 L.Ed.2d 49 (1986).

b. *Faragher v. City of Boca Raton*, 524 U.S. 725, 118 S.Ct. 2275, 141 L.Ed.2d 662 (1998).

Case 2.1 Continued

In the Words of the Court . . .
DAMRELL, District J.

* * * *

* * * [An] employer may raise an affirmative defense [against charges of sexual harassment]. * * * The defense comprises two necessary elements: (a) that the employer exercised reasonable care to prevent and correct promptly any sexually harassing behavior, and (b) that the plaintiff employee unreasonably failed to take advantage of any preventive or corrective opportunities provided by the employer or to avoid harm otherwise.

* * * *

* * * AGCO exercised reasonable care to prevent sexual harassment by maintaining and distributing a policy prohibiting sexual harassment and by providing a mechanism for employees to report such conduct directly to the Human Resources Department. Moreover, AGCO immediately investigated plaintiff's complaints and acted to correct the same. Conversely, plaintiff unreasonably failed to take advantage of the preventive and corrective opportunities provided by AGCO or to otherwise avoid harm.

Decision and Remedy   The court issued a summary judgment in AGCO's favor regarding the Title VII claim. The court held that an employer's policy and procedure concerning sexual harassment, and an employee's delay in using the procedure, can constitute a defense to a charge of harassment.

For Critical Analysis—Economic Consideration   *What might have been the result in this case if AGCO had not had a sexual-harassment policy and reporting procedure?*

CORPORATE RESTRUCTURING AND EMPLOYEE WELFARE   Suppose that our hypothetical firm, the Farris Company, decided to reduce its costs by downsizing and restructuring its operations. Among other things, this would allow Farris to cut back on its overhead by consolidating various supervisory and managerial positions. Yet which employees should Farris retain, and which employees should Farris let go? Should the firm retain its highly paid employees who have worked for—and received annual raises from—the firm for years? Alternatively, in the interests of cutting costs, should it retain (or hire) younger, less experienced persons at lower salaries?

The firm would not necessarily be acting illegally if it pursued the second option. Unless a fired employee can prove that the employer has breached an employment contract or violated the Age Discrimination in Employment Act (ADEA) of 1967, the employee normally will not have a cause of action against the employer. The ADEA prohibits discrimination against workers forty years old and older on the basis of their age (see this chapter's *Inside the Legal Environment* on the next page for a further discussion of age discrimination). Farris, though, can always say that lack of performance or ability, not age, was the deciding factor.

In deciding this issue, remember that Farris must keep its eye on its profit margin. If it does not, the firm may fail, and the shareholders will lose their investments. Furthermore, why should the firm retain highly paid employees if it can obtain essentially the same work output for a lower price by retaining

Inside the Legal Environment

Protection for Older Workers

The Age Discrimination in Employment Act (ADEA) of 1967, as amended by the Older Workers Benefit Protection Act (OWBPA) of 1990, allows employers to obtain releases from employees—contracts in which the employees agree not to bring legal proceedings against the employers under the ADEA—in return for receiving severance benefits. The OWBPA sets forth specific requirements that employers must meet when drafting such contracts, however. An employee, for example, must sign the release "knowingly and voluntarily" and must be given forty-five days to decide whether to sign the release.

Whether Sears Roebuck & Company had violated the OWBPA was at issue in a recent case brought by a former Sears employee, Thomas Long. Long had worked for Sears for thirty years when he and several other employees in the Home Improvement Products and Services (HIPS) division of Sears were told that the company was permanently disbanding the HIPS division. Sears promised HIPS employees that it would try to transfer them to other positions with the company and that preference would be given to long-term HIPS employees with satisfactory performance ratings. Those employees who were not transferred would be laid off, as Long ultimately was, even though he had actively sought a transfer within Sears.

Long was offered a severance package, including $39,000 in severance benefits, in return for signing a release in which he agreed to waive all claims against Sears under the ADEA. Although Long accepted the benefits and signed the release, he later sued Sears for age discrimination and for violating the OWBPA. Long claimed that following his layoff, Sears retrained younger employees with less seniority to work in other departments, and, contrary to its representations, Sears did not permanently disband its HIPS division. Long also claimed that he had not knowingly or voluntarily signed the release; rather, he had been pressured by his supervisor into signing it.

A central issue before the court was whether Long had to "tender back" the $39,000 in order to be able to bring an action against Sears or whether Long

An elderly employee works at a fast-food restaurant. What laws protect older workers from discrimination?

could go forward with the suit and simply deduct the $39,000 from any damage award he received. Ultimately, a federal appellate court held against the "tender-back" requirement. The court ruled that to apply the requirement in such circumstances would mean that "[n]o matter how egregiously releases might violate the requirements of the [OWBPA], employees would be precluded from challenging them unless they somehow . . . come up with the money they were given when allegedly forced into retirement." In the appellate court's eyes, employees whose releases were defective under the OWBPA would, in effect, be "no better off than before the OWBPA was enacted."[a]

For Critical Analysis: *When an older employee, such as Long, is laid off, does that person have any real choice when deciding whether or not to accept severance pay and sign a required release?*

---

a. *Long v. Sears Roebuck & Co.,* 105 F.3d 1529 (3d Cir. 1997).

its less highly paid employees? Does Farris owe an ethical duty to its employees who have served the firm loyally over a long period of time? Most people would say yes. Should this duty take precedence over Farris's duty to the firm's owners to maintain or increase the profitability of the firm? Would your answer be the same if the firm faced imminent bankruptcy if it could not lower its operating costs? What if long-time employees were willing to take a slight reduction in pay to help the firm through its financial difficulties? What if they were not?

In the following case, an employer was confronted with a dwindling market and decreasing sales. The employer decided to reduce its costs of doing business by eliminating some of its obligations to its employees.

Case 2.2 ● Varity Corp. v. Howe

Supreme Court of the United States, 1996.
516 U.S. 489, 116 S.Ct. 1065,
134 L.Ed.2d 130.
**http://laws.findlaw.com/US/
000/U10206.html**[a]

Historical and Economic Setting *Since 1950, the number of U.S. farms has declined as small farms have been driven out of business by corporate agribusinesses with assets that small farmers cannot match. Between 1980 and 1996, the number of farms decreased by over 14 percent, to less than 2 million, even as the average acreage per farm increased by 10 percent, to nearly 470 acres. Agribusinesses require fewer workers than do small farms, and thus, the total farm population also decreased by 24 percent in the 1980s. Fewer farmers means a smaller market for those who cater to it.*

Background and Facts Varity Corporation manufactures and sells farm implements. In 1986,

a. This is a page within the Web site of FindLaw. In addition to its own databases, FindLaw provides links to other legal resources on the Internet.

Varity set up a subsidiary, Massey Combines Corporation (MCC), to market its self-propelled combines and four-wheel-drive tractors. The sales of both products were at an all-time low. Varity convinced current and former employees who were, or had been, involved with the products to accept a transfer of their jobs and retirement benefit plans to MCC. Varity did not tell those employees that it expected MCC to fail. Within two years, MCC failed. Among other consequences, some retirees stopped receiving benefits. The retirees and other ex-employees sued Varity in a federal district court under the Employee Retirement Income Security Act of 1974 (ERISA).[b] They claimed that Varity owed them a fiduciary duty, which it had breached.[c] The court ruled in their favor, and the U.S. Court of Appeals for the Eighth Circuit affirmed the decision. Varity then appealed to the United States Supreme Court.

b. 29 U.S.C. Sections 1001–1461. See Chapter 17.
c. A *fiduciary* is a party who, because of something that he or she has undertaken to do, has a duty to act primarily for another's benefit.

In the Words of the Court . . .
JUSTICE BREYER delivered the opinion of the Court.

* * * *

* * * ERISA requires a "fiduciary" to "discharge his duties with respect to a plan solely in the interest of the participants and beneficiaries." To participate knowingly and significantly in deceiving a plan's beneficiaries in order to save the employer money at the beneficiaries' expense, is not to act "solely in the interest of the participants and beneficiaries." As other courts have held, "[l]ying is inconsistent with the duty of loyalty owed by all fiduciaries * * * ."

Decision and Remedy The United States Supreme Court affirmed the decision of the lower court. Varity breached its fiduciary duty to its employees with respect to their retirement benefits.

For Critical Analysis—Ethical Consideration *Should a company continue to market a slow-selling line of products for the sole purpose of employing those who work on the products?*

> **"A man cannot shift his misfortunes to his neighbor's shoulders."**
>
> Oliver Wendell Holmes, Jr.,
> 1841–1935
> (Associate justice of the United States
> Supreme Court, 1902–1932)

Duty to Consumers

Clearly, a corporation has a duty to the users of its products. This is not just an ethical duty but a legal one as well—as you will read in later chapters of this book. Sometimes, though, firms find it difficult to know exactly how the law will apply to certain uses, or misuses, of their products. Another issue with respect to corporate social responsibility has to do with the extent to which a corporation has an ethical duty beyond those obligations mandated by law.

FORESEEABLE PRODUCT MISUSES   Generally, whenever a corporation markets a product, the law imposes a duty on the firm to warn consumers, among other things, of the harms that can result from *foreseeable* misuses. When a risk is "open and obvious," however, courts tend to hold that no warning is necessary. Sharp knives, for example, can obviously injure their users. Courts normally decide whether a particular risk is "open and obvious" on a case-by-case basis, and courts often disagree on whether certain types of risks are open and obvious. Businesspersons thus find it difficult to predict how a court might rule in deciding whether a particular risk is open and obvious or whether consumers should be warned of that risk.

The following case involves an allegation that the warning on an aerosol can of butane failed to warn consumers of the danger of inhaling the contents of the can.

Case 2.3 ● Pavlik v. Lane Ltd./Tobacco Exporters International

United States Court of Appeals,
Third Circuit, 1998.
135 F.3d 876.
http://www.law.vill.edu/Fed-Ct/
Circuit/3d/February98.html[a]

Historical and Cultural Setting   *It is human nature to play Monday morning quarterback—to second-guess the choices that others make after the consequences of those choices become fact. Sometimes, such hindsight consists of superimposing what one person believes is common knowledge onto another's set of beliefs and assumptions. This can occur when adults assume that children know what adults know—that an oven is hot, for example. A child has to be warned that an oven is hot, and even then he or she may not appreciate the danger, or the seriousness of the danger,*

depending on the context of the warning. Judges, in particular, have to avoid the temptation to impose their own assumptions about what is common knowledge onto the parties in the cases that come before them.

Background and Facts   Butane is a fuel for cigarette lighters. Zeus brand butane is distributed in small aerosol cans by Lane Limited/Tobacco Exporters International (Lane). On each can is the warning "DO NOT BREATHE SPRAY." Twenty-year-old Stephen Pavlik died from intentionally inhaling the contents of one of the cans. His father, George Pavlik, filed a suit in a federal district court against Lane and others, claiming in part that the statement on the can did not adequately warn users of the hazards of butane inhalation. The court issued a summary judgment in the defendants' favor, reasoning in part that Stephen must have been aware of the dangers of inhaling butane and that a more specific warning would not have affected his conduct. George Pavlik appealed to the U.S. Court of Appeals for the Third Circuit.

a. This is the "February Decisions" page within the collection of "1998 Decisions" of the U.S. Court of Appeals for the Third Circuit available at the Web site of the Center for Information Law and Policy. Scroll down the list of cases to the entry for the *Pavlik* case. Click on the link to access the opinion.

In the Words of the Court . . .
BECKER, Chief Judge.

Case 2.3 Continued

* * * *

* * * [A]n otherwise properly designed product may still be unreasonably dangerous (and therefore "defective") for strict liability purposes if the product is distributed without sufficient warnings to apprise the ultimate user of the latent dangers in the product.

* * * *

* * * [W]e have serious doubts that the Zeus warning sufficiently warns users of the potentially fatal consequences of butane inhalation, and we are not convinced of its adequacy * * * . More specifically, the "DO NOT BREATHE SPRAY" warning appears to give the user no notice of the serious nature of the danger posed by inhalation, intentional or otherwise, and no other language on the Zeus can does so. Yet, we similarly cannot find that such a directive is inadequate as a matter of law, and so we must leave the question for the jury.

Decision and Remedy   The U.S. Court of Appeals for the Third Circuit held that it was not clear that Stephen was fully aware of the dangers of inhaling butane, based on the label on the Zeus cans. The court reversed the judgment of the lower court and remanded the case for trial.

For Critical Analysis—Cultural Consideration   *Would it have made any difference to the outcome in this case if Stephen's parents had warned him of the dangers of inhaling butane?*

UNFORESEEABLE PRODUCT MISUSES   Sometimes, unforeseeable product misuses pose ethical dilemmas for manufacturers. • **Example 2.10** Suppose that the Farris Company learns that one of its products—glue—is being inhaled by thousands of children in several Latin American countries. The health consequences of this misuse can include future kidney disease and brain damage. Consumer activists have launched a media campaign against Farris, accusing it of being unethical by marketing its glue in those countries when such harms result. What is Farris's responsibility in this situation? On the one hand, it has not violated any law and to cease selling the product in those areas would significantly cut into its profits. On the other hand, suspending sales would reduce the suffering of children, and if Farris ignores the public outcry, the continued adverse publicity could also cause the firm to lose sales—and thus profits. Farris's solution will rest on the "ethical weight" it attaches to each of these factors.[3]•

Duty to Society

In some circumstances, the community in which a business enterprise is located has a substantial stake in the firm. Assume, for example, that the Farris

---

3. When the H. B. Fuller Company faced this situation a few years ago, its solution was to suspend sales of its glues in some Latin American countries but not others. Fuller's critics contended that it should have suspended sales in all of the Latin American countries in which the product was being misused.

Ethical Issue 2.1

Do firms have a duty to prevent criminal misuses of their products?

Should pesticide manufacturers be held liable when their products are used to create bombs that cause destruction? Should service stations be held liable for selling gasoline to purchasers who then use the gas to set buildings on fire? Such questions have come before the courts on several occasions. In a recent Colorado case, for example, the plaintiff was injured when, after an argument with a man, the man went to a gas station, bought a cupful of gasoline, threw it on the plaintiff, and set her on fire. The plaintiff argued that the defendant gas station was negligent because it should have foreseen, based on the man's behavior and appearance, that selling him a cupful of gas could create a risk that he might harm someone with it. Routinely, the courts have held that such criminal uses of products are unforeseeable misuses for which the manufacturers of the products cannot be held liable. In the Colorado case, a Colorado appellate court also reached this conclusion. The court stated that the risk that a purchaser of gasoline would intentionally throw it on a victim and set the victim on fire was not reasonably foreseeable.[a]

a. *Walcott v. Total Petroleum, Inc.*, 964 P.2d 609 (Colo.App. 1998).

> **"Responsibility walks hand in hand with capacity and power."**
>
> Josiah G. Holland, 1819–1881
> (American author and editor)

Company employs two thousand workers at one of its plants. If the company decides that it would be profitable to close the plant or move it to another location, the employees—and the community—would suffer as a result. Today, to be considered socially responsible, a corporation must take both employees' needs and community needs into consideration when making such a decision.

Perhaps the most disputed area in the controversy surrounding corporate social responsibility is the nature of a corporation's duty to society at large. Generally, the question turns less on whether corporations owe a duty to society than on how that duty can best be fulfilled.

PROFIT MAXIMIZATION   Those who contend that corporations should attend to the goal of profit maximization would argue that it is by generating profits that a firm can best contribute to society. Society benefits by profit-making activities, because profits can only be realized when a firm markets products or services that are desired by society. These products and services enhance the standard of living, and the profits accumulated by successful business firms generate national wealth. Our laws and court decisions promoting trade and commerce reflect the public policy that the fruits of commerce (income and wealth) are desirable and good. Because our society values income and wealth as ethical goals, corporations, by contributing to income and wealth, automatically are acting ethically.

Furthermore, profit maximization results in the efficient allocation of resources. Capital, labor, raw materials, and other resources are directed to the production of those goods and services most desired by society. If capital were directed toward a social goal instead of being reinvested in the corporation, the business operation would become less efficient. For example, if an automobile company contributes $1 million annually to the United Way, that contribution represents $1 million that is not reinvested in making better and safer cars.

Those arguing for profit maximization as a corporate goal also point out that it would be inappropriate to use the power of the corporate business world to fashion society's goals by promoting social causes. Determinations as to what exactly is in society's best interest are essentially political questions, and therefore the public, through the political process, should have a say in making those determinations. The legislature—not the corporate board-room—is thus the appropriate forum for such decisions.

CRITICS OF PROFIT MAXIMIZATION   Critics of the profit-maximization view believe that corporations should become actively engaged in seeking and furthering solutions to social problems. Because so much of the wealth and power of this country is controlled by business, business in turn has a responsibility to society to use that wealth and power in socially beneficial ways. Corporations should therefore promote human rights, strive for equal treatment of minorities and women in the workplace, take care to preserve the environment, and generally not profit from activities that society has deemed unethical. The critics also point out that it is ethically irresponsible to leave decisions concerning social welfare up to the government, because many social needs are not being met sufficiently through the political process.

CORPORATE PHILANTHROPY VERSUS CORPORATE PROCESS   Since the nineteenth century and the emergence of large business enterprises in America, corporations have generally contributed some of their shareholders' wealth to meet social needs. Frequently, corporations establish separate nonprofit foundations for this purpose. For example, Honda, Inc., created the American Honda Education Corporation, through which it donated $40 million over a ten-year period to launch and support the Eagle Rock School in Estes Park, Colorado. This school and educator training center gives preference to students who have not been able to succeed in the more rigid, highly structured public school systems. Today, virtually all major corporations routinely donate to hospitals, medical research, the arts, universities, and programs that benefit society.

Increasingly, however, corporations are being judged less on the basis of their philanthropic activities than on their practices, or corporate process. Corporate process, in this sense, refers to how a corporation conducts its affairs at all levels of operation. Does it establish and effectively implement ethical policies and take those policies seriously? Does it deal ethically with its shareholders? Does it consider the needs of its employees—for day-care facilities or flexible working hours, for example? Does it promote equal opportunity in the workplace for women, minority groups, and persons with disabilities? Do the corporation's suppliers, particularly those from developing countries, protect the human rights of their employees (provide for safety in the workplace or pay a decent wage, for example)? Does the corporation investigate complaints about its products promptly and, if necessary, take action to improve them?

For many, the answers to these and similar questions are the key factors in determining whether a corporation is socially responsible and responsive to society's needs. From this perspective, no matter how much a corporation may contribute to worthy causes, it will not be socially responsible if it fails to observe ethical standards in its day-to-day activities.

> "The highest morality almost always is the morality of process."
>
> Alexander M. Bickel, 1924–1974
> (Rumanian-American legal scholar)

It Pays to Be Ethical

Most corporations today have learned that it pays to be ethically responsible—even if it means less profits in the short run (and it often does). Today's corporations are subject to more intensive scrutiny—both by government agencies and the public—than they ever were in the past. If a corporation fails to conduct its operations ethically or respond quickly to an ethical crisis, its goodwill and reputation (and thus future profits) will likely suffer as a result. For this reason, many firms today, instead of aiming for *maximum profits,* aim for *optimum profits*—profits that can be realized while staying within legal and ethical limits. Notice how Costco's Code of Ethics (see the fold-out exhibit in this chapter) stresses both legal and ethical duties.

There are other reasons as well for a corporation to behave ethically. Companies that demonstrate a commitment to ethical behavior—by implementing ethical programs, complying with environmental regulations, and promptly investigating product complaints, for example—often receive more lenient treatment from government agencies or the courts, as mentioned earlier in this chapter. Furthermore, by keeping their own houses in order, corporations may be able to avoid the necessity for the government to do so—through new laws and regulations.

Additionally, investors may shy away from a corporation's stock if the corporation is perceived to be socially irresponsible. Since the 1970s, certain investment funds have guaranteed to the purchasers of their shares that they will only invest in companies that are socially responsible. These "ethical" investment funds base their investments on various ethical criteria. For example, some funds invest money only in corporations that are "environmentally kind"; others invest only in corporations that ensure fair treatment for their employees or the employees of their suppliers in foreign countries.

Ethics in the Global Context

Given the varied cultures and religions of the world's nations, one should not be surprised that frequent conflicts in ethics arise between foreign and U.S. businesspersons. • **Example 2.11** In Islamic (Muslim) countries the consumption of alcohol and certain foods is forbidden by the Koran (the sayings of the prophet Mohammed, which lie at the heart of Islam and Islamic law). It would be thoughtless and imprudent to invite a Saudi Arabian business contact out for a drink.•

The role played by women in other countries also may present some difficult ethical problems for firms doing business internationally. Equal employment opportunity is a fundamental public policy in the United States, and Title VII of the Civil Rights Act of 1964 prohibits discrimination against women in the employment context (see Chapter 18). Some other countries, however, offer little protection for women against gender discrimination in the workplace, including sexual harassment.

We look here at how laws governing workers in other countries, particularly in the developing countries, have created some especially difficult ethical problems for U.S. sellers of goods manufactured in foreign countries. We also examine some of the ethical ramifications of a U.S. law that prohibits American businesspersons from bribing foreign officials to obtain favorable business contracts.

Monitoring the Employment Practices of Foreign Suppliers

Suppose that the Farris Company, to save costs, contracts with companies in developing nations to manufacture some of its products, because the wage rates in those nations are significantly lower than in the United States. Further suppose that one of the foreign companies exploits its workers—it hires women and children at below-minimum-wage rates and requires its employees to work long hours in a workplace full of health hazards. Additionally, the company's supervisors routinely engage in workplace conduct that is offensive to women.

What is the Farris Company's ethical responsibility in this situation? Should it refuse to deal with these suppliers (and sacrifice profits)? Should it use these suppliers' services but only on the condition that the suppliers allow Farris employees to monitor the suppliers' workplaces to make sure that the workers are not being mistreated?

At one time, society's concept of ethical business behavior did not include concerns over other nations' employment laws and practices. Today, however, the situation has changed. Few activities of business firms go overlooked by interest groups supporting human rights on a worldwide level. If a company such as Farris fails to take steps to protect foreign workers' rights, its reputation as an ethically responsible firm may be damaged—and its profits significantly affected—by the adverse publicity sponsored by such interest groups. (For a further discussion of this issue, see this chapter's *Legal E-nvironment: Corporate Social Responsibility* on pages 54 and 55.)

> **Remember** Changing ethical notions about social responsibility often motivate lawmakers to enact or repeal laws.

The Foreign Corrupt Practices Act

Another ethical problem in international business dealings has to do with the legitimacy of certain side payments to government officials. In the United States, the majority of contracts are formed within the private sector. In many foreign countries, however, decisions on most major construction and manufacturing contracts are made by government officials because of extensive government regulation and control over trade and industry. Side payments to

International Perspective

International Standards for Social Accountability

The International Standards Organization (ISO) has created standards for environmental auditing that have been widely adopted by corporate managers around the world. When such standards are issued or revised, they are given a number, such as ISO14001. Recently, the Council on Economic Priorities Accreditation Agency (CEPAA) used the ISO's model for its new human rights standards, called Social Accountability 8000 (SA8000). These standards call on corporate leaders to restrict child labor and forced labor, limit workweeks to forty-eight hours, respect workers' rights to form unions, provide safe working conditions, and pay wages that meet basic needs. By adopting these standards and agreeing to "Social Accountability audits," firms can demonstrate their commitment to international human rights and help to dispel stories that they make profits by using "sweatshop labor."

For Critical Analysis: *Can an American corporation be compelled to respect the human rights of workers in factories located in other nations?*

government officials in exchange for favorable business contracts are not unusual in such countries, nor are they considered to be unethical. In the past, U.S. corporations doing business in developing countries largely followed the dictum, "When in Rome, do as the Romans do."

In the 1970s, however, the U.S. press, and government officials as well, uncovered a number of business scandals involving large side payments by American corporations to foreign representatives for the purpose of securing advantageous international trade contracts. In response to this unethical behavior, Congress passed the Foreign Corrupt Practices Act (FCPA) in 1977, which prohibits American businesspersons from bribing foreign officials to secure advantageous contracts. The act, which is the subject of this chapter's *Landmark in the Legal Environment* on page 56, made it difficult for American companies to compete as effectively as they otherwise might have in the global marketplace.

Legal *e*-nvironment

Corporate Social Responsibility

In *The Gospel of Wealth and Other Timely Essays,* published in 1889, the industrialist Andrew Carnegie argued that a holder of corporate wealth should consider all corporate surplus revenues simply as "trust funds." These funds, contended Carnegie, should be administered in a way that would "produce the most beneficial results for the community." Thus was born the concept of corporate philanthropy, which for some time was equated with corporate social responsibility.

As mentioned elsewhere in this chapter, today corporate philanthropy is not enough. Largely as a result of social movements during the 1960s and 1970s (movements focusing on civil rights, gender equality, and consumer and environmental protection), groups concerned with corporate social responsibility began to focus on corporate practices and whether those practices were ethical. These groups started to scrutinize corporate behavior closely and to campaign—through media ads, boycotts, and the like—against companies whose actions were perceived as unethical.

Enter the Internet

In recent years, the Internet has made it possible for business conduct to come under closer public scrutiny than ever before. Human rights activists and other interest groups concerned with unethical business behavior no longer have to spend years getting organized and soliciting funds to pay for their operating expenses, for distributing literature, and for costly media ads exposing unethical business practices.

Today, such groups can plead their causes on the Internet. They can publish online, at virtually no cost, reports about unethical business practices. They can invite other Internet users to donate to their causes or join in their missions in other ways—by telephoning or sending letters to a company, for example, as part of a pressure campaign against the firm to cease its unethical behavior. Indeed, many sites invite users to simply print out letters that have already been drafted, sign the letters, and send them to the targeted firm.

Corporate Watch Groups

There is an expanding number of interest groups online whose sole aim is to hold corporations accountable for their actions by exposing, via online publications, what these groups deem to be unethical corporate practices. Many of these "corporate watch" groups focus on the impact of corporate activities on the environment (for a discussion of some of these sites, see the *Legal E-nvironment* feature in Chapter 21). Others are more concerned with corporate "influence peddling" through contributions to political candidates (see, for example, *INFACT*'s Web site at **http://www.infact.org**). Still others are focused on human rights issues (see, for instance, the Web site of Human Rights Watch at **http://www.hrw.org**). A number of online groups also investigate and report on the impact of specific business actions that affect the welfare of workers in factories located abroad that produce or assemble goods

Legal *e*-nvironment

Activist groups increasingly are holding American companies accountable for their actions, no matter where those actions take place. Given the speed of global communications via the Internet, an online group such as Corporate Watch can organize a worldwide campaign very quickly against a company that, in the group's eyes, mistreats its workers or engages in other types of unethical behavior.

CORPORATE WATCH
THE WATCHDOG ON THE WEB

DISPATCH
Climate Justice Summit Provides Alternative Vision
Updated: 11/22/2000

Community groups from around the world hold watershed meeting linking local activism with global climate change.
Full Story | Full Coverage

Colorful protests at climate negotiations.
Photo Credit: Rod Harbinson/ASEED

GREENWASH AWARD
Shell: "Clouding the Issue"
Updated: 11/16/2000

Shell wants you to believe that they're working to curb climate change. But Greenwash Guru Kenny Bruno takes a deeper look at Shell's latest ad campaign and finds they're full of hot air.
Full Story | Full Archive

CLOUD THE ISSUE

OR CLEAR THE AIR?

Shell's ad on global warming

Take Action
Posted: 10/11/2000

Save Brazil's Wetlands from Corporate Predators!

DonateNow!
Secure donations by eGRANTS.org

Headlines
Updated: 11/22/2000

Netherlands: Anger at US Boils Over at Climate Talks

Netherlands: Oil Companies Wreak Destruction from Arctic Circle to Nigeria

India: Three Dead in Protests Against Industry Shut Down

Colombia: Monsanto, US War on Drugs Poison Environment

France: Yahoo! Ordered To Block Users

USA: United Farm Workers Call Off Grape Boycott

Check out more

for American companies (as an example, see the Web site of Responsibility, Inc., at **http://www.responsibilityinc.com**).

Calls to action made by online corporate watch groups can be particularly effective. Consider the activities of just one of these online groups—Corporate Watch (at **http://www.corpwatch.org**). Corporate Watch recently launched an online campaign against L. V. Myles, a factory located in Port-au-Prince, Haiti, which assembles clothing for several U.S. firms, including the Disney Company. Corporate Watch reported online that workers at the factory were paid about half of the basic living wage, and women were allegedly subjected to sexual harassment from their supervisors. When a flier protesting the

abusive working conditions was circulated throughout the factory, management responded by firing a number of workers who were suspected of being responsible for the flier. Management ceased firing workers, however, after it was bombarded with faxes, e-mail and printed letters, and telephone calls from concerned U.S. citizens, who were alerted to the situation by Corporate Watch and various other online groups.

For Critical Analysis: *Using the Internet, a small handful of activists can bring significant pressure to bear on a corporation that, in the opinion of those activists, is acting unethically. What are the implications of this development for corporate ethical decision making?*

Other Nations Denounce Bribery

For twenty years, the FCPA was the only law of its kind in the world, despite attempts by U.S. political leaders to convince other nations to pass similar legislation. That situation is now changing. In 1997, the Organization for Economic Cooperation and Development, to which twenty-six of the world's leading industrialized nations belong, signed a convention (treaty) that made the bribery of foreign public officials a serious crime. Each signatory is obligated to enact legislation within its nation in accordance with the treaty. The agreement will not only improve the ethical climate in international trade but also level the playing field for U.S businesspersons.

Landmark in the Legal Environment

The Foreign Corrupt Practices Act of 1977

The Foreign Corrupt Practices Act (FCPA) of 1977 is divided into two major parts. The first part applies to all U.S. companies and their directors, officers, shareholders, employees, and agents. This part of the FCPA prohibits the bribery of most officials of foreign governments if the purpose of the payment is to get the official to act in his or her official capacity to provide business opportunities.

The FCPA does not prohibit payment of substantial sums to minor officials whose duties are ministerial. These payments are often referred to as "grease," or facilitating payments. They are meant to ensure that administrative services that might otherwise be performed at a slow pace are sped up. Thus, for example, if a firm makes a payment to a minor official to speed up an import licensing process, the firm has not violated the FCPA. Generally, the act, as amended, permits payments to foreign officials if such payments are lawful within the foreign country. The act also does not prohibit payments to private foreign companies or other third parties unless the American firm knows that the payments will be passed on to a foreign government in violation of the FCPA.

The second part of the FCPA is directed toward accountants, because in the past bribes were often concealed in corporate financial records. All companies must keep detailed records that "accurately and fairly" reflect the company's financial activities. In addition, all companies must have an accounting system that provides "reasonable assurance" that all transactions entered into by the company are accounted for and legal. These requirements assist in detecting illegal bribes. The FCPA further prohibits any person from making false statements to accountants or false entries in any record or account.

In 1988, the FCPA was amended to provide that business firms that violated the act may be fined up to $2 million. Individual officers or directors who violate the FCPA may be fined up to $100,000 (the fine cannot be paid by the company) and may be imprisoned for up to five years.

For Critical Analysis: *The FCPA did not change international trade practices in other countries, but it effectively tied the hands of American firms trying to secure foreign contracts. In passing the FCPA, did Congress give too much weight to ethics and too little weight to international economic realities?*

Key Terms

business ethics 36	cost-benefit analysis 39	principle of rights 38
categorical imperative 38	ethics 36	utilitarianism 39
corporate social responsibility 42		

Chapter Summary • Ethics and Social Responsibility

The Nature of Business Ethics (See pages 36–37.)	Ethics can be defined as the study of what constitutes right or wrong behavior. Business ethics focuses on how moral and ethical principles are applied in the business context. The law reflects society's convictions on what constitutes right or wrong behavior. The law has its limits, though, and some actions may be legal yet not be ethical.
Sources of Ethical Standards (See pages 37–39.)	1. **Duty-based ethics**—Ethics based on religious beliefs; philosophical reasoning, such as that of Immanuel Kant; and the principle of rights.

Chapter Summary • Ethics and Social Responsibility

Sources of Ethical Standards—continued	2. **Outcome-based ethics (utilitarianism)**—Ethics based on philosophical reasoning, such as that of John Stuart Mill.

Ethical Decision Making
(See pages 39–42.)

Most major companies today, before undertaking an action, consider the following three questions:

1. **Is the contemplated action profitable?** This question is foremost, and if an action would not be profitable, it probably will not be undertaken. If the action would be profitable, then the decision makers consider the second and third questions listed below.

2. **Is the contemplated action legal?** Compliance with the law is regarded as the *moral minimum* for businesses. Determining whether an action is legal is not always easy, however, because of the numerous laws regulating business activity and the many "gray areas" in the law.

3. **Is the contemplated action ethical?** In evaluating this question, company decision makers are guided by their own ethical principles and reasoning processes, their company's ethical policies and code of conduct, and, to some extent, by public opinion.

Corporate Social Responsibility
(See pages 42–52.)

Corporate social responsibility rests on the assumption that corporations should conduct their affairs in a socially responsible manner. Corporations are perceived to hold duties to the following groups:

1. **Shareholders**—Because the shareholders are the owners of the corporation, directors and officers have a duty to act in the shareholders' interest (maximize profits).

2. **Employees**—Employers have numerous legal duties to employees, including the duty to provide employees with a safe workplace and to refrain from discriminating against employees on the basis of race, color, national origin, gender, religion, age, or disability.

3. **Consumers**—Corporate directors and officers have a legal duty to the users of their products. Controversy exists over the point at which corporate responsibility for consumer safety ends and consumer responsibility begins.

4. **Society**—Most people hold that a corporation has a duty to the community in which it operates. The corporation should consider the needs of the community when making decisions that substantially affect the welfare of the community. Most people hold that a corporation also has a duty to society in general, but they differ in their ideas on how corporations can best fulfill this duty. One view is that corporations serve society's needs most effectively by maximizing profits because profits generally increase national wealth and social welfare. Another view holds that corporations, because they control so much of the country's wealth and power, should use that wealth and power in socially beneficial ways and not engage in actions that society deems unethical. It is difficult to measure corporate social responsibility because different yardsticks are used. Traditionally, corporate philanthropy has been utilized as a means of measuring corporate social responsibility. Increasingly, corporate process—how a corporation conducts its business on a day-to-day basis—is a key factor in determining whether a corporation is socially responsible.

(Continued)

Chapter Summary • Ethics and Social Responsibility, *Continued*

Ethics in the Global Context (See pages 52–56.)	There are many cultural, religious, and legal differences among nations. Notable differences relate to the role of women in society, employment laws governing workplace conditions, and the practice of giving side payments to foreign officials to secure favorable contracts.

For Review

1. What is ethics? What is business ethics?

2. What are some sources of ethical standards?

3. What questions are considered in ethical business decision making?

4. To what groups does a corporation owe duties? Why do these duties sometimes come into conflict?

5. What is the difference between maximum profits and optimum profits?

Questions and Case Problems

2–1. Business Ethics. Some business ethicists maintain that whereas personal ethics has to do with right or wrong behavior, business ethics is concerned with appropriate behavior. In other words, ethical behavior in business has less to do with moral principles than with what society deems to be appropriate behavior in the business context. Do you agree with this distinction? Do personal and business ethics ever overlap? Should personal ethics play any role in ethical business decision making?

2–2. Ethical Decision Making. Assume that you are a high-level manager for a shoe manufacturer. You know that your firm could increase its profit margin by producing shoes in Indonesia, where you could hire women for $100 a month to assemble them. You also know, however, that a competing shoe manufacturer recently was accused by human rights advocates of engaging in exploitative labor practices because the manufacturer sold shoes made by Indonesian women for similarly low wages. You personally do not believe that paying $100 a month to Indonesian women is unethical, because you know that in that country, $100 a month is a better-than-average wage rate. Assuming that the decision is yours to make, should you have the shoes manufactured in Indonesia and make higher profits for your company? Should you instead avoid the risk of negative publicity and the consequences of that publicity for the firm's reputation and subsequent profits? Are there other alternatives? Discuss fully.

2–3. Ethical Decision Making. In recent years, human rights groups, environmental activists, and other interest groups concerned with unethical business practices have conducted publicity campaigns against various corporations that those groups feel have engaged in unethical practices. Do you believe that a small group of well-organized activists should dictate how a major corporation should conduct its affairs? Discuss fully.

2–4. Duty to Consumers. Two eight-year-old boys, Douglas Bratz and Bradley Baughn, were injured while riding a mini-trail bike manufactured by Honda Motor Co. Bratz, who was driving the bike while Baughn rode as a passenger behind him, ran three stop signs and then collided with a truck. Bratz did not see the truck because, at the time of the accident, he was looking behind him at a girl chasing them on another mini-trail bike. Bratz wore a helmet, but it flew off on impact because it was unfastened. Baughn was not wearing a helmet. The owner's manual for the mini-trail bike stated in bold print that the bike was intended for off-the-road use only and urged users to "Always Wear a Helmet." A prominent label on the bike itself also warned that the bike was for off-the-road use only and that it should not be used on public streets or highways. In addition, Bratz's father had repeatedly told the boy not to ride the bike in the street. The parents of the injured boys sued Honda, alleging that the mini-trail bike was unreasonably dangerous. Honda claimed it had sufficiently warned consumers of potential dangers that could result if the bike was not used as directed. Should Honda be held responsible for the boys' injuries? Why or why not? [*Baughn v. Honda Motor Co.,* 107 Wash.2d 127, 727 P.2d 655 (1986)]

2–5. Duty to Consumers. The Seven-Up Co., as part of a marketing scheme, placed two glass bottles of "Like" cola on the front entrance of the Gruenemeier residence. Russell Gruenemeier, a nine-year-old boy, began playing while holding one of the bottles. He tripped and fell, and the bottle broke, severely cutting his right eye and causing him to eventually lose his eyesight in the eye. Russell's mother brought an action against the Seven-Up Co. for damages, claiming that the cause of Russell's injury was Seven-Up's negligence. She claimed that the company was negligent because it placed potentially dangerous instrumentalities—glass bottles—within the reach of small children and that the firm should have used unbreakable bottles for its marketing scheme. Are glass bottles so potentially dangerous that the Seven-Up Co. should be held liable for the boy's harm? If you were the judge, how would you decide the issue? [*Gruenemeier v. Seven-Up Co.,* 229 Neb. 267, 426 N.W.2d 510 (1988)]

2–6. Duty to Consumers. The father of an eleven-year-old child sued the manufacturer of a jungle gym because the manufacturer had failed to warn users of the equipment that they might fall off the gym and get hurt, as the boy did in this case. The father also claimed that the jungle gym was unreasonably dangerous because, as his son began to fall and reached frantically for a bar to grasp, there was no bar within reach. The father based his argument in part on a previous case involving a plaintiff who was injured as a result of somersaulting off a trampoline. In that case [*Pell v. Victor J. Andrew High School,* 123 Ill.App.3d 423, 462 N.E.2d 858, 78 Ill.Dec. 739 (1984)], the court had held that the trampoline's manufacturer was liable for the plaintiff's injuries because it had failed to warn of the trampoline's propensity to cause severe spinal cord injuries if it was used for somersaulting. Should the court be convinced by the father's arguments? Why or why not? [*Cozzi v. North Palos Elementary School District No. 117,* 232 Ill.App.3d 379, 597 N.E.2d 683, 173 Ill.Dec. 709 (1992)]

2–7. Duty to Employees. Matt Theurer, an eighteen-year-old high school senior, worked part-time at a McDonald's restaurant in Oregon. Theurer volunteered to work an extra shift one day, in addition to his regular shifts (one preceding and one following the extra shift). After working about twelve hours during a twenty-four-hour period, Theurer told the manager that he was tired and asked to be excused from his next regularly scheduled shift so that he could rest. The manager agreed. While driving home from work, Theurer fell asleep at the wheel and crashed into a van driven by Frederic Faverty. Theurer died, and Faverty was severely injured. Faverty sued McDonald's, alleging, among other things, that McDonald's was negligent in permitting Theurer to drive a car when it should have known that Theurer was too tired to drive safely. Do employers have a duty to prevent fatigued employees from driving home from work? Should such a duty be imposed on them? How should the court decide this issue? How would you decide the issue if you were the judge? [*Faverty v. McDonald's Restaurants of Oregon, Inc.,* 133 Or.App. 514, 892 P.2d 703 (1994)]

2–8. Duty to Consumers. Isuzu Motors America, Inc., does not warn its customers of the danger of riding unrestrained in the cargo beds of its pickup trucks. Seventeen-year-old Donald Josue was riding unrestrained in the bed of an Isuzu truck driven by Iaone Frias. When Frias lost control of the truck, it struck a concrete center divider. Josue was ejected and his consequent injuries rendered him a paraplegic. Josue filed a suit in a Hawaii state court against Isuzu, asserting a variety of legal claims based on its failure to warn of the danger of riding in the bed of the truck. Should Isuzu be held liable for Josue's injuries? Why or why not? [*Josue v. Isuzu Motors America, Inc.,* 87 Haw. 413, 958 P.2d 535 (1998)]

A Question of Ethics and Social Responsibility

2–9. Hazen Paper Co. manufactured paper and paperboard for use in such products as cosmetic wrap, lottery tickets, and pressure-sensitive items. Walter Biggins, a chemist hired by Hazen in 1977, developed a water-based paper coating that was both environmentally safe and of superior quality. By the mid-1980s, the company's sales had increased dramatically as a result of its extensive use of "Biggins Acrylic." Because of this, Biggins thought he deserved a substantial raise in salary, and from 1984 to 1986, Biggins's persistent requests for a raise became a bone of contention between him and his employers. Biggins ran a business on the side, which involved cleaning up hazardous wastes for various companies. Hazen told Biggins that unless he signed a "confidentiality agreement" promising to restrict his outside activities during the time he was employed by Hazen and for a limited time afterward, he would be fired. Biggins said he would sign the agreement only if Hazen raised his salary to $100,000. Hazen refused to do so, fired Biggins, and hired a younger man to replace him. At the time of his discharge in 1986, Biggins was sixty-two years old, had worked for the company nearly ten years, and was just a few weeks away from being entitled to pension rights worth about $93,000. In view of these circumstances, evaluate and answer the following questions. [*Hazen Paper Co. v. Biggins,* 507 U.S. 604, 113 S.Ct. 1701, 123 L.Ed.2d 338 (1993)]

1. Did the company owe an ethical duty to Biggins to increase his salary, given the fact that its sales increased dramatically as a result of Biggins's efforts and ingenuity in developing the coating? If you were one of the company's executives, would you have raised Biggins's salary? Why or why not?
2. Generally, what public policies come into conflict in cases involving employers who, for reasons of cost and efficiency of operations, fire older, higher-paid workers and replace them with younger, lower-paid workers? If you were an employer facing the need to cut back on personnel to save costs, what would you do, and on what ethical premises would you justify your decision?

For Critical Analysis

2–10. If a firm engages in "ethically responsible" behavior solely for the purpose of gaining profits from the goodwill it generates, the "ethical" behavior is essentially a means toward a self-serving end (profits and the accumulation of wealth). In this situation, is the firm acting unethically in any way? Should motive or conduct carry greater weight on the ethical scales in this situation?

Interacting with the Internet

■ For updated links to resources available on the Web, as well as a variety of other materials, visit this text's Web site at

http://leet.westbuslaw.com

■ The Web site of DePaul University's Institute for Business and Professional Ethics includes several examples of the types of ethical issues that can arise in the business context. Go to

http://condor.depaul.edu/ethics/ biz17.html

■ You can find articles on issues relating to shareholders and corporate accountability at the Corporate Governance Web site. Go to

http://www.corpgov.net

■ Numerous online groups focus on the activities of various corporations from an ethical perspective. A good starting point for locating these kinds of Web sites is Baobab's Corporate Power Information Center at

http://www.baobabcomputing.com/ corporatepower

Online Legal Research Exercises

Go to **http://leet. westbuslaw.com**, the Web site that accompanies this text. Select "Interactive Study Center," and then click on "Chapter 2." There you will find the following Internet research exercises that you can perform to learn more about ethics and business decision making:

Activity 2–1: Ethics in Business
Activity 2–2: Environmental Self-Audits

Before the Test

Go to **http://leet.westbuslaw. com**, the Web site that accompanies this text. Select "Interactive Quizzes." You will find a number of interactive questions relating to this chapter.

The American Court System

contents

chapter objectives

After reading this chapter, you should be able to:

1. Explain the concepts of jurisdiction and venue.

2. State the requirements for federal jurisdiction.

3. Identify the basic components of the federal and state court systems.

4. Compare and contrast the functions of trial courts and appellate courts.

5. Discuss the various steps involved in an appeal.

> "The Judicial Department comes home in its effects to every man's fireside: it passes on his property, his reputation, his life, his all."
>
> John Marshall, 1755–1835
> (Chief Justice of the United States
> Supreme Court, 1801–1835)

As Chief Justice John Marshall remarked in the quotation alongside, ultimately, we are all affected by what the courts say and do. This is particularly true in the business world—nearly every businessperson faces either a potential or an actual lawsuit at some time or another in his or her career. For this reason, anyone contemplating a career in business will benefit from an understanding of American court systems, including the mechanics of lawsuits.

In this chapter, after examining the judiciary's overall role in the American governmental scheme, we discuss some basic requirements that must be met before a party may bring a lawsuit before a particular court. We then look at the court systems of the United States in some detail and, to clarify judicial procedures, follow a hypothetical case through a state court system. Even though there are fifty-two court systems—one for each of the fifty states, one for the District of Columbia, plus a federal system—similarities abound. Keep in mind that the federal courts are not superior to the state courts; they are simply an independent system of courts, which derives its authority from Article III, Section 2, of the U.S. Constitution. The chapter concludes with an overview of some alternative methods of settling disputes.

Note that technological developments are affecting court procedures just as they are affecting all other areas of the law. This important topic will be explored in detail in Chapter 7.

The Judiciary's Role in American Government

As you learned in Chapter 1, the body of American law is vast and complex. It includes the federal and state constitutions, statutes passed by legislative bodies, administrative law, and the case decisions and legal principles that form the common law. These laws would be meaningless, however, without the courts to interpret and apply them. This is the essential role of the judiciary—the courts—in the American governmental system: to interpret and apply the law.

As the branch of government entrusted with interpreting the laws, the judiciary can decide, among other things, whether the laws or actions of the other two branches are constitutional. The process for making such a determination is known as **judicial review.** The power of judicial review enables the judicial branch to act as a check on the other two branches of government, in line with the checks-and-balances system established by the U.S. Constitution.

Judicial Review The process by which a court decides on the constitutionality of legislative enactments and actions of the executive branch.

The power of judicial review was not mentioned in the Constitution, but the concept was not new at the time the nation was founded. Indeed, prior to 1789 state courts had already overturned state legislative acts that conflicted with state constitutions. Additionally, many of the founders expected the United States Supreme Court to assume a similar role with respect to the federal Constitution. Alexander Hamilton and James Madison both emphasized the importance of judicial review in their essays urging the adoption of the new Constitution.

The doctrine of judicial review was not legally established, however, until 1803, when the United States Supreme Court rendered its decision in *Marbury v. Madison.*[1] In that case, the Supreme Court stated, "It is emphatically the province and duty of the Judicial Department to say what the law is. . . . If two

---

1. 5 U.S. (1 Cranch) 137, 2 L.Ed. 60 (1803).

laws conflict with each other, the courts must decide on the operation of each. . . . So if the law be in opposition to the Constitution . . . [t]he Court must determine which of these conflicting rules governs the case. This is the very essence of judicial duty." Since the *Marbury v. Madison* decision, details of which are offered in this chapter's *Landmark in the Legal Environment,* the power of judicial review has remained unchallenged. Today, this power is exercised by both federal and state courts.

Landmark in the Legal Environment

Marbury v. Madison (1803)

In the edifice of American law, the *Marbury v. Madison* decision in 1803 can be viewed as the keystone of the constitutional arch. The facts of the case were as follows: John Adams, who had lost his bid for reelection to Thomas Jefferson in 1800, feared the Jeffersonians' antipathy toward business and toward a strong central government. Adams thus worked feverishly to "pack" the judiciary with loyal Federalists (those who believed in a strong national government) by appointing what came to be called "midnight judges" just before Jefferson took office. All of the fifty-nine judicial appointment letters had to be certified and delivered, but Adams's secretary of state (John Marshall) had only succeeded in delivering forty-two of them by the time Jefferson took over as president. Jefferson, of course, refused to order his secretary of state, James Madison, to deliver the remaining commissions.

William Marbury and three others to whom the commissions had not been delivered sought a writ of *mandamus* (an order directing a government official to fulfill a duty) from the United States Supreme Court, as authorized by Section 13 of the Judiciary Act of 1789. As fate would have it, John Marshall had stepped down as Adams's secretary of state only to become chief justice of the Supreme Court. Marshall faced a dilemma: If he ordered the commissions delivered, the new secretary of state (Madison) could simply refuse to deliver them—and the Court had no way to compel action, because it had no police force. At the same time, if Marshall simply allowed the new administration to do as it wished, the Court's power would be severely eroded.

Marshall masterfully fashioned a decision that did not require anyone to do anything but at the same

James Madison. If Madison had delivered the commissions of the Federalist judges, would the United States Supreme Court today have the power of judicial review?

time enlarged the power of the Supreme Court. He stated that the highest court did not have the power to issue a writ of *mandamus* in this particular case. Marshall pointed out that although the Judiciary Act of 1789 specified that the Supreme Court could issue writs of *mandamus* as part of its original jurisdiction, Article III of the Constitution, which spelled out the Court's original jurisdiction, did not mention writs of *mandamus.* Because Congress did not have the right to expand the Supreme Court's jurisdiction, this section of the Judiciary Act of 1789 was unconstitutional—and thus void. The decision still stands today as a judicial and political masterpiece.

For Critical Analysis: *What might result if the courts could not exercise the power of judicial review?*

International Perspective

Judicial Review across Nations

The concept of judicial review was pioneered by the United States. Today, however, all established constitutional democracies have some type of judicial review—the power to rule on the constitutionality of laws—but its form varies from country to country. For example, Canada's Supreme Court can exercise judicial review but is barred from doing so if a law includes a provision explicitly prohibiting such review. France has a Constitutional Council that rules on the constitutionality of laws before the laws take effect. Laws can be referred to the council for prior review by the president, prime minister, and the heads of the two chambers of parliament. Prior review is also an option in Germany and Italy, if requested by the national or a regional government. In contrast, the United States Supreme Court does not give advisory opinions; rather, there must be an actual dispute concerning an issue before the Supreme Court can render a decision on the matter.

For Critical Analysis: *In any country in which a constitution sets forth the basic powers and structure of government, some government branch or unit has to decide on whether laws enacted by government are consistent with that constitution. Is this task best handled by the courts? Can you think of a better alternative?*

Basic Judicial Requirements

Before a lawsuit can be brought before a court, certain requirements must first be met. These requirements relate to jurisdiction, venue, and standing to sue. We examine each of these important concepts here.

Jurisdiction

Jurisdiction The authority of a court to hear and decide a specific action.

In Latin, *juris* means "law," and *diction* means "to speak." Thus, "the power to speak the law" is the literal meaning of the term **jurisdiction.** Before any court can hear a case, it must have jurisdiction over the person against whom the suit is brought or over the property involved in the suit. The court must also have jurisdiction over the subject matter.

JURISDICTION OVER PERSONS   Generally, a court can exercise personal jurisdiction (*in personam* jurisdiction) over residents of a certain geographical area. A state trial court, for example, normally has jurisdictional authority over residents of a particular area of the state, such as a county or district. A state's highest court (often called the state supreme court)[2] has jurisdictional authority over all residents within the state.

Long Arm Statute A state statute that permits a state to obtain personal jurisdiction over nonresident defendants. A defendant must have certain "minimum contacts" with that state for the statute to apply.

In some cases, under the authority of a state **long arm statute,** a court can exercise personal jurisdiction over nonresident defendants as well. Before a court can exercise jurisdiction over a nonresident under a long arm statute, though, it must be demonstrated that the nonresident had sufficient contacts, or *minimum contacts*, with the state to justify the jurisdiction.[3] ● **Example 3.1** If an individual has committed a wrong within the state, such as causing an automobile accident or selling defective goods, a court can usually exercise ju-

2. As will be discussed shortly, a state's highest court is often referred to as the state supreme court, but there are exceptions. For example, in New York, the supreme court is a trial court.
3. The minimum-contacts standard was established in *International Shoe Co. v. State of Washington,* 326 U.S. 310, 66 S.Ct. 154, 90 L.Ed. 95 (1945).

risdiction even if the person causing the harm is located in another state. Similarly, a state may exercise personal jurisdiction over a nonresident defendant who is sued for breaching a contract that was formed within the state.•

In regard to corporations, the minimum-contacts requirement is usually met if the corporation does business within the state. • **Example 3.2** Suppose that a corporation incorporated under the laws of Maine and headquartered in that state has a sales office in Georgia. Does this corporation have sufficient minimum contacts with the state of Georgia to allow a Georgia court to exercise jurisdiction over the Maine corporation? Yes, it does. If the Maine corporation advertises and sells its products in Georgia, those activities may also suffice to meet the minimum-contacts requirement.•

In the following case, the issue was whether phone calls and letters constituted sufficient minimum contacts to give a court jurisdiction over a nonresident defendant.

Case 3.1 ● Cole v. Mileti

United States Court of Appeals, Sixth Circuit, 1998.
133 F.3d 433.
http://www.law.emory.edu/
6circuit/jan98/index.html[a]

Historical and Economic Setting *A movie production company is expensive to operate. Over the several years it can take to produce a film, there are many expenses, including maintaining an office and hiring professionals of all kinds. Newcomers to the industry make many of the same wrong moves that are the pitfalls of all businesses. For a novice producer or investor, there is the uncertainty of not knowing what you are doing and the danger of being outnegotiated*

---

a. This is a page at the Web site of the Emory University School of Law that lists the published opinions of the U.S. Court of Appeals for the Sixth Circuit for January 1998. Scroll down the list of cases to the *Cole* case. To access the opinion, click on the case name.

by those who prey on a novice's ignorance. Finally, once a film is made, there is the audience, which may not choose to see it.

Background and Facts Nick Mileti, a resident of California, co-produced a movie called *Streamers* and organized a corporation, Streamers International Distributors, Inc., to distribute the film. Joseph Cole, a resident of Ohio, bought two hundred shares of Streamers stock. Cole also lent the firm $475,000, which he borrowed from Equitable Bank of Baltimore. The film was unsuccessful. Mileti agreed to repay Cole's loan in a contract arranged through phone calls and correspondence between California and Ohio. When Mileti did not repay the loan, the bank sued Cole, who in turn filed a suit against Mileti in a federal district court in Ohio. The court entered a judgment against Mileti. He appealed to the U.S. Court of Appeals for the Sixth Circuit, arguing in part that the district court's exercise of jurisdiction over him was unfair.

In the Words of the Court . . .
MERRITT, Circuit Judge.

* * * *

* * * [There is] a three-part test to determine whether specific jurisdiction exists over a nonresident defendant like Mileti. First, the defendant must purposefully avail himself of the privilege of conducting activities within the forum state; second, the cause of action must arise from the defendant's activities there; and third, the acts of the defendant or consequences caused by the defendant must have a substantial enough connection with the forum state to make its exercise of jurisdiction over the defendant fundamentally fair.

(Continued)

Case 3.1 Continued

If, as here, a nonresident defendant transacts business by negotiating and executing a contract via telephone calls and letters to an Ohio resident, then the defendant has purposefully availed himself of the forum by creating a continuing obligation in Ohio. Furthermore, if the cause of action is for breach of that contract, as it is here, then the cause of action naturally arises from the defendant's activities in Ohio. Finally, when we find that a defendant like Mileti purposefully availed himself of the forum and that the cause of action arose directly from that contact, we presume the specific assertion of personal jurisdiction was proper.

Decision and Remedy The U.S. Court of Appeals for the Sixth Circuit held that the district court could exercise personal jurisdiction over Mileti. The appellate court reasoned that a federal district court in Ohio can exercise personal jurisdiction over a resident of California who does business in Ohio via phone calls and letters.

For Critical Analysis—Economic Consideration *Why might a defendant prefer to be sued in one state rather than in another?*

JURISDICTION OVER PROPERTY A court can also exercise jurisdiction over property that is located within its boundaries. This kind of jurisdiction is known as *in rem* jurisdiction, or "jurisdiction over the thing." • **Example 3.3** Suppose that a dispute arises over the ownership of a boat in dry dock in Fort Lauderdale, Florida. The boat is owned by an Ohio resident, over whom a Florida court cannot normally exercise personal jurisdiction. The other party to the dispute is a resident of Nebraska. In this situation, a lawsuit concerning the boat could be brought in a Florida state court on the basis of the court's *in rem* jurisdiction.•

JURISDICTION OVER SUBJECT MATTER Jurisdiction over subject matter is a limitation on the types of cases a court can hear. In both the federal and state court systems, there are courts of *general* (unlimited) *jurisdiction* and courts of *limited jurisdiction*. An example of a court of general jurisdiction is a state trial court or a federal district court. An example of a state court of limited jurisdiction is a probate court. **Probate courts** are state courts that handle only matters relating to the transfer of a person's assets and obligations after that person's death, including matters relating to the custody and guardianship of children. An example of a federal court of limited subject-matter jurisdiction is a bankruptcy court. **Bankruptcy courts** handle only bankruptcy proceedings, which are governed by federal bankruptcy law (discussed in Chapter 23). In contrast, a court of general jurisdiction can decide a broad array of cases.

A court's jurisdiction over subject matter is usually defined in the statute or constitution creating the court. In both the federal and state court systems, a court's subject-matter jurisdiction can be limited not only by the subject of the lawsuit but also by the amount of money in controversy, by whether a case is a felony (a more serious type of crime) or a misdemeanor (a less serious type of crime), or by whether the proceeding is a trial or an appeal.

Probate Court A state court of limited jurisdiction that conducts proceedings relating to the settlement of a deceased person's estate.

Bankruptcy Court A federal court of limited jurisdiction that handles only bankruptcy proceedings. Bankruptcy proceedings are governed by federal bankruptcy law.

ORIGINAL AND APPELLATE JURISDICTION The distinction between courts of original jurisdiction and courts of appellate jurisdiction normally lies in whether the case is being heard for the first time. Courts having original jurisdiction are courts of the first instance, or trial courts—that is, courts in which lawsuits begin, trials take place, and evidence is presented. In the federal court system, the *district courts* are trial courts. In the various state court systems, the trial courts are known by various names, as will be discussed shortly.

The key point here is that normally, any court having original jurisdiction is known as a trial court. Courts having appellate jurisdiction act as reviewing courts, or appellate courts. In general, cases can be brought before appellate courts only on appeal from an order or a judgment of a trial court or other lower court.

JURISDICTION OF THE FEDERAL COURTS Because the federal government is a government of limited powers, the jurisdiction of the federal courts is limited. Article III of the U.S. Constitution establishes the boundaries of federal judicial power. Section 2 of Article III states that "[t]he judicial Power shall extend to all Cases, in Law and Equity, arising under this Constitution, the Laws of the United States, and Treaties made, or which shall be made, under their Authority."

Whenever a plaintiff's cause of action is based, at least in part, on the U.S. Constitution, a treaty, or a federal law, then a **federal question** arises, and the case comes under the judicial power of the federal courts. Any lawsuit involving a federal question can originate in a federal court. People who claim that their constitutional rights have been violated can begin their suits in a federal court.

Federal district courts can also exercise original jurisdiction over cases involving **diversity of citizenship.** Such cases may arise between (1) citizens of different states, (2) a foreign country and citizens of a state or of different states, or (3) citizens of a state and citizens or subjects of a foreign country. The amount in controversy must be more than $75,000 before a federal court can take jurisdiction in such cases. For purposes of diversity jurisdiction, a corporation is a citizen of both the state in which it is incorporated and the state in which its principal place of business is located. A case involving diversity of citizenship can be filed in the appropriate federal district court, or, if the case starts in a state court, it can sometimes be transferred to a federal court. A large percentage of the cases filed in federal courts each year are based on diversity of citizenship.

Note that in a case based on a federal question, a federal court will apply federal law. In a case based on diversity of citizenship, however, a federal court will apply the relevant state law (which is often the law of the state in which the court sits).

EXCLUSIVE VERSUS CONCURRENT JURISDICTION When both federal and state courts have the power to hear a case, as is true in suits involving diversity of citizenship, **concurrent jurisdiction** exists. When cases can be tried only in federal courts or only in state courts, exclusive jurisdiction exists. Federal courts have **exclusive jurisdiction** in cases involving federal crimes, bankruptcy, patents, and copyrights; in suits against the United States; and in some areas of admiralty law (law governing transportation on the seas and ocean waters). States also have exclusive jurisdiction in certain subject matters—for example, in divorce and adoption. The concepts of concurrent and exclusive jurisdiction are illustrated in Exhibit 3–1 on the next page.

Federal Question A question that pertains to the U.S. Constitution, acts of Congress, or treaties. A federal question provides a basis for federal jurisdiction.

Diversity of Citizenship Under Article III, Section 2, of the Constitution, a basis for federal district court jurisdiction over a lawsuit between (1) citizens of different states, (2) a foreign country and citizens of a state or of different states, or (3) citizens of a state and citizens or subjects of a foreign country. The amount in controversy must be more than $75,000 before a federal district court can take jurisdiction in such cases.

Concurrent Jurisdiction Jurisdiction that exists when two different courts have the power to hear a case. For example, some cases can be heard in a federal or a state court.

Exclusive Jurisdiction Jurisdiction that exists when a case can be heard only in a particular court or type of court.

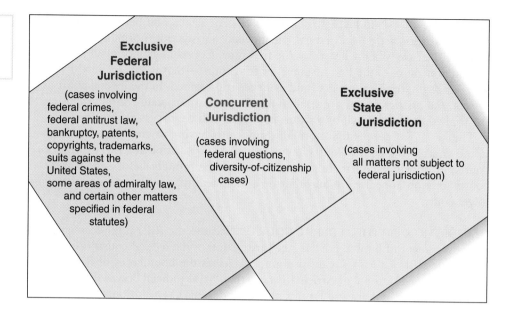

**Exclusive
Federal
Jurisdiction**

(cases involving
federal crimes,
federal antitrust law,
bankruptcy, patents,
copyrights, trademarks,
suits against the
United States,
some areas of admiralty law,
and certain other matters
specified in federal
statutes)

**Concurrent
Jurisdiction**

(cases involving
federal questions,
diversity-of-citizenship
cases)

**Exclusive
State
Jurisdiction**

(cases involving
all matters not subject to
federal jurisdiction)

When a case can be brought in more than one court, such as in a state court or a federal court, the choice is up to the party bringing the suit. Normally, the party's attorney helps the client decide this issue. The lawyer might prefer to bring the suit in a state court for any number of reasons. The lawyer may expect that the state court's judge or jury will be more sympathetic to the client and the case, or the lawyer may want to avoid some aspect of federal practice or procedural rule that does not exist in the state court. The lawyer may simply have more experience litigating cases in the state court. The attorney may prefer to sue in a federal court for similar reasons. Jurisdictional issues also may play a role in the decision. Note that attorneys have an ethical (and legal) obligation to serve their clients' best interests, and thus care must be taken in choosing the forum (court) in which the client's case will be heard—particularly if the attorney believes that the choice may affect the outcome of the case.

Venue

Venue The geographical district in which an action is tried and from which the jury is selected.

Jurisdiction has to do with whether a court has authority to hear a case involving specific persons, property, or subject matter. **Venue**[4] is concerned with the most appropriate location for a trial. Two state courts (or two federal courts) may have the authority to exercise jurisdiction over a case, but it may be more appropriate or convenient to hear the case in one court than in the other.

Basically, the concept of venue reflects the policy that a court trying a suit should be in the geographical neighborhood (usually the county) in which the incident leading to the lawsuit occurred or in which the parties involved in the lawsuit reside. Pretrial publicity or other factors, though, may require a change of venue to another community, especially in criminal cases in which the defendant's right to a fair and impartial jury has been impaired. • **Example 3.4** A change of venue from Oklahoma City to Denver, Colorado, was ordered for

---

4. Pronounced *ven*-yoo.

the trials of Timothy McVeigh and Terry Nichols, who had been indicted in connection with the 1995 bombing of the Alfred P. Murrah Federal Building in Oklahoma City.•

Standing to Sue

Before a person can bring a lawsuit before a court, the party must have **standing to sue,** or a sufficient "stake" in a matter to justify seeking relief through the court system. In other words, a party must have a legally protected and tangible interest at stake in the litigation in order to have standing. The party bringing the lawsuit must have suffered a harm, or have been threatened by a harm, as a result of the action about which he or she complained. At times, a person will have standing to sue on behalf of another person. • **Example 3.5** Suppose that a child suffered serious injuries as a result of a defectively manufactured toy. Because the child is a minor, a lawsuit could be brought on his or her behalf by another person, such as the child's parent or legal guardian.•

Standing to sue also requires that the controversy at issue be a **justiciable**[5] **controversy**—a controversy that is real and substantial, as opposed to hypothetical or academic. • **Example 3.6** In the above example, the child's parent could not sue the toy manufacturer merely on the ground that the toy was defective. The issue would become justiciable only if the child had actually been injured due to the defect in the toy as marketed. In other words, the parent normally could not ask the court to determine, for example, what damages might be obtained if the child had been injured, because this would merely be a hypothetical question.•

Meeting standing requirements is not always easy. In the following case, for example, an environmental organization sued a company for allegedly discharging pollutants into waterways beyond the amount allowed by the Environmental Protection Agency. At issue in the case was whether the organization had standing to sue under federal environmental laws.

Standing to Sue The requirement that an individual must have a sufficient stake in a controversy before he or she can bring a lawsuit. The plaintiff must demonstrate that he or she either has been injured or threatened with injury.

Justiciable Controversy A controversy that is not hypothetical or academic but real and substantial; a requirement that must be satisfied before a court will hear a case.

5. Pronounced jus-*tish*-uh-bul.

Case 3.2 • Friends of the Earth, Inc. v. Crown Central Petroleum Corp.

United States Court of Appeals, Fifth Circuit, 1996.
95 F.3d 358.
http://www.ca5.uscourts.gov/oparchdt.cfm?Year-1996[a]

Historical and Environmental Setting
In the early 1970s, the Sierra Club, a conservation or-

ganization, challenged the Environmental Protection Agency's approval of locating a ski complex near a national wilderness area. The court refused to consider the challenge on the ground that the Sierra Club did not show that it had standing to bring the suit. The United States Supreme Court upheld this decision.[b] The Sierra Club amended its complaint to allege that some of its members used, hiked in, and enjoyed the wilderness area that the development threatened. It

a. This is the "Opinions Archive by Date Released" page within the Web site of the U.S. Courts of the Fifth Judicial Circuit. Click on "1996." When the link opens, click on "September." When that link opens, click on "September 3." From the list of cases that appears, click on the appropriate case name to access the opinion.

b. *Sierra Club v. Morton,* 405 U.S. 727, 92 S.Ct. 1361, 31 L.Ed.2d 636 (1972).

(Continued)

Case 3.2 Continued

also alleged that the ski complex compromised these members' enjoyment of the area. The court then agreed to hear the case. In 1972, Congress incorporated this same test for standing into the Federal Water Pollution Control Act.

Background and Facts Crown Central Petroleum Corporation does business as La Gloria Oil & Gas Company. Under a permit issued by the Environmental Protection Agency (EPA), La Gloria's oil refinery discharges storm-water run-off into Black Fork Creek. Black Fork Creek flows into Prairie Creek, which flows into the Neches River, which flows into Lake Palestine eighteen miles downstream. Friends of

the Earth, Inc. (FOE), is a not-for-profit corporation dedicated to the protection of the environment. FOE filed a suit in a federal district court against La Gloria under the Federal Water Pollution Control Act.[c] FOE claimed that La Gloria had violated its EPA permit and that this conduct had directly affected "the health, economic, recreational, aesthetic and environmental interests of FOE's members" who used the lake. La Gloria filed a motion for summary judgment, arguing that FOE lacked standing to bring the suit. The court granted the motion, and FOE appealed.

_____
c. 33 U.S.C. Sections 1251–1387.

In the Words of the Court . . .
PATRICK E. HIGGINBOTHAM, Circuit Judge:

* * * *

To demonstrate that FOE's members have standing, FOE must show that * * * the injury is "fairly traceable" to the defendant's actions * * * .

* * * *

* * * FOE offered no competent evidence that La Gloria's discharges have made their way to Lake Palestine or would otherwise affect Lake Palestine. * * * FOE and its members relied solely on the truism that water flows downstream and inferred therefrom that any injury suffered downstream is "fairly traceable" to unlawful discharges upstream. At some point this common sense observation becomes little more than surmise. At that point certainly the requirements [for standing] are not met.

Decision and Remedy The U.S. Court of Appeals for the Fifth Circuit affirmed the lower court's decision. FOE lacked standing to bring a suit against La Gloria.

For Critical Analysis—Social Consideration *What might result if the courts did not impose the requirement of standing to sue?*

The State and Federal Court Systems

> **"The perfect judge fears nothing—he could go front to front before God."**
>
> Walt Whitman, 1819–1892
> (American poet)

As mentioned earlier in this chapter, each state has its own court system. Additionally, there is a system of federal courts. Although state court systems differ, Exhibit 3–2 illustrates the basic organizational structure characteristic of the court systems in many states. The exhibit also shows how the federal court system is structured. We turn now to an examination of these court systems, beginning with the state courts.

Technology is affecting all areas of government, and the judiciary is no exception. Today's courts are becoming increasingly "wired," and there is little doubt that in the future we will see more court proceedings being conducted via the Internet—as discussed in this chapter's feature, *Legal E-nvironment: Toward a Virtual Courtroom* on page 72.

Exhibit 3-2 Federal Courts and State Court Systems

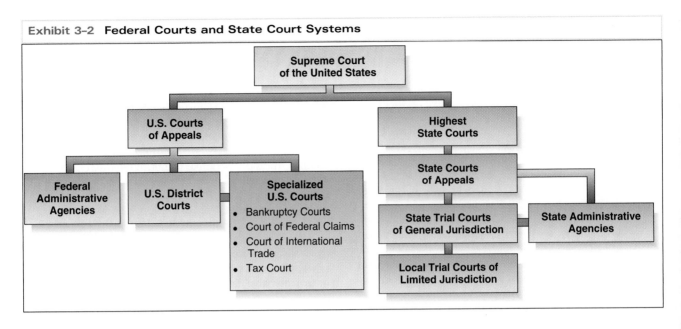

State Court Systems

Typically a state court system will include several levels, or tiers, of courts. As indicated in Exhibit 3–2, state courts may include (1) trial courts of limited jurisdiction, (2) trial courts of general jurisdiction, (3) appellate courts, and (4) the state's highest court (often called the state supreme court). Judges in the state court system are usually elected by the voters for a specified term.

Generally, any person who is a party to a lawsuit has the opportunity to plead the case before a trial court and then, if he or she loses, before at least one level of appellate court. Finally, if a federal statute or federal constitutional issue is involved in the decision of the state supreme court, that decision may be further appealed to the United States Supreme Court.

TRIAL COURTS   Trial courts are exactly what their name implies—courts in which trials are held and testimony taken. State trial courts have either general or limited jurisdiction. Trial courts that have general jurisdiction as to subject matter may be called county, district, superior, or circuit courts.[6] The jurisdiction of these courts is often determined by the size of the county in which the court sits. State trial courts of general jurisdiction have jurisdiction over a wide variety of subjects, including both civil disputes and criminal prosecutions. In some states, trial courts of general jurisdiction may hear appeals from courts of limited jurisdiction.

Some courts of limited jurisdiction are called special inferior trial courts or minor judiciary courts. **Small claims courts** are inferior trial courts that hear only civil cases involving claims of less than a certain amount, such as $5,000 (the amount varies from state to state). Suits brought in small claims courts are generally conducted informally, and lawyers are not required. In a minority of states, lawyers are not even allowed to represent people in small claims courts for most purposes. Another example of an inferior trial court is a local municipal court that hears mainly traffic cases. Decisions of small claims courts

Small Claims Courts
Special courts in which parties may litigate small claims (usually, claims involving $5,000 or less). Attorneys are not required in small claims courts, and in many states attorneys are not allowed to represent the parties.

---

6. The name in Ohio is court of common pleas; the name in New York is supreme court.

Legal *e*-nvironment

Toward a Virtual Courtroom

Most courts in the United States now have sites on the Web. Of course, it is up to each court to decide what to make available at its site. Some courts display only the names of court personnel and office phone numbers. Others add court rules and forms. Some include judicial decisions, although generally the sites do not include archives of old decisions. Instead, the time within which decisions are available online is limited. For example, California keeps opinions online for only sixty days. Generally, except for the decisions of the United States Supreme Court and some opinions in classic cases, few court decisions that predate the 1990s are available online free of charge.

At some point in the future, we may see the use of *virtual courtrooms,* in which judicial proceedings take place totally via the Internet. Already, a number of courts allow parties to file court documents, such as those initiating a lawsuit, electronically.

Electronic Filing

The federal court system first experimented with an electronic filing system in January 1996, in an asbestos case heard by a federal court in Ohio. Currently, more than a dozen federal courts permit attorneys to file documents electronically in certain types of cases. At last count, more than 130,000 documents in approximately 10,000 cases had been filed electronically in federal courts.

State and local courts also are setting up electronic court filing systems. Since late 1997, the Pima County, Arizona, court system has been accepting filings of litigation documents via e-mail. In 1998, the supreme court of the state of Washington also began to accept online filings of litigation documents. Electronic filing projects are also being developed in other states, including Kansas, Virginia, Utah, and Michigan. Notably, the judicial branch of the state of Colorado recently decided to implement the first statewide court e-filing system in the United States. When implementation is complete, an Internet-based service will allow all Colorado civil courts to accept legal filings electronically. In California, Florida, and a few other states, some court clerks offer docket information and other searchable databases online.

Virtual Courtrooms

In the future, it is possible that litigation will also be conducted entirely via the Internet. The parties to a case could meet online to make their arguments and present their evidence. This might be done with e-mail submissions, through video cameras, in designated "chat" rooms, at closed sites, or through the use of any other Internet facility. These courtrooms could be efficient and economical. It is possible that we will also see the use of virtual lawyers, judges, and juries.

For Critical Analysis: *Some individuals are concerned about the possibility that people will have less respect for the law if litigation is conducted via the Internet instead of in traditional courtrooms. Do you agree? Why or why not?*

---

and municipal courts may be appealed to a state trial court of general jurisdiction.

Other courts of limited jurisdiction as to subject matter include domestic relations courts, which handle only divorce actions and child-custody cases, and probate courts, as mentioned earlier.

COURTS OF APPEALS Every state has at least one court of appeals (appellate court, or reviewing court), which may be an intermediate appellate court or the state's highest court. About three-fourths of the states have intermediate appellate courts. Generally, courts of appeals do not conduct new trials, in which evidence is submitted to the court and witnesses are examined. Rather, an appellate court panel of three or more judges reviews the record of the case on appeal, which includes a transcript of the trial proceedings, and the panel determines whether the trial court committed an error.

Usually, appellate courts do not look at questions of *fact* (such as whether a party did, in fact, commit a certain action, such as burning a flag) but at questions of *law* (such as whether the act of flag-burning is a form of speech protected by the First Amendment to the Constitution). Only a judge, not a jury, can rule on questions of law. Appellate courts normally defer to a trial court's findings on questions of fact because the trial court judge and jury were in a better position to evaluate testimony—by directly observing witnesses' gestures, demeanor, and nonverbal behavior during the trial. At the appellate level, the judges review the written transcript of the trial, which does not include these nonverbal elements.

An appellate court will challenge a trial court's finding of fact only when the finding is clearly erroneous (that is, when it is contrary to the evidence presented at trial) or when there is no evidence to support the finding. • **Example 3.7** If a jury concluded that a manufacturer's product harmed the plaintiff but no evidence was submitted to the court to support that conclusion, the appellate court would hold that the trial court's decision was erroneous. The options exercised by appellate courts will be further discussed later in this chapter.•

STATE SUPREME (HIGHEST) COURTS   The highest appellate court in a state is usually called the supreme court but may be called by some other name. For example, in both New York and Maryland, the highest state court is called the court of appeals. The decisions of each state's highest court on all questions of state law are final. Only when issues of federal law are involved can a decision made by a state's highest court be overruled by the United States Supreme Court.

> **Be Careful** The decisions of a state's highest court are final on questions of state law.

The Federal Court System

The federal court system is basically a three-tiered model consisting of (1) U.S. district courts (trial courts of general jurisdiction) and various courts of limited jurisdiction, (2) U.S. courts of appeals (intermediate courts of appeals), and (3) the United States Supreme Court.

Unlike state court judges, who are usually elected, federal court judges—including the justices of the Supreme Court—are appointed by the president of the United States and confirmed by the U.S. Senate. All federal judges receive lifetime appointments (because under Article III they "hold their offices during Good Behavior").

U.S. DISTRICT COURTS   At the federal level, the equivalent of a state trial court of general jurisdiction is the district court. There is at least one federal district court in every state. The number of judicial districts can vary over time, primarily owing to population changes and corresponding caseloads. Currently, there are ninety-four federal judicial districts.

U.S. district courts have original jurisdiction in federal matters. Federal cases typically originate in district courts. There are other courts with original, but special (or limited), jurisdiction, such as the federal bankruptcy courts and others shown in Exhibit 3–2 on page 71.

U.S. COURTS OF APPEALS   In the federal court system, there are thirteen U.S. courts of appeals—also referred to as U.S. circuit courts of appeals. The federal courts of appeals for twelve of the circuits, including the U.S. Court of

> "I am unaware that any nation of the globe has hitherto organized a judicial power in the same manner as the Americans. . . . A more imposing judicial power was never constituted by any people."
>
> Alexis de Tocqueville, 1805–1859
> (French historian and statesman)

Appeals for the District of Columbia Circuit, hear appeals from the federal district courts located within their respective judicial circuits. The Court of Appeals for the Thirteenth Circuit, called the Federal Circuit, has national appellate jurisdiction over certain types of cases, such as cases involving patent law and cases in which the U.S. government is a defendant.

The decisions of the circuit courts of appeals are final in most cases, but appeal to the United States Supreme Court is possible. Exhibit 3–3 shows the geographical boundaries of U.S. circuit courts of appeals and the boundaries of the U.S. district courts within each circuit.

THE UNITED STATES SUPREME COURT   The highest level of the three-tiered model of the federal court system is the United States Supreme Court. According to the language of Article III of the U.S. Constitution, there is only one national Supreme Court. All other courts in the federal system are considered "inferior." Congress is empowered to create other inferior courts as it deems necessary. The inferior courts that Congress has created include the second tier in our model—the U.S. courts of appeals—as well as the district courts and any other courts of limited, or specialized, jurisdiction.

The United States Supreme Court consists of nine justices. Although the United States Supreme Court has original, or trial, jurisdiction in rare instances (set forth in Article III, Section 2), most of its work is as an appeals

> **"We are not final because we are infallible, but we are infallible only because we are final."**
>
> Robert H. Jackson, 1892–1954
> (Associate justice of the United States Supreme Court, 1941–1954)

Exhibit 3–3   U.S. Courts of Appeals and U.S. District Courts

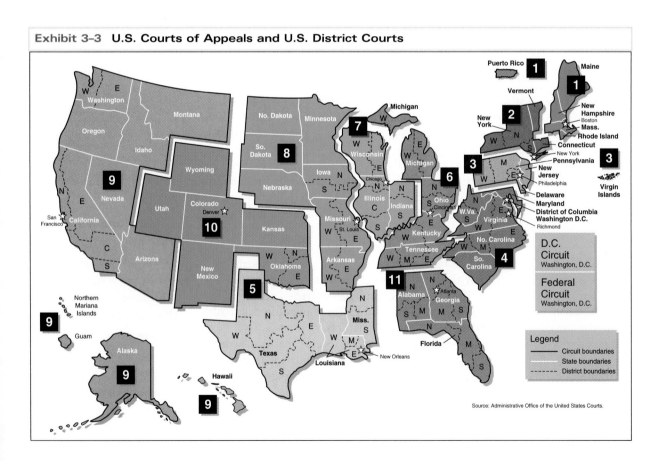

Source: Administrative Office of the United States Courts.

The justices of the United States Supreme Court as of early 2001 are, seated left to right, Antonin Scalia, John Paul Stevens, Chief Justice William H. Rehnquist, Sandra Day O'Connor, and Anthony M. Kennedy; and standing left to right, Ruth Bader Ginsburg, David H. Souter, Clarence Thomas, and Stephen Breyer. Does the fact that these justices are appointed for life have any effect on the decisions they reach in the cases they hear?

court. The Supreme Court can review any case decided by any of the federal courts of appeals, and it also has appellate authority over some cases decided in the state courts.

To bring a case before the Supreme Court, a party requests the Court to issue a writ of *certiorari*. A **writ of *certiorari***[7] is an order issued by the Supreme Court to a lower court requiring the latter to send it the record of the case for review. The Court will not issue a writ unless at least four of the nine justices approve of it. This is called the **rule of four.** Whether the Court will issue a writ of *certiorari* is entirely within its discretion. The Court is not required to issue one, and most petitions for writs are denied. (Thousands of cases are filed with the Supreme Court each year, yet it hears, on average, less than one hundred of these cases.[8]) A denial is not a decision on the merits of a case, nor does it indicate agreement with the lower court's opinion. Furthermore, a denial of the writ has no value as a precedent.

Writ of *Certiorari* A writ from a higher court asking the lower court for the record of a case.

Rule of Four A rule of the United States Supreme Court under which the Court will not issue a writ of *certiorari* unless at least four justices approve of the decision to issue the writ.

Typically, the petitions granted by the Court involve cases that raise important constitutional questions or cases that conflict with other state or federal court decisions. Similarly, if federal appellate courts are rendering inconsistent opinions on an important issue, the Supreme Court may review the case and issue a decision to define the law on the matter.

Following a State Court Case

To illustrate the procedures that would be followed in a civil lawsuit brought in a state court, we present a hypothetical case and follow it through the state court system. The case involves an automobile accident in which Kevin Anderson, driving a Mercedes, struck Lisa Marconi, driving a Ford Taurus.

---

7. Pronounced sur-shee-uh-*rah*-ree.
8. From the mid-1950s through the early 1990s, the Supreme Court reviewed more cases per year than it has in the last few years. In the Court's 1982–1983 term, for example, the Court issued opinions in 151 cases. In contrast, since the mid-1990s, the Court has issued opinions in only about 80 to 90 cases each term.

The accident occurred at the intersection of Wilshire Boulevard and Rodeo Drive in Beverly Hills, California. Marconi suffered personal injuries, incurring medical and hospital expenses as well as lost wages for four months. Anderson and Marconi are unable to agree on a settlement, and Marconi sues Anderson. Marconi is the plaintiff, and Anderson is the defendant. Both are represented by lawyers.

During each phase of the **litigation** (the process of working a lawsuit through the court system), Marconi and Anderson will be required to observe strict procedural requirements. A large body of law—procedural law—establishes the rules and standards for determining disputes in courts. Procedural rules are very complex, and they vary from court to court. There is a set of federal rules of procedure and various sets of rules for state courts. Additionally, the applicable procedures will depend on whether the case is a civil or criminal proceeding. Generally, the Marconi-Anderson civil lawsuit will involve the procedures discussed in the following subsections. Keep in mind that attempts to settle the case may be ongoing throughout the trial.

Litigation The process of resolving a dispute through the court system.

The Pleadings

The complaint and answer (and the counterclaim and reply)—all of which are discussed below—taken together are called the **pleadings**. The pleadings inform each party of the claims of the other and specify the issues (disputed questions) involved in the case.

Pleadings Statements made by the plaintiff and the defendant in a lawsuit that detail the facts, charges, and defenses involved in the litigation; the complaint and answer are part of the pleadings.

THE PLAINTIFF'S COMPLAINT Marconi's suit against Anderson commences when her lawyer files a **complaint** with the appropriate court. The complaint contains a statement alleging (asserting to the court, in a pleading) the facts necessary for the court to take jurisdiction, a brief summary of the facts necessary to show that the plaintiff is entitled to a remedy, and a statement of the remedy the plaintiff is seeking. Exhibit 3–4 illustrates how the complaint

Complaint The pleading made by a plaintiff alleging wrongdoing on the part of the defendant; the document that, when filed with a court, initiates a lawsuit.

Ethical Issue 3.1

Are confidential settlement agreements contrary to the public interest?

One of the major advantages of a settlement agreement, aside from avoiding litigation costs, is confidentiality. A defendant manufacturer, for example, might place a high value on keeping allegations that its product is defective from reaching the public or other potential plaintiffs. In the past, the courts tended to approve settlement agreements, including confidentiality provisions, with few objections. This tradition is now changing. Increasingly, "sunshine in government" or "sunshine in litigation" laws and court rules are imposing requirements on the courts that make it difficult for parties to obtain a court's consent to a confidentiality agreement. This is particularly true when the agreement relates to disputes concerning products or practices that may be harmful to the public. Clearly, shielding the public from knowledge of harmful products or services by means of confidentiality agreements may not be in the public interest. Yet limiting the availability of confidentiality agreements may not be in the public interest either, because it makes settlements less attractive for many litigants. As a result, more cases will go to trial and an already strained court system will be even more heavily burdened.

Exhibit 3–4 Example of a Typical Complaint

IN THE LOS ANGELES MUNICIPAL COURT
FOR THE LOS ANGELES JUDICIAL DISTRICT

CIVIL NO. 1–1026

Lisa Marconi
_____
Plaintiff

v.

COMPLAINT

Kevin Anderson
_____
Defendant

Comes now the plaintiff and for her cause of action against the defendant alleges and states as follows:

1. The jurisdiction of this court is based on Section 86 of the California Civil Code.
2. This action is between plaintiff, a California resident living at 1434 Palm Drive, Anaheim, California, and defendant, a California resident living at 6950 Garrison Avenue, Los Angeles, California.
3. On September 10, 2001, plaintiff, Lisa Marconi, was exercising good driving habits and reasonable care in driving her car through the intersection of Rodeo Drive and Wilshire Boulevard when defendant, Kevin Anderson, negligently drove his vehicle through a red light at the intersection and collided with plaintiff's vehicle. Defendant was negligent in the operation of the vehicle as to:

    a. Speed,
    b. Lookout,
    c. Management and control.

4. As a result of the collision plaintiff suffered severe physical injury that prevented her from working and property damage to her car. The costs she incurred included $10,000 in medical bills, $9,000 in lost wages, and $5,000 for automobile repairs.

WHEREFORE, plaintiff demands judgment against the defendant for the sum of $24,000 plus interest at the maximum legal rate and the costs of this action.

By _____ *Roger Harrington* _____
Roger Harrington
Attorney for the Plaintiff
800 Orange Avenue
Anaheim, CA 91426

might read in the Marconi-Anderson case. Complaints may be lengthy or brief, depending on the complexity of the case.

After the complaint has been filed, the sheriff, a deputy of the county, or another *process server* (one who delivers a complaint and summons) serves a **summons** and a copy of the complaint on defendant Anderson. The summons notifies Anderson that he must file an answer to the complaint with both

Summons A document informing a defendant that a legal action has been commenced against him or her and that the defendant must appear in court on a certain date to answer the plaintiff's complaint. The document is delivered by a sheriff or any other person so authorized.

the court and the plaintiff's attorney within a specified time period (usually twenty to thirty days). The summons also informs Anderson that failure to answer may result in a **default judgment** for the plaintiff, meaning the plaintiff will be awarded the damages alleged in her complaint.

Default Judgment A judgment entered by a court against a defendant who has failed to appear in court to answer or defend against the plaintiff's claim.

Answer Procedurally, a defendant's response to the plaintiff's complaint.

THE DEFENDANT'S ANSWER The defendant's **answer** either admits the statements or allegations set forth in the complaint or denies them and outlines any defenses that the defendant may have. If Anderson admits to all of Marconi's allegations in his answer, the court will enter a judgment for Marconi. If Anderson denies any of Marconi's allegations, the litigation will go forward.

Anderson can deny Marconi's allegations and set forth his own claim that Marconi was in fact negligent and therefore owes him money for damages to his Mercedes. This is appropriately called a **counterclaim.** If Anderson files a counterclaim, Marconi will have to answer it with a pleading, normally called a **reply,** which has the same characteristics as an answer.

Counterclaim A claim made by a defendant in a civil lawsuit against the plaintiff. In effect, the defendant is suing the plaintiff.

Reply Procedurally, a plaintiff's response to a defendant's answer.

Anderson can also admit the truth of Marconi's complaint but raise new facts that may result in dismissal of the action. This is called raising an affirmative defense. For example, Anderson could assert the expiration of the time period under the relevant statute of limitations (a state or federal statute that sets the maximum time period during which a certain action can be brought or rights enforced) as an affirmative defense.

Motion to Dismiss A pleading in which a defendant asserts that the plaintiff's claim fails to state a cause of action (that is, has no basis in law) or that there are other grounds on which a suit should be dismissed.

MOTION TO DISMISS A **motion to dismiss** requests the court to dismiss the case for stated reasons. The motion to dismiss is often made by a defendant before filing an answer to the plaintiff's complaint. Grounds for dismissal of a case include improper delivery of the complaint and summons, improper venue, and the plaintiff's failure to state a claim for which a court could grant relief (a remedy). For example, if Marconi had suffered no injuries or losses as a result of Anderson's negligence, Anderson could move to have the case dismissed because Marconi had not stated a claim for which relief could be granted.

If the judge grants the motion to dismiss, the plaintiff generally is given time to file an amended complaint. If the judge denies the motion, the suit will go forward, and the defendant must then file an answer. Note that if Marconi wishes to discontinue the suit because, for example, an out-of-court settlement has been reached, she can likewise move for dismissal. The court can also dismiss the case on its own motion. (Occasionally, a judge will dismiss a case to sanction a party for failing to preserve evidence relevant to the litigation. See this chapter's *Inside the Legal Environment* for a discussion of this issue.)

Pretrial Motions

Either party may attempt to get the case dismissed before trial through the use of various pretrial motions. We have already mentioned the motion to dismiss. Two other important pretrial motions are the motion for judgment on the pleadings and the motion for summary judgment.

Motion for Judgment on the Pleadings A motion by either party to a lawsuit at the close of the pleadings requesting the court to decide the issue solely on the pleadings without proceeding to trial. The motion will be granted only if no facts are in dispute.

At the close of the pleadings, either party may make a **motion for judgment on the pleadings,** or on the merits of the case. The judge will grant the motion only when there is no dispute over the facts of the case and the only issue to be resolved is a question of law. In deciding on the motion, the judge may only consider the evidence contained in the pleadings.

Inside the Legal Environment

Evidence Spoliation

Omnia praesumuntur contra spoliatorem (Latin for "all things are presumed against the destroyer") is an age-old legal maxim. It means that when a party loses or destroys evidence relating to a lawsuit, the presumption arises that the evidence was harmful to the "spoliator"—the party that lost or destroyed the evidence. Courts in most states hold that the jury may—but is not compelled to—infer or presume that any evidence that has been destroyed would have been adverse to the spoliator.

Courts can also impose more severe sanctions—including fines, the dismissal of a lawsuit, or the entry of a default judgment for the opposing party—for evidence spoliation. Traditionally, courts have imposed these harsher sanctions only when evidence is *intentionally* destroyed. Increasingly, however, even parties that accidentally destroy or inadvertently fail to preserve relevant evidence may face similar sanctions. In one case, for example, the plaintiff, Jordan Miller, purchased a Cessna twin-engine airplane from Mid-Continent Aircraft Service and Jet Center Tulsa, Inc. (collectively, MCAS). When landing the aircraft after his first flight, the left landing gear collapsed, causing major damage to the airplane. A Federal Aviation Administration (FAA) investigator who inspected the airplane shortly after the crash reported that the landing gear was defective. Inspectors for Miller's insurance company concluded likewise.

When Miller sued MCAS to recover damages, MCAS requested that it be allowed to inspect the defective landing gear. As it turned out, the various companies involved in making repairs to the plane had either lost or destroyed all but one of the component parts of the left landing gear. Notwithstanding the FAA inspector's report, the insurance company's findings, and testimony from those repairing the plane, the court dismissed Miller's case. To allow the case to go forward, stated the court, would be prejudicial to MCAS because it could not conduct its own inspection of the gear.[a]

Notably, the spoliation of evidence can give rise not only to court sanctions but also, in some states, to tort lawsuits. (As will be discussed in Chapter 4, under tort

A man shreds a document with the help of a document shredder. What other actions, besides shredding documents, might be involved in evidence spoliation?

law, a party who suffers harm as a result of another's wrongful act, or *tort,* may sue to obtain money damages.) Some of these states limit the tort to the intentional destruction of evidence. Others, however, allow private actions against spoliators even though the spoliation may have been accidental.

Avoiding court-imposed sanctions or tort liability for evidence spoliation is particularly challenging with respect to electronic evidence, including e-mail. If a firm retains back-up copies of all e-mail messages, it may face significant time costs in sorting through those messages to satisfy a request for documents during discovery. At the same time, if it deletes (destroys) e-mail that could be crucial evidence in bringing or defending against a lawsuit, it may face significant sanctions.

One of the murkiest aspects of spoliation law is determining when the obligation to preserve evidence arises. Clearly, once a summons has been served on a defendant, the defendant is obligated to preserve all evidence relevant to the plaintiff's claim. Beyond this requirement, however, there are few guidelines, and

a. *Miller v. Mid-Continent Aircraft Service, Inc.,* 139 F.3d 912 (10th Cir. 1998).

(Continued)

Inside the Legal Environment

generally the courts decide the issue on a case-by-case basis. As a practical matter, any businessperson today should seek legal advice when establishing a document-retention policy, with respect to both paper and electronic documents.

For Critical Analysis: *Is it fair to impose severe sanctions, such as the dismissal of a case, on those who inadvertently lose or destroy evidence relevant to a lawsuit?*

Motion for Summary Judgment A motion requesting the court to enter a judgment without proceeding to trial. The motion can be based on evidence outside the pleadings and will be granted only if no facts are in dispute.

In contrast, in a **motion for summary judgment** the court may consider evidence outside the pleadings, such as sworn statements (affidavits) by parties or witnesses or other documents relating to the case. A motion for summary judgment can be made by either party. As with the motion for judgment on the pleadings, a motion for summary judgment will be granted only if there are no genuine questions of fact and the only question is a question of law.

Deciding whether a certain issue presents a question of fact or a question of law is not always easy, and judges sometimes disagree on whether summary judgment is appropriate in a given proceeding. The following case illustrates this point.

Case 3.3 ● Metzgar v. Playskool, Inc.

United States Court of Appeals, Third Circuit, 1994. 30 F.3d 459.

Company Profile *Hasbro, Inc. (http://www.hasbro.com) is the world's largest toy maker. Hasbro manufactures and sells many of the most famous, biggest-selling toys—including games, puzzles, and baby items—on the U.S. and world markets. Hasbro products include Cabbage Patch Kids, G.I. Joe, Lincoln Logs, Mr. Potato Head, Monopoly, Scrabble, Trivial Pursuit, Twister, and Yahtzee. Hasbro brand names include Hasbro, Kenner, Milton Bradley, Parker Brothers, Tonka, and Playskool.*

Background and Facts Ronald Metzgar placed his fifteen-month-old son Matthew, awake and healthy, in his playpen. Ronald left the room for five minutes and on his return found Matthew lifeless. A purple toy block had lodged in the boy's throat, choking him to death. Ronald called 911, but efforts to revive Matthew were to no avail. There was no warning of a choking hazard on the box containing the block. Matthew's parents sued Playskool, Inc., the manufacturer of the block, and others in a federal district court. They alleged, among other things, negligence[a] in failing to warn of the hazard of the block. Playskool filed a motion for summary judgment, arguing that the danger of a young child choking on a small block was obvious. The court entered a summary judgment in favor of Playskool. The parents appealed.

---

a. *Negligence* is a failure to use the standard of care that a reasonable person would exercise in similar circumstances. See Chapter 9.

In the Words of the Court . . .
MANSMANN, Circuit Judge.

* * * *

* * * For a risk to be deemed obvious for purposes of a failure to warn claim, * * * there must be general consensus within the relevant community. We cannot see how the purple Playskool block can be deemed as

Case 3.3 Continued

a matter of law an obvious safety hazard in the eyes of the relevant community, when Playskool itself believed the block was safe for its intended use. Furthermore, Matthew's parents * * * testified that they did not believe that the product posed an obvious threat of asphyxiation to Matthew. Moreover, the defendant did not proffer any evidence tending to show that the danger of asphyxiation was obvious.

Under a negligence theory, although a failure to warn claim may be defeated if the risk was obvious or known, the question of obviousness is more properly submitted to a jury than disposed on motion for summary judgment. The court's role in deciding a motion for summary judgment is merely to decide whether there is a genuine issue of material fact for trial. The district court's dismissal of Metzgars' negligence claim on the basis of its determination that the danger to Matthew was obvious was tantamount to holding that no reasonable jury could conclude otherwise. Based on the evidence of record, we cannot agree.

Decision and Remedy The U.S. Court of Appeals for the Third Circuit held that the question of obviousness in this case was not a proper subject for summary judgment and remanded the case for a trial.

For Critical Analysis—Social Consideration *When a case requires a determination of such matters as community standards, summary judgment is not considered appropriate. Such matters are given to juries to determine. Why?*

Discovery

Before a trial begins, each party can use a number of procedural devices to obtain information and gather evidence about the case from the other party or from third parties. The process of obtaining such information is known as **discovery.** Discovery includes gaining access to witnesses, documents, records, and other types of evidence.

The Federal Rules of Civil Procedure and similar rules in the states set forth the guidelines for discovery activity. The rules governing discovery are designed to make sure that a witness or a party is not unduly harassed, that privileged material (communications that need not be presented in court) is safeguarded, and that only matters relevant to the case at hand are discoverable.

Discovery prevents surprises at trial by giving parties access to evidence that might otherwise be hidden. This allows both parties to learn as much as they can about what to expect at a trial before they reach the courtroom. It also serves to narrow the issues so that trial time is spent on the main questions in the case. Currently, the trend is toward allowing more discovery and thus fewer surprises.[9]

Discovery A phase in the litigation process during which the opposing parties may obtain information from each other and from third parties prior to trial.

DEPOSITIONS AND INTERROGATORIES Discovery can involve the use of depositions or interrogatories, or both. **Depositions** are sworn testimony by

Deposition The testimony of a party to a lawsuit or a witness taken under oath before a trial.

---

9. This is particularly evident in the 1993 revision of the Federal Rules of Civil Procedure. The revised rules provide that each party must disclose to the other, on an ongoing basis, the types of evidence that will be presented at trial, the names of witnesses that may or will be called, and so on.

a party to the lawsuit or any witness. The person being deposed (the deponent) answers questions asked by the attorneys, and the questions and answers are recorded by an authorized court official and sworn to and signed by the deponent. (Occasionally, written depositions are taken when witnesses are unable to appear in person.) The answers given to depositions will, of course, help the attorneys prepare their cases. They can also be used in court to impeach (challenge the credibility of) a party or a witness who changes testimony at the trial. In addition, the answers given in a deposition can be used as testimony if the witness is not available at trial.

Interrogatories A series of written questions for which written answers are prepared and then signed under oath by a party to a lawsuit, usually with the assistance of the party's attorney.

Interrogatories are written questions for which written answers are prepared and then signed under oath. The main difference between interrogatories and written depositions is that interrogatories are directed to a party to the lawsuit (the plaintiff or the defendant), not to a witness, and the party can prepare answers with the aid of an attorney. The scope of interrogatories is broader, because parties are obligated to answer questions, even if it means disclosing information from their records and files.

OTHER INFORMATION   A party can serve a written request to the other party for an admission of the truth of matters relating to the trial. Any matter admitted under such a request is conclusively established for the trial. For example, Marconi can ask Anderson to admit that he was driving at a speed of forty-five miles an hour. A request for admission saves time at trial, because the parties will not have to spend time proving facts on which they already agree.

A party can also gain access to documents and other items not in his or her possession in order to inspect and examine them. Likewise, a party can gain "entry upon land" to inspect the premises. Anderson's attorney, for example, normally can gain permission to inspect and duplicate Marconi's car repair bills.

When the physical or mental condition of one party is in question, the opposing party can ask the court to order a physical or mental examination. If the court is willing to make the order, which it will do only if the need for the information outweighs the right to privacy of the person to be examined, the opposing party can obtain the results of the examination.

Pretrial Conference

Either party or the court can request a pretrial conference, or hearing. Usually, the hearing consists of an informal discussion between the judge and the opposing attorneys after discovery has taken place. The purpose of the hearing is to explore the possibility of a settlement without trial and, if this is not possible, to identify the matters that are in dispute and to plan the course of the trial.

Jury Selection

Take Note A prospective juror cannot be excluded solely on the basis of his or her race or gender.

A trial can be held with or without a jury. If there is no jury, the judge determines the truth of the facts alleged in the case. The Seventh Amendment to the U.S. Constitution guarantees the right to a jury trial for cases in federal courts when the amount in controversy exceeds $20. Most states have similar guarantees in their own constitutions (although the threshold dollar amount is higher than $20). The right to a trial by jury does not have to be exercised,

Ethical Issue 3.2

Are jurors underpaid for their services?

When David Olson was selected as a juror in the Minnesota trial against the major tobacco companies, little did he realize the consequences he would pay for fulfilling his civic duty. For the four months he served on the jury (before the case was settled, in early 1998), he was paid $30 a day by the court and nothing by his employer. A single father with two children, Olson ended up defaulting on credit-card payments, struggling to obtain food for his family, and refinancing his home to avoid losing it. Yet Olson's $30 a day was in the upper range ($30 to $40 per day) of juror fees paid by state courts. Some states pay much less—Texas, for example, pays only $6 per day. Although some programs are under way to increase juror pay in long trials, most jurors in U.S. courtrooms continue to experience what one economist has referred to as the only remaining form of involuntary servitude in the United States.

and many cases are tried without a jury. In most states and in federal courts, one of the parties must request a jury, or the right is presumed to be waived.

Before a jury trial commences, a jury must be selected. The jury-selection process is known as **voir dire.**[10] In most jurisdictions, *voir dire* consists of oral questions that attorneys for the plaintiff and the defendant ask a group of prospective jurors (one at a time) to determine whether a potential jury member is biased or has any connection with a party to the action or with a prospective witness.

During *voir dire,* a party may challenge a certain number of prospective jurors *peremptorily*—that is, ask that an individual not be sworn in as a juror without providing any reason. Alternatively, a party may challenge a prospective juror *for cause*—that is, provide a reason why an individual should not be sworn in as a juror. If the judge grants the challenge, the individual is asked to step down. A prospective juror may not be excluded from the jury by the use of discriminatory challenges, however, such as those based on racial criteria[11] or gender.[12]

Voir Dire French verbs that mean, literally, "to see" and "to speak." In jury trials, the phrase refers to the process in which the attorneys question prospective jurors to determine whether they are biased or have any connection with a party to the action or with a prospective witness.

At the Trial

At the beginning of the trial, the attorneys present their opening arguments, setting forth the facts that they expect to provide during the trial. Then the plaintiff's case is presented. In our hypothetical case, Marconi's lawyer would introduce evidence (relevant documents, exhibits, and the testimony of witnesses) to support Marconi's position. The defendant has the opportunity to challenge any evidence introduced and to cross-examine any of the plaintiff's witnesses.

"Proceed. You have my biased attention."

Learned Hand, 1872–1961 (American jurist)

---

10. Pronounced vwahr *deehr.* Literally, these French verbs mean "to see, to speak." During the *voir dire* phase of litigation, attorneys do in fact see the prospective jurors speak. In legal language, however, the phrase refers to the process of interrogating prospective jurors to learn about their backgrounds, attitudes, and so on.
11. *Batson v. Kentucky,* 476 U.S. 79, 106 S.Ct. 1712, 90 L.Ed.2d 69 (1986).
12. *J.E.B. v. Alabama ex rel. T.B.,* 511 U.S. 127, 114 S.Ct. 1419, 128 L.Ed.2d 89 (1994). (*Ex rel.* is Latin for *ex relatione.* The phrase refers to an action brought on behalf of the state, by the attorney general, at the instigation of an individual who has a private interest in the matter.)

Motion for a Directed Verdict In a jury trial, a motion for the judge to take the decision out of the hands of the jury and direct a verdict for the moving party on the ground that the other party has not produced sufficient evidence to support his or her claim.

At the end of the plaintiff's case, the defendant's attorney has the opportunity to ask the judge to direct a verdict for the defendant on the ground that the plaintiff has presented no evidence that would justify the granting of the plaintiff's remedy. This is called a **motion for a directed verdict** (known in federal courts as a *motion for judgment as a matter of law*). If the motion is not granted (it seldom is), the defendant's attorney then presents the evidence and witnesses for the defendant's case. The defendant's attorney may also make a motion for a directed verdict. The plaintiff's attorney can challenge any evidence introduced and cross-examine the defendant's witnesses.

After the defense concludes its presentation, the attorneys give their closing arguments, each urging a verdict in favor of his or her client. The judge instructs the jury in the law that applies to the case (these instructions are often called *charges*), and the jury retires to the jury room to deliberate a verdict. In the Marconi-Anderson case, the jury will not only decide for the plaintiff or for the defendant but, if it finds for the plaintiff, will also decide on the amount of the **award** (the money to be paid to her).

Award The amount of money awarded to a plaintiff in a civil lawsuit as damages.

Posttrial Motions

After the jury has rendered its verdict, either party may make a posttrial motion. If Marconi wins, and Anderson's attorney has previously moved for a directed verdict, Anderson's attorney may make a **motion for judgment *n.o.v.*** (from the Latin *non obstante veredicto,* which means "notwithstanding the verdict"—called a *motion for judgment as a matter of law* in the federal courts) in Anderson's favor on the ground that the jury verdict in favor of Marconi was unreasonable and erroneous. If the judge decides that the jury's verdict was reasonable in light of the evidence presented at trial, the motion will be denied. If the judge agrees with Anderson's attorney, then he or she will set the jury's verdict aside and enter a judgment in favor of Anderson.

Motion for Judgment *N.O.V.* A motion requesting the court to grant judgment in favor of the party making the motion on the ground that the jury verdict against him or her was unreasonable and erroneous.

Alternatively, Anderson could make a **motion for a new trial,** requesting the judge to set aside the adverse verdict and to hold a new trial. The motion will be granted if the judge is convinced, after looking at all the evidence, that the jury was in error but does not feel it is appropriate to grant judgment for the other side. A new trial may also be granted on the ground of newly discovered evidence, misconduct by the participants or the jury during the trial, or error by the judge.

Motion for a New Trial A motion asserting that the trial was so fundamentally flawed (because of error, newly discovered evidence, prejudice, or other reason) that a new trial is necessary to prevent a miscarriage of justice.

In the following case, the defendants filed a motion for a new trial based on the plaintiff's attorney's "improper and inflammatory" remarks.

Case 3.4 ● LeBlanc v. American Honda Motor Co.

Supreme Court of New Hampshire, 1997.
141 N.H. 579,
688 A.2d 556.
**http://www.state.nh.us/
courts/supreme/opinions/9701/
honda.htm[a]**

---

a. This is a page within the collection of New Hampshire Supreme Court opinions available at the Web site of the New Hampshire state government.

Historical and Social Setting *One of the principles on which the United States was founded is that all persons are created equal and are entitled to have their individual dignity respected. This guarantee is in our federal and state constitutions, and there have been continual efforts by legislative enactments and judicial decisions to purge our society of racial and other prejudices. Despite these efforts, such biases still appear to influence decisions by many people who would*

Case 3.4 Continued

deny equal respect to those of us of a different race, religion, or ethnic origin.

Background and Facts While riding on a snowmobile, Thomas LeBlanc was injured when the snowmobile collided with an off-road vehicle manufactured by American Honda Motor Company (a subsidiary of a Japanese corporation). LeBlanc sued Honda and the driver in a New Hampshire state court. During the trial, LeBlanc's lawyer, Vincent Martina, asked Honda's expert witness if he had ever wondered why the Honda vehicle was "red, white, and blue, the color of the American flag." During his closing argument, Martina told the jury that the case was not about "Pearl Harbor or the Japanese prime minister saying Americans are lazy and stupid. * * * What this case is about is not American xenophobia; it's about corporate greed." When the jury returned a verdict in favor of LeBlanc, Honda filed a motion for a new trial, which the court denied. Honda appealed to the Supreme Court of New Hampshire, arguing in part that Martina's remarks so tainted the proceedings as to deprive Honda of a fair trial.

In the Words of the Court . . .
BROCK, Chief Justice.

* * * *

* * * To justify a [new trial], remarks or * * * conduct must be more than merely inadmissible; they must constitute an irreparable injustice * * * .

* * * *

* * * [A] new trial may be warranted where counsel attempts to appeal to the sympathies, passions, and prejudices of jurors grounded in race or nationality, by reference to the opposing party's religious beliefs or lack thereof, or by reference to a party's social or economic condition or status. Such an appeal was attempted in this case.

* * * It is true that counsel's closing reference was brief. At the same time, when an elephant has passed through the courtroom one does not need a forceful reminder.

Decision and Remedy The Supreme Court of New Hampshire reversed the decision in favor of LeBlanc and remanded the case for a new trial. The court held that remarks made during a trial to cultivate in the jury a racial and national bias constitute sufficient grounds for a new trial.

For Critical Analysis—Social Consideration *If a trial judge tells a jury to ignore a lawyer's remarks, it is presumed that the jury does not consider them. Do you think that is a valid presumption?*

The Appeal

Assume here that any posttrial motion is denied, and Anderson appeals the case. (If Marconi wins but receives a smaller money award than she sought, she can appeal also.) A notice of appeal must be filed with the clerk of the trial court within a prescribed time. Anderson now becomes the appellant, or petitioner, and Marconi becomes the appellee, or respondent.

FILING THE APPEAL Anderson's attorney files with the appellate court the record on appeal, which includes the pleadings, the trial transcript, the judge's ruling on motions made by the parties, and other trial-related documents. Anderson's attorney will also file with the reviewing court a condensation of the record, known as an abstract, which is filed with the reviewing court along

Brief A formal legal document submitted by the attorney for the appellant or the appellee (in answer to the appellant's brief) to an appellate court when a case is appealed. The appellant's brief outlines the facts and issues of the case, the judge's rulings or jury's findings that should be reversed or modified, the applicable law, and the arguments on the client's behalf.

with the brief. The **brief** is a formal legal document outlining the facts and issues of the case, the judge's rulings or jury's findings that should be reversed or modified, the applicable law, and arguments on Anderson's behalf (citing applicable statutes and relevant cases as precedents).

Marconi's attorney will file an answering brief. Anderson's attorney can file a reply to Marconi's brief, although it is not required. The reviewing court then considers the case.

APPELLATE REVIEW   As mentioned earlier, a court of appeals does not hear evidence. Rather, it reviews the record for errors of law. Its decision concerning a case is based on the record on appeal, the abstracts, and the attorneys' briefs. The attorneys can present oral arguments, after which the case is taken under advisement. In general, appellate courts do not reverse findings of fact unless the findings are unsupported or contradicted by the evidence.

If the reviewing court believes that an error was committed during the trial or that the jury was improperly instructed, the judgment will be *reversed.* Sometimes the case will be *remanded* (sent back to the court that originally heard the case) for a new trial. ● Example 3.8 A case may be remanded for several reasons. For instance, if the appellate court decided that a judge improperly granted summary judgment, the case would be remanded for trial. If an appellate court decided that the trial jury's award of damages was too high, the case would be remanded with instructions to reduce the damages award.● In most cases, the judgment of the lower court is *affirmed,* resulting in the enforcement of the court's judgment or decree.

If the reviewing court is an intermediate appellate court, the losing party normally may appeal to the state supreme court (the highest state court). Such a petition corresponds to a petition for a writ of *certiorari* in the United States Supreme Court. If the petition is granted, new briefs must be filed before the state supreme court, and the attorneys may be allowed or requested to present oral arguments. Like the intermediate appellate courts, the supreme court may reverse or affirm the appellate court's decision or remand the case. At this point, unless a federal question is at issue, the case has reached its end.

Key Terms

Chapter Summary • The American Court System

The Judiciary's Role in American Government (See pages 62–64.)	The role of the judiciary—the courts—in the American governmental system is to interpret and apply the law. Through the process of judicial review—determining the constitutionality of laws—the judicial branch acts as a check on the executive and legislative branches of government. The power of judicial review was established by Chief Justice John Marshall in *Marbury v. Madison* (1803).

Basic Judicial Requirements (See pages 64–70.)

1. **Jurisdiction**—Before a court can hear a case, it must have jurisdiction over the person against whom the suit is brought or the property involved in the suit, as well as jurisdiction over the subject matter.

    a. Limited versus general jurisdiction—Limited jurisdiction exists when a court is limited to a specific subject matter, such as probate or divorce. General jurisdiction exists when a court can hear any kind of case.

    b. Original versus appellate jurisdiction—Original jurisdiction exists with courts that have authority to hear a case for the first time (trial courts). Appellate jurisdiction exists with courts of appeals, or reviewing courts; generally, appellate courts do not have original jurisdiction.

    c. Federal jurisdiction—Arises (1) when a federal question is involved (when the plaintiff's cause of action is based, at least in part, on the U.S. Constitution, a treaty, or a federal law) or (2) when a case involves diversity of citizenship (citizens of different states, for example) and the amount in controversy exceeds $75,000.

    d. Concurrent versus exclusive jurisdiction—Concurrent jurisdiction exists when two different courts have authority to hear the same case. Exclusive jurisdiction exists when only state courts or only federal courts have authority to hear a case.

2. **Venue**—Venue has to do with the most appropriate location for a trial, which is usually the geographical area in which the event leading to the dispute took place or where the parties reside.

3. **Standing to sue**—A requirement that a party must have a legally protected and tangible interest at stake sufficient to justify seeking relief through the court system. The controversy at issue must also be a justiciable controversy—one that is real and substantial, as opposed to hypothetical or academic.

The State and Federal Court Systems (See pages 70–75.)

1. **Trial courts**—Courts of original jurisdiction, in which legal actions are initiated.

    a. State—Courts of general jurisdiction can hear any case; courts of limited jurisdiction include divorce courts, probate courts, traffic courts, small claims courts, and so on.

    b. Federal—The federal district court is the equivalent of the state trial court. Federal courts of limited jurisdiction include the U.S. Tax Court, the U.S. Bankruptcy Court, and the U.S. Court of Federal Claims.

2. **Intermediate appellate courts**—Courts of appeals, or reviewing courts; generally without original jurisdiction. Many states have an intermediate appellate court; in the federal court system, the U.S. circuit courts of appeals are the intermediate appellate courts.

3. **Supreme (highest) courts**—Each state has a supreme court, although it may be called by some other name, from which appeal to the United States Supreme

(Continued)

Chapter Summary • The American Court System, *Continued*

The State and Federal Court Systems—continued

Court is only possible if a federal question is involved. The United States Supreme Court is the highest court in the federal court system and the final arbiter of the Constitution and federal law.

Following a State Court Case
(See pages 75–86.)

Rules of procedure prescribe the way in which disputes are handled in the courts. Rules differ from court to court, and separate sets of rules exist for federal and state courts, as well as for criminal and civil cases. A sample civil court case in a state court would involve the following procedures:

1. **The pleadings—**

   a. Complaint—Filed by the plaintiff with the court to initiate the lawsuit; served with a summons on the defendant.

   b. Answer—Admits or denies allegations made by the plaintiff; may assert a counterclaim or an affirmative defense.

   c. Motion to dismiss—A request to the court to dismiss the case for stated reasons, such as the plaintiff's failure to state a claim for which relief can be granted.

2. **Pretrial motions (in addition to the motion to dismiss)—**

   a. Motion for judgment on the pleadings—May be made by either party; will be granted if the parties agree on the facts and the only question is how the law applies to the facts. The judge bases the decision solely on the pleadings.

   b. Motion for summary judgment—May be made by either party; will be granted if the parties agree on the facts. The judge applies the law in rendering a judgment. The judge can consider evidence outside the pleadings when evaluating the motion.

3. **Discovery—**The process of gathering evidence concerning the case. Discovery involves depositions (sworn testimony by a party to the lawsuit or any witness), interrogatories (written questions and answers to these questions made by parties to the action with the aid of their attorneys), and various requests (for admissions, documents, medical examinations, and so on).

4. **Pretrial conference—**Either party or the court can request a pretrial conference to identify the matters in dispute after discovery has taken place and to plan the course of the trial.

5. **Trial—**Following jury selection *(voir dire),* the trial begins with opening statements from both parties' attorneys. The following events then occur:

   a. The plaintiff's introduction of evidence (including the testimony of witnesses) supporting the plaintiff's position. The defendant's attorney can challenge evidence and cross-examine witnesses.

   b. The defendant's introduction of evidence (including the testimony of witnesses) supporting the defendant's position. The plaintiff's attorney can challenge evidence and cross-examine witnesses.

   c. Closing arguments by attorneys in favor of their respective clients, the judge's instructions to the jury, and the jury's verdict.

6. **Posttrial motions—**

   a. Motion for judgment *n.o.v.* ("notwithstanding the verdict")—Will be granted if the judge is convinced that the jury was in error.

Chapter Summary • The American Court System

Following a State Court Case—continued

    b. Motion for a new trial—Will be granted if the judge is convinced that the jury was in error; can also be granted on the grounds of newly discovered evidence, misconduct by the participants during the trial, or error by the judge.

7. Appeal—Either party can appeal the trial court's judgment to an appropriate court of appeals. After reviewing the record on appeal, the abstracts, and the attorneys' briefs, the appellate court holds a hearing and renders its opinion.

For Review

1. What is judicial review? How and when was the power of judicial review established?

2. Before a court can hear a case, it must have jurisdiction. Over what must it have jurisdiction? In what circumstances does a federal court have jurisdiction?

3. What is the difference between a trial court and an appellate court?

4. In a lawsuit, what are the pleadings? What is discovery?

5. What are the steps involved in an appeal?

Questions and Case Problems

3–1. Courts of Appeals. Appellate courts normally see only written transcripts of trial proceedings when they are reviewing cases. Today, in some states, videotapes are being used as the official trial reports. If the use of videotapes as official reports continues, will this alter the appellate process? Should it? Discuss fully.

3–2. Discovery. In the past, the rules of discovery were very restrictive, and trials often turned on elements of surprise. For example, a plaintiff would not necessarily know until the trial what the defendant's defense was going to be. Within the last twenty-five years, however, new rules of discovery have substantially changed all this. Now each attorney can discover practically all the evidence that the other will be presenting at trial, with the exception of certain information—namely, the opposing attorney's work product. *Work product* is not a clear concept. Basically, it includes all the attorney's thoughts on the case. Can you see any reason why such information should not be made available to the opposing attorney? Discuss fully.

3–3. Motions. When and for what purpose are each of the following motions made? Which of them would be appropriate if a defendant claimed that the only issue between the parties was a question of law and that the law was favorable to the defendant's position?

    (a) A motion for judgment on the pleadings.

    (b) A motion for a directed verdict.

    (c) A motion for summary judgment.

    (d) A motion for judgment *n.o.v.*

3–4. Peremptory Challenges. During *voir dire*, the parties or their attorneys select those persons who will serve as jurors during the trial. The parties are prohibited, however, from excluding potential jurors on the basis of race or other discriminatory criteria. An issue concerns whether the prohibition against discrimination extends to potential jurors who have physical or mental disabilities. Federal law prohibits discrimination against an otherwise qualified person with a disability when that person could be accommodated without too much difficulty. Should this law also apply to the jury-selection process? For example, should parties be prohibited from excluding blind persons, through either challenges for cause or peremptory challenges, from serving on juries? Discuss.

3–5. Jurisdiction. Marya Callais, a citizen of Florida, was walking near a busy street in Tallahassee, Florida, one day when a large crate flew off a passing truck and hit her, resulting in numerous injuries. She incurred a great deal of pain and suffering, plus significant medical expenses, and she could not work for six months. She wants to sue the trucking firm for $300,000 in damages. The firm's headquarters are in Georgia, although the company does business in Florida. In what court might Callais bring suit—a Florida state court, a Georgia state court, or a federal court? What factors might influence her decision?

3-6. Jurisdiction.   George Rush, a New York resident and columnist for the New York *Daily News,* wrote a critical column about Berry Gordy, the founder and former president of Motown Records. Gordy, a California resident, filed a suit in a California state court against Rush and the newspaper (the defendants), alleging defamation (a civil wrong, or tort, that occurs when the publication of false statements harms a person's good reputation). Most of the newspaper's subscribers are in the New York area, and the paper covers mostly New York events. Thirteen copies of its daily edition are distributed to California subscribers, however, and the paper does cover events that are of nationwide interest to the entertainment industry. Because of its focus on entertainment, the newspaper also routinely sends reporters to California to gather news from California sources. Can a California state court exercise personal jurisdiction over the New York defendants in this case? What factors will the court consider in deciding this question? If you were the judge, how would you decide the issue, and why? Discuss fully. [*Gordy v. Daily News, L.P.,* 95 F.3d 829 (9th Cir. 1996)]

3-7. Motion for a New Trial.   Washoe Medical Center, Inc., admitted Shirley Swisher for the treatment of a fractured pelvis. During her stay, Swisher suffered a fatal fall from her hospital bed. Gerald Parodi, the administrator of her estate, and others filed an action against Washoe in which they sought damages for the alleged lack of care in treating Swisher. During *voir dire,* when the plaintiffs' attorney returned a few minutes late from a break, the trial judge led the prospective jurors in a standing ovation. The judge joked with one of the prospective jurors, whom he had known in college, about the judge's fitness to serve as a judge and personally endorsed another prospective juror's business. After the trial, the jury returned a verdict in favor of Washoe. The plaintiffs moved for a new trial, but the judge denied the motion. The plaintiffs then appealed, arguing that the tone set by the judge during *voir dire* prejudiced their right to a fair trial. Should the appellate court agree? Why or why not? [*Parodi v. Washoe Medical Center,* Inc., 111 Nev. 365, 892 P.2d 588 (1995)]

3-8. Standing.   Blue Cross and Blue Shield insurance companies (the Blues) provide 68 million Americans with health-care financing. The Blues have paid billions of dollars for care attributable to illnesses related to tobacco use. In an attempt to recover some of this amount, the Blues filed a suit in a federal district court against tobacco companies and others, alleging fraud, among other things. The Blues claimed that beginning in 1953, the defendants conspired to addict millions of Americans, including members of Blue Cross plans, to cigarettes and

other tobacco products. The conspiracy involved misrepresentation about the safety of nicotine and its addictive properties, marketing efforts targeting children, and agreements not to produce or market safer cigarettes. Their success caused lung, throat, and other cancers, as well as heart disease, stroke, emphysema, and other illnesses. The defendants asked the court to dismiss the case on the ground that the plaintiffs did not have standing to sue. Do the Blues have standing in this case? Why or why not? [*Blue Cross and Blue Shield of New Jersey, Inc. v. Philip Morris, Inc.,* 36 F.Supp.2d 560 (E.D.N.Y. 1999)]

3-9. Discovery.   Advance Technology Consultants, Inc. (ATC), contracted with RoadTrac, L.L.C., to provide software and client software systems for the products for global positioning satellite system (GPS) technology being developed by RoadTrac. RoadTrac agreed to provide ATC hardware with which ATC's software would interface. Problems soon arose, however. ATC claimed that RoadTrac's hardware was defective, making it difficult to develop the software. RoadTrac contended that its hardware was fully functional and that ATC simply failed to provide supporting software. ATC told RoadTrac that it considered their contract terminated. RoadTrac filed a suit in a Georgia state court against ATC, charging, among other things, breach of contract. During discovery, RoadTrac requested ATC's customer lists and marketing procedures. Before producing this material, ATC asked the court to limit RoadTrac's use of the information. Meanwhile, RoadTrac and ATC had become competitors in the GPS industry. How should the court rule regarding RoadTrac's discovery request? [*Advance Technology Consultants, Inc. v. RoadTrac, L.L.C.,* 236 Ga.App. 582, 512 S.E.2d 27 (1999)]

A Question of Ethics and Social Responsibility

3-10.   The state of Alabama, on behalf of a mother (T.B.), brought a paternity suit against the alleged father (J.E.B.) of T.B.'s child. During jury selection, the state, through peremptory challenges, removed nine of the ten prospective male jurors. J.E.B.'s attorney struck the final male from the jury pool. As a result of these peremptory strikes, the final jury consisted of twelve women. When the jury returned a verdict in favor of the mother, the father appealed. The father argued that eliminating men from the jury constituted gender discrimination and violated his rights to equal protection and due process (see Chapter 6). The father requested the court to extend the principle enunciated in *Batson v. Kentucky* (cited in footnote 11 of this chapter), which prohibited peremptory strikes based solely on race, to include gender-based strikes. The appellate court refused to do so. [*J.E.B. v. Alabama ex rel. T.B.,* 511 U.S. 127, 114 S.Ct. 1419, 128 L.Ed.2d 89 (1994)]

1. Do you agree with J.E.B. that the state's exercise of its peremptory challenges violated his right to equal protection and due process? Why or why not?
2. If you were the judge, how would you rule?
3. The late Supreme Court Justice Thurgood Marshall urged, when the Court was reviewing the *Batson* case, that peremptory challenges be banned entirely. Do you agree with this proposal? Discuss.

For Critical Analysis

3–11. American courts are forums for adversarial justice, in which attorneys defend the interests of their respective clients before the court. This means that an attorney may end up claiming before a court that his or her client is innocent, even though the attorney knows that the client acted wrongfully. Is it ethical for attorneys to try to "deceive" the court in these situations? Can the adversarial system of justice really lead to "truth"?

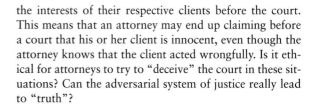

Interacting with the Internet

■ For updated links to resources available on the Web, as well as a variety of other materials, visit this text's Web site at

http://leet.westbuslaw.com

■ The decisions of the United States Supreme Court and of all of the U.S. courts of appeals are now published online shortly after the decisions are rendered (often within hours). You can find these decisions and obtain information about the federal court system by accessing the Federal Court Locator at

http://ls.law.vill.edu/Locator/fedcourt.htm

■ For information on the justices of the United States Supreme Court, links to opinions they have authored, and other information about the Supreme Court, go to

http://oyez.nwu.edu

■ The Web site for the federal courts offers information on the federal court system and links to all federal courts at

http://www.uscourts.gov

■ The National Center for State Courts (NCSC) offers links to the Web pages of all state courts. Go to

http://www.ncsc.dni.us/court/sites/courts.htm

■ If you are interested in learning more about the Federal Rules of Civil Procedure (FRCP) and the Federal Rules of Evidence (FRE), they can now be accessed via the Internet at the following Web site:

http://www.cornell.edu

■ You can find information on the federal court system, including its history and the origins of the doctrine of judicial review, at

http://www.usscplus.com/info

■ To access the Supreme Court's official Web site, on which Supreme Court decisions are made available within hours of their release, go to

http://supremecourtus.gov

■ Several Web sites offer searchable databases of Supreme Court decisions. You can access Supreme Court cases since 1970 at FindLaw's site:

http://www.findlaw.com

■ The following Web site also offers an easily searchable index to Supreme Court opinions, including some important historic decisions:

http://supct.law.cornell.edu/supct/index.html

■ Court TV's Web site offers information ranging from its program schedule and how you can find Court TV in your area to famous cases and the wills of famous people. For each case it includes on the site, it gives a complete history as well as selected documents filed with the court and court transcripts. You can access this site at

http://www.courttv.com

Online Legal Research Exercises

Go to http://leet. westbuslaw.com, the Web site that accompanies this text. Select "Interactive Study Center," and then click on "Chapter 3." There you will find the following Internet exercises that you can perform to learn more about the role of American courts and court procedures.

Activity 3–1: The Judiciary's Role in American Government
Activity 3–2: Civil Procedure

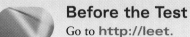

Before the Test

Go to http://leet. westbuslaw.com, the Web site that accompanies this text. Select "Interactive Quizzes." You will find a number of interactive questions relating to this chapter.

Legal Representation and Alternative Dispute Resolution

chapter objectives

After reading this chapter, you should be able to:

1. Describe the role of attorneys in the dispute-resolution process.

2. List the differences between litigation and the other forms of dispute resolution.

3. Discuss the processes of negotiation and mediation.

4. Identify the steps in the arbitration process.

5. Define summary jury trials and mini-trials.

contents

Despite Bentham's sentiments to the contrary (expressed in the quotation alongside), all persons, *including* lawyers, are expected to know the law so as to conduct themselves in an appropriate manner. Laws are passed to promote the public welfare. Every law implicitly or explicitly recognizes a particular legal right or punishes a specific kind of behavior. Some laws restrict the actions of individuals, while others authorize persons to behave in a certain way. Each law necessarily involves a parceling out of rights and duties. Often the same person possesses both rights and duties, but the rights are useless unless persons who are deprived of them or who are otherwise injured can be compensated for the injury. Because there is no mechanism in our legal system that automatically transfers assets from a wrongdoer to the victim, victims must insist that their legal rights be enforced if they are to have any hope of recovering damages—usually in the form of a cash payment—for their injuries.

Attorneys and Dispute Resolution

When a person has suffered an injury for which he or she seeks compensation, that person may wish to seek the advice of an **attorney.** An attorney is a person who has received a law degree and has been licensed by one or more states to practice law. An attorney is often hired to represent the interests of a client in a legal proceeding or to review particular legal documents, such as a contract to purchase or lease a home. Despite the diversity of legal issues that attorneys may confront on a day-to-day basis, they share a common approach to the law because their education nearly always involves an in-depth study of basic legal principles and concepts, rather than a memorization of existing laws (which frequently change). Consequently, all attorneys use similar research and analytical techniques.

Attorney A person who has received a law degree and has been licensed by one or more states to practice law.

The Roles of an Attorney

An attorney must fulfill several different roles to represent the interests of a client effectively. Although law school training provides a general background from which to approach a given legal matter and research the law, attorneys also research the extent to which the client's position is supported by that law. The attorney must also verify that the facts support the client's position. In a legal matter involving illegal activities, the attorney may uncover evidence that contradicts the client's position or even directly implicates the client in criminal conduct. In such cases, the attorney is not required to disclose the client's complicity, but the attorney may not knowingly assist the client in any way that would facilitate the perpetration of a crime.

ADVISER   If a client comes to an attorney for advice on how to avoid a particular problem in the future, the attorney will counsel the client as to what practices should be changed and what measures should be taken to head off potential problems. Here the attorney will find it necessary to practice **preventive law** and play the role of adviser, spotting possible legal land mines before they harm the client. Because there is more than one way to deal with most legal problems, the attorney will have to investigate the full range of possible solutions and then suggest a preferred alternative.

Preventive Law The law that an attorney practices when he or she plays the role of an adviser for a client, spotting possible legal problems and suggesting preventive measures before the problems harm the client.

● **Example 4.1** Primo Electronics wants to buy fifty Adco computers from Wadel Wholesalers, Inc. Wadel is willing to sell. Wadel agrees to ship the computers to Primo, but Wadel does not want to pay for any damage to the computers that may occur while they are in transit. Wadel's attorney might suggest that Wadel obtain insurance to cover the risk of any damage to the computers. The attorney might alternatively suggest that a clause be included in the contract under which Primo agrees to assume the risk of damage. ●

DRAFTER   Because the attorney must handle a client's legal affairs, the attorney may be called on to draft documents and instruments ranging from leases and contracts to promissory notes and mortgages. Words are the lawyer's tools. Most attorneys find that they must familiarize themselves with several areas of the law to draft competent documents. The form of a document, particularly the extent to which it complies with certain legal formalities, may be as important as the document's content. Yet an attorney cannot draft a document for a client without knowing something about the content and the client's goals and objectives. In the case of a corporate client, the attorney often finds that he or she can draft a more effective document by becoming familiar with the corporation's operations and future plans.

● **Example 4.2** Wadel's attorney can draft a more effective contract by knowing that Wadel wishes to avoid liability for any damage to the Adco computers while they are being shipped to Primo. If the attorney knows that Wadel wishes to avoid liability in all similar future transactions, he or she might draft a basic contract form that Wadel could use in the Primo deal and in future transactions. ●

NEGOTIATOR   An attorney is often required to negotiate the terms of a particular agreement or settlement on behalf of his or her client. Negotiation is the art of persuasion. The attorney must marshal the strongest arguments in

An attorney advises her client. Can an attorney's skill as an advocate and an adviser have more effect than the facts in a client's case?

favor of the client and bring them to bear on the opposing side to produce the most favorable results. Most transactions involving significant sums of money are preceded by lengthy negotiations in which the terms of the deal and any accompanying details are hammered out. Although the client may choose to conduct certain business negotiations without the attorney present, the client will want to confer with the attorney throughout the course of the negotiations. A properly negotiated contract can prevent many legal disputes and costs in the future.

ADVOCATE   Sometimes a lawyer must represent a client in court. If two parties are unable to resolve their dispute over a particular matter—such as whether the delivery of a defective item should obligate the buyer to pay for that item—then they may wish to solve their problem in court. Both parties will usually hire attorneys to present their respective positions to a jury. This advocacy role is perhaps the most demanding one for attorneys to fulfill because the litigation of even minor claims requires that the attorney be prepared to deal with any potential difficulties, ranging from witnesses who knowingly offer false testimony to a last-minute revelation of damaging evidence. A court proceeding, particularly one that involves high stakes, can be mentally and emotionally draining. The successful advocate will maintain the necessary presence of mind to deal with or minimize any problems that may arise.

The Attorney-Client Relationship

For many individuals and businesses, relationships with attorneys last for decades. Thus, it is important that clients seek attorneys who are knowledgeable in the areas of the law that are needed to address their concerns. The client and attorney should communicate well—the attorney should perceive which issues are of foremost concern to the client and address those issues. The attorney should keep the client informed of developments in the law that affect the client's concerns. Most important, the attorney should advise the client of possible actions to take and then act according to the client's choice.

> **"A lawyer's opinion is worth nothing unless paid for."**
>
> (Proverb)

SELECTING AN ATTORNEY   In some situations, attorneys are allowed to include information about their areas of specialization in advertisements aimed at the general public. Also, a person interested in pursuing a legal claim should ask friends or relatives to recommend an attorney. If they cannot suggest an attorney who practices in the desired area of law, then the individual can call the local or state bar association to obtain the names of several lawyers. If this approach proves unsatisfactory, the local telephone directory may be scanned for possible selections. If all these steps are unsuccessful, a professional directory should be consulted. Most libraries have copies of the *Martindale-Hubbell Law Directory,* which features professional biographies of nearly all the attorneys engaged in private practice throughout the country; the listings also include areas of concentration, as well as bank references and representative clients. The *Martindale-Hubbell Law Directory* and other sources for selecting an attorney can also be found on the Internet.

ESTABLISHING THE RELATIONSHIP   Having selected an attorney, the client should make an appointment to see the attorney as soon as possible. Even a company that maintains an in-house attorney usually seeks outside counsel when the matter involves a particular area of expertise outside the range of the company attorney. Undue delay may cost the client the opportunity of pursuing legal action or may, alternatively, increase the potential liability of the client. Although it is preferable that a client consult a lawyer before becoming involved in a legal dispute, many people put off the decision to hire a lawyer until the matter has become aggravated. In many cases, this procrastination prevents a simple, relatively inexpensive solution to the matter.

Once the decision to hire an attorney has been made, the client must disclose any relevant information so that the attorney can formulate the strongest possible plan of attack or the best defense.

THE ATTORNEY-CLIENT PRIVILEGE Attorneys can best serve their clients only when they know all the relevant facts. The **attorney-client privilege** protects any relevant confidential communications from compelled disclosure—that is, courts and other government institutions cannot require that the communications be divulged. The privilege protects communications between an attorney and client made for the purpose of furnishing or obtaining professional legal advice or assistance. Thus, as long as the client's present legal matters are being discussed, the attorney cannot reveal the contents of these discussions even if, for example, the client confesses to having committed a string of robberies in the past. This privilege may be waived only by the client.

Note that privileged information is *confidential* information. If confidential information is disclosed to others, it is no longer confidential and can no longer be considered privileged. Thus, if an attorney-client conversation is overheard by a third party, such as a janitor or someone walking down a hall, the information exchanged in the conversation is no longer confidential and thus no longer privileged. The presence of the client's spouse will not affect the attorney-client privilege, however, even if he or she is not a part of the discussion. Similarly, this privilege will continue to exist if the attorney's paralegal or other staff member hears the conversation, because the staff member will assist the attorney in preparing the client's case. (See this chapter's *Legal E-nvironment* on the next page for an examination of whether e-mail communications between attorneys and their clients are confidential.)

The Role of the Court

The adversarial nature of our legal system pits the attorneys for the opposing parties against each other; the assumption is that the search for the truth will best be facilitated by the presentation of competing arguments and evidence. The dispute must be a real one, however, in which tangible injury has been suffered or there is an immediate threat of harm; the courts will not consider hypothetical questions. • **Example 4.3** A court will hear a dispute between you and your neighbor over whether his weekend barbecues constitute a nuisance that should be stopped. The court will not entertain questions of law relating to nuisances from two persons who are interested purely in discussing the law's theoretical implications.•

Although the courts allow attorneys great leeway in defining the issues and presenting the relevant evidence, the court itself is responsible for making sure that the trial is conducted in a proper and dignified manner. The court does not usually interview witnesses or ask many questions about particular evidence, but it will prevent the parties from straying too far from the issues being

Attorney-Client Privilege
Protected communications between an attorney and client made for the purpose of furnishing or obtaining professional legal advice or assistance. Courts and other government institutions cannot require disclosure of the communications.

A judge listens as an attorney appeals to the jury during a trial. Can a judge in a jury trial influence the outcome of the case? In what way? Should an individual or a company consider such factors when deciding whether to file a lawsuit?

Legal *e*-nvironment

The Confidentiality of E-Mail

An attorney who breaches his or her duty to preserve the confidentiality of client information may face serious consequences, including liability to the client for damages caused by the breach and the possibility of disciplinary action by the state bar association. The widespread use of the Internet by lawyers to communicate with their clients has thus raised a significant question: Does communicating with a client via e-mail constitute a violation of the confidentiality rule? Because the law is not yet settled on the issue of e-mail as a confidential mode of communication, legal professionals should consider encrypting their e-mail messages to or about clients, using disclaimers, and discussing this issue with their clients.

Bar Associations Address the Issue

Although the courts have not yet addressed this question, bar associations in several states have rendered ethical opinions on the subject. Among the first to do so was South Carolina, which concluded in 1994 that lawyers should not use e-mail for sensitive client communications because it is possible for e-mail to be intercepted. For the next few years, there seemed to be a growing consensus that only encrypted communications (encoded messages, using encryption software) with clients could be considered confidential.

Since 1997, however, several states have reached the opposite conclusion. For example, when the Vermont state bar's ethics panel considered the issue, it reasoned that since "(a) e-mail privacy is no less to be expected than in ordinary phone calls, and (b) unauthorized interception is illegal, a lawyer does not violate [the confidentiality rule] by communicating with a client by e-mail . . . without encryption."

The panel went on to say that in various instances "of a very sensitive nature, encryption might be prudent, in which case ordinary phone calls would obviously be deemed inadequate." This reasoning is typical of state bar ethics committees in about two dozen other states, including Illinois, Arizona, and even South Carolina—which reversed its earlier opinion when it revisited the issue later.

In 1999, the American Bar Association (ABA) issued an opinion on the matter. According to the ABA's Standing Committee on Ethics and Professional Responsibility, "a lawyer may transmit information relating to the representation of a client by unencrypted e-mail" without violating the ABA's rules governing attorney conduct. The committee went on to state that plain, unencrypted e-mail "affords a reasonable expectation of privacy from a technological and legal standpoint." According to one commentator, when this announcement was made, the "sigh of relief" among attorneys was "almost audible."[a]

Attorneys Remain Concerned

Notwithstanding the ABA's opinion, attorneys remain concerned. Although the ABA's opinions wield considerable influence, it is entirely possible that a court may arrive at a different conclusion. For this reason, many attorneys remain cautious when communicating with clients over the Internet. Encrypting e-mail and files that are transmitted over the Internet is one way to avoid confidentiality problems. Another is to add disclaimers to e-mail indicating that the communications may not be secure. Finally, some legal ethicists suggest that lawyers should discuss the issue with their clients and let the clients decide on how sensitive information should be exchanged.

For Critical Analysis: *In terms of privacy and confidentiality, what is the difference between cell phone conversations and e-mail communications?*

---

a. Wendy R. Leibowitz, "E-Mail Ethics Evolving," *National Law Journal*, May 17, 1999, p. A17.

---

litigated. It will also monitor the methods used by the attorneys in questioning witnesses and rule on various motions made by the attorneys regarding, for example, the introduction of new evidence. Although the role of the jury is to determine the relevant facts in a case, the judge, by virtue of the instructions that he or she gives to the jury members before they begin deliberating their formal decision, called a **verdict**, determines in part whether those facts support the position of the plaintiff or the defendant.

Verdict A formal decision made by a jury.

The Decision to File a Lawsuit

Before an individual or a company decides to file a complaint and thus initiate legal proceedings against a defendant, it must be determined, in consultation with an attorney, (1) whether the law provides an adequate remedy for the claim, (2) who can reasonably be expected to prevail in the lawsuit, and (3) whether the expected benefit is sufficient to compensate for any costs and expenses as well as any lost business.

In deciding whether to pursue a legal claim or right, the prospective **litigant** must consider a number of questions that relate not only to the desirability of the suit itself but also to whether such an action will help or hinder the person's long-term objectives. Filing a lawsuit may permanently rupture a long-standing personal or business relationship, so careful attention will have to be given to whether the expected gains resulting from a successful court case outweigh the potential costs. Any such cost-benefit analysis is further muddied when both parties have strong legal support for their particular positions. In such cases, the verdict may turn on a party's demeanor or some other irrelevant factor. Although an attorney will take all reasonable measures to present the strongest possible case on behalf of a client, there are other factors, such as the client's appearance or voice, that are beyond the control of even the most talented attorney.

Litigant A party to a lawsuit.

ADEQUACY OF THE REMEDY The fact that a company has been adversely affected by the actions of a competitor will not necessarily give rise to a claim for **damages,** because the law grants remedies only for certain types of conduct. In general, the courts will not grant a particular type of relief simply because a company wishes to be insulated from the pressures of a competitive market.

Damages Money sought as a remedy for a breach of contract or for a tortious act.

• **Example 4.4** Suppose that the Sparkling Cola Company is able to convince Red Castle, a nationwide chain of fast-food restaurants, to use its cola products instead of those offered by Red Castle's long-time supplier, the Effervescent Cola Company, based on favorable consumer taste tests and Sparkling's willingness to undersell Effervescent. Effervescent will probably not be able to sue Sparkling for interfering with its contractual relationship with Red Castle simply because it lost a customer to a competitor having a better product. In contrast, if Sparkling convinces Red Castle to stop using Effervescent's products by spreading false rumors about the quality of the products or labor problems at Effervescent's manufacturing plants, Effervescent can seek to recover damages from Sparkling based on a variety of legal theories, including defamation and wrongful interference with a contractual relationship (discussed in Chapter 9). In such a situation, it would clearly be in Effervescent's interest to seek damages, because Sparkling might otherwise continue spreading false rumors about its products to Effervescent's remaining customers.•

CHANCES OF WINNING THE SUIT Once a party, such as Effervescent, has determined that there is a remedy for the particular injury it has suffered, the next factor to consider is the likelihood that the company will be able to win the lawsuit. Although jury trials always have an element of unpredictability (jurors may disregard important facts and give undue weight to trivial facts), any assessment by the company of its chances of prevailing in court will depend on the applicable laws and the outcomes of any factually similar cases. The client company and its attorney will also have to consider whether there is enough evidence to convince a court to rule in its favor and whether the other party can offer any **defenses,** or excuses, to justify its actions. Finally, the company will have to consider whether its own actions could significantly reduce its chances of prevailing in court.

Defense That which a defendant offers and alleges in an action or suit as a reason why the plaintiff should not recover or establish what he or she seeks.

VALUE OF THE REMEDY Assuming that the client and the client's attorney have determined that they stand a very good chance of winning their suit against the defendant, they will then have to decide whether the relief that they would probably receive is worth the time and expense of the litigation.

Legal Fees. One factor to be considered is, of course, the cost of the attorney's time—the legal fees that the client will have to pay to collect damages from the defendant. Attorneys base their fees on such factors as the difficulty of a matter, the amount of time involved, the experience and skill of the attorney in the particular area of the law, and the cost of doing business. In the United States, legal fees range from $60 per hour to $450 per hour (the average fee per hour is between $140 and $160). Not included in attorneys' fees are such expenses as court filing charges and other costs directly related to a case.

A particular legal matter may include one or a combination of several types of fees. *Fixed fees* may be charged for the performance of such services as drafting a simple will. *Hourly fees* may be computed for matters that involve an indeterminate period of time. Any case brought to trial, for example, may involve an expenditure of time that cannot be precisely estimated in advance. *Contingent fees* are fixed as a percentage (between 25 and 40 percent) of a client's recovery in certain types of lawsuits, such as personal injury. If the lawsuit is unsuccessful, the attorney receives no fee. The client will, however, have to pay the court fees and any other expenses incurred by the attorney (such as travel expenses, copying expenses, and so on—often called out-of-pocket costs) on the client's behalf.

Many state and federal statutes allow for an award of attorneys' fees in certain legal actions, such as probate matters. In these cases, a judge sets the amount of the fee, based on such factors as the results obtained by the attorney and the fee customarily charged for similar services. In some cases, a client may receive an award of attorneys' fees as part of his or her recovery.

Settlement Consideration. A client's decision as to how much money he or she can afford to invest in the resolution of a particular legal problem is frequently the most important factor in determining the extent to which an attorney will pursue a resolution. If a client decides that he or she can afford a lengthy trial and one or more appeals, an attorney may pursue those actions. Often, once a client learns the extent of the costs involved in litigating a claim, he or she will be more willing to settle the claim instead of going to trial.

• **Example 4.5** If the litigation is expected to be extremely costly, then in our earlier example, Effervescent may wish to consider alternative approaches, such as settling with Sparkling out of court, submitting the dispute to a third party (not a member of the judiciary), or doing nothing at all. Effervescent will also have to decide whether Sparkling has the financial resources to satisfy a court judgment and whether the enforcement of the judgment will be excessively expensive.•

The Decision to Defend against a Lawsuit

The plaintiff is not the only one that must consider the merits of becoming involved in a lawsuit. The defendant does not usually wish to be involved in a lawsuit, and there are a number of issues that the defendant must consider before deciding to battle the plaintiff in court. These issues include (1) whether the relationship it has with the plaintiff is too valuable to risk by becoming involved in an adversarial proceeding, (2) whether the publicity surrounding a trial would appreciably damage its reputation or image, and (3) whether the claim can be settled in a less costly manner.

VALUE OF A BUSINESS RELATIONSHIP   In some cases, the defendant will not have to worry about the potential disruption of any business relationship because it has no commercial association with the plaintiff. But even in the case of a competitor, a company might be reluctant to become involved in litigation because of the effect a court battle might have on possible joint ventures or mutually beneficial research and development programs.

• **Example 4.6** Because Sparkling is highly competitive with Effervescent, it is not likely to place a very great value on the effect a vigorous courtroom defense will have on their relationship. Consequently, Sparkling will be more inclined to consider litigation as a viable strategy for resolving the dispute. The story might be very different if the suit were filed by Bob's Beef Wagon, a regional restaurant chain and long-time purchaser of Sparkling products. In that situation, Sparkling would consider the value of Bob's business very seriously and investigate alternative solutions before deciding to become involved in a court trial.•

POTENTIAL DAMAGE TO A COMPANY'S REPUTATION   Because trials are public proceedings, they may be covered, if the case is sufficiently noteworthy, by newspaper, magazine, radio, and television journalists. This means that any statements made by either side, as well as any testimony or evidence, may be publicized by the media. • **Example 4.7** If the case between Effervescent and Sparkling involves numerous unflattering allegations regarding unethical business practices and poor product quality, then Sparkling will have to consider the likelihood that these charges will be publicized throughout the country. Sparkling's attorney may also remind the company that the charges themselves—rather than the actual truth of the charges—will dominate the media coverage. Furthermore, Sparkling will have to consider the harm to its image as a model corporate citizen that might result from a verdict for the plaintiff (Effervescent).• In general, the cost of satisfying a judgment might understate the true cost of the legal dispute, because the publicity might negate the positive public image that Sparkling has achieved through its advertising campaigns.

OTHER FORMS OF RESOLUTION   Even though a defendant may have been served with a complaint by the plaintiff's attorney, this does not preclude the defendant from exploring alternative methods of settling the dispute. These methods include an out-of-court settlement. The attractiveness of an out-of-court settlement may be directly related to the amount of publicity given to the case and its effect on public attitudes toward the company. Because the terms of out-of-court settlements are normally not made available to the public, they provide a means by which a company may "buy" its way out of a lawsuit and avoid the attendant publicity.

● **Example 4.8** Sparkling's receptiveness to an out-of-court settlement would depend on its own perception about the strength of its case. If it believes that Effervescent has filed the lawsuit merely to harass it, then it might prefer to risk litigating the claims. Alternatively, Sparkling might propose to Effervescent that they submit the matter to arbitration. In *arbitration,* which will be discussed more fully later in this chapter, the parties agree to let a neutral third party decide the issue. Both parties might prefer arbitration as a solution for avoiding the incessant delays and higher costs of courtroom litigation. Because the terms of the arbitration agreement would not be released to the public, both companies could avoid having their images sullied by the press.●

The Search for Alternatives to Litigation

A number of solutions have been proposed, and some have been implemented, to reduce the congestion in our court system and to reduce the litigation costs facing all members of society. The enforcement of arbitration clauses, the use of court-referred arbitration and mediation, and the emergence of an increasing number of private forums for dispute resolution have all helped to reduce the caseload of the courts.

Another solution to the problem involves putting caps on damage awards, particularly for pain and suffering. Without the probability of obtaining multimillion-dollar judgments for pain and suffering, some potential litigants will be deterred from undertaking lawsuits to obtain damages. Another avenue of attack is to penalize those who bring frivolous lawsuits. Rule 11 of the Federal Rules of Civil Procedure allows for disciplinary sanctions against lawyers and litigants who bring frivolous lawsuits in federal courts.

The parties to a controversy and their attorneys negotiate to resolve the dispute. When should a third party be brought in to mediate?

Many courts require mediation or arbitration before a case goes to trial. There are proposals to reduce delay and expenses in federal civil cases further, and proposals are being considered by the states as well. Some of the proposals can be viewed as case-management plans. One suggested program, for example, would require each federal district court to implement procedures for placing cases on different tracks, with simple cases being handled more quickly than complex ones.

Politics and Law

Because reforms of any system affect individuals and groups differently, they seldom are accomplished easily and quickly. Reform of the court system is a prime example. At the federal level, members of Congress long have been concerned with bringing court costs and delay under control. These concerns gave rise to the enactment of legislation in the early 1990s that required the federal courts to develop a plan to cut costs and reduce delay within the federal judicial system.

New Methods and Arrangements

The search for alternative means to resolve disputes has produced several distinct methods and arrangements. These range from neighbors' sitting down over a cup of coffee to work out their differences to huge multinational corporations' agreeing to resolve a dispute through a formal hearing before a panel of experts. All of these alternatives to traditional litigation make up what is broadly termed alternative dispute resolution.

Alternative dispute resolution (ADR) describes any procedure or device for resolving disputes other than the traditional judicial process. ADR is normally a less expensive and less time-consuming process than formal litigation. In some cases, it also has the advantage of being more private. Except in cases involving court-annexed arbitration (discussed later in this chapter), no public record of ADR proceedings is created; only the parties directly involved are privy to the information presented during the process. This is a particularly important consideration in many business disputes, because such cases may involve sensitive commercial information.

Alternative Dispute Resolution (ADR) The resolution of disputes in ways other than those involved in the traditional judicial process. Negotiation, mediation, and arbitration are forms of ADR.

Negotiation and Mediation

Alternative dispute resolution methods differ in the degree of formality involved and the extent to which third parties participate in the process. Generally, negotiation is the least formal method and involves no third parties. Mediation may be similarly informal but does involve the participation of a third party.

Negotiation

In the process of **negotiation,** the parties come together informally, with or without attorneys to represent them. Within this informal setting, the parties air their differences and try to reach a settlement or resolution without the involvement of independent third parties. Because no third parties are involved and because of the informal setting, negotiation is the simplest form of ADR. Even if a lawsuit has been initiated, the parties may continue to negotiate their differences at any time during the litigation process and settle their dispute.

Negotiation In regard to dispute settlement, a process in which parties attempt to settle their dispute without going to court, with or without attorneys to represent them.

Less than 10 percent of all corporate lawsuits, for example, end up in trial—the rest are settled beforehand.

PREPARATION FOR NEGOTIATION　Because so many disputes are settled through negotiation, in spite of the informality of this means of dispute resolution, each party must carefully prepare his or her side of the case. The elements of the dispute should be considered, documents and other evidence should be collected, and witnesses should be prepared to testify. Negotiating from a well-prepared position improves the odds of obtaining a favorable result. Even if a dispute is not resolved through negotiation, preparation for negotiation will reduce the effort required to prepare for the next step in the dispute-resolution process.

"ASSISTED NEGOTIATION"　To facilitate negotiation, various forms of what might be called "assisted negotiation" have been employed. Forms of ADR associated with the negotation process include mini-trials and early neutral case evaluation. Another form of assisted negotiation—the summary jury trial—is discussed later in this chapter.

A **mini-trial** is a private proceeding in which each party's attorney briefly argues the party's case before the other party. Typically, a neutral third party, who acts as an adviser and an expert in the area being disputed, is also present. If the parties fail to reach an agreement, the adviser renders an opinion as to how a court would likely decide the issue. The proceeding assists the parties in determining whether they should negotiate a settlement of the dispute or take it to court.

In **early neutral case evaluation,** the parties select a neutral third party (generally an expert in the subject matter of the dispute) to evaluate their respective positions. The parties explain their positions to the case evaluator however they wish. The evaluator then assesses the strengths and weaknesses of the parties' positions, and this evaluation forms the basis for negotiating a settlement.

Disputes may also be resolved in a friendly, nonadversarial manner through **conciliation,** in which a third party assists parties to a dispute in reconciling their differences. The conciliator helps to schedule negotiating sessions and carries offers back and forth between the parties when they refuse to face each other in direct negotiations. Technically, conciliators are not supposed to recommend solutions. In practice, however, they often do. In contrast, a mediator is expected to propose solutions.

Mediation

Mediation is similar to negotiation. In the mediation process, as in negotiation, the parties themselves must reach agreement about their dispute. The major difference between negotiation and mediation is that the latter involves a third party, called a mediator. The **mediator** assists the parties in reaching a mutually acceptable agreement. The mediator talks face to face with the parties and allows them to discuss their disagreement, usually in an informal environment. The mediator's role, however, is limited to assisting the parties. The mediator does not decide a controversy; he or she only facilitates the process by helping the parties more quickly find common ground on which they can begin to reach an agreement for themselves.

Mini-Trial　A private proceeding in which each party to a dispute argues its position before the other side and vice versa. A neutral third party may be present and act as an adviser if the parties fail to reach an agreement.

Early Neutral Case Evaluation　A form of alternative dispute resolution in which a neutral third party evaluates the strengths and weaknesses of the disputing parties' positions; the evaluator's opinion forms the basis for negotiating a settlement.

Conciliation　A form of alternative dispute resolution in which the parties reach an agreement themselves with the help of a neutral third party, called a conciliator, who facilitates the negotiations.

Mediation　A method of settling disputes outside of court by using the services of a neutral third party, called a mediator. The mediator acts as a communicating agent between the parties and suggests ways in which the parties can resolve their dispute.

Mediator　A person who attempts to reconcile the differences between two or more parties.

ADVANTAGES OF MEDIATION Few procedural rules are involved in the mediation process—far fewer than in a courtroom setting. The proceedings can be tailored to fit the needs of the parties—the mediator can be told to maintain a diplomatic role or be asked to express an opinion about the dispute, lawyers can be excluded from the proceedings, and the exchange of a few documents can replace the more expensive and time-consuming process of pretrial discovery. Disputes are often settled much more quickly in mediation than in formal litigation.[1]

There are other benefits. Because the parties reach agreement by mutual consent, the bitterness that often flows from the winner-take-all outcome of a formal trial decision is avoided. Hard feelings are also minimized by the less stressful environment provided by mediation; the absence of the formal rules and adversarial tone of courtroom proceedings lessens the hostility the parties may feel toward one another. Minimizing hard feelings can be very important when the parties have to go on working with one another while the controversy is being resolved or after it has been settled. This is frequently the case when two businesses—say, a supplier and a purchaser—have a long-standing, mutually beneficial relationship that they would like to preserve despite their disagreement. Similar considerations are found in the context of management and labor disputes; employee disciplinary matters and grievances are subjects that invite mediation as an alternative to formal litigation.

Another important benefit of mediation is that the mediator is selected by the parties. In litigation, the parties have no control over the selection of a judge. In mediation, the parties may choose a mediator on the basis of expertise in a particular field as well as for fairness and impartiality. To the degree that the mediator has these attributes, he or she will more effectively aid the parties in reaching an agreement over their dispute.

DISADVANTAGES OF MEDIATION Mediation is not without disadvantages. A mediator is likely to charge a fee. (This can be split between the parties, though, and thus may represent less expense than would both sides' hiring lawyers.)

Informality and the absence of a third party referee can also be a detriment. (Remember that a mediator can only help the parties reach a decision, not make a decision for them.) Without a deadline hanging over the parties' heads, and without the threat of sanctions if they fail to negotiate in good faith, they may be less willing to make concessions or otherwise strive honestly and diligently to reach a settlement. This can slow the process or even cause it to fail.

Arbitration

A third method of dispute resolution combines the advantages of third party decision making—as provided by judges and juries in formal litigation—-with the speed and flexibility inherent in rules of procedure and evidence less rigid than those governing courtroom litigation. This is the process of **arbitration**—the settling of a dispute by an impartial third party (other than a court) who renders a legally binding decision. The third party who renders the decision is called an **arbitrator.**

Arbitration The settling of a dispute by submitting it to a disinterested third party (other than a court), who renders a decision. The decision may or may not be legally binding.

Arbitrator A disinterested party who, by prior agreement of the parties submitting their dispute to arbitration, has the power to resolve the dispute and (generally) bind the parties.

---

1. In Florida alone, as many as fifty thousand disputes that might have ended up in court are instead resolved through mediation each year. Florida's insurance commissioner used mediation to resolve hundreds of insurance claims stemming from 1992's Hurricane Andrew.

International Perspective

ADR in Japan and China

The United States is not the only country that encourages mediation, arbitration, and other forms of ADR. Japan, for example, has recently authorized the establishment of neutral panels to act as mediators in product liability suits (suits brought by plaintiffs who have allegedly been injured by a seller's defective product—see Chapter 10). Several industries, including those manufacturing and selling housing materials, automobiles, and appliances, have set up such panels, which follow guidelines published by the Japanese Ministry of International Trade and Industry.

Since the mid-1990s, China has also made it simpler for disputes to be settled through ADR. Under Chinese law, although most disputes can be arbitrated, family matters (such as those relating to marriage, adoption, and financial support) cannot be submitted for arbitration. Such disputes will continue to be handled by the relevant administrative agencies of the Chinese government.

For Critical Analysis: *Do you see any reason why certain types of disputes, such as those involving family matters, should not be decided by arbitration?*

When a dispute arises, the parties can agree to settle their differences informally through arbitration rather than formally through the court system. Alternatively, the parties may agree ahead of time that, if a dispute should arise, they will submit to arbitration rather than bring a lawsuit. Both parties are obligated to follow the arbitrator's decision regardless of whether or not they agree with it; this is what is meant by saying the decision is legally binding.

The federal government and many state governments favor arbitration over litigation. The federal policy favoring arbitration is embodied in the Federal Arbitration Act (FAA) of 1925.[2] The FAA requires that courts give deference to all voluntary arbitration agreements in cases governed by federal law. Virtually any dispute can be the subject of arbitration. A voluntary agreement to arbitrate a dispute normally will be enforced by the courts if the agreement does not compel an illegal act or contravene public policy.

The Federal Arbitration Act

The Federal Arbitration Act does not establish a set arbitration procedure. The parties themselves must agree on the manner of resolving their dispute. The FAA provides the means for enforcing the arbitration procedure that the parties have established for themselves.

Section 4 allows a party to petition a federal district court for an order compelling arbitration under an agreement to arbitrate a dispute. If the judge is "satisfied that the making of the agreement for arbitration or the failure to comply therewith is not in issue, the court shall make an order directing the parties to proceed with arbitration in accordance with the terms of the agreement."

Under Section 9 of the FAA, the parties to the arbitration may agree to have the arbitrator's decision confirmed in a federal district court. Through confirmation, one party obtains a court order directing another party to comply with the terms of the arbitrator's decision. Section 10 establishes the grounds by which the arbitrator's decision may be set aside (canceled). The grounds for setting aside a decision are limited to misconduct, fraud, corruption, or abuse

---

2. 9 U.S.C. Sections 1–15.

of power in the arbitration process itself; a court will not review the merits of the dispute or the arbitrator's judgment.

The FAA covers any arbitration clause in a contract that involves interstate commerce. Business activities that have even remote connections or minimal effects on commerce between two or more states are considered to be included. Thus, arbitration agreements involving transactions only slightly connected to the flow of interstate commerce may fall under the FAA, even if the parties, at the time of contracting, did not expect their arbitration agreement to involve interstate commerce.[3]

In the following case, an employer asked a court to issue an order compelling an ex-employee to submit to arbitration under an arbitration agreement that the parties had signed. Under that agreement, it was the employer's responsibility to establish the procedure and the rules for the arbitration. Those rules were the focus of the court's consideration of the employer's request.

---

3. *Allied-Bruce Terminix Cos., Inc. v. Dobson,* 513 U.S. 265, 115 S.Ct. 834, 130 L.Ed.2d 753 (1995).

Case 4.1 ● Hooters of America, Inc. v. Phillips

United States Court of Appeals, Fourth Circuit, 1999.
173 F.3d 933.
http://www.law.emory.edu/4circuit[a]

Company Profile *The first Hooters restaurant was opened in Clearwater, Florida, in 1983, by six friends, all of whom had business experience but none of whom had restaurant experience. The following year, they sold the rights to expand the business under the Hooters name to Hooters of America, Inc. (http://www.hooters.com). Today, Hooters of America owns or licenses more than two hundred restaurants in forty-two states, as well as Argentina, the Bahamas, Canada, Mexico, the United Kingdom, and other countries. The menu includes spicy chicken wings and sandwiches.*

Background and Facts In 1989, Annette Phillips was hired by Hooters of Myrtle Beach (HOMB), a franchisee of Hooters of America, Inc., to work as a bartender at a Hooters restaurant in Myrtle Beach, South Carolina. Five years later, Hooters imple-

mented an alternative dispute-resolution program. The company conditioned eligibility for raises, transfers, and promotions on an employee's signing an "agreement to arbitrate employment-related disputes," which specifically included claims of sexual harassment. The agreement stated that the arbitration was subject to "the company's rules and procedures for alternative resolution of employment-related disputes, as promulgated by the company from time to time." The employees were not given a copy of these rules. Phillips signed the agreement. In June 1996, Gerald Brooks, a Hooters's official and the brother of HOMB's principal owner, allegedly sexually harassed Phillips by grabbing and slapping her buttocks. After appealing to her manager for help and being told to "let it go," she quit her job. Phillips threatened to sue, claiming that the attack and the restaurant's failure to address it violated her rights.[b] Hooters responded that she was required to submit her claim to arbitration. Phillips refused. Hooters filed a suit in a federal district court against Phillips to compel arbitration under Section 4 of the FAA. The court denied Hooters's request. The company appealed to the U.S. Court of Appeals for the Fourth Circuit.

---

a. In the "Listing by Month of Decision" section, click on "1999 Decisions." When the list opens, click on "April." On that page, scroll down the list of cases to the name of the case and click on it to access the opinion. This Web site is sponsored by Emory University.

b. Phillips claimed specifically that Hooters violated her rights under Title VII of the Civil Rights Act of 1964. This law is discussed more fully in Chapter 18.

In the Words of the Court . . .
WILKINSON, Chief Judge.

* * * *

(Continued)

Case 4.1 Continued

Hooters and Phillips agreed to settle any disputes between them not in a judicial forum, but in another neutral forum—arbitration. Their agreement provided that Hooters was responsible for setting up such a forum by promulgating arbitration rules and procedures. * * *

The Hooters rules when taken as a whole, however, are so one-sided that their *only possible purpose is to undermine the neutrality of the proceeding.* The rules require the employee to provide the company notice of her claim at the outset, including "the nature of the Claim" and "the specific act(s) or omissions(s) which are the basis of the Claim." Hooters, on the other hand, is not required to file any responsive pleadings or to [provide] notice [of] its defenses. Additionally, at the time of filing this notice, the employee must provide the company with a list of all fact witnesses with a brief summary of the facts known to each. The company, however, is not required to reciprocate. [Emphasis added.]

The Hooters rules also provide a mechanism for selecting a panel of three arbitrators that is crafted to ensure a biased decision maker. The employee and Hooters each select an arbitrator, and the two arbitrators in turn select a third. Good enough, except that the employee's arbitrator and the third arbitrator must be selected from a list of arbitrators created exclusively by Hooters. This gives Hooters control over the entire panel and places no limits whatsoever on whom Hooters can put on the list. Under the rules, Hooters is free to devise lists of partial arbitrators who have existing relationships, financial or familial, with Hooters and its management. In fact, the rules do not even prohibit Hooters from placing its managers themselves on the list. Further, nothing in the rules restricts Hooters from punishing arbitrators who rule against the company by removing them from the list. Given the unrestricted control that one party (Hooters) has over the panel, the selection of an impartial decision maker would be a surprising result.

* * * *

In addition, the rules provide that upon 30 days notice Hooters, but not the employee, may cancel the agreement to arbitrate. Moreover, Hooters reserves the right to modify the rules, "in whole or in part," whenever it wishes and "without notice" to the employee. Nothing in the rules even prohibits Hooters from changing the rules in the middle of an arbitration proceeding.

Decision and Remedy The U.S. Court of Appeals for the Fourth Circuit held that Hooters's issuance of "so many biased rules" created "a sham system unworthy even of the name of arbitration," in violation of the parties' contract to arbitrate. The court affirmed the judgment of the lower court.

For Critical Analysis—Ethical Consideration *Increasingly, employers are including arbitra-tion clauses in contracts with their employees. Some argue that while it may be fair to enforce such clauses in contracts between parties of equal bargaining strength, it is not fair to enforce them in employment contracts—because employees usually have no right to negotiate the terms of the contract. Do you agree with this argument? Explain.*

State Arbitration Statutes

Virtually all states follow the federal approach to voluntary arbitration. Thirty-four states and the District of Columbia have adopted the Uniform Arbitration

Act, which was drafted by the National Conference of Commissioners on Uniform State Laws in 1955. Those states that have not adopted the uniform act nonetheless follow many of the practices specified in it.

Under the uniform act, the basic approach is to give full effect to voluntary agreements to arbitrate disputes between private parties. The act supplements private arbitration agreements by providing explicit procedures and remedies for enforcing arbitration agreements. The uniform act does not, however, dictate the terms of the agreement. Moreover, under both federal and state statutes, the parties are afforded considerable latitude in deciding the subject matter of the arbitration and the methods for conducting the arbitration process. In the absence of a controlling statute, the rights and duties of the parties are established and limited by their agreement.

The Arbitration Process

The arbitration process begins with a *submission.* **Submission** is the act of referring a dispute to an arbitrator. The next step is the *hearing,* in which evidence and arguments are presented to the arbitrator. The process culminates in an *award,* which is the decision of the arbitrator.

The right to appeal the award to a court of law is limited. If the award was made under a voluntary arbitration agreement, a court normally will not set it aside even if it was the result of an erroneous determination of fact or an incorrect interpretation of law by the arbitrator.

This limitation is based on at least two grounds. First, if an award is not treated as final, rather than speeding up the dispute-resolution process, arbitration would merely add one more layer to the process of litigation. Second, the basis of arbitration—the freedom of parties to agree among themselves how to settle a controversy—supports treating an award as final. Having had the opportunity to frame the issues and to set out the manner for resolving the dispute, one party should not complain if the result was not what that party had hoped it would be.

Submission An agreement by two or more parties to refer any disputes they may have under their contract to a disinterested third party, such as an arbitrator, who has the power to render a binding decision.

International Perspective

International Arbitration

International standards for the recognition of arbitration agreements and awards were set by the United Nations Convention on the Recognition and Enforcement of Foreign Arbitral Awards,[a] which has been signed by seventy-three countries, including the United States. Article V(2) of the convention creates an exception to enforcement of arbitration clauses that are "contrary to the public policy" of the relevant country. Thus, the resolution of a case will depend on the strength of a public policy in a given country. International organizations that handle arbitration matters include the United Nations Commission on International Trade Laws, the London Court of International Arbitration, the Euro-Arab Chamber of Commerce, the International Chamber of Commerce in Paris, and the International Trademark Association.

For Critical Analysis: *Should businesspersons evaluate the policies of different countries before deciding where to arbitrate their disputes?*

a. June 10, 1958, 21 U.S.T. 2517 (also known as the New York Convention).

SUBMISSION The parties may agree to submit questions of fact, questions of law, or both to the arbitrator. The parties may even agree to leave the interpretation of the arbitration agreement to the arbitrator. In the case of an existing agreement to arbitrate, the clause itself is the submission to arbitration. The submission typically states the identities of the parties, the nature of the dispute to be resolved, the monetary amounts involved in the controversy, the place at which the arbitration is to take place, and the intention of the parties to be bound by the arbitrator's award. Exhibit 4–1 contains a sample submission form.

Most states require that an agreement to submit a dispute to arbitration be in writing. Moreover, because the goal of arbitration is speed and efficiency in resolving controversies, most states require that matters be submitted within a definite period of time, generally six months from the date on which the dispute arises.

THE HEARING Because the parties are free to construct the method by which they want their dispute resolved, they must state the issues that will be submitted and the powers that the arbitrator will exercise. The arbitrator may be given power at the outset of the process to establish rules that will govern the proceedings. Typically, these rules are much less restrictive than those governing formal litigation. Regardless of who establishes the rules, the arbitrator will apply them during the course of the hearing.

Restrictions on the kind of evidence and the manner in which it is presented may be less rigid in arbitration, partly because the arbitrator is likely to be an expert in the subject matter involved in the controversy. Restrictions may also be less stringent because there is less fear that the arbitrator will be swayed by improper evidence. In contrast, evidence in a jury trial must sometimes be presented twice: once to the judge, outside the presence of the jury, to determine if the evidence may be heard by the jury, and—depending on the judge's ruling—again, to the jury.

In the typical hearing format, the parties begin as they would at trial by presenting opening arguments to the arbitrator and stating what remedies should or should not be granted. After the opening statements have been made, evidence is presented. Witnesses may be called and examined by both sides. After all the evidence has been presented, the parties give their closing arguments. On completion of the closing arguments, the arbitrator closes the hearing.

THE AWARD After each side has had an opportunity to present evidence and to argue its case, the arbitrator reaches a decision. The final decision of the arbitrator is called an **award,** even if no money is conferred on a party as a result of the proceedings. Under most statutes, the arbitrator must render an award within thirty days of the close of the hearing.

In most states, the award need not state the arbitrator's findings regarding factual questions in the case. Nor must the award state the conclusions that the arbitrator reached on any questions of law that may have been presented. All that is required for the award to be valid is that it completely resolve the controversy.

Most states do, however, require that the award be in writing, regardless of whether any conclusions of law or findings of fact are included. If the arbitrator does state his or her legal conclusions and factual findings, then a letter or an opinion will be drafted containing the basis for the award. Even when there

Award In the context of litigation, the amount of money awarded to a plaintiff in a civil lawsuit as damages. In the context of arbitration, the arbitrator's decision.

Exhibit 4–1   Sample Submission Form

American Arbitration Association

SUBMISSION TO DISPUTE RESOLUTION

Date: _____

The named parties hereby submit the following dispute for resolution under the _____
_____ Rules* of the American Arbitration Association:

Procedure Selected: ☐ Binding arbitration   ☐ Mediation settlement
                      ☐ Other _____
                              (Describe)

FOR INSURANCE CASES ONLY:

_____   _____ to _____   _____
Policy Number   Effective Dates   Applicable Policy Limits

_____   _____
Date of Incident   Location

Insured: _____   Claim Number: _____

Name(s) of Claimant(s)	Check if a Minor	Amount Claimed
_____	☐	_____
_____	☐	_____

Nature of Dispute and/or Injuries Alleged (attach additional sheets if necessary):

Place of Hearing: _____

We agree that, if binding arbitration is selected, we will abide by and perform any award rendered hereunder and that a judgment may be entered on the award.

To Be Completed by the Claimant	*To Be Completed by the Respondent*
_____	_____
Name of Party	Name of Party
_____	_____
Address	Address
_____	_____
City, State, and ZIP Code	City, State, and ZIP Code
( ) _____	( ) _____
Telephone Fax	Telephone Fax
_____	_____
Signature†	Signature†
_____	_____
Name of Party's Attorney or Representative	Name of Party's Attorney or Representative
_____	_____
Address	Address
_____	_____
City, State, and ZIP Code	City, State, and ZIP Code
( ) _____	( ) _____
Telephone Fax	Telephone Fax
_____	_____
Signature†	Signature†

Please file three copies with the AAA.

* If you have a question as to which rules apply, please contact the AAA.
† Signatures of all parties are required for arbitration.

Form G1-7/90

is no statutory requirement that the arbitrator state the factual and legal basis for the award, the parties may impose the requirement in their submission or in their predispute agreement to arbitrate.

Enforcement of Agreements to Submit to Arbitration

The role of the courts in the arbitration process is limited. One important role is played at the prearbitration stage. A court may be called on to order one party to an arbitration agreement to submit to arbitration under the terms of the agreement. The court in this role is essentially interpreting a contract. The court must determine to what the parties have committed themselves before ordering that they submit to arbitration.

> **Remember** Litigation—even of a dispute over whether a particular matter should be submitted to arbitration—can be time consuming and expensive.

THE ISSUE OF ARBITRABILITY When a dispute arises as to whether or not the parties have agreed in an arbitration clause to submit a particular matter to arbitration, one party may file suit to compel arbitration. The court before which the suit is brought will not decide the basic controversy but must decide the issue of arbitrability—that is, whether the issue is one that must be resolved through arbitration. If the court finds that the subject matter in controversy is covered by the agreement to arbitrate, then a party may be compelled to arbitrate the dispute involuntarily.

Although the parties may agree to submit the issue of arbitrability to an arbitrator, the agreement must be explicit; a court will never *infer* an agreement to arbitrate. Unless a court finds an *explicit* agreement to have the arbitrator decide whether a dispute is arbitrable, the court will decide the issue. This is an important initial determination, because no party will be ordered to submit to arbitration unless the court is convinced that the party has consented to do so.

COMPULSORY ARBITRATION Are violations of rights granted by statutes appropriate subjects for arbitration? For example, should a court order the arbitration of a claim involving an alleged violation of a federal statute protecting an employee from employment discrimination?

In one important case, the United States Supreme Court held that a claim brought under the Age Discrimination in Employment Act (ADEA) of 1967 (discussed in Chapter 18) could be subject to compulsory arbitration.[4] The plaintiff in the case, Robert Gilmer, had been discharged from his employment at the age of sixty-two. Gilmer sued his employer, claiming that he was a victim of age discrimination. The employer argued that Gilmer had to submit the dispute to arbitration because he had agreed, as part of a required registration application to be a securities representative with the New York Stock Exchange, to arbitrate "any dispute, claim, or controversy" relating to his employment. The Supreme Court held that Gilmer, by agreeing to arbitrate any dispute, had waived his right to sue. (For a further discussion of compulsory arbitration in the employment context, see this chapter's *Inside the Legal Environment* on page 114.)

Note that Gilmer had waived his *own* rights in a broadly worded arbitration clause. In the following case, the Supreme Court addresses the question of whether a union, in an equally broadly worded arbitration clause, can waive the rights of the employees whom it represents.

---

4. *Gilmer v. Interstate/Johnson Lane Corp.*, 500 U.S. 20, 111 S.Ct. 1647, 114 L.Ed.2d 26 (1991).

Case 4.2 ● Wright v. Universal Maritime Service Corp.

Supreme Court of the United States, 1998.
525 U.S. 70,
119 S.Ct. 391,
142 L.Ed.2d 361.
http://supct.law.cornell.edu/
supct/html/97-156.ZS.html[a]

Background and Facts Ceasar Wright was a longshoreman and a member of the International Longshoremen's Association (ILA). The ILA supplies workers to Universal Maritime Service Corporation and other members of the South Carolina Stevedores Association (SCSA). A collective bargaining agreement (CBA) between the ILA and the SCSA provided for the arbitration of "matters under dispute" in one clause and "all matters affecting wages, hours, and other terms and conditions of employment" in another. Still another clause stated that "[a]nything not contained in this Agreement shall not be construed as being part of this Agreement." Wright suffered a job-related injury that resulted in a disability. When a physician approved Wright's return to work, the SCSA members refused to hire him because of the disability. Wright filed a suit in a federal district court against Universal and others, on the ground that they had discriminated against him in violation of the Americans with Disabilities Act (ADA) of 1990 (see Chapter 18). The defendants argued that the suit should be dismissed because Wright had not submitted his claim to arbitration. The district court ruled in the defendants' favor, and the U.S. Court of Appeals for the Fourth Circuit affirmed this ruling. Wright appealed to the United States Supreme Court.

---

a. This page is part of the Supreme Court Collection of cases maintained by the Legal Information Institute, which is part of Cornell Law School. In the right-hand frame, in the "Arranged by party name" list, in the "1998" links, click on "1st party." On that page, scroll down to the case name and click on it to access the case.

In the Words of the Court . . .
Justice SCALIA delivered the opinion of the Court.

* * * *

* * * In [a previous case] we stated that a union could waive its officers' statutory right * * * to be free of antiunion discrimination, but we held that such a waiver must be *clear and unmistakable.* * * * [Emphasis added.]

* * * [T]he right to a federal judicial forum is of sufficient importance to be protected against a less-than-explicit union waiver in a CBA. The CBA in this case does not meet that standard. Its arbitration clause is very general, providing for arbitration of "[m]atters under dispute"—which could be understood to mean matters in dispute under the contract. And the remainder of the contract contains no explicit incorporation of statutory antidiscrimination requirements. The Fourth Circuit relied upon the fact that the equivalently broad arbitration clause in *Gilmer v. Interstate/Johnson Lane Corp.*—applying to "any dispute, claim or controversy"—was held to embrace federal statutory claims. But *Gilmer* involved an individual's waiver of his own rights, rather than a union's waiver of the rights of represented employees—and hence the "clear and unmistakable" standard was not applicable.

* * * *

We hold that the collective-bargaining agreement in this case does not contain a clear and unmistakable waiver of the covered employees' rights to a judicial forum for federal claims of employment discrimination. We do not reach the question whether such a waiver would be enforceable.

(Continued)

Case 4.2 Continued

Decision and Remedy The Supreme Court held that the arbitration clause in the CBA did not clearly waive the union members' right to have a court rule on federal claims of employment discrimination. Thus, Wright was not required to submit his claim to arbitration. The Court did not decide whether such a waiver would be enforceable if it were clear. The Court vacated the judgment of the lower court and remanded the case.

For Critical Analysis—Ethical Consideration *Does compulsory arbitration contradict the public policy enunciated in statutes specifically designed to protect employees' rights, such as the right to be free from discrimination (see Chapter 18)?*

Inside the Legal Environment

Arbitration Clauses in Employment Contracts

Arbitration is normally simpler, speedier, and less costly than litigation. For that reason, business owners and managers today often include arbitration clauses in their contracts, including employment contracts. But what happens if a job candidate whom you wish to hire (or an existing employee whose contract is being renewed) objects to one or more of the provisions in an arbitration clause? If you insist that signing the agreement to arbitrate future disputes is a mandatory condition of employment, will such a clause be enforceable?

The *Gilmer* Precedent

The majority of courts have followed the precedent set by the United States Supreme Court in its 1991 *Gilmer* decision. As discussed elsewhere in this chapter, in that case the Court held that an employee's claim of age discrimination was arbitrable, even though the employee alleged that the employer had violated a statute specifically protecting employees from this form of discrimination. The Court reasoned that because the Federal Arbitration Act (FAA) favors the arbitration of disputes, arbitration clauses in employment contracts should be enforced unless it can be shown that Congress, in enacting a particular statute, intended otherwise.

Closer Scrutiny of Mandatory Arbitration Clauses

Recently, however, a number of courts have been looking more closely at the issue of mandatory arbitration.

Arbitration clauses that require the employee to pay the arbitrator's fee and other costs, that bar employees from seeking punitive damages, or that fail in other ways to protect the employees' interests and due process rights sufficiently have been deemed unenforceable by some courts. The Circuit Court of Appeals for the Ninth Circuit has gone even further. In 1998, that court ruled that the legislative history of Title VII of the Civil Rights Act of 1964 does not support arbitration as the exclusive forum for the resolution of discrimination disputes.[a] A year later, the Ninth Circuit held that the Federal Arbitration Act does not apply to employment contracts.[b]

Although the United States Supreme Court addressed the issue of mandatory arbitration in a 1998 case (see Case 4.2), the Court's ruling was narrowly tailored. The Court held that the clause in question, which was included in a collective bargaining contract, did not contain a "clear and unmistakable waiver of the covered employees' rights to a judicial forum for federal claims of employment discrimination" and therefore was unenforceable. The Court did not decide the question of whether a contract that *did* contain a "clear and unmistakable waiver" of the employees' rights would be enforceable.

For Critical Analysis: *Why might victims of employment discrimination prefer to litigate their claims in a judicial forum rather than having them arbitrated, even assuming that arbitration proceedings would be unbiased and would not violate due process rights?*

---

a. *Duffield v. Robertson Stephens Co.*, 144 F.3d 1182 (9th Cir. 1998).

b. *Circuit City Stores, Inc. v. Adams*, 194 F.3d 1070 (9th Cir. 1999).

Setting Aside an Arbitration Award

After the arbitration has been concluded, the losing party may appeal the arbitrator's award to a court, or the winning party may seek a court order compelling the other party to comply with the award. The scope of review in either situation is much more restricted than in an appellate court's review of a trial court decision. The court does not look at the merits of the underlying dispute, and the court will not add to or subtract from the remedies provided by the award. The court's role is limited to determining whether there exists a valid award. If so, the court will order the parties to comply with the terms. The general view is that because the parties were free to frame the issues and set the powers of the arbitrator at the outset, they cannot complain about the result.

FACT FINDINGS AND LEGAL CONCLUSIONS The arbitrator's fact findings and legal conclusions are normally final. That the arbitrator may have erred in a ruling during the hearing or made an erroneous fact finding is normally no basis for setting aside an award: the parties agreed that the arbitrator would be the judge of the facts. Similarly, no matter how obviously the arbitrator was mistaken in a conclusion of law, the award is normally nonetheless binding: the parties agreed to accept the arbitrator's interpretation of the law. A court will not look at the merits of the dispute, the sufficiency of the evidence presented, or the arbitrator's reasoning in reaching a particular decision.

This approach is consistent with the underlying view of all voluntary arbitration—that its basis is really contract law. If the parties freely contract with one another, courts will not interfere simply because one side feels that it received a bad bargain. Any party challenging an award must face the presumption that a final award is valid. But is an award final or binding if the parties did not agree that it would be? That was the issue in the following case.

Case 4.3 ● Orlando v. Interstate Container Corp.

United States Court of Appeals,
Third Circuit, 1996.
100 F.3d 296.

Background and Facts Joseph Orlando, an employee of Interstate Container Corporation, underwent heart bypass surgery. For several months, he did not work but collected disability benefits, in part as provided by a collective bargaining agreement.[a] When his condition improved, he asked to return to work, but Interstate denied his request. He filed a complaint with the company, which, under the collective bargaining agreement, went to arbitration, culminating in an arbitrator's decision in Interstate's favor. The agreement did not state that the arbitrator's decision would be "final" or "binding," however. In Orlando's subsequent suit against Interstate, a federal district court ruled that the decision was not binding. Interstate appealed.

a. A collective bargaining agreement is a contract negotiated by employees and their employer concerning the terms and conditions of employment. See Chapter 19.

In the Words of the Court . . .
WEIS, Circuit Judge.

* * * *

[Interstate] argues that because the contract makes arbitration mandatory, it must necessarily be final as well. That argument finds support in the policy

(Continued)

Case 4.3 Continued

favoring arbitration as a means of resolving disputes, but fails to meet the requirement of authorization by agreement of the parties. * * *

* * * *

* * * [W]e must give full credit to the language the parties have chosen to include—or not include—in their agreement.

Collective bargaining agreements almost invariably explain that arbitration proceedings will be "final," "binding," or "exclusive," or use other words to that effect. This agreement was drafted by parties well-versed in labor matters and cognizant [aware] of that convention. The omission of any indication that arbitration proceedings should be final and binding leads us to conclude that, if we nevertheless declared them to be so, we would not be enforcing the will of the parties, as expressed in their agreement.

Decision and Remedy The U.S. Court of Appeals for the Third Circuit affirmed the lower court's decision. The award was not final or binding because the parties did not agree that it would be.

For Critical Analysis—Economic Consideration *Why might a party insist on the enforcement of an award that is against public policy?*

PUBLIC POLICY AND ILLEGALITY   In keeping with contract law principles, no award will be enforced if compliance with the award would result in the commission of a crime or would conflict with some greater social policy mandated by statute. A court will not overturn an award, however, simply because the arbitrator was called on to resolve a dispute involving a matter of significant public concern.[5] For an award to be set aside, it must call for some action on the part of the parties that would conflict with or in some way undermine public policy.[6]

DEFECTS IN THE ARBITRATION PROCESS   There are some bases for setting aside an award when there is a defect in the arbitration process. These bases are typified by those set forth in the Federal Arbitration Act. Section 10 of the act provides four grounds on which an arbitration award may be set aside:

1. The award was the result of corruption, fraud, or other "undue means."
2. The arbitrator exhibited bias or corruption.
3. The arbitrator refused to postpone the hearing despite sufficient cause, refused to hear evidence pertinent and material to the dispute, or otherwise acted to substantially prejudice the rights of one of the parties.
4. The arbitrator exceeded his or her powers or failed to use them to make a mutual, final, and definite award.

The first three bases for setting aside the award include actions or decisions that are more than simply mistakes in judgment. Each requires some "bad faith" on the part of the arbitrator. Bad faith actions or decisions are ones that

---

5. See, for example, *Faherty v. Faherty,* 97 N.J. 99, 477 A.2d 1257 (1984).
6. See, for example, *Meehan v. Nassau Community College,* 647 N.Y.S.2d 865 (App.Div. 2 Dept. 1996).

affect the integrity of the arbitration process. The honesty and impartiality, rather than the judgment, of the arbitrator are called into question.

Sometimes it is difficult to make the distinction between honest mistakes in judgment and actions or decisions made in bad faith. A bribe is clearly the kind of "undue means" included in the first basis for setting aside an award. Letting only one side argue its case is likewise a clear violation of the second basis.

Meetings between the arbitrator and one party outside the presence of the other party also taint the arbitration process. Although meetings might not involve the kind of corruption that results from taking a bribe, they do affect the integrity of the process; the third basis for setting aside an award is meant to protect against this.

Not every refusal by an arbitrator to admit certain evidence is grounds for setting aside an award under the third basis. As noted, to provide a basis for overturning an award, the arbitrator's decision must be more than an error in judgment, no matter how obviously incorrect that judgment might appear to another observer. The decision must be so obviously wrong or unfair as to imply bias or corruption. Otherwise, the decision normally cannot be a basis for setting aside an award.

The fourth basis for setting aside an award is that the arbitrator exceeded his or her powers in arbitrating the dispute. This issue involves the question of arbitrability. An arbitrator exceeds his or her powers and authority by attempting to resolve an issue that is not covered by the agreement to submit to arbitration.

In the following case, a party to an arbitration proceeding asked a court to set aside the award.

Case 4.4 ● Garvey v. Roberts

United States Court of Appeals,
Ninth Circuit, 2000.
203 F.3d 580.
http://www.ca9.uscourts.gov[a]

Background and Facts In 1986, 1987, and 1988, the Major League Baseball Players Association complained that the Major League Baseball Clubs had engaged in collusion to underpay some of the players. The grievance was submitted to arbitration before a panel chaired by Thomas Roberts. During a hearing in 1986, Ballard Smith, the president of the San Diego Padres, testified that there had been no collusion. Roberts's panel rejected this testimony as false. The Association and the Clubs entered into a settlement agreement, under which the Clubs set up a

fund of $280 million to be distributed to players who suffered losses due to the collusion and the Association established a framework for evaluating each player's claim. A player could challenge the Association's recommendation in binding arbitration. Steve Garvey, who had played for the Padres between 1983 and 1987 under a contract, filed a claim for damages, alleging that the Padres would have extended his contract for the 1988 and 1989 seasons but for the collusion. Roberts, the arbitrator in Garvey's case, denied the claim. Roberts cited Smith's testimony in the 1986 hearing that the Padres were not interested in extending Garvey's contract. Roberts rejected Smith's admission, in a 1996 letter, that he had not told the truth during those hearings and that he had made Garvey an offer that was withdrawn due to the collusion. Garvey filed a suit in a federal district court against Roberts and the Association to have the arbitrator's award set aside. The court ruled in the defendants' favor. Garvey appealed to the U.S. Court of Appeals for the Ninth Circuit.

---

a. In the right column, click on "Appeals Court Decisions." On the page, click on "2000." In the expanded list, click on "February." In that list, scroll to the name of the case and click on it to access the opinion.

(Continued)

Case 4.4 Continued

In the Words of the Court . . .
REINHARDT, Circuit Judge.

* * * *

* * * We overturn an arbitrator's award only when it is clear from the arbitral opinion or award that the arbitrator * * * disregarded what the parties put before him and instead followed his own whims or biases.

* * * *

Under ordinary circumstances, we would accept a conclusion by the arbitrator that Smith told the truth in his 1986 testimony and lied in his 1996 letter even if that conclusion were clearly erroneous. We are presented, however, with the extraordinary circumstance in which the arbitrator's own rulings make clear that, more than being simply erroneous, his finding is completely inexplicable and borders on the irrational. * * *

* * * [At] the collusion proceedings * * *, the panel of arbitrators headed by Arbitrator Roberts had previously ruled that the 1986 testimony by the owners, including Smith, was untruthful. The owners' testimony during those hearings had been designed for the sole purpose of convincing the arbitrators that no collusion had taken place, and the arbitrators had concluded that the owners' testimony was not true. In light of that conclusion, Arbitrator Roberts' determination in Garvey's individual claim proceeding that Smith's (false) 1986 collusion testimony somehow precluded the crediting of his (truthful) confession in 1996 is, to say the least, bizarre.

The owners' mendacity [lies] in their 1980's collusive efforts to depress the ballplayers' income was in many ways as damaging to baseball as the Black Sox scandal of 1919.[b] The scope of the owners' deceit and fabrications in their 1980's effort to cheat their employees out of their rightful wages was wholly unprecedented, as was the financial injury suffered by the ballplayers. That the arbitrator would in these circumstances rely on Smith's statements made in the collusion hearing, and on the basis of those false statements reject Smith's later effort to remedy the injury he had caused, surpasses understanding. The only inference that can fairly be drawn from the arbitrator's current crediting of Smith's earlier perjurious testimony is that the arbitrator was attempting to dispense his own brand of industrial justice. For this reason, we decline to enforce his award.

Decision and Remedy The U.S. Court of Appeals for the Ninth Circuit reversed the ruling of the lower court and remanded the case with directions to set aside the arbitrator's award. The arbitrator had improperly attempted "to dispense his own brand of industrial justice" by granting credibility to testimony that he had earlier declared to be false.

For Critical Analysis—Ethical Consideration What did the court mean when it stated that "we would accept a conclusion by the arbitrator that

Smith told the truth in his 1986 testimony and lied in his 1996 letter even if that conclusion were clearly erroneous"? Is it fair for the courts to give such deference to arbitrators' findings of facts?

————
b. In the 1919 World Series, the Chicago White Sox lost to the Cincinnati Reds under circumstances that led to the indictment of eight Chicago players—named the "Black Sox"—on charges of accepting bribes from gamblers to lose the games.

WAIVER Although a defect in the arbitration process is sufficient grounds for setting aside an award, a party sometimes forfeits the right to challenge an award by failing to object to the defect in a timely manner. The party must object when he or she learns of the problem. After making the objection, the party can still proceed with the arbitration process and still challenge the award in court after the arbitration proceedings have concluded. If, however, a party makes no objection and proceeds with the arbitration process, then a later court challenge to the award may be denied on the ground that the party *waived* the right to challenge the award on the basis of the defect.

Frequently, this occurs when a party fails to object that an arbitrator is exceeding his or her powers in resolving a dispute because the subject matter is not arbitrable or because the party did not agree to arbitrate the dispute. The question of arbitrability is one for the courts to decide. If a party does not object on this issue at the first demand for arbitration, however, a court may consider the objection waived.

CONFLICTS OF LAW Parties are afforded wide latitude in establishing the manner in which their disputes will be resolved. Nevertheless, an agreement to arbitrate may be governed by the Federal Arbitration Act (FAA) or one of the many state arbitration acts, even though the parties do not refer to a statute in their agreement. Recall that the FAA covers any arbitration clause in a contract that involves interstate commerce. Frequently, however, transactions involving interstate commerce also have substantial connections to particular states, which may in turn have their own arbitration acts. In such situations, unless the FAA and state arbitration law are nearly identical, the acts may conflict. How are these conflicts to be resolved?

As a general principle, the supremacy clause and the commerce clause of the U.S. Constitution are the bases for giving federal law preeminence; when there is a conflict, state law is preempted by federal law. Thus, in cases of arbitration, the strong federal policy favoring arbitration can override a state's laws that might be more favorable to normal litigation.

CHOICE OF LAW Notwithstanding federal preemption of conflicting state laws, the Federal Arbitration Act has been interpreted as allowing the parties to choose a particular state law to govern their arbitration agreement. The parties may choose to have the laws of a specific state govern their agreement by including in the agreement a *choice-of-law clause*. The FAA does not mandate any particular set of rules that parties must follow in arbitration; the parties are free to agree on the manner best suited to their needs. Consistent with this view that arbitration is at heart a contractual matter between private parties, the United States Supreme Court has upheld arbitration agreements containing choice-of-law provisions.

Disadvantages of Arbitration

Arbitration has some disadvantages. The result in any particular dispute can be unpredictable, in part because arbitrators do not need to follow any previous cases in rendering their decisions. Unlike judges, arbitrators do not have to issue written opinions or facilitate a participant's appeal to a court. Arbitrators must decide disputes according to whatever rules have been provided by the parties, regardless of how unfair those rules may be. In some cases, arbitration can be nearly as expensive as litigation. In part, this is because both sides must prepare their cases for presentation before a third party decision maker, just as they would have to do to appear in court. Discovery is usually not available in arbitration, however, which means that during the hearing the parties must take the time to question witnesses whom, in a lawsuit, they would not need to call.[7]

The Integration of ADR and Formal Court Procedures

Because of the congestion within the judicial system, many jurisdictions at both the state and federal levels are integrating alternative dispute resolution into the formal legal process. Utilizing methods such as arbitration and mediation within the traditional framework may relieve the logjams afflicting most of the nation's court systems.

Court-Mandated ADR

Increasingly, courts are requiring that parties attempt to settle their differences through some form of ADR before proceeding to trial. Several federal district courts now encourage nonbinding arbitration for cases involving amounts less than $100,000. Less than 10 percent of the cases referred for arbitration ever go to trial. Today, about half of all federal courts have adopted formal rules regarding the use of ADR, and many other courts without such rules use ADR procedures.

Most states have adopted programs that allow them to refer certain types of cases for negotiation, mediation, or arbitration. Typically—as in California and Hawaii—court systems have adopted mandatory mediation or nonbinding arbitration programs for certain types of disputes, usually involving less than a specified threshold dollar amount.[8] Only if the parties fail to reach an agreement, or if one of the parties disagrees with the decision of a third party mediating or arbitrating the dispute, will the case be heard by a court. South Carolina was the first state to institute a voluntary arbitration program at the appellate court level. In the South Carolina system, litigants must waive a court hearing when requesting arbitration. All decisions by the arbitrators are final and binding.

Court-Annexed Arbitration

Court-annexed arbitration differs significantly from the voluntary arbitration process discussed above. There are some disputes that courts will not allow to go to arbitration. Most states, for example, do not allow court-annexed arbitration in disputes involving title to real estate or in cases in which a court's equity powers are involved.

A FUNDAMENTAL DIFFERENCE The fundamental difference between voluntary arbitration and court-annexed arbitration is the finality and reviewability

---

7. One notable dispute concerning computer chip technology lasted more than seven years and cost the participants more than $100 million. See *Advanced Micro Devices, Inc. v. Intel Corp.,* 9 Cal.4th 362, 885 P.2d 994, 36 Cal.Rptr.2d 581 (1994).
8. Hawaii, for example, has a program of mandatory, nonbinding arbitration for disputes involving less than $150,000.

of the award. With respect to court-annexed arbitration, either party may reject the award for any reason. In the event that one of the parties does reject the award, the case will proceed to trial, and the court will hear the case *de novo*—that is, the court will reconsider all the evidence and legal questions as though no arbitration had occurred.

Everyone who has a recognizable cause of action or against whom such an action is brought is entitled to have the issue decided in a court of law. Because court-annexed arbitration is not voluntary, there must be some safeguard against using it in a way that denies an individual his or her day in court. This safeguard is provided by permitting either side to reject the award regardless of the reason for so doing.

The party rejecting the award may be penalized, however. Many statutes providing for court-annexed arbitration impose court costs and fees on a party who rejects an arbitration award but does not improve his or her position by going to trial. Thus, for example, if a party rejects an arbitration award, and the award turns out to be more favorable to that party than the subsequent jury verdict, the party may be compelled to pay the costs of the arbitration or some fee for the costs of the trial.

In court-annexed arbitration, discovery of evidence occurs before the hearing. After the hearing has commenced, a party seeking to discover new evidence must usually secure approval from the court that mandated the arbitration. This is intended to prevent the parties from using arbitration as a means of previewing each other's cases and then rejecting the arbitrator's award.

THE ROLE OF THE ARBITRATOR   Notwithstanding the differences between voluntary and court-annexed arbitration, the role of the arbitrator is essentially the same in both types of proceedings. The arbitrator determines issues of both fact and law. The arbitrator also makes all decisions concerning applications of the rules of procedure and evidence during the hearing.

WHICH RULES APPLY   Regarding the rules of evidence, there are differences among the states. Most states impose the same rules of evidence on an arbitration hearing as on a trial. Other states, such as New Jersey, allow all evidence relevant to the dispute regardless of whether the evidence would be admissible at trial. Still other jurisdictions, such as Washington, leave it to the arbitrator to decide what evidence is admissible.

WAIVER   Once a court directs that a dispute is to be submitted to court-annexed arbitration, the parties must proceed to arbitration. As noted above, either side may reject the award that results from the arbitration for any reason. If a party fails to appear at or participate in the arbitration proceeding as directed by the court, however, that failure constitutes a waiver of the right to reject the award.

Court-Related Mediation

Mediation is proving to be more popular than arbitration as a court-related method of ADR. No federal court has adopted an arbitration program since 1991, while mediation programs continue to increase in number in both federal and state courts. Today, more court systems offer or require mediation, rather than arbitration, as an alternative to litigation.

> **Be Aware**   Arbitration can be voluntary, but in some cases, it may be mandatory, and although an arbitrator's decision may be nonbinding, in some cases, the parties are bound.

Mediation is often used in disputes relating to employment law, environmental law, product liability, and franchises. One of the most important business advantages of mediation is the lower cost, which can be 25 percent (or less) of the expense of litigation. Another advantage is the speed with which a dispute can go through mediation (possibly one or two days) compared with arbitration (possibly months) or litigation (possibly years).

Part of the popularity of mediation is that its goal, unlike that of litigation and some other forms of ADR, is for opponents to work out a resolution that benefits both sides. The rate of participants' satisfaction with the outcomes in mediated disputes is high. In New Hampshire, for example, where mediation is mandatory for all civil cases in most state trial courts, as many as 70 percent of the participants report satisfaction with the results.

Summary Jury Trials

Another means by which the courts have integrated alternative dispute resolution methods into the traditional court process is through the use of summary jury trials. A **summary jury trial** is a mock trial that occurs in a courtroom before a judge and jury. Evidence is presented in an abbreviated form, along with each side's major contentions. The jury then presents a verdict.

The fundamental difference between a traditional trial and a summary jury trial is that in the latter, the jury's verdict is only advisory. The goal of a summary jury trial is to give each side an idea of how it would fare in a full-blown jury trial with a more elaborate and detailed presentation of evidence and arguments. At the end of the summary jury trial, the presiding judge meets with the parties and may encourage them to settle their dispute without going through a standard jury trial.

Summary Jury Trial (SJT)
A method of settling disputes in which a trial is held, but the jury's verdict is not binding. The verdict acts only as a guide to both sides in reaching an agreement during the mandatory negotiations that immediately follow the summary jury trial.

ADR and Mass Torts

A *tort* is a civil wrong that does not arise from a breach of contract. (Torts are discussed in detail in Chapter 9. Breach of contract is discussed in Chapter 13.) *Mass tort* is the term applied to civil lawsuits that share such features as scientific or technological complexity and a large number of participants. Such cases often feature a high degree of emotional involvement on the part of the claimants, who may suffer from severe or life-threatening injuries, and on the part of the defendants, whose financial existence may be at stake. Examples of mass torts include litigation involving Agent Orange, the Dalkon Shield, the prescription drug DES, heart valves, and asbestos.

In the 1990s, there was an explosion in the number of mass torts. For example, more than 300,000 claims were filed in asbestos-related litigation—in the mid-1990s, new claims were filed at the rate of 5,000 every month. Such claims are overwhelming our civil justice system. In attempts to clear the courts, some judges in mass tort cases turn to methods of alternative dispute resolution, including mediation, arbitration, mini-trials, and summary jury trials. ADR may be used to assess the validity or the value of the claims or to sort out or resolve the scientific, technological, or medical issues. ADR may be used to settle large numbers of claims in a speedy, efficient, cost-effective manner. Once a settlement is reached, a neutral third party may coordinate payments to claimants. There may even be provision for an ADR appeals process.

ADR Forums and Services

Services facilitating dispute resolution outside the courtroom are provided by both government agencies and private organizations.

Nonprofit Organizations

The major source of private arbitration services is the American Arbitration Association (AAA). Most of the largest law firms in the nation are members of this association. Founded in 1926, the AAA now settles more than 80,000 disputes a year and has offices in every state. Cases brought before the AAA are heard by an expert or a panel of experts—of whom usually about half are lawyers—in the area relating to the dispute. To cover its costs, this nonprofit organization charges a fee, paid by the party filing the claim. In addition, each party to the dispute pays a price for each hearing day, as well as a special additional fee in cases involving personal injuries or property loss.

In addition to the AAA, hundreds of other state and local nonprofit organizations provide arbitration services. For example, the Arbitration Association of Florida provides ADR services in that state. The Better Business Bureau (BBB) offers ADR programs to aid in the resolution of certain types of disagreements. The BBB's programs include a mediation program called ComputerCare, through which buyers and sellers of computer equipment and software can settle their disputes. Many industries—including the insurance, automobile, and securities industries—also now have mediation or arbitration programs to facilitate timely and inexpensive settlement of claims.

For-Profit Organizations

Those who seek to settle their disputes quickly can turn to private, for-profit organizations to act as mediators or arbitrators. The leading firm in this private system of justice is JAMS/Endispute, which is based in Santa Ana, California. The private system of justice includes hundreds of firms throughout the country offering dispute-resolution services by hired judges. Procedures in these private courts are fashioned to meet the desires of the clients seeking their services. For example, the parties might decide on the date of the hearing, the presiding judge, whether the judge's decision will be legally binding, and the site of the hearing—which could be a conference room, a law school office, or a leased courtroom complete with flag and Bible. The judges may follow procedures similar to those of the federal courts and use similar rules. Each party to the dispute may pay a filing fee and a designated fee for a half-day hearing session or a special, one-hour settlement conference.

There are also international organizations, such as the International Chamber of Commerce, that provide forums for the arbitration of disputes between parties to international contracts. These organizations, as well as some of the advantages and disadvantages of arbitrating disputes in the international context, will be discussed in Chapter 25.

Finally, a growing number of firms are offering dispute-resolution services online. We will examine this development in Chapter 5.

Key Terms

Chapter Summary • Legal Representation and Alternative Dispute Resolution

Attorneys and Dispute Resolution
(See pages 94–102.)

1. **Roles of an attorney**—Adviser (advises a client on steps to take to avoid possible legal problems), drafter (writes contracts and other documents for clients), negotiator (persuades, argues, or settles with another party on a client's behalf), and advocate (presents a client's position in court).

2. **Attorney-client relationship**—A client must disclose all relevant information to his or her attorney so the attorney can determine the best course of action. The attorney must keep the information confidential—the attorney-client privilege prevents a court and other government bodies from compelling disclosure of the information.

3. **Decision to file a lawsuit**—Factors include whether the law provides a remedy, whether the person can expect to prevail, and whether the expected benefit will compensate for expenses and other costs, including any business lost as a result of the lawsuit and accompanying publicity.

4. **Decision to defend against a lawsuit**—Factors include whether the relationship with the plaintiff is too valuable to risk, whether the publicity surrounding a trial would damage the defendant's reputation or image, and whether the dispute could be resolved in a less costly manner.

Alternative Dispute Resolution (ADR)
(See pages 103–123.)

ADR is a less costly, less time-consuming, and increasingly attractive alternative to litigation in the courts. Forms of ADR include the following:

1. **Negotiation**—The parties come together, with or without attorneys to represent them, and try to reach a settlement without the involvement of a third party.

2. **Mediation**—The parties themselves reach an agreement with the help of a third party, called a mediator, who proposes solutions.

3. **Arbitration**—A more formal method of ADR in which the parties submit their dispute to a neutral third party, the arbitrator, who renders a decision, which may or may not be legally binding, depending on the circumstances. Some courts refer certain cases for arbitration before allowing the cases to proceed to trial; in most cases, this kind of arbitration is nonbinding on the parties.

4. **Summary jury trial**—A kind of trial in which litigants present their arguments and evidence and the jury renders a nonbinding verdict.

5. **Mini-trial**—A private proceeding in which each party's attorney argues the party's case before the other party. Often, a neutral third party acts as an adviser and renders an opinion on how a court would likely decide the issue.

6. **ADR forums**—Both government agencies and private firms provide ADR services. Private firms include both nonprofit and for-profit organizations.

For Review

1. What roles do attorneys play in resolving disputes?
2. What are some of the similarities and differences between litigation and other forms of dispute resolution?
3. How do the processes of negotiation and mediation differ?
4. What are the steps in the arbitration process?
5. What are the differences between voluntary arbitration and court-annexed arbitration?

Questions and Case Problems

4–1. Arbitration. In an arbitration proceeding, the arbitrator need not be a judge or even a lawyer. How, then, can the arbitrator's decision have the force of law and be binding on the parties involved?

4–2. Choice of Law. Two private U.S. corporations enter into a joint-venture agreement to conduct mining operations in the newly formed Middle Eastern nation of Euphratia. As part of the agreement, the companies include an arbitration clause and a choice-of-law provision. The first states that any controversy arising out of the performance of the agreement will be settled by arbitration. The second states that the agreement is to be governed by the laws of the location of the venture, Euphratia. A dispute arises, and the parties discontinue operations. One of the parties claims sole ownership to the Euphratian mines and orders the other party to remove its equipment from the mines. The other party disputes the claim of sole ownership and seeks an order from a U.S. federal court compelling the parties to submit to arbitration over the ownership issue and alleged breaches of the joint-venture agreement. How should the court rule if the laws of Euphratia state that, whereas arbitration agreements are to be enforced generally, matters of ownership of natural resources can only be resolved in a Euphratian court of law? Does it matter that two U.S. companies engaged in international commerce would be governed by the Federal Arbitration Act?

4–3. Confirmation of Award. Two brothers, both of whom are certified public accountants (CPAs), form a professional association to provide tax-accounting services to the public. They also agree, in writing, that any disputes that arise between them over matters concerning the association will be submitted to an independent arbitrator, whom they designate to be their father, who is also a CPA. A dispute arises, and the matter is submitted to the father for arbitration. During the course of arbitration, which occurs over several weeks, the father asks the older brother, who is visiting one evening, to explain a certain entry in the brothers' association accounts. The younger brother learns of the discussion at the next

meeting for arbitration; he says nothing about it, however. The arbitration is concluded in favor of the older brother, who seeks a court order compelling the younger brother to comply with the award. The younger brother seeks to set aside the award, claiming that the arbitration process was tainted by bias because "Dad always liked my older brother best." The younger brother also seeks to have the award set aside on the basis of improper conduct in that matters subject to arbitration were discussed between the father and older brother without the younger brother's being present. Should a court confirm the award or set it aside? Why?

4–4. Calculation of Award. After resolving their dispute, the two brothers encountered in Problem 4–3 above decide to resume their tax-accounting practice according to the terms of their original agreement. Again a dispute arises, and again it is decided by the father (now retired except for numerous occasions on which he acts as an arbitrator) in favor of the older brother. The older brother files a petition to enforce the award. The younger brother seeks to set aside the award and offers evidence that the father, as arbitrator, made a gross error in calculating the accounts that were material to the dispute being arbitrated. If the court is convinced that the father erred in the calculations, should the award be set aside? Why?

4–5. Compelling Arbitration. In 1981, AT&T laid off seventy-nine workers in the Chicago area, purportedly because of a slowdown in economic activity. The Communications Workers of America, a union representing some AT&T workers, argued that there was no lack of work and objected to the layoffs as violations of the terms of a collective bargaining agreement between the union and AT&T. The agreement provided that "differences arising with respect to the interpretation of this contract or the performance of any obligation" under the agreement would be resolved through arbitration. The agreement reserved to AT&T the free exercise of managerial functions such as hiring and firing employees. The agreement conditioned such decision making on compliance with the terms of the contract but expressly excluded disputes over those decisions from arbitration. AT&T relied on this exclusion to avoid the union's demand for arbitration over the layoffs. The union sought a court order to compel arbitration. The court held that the issue of whether the dispute over the layoffs was subject to arbitration should be decided by the arbitrator and ordered the parties to submit the question to the arbitrator. An appellate court affirmed the holding, and AT&T appealed to the United States Supreme Court. How should the Court rule? Discuss fully. [*AT&T Technologies v. Communications Workers of America*, 475 U.S. 643, 106 S.Ct. 1415, 89 L.Ed.2d 648 (1990)]

4–6. Arbitration. Randall Fris worked as a seaman on an Exxon Shipping Co. oil tanker for eight years without incident. One night, he boarded the ship for duty while intoxicated, in violation of company policy. This policy also allowed Exxon to discharge employees who were intoxicated and thus unfit for work. Exxon discharged Fris. Under a contract with Fris's union, the discharge was submitted to arbitration. The arbitrators ordered Exxon to reinstate Fris on an oil tanker. Exxon filed a suit against the union, challenging the award as contrary to public policy, which opposes having intoxicated persons operate seagoing vessels. Can a court set aside an arbitration award on the ground that the award violates public policy? Should the court set aside the award in this case? Explain. [*Exxon Shipping Co. v. Exxon Seamen's Union*, 11 F.3d 1189 (3d Cir. 1993)]

4–7. Arbitration. Phillip Beaudry, who suffered from mental illness, worked in the Department of Income Maintenance for the state of Connecticut. Beaudry was fired from his job when it was learned that he had misappropriated approximately $1,640 in state funds. Beaudry filed a complaint with his union, Council 4 of the American Federation of State, County, and Municipal Employees (AFSCME), and eventually the dispute was submitted to an arbitrator. The arbitrator concluded that Beaudry had been dismissed without "just cause," because Beaudry's acts were caused by his mental illness and "were not willful or volitional or within his capacity to control." Because Beaudry was disabled, the employer was required, under state law, to transfer him to a position that he was competent to hold. The arbitrator awarded Beaudry reinstatement, back pay, seniority, and other benefits. The state appealed the decision to a court. What public policies must the court weigh in making its decision? How should the court rule? [*State v. Council 4, AFSCME*, 27 Conn.App. 635, 608 A.2d 718 (1992)]

4–8. Arbitration. Stephanie Prince was an employee of Coca-Cola Bottling Co. of New York, Inc. (CNY), and a member of the Soft Drink and Brewery Workers Union. An agreement between CNY and the Union set out a procedure to follow in the event of a dispute between an employee and CNY relating to "any matter whatsoever, including the meaning, interpretation, application or violation of this Agreement." In this context, the agreement mentioned some employment laws but did not mention federal discrimination laws. After the Union was notified, and if the grievance was not resolved within thirty days, the dispute was to be submitted to arbitration. Prince reported to the Union, which told CNY, that she was being sexually harassed by her supervisors, Michael Drake and Leonard Erlanger. When no action was taken and Prince was subject to retaliatory behavior by Drake and Erlanger, she filed a complaint with the Equal Employment Opportunity Commission. The supervisors retaliated again by ordering her to leave the workplace and "stay home." Prince filed a suit in a federal district court against CNY and the supervisors, alleging, among other things, violations of federal discrimination law. CNY responded that its agreement with the Union required Prince to submit her claim to arbitration. Is CNY right? In whose favor should the court rule? Why? [*Prince. v. Coca-Cola Bottling Co. of New York, Inc.*, 37 F.Supp.2d 289 (S.D.N.Y. 1999)]

4–9. Arbitration. New York State revised its New Car Lemon Law to allow consumers who complained of purchasing a "lemon" to have their disputes arbitrated before a professional arbitrator appointed by the New York attorney general. Before this revision, the Lemon Law allowed for arbitration of disputes, but the forum in which arbitration took place was sponsored by trade associations within the automobile industry, and consumers often complained of unfair awards. The revised law also provided that consumers could choose between two options: arbitration before a professional arbitrator and suing the manufacturer in court. Manufacturers, however, were compelled to arbitrate claims, if a consumer chose to do so, and could not resort to the courts. Trade associations representing automobile manufacturers and importers brought an action seeking a declaration that the alternative arbitration mechanism of the Lemon Law was unconstitutional because it deprived them of their right to trial by jury. How will the court decide? Discuss. [*Motor Vehicle Manufacturers Association of the United States v. State*, 75 N.Y.2d 175, 550 N.E.2d 919, 551 N.Y.S.2d 470 (1990)]

A Question of Ethics and Social Responsibility

4–10. Linda Bender, in her application for registration as a stockbroker with A. G. Edwards & Sons, Inc., agreed to submit any disputes with her employer to arbitration. Bender later sued her supervisor and employer (the defendants) for sexual harassment in violation of Title VII of the Civil Rights Act of 1964, which prohibits, among other things, employment discrimination based on gender. The defendants requested the court to compel arbitration. The district court judge refused to do so, holding that Bender could not be forced to waive her right to adjudicate Title VII claims in a federal court. The appellate court reversed, ruling that Title VII claims are arbitrable. The court held that compelling Bender to submit her claim for arbitration did not deprive her of the right to a judicial forum, because if the arbitration proceedings were somehow legally deficient, she could still take her case to a federal court for review. [*Bender v. A. G. Edwards & Sons, Inc.*, 971 F.2d 698 (11th Cir. 1992)]

1. Does the right to a postarbitration judicial forum equate to the right to initial access to a judicial forum in employment disputes?
2. Should the fact that reviewing courts rarely set aside arbitrators' awards have any bearing on the arbitrability of certain types of claims, such as those brought under Title VII?

Case Briefing Assignment

4–11. Examine Case A.1 [*Rodriguez de Quijas v. Shearson/American Express, Inc.*, 490 U.S. 477, 109 S.Ct. 1917, 104 L.Ed.2d 379 (1989)] in Appendix A. The case has been excerpted there in great detail. Review and then brief the case, making sure that your brief answers the following questions.

1. What is the legislative policy "embodied in the Arbitration Act"?
2. How did the Court reconcile the protections afforded investors under the Securities Act and the legislative policy advanced by the Arbitration Act? Did the Court believe that by submitting to arbitration, investors forgo "substantive rights" given under the Securities Act?

For Critical Analysis

4–12. The attorney-client privilege protects disclosure of communications. Therefore, a client cannot be compelled to answer such a question as, "What did you tell your attorney about the accident?" Imagine, however, that the client is asked, "Did you see that the light was red?" Should the client be allowed to refuse to answer on the ground that he or she disclosed that fact to the attorney?

Interacting with the Internet

■ For updated links to resources available on the Web, as well as a variety of other materials, visit this text's Web site at

http://leet.westbuslaw.com

■ For information on alternative dispute resolution, go to the American Arbitration Association's Web site at

http://www.adr.org

■ Information on the rules and procedures used in mediation and arbitration can be accessed at

http://legal.gsa.gov/legal89.htm

Online Legal Research Exercises

Go to **http://leet. westbuslaw.com**, the Web site that accompanies this text. Select "Interactive Study Center," and then click on "Chapter 4." There you will find the following Internet research exercise that you can perform to learn more about alternative dispute resolution:

Activity 4–1: Alternative Dispute Resolution

Before the Test

Go to **http://leet. westbuslaw.com**, the Web site that accompanies this text. Select "Interactive Quizzes." You will find a number of interactive questions relating to this chapter.

E-Commerce and Dispute Resolution

contents

chapter objectives

After reading this chapter, you should be able to:

1. Describe how the courts are dealing with jurisdictional issues with respect to cyberspace transactions.

2. Identify the types of disputes that are classified as "e-commerce disputes."

3. Discuss the role and function of the Internet Corporation for Assigned Names and Numbers (ICANN) in settling e-commerce disputes.

4. Indicate what legal principles apply in the online resolution of most disputes.

5. Summarize some of the advantages and disadvantages of online dispute resolution.

E-commerce can include any business transaction that occurs in cyberspace, whether it involves a sale from business to business (B2B) or business to consumer (B2C). For B2B and B2C transactions, cyberspace offers buyers convenient marketplace accessibility twenty-four hours a day, seven days a week (24/7), and gives sellers access to an enormous customer base. At the same time, with the growth of e-commerce has come an increase in the number of disputes that traditional dispute-resolution systems were not designed to handle. With respect to the judicial resolution of disputes, a basic problem created by e-commerce has to do with jurisdiction. After all, e-businesses and their customers are located in all parts of the world and conduct transactions with little regard for geographic boundaries. A threshold issue is thus jurisdictional in nature.

In Chapters 3 and 4, we looked at the various forms of dispute resolution that have been used to resolve disagreements that traditionally have arisen in the business context. In this chapter, we first look at how the courts are deciding jurisdictional questions with respect to cyberspace transactions. In the remainder of the chapter, we will discuss the types of disputes that most commonly arise in e-commerce and some of the methods that are being used to resolve these issues outside the judicial process.

> **E-commerce** A business transaction that occurs in cyberspace. Cyberspace is the virtual world within which computer-based networks operate.

Jurisdiction in Cyberspace

The Internet's capacity to bypass political and geographic boundaries makes it revolutionary. This ability undercuts the traditional basis for a court to assert personal jurisdiction. This basis includes the contacts a party has with a court's geographic jurisdiction. For a court to compel a defendant to come before the court, there must be at least minimum contacts—the presence of a salesperson within the state, for example. Are there sufficient minimum contacts if the only connection to a jurisdiction is an ad on the Web originating from a remote location?

> **Remember** State long arm statutes allow courts to exercise personal jurisdiction over nonresident defendants *if* it can be demonstrated that the nonresident had sufficient ("minimum") contacts with the state.

• **Example 5.1** Adam lives in Florida. Carol, who lives in New York and has never been to Florida or done business with anyone in Florida, advertises her business on the Web. Carol's home page has received hundreds of "hits" by residents of Florida. Adam files a suit against Carol in a Florida state court. Can the court compel Carol to appear?

On the one hand, it could be argued that Carol knows (or should know) that her Web site could be accessed by residents of Florida, and by advertising her business on the Web, she should reasonably expect to be called into court there. If this reasoning is applied, then setting up a Web site could subject the owner to a suit anywhere that the site can be accessed. Some courts have upheld exercises of jurisdiction on the basis of the accessibility of a Web page.[1]

On the other hand, it could be argued that it is not possible for Carol to set up a Web page that excludes residents of Florida (or of any other specific jurisdiction). With this in mind, it would seem unreasonable and unfair to subject Carol to the possible personal jurisdiction of every court in the United States and maybe the world. For this reason, some courts have concluded that without more, a presence on the Web is not enough to support jurisdiction over nonresident defendants.[2]•

---

1. See, for example, *Minnesota v. Granite Gates Resorts, Inc.,* 568 N.W.2d 715 (Minn.App. 1997), aff'd 576 N.W.2d 747 (Minn. 1998).
2. See, for example, *Weber v. Jolly Hotels,* 977 F.Supp. 327 (D.N.J. 1997).

Recently, a new standard is becoming generally accepted for evaluating the exercise of jurisdiction based on contacts over the Internet. This standard is a "sliding scale." On this scale, a court's exercise of personal jurisdiction depends on the amount of business that an individual or firm transacts over the Internet. The standard is explained more fully in the following case.

Case 5.1 ● Zippo Manufacturing Co. v. Zippo Dot Com, Inc.

United States District Court,
Western District of Pennsylvania, 1997.
952 F.Supp. 1119.
http://zeus.bna.com/
e-law/cases/zippo.html[a]

Historical and Technological Setting *In a case decided before 1960, the United States Supreme Court noted that "[a]s technological progress has increased the flow of commerce between States, the need for jurisdiction has undergone a similar increase."[b] Twenty-seven years later, the Court observed that jurisdiction could not be avoided "merely because the defendant did not physically enter the forum state. * * * [I]t is an inescapable fact of modern commercial life that a substantial amount of commercial business is transacted solely by mail and wire communications across state lines."[c]*

a. This is a page in the "Electronic Commerce & Law Report" library.
b. *Hanson v. Denckla,* 357 U.S. 235, 78 S.Ct. 1228, 2 L.Ed.2d 1283 (1958).
c. *Burger King Corp. v. Rudzewicz,* 471 U.S. 462, 105 S.Ct. 2174, 85 L.Ed.2d 528 (1985).

Background and Facts Zippo Manufacturing Company (ZMC) makes, among other things, "Zippo" lighters. Zippo Dot Com, Inc. (ZDC), operates a Web page and an Internet subscription news service. ZDC has the exclusive right to use the domain names "zippo.com," "zippo.net," and "zipponews.com." ZMC is based in Pennsylvania. ZDC is based in California, and its contacts with Pennsylvania have occurred almost exclusively over the Internet. Two percent of its subscribers (3,000 of 140,000) are Pennsylvania residents who contracted over the Internet to receive its service. Also, ZDC has agreements with seven Internet service providers in Pennsylvania to permit their subscribers to access the service. ZMC filed a suit in a federal district court against ZDC, alleging trademark infringement and other claims, based on ZDC's use of the word "Zippo." ZDC filed a motion to dismiss for lack of personal jurisdiction.

In the Words of the Court . . .
McLAUGHLIN, District Judge.

* * * *

* * * *[T]he likelihood that personal jurisdiction can be constitutionally exercised is directly proportionate to the nature and quality of commercial activity that an entity conducts over the Internet.* * * * At one end of the spectrum are situations where a defendant clearly does business over the Internet. If the defendant enters into contracts with residents of a foreign jurisdiction that involve the knowing and repeated transmission of computer files over the Internet, personal jurisdiction is proper. At the opposite end are situations where a defendant has simply posted information on an Internet Web site which is accessible to users in foreign jurisdictions. A passive Web site that does little more than make information available to those who are interested in it is not grounds for the exercise of personal jurisdiction. The middle ground is occupied by interactive Web sites where a user can exchange information with the host computer. In these cases, the exercise of jurisdiction is determined by examining the level of interactivity and commercial nature of the exchange of information that occurs on the Web site. [Emphasis added.]

Case 5.1 Continued

* * * *

* * * We are being asked to determine whether [ZDC's] conducting of electronic commerce with Pennsylvania residents constitutes * * * doing business in Pennsylvania. We conclude that it does. [ZDC] has contracted with approximately 3,000 individuals and seven Internet access providers in Pennsylvania. The intended object of these transactions has been the downloading of the electronic messages that form the basis of this suit in Pennsylvania.

Decision and Remedy The court held that it has jurisdiction over parties that conduct substantial business in its jurisdiction exclusively over the Internet. The court concluded that ZDC fits this description and denied the motion to dismiss.

For Critical Analysis—Technological Consideration *Is the court in this case applying traditional jurisdictional rules to cyberspace or creating new rules? Explain.*

E-Commerce Disputes

Any dispute that arises in e-commerce can be classified as an **e-commerce dispute**. The remaining pages of this chapter focus on the most common of these disputes and how they are being resolved.

E-commerce Dispute A dispute that arises from business conducted in cyberspace.

Common Disputes

According to the Federal Trade Commission (FTC), two types of disputes make up more than half of the cyberspace complaints received by the FTC: disagreements over the rights to domain names (domain names will be discussed shortly), and disagreements over the quality of goods sold over the Internet, including complaints related to auction Web sites. Exhibit 5–1 compares the total number of Internet-related complaints and the number of on-line auction–related complaints that the FTC received in a recent year. According to at least one survey, as many as 40 percent of online consumers have experienced problems with at least one e-commerce transaction.

Online Dispute Resolution (ODR) The resolution of a dispute in cyberspace.

Online Dispute Resolution

Considering the potentially large number of e-commerce disputes, why aren't the courts overwhelmed with such cases? Part of the answer is that many of these disputes, even those concerning domain names, involve small amounts of money and parties in distant locations. To settle these conflicts, **online dispute resolution (ODR)** is now possible.

ODR is essentially a form of alternative dispute resolution (ADR). Among the factors that distinguish ODR from the forms of ADR discussed in Chapter 4 is the fact that in ODR the complaint, response, evidence, decision, and opinion are all communicated through cyberspace. Traditional forms of ADR, in contrast, require a face-to-face presentation. Resolving disputes through the courts (see Chapter 3) is even more restrictive, requiring the satisfaction of jurisdictional elements and a physical presence in a specific location—even if some of the papers are filed online.

**Exhibit 5–1
Internet-Related
Consumer
Complaints**

Internet-
related
complaints
received
by the FTC
in 1999
(18,622)

Auction-
related
complaints
(10,688)

Other distinguishing features of ODR include its 24/7 accessibility and its application of commonly accepted general legal principles when resolving disputes. In contrast, in traditional arbitration proceedings, the parties normally agree on which state's or nation's law will apply. In court proceedings, of course, an established body of law, including case precedents, is applied. Exhibit 5–2 illustrates how ODR fits into the universe of "all e-commerce disputes."

Online Resolution of Domain Name Disputes

Domain Name
The last part of an Internet address, such as "westlaw.com." The top level (the part of the name to the right of the period) represents the type of entity that operates the site ("com" is an abbreviation for "commercial"). The second level (the part of the name to the left of the period) is chosen by the entity.

A **domain name** is part of an Internet address, such as "westlaw.com." The top level domain (TLD) is the part of the name to the right of the period and represents the type of entity that operates the site ("com" is an abbreviation for "commercial"). The second level (the part of the name to the left of the period) is chosen by the entity registering the domain name.

Disputes that have arisen over the use of the same, or similar, domain names have involved parties' attempts to profit from the goodwill of a competitor, to sell pornography, to offer for sale another party's name, and to otherwise *infringe on* (use without authorization) others' trademarks. As you will read in Chapter 11, a *trademark* is a distinctive mark affixed to goods to identify the goods and their origin. A *service mark* is a distinctive mark used in the sale or advertising of services. A *trade name,* such as the name of a business, can also be protected under trademark law if the business's name is the same as its trademarked product. Once established, the owner of a mark is entitled to its exclusive use.

In the real world, one business can often use the same name as another without causing any conflict, particularly if the businesses are small, their goods or services are different, and the areas within which they do business are separate. In cyberspace, however, no two businesses can use the same domain name.

Exhibit 5–2
Online Dispute Resolution

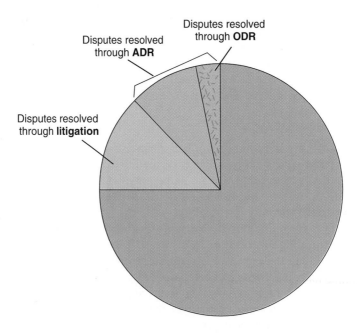

All E-Commerce Disputes

Ethical Issue 5.1

Is litigating a domain name dispute sometimes a better option than ODR?

ODR can be an effective and relatively inexpensive way to settle disputes. Nonetheless, companies involved in domain name disputes sometimes prefer to go to court. To understand why, consider an example. Suppose that a company produces filtering software that parents can purchase to block their children's access to certain Web sites. The company learns that its domain name is being used to link Internet users to a pornography site. Assuming that the company can discover the identity of the offending site's owner (this is often difficult to do), how should it proceed to resolve the problem? If the dispute is mediated or arbitrated, the offending site will continue to operate until a decision is made. If the company sues the offender, however, it can ask the court for a preliminary injunction ordering the offender to close down the site until the court renders its decision on the matter.

Litigation may be advantageous in other types of domain name disputes as well. For example, as you will read in Chapter 11, recently enacted federal legislation provides that a company can collect up to $100,000 in damages in a successful lawsuit against a *cybersquatter* (one who registers the company's mark as a domain name and then offers to forfeit the name for a sum of money). The possibility of damages may make litigation more attractive than ODR for such complaints.

The Dot.Com Explosion

The emergence of e-commerce on a world scale during the 1990s led to a number of problems relating to domain names. For one thing, of the seven TLDs then available, only one—*.com*—was commonly used by commercial enterprises. The others *(.org, .net, .edu, .int, .mil, .gov)* were initially provided for use by nonprofit organizations, Internet service providers, educational institutions, international organizations, the military, and government agencies, respectively. Additionally, there were about two hundred nation-specific TLDs, such as *.us* for the United States or *.fr* for France.

As e-commerce expanded, the *.com* TLD became widely used by businesses on the Web. In fact, by 1998 nearly 85 percent of registered domain names used the *.com* TLD.[3] Competition among individuals and firms with identical or similar names and products for the second level domains preceding the *.com* TLD led, understandably, to disputes over domain name rights. •**Example 5.2** Madonna, the well-known singer, recently learned that fans who went to the madonna.com site on the Web ended up at a pornography site operated by Dan Parisi, who had registered earlier for the domain name. Madonna claimed that Parisi was cybersquatting.• Disputes such as that between Madonna and Parisi have become increasingly common. (For another common type of dispute involving domain names, see this chapter's *Inside the Legal Environment: Dealing with Cybergripers* on the next page.)

The problem is, because cyberspace is international in scope, litigating such disputes can be exceedingly cumbersome and costly. As a result, new ways of settling such disputes have been devised and are now being implemented. At the forefront of this development is the Internet Corporation for Assigned

3. Lee B. Burgunder, *Legal Aspects of Managing Technology,* 2d ed. (Cincinnati: South-Western College Publishing, 2001), p. 434.

Inside the Legal Environment

Dealing with Cybergripers

A recurring challenge for owners of trademarks has to do with Web sites—often referred to "cybergriping" or "sucks" sites—that are established solely for the purpose of criticizing the products or services sold by owners of the marks. For example, walmartsucks.com is a site devoted to critical comments on Wal-Mart's policies and services. Is there anything online businesses can do to ward off these cyber attacks on their reputations and goodwill?

Trademark Protection versus Free Speech Rights

There is little that trademark owners can do to protect themselves against these sites, because, in the United States at least, the courts have been reluctant to hold that such domain names infringe on the trademark owners' rights. After all, one of the primary reasons trademarks are protected under U.S. law is to prevent customers from becoming confused over the origins of the goods for sale—and a cybergriping site would certainly not create such confusion. Furthermore, American courts give extensive protection to free speech rights, including the right to express opinions about companies and their products. Of course, when such opinions are defamatory—consisting of false statements that are harmful to the reputation of

another—a trademark owner may have recourse under tort law (see Chapter 9).

Preventive Tactics

Many businesses have concluded that while they cannot control what people say about them, they can make it more difficult for them to say it—by signing up for insulting domain names before the cybergripers can register them. For example, United Parcel Service (UPS) recently registered UPSstinks.com, IHateUPS.com, UPSBites.com, and a number of other names. According to Ram Mohan, the founder of the Internet research site Company Sleuth, "Tech-savvy companies used to do this occasionally, but now it's more mainstream, almost standard." Indeed, a study by Company Sleuth of recent domain name registrations revealed that in August 2000 nearly 250 companies had registered domain names containing "stinks," "bites," "sucks," or similarly disparaging words. Wal-Mart alone registered for more than two hundred anti–Wal-Mart names.[a]

For Critical Analysis: *Given the extensive number of insulting words in the English language, are businesses that register multiple (insulting) domain names to ward off potential criticism fighting a losing battle? Is it fair for businesses to register domain names that they will never use for the sole purpose of squelching critical cyber speech?*

---

a. David Stretfield, "Making Bad Names for Themselves: Firms Preempt Critics with Nasty Domains," *The Washington Post*, September 8, 2000, p. A1.

Names and Numbers (ICANN). ICANN's services include efforts to address these disputes.[4]

Internet Corporation for Assigned Names and Numbers

The Internet Corporation for Assigned Names and Numbers (ICANN) is a nonprofit corporation that the federal government set up to oversee the distribution of domain names. Because of its importance in establishing domain name policies and dispute-resolution procedures, ICANN is presented as this chapter's *Landmark in the Legal Environment*.

ICANN'S SERVICES To obtain relief from a party engaged in trademark infringement, a mark's owner was at one time limited primarily to filing a suit

---

4. See ICANN's Uniform Domain Name Dispute Resolution Policy at **http://www.icann. org/udrp.udrp-policy-24oct99.htm**. This policy is also discussed below.

Landmark in the Legal Environment

Internet Corporation for Assigned Names and Numbers (ICANN)

In 1997, the U.S. government directed the secretary of the Department of Commerce to privatize the domain name system in a manner that increased competition and facilitated international participation in its management. The end result of the Commerce Department's efforts was the creation, in October 1998, of the Internet Corporation for Assigned Names and Numbers (ICANN), a private, nonprofit organization, to act as a technical coordination body for the Internet.

Domain Name Registration

Part of the impetus behind ICANN's creation was to remove domain name registration oversight from the U.S. government to a private organization that could work to serve the broader interests of the international community. Previously, because the Internet developed from a U.S. military and research network, domain name registration had been under the direction of U.S. government organizations. From 1993 to 1998, Network Solutions, Inc. (NSI), under a contract with the U.S. government, exclusively controlled the allocation of domain names.

As the Internet became global in scope, there was a growing sentiment that other organizations, in addition to NSI, should be allowed to provide domain name registration services. ICANN has already authorized numerous other organizations to register domain names.

Domain Name Dispute-Resolution Policy and Rules

In October 1999, ICANN adopted the Uniform Domain Name Dispute Resolution Policy (UDRP) and a set of accompanying rules to be used in resolving domain name disputes. The UDRP, which took effect in January 2000, applies to all domain names that were in existence at that time as well as to subsequently registered domain names. As discussed elsewhere in this chapter, ICANN's policy and rules provide specific guidelines for resolving domain name disputes.

In November 2000, ICANN announced that it had selected seven registry operators for new top level domains (TLDs). Pending final approval of agreements with each operator, the new TLDs that will be available for use in domain names in the future are the following: *.aero, .biz, .coop, .info, .museum, .name,* and *.pro.* Generally, these TLDs reflect the names of the registrars. For example, the registrar for *.coop* is the National Cooperative Business Association, and the registrar for *.pro* is RegistryPro, Ltd. Some had hoped that any new TLDs adopted by ICANN would be more descriptive of the specific types of businesses or organizations—for example, *.shop* or *.travel.* Possibly, such descriptive TLDs may be adopted in the future.

For Critical Analysis: *In the past, disputes have been decided in court or by arbitrators under the law of a particular jurisdiction. ICANN's dispute-resolution policy and rules, however, are independent of any particular jurisdiction and are not governed by any one nation's laws, including case precedents. How, then, in cases decided under ICANN's rules, should arbitrating panels decide how the rules should be interpreted and applied?*

in a court with appropriate jurisdiction. ICANN began operating an online arbitration system on January 1, 2000, to resolve domain name disputes. Now, if trademark infringement involves a domain name, instead of, or in addition to, filing a suit, a party may submit a complaint to an ICANN-approved dispute-resolution provider.

ICANN refers to these dispute-resolution proceedings as *administrative proceedings* and to the arbitrator, or arbitrators, as the **panel.** To initiate an administrative proceeding, the complainant chooses one of four services that ICANN has approved: the National Arbitration Forum, eResolution, the World Intellectual Property Organization Arbitration and Mediation Center (WIPO Center, discussed later in this chapter), or the CPR Institute for Dispute

Panel An arbitrator, or arbitrators, appointed to make a decision regarding a domain name complaint in an online dispute-resolution proceeding governed by the policy and rules of the Internet Corporation for Assigned Names and Numbers (ICANN). An ICANN-approved dispute-resolution service provider appoints the panelists.

Resolution. Each service appoints its own arbitrators to a panel. The panelists include former judges, law professors, lawyers, and nonlawyers.

What is the legal effect of a decision and order in a dispute resolved by one of these services? That was the question in the following case.

Case 5.2 ● Weber-Stephen Products Co. v. Armitage Hardware and Building Supply, Inc.

United States District Court,
Northern District of Illinois, 2000.
__ F.Supp.2d __.

Background and Facts Armitage Hardware and Building Supply, Inc., owned a number of domain names. Weber-Stephen Products Company believed that the names included Weber-Stephen's registered trademarks and service marks and that Armitage was using these marks in a deceptive, confusing, and misleading manner, intentionally and in bad faith. Weber-Stephen initiated an administrative proceeding with the WIPO Center, one of the ICANN-approved dispute-resolution providers. Weber-Stephen asked a WIPO Center panel to resolve the issue of whether Armitage was using its domain names in bad faith. Weber-Stephen also asked that Armitage's domain names either be transferred to Weber-Stephen or be canceled. The next day, Weber-Stephen filed a suit in a federal district court against Armitage, alleging violations of the law, including trademark infringement. In response, Armitage asked the court to declare the WIPO Center proceeding nonbinding and stay (postpone) the suit or, if the proceeding was ruled to be binding, to stay that proceeding to consider whether Armitage could be compelled to participate. (Recall that under the Federal Arbitration Act, when an arbitrator's decision is binding, a court's review of that decision is more limited than if the decision is nonbinding.)

In the Words of the Court . . .
ASPEN, Chief J. [Judge]

* * * *

No federal court has yet considered the legal effect of a WIPO proceeding. However, the ICANN [Uniform Domain Name Dispute Resolution Policy, discussed elsewhere in this chapter] and its accompanying rules do contemplate the possibility of parallel proceedings in federal court. First, the Policy provides that ICANN will cancel or transfer domain name registrations upon "our receipt of an order from a court * * * of competent jurisdiction, requiring such action * * *." Also, the procedural rules governing the Policy provide that if legal proceedings are initiated prior to or during an administrative proceeding with regard to a domain name dispute that is the subject of the administrative complaint, the panel has the discretion to decide whether to suspend or terminate the administrative proceeding or whether to proceed and make a decision. And the language of the Policy suggests that the administrative panels' decisions are not intended to be binding on federal courts. For example, under the heading "Availability of Court Proceedings," the ICANN Policy provides:

> * * * [If we receive] official documentation (such as a copy of a complaint, file-stamped by the clerk of the court) that you have commenced a lawsuit against the complainant in a jurisdiction to which the complainant has submitted * * *, we will not implement the Administrative Panel's decision, and we will take no further action, until we receive (i) evidence satisfactory to us of a resolution between the parties; (ii) evidence satisfactory to us that your lawsuit has been dismissed or withdrawn; or (iii) a copy of an order from such court dismissing your lawsuit or ordering that you do not have the right to continue to use your domain name.

Case 5.2 Continued

Furthermore, Armitage's counsel sent an e-mail inquiry to <domain.disputes @wipo.int>, and the response from the WIPO Arbitration and Mediation Center said that the administrative panel's determination would be binding on the registrar[a] of the domain name, but that "[t]his decision is not binding upon a court, and a court may give appropriate weight to the Administrative Panel's decision." * * *

We conclude that this Court is not bound by the outcome of the ICANN administrative proceedings. But at this time we decline to determine the precise standard by which we would review the panel's decision, and what degree of deference [respect, willingness to abide by] (if any) we would give that decision. Neither the ICANN Policy nor its governing rules dictate to courts what weight should be given to a panel's decision, and the WIPO e-mail message stating that "a court may give appropriate weight to the Administrative Panel's decision" confirms the breadth of our discretion.

Because both parties to this case have adequate avenues of recourse should they be unhappy with the administrative panel's imminent decision, we find no need to stay the pending ICANN administrative action. Instead, we hereby stay this case pending the outcome of those proceedings.

Decision and Remedy The court held that the outcome of an ICANN administrative proceeding was not binding on the court, but it did not decide to what extent it would defer to the WIPO Center panel's decision. The court stayed its own proceedings until the panel issued its decision.

For Critical Analysis—Economic Consideration *Sometimes, a party establishes a domain name as an address for a Web site before the name's owner can take legal action. When this occurs and the owner files a suit, it may be some time before the dispute is resolved in court. Is there anything the owner might do in the meantime to prevent the other party from profiting from—or harming—the reputation and goodwill associated with the owner's mark?*

---

a. A *registrar* is the entity through which a company or individual registers a domain name.

ICANN'S DISPUTE-RESOLUTION PROCEDURE All of ICANN's approved dispute-resolution providers follow ICANN's prescribed procedure.[5] As indicated by the events in the *Weber-Stephen* case discussed above, a complaint is filed with one of the four approved services, and the party against whom the complaint is made is given the opportunity to file an answer. Both the complaint and the answer are submitted online, although hard copies are also delivered to the provider. A decision is issued, also online, in sixty days or less. The decision may be appealed to a court. The steps in a typical proceeding are illustrated in Exhibit 5–3 on page 142.

ICANN's Uniform Domain Name Dispute Resolution Policy includes three elements that must be proved to have a domain name transferred or canceled. These elements are the following:

> **Contrast** Under most statutes that apply to traditional arbitration proceedings, the arbitrator's award, or decision in the case, must be rendered within thirty days after the close of the hearing—see Chapter 4.

1. The challenged domain name must be identical or confusingly similar to a trademark or service mark in which the complainant has rights.

---

5. See ICANN's Rules for Uniform Domain Name Dispute Resolution Policy at http://www. icann.org/udrp/udrp-rules-24oct99.htm.

2. The party against whom the complaint is made must have no rights or legitimate interests in the domain name.
3. The challenged domain name must be registered and be used in bad faith.[6]

The issue in the following case was whether these elements were proved.

_____
6. ICANN's Uniform Domain Name Dispute Resolution Policy Rule 4(a).

Case 5.3 ● Blue Max Technology v. Compudigital Industries

National Arbitration Forum, 2000.
Claim No. FA0007000095107.
http://www.icann.org/udrp/
proceedings-list-name.htm[a]

Background and Facts In 1969, International Instrumentation, Inc., began manufacturing computer-related products under the brand name "Blue Max" and registered this name as a trademark. Over the next twenty-five years, the product name came to have more widespread recognition than the company name. For this reason, in 1998 the firm reincorporated itself under the name Blue Max Technology.

_____
a. This Web site is maintained by ICANN. Scroll down the "Domain Name" column to "bluemax.com." In the corresponding box in the "Status/Panel Decision" column, click on "Name transfer" to access this decision.

Blue Max uses the domain name "bluemax.net" to promote its services on the Internet. Compudigital Industries registered the domain name "bluemax.com" in 1996. In early 1999, Compudigital used this name to link users to a test Web page for an auction site that was under construction. Before the end of the year, Compudigital stopped using the name completely. Blue Max contacted Compudigital and was told that the firm was not using, and did not plan to use, the name. Blue Max offered up to $10,000 for the name. Compudigital refused the offer and forced Blue Max into a bidding war with another party. Blue Max filed a complaint with the National Arbitration Forum (NAF), an ICANN-approved dispute-resolution provider. Despite notices sent by mail, e-mail, and fax, Compudigital did not respond. Blue Max asked the NAF panel to order the domain name "bluemax.com" transferred to Blue Max.

In the Words of the Panel . . .
Honorable[b] James A. CARMODY, as Panelist.

*   *   *   *

*   *   * [T]he ICANN Uniform Domain Name Dispute Resolution Policy ("Policy") directs that the complainant must prove each of the following three elements to support a claim that a domain name should be cancelled or transferred:

Identical and/or Confusingly Similar
The Complainant [Blue Max] has *   *   * rights in the mark BLUE MAX. The Respondent's [Compudigital's] domain name is identical to the Complainant's mark.

Rights or Legitimate Interests
*   *   *   *

The domain name in question is not a mark by which the Respondent is commonly known. Rather, the Respondent is associated with the domain name Compudigital Industries. The Respondent has *   *   * not argued that it is using the domain name in connection with a bona fide offering of goods

_____
b. "Honorable" is a title of courtesy for an official or a judge. In this case, James Carmody is a retired judge.

Case 5.3 Continued

and services or is making a legitimate noncommercial or fair use of the site. Failure to respond to the Complaint permits the inference that the use of the Complainant's mark is misleading and Respondent has no rights or legitimate interests in the domain name in question.

Registration and Use in Bad Faith
* * * *

The Respondent used the domain name to attract users to the auction site prior to 1999. Attracting users to a website or other on-line location by creating a likelihood of confusion with the Complainant's mark as to the source of the website is evidence of bad faith registration and use.

The Respondent also is now passively holding the domain name without use. The Respondent * * * admitted that the domain name was not in use and was not to be used in the immediate future. This is evidence of bad faith.

The Respondent used the domain name for a profit by offering it for sale to the Complainant and the Complainant's competitors for valuable consideration in excess of out-of-pocket expenses.

Based on the above, the panel concludes that the Respondent registered and used the domain name in bad faith.
* * * *

Having established all three elements * * *, it is the decision of the panel that the requested relief be granted.

Accordingly, for all of the foregoing reasons, it is ordered that the domain name, "BLUEMAX.COM" be transferred from the Respondent to the Complainant.

Decision and Remedy The NAF panel concluded that Blue Max established all of the elements under ICANN's policy to have a domain name transferred or cancelled. The panel ordered the name "bluemax.com" transferred to Blue Max.

For Critical Analysis—Ethical Consideration *"Proving bad faith in the registration and use of a domain name is impossible to do because whether someone acts in good or bad faith is ultimately a subjective decision." Do you agree with this statement? Why or why not? Were the criteria used by the panel deciding this case subjective or objective in nature?*

World Intellectual Property Organization Arbitration and Mediation Center

The World Intellectual Property Organization Arbitration and Mediation Center (WIPO Center) is part of the International Bureau of the World Intellectual Property Organization. Since 1994, the WIPO Center has arbitrated and mediated international commercial disputes between private parties. The WIPO Center focuses particularly on the resolution of disputes that relate to cyberspace and e-commerce. This includes disputes that arise from the use of domain names (such as the dispute between Madonna and Parisi mentioned in Example 5.2 on page 133, which the WIPO Center agreed to arbitrate) and other conflicts that relate to intellectual property.

The WIPO Center offers four dispute-resolution services. Each has different advantages and legal effects.

1. *Arbitration* is the WIPO Center's service in which the outcome is binding on the parties. There may be one arbitrator or a team of arbitrators. Once a party agrees to arbitration, he or she cannot unilaterally withdraw.
2. *Expedited arbitration* is a speedier, less expensive form of arbitration, with a single arbitrator and condensed proceedings.
3. *Mediation* involves a neutral third party who helps the disputing parties to resolve their differences but who cannot impose a settlement. Any party may withdraw at any time.
4. *Mediation followed by arbitration* requires the parties to attempt a resolution through mediation within a certain time. If no settlement is reached, either party can refer the dispute to arbitration for a binding decision.

The WIPO Center is an ICANN-approved service and follows ICANN's dispute-resolution procedure and policy when they apply. The following proceeding illustrates the WIPO Center's application of the ICANN rules.

> **Realize** Mediation followed by arbitration, often referred to as "mediation-arbitration" or "med-arb," is not new. For some years, this combination of traditional ADR methods has been used by parties to resolve their disputes.

Case 5.4 ● AT&T Corp. v. Alamuddin

World Intellectual Property Organization Arbitration and Mediation Center, 2000. Case No. D2000-0249.
http://www.icann.org/udrp/proceedings-list-name.htm[a]

Company Profile *For more than a century, AT&T Corporation (http://www.att.com) has created, provided, distributed, advertised, and sold telecommunications and related goods and services in the United States and abroad. Today, these goods and services include Internet access, e-mail, and Web hosting services. AT&T serves more than 80 million customers—consumers, businesses, and governments—with more than 150,000 employees and annual revenue of more than $64 billion. AT&T operates the world's largest, most sophisticated communications network and has one of the largest digital wireless networks in North America.*

Background and Facts AT&T owns the trademarks "AT&T" and "ATT" (as in "1 800 Call ATT"),

in which it invests money and effort for advertising and promotion. AT&T's registered domain names, including "ATT.com," "ATT.net," and "ATTWIRELESS.com," use these trademarks. In 1998, Tala Alamuddin, a British citizen living in Singapore, registered the domain name "ATT2000.com." At that address, Alamuddin set up a Web site that stated, "This URL is for sale." When contacted by AT&T, Alamuddin said that if the corporation wanted "ATT2000.com," it would have to pay for it. AT&T filed a complaint against Alamuddin with the WIPO Center, asking for the transfer of "ATT2000.com." AT&T argued in part that the domain name was confusingly similar to its trademarks and that Alamuddin showed bad faith in attempting to sell the name. Alamuddin responded in part that she originally planned the Web site to sell Asian clothing and other items related to the millennium, and that she bought supplies and made contacts toward this end, but that she dropped this plan when she got a full-time job. She claimed that "ATT2000" signified her given name ("Tala") and the new millennium ("2000"). AT&T asserted that this claim "defies credibility."

---

a. Scroll down the "Domain Name" column to "att2000.com." In the corresponding box in the "Status/Panel Decision" column, click on "Name transfer" to access this decision.

In the Words of the Panel . . .
Hon. Sir Ian BARKER Q.C. [Queen's Counsel, a special type of attorney in the United Kingdom], Presiding Panelist.

* * * *

The Panel finds no evidence that the Respondent [Alamuddin], before receiving notice of the dispute, used or demonstrably prepared to use the

Case 5.4 Continued

domain name in connection with a *bona fide* offering of services without intent for commercial gain. The Respondent claims that she had purchased stock and made contacts, yet she has provided no supporting documents. She no longer wishes to conduct an Internet mail-order business in Asian clothing and curios. She wants to retain the name, but gives no reason why. There is no evidence that she is known by the domain name. The submission that ATT somehow reflects her given name of Tala is pathetic. The Panel therefore decides that the Respondent has no rights or legitimate interests in respect of the domain name.

* * * *

The Internet is a worldwide institution and persons accessing any website can come from any country. It must be assumed that some hits on the Respondent's website could come from persons living in countries where there is a registered AT&T mark (which include the United Kingdom). These persons could easily have had dealings with the Complainant [AT&T] or its websites or else have encountered AT&T, which is inevitable for anyone who has lived in the United States, even as a visitor. They could easily conclude that the domain site had something to do with the Complainant's operations in the year 2000. Geographical destinations can be irrelevant to users of the Internet.

There is evidence that the Respondent offered to sell the domain name to the Complainant "as part of an acceptable cash settlement." Many cases decided by WIPO Center panels have concluded that such behaviour constitutes use of the Complainant's mark in bad faith. * * *

The Panel accordingly determines that the Respondent has registered and used the Complainant's mark in bad faith.

* * * *

The Panel has determined that, under [ICANN's Uniform Domain Name Dispute Resolution] Policy, the Complainant has proved its case. Accordingly, the Complainant is entitled to the limited relief which this Panel is empowered to give.

Decision and Remedy The WIPO Center panel decided that "ATT2000.com" was confusingly similar to AT&T's trademarks, and that Alamuddin had no legitimate rights in the name, which she was using in bad faith. The panel ordered a transfer of the name to AT&T.

For Critical Analysis—Economic Consideration *Suppose that the "ATT" in* "ATT2000.com" *did represent Alamuddin's business name, that she was actually using the Web site to market products, and that there was no evidence of bad faith in her use of the domain name. Is there anything AT&T could do in this situation to prevent Alamuddin's use of the name?*

Online Resolution of Other Disputes

E-commerce transactions take place rapidly. Personal contact is minimal, and when a mistake or a misunderstanding occurs, resolving the dispute can be time consuming and expensive. The Internet provides new opportunities for the resolution of these disputes.

As one example, consider **newsgroups**. Newsgroups are discussion groups to which participants go to post and read messages. A dispute that, in the real

Newsgroup A discussion group operated according to certain Internet formats and rules. Like a bulletin board, a newsgroup is a location to which participants go to read and post messages.

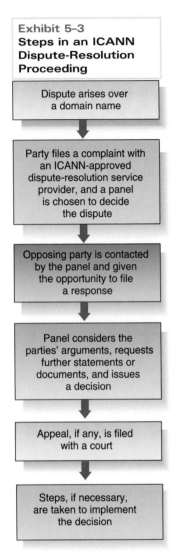

Exhibit 5–3

Steps in an ICANN Dispute-Resolution Proceeding

Dispute arises over a domain name

⬇

Party files a complaint with an ICANN-approved dispute-resolution service provider, and a panel is chosen to decide the dispute

⬇

Opposing party is contacted by the panel and given the opportunity to file a response

⬇

Panel considers the parties' arguments, requests further statements or documents, and issues a decision

⬇

Appeal, if any, is filed with a court

⬇

Steps, if necessary, are taken to implement the decision

world, could be resolved only through litigation, or even not at all, may be resolved within the virtual world of the newsgroup, with or without the assistance of others, inexpensively, and quickly, by parties who do not need to meet face to face. Newsgroups and other capabilities of the Internet make cyberspace a unique vehicle for dispute resolution.

When a dispute develops for which outside help is needed, there are an increasing number of Web sites that offer assistance. These alternatives may be best for resolving small- to medium-sized business liability claims, which may not be worth the expense of litigation or traditional methods of alternative dispute resolution. In most of the online forums, there is no automatic application of the law of any specific jurisdiction. Instead, results are often based on general, universal legal principles.

Negotiation Services

CyberSettle.com., Inc., clickNsettle.com, U.S. Settlement Corp. (ussettle.com), and other Web-based firms offer online forums to negotiate monetary settlements through "blind bidding." These services are useful for, among other parties, insurance companies and their claimants to work out settlements.

An online negotiation service does not evaluate the merits of a claim that is presented to it. Instead, the parties to a dispute may agree to submit offers to settle the dispute. If the offers fall within a previously agreed-on range, the dispute will be settled, and the parties will split the difference. Special software is used to filter, and keep secret, any offers that are not within the range. If there is no agreed-on range, typically an offer includes a deadline within which the other party must respond before the offer expires. The parties can drop the negotiations at any time.

Such cyber resolution of disputes, or e-resolution, is generally more practical than litigation. Notice is given by e-mail. Password-protected access is possible twenty-four hours a day, seven days a week (24/7). Fees are sometimes nominal and otherwise low (often 2 percent to 4 percent, or less, of the disputed amount).

Mediation Providers

Mediation providers have also tried resolving disputes online. Most notable have been the efforts of eBay, a Web-based auction site, to provide mediation services for its sellers and buyers whose transactions result in disputes. In general, online mediation is the same as offline mediation, except that the parties never see each other. Everything is done via e-mail.

ONLINE OMBUDS OFFICE To test the capability of an online service to mediate disputes between its customers, eBay initiated a pilot program with the Online Ombuds Office (OOO). A dissatisfied customer could request the service through eBay's Web page. Most of the disputes involved goods that were not received, were damaged in transit, or were not what the buyer expected.

The University of Massachusetts's Center for Information Technology and Dispute Resolution ran the OOO. The OOO worked with the World Organization of Webmasters to resolve online disputes involving its members. Another of the OOO's services has been to mediate online domain name disputes. The OOO has also resolved disputes among newsgroup participants, business competitors, and Internet service providers and their customers.

Be Aware Negotiation is a method of dispute settlement that does not involve a third party; rather the parties to the dispute, perhaps with the help of their attorneys, reach an agreement. In the online environment, the parties are still in charge—even though a third party provides an online forum for the negotiations.

SQUARETRADE At the end of the OOO pilot program, eBay continued its mediation services with SquareTrade, another online mediation provider. SquareTrade resolves, currently for no charge, disputes involving $100 or more between eBay customers. The mediators try to do more than offer opinions, attempting to negotiate a settlement.

SquareTrade also resolves disputes between other parties. SquareTrade uses Web-based software that walks participants through a five-step e-resolution process. A complaint is filed, and the other party is notified. Negotiation between the parties occurs on a secure page within SquareTrade's Web site. The parties may consult a mediator. The case is resolved. The entire process takes as little as ten to fourteen days, and there is no fee unless the parties use a mediator.

Other Web firms—for example, Resolution Forum, Inc., discussed below—offer similar services and often offer other forms of dispute resolution as well. As with offline methods of dispute resolution, any party may appeal to a court at any time.

Arbitration Programs

A number of companies offer online arbitration programs. As explained earlier in this chapter, among the conflicts that these firms arbitrate are domain name disputes. Any e-commerce dispute may be appropriate for arbitration, however. Companies that offer online arbitration programs include Resolution Forum, Inc., and the Virtual Magistrate Project.

RESOLUTION FORUM, INC. Resolution Forum, Inc. (RFI), is a nonprofit organization associated with the Center for Legal Responsibility at South Texas College of Law. RFI offers arbitration services through its CAN-WIN conferencing system. Using standard browser software and an RFI password, the parties to a dispute access an online conference room. When multiple parties are involved, private communications and break-out sessions are possible via private messaging facilities. RFI also offers mediation services.

VIRTUAL MAGISTRATE PROJECT The Virtual Magistrate Project (VMAG) is affiliated with the American Arbitration Association, Chicago-Kent College of Law, Cyberspace Law Institute, National Center for Automated Information Research, and other organizations. VMAG offers arbitration for disputes involving users of online systems; victims of wrongful messages, postings, and files; and system operators subject to complaints or similar demands. VMAG arbitrates online-related contract, intellectual property, personal property, real property, and tort disputes.

VMAG attempts to resolve a dispute within seventy-two hours. A complaint is submitted online and reviewed for appropriateness. Proceedings occur in a password-protected online newsgroup setting. Private e-mail among the participants is possible. A VMAG arbitrator's decision is issued in a written opinion. A party may appeal the outcome to a court.

Unlike offline arbitration, in which the results are usually kept private, a VMAG arbitrator's decision is made public. This may include the messages, postings, and other parts of the file of a case. This material is available through a Web site maintained by the Center for Law and Information Policy at Villanova Law School.

Other Methods of Online Dispute Resolution

Other methods of online dispute resolution (ODR) have begun to emerge. The most innovative services combine characteristics of traditional forms of dispute resolution, including the judicial system, with qualities of cyberspace forums. These hybrid programs illustrate the current state of dispute-resolution techniques and indicate the direction toward which they may evolve.

• **Example 5.3** iCourthouse offers ODR by jury. Unlike juries in the judicial system, however, iCourthouse juries consist of volunteers who choose whether they want to serve and which, and how many, cases they want to decide. The jury is free to the parties with the dispute.

To initiate a case, a party registers, files his or her claim, and receives a case number and a password. This party and his or her opponent post their arguments and submit their evidence, which can include audio and video media. Jurors review the evidence, ask questions, make comments, and render their verdicts. The parties are given a verdict summary that includes the jurors' comments about the case.

For a fee, the parties can select their jurors, which can be any number the parties choose. The jurors deliberate in a chat room where the parties and their attorneys "listen in." Unless otherwise agreed, all decisions are nonbinding and the parties can still go to court. According to iCourthouse, however, no one has. •

The Future of E-Commerce Dispute Resolution

The evolving methods of online dispute resolution (ODR) provide a glimpse of the future of e-commerce dispute resolution. These methods were among the topics at a seminar hosted by the U.S. Department of Commerce and the Federal Trade Commission in June 2000.[7] During the seminar, a group of U.S. companies heavily involved in e-commerce proposed, for those who do business in cyberspace, new guidelines that included proposals for the resolution of e-commerce disputes. These proposals are discussed in this chapter's *Legal E-nvironment* feature.

As explained in this chapter, ODR approaches traditional conflict resolution in innovative ways. These innovations illustrate how all methods of dispute resolution can change to make efficient use of the speed and intelligence available in the technology of cyberspace. For this transformation to happen, however, the advantages of ODR must come to outweigh the disadvantages.

The Advantages of ODR

Online dispute resolution (ODR) has some advantages over more traditional forms of dispute resolution. For instance, the use of computers makes ODR faster, more convenient, and more efficient. Access to ODR services is possible twenty-four hours a day, seven days a week. The results are easily publicized. ICANN, for example, posts all of its decisions online. The cost is low compared to the higher expense of litigation (which, in a domain name dispute, for example, can cost more than $50,000). In fact, ODR is often free.

---

7. For more information about this workshop, go to the International Trade Administration's Web site at **http://www.ita.doc.gov** or to the FTC's Web site at **http://www.ftc.gov**.

Legal *e*-nvironment

ODR Guidelines for E-Commerce

The International Trade Administration, an agency of the U.S. Department of Commerce, and the Federal Trade Commission (FTC) sponsored a public workshop, in June 2000, titled "Alternative Dispute Resolution for Consumer Transactions in the Borderless Online Marketplace." The participants reviewed the use of, and the developments, obstacles, and issues associated with, alternative dispute resolution (ADR) and online dispute resolution (ODR) in e-commerce.

The Electronic Commerce and Consumer Protection Group

On the first day of the June 2000 workshop, a consortium of seven U.S. companies with an important stake in e-commerce proposed their own *Guidelines for Merchant-to-Consumer Transactions* in cyberspace. The companies that issued the proposals included America Online, Inc., AT&T Corporation, Dell Computer Corporation, International Business Machines Corporation (IBM), Microsoft Corporation, Network Solutions, Inc., and Time Warner, Inc. These firms called themselves the Electronic Commerce and Consumer Protection Group (the Group).

The Group's Guidelines

The group's voluntary guidelines focused on protection for consumers who make purchases online. The guidelines included the following:

- Consumers should have a prompt, easy, and effective way to contact merchants.
- Merchants should not engage in deceptive, fraudulent, or misleading practices.
- Merchants should provide consumers with the opportunity to review their transactions before

the transactions become binding. Merchants should also employ return and refund policies.
- Merchants should make "reasonable efforts" to ensure the security of consumer information and adopt privacy policies that are consistent with existing industry standards and legal requirements.
- Third party ODR should be implemented, but it should be nonbinding to avoid undercutting consumers' existing legal rights.

The primary emphasis was on the proposal for ODR. "The goal is to resolve [e-commerce disputes] in a manner that reflects that the monetary value of these disputes, while important to individual consumers, is often small in amount," the Group stated. "Therefore, traditional court-based solutions, including small claims courts, particularly for people who live in different countries, are by and large impractical."

The Group recognized that ODR would reduce the costs and complications for both consumers and businesses. In turn, this should foster competition among businesses and lead to more choices for consumers.

The Group hopes that its guidelines lead to a permanent framework for consumer protection and the growth of e-commerce. The guidelines can be read at **http://www.ecommercegroup.guidelines.htm**.

For Critical Analysis: *Some favor the adoption of these guidelines, because, if widely employed, they would likely reduce some of the uncertainty in e-commerce and increase consumers' willingness to buy online. Others criticize the guidelines because, among other things, they do not apply to online auctions, do not encourage limits on consumer liability (such as limits that apply in cases of credit-card fraud), and do not require that merchants be bound by any ODR results; at the same time, they require that consumers use ODR before going to court. Is it possible to draft proposals that both the proponents and the critics of these guidelines would support?*

The Internet's low cost and speed of communication make it easier for parties to negotiate a resolution without the use of a third party. The low cost also makes this form of dispute resolution attractive to those with low-value disputes, such as those arising from transactions in Web auctions. Eventually, government agencies and other entities that deal with large numbers of disputes may turn to ODR as an effective vehicle for resolving those disputes.

The Disadvantages of ODR

There are disadvantages to ODR. For instance, ODR is not yet widely accepted. Also, efficiency, speed, and low cost could be an obstacle to a party who wants to wear out his or her opponent in a long, expensive, contentious battle.

There are no sheriffs to execute ODR judgments, which means that, unlike the orders in cases decided by courts, the results in cases decided in extrajudicial, online forums are not directly enforceable. There are also issues of jurisdiction, which have not been finally solved. For example, should cyberspace have its own jurisdiction, or should it link to the physical locations of the parties?

Finally, the technology has some disadvantages. E-mail is not sufficient for resolving all types of disputes. Software for smoother and more visual interaction needs to be developed.

Key Terms

domain name 132	newsgroup 141	panel 135
e-commerce 129	online dispute resolution	
e-commerce dispute 131	(ODR) 131	

Chapter Summary • E-Commerce and Dispute Resolution

Jurisdiction in Cyberspace (See pages 129–131.)	Traditionally, geographic and political boundaries have played a key role in determining a court's jurisdiction. The Internet, because it extends beyond geographic and political boundaries, has undercut this traditional basis for a court to assert personal jurisdiction. Slowly, the courts are developing a standard for evaluating the exercise of jurisdiction based on contacts made over the Internet.
E-Commerce Disputes (See pages 131–132.)	1. **Common disputes**—Common types of cyberspace complaints include disputes over the rights to domain names and disagreements over the quality of goods sold over the Internet, including via auction sites. 2. **Online dispute resolution (ODR)**—A form of alternative dispute resolution (ADR) that is distinguished from other forms of ADR primarily by the fact that the complaint, response, evidence, decision, and opinion are all communicated through cyberspace.
Online Resolution of Domain Name Disputes (See pages 132–141.)	1. **The "dot.com explosion"**—Although there are several top level domains (TLDs) available for use in domain names (Internet addresses), generally only one (.com) can be used by commercial enterprises. As e-commerce expanded, the "dot.com explosion" led to numerous disputes over rights to particular domain names. 2. **The Internet Corporation for Assigned Names and Numbers (ICANN)**—The ICANN is a nonprofit corporation set up by the federal government to oversee the distribution of domain names. Among other things, ICANN has developed a policy and rules for settling domain name disputes.

Chapter Summary • E-Commerce and Dispute Resolution

Online Resolution of Domain Name Disputes—continued

3. **ICANN's services**—ICANN-approved dispute resolution providers (such as the World Intellectual Property Organization Arbitration and Mediation Center, or WIPO Center) follow ICANN's prescribed procedure for settling domain name disputes through administrative proceedings conducted by arbitrators. The complaint, answer, and decision are all transmitted online.

Online Resolution of Other Disputes
(See pages 141–144.)

1. **Negotiation services**—Several Web-based firms now offer online forums through which disputes are negotiated and settled, using such methods as "blind bidding" procedures. The e-resolution of disputes through these forums is practical because such forums are available on a 24/7 basis and require only nominal or low fees.

2. **Mediation providers**—Online mediation services are also available to help parties settle disputes arising out of online transactions, such as disputes over goods sold at auction sites, as well as disputes over domain names.

3. **Arbitration programs**—A number of companies offer online arbitration programs to decide the outcome of conflicts concerning e-commerce transactions, including domain name disputes.

4. **Hybrid programs**—Other online innovative services combine characteristics of traditional dispute resolution, including the judicial system, with qualities of cyberspace forums. For example, iCourthouse offers ODR by jury—in which a volunteer online jury deliberates in a chat room and submits a nonbinding verdict in the case.

The Future of E-Commerce and Dispute Resolution
(See pages 144–146.)

In the future, ODR may come into widespread use—depending on whether the advantages of ODR come to outweigh the disadvantages.

1. **Advantages of ODR**—The advantages of ODR include convenience, efficiency, 24/7 access, easily published results, and low cost.

2. **Disadvantages of ODR**—The disadvantages of ODR include the lack of widespread acceptance of this form of dispute resolution, the fact that some parties prefer long-drawn-out and costly legal proceedings to wear out opponents, the fact that ODR judgments are not directly enforceable, and the challenges presented by jurisdictional issues.

For Review

1. What standard are the courts developing for evaluating the exercise of jurisdiction based on contacts via the Internet?
2. What disputes can be classified as "e-commerce disputes"?
3. What is the Internet Corporation for Assigned Names and Numbers (ICANN), and according to ICANN's rules, what is the legal effect of a decision rendered by an arbitrator?
4. What legal principles apply in the online resolution of most disputes?
5. State some of the advantages and disadvantages of online dispute resolution.

Questions and Case Problems

5–1. Domain Names. Urban Sport, Inc., is a nationally renowned manufacturer and retailer of clothing and other items under its "Urban Sport" trademark. Urban Sport registered the mark with the U.S. Patent and Trademark Office in 1990. Urban Sport's domain name for its e-commerce business is "urbansports.com." In

1996, Frank registered thirty domain names, including "urbansport.com" and other names that contain the registered trademarks of other entities, with Network Solutions, Inc. Frank used the names to funnel Internet traffic to his Web site at **http://www.names-for-sale.com**, where he offered to sell each of the names to the highest bidder. Urban Sport filed a complaint with the National Arbitration Forum (NAF), seeking to have the "urbansport.com" name transferred to the firm. What standards will the NAF apply in considering Urban Sport's case? What should the NAF decide, and why?

5–2. Online Dispute Resolution. On a Web-based auction site, Beth advertises a laptop computer for sale "as is" to the highest bidder. After a brief online discussion with Beth about the qualities of the computer, Adam submits a bid. Adam's bid is the highest offer, and Beth ships the computer to him, insured and packed in bubble-wrap and packing peanuts. Ten days later, Adam begins sending e-mail complaints to Beth about an inadequate processor, insufficient memory, and a cracked case. He threatens to complain about the deal in every chat room on the Web unless she refunds his money. Which ODR forum is the most appropriate for resolving the dispute between Beth and Adam, and why? What might be a good resolution of this dispute?

5–3. Online Dispute Resolution. Which method of ODR would be most appropriate for resolving each of the following disputes, and why?

(a) The ad for Local Network Systems Design, Inc., in the city telephone directory is in the wrong classification and the publisher refuses to fix it.

(b) A former employee of Standard Personnel Corporation claims that the company wrongfully fired her.

(c) American Bicycle Company's landlord postpones repairing a leaky roof, which causes American Bicycle to lose some of its merchandise in a storm.

5–4. Online Dispute Resolution. Reliable Accounting & Payroll Service contracts with Superior Contractors Corporation to build an office building. Superior subcontracts the telephone wiring to Town Electricians, Inc. Reliable contracts separately with Town Electricians to include computer network wiring in the new building. Before Town Electricians finishes its part of the job, Reliable pays Superior, and Superior pays the subcontractor. Town Electricians goes out of business. Reliable wants Superior to either finish the wiring or make good the amount that Reliable paid to Town Electricians. Superior refuses. Reliable submits a description of the situation to iCourthouse. Describe the process by which this dispute would be resolved on iCourthouse. What are the advantages and disadvantages of this type of dispute resolution?

5–5. Domain Names. BroadBridge Media, L.L.C., sells an Internet-based system through which a client can control its customer's use of the content on a compact disc (CD). BroadBridge's technology converts and compresses analog audio information into digital information and burns it onto a CD. A customer accesses the CD by going to a particular Web site and downloading certain information. Before 2000, BroadBridge distributed more than 4.5 million compact discs under the trademark "HyperCD," and the domain name and e-mail address "hypercd.com." HyperCD was registered as a trademark with the U.S. Patent and Trademark Office in 1997, but BroadBridge failed to renew its domain name and e-mail registration, which lapsed on March 1, 2000. Three weeks later, Creation Technologies, Inc. (CTI), which was developing similar technology, registered "hypercd.com" as a domain name. BroadBridge offered to pay CTI up to $7,000 for its transfer of the name back to BroadBridge, but CTI refused to accept less than $46,000. BroadBridge filed a complaint with ICANN and, two days later, a suit in a federal district court, against CTI. CTI responded to the suit in part by arguing that filing a complaint with ICANN prohibits the filing of a suit. Is CTI correct? How should the court rule? [*BroadBridge Media, L.L.C. v. Hypercd.com*, 106 F.Supp.2d 505 (S.D.N.Y. 2000)]

5–6. Domain Names. Pure Color contracted with Sabin and Associates for Sabin to design and sell a Web site to Pure Color with the domain name "PURECOLOR.COM" for $7,500. As part of the deal, Sabin promised to transfer that name to Pure Color and gave the firm a signed "Domain Name Assignment Agreement." When Pure Color contacted Network Solutions, Inc., the registrar refused to transfer the name because the agreement was not notarized. Meanwhile, Sabin, which had not finished the work for Pure Color, disappeared—its phone was disconnected and its mail went unanswered—but the incomplete Web site remained on the Internet. Pure Color obtained a different domain name and a new Web site, and filed a complaint with the National Arbitration Forum. Pure Color contended that Sabin "highjacked" the PURECOLOR.COM domain name, which was identical to Pure Color's trademark. Pure Color asked that the name be transferred to the complainant. What should the arbitrator decide, and why? [*Pure Color v. Sabin and Associates*, NAF Case No. FA0006000095009 (2000)]

5–7. Domain Names. Metalco, a Jordanian firm in the business of heating equipment, began using "METALCO" as a trademark in 1975 and registered the mark with the Jordanian Registrar of Trade Names in 1976. Metalco registered the domain name "METALCO.COM" with Network Solutions, Inc., in January 1998. In applying to register the name, Metalco warranted that its use of the name would not infringe on the rights of any third party. AMRGI, Inc., a U.S. firm in the business of metal fence and railing panels, posts, stays, and gates, began using "METALCO" as a trademark in 1994, but did not register the mark until February 1999. One year later, AMRGI filed a complaint with the National Arbitration Forum, seeking to have the domain name METALCO.COM transferred to AMRGI. The complainant argued that Metalco's use of the name infringed on AMRGI's trademark. Metalco responded that AMRGI's use of METALCO as a trademark infringed on Metalco's rights, and asked to have AMRGI's trademark registration canceled. How should the arbitrator resolve this dispute? Explain. [*AMRGI, Inc. v. Metalco,* NAF Case No. FA0006000095016 (2000)]

A Question of Ethics and Social Responsibility

5–8. Gordon Sumner is a musician, who since at least 1978 has been known professionally as "Sting." Sumner has used that name worldwide in recording music and performing concerts. In 1995, Michael Urvan registered the domain name "sting.com" with Network Solutions, Inc., and linked the name to various Web sites, most of which were under construction. When contacted by Sumner, Urvan offered to sell the name for $25,000. Sumner filed a complaint with the World Intellectual Property Organization Arbitration and Mediation Center (WIPO Center), asking that the name be transferred to him or that Urvan's registration be canceled. Sumner asserted that the name "Sting" was synonymous in the public mind with his activities as a musician. Urvan responded that there were twenty registered trademarks with the word "sting," none of which were owned by Sumner. Urvan added that the word "sting" is a common word, that he was not Sumner's competitor, and that there was no confusion between him and Sumner. [*Sumner v. Urvan,* WIPO Case No. D2000-0596 (2000)]

1. If the WIPO Center arbitrators apply ICANN's dispute-resolution policy, what elements must Sumner prove in order to have the "sting.com" domain name registered by Urvan transferred to Sumner? What ethical precepts, if any, underlie each of these elements?
2. In deciding the matter, will the WIPO Center arbitrators be at all influenced by Urvan's offer to sell Sumner the "sting.com" name for $25,000? Explain.
3. Generally, in whose favor do you think the WIPO Center will rule? Why?

For Critical Analysis

5–9. In both court litigation and traditional arbitration forums, evidence, including testimony, normally is presented to the judge or arbitrator in a physical, face-to-face manner. In contrast, in ODR evidence is submitted online. Is it possible that this difference in the way evidence is presented could influence the outcome of the case? Why or why not?

Interacting with the Internet

■ For updated links to resources available on the Web, as well as a variety of other materials, visit this text's Web site at

http://leet.westbuslaw.com

■ ICANN's Web site can be found at

http://www.icann.com

■ Additional information about the WIPO Center can be found at

http://arbiter.wipo.int/center/ index.html

■ The page on the Web site of eBay through which the Web auction firm's ODR service can be accessed is

http://pages.ebay.com/services/ buyandsell/disputeres.html

■ More information about the Online Ombuds Office (OOO) operated by the University of Massachusetts's Center for Information Technology and Dispute Resolution can be found at

http://aaron.sbs.umass.edu/center/ ombuds/database.html

■ SquareTrade's Web site is located at

http://SquareTrade.com

■ To learn more about negotiation services available on the Web, go to

http://clicknsettle.com

and

http://www.cybersettle.com

(Continued)

■ Information on iCourthouse can be found on the Web at   **http://www.i-courthouse.com**

Online Legal Research Exercises

Go to **http://leet. westbuslaw.com**, the Web site that accompanies this text. Select "Interactive Study Center," and then click on "Chapter 5." There you will find the following Internet research exercise that you can perform to learn more about online dispute resolution:

Activity 5–1: Online Dispute Resolution

Before the Test

Go to **http://leet. westbuslaw.com**, the Web site that accompanies this text. Select "Interactive Quizzes." You will find a number of interactive questions relating to this chapter.

Unit I Cumulative Hypothetical Problem

Korman, Inc., a toy manufacturer, has its head-quarters in Minneapolis, Minnesota. It markets its toys throughout the United States, as well as in overseas markets. Recently, Korman has placed on the market a new line of dolls that has been a great commercial success.

1. Jan's Toy Mart, the California distributor of Korman toys, claims that Korman breached its contract with the company. What factors should Jan's Toy Mart consider in deciding whether to sue Korman? What alternatives to litigation might the company pursue to settle the dispute with Korman?

2. If Jan's Toy Mart brought a suit against Korman in a California state court, could that court exercise jurisdiction over Korman? Would your answer be the same if Jan's Toy Mart had purchased the toys online from Korman's Web site? Explain.

3. Suppose that in its contract with Korman, Jan's Toy Mart agreed to submit any dispute that arose between the two companies to binding arbitration. Following the arbitration hearing, the arbitrator concludes that Korman did not breach the contract. Jan's Toy Mart is unsatisfied with the arbitrator's award. Can Jan's Toy Mart appeal the arbitrator's decision to a court?

4. Korman has learned that Johann Klein, a German citizen, registered the domain name "korman.com" after Korman's toys became popular but before Korman had registered for a domain name. Klein does not use the domain name, and Korman has offered Klein $10,000 to transfer the site to Korman. Klein, however, tells Korman that he will not give up his rights to the domain name unless Korman pays him $25,000, which Korman refuses to do. What might Korman do to obtain the domain name without paying Klein $25,000?

5. Korman launches a series of ads showing children fighting with one another to play with Korman's dolls. A number of groups, including parent-teacher associations and groups concerned with the rights and welfare of children, believe that the ads are too violent and should be withdrawn. These groups have organized a media campaign against Korman. Recently, they picketed Korman's headquarters in Minneapolis, bearing such signs as "Korman Teaches Hate" and "Stop the Violence." The ads, however, have led to a dramatic increase in sales of the dolls. If you were a Korman executive, would you recommend that the company withdraw the ads? What factors would Korman's directors need to consider in making this decision?

The Public Environment

chapter

6

Constitutional Authority to Regulate Business

contents

chapter objectives

After reading this chapter, you should be able to:

1. Describe the form of government created by the U.S. Constitution.

2. Explain the relationship between the national government and state governments as set forth in the Constitution.

3. Identify the constitutional basis for the regulatory power of the federal government.

4. Summarize the fundamental rights protected by the First Amendment.

5. Give some examples of how other constitutional protections affect business.

The U.S. Constitution is brief.[1] It consists of only about seven thousand words, which is less than one-third of the number of words in the average state constitution. Perhaps its brevity explains why it has proved to be so "marvelously elastic," as Franklin Roosevelt pointed out in the quotation alongside, and why it has survived for over two hundred years—longer than any other written constitution in the world.

Laws that govern business have their origin in the lawmaking authority granted by this document, which is the supreme law in this country. As mentioned in Chapter 1, neither Congress nor any state may pass a law that conflicts with the Constitution.

In this chapter, we first look at some basic constitutional concepts and clauses and their significance for business. Then we examine how certain fundamental freedoms guaranteed by the Constitution affect businesspersons and the workplace.

> "The United States Constitution has proved itself the most marvelously elastic compilation of rules of government ever written."
>
> Franklin D. Roosevelt, 1882–1945
> (Thirty-second president of the United States, 1933–1945)

The Constitutional Powers of Government

Following the Revolutionary War, the states created a *confederal* form of government. The Articles of Confederation, which went into effect in 1781, established a confederation of independent states and a central (national) government that could exercise only very limited powers. The sovereign power, or supreme authority to govern, rested largely with the states. The limitation on the central government's powers reflected a basic tenet of the American Revolution—that a national government should not have unlimited power that could be used to tyrannize over the states.

The confederation, however, faced serious problems. For one thing, laws passed by the various states hampered national commerce and foreign trade by preventing the free movement of goods and services. By 1784, the nation faced a serious economic depression. Many who could not afford to pay their debts were thrown into "debtors' prisons." By 1786, a series of uprisings by farmer debtors were difficult to control because the national government did not have the authority to demand revenues (by levying taxes, for example) to support a militia.

Because of these problems, a national convention was called to amend the Articles of Confederation. Instead of amending the articles, however, the delegates to the convention wrote the U.S. Constitution, which, after its ratification by the states in 1789, became the basis for an entirely new form of government. Many of the provisions of the Constitution, including those discussed in the following pages, were shaped by the delegates' experiences during the confederal era (1781–1789).

Federalism and the Separation of Powers

The new government created by the Constitution reflected a series of compromises made by delegates to the convention on various issues. Some delegates wanted sovereign power to remain with the states; others wanted the national government alone to exercise sovereign power. The end result was a compromise—a **federal form of government** in which the national government and the states *share* sovereign power. The Constitution expressly delegated certain powers to the national government and reserved all other powers to the states.

Federal Form of Government A system of government in which the states form a union and the sovereign power is divided between a central government and the member states.

---

1. See Appendix B for the full text of the U.S. Constitution.

The relationship between the national government and the state governments is a partnership. Neither partner is superior to the other except within the particular area of exclusive authority granted to it under the Constitution.

To prevent the possibility that the national government might use its power arbitrarily, the Constitution divided the national government's powers among the three branches of government. The legislative branch makes the laws, the executive branch enforces the laws, and the judicial branch interprets the laws. Each branch performs a separate function, and no branch may exercise the authority of another branch. Additionally, a system of **checks and balances** allows each branch to limit the actions of the other two branches, thus preventing any one branch from exercising too much power. Some examples of these checks and balances are the following:

Checks and Balances
The national government is composed of three separate branches: the executive, the legislative, and the judicial branches. Each branch of the government exercises a check on the actions of the others.

1. The legislative branch (Congress) can enact a law, but the executive branch (the president) has the constitutional authority to veto that law.
2. The executive branch is responsible for foreign affairs, but treaties with foreign governments require the advice and consent of the Senate.
3. Congress determines the jurisdiction of the federal courts and the president appoints federal judges, with the advice and consent of the Senate, but the judicial branch has the power to hold actions of the other two branches unconstitutional.[2]

The Commerce Clause

To prevent states from establishing laws and regulations that would interfere with trade and commerce among the states, the Constitution expressly delegated to the national government the power to regulate interstate commerce. Article I, Section 8, of the U.S. Constitution expressly permits Congress "[t]o

---

2. See the *Landmark in the Legal Environment* in Chapter 3 on *Marbury v. Madison,* 5 U.S. (1 Cranch) 137, 2 L.Ed. 60 (1803), a case in which the doctrine of judicial review was clearly enunciated by Chief Justice John Marshall.

Ethical Issue 6.1

Should nine unelected justices make the law?

The checks and balances built into the Constitution were designed to keep any one branch of government from exercising too much power. Among these checks is the judiciary's power to hold unconstitutional the laws and actions of the other two branches. Yet some claim that this power gives federal judges, particularly the justices who sit on the United States Supreme Court, too much control over national laws and policies, the making of which the framers of the Constitution en-

trusted to Congress. Because members of Congress are elected, the people have some say in the lawmaking process. But the people have little say in the decisions made by federal judges, who are not elected but appointed—albeit with the advice and consent of the Senate, an elected body.

In the early years of the nation, there was little concern about the Supreme Court wielding too much power. In fact, Alexander Hamilton spoke of the judicial branch (the Supreme Court) as "the least dangerous branch" of government because the Court had no enforcement powers and—in those days—little stature in the eyes of the public. Today, although it still has no enforcement powers, its stature in the eyes of the public allows it to influence national affairs to an extent that the founders could not possibly have foreseen.

regulate Commerce with foreign Nations, and among the several States, and with the Indian Tribes." This clause, referred to as the **commerce clause,** has had a greater impact on business than any other provision in the Constitution.

For some time, the commerce power was interpreted as being limited to *interstate* commerce (commerce among the states) and not applicable to *intrastate* commerce (commerce within the states). In 1824, however, in *Gibbons v. Ogden* (see the *Landmark in the Legal Environment*), the United States Supreme Court held that commerce within states could also be regulated by the national government as long as the commerce *substantially affected* commerce involving more than one state.

THE BREADTH OF THE COMMERCE CLAUSE In *Gibbons v. Ogden,* the commerce clause was expanded to regulate activities that "substantially affect interstate commerce." As the nation grew and faced new kinds of problems, the commerce clause became a vehicle for the additional expansion of national-government regulatory powers. Even activities that seemed purely local came under the regulatory reach of the national government if those activities were deemed to substantially affect interstate commerce. ● **Example 6.1** In 1942, in *Wickard v. Filburn,*[3] the Supreme Court held that wheat production

> **Commerce Clause** The provision in Article I, Section 8, of the U.S. Constitution that gives Congress the power to regulate interstate commerce.

> **"We are under a Constitution, but the Constitution is what judges say it is."**
>
> Charles Evans Hughes, 1862–1948
> (American jurist)

---

3. 317 U.S. 111, 63 S.Ct. 82, 87 L.Ed. 122 (1942).

Landmark in the Legal Environment

Gibbons v. Ogden (1824)

The commerce clause, which is found in Article I, Section 8, of the U.S. Constitution, gives Congress the power "to regulate Commerce with foreign Nations, and among the several States, and with the Indian Tribes." What exactly does "to regulate commerce" mean? What does "commerce" entail? These questions came before the United States Supreme Court in 1824 in the case of *Gibbons v. Ogden.*[a]

The background of the case was as follows. Robert Fulton, inventor of the steamboat, and Robert Livingston, who was then American minister to France, secured a monopoly on steam navigation on the waters in the state of New York from the New York legislature in 1803. Fulton and Livingston licensed Aaron Ogden, a former governor of New Jersey and a U.S. senator, to operate steam-powered ferryboats between New York and New Jersey. Thomas Gibbons, who had obtained a license from the U.S. government to operate boats in interstate waters, com-

peted with Ogden without New York's permission. Ogden sued Gibbons. The New York state courts granted Ogden an injunction, prohibiting Gibbons from operating in New York waters. Gibbons appealed the decision to the United States Supreme Court.

Sitting as chief justice on the Supreme Court was John Marshall, an advocate of a strong national government. In his decision, Marshall defined the word *commerce* as used in the commerce clause to mean all commercial intercourse—that is, all business dealings that affect more than one state. The Court ruled against Ogden's monopoly, reversing the injunction against Gibbons. Marshall used this opportunity not only to expand the definition of commerce but also to validate and increase the power of the national legislature to regulate commerce. Said Marshall, "What is this power? It is the power . . . to prescribe the rule by which commerce is to be governed." Marshall held that the power to regulate interstate commerce was an exclusive power of the national government and that this power included the power to regulate any intrastate commerce that substantially affects interstate commerce.

For Critical Analysis: *What might have resulted if the Court had held otherwise—that the national government did not have the exclusive power to regulate interstate commerce?*

---

a. 22 U.S. (9 Wheat.) 1, 6 L.Ed. 23 (1824).

> **Recall** Any law in violation of the U.S. Constitution will not be enforced.

by an individual farmer intended wholly for consumption on his own farm was subject to federal regulation. The Court reasoned that the home consumption of wheat reduced the demand for wheat and thus could have a substantial effect on interstate commerce.●

Today, at least theoretically, the power over commerce authorizes the national government to regulate every commercial enterprise in the United States. Federal (national) legislation governs virtually every major activity conducted by businesses—from hiring and firing decisions, to workplace safety, to competitive practices, to how they compete for business, to how they finance their enterprises.

Only rarely has the Supreme Court limited the regulatory reach of the national government under the commerce power. One of these occasions was in 1995, when the Court held—for the first time in sixty years—that Congress had exceeded its regulatory authority under the commerce clause when it passed the Gun-Free School Zones Act in 1990. The Court stated that the act, which banned the possession of guns within one thousand feet of any school, was unconstitutional because it attempted to regulate an area that had "nothing to do with commerce."[4]

Generally, today's Supreme Court has indicated a willingness to rein in the constitutional powers of the national government to a far greater extent than the Court has during the past six decades. In addition to restricting the national government's regulatory reach under the commerce clause, the Court issued a number of decisions in the late 1990s and early 2000s that significantly enhanced the sovereign powers of the states within the federal system.[5] The following landmark case involves an earlier challenge to the scope of the national government's constitutional authority to regulate local activities.

---

4. 514 U.S. 549, 115 S.Ct. 1624, 131 L.Ed.2d 626 (1995).
5. See, for example, *Printz v. United States,* 521 U.S. 898, 117 S.Ct. 2365, 138 L.Ed.2d 914 (1997); and *Alden v. Maine,* 527 U.S. 706, 119 S.Ct. 2240, 144 L.Ed.2d 636 (1999).

Case 6.1 ● Heart of Atlanta Motel v. United States

Supreme Court of the United States, 1964.
379 U.S. 241,
85 S.Ct. 348,
13 L.Ed. 2d 258.
http://supct.law.cornell.edu/ supct/cases/name.htm[a]

Historical and Social Setting *In the first half of the twentieth century, state governments sanctioned*

segregation on the basis of race. In 1954, the United States Supreme Court decided that racially segregated school systems violated the Constitution. In the following decade, the Court ordered an end to racial segregation imposed by the states in other public facilities, such as beaches, golf courses, buses, parks, auditoriums, and courtroom seating. Privately owned facilities that excluded or segregated African Americans and others on the basis of race were not subject to the same constitutional restrictions, however. Congress passed the Civil Rights Act of 1964 to prohibit racial discrimination in "establishments affecting interstate commerce." These facilities included "places of public accommodation."

Background and Facts The owner of the Heart of Atlanta Motel, in violation of the Civil Rights

---

a. This is the "Historic Supreme Court Decisions—by Party Name" page within the "Caselists" collection of the Legal Information Institute available at its site on the Web. Click on the "H" link or scroll down the list of cases to the entry for the *Heart of Atlanta* case. Click on the case name. When the link opens, click on one of the choices to read the "Syllabus," the "Full Decision," or the "Edited Decision."

Case 6.1 Continued

Act of 1964, refused to rent rooms to African Americans. The motel owner brought an action in a federal district court to have the act declared unconstitutional, alleging that Congress had exceeded its constitutional authority to regulate commerce by enacting the act. The owner argued that his motel was not engaged in interstate commerce but was "of a purely local character." The motel, however, was accessible to state and interstate highways. The owner advertised nationally, maintained billboards throughout the state, and accepted convention trade from outside the state (75 percent of the guests were residents of other states). The court sustained the constitutionality of the act and enjoined (prohibited) the owner from discriminating on the basis of race. The owner appealed. The case ultimately went to the United States Supreme Court.

In the Words of the Court . . .
Mr. Justice CLARK delivered the opinion of the Court.

* * * *

While the Act as adopted carried no congressional findings, the record of its passage through each house is replete with evidence of the burdens that discrimination by race or color places upon interstate commerce * * * . This testimony included the fact that our people have become increasingly mobile with millions of all races traveling from State to State; that Negroes in particular have been the subject of discrimination in transient accommodations, having to travel great distances to secure the same; that often they have been unable to obtain accommodations and have had to call upon friends to put them up overnight. * * * These exclusionary practices were found to be nationwide, the Under Secretary of Commerce testifying that there is "no question that this discrimination in the North still exists to a large degree" and in the West and Midwest as well * * * . This testimony indicated a qualitative as well as quantitative effect on interstate travel by Negroes. The former was the obvious impairment of the Negro traveler's pleasure and convenience that resulted when he continually was uncertain of finding lodging. As for the latter, there was evidence that this uncertainty stemming from racial discrimination had the effect of discouraging travel on the part of a substantial portion of the Negro community * * * . We shall not burden this opinion with further details since the voluminous testimony presents overwhelming evidence that discrimination by hotels and motels impedes interstate travel.

* * * *

It is said that the operation of the motel here is of a purely local character. But, assuming this to be true, "if it is interstate commerce that feels the pinch, it does not matter how local the operation that applies the squeeze." * * * Thus the power of Congress to promote interstate commerce also includes the power to regulate the local incidents thereof, including local activities in both the States of origin and destination, which might have a substantial and harmful effect upon that commerce.

Decision and Remedy The United States Supreme Court upheld the constitutionality of the Civil Rights Act of 1964. The power of Congress to regulate interstate commerce permitted the enactment of legislation that could halt local discriminatory practices.

For Critical Analysis—Political Consideration *Suppose that only 5 percent of the motel's guests—or even 2 or 1 percent—were from out of state. In such a situation, would the Court still have been justified in regulating the motel's activities?*

THE REGULATORY POWERS OF THE STATES

As part of their inherent sovereignty, state governments have the authority to regulate affairs within their borders. State regulatory powers are often referred to as **police powers**. The term does not relate solely to criminal law enforcement but also to the right of state governments to regulate private activities to protect or promote the public order, health, safety, morals, and general welfare. Fire and building codes, antidiscrimination laws, parking regulations, zoning restrictions, licensing requirements, and thousands of other state statutes covering virtually every aspect of life have been enacted pursuant to a state's police powers.

Police Powers Powers possessed by states as part of their inherent sovereignty. These powers may be exercised to protect or promote the public order, health, safety, morals, and general welfare.

Generally, laws enacted pursuant to a state's police powers carry a strong presumption of validity. If a state law substantially burdens interstate commerce, however, it will be held to violate the commerce clause of the Constitution—which authorizes only the national government to regulate trade and commerce among the states. When state regulations impinge on interstate commerce, courts must balance the state's interest in the merits and purposes of the regulation against the burden placed on interstate commerce.

• **Example 6.2** In *Raymond Motor Transportation, Inc. v. Rice,*[6] the issue concerned Wisconsin administrative regulations that limited the length of trucks traveling on its highways. The United States Supreme Court weighed the burden on interstate commerce against the benefits created by the regulations

6. 434 U.S. 429, 98 S.Ct. 787, 54 L.Ed.2d 664 (1978).

Hazardous waste is deposited at a burial site. Can the state in which this site is located regulate this activity? If so, and if those regulations impinge on interstate commerce, will they be held unconstitutional?

and concluded that the challenged regulations "place a substantial burden on interstate commerce and they cannot be said to make more than the most speculative contribution to highway safety." Because courts balance the interests involved, it is extremely difficult to predict the outcome in a particular case.

Local governments, including cities, also exercise police powers. Local governments derive their authority to regulate their communities from the state, because they are creatures of the state. In other words, they cannot come into existence unless authorized by the state to do so. The following case concerns whether it is reasonable for a local government to impose a duty on property owners to keep clear the strips of government-owned land between the streets and the adjoining property.

Case 6.2 ● J. E. Goodenow v. City Council of Maquoketa, Iowa

Supreme Court of Iowa, 1998.
574 N.W.2d 18.
http://www.iowabar.org/
IowaSupremeCourt.nsf[a]

Historical and Environmental Setting *The ditches that line roads are generally designed to channel water that runs off those right-of-ways during storms and other severe weather. At one time, those who lived in a community maintained the right-of-ways that ran through it and kept them clear. As cities developed, the bulk of the work was given to local government departments, but the owners of the adjoining property were sometimes expected to clear the ditches. Steep, rolling ditches cannot be mowed with a push mower or riding mower, but require a ro-*

tary mower or a sickle bar attached to a utility tractor and heavy-duty weed eaters. This equipment can cost tens of thousands of dollars to buy and hundreds of dollars a month in man-hours to use.

Background and Facts Two-thirds of the Goodenow family farm is located within the city limits of Maquoketa, Iowa. At one time, the city mowed all of its right-of-ways, including the grass and weeds between its streets and the edge of the Goodenow property (and the property of other landowners). This included the hard-to-mow ditches that border the Goodenow farm. When the city enacted an ordinance to require the owners of the adjoining property to mow these strips, the owners of the Goodenow farm did not comply. Instead, they appealed to the city council, which refused to exempt them from the ordinance. John Goodenow, and others, filed a petition in an Iowa state court against the city, and others, asking the court to prevent enforcement of the ordinance. The court issued a summary judgment in favor of the defendants. The plaintiffs appealed.

a. This is a page within a collection of Iowa state court cases made available on the Web by the Iowa State Bar Association. Click on the "Date" link. When the "Date" page opens, scroll down the list to the *Goodenow* case, which was decided on January 21, 1998. Click on the number preceding the date to access the opinion.

In the Words of the Court . . .
McGIVERIN, Chief Justice.

* * * *

* * * We believe that the [ordinance is] designed to maintain the height of weeds and grasses along the boulevard of city streets to ensure adequate view of the road and access thereto, especially at or near intersections, and to prevent vegetation from becoming unsightly and unsafe to the public. * * * In other words the statute was enacted for the public safety, which has always been regarded as a proper subject of police power. * * *

We further note that [a] law does not become unconstitutional because it works a hardship. Additionally, the fact that one must make substantial expenditures to comply with regulatory statutes does not raise constitutional barriers.

We therefore conclude that * * * the Maquoketa city ordinances promote and protect the public health, safety, and welfare of persons who

(Continued)

Case 6.2 Continued

travel the city streets, and that the enactments are reasonably related to achieving those goals. The enactments thus constitute valid exercises of police power * * *.

Decision and Remedy The Supreme Court of Iowa affirmed the decision of the lower court. The state supreme court held that the ordinance constituted a valid exercise of police power.

For Critical Analysis—Social Consideration *Should all citizens be considered obligated to render some unpaid service to their states?*

The Supremacy Clause

Supremacy Clause The provision in Article VI of the Constitution that provides that the Constitution, laws, and treaties of the United States are "the supreme Law of the Land." Under this clause, state and local laws that directly conflict with federal law will be rendered invalid.

Article VI of the Constitution provides that the Constitution, laws, and treaties of the United States are "the supreme Law of the Land." This article, commonly referred to as the **supremacy clause,** is important in the ordering of state and federal relationships. When there is a direct conflict between a federal law and a state law, the state law is rendered invalid. Because some powers are concurrent (shared by the federal government and the states), however, it is necessary to determine which law governs in a particular circumstance.

When Congress chooses to act exclusively in a concurrent area, it is said to have *preempted* the area. In this circumstance, a valid federal statute or regulation will take precedence over a conflicting state or local law or regulation on the same general subject. Congress, however, rarely makes clear its intent to preempt an entire subject area against state regulation; consequently, the courts must determine whether Congress intended to exercise exclusive dominion over a given area. Consideration of **preemption** often occurs in the commerce clause context.

Preemption A doctrine under which certain federal laws preempt, or take precedence over, conflicting state or local laws.

No single factor is decisive as to whether a court will find preemption. Generally, congressional intent to preempt will be found if a federal law regulating an activity is so pervasive, comprehensive, or detailed that the states have no room to regulate in that area. Also, when a federal statute creates an agency—such as the National Labor Relations Board—to enforce the law, matters that may come within the agency's jurisdiction will likely preempt state laws.

The Taxing and Spending Powers

Article I, Section 8, provides that Congress has the "Power to lay and collect Taxes, Duties, Imposts, and Excises." Section 8 further provides that "all Duties, Imposts and Excises shall be uniform throughout the United States." The requirement of uniformity refers to uniformity among the states, and thus Congress may not tax some states while exempting others.

Traditionally, if Congress attempted to regulate indirectly, by taxation, an area over which it had no authority, the tax would be invalidated by the courts. Today, however, if a tax measure bears some reasonable relationship to revenue production, it is generally held to be within the national taxing power. Moreover, the expansive interpretation of the commerce clause almost always provides a basis for sustaining a federal tax.

Under Article I, Section 8, Congress has the power "to pay the Debts and provide for the common Defence and general welfare of the United States." Through the spending power, Congress disposes of the revenues accumulated from the taxing power. Congress can spend revenues not only to carry out its enumerated powers but also to promote any objective it deems worthwhile, so long as it does not violate the Constitution or its amendments. For example, Congress could not condition welfare payments on the recipients' political views. The spending power necessarily involves policy choices, with which taxpayers may disagree.

States also have the authority, as part of their police powers, to impose income taxes on their citizens and sales and other types of taxes on intrastate activities, and to spend those revenues to provide for the general welfare. In recent years, one of the most significant questions facing U.S. governments at all levels is whether Internet transactions should be taxed (see this chapter's *Legal E-nvironment* for a discussion of this issue).

Legal *e*-nvironment

Taxation Issues and Global E-Commerce

At the heart of any government's authority to regulate are its taxing and spending powers. The government that is deprived of its ability to tax income is a government that loses its strength. Yet increasingly, activities that traditionally have been subject to taxation, such as the purchase and sale of goods and services, are avoiding such taxation because these activities take place via the Internet.

A Moratorium on Internet Taxation

Every year, consumers purchase more goods and services—ranging from automobiles to software to CDs to objects of art—from online merchants. Business-to-business sales are also increasing at a rapid rate, as you will read in the *Legal E-nvironment* feature in Chapter 14. Some contend that one of the major reasons for the dramatic increase in e-commerce in the United States is the passage of the Internet Tax Freedom Act (ITFA) of 1998, which imposed a three-year moratorium (to expire in 2001) on the taxation of Internet sales and services. (Congress is currently considering legislation that, if passed, would extend the moratorium to 2006.)

Not surprisingly, online merchants, Internet companies, and various other business coalitions support the tax moratorium. They argue that Internet taxation would constrain the growth of e-commerce. Others, however, are not so sure that a tax-free Internet is in the best interests of the nation.

The Problem Facing Governments

For most state governments, taxes, and particularly sales taxes, are major sources of income. Typically, between 35 and 40 percent of state revenues are obtained through sales taxes. Today, however, some states are facing declining sales tax revenues. In part, this is because of the growth in direct-marking sales made via mail order or the Internet. In a direct-marketing transaction, a seller, such as an online merchant, sells goods directly to consumers located around the country or even in another country. The problem for the states is that their ability to impose tax obligations on out-of-state sellers is limited.

Consider that simple sales transactions are often hard to trace in the expanding world of e-commerce. If a U.S. customer orders a product from a Peruvian company with a Guatemalan factory and uses funds in an offshore bank to pay for the purchase, the transaction becomes difficult, if not impossible, to tax. Where did the transaction actually take place? Where was the product ordered? As more corporations become spread out throughout the world and as communications and encryption become more sophisticated, similar transactions will become commonplace and even more complicated. Thus, governments will lose, little by little, their ability to tax such transactions.

Taxes on income present similar problems. At both the state and national level, income taxes constitute an important source of revenue. Yet before governments can tax income, they must know where the income is earned and by whom—which is not always easy when the income is derived through Internet transactions.

For Critical Analysis: *Is it unfair for states to impose sales taxes on goods sold through traditional outlets—such as those located in downtown areas or shopping malls—but not on similar goods sold by online direct marketers? Would your answer be the same if you knew that the taxation of goods sold online would stifle the growth of e-commerce?*

Business and the Bill of Rights

The importance of a written declaration of the rights of individuals eventually caused the first Congress of the United States to submit twelve amendments to the Constitution to the states for approval. The first ten of these amendments, commonly known as the **Bill of Rights**, were adopted in 1791 and embody a series of protections for the individual against various types of interference by the federal government.[7] Some constitutional protections apply to business entities as well. For example, corporations exist as separate legal entities, or legal persons, and enjoy many of the same rights and privileges as natural persons do. Summarized here are the protections guaranteed by these ten amendments (see the Constitution in Appendix B for the complete text of each amendment):

Bill of Rights The first ten amendments to the U.S. Constitution.

1. The First Amendment guarantees the freedoms of religion, speech, and the press and the rights to assemble peaceably and to petition the government.
2. The Second Amendment guarantees the right to keep and bear arms.
3. The Third Amendment prohibits, in peacetime, the lodging of soldiers in any house without the owner's consent.
4. The Fourth Amendment prohibits unreasonable searches and seizures of persons or property.
5. The Fifth Amendment guarantees the rights to indictment by grand jury, to due process of law, and to fair payment when private property is taken for public use. The Fifth Amendment also prohibits compulsory self-incrimination and double jeopardy (trial for the same crime twice).
6. The Sixth Amendment guarantees the accused in a criminal case the right to a speedy and public trial by an impartial jury and with counsel. The accused has the right to cross-examine witnesses against him or her and to solicit testimony from witnesses in his or her favor.
7. The Seventh Amendment guarantees the right to a trial by jury in a civil case involving at least twenty dollars.[8]
8. The Eighth Amendment prohibits excessive bail and fines, as well as cruel and unusual punishment.
9. The Ninth Amendment establishes that the people have rights in addition to those specified in the Constitution.
10. The Tenth Amendment establishes that those powers neither delegated to the federal government nor denied to the states are reserved for the states.

Be Careful Although most of these rights apply to actions of the states, some of them apply only to actions of the federal government.

Limitations on Government

Realize that the Bill of Rights protects citizens against *government* actions. It does not protect persons against actions undertaken by other individuals or groups, however. For example, suppose that a government agency ordered its employees to undergo random drug testing, even though there was no cause to suspect that any employee was using illegal drugs. A court could hold that such drug testing violated the Fourth Amendment's prohibition against unreasonable searches and seizures. If a private company issued a similar order, an employee subject to the order could not look to the Fourth Amendment for protection. Other laws, however, such as a state constitutional provision relating to employee privacy rights, might apply.

As originally intended, the Bill of Rights limited only the powers of the national government. Over time, however, the Supreme Court "incorporated"

---

7. One of these proposed amendments was ratified 203 years later (in 1992) and became the Twenty-seventh Amendment to the Constitution. See Appendix B.
8. Twenty dollars was forty days' pay for the average person when the Bill of Rights was written.

Police search a crack house in Florida. Do the owners and occupants of such houses receive protection from unreasonable searches and seizures under the U.S. Constitution? Should they?

most of these rights into the protections against state actions afforded by the Fourteenth Amendment to the Constitution. That amendment, passed in 1868 after the Civil War, provides in part that "[n]o State shall . . . deprive any person of life, liberty, or property, without due process of law." Starting in 1925, the Supreme Court began to define various rights and liberties guaranteed in the national Constitution as constituting "due process of law," which was required of state governments under the Fourteenth Amendment. Today, most of the rights and liberties set forth in the Bill of Rights apply to state governments as well as to the national government.

We will look closely at several of the amendments in the above list in Chapter 8, in the context of criminal law and procedures. Here we examine two important guarantees of the First Amendment—freedom of speech and freedom of religion. These and other First Amendment freedoms (of the press, assembly, and petition) have all been applied to the states through the due process clause of the Fourteenth Amendment. As you read through the following pages, keep in mind that none of these (or other) constitutional freedoms confers an absolute right. Ultimately, it is the United States Supreme Court, as the final interpreter of the Constitution, that gives meaning to these rights and determines their boundaries.

The First Amendment—Freedom of Speech

Freedom of speech is the most prized freedom that Americans have. Indeed, it forms the basis for our democratic form of government, which could not exist if people could not express freely their political opinions and criticize government actions or policies. Because of its importance, the courts traditionally have protected this right to the fullest extent possible.

The courts also protect **symbolic speech**—gestures, movements, articles of clothing, and other forms of nonverbal expressive conduct. For example, the Supreme Court has held that the burning of the American flag to protest government policies is a constitutionally protected form of expression.[9] Similarly, the Court has ruled that the placing of a burning cross in another's front yard as a gesture of hate is protected under the First Amendment.[10] In

> **"It is by the goodness of God that in our country we have three unspeakably precious things: freedom of speech, freedom of conscience, and the prudence never to practice either of them."**
>
> Mark Twain (Samuel Clemens), 1835–1910
> (American author and humorist)

Symbolic Speech
Nonverbal expressions of beliefs. Symbolic speech, which includes gestures, movements, and articles of clothing, is given substantial protection by the courts.

9. See *Texas v. Johnson,* 491 U.S. 397, 109 S.Ct. 2533, 105 L.Ed.2d 342 (1989).
10. *R.A.V. v. City of St. Paul, Minnesota,* 505 U.S. 377, 112 S.Ct. 2538, 120 L.Ed.2d 305 (1992).

> **Remember** The First Amendment guarantee of freedom of speech only applies to *government* restrictions on speech.

the interests of curbing violence in our society, many Americans have concluded that the courts should give more weight to community interests when deciding cases involving free speech and other First Amendment freedoms. (See this chapter's *Inside the Legal Environment* for a discussion of this issue.)

CORPORATE POLITICAL SPEECH   Political speech by corporations also falls within the protection of the First Amendment. • **Example 6.3** In *First National Bank of Boston v. Bellotti,* national banking associations and business corporations sought United States Supreme Court review of a Massachusetts statute that prohibited corporations from making political contributions or expenditures that individuals were permitted to make. The Court ruled that the Massachusetts law was unconstitutional because it violated the right of corporations to freedom of speech.[11]• Similarly, the Court has held that a law forbidding a corporation from using bill inserts to express its views on controversial issues violates the First Amendment.[12] Although in 1990 a more conservative Supreme Court reversed this trend somewhat,[13] corporate political speech continues to be given significant protection under the First Amendment.

---

11. 435 U.S. 765, 98 S.Ct. 1407, 55 L.Ed.2d 707 (1978).
12. *Consolidated Edison Co. v. Public Service Commission,* 447 U.S. 530, 100 S.Ct. 2326, 65 L.Ed.2d 319 (1980).
13. See *Austin v. Michigan Chamber of Commerce,* 494 U.S. 652, 110 S.Ct. 1391, 108 L.Ed.2d 652 (1990), in which the Court upheld a state law prohibiting corporations from using general corporate funds for independent expenditures in state political campaigns.

Inside the Legal Environment

Individual Rights versus Community Interests

Traditionally, the courts have given the fullest protection possible to free speech and other First Amendment freedoms, even when the result is to allow "hate speech" or "hate crimes" that interfere with the security and welfare of a community. For example, the Minnesota Supreme Court recently concluded that even though a man rode a horse through a gay pride parade and shouted antigay slogans, he cannot be prosecuted under a Minnesota "hate crime" statute because the statute violates the First Amendment.[a] The statute criminalized "harassing conduct" that caused a victim to feel "oppressed, persecuted or intimidated." The court concluded that the statute sweeps too broadly because it also criminalizes protected "expressive activity," such as an employer who chastises a worker for tardiness or a law professor who drills a student with the Socratic method.

In a few cases, however, the courts have shown a willingness to take community concerns into consideration when deciding First Amendment cases. For example, the Supreme Court of California recently concluded that the First Amendment right to "peaceably assemble" does not outweigh the community's interests in curbing gang-related violence.[b] According to that court, gang members can be enjoined (prevented) from associating with each other under a Los Angeles "public nuisance" ordinance even though they have not been convicted of a crime.

The Supreme Court of Illinois also recently upheld a Chicago ordinance designed to prevent gangs from loitering on the streets. The ordinance stated that "[w]henever a police officer observes a person who he reasonably believes to be a criminal street gang member loitering in any public place with one or more other persons, he shall order all such persons to disperse and remove themselves from the area."[c]

For Critical Analysis: *Should ordinances prohibiting gangs from assembling on streets be permissible restraints on First Amendment freedoms?*

---

b. *People ex rel. Gallo v. Acuna,* 14 Cal.4th 1090, 929 P.2d 596, 60 Cal.Rptr.2d 277 (1997).
c. *Chicago v. Morales,* 177 Ill.2d 440, 687 N.E.2d 53, 227 Ill.Dec. 130 (1997).

---

a. *State v. Machholz,* 574 N.W.2d 415 (Minn. 1998).

COMMERCIAL SPEECH—ADVERTISING   The courts also give substantial protection to "commercial" speech, which consists of speech and communications—primarily advertising—made by business firms. The protection given to commercial speech under the First Amendment is not as extensive as that afforded to noncommercial speech, however. A state may restrict certain kinds of advertising, for example, in the interest of protecting consumers from being misled by the advertising practices. States also have a legitimate interest in the beautification of roadsides, and this interest allows states to place restraints on billboard advertising.

Generally, a restriction on commercial speech will be considered valid as long as it meets the following three criteria: (1) it must seek to implement a substantial government interest, (2) it must directly advance that interest, and (3) it must go no further than necessary to accomplish its objective. At issue in the following case was whether a government agency's decision to prohibit the inclusion of a certain illustration on beer labels unconstitutionally restricted commercial speech.

Case 6.3 ● Bad Frog Brewery, Inc. v. New York State Liquor Authority

United States Court of Appeals, Second Circuit, 1998. 134 F.3d 87. http://www.tourolaw.edu/ 2ndCircuit/January98/ 97-79490.html[a]

Historical and Cultural Setting   *Hand gestures signifying insults have been in use throughout the world for centuries. Hand gestures regarded as insults in some countries include an extended right thumb, an extended little finger, raised index and middle fingers, and gestures effected with two hands. A gesture using the extended middle finger of either hand (sometimes referred to as "giving the finger" or "flipping the bird") is generally acknowledged to convey an obscene, offensive message: a suggestion to have intercourse with one's self. This gesture is said to have been used by Diogenes (a Greek philosopher in the fourth century* B.C.E. *who was known for his disregard of social niceties) to insult Demosthenes (a Greek statesman and contemporary of Diogenes).*[b]

Background and Facts   Bad Frog Brewery, Inc., makes and sells alcoholic beverages. Some of the beverages feature labels that display a drawing of a frog making the gesture generally known as "giving the

finger." Bad Frog's authorized New York distributor, Renaissance Beer Company, applied to the New York State Liquor Authority (NYSLA) for brand label

Different labels on beer bottles are displayed. Can a brewery use any type of label on its beer? If not, what are the constraints?

---

a. This page is part of a Web site maintained by the Touro College Jacob D. Fuchsberg Law Center in Huntington, New York.

b. Betty J. Bauml and Franz H. Bauml, *Dictionary of Worldwide Gestures*, 2d ed. (Lanham, Md.: Scarecrow Press, 1997), p. 159.

(Continued)

Case 6.3 Continued

approval, as required by state law before the beer could be sold in New York. The NYSLA denied the application, in part because "the label could appear in grocery and convenience stores, with obvious exposure on the shelf to children of tender age." Bad Frog filed a suit in a federal district court against the NYSLA, asking for, among other things, an injunction against the denial of Bad Frog's application. The court granted a summary judgment in favor of the NYSLA. Bad Frog appealed to the U.S. Court of Appeals for the Second Circuit.

In the Words of the Court . . .
JON O. NEWMAN, Circuit Judge:

* * * *

* * * [T]o support its asserted power to ban Bad Frog's labels [NYSLA advances] * * * the State's interest in "protecting children from vulgar and profane advertising" * * * .

[This interest is] substantial * * * . States have a compelling interest in protecting the physical and psychological well-being of minors * * * .

* * * *

* * * NYSLA endeavors to advance the state interest in preventing exposure of children to vulgar displays by taking only the limited step of barring such displays from the labels of alcoholic beverages. In view of the wide currency of vulgar displays throughout contemporary society, including comic books targeted directly at children, barring such displays from labels for alcoholic beverages cannot realistically be expected to reduce children's exposure to such displays to any significant degree.

* * * If New York decides to make a substantial effort to insulate children from vulgar displays in some significant sphere of activity, at least with respect to materials likely to be seen by children, NYSLA's label prohibition might well be found to make a justifiable contribution to the material advancement of such an effort, but its currently isolated response to the perceived problem, applicable only to labels on a product that children cannot purchase, does not suffice. * * * [A] state must demonstrate that its commercial speech limitation is part of a substantial effort to advance a valid state interest, not merely the removal of a few grains of offensive sand from a beach of vulgarity.

* * * *

* * * Even if we were to assume that the state materially advances its asserted interest by shielding children from viewing the Bad Frog labels, it is plainly excessive to prohibit the labels from all use, including placement on bottles displayed in bars and taverns where parental supervision of children is to be expected. Moreover, to whatever extent NYSLA is concerned that children will be harmfully exposed to the Bad Frog labels when wandering without parental supervision around grocery and convenience stores where beer is sold, that concern could be less intrusively dealt with by placing restrictions on the permissible locations where the appellant's products may be displayed within such stores.

Decision and Remedy The U.S. Court of Appeals for the Second Circuit reversed the judgment of the district court and remanded the case for the entry of a judgment in favor of Bad Frog. The NYSLA's ban on the use of the labels lacked a "reasonable fit" with the state's interest in shielding minors from vulgarity, and the NYSLA did not adequately consider alternatives to the ban.

For Critical Analysis—Social Consideration *Whose interests are advanced by the banning of certain types of advertising?*

UNPROTECTED SPEECH   The United States Supreme Court has made it clear that certain types of speech will not be given any protection under the First Amendment. Speech that harms the good reputation of another, or defamatory speech (see Chapter 9), will not be protected. Speech that violates criminal laws (such as threatening speech) is not constitutionally protected. Other unprotected speech includes "fighting words," or words that are likely to incite others to respond violently.

The Supreme Court has also held that obscene speech is not protected by the First Amendment. The Court has grappled from time to time with the problem of trying to establish an objective definition of obscene speech. In a 1973 case, *Miller v. California*,[14] the Supreme Court created a test for legal obscenity, which involved a set of requirements that must be met for material to be legally obscene. Under this test, material is obscene if (1) the average person finds that it violates contemporary community standards; (2) the work taken as a whole appeals to a prurient interest in sex; (3) the work shows patently offensive sexual conduct; and (4) the work lacks serious redeeming literary, artistic, political, or scientific merit.

Because community standards vary widely, the *Miller* test has had inconsistent applications, and obscenity remains a constitutionally unsettled issue. Numerous state and federal statutes make it a crime to disseminate obscene materials, however, and such laws have often been upheld by the Supreme Court, including laws prohibiting the sale and possession of child pornography.[15]

A challenging legal issue today is how to regulate the availability of obscene materials on the Internet. In 1996, Congress enacted the Communications Decency Act in an effort to protect minors from harmful materials on the Internet. The act made it a crime to make available to minors online any "obscene or indecent" message that "depicts or describes, in terms patently offensive as measured by contemporary community standards, sexual or excretory activities or organs." The United States Supreme Court ruled that the act was unconstitutional, because of its broad restriction on speech. The Court stated that the "general, undefined terms 'indecent' and 'patently offensive' cover large amounts of nonpornographic material with serious educational or other value.[16]

Communication Decency Act

The First Amendment—Freedom of Religion

The First Amendment states that the government may neither establish any religion nor prohibit the free exercise of religious practices. The first part of this constitutional provision is referred to as the **establishment clause,** and the second part is known as the **free exercise clause.** Government action, both federal and state, must be consistent with this constitutional mandate.

THE ESTABLISHMENT CLAUSE   The establishment clause prohibits the government from establishing a state-sponsored religion, as well as from passing laws that promote (aid or endorse) religion or that show a preference for one religion over another. The establishment clause does not require a complete separation of church and state, however. On the contrary, it requires the government to accommodate religions.

Establishment Clause
The provision in the First Amendment to the Constitution that prohibits Congress from creating any law "respecting an establishment of religion."

Free Exercise Clause
The provision in the First Amendment to the Constitution that prohibits Congress from making any law "prohibiting the free exercise" of religion.

14. 413 U.S. 15, 93 S.Ct. 2607, 37 L.Ed.2d 419 (1973).
15. For example, see *Osborne v. Ohio,* 495 U.S. 103, 110 S.Ct. 1691, 109 L.Ed.2d 98 (1990).
16. *Reno v. American Civil Liberties Union,* 521 U.S. 844, 117 S.Ct. 2329, 138 L.Ed.2d 874 (1997). A further attempt by the government to regulate Internet speech, the 1998 Child Online Protection Act, met a similar fate; in 1999 a federal district court ordered that it not be implemented—see *American Civil Liberties Union v. Reno,* 31 F.Supp.2d 473 (E.D.Pa. 1999).

International Perspective

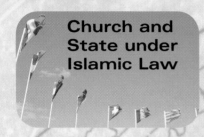

Church and State under Islamic Law

Today, Muslims constitute over one-half of the population in thirty-five nations, a significant portion of the population in twenty-one other nations, and nearly one-fourth of the global population. The Muslim faith (Islam) is one of the great religions of the world. Increasingly, American businesspersons deal with Muslims in the international marketplace. Yet Americans who would like to understand Islamic law often find it difficult to do so.

This is not really surprising, given the American legal tradition in which church and state are separate entities. Indeed, for many Americans the idea of a state-sponsored religion is regarded as somehow inherently evil. Islamic law, in contrast, does not provide for the separation of church and state—law and religion are one and the same concept. The Islamic religion controls Islamic law and regulates all public and private matters. The governments of Islamic nations, such as Iraq and Iran, are to a large extent "theocracies" that govern in accordance with religious principles.

Islamic law does not provide for the separation of church and state. Are there aspects of religion that permeate the American political and legal systems?

This lack of any separation between church and state is perhaps the most difficult aspect of Islamic law for Americans to grasp.

For Critical Analysis: *Is the union of religion and law incompatible with a democratic form of government?*

The establishment clause covers all conflicts about such matters as the legality of state and local government support for a particular religion, government aid to religious organizations and schools, the government's allowing or requiring school prayers, and the teaching of evolution versus fundamentalist theories of creation. The Supreme Court has held that to be constitutional, a government law or policy must be secular in aim, must not have the primary effect of advancing or inhibiting religions, and must not create "an excessive government entanglement with religion."[17] Generally, federal or state regulation that does not promote religion or place a significant burden on religion is constitutional even if it has some impact on religion.

● Example 6.4 "Sunday closing laws" make the performance of some commercial activities on Sunday illegal. These statutes, also known as "blue laws" (from the color of the paper on which an early Sunday law was written), have been upheld on the ground that it is a legitimate function of government to provide a day of rest. The United States Supreme Court has held that the closing laws, although originally of a religious character, have taken on the secular purpose of promoting the health and welfare of workers.[18] Even though Sunday closing laws admittedly make it easier for Christians to attend religious services, the Court has viewed this effect as an incidental, not a primary, purpose of Sunday closing laws. ●

---

17. *Lemon v. Kurtzman,* 403 U.S. 602, 91 S.Ct. 2105, 29 L.Ed.2d 745 (1971).
18. *McGowan v. Maryland,* 366 U.S. 420, 81 S.Ct. 1101, 6 L.Ed.2d 393 (1961).

Ethical Issue 6.2

Do religious displays on public property violate the establishment clause?

The thorny issue of whether religious displays on public property violate the establishment clause often arises during the holiday season. Time and again, the courts have wrestled with this issue, but it has never been resolved in a way that satisfies everyone. In a 1984 case, the United States Supreme Court decided that a city's official Christmas display, which included a crèche (Nativity scene), did not violate the establishment clause because it was just one part of a larger holiday display that featured secular symbols, such as reindeer and candy canes.[a] In a later case, the Court held that the presence of a crèche within a county courthouse violated the establishment clause because it was not in close proximity to nonreligious symbols, including a Christmas tree, which were located outside, on the building's steps. The presence of a menorah (a nine-branched candelabrum used in celebrating Chanukah) on the building's steps, however, did not violate the establishment clause because the menorah was situated in close proximity to the Christmas tree.[b] The courts continue to apply this reasoning in cases involving similar issues.

a. *Lynch v. Donnelly,* 465 U.S. 668, 104 S.Ct. 1355, 79 L.Ed.2d 604 (1984).
b. See, for example, *County of Allegheny v. American Civil Liberties Union,* 492 U.S. 573, 109 S.Ct. 3086, 106 L.Ed.2d 472 (1989).

THE FREE EXERCISE CLAUSE   The free exercise clause guarantees that a person can hold any religious belief that he or she wants; or a person can have no religious belief. When religious *practices* work against public policy and the public welfare, however, the government can act. For example, regardless of a child's or parent's religious beliefs, the government can require certain types of vaccinations. Similarly, although children of Jehovah's Witnesses are not required to say the Pledge of Allegiance at school, their parents cannot prevent them from accepting medical treatment (such as blood transfusions) if in fact their lives are in danger. Additionally, public school students can be required to study from textbooks chosen by school authorities.

For business firms, an important issue involves the accommodation that businesses must make for the religious beliefs of their employees. For example, if an employee's religion prohibits him or her from working on a certain day of the week or at a certain type of job, the employer must make a reasonable attempt to accommodate these religious requirements. Employers must reasonably accommodate an employee's religious beliefs even if the beliefs are not based on the tenets or dogma of a particular church, sect, or denomination. The only requirement is that the belief be religious in nature and sincerely held by the employee. (We will look further at this issue in Chapter 18, in the context of employment discrimination.)

Due Process and Equal Protection

Two other constitutional guarantees of great significance to Americans are mandated by the due process clauses of the Fifth and Fourteenth Amendments and the equal protection clause of the Fourteenth Amendment.

Due Process

Both the Fifth and the Fourteenth Amendments provide that no person shall be deprived "of life, liberty, or property, without due process of law." The

Due Process Clause The provisions of the Fifth and Fourteenth Amendments to the Constitution that guarantee that no person shall be deprived of life, liberty, or property without due process of law. Similar clauses are found in most state constitutions.

due process clause of each of these constitutional amendments has two aspects—procedural and substantive.

PROCEDURAL DUE PROCESS Procedural due process requires that any government decision to take life, liberty, or property must be made fairly. For example, fair procedures must be used in determining whether a person will be subjected to punishment or have some burden imposed on him or her. Fair procedure has been interpreted as requiring that the person have at least an opportunity to object to a proposed action before a fair, neutral decision maker (which need not be a judge). Thus, for example, if a driver's license is construed as a property interest, some sort of opportunity to object to its suspension or termination by the state must be provided.

SUBSTANTIVE DUE PROCESS Substantive due process focuses on the content, or substance, of legislation. If a law or other governmental action limits a *fundamental right,* it will be held to violate substantive due process unless it promotes a compelling or overriding state interest. Fundamental rights include interstate travel, privacy, voting, and all First Amendment rights. Compelling state interests could include, for example, the public's safety. • **Example 6.5** Laws designating speed limits may be upheld even though they affect interstate travel, if they are shown to reduce highway fatalities, because the state has a compelling interest in protecting the lives of its citizens.•

In situations not involving fundamental rights, a law or action does not violate substantive due process if it rationally relates to any legitimate governmental end. It is almost impossible for a law or action to fail the "rationality" test. Under this test, virtually any business regulation will be upheld as reasonable—the United States Supreme Court has sustained insurance regulations, price and wage controls, banking controls, and controls of unfair competition and trade practices against substantive due process challenges.

• **Example 6.6** If a state legislature enacted a law imposing a fifteen-year term of imprisonment without a trial on all businesspersons who appeared in their own television commercials, the law would be unconstitutional on both substantive and procedural grounds. Substantive review would invalidate the legislation because it abridges freedom of speech. Procedurally, the law is unfair because it imposes the penalty without giving the accused a chance to defend his or her actions.• The lack of procedural due process will cause a court to invalidate any statute or prior court decision. Similarly, a denial of substantive due process requires courts to overrule any state or federal law that violates the Constitution.

> "What is due process of law depends on circumstances. It varies with the subject matter and necessities of the situation."
>
> Oliver Wendell Holmes, Jr., 1841–1935
> (Associate justice of the United States Supreme Court, 1902–1932)

Equal Protection

Under the Fourteenth Amendment, a state may not "deny to any person within its jurisdiction the equal protection of the laws." The United States Supreme Court has used the due process clause of the Fifth Amendment to make the **equal protection clause** applicable to the federal government as well. Equal protection means that the government must treat similarly situated individuals in a similar manner.

Both substantive due process and equal protection require review of the substance of the law or other governmental action rather than review of the procedures used. When a law or action limits the liberty of all persons to do something, it may violate substantive due process; when a law or action limits

Equal Protection Clause The provision in the Fourteenth Amendment to the Constitution that guarantees that no state will "deny to any person within its jurisdiction the equal protection of the laws." This clause mandates that the state governments treat similarly situated individuals in a similar manner.

the liberty of some persons but not others, it may violate the equal protection clause. • **Example 6.7** If a law prohibits all persons from buying contraceptive devices, it raises a substantive due process question; if it prohibits only unmarried persons from buying the same devices, it raises an equal protection issue.•

Basically, in determining whether a law or action violates the equal protection clause, a court will consider questions similar to those previously noted as applicable in a substantive due process review. Under an equal protection inquiry, when a law or action distinguishes between or among individuals, the basis for the distinction—that is, the classification—is examined. Depending on the classification, the courts apply different levels of scrutiny, or "tests," to determine whether the law or action violates the equal protection clause.

MINIMAL SCRUTINY—THE "RATIONAL BASIS" TEST   Generally, laws regulating economic and social matters are presumed to be valid and are subject to only minimal scrutiny. A classification will be considered valid if there is any conceivable "rational basis" on which the classification might relate to any legitimate government interest. It is almost impossible for a law or action to fail the rational basis test.

• **Example 6.8** A city ordinance that in effect prohibits all pushcart vendors except a specific few from operating in a particular area of the city will be upheld if the city proffers a rational basis—perhaps regulation and reduction of traffic in the particular area—for the ordinance. In contrast, a law that provides unemployment benefits only to people over six feet tall would violate the guarantee of equal protection. There is no rational basis for determining the distribution of unemployment compensation on the basis of height. Such a distinction could not further any legitimate government objective.•

In the following case, the court applied the rational basis test to consider the constitutionality of a government-imposed dress code for cab drivers.

Case 6.4 ● Bah v. City of Atlanta

United States Court of Appeals, Eleventh Circuit, 1997.
103 F.3d 964.
http://www.law.emory.edu/
11circuit/jan97/96-8095.
opa.html[a]

Historical and Social Setting *In the first third of the twentieth century, dress codes were imposed in a variety of occupations. When particular clothing was not expressly required, there were social norms that dictated appropriate dress. Suits were often considered proper attire for men, for example, even in casual situations. After World War II, men began to stop wearing hats. This started a trend toward more casual dress. In the 1960s, the trend accelerated, with an explosion of flamboyant, individual styles of dress and casual clothes, such as denim. By the 1990s, the di-*

verse cultural background of Americans was influencing this fashion mix.

Background and Facts The Atlanta City Council adopted a dress code for cab drivers that required them, while driving a cab, to wear "shoes which entirely cover the foot (no sandals) and dark pants to ankle length or dark skirt or dress and solid white or light blue shirt or solid white or light blue blouse with sleeves and folded collar. * * * If a hat is worn, it shall be a base-ball style cap with an Atlanta or taxicab theme."[b] Mohamed Bah, a cab driver, was cited for violating the code and filed a suit in a federal district court against the city. Bah contended in part that the code violated the equal protection clause and asked the court to enjoin its enforcement. The city offered several reasons for the

a. This is a page within an online library of court decisions maintained by the Hugh F. Macmillan Law Library at Emory University School of Law in Atlanta, Georgia.

b. Atlanta Code of Ordinances Section 14-8005(d)(2). The Atlanta Code of Ordinances was renumbered in 1996. This is the prior number for this section, which is the number that the court cited in this case.

(Continued)

Case 6.4 Continued

code, including "public safety," "identification of gypsy taxicab drivers," and "promoting a safe image." The court issued the injunction. The city appealed to the U.S. Court of Appeals for the Eleventh Circuit.

In the Words of the Court . . .
PER CURIAM [by the whole court]:

* * * *

* * * Bah does not contend * * * that the dress code burdens a fundamental right or targets a suspect class. Both Bah and the City agree that rational basis is the appropriate level of scrutiny.

[Other courts have stated that in] a rational basis analysis, the legislative enactment carries a "strong presumption of validity." Review of enactments must be a "paradigm of judicial restraint." "[T]hose attacking the rationality of the legislative classification have the burden to negate every conceivable basis which might support it." * * *

Following these decisional directives, we readily conclude that the district court erred in finding that the dress code is not rationally related to a legitimate government interest. * * *

[E]ven if the district court was correct in rejecting the two reasons it discussed—public safety and identification of gypsy taxicab drivers—there is another reason for the dress code that is rationally related to a legitimate government interest. As the City explained in the district court and this Court, the dress code is rationally related to its legitimate interest in promoting a safe image. Drivers of vehicles for hire, particularly taxicab drivers, are often among the first people that out-of-town visitors encounter. Such visitors often find themselves getting into a vehicle for hire driven by a total stranger, sometimes at night and sometimes while they are alone. It is in the City's interest to promote a safe appearance and image, and a rational way to do that is by prescribing that its self-styled "ambassadors" wear innocuous, conventional, relatively uniform clothing.

Decision and Remedy   The U.S. Court of Appeals for the Eleventh Circuit reversed the decision of the lower court and remanded the case. The appellate court held that the dress code was rationally related to a legitimate government objective and thus did not violate the equal protection clause.

For Critical Analysis—Social Consideration   *Would it be constitutional to impose a dress code on others who are licensed by the city and who deal with out-of-town visitors—food servers, bellhops, and outdoor vendors, for example?*

INTERMEDIATE SCRUTINY   A harder standard to meet, that of "intermediate scrutiny," is applied in cases involving discrimination based on gender or legitimacy. Laws using these classifications must be substantially related to important government objectives. • **Example 6.9** An important government objective is preventing illegitimate teenage pregnancies. Because males and females are not similarly situated in this circumstance—only females can become pregnant—a law that punishes men but not women for statutory rape will be upheld. A state law requiring illegitimate children to bring paternity suits within six years of their births, however, will be struck down if legitimate children are allowed to seek support from their parents at any time.•

STRICT SCRUTINY   The most difficult standard to meet is that of "strict scrutiny." Very few cases survive strict-scrutiny analysis. Strict scrutiny is applied when a law or action inhibits some persons' exercise of a fundamental right or is based on a suspect trait (such as race, national origin, or citizenship status). Strict scrutiny means that the court will examine the law or action involved very closely, and the law or action will be allowed to stand only if it is *necessary to promote a compelling state interest.*

• **Example 6.10** Suppose that a city gives preference to minority applicants in awarding construction contracts. Because the policy is based on suspect traits (race and national origin), it will violate the equal protection clause *unless* it is necessary to promote a compelling state interest. Courts have often held that states have a compelling interest in remedying past unconstitutional or illegal discrimination. The Supreme Court has declared, however, that such programs must be narrowly tailored. In other words, the city must identify the past unconstitutional or illegal discrimination against minority construction firms that it is attempting to correct, go no further than necessary to remedy the problem, and change or drop its program once it has succeeded in correcting the problem.[19] •

Privacy Rights

Today, virtually all institutions and professionals with which an individual has dealings—including schools, physicians and dentists, insurance companies, mail-order houses, firms engaged in online marketing, banking institutions, credit-card companies, and mortgage firms—obtain information about that individual, store it in their computer files, and, in many cases, sell it for a price. In addition, numerous government agencies, such as the Census Bureau, the Social Security Administration, and the Internal Revenue Service, collect and store data concerning individuals' incomes, expenses, marital status, and other personal history and habits. Any time an individual applies for a driver's license, a credit card, or even telephone service, information concerning that individual is gathered and stored. Frequently, this personal information finds its way to credit bureaus, online and other marketing departments and firms, or other organizations without the permission or even the knowledge of the individuals involved. An area of pressing concern today is how to secure privacy rights in an online world.

Although there is no specific guarantee of a right to privacy in the Constitution, such a right has been derived from guarantees found in the First, Third, Fourth, Fifth, and Ninth Amendments. Furthermore, a personal right to privacy has been held to be so fundamental as to be applicable at both the state and the federal levels. Additionally, invasion of another's privacy is a civil wrong (see Chapter 9), and over the last several decades legislation has been passed at the federal level to protect the privacy of individuals in several areas of concern. In the business context, issues of privacy often arise in the employment context, a topic we will cover in detail in Chapter 17.

---

19. *Adarand Constructors, Inc. v. Peña,* 515 U.S. 200, 115 S.Ct. 2097, 132 L.Ed.2d 158 (1995).

Key Terms

Bill of Rights 162	equal protection clause 170	police powers 158
checks and balances 154	establishment clause 167	preemption 160
commerce clause 155	federal form of government 153	supremacy clause 160
due process clause 170	free exercise clause 167	symbolic speech 163

Chapter Summary • Constitutional Authority to Regulate Business

The Constitutional Powers of Government (See pages 153–154.)	The U.S. Constitution established a federal form of government, in which government powers are shared by the national government and the state governments. At the national level, government powers are divided among the legislative, executive, and judicial branches.
The Commerce Clause (See pages 154–160.)	1. **The breadth of the commerce clause**—The commerce clause expressly permits Congress to regulate commerce. Over time, courts expansively interpreted this clause, and today the commerce power authorizes the national government, at least theoretically, to regulate every commercial enterprise in the United States. 2. **The regulatory powers of the states**—Under their police powers, state governments may regulate private activities to protect or promote the public order, health, safety, morals, and general welfare. If state regulations substantially interfere with interstate commerce, they will be held to violate the commerce clause of the U.S. Constitution.
The Supremacy Clause (See page 160.)	The U.S. Constitution provides that the Constitution, laws, and treaties of the United States are "the supreme Law of the Land." Whenever a state law directly conflicts with a federal law, the state law is rendered invalid.
The Taxing and Spending Powers (See pages 160–161.)	The U.S. Constitution gives Congress the power to impose uniform taxes throughout the United States and to spend revenues accumulated from the taxing power. Congress can spend revenues to promote any objective it deems worthwhile, so long as it does not violate the Bill of Rights.
Business and the Bill of Rights (See pages 162–169.)	The Bill of Rights, which consists of the first ten amendments to the U.S. Constitution, was adopted in 1791 and embodies a series of protections for individuals—and in some cases, business entities—against various types of interference by the federal government. Freedoms guaranteed by the First Amendment that affect businesses include the following: 1. **Freedom of speech**—Speech, including symbolic speech, is given the fullest possible protection by the courts. Corporate political speech and commercial speech also receive substantial protection under the First Amendment. Certain types of speech, such as defamatory speech and lewd or obscene speech, are not protected under the First Amendment. 2. **Freedom of religion**—Under the First Amendment, the government may neither establish any religion (the establishment clause) nor prohibit the free exercise of religion (the free exercise clause).
Due Process and Equal Protection (See pages 169–173.)	1. **Due process**—Both the Fifth and the Fourteenth Amendments provide that no person shall be deprived of "life, liberty, or property, without due process of law." Procedural due process requires that any government decision to take life, liberty, or property must be made fairly, using fair procedures. Substantive due process focuses on the content of legislation. Generally, a law that is not compatible with the Constitution violates substantive due process unless the law promotes a compelling state interest, such as public safety. 2. **Equal protection**—Under the Fourteenth Amendment, a state may not "deny to any person within its jurisdiction the equal protection of the laws." A law or action that limits the liberty of some persons but not others may violate the equal protection clause. Such a law may be deemed valid, however, if there is a rational basis for the discriminatory treatment of a given group or if the law substantially relates to an important government objective.

Chapter Summary • Constitutional Authority to Regulate Business

Privacy Rights
(See page 173.)

There is no specific guarantee of a right to privacy in the Constitution, but such a right has been derived from guarantees found in other constitutional amendments.

For Review

1. What is the basic structure of the U.S. government?

2. What constitutional clause gives the federal government the power to regulate commercial activities among the various states?

3. What constitutional clause allows laws enacted by the federal government to take priority over conflicting state laws?

4. What is the Bill of Rights? What freedoms are guaranteed by the First Amendment?

5. Where in the Constitution can the due process clause be found?

Questions and Case Problems

6–1. Government Powers. The framers of the Constitution feared the twin evils of tyranny and anarchy. Discuss how specific provisions of the Constitution and the Bill of Rights reflect these fears and protect against both of these extremes.

6–2. Commercial Speech. A mayoral election is about to be held in a large U.S. city. One of the candidates is Luis Delgado, and his campaign supporters wish to post campaign signs on lampposts and utility posts throughout the city. A city ordinance, however, prohibits the posting of any signs on public property. Delgado's supporters contend that the city ordinance is unconstitutional, because it violates their rights to free speech. What factors might a court consider in determining the constitutionality of this ordinance?

6–3. Commerce Clause. Suppose that Georgia enacts a law requiring the use of contoured rear-fender mudguards on trucks and trailers operating within its state lines. The statute further makes it illegal for trucks and trailers to use straight mudguards. In thirty-five other states, straight mudguards are legal. Moreover, in the neighboring state of Florida, straight mudguards are explicitly required by law. There is some evidence suggesting that contoured mudguards might be a little safer than straight mudguards. Discuss whether this Georgia statute would violate the commerce clause of the U.S. Constitution.

6–4. Freedom of Religion. A business has a backlog of orders, and to meet its deadlines, management decides to run the firm seven days a week, eight hours a day. One of the employees, Marjorie Tollens, refuses to work on Saturday on religious grounds. Her refusal to

work means that the firm may not meet its production deadlines and may therefore suffer a loss of future business. The firm fires Tollens and replaces her with an employee who is willing to work seven days a week. Tollens claims that her employer, in terminating her employment, violated her constitutional right to the free exercise of her religion. Do you agree? Why or why not?

6–5. Equal Protection. In 1988, the Nebraska legislature enacted a statute that required any motorcycle operator or passenger on Nebraska's highways to wear a protective helmet. Eugene Robotham, a licensed motorcycle operator, sued the state of Nebraska to block enforcement of the law. Robotham asserted, among other things, that the statute violated the equal protection clause, because it placed requirements on motorcyclists that were not imposed on other motorists. Will the court agree with Robotham that the law violates the equal protection clause? Why or why not? [*Robotham v. State*, 241 Neb. 379, 488 N.W.2d 533 (1992)]

6–6. Commerce Clause. Taylor owned a bait business in Maine and arranged to have live baitfish imported into the state. The importation of the baitfish violated a Maine statute. Taylor was charged with violating a federal statute that makes it a federal crime to transport fish in interstate commerce in violation of state law. Taylor moved to dismiss the charges on the ground that the Maine statute unconstitutionally burdened interstate commerce. Maine intervened to defend the validity of its statute, arguing that the law legitimately protected the state's fisheries from parasites and nonnative species that might be included in shipments of live baitfish. Were Maine's interests in protecting its fisheries from parasites and nonnative species sufficient to justify the burden placed on interstate commerce by the Maine statute? Discuss. [*Maine v. Taylor*, 477 U.S. 131, 106 S.Ct. 2440, 91 L.Ed.2d 110 (1986)]

6–7. Freedom of Religion. Isaiah Brown was the director of the information services department for Polk County, Iowa. During department meetings in his office, he allowed occasional prayers and, in addressing one meeting, referred to Bible passages related to sloth and "work ethics." There was no apparent disruption of the work routine, but the county administrator reprimanded Brown. Later, the administrator ordered Brown to remove from his office all items with a religious connotation. Brown sued the county, alleging that the reprimand and the order violated, among other things, the free exercise clause of the First Amendment. Could the county be held liable for violating Brown's constitutional rights? Discuss. [*Brown v. Polk County, Iowa*, 61 F.3d 650 (8th Cir. 1995)]

6–8. Equal Protection. With the objectives of preventing crime, maintaining property values, and preserving the quality of urban life, New York City enacted an ordinance to regulate the locations of commercial establishments that featured adult entertainment. The ordinance expressly applied to female, but not male, topless entertainment. Adele Buzzetti owned the Cozy Cabin, a New York City cabaret, that featured female topless dancers. Buzzetti and an anonymous dancer filed a suit in a federal district court against the city, asking the court to block the enforcement of the ordinance. The plaintiffs argued in part that the ordinance violated the equal protection clause. Under the equal protection clause, what standard applies to the court's consideration of this ordinance? Under this test, how should the court rule? Why? [*Buzzetti v. City of New York*, 140 F.3d 134 (2d Cir. 1998)]

6–9. Free Speech. The City of Tacoma, Washington, enacted an ordinance that prohibited the playing of car sound systems at a volume that would be "audible" at a distance greater than fifty feet. Dwight Holland was arrested and convicted for violating the ordinance. The conviction was later dismissed but Holland filed a civil suit in a Washington state court against the city. He claimed in part that the ordinance violated his freedom of speech under the First Amendment. On what basis might the court conclude that this ordinance is constitutional? (Hint: In playing a sound system, was Holland actually expressing himself?) [*Holland v. City of Tacoma*, 90 Wash.App. 533, 954 P.2d 290 (1998)]

6–10. Free Speech. The members of Greater New Orleans Broadcasting Association, Inc., operate radio and television stations in New Orleans. They wanted to broadcast ads for private, for-profit casinos that are legal in Louisiana. A federal statute banned casino advertising, but other federal statutes exempted ads for tribal, government, nonprofit, and "occasional

and ancillary" commercial casinos. The association filed a suit in a federal district court against the federal government, asking the court to hold that the statute, as it applied to their ads, violated the First Amendment. The government argued that the ban should be upheld, because "[u]nder appropriate conditions, some broadcast signals from Louisiana broadcasting stations may be heard in neighboring states including Texas and Arkansas," where private casino gambling is unlawful. What is the test for whether a regulation of commercial speech violates the First Amendment? How might it apply in this case? How should the court rule? [*Greater New Orleans Broadcasting Association, Inc. v. United States*, 527 U.S. 173, 119 S.Ct. 1923, 144 L.Ed.2d 161 (1999)]

A Question of Ethics and Social Responsibility

6–11. Carol Elewski, a resident of Syracuse, New York, brought an action to enjoin (prevent) the city from displaying a crèche in a city park during the holidays. The crèche, accompanied by a religious banner, was situated at the foot of a decorated evergreen tree and surrounded by sawhorse barricades containing the names of the mayor and a municipal agency. The downtown merchants supported the display to attract shoppers. There were secular decorations in neighboring areas of the park, and a menorah was displayed in another city park located a block away. In view of these facts, consider the following questions. [*Elewski v. City of Syracuse*, 123 F.3d 51 (2d Cir. 1997)]

1. Does the display of the crèche and the religious banner on city property violate the establishment clause? How might the precedents established by the Supreme Court on this issue (see *Ethical Issue 6.2*) apply to this set of facts?
2. Are the crèche and the menorah in close enough proximity to be considered part of one "display"?
3. How can a city avoid the appearance of endorsing one religion over another if it includes symbols from some religions—but not all religions—in its seasonal displays?

Case Briefing Assignment

6–12. Examine Case A.2 [*Austin v. Berryman*, 878 F.2d 786 (4th Cir. 1989)] in Appendix A. The case has been excerpted there in great detail. Review and then brief the case, making sure that you include answers to the following questions in your brief.

1. Who were the plaintiff and defendant in this action?
2. Why did Austin claim that she had been forced to leave her job?

3. Why was Austin refused state unemployment benefits?
4. Did the state's refusal to give Austin unemployment compensation violate her rights under the free exercise clause of the First Amendment?
5. What logic or reasoning did the court employ in arriving at its conclusion?

For Critical Analysis

6–13. In recent years, many people have criticized the film and entertainment industries for promoting violence by exposing the American public, and particularly American youth, to extremely violent films and song lyrics. Do you think that the right to free speech can (or should) be traded off to reduce violence in America?

Interacting with the Internet

■ For updated links to resources available on the Web, as well as a variety of other materials, visit this text's Web site at

http://leet.westbuslaw.com

■ For an online version of the Constitution that provides hypertext links to amendments and other changes, go to

http://www.law.cornell.edu/ constitution/constitution. overview.html

■ An ongoing debate in the United States is whether the national government exercises too much regulatory control over intrastate affairs. To find current articles on this topic, go to

http://www.vote-smart.org/ issues/FEDERALISM_STATES_RIGHTS

■ For discussions of current issues involving the rights and liberties contained in the Bill of Rights, go to the Web site of the American Civil Liberties Union at

http://www.aclu.org

■ Summaries and the full texts of constitutional law decisions by the United States Supreme Court are included at the following site:

http://oyez.nwu.edu

Online Legal Research Exercises

Go to **http://leet.west buslaw.com**, the Web site that accompanies this text. Select "Interactive Study Center," and then click on "Chapter 6." There you will find the following Internet research exercises that you can perform to learn more about free speech issues:

Activity 6–1: Flag Burning
Activity 6–2: Begging and the First Amendment

Before the Test

Go to **http://leet.westbus law.com**, the Web site that accompanies this text. Select "Interactive Quizzes." You will find a number of interactive questions relating to this chapter.

<table>
<tr><td>

chapter

7

</td><td>

Powers and Functions of Administrative Agencies

</td></tr>
</table>

---

chapter objectives

After reading this chapter, you should be able to:

1. Explain the rulemaking function of administrative agencies.

2. Describe the investigation and adjudication functions of agencies.

3. Identify how agency authority is held in check.

4. List laws that make agencies more accountable to the public.

5. Discuss the relation between state and federal agencies.

As the opening quotation suggests, government agencies established to administer the law have a tremendous impact on the day-to-day operation of the government and the economy. In the early years of our nation, the United States had a relatively simple, nonindustrial economy that required little regulation. Because administrative agencies often create and enforce such regulations, there were relatively few such agencies. Today, however, there are rules covering virtually every aspect of a business's operation. Consequently, agencies have multiplied. • Example 7.1 At the federal level, the Securities and Exchange Commission regulates the firm's capital structure and financing, as well as its financial reporting. The National Labor Relations Board oversees relations between the firm and any unions with which it may deal. The Equal Employment Opportunity Commission also regulates employment relationships. The Environmental Protection Agency and the Occupational Safety and Health Administration affect the way the firm manufactures its products. The Federal Trade Commission affects the way it markets these products.•

Added to this layer of federal regulation is a second layer of state regulation that, when not preempted by federal legislation, may cover many of the same activities or regulate independently those activities not covered by federal regulation. Finally, agency regulations at the county or municipal level also affect certain types of business activities. (Increasingly, administrative agencies at all levels of government are delivering services via the Internet—see this chapter's *Legal E-nvironment* on the next page for a discussion of this development.)

Administrative agencies issue rules, orders, and decisions. These regulations make up the body of *administrative law.* You were introduced briefly to some of the main principles of administrative law in Chapter 1. In the following pages, these principles are presented in much greater detail.

Agency Creation and Powers

Congress creates federal administrative agencies. Because Congress cannot possibly oversee the actual implementation of all the laws it enacts, it must delegate such tasks to others, particularly when the issues relate to highly technical areas, such as air and water pollution. By delegating some of its authority to make and implement laws, Congress can monitor indirectly a particular area in which it has passed legislation without becoming bogged down in the details relating to enforcement—details that are often best left to specialists.

Enabling Legislation

To create an administrative agency, Congress passes **enabling legislation,** which specifies the name, purposes, functions, and powers of the agency being created. Federal administrative agencies may exercise only those powers that Congress has delegated to them in enabling legislation. Through similar enabling acts, state legislatures create state administrative agencies.

For example, Congress created the Federal Trade Commission (FTC) in the Federal Trade Commission Act of 1914.[1] The act prohibits unfair and deceptive trade practices. It also describes the procedures that the agency must follow to charge persons or organizations with violations of the act, and it

> "[P]erhaps more values today are affected by [administrative] decisions than by those of all the courts."
>
> Robert H. Jackson, 1892–1954
> (Associate justice of the United States Supreme Court, 1941–1954)

Enabling Legislation
Statutes enacted by Congress that authorize the creation of an administrative agency and specify the name, composition, and powers of the agency being created.

---

1. 15 U.S.C. Sections 41–58.

Legal *e*-nvironment

Government via the Web

Most large cities and all of the agencies of the federal government offer information and assistance via the Internet. Today, most local governments have Web sites on which they list public meeting schedules, post public documents, and offer other services to their citizens. Americans can also access virtually all state and national government agencies online. Among other things, they can find information on state and national parks, the rules for naturalization and immigration, and decisions rendered by state and federal courts.

EZ Government on the Web

Due to security issues and the high level of technology needed, far fewer interactive applications are available to citizens at government agency Web sites than can be found in the world of e-commerce. Nevertheless, their number is growing. Increasingly, state and local government agencies are allowing citizens to use the Internet for a variety of transactions, such as paying for parking tickets or renewing driver's licenses. In Riverside, California, tax bills are payable through the Internet. In Atlanta, citizens can pay parking tickets, renew their driver's licenses, and obtain building permits by going online. In Maryland, some professionals can renew their licenses by visiting a state government site.

In 2000, the federal government launched an interactive Web site (Pay.gov) that will allow Americans to conduct any number of transactions online. These transactions will include applying for passports, paying off student loans, and filing forms with the Immigration and Naturalization Service.

Online Government Is Less Costly

Today, businesses and individuals do about $600 billion in transactions with federal, state, and local governments each year. A tiny fraction—less than 1 percent—of these funds changes hands over the Internet. That amount will increase sharply over the next decade, providing a number of benefits to taxpayers. Besides being more convenient, a "virtual government" would be less costly. The state of Maryland, for example, saved $1.6 million when 40 percent of its 250,000 professionals renewed their licenses online. Arizona saves $5 every time a citizen renews her or his vehicle registration via the Internet. Eventually, those savings are passed on to the taxpayer.

For Critical Analysis: *Which government agencies, at all levels of government, are most likely to continue to render services in person? Which are most likely to conduct their functions online?*

---

provides for judicial review of agency orders. The act grants the FTC the power to

- Create "rules and regulations for the purpose of carrying out the Act."
- Conduct investigations of business practices.
- Obtain reports from interstate corporations concerning their business practices.
- Investigate possible violations of federal antitrust statutes.[2]
- Publish findings of its investigations.
- Recommend new legislation.
- Hold trial-like hearings to resolve certain kinds of trade disputes that involve FTC regulations or federal antitrust laws.

The commission that heads the FTC is composed of five members, each of whom the president appoints, with the advice and consent of the Senate, for a term of seven years. The president designates one of the commissioners to be chairperson. Various offices and bureaus of the FTC undertake different ad-

---

2. The FTC shares this task with the Antitrust Division of the U.S. Department of Justice.

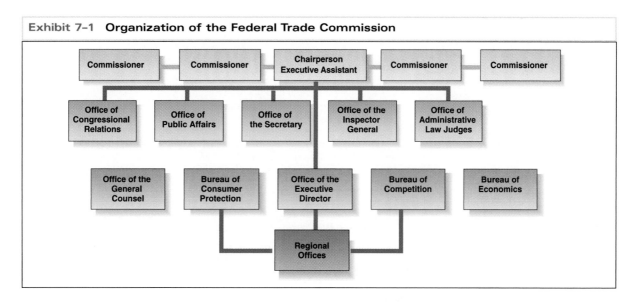

Exhibit 7-1 Organization of the Federal Trade Commission

ministrative activities for the agency. The organization of the FTC is illustrated in Exhibit 7–1 above.

Types of Agencies

There are two basic types of administrative agencies: executive agencies and independent regulatory agencies. Federal **executive agencies** include the cabinet departments of the executive branch, which were formed to assist the president in carrying out executive functions, and the subagencies within the cabinet departments. The Occupational Safety and Health Administration, for example, is a subagency within the Department of Labor. Exhibit 7–2 on page 182 lists the cabinet departments and their most important subagencies.

All administrative agencies are part of the executive branch of government, but **independent regulatory agencies** are outside the major executive departments. The Federal Trade Commission and the Securities and Exchange Commission are examples of independent regulatory agencies. These and other selected independent regulatory agencies, as well as their principal functions, are listed in Exhibit 7–3 on page 183.

The significant difference between the two types of agencies lies in the accountability of the regulators. Agencies that are considered part of the executive branch are subject to the authority of the president, who has the power to appoint and remove federal officers. In theory, this power is less pronounced in regard to independent agencies, whose officers serve for fixed terms and cannot be removed without just cause. In practice, however, the president's power to exert influence over independent agencies is often considerable.

Agency Powers and the Constitution

Administrative agencies occupy an unusual niche in the American legal scheme, because they exercise powers that are normally divided among the three branches of government. • **Example 7.2** In the FTC's enabling legislation discussed above, the FTC's grant of power incorporates functions associated with the legislature (rulemaking), the executive branch (enforcement of the rules), and the courts (adjudication, or the formal resolution of disputes).•

Executive Agency An administrative agency that is either a cabinet department or a subagency within a cabinet department. Executive agencies fall under the authority of the president, who has the power to appoint and remove federal officers.

Independent Regulatory Agency An administrative agency that is not considered part of the government's executive branch and is not subject to the authority of the president. Agency officials cannot be removed without cause.

Exhibit 7–2 **Executive Departments and Important Subagencies**

DEPARTMENT	DATE FORMED	IMPORTANT SUBAGENCIES
State	1789	Passport Office; Bureau of Diplomatic Security; Foreign Service; Bureau of Human Rights and Humanitarian Affairs; Bureau of Consular Affairs; Bureau of Intelligence and Research
Treasury	1789	Internal Revenue Service; Bureau of Alcohol, Tobacco, and Firearms; U.S. Secret Service; U.S. Mint; Customs Service
Interior	1849	U.S. Fish and Wildlife Service; National Park Service; Bureau of Indian Affairs; Bureau of Land Management
Justice	1870[a]	Federal Bureau of Investigation; Drug Enforcement Administration; Bureau of Prisons; U.S. Marshals Service; Immigration and Naturalization Service
Agriculture	1889	Soil Conservation Service; Agricultural Research Service; Food Safety and Inspection Service; Federal Crop Insurance Corporation; Farmers Home Administration
Commerce	1913[b]	Bureau of the Census; Bureau of Economic Analysis; Minority Business Development Agency; Patent and Trademark Office; National Oceanic and Atmospheric Administration; U.S. Travel and Tourism Administration
Labor	1913[b]	Occupational Safety and Health Administration; Bureau of Labor Statistics; Employment Standards Administration; Office of Labor-Management Standards; Employment and Training Administration
Defense	1949[c]	National Guard; Defense Investigative Service; National Security Agency; Joint Chiefs of Staff; Departments of the Air Force, Navy, Army
Housing and Urban Development	1965	Assistant Secretary for Community Planning and Development; Government National Mortgage Association; Assistant Secretary for Housing—Federal Housing Commissioner; Assistant Secretary for Fair Housing and Equal Opportunity
Transportation	1967	Federal Aviation Administration; Federal Highway Administration; National Highway Traffic Safety Administration; U.S. Coast Guard; Federal Transit Administration
Energy	1977	Office of Civilian Radioactive Waste Management; Bonneville Power Administration; Office of Nuclear Energy; Energy Information Administration; Office of Conservation and Renewable Energy
Health and Human Services	1980[d]	Food and Drug Administration; Health Care Financing Administration; Public Health Service
Education	1980[e]	Office of Special Education and Rehabilitation Services; Office of Elementary and Secondary Education; Office of Postsecondary Education; Office of Vocational and Adult Education
Veterans' Affairs	1989	Veterans Health Administration; Veterans Benefits Administration; National Cemetery System

a. Formed from the Office of the Attorney General (created in 1789).
b. Formed from the Department of Commerce and Labor (created in 1903).
c. Formed from the Department of War (created in 1789) and the Department of the Navy (created in 1798).
d. Formed from the Department of Health, Education, and Welfare (created in 1953).
e. Formed from the Department of Health, Education, and Welfare (created in 1953).

Exhibit 7–3 Selected Independent Regulatory Agencies

NAME	DATE FORMED	PRINCIPAL DUTIES
Federal Reserve System Board of Governors (Fed)	1913	Determines policy with respect to interest rates, credit availability, and the money supply.
Federal Trade Commission (FTC)	1914	Prevents businesses from engaging in unfair trade practices; stops the formation of monopolies in the business sector; protects consumer rights.
Securities and Exchange Commission (SEC)	1934	Regulates the nation's stock exchanges, in which shares of stock are bought and sold; enforces the securities laws, which require full disclosure of the financial profiles of companies that wish to sell stock and bonds to the public.
Federal Communications Commission (FCC)	1934	Regulates all communications by telegraph, cable, telephone, radio, satellite, and television.
National Labor Relations Board (NLRB)	1935	Protects employees' rights to join unions and bargain collectively with employers; attempts to prevent unfair labor practices by both employers and unions.
Equal Employment Opportunity Commission (EEOC)	1964	Works to eliminate discrimination in employment based on religion, gender, race, color, disability, national origin, or age; investigates claims of discrimination.
Environmental Protection Agency (EPA)	1970	Undertakes programs aimed at reducing air and water pollution; works with state and local agencies to help fight environmental hazards. (It has been suggested recently that its status be elevated to that of a department.)
Nuclear Regulatory Commission (NRC)	1975	Ensures that electricity-generating nuclear reactors in the United States are built and operated safely; regularly inspects operations of such reactors.

The constitutional principle of *checks and balances* allows each branch of government to act as a check on the actions of the other two branches. Furthermore, the Constitution authorizes only the legislative branch to create laws. Yet administrative agencies, to which the Constitution does not specifically refer, make **legislative rules,** or *substantive rules,* that are as legally binding as laws that Congress passes.

Courts generally hold that Article I of the U.S. Constitution authorizes delegating such powers to administrative agencies. In fact, courts generally hold that Article I is the basis for all administrative law. Section 1 of that article grants all legislative powers to Congress and requires Congress to oversee the implementation of all laws. Article I, Section 8, gives Congress the power to make all laws necessary for executing its specified powers. The courts interpret these passages, under what is known as the **delegation doctrine,** as granting Congress the power to establish administrative agencies that can create rules for implementing those laws.

The three branches of government exercise certain controls over agency powers and functions, as is discussed later in this chapter, but in many ways administrative agencies function independently. For this reason, administrative agencies, which constitute the **bureaucracy,** are sometimes referred to as the "fourth branch" of the American government.

Legislative Rule An administrative agency rule that carries the same weight as a congressionally enacted statute.

Delegation Doctrine A doctrine based on Article I, Section 8, of the U.S. Constitution, which has been construed to allow Congress to delegate some of its power to make and implement laws to administrative agencies.

Bureaucracy The organizational structure, consisting of government bureaus and agencies, through which the government implements and enforces the laws.

Administrative Process

The three functions mentioned previously—rulemaking, enforcement, and adjudication—make up what is called the administrative process. **Administrative process** involves the administration of law by administrative agencies, in contrast to **judicial process,** which involves the administration of law by the courts.

The Administrative Procedure Act (APA) of 1946[3] imposes procedural requirements that all federal agencies must follow in their rulemaking, adjudication, and other functions. The APA is such an integral part of the administrative process that its application will be examined as we go through the basic functions carried out by administrative agencies.

Rulemaking

A major function of an administrative agency is **rulemaking**—the formulation of new regulations. In an agency's enabling legislation, Congress confers the agency's power to make rules. • **Example 7.3** The Occupational Safety and Health Act of 1970 authorized the Occupational Health and Safety Administration (OSHA) to develop and issue rules governing safety in the workplace. In 1991, OSHA deemed it in the public interest to issue a new rule regulating the health-care industry to prevent the spread of such diseases as acquired immune deficiency syndrome (AIDS). OSHA created a rule specifying various standards—on how contaminated instruments should be handled, for example—with which employers in that industry must comply.•

In formulating rules, administrative agencies follow specific rulemaking procedures required under the APA. We look here at the most common rulemaking procedure, called **notice-and-comment rulemaking.** This procedure involves three basic steps: notice of the proposed rulemaking, a comment period, and the final rule.

NOTICE OF THE PROPOSED RULEMAKING   When a federal agency decides to create a new rule, the agency publishes a notice of the proposed rulemaking proceedings in the *Federal Register,* a daily publication of the executive branch that prints government orders, rules, and regulations. The notice states where and when the proceedings will be held, the agency's legal authority for making the rule (usually its enabling legislation), and the terms or subject matter of the proposed rule.

COMMENT PERIOD   Following the publication of the notice of the proposed rulemaking proceedings, the agency must allow ample time for persons to comment in writing on the proposed rule. The purpose of this comment period is to give interested parties the opportunity to express their views on the proposed rule in an effort to influence agency policy. The comments may be in writing or, if a hearing is held, may be given orally. The agency need not respond to all comments, but it must respond to any significant comments that bear directly on the proposed rule. The agency responds by either modifying its final rule or explaining, in a statement accompanying the final rule, why it did not make any changes. In some circumstances, particularly when the procedure being used in a specific instance is less formal, an agency may accept

---

3. 5 U.S.C. Sections 551–706.

Administrative Process The procedure used by administrative agencies in the administration of law.

Judicial Process The procedures relating to, or connected with, the administration of justice through the judicial system.

Rulemaking The actions undertaken by administrative agencies when formally adopting new regulations or amending old ones. Under the Administrative Procedure Act, rulemaking includes notifying the public of proposed rules or changes and receiving and considering the public's comments.

Notice-and-Comment Rulemaking A procedure in agency rulemaking that requires (1) notice, (2) opportunity for comment, and (3) a published draft of the final rule.

"In some respects matters of procedure constitute the very essence of ordered liberty under the Constitution."

Wiley B. Rutledge, 1894–1949
(Associate justice of the United States Supreme Court, 1943–1949)

comments after the comment period is closed. The agency should summarize these *ex parte* comments for possible review.

THE FINAL RULE   After the agency reviews the comments, it drafts the final rule and publishes it in the *Federal Register.* The final rule is later compiled with the rules and regulations of other federal administrative agencies in the *Code of Federal Regulations* (C.F.R.). Final rules have binding legal effect unless the courts later overturn them.

In the following case, AT&T Corporation and other established local telephone service providers asked the United States Supreme Court to overturn a Federal Communications Commission (FCC) rule issued to implement part of the Telecommunications Act of 1996. The Court considered the FCC's interpretation of certain terms in the act that the agency made in formulating its rule. This illustrates the interpretation and application of statutory terms that any agency must make in its rulemaking.

Case 7.1 ● AT&T Corp. v. Iowa Utilities Board

Supreme Court of the United States, 1999.
525 U.S. 366,
119 S.Ct. 721,
142 L.Ed.2d 835.
http://supct.law.cornell.edu/
supct/supct.January.1999.html[a]

Historical and Social Setting   *Until the 1990s, local phone service was thought to be a natural monopoly. States typically granted an exclusive franchise in each local service area to a local exchange carrier (LEC), which owned, among other things, the local loops (wires connecting telephones to switches), the switches (equipment directing calls to their destinations), and the transport trunks (wires carrying calls between switches) that constituted a local exchange network. When technological advances made competition among multiple providers of local service seem possible, however, Congress enacted the Telecommunications Act of 1996 to end the state-sanctioned monopolies.*

Background and Facts   The act required existing LECs to, among other things, share elements of their networks (loops, switches, and trunks) with their

new competitors. The act ordered the Federal Communications Commission (FCC) to issue rules to implement this requirement. In deciding which elements to make available, the FCC was directed to consider whether access to each element was "necessary" and whether a lack of access would "impair" a competitor's ability to provide service. The FCC concluded that access was "necessary" even if a competitor could substitute an element from another source, and that "impairment" occurred if access was denied and a competitor had any increase in cost or decrease in quality. The FCC issued Rule 319, requiring the LECs to give their new competitors access to seven specific network elements.[b] The LECs, including AT&T Corporation, and others filed suits in courts across the United States to challenge the FCC's new rules, including Rule 319. The suits were combined into a single case in the U.S. Court of Appeals for the Eighth Circuit, which held, among other things, that the FCC's interpretations of "necessary" and "impair" were reasonable. The LECs appealed to the United States Supreme Court.

---

a. This page is part of the database of United States Supreme Court opinions maintained by the Legal Information Institute of Cornell Law School. On this page, click on the case title to access the opinion.

b. 47 C.F.R. Section 51.319. The seven elements included "the local loop, the network interface device, switching capability, interoffice transmission facilities, signaling networks and call-related databases, operations support systems functions, and operator services and directory assistance."

In the Words of the Court . . .
Justice SCALIA delivered the opinion of the Court.

* * * *

* * * [T]he [Telecommunications] Act requires the FCC to apply some limiting standard, rationally related to the goals of the Act, which it has

(Continued)

Case 7.1 Continued

simply failed to do. * * * [I]t is hard to imagine when [an LEC's] failure to give access to the element[s] would not constitute an "impairment" under [the FCC's] standard. * * * [T]hat judgment allows [competitors], rather than the [FCC], to determine whether access to [the] elements is necessary, and whether the failure to obtain access to [the] elements would impair the ability to provide services. The [FCC] cannot, consistent with the statute, [ignore] the availability of elements outside the [LEC's] network. That failing alone would require [Rule 319] to be set aside. In addition, however, the [FCC's] assumption that any increase in cost (or decrease in quality) imposed by denial of a network element renders access to that element "necessary," and causes the failure to provide that element to "impair" the [competitor's] ability to furnish its desired services, is simply not in accord with the ordinary and fair meaning of those terms. [A competitor] whose anticipated annual profits from the proposed service are reduced [by only 1 percent] of [its] investment has perhaps been "impaired" in its ability to amass earnings, but has not * * * been "impair[ed] * * * in its ability to provide the services it seeks to offer"; and it cannot realistically be said that the network element enabling it to [increase] its profits [by 1 percent] is "necessary." In a world of perfect competition, in which all carriers are providing their service at marginal [incremental] cost, the [FCC's] total equating of increased cost (or decreased quality) with "necessity" and "impairment" might be reasonable; but it has not established the existence of such an ideal world.

Decision and Remedy The United States Supreme Court concluded that the FCC did not interpret the terms of the Telecommunications Act in a "reasonable fashion" and vacated Rule 319. The Court indicated that the FCC should consider the availability, to competitors, of elements outside the LECs' networks.

For Critical Analysis—Political Consideration *Why doesn't Congress always define specifically what an administrative agency is to consider when making rules?*

Investigation

Administrative agencies conduct investigations of the entities that they regulate. Agencies investigate a wide range of activities, including coal mining, automobile manufacturing, and the industrial discharge of pollutants into the environment. A typical agency investigation occurs during the rulemaking process to obtain information about a certain individual, firm, or industry. The purpose of such an investigation is to avoid issuing a rule that is arbitrary and capricious and instead to issue a rule based on a consideration of relevant factors. After final rules are issued, agencies conduct investigations to monitor compliance with those rules. A typical agency investigation of this kind might begin when a citizen reports a possible violation.

INSPECTIONS AND TESTS Many agencies gather information through on-site inspections. Sometimes, inspecting an office, a factory, or some other business facility is the only way to obtain the evidence needed to prove a regulatory violation. At other times, an inspection or test is used in place of a formal hearing to show the need to correct or prevent an undesirable condition. Administrative inspections and tests cover a wide range of activities, including safety inspections of underground coal mines, safety tests of commercial equipment and automobiles, and environmental monitoring of factory emissions. An agency may also ask a firm or individual to submit certain documents or records to the agency for examination.

Normally, business firms comply with agency requests to inspect facilities or business records, because it is in any firm's interest to maintain a good relationship with regulatory bodies. In some instances, however, such as when a firm thinks an agency's request is unreasonable and may be detrimental to the firm's interest, the firm may refuse to comply with the request. In such situations, an agency may resort to the use of a subpoena or a search warrant.

SUBPOENAS   There are two basic types of subpoenas. The subpoena *ad testificandum* ("to testify") is the technical term for an ordinary subpoena. It is a writ, or order, compelling a witness to appear at an agency hearing. The subpoena *duces tecum* ("bring it with you") compels an individual or organization to hand over books, papers, records, or documents to the agency. An administrative agency may use either type of subpoena to obtain testimony or documents.

There are limits on what an agency can demand. To determine whether an agency is abusing its discretion in its pursuit of information as part of an investigation, a court may consider such factors as the following:

- The purpose of the investigation. An investigation must have a legitimate purpose. An improper purpose is, for example, harassment.
- The relevancy of the information being sought. Information is relevant if it reveals that the law is being violated or if it assures the agency that the law is not being violated.
- The specificity of the demand for testimony or documents. A subpoena must, for example, adequately describe the material being sought.
- The burden of the demand on the party from whom the information is sought. In responding to a request for information, a party must bear the costs of, for example, copying the documents that must be handed over, but a business is generally protected from revealing such information as trade secrets.

In the following case, former bank directors challenged the right of an administrative agency to subpoena their personal financial records. The court considered the extent of the agency's investigative powers.

Case 7.2 ● Federal Deposit Insurance Corp. v. Wentz

United States Court of Appeals, Third Circuit, 1995. 55 F.3d 905.

Historical and Economic Setting

Congress created the Federal Deposit Insurance Corporation (FDIC) in 1933 to help prevent commercial bank failures and to protect bank customers' ac- *counts. In 1992, nearly five hundred banks failed. More than half of all bank failures can be attributed to agricultural loans, when the failure of farms leads to default on the loans. Fraud also often plays a role, particularly in nonagricultural states. When a bank fails, the FDIC covers each depositor's loss up to $100,000 and then sells the bank's assets, or takes other steps, to regain some of those funds.*

(Continued)

Case 7.2 Continued

Background and Facts Sidney Wentz and Natalie Koether were directors of the Howard Savings Bank of Livingston, New Jersey, when it was declared insolvent in October 1992. The Federal Deposit Insurance Corporation (FDIC) was appointed receiver. In April 1993, the FDIC issued subpoenas *duces tecum* to Wentz, Koether, and others, seeking, among other things, their personal financial records. The directors refused to comply. The FDIC asked a federal district court to enforce the subpoenas, arguing that the records were needed to assess any bank losses that might be due to any breach of the directors' fiduciary duties. The court ordered the directors to produce only those records showing additions to or reductions in their assets. The directors appealed, contending that this order intruded on their privacy.

In the Words of the Court . . .
WEIS, Circuit Judge.

* * * *

When personal documents of individuals, as contrasted with business records of corporations, are the subject of an administrative subpoena, privacy concerns must be considered. * * * [R]elevant factors [include] such matters as the type of record requested, the information that it might contain, the potential for harm and subsequent nonconsensual disclosure, the adequacy of safeguards to prevent unauthorized disclosure, the degree of need for access, * * * and the presence of recognizable public interests justifying access.

* * * *

In applying [these] factors * * * , there is a significant public interest in promptly resolving the affairs of insolvent banks on behalf of their creditors and depositors, many of whom have lost significant sums of money and are often left with little hope for recovery. * * *

The FDIC has shown a reasonable need for gaining access to the directors' records in order to determine whether they reveal breaches of fiduciary duties through the improper channeling of bank funds for personal benefit. Moreover, the directors have not produced any evidence to show that the information contained in their personal financial records "is of such a high degree of sensitivity that the intrusion could be considered severe or that the [directors] are likely to suffer any adverse effects from disclosure to [FDIC] personnel." Finally, we observe that regulatory provisions have been promulgated to guard against subsequent unauthorized disclosure of the subpoenaed information.

Decision and Remedy The U.S. Court of Appeals for the Third Circuit affirmed the district court's order.

For Critical Analysis—Economic Consideration *If the FDIC covers most of the cus-* *tomers' losses, why would anyone care whether the bank directors channeled some bank funds for their personal benefit?*

SEARCH WARRANTS The Fourth Amendment protects against unreasonable searches and seizures by requiring that in most instances a physical search for evidence must be conducted under the authority of a search warrant. An agency's search warrant is an order directing law enforcement officials to search a specific place for a specific item and present it to the agency. Although it was once thought that administrative inspections were exempt from the warrant requirement, the United States Supreme Court held in *Marshall v. Barlow's, Inc.,*[4] that the requirement does apply to the administrative process.

Agencies can conduct warrantless searches in several situations. Warrants are not required to conduct searches in highly regulated industries. Firms that sell firearms or liquor, for example, are automatically subject to inspections without warrants. Sometimes, a statute permits warrantless searches of certain types of hazardous operations, such as coal mines. Also, a warrantless inspection in an emergency situation is normally considered reasonable.

Adjudication

After conducting an investigation of a suspected rule violation, an agency may begin to take administrative action against an individual or organization. Most administrative actions are resolved through negotiated settlements at their initial stages, without the need for formal **adjudication** (the resolution of the dispute through a hearing conducted by the agency).

Adjudication The act of rendering a judicial decision. In an administrative process, the proceeding in which an administrative law judge hears and decides on issues that arise when an administrative agency charges a person or a firm with violating a law or regulation enforced by the agency.

NEGOTIATED SETTLEMENTS   Depending on the agency, negotiations may take the form of a simple conversation or a series of informal conferences. Whatever form the negotiations take, their purpose is to rectify the problem to the agency's satisfaction and eliminate the need for additional proceedings.

Settlement is an appealing option to firms for two reasons. First, regulated industries often do not want to appear to the regulating agency to be uncooperative. Second, litigation can be very expensive. To conserve their own resources and avoid formal actions, administrative agencies devote a great deal of effort to giving advice and negotiating solutions to problems.

FORMAL COMPLAINTS   If a settlement cannot be reached, the agency may issue a formal complaint against the suspected violator. • **Example 7.4** The Environmental Protection Agency (EPA) finds that Acme Manufacturing, Inc., is polluting groundwater in violation of federal pollution laws. The EPA issues a complaint against the violator in an effort to bring the plant into compliance with federal regulations.• This complaint is a public document, and a press release may accompany it. The party charged in the complaint responds by filing an *answer* to the allegations. If the charged party and the agency cannot agree on a settlement, the case is heard in a trial-like setting before an **administrative law judge (ALJ)**. The formal adjudication process is described below and illustrated graphically in Exhibit 7–4 on the next page.

Administrative Law Judge (ALJ) One who presides over an administrative agency hearing and who has the power to administer oaths, take testimony, rule on questions of evidence, and make determinations of fact.

THE ROLE OF THE ADMINISTRATIVE LAW JUDGE   The ALJ presides over the hearing and has the power to administer oaths, take testimony, rule on questions of evidence, and make determinations of fact. Although formally the ALJ works for the agency prosecuting the case, the law requires an ALJ to be an unbiased adjudicator (judge).

Certain safeguards prevent bias on the part of the ALJ and promote fairness in the proceedings. For example, the Administrative Procedure Act requires that the ALJ be separate from the agency's investigative and prosecutorial staff. The APA also prohibits *ex parte* (private) communications between the ALJ and any party to an agency proceeding, including a party charged with a

---

4. 436 U.S. 307, 98 S.Ct. 1816, 56 L.Ed.2d 305 (1978).

Exhibit 7–4
The Process
of Formal
Administrative
Adjudication

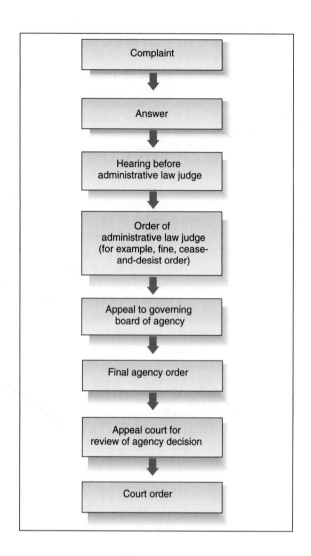

Exhibit 7–4
The Process of Formal Administrative Adjudication

complaint and the agency itself. Finally, provisions of the APA protect the ALJ from agency disciplinary actions unless the agency can show good cause for such an action.

HEARING PROCEDURES   Hearing procedures vary widely from agency to agency. Administrative agencies generally can exercise substantial discretion over the type of hearing procedures that will be used. Frequently, disputes are resolved through informal adjudication proceedings. • **Example 7.5** The Federal Trade Commission (FTC) charges Good Foods, Inc., with deceptive advertising. Representatives of Good Foods and of the FTC, their counsel, and the ALJ meet at a table in a conference room to resolve the dispute informally.•

A formal adjudicatory hearing, in contrast, resembles a trial in many respects. Prior to the hearing, the parties are permitted to undertake extensive discovery proceedings (involving depositions, interrogatories, and requests for documents or other information, as described in Chapter 3). During the hearing, the parties may give testimony, present other evidence, and cross-examine adverse witnesses.

A significant difference between a trial and an administrative agency hearing, though, is that normally, much more information, including hearsay (secondhand information offered for its truth), can be introduced as evidence during an administrative hearing.

AGENCY ORDERS   Following a hearing, the ALJ renders an **initial order**, or decision, on the case. Either party may appeal the ALJ's decision to the board or commission that governs the agency. • **Example 7.6** National Warehouse Corporation is charged with violations of the Occupational Safety and Health Act, and an ALJ from the Occupational Health and Safety Administration (OSHA) imposes penalties on National Warehouse. If the firm is dissatisfied with the ALJ's decision, it may appeal the decision to the commission that governs OSHA. If the firm is dissatisfied with the commission's decision, it may appeal the decision to a federal court of appeals.• If no party appeals the case, the ALJ's decision becomes the **final order** of the agency. If a party does appeal the case, the final order comes from the commission's decision or that of the reviewing court. If a party appeals and the commission and the court decline to review the case, the ALJ's decision also becomes final. This point, as well as the role of common sense in an administrative decision, is illustrated in the following case.

Initial Order An administrative agency's first, or initial, decision in a matter other than rulemaking.

Final Order The final decision of an administrative agency on an issue. If no appeal is taken, or if the case is not reviewed or considered anew by the agency commission, the administrative law judge's initial order becomes the final order of the agency.

Case 7.3 ● Buck Creek Coal, Inc. v. Federal Mine Safety and Health Administration

United States Court of Appeals, Seventh Circuit, 1995. 52 F.3d 133.

Historical and Environmental Setting *Historically, three fossil fuels—coal, oil, and natural gas—have accounted for the bulk of U.S. energy production. Of those three fuels, coal accounted for the largest share of energy production in the 1980s. It is estimated that U.S. coal production could be sustained at present levels for more than two hundred years. Some of the richest U.S. coal deposits are in the Appalachian Mountains and in the southern half of Indiana.*

Background and Facts Buck Creek Coal, Inc., operates a coal mine in Sullivan County, Indiana.

When James Holland, an inspector for the Mine Safety and Health Administration (MSHA), inspected the mine, he noted an accumulation of loose coal and coal dust in the feeder area, where mined coal is transferred from mine shuttle cars to conveyor belts. Holland issued a citation, charging Buck Creek with violations of federal regulations that require mine operators to keep feeder areas clean. After hearing evidence from both sides, an ALJ found that the evidence supported Holland's conclusions and fined Buck Creek $2,000. Buck Creek asked the Federal Mine Safety and Health Review Commission to review the ALJ's conclusions. When the Commission declined, Buck Creek sought review in the courts.

In the Words of the Court . . .
ILANA DIAMOND ROVNER, Circuit Judge.
    * * * *
    * * * [The ALJ] made these findings, based primarily on the testimony of Inspector Holland: "[T]here were substantial accumulations of loose coal, coal fines and float coal dust, in the feeder area * * *. A heated roller turning in that combustible material could easily be an ignition source which could in turn cause a fire. * * * [I]n the event of a fire, smoke and gas inhalation by miners in the area would cause a reasonably serious injury requiring medical

(Continued)

Case 7.3 Continued

attention." * * * [N]o further evidence was necessary to support the ALJ's conclusion. First, * * * Inspector Holland [is] a federal mine inspector with 32 years of mining experience who specializes in mine ventilation. Nor was anything more than Inspector Holland's opinion necessary to support the common sense conclusion that a fire burning in an underground coal mine would present a serious risk of smoke and gas inhalation to miners who are present. * * * [F]ire is one of the primary safety concerns that has motivated federal regulation of the coal mining industry.

Nor has Buck Creek identified any evidence that tends to undermine the ALJ's conclusion. * * * Buck Creek has relied mainly on * * * testimony [that] pertained to Buck Creek's fire safety systems. * * * The fact that Buck Creek has safety measures in place * * * does not mean that fires do not pose a serious safety risk to miners. Indeed, the precautions are * * * in place * * * precisely because of the significant dangers associated with coal mine fires.

Decision and Remedy The U.S. Court of Appeals for the Seventh Circuit denied Buck Creek's petition for review. The ALJ's conclusions became the final order for the agency.

For Critical Analysis—Social Consideration *What role does common sense play in the application and review of administrative rulings?*

> **"Absolute discretion . . . is more destructive of freedom than any of man's other inventions."**
>
> William O. Douglas, 1892–1954
> (Associate justice of the United States
> Supreme Court, 1939–1975)

Limitations on Agency Powers

Combining the functions normally divided among the three branches of government into an administrative agency concentrates considerable power in a single organization. Because of this concentration of authority, one of the major policy objectives of the government is to control the risks of arbitrariness and overreaching by administrative agencies without hindering the effective use of agency power to deal with particular problem areas, as Congress intends.

The judicial branch of the government exercises control over agency powers through the courts' review of agency actions. The executive and legislative branches of government also exercise control over agency authority.

Judicial Controls

The APA provides for judicial review of most agency decisions. As discussed above, if a charged party is dissatisfied with an agency's order, it can appeal the decision to a federal appeals court. Agency actions are not automatically subject to judicial review, however. Parties seeking review must demonstrate that they meet certain requirements, including those listed here:

- The action must be *reviewable* by the court. The APA creates a presumption that agency actions are reviewable, making this requirement easy to satisfy.
- The party must have *standing to sue* the agency (the party must have a direct stake in the outcome of the judicial proceeding).
- The party must have *exhausted all possible administrative remedies*. Each agency has its "chain of review," and the party must follow agency

appeal procedures before a court will deem that administrative remedies have been exhausted.

- There must be an *actual controversy* at issue. Courts will not review cases before it is necessary to decide them.

Recall from Chapter 3 that appellate courts normally defer to the decisions of trial courts on questions of fact. In reviewing administrative actions, the courts are similarly reluctant to review the factual findings of agencies. In most cases, the courts accept the facts as found in the agency proceedings. Normally, when a court reviews an administrative agency decision, the court considers the following types of issues:

- Whether the agency has exceeded its authority under its enabling legislation.
- Whether the agency has properly interpreted laws applicable to the agency action under review.
- Whether the agency has violated any constitutional provisions.
- Whether the agency has acted in accordance with procedural requirements of the law.
- Whether the agency's actions were arbitrary, capricious, or an abuse of discretion.
- Whether any conclusions drawn by the agency are not supported by substantial evidence.

The issue in the following case was whether an agency's action was arbitrary and capricious.

Case 7.4 ● Sierra Club v. Thomas

United States Court of Appeals, Sixth Circuit, 1997.
105 F.3d 248.
http://www.law.emory.edu/
6circuit/jan97/index.html[a]

Historical and Political Setting *Congress enacted the National Forest Management Act of 1976[b] out of concern that timber production was becoming the dominant policy of the U.S. Forest Service. Congress believed that, if left unregulated, the Forest Service would manage the national forests as "tree farms." The act required the Forest Service to develop formal "Land and Resource Management Plans" for the national forests. Congress hoped that this would inhibit agency discretion and ensure forest preservation*

and productivity. Among other things, the act imposed limitations on timber harvesting by restricting the use of clearcutting unless that was the optimum method for harvesting. Clearcutting involves the removal of all trees within areas ranging in size from fifteen to thirty acres.

Background and Facts The Forest Service issued a plan for cutting timber from the Wayne National Forest. Most of the cutting was to be done by a technique known as even-aged management, which requires clearcutting. The Sierra Club challenged the plan in an appeal to Jack Ward Thomas, chief of the Forest Service. When Thomas affirmed the plan, the Sierra Club and others filed a suit in a federal district court against Thomas and others, arguing that the plan was arbitrary and capricious because, in making it, the Forest Service had not complied with the National Forest Management Act. The court granted the Forest Service's motion for summary judgment, and the Sierra Club appealed.

a. This is a page, within the Web site of the Emory University School of Law, that lists the published opinions of the U.S. Court of Appeals for the Sixth Circuit for January 1997. Scroll down the list of cases to the *Sierra Club* case. Click on the case name to access the opinion.

b. 16 U.S.C. Sections 1600–1614.

(Continued)

Case 7.4 Continued

In the Words of the Court . . .
BOYCE F. MARTIN, JR., Chief Judge.

* * * *

* * * The Forest Service argues that its even-aged management plan is based on evidence that timbering will provide new opportunities for recreation that will, in turn, preserve and enhance the diversity of plant and animal communities in the Wayne National Forest. Most recreation does not require timber harvesting, however. Further, as the Forest Service's own records reflect, the Wayne is surrounded by and intermingled with privately held land which already contains an abundance of diverse plant and animal life. Timbering simply does not promote the kind of recreational activities that are in demand in the Wayne; in fact, recreation like fishing and hiking is harmed by clearcutting. The planners also failed to recognize that cutting is unlikely to stimulate new and valuable forms of recreation because much of the Wayne has already been cut or developed. In that particular environment, clearcutting loses its value.

* * * The National Forest Management Act * * * contemplates that even-aged management techniques will be used only in exceptional circumstances. Yet, the defendants would utilize even-aged management logging as if it were the statutory rule, rather than the exception. By arbitrarily undervaluing the recreational value of wilderness, the Forest Service created a very distorted picture of the Wayne National Forest. Based on false premises such as these, the Forest Service improperly concluded that clearcutting was necessary.

Decision and Remedy The U.S. Court of Appeals for the Sixth Circuit concluded that the Forest Service plan was arbitrary and capricious. The court reversed the lower court's decision and remanded the case.

For Critical Analysis—Economic Consideration *Why isn't every agency action subject to automatic judicial review?*

Executive Controls

The executive branch of government exercises control over agencies both through the president's powers to appoint federal officers and through the president's veto powers. The president may veto enabling legislation presented by Congress or congressional attempts to modify an existing agency's authority.

Legislative Controls

Congress also exercises authority over agency powers. Through enabling legislation, Congress gives power to an agency. Of course, an agency may not exceed the power that Congress delegates to it. Through subsequent legislation, Congress can take away that power or even abolish an agency altogether. Legislative authority is required to fund an agency, and enabling legislation usually sets certain time and monetary limits relating to the funding of particular programs. Congress can always revise these limits.

In addition to its power to create and fund agencies, Congress has the authority to investigate the implementation of its laws and the agencies that it has created. Individual legislators may also affect agency policy through their "casework" activities, which involve attempts to help their constituents deal with agencies.

Inside the Legal Environment

Business Opportunity Scams

This is how it starts: a promise of big income for a few hours of easy work—"No Experience Necessary!" The promise appears in an ad in a newspaper or a magazine, or a commercial on television or radio, urging you to "Act Now!" The work may be said to take "only a little of your spare time" tending video games or pay phones, or stocking vending machines or display racks for anything from car wax and cookies to herbal pills and pizza. It sounds too good to be true—and it is. Such deals cost innocent investors more than $100 million a year.

If you agree to take advantage of one of these so-called "opportunities," it may end up taking advantage of you. To obtain the display racks and inventory, for example, you may be asked to make a large down payment or to buy a large amount of start-up product. To convince you of the "Easy Money!" claims, a seller may cite a government report or include testimonials from "satisfied dealers." The promises of profitability are usually empty—the report may not exist and the testimonials will be hand-picked for what they say.

One item that a scam artist will not provide is the document that the Federal Trade Commission (FTC) requires under its business opportunity disclosure rule.[a] Basically, this rule applies to deals that cost an investor $500 or more in the first six months and in which the seller agrees to handle such matters as finding locations. The document must include an audited financial statement and must cover, among other things, the seller's business history. If an ad claims that a product will be profitable, a prospective buyer is entitled to written proof. The document must also state the following: "To protect you, we've required your [seller] to give you this information. We haven't checked it, and don't know if it's correct. * * * If you find anything you think may be wrong or anything important that's been left out, you should let us know about it. It may be against the law."

Such information might have helped the individual who invested $12,000 in popcorn vending machines that return less than $30 per month. It might have helped the person who invested more than $13,000 in video games that broke down in less than ninety days, or the two investors who lost $72,000 in hot-pizza vending machines. Other buyers have lost as much as $40,000 each in display-rack frauds involving such items as greeting cards and CD-ROM disks.

In response to an astounding increase in such bogus moneymaking schemes, the FTC initiated Project Telesweep in 1995. A team of FTC employees, pretending to be potential entrepreneurs, began answering the ads that boasted big returns on such business "opportunities" as those listed above. After identifying the frauds and accumulating evidence, the FTC joined the U.S. Department of Justice, the North American Securities Administrators Association, and the attorneys general of twenty states to bring legal actions against more than one hundred business opportunity scams for violations of state and federal law, including the FTC disclosure rule.

For Critical Analysis: *What should a potential entrepreneur do to protect himself or herself from fraudulent business opportunities?*

a. 16 C.F.R. Section 436.1.

Congress also has the power to "freeze" the enforcement of most federal regulations before the regulations take effect. Under the Small Business Regulatory Enforcement Fairness Act of 1996,[5] all federal agencies must submit final rules to Congress before the rules become effective. If, within sixty days, Congress passes a joint resolution of disapproval concerning a rule, enforcement of the regulation is frozen while the rule is reviewed by congressional committees.

Other legislative checks on agency actions include the Administrative Procedure Act, discussed earlier in this chapter, and the laws discussed in the next section.

---

5. 5 U.S.C. Sections 801–808.

Ethical Issue 7.1

Should Congress and the courts rein in agency rulemaking powers?

Of increasing concern today is the extent to which unelected rulemakers in administrative agencies are creating national policy. Some claim that Congress should limit the rulemaking authority of administrative agencies by not leaving so many "gaps" in legislation to be filled by agency rules. Others would like the courts to scrutinize agency findings and actions more closely when reviewing agency orders, rather than deferring to the conclusions of agency rulemakers. Indeed, some observers believe that a recent United States Supreme Court decision may indicate a greater willingness on the part of the Court to rein in agency powers. The Court ruled that the Food and Drug Administration (FDA) exceeded its authority when it issued rules calling for restrictions on the marketing and sale of tobacco products to youth. According to the Court, Congress had not explicitly authorized the FDA to regulate tobacco products because nicotine did not meet the definitional requirements for a "drug" under the Federal Food, Drug, and Cosmetic Act—the statutory authority for the FDA's rules.[a]

a. *Food and Drug Administration v. Brown & Williamson Tobacco Corp.*, 529 U.S. 120, 120 S.Ct. 1291, 146 L.Ed.2d 121 (2000).

> **"Law . . . is a human institution, created by human agents to serve human ends."**
>
> Harlan F. Stone, 1872–1946
> (Chief justice of the United States Supreme Court, 1941–1946)

Public Accountability

As a result of growing public concern over the powers exercised by administrative agencies, Congress passed several laws to make agencies more accountable through public scrutiny. We discuss here the most significant of these laws.

Freedom of Information Act

Enacted in 1966, the Freedom of Information Act (FOIA)[6] requires the federal government to disclose certain "records" to "any person" on request, even without any reason being given for the request. The FOIA exempts certain types of records. For other records, though, a request that complies with the FOIA procedures need only contain a reasonable description of the information sought (see Exhibit 7–5). An agency's failure to comply with a request may be challenged in a federal district court. The media, industry trade associations, public-interest groups, and even companies seeking information about competitors rely on these FOIA provisions to obtain information from government agencies.

Government-in-the-Sunshine Act

Congress passed the Government-in-the-Sunshine Act,[7] or open meeting law, in 1976. It requires that "every portion of every meeting of an agency" be open to "public observation." The act also requires procedures to ensure that the public is provided with adequate advance notice of the agency's scheduled meeting and agenda. As with the FOIA, the Sunshine Act contains certain exceptions. Closed meetings are permitted when (1) the subject of the meeting concerns accusing any person of a crime, (2) open meetings would frustrate

6. 5 U.S.C. Section 552.
7. 5 U.S.C. Section 552b.

Exhibit 7–5
**Sample Letter
Requesting
Information
from an Executive
Department or
Agency**

Date

Agency Head or FOIA Officer
Title
Name of Agency
Address of Agency
City, State, Zip

Re: Freedom of Information Act Request.

Dear _____ :
　Under the provisions of the Freedom of Information Act, 5 U.S.C. Section 552, I am requesting access to

_____

[identify the records as clearly as possible].
　[Optional] I am requesting this information because

_____　_____

[state the reason for your request if you think it will assist you in obtaining the information].
　If there are any fees for searching for, or copying, the records I have requested, please inform me before you fill the request [or:] please supply the records without informing me if the fees do not exceed $ _____ .
　[or:] As you know, the act permits you to reduce or waive fees when the release of the information is considered as "primarily benefiting the public." I believe that this request fits that category, and I therefore ask that you waive any fees.
　If all or any part of this request is denied, please cite the specific exemption(s) that you think justifies your refusal to release the information, and inform me of the appeal procedures available to me under the law.
　I would appreciate your handling this request as quickly as possible, and I look forward to hearing from you within 10 days, as the law stipulates.

Sincerely,
[Signature]
Name
Address
City, State, Zip

Source: U.S. Congress, House Committee on Government Operations, *A Citizen's Guide on How to Use the Freedom of Information Act and the Privacy Act Requesting Government Documents,* 95th Congress, 1st session, 1977.

implementation of future agency actions, or (3) the subject of the meeting involves matters relating to future litigation or rulemaking. Courts interpret these exceptions to allow open access whenever possible.

Regulatory Flexibility Act

Concern over the effects of regulation on the efficiency of businesses, particularly smaller ones, led Congress to pass the Regulatory Flexibility Act in 1980.[8] Under this act, whenever a new regulation will have a "significant

---

8. 5 U.S.C. Sections 601–612.

impact upon a substantial number of small entities," the agency must conduct a regulatory flexibility analysis. The analysis must measure the cost that the rule would impose on small businesses and must consider less burdensome alternatives. The act also contains provisions to alert small businesses about forthcoming regulations. The act relieved some record-keeping burdens for small businesses, especially with regard to hazardous waste management.

Small Business Regulatory Enforcement Fairness Act

As mentioned above, the Small Business Regulatory Enforcement Fairness Act (SBREFA) of 1996 allows Congress to review new federal regulations for at least sixty days before they take effect. This period gives opponents of the rules time to present their arguments to Congress.

The SBREFA also authorizes the courts to enforce the Regulatory Flexibility Act. This helps to ensure that federal agencies, such as the Internal Revenue Service, consider ways to reduce the economic impact of new regulations on small businesses. Federal agencies are required to prepare guides that explain in "plain English" how small businesses can comply with federal regulations.

At the Small Business Administration, the SBREFA set up the National Enforcement Ombudsman to receive comments from small businesses about their dealings with federal agencies. Based on these comments, Regional Small Business Fairness Boards rate the agencies and publicize their findings.

Finally, the SBREFA allows small businesses to recover their expenses and legal fees from the government when an agency makes demands for fines or penalties that a court considers excessive.

State Administrative Agencies

Although much of this chapter deals with federal administrative agencies, state agencies also play a significant role in regulating activities within the states. Many of the factors that encouraged the proliferation of federal agencies also fostered the growing presence of state agencies. For example, the reasons for the growth of administrative agencies at all levels of government include the inability of Congress and state legislatures to oversee the actual implementation of their laws and the greater technical competence of the agencies.

Parallel Agencies

Commonly, a state creates an agency as a parallel to a federal agency to provide similar services on a more localized basis. • **Example 7.7** The Pennsylvania Department of Public Welfare shoulders some of the same responsibilities at the state level as the Social Security Administration does at the federal level. The New York Department of Taxation and Finance performs, on a statewide basis, duties that resemble those performed by the Internal Revenue Service on a nationwide basis. The Minnesota Pollution Control Agency parallels the federal Environmental Protection Agency.• Not all federal agencies have parallel state agencies, however. For example, the Federal Bureau of Investigation and the Nuclear Regulatory Commission have no parallel agencies at the state level.

Conflicts between Parallel Agencies

If the actions of parallel state and federal agencies conflict, the actions of the federal agency will prevail. • **Example 7.8** The Federal Aviation Administration

(FAA) specifies the hours during which airplanes may land at and depart from airports. A California state agency issues inconsistent regulations governing the same activities. In a proceeding initiated by Interstate Distribution Corporation, an air transport company, to challenge the state rules, the FAA regulations would be held to prevail.● The priority of federal law over conflicting state laws is based on the supremacy clause of the U.S. Constitution. This clause, which is found in Article VI of the Constitution, states that the Constitution and "the Laws of the United States which shall be made in Pursuance thereof . . . shall be the supreme Law of the Land."

Key Terms

adjudication 189	enabling legislation 179	judicial process 184
administrative law judge (ALJ) 189	executive agency 181	legislative rule 183
administrative process 184	final order 191	notice-and-comment rulemaking 184
bureaucracy 183	independent regulatory agency 181	rulemaking 184
delegation doctrine 183	initial order 191	

Chapter Summary ● Powers and Functions of Administrative Agencies

Agency Creation and Powers (See pages 179–183.)	1. Under the U.S. Constitution, Congress may delegate the task of implementing its laws to government agencies. By delegating the task, Congress may indirectly monitor an area in which it has passed legislation without becoming bogged down in the details relating to enforcement of the legislation.
	2. Administrative agencies are created by enabling legislation, which usually specifies the name, composition, and powers of the agency.
	3. Administrative agencies exercise enforcement, rulemaking, and adjudicatory powers.
Administrative Process— Rulemaking (See pages 184–186.)	1. Agencies are authorized to create new regulations—their rulemaking function. This power is conferred on an agency in the enabling legislation.
	2. Agencies may create legislative rules, which are as important as formal acts of Congress.
	3. Notice-and-comment rulemaking, the most common rulemaking procedure, begins with the publication of the proposed regulation in the *Federal Register*. Publication of the notice is followed by a comment period to allow private parties to comment on the proposed rule.
Administrative Process— Investigation (See pages 186–188.)	1. Administrative agencies investigate the entities that they regulate. Investigations are conducted during the rulemaking process to obtain information and after rules are issued to monitor compliance.
	2. The most important investigative tools available to an agency are the following:
	a. Inspections and tests—Used to gather information and to correct or prevent undesirable conditions.

(Continued)

Chapter Summary • Powers and Functions of
Administrative Agencies, *Continued*

Administrative Process— Investigation— continued	**b.** Subpoenas—Orders that direct individuals to appear at a hearing or to hand over specified documents.
	3. Limits on administrative investigations include the following:
	a. The investigation must be for a legitimate purpose.
	b. The information sought must be relevant, and the investigative demands must be specific and not unreasonably burdensome.
	c. The Fourth Amendment protects companies and individuals from unreasonable searches and seizures by requiring search warrants in most instances.
Administrative Process— Adjudication (See pages 189–192.)	**1.** After a preliminary investigation, an agency may initiate an administrative action against an individual or organization by filing a complaint. Most such actions are resolved at this stage before they go through the formal adjudicatory process.
	2. If there is no settlement, the case is presented to an administrative law judge (ALJ) in a proceeding similar to a trial.
	3. After a case is concluded, the ALJ renders an initial order that may be appealed by either party in federal appeals court. If no appeal is taken or the case is not reviewed, then the order becomes the final order of the agency. It may direct the charged party to pay damages, or it may forbid the party from carrying on some specified activity.
Limitations on Agency Powers (See pages 192–196.)	**1. Judicial controls**—Administrative agencies are subject to the judicial review of the courts. A court may review whether—
	a. An agency has exceeded the scope of its enabling legislation.
	b. An agency has properly interpreted the laws.
	c. An agency has violated the U.S. Constitution.
	d. An agency has complied with all applicable procedural requirements.
	e. An agency's actions are arbitrary or capricious, or an abuse of discretion.
	f. An agency's conclusions are not supported by substantial evidence.
	2. Executive controls—The president can control administrative agencies through appointments of federal officers and through vetoes of legislation creating or affecting agency powers.
	3. Legislative controls—Congress can give power to an agency, take it away, increase or decrease the agency's finances, or abolish the agency. The Administrative Procedure Act of 1946 also limits agencies.
Public Accountability (See pages 196–198.)	**1. Freedom of Information Act of 1966**—Requires the government to disclose records to "any person" on request.
	2. Government-in-the-Sunshine Act of 1976—Requires the following:
	a. "[E]very portion of every meeting of an agency" must be open to "public observation."
	b. Procedures must be implemented to ensure that the public is provided with adequate advance notice of the agency's scheduled meeting and agenda.

Chapter Summary • Powers and Functions of Administrative Agencies

Public Accountability— continued	**3. Regulatory Flexibility Act of 1980**—Requires a regulatory flexibility analysis whenever a new regulation will have a "significant impact upon a substantial number of small entities."
	4. Small Business Regulatory Enforcement Fairness Act of 1996—Allows Congress to review new federal regulations. Requires federal agencies to explain in "plain English" how to comply with regulations. Established Regional Small Business Fairness Boards to rate agencies from a small-business perspective. Provides for the recovery of expenses and fees when an agency imposes an excessive penalty.
State Administrative Agencies (See pages 198–199.)	**1.** States create agencies that parallel federal agencies to provide similar services on a more localized basis.
	2. If the actions of parallel state and federal agencies conflict, the actions of the federal agency will prevail.

For Review

1. How are federal administrative agencies created?
2. What are the three operations that make up the basic functions of most administrative agencies?
3. What sequence of events must normally occur before an agency rule becomes law?
4. How do administrative agencies enforce their rules?
5. How do the three branches of government limit the power of administrative agencies?

Questions and Case Problems

7–1. Rulemaking Procedures. Assume that the Securities and Exchange Commission (SEC) has a policy not to enforce rules prohibiting insider trading except when the insiders make monetary profits for themselves. Then the SEC modifies this policy by a determination that the agency has the statutory authority to bring an enforcement action against an individual even if he or she does not personally profit from the insider trading. In modifying the policy, the SEC does not conduct a rulemaking but simply announces its new decision. A securities organization objects and says that the policy was unlawfully developed without opportunity for public comment. In a lawsuit challenging the new policy, should the policy be overruled under the Administrative Procedure Act? Discuss.

7–2. Rulemaking Procedures. Assume that the Food and Drug Administration (FDA), using proper procedures, adopts a rule describing its future investigations. This new rule covers all future cases in which the FDA wants to regulate food additives. Under the new rule, the FDA says that it will not regulate food additives with-

out giving food companies an opportunity to cross-examine witnesses. Some time later, the FDA wants to regulate methylisocyanate, a food additive. In doing so, the FDA undertakes an informal rulemaking procedure, without cross-examination, and regulates methylisocyanate. Producers protest, saying that the FDA promised cross-examination. The FDA responds that the Administrative Procedure Act does not require such cross-examination and that it could freely withdraw the promise made in its new rule. If the producers challenge the FDA in a court, on what basis would the court rule in their favor?

7–3. Rulemaking and Adjudication Powers. For decades, the Federal Trade Commission (FTC) resolved fair trade and advertising disputes through individual adjudications. In the 1960s, the FTC began promulgating rules that defined fair and unfair trade practices. In cases involving violations of these rules, the due process rights of participants were more limited and did not include cross-examination. This was because, although anyone found violating a rule would receive a full adjudication, the legitimacy of the rule itself could not be challenged in the adjudication. Any party charged with violating a rule was almost certain to lose the adjudication. Affected parties complained to a court, arguing that their rights before the FTC were unduly limited by the new rules. What will the court examine to determine whether to uphold the new rules?

7–4. Rulemaking Procedures. The Atomic Energy Commission (AEC) was engaged in rulemaking proceedings for nuclear reactor safety. An environmental group sued the commission, arguing that its proceedings were inadequate. The commission had carefully complied with all requirements of the Administrative Procedure Act. The environmentalists argued, however, that the very hazardous and technical nature of the reactor safety issue required elaborate procedures above and beyond those of the act. A federal court of appeals agreed and overturned the AEC rules. The commission appealed the case to the United States Supreme Court. Under what circumstances should an agency have to do more than comply with the Administrative Procedure Act? [*Vermont Yankee Nuclear Power Corp. v. Natural Resources Defense Council, Inc.,* 435 U.S. 519, 98 S.Ct. 1197, 55 L.Ed.2d 460 (1978)]

7–5. Agency Investigations. A state statute required vehicle dismantlers—persons whose business includes dismantling automobiles and selling the parts—to be licensed and to keep records regarding the vehicles and parts in their possession. The statute also authorized warrantless administrative inspections; that is, without first obtaining a warrant, agents of the state department of motor vehicles or police officers could inspect a vehicle dismantler's license and records, as well as vehicles on the premises. Pursuant to this statute, police officers entered an automobile junkyard and asked to see the owner's license and records. The owner replied that he did not have the documents. The officers inspected the premises and discovered stolen vehicles and parts. Charged with possession of stolen property and unregistered operation as a vehicle dismantler, the junkyard owner argued that the warrantless inspection statute was unconstitutional under the Fourth Amendment. The trial court disagreed, reasoning that the junkyard business was a highly regulated industry. On appeal, the highest state court concluded that the statute had no truly administrative purpose and impermissibly authorized searches only to discover stolen property. The state appealed to the United States Supreme Court. Should the Court uphold the statute? Discuss. [*New York v. Burger,* 482 U.S. 691, 107 S.Ct. 2636, 96 L.Ed.2d 601 (1987)]

7–6. *Ex Parte* Comments. In 1976, the Environmental Protection Agency (EPA) proposed a rule establishing new standards for coal-fired steam generators. The agency gave notice and received comments in the manner prescribed by the Administrative Procedure Act. After the public comments had been received, the EPA received informal suggestions from members of Congress and other federal officials. In 1979, the EPA published its final standards. Several environmental groups protested these standards, arguing that they were too lax. As part of this protest, the groups complained that political influence from Congress and other federal officials had encouraged the EPA to relax the proposed standards. The groups went on to argue that these *ex parte* comments were themselves illegal or that such comments at least should have been summarized in the record. What will the court decide? Discuss fully. [*Sierra Club v. Costle,* 657 F.2d 298 (D.C.Cir. 1981)]

7–7. Arbitrary and Capricious Test. In 1977, the Department of Transportation (DOT) adopted a passive-restraint standard (known as Standard 208) that required new cars to have either air bags or automatic seat belts. By 1981, it had become clear that all the major auto manufacturers would install automatic seat belts to comply with this rule. The DOT determined that most purchasers of cars would detach their automatic seat belts, thus making them ineffective. Consequently, the department repealed the regulation. State Farm Mutual Automobile Insurance Co. and other insurance companies sued in the District of Columbia Circuit Court of Appeals for a review of the DOT's repeal of the regulation. That court held that the repeal was arbitrary and capricious because the DOT had reversed its rule without sufficient support. The motor vehicle manufacturers then appealed this decision to the United States Supreme Court. What will result? Discuss. [*Motor Vehicle Manufacturers Association v. State Farm Mutual Automobile Insurance Co.,* 463 U.S. 29, 103 S.Ct. 2856, 77 L.Ed.2d 443 (1983)]

7–8. Judicial Review. American Message Centers (AMC) provides answering services to retailers. Calls to a retailer are automatically forwarded to AMC, which pays for the calls. AMC obtains telephone service at a discount from major carriers, including Sprint. Sprint's tariff (a public document setting out rates and rules relating to Sprint's services) states that the "subscriber shall be responsible for the payment of all charges for service." When AMC learned that computer hackers had obtained the access code for AMC's lines and had made nearly $160,000 in long-distance calls, it asked Sprint to absorb the cost. Sprint refused. AMC filed a complaint with the Federal Communications Commission (FCC), claiming in part that Sprint's tariff was vague and ambiguous, in violation of the Communications Act of 1934 and FCC rules. These laws require that a carrier's tariff "clearly and definitely" specify any "exceptions or conditions which in any way affect the rates named in the tariff." The FCC rejected AMC's complaint. AMC appealed the FCC's decision to a federal appellate court, claiming that the FCC's decision to reject AMC's complaint was arbitrary and capricious. What should the court decide? Discuss fully. [*American Message Centers v. Federal Communications Commission,* 50 F.3d 35 (D.C.Cir. 1995)]

7–9. Rulemaking. The Occupational Safety and Health Administration (OSHA) is part of the U.S. Department of Labor. OSHA issued a "Directive" under which each employer in selected industries was to be inspected unless it adopted a "Comprehensive Compliance Program (CCP)"—a safety and health program designed to meet standards that in some respects exceeded those otherwise required by law. The Chamber of Commerce of the United States objected to the Directive and filed a petition for review with the U.S. Court of Appeals for the District of Columbia Circuit. The Chamber claimed, in part, that OSHA did not use proper rulemaking procedures in issuing the Directive. OSHA argued that it was not required to follow those procedures because the Directive itself was a "rule of procedure." OSHA claimed that the rule did not "alter the rights or interests of parties, although it may alter the manner in which the parties present themselves or their viewpoints to the agency." What are the steps of the most commonly used rulemaking procedure? Which steps are missing in this case? In whose favor should the court rule? Why? [*Chamber of Commerce of the United States v. U.S. Department of Labor,* 74 F.3d 206 (D.C.Cir. 1999)]

A Question of Ethics and Social Responsibility

7–10. The Marine Mammal Protection Act was enacted in 1972 to reduce incidental killing and injury of marine mammals during commercial fishing operations. Under the act, commercial fishing vessels are required to allow an employee of the National Oceanic and Atmospheric Administration (NOAA) to accompany the vessels to conduct research and observe operations. In December 1986, after NOAA had adopted a new policy of recruiting female as well as male observers, NOAA notified Caribbean Marine Services Co. that female observers would be assigned to accompany two of the company's fishing vessels on their next voyages. The owners and crew members of the ships (the plaintiffs) moved for an injunction against the implementation of the NOAA directive. The plaintiffs contended that the presence of a female on board a fishing vessel would be very awkward, because the female would have to share the crew's quarters, and crew members enjoyed little or no privacy with respect to bodily functions. Further, they alleged that the presence of a female would be disruptive to fishing operations, because some of the crew members were "crude" men with little formal education who might harass or sexually assault a female observer, and the officers would therefore have to devote time to protecting the female from the crew. Finally, the plaintiffs argued that the presence of a female observer could destroy morale and distract the crew, thus affecting the crew's efficiency and decreasing the vessel's profits. [*Caribbean Marine Services Co. v. Baldrige,* 844 F.2d 668 (9th Cir. 1988)]

1. In general, do you think that the public policy of promoting equal employment opportunity should override the concerns of the vessel owners and crew? If you were the judge, would you grant the injunction? Why or why not?
2. The plaintiffs pointed out that fishing voyages could last three months or longer. Would the length of a particular voyage affect your answer to the preceding question?
3. The plaintiffs contended that even if the indignity of sharing bunk rooms and toilet facilities with a female observer could be overcome, the observer's very presence in the common areas of the vessel, such as the dining area, would unconstitutionally infringe on the crew members' right to privacy in these areas. Evaluate this claim.

For Critical Analysis

7–11. Does Congress delegate too much power to federal administrative agencies? Do the courts defer too much to Congress in its grant of power to those agencies? What are the alternatives to the agencies that we encounter in every facet of our lives?

Interacting with the Internet

■ For updated links to resources available on the Web, as well as a variety of other materials, visit this text's Web site at

http://leet.westbuslaw.com

■ The Federal Web Locator permits searches for the names of federal administrative agencies and provides links to agency-related information. Go to

http://www.infoctr.edu/fwl

■ The Web site of the U.S. Government Printing Office, called GPO Access, offers free online access to all of its databases, including the *Federal Register,* at

http://www.access.gpo.gov/su_docs

Online Legal Research Exercises

Go to **http://leet.westbus law.com**, the Web site that accompanies this text. Select "Interactive Study Center," and then click on "Chapter 7." There you will find the following Internet research exercise that you can perform to learn more about how to obtain information from government agencies:

Activity 7–1: The Freedom of Information Act

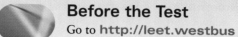

Before the Test

Go to **http://leet.westbus law.com**, the Web site that accompanies this text. Select "Interactive Quizzes." You will find a number of interactive questions relating to this chapter.

Criminal Wrongs

chapter objectives

After reading this chapter, you should be able to:

1. Explain the difference between criminal offenses and other types of wrongful conduct.

2. Indicate the essential elements of criminal liability.

3. Describe the constitutional safeguards that protect the rights of persons accused of crimes.

4. Identify and define the crimes that affect business.

5. Summarize the defenses to criminal liability.

Various sanctions are used to bring about a society in which individuals engaging in business can compete and flourish. These sanctions include damages for various types of tortious conduct (as discussed in the preceding chapters), damages for breach of contract (to be discussed in Chapter 13), and the equitable remedies discussed in Chapter 1. Additional sanctions are imposed under criminal law. Many statutes regulating business provide for criminal as well as civil sanctions. Therefore, criminal law joins civil law as an important element in the legal environment of business.

In this chapter, following a brief summary of the major differences between criminal and civil law, we look at how crimes are classified and what elements must be present for criminal liability to exist. We then focus on crimes affecting business and the defenses that can be raised to avoid liability for criminal actions. In the remainder of the chapter, we examine criminal procedural law, which attempts to ensure that a criminal defendant's right to "due process of law" (see quotation alongside) is enforced.

Civil Law and Criminal Law

Remember from Chapter 1 that *civil law* spells out the duties that exist between persons or between citizens and their governments, excluding the duty not to commit crimes. Contract law, for example, is part of civil law. The whole body of tort law, which deals with the infringement by one person on the legally recognized rights of another, is also an area of civil law.

Criminal law, in contrast, has to do with crime. A **crime** can be defined as a wrong against society proclaimed in a statute and, if committed, punishable by society through fines and/or imprisonment—and, in some cases, death. As mentioned in Chapter 1, because crimes are *offenses against society as a whole,* they are prosecuted by a public official, such as a district attorney (D.A.), not by victims.

Crime A wrong against society proclaimed in a statute and, if committed, punishable by society through fines, removal from public office, and/or imprisonment—and, in some cases, death.

Key Differences between Civil Law and Criminal Law

Because the state has extensive resources at its disposal when prosecuting criminal cases, there are numerous procedural safeguards to protect the rights of defendants. One of these safeguards is the higher standard of proof that applies in a criminal case. In a civil case the plaintiff usually must prove his or her case by a *preponderance of the evidence.* Under this standard, the plaintiff must convince the court that, based on the evidence presented by both parties, it is more likely than not that the plaintiff's allegation is true.

In a criminal case, in contrast, the state must prove its case **beyond a reasonable doubt.** Every juror in a criminal case must be convinced, beyond a reasonable doubt, of the defendant's guilt. The higher standard of proof in criminal cases reflects a fundamental social value—a belief that it is worse to convict an innocent individual than to let a guilty person go free. We will look at other safeguards later in the chapter, in the context of criminal procedure.

Beyond a Reasonable Doubt The standard of proof used in criminal cases. If there is any reasonable doubt that a criminal defendant did not commit the crime with which he or she has been charged, then the verdict must be "not guilty."

Civil Liability for Criminal Acts

Those who commit crimes may be subject to both civil and criminal liability.
• **Example 8.1** Joe is walking down the street, minding his own business, when suddenly a person attacks him. In the ensuing struggle, the attacker stabs Joe

several times, seriously injuring him. A police officer restrains and arrests the wrongdoer. In this situation, the attacker may be subject both to criminal prosecution by the state and to a tort lawsuit brought by Joe.● Exhibit 8–1 illustrates how the same wrongful act can result in both a civil (tort) action—an action under tort law, which will be discussed in Chapter 9—and a criminal action against the wrongdoer.

Classification of Crimes

Depending on their degree of seriousness, crimes are classified as felonies or misdemeanors. **Felonies** are serious crimes punishable by death or by imprisonment in a federal or state penitentiary for more than a year. The Model Penal Code[1] provides for four degrees of felony: (1) capital offenses, for which the maximum penalty is death; (2) first degree felonies, punishable by a maximum penalty of life imprisonment; (3) second degree felonies, punishable by

Felony A crime—such as arson, murder, rape, or robbery—that carries the most severe sanctions, which range from one year in a state or federal prison to the death penalty.

---

1. The American Law Institute issued the Official Draft of the Model Penal Code in 1962. The Model Penal Code is not a uniform code. Uniformity of criminal law among the states is not as important as uniformity in other areas of the law. Types of crimes vary with local circumstances, and it is appropriate that punishments vary accordingly. The Model Penal Code contains four parts: (1) general provisions, (2) definitions of special crimes, (3) provisions concerning treatment and corrections, and (4) provisions on the organization of correction.

Exhibit 8–1   Tort Lawsuit and Criminal Prosecution for the Same Act

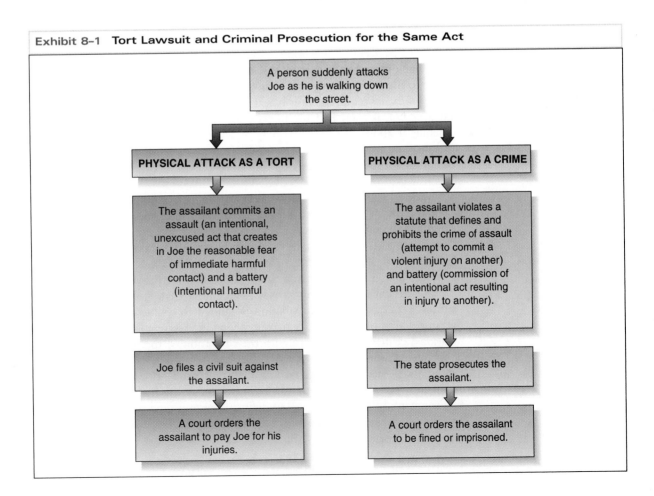

a maximum of ten years' imprisonment; and (4) third degree felonies, punishable by a maximum of five years' imprisonment.

Under federal law and in most states, any crime that is not a felony is considered a **misdemeanor.** Misdemeanors are crimes punishable by a fine or by confinement for up to a year. If incarcerated (imprisoned), the guilty party goes to a local jail instead of a prison. Disorderly conduct and trespass are common misdemeanors. Some states have different classes of misdemeanors. For example, in Illinois misdemeanors are either Class A (confinement for up to a year), Class B (not more than six months), or Class C (not more than thirty days). Whether a crime is a felony or a misdemeanor can also determine whether the case is tried in a magistrate's court (for example, by a justice of the peace) or in a general trial court.

In most jurisdictions, **petty offenses** are considered to be a subset of misdemeanors. Petty offenses are minor violations, such as driving under the influence of alcohol or violations of building codes. Even for petty offenses, however, a guilty party can be put in jail for a few days, fined, or both, depending on state or local law.

Misdemeanor A lesser crime than a felony, punishable by a fine or incarceration in a jail for up to one year.

Petty Offense In criminal law, the least serious kind of criminal offense, such as a traffic or building-code violation.

Criminal Liability

Two elements must exist simultaneously for a person to be convicted of a crime: (1) the performance of a prohibited act and (2) a specified state of mind or intent on the part of the actor. Every criminal statute prohibits certain behavior. Most crimes require an act of *commission;* that is, a person must *do* something in order to be accused of a crime.[2] In some cases, an act of *omission* can be a crime, but only when a person has a legal duty to perform the omitted act. Failure to file a tax return is an example of an omission that is a crime.

The *guilty act* requirement is based on one of the premises of criminal law—that a person is punished for harm done to society. Thinking about killing someone or about stealing a car may be wrong, but the thoughts do no harm until they are translated into action. Of course, a person can be punished for attempting murder or robbery, but normally only if he or she took substantial steps toward the criminal objective.

A *wrongful mental state*[3] is as necessary as a wrongful act in establishing criminal liability. What constitutes such a mental state varies according to the wrongful action. For murder, the act is the taking of a life, and the mental state is the intent to take life. For theft, the guilty act is the taking of another person's property, and the mental state involves both the knowledge that the property belongs to another and the intent to deprive the owner of it.

Criminal liability typically arises for actions that violate state criminal statutes. Federal criminal jurisdiction is limited to crimes that occur outside the jurisdiction of any state, crimes involving interstate commerce or communications, crimes that interfere with the operation of the federal government or its agents, and crimes directed at citizens or property located outside the United States. Federal jurisdiction also exists if a federal law or a federal government agency (such as the U.S. Department of Justice or the federal Environmental Protection Agency) defines a certain type of action as a crime. Today, businesspersons are subject to criminal penalties under numerous fed-

---

2. Called the *actus reus* (pronounced *ak*-tuhs *ray*-uhs), or "guilty act."
3. Called the *mens rea* (pronounced mehns *ray*-uh), or "evil intent."

eral laws and regulations. We will examine many of these laws in later chapters of this text.

Regardless of the type of criminal activity involved, generally the rule is that without the intent required by law for a particular crime, there is no crime. At issue in the following case is whether the required intent for a crime was present.

Case 8.1 ● In re Gavin T.

California Court of Appeal,
First District, Division 5, 1998.
66 Cal.App.4th 238,
77 Cal.Rptr.2d 701.

Historical and Social Setting

Many observers believe that public education deteriorated between the 1950s and the 1990s. Some commentators blame this deterioration on changing achievement standards. Others fault a societal mistrust of institutional authority in general. Suggestions for improving education and the educational environment also range across a wide spectrum. Despite these differences, however, a safe environment is generally considered a necessity for a quality education. A safe environment might be defined as one in which there is little crime or unruly behavior. Discipline is seen as a key to creating a safe environment.

Background and Facts On the grounds of a school, Gavin T., a fifteen-year-old student, was eating lunch. He threw a half-eaten apple toward the outside wall of a classroom some distance away. The apple sailed through a slowly closing door and struck a teacher who was in the room. The teacher was knocked to the floor and lost consciousness for a few minutes. Gavin was charged, in a California state court, with assault by "any means of force likely to produce great bodily injury." The court found that he did not intend to hit the teacher but only intended to see the apple splatter against the outside wall. To send a "message" to his classmates that his actions were wrong, however, the court convicted him of the charge. Gavin appealed.

In the Words of the Court . . .
PETERSON, Presiding Justice.

* * * *

* * * [I]t is black letter law that one cannot unintentionally commit the crime of assault. In order to be found guilty of a criminal assault, one must have either the intent to batter, hit, strike, or wrongfully touch a victim; or one must have a general criminal intent to do an act which is inherently dangerous to human life—such as firing a cannon at an inhabited castle, or driving an elephant into a crowded judicial conference.

* * * *

Here, there was * * * no evidence that appellant intended to strike the teacher with a discarded apple core; and all the evidence and circumstances showed the contrary. In the absence of any sufficient evidence of an intent to touch or strike the victim, the [lower] court rightly found appellant had no such intent, and that he merely intended to watch the discarded apple splatter against the wall. Such an urge may have been juvenile and, therefore, rather appropriate to appellant's age; but it did not constitute a criminal intent to batter the victim or a general criminal intent to act in a manner inherently dangerous to human life.

Decision and Remedy The state intermediate appellate court vacated the order of the lower court and remanded the case with instructions to dismiss it. The appellate court held that a defendant cannot be convicted of assault without having had the intent to commit the crime.

For Critical Analysis—Ethical Consideration *If the lower court's "message" to Gavin and his classmates was that reckless behavior would not be condoned, what was the appellate court's message to the lower court?*

Corporate Criminal Liability

At one time, it was thought that a corporation could not incur criminal liability because, although a corporation is a legal person, it can act only through its agents (corporate directors, officers, and employees). Therefore, the corporate entity itself could not "intend" to commit a crime. Under modern criminal law, however, a corporation may be held liable for crimes. Obviously, corporations cannot be imprisoned, but they can be fined or denied certain legal privileges (such as a license). Today, corporations are normally liable for the crimes committed by their agents and employees within the course and scope of their employment.

Corporate directors and officers are personally liable for the crimes they commit, regardless of whether the crimes were committed for their personal benefit or on the corporation's behalf. Additionally, corporate directors and officers may be held liable for the actions of employees under their supervision. Under what has become known as the "responsible corporate officer" doctrine, a court may impose criminal liability on a corporate officer regardless of whether he or she participated in, directed, or even knew about a given criminal violation.

● **Example 8.2** In *United States v. Park,*[4] the chief executive officer of a national supermarket chain was held personally liable for sanitation violations in corporate warehouses, in which the food was exposed to contamination by rodents. The court imposed personal liability on the corporate officer not because he intended the crime or even knew about it. Rather, liability was imposed because the officer was in a "responsible relationship" to the corporation and had the power to prevent the violation.● Since the *Park* decision, courts have applied this "responsible corporate officer" doctrine on a number of occasions to hold corporate officers liable for their employees' statutory violations.

The following case illustrates that corporate officers and supervisors who oversee operations causing environmental harm may be held liable under the criminal provisions of environmental statutes. (The statute involved in this case—the federal Clean Water Act—will be discussed in Chapter 21.)

---

4. 421 U.S. 658, 95 S.Ct. 1903, 44 L.Ed.2d 489 (1975).

Case 8.2 ● United States v. Hanousek

United States Court of Appeals,
Ninth Circuit, 1999.
176 F.3d 1116.
http://www.ca9.uscourts.gov[a]

Background and Facts Edward Hanousek worked for Pacific & Arctic Railway and Navigation Company (P&A) as a roadmaster of the White Pass & Yukon Railroad in Alaska. Hanousek was responsible "for every detail of the safe and efficient maintenance and construction of track, structures, and marine facilities of the entire railroad," including special projects. One project was a rock quarry, known as "6-mile," above the Skagway River. Next to the quarry, and just beneath the surface, ran a high-pressure oil pipeline owned by Pacific & Arctic Pipeline, Inc., P&A's sister company. When the quarry's backhoe operator punctured the pipeline, an estimated 1,000 to 5,000 gallons of oil were discharged into the river. Hanousek was charged with, among other things, negligently discharging a harmful quantity of oil into a nav-

---

a. The U.S. Court of Appeals for the Ninth Circuit maintains this Web site. Click on the "OPINIONS" oval. From that page, click on the "1999" icon, and when the menu opens, click on "March." Scroll down to "USA V HANOUSEK" and click on the case name to access the case.

Case 8.2 Continued

igable water of the United States in violation of the criminal provisions of the Clean Water Act (CWA). After a trial in a federal district court, a jury convicted Hanousek, and the court imposed a sentence of six months' imprisonment, six months in a halfway house, six months' supervised release, and a fine of $5,000. Hanousek appealed to the U.S. Court of Appeals for the Ninth Circuit, arguing in part that the statute under which he was convicted violated his right to due process because he was not aware of what the CWA required.

In the Words of the Court . . .
DAVID R. THOMPSON, Circuit Judge.

* * * *

The criminal provisions of the CWA [Clean Water Act] constitute public welfare legislation. Public welfare legislation is designed to protect the public from potentially harmful or injurious items and may render criminal a type of conduct that a reasonable person should know is subject to stringent public regulation and may seriously threaten the community's health or safety.

It is well established that a public welfare statute may subject a person to criminal liability for his or her ordinary negligence without violating due process. [Emphasis added.]

* * * [W]here * * * dangerous or deleterious devices or products or obnoxious waste materials are involved, the probability of regulation is so great that anyone who is aware that he is in possession of them or dealing with them must be presumed to be aware of the regulation.

Hanousek argues that * * * he was simply the roadmaster of the White Pass & Yukon railroad charged with overseeing a rock-quarrying project and was not in a position to know what the law required under the CWA. * * * In the context of a public welfare statute, as long as a defendant knows he is dealing with a dangerous device of a character that places him in responsible relation to a public danger, he should be alerted to the probability of strict regulation. * * * Hanousek * * * does not dispute that he was aware that a high-pressure petroleum products pipeline owned by Pacific & Arctic's sister company ran close to the surface next to the railroad tracks at 6-mile, and does not argue that he was unaware of the dangers a break or puncture of the pipeline by a piece of heavy machinery would pose. Therefore, Hanousek should have been alerted to the probability of strict regulation.

In light of [the fact] that the criminal provisions of the CWA constitute public welfare legislation, and the fact that a public welfare statute may impose criminal penalties for ordinary negligent conduct without offending due process, we conclude that [the CWA] does not violate due process by permitting criminal penalties for ordinary negligent conduct.

Decision and Remedy The U.S. Court of Appeals for the Ninth Circuit affirmed Hanousek's conviction. A corporate manager who has responsibility for operations with the potential to cause harm can be held criminally liable for harm that results even if he or she does not actually know of the specific statute under which liability may be imposed.

For Critical Analysis—Social Consideration *As you read earlier in this chapter, one of the essential elements of criminal liability is intent. How can you square the criminal provisions of the Clean Water Act with this intent requirement?*

Types of Crimes

The number of actions that are designated as criminal is nearly endless. Federal, state, and local laws provide for the classification and punishment of hundreds of thousands of different criminal acts. Generally, though, criminal acts can be grouped into six broad categories: violent crime (crimes against persons), property crime, public order crime, white-collar crime, organized crime, and computer crime.

Violent Crime

Some types of crime are called *violent crimes,* or crimes against persons, because they cause others to suffer harm or death. Murder is a violent crime. So is sexual assault, or rape. Assault and battery, which can be civil wrongs, are also classified as violent crimes. **Robbery**—defined as the taking of money, personal property, or any other article of value from a person by means of force or fear—is also a violent crime. Typically, states have more severe penalties for *aggravated robbery*—robbery with the use of a deadly weapon.

Each of these violent crimes is further classified by degree, depending on the circumstances surrounding the criminal act. These circumstances include the intent of the person committing the crime, whether a weapon was used, and (in cases other than murder) the level of pain and suffering experienced by the victim.

Robbery The act of forcefully and unlawfully taking personal property of any value from another; force or intimidation is usually necessary for an act of theft to be considered a robbery.

Property Crime

The most common type of criminal activity is property crime, or those crimes in which the goal of the offender is some form of economic gain or the damaging of property. Robbery is a form of property crime, as well as a violent crime, because the offender seeks to gain the property of another. We look here at a number of other crimes that fall within the general category of property crime.

BURGLARY   At common law, **burglary** was defined as breaking and entering the dwelling of another at night with the intent to commit a felony. Originally, the definition was aimed at protecting an individual's home and its occupants. Most state statutes have eliminated some of the requirements found in the common law definition. The time at which the breaking and entering occurs, for example, is usually immaterial. State statutes frequently omit the element of breaking, and some states do not require that the building be a dwelling. *Aggravated burglary*—which is defined as burglary with the use of a deadly weapon, burglary of a dwelling, or both—incurs a greater penalty.

Burglary The unlawful entry or breaking into a building with the intent to commit a felony. (Some state statutes expand this to include the intent to commit any crime.)

LARCENY   Any person who wrongfully or fraudulently takes and carries away another person's personal property is guilty of **larceny**. Larceny includes the fraudulent intent to deprive an owner permanently of property. Many business-related larcenies entail fraudulent conduct. Whereas robbery involves force or fear, larceny does not. Therefore, picking pockets is larceny, not robbery.

In most states, the definition of property that is subject to larceny statutes has been expanded to cover relatively new forms of theft. • **Example 8.3** Stealing computer programs may constitute larceny even though the "property" consists of magnetic impulses. Stealing computer time may also be considered larceny. So, too, may the theft of natural gas. Trade secrets may be

Larceny The wrongful taking and carrying away of another person's personal property with the intent to permanently deprive the owner of the property. Some states classify larceny as either grand or petit, depending on the property's value.

subject to larceny statutes. Intercepting cellular phone calls to obtain another's phone card number—and then using that number to place long-distance calls, often overseas—is a form of property theft.• These types of larceny are covered by "theft of services" statutes in many jurisdictions.

The common law makes a distinction between grand and petit larceny based on the value of the property taken. Many states have abolished this distinction, but in those that have not, grand larceny (theft above a certain amount) is a felony and petit larceny, a misdemeanor.

ARSON The willful and malicious burning of a building (and in some states, personal property) owned by another is the crime of **arson**. At common law, arson applied only to burning down another person's house. The law was designed to protect human life. Today, arson statutes have been extended to cover the destruction of any building, regardless of ownership, by fire or explosion.

Every state has a special statute that covers a person's burning a building for the purpose of collecting insurance. • **Example 8.4** If Shaw owns an insured apartment building that is falling apart and sets fire to it himself or pays someone else to do so, he is guilty not only of arson but also of defrauding insurers, which is an attempted larceny. Of course, the insurer need not pay the claim when insurance fraud is proved.•

RECEIVING STOLEN GOODS It is a crime to receive stolen goods. The recipient of such goods need not know the true identity of the owner or the thief. All that is necessary is that the recipient knows or should know that the goods are stolen, which implies an intent to deprive the owner of those goods.

FORGERY The fraudulent making or altering of any writing in a way that changes the legal rights and liabilities of another is **forgery**. • **Example 8.5** If, without authorization, Severson signs Bennett's name to the back of a check made out to Bennett, Severson is committing forgery.• Forgery also includes changing trademarks, falsifying public records, counterfeiting, and altering a legal document.

OBTAINING GOODS BY FALSE PRETENSES It is a criminal act to obtain goods by false pretenses—for example, to buy groceries with a check, knowing that one has insufficient funds to cover it. Using another's credit-card number to obtain goods is another example of obtaining goods by false pretenses. Statutes dealing with such illegal activities vary widely from state to state. • **Example 8.6** In some states an intent to defraud must be proved before a person is criminally liable for writing a bad check. Some states define the theft and use of another's credit card as a separate crime, while others consider credit-card crime as a form of forgery.•

Public Order Crime

Historically, societies have always outlawed activities that are considered contrary to public values and morals. Today, the most common public order crimes include public drunkenness, prostitution, gambling, and illegal drug use. These crimes are sometimes referred to as *victimless crimes* because they harm only the offender. From a broader perspective, however, they are deemed detrimental to society as a whole because they often create an environment that may give rise to property and violent crimes.

"A large number of houses deserve to be burnt."

H.G. Wells, 1866–1946
(English author)

Arson The intentional burning of another's dwelling. Some statutes have expanded this to include any real property regardless of ownership and the destruction of property by other means—for example, by explosion.

Forgery The fraudulent making or altering of any writing in a way that changes the legal rights and liabilities of another.

White-Collar Crime

Crimes occurring in the business context are popularly referred to as white-collar crimes. Although there is no official definition of **white-collar crime,** the term is commonly used to mean an illegal act or series of acts committed by an individual or business entity using some nonviolent means to obtain a personal or business advantage. Usually, this kind of crime takes place in the course of a legitimate business occupation. The crimes discussed next normally occur only in the business environment and thus fall into the category of white-collar crimes. Note, though, that certain property crimes, such as larceny and forgery, may also fall into this category if they occur within the business context.

EMBEZZLEMENT   When a person entrusted with another person's property or funds fraudulently appropriates that property or those funds, **embezzlement** occurs. Typically, embezzlement involves an employee who steals funds from his or her employer. Banks face this problem, and so do a number of businesses in which corporate officers or accountants "doctor" the books to cover up the fraudulent conversion of funds for their own benefit. Embezzlement is not larceny, because the wrongdoer does not physically take the property from the possession of another, and it is not robbery, because no force or fear is used.

It does not matter whether the accused takes the money from the victim or from a third person. • **Example 8.7** If, as the financial officer of a large corporation, Carlson pockets a certain number of checks from third parties that were given to her to deposit into the corporate account, she is embezzling.•

Ordinarily, an embezzler who returns what has been taken will not be prosecuted, because the owner usually will not take the time to make a complaint, give depositions, and appear in court. That the accused intended eventually to return the embezzled property, however, does not constitute a sufficient defense to the crime of embezzlement.

MAIL AND WIRE FRAUD   One of the most potent weapons against white-collar criminals is the Mail Fraud Act of 1990.[5] Under this act, it is a federal crime to use the mails to defraud the public. Illegal use of the mails must involve (1) mailing or causing someone else to mail a writing—something written, printed, or photocopied—for the purpose of executing a scheme to defraud and (2) contemplating or organizing a scheme to defraud by false pretenses. If, for example, Johnson advertises by mail the sale of a cure for cancer that he knows to be fraudulent because it has no medical validity, he can be prosecuted for fraudulent use of the mails.

Federal law also makes it a crime (wire fraud) to use wire, radio, or television transmissions to defraud.[6] Violators may be fined up to $1,000, imprisoned for up to five years, or both. If the violation affects a financial institution, the violator may be fined up to $1 million, imprisoned for up to thirty years, or both.

BRIBERY   Basically, three types of bribery are considered crimes: commercial bribery, bribery of public officials, and bribery of foreign officials. As an element of the crime of bribery, intent must be present and proved. The bribe can

---

5. 18 U.S.C. Sections 1341–1342.
6. 18 U.S.C. Section 1343.

be anything the recipient considers to be valuable. Realize that the *crime of bribery occurs when the bribe is offered*. It does not matter whether the person to whom the bribe is offered accepts the bribe or agrees to perform whatever action is desired by the person offering the bribe. *Accepting a bribe* is a separate crime.

Typically, people make commercial bribes to obtain proprietary information, cover up an inferior product, or secure new business. Industrial espionage sometimes involves commercial bribes. For example, a person in one firm may offer an employee in a competing firm some type of payoff in exchange for trade secrets or pricing schedules. So-called kickbacks, or payoffs for special favors or services, are a form of commercial bribery in some situations.

The attempt to influence a public official to act in a way that serves a private interest is a crime. Bribing foreign officials to obtain favorable business contracts is also a crime. This crime was discussed in detail in Chapter 2, along with the Foreign Corrupt Practices Act of 1977, which was passed to curb the use of bribery by American businesspersons in securing foreign contracts.

BANKRUPTCY FRAUD   Today, federal bankruptcy law (see Chapter 15) allows individuals and businesses to be relieved of oppressive debt through bankruptcy proceedings. Numerous white-collar crimes may be committed during the many phases of a bankruptcy action. A creditor, for example, may file a false claim against the debtor, which is a crime. Also, a debtor may fraudulently transfer assets to favored parties before or after the petition for bankruptcy is filed. For example, a company-owned automobile may be "sold" at a bargain price to a trusted friend or relative. Closely related to the crime of fraudulent transfer of property is the crime of fraudulent concealment of property, such as the hiding of gold coins.

INSIDER TRADING   An individual who obtains "inside information" about the plans of publicly held corporations can often make stock-trading profits by using the information to guide decisions relating to the purchase or sale of corporate securities. *Insider trading* is a violation of securities law and will be considered more fully in Chapter 24. At this point, it may be said that one who possesses inside information and who has a duty not to disclose it to outsiders may not profit from the purchase or sale of securities based on that information until the information is available to the public.

THE THEFT OF TRADE SECRETS   As will be discussed in Chapter 11, trade secrets constitute a form of intellectual property that for many businesses can be extremely valuable. The Economic Espionage Act of 1996[7] makes the theft of trade secrets a federal crime. The act also makes it a federal crime to buy or possess another person's trade secrets, knowing that the trade secrets were stolen or otherwise acquired without the owner's authorization.

Violations of the act can result in steep penalties. The act provides that an individual who violates the act can be imprisoned for up to ten years and fined up to $500,000. If a corporation or other organization violates the act, it can be fined up to $5 million. Additionally, the law provides that any property acquired as a result of the violation and any property used in the commission of the violation is subject to criminal forfeiture—meaning that the government

---

7. 18 U.S.C. Sections 1831–1839.

can take the property. A theft of trade secrets conducted via the Internet, for example, could result in the forfeiture of every computer, printer, or other device used to commit or facilitate the violation.

Organized Crime

White-collar crime takes place within the confines of the legitimate business world. Organized crime, in contrast, operates *illegitimately* by satisfying the public's demand for illegal goods and services. For organized crime, the traditional preferred markets are gambling, prostitution, illegal narcotics, pornography, and loan sharking (lending money at higher than legal interest rates), along with more recent ventures into counterfeiting and credit-card scams.

Money Laundering Falsely reporting income that has been obtained through criminal activity as income obtained through a legitimate business enterprise—in effect, "laundering" the "dirty money."

MONEY LAUNDERING The profits from organized crime and other illegal activities amount to billions of dollars a year, particularly the profits from illegal drug transactions and, to a lesser extent, from racketeering, prostitution, and gambling. Under federal law, banks, savings and loan associations, and other financial institutions are required to report currency transactions of over $10,000. Consequently, those who engage in illegal activities face difficulties in depositing their cash profits from illegal transactions.

As an alternative to simply placing cash from illegal transactions in bank deposits, wrongdoers and racketeers have invented ways to launder "dirty" money to make it "clean." This **money laundering** is done through legitimate businesses. • Example 8.8 A successful drug dealer might become a partner with a restaurateur. Little by little, the restaurant shows an increasing profit. As a shareholder or partner in the restaurant, the wrongdoer is able to report the "profits" of the restaurant as legitimate income on which federal and state taxes are paid. The wrongdoer can then spend those monies without worrying about whether his or her lifestyle exceeds the level possible with his or her reported income.•

The Federal Bureau of Investigation estimates that organized crime alone has invested tens of billions of dollars in as many as a hundred thousand business establishments in the United States for the purpose of money laundering. Globally, it is estimated that $300 billion in illegal money moves through the world banking system every year.

RICO In 1970, in an effort to curb the apparently increasing entry of organized crime into the legitimate business world, Congress passed the Racketeer Influenced and Corrupt Organizations Act (RICO).[8] The act, which was enacted as part of the Organized Crime Control Act, makes it a federal crime to (1) use income obtained from racketeering activity to purchase any interest in an enterprise, (2) acquire or maintain an interest in an enterprise through racketeering activity, (3) conduct or participate in the affairs of an enterprise through racketeering activity, or (4) conspire to do any of the preceding activities.

Racketeering activity is not a new type of substantive crime created by RICO; rather, RICO incorporates by reference twenty-six separate types of federal crimes and nine types of state felonies[9] and declares that if a person commits two of these offenses, he or she is guilty of "racketeering activity." The act provides for both civil and criminal liability.

---

8. 18 U.S.C. Sections 1961–1968.
9. See 18 U.S.C. Section 1961(1)(A).

CIVIL LIABILITY UNDER RICO   The penalties for violations of the RICO statute are harsh. In the event of a violation, the statute permits the government to seek civil penalties, including the divestiture of a defendant's interest in a business (called forfeiture) or the dissolution of the business. Perhaps the most controversial aspect of RICO is that in some cases, private individuals are allowed to recover three times their actual losses (treble damages), plus attorneys' fees, for business injuries caused by a violation of the statute.

The broad language of RICO has allowed it to be applied in cases that have little or nothing to do with organized crime, and an aggressive trial attorney may attempt to show that any business fraud constitutes "racketeering activity." In its 1985 decision in *Sedima, S.P.R.L. v. Imrex Co.,*[10] the United States Supreme Court interpreted RICO broadly and set a significant precedent for subsequent applications of the act. Plaintiffs have used the RICO statute in numerous commercial fraud cases because of the inviting prospect of being awarded treble damages if they win. The most frequent targets of civil RICO lawsuits are insurance companies, employment agencies, commercial banks, and stockbrokerage firms.

One of the requirements of RICO is that there be more than one offense—there must be a "pattern of racketeering activity." What constitutes a "pattern" has been the subject of much litigation. According to the interpretation of some courts, a pattern must involve, among other things, continued criminal activity. This is known as the "continuity" requirement. Part of this requirement is that the activity occur over a "substantial" period of time.

Computer Crime Any act that is directed against computers and computer parts, that uses computers as instruments of crime, or that involves computers and constitutes abuse.

CRIMINAL LIABILITY UNDER RICO   Many criminal RICO offenses, such as gambling, arson, and extortion, have little, if anything, to do with normal business activities. But securities fraud (involving the sale of stocks and bonds) and mail and wire fraud also may constitute criminal RICO violations, and RICO has become an effective tool in attacking these white-collar crimes in recent years. Under the criminal provisions of RICO, any individual found guilty of a violation is subject to a fine of up to $25,000 per violation, imprisonment for up to twenty years, or both.

Computer Crime

The American Bar Association defines **computer crime** as any act that is directed against computers and computer parts, that uses computers as instruments of crime, or that involves computers and constitutes abuse. A variety of different types of crime can be committed with or against computers, including the cyber crimes discussed in this chapter's *Legal E-nvironment* on page 218. The dependence of businesses on computer operations has left firms vulnerable to sabotage, fraud, embezzlement, and the theft of proprietary data, such as trade secrets or other intellectual property (discussed in Chapter 11).

Many computer crimes fall into the broad category of financial crimes. Computer networks provide opportunities for employees and others to commit crimes that can involve serious economic losses. ● **Example 8.9** Employees of accounting and computer departments can transfer monies among accounts with little effort and often with less risk than that involved in transactions evidenced by paperwork.● The potential for crime in the area of financial transactions is great; most monetary losses from computer crime are suffered in this area.

Two people work together on a computer. If the work being done is copied by another employee without permission and given to a business competitor, what crime has been committed?

---

10. 473 U.S. 479, 105 S.Ct. 3275, 87 L.Ed.2d 346 (1985).

Legal *e*-nvironment

Crime Control versus Civil Liberties

Cyber crimes—crimes committed via the Internet—understandably raise new legal questions. Given the unique nature of the Internet, a threshold issue with respect to any legal action has to do with jurisdiction, a topic discussed in Chapter 5. Other problematic concerns relate to the difficulty of applying traditional laws, which were designed to protect persons from physical harm or to safeguard their physical property, to crimes committed in cyberspace. For example, a federal statute makes it illegal to threaten physical violence to property. A threat to delete computer files, however, does not involve physical violence to property. We look here at yet another perplexing problem facing lawmakers today—the difficulty of detecting and prosecuting cyber crimes.

Investigating and Prosecuting Cyber Crimes

The online environment makes it difficult to identify and prosecute those who commit cyber crimes. Cyber criminals do not leave physical traces, such as fingerprints or DNA samples, as evidence of their crimes. Even electronic "footprints" can be hard to find and follow. For example, e-mail may be sent through a remailer, an online service that guarantees that a message cannot be traced to its source.

In spite of all these difficulties, law enforcement officials have been able to discover the identities of those who commit cyber wrongs, such as hackers who access others' databases without authorization and programmers who create and transmit online destructive viruses. Governments in some countries, such as Russia, have succeeded in controlling Internet crime to some extent by monitoring the e-mail and other electronic transmissions of users of certain Internet service providers. In the United States, however, any government attempt to monitor Internet use to detect criminal conspiracies or activities would likely be challenged as violating the constitutional rights of Americans.

The FBI's Carnivore Program

Consider the Carnivore program launched by the Federal Bureau of Investigation (FBI) in 1999. The program was established to monitor e-mail and other online transmissions to and from particular criminal suspects. Although the FBI states that the program is used only under court order and is closely supervised by officials in the Department of Justice, it has nonetheless elicited a great deal of controversy. Critics claim that this unprecedented form of communications surveillance is a threat to Americans' privacy rights because in addition to targeting criminal suspects, the government could also monitor the communications of innocent citizens. As a result of public concern over the program, Congress held hearings to see if the program can be justified.

For Critical Analysis: *Should Americans be willing to sacrifice some of their civil liberties in order to allow the government to protect them from cyber crimes, including online terrorist conspiracies that threaten U.S. national security?*

> **BE AWARE** Technological change is one of the primary factors that lead to new types of crime.

The theft of computer equipment and the theft of goods with the aid of computers (such as by manipulating inventory records to disguise the theft of goods) are subject to the same criminal and tort laws as thefts of other physical property. In many jurisdictions, the unauthorized use of computer data or services is considered larceny. Other computer crimes include vandalism and destructive programming. A knowledgeable individual, such as an angry employee whose job has just been terminated, can do a considerable amount of damage to computer data and files. Destructive programming in the form of "viruses" presents an ongoing problem for businesspersons and other computer users today.

Defenses to Criminal Liability

Among the most important defenses to criminal liability are infancy, intoxication, insanity, mistake, consent, duress, justifiable use of force, entrapment, and the statute of limitations. Many of these defenses involve assertions that the intent requirement for criminal liability is lacking. Also, in some cases, defendants are given immunity and thus relieved, at least in part, of criminal liability for crimes they committed. We look at each of these defenses here.

Note that procedural violations (such as obtaining evidence without a valid search warrant) may operate as defenses also—because evidence obtained in violation of a defendant's constitutional rights normally may not be admitted in court. If the evidence is suppressed, then there may be no basis for prosecuting the defendant. (Criminal procedures will be discussed later in this chapter.)

Infancy

The term *infant,* as used in the law, refers to any person who has not yet reached the age of majority (see Chapter 12). In all states, certain courts handle cases involving children who are alleged to have violated the law. In some states, juvenile courts handle children's cases exclusively. In other states, however, courts that handle children's cases may also have jurisdiction over other matters.

Originally, juvenile court hearings were informal, and lawyers were rarely present. Since 1967, however, when the United States Supreme Court ordered that a child charged with delinquency must be allowed to consult with an attorney before being committed to a state institution,[11] juvenile court hearings have become more formal. In some states, a child will be treated as an adult and tried in a regular court if he or she is above a certain age (usually fourteen) and is guilty of a felony, such as rape or murder.

Intoxication

The law recognizes two types of intoxication, whether from drugs or from alcohol: *involuntary* and *voluntary.* Involuntary intoxication occurs when a person either is physically forced to ingest or inject an intoxicating substance or is unaware that a substance contains drugs or alcohol. Involuntary intoxication is a defense to a crime if its effect was to make a person incapable of obeying the law or incapable of understanding that the act committed was wrong. There is controversy as to whether voluntary intoxication is a defense when the defendant was *extremely* intoxicated when committing the wrong. In the following case, the United States Supreme Court had to decide whether a state law banning the introduction at trial of evidence of intoxication violated the defendant's constitutional right to due process of law.

---

11. *In re Gault,* 387 U.S. 1, 87 S.Ct. 1428, 18 L.Ed.2d 527 (1967).

Case 8.3 ● Montana v. Egelhoff

Supreme Court of the United States, 1996.
518 U.S. 37,
116 S.Ct. 2013,
135 L.Ed.2d 361.
**http://supct.law.cornell.edu/
supct/html/95-566.ZS.html**[a]

---

a. This is a page within the "Historic Supreme Court Decisions" collection of the Legal Information Institute (LII) and Project Hermes available at the LII site on the Web. Read the opinion beginning with the syllabus on this page or click on a link to take advantage of one of the other options.

Historical and Social Setting *Using voluntary drug or alcohol intoxication as a defense is based on the theory that extreme levels of intoxication may negate the state of mind that a crime requires. Many courts are reluctant to allow voluntary intoxication as a defense to a crime, however. After all, the defendant, by definition, voluntarily chose to put himself or herself into an intoxicated state.*

Background and Facts James Egelhoff was charged in a Montana state court with two counts of
(Continued)

Case 8.3 Continued

deliberate homicide. Egelhoff claimed that he had been intoxicated at the time the incident occurred and therefore he lacked the mental state required for commission of the crime of murder. Under a state statute, the jury was told not to consider his intoxication in determining whether he had lacked the required mental state. The jury found him guilty, and he appealed. The Montana Supreme Court reversed, reasoning that a defendant has a right, under the Constitution's due process clause, to have a jury consider evidence of voluntary intoxication in deciding whether he or she had the requisite mental state. The state appealed to the United States Supreme Court.

In the Words of the Court . . .
Justice SCALIA announced the judgment of the Court * * * .

* * * *

* * * [The] stern rejection of inebriation [drunkenness] as a defense became a fixture of early American law * * * .

* * * *

* * * Over the course of the 19th century, courts carved out an exception * * * .

* * * *

* * * [O]ne-fifth of the States either never adopted the [exception] or have recently abandoned it.

* * * [P]rohibiting consideration of voluntary intoxication in the determination of *mens rea* * * * has considerable justification * * * . [For example, d]isallowing consideration of voluntary intoxication has the effect of increasing the punishment for all unlawful acts committed in that state, and thereby deters drunkenness or irresponsible behavior while drunk. * * *

* * * *

* * * [T]he rule allowing a jury to consider evidence of a defendant's voluntary intoxication where relevant to *mens rea* * * * has not received sufficiently uniform and permanent allegiance to qualify as fundamental, especially since it displaces a lengthy common-law tradition which remains supported by valid justifications today.

Decision and Remedy The Supreme Court held that Montana's ban did not violate the Constitution's due process clause. The Court reversed the state supreme court's decision.

For Critical Analysis—Social Consideration *Do you agree that disallowing voluntary intoxication as a defense "deters drunkenness or irresponsible behavior while drunk"? Why or why not?*

> **"Insanity is often the logic of an accurate mind overtaxed."**
>
> Oliver Wendell Holmes, Jr.,
> 1841–1935
> (Associate justice of the United States
> Supreme Court, 1902–1932)

Insanity

Just as a child is often judged incapable of the state of mind required to commit a crime, so also may be someone suffering from a mental illness. Thus, insanity may be a defense to a criminal charge. The courts have had difficulty deciding what the test for legal insanity should be, and psychiatrists as well as lawyers are critical of the tests used. Almost all federal courts and some states use the relatively liberal standard set forth in the Model Penal Code:

> A person is not responsible for criminal conduct if at the time of such conduct as a result of mental disease or defect he lacks substantial capacity either to appreciate the wrongfulness of his conduct or to conform his conduct to the requirements of the law.

Some states use the *M'Naghten* test,[12] under which a criminal defendant is not responsible if, at the time of the offense, he or she did not know the nature and quality of the act or did not know that the act was wrong. Other states use the irresistible-impulse test. A person operating under an irresistible impulse may know an act is wrong but cannot refrain from doing it.

Mistake

Everyone has heard the saying, "Ignorance of the law is no excuse." Ordinarily, ignorance of the law or a mistaken idea about what the law requires is not a valid defense. In some states, however, that rule has been modified. Criminal defendants who claim that they honestly did not know that they were breaking a law may have a valid defense if (1) the law was not published or reasonably made known to the public or (2) the defendant relied on an official statement of the law that was erroneous.

Compare "Ignorance" is a lack of information. "Mistake" is a confusion of information.

A *mistake of fact,* as opposed to a *mistake of law,* operates as a defense if it negates the mental state necessary to commit a crime. • **Example 8.10** If Oliver Wheaton mistakenly walks off with Julie Tyson's briefcase because he thinks it is his, there is no theft. Theft requires knowledge that the property belongs to another. (If Wheaton's act causes Tyson to incur damages, however, Wheaton may be subject to tort liability for trespass to personalty or conversion.)•

Consent

What if a victim consents to a crime or even encourages the person intending a criminal act to commit it? The law allows **consent** as a defense if the consent cancels the harm that the law is designed to prevent. In each case, the question is whether the law forbids an act that was committed against the victim's will or forbids the act without regard to the victim's wish. The law forbids murder, prostitution, and drug use regardless of whether the victim consents to it. Also, if the act causes harm to a third person who has not consented, there is no escape from criminal liability. Consent or forgiveness given after a crime has been committed is not really a defense, though it can affect the likelihood of prosecution. Consent operates as a defense most successfully in crimes against property.

Consent Voluntary agreement to a proposition or an act of another. A concurrence of wills.

Duress

Duress exists when the *wrongful threat* of one person induces another person to perform an act that he or she would not otherwise perform. In such a situation, duress is said to negate the mental state necessary to commit a crime. For duress to qualify as a defense, the following requirements must be met:

Duress Unlawful pressure brought to bear on a person, causing the person to perform an act that he or she would not otherwise perform.

1. The threat must be of serious bodily harm or death.
2. The harm threatened must be greater than the harm caused by the crime.
3. The threat must be immediate and inescapable.
4. The defendant must have been involved in the situation through no fault of his or her own.

Justifiable Use of Force

Probably the most well-known defense to criminal liability is **self-defense.** Other situations, however, also justify the use of force: the defense of one's

Self-Defense The legally recognized privilege to protect one's self or property against injury by another. The privilege of self-defense protects only acts that are reasonably necessary to protect oneself, one's property, or another person.

---

12. A rule derived from *M'Naghten's Case,* 8 Eng.Rep. 718 (1843).

dwelling, the defense of other property, and the prevention of a crime. In all of these situations, it is important to distinguish between the use of deadly and nondeadly force. *Deadly force* is likely to result in death or serious bodily harm. *Nondeadly force* is force that reasonably appears necessary to prevent the imminent use of criminal force.

Generally speaking, people can use the amount of nondeadly force that seems necessary to protect themselves, their dwellings, or other property or to prevent the commission of a crime. Deadly force can be used in self-defense if there is a *reasonable belief* that imminent death or grievous bodily harm will otherwise result, if the attacker is using unlawful force (an example of lawful force is that exerted by a police officer), and if the defender has not initiated or provoked the attack. Deadly force normally can be used to defend a dwelling only if the unlawful entry is violent and the person believes deadly force is necessary to prevent imminent death or great bodily harm or—in some jurisdictions—if the person believes deadly force is necessary to prevent the commission of a felony (such as arson) in the dwelling.

Entrapment

Entrapment In criminal law, a defense in which the defendant claims that he or she was induced by a public official—usually an undercover agent or police officer—to commit a crime that he or she would otherwise not have committed.

Entrapment is a defense designed to prevent police officers or other government agents from encouraging crimes in order to apprehend persons wanted for criminal acts. In the typical entrapment case, an undercover agent *suggests* that a crime be committed and somehow pressures or induces an individual to commit it. The agent then arrests the individual for the crime.

For entrapment to be considered a defense, both the suggestion and the inducement must take place. The defense is intended not to prevent law enforcement agents from setting a trap for an unwary criminal but rather to prevent them from pushing the individual into it. The crucial issue is whether a person who committed a crime was predisposed to commit the crime or did so because the agent induced it.

Statute of Limitations

With some exceptions, such as for the crime of murder, statutes of limitations apply to crimes just as they do to civil wrongs. In other words, criminal cases must be prosecuted within a certain number of years. If a criminal action is brought after the statutory time period has expired, the accused person can raise the statute of limitations as a defense.

Immunity

Plea Bargaining The process by which a criminal defendant and the prosecutor in a criminal case work out a mutually satisfactory disposition of the case, subject to court approval; usually involves the defendant's pleading guilty to a lesser offense in return for a lighter sentence.

At times, the state may wish to obtain information from a person accused of a crime. Accused persons are understandably reluctant to give information if it will be used to prosecute them, and they cannot be forced to do so. The privilege against self-incrimination is granted by the Fifth Amendment to the Constitution, which reads, in part, "nor shall [any person] be compelled in any criminal case to be a witness against himself." In cases in which the state wishes to obtain information from a person accused of a crime, the state can grant *immunity* from prosecution or agree to prosecute for a less serious offense in exchange for the information. Once immunity is given, the person can no longer refuse to testify on Fifth Amendment grounds, because he or she now has an absolute privilege against self-incrimination.

Often a grant of immunity from prosecution for a serious crime is part of the **plea bargaining** between the defendant and the prosecuting attorney. The defendant may be convicted of a lesser offense, while the state uses the defendant's testimony to prosecute accomplices for serious crimes carrying heavy penalties.

Constitutional Safeguards and Criminal Procedures

Criminal law brings the power of the state, with all its resources, to bear against the individual. Criminal procedures are designed to protect the constitutional rights of individuals and to prevent the arbitrary use of power on the part of the government.

The U.S. Constitution provides specific safeguards for those accused of crimes. Most of these safeguards protect individuals against state government actions, as well as federal government actions, by virtue of the due process clause of the Fourteenth Amendment. These safeguards are set forth in the Fourth, Fifth, Sixth, and Eighth Amendments.

Fourth Amendment Protections

The Fourth Amendment protects the "right of the people to be secure in their persons, houses, papers, and effects." Before searching or seizing private property, law enforcement officers must obtain a **search warrant**—an order from a judge or other public official authorizing the search or seizure.

Search Warrant An order granted by a public authority, such as a judge, that authorizes law enforcement personnel to search particular premises or property.

SEARCH WARRANTS AND PROBABLE CAUSE To obtain a search warrant, the officers must convince a judge that they have reasonable grounds, or **probable cause,** to believe a search will reveal a specific illegality. Probable cause requires law enforcement officials to have trustworthy evidence that would convince a reasonable person that the proposed search or seizure is more likely justified than not. Furthermore, the Fourth Amendment prohibits general warrants. It requires a particular description of that which is to be searched or seized. General searches through a person's belongings are impermissible. The search cannot extend beyond what is described in the warrant.

Probable Cause Reasonable grounds to believe the existence of facts warranting certain actions, such as the search or arrest of a person.

There are exceptions to the requirement of a search warrant, as when it is likely that the items sought will be removed before a warrant can be obtained. For example, if a police officer has probable cause to believe an automobile contains evidence of a crime and it is likely that the vehicle will be unavailable by the time a warrant is obtained, the officer can search the vehicle without a warrant.

SEARCHES AND SEIZURES IN THE BUSINESS CONTEXT Constitutional protection against unreasonable searches and seizures is important to businesses and professionals. As federal and state regulation of commercial activities increased, frequent and unannounced government inspections were conducted to ensure compliance with the regulations. Such inspections were at times extremely disruptive. In *Marshall v. Barlow's, Inc.,*[13] the United States Supreme Court held that government inspectors do not have the right to enter business premises without a warrant, although the standard of probable cause is not the same as that required in nonbusiness contexts. The existence of a general and neutral enforcement plan will justify issuance of the warrant.

Lawyers and accountants frequently possess the business records of their clients, and inspecting these documents while they are out of the hands of their true owners also requires a warrant. No warrant is required, however, for

---

13. 436 U.S. 307, 98 S.Ct. 1816, 56 L.Ed.2d 305 (1978).

seizures of spoiled or contaminated food. Nor are warrants required for searches of businesses in such highly regulated industries as liquor, guns, and strip mining. General manufacturing is not considered to be one of these highly regulated industries, however.

Of increasing concern to many employers is how to maintain a safe and efficient workplace without jeopardizing the Fourth Amendment rights of employees "to be secure in their persons." Requiring employees to undergo random drug tests, for example, may be held to violate the Fourth Amendment. In Chapter 17, we discuss Fourth Amendment issues in the employment context, as well as the privacy rights of employees in general, in detail.

Fifth Amendment Protections

The Fifth Amendment offers significant protections for accused persons. One is the requirement that no one can be deprived of "life, liberty, or property without due process of law." Two other important Fifth Amendment provisions protect persons against double jeopardy and self-incrimination.

DUE PROCESS OF LAW   Remember from Chapter 6 that *due process of law* has both procedural and substantive aspects. Procedural due process requirements underlie criminal procedures. Basically, the law must be carried out in a fair and orderly way. In criminal cases, due process means that defendants should have an opportunity to object to the charges against them before a fair, neutral decision maker, such as a judge. Defendants must also be given the opportunity to confront and cross-examine witnesses and accusers and to present their own witnesses.

Double Jeopardy A situation occurring when a person is tried twice for the same criminal offense; prohibited by the Fifth Amendment to the Constitution.

DOUBLE JEOPARDY   The Fifth Amendment also protects persons from **double jeopardy** (being tried twice for the same criminal offense). The prohibition against double jeopardy means that once a criminal defendant is acquitted (found "not guilty") of a particular crime, the government may not reindict the person and retry him or her for the same crime. The prohibition against double jeopardy does not preclude the crime victim from bringing a civil suit against the same person to recover damages, however. For example, a person found "not guilty" of assault and battery in a criminal case may be sued by the victim in a civil tort case for damages. Additionally, a state's prosecution of a crime will not prevent a separate federal prosecution relating to the same activity, and vice versa. For example, a person who is prosecuted for assault and battery in a state court may be prosecuted in a federal court for civil rights violations resulting from the same action.

Be Aware The Fifth Amendment protection against self-incrimination does not cover partnerships or corporations.

Self-Incrimination The giving of testimony that may subject the testifier to criminal prosecution. The Fifth Amendment to the Constitution protects against self-incrimination by providing that no person "shall be compelled in any criminal case to be a witness against himself."

SELF-INCRIMINATION   The Fifth Amendment guarantees that no person "shall be compelled in any criminal case to be a witness against himself." Thus, in any criminal proceeding, an accused person cannot be compelled to give testimony that might subject him or her to any criminal prosecution.

The Fifth Amendment's guarantee against **self-incrimination** extends only to natural persons. Because a corporation is a legal entity and not a natural person, the privilege against self-incrimination does not apply to it. Similarly, the business records of a partnership do not receive Fifth Amendment protection.[14] When a partnership is required to produce these records, it must give the information even if it incriminates the persons who constitute the business

---

14. The privilege has been applied to some small family partnerships. See *United States v. Slutsky*, 352 F.Supp. 1005 (S.D.N.Y. 1972).

International Perspective

The Fifth Amendment and Foreign Governments

The Fifth Amendment to the U.S. Constitution allows defendants or witnesses in criminal cases to refuse to answer certain questions if their answers may be self-incriminating and lead to future government prosecutions against them. But what if a person fears that a foreign government may bring a criminal prosecution against him or her as a result of statements made in a U.S. legal proceeding? Can that person "take the Fifth"? This question recently came before the United States Supreme Court in *United States v. Balsys.*[a] The case

a. 524 U.S. 666, 118 S.Ct. 2218, 141 L.Ed.2d 575 (1998).

involved a resident alien, Aloyzas Balsys, who was requested to testify before the Justice Department's Office of Special Investigations (OSI). The OSI sought to determine whether Balsys had lied on his immigration application about his activities during World War II. Balsys asserted the Fifth Amendment privilege against self-incrimination, contending that compliance with the OSI's request could subject him to prosecution for war crimes by foreign governments, such as Germany or Israel. The Supreme Court held that Balsys's concern with foreign prosecution was beyond the scope of the Fifth Amendment, which applied only to possible federal or state government prosecutions in the United States. Therefore, Balsys could not avoid complying with the OSI's request on Fifth Amendment grounds.

For Critical Analysis: *How would you argue in support of the Supreme Court's conclusion in this case?*

---

entity. Sole proprietors and sole practitioners (those who fully own their businesses) who have not incorporated cannot be compelled to produce their business records. These individuals have full protection against self-incrimination, because they function in only one capacity; there is no separate business entity.

> "A search is not to be made legal by what it turns up."
>
> Robert H. Jackson, 1892–1954
> (Associate justice of the United States Supreme Court, 1941–1954)

Protections under the Sixth Amendment and Eighth Amendment

The Sixth Amendment guarantees several important rights for criminal defendants: the right to a speedy trial, the right to a jury trial, the right to a public trial, the right to confront witnesses, and the right to counsel. The Eighth Amendment prohibits excessive bails and fines, and cruel and unusual punishment.

Ethical Issue 8.1

Can asset forfeitures violate the Eighth Amendment?

Questions of fairness often arise in asset forfeiture proceedings under RICO or other laws because sometimes the punishment (the value of the assets forfeited) can be grossly disproportionate to the crime. For example, suppose that a U.S. citizen boards an international flight carrying $357,144 but does not declare that he or she is carrying that amount (in violation of

a federal law that requires the reporting of any transport of more than $10,000 in U.S. currency). Should the entire amount ($357,144) be subject to forfeiture, even though the funds were legally acquired and were being transported to pay a legal debt? If so, would the forfeiture violate the "excessive fines" clause of the Eighth Amendment? In 1998, addressing this issue for the first time, the United States Supreme Court gave some guidance to the lower courts on this issue. The Court held that "a punitive forfeiture violates the Excessive Fines Clause if it is grossly disproportional to the gravity of a defendant's offense."[a]

a. *United States v. Bajakajian,* 524 U.S. 321, 118 S.Ct. 2028, 141 L.Ed.2d 314 (1998).

The Exclusionary Rule and the *Miranda* Rule

Two other procedural protections for criminal defendants are the exclusionary rule and the *Miranda* rule.

Exclusionary Rule In criminal procedure, a rule under which any evidence that is obtained in violation of the accused's constitutional rights guaranteed by the Fourth, Fifth, and Sixth Amendments, as well as any evidence derived from illegally obtained evidence, will not be admissible in court.

THE EXCLUSIONARY RULE Under what is known as the **exclusionary rule,** all evidence obtained in violation of the constitutional rights spelled out in the Fourth, Fifth, and Sixth Amendments normally must be excluded from the trial, as well as all evidence derived from the illegally obtained evidence. Illegally obtained evidence is known as the "fruit of the poisonous tree." For example, if a confession is obtained after an illegal arrest, the arrest is "the poisonous tree," and the confession, if "tainted" by the arrest, is the "fruit."

The purpose of the exclusionary rule is to deter police from conducting warrantless searches and other misconduct. The rule is sometimes criticized because it can lead to injustice. Many a defendant has "gotten off on a technicality" because law enforcement personnel failed to observe procedural requirements. Even though a defendant may be obviously guilty, if the evidence of that guilt is obtained improperly (without a valid search warrant, for example), it normally cannot be used against the defendant in court.

Note A person may be convicted despite police misconduct, because evidence obtained independently of the misconduct is admissible.

THE *MIRANDA* RULE In *Miranda v. Arizona,* the United States Supreme Court established the rule that individuals who are arrested must be informed of certain constitutional rights, including their Fifth Amendment right to remain silent and their Sixth Amendment right to counsel. If the arresting officers fail to inform a criminal suspect of these constitutional rights, any statements the suspect makes normally will not be admissible in court. Because of its importance in criminal procedure, the *Miranda* case is presented as this chapter's *Landmark in the Legal Environment.*

Police officers take a suspect into custody. Why must a criminal suspect be informed of his or her legal rights?

EXCEPTIONS TO THE *MIRANDA* RULE As part of a continuing attempt to balance the rights of accused persons against the rights of society, the Supreme Court has made a number of exceptions to the *Miranda* ruling. In 1984, for example, the Court recognized a "public safety" exception to the *Miranda* rule. The need to protect the public warranted the admissibility of statements made by the defendant (in this case, indicating where he placed the gun) as evidence in a trial, even when the defendant had not been informed of his *Miranda* rights.[15]

In 1986, the Court further held that a confession need not be excluded even though the police failed to inform a suspect in custody that his attorney had tried to reach him by telephone.[16] In an important 1991 decision, the Court stated that a suspect's conviction will not be automatically overturned if the suspect was coerced into making a confession. If the other evidence admitted at trial was strong enough to justify the conviction without the confession, then the fact that the confession was obtained illegally can be, in effect, ignored.[17] In yet another case, in 1994, the Supreme Court ruled that a suspect must unequivocally and assertively state his right to counsel in order to stop police questioning. Saying, "Maybe I should talk to a lawyer" during an interrogation

---

15. *New York v. Quarles,* 467 U.S. 649, 104 S.Ct. 2626, 81 L.Ed.2d 550 (1984).
16. *Moran v. Burbine,* 475 U.S. 412, 106 S.Ct. 1135, 89 L.Ed.2d 410 (1986).
17. *Arizona v. Fulminante,* 499 U.S. 279, 111 S.Ct. 1246, 113 L.Ed.2d 302 (1991).

Landmark in the Legal Environment

Miranda v. Arizona (1966)

The United States Supreme Court's decision in *Miranda v. Arizona*[a] has been cited in more court decisions than any other case in the history of American law. Through television shows and other media, the case has also become familiar to most of America's adult population. The case arose after Ernesto Miranda was arrested in his home, on March 13, 1963, for the kidnapping and rape of an eighteen-year-old woman. Miranda was taken to a Phoenix, Arizona, police station and questioned by two police officers. Two hours later, the officers emerged from the interrogation room with a written confession signed by Miranda. The confession was admitted into evidence at the trial, and Miranda was convicted and sentenced to prison for twenty to thirty years.

Miranda appealed the decision, claiming that he had not been informed of his constitutional rights. He did not claim that he was innocent of the crime or that his confession was false or made under duress. He only claimed that he would not have confessed to the crime if he had been advised of his right to remain silent and to have an attorney. Nonetheless, the Supreme Court of Arizona held that Miranda's constitutional rights had not been violated and affirmed his conviction. In forming its decision, the court emphasized the fact that Miranda had not specifically requested an attorney. The *Miranda* case was subsequently consolidated with three other cases involving similar issues and reviewed by the United States Supreme Court.

In its decision, the Supreme Court stated that whenever an individual is taken into custody, "the following measures are required: He must be warned prior to any questioning that he has the right to remain silent, that anything he says can be used against him in a court of law, that he has the right to the presence of an attorney, and that if he cannot afford an attorney one will be appointed for him prior to any questioning if he so desires." If the accused waives his or her rights to remain silent and to have counsel present, the government must be able to demonstrate that the waiver was made knowingly, intelligently, and voluntarily.

Today, both on television and in the real world, police officers routinely advise suspects of their "*Miranda* rights" on arrest. When Ernesto Miranda himself was later murdered, the suspected murderer was "read his *Miranda* rights."

For Critical Analysis: *Why should defendants who have admitted that they are guilty be allowed to avoid criminal liability because of procedural violations?*

a. 384 U.S. 436, 86 S.Ct. 1602, 16 L.Ed.2d 694 (1966).

---

after being taken into custody is not enough. The Court held that police officers are not required to decipher the suspect's intentions in such situations.[18]

SECTION 3501 OF THE OMNIBUS CRIME CONTROL ACT OF 1968   In 1999, the U.S. Court of Appeals for the Fourth Circuit stunned the nation's legal establishment by enforcing a long-forgotten provision, Section 3501, of the Omnibus Crime Control Act of 1968. Congress passed the act two years after the Supreme Court's *Miranda* decision in an attempt to reinstate a rule that had been in effect for 180 years before *Miranda*—namely, that statements by defendants can be used against them as long as they are voluntarily made.

The Justice Department immediately disavowed Section 3501 as unconstitutional and continues to hold this position. The Fourth Circuit, however, could see no reason not to enforce the provision. According to that court, Congress has the "unquestioned power to establish the rules of procedure and evidence in federal courts," and there is no explicit constitutional requirement

> **Remember** Once a suspect has been informed of his or her rights, anything that person says can be used as evidence in a trial.

---

18. *Davis v. United States*, 512 U.S. 452, 114 S.Ct. 2350, 129 L.Ed.2d 362 (1994).

that defendants be told of their rights to counsel and to remain silent.[19] Not surprisingly, the Fourth Circuit's decision led to substantial controversy. In 2000, however, the United States Supreme Court resolved the issue by holding that the *Miranda* rights enunciated by the Court in the 1966 *Miranda* case were constitutionally based and thus could not be overruled by a legislative act.[20]

Criminal Process

As mentioned, a criminal prosecution differs significantly from a civil case in several respects. These differences reflect the desire to safeguard the rights of the individual against the state. Exhibit 8–2 summarizes the major steps in processing a criminal case. We discuss below in more detail three phases of the criminal process—arrest, indictment or information, and trial.

Arrest

Before a warrant for arrest can be issued, there must be probable cause for believing that the individual in question has committed a crime. As discussed earlier, *probable cause* can be defined as a substantial likelihood that the person has committed or is about to commit a crime. Note that probable cause involves a likelihood, not just a possibility. Arrests may sometimes be made without a warrant if there is no time to get one, as when a police officer observes a crime taking place, but the action of the arresting officer is still judged by the standard of probable cause.

Indictment or Information

Indictment A charge by a grand jury that a named person has committed a crime.

Grand Jury A group of citizens called to decide, after hearing the state's evidence, whether a reasonable basis (probable cause) exists for believing that a crime has been committed and whether a trial ought to be held.

Information A formal accusation or complaint (without an indictment) issued in certain types of actions (usually criminal actions involving lesser crimes) by a law officer, such as a magistrate.

Individuals must be formally charged with having committed specific crimes before they can be brought to trial. If issued by a grand jury, this charge is called an **indictment**.[21] A **grand jury** usually consists of a greater number of jurors than the ordinary trial jury. A grand jury does not determine the guilt or innocence of an accused party; rather, its function is to determine, after hearing the state's evidence, whether a reasonable basis (probable cause) exists for believing that a crime has been committed and whether a trial ought to be held.

Usually, grand juries are called in cases involving serious crimes, such as murder. For lesser crimes, an individual may be formally charged with a crime by what is called an **information,** or criminal complaint. An information will be issued by a magistrate (a public official vested with judicial authority) if the magistrate determines that there is sufficient evidence to justify bringing the individual to trial.

Trial

At a criminal trial, the accused person does not have to prove anything; the entire burden of proof is on the prosecutor (the state). As mentioned earlier, the prosecution must show that, based on all the evidence presented, the defendant's guilt is established *beyond a reasonable doubt*. If there is any reasonable doubt that a criminal defendant did not commit the crime with which he or she has been charged, then the verdict must be "not guilty." Note that giving

---

19. *United States v. Dickerson,* 97 F.3d 4750 (4th Cir. 1999).
20. *Dickerson v. United States,* ___ U.S. ___, 120 S.Ct. 2326, 147 L.Ed.2d 405 (2000).
21. Pronounced in-*dyte*-ment.

Exhibit 8-2 Major Steps in Processing a Criminal Case

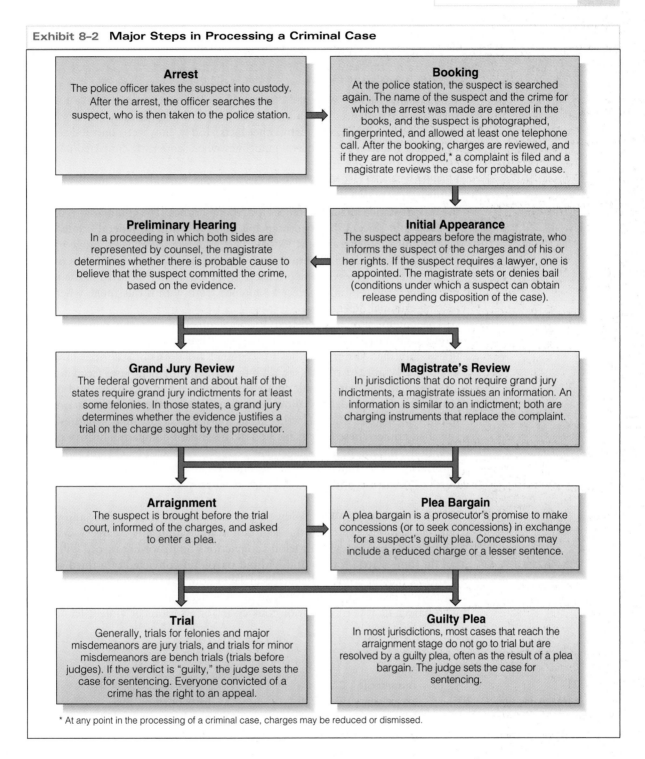

Arrest
The police officer takes the suspect into custody. After the arrest, the officer searches the suspect, who is then taken to the police station.

Booking
At the police station, the suspect is searched again. The name of the suspect and the crime for which the arrest was made are entered in the books, and the suspect is photographed, fingerprinted, and allowed at least one telephone call. After the booking, charges are reviewed, and if they are not dropped,* a complaint is filed and a magistrate reviews the case for probable cause.

Preliminary Hearing
In a proceeding in which both sides are represented by counsel, the magistrate determines whether there is probable cause to believe that the suspect committed the crime, based on the evidence.

Initial Appearance
The suspect appears before the magistrate, who informs the suspect of the charges and of his or her rights. If the suspect requires a lawyer, one is appointed. The magistrate sets or denies bail (conditions under which a suspect can obtain release pending disposition of the case).

Grand Jury Review
The federal government and about half of the states require grand jury indictments for at least some felonies. In those states, a grand jury determines whether the evidence justifies a trial on the charge sought by the prosecutor.

Magistrate's Review
In jurisdictions that do not require grand jury indictments, a magistrate issues an information. An information is similar to an indictment; both are charging instruments that replace the complaint.

Arraignment
The suspect is brought before the trial court, informed of the charges, and asked to enter a plea.

Plea Bargain
A plea bargain is a prosecutor's promise to make concessions (or to seek concessions) in exchange for a suspect's guilty plea. Concessions may include a reduced charge or a lesser sentence.

Trial
Generally, trials for felonies and major misdemeanors are jury trials, and trials for minor misdemeanors are bench trials (trials before judges). If the verdict is "guilty," the judge sets the case for sentencing. Everyone convicted of a crime has the right to an appeal.

Guilty Plea
In most jurisdictions, most cases that reach the arraignment stage do not go to trial but are resolved by a guilty plea, often as the result of a plea bargain. The judge sets the case for sentencing.

* At any point in the processing of a criminal case, charges may be reduced or dismissed.

a verdict of "not guilty" is not the same as stating that the defendant is innocent; it merely means that not enough evidence was properly presented to the court to prove guilt beyond all reasonable doubt.

Courts have complex rules about what types of evidence may be presented and how the evidence may be brought out in criminal cases, especially in jury trials. These rules are designed to ensure that evidence in trials is relevant, reliable, and not prejudicial against the defendant.

Sentencing Guidelines

Traditionally, persons who had committed the same crime might have received very different sentences, depending on the judge hearing the case, the jurisdiction in which it was heard, and many other facts. Today, however, court judges typically must follow state or federal guidelines when sentencing convicted persons.

FEDERAL SENTENCING GUIDELINES At the federal level, the Sentencing Reform Act created the U.S. Sentencing Commission, which was charged with the task of standardizing sentences for federal crimes. The commission fulfilled its task, and since 1987 its sentencing guidelines for all federal crimes have been applied by federal court judges. The guidelines establish a range of possible penalties for each federal crime. Depending on the defendant's criminal record, the seriousness of the offense, and other factors specified in the guidelines, federal judges must select a sentence from within this range when sentencing criminal defendants.

The commission also created specific guidelines for the punishment of crimes committed by corporate employees (white-collar crimes). These guidelines established stiffer penalties for criminal violations of securities laws (see Chapter 24), antitrust laws (see Chapter 23), employment laws (see Chapters 17–19), mail and wire fraud, commercial bribery, and kickbacks and money laundering. The guidelines allow federal judges to take into consideration a number of factors when selecting from the range of possible penalties for a specified crime. These factors include the defendant company's history of past violations, the extent of management's cooperation with federal investigators, and the extent to which the firm has undertaken specific programs and procedures to prevent criminal activities by its employees.

"THREE STRIKES" LAWS Many states have enacted "three strikes and you're out" legislation. Typically, this legislation states that any "career" criminal who already has two violent felony convictions on his or her record will go to jail (in some states, for life and without parole) if convicted of a third similar felony. A federal crime bill enacted in 1994 adopted this provision as well. A California law, enacted in 1994, requires longer prison sentences for felons who have had at least one prior conviction for a serious or violent felony.

Key Terms

arson 213	entrapment 222	money laundering 216
beyond a reasonable doubt 206	exclusionary rule 226	petty offense 208
burglary 212	felony 207	plea bargaining 222
computer crime 217	forgery 213	probable cause 223
consent 221	grand jury 228	robbery 212
crime 206	indictment 228	search warrant 223
double jeopardy 224	information 228	self-defense 221
duress 221	larceny 212	self-incrimination 224
embezzlement 214	misdemeanor 208	white-collar crime 214

Chapter Summary • Criminal Wrongs

Civil Law and Criminal Law (See pages 206–207.)	1. **Civil law**—Spells out the duties that exist between persons or between citizens and their governments, excluding the duty not to commit crimes.
	2. **Criminal law**—Has to do with crimes, which are defined as wrongs against society proclaimed in statutes and, if committed, punishable by society through fines, removal from public office, and/or imprisonment—and, in some cases, death. Because crimes are *offenses against society as a whole*, they are prosecuted by a public official, not by victims.
	3. **Key differences**—An important difference between civil and criminal law is that the standard of proof is higher in criminal cases.
	4. **Civil liability for criminal acts**—A criminal act may give rise to both criminal liability and tort liability (see Exhibit 8–1 for an example of criminal and tort liability for the same act).
Classification of Crimes (See pages 207–208.)	1. **Felonies**—Serious crimes punishable by death or by imprisonment in a penitentiary for more than one year.
	2. **Misdemeanors**—Under federal law and in most states, any crime that is not a felony.
Criminal Liability (See pages 208–209.)	1. **Guilty act**—In general, some form of harmful act must be committed for a crime to exist.
	2. **Intent**—An intent to commit a crime, or a wrongful mental state, is required for a crime to exist.
Corporate Criminal Liability (See pages 210–211.)	1. **Liability of corporations**—Corporations normally are liable for the crimes committed by their agents and employees within the course and scope of their employment. Corporations cannot be imprisoned, but they can be fined or denied certain legal privileges.
	2. **Liability of corporate officers and directors**—Corporate directors and officers are personally liable for the crimes they commit and may be held liable for the actions of employees under their supervision.
Types of Crimes (See pages 212–218.)	1. **Violent crime**—Crimes that cause others to suffer harm or death. Examples are murder, assault and battery, sexual assault (rape), and robbery.
	2. **Property crime**—Crimes in which the goal of the offender is some form of economic gain or the damaging of property; the most common form of crime. Examples include burglary, larceny, arson, receiving stolen goods, forgery, and obtaining goods by false pretenses.
	3. **Public order crime**—Crimes contrary to public values and morals, such as public drunkenness, prostitution, gambling, and illegal drug use.
	4. **White-collar crime**—An illegal act or series of acts committed by an individual or business entity using some nonviolent means to obtain a personal or business advantage; usually committed in the course of a legitimate occupation. Embezzlement, mail and wire fraud, bribery, bankruptcy fraud, insider trading, and the theft of trade secrets are examples of white-collar crime.
	5. **Organized crime**—A form of crime conducted by groups operating illegitimately to satisfy the public's demand for illegal goods and services, such as narcotics or

(Continued)

Chapter Summary • Criminal Wrongs, *Continued*

Types of Crimes—continued	pornography. Money laundering involves the establishment of legitimate enterprises through which "dirty" money (obtained through criminal activities, such as organized crime) can be "laundered" (made to appear as legitimate income). The Racketeer Influenced and Corrupt Organizations Act (RICO) of 1970 makes it a federal crime to (a) use income obtained from racketeering activity to purchase any interest in an enterprise, (b) acquire or maintain an interest in an enterprise through racketeering activity, (c) conduct or participate in the affairs of an enterprise through racketeering activity, or (d) conspire to do any of the preceding activities. RICO provides for both civil and criminal liability.
	5. **Computer crime**—Any act that is directed against computers and computer parts, that uses computers as instruments of crime, or that involves computers and constitutes abuse. Computer crime includes virtually all crimes involving computer use or abuse, including financial crimes (such as embezzlement), the theft of computer equipment, the theft of goods or services with the aid of computers, and destructive programming (such as viruses).
Defenses to Criminal Liability (See pages 218–223.)	1. Infancy. 6. Duress. 2. Intoxication. 7. Justifiable use of force. 3. Insanity. 8. Entrapment. 4. Mistake. 9. Statute of limitations. 5. Consent. 10. Immunity.
Constitutional Safeguards and Criminal Procedures (See pages 223–228.)	1. **Fourth Amendment**—Provides protection against unreasonable searches and seizures and requires that no warrants for a search or an arrest can be issued without probable cause.
	2. **Fifth Amendment**—Requires due process of law, prohibits double jeopardy, and protects against self-incrimination.
	3. **Sixth Amendment**—Provides guarantees of a speedy trial, a trial by jury, a public trial, the right to confront witnesses, and the right to counsel.
	4. **Eighth Amendment**—Prohibits excessive bail and fines, and cruel and unusual punishment.
	5. **Exclusionary rule**—A criminal procedural rule that prohibits the introduction at trial of all evidence obtained in violation of constitutional rights, as well as any evidence derived from the illegally obtained evidence.
	6. *Miranda* **rule**—A rule set forth by the Supreme Court in *Miranda v. Arizona* that individuals who are arrested must be informed of certain constitutional rights, including their right to counsel.
Criminal Process (See pages 228–230.)	1. **Arrest, indictment, and trial**—Procedures governing arrest, indictment, and trial for a crime are designed to safeguard the rights of the individual against the state. See Exhibit 8–2 for the steps involved in prosecuting a criminal case.
	2. **Sentencing guidelines**—Both the federal government and the states have established sentencing laws or guidelines. The federal sentencing guidelines indicate a range of penalties for each federal crime; federal judges must abide by these guidelines when imposing sentences on those convicted of federal crimes. "Three strikes" laws have been passed by many states as well as the federal government.

For Review

1. What is the difference between criminal law and civil law?

2. What two elements must exist before a person can be held liable for a crime? Can a corporation be liable for crimes?

3. List and describe the various types of crimes. Give examples of each type.

4. What defenses might be raised by criminal defendants to avoid liability for criminal acts?

5. What constitutional safeguards exist to protect persons accused of crimes? What are the basic steps in the criminal process?

Questions and Case Problems

8–1. Criminal versus Civil Trials. In criminal trials, the defendant must be proved guilty beyond a reasonable doubt, whereas in civil trials, the defendant need only be proved guilty by a preponderance of the evidence. Discuss why a higher standard of proof is required in criminal trials.

8–2. Types of Crimes. The following situations are similar (all involve the theft of Makoto's television set), yet they represent three different crimes. Identify the three crimes, noting the differences among them.

(a) While passing Makoto's house one night, Sarah sees a portable television set left unattended on Makoto's lawn. Sarah takes the television set, carries it home, and tells everyone she owns it.

(b) While passing Makoto's house one night, Sarah sees Makoto outside with a portable television set. Holding Makoto at gunpoint, Sarah forces him to give up the set. Then Sarah runs away with it.

(c) While passing Makoto's house one night, Sarah sees a portable television set in a window. Sarah breaks the front-door lock, enters, and leaves with the set.

8–3. Types of Crimes. Which, if any, of the following crimes necessarily involve illegal activity on the part of more than one person?

(a) Bribery.

(b) Forgery.

(c) Embezzlement.

(d) Larceny.

(e) Receiving stolen property.

8–4. Double Jeopardy. Armington, while robbing a drugstore, shot and seriously injured a drugstore clerk, Jennings. Armington was subsequently convicted in a criminal trial of armed robbery and assault and battery. Jennings later brought a civil tort suit against Armington for damages. Armington contended that he could not be tried again for the same crime, as that would constitute double jeopardy, which is prohibited by the Fifth Amendment to the Constitution. Is Armington correct? Explain.

8–5. Receiving Stolen Property. Rafael stops Laura on a busy street and offers to sell her an expensive wristwatch for a fraction of its value. After some questioning by Laura, Rafael admits that the watch is stolen property, although he says he was not the thief. Laura pays for and receives the wristwatch. Has Laura committed any crime? Has Rafael? Explain.

8–6. Embezzlement. Slemmer, who had been a successful options trader, gave lectures to small groups about stock options. Several persons who attended his lectures decided to invest in stock options and have Slemmer advise them. They formed an investment club called Profit Design Group (PDG). Slemmer set up an account for PDG with a brokerage firm. Slemmer had control of the PDG account and could make decisions on which stock options to buy or sell. He was not authorized to withdraw money from the account for his own benefit. Nonetheless, he withdrew money from the PDG account to make payments on personal loans. Slemmer made false representations to the members of PDG, and he eventually lost all the money in their account. A jury found him guilty of first degree theft by embezzlement. Slemmer objected to the trial court's failure to instruct the jury that an intent to permanently deprive was an element of the crime charged. Is intent to permanently deprive another of property a required element for the crime of embezzlement? Discuss fully. [*State v. Slemmer*, 48 Wash.App. 48, 738 P.2d 281 (1987)]

8–7. Self-Defense. Bernardy came to the defense of his friend Harrison in a fight with Wilson. Wilson started the fight, and after Harrison knocked Wilson down, Bernardy (who was wearing tennis shoes) kicked Wilson several times in the head. Bernardy stated that he did so because he believed an onlooker, Gowens, would join forces with Wilson against Harrison. Bernardy maintained that his use of force was justifiable because he was protecting another (Harrison) from injury. Discuss whether Bernardy's use of force to protect Harrison from harm was justified. [*State v. Bernardy*, 25 Wash.App. 146, 605 P.2d 791 (1980)]

8–8. Criminal Liability. In January 1988, David Ludvigson was hired as chief executive officer of Leopard Enterprises, a group of companies that owned funeral homes and cemeteries in Iowa and sold "pre-need" funeral contracts. Under Iowa law, 80 percent of monies obtained under such a contract must be set aside in trust until the death of the person for whose benefit the funds were paid. Shortly after Ludvigson was hired, the firm began having financial difficulties. Ludvigson used money from these contracts to pay operating expenses until the company went bankrupt and was placed in receivership. Ludvigson was charged and found guilty on five counts of second degree theft stemming from the misappropriation of these funds. He appealed, alleging, among other things, that because none of the victims whose trust funds were used to cover operating expenses was denied services, no injury was done and thus no crime was committed. Will the court agree with Ludvigson? Explain. [*State v. Ludvigson,* 482 N.W.2d 419 (Iowa 1992)]

8–9. Defenses to Criminal Liability. The Child Protection Act of 1984 makes it a crime to receive knowingly through the mails sexually explicit depictions of children. After this act was passed, government agents found Keith Jacobson's name on a bookstore's mailing list. (Jacobson previously had ordered and received from a bookstore two *Bare Boys* magazines containing photographs of nude preteen and teenage boys.) To test Jacobson's willingness to break the law, government agencies sent mail to him, through five fictitious organizations and a bogus pen pal, over a period of two and a half years. Many of these "organizations" claimed that they had been founded to protect sexual freedom, freedom of choice, and so on. Jacobson eventually ordered a magazine. He testified at trial that he ordered the magazine because he was curious about "all the trouble and the hysteria over pornography and I wanted to see what the material was." When the magazine was delivered, he was arrested for violating the 1984 act. What defense discussed in this chapter might Jacobson raise to avoid criminal liability under the act? Explain fully. [*Jacobson v. United States,* 503 U.S. 540, 112 S.Ct. 1535, 118 L.Ed.2d 174 (1992)]

8–10. Searches and Seizures. The city of Ferndale enacted an ordinance regulating massage parlors. Among other things, the ordinance provided for periodic inspections of the establishments by "[t]he chief of police or other authorized inspectors from the City."

Operators and employees of massage parlors in Ferndale filed a suit in a Michigan state court against the city. The plaintiffs pointed out that the ordinance did not require a warrant to conduct a search and argued in part that this was a violation of the Fourth Amendment. On what ground might the court uphold the ordinance? Do massage parlors qualify on this ground? Why or why not? [*Gora v. City of Ferndale,* 456 Mich. 704, 576 N.W.2d 141 (1998)]

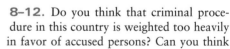

A Question of Ethics and Social Responsibility

8–11. A troublesome issue concerning the constitutional privilege against self-incrimination has to do with "jail plants"—that is, placing undercover police officers in cells with criminal suspects to gain information from the suspects. For example, in one case the police placed an undercover agent, Parisi, in a jail cell block with Lloyd Perkins, who had been imprisoned on charges unrelated to the murder that Parisi was investigating. When Parisi asked Perkins if he had ever killed anyone, Perkins made statements implicating himself in the murder. Perkins was then charged with the murder. [*Illinois v. Perkins,* 496 U.S. 914, 110 S.Ct. 2394, 110 L.Ed.2d 243 (1990)]

1. Review the discussion of *Miranda v. Arizona* in this chapter's *Landmark in the Legal Environment.* Should Perkins's statements be suppressed—that is, not be treated as admissible evidence at trial—because he was not "read his rights," as required by the *Miranda* decision, prior to making his self-incriminating statements? Does *Miranda* apply to Perkins's situation?

2. Do you think that it is fair for the police to resort to trickery and deception to bring those who have committed crimes to justice? Why or why not? What rights or public policies must be balanced in deciding this issue?

For Critical Analysis

8–12. Do you think that criminal procedure in this country is weighted too heavily in favor of accused persons? Can you think of a fairer way to balance the constitutional rights of accused persons against the right of society to be protected against criminal behavior? Explain.

Interacting with the Internet

■ For updated links to resources available on the Web, as well as a variety of other materials, visit this text's Web site at

http://leet.westbuslaw.com

■ The Bureau of Justice Statistics in the U.S. Department of Justice offers an impressive collection of statistics on crime at the following Web site:

http://www.ojp.usdoj.gov/bjs

■ For summaries of famous criminal cases and documents relating to these trials, go to Court TV's Web site at

http://www.courttv.com/index.html

■ If you would like to learn more about criminal procedures, the following site offers an "Anatomy of a Murder: A Trip through Our Nation's Legal Justice System":

**http://tqd.advanced.org/
2760/home.htm**

■ At the previously mentioned site, you can also find a glossary of terms used in criminal law, view actual forms that are filled out during the course of an arrest, and learn about some controversial issues in criminal law.

Many state criminal codes are now online. To find your state's code, go to

http://www.findlaw.com

and select "State" under the link to "Laws: Cases and Codes."

■ You can learn about some of the constitutional questions raised by various criminal laws and procedures by going to the Web site of the American Civil Liberties Union at

http://www.aclu.org

■ The text of the U.S. Sentencing Guidelines Manual is online at

http://www.ussc.gov

Online Legal Research Exercises

Go to **http://leet. westbuslaw.com**, the Web site that accompanies this text. Select "Interactive Study Center," and then click on "Chapter 8." There you will find the following Internet research exercise that you can perform to learn more about criminal procedures:

Activity 8–1: Revisiting *Miranda*

Before the Test

Go to **http://leet. westbuslaw.com**, the Web site that accompanies this text. Select "Interactive Quizzes." You will find a number of interactive questions relating to this chapter.

Unit II Cumulative Hypothetical Problem

Jonatron, Inc., a battery manufacturer, has its headquarters in New Carlisle, Indiana.

1. Suppose that Jonatron does business only within the state of Indiana. A Jonatron employee claims that the company has violated a federal employment law. Jonatron argues that it is not liable because the law applies only to employees of companies that are engaged in interstate commerce. What might a court decide? Discuss fully.

2. The Occupational Safety and Health Administration (OSHA) has proposed a new safety rule governing the handling of certain materials in the workplace, including those used by Jonatron in its manufacturing operations. Jonatron concludes that the rule, which will involve substantial compliance costs, will not significantly increase workplace safety. Jonatron sends a letter to OSHA indicating its objections to the proposed rule and enclosing research reports and other data supporting those objections. Does OSHA have any obligation to consider these objections? What procedures must OSHA follow when it makes new rules, such as this one?

3. The head of Jonatron's accounting department, Roy Olson, has to pay his daughter's college tuition within a week, or his daughter will not be able to continue taking classes. The payment due is over $20,000. Roy would be able to make the payment in two months, but cannot do so until then. The college refuses to wait that long. In desperation, Roy—through a fictitious bank account and some clever accounting—"borrows" funds from Jonatron. Before Roy can pay back the borrowed funds, an auditor discovers what Roy did. Jonatron's president alleges that Roy has "stolen" company funds and informs the police of the theft. Has Roy committed a crime? If so, what crime did he commit? Explain.

The Private Environment

chapter 9

Torts

contents

chapter objectives

After reading this chapter, you should be able to:

1. Explain how torts and crimes differ.

2. State the purpose of tort law.

3. Identify some intentional torts against persons and business relationships.

4. Describe some intentional torts against property.

5. Name the four elements of negligence.

As Scott Turow's statement in the quotation alongside indicates, **torts** are wrongful actions.[1] Through tort law, society compensates those who have suffered injuries as a result of the wrongful conduct of others. Although some torts, such as assault and trespass, originated in the English common law, the field of tort law continues to expand as new ways to commit wrongs are discovered and new conceptions of what is right and wrong in a social or business context emerge.

Tort law covers a wide variety of injuries. Society recognizes an interest in personal physical safety, and tort law provides remedies for acts that cause physical injury or that interfere with physical security and freedom of movement. Society recognizes an interest in protecting real and personal property, and tort law provides remedies for acts that cause destruction or damage to property. Society also recognizes an interest in protecting certain intangible interests, such as personal privacy, family relations, reputation, and dignity, and tort law provides remedies for invasion of these protected interests.

Many of the lawsuits brought by or against business firms are based on the tort theories discussed in this chapter. Some of the torts examined here can occur in any context, including the business environment. Others traditionally have been referred to as **business torts,** which are defined as wrongful interferences with the business rights of others. Included in business torts are such vaguely worded concepts as *unfair competition* and *wrongfully interfering with the business relations of others.*

The Basis of Tort Law

Two notions serve as the basis of all torts: wrongs and compensation. Tort law recognizes that some acts are wrong because they cause injuries to others. Of course, a tort is not the only type of wrong that exists in the law; crimes also involve wrongs. A crime, however, is an act so reprehensible that it is considered a wrong against the state or against society as a whole, as well as against the individual victim. Therefore, the *state* prosecutes and punishes (through fines and/or imprisonment—and possibly death) persons who commit criminal acts. A tort action, in contrast, is a civil action in which one person brings a personal suit against another to obtain compensation (money **damages**) or other relief for the harm suffered.

Some torts provide a basis for a criminal prosecution as well as a tort action. We discussed how the same act can give rise to liability under both tort law and criminal law in Chapter 8.

In deciding tort cases, courts frequently refer to the second edition of the *Restatement of the Law of Torts,* commonly referred to as the *Restatement (Second) of Torts.* As discussed in Chapter 1, although the *Restatements of the Law* are secondary sources of law, they are valuable summaries of common law principles, and judges often rely on them when making decisions. The American Law Institute (ALI), which drafts and publishes the *Restatements,* is currently revising the *Restatement (Second) of Torts.* To date, the only published portion of the revision concerns product liability law (mentioned later in this chapter). Because of its importance to the legal community, the *Restatement (Third) of Torts: Products Liability* is discussed in detail in Chapter 10 in the context of product liability law.

> **"Tort more or less means 'wrong' . . . . One of my friends [in law school] said that Torts is the course which proves that your mother was right."**
>
> Scott Turow, 1949–
> (American lawyer and author)

Tort A civil wrong not arising from a breach of contract. A breach of a legal duty that proximately causes harm or injury to another.

Business Tort The wrongful interference with another's business rights.

Damages Money sought as a remedy for a breach of contract or a tortious action.

---

1. The term *tort* is French for "wrong."

Intentional Torts against Persons and Business Relationships

Intentional Tort A wrongful act knowingly committed.

Tortfeasor One who commits a tort.

An **intentional tort,** as the term implies, requires *intent.* The **tortfeasor** (the one committing the tort) must intend to commit an act, the consequences of which interfere with the personal or business interests of another in a way not permitted by law. An evil or harmful motive is not required—in fact, the actor may even have a beneficial motive for committing what turns out to be a tortious act. In tort law, intent only means that the actor intended the consequences of his or her act or knew with substantial certainty that certain consequences would result from the act. The law generally assumes that individuals intend the *normal* consequences of their actions. Thus, forcefully pushing another—even if done in jest and without any evil motive—is an intentional tort (if injury results), because the object of a strong push can ordinarily be expected to go flying.

This section discusses intentional torts against persons and business relationships, which include assault and battery, false imprisonment, infliction of emotional distress, defamation, invasion of the right to privacy, appropriation, misrepresentation, and wrongful interference.

Assault and Battery

Assault Any word or action intended to make another person fearful of immediate physical harm; a reasonably believable threat.

Any intentional, unexcused act that creates in another person a reasonable apprehension or fear of immediate harmful or offensive contact is an **assault.** Apprehension is not the same as fear. If a contact is such that a reasonable person would want to avoid it, and if there is a reasonable basis for believing that the contact will occur, then the plaintiff suffers apprehension whether or not he or she is afraid. The interest protected by tort law concerning assault is the freedom from having to expect harmful or offensive contact. The occurrence of apprehension is enough to justify compensation.

Battery The unprivileged, intentional touching of another.

The *completion* of the act that caused the apprehension, if it results in harm to the plaintiff, is a **battery,** which is defined as an unexcused and harmful or offensive physical contact *intentionally* performed. For example, suppose that Ivan threatens Jean with a gun, then shoots her. The pointing of the gun at Jean is an assault; the firing of the gun (if the bullet hits Jean) is a battery. The interest protected by tort law concerning battery is the right to personal security and safety. The contact can be harmful, or it can be merely offensive (such as an unwelcome kiss). Physical injury need not occur. The contact can involve any part of the body or anything attached to it—for example, a hat or other item of clothing, a purse, or a chair or an automobile in which one is sitting. Whether the contact is offensive or not is determined by the *reasonable person* standard.[2] The contact can be made by the defendant or by some force the defendant sets in motion—for example, a rock thrown, food poisoned, or a stick swung.

COMPENSATION   If the plaintiff shows that there was contact, and the jury agrees that the contact was offensive, the plaintiff has a right to compensation. There is no need to show that the defendant acted out of malice; the person could have just been joking or playing around. The underlying motive does not matter, only the intent to bring about the harmful or offensive contact to

---

2. The reasonable person standard is an objective test of how a reasonable person would have acted under the same circumstances. See "The Duty of Care and Its Breach" later in this chapter.

the plaintiff. In fact, proving a motive is never necessary (but is sometimes relevant). A plaintiff may be compensated for the emotional harm or loss of reputation resulting from a battery, as well as for physical harm.

DEFENSES TO ASSAULT AND BATTERY A number of legally recognized **defenses** (reasons why plaintiffs should not obtain what they are seeking) can be raised by a defendant who is sued for assault or battery, or both:

1. *Consent.* When a person consents to the act that damages him or her, there is generally no liability (legal responsibility) for the damage done.
2. *Self-defense.* An individual who is defending his or her life or physical well-being can claim self-defense. In situations of both *real* and *apparent* danger, a person may use whatever force is *reasonably* necessary to prevent harmful contact.
3. *Defense of others.* An individual can act in a reasonable manner to protect others who are in real or apparent danger.
4. *Defense of property.* Reasonable force may be used in attempting to remove intruders from one's home, although force that is likely to cause death or great bodily injury can never be used just to protect property.

> **Defense** That which a defendant offers and alleges in an action or suit as a reason why the plaintiff should not recover or establish what he or she seeks.

> **Be Aware** Some of these same defenses can be raised by a defendant who is sued for other torts.

False Imprisonment

False imprisonment is defined as the intentional confinement or restraint of another person's activities without justification. False imprisonment interferes with the freedom to move without restraint. The confinement can be accomplished through the use of physical barriers, physical restraint, or threats of physical force. Moral pressure or threats of future harm do not constitute false imprisonment. It is essential that the person being restrained not comply with the restraint willingly.

Businesspersons are often confronted with suits for false imprisonment after they have attempted to confine a suspected shoplifter for questioning. Under the "privilege to detain" granted to merchants in some states, a merchant can use the defense of *probable cause* to justify delaying a suspected shoplifter. Probable cause exists when the evidence to support the belief that a person is guilty outweighs the evidence against that belief. The detention, however, must be conducted in a *reasonable* manner and for only a *reasonable* length of time. At issue in the following case was whether a store's detention of a suspected shoplifter was reasonable.

Case 9.1 ● Wal-Mart Stores, Inc. v. Resendez

Supreme Court of Texas, 1998.
962 S.W.2d 539.
http://www.supreme.courts.
state.tx.us/scopn.htm[a]

Company Profile *Wal-Mart Stores, Inc., is the world's leading retail firm—larger than J. C.*

Penney *Company, Kmart Corporation, and Sears, Roebuck and Company combined. Wal-Mart is also the second largest grocer and the second largest chain of warehouse stores in the United States. With more than 3,400 Wal-Mart stores, Sam's Club membership-only warehouse stores, and Wal-Mart Supercenter stores, the company accounts for 15 percent of U.S. general merchandise, apparel, and furniture sales.*

---

a. The opinion in this case can be downloaded from this page within the Web site "Texas Judiciary Online," the home page of the Texas state courts. The case's date, which is needed to download the case, is February 13, 1998.

(Continued)

Case 9.1 Continued

Background and Facts   In a Wal-Mart store, Raul Salinas, a store security guard, saw Lucia Resendez, a customer, eating from a bag of peanuts marked with a Wal-Mart price sticker. Salinas saw Resendez discard the empty bag in the store. After she left, he determined that she had not paid for a bag of peanuts. He followed her into the parking lot and accused her of taking the peanuts without paying. She protested that she had purchased them the day before at another Wal-Mart store and said that she could provide the receipt. They went back into the store, where she was detained. Less than fifteen minutes later, a police officer arrived and arrested her. She was convicted of misdemeanor theft. When the conviction was overturned on appeal, Resendez filed a suit in a Texas state court against Wal-Mart, alleging, among other things, false imprisonment. The court entered a judgment in Resendez's favor, which the state intermediate appellate court affirmed. Wal-Mart appealed to the Texas Supreme Court.

In the Words of the Court . . .
PER CURIAM [by the whole court]:

* * * *

* * * [Under a state statute, the] "shopkeeper's privilege" expressly grants an employee the authority of law to detain a customer to investigate the ownership of property in a reasonable manner and for a reasonable period of time if the employee has a reasonable belief that the customer has stolen or is attempting to steal store merchandise.

There was no evidence to support the contention that the detention occurred for an unreasonable period of time. * * * [T]he ten to fifteen minute detention in this case was not unreasonable * * * . Also, no evidence exists that the detention occurred in an unreasonable manner. The only question is whether it was reasonable for Salinas to believe that Resendez had stolen the peanuts. It was.

* * * Based upon the undisputed facts—Resendez * * * was * * * seen eating from a bag of peanuts marked with a Wal-Mart price sticker, and she did not pay for the peanuts on leaving the store—probable cause existed to believe that the peanuts were stolen property. * * * [T]he undisputed facts of this case establish that Salinas had the authority of law to detain Resendez and therefore she was not falsely imprisoned.

* * * *

* * * The [shopkeeper's] privilege does not require the detainer to confirm or refute the detainee's claims, nor does it prevent the detainer from holding the suspected shoplifter for a reasonable time in order to deliver her to the police.

Decision and Remedy   The Texas Supreme Court reversed the decision of the lower court and entered a judgment for Wal-Mart. The state supreme court held that Wal-Mart detained Resendez for a reasonable period of time, in a reasonable manner, and under a reasonable belief that she had stolen store merchandise.

For Critical Analysis—Social Consideration   *What might be the result for society if businesses were held liable every time they detained a customer?*

Infliction of Emotional Distress

The tort of *infliction of emotional distress* can be defined as an intentional act that amounts to extreme and outrageous conduct resulting in severe emotional distress to another.[3] ● **Example 9.1** A prankster telephones an individual and says that the individual's spouse has just been in a horrible accident. As a result, the individual suffers intense mental pain or anxiety. The caller's behavior is deemed to be extreme and outrageous conduct that exceeds the bounds of decency accepted by society and is therefore **actionable** (capable of serving as the ground for a lawsuit).●

The tort of infliction of emotional distress poses several problems for the courts. One problem is the difficulty of proving the existence of emotional suffering. For this reason, some courts require that the emotional distress be evidenced by some physical symptom or illness or some emotional disturbance that can be documented by a psychiatric consultant or other medical professional.

Another problem is that emotional distress claims must be subject to some limitation, or they could flood the courts with lawsuits. A society in which individuals are rewarded if they are unable to endure the normal emotional stresses of day-to-day living is obviously undesirable. Therefore, the law usually holds that indignity or annoyance alone is not enough to support a lawsuit based on infliction of emotional distress. Repeated annoyances (such as those experienced by a person who is being stalked), however, coupled with threats, are enough. In the business context, the repeated use of extreme methods to collect a delinquent account may be actionable.

In the following case, the court looked at one of the requirements that plaintiffs must meet to establish an emotional distress claim.

> **Actionable** Capable of serving as the basis of a lawsuit. An actionable claim can be pursued in a lawsuit or other court action.

---

3. *Restatement (Second) of Torts*, Section 46, Comment d.

Case 9.2 ● Roach v. Stern

Supreme Court of New York,
Appellate Division,
Second Department, 1998.
675 N.Y.S.2d 133.

Historical and Social Setting

What some persons may consider extreme and outrageous, others may consider humorous or insightful. Never has this been truer than in the case of Howard Stern. Stern is a talk-show host whose style is to ask irreverent questions and make off-color jokes. The subjects of his interviews—and the objects of his comments—include celebrities and less well-known personalities with offbeat interests. The Howard Stern Show is broadcast on radio and on television. The show is popular—the radio broadcasts alone have more than 16 million weekly listeners. Stern's style can be controversial, however. Over the years, the Federal Communications Commission has fined his employer, Infinity Broadcasting, Inc., more than $2 million for indecency.

Background and Facts Deborah Roach—known as "Debbie Tay"—was a perennial guest on *The Howard Stern Show,* on which she discussed her pur-

ported sexual encounters with female aliens. Tay used the notoriety to launch her own cable television show. After her death from a drug overdose at the age of twenty-seven, her sister Melissa Driscol had the body cremated and gave a portion of the remains to Tay's friend Chaunce Hayden. Shortly afterward, Tay's brother Jeff Roach learned that Hayden was to appear on Stern's show and asked the producer to cancel the appearance. Hayden went on as planned, and during his appearance, the participants in the program handled and joked about Tay's remains. For example, Stern held up bone fragments while he guessed whether they came from Tay's skull or ribs. Tay's brother and sister filed a suit in a New York state court against Stern and others, seeking $8 million in damages for, among other things, intentional infliction of emotional distress. The defendants filed a motion to dismiss, contending that the conduct at issue was not particularly shocking, in light of Stern's reputation for vulgar humor and Tay's actions during her guest appearances on his show. The court granted the motion, and the plaintiffs appealed.

(Continued)

Case 9.2 Continued

In the Words of the Court . . .
MEMORANDUM BY THE COURT.

* * * *

* * * In order to impose liability for this intentional tort, the conduct complained of must be so outrageous in character, and so extreme in degree, as to go beyond all possible bounds of decency, and to be regarded as atrocious, and utterly intolerable in a civilized community. The element of outrageous conduct is rigorous, and difficult to satisfy, and its purpose is to filter out trivial complaints and assure that the claim of severe emotional distress is genuine. * * *

Upon our review of the allegations in the case at bar, we conclude that the Supreme Court erred in determining that the element of outrageous conduct was not satisfied * * * . Although the defendants contend that the conduct at issue was not particularly shocking, in light of Stern's reputation for vulgar humor and Tay's actions during her guest appearances on his program, a jury might reasonably conclude that the manner in which Tay's remains were handled, for entertainment purposes and against the express wishes of her family, went beyond the bounds of decent behavior.

We further conclude that the remaining elements necessary to establish a cause of action to recover damages for the intentional infliction of emotional distress were also sufficiently pleaded in the complaint.

Decision and Remedy The state intermediate appellate court reversed the decision of the lower court and remanded the case for trial. The court held that a jury could reasonably conclude the manner in which Tay's remains were handled could constitute intentional infliction of emotional distress.

For Critical Analysis—Social Consideration *What would be the result for society if broadcasters such as Howard Stern were never held liable for any distress caused by their broadcasts?*

Defamation

Defamation Anything published or publicly spoken that causes injury to another's good name, reputation, or character.

Slander Defamation in oral form.

Libel Defamation in writing or other form (such as in a videotape) having the quality of permanence.

Defamation of character involves wrongfully hurting a person's good reputation. The law has imposed a general duty on all persons to refrain from making false, defamatory statements about others. Breaching this duty orally involves the tort of **slander**; breaching it in writing involves the tort of **libel**. The tort of defamation also arises when a false statement is made about a person's product, business, or title to property.

The common law defines four types of false utterances that are considered slander *per se* (meaning that no proof of injury or harm is required for these false utterances to be actionable):

1. A statement that another has a loathsome communicable disease.
2. A statement that another has committed improprieties while engaging in a profession or trade.
3. A statement that another has committed or has been imprisoned for a serious crime.
4. A statement that an unmarried woman is unchaste.

THE PUBLICATION REQUIREMENT   The basis of the tort of defamation is the publication of a statement or statements that hold an individual up to contempt, ridicule, or hatred. *Publication* here means that the defamatory statements are communicated to persons other than the defamed party. • **Example 9.2** If Thompson writes Andrews a private letter accusing him of embezzling funds, the action does not constitute libel. If Peters calls Gordon dishonest, unattractive, and incompetent when no one else is around, the action does not constitute slander. In neither case was the message communicated to a third party.•

The courts have generally held that even dictating a letter to a secretary constitutes publication, although the publication may be privileged (privileged communications will be discussed shortly). Moreover, if a third party overhears defamatory statements by chance, the courts usually hold that this also constitutes publication. Defamatory statements made via the Internet are also actionable. (For a discussion of liability for online defamation, see this chapter's *Legal E-nvironment* feature on the next page.) Note further that any individual who republishes or repeats defamatory statements is liable even if that person reveals the source of such statements.

DEFENSES AGAINST DEFAMATION   Truth is normally an absolute defense against a defamation charge. In other words, if the defendant in a defamation suit can prove that his or her allegedly defamatory statements were true, the defendant will not be liable.

Another defense that is sometimes raised is that the statements were **privileged** communications, and thus the defendant is immune from liability. Privileged communications are of two types: absolute and qualified. Only in judicial proceedings and certain legislative proceedings is *absolute* privilege granted. For example, statements made in the courtroom by attorneys and judges during a trial are absolutely privileged. So are statements made by legislators during congressional floor debate, even if the legislators make such statements maliciously—that is, knowing them to be untrue. An absolute privilege is granted in these situations because judicial and legislative personnel deal with matters that are so much in the public interest that the parties involved should be able to speak out fully and freely without restriction.

In general, false and defamatory statements that are made about *public figures* (those who exercise substantial governmental power and any persons in the public limelight) and that are published in the press are privileged if they are made without **actual malice**.[4] To be made with actual malice, a statement must be made *with either knowledge of falsity or a reckless disregard of the truth*. Statements made about public figures, especially when they are made via a public medium, are usually related to matters of general public interest; they are made about people who substantially affect all of us. Furthermore, public figures generally have some access to a public medium for answering disparaging (belittling, discrediting) falsehoods about themselves; private individuals do not. For these reasons, public figures have a greater burden of proof in defamation cases (they must prove actual malice) than do private individuals.

> "Reputation, reputation, reputation! Oh, I have lost my reputation! I have lost the immortal part of myself, and what remains is bestial."
>
> William Shakespeare, 1564–1616 (English dramatist and poet)

Privilege In tort law, the ability to act contrary to another person's right without that person's having legal redress for such acts. Privilege may be raised as a defense to defamation.

Actual Malice In a defamation suit, a statement made about a public figure normally must be made with either knowledge of its falsity or a reckless disregard of the truth (actual malice) for liability to be incurred.

> "Truth is generally the best vindication against slander."
>
> Abraham Lincoln, 1809–1865 (Sixteenth president of the United States, 1861–1865)

---

4. *New York Times Co. v. Sullivan,* 376 U.S. 254, 84 S.Ct. 710, 11 L.Ed.2d 686 (1964).

Legal *e*-nvironment

Defamation Online: Who Is Liable?

Online forums allow anyone—customers, employees, or crackpots—to complain about a business firm. The complaint could concern the firm's personnel, policies, practices, or products, and it might have an impact on the business of the firm. This is possible whether or not the complaint is justified and whether or not it is true.

If a statement is not true, it may constitute defamation. Defamation is any published or publicly spoken false statement that causes injury to another's good name, reputation, or character. Like other torts, defamation is governed by state law, and the elements of the tort can vary from state to state. As discussed elsewhere in this chapter, generally a plaintiff must show that a statement was false, was not subject to a privilege, was communicated to a third person, and resulted in damage to the plaintiff. A public figure must also show that the statement was made with actual malice.

Internet Service Providers Are Exempt from Liability

Newspapers, magazines, and television and radio stations may be held liable for defamatory remarks that they disseminate, even if those remarks are prepared or created by others. Under the Communications Decency Act (CDA) of 1996, however, Internet service providers (ISPs), or "interactive computer service providers," are not liable with respect to such material.[a] An ISP typically provides access to the Internet through a local phone number and may provide other services, including access to databases available only to the ISP's sub-

scribers. One of the most well known ISPs is America Online, Inc. (AOL). In defamation suits involving online statements, the courts have focused chiefly on such issues as determining who would be held liable.

A Case in Point

Under a licensing agreement with America Online, Inc. (AOL), the *Drudge Report,* an online political publication, was made available free to all AOL subscribers. According to the agreement, AOL could remove content that it determined was in violation of AOL's "standard terms of service." One issue of the *Drudge Report* contained an article charging that Sidney Blumenthal, an assistant to the president of the United States, "has a spousal abuse past that has been effectively covered up." Blumenthal's spouse, Jacqueline Blumenthal, also worked in the White House as the director of a presidential commission. When the *Report's* editor, Matt Drudge, learned that the article was false, he printed a retraction and publicly apologized to the Blumenthals. The Blumenthals, however, filed a suit in a federal district court against Drudge, AOL, and others, alleging in part that the original remarks were defamatory. AOL filed a motion for summary judgment.

The court granted AOL's motion for summary judgment. The court held that under the CDA, an Internet service provider (ISP) is not liable for failing to edit, withhold, or restrict access to defamatory remarks which it disseminates but which it did not create. The court stated that if it were writing on a "clean slate," it would agree with the Blumenthals. But, said the court, "Congress has made a different policy choice by providing immunity even where the interactive service provider has an active, even aggressive role in making available content prepared by others."[b]

For Critical Analysis: *What considerations might have led Congress to exempt ISPs from liability for defamation?*

a. 47 U.S.C. Section 230.

b. *Blumenthal v. Drudge,* 992 F.Supp. 44 (D.C. 1998).

Invasion of the Right to Privacy

A person has a right to solitude and freedom from prying public eyes—in other words, to privacy. Four acts qualify as an invasion of that privacy:

1. *The use of a person's name, picture, or other likeness for commercial purposes without permission.* This tort, which is usually referred to as the tort of appropriation, will be examined in the next chapter.

2. *Intrusion in an individual's affairs or seclusion.* For example, invading someone's home or illegally searching someone's briefcase is an invasion of privacy. The tort has been held to extend to eavesdropping by wiretap, the unauthorized scanning of a bank account, compulsory blood testing, and window peeping.

3. *Publication of information that places a person in a false light.* This could be a story attributing to the person ideas not held or actions not taken by the person. (Publishing such a story could involve the tort of defamation as well.)

4. *Public disclosure of private facts about an individual that an ordinary person would find objectionable.* A newspaper account of a private citizen's sex life or financial affairs could be an actionable invasion of privacy.

As discussed in Chapter 6, the Supreme Court has held that a fundamental right to privacy is also implied by various amendments to the U.S. Constitution. This right protects individuals against *government* intrusion into their lives. The tort of invasion of privacy protects people against intrusions by other persons.

Appropriation

The use of another person's name, likeness, or other identifying characteristic, without permission and for the benefit of the user, constitutes the tort of **appropriation.** Under the law, normally an individual's right to privacy includes the right to the exclusive use of his or her identity. • Example 9.3 In a case involving a Ford Motor Company television commercial in which a Bette Midler "sound-alike" sang a song that Midler had made famous, the court held that Ford "for their own profit in selling their product did appropriate part of her identity."[5]•

• Example 9.4 A court ruled similarly in a case brought by Vanna White, the hostess of the popular television game show *Wheel of Fortune,* against Samsung Electronics America, Inc. Without White's permission, Samsung included in an advertisement for Samsung videocassette recorders a depiction of a robot dressed in a wig, gown, and jewelry, posed in a setting that resembled the *Wheel of Fortune* set, in a stance for which White is famous. The court held in White's favor, holding that the tort of appropriation does not require the use of a celebrity's name or likeness. The court stated that Samsung's robot ad left "little doubt" as to the identity of the celebrity that the ad was meant to depict.[6]•

Cases of wrongful appropriation, or misappropriation, may also involve the rights of those who invest time and money in the creation of a special system, such as a method of broadcasting sports events. Commercial misappropriation may also occur when a person takes and uses the property of another for the sole purpose of capitalizing unfairly on the goodwill or reputation of the property owner.

Appropriation The use of a person's name, likeness, or other identifying characteristic, without permission and for the benefit of the user.

Misrepresentation (Fraud)

A misrepresentation leads another to believe in a condition that is different from the condition that actually exists. This is often accomplished through a false or

5. *Midler v. Ford Motor Co.,* 849 F.2d 460 (9th Cir. 1988).
6. *White v. Samsung Electronics America, Inc.,* 971 F.2d 1395 (9th Cir. 1992).

an incorrect statement. Misrepresentations may be innocently made by someone who is unaware of the existing facts. In the context of contract law (discussed in Chapters 12 and 13), innocent misrepresentation can serve as a basis for contract cancellation. Normally, a victim of innocent misrepresentation cannot seek damages, however. The tort of **fraudulent misrepresentation,** or fraud, however, involves intentional deceit for personal gain. The tort includes several elements:

Fraudulent Misrepresentation Any misrepresentation, either by misstatement or omission of a material fact, knowingly made with the intention of deceiving another and on which a reasonable person would and does rely to his or her detriment.

1. Misrepresentation of facts or conditions with knowledge that they are false or with reckless disregard for the truth.
2. Intent to induce another to rely on the misrepresentation.
3. Justifiable reliance by the deceived party.
4. Damages suffered as a result of the reliance.
5. Causal connection between the misrepresentation and the injury suffered.

Puffery A salesperson's often exaggerated claims concerning the quality of property offered for sale. Such claims involve opinions rather than facts and are not considered to be legally binding promises or warranties.

For fraud to occur, more than mere **puffery,** or *seller's talk,* must be involved. Fraud exists only when a person represents as a fact something he or she knows is untrue. For example, it is fraud to claim that a building does not leak when one knows it does. Facts are objectively ascertainable, whereas seller's talk is not. "I am the best accountant in town" is seller's talk. The speaker is not trying to represent something as fact, because the term *best* is a subjective, not an objective, term.[7]

Normally, the tort of misrepresentation or fraud occurs only when there is reliance on a *statement of fact.* Sometimes, however, reliance on a *statement of opinion* may involve the tort of misrepresentation if the individual making the statement of opinion has a superior knowledge of the subject matter. For example, when a lawyer makes a statement of opinion about the law in a state in which the lawyer is licensed to practice, a court would construe reliance on such a statement to be equivalent to reliance on a statement of fact.

Wrongful Interference

Torts involving wrongful interference with another's business rights generally fall into two categories—interference with a contractual relationship and interference with a business relationship.

WRONGFUL INTERFERENCE WITH A CONTRACTUAL RELATIONSHIP The body of tort law relating to *wrongful interference with a contractual relationship* has increased greatly in recent years. A landmark case in this area involved an opera singer, Joanna Wagner, who was under contract to sing for a man named Lumley for a specified period of years. A man named Gye, who knew of this contract, nonetheless "enticed" Wagner to refuse to carry out the agreement, and Wagner began to sing for Gye. Gye's action constituted a tort, because it interfered with the contractual relationship between Wagner and Lumley. (Of course, Wagner's refusal to carry out the agreement also entitled Lumley to sue Wagner for breach of contract.)[8]

In principle, any lawful contract can be the basis for an action of this type. The plaintiff must prove that the defendant actually knew of the contract's existence and *intentionally induced* the breach of the contractual relationship, not merely that the defendant reaped the benefits of a broken contract.

---

7. In contracts for the sale of goods, Article 2 of the Uniform Commercial Code (see Chapter 12) distinguishes, for warranty purposes, between statements of opinion ("puffery") and statements of fact.
8. *Lumley v. Gye,* 118 Eng.Rep. 749 (1853).

• **Example 9.5** Suppose that Carlin has a contract with Sutter that calls for Sutter to do gardening work on Carlin's large estate every week for fifty-two weeks at a specified price per week. Mellon, who needs gardening services, contacts Sutter and offers to pay Sutter a wage that is substantially higher than that offered by Carlin—although Mellon knows nothing about the Sutter-Carlin contract. Sutter breaches his contract with Carlin so that he can work for Mellon. Carlin cannot sue Mellon, because Mellon knew nothing of the Sutter-Carlin contract and was totally unaware that the higher wage he offered induced Sutter to breach that contract.•

Three elements are necessary for wrongful interference with a contractual relationship to occur:

1. A valid, enforceable contract must exist between two parties.
2. A third party must know that this contract exists.
3. This third party must *intentionally* cause one of the two parties to the contract to breach the contract, and the interference must be for the purpose of advancing the economic interest of the third party.

The contract may be between a firm and its employees or a firm and its customers, suppliers, competitors, or other parties. Sometimes a competitor of a firm draws away a key employee. If the original employer can show that the competitor induced the breach of the employment contract—that is, that the employee would not normally have broken the contract—damages can be recovered.

• **Example 9.6** In a famous case in the 1980s, Texaco, Inc., was found to have wrongfully interfered with an agreement between the Pennzoil Company and the Getty Oil Company. After Pennzoil had agreed to purchase a portion of Getty Oil, Texaco made an offer to purchase Getty Oil, and Getty Oil accepted Texaco's offer. Pennzoil then successfully sued Texaco for wrongful interference with Pennzoil's contractual relationship with Getty Oil.[9]•

WRONGFUL INTERFERENCE WITH A BUSINESS RELATIONSHIP   Individuals devise countless schemes to attract business, but they are forbidden by the courts to interfere unreasonably with another's business in their attempts to gain a share of the market. There is a difference between *competitive practices* and *predatory behavior*. The distinction usually depends on whether a business is attempting to attract customers in general or to solicit only those customers who have already shown an interest in the similar product or service of a specific competitor.

• **Example 9.7** If a shopping center contains two shoe stores, an employee of Store A cannot be positioned at the entrance of Store B for the purpose of diverting customers to Store A. This type of activity constitutes the tort of wrongful interference with a business relationship, often referred to as interference with a prospective (economic) advantage, and it is commonly considered to be an unfair trade practice. If this type of activity were permitted, Store A would reap the benefits of Store B's advertising.•

---

9. *Texaco, Inc. v. Pennzoil Co.*, 725 S.W.2d 768 (Tex.App.—Houston [1st Dist.] 1987, writ ref'd n.r.e.). (Generally, a complete Texas Court of Appeals citation includes a writ-of-error history showing the Texas Supreme Court's disposition of the case. In this case, "writ ref'd n.r.e." is an abbreviation for "writ refused, no reversible error," which means that Texas's highest court refused to grant the appellant's request to review the case, because the court did not consider there to be any reversible error.)

Generally, a plaintiff must prove the following elements to recover damages for the tort of wrongful interference with a business relationship:

1. There was an established business relationship.
2. The tortfeasor, by use of predatory methods, *intentionally* caused this business relationship to end.
3. The plaintiff suffered damages as a result of the tortfeasor's actions.

DEFENSES TO WRONGFUL INTERFERENCE   A person will not be liable for the tort of wrongful interference with a contractual or business relationship if it can be shown that the interference was justified, or permissible. Bona fide competitive behavior is a permissible interference even if it results in the breaking of a contract.

  • **Example 9.8** If Jerrod's Meats advertises so effectively that it induces Sam's Restaurant to break its contract with Burke's Meat Company, Burke's Meat Company will be unable to recover against Jerrod's Meats on a wrongful interference theory. • After all, the public policy that favors free competition in advertising definitely outweighs any possible instability that such competitive activity might cause in contractual relations. Therefore, although luring customers away from a competitor through aggressive marketing and advertising strategies obviously interferes with the competitor's relationship with its customers, such activity is permitted by the courts.

Intentional Torts against Property

Intentional torts against property include trespass to land, trespass to personal property, and conversion. These torts are wrongful actions that interfere with individuals' legally recognized rights with regard to their land or personal property. The law distinguishes real property from personal property. *Real property* is land and things "permanently" attached to the land. *Personal property* consists of all other items, which are basically movable. Thus, a house and lot are real property, whereas the furniture inside a house is personal property. Money and stocks and bonds are also personal property.

Trespass to Land

Trespass to Land The entry onto, above, or below the surface of land owned by another without the owner's permission or legal authorization.

A **trespass to land** occurs whenever a person, without permission, enters onto, above, or below the surface of land that is owned by another; causes anything to enter onto the land; remains on the land; or permits anything to remain on it. Actual harm to the land is not an essential element of this tort because the tort is designed to protect the right of an owner to exclusive possession of his or her property. Common types of trespass to land include walking or driving on the land, shooting a gun over the land, throwing rocks at a building that belongs to someone else, building a dam across a river and thus causing water to back up on someone else's land, and placing part of one's building on an adjoining landowner's property.

TRESPASS CRITERIA, RIGHTS, AND DUTIES   Before a person can be a trespasser, the owner of the real property (or other person in actual and exclusive possession of the property) must establish that person as a trespasser. For example, "posted" trespass signs expressly establish as a trespasser a person who ignores these signs and enters onto the property. A guest in your home is not a trespasser—unless he or she has been asked to leave but refuses. Any person who enters onto your property to commit an illegal act (such as a thief entering a lumberyard at night to steal lumber) is established impliedly as a trespasser, without posted signs.

At common law, a trespasser is liable for damages caused to the property and generally cannot hold the owner liable for injuries sustained on the premises. This common law rule is being abandoned in many jurisdictions in favor of a "reasonable duty of care" rule that varies depending on the status of the parties; for example, a landowner may have a duty to post a notice that the property is patrolled by guard dogs. Futhermore, under the "attractive nuisance" doctrine, children do not assume the risks of the premises if they are attracted to the premises by some object, such as a swimming pool, an abandoned building, or a sand pile. Trespassers normally can be removed from the premises through the use of reasonable force without the owner's being liable for assault and battery.

A sign warns trespassers. Should a trespasser be allowed to recover from a landowner for injuries sustained on the premises?

DEFENSES AGAINST TRESPASS TO LAND   Trespass to land involves wrongful interference with another person's real property rights. If it can be shown that the trespass was warranted, however, as when a trespasser enters to assist someone in danger, a defense exists. Another defense exists when the trespasser can show that he or she had a license to come onto the land. A *licensee* is one who is invited (or allowed to enter) onto the property of another for the licensee's benefit. A person who enters another's property to read an electric meter, for example, is a licensee. When you purchase a ticket to attend a movie or sporting event, you are licensed to go onto the property of another to view that movie or event. Note that licenses to enter on another's property are *revocable* by the property owner. If a property owner asks a meter reader to leave and the meter reader refuses to do so, the meter reader at that point becomes a trespasser.

Trespass to Personal Property

Whenever any individual unlawfully harms the personal property of another or otherwise interferes with the personal property owner's right to exclusive possession and enjoyment of that property, **trespass to personal property**— also called *trespass to personalty*[10]—occurs. If a student takes another student's business law book as a practical joke and hides it so that the owner is unable to find it for several days prior to a final examination, the student has engaged in a trespass to personal property.

If it can be shown that trespass to personal property was warranted, then a complete defense exists. Most states, for example, allow automobile repair shops to hold a customer's car (under what is called an *artisan's lien,* discussed in Chapter 15) when the customer refuses to pay for repairs already completed.

Trespass to Personal Property The unlawful taking or harming of another's personal property; interference with another's right to the exclusive possession of his or her personal property.

Conversion

Whenever personal property is wrongfully taken from its rightful owner or possessor and placed in the service of another, the act of **conversion** occurs. Conversion is defined as any act depriving an owner of personal property without that owner's permission and without just cause. When conversion

Conversion The wrongful taking or retaining possession of a person's personal property and placing it in the service of another.

---

10. Pronounced *per*-sun-ul-tee.

occurs, the lesser offense of trespass to personal property usually occurs as well. If the initial taking of the property was unlawful, there is trespass; retention of that property is conversion. If the initial taking of the property was permitted by the owner or for some other reason is not a trespass, failure to return it may still be conversion. Conversion is the civil side of crimes related to theft. A store clerk who steals merchandise from the store commits a crime and engages in the tort of conversion at the same time.

Even if a person mistakenly believed that he or she was entitled to the goods, a tort of conversion may occur. In other words, good intentions are not a defense against conversion; in fact, conversion can be an entirely innocent act. Someone who buys stolen goods, for example, is guilty of conversion even if he or she did not know that the goods were stolen. If the true owner brings a tort action against the buyer, the buyer must either return the property to the owner or pay the owner the full value of the property, despite having already paid money to the thief.

A successful defense against the charge of conversion is that the purported owner does not in fact own the property or does not have a right to possess it that is superior to the right of the holder. Necessity is another possible defense against conversion. • **Example 9.9** If Abrams takes Mendoza's cat, Abrams is guilty of conversion. If Mendoza sues Abrams, Abrams must return the cat or pay damages. If, however, the cat has rabies and Abrams took the cat to protect the public, Abrams has a valid defense—necessity (and perhaps even self-defense, if he can prove that he was in danger because of the cat).•

> **Keep in Mind** In tort law, the underlying motive for an act does not matter. What matters is the intent to do the act that results in the tort.

Disparagement of Property

> **Disparagement of Property** Occurs when economically injurious falsehoods are made about another's product or property.

Disparagement of property occurs when economically injurious falsehoods are made not about another's reputation but about another's product or property. *Disparagement of property* is a general term for torts that can be more specifically referred to as *slander of quality* or *slander of title*.

> **Slander of Quality (Trade Libel)** Publishing false information about another's product.

SLANDER OF QUALITY   Publishing false information about another's product, alleging it is not what its seller claims, constitutes the tort of **slander of quality**. This tort has also been given the name **trade libel**. The plaintiff must prove that actual damages proximately resulted from the slander of quality. That is, it must be shown not only that a third person refrained from dealing with the plaintiff because of the improper publication but also that the plaintiff suffered damages because the third person refrained from dealing with him or her. The economic calculation of such damages—they are, after all, conjectural—is often extremely difficult.

It is possible for an improper publication to be both a slander of quality and a defamation. For example, a statement that disparages the quality of a product may also, by implication, disparage the character of a person who would sell such a product. In one case, for instance, the claim that a product that was marketed as a sleeping aid contained "habit-forming drugs" was held to constitute defamation.[11]

SLANDER OF TITLE   When a publication falsely denies or casts doubt on another's legal ownership of property, and when this results in financial loss to

---

11. *Harwood Pharmacal Co. v. National Broadcasting Co.*, 9 N.Y.2d 460, 174 N.E.2d 602, 214 N.Y.S.2d 725 (1961).

the property's owner, the tort of **slander of title** may exist. Usually, this is an intentional tort in which someone knowingly publishes an untrue statement about another's ownership of certain property with the intent of discouraging a third person from dealing with the person slandered. For example, it would be difficult for a car dealer to attract customers after competitors published a notice that the dealer's stock consisted of stolen autos.

Slander of Title Occurs when someone knowingly publishes an untrue statement about another's ownership of property.

Unintentional Torts (Negligence)

The tort of **negligence** occurs when someone suffers injury because of another's failure to live up to a required *duty of care*. In contrast to intentional torts, in torts involving negligence, the tortfeasor neither wishes to bring about the consequences of the act nor believes that they will occur. The actor's conduct merely creates a *risk* of such consequences. If no risk is created, there is no negligence.

Negligence The failure to exercise the standard of care that a reasonable person would exercise in similar circumstances.

Many of the actions discussed in the section on intentional torts constitute negligence if the element of intent is missing. • **Example 9.10** If Juarez intentionally shoves Natsuyo, who falls and breaks an arm as a result, Juarez will have committed the intentional tort of assault and battery. If Juarez carelessly bumps into Natsuyo, however, and she falls and breaks an arm as a result, Juarez's action will constitute negligence. In either situation, Juarez has committed a tort.•

Drawing by Maslin; © 1990 The New Yorker Magazine, Inc.

"To answer your question. Yes, if you shoot an arrow into the air and it falls to earth you should know not where, you could be liable for any damage it may cause."

In examining a question of negligence, one should ask four questions:

1. Did the defendant owe a duty of care to the plaintiff?
2. Did the defendant breach that duty?
3. Did the plaintiff suffer a legally recognizable injury as a result of the defendant's breach of the duty of care?
4. Did the defendant's breach cause the plaintiff's injury?

Each of these elements of negligence is discussed in this section.

The Duty of Care and Its Breach

Duty of Care The duty of all persons, as established by tort law, to exercise a reasonable amount of care in their dealings with others. Failure to exercise due care, which is normally determined by the "reasonable person standard," constitutes the tort of negligence.

The concept of a **duty of care** arises from the notion that if we are to live in society with other people, some actions can be tolerated and some cannot; some actions are right and some are wrong; and some actions are reasonable and some are not. The basic principle underlying the duty of care is that people are free to act as they please so long as their actions do not infringe on the interests of others.

When someone fails to comply with the duty of exercising reasonable care, a potentially tortious act may have been committed. Failure to live up to a standard of care may be an act (setting fire to a building) or an omission (neglecting to put out a campfire). It may be a careless act or a carefully performed but nevertheless dangerous act that results in injury. Courts consider the nature of the act (whether it is outrageous or commonplace), the manner in which the act is performed (cautiously versus heedlessly), and the nature of the injury (whether it is serious or slight) in determining whether the duty of care has been breached.

Reasonable Person Standard The standard of behavior expected of a hypothetical "reasonable person." The standard against which negligence is measured and that must be observed to avoid liability for negligence.

THE REASONABLE PERSON STANDARD   Tort law measures duty by the **reasonable person standard**. In determining whether a duty of care has been breached, the courts ask how a reasonable person would have acted in the same circumstances. The reasonable person standard is said to be (though in an absolute sense it cannot be) objective. It is not necessarily how a particular person would act. It is society's judgment on how people *should* act. If the so-called reasonable person existed, he or she would be careful, conscientious, even tempered, and honest. This hypothetical reasonable person is frequently used by the courts in decisions relating to other areas of law as well.

That individuals are required to exercise a reasonable standard of care in their activities is a pervasive concept in business law, and many of the issues dealt with in subsequent chapters of this text have to do with this duty. What constitutes reasonable care varies, of course, with the circumstances.

THE DUTY OF LANDOWNERS   Landowners are expected to exercise reasonable care to protect from harm persons coming onto their property. As mentioned earlier, in some jurisdictions, landowners are held to owe a duty to protect even trespassers against certain risks. Landowners who rent or lease premises to tenants are expected to exercise reasonable care to ensure that the tenants and their guests are not harmed in common areas, such as stairways, entryways, laundry rooms, and the like.

Business Invitees Those people, such as customers or clients, who are invited onto business premises by the owner of those premises for business purposes.

Retailers and other firms that explicitly or implicitly invite persons to come onto their premises are usually charged with a duty to exercise reasonable care to protect those persons, who are considered **business invitees**. For example, if you entered a supermarket, slipped on a wet floor, and sustained injuries as a result, the owner of the supermarket would be liable for damages if when

Ethical Issue 9.1

Does a person's duty of care include a duty to come to the aid of a stranger in peril?

Suppose that you are walking down a city street and notice that a pedestrian is about to step directly in front of an oncoming bus. Do you have a legal duty to warn that individual? No. Although most people would probably concede that in this situation, the observer has an *ethical* or *moral* duty to warn the other, tort law does not impose a general duty to rescue others in peril.

People involved in special relationships, however, have been held to have a duty to rescue other parties within the relationship. A married person, for example, has a duty to rescue his or her child or spouse if either is in danger. Other special relationships, such as those between teachers and students or hiking and hunting partners, may also give rise to a duty to rescue. In addition, if a person who has no duty to rescue undertakes to rescue another, then the rescuer is charged with a duty to follow through with due care on the rescue attempt.

you slipped there was no sign warning that the floor was wet. A court would hold that the business owner was negligent because the owner failed to exercise a reasonable degree of care in protecting the store's customers against foreseeable risks about which the owner knew or *should have known*. That a patron might slip on the wet floor and be injured as a result was a foreseeable risk, and the owner should have taken care to avoid this risk or to warn the customer of it. The landowner also has a duty to discover and remove any hidden dangers that might injure a customer or other invitee.

Some risks, of course, are so obvious that the owner need not warn of them. For instance, a business owner does not need to warn customers to open a door before attempting to walk through it. Other risks, however, even though they may seem obvious to a business owner, may not be so in the eyes of another, such as a child. For example, a hardware store owner may not think it is necessary to warn customers that a stepladder leaning against the back wall of the store could fall down and harm them. It is possible, though, that a child could tip the ladder over and be hurt as a result and that the store could be held liable.

In the following case, the court had to decide whether a store owner should be held liable for a customer's injury on the premises. The question was whether the owner had notice of the condition that led to the customer's injury.

Case 9.3 ● Martin v. Wal-Mart Stores, Inc.

United States Court of Appeals, Eighth Circuit, 1999.
183 F.3d 770.

Background and Facts Harold Martin was shopping in the sporting goods department of a Wal-Mart store. There was one employee in the department at that time. In front of the sporting goods section, in the store's main aisle (which the employees referred to as "action alley"), there was a large display of stacked cases of shotgun shells. On top of the cases were individual boxes of shells. Shortly after the sporting goods employee walked past the display, Martin did so, but Martin slipped on some loose shotgun shell pellets and fell to the floor. He immediately lost feeling in, and control of, his legs. Sensation and control returned, but during the next week, he lost the use of his legs several times for periods of ten to fifteen minutes. Eventually, sensation and control did not return to the front half of his left foot. Doctors diagnosed the condition as permanent. Martin filed a suit against

(Continued)

Case 9.3 Continued

Wal-Mart in a federal district court, seeking damages for his injury. The jury found in his favor, and the court denied Wal-Mart's motion for a directed verdict. Wal-Mart appealed to the U.S. Court of Appeals for the Eighth Circuit.

In the Words of the Court . . .
BEAM, Circuit J. [Judge]

* * * *

* * * [T]he traditional rule * * * required a plaintiff in a slip and fall case to establish that the defendant store had either actual or constructive notice of the dangerous condition. The defendant store [was] deemed to have actual notice if it [was] shown that an employee created or was aware of the hazard. Constructive notice could be established by showing that the dangerous condition had existed for a sufficient length of time that the defendant should reasonably have known about it.

* * * *

* * * [R]etail store operations have evolved since the traditional liability rules were established. In modern self-service stores, customers are invited to traverse the same aisles used by the clerks to replenish stock, they are invited to retrieve merchandise from displays for inspection, and to place it back in the display if the item is not selected for purchase. Further, a customer is enticed to look at the displays, thus reducing the chance that the customer will be watchful of hazards on the floor. * * * [C]ustomers may take merchandise into their hands and may then lay articles that no longer interest them down in the aisle. * * * The risk of items creating dangerous conditions on the floor, previously created by employees, is now created by other customers as a result of the store's decision to employ the self-service mode of operation. * * * Thus, in slip and fall cases in self-service stores, the inquiry of whether the danger existed long enough that the store should have reasonably known of it (constructive notice) is made in light of the fact that the store has notice that certain dangers arising through customer involvement are likely to occur, and the store has a duty to anticipate them.

* * * *

Wal-Mart * * * claims that Martin * * * failed to establish that Wal-Mart had actual or constructive notice of the pellets in the action aisle. We disagree. We find there is substantial evidence of constructive notice in the record. Martin slipped on shotgun shell pellets on the floor which were next to a large display of shotgun shells immediately abutting the sporting goods department. The chance that merchandise will wind up on the floor (or merchandise will be spilled on the floor) in the department in which that merchandise is sold or displayed is exactly the type of foreseeable risk [that is part of the self-service exception to the traditional rule]. Under [this exception], Wal-Mart has notice that merchandise is likely to find its way to the floor and create a dangerous condition, and *it must exercise due care to discover this hazard and warn customers or protect them from the danger.* * * * Even assuming that the hazard was created by a customer, a jury could easily find, given that it had notice that merchandise is often mishandled or mislaid by customers in a manner that can create dangerous conditions, that, had Wal-Mart exercised due care under the circumstances, it would have discovered the shotgun pellets on the floor. [Emphasis added.]

Case 9.3 Continued

Decision and Remedy The U.S. Court of Appeals for the Eighth Circuit affirmed the judgment of the lower court. There was sufficient evidence for a jury to find that Wal-Mart had constructive notice of the pellets on the floor in the main aisle.

For Critical Analysis—Social Consideration *If you managed a self-service store such as Wal-Mart, what steps might you take to exercise "due care" in maintaining the safety of the premises?*

THE DUTY OF PROFESSIONALS If an individual has knowledge, skill, or intelligence superior to that of an ordinary person, the individual's conduct must be consistent with that status. Professionals—including physicians, dentists, psychiatrists, architects, engineers, accountants, lawyers, and others—are required to have a standard minimum level of special knowledge and ability. Therefore, in determining what constitutes reasonable care in the case of professionals, their training and expertise is taken into account. In other words, an accountant cannot defend against a lawsuit for negligence by stating, "But I was not familiar with that principle of accounting."

If a professional violates his or her duty of care toward a client, the professional may be sued for **malpractice**. For example, a patient might sue a physician for *medical malpractice*. A client might sue an attorney for *legal malpractice*.

Malpractice Professional misconduct or the lack of the requisite degree of skill as a professional. Negligence—the failure to exercise due care—on the part of a professional, such as a physician, is commonly referred to as malpractice.

The Injury Requirement and Damages

For a tort to have been committed, the plaintiff must have suffered a *legally recognizable* injury. To recover damages (receive compensation), the plaintiff must have suffered some loss, harm, wrong, or invasion of a protected interest. Essentially, the purpose of tort law is to compensate for legally recognized injuries resulting from wrongful acts. If no harm or injury results from a given negligent action, there is nothing to compensate—and no tort exists.

• **Example 9.11** If you carelessly bump into a passerby, who stumbles and falls as a result, you may be liable in tort if the passerby is injured in the fall. If the person is unharmed, however, there normally could be no suit for damages, because no injury was suffered. Although the passerby might be angry and suffer emotional distress, few courts recognize negligently inflicted emotional distress as a tort unless it results in some physical disturbance or dysfunction.•

As already mentioned, the purpose of tort law is not to punish people for tortious acts but to compensate the injured parties for damages suffered. Occasionally, however, damages awarded in tort lawsuits include both **compensatory damages** (which are intended to reimburse a plaintiff for actual losses—to make the plaintiff whole) and **punitive damages** (which are intended to punish the wrongdoer and deter others from similar wrongdoing). The damages awarded do not depend on whether the tort was intentional or negligent, although punitive damages are awarded more often in cases involving intentional torts.

Compensatory Damages A money award equivalent to the actual value of injuries or damages sustained by the aggrieved party.

Punitive Damages Money damages that may be awarded to a plaintiff to punish the defendant and deter future similar conduct.

Causation

Another element necessary to a tort is *causation*. If a person fails in a duty of care and someone suffers injury, the wrongful activity must have caused the harm for a tort to have been committed.

International Perspective

Tort Liability in Europe

In contrast to U.S. courts, courts in Europe generally limit damages to compensatory damages, and punitive damages are virtually unheard of in European countries such as Germany. Even when plaintiffs do win compensatory damages, generally the amount they receive is much less than it would be in a similar case brought in the United States. In part, this is because governments in Europe usually provide for health care and have relatively generous Social Security payments. Yet it is also because European courts tend to view the duty of care and the concept of risk differently than U.S. courts do. In the United States, if a swimmer is injured while falling off a high diving board, a court may decide that the pool owner should be held liable, given that such falls are a foreseeable risk. If punitive damages are awarded, they could total millions of dollars. In a similar situation in Europe, a court might hold that the plaintiff, not the pool owner, was responsible for the injury.

For Critical Analysis: *Punitive damages are an important element in American tort litigation. Why is this? What do awards of punitive damages achieve?*

> "There's no limit to how complicated things can get, on account of one thing always leading to another."
>
> E. B. White, 1899–1985
> (American author)

Causation in Fact An act or omission without which an event would not have occurred.

Proximate Cause Legal cause; exists when the connection between an act and an injury is strong enough to justify imposing liability.

CAUSATION IN FACT AND PROXIMATE CAUSE   In deciding whether there is causation, the court must address two questions:

1. *Is there causation in fact?* Did the injury occur because of the defendant's act, or would it have occurred anyway? If an injury would not have occurred without the defendant's act, then there is causation in fact. **Causation in fact** can usually be determined by the use of the *but for* test: "but for" the wrongful act, the injury would not have occurred. Theoretically, causation in fact is limitless. One could claim, for example, that "but for" the creation of the world, a particular injury would not have occurred. Thus, as a practical matter, the law has to establish limits, and it does so through the concept of proximate cause.

2. *Was the act the proximate cause of the injury?* **Proximate cause,** or legal cause, exists when the connection between an act and an injury is strong enough to justify imposing liability. In most cases, the connection between the defendant's negligence and the plaintiff's harm will be clear, and the element of proximate cause will be easily satisfied—as when a construction crew leaves a ditch unprotected and someone falls into the ditch. At other times, determining whether the defendant's action was the proximate cause of the plaintiff's harm is less clear. • **Example 9.12** Ackerman carelessly leaves a campfire burning. The fire not only burns down the forest but also sets off an explosion in a nearby chemical plant that spills chemicals into a river, killing all the fish for a hundred miles downstream and ruining the economy of a tourist resort. Should Ackerman be liable to the resort owners? To the tourists whose vacations were ruined? These are questions of proximate cause that a court must decide. •

Probably the most cited case on proximate cause is the *Palsgraf* case, discussed in the following *Landmark in the Legal Environment.* The question before the court was as follows: Does a defendant's duty of care extend only to those who may be injured as a result of a foreseeable risk, or does it extend also to a person whose injury could not reasonably be foreseen?

Landmark in the Legal Environment

Palsgraf v. Long Island Railroad Co. (1928)

In 1928, the New York Court of Appeals (that state's highest court) issued its decision in *Palsgraf v. Long Island Railroad Co.*,[a] a case that has become a landmark in negligence law with respect to proximate cause.

The facts of the case were as follows. The plaintiff, Palsgraf, was waiting for a train on a station platform. A man carrying a small package wrapped in newspaper was rushing to catch a train that had begun to move away from the platform. As the man attempted to jump aboard the moving train, he seemed unsteady and about to fall. A railroad guard on the train car reached forward to grab him, and another guard on the platform pushed him from behind to help him board the train. In the process, the man's package fell on the railroad tracks and exploded, because it contained fireworks. The repercussions of the explosion caused scales at the other end of the train platform to fall on Palsgraf, who was injured as a result. She sued the railroad company for damages in a New York state court.

At the trial, the jury found that the railroad guards were negligent in their conduct. On appeal, the question before the New York Court of Appeals was whether the conduct of the railroad guards was the proximate cause of Palsgraf's injuries. In other words, did the guards' duty of care extend to Palsgraf, who was outside the zone of danger and whose injury could not reasonably have been foreseen?

The court stated that the question of whether the guards were negligent *with respect to Palsgraf* depended on whether her injury was *reasonably foreseeable* to the railroad guards. Although the guards may have acted negligently with respect to the man boarding the train, this has no bearing on the question of their negligence with respect to Palsgraf. This is not a situation in which a person commits an act so potentially harmful (for example, firing a gun at a building) that he or she would be held responsible for any harm that resulted. The court stated that here, "by concession, there was nothing in the situation to suggest to the most cautious mind that the parcel wrapped in newspaper would spread wreckage through the station." The court thus concluded that the railroad guards were not negligent with respect to Palsgraf and not liable for her injuries.

For Critical Analysis: *If the guards knew that the package contained fireworks, would the court have ruled differently? Would it matter that the guards were motivated by a desire to help the man board the train and not by a desire to harm anyone?*

a. 248 N.Y. 339, 162 N.E. 99 (1928).

FORESEEABILITY   Since the *Palsgraf* case, the courts have used *foreseeability* as the test for proximate cause. The railroad guards were negligent, but the railroad's duty of care did not extend to Palsgraf, because her injury was unforeseeable. If the victim of the harm or the consequences of the harm done are unforeseeable, there is no proximate cause. Of course, it is foreseeable that people will stand on railroad platforms and that objects attached to the platforms will fall as the result of explosions nearby; however, this is not a chain of events against which a reasonable person would usually guard.

It is difficult to predict when a court will say that something is foreseeable and when it will say that something is not. How far a court stretches foreseeability is determined in part by the extent to which the court is willing to stretch the defendant's duty of care. (See this chapter's *Inside the Legal Environment* on the next page for a further discussion of this topic.)

SUPERSEDING CAUSE   An independent intervening force may break the connection between a wrongful act and an injury to another. If so, it acts as a *superseding cause*—that is, the intervening force or event sets aside, or

> **Note** Proximate cause can be thought of as a question of social policy. Should the defendant be made to bear the loss instead of the plaintiff?

Inside the Legal Environment

How Far Should Foreseeability Extend?

Foreseeability is an important element in tort law because it establishes an outer limit on the duty of care. In a tort case, the defendant's duty of care is usually held to extend only to those who might foreseeably be harmed or placed at risk by the defendant's action. If a defendant could not reasonably foresee that his or her actions would place the plaintiff at risk, then it would be unfair to hold the defendant liable for the plaintiff's injury.

Deciding whether a given risk is reasonably foreseeable is not easy, and it is difficult to predict how the courts might hold in particular cases. Consider an example. On the evening of March 28, 1990, Tonya Brown was using a pay telephone located on the corner of a busy intersection in the city of Flint, Michigan. Tonya Brown's friend, Anita Addison, stood nearby. Suddenly, a car driven by Ruby Greer veered out of control as she attempted to make a left turn and crashed into both girls at the phone booth, causing Brown to lose both legs and Addison to suffer permanent brain damage. Brown and Addison's guardian (on behalf of Addison) sued Michigan Bell Telephone, Inc., for damages.

The plaintiffs argued that Michigan Bell should have foreseen the possibility of a car veering off the road near that busy intersection and that Michigan Bell should therefore have placed its phone booth in a "safer" area. Michigan Bell contended that this accident was in no way foreseeable. The telephone company pointed out that Ruby Greer had never driven a car before, had no driver's license, was high on crack cocaine, and was in a frightened state—she was fleeing the scene of a nearby robbery. Michigan Bell also pointed out that its phone booth at that intersection had never before been hit by a car. Nonetheless, a Michigan appellate court concluded that the accident was foreseeable and therefore the defendant owed a duty of care (and monetary damages for violating that duty of care) to the plaintiffs.[a]

Plaintiffs who crash into utility poles near roadways have made similar claims. In 1998, the Supreme Court of Mississippi held that Mississippi Power and Light Company could be held liable for the injuries suffered by a plaintiff whose car ran off the road and hit an electrical utility pole. Even though the driver had been drinking, the court held that the utility company should have foreseen that, for whatever reason, drivers may veer off the road and hit utility poles that are placed too close to roadways.[b]

For Critical Analysis: *In regard to the Michigan Bell case, the defendant telephone company was much "wealthier" than the driver of the car that crashed into the phone booth (who was, according to the court, "impecunious"—meaning that she had no money). Should wealth ("deep pockets") enter into the picture when making decisions regarding tort liability?*

---

a. *Brown v. Michigan Bell Telephone, Inc.*, 225 Mich.App. 617, 572 N.W.2d 33 (1998).

b. *Mississippi Power & Light Co. v. Lumpkin*, 1998 WL 80164 (Miss. 1998).

---

replaces, the original wrongful act as the cause of the injury. • Example 9.13 Suppose that Derrick keeps a can of gasoline in the trunk of his car. The presence of the gasoline creates a foreseeable risk and is thus a negligent act. If Derrick's car skids and crashes into a tree, causing the gasoline can to explode, Derrick would be liable for injuries sustained by passing pedestrians because of his negligence. If the explosion had been caused by lightning striking the car, however, the lightning would supersede Derrick's original negligence as a cause of the damage, because the lightning was not foreseeable.•

In negligence cases, the negligent party will often attempt to show that some act has intervened after his or her action and that this second act was the proximate cause of injury. Typically, in cases in which an individual takes a defensive action, such as swerving to avoid an oncoming car, the original wrongdoer will not be relieved of liability even if the injury actually resulted from the attempt to escape harm. The same is true under the "danger invites rescue" doctrine. Under this doctrine, if Lemming commits an act that endangers Salter and Yokem sustains an injury trying to protect Salter, then Lemming will be liable for Yokem's injury, as well as for any injuries Salter may sustain. Rescuers can injure themselves, or the person rescued, or even a stranger, but the original wrongdoer will still be liable.

Defenses to Negligence

Defendants often defend against negligence claims by asserting that the plaintiffs failed to prove the existence of one or more of the required elements for negligence. A defendant may also assert that an intervening force should be deemed a superseding cause, thus relieving the defendant of liability. Additionally, there are three basic *affirmative* defenses in negligence cases (defenses that defendants can use to avoid liability even if the facts are as the plaintiffs state). These defenses are (1) assumption of risk, (2) superseding cause, and (3) contributory negligence.

ASSUMPTION OF RISK   A plaintiff who voluntarily enters into a risky situation, knowing the risk involved, will not be allowed to recover. This is the defense of **assumption of risk**. The requirements of this defense are (1) knowledge of the risk and (2) voluntary assumption of the risk.

The risk can be assumed by express agreement, or the assumption of risk can be implied by the plaintiff's knowledge of the risk and subsequent conduct. For example, a driver entering a race knows that there is a risk of being killed or injured in a crash. Of course, the plaintiff does not assume a risk different from or greater than the risk normally carried by the activity. In our example, the race driver would not assume the risk that the banking in the curves of the racetrack will give way during the race because of a construction defect.

Risks are not deemed to be assumed in situations involving emergencies. Neither are they assumed when a statute protects a class of people from harm and a member of the class is injured by the harm. • **Example 9.14** Employees are protected by statute from harmful working conditions and therefore do not assume the risks associated with the workplace. If an employee is injured, he or she will generally be compensated regardless of fault under state workers' compensation statutes (discussed in Chapter 17).•

In the following case, a gas company worker was severely injured in a natural gas explosion that occured during an attempt to repair a gas leak. The question before the court was whether the worker should be barred from recovering for the injury by the defense of assumption of risk.

> **Note** The concept of superseding cause is not a question of physics but is, like proximate cause, a question of responsibility.

Assumption of Risk A doctrine whereby a plaintiff may not recover for injuries or damages suffered from risks he or she knows of and to which he or she assents. A defense against negligence that can be used when the plaintiff has knowledge of and appreciates a danger and voluntarily exposes himself or herself to the danger.

Case 9.4 ● Crews v. Hollenbach

Court of Special Appeals
of Maryland, 1999.
126 Md.App. 609,
730 A.2d 742.

Background and Facts   Maryland Cable Partners, Limited Partnership,[a] hired Excalibur Cable Communications, Inc., to install cable lines in Bowie, Maryland. Byers Engineering Company was retained to locate the buried utility lines in the area where the cable lines were to be buried. Excalibur hired Honcho & Sons, Inc., to do the excavation. While Honcho's employee John Hollenbach was digging a hole, he struck a natural gas line owned by Washington Gas Company. Neither the police nor the fire department was promptly notified. Eventually, someone who smelled gas a mile and a half away contacted the fire department. Washington Gas was notified more than

---

a. A limited partnership is a special form of a business organization. See Chapter 16.

(Continued)

Case 9.4 Continued

two hours later and dispatched a crew to fix the leak. The foreman was Lee James Crews. While Crews and his co-workers were attempting to repair the leak, an explosion occurred, severely injuring Crews. He filed a suit in a Maryland state court against Hollenbach and the others. The defendants filed a motion for summary judgment, claiming that Crews had assumed the risk of a gas explosion by virtue of his occupation. The court granted the motion. Crews appealed to a state intermediate appellate court.

In the Words of the Court . . .
HOLLANDER, Judge.

* * * *

Appellant complains that there are issues relevant to whether he * * * assumed the risk, which the trial court did not consider and that the record did not address, such as the nature of the risk, whether appellant had a choice to respond to the scene, and whether appellant knew that the gas had been leaking for some two hours when he arrived at the scene. It is clear to us that these matters, including the apparent delay of some two hours in reporting the gas leak, do not defeat the application of the doctrine of * * * assumption of risk.

There is no basis to conclude that a gas company is always promptly advised about a possible gas leak. Indeed, it seems just as likely that a gas company would not immediately learn about a gas leak, for any number of reasons. To illustrate, a line could develop a leak in the middle of the night, and no one might realize it until hours later. * * * When a gas leak repairman accepts a position with the gas company, he does not assume only those risks associated with the least dangerous gas leak, or one that is reported within minutes of the occurrence. Rather, he assumes the dangers associated with gas leaks generally. * * *

* * * *

* * * [T]he risk of an explosion from a gas leak is precisely within the scope of dangers intrinsic to the occupation of a gas leak repairman, much like a helicopter crash for a helicopter rescue team, an animal bite for a veterinarian, or a fireman's fall down an elevator shaft [while fighting a fire]. As appellant acknowledged in his deposition, "any type of gas leak or odor is always dangerous," because a fire could always "start behind natural gas." Thus, * * * appellant had reason to anticipate the danger. Indeed, Crews admitted that when working on a volatile natural gas leak "anything can set it off, gravels [sic] or rocks that hit together, hitting metal."

Crews "accept[ed] that responsibility when * * * [he] first got hired." Clearly, there was a direct causal relationship between the performance of appellant's duties as a gas leak repairman and the cause of his injury. Because appellant knew that his occupation carried with it certain risks, *he may not now be heard to complain when one of those job-related foreseeable risks materialized.* Under such circumstances, we agree with the trial court that appellant was barred from recovery. [Emphasis added.]

Decision and Remedy The state intermediate appellate court affirmed the ruling of the lower court. The appellate court held that Crews accepted the responsibility as a gas leak repairman to fix leaks in the face of dangers, including an explosion. By virtue of his employment, Crews was thus barred from recovering for his injury by the defense of assumption of risk.

For Critical Analysis—Social Consideration *Whether Hollenbach was negligent in striking the gas line was not an issue in this case. Why is this?*

SUPERSEDING CAUSE An unforeseeable intervening event may break the causal connection between a wrongful act and an injury to another. If so, it acts as a *superseding cause*—that is, it relieves a defendant of liability for injuries caused by the intervening event. • **Example 9.15** Suppose that Derrick, while riding his bicycle, negligently hits Julie, who is walking on a sidewalk. As a result of the impact, Julie falls and fractures her hip. While she is waiting for help to arrive, a vehicle on the street in front of Julie swerves to avoid an oncoming car, comes onto the sidewalk, and runs over Julie's legs. Derrick will be liable for damages caused by Julie's fractured hip, but normally he will not be liable for the wounds caused by the vehicle—because the risk of a vehicle coming onto the sidewalk and injuring Julie was not foreseeable.•

CONTRIBUTORY NEGLIGENCE Traditionally, under the common law, if a plaintiff's own negligence contributed to his or her injury, the defendant could raise the defense of **contributory negligence**. Contributory negligence on the part of the plaintiff was a complete defense to liability for negligence. Today, contributory negligence can be used as a defense in only a very few states.

In those jurisdictions that do allow the defense of contributory negligence, the *last clear chance* doctrine can excuse the effect of a plaintiff's negligence. The last clear chance doctrine allows the plaintiff to recover full damages despite his or her failure to exercise care. This rule operates when, through his or her own negligence, the plaintiff is endangered (or his or her property is endangered) by a defendant who has an opportunity to avoid causing damage but fails to take advantage of that opportunity. • **Example 9.16** If Murphy walks across the street against the light, and Lewis, a motorist, sees her in time to avoid hitting her but hits her anyway, Lewis (the defendant) is not permitted to use Murphy's (the plaintiff's) prior negligence as a defense. The defendant negligently missed the opportunity to avoid injuring the plaintiff.•

Neither the complete defense of contributory negligence nor the last clear chance doctrine applies in states that have adopted a comparative negligence standard, as the majority of states have done. Under the doctrine of **comparative negligence,** both the plaintiff's negligence and the defendant's negligence are taken into consideration, and damages are awarded accordingly. Some jurisdictions have adopted a "pure" form of comparative negligence that allows the plaintiff to recover damages even if his or her fault is greater than that of the defendant. For example, if the plaintiff was 80 percent at fault and the defendant was 20 percent at fault, the plaintiff may recover 20 percent of his or her damages. Many states' comparative negligence statutes, however, contain a "50 percent" rule, under which the plaintiff recovers nothing if he or she was more than 50 percent at fault.

Special Negligence Doctrines and Statutes

There are a number of special doctrines and statutes relating to negligence. One of these doctrines involves the concept of **negligence *per se*** (*per se* means "in or of itself"). Negligence *per se* may occur if an individual violates a statute or an ordinance providing for a criminal penalty and that violation causes another to be injured. The injured person must prove (1) that the statute clearly sets out what standard of conduct is expected, when and where it is expected, and of whom it is expected; (2) that he or she is in the class intended to be protected by the statute; and (3) that the statute was designed to prevent the type of injury that he or she suffered. The standard of conduct

A bungee jumper leaps from a platform. If the jumper is injured and sues the operator of the jump for negligence, what defenses might the operator use to avoid liability?

Contributory Negligence
A theory in tort law under which a complaining party's own negligence contributed to or caused his or her injuries. Contributory negligence is an absolute bar to recovery in a minority of jurisdictions.

Comparative Negligence
A theory in tort law under which the liability for injuries resulting from negligent acts is shared by all persons who were guilty of negligence (including the injured party), on the basis of each person's proportionate carelessness.

Negligence *Per Se* An action or failure to act in violation of a statutory requirement.

required by the statute is the duty that the defendant owes to the plaintiff, and a violation of the statute is the breach of that duty.

● **Example 9.17** A statute may require a landowner to keep a building in a safe condition and may also subject the landowner to a criminal penalty, such as a fine, if the building is not kept safe. The statute is meant to protect those who are rightfully in the building. Thus, if the owner, without a sufficient excuse, violates the statute and a tenant is thereby injured, then a majority of courts will hold that the owner's unexcused violation of the statute conclusively establishes a breach of a duty of care—that is, that the owner's violation is negligence *per se*.●

Statutes may also prescribe duties and responsibilities in certain circumstances. For example, most states now have what are called **Good Samaritan statutes,** under which persons who are aided voluntarily by others cannot turn around and sue the "Good Samaritans" for negligence. These laws were passed largely to protect physicians and medical personnel who voluntarily render their services in emergency situations to those in need, such as individuals hurt in car accidents. Many states have also passed **dram shop acts,** under which a tavern owner or bartender may be held liable for injuries caused by a person who became intoxicated while drinking at the bar or who was already intoxicated when served by the bartender. In some states, statutes impose liability on *social hosts* (persons hosting parties) for injuries caused by guests who became intoxicated at the hosts' homes. Under these statutes, it is unnecessary to prove that the tavern owner, bartender, or social host was negligent.

Good Samaritan Statutes
State statutes that provide that persons who provide emergency services to, or rescue, others in peril—unless they do so recklessly, thus causing further harm—cannot be sued for negligence.

Dram Shop Acts State statutes that impose liability on the owners of bars and taverns, as well as those who serve alcoholic drinks to the public, for injuries resulting from accidents caused by intoxicated persons when the sellers or servers of alcoholic drinks contributed to the intoxication.

Ethical Issue 9.2

Should social hosts be liable for injuries caused by intoxicated guests?

Many people question the fairness of imposing liability on social hosts for injuries causes by intoxicated guests. Currently, nearly half of the states allow plaintiffs injured in car accidents to sue social hosts—those who served alcoholic beverages to the defendants. Some courts fashion the definition of "social host" broadly. For example, in a New York case the court held that the father of a minor who hosted a "bring your own keg" party could be held liable for injuries caused by an intoxicated guest.[a] In some states and jurisdictions, however, courts refuse to hold social hosts liable in these situations. In one case, the Illinois Supreme Court declared that it would not open that "Pandora's Box of unlimited liability" in which plaintiffs' attorneys could "drag into court any and all adults who may qualify as a social host." The court declared that the victims of drunk driving "have always had, and will continue to have, a civil remedy. They can sue the drunk driver, who is undoubtedly at fault."[b]

---

a. *Rust v. Reyer,* 693 N.E.2d 1074, 670 N.Y.S.2d 822 (1998).

b. *Charles v. Seigfried,* 165 Ill.2d 482, 651 N.E.2d 154, 209 Ill.Dec. 226 (1995).

Key Terms

Chapter Summary   • Torts

Intentional Torts against Persons and Business Relationships (See pages 240–250.)	1. **Assault and battery**—An assault is an unexcused and intentional act that causes another person to be apprehensive of immediate harm. A battery is an assault that results in physical contact.
	2. **False imprisonment**—The intentional confinement or restraint of another person's movement without justification.
	3. **Infliction of emotional distress**—An intentional act that amounts to extreme and outrageous conduct resulting in severe emotional distress to another.
	4. **Defamation (libel or slander)**—A false statement of fact, not made under privilege, that is communicated to a third person and that causes damage to a person's reputation. For public figures, the plaintiff must also prove actual malice.
	5. **Invasion of the right to privacy**—The use of a person's name or likeness for commercial purposes without permission, wrongful intrusion into a person's private activities, publication of information that places a person in a false light, or disclosure of private facts that an ordinary person would find objectionable.
	6. **Appropriation**—The use of another person's name, likeness, or other identifying characteristic, without permission and for the benefit of the user.
	7. **Misrepresentation (fraud)**—A false representation made by one party, through misstatement of facts or through conduct, with the intention of deceiving another and on which the other reasonably relies to his or her detriment.
	8. **Wrongful interference with a contractual or a business relationship**—The knowing, intentional interference by a third party with an enforceable contractual relationship or an established business relationship between other parties for the purpose of advancing the economic interests of the third party.
Intentional Torts against Property (See pages 250–253.)	1. **Trespass to land**—The invasion of another's real property without consent or privilege. Specific rights and duties apply once a person is expressly or impliedly established as a trespasser.

(Continued)

Chapter Summary • Torts, *Continued*

Intentional Torts against Property— continued	**2. Trespass to personal property**—Unlawfully damaging or interfering with the owner's right to use, possess, or enjoy his or her personal property.
	3. Conversion—A wrongful act in which personal property is taken from its rightful owner or possessor and placed in the service of another.
	4. Disparagement of property—Any economically injurious falsehood that is made about another's product or property; an inclusive term for the torts of *slander of quality* and *slander of title*.
Unintentional Torts—Negligence (See pages 253–264.)	**1. Negligence**—The careless performance of a legally required duty or the failure to perform a legally required act. Elements that must be proved are that a legal duty of care exists, that the defendant breached that duty, and that the breach caused damage or injury to another.
	2. Defenses to negligence—The basic affirmative defenses in negligence cases are (a) assumption of risk, (b) contributory negligence, and (c) comparative negligence.
	3. Special negligence doctrines and statutes—
	a. Negligence *per se*—A type of negligence that may occur if a person violates a statute or an ordinance providing for a criminal penalty and the violation causes another to be injured.
	b. Dram shop acts and Good Samaritan statutes—Examples of special negligence statutes that prescribe duties and responsibilities in certain circumstances.

For Review

1. What is the function of tort law?
2. What are some examples of torts against persons or business relationships?
3. What are some examples of torts against property?
4. What are the four elements of negligence?
5. What defenses are available in an action for negligence?

Questions and Case Problems

9–1. Defenses to Negligence. Corinna was riding her bike on a city street. While she was riding, she frequently looked behind her to verify that the books that she had fastened to the rear part of her bike were still attached. On one occasion while she was looking behind her, she failed to notice a car that was entering an intersection just as she was crossing it. The car hit her, causing her to sustain numerous injuries. Three eyewitnesses stated that the driver of the car had failed to stop at the stop sign before entering the intersection. Corinna sued the driver of the car for negligence. What defenses might the defendant driver raise in this lawsuit? Discuss fully.

9–2. Liability to Business Invitees. Kim went to Ling's Market to pick up a few items for dinner. It was a rainy, windy day, and the wind had blown water through the door of Ling's Market each time the door opened. As Kim entered through the door, she slipped and fell in the approximately one-half inch of rainwater that had accumulated on the floor. The manager knew of the weather conditions but had not posted any sign to warn customers of the water hazard. Kim injured her back as a result of the fall and sued Ling's for damages. Can Ling's be held liable for negligence in this situation? Discuss.

9–3. Negligence. In which of the following situations will the acting party be liable for the tort of negligence? Explain fully.

(a) Mary goes to the golf course on Sunday morning, eager to try out a new set of golf clubs she has just purchased. As she tees off on the first hole, the head of her club flies off and injures a nearby golfer.

(b) Mary's doctor gives her some pain medication and tells her not to drive after she takes it, as the medication induces drowsiness. In spite of the doctor's warning, Mary decides to drive to the store while on the medication. Owing to her lack of alertness, she fails to stop at a traffic light and crashes into another vehicle, in which a passenger is injured.

9–4. Causation. Ruth carelessly parks her car on a steep hill, leaving the car in neutral and failing to engage the parking brake. The car rolls down the hill, knocking down an electric line. The sparks from the broken line ignite a grass fire. The fire spreads until it reaches a barn one mile away. The barn houses dynamite, and the burning barn explodes, causing part of the roof to fall on and injure a passing motorist, Jim. Can Jim recover from Ruth? Why or why not?

9–5. Trespass to Land. During a severe snowstorm, Yoshiko parked his car in a privately owned parking lot. The car was later towed from the lot, and Yoshiko had to pay $100 to the towing company to recover his car. Yoshiko sued the owner of the parking lot, Icy Holdings, Inc., to get back the $100 he had paid. Icy Holdings claimed that notwithstanding the severe snowstorm, Yoshiko's parking of his car on its property constituted trespass, and therefore Icy Holdings did not act wrongfully in having the car towed off the lot. Discuss whether Yoshiko can recover his $100.

9–6. Negligence _Per Se._ A North Carolina Department of Transportation regulation prohibits the placement of telephone booths within public rights of way. Despite this regulation, GTE South, Inc., placed a booth in the right of way near the intersection of Hillsborough and Sparger Roads in Durham County. Laura Baldwin was using the booth when an accident at the intersection caused a dump truck to cross the right of way and smash into the booth. To recover for her injuries, Baldwin filed a suit in a North Carolina state court against GTE and others. Was Baldwin within the class of persons protected by the regulation? If so, did GTE's placement of the booth constitute negligence _per se_? [_Baldwin v. GTE South, Inc.,_ 335 N.C. 544, 439 S.E.2d 108 (1995)]

9–7. Duty of Care. As pedestrians exited at the close of an arts and crafts show, Jason Davis, an employee of the show's producer, stood near the exit. Suddenly and without warning, Davis turned around and collided with Yvonne Esposito, an eighty-year-old woman. Esposito was knocked to the ground, fracturing her hip. After hip-replacement surgery, she was left with a permanent physical impairment. Esposito filed a suit in a federal district court against Davis and others, alleging negligence. What are the factors that indicate whether or not Davis owed Esposito a duty of care? What do those factors indicate in these circumstances? [_Esposito v. Davis,_ 47 F.3d 164 (5th Cir. 1995)]

9–8. Duty to Business Invitees. Flora Gonzalez visited a Wal-Mart store. While walking in a busy aisle from the store's cafeteria toward a refrigerator, Gonzalez stepped on some macaroni that came from the cafeteria. She slipped and fell, sustaining injuries to her back, shoulder, and knee. She filed a suit in a Texas state court against Wal-Mart, alleging that the store was negligent. She presented evidence that the macaroni had "a lot of dirt" and tracks through it and testified that the macaroni "seemed like it had been there awhile." What duty does a business have to protect its patrons from dangerous conditions? In Gonzalez's case, should Wal-Mart be held liable for a breach of that duty? Why or why not? [_Wal-Mart Stores, Inc. v. Gonzalez,_ 968 S.W.2d 934 (Tex.Sup. 1998)]

9–9. Duty of Landowners. The Oklahoma State Board of Cosmetology inspected the equipment of the Poteau Beauty College and found it to be in satisfactory condition. A month later, Marilyn Sue Weldon, a student at Poteau, was injured when a salon chair failed to work properly. Weldon had washed the hair of a woman with the chair in a reclining position. The chair did not spring back, and due to a previous injury, the client had to be helped into an upright position. The chair was close to a manicure table, and in maneuvering around the table, Weldon twisted her back. Weldon filed a suit in an Oklahoma state court against Charles Dunn and other owners of Poteau, claiming in part that the college was negligent. Assuming that Weldon was a business invitee, what duty did Poteau, as the owner of the premises, owe to her? On what basis might the court rule that Poteau was not liable? [_Weldon v. Dunn,_ 962 P.2d 1273 (Okla.Sup. 1998)]

9–10. Misappropriation. The United States Golf Association (USGA) was founded in 1894. In 1911, the USGA developed the Handicap System, which was designed to enable individual golfers of different abilities to compete fairly with one another. The USGA revised the system and implemented new handicap formulas between 1987 and 1993. The USGA permits any entity to use the system free of charge as long as it complies with the USGA's procedure for peer review through authorized golf associations of the handicaps issued to individual golfers. In 1991, Arroyo Software Corp. began marketing software known as EagleTrak, which incorporated the USGA's system, and used its name in Arroyo's ads without the USGA's permission. Arroyo's EagleTrak did not incorporate any means for obtaining peer review of handicap computations. The USGA filed a suit in a California state court against Arroyo, alleging, among other things, misappropriation. The USGA asked the court to stop Arroyo's use of its system. Should the court grant the injunction? Why or why not? [*United States Golf Association v. Arroyo Software Corp.*, 69 Cal.App.4th 607, 81 Cal.Rptr.2d 708 (1999)]

A Question of Ethics and Social Responsibility

9–11. Patsy Slone, while a guest at the Dollar Inn, a hotel, was stabbed in the thumb by a hypodermic needle concealed in the tube of a roll of toilet paper. Slone, fearing that she might have been exposed to the virus that causes acquired immune deficiency syndrome (AIDS), sued the hotel for damages to compensate her for the emotional distress she suffered after the needle stab. An Indiana trial court held for Slone and awarded her $250,000 in damages. The hotel appealed, and one of the issues before the court was whether Sloane had to prove that she was actually exposed to AIDS to recover for emotional distress. The appellate court held that she did not and that her fear of getting AIDS was reasonable in these circumstances. [*Slone v. Dollar Inn, Inc.*, 395 N.E.2d 185 (Ind.App. 1998)]

1. Should the plaintiff in this case have been required to show that she was actually exposed to the AIDS virus in order to recover for emotional distress? Should she have been required to show that she actually acquired the AIDS virus as a result of the needle stab?

2. In some states, plaintiffs are barred from recovery in emotional distress cases unless the distress is evidenced by some kind of physical illness. Is this fair?

Case Briefing Assignment

9–12. Examine Case A.3 [*Burlingham v. Mintz*, 891 P.2d 527 (Mont. 1995)] in Appendix A. The case has been excerpted there in great detail. Review and then brief the case, making sure that you include answers to the following questions in your brief.

1. Who were the plaintiff and defendant in this action?
2. Describe the events that led up to this lawsuit.
3. What was the central issue on appeal?
4. How did the state supreme court rule on this issue and dispose of the case?

For Critical Analysis

9–13. What general principle underlies the common law doctrine that business owners have a duty of care toward their customers? Does the duty of care unfairly burden business owners? Why or why not?

Interacting with the Internet

■ For updated links to resources available on the Web, as well as a variety of other materials, visit this text's Web site at

> http://leet.westbuslaw.com

■ You can find cases and articles on torts, including business torts, in the tort law library at the Internet Law Library's Web site. Go to

> http://www.lawguru-com/
> ilawlib/index.com

Online Legal Research Exercises

Go to **http://leet. westbuslaw.com**, the Web site that accompanies this text. Select "Interactive Study Center," and then click on "Chapter 9." There you will find the following Internet research exercises that you can perform to learn more about privacy rights in an online world and the elements of negligence:

Activity 9–1: Privacy Rights in Cyberspace
Activity 9–2: Negligence and the *Titanic*

Before the Test

Go to **http://leet.westbuslaw. com**, the Web site accompanying this text. Select "Interactive Quizzes." You will find a number of interactive questions relating to this chapter.

chapter

10

Strict Liability and Product Liability

chapter objectives

After reading this chapter, you should be able to:

1. Explain what is meant by strict liability.

2. Describe the types of warranties that may arise in a sales or lease transaction.

3. Discuss how negligence and misrepresentation can provide a basis for a product liability action.

4. List the requirements for an action in strict product liability.

5. Summarize the defenses that can be raised against product liability claims.

Product liability refers to the liability incurred by manufacturers and sellers of products when product defects cause injury or property damage to consumers, users, or bystanders (people in the vicinity of the product). Product liability encompasses the tort theories of negligence and misrepresentation, which were discussed in Chapter 9. For example, as indicated in the quotation alongside, if a product is defective because of the manufacturer's negligence, an injured user of the product can sue the manufacturer for negligence in a product liability suit. If a user is injured by a product as a result of the seller's fraudulent misrepresentation of the nature of that product, the basis of the product liability suit is fraud. In the last several decades, the doctrine of *strict liability* often has been applied in product liability suits. Product liability can also be based on warranty law. In this chapter, we examine each of these bases for product liability.

> "If the nature of a thing is such that it is reasonably certain to place life and limb in peril when negligently made, it is then a thing of danger."
>
> Benjamin N. Cardozo, 1870–1938
> (Associate justice of the United States Supreme Court, 1932–1938)

The Doctrine of Strict Liability

An important doctrine in tort law is **strict liability,** or *liability without fault.* Intentional torts and torts of negligence involve acts that depart from a reasonable standard of care and cause injuries. Under the doctrine of strict liability, liability for injury is imposed for reasons other than fault. Strict liability for damages proximately caused by an abnormally dangerous or exceptional activity is one application of this doctrine. Courts apply the doctrine of strict liability in such cases because of the extreme risk of the activity. • **Example 10.1** Even if blasting with dynamite is performed with all reasonable care, there is still a risk of injury. Balancing that risk against the potential for harm, it seems reasonable to ask the person engaged in the activity to pay for injuries caused by that activity. Although there is no fault, there is still responsibility because of the dangerous nature of the undertaking.•

There are other applications of the strict liability principle. Persons who keep dangerous animals, for example, are strictly liable for any harm inflicted by the animals. In the business context, a significant application of strict liability is in the area of product liability. We will discuss what is known as *strict product liability* later in this chapter.

Product Liability The legal liability of manufacturers, sellers, and lessors of goods to consumers, users, and bystanders for injuries or damages that are caused by the goods.

Strict Liability Liability regardless of fault. In tort law, strict liability is imposed on a merchant who introduces into commerce a good that is unreasonably dangerous when in a defective condition.

Warranty Law

Today, warranty law is an important part of the entire spectrum of laws relating to product liability. Most goods are covered by some type of warranty designed to protect consumers. The concept of warranty is based on the seller's assurance to the buyer that the goods will meet certain standards. Because a warranty imposes a duty on the seller, a breach of the warranty is a breach of the seller's promise.

The Uniform Commercial Code (UCC) designates five types of warranties that can arise in a contract for the sale of goods. These include express and implied warranties. A seller can create an **express warranty** by making a representation concerning the quality, condition, description, or performance potential of goods at such a time that the buyer could have relied on the representation when he or she agreed to the contract. These representations may be made in advertisements or by a salesperson.

Express Warranty A promise, ancillary to an underlying sales agreement, that is included in the written or oral terms of the sales agreement under which the promisor assures the quality, description, or performance of the goods.

Realize that sellers are allowed to "huff and puff" their wares as they like. Sellers' statements of opinion (such as "this car is a gem") are known as *puffery,* as noted in Chapter 9 in the discussion of the tort of misrepresentation. Normally, a seller's statement of *opinion* does not constitute an express warranty. If a seller makes a statement of *fact,* however, such as "this car has a new engine," this may create an express warranty if the statement goes to the "basis of the bargain"—that is, was essential to the buyer's decision to purchase the car. As you will read in this chapter's *Inside the Legal Environment,* the line distinguishing puffery from statements that constitute express warranties is often blurred.

An **implied warranty of merchantability** that goods are "reasonably fit for the ordinary purposes for which such goods are used" arises automatically in a sale of goods by a merchant who deals in such goods. An **implied warranty of fitness for a particular purpose** arises when any seller—merchant or nonmerchant—knows the particular purpose for which a buyer will use the goods and knows that the buyer is relying on the seller's skill and judgment to select suitable goods.

Consumers, purchasers, and even users of goods can recover *from any seller* for losses resulting from breach of implied and express warranties. A manufacturer is a *seller.* Therefore, a person who purchases goods from a retailer can recover from the retailer or the manufacturer if the goods are not merchantable, because in most states *privity of contract* (the legal connection that exists between contracting parties) is no longer a prerequisite for recovery for personal injuries for a breach of warranty. That is, a product purchaser may sue not only the firm from which he or she purchased a product but also a third party—the manufacturer of the product—in product liability.

Product Liability Based on Negligence

In Chapter 9, *negligence* was defined as the failure to exercise the degree of care that a reasonable, prudent person would have exercised under the circumstances. If a manufacturer fails to exercise "due care" to make a product safe, a person who is injured by the product may sue the manufacturer for negligence.

Due care must be exercised in designing the product, in selecting the materials, in using the appropriate production process, in assembling the product, and in placing adequate warnings on the label informing the user of dangers of which an ordinary person might not be aware. The duty of care also extends to the inspection and testing of any purchased products that are used in the final product sold by the manufacturer.

As with a product liability action based on warranty law, an action based on negligence does not require privity of contract between the injured plaintiff and the negligent defendant-manufacturer. Section 395 of the *Restatement (Second) of Torts* states as follows:

> A manufacturer who fails to exercise reasonable care in the manufacture of a chattel [movable good] which, unless carefully made, he should recognize as involving an unreasonable risk of causing physical harm to those who lawfully use it for a purpose for which the manufacturer should expect it to be used and to those whom he should expect to be endangered by its probable use, is subject to liability for physical harm caused to them by its lawful use in a manner and for a purpose for which it is supplied.

Implied Warranty of Merchantability A presumed promise by a merchant seller of goods that the goods are reasonably fit for the general purpose for which they are sold, are properly packaged and labeled, and are of proper quality.

Implied Warranty of Fitness for a Particular Purpose A presumed promise made by a merchant seller of goods that the goods are fit for the particular purpose for which the buyer will use the goods. The seller must know the buyer's purpose and know that the buyer is relying on the seller's skill and judgment to select suitable goods.

Recall The elements of negligence include a duty of care, a breach of the duty, and an injury to the plaintiff proximately caused by the breach.

Inside the Legal Environment

Sometimes, "Puffery" Becomes the "Basis of the Bargain"

It could be said that every salesperson would like every statement that he or she makes to be deemed puffery, whereas every consumer would like every statement made by a salesperson to constitute an express warranty. The UCC sets forth the kind of statements that will constitute express warranties [UCC 2–313(1)].[a] The UCC also states that "an affirmation merely of the value of the goods or a statement purporting to be merely the seller's opinion or commendation of the goods does not create a warranty" [UCC 2–313(2)]. The latter provision has been called the "puffing"

_____
a. See Appendix D for the text of this provision.

A car salesperson and potential buyers review the terms of a deal. Does everything a salesperson says about a product constitute part of the "basis of the bargain"?

exception to UCC 2–313. In the real world, however, there is often no bright line that separates statements that amount to mere puffery and statements that form express warranties.

Consider the statements made by an Illinois used-car dealer to Michael and Carla Weng about a used car that they ultimately purchased. The salesperson assured the Wengs that the car was "in good condition," was "a good reliable car," was "mechanically sound," and had "no problems." The salesperson later stated that he was merely giving his opinion. The Wengs, however, believed that his words constituted an express warranty, and when the car proved not to be in good condition, reliable, or mechanically sound, the Wengs sued the dealer for breach of warranty.

At trial, the Wengs lost. The trial court concluded that the Wengs should have realized that the salesperson's statements were mere puffery. After all, the car cost only $800, was ten years old, and had almost 100,000 miles on it. On appeal, however, the Wengs prevailed. The reviewing court believed that the salesperson's statement that the car was "in good condition" was an affirmation of fact and therefore created an express warranty. The court reasoned that the salesperson's statements, even if the buyers had not relied on them, became "part of the basis of the bargain." Therefore, stated the appellate court, "It is not necessary . . . for the buyer to show reasonable reliance upon the seller's affirmations in order to make the affirmations part of the basis of the bargain . . . . This burden is upon the seller to establish by clear, affirmative proof that the affirmations _did not become part of the basis of the bargain._" [Emphasis added] According to the court, the seller did not meet this burden of proof.[b]

For Critical Analysis: _In reading the court's words, is there really a clear line between language considered to be mere puffing and language considered to create an express warranty?_

_____
b. _Weng v. Allison,_ 287 Ill.App.3d 535, 678 N.E.2d 1254, 223 Ill.Dec. 123 (1997).

In other words, a manufacturer is liable for its failure to exercise due care to any person who sustained an injury proximately caused by a negligently made (defective) product, regardless of whether the injured person is in privity of contract with the negligent defendant-manufacturer or lessor. Relative to the long history of the common law, this exception to the privity requirement is a fairly recent development, dating to the early part of the twentieth century.

A leading case in this respect is *MacPherson v. Buick Motor Co.,* which we present as this chapter's *Landmark in the Legal Environment.*

Product Liability Based on Misrepresentation

When a fraudulent misrepresentation has been made to a user or consumer, and that misrepresentation ultimately results in an injury, the basis of liability may be the tort of fraud. For example, the intentional mislabeling of packaged cosmetics and the intentional concealment of a product's defects would constitute fraudulent misrepresentation.

Nonfraudulent misrepresentation, which occurs when a merchant *innocently* misrepresents the character or quality of goods, can also provide a basis of liability. In this situation, the plaintiff does not have to prove that the misrepresentation was made knowingly. • **Example 10.2** A famous example involved a drug manufacturer and a victim of addiction to a prescription medicine called Talwin. The manufacturer, Winthrop Laboratories, a division of Sterling Drug, Inc., innocently indicated to the medical profession that the drug was not physically addictive. Using this information, a physician prescribed the drug for his patient, who developed an addiction that turned out

---

Landmark in the Legal Environment

MacPherson v. Buick Motor Co. (1916)

In the landmark case of *MacPherson v. Buick Motor Co.,*[a] the New York Court of Appeals—New York's highest court—dealt with the liability of a manufacturer that failed to exercise reasonable care in manufacturing a finished product. The case was brought by Donald MacPherson, who suffered injuries while riding in a Buick automobile that suddenly collapsed because one of the wheels was made of defective wood. The spokes crumbled into fragments, throwing MacPherson out of the vehicle and injuring him.

MacPherson had purchased the car from a Buick dealer, but he brought suit against the manufacturer, Buick Motor Company. The wheel itself had not been made by Buick; it had been bought from another manufacturer. There was evidence, though, that the defects could have been discovered by reasonable inspection by Buick and that no such inspection had taken place. MacPherson charged Buick with negligence for putting a human life in imminent danger. The major issue before the court was whether Buick

owed a duty of care to anyone except the immediate purchaser of the car (that is, the Buick dealer).

In deciding the issue, Justice Benjamin Cardozo stated that "[i]f the nature of a thing is such that it is reasonably certain to place life and limb in peril when negligently made, it is then a thing of danger. . . . If to the element of danger there is added knowledge that the thing will be used by persons other than the purchaser, and used without new tests, then, irrespective of contract, the manufacturer of this thing of danger is under a duty to make it carefully." The court concluded that "[b]eyond all question, the nature of an automobile gives warning of probable danger if its construction is defective. This automobile was designed to go 50 miles an hour. Unless its wheels were sound and strong, injury was almost certain."

Although Buick had not manufactured the wheel itself, the court held that Buick had a duty to inspect the wheels and that Buick "was responsible for the finished product." Therefore, Buick was liable to MacPherson for the injuries he sustained when he was thrown from the car.

For Critical Analysis: *To what extent, if any, have technological developments contributed to the courts' placing less emphasis on the doctrine of* caveat emptor *("let the buyer beware") and more emphasis on the doctrine of* caveat venditor *("let the seller beware")?*

---

a. 217 N.Y. 382, 111 N.E. 1050 (1916).

to be fatal. Even though the addiction was a highly uncommon reaction resulting from the victim's unusual susceptibility to this product, the drug company was still held liable.[1] •

Whether fraudulent or nonfraudulent, the misrepresentation must be of a material fact (a fact concerning the quality, nature, or appropriate use of the product on which a normal buyer may be expected to rely). There must also have been an intent to induce the buyer's reliance on the misrepresentation. Misrepresentation on a label or advertisement is enough to show an intent to induce the reliance of anyone who may use the product. The buyer also must rely on the misrepresentation. If the buyer is not aware of the misrepresentation or if it does not influence the transaction, there is no liability.

Strict Product Liability

Under the doctrine of strict liability, discussed earlier in this chapter, people may be liable for the results of their acts regardless of their intentions or their exercise of reasonable care. Under this doctrine, liability does not depend on privity of contract. The injured party does not have to be the buyer or a third party beneficiary, as required under contract warranty theory. Indeed, this type of liability in law is not governed by the provisions of the UCC because it is a tort doctrine, not a principle of the law relating to sales contracts.

Strict Product Liability and Public Policy

Strict product liability is imposed by law as a matter of public policy. This policy rests on the threefold assumption that (1) consumers should be protected against unsafe products; (2) manufacturers and distributors should not escape liability for faulty products simply because they are not in privity of contract with the ultimate user of those products; and (3) manufacturers, sellers, and lessors of products are generally in a better position than consumers to bear the costs associated with injuries caused by their products—costs that they can ultimately pass on to all consumers in the form of higher prices.

California was the first state to impose strict product liability in tort on manufacturers. In the landmark decision that follows, the California Supreme Court sets out the reason for applying tort law rather than contract law to cases in which consumers are injured by defective products.

> "The assault upon the citadel of privity [of contract] is proceeding in these days apace."
>
> Benjamin Cardozo, 1870–1938
> (Associate justice of the United States
> Supreme Court, 1932–1938)

---

1. *Crocker v. Winthrop Laboratories, Division of Sterling Drug, Inc.,* 514 S.W.2d 429 (Tex. 1974).

Case 10.1 ● Greenman v. Yuba Power Products, Inc.

Supreme Court of California, 1962.
59 Cal.2d 57,
377 P.2d 897,
27 Cal.Rptr. 697.
http://mcs.newpaltz.edu/
~zuckerman/cases/green1.htm[a]

---

a. This case is included within the Web site for an "Introduction to Law" course taught by Paul Zuckerman, a professor with the State University of New York at New Paltz.

Historical and Social Setting *From the earliest days of the common law, English courts applied a doctrine of strict liability. Often, persons whose conduct resulted in the injury of another were held liable for damages, even if they had not intended to injure anyone and had exercised reasonable care. This approach was abandoned around 1800 in favor of the fault approach, in which an action was considered tortious only if it was wrongful or blameworthy in some*

(Continued)

Case 10.1 Continued

respect. Strict liability began to be reapplied to manufactured goods in several landmark cases in the 1960s, a decade during which many traditional assumptions were being challenged.

Background and Facts Greenman, the plaintiff, wanted a Shopsmith—a combination power tool that could be used as a saw, drill, and wood lathe—after seeing a Shopsmith demonstrated by a retailer and studying a brochure prepared by the manufacturer. The plaintiff's wife bought and gave him one for Christmas. More than a year later, a piece of wood flew out of the lathe attachment of the Shopsmith while the plaintiff was using it, inflicting serious injuries on him. About ten and a half months later, the plaintiff filed a suit in a California state court against both the retailer and the manufacturer for breach of warranties and negligence. The trial court jury found for the plaintiff. The case was ultimately appealed to the Supreme Court of California.

In the Words of the Court . . .
TRAYNOR, Justice.

* * * *

Plaintiff introduced substantial evidence that his injuries were caused by defective design and construction of the Shopsmith. * * * The jury could therefore reasonably have concluded that the manufacturer negligently constructed the Shopsmith. The jury could also reasonably have concluded that statements in the manufacturer's brochure were untrue, that they constituted express warranties, and that plaintiff's injuries were caused by their breach.

* * * *

[But] to impose strict liability on the manufacturer under the circumstances of this case, it was not necessary for plaintiff to establish an express warranty * * * . A manufacturer is strictly liable in tort when an article he places on the market, knowing that it is to be used without inspection for defects, proves to have a defect that causes injury to a human being. * * *

* * * *

* * * The purpose of such liability is to insure that the costs of injuries resulting from defective products are borne by the manufacturers * * * rather than by the injured persons who are powerless to protect themselves.

Decision and Remedy The Supreme Court of California upheld the jury verdict for the plaintiff. The manufacturer was held strictly liable in tort for the harm caused by its unsafe product.

For Critical Analysis—Ethical Consideration *What ethical doctrine underlies the doctrine of strict liability?*

Requirements for Strict Liability

Section 402A of the *Restatement (Second) of Torts* indicates how it was envisioned that the doctrine of strict liability should be applied. It was issued in 1964, and during the decade following its release it became a widely accepted statement of the liabilities of sellers of goods (including manufacturers, processors, assemblers, packagers, bottlers, wholesalers, distributors, retailers, and lessors). Section 402A states as follows:

(1) One who sells any product in a defective condition unreasonably dangerous to the user or consumer or to his property is subject to liability for physical harm thereby caused to the ultimate user or consumer or to his property, if

If a child is injured by a toy, does he or she (through his or her parents) have a cause of action against the manufacturer?

(a) the seller is engaged in the business of selling such a product, and
(b) it is expected to and does reach the user or consumer without substantial change in the condition in which it is sold.
(2) The rule stated in Subsection (1) applies although
(a) the seller has exercised all possible care in the preparation and sale of his product, and
(b) the user or consumer has not bought the product from or entered into any contractual relation with the seller.

The bases for an action in strict liability as set forth in Section 402A of the *Restatement (Second) of Torts,* and as the doctrine came to be commonly applied, can be summarized as a series of six requirements, which are listed here. Depending on the jurisdiction, if these requirements were met, a manufacturer's liability to an injured party could be virtually unlimited.[2]

1. The product must be in a defective condition when the defendant sells it.
2. The defendant must normally be engaged in the business of selling (or otherwise distributing) that product.
3. The product must be unreasonably dangerous to the user or consumer because of its defective condition (in most states).
4. The plaintiff must incur physical harm to self or property by use or consumption of the product.
5. The defective condition must be the proximate cause of the injury or damage.
6. The goods must not have been substantially changed from the time the product was sold to the time the injury was sustained.

Thus, under these requirements, in any action against a manufacturer, seller, or lessor, the plaintiff does not have to show why or in what manner the

---

2. Some states have enacted what are called *statutes of repose.* Basically, these statutes provide that after a specific statutory period of time from the date of manufacture or sale, a plaintiff is precluded from pursuing a cause of action for injuries or damages sustained from a product, even though the product is defective. The states of Illinois, Indiana, Alabama, Tennessee, Florida, Texas, and Nebraska are illustrative.

product became defective. To recover damages, however, the plaintiff must show that the product was so "defective" as to be "unreasonably dangerous"; that the product caused the plaintiff's injury; and that at the time the injury was sustained, the condition of the product was essentially the same as when it left the hands of the defendant manufacturer, seller, or lessor.

A court could consider a product so defective as to be an **unreasonably dangerous product** if either (1) the product was dangerous beyond the expectation of the ordinary consumer or (2) a less dangerous alternative was economically feasible for the manufacturer, but the manufacturer failed to produce it. As will be discussed in the next section, a product may be unreasonably dangerous due to a flaw in the manufacturing process, a design defect, or an inadequate warning.

Unreasonably Dangerous Product In product liability, a product that is defective to the point of threatening a consumer's health and safety. A product will be considered unreasonably dangerous if it is dangerous beyond the expectation of the ordinary consumer or if a less dangerous alternative was economically feasible for the manufacturer, but the manufacturer failed to produce it.

Market-Share Liability

Generally, in all cases involving product liability, a plaintiff must prove that the defective product that caused his or her injury was the product of a specific defendant. In the last decade or so, in cases in which plaintiffs could not prove which of many distributors of a harmful product supplied the particular product that caused the plaintiffs' injuries, courts have dropped this requirement.

• **Example 10.3** Market-share liability has been imposed in several cases involving DES (diethylstilbestrol), a drug administered in the past to prevent miscarriages. DES's harmful character was not realized until, a generation later, daughters of the women who had taken DES developed health problems, including vaginal carcinoma, that were linked to the drug. Partly because of the passage of time, a plaintiff-daughter often could not prove which pharmaceutical company—out of as many as three hundred—had marketed the DES her mother had ingested. In these cases, some courts applied market-share liability, holding that all firms that manufactured and distributed DES during the period in question were liable for the plaintiffs' injuries in proportion to the firms' respective shares of the market.[3] •

Market-share liability has also been applied in other situations. • **Example 10.4** In one case, a plaintiff who was a hemophiliac received injections of a blood protein known as antihemophiliac factor (AHF) concentrate. The plaintiff later tested positive for the AIDS (acquired immune deficiency syndrome) virus. Because it was not known which manufacturer was responsible for the particular AHF received by the plaintiff, the court held that all of the manufacturers of AHF could be held liable under a market-share theory of liability.[4] •

Other Applications of Strict Liability

Although the drafters of the *Restatement (Second) of Torts*, Section 402A, did not take a position on bystanders, all courts extend the strict liability of manufacturers and other sellers to injured bystanders. • **Example 10.5** In one case, an automobile manufacturer was held liable for injuries caused by the explosion of a car's motor. A cloud of steam that resulted from the explosion caused multiple collisions because other drivers could not see well.[5] •

---

3. See, for example, *Martin v. Abbott Laboratories,* 102 Wash.2d 581, 689 P.2d 368 (1984).
4. *Smith v. Cutter Biological, Inc.,* 72 Haw. 416, 823 P.2d 717 (1991).
5. *Giberson v. Ford Motor Co.,* 504 S.W.2d 8 (Mo. 1974).

The rule of strict liability also is applicable to suppliers of component parts. • **Example 10.6** General Motors buys brake pads from a subcontractor and puts them in Chevrolets without changing their composition. If those pads are defective, both the supplier of the brake pads and General Motors will be held strictly liable for the damages caused by the defects.•

Restatement (Third) of Torts: Products Liability

Because Section 402A of the *Restatement (Second) of Torts* did not clearly define such terms as "defective" and "unreasonably dangerous," they have been subject to different interpretations by different courts. Also, over the years, issues that had not even been imagined when Section 402A was written became points of contention and debate in the courts. These circumstances led to complex and confusing legal principles in the area of product liability and made it difficult to predict how a court might decide a certain case.

In the early 1990s, the American Law Institute (ALI) began drafting a new restatement of the principles and policies underlying product liability law. In particular, the ALI attempted to respond to questions that had not been part of the legal landscape thirty-five years before. The result was the *Restatement (Third) of Torts: Products Liability.* The final draft of the new *Restatement* was released in 1997, after five years of planning, drafting, and debating. The question now is whether state courts will adopt this new *Restatement* as rapidly as they did the *Restatement (Second) of Torts,* which spread the doctrine of strict liability throughout the United States in the late 1960s and early 1970s.

The law categorizes product defects into three types: manufacturing defects, design defects, and warning defects—each of which will be discussed shortly. The *Restatement (Third) of Torts: Products Liability* defines the three types of defects and integrates the applicable legal principles into the definitions. By defining defects in such a way, the new *Restatement* does away with some of the hard-to-understand distinctions that developed when different theories of liability were applied to the same defects.

• **Example 10.7** In one case a court upheld a verdict that found a product "not defective" on a theory of strict liability but its manufacturer liable for harm caused by the product on a theory of breach of warranty.[6] The court based its decision on the different tests that exist under the different legal theories.• The new *Restatement* sets out a single test for each type of defect to be applied regardless of the type of legal claim.

Manufacturing Defects

According to Section 2(a) of the new *Restatement,* a product "contains a manufacturing defect when the product departs from its intended design even though all possible care was exercised in the preparation and marketing of the product." This statement imposes liability on the manufacturer (and on the wholesaler and retailer) whether or not the manufacturer acted "reasonably." This is strict liability, or liability without fault.

---

6. See, for example, *Denny v. Ford Motor Co.,* 87 N.Y.2d 248, 662 N.E.2d 730, 639 N.Y.S.2d 250 (1995). The *Restatement* has not eliminated all of these distinctions, however, because in some cases they may be necessary.

Design Defects

A determination that a product has a design defect (or a warning defect, discussed later in this chapter) can affect all of the units of a product. A product "is defective in design when the foreseeable risks of harm posed by the product could have been reduced or avoided by the adoption of a reasonable alternative design by the seller or other distributor, or a predecessor in the commercial chain of distribution, and the omission of the alternative design renders the product not reasonably safe."[7]

Different states have applied different tests to determine whether a product has a design defect under the *Restatement (Second) of Torts,* Section 402A. There has been much controversy about the different tests, particularly over one that focused on the "consumer expectations" concerning a product. The test prescribed by the *Restatement (Third) of Torts: Products Liability* focuses on a product's actual design and the reasonableness of that design.

To succeed in a product liability suit alleging a design defect, a plaintiff has to show that there is a reasonable alternative design. In other words, a manufacturer or other defendant is liable only when the harm was reasonably preventable. According to the Official Comments accompanying the new *Restatement,* factors that a court may consider on this point include

> the magnitude and probability of the foreseeable risks of harm, the instructions and warnings accompanying the product, and the nature and strength of consumer expectations regarding the product, including expectations arising from product portrayal and marketing. The relative advantages and disadvantages of the product as designed and as it alternatively could have been designed may also be considered. Thus, the likely effects of the alternative design on production costs; the effects of the alternative design on product longevity, maintenance, repair, and esthetics; and the range of consumer choice among products are factors that may be taken into account.

Note that "consumer expectations," instead of being the whole test, is only one factor taken into consideration. Another factor is the warning that accompanies a product. Can a warning insulate a manufacturer from liability for the harm caused by a design defect? That was the issue in the following case.

---

7. *Restatement (Third) of Torts: Products Liability,* Section 2(b).

Case 10.2 ● Rogers v. Ingersoll-Rand Co.

United States Court of Appeals, District of Columbia Circuit, 1998. 144 F.3d 841. http://laws.findlaw.com/DC/977131A.html[a]

Company Profile *Ingersoll-Rand Company is a manufacturer of air compressors, construction and mining equipment, bearings and precision components, tools, locks and architectural hardware, and industrial machinery. The company also makes Bobcat skid-steer loaders, Blaw-Knox pavers, Club Car golf carts and light utility vehicles, and Thermo King transport temperature control systems. In joint ventures with other firms, Ingersoll-Rand is a supplier of pumps and hydrocarbon processing equipment and services. Ingersoll-Rand distributes its products in more than one hundred countries. Forty percent of its sales are outside the United States.*

Background and Facts Among the equipment that Ingersoll-Rand makes is a milling machine. In the maintenance manual that accompanies the machine are warnings that users should stay ten feet away from the rear of the machine when it is operating, verify that the back-up alarm is working, and

---

a. This is a page within the Web site of FindLaw, a resource for Internet legal sources.

Case 10.2 Continued

check the area for the presence of others. There is also a sign on the machine that tells users to stay ten feet away. While using the machine to strip asphalt from a road being repaved, Terrill Wilson backed up. The alarm did not sound, and Cosandra Rogers, who was standing with her back to the machine, was run over and maimed. Rogers filed a suit in a federal district court against Ingersoll-Rand, alleging in part strict liability on the basis of a design defect. The jury awarded Rogers $10.2 million in compensatory damages and $6.5 million in punitive damages. Ingersoll-Rand appealed, emphasizing the adequacy of its warnings.

In the Words of the Court . . .
SENTELLE, Justice.

* * * *

* * * Under [a risk-utility balancing] test [in a defective design case], a plaintiff must show the risks, costs and benefits of the product in question and alternative designs, and that the magnitude of the danger from the product outweighed the costs of avoiding danger. * * *

[Ingersoll-Rand argues that] the adequacy of its warnings [should be] the sole consideration in the risk-utility analysis. As Ingersoll-Rand would have it, once the jury evaluates the milling machine's warnings and finds them adequate, its job is over; it "should find for [the] defendant." * * * [T]he "warnings" defense would have instructed the jury that adequate warnings trump all other factors—including the "magnitude of the danger from the product" * * * .

* * * *

We do not mean to dispute that warnings may tip the balance in a manufacturer's favor in individual cases. On the other hand, warnings need not be the [decisive] factor in every case. Here, for example, it seems reasonably foreseeable that a worker with her back to a milling machine would be in no position to "heed" a sign on the machine instructing her to keep ten feet away. Under these circumstances, a manufacturer may have a heightened responsibility to incorporate additional safety features to guard against foreseeable harm.

Decision and Remedy The U.S. Court of Appeals for the District of Columbia Circuit upheld the jury's award. The court held that an adequate warning cannot immunize a manufacturer from any liability caused by a defectively designed product.

For Critical Analysis—Technological Consideration *What other safety features might a manufacturer use in these circumstances?*

Warning Defects

Product warnings and instructions alert consumers to the risks of using a product. A "reasonableness" test applies to this material. A product "is defective because of inadequate instructions or warnings when the foreseeable risks of harm posed by the product could have been reduced or avoided by the provision of reasonable instructions or warnings by the seller or other distributor, or a predecessor in the commercial chain of distribution, and the omission of the instructions or warnings renders the product not reasonably safe."[8]

---

8. *Restatement (Third) of Torts: Products Liability,* Section 2(c).

Important factors for a court to consider under the *Restatement (Third) of Torts: Products Liability* include the risks of a product, the "content and comprehensibility" and "intensity of expression" of warnings and instructions, and the "characteristics of expected user groups."[9] For example, children would likely respond more readily to bright, bold, simple warning labels, while educated adults might need more detailed information.

There is no duty to warn about risks that are obvious or commonly known. Warnings about such risks do not add to the safety of a product and could even detract from it by making other warnings seem less significant. The obviousness of a risk and a user's decision to proceed in the face of that risk may be a defense in a product liability suit based on a warning defect. (This defense and other defenses in product liability suits are discussed later in this chapter.)

Generally, a seller must warn those who purchase its product of the harm that can result from the foreseeable misuse of the product as well. The key is the *foreseeability* of the misuse. According to the Official Comments accompanying the new *Restatement,* sellers "are not required to foresee and take precautions against every conceivable mode of use and abuse to which their products might be put."

Most states already apply the test outlined here to product warnings and instructions. Generally, everyone also agrees that despite the duty to warn, some risk is unavoidable and the users of a product bear some responsibility to prevent injury or damage. The difficult question facing business owners and managers, as noted in Chapter 2, is how to determine when a court might find a particular use foreseeable.

---

9. *Restatement (Third) of Torts: Products Liability,* Section 2, Comment h.

Ethical Issue 10.1

Should consumers be warned that hot coffee can cause severe burns?

In the last few years, a number of plaintiffs who have sustained burns due to coffee spills have alleged that the sellers of the coffee should have warned customers about the dangers of hot coffee. The problem is, what would such a warning entail? Should the warning state that coffee is served hot, or that hot coffee can cause burns? Coffee drinkers are already aware of these dangers, and plaintiffs in several coffee cases have conceded that they seek out hot coffee, know it can burn, and take precautions as a result.[a] What is not commonly known, though, is just how severe burns caused by coffee spills can be. Should manufacturers of coffee makers and sellers of hot coffee warn consumers of the severity of burns that can be caused by hot coffee? In one case addressing this issue, the court pointed out that such a warning would be self-defeating. In addition to having to deliver a "medical education" with every cup of coffee served, said the court, the warning would have to address such things as "the risk of burns in real life, starting with the number of cups of coffee sold annually, the number of these that spill (broken down by location, such as home, restaurant, and car), and the probability that any given spill will produce a severe (as opposed to a mild or average) burn." According to the court, such a detailed warning, which would be equivalent to the package insert that comes with drugs, would only obscure the principal point—that precautions should be taken to avoid spills.[b]

---

a. See, for example, *Greene v. Boddie-Noell Enterprises, Inc.,* 966 F.Supp. 416 (W.D.Va. 1997); and *Barnett v. Leiserv, Inc.,* 137 F.3d 1356 (11th Cir. 1997).

b. *McMahon v. Bunn-O-Matic Corp.,* 150 F.3d 651 (7th Cir. 1998).

Defenses to Product Liability

There are several defenses that manufacturers, sellers, or lessors can raise to avoid liability for harms caused by their products. We look at some of these defenses here.

Assumption of Risk

Assumption of risk can sometimes be used as a defense in a product liability action. For example, if a buyer fails to heed a product recall by the seller, a court might conclude that the buyer assumed the risk caused by the defect that led to the recall. To establish such a defense, the defendant must show that (1) the plaintiff knew and appreciated the risk created by the product defect and (2) the plaintiff voluntarily assumed the risk, even though it was unreasonable to do so. (See Chapter 9 for a more detailed discussion of assumption of risk.)

> **Be Careful** A defendant cannot successfully claim that the plaintiff assumed a risk different from or greater than the risk normally associated with the product.

Product Misuse

Similar to the defense of voluntary assumption of risk is that of misuse of the product. Here, the injured party *does not know that the product is dangerous for a particular use* (contrast this with assumption of risk), but the use is not the one for which the product was designed. The courts have severely limited this defense, however. Even if the injured party does not know about the inherent danger of using the product in a wrong way, if the misuse is foreseeable, the seller must take measures to guard against it.

Comparative Negligence

Developments in the area of comparative negligence (discussed in Chapter 9) have even affected the doctrine of strict liability—the most extreme theory of product liability. Whereas previously the plaintiff's conduct was not a defense to strict liability, today many jurisdictions consider the negligent or intentional actions of both the plaintiff and the defendant in the apportionment of liability and damages. This means that even if a product was misused by the plaintiff, the plaintiff may nonetheless be able to recover at least some damages for injuries caused by the defendant's defective product.

Commonly Known Dangers

The dangers associated with certain products (such as sharp knives and guns) are so commonly known that manufacturers need not warn users of those dangers. If a defendant succeeds in convincing the court that a plaintiff's injury resulted from a *commonly known danger,* the defendant normally will not be liable.

 • **Example 10.8** A classic case on this issue involved a plaintiff who was injured when an elastic exercise rope that she had purchased slipped off her foot and struck her in the eye, causing a detachment of the retina. The plaintiff claimed that the manufacturer should be liable because it had failed to warn users that the exerciser might slip off a foot in such a manner. The court stated that to hold the manufacturer liable in these circumstances "would go beyond the reasonable dictates of justice in fixing the liabilities of manufacturers." After all, stated the court, "[a]lmost every physical object can be inherently dangerous or potentially dangerous in a sense. . . . A manufacturer cannot manufacture a knife that will not cut or a hammer that will not mash a thumb or a stove that will not burn a finger. The law does not require [manufacturers] to warn of such common dangers."[10]●

A related defense is the *knowledgeable user* defense. If a particular danger (such as electrical shock) is or should be commonly known by particular users of the product (such as electricians), the manufacturer of electrical equipment need not warn these users of the danger. The following case illustrates this concept.

---

10. *Jamieson v. Woodward & Lothrop*, 247 F.2d 23, 101 D.C.App. 32 (1957).

Case 10.3 ● Travelers Insurance Co. v. Federal Pacific Electric Co.

Supreme Court of New York,
Appellate Division,
First Department, 1995.
211 A.D.2d 40,
625 N.Y.S.2d 121.

Company Profile *Federal Pacific Electric Company makes electrical equipment, including Stab-Lok circuit breakers. Reliance Electric Company bought Federal from UV Industries Liquidating Trust, Inc., in 1979. In 1980, Federal revealed that it had obtained Underwriters Laboratories (UL) certification for its Stab-Lok circuit breakers by cheating on UL tests. Reliance sued UV Industries. A cash settlement ended the lawsuit in 1984. Two years later, Reliance sold Federal to the Challenger Electric Equipment Corporation. The federal Consumer Product Safety Commission later concluded that the Stab-Lok circuit breakers "did not present a serious risk of injury."*

Background and Facts A water pipe burst, flooding a switchboard at the offices of RCA Global Communications, Inc. This tripped the switchboard circuit breakers. RCA employees assigned to reactivate the switchboard included an electrical technician with twelve years of on-the-job training, a licensed electrician, and an electrical engineer with twenty years of experience who had studied power engineering in college. The employees attempted to switch one of the circuit breakers back on without testing for short circuits, which they later admitted they knew how to do and should have done. The circuit breaker failed to engage but ignited an explosive fire. RCA filed a claim with its insurer, the Travelers Insurance Company. Travelers paid the claim and filed a suit in a New York state court against, among others, the Federal Pacific Electric Company, the supplier of the circuit breakers. Travelers alleged that Federal had been negligent in failing to give RCA adequate warnings and instructions regarding the circuit breakers. The court apportioned 15 percent of the responsibility for the fire to Federal. Federal appealed.

In the Words of the Court . . .
NARDELLI, Justice.

* * * *

* * * [T]here is "no necessity to warn a customer already aware—through common knowledge or learning—of a specific hazard" and, in the proper case, the court can decide as a matter of law that there is no duty to warn or that the duty has been discharged. * * *

* * * *

Given the * * * common knowledge of the minimal accepted practices in the field and the level of expertise, training and experience of the RCA electricians which encompassed the specific situation they faced, the * * * court should have found that there was no necessity on the part of Federal to warn RCA, which was already aware of the specific hazard, and the court should have granted Federal's motion entering judgment in its favor * * * .

Decision and Remedy The Supreme Court of New York, Appellate Division, reversed the judgment of the lower court and dismissed the complaint against Federal.

For Critical Analysis—Technological Consideration *What might have been the result in this case if the training, experience, and expertise of the employees dispatched to check the circuit breakers had been with a different, out-of-date technology?*

Other Defenses

A defendant can also defend against product liability by showing that there is no basis for the plaintiff's claim. Suppose that a plaintiff alleges that a seller breached an implied warranty. If the seller can prove that he or she effectively disclaimed all implied warranties, the plaintiff cannot recover. Similarly, in a product liability case based on negligence, a defendant who can show that the plaintiff has not met the requirements (such as causation) for an action in negligence will not be liable. In regard to strict product liability, a defendant could claim that the plaintiff failed to meet one of the requirements for an action in strict liability. If the defendant establishes that the goods have been subsequently altered, the defendant will not be held liable.

Key Terms

express warranty 271	implied warranty of	strict liability 271
implied warranty of fitness for a	merchantability 272	unreasonably dangerous
particular purpose 272	product liability 271	product 278

Chapter Summary • Strict Liability and Product Liability

The Doctrine of Strict Liability (See page 271.)	Under the doctrine of strict liability, a person may be held liable, regardless of the degree of care exercised, for damages or injuries caused by his or her product or activity. Strict liability includes liability for harms caused by abnormally dangerous activities, by wild animals, and by defective products (product liability).
Warranty Law (See pages 271–272.)	Under the Uniform Commercial Code, certain warranties can arise in a contract for a sale of goods. These include express warranties, an implied warranty of merchantability, and an implied warranty of fitness for a particular purpose. Consumers and others can recover from any seller for losses resulting from a breach of these warranties.
Product Liability Based on Negligence (See pages 272–274.)	1. Due care must be used by the manufacturer in designing the product, selecting materials, using the appropriate production process, assembling and testing the product, and placing adequate warnings on the label or product. 2. Privity of contract is not required. A manufacturer is liable for failure to exercise due care to any person who sustains an injury proximately caused by a negligently made (defective) product.
Product Liability Based on Misrepresentation (See pages 274–275.)	Fraudulent misrepresentation of a product may result in product liability based on the tort of fraud.
Strict Liability— Requirements (See pages 275–278.)	1. The defendant must sell the product in a defective condition. 2. The defendant must normally be engaged in the business of selling that product. 3. The product must be unreasonably dangerous to the user or consumer because of its defective condition (in most states).

(Continued)

Chapter Summary • Strict Liability and Product Liability, *Continued*

Strict Liability—Requirements— continued	**4.** The plaintiff must incur physical harm to self or property. **5.** The defective condition must be the proximate cause of the injury or damage. **6.** The goods must not have been substantially changed from the time the product was sold to the time the injury was sustained.
Market-Share Liability (See page 278.)	In cases in which plaintiffs cannot prove which of many distributors of a defective product supplied the particular product that caused the plaintiffs' injuries, some courts have applied market-share liability. All firms that manufactured and distributed the harmful product during the period in question are then held liable for the plaintiffs' injuries in proportion to the firms' respective shares of the market, as directed by the court.
Other Applications of Strict Liability (See pages 278–279.)	**1.** Manufacturers and other sellers are liable for harms suffered by injured bystanders due to defective products. **2.** Suppliers of component parts are strictly liable for defective parts that, when incorporated into a product, cause injuries to users.
Restatement (Third) of Torts: Products Liability (See pages 279–282.)	There are three basic ways in which a product may be defective: **1.** In its manufacture. **2.** In its design. **3.** In the instructions or warnings that come with it.
Defenses to Product Liability (See pages 283–285.)	**1. Assumption of risk**—The user or consumer knew of the risk of harm and voluntarily assumed it. **2. Product misuse**—The user or consumer misused the product in a way unforeseeable by the manufacturer. **3. Comparative negligence and liability**—Liability may be distributed between plaintiff and defendant under the doctrine of comparative negligence if the plaintiff's misuse of the product contributed to the risk of injury. **4. Commonly known dangers**—If a defendant succeeds in convincing the court that a plaintiff's injury resulted from a commonly known danger, such as the danger associated with using a sharp knife, the defendant will not be liable. **5. Other defenses**—A defendant can also defend against a strict liability claim by showing that there is no basis for the plaintiff's claim (that the plaintiff has not met the requirements for an action in negligence).

For Review

1. How does the doctrine of strict liability differ from the tort doctrines discussed in Chapter 9?

2. What factors determine whether a seller's or lessor's statement constitutes an express warranty or merely "puffing"?

3. Discuss whether a manufacturer can be held liable to any person who suffers an injury proximately caused by the manufacturer's negligently made product.

4. What are the elements of a cause of action in strict product liability?

5. What defenses to liability can be raised in a product liability lawsuit?

Questions and Case Problems

10–1. Product Liability. Under what contract theory can a seller be held liable to a consumer for physical harm or property damage that is caused by the goods sold? Under what tort theories can the seller be held liable?

10–2. Product Liability. Carmen buys a television set manufactured by AKI Electronics. She is going on vacation, so she takes the set to her mother's house for her mother to use. Because the set is defective, it explodes, causing considerable damage to her mother's house. Carmen's mother sues AKI for the damages to her house. Discuss the theories under which Carmen's mother can recover from AKI.

10–3. Product Liability. George Nesselrode lost his life in an airplane crash. The plane had been manufactured by Beech Aircraft Corp. and sold to Executive Beechcraft, Inc. Shortly before the crash occurred, Executive Beechcraft had conducted a routine inspection of the plane and found that some of the parts needed to be replaced. The new parts were supplied by Beech Aircraft but installed by Executive Beechcraft. These particular airplane parts could be installed backward, and if they were, the plane would crash. Nesselrode's crash resulted from just such an incorrect installation of the airplane parts. Nesselrode's wife, Jane, and three daughters sued Executive Beechcraft, Beech Aircraft, and Gerald Hultgren, the pilot who had flown the plane, for damages. Beech Aircraft claimed that it was not at fault because it had not installed the parts. Will Beech Aircraft be held liable for Nesselrode's death? Discuss. [*Nesselrode v. Executive Beechcraft, Inc.,* 707 S.W.2d 371 (Mo. 1986)]

10–4. Strict Liability. Embs was buying some groceries at Stamper's Cash Market. Unnoticed by her, a carton of 7-Up was sitting on the floor at the edge of the produce counter about one foot from where she was standing. Several of the 7-Up bottles exploded. Embs's leg was injured severely enough that she had to be taken to the hospital by a managing agent of the store. Embs sued the manufacturer of 7-Up, Pepsi-Cola Bottling Co. of Lexington, Kentucky, Inc., claiming that the manufacturer should be held strictly liable for the harm caused by its products. The trial court dismissed her claim. On appeal, what will the court decide? Discuss fully. [*Embs v. Pepsi-Cola Bottling Co. of Lexington, Kentucky, Inc.,* 528 S.W.2d 703 (Ky.App. 1975)]

10–5. Defenses to Product Liability. The Campbell Soup Co. manufactured, sold, and shipped packages of chicken-flavored Campbell's Ramen Noodle Soup to a distributor. The distributor sold and shipped the packages to Associated Grocers. Associated Grocers shipped the packages to Warehouse Foods, a retail grocer. Six weeks after Campbell first shipped the soup to the distributor, Warehouse Foods sold a packet of the soup to Kathy Jo Gates. Gates prepared the soup. Halfway through eating her second bowl, she discovered beetle larvae in the noodles. She filed a product liability suit against Campbell and others. Gates argued, in effect, that the mere presence of the bugs in the soup was sufficient to hold Campbell strictly liable. How might Campbell defend itself? [*Campbell Soup Co. v. Gates,* 319 Ark. 54, 889 S.W.2d 750 (1994)]

10–6. Product Liability. John Whitted bought a Chevrolet Nova from General Motors Corp. (GMC). Six years later, Whitted crashed the Nova into two trees. During the impact, the seat belt broke, and Whitted was thrust against the steering wheel, which broke, and the windshield, which shattered. He suffered fractures in his left arm and cuts to his forehead. Whitted sued GMC and the manufacturer, asserting, among other things, that because the seat belt broke, the defendants were strictly liable for his injuries. What does Whitted have to show in order to prove his case? [*Whitted v. General Motors Corp.,* 58 F.3d 1200 (7th Cir. 1995)]

10–7. Implied Warranty of Merchantability. Marilyn Keaton entered an A.B.C. Drug store to buy a half-gallon bottle of liquid bleach. The bottles were stacked at a height above her eye level. She reached up, grasped the handle of one of the bottles, and began pulling it down from the shelf. The cap was loose, however, causing bleach to splash into her face, injuring her eye. Keaton filed a suit in a Georgia state court against A.B.C., alleging, in part, breach of the implied warranty of merchantability. She claimed that the bleach had not been adequately packaged. A.B.C. argued, in part, that Keaton had failed to exercise care for her own safety. Had A.B.C. breached the implied warranty of merchantability? Discuss. [*Keaton v. A.B.C. Drug Co.,* 266 Ga. 385, 467 S.E.2d 558 (1996)]

10–8. Failure to Warn. When Mary Bresnahan drove her Chrysler LeBaron, she sat very close to the steering wheel—less than a foot away from the steering-wheel enclosure of the driver's side air bag. At the time, Chrysler did not provide any warning that a driver should not sit close to the air bag. In an accident with another car, Bresnahan's air bag deployed. The bag caused her elbow to strike the windshield pillar and fracture in three places, resulting in repeated surgery and physical therapy. Bresnahan filed a suit in a California state court against Chrysler to recover for her injuries, alleging in part that they were caused by Chrysler's failure to warn consumers about sitting near the air bag. At the trial, an expert testified that the air bag was not intended to prevent arm injuries, which were "a predictable, incidental consequence" of the bag's deploying. Should Chrysler pay for Bresnahan's injuries? Why or why not? [*Bresnahan v. Chrysler Corp.*, 76 Cal.Rptr.2d 804, 65 Cal.App.4th 1149 (1998)]

10–9. Product Liability. New England Ecological Development, Inc. (NEED), a recycling station in Rhode Island, needed a conveyor belt system and gave the specifications to Colmar Belting Co. Colmar did not design or make belts but distributed the component parts. For this system, Emerson Power Transmission Corp. (EPT) manufactured the wing pulley, a component of the nip point (the point at which a belt moves over the stationary part of the system). Kenneth Butler, a welder, assembled the system with assistance from Colmar. Neither Colmar nor EPT recommended the use of a protective shield to guard the nip point, and as finally built, NEED's system did not have a shield. Later, as Americo Buonanno, a NEED employee, was clearing debris from the belt, his arm was pulled into the nip point. The arm was severely crushed and later amputated at the elbow. Buonanno filed a suit in a Rhode Island state court against Colmar and EPT, alleging in part strict liability. The defendants filed a motion for summary judgment, arguing that as sellers of component parts, they had no duty to ensure the proper design of the final product. On what grounds might the court deny the motion? [*Buonanno v. Colmar Belting Co.*, 733 A.2d 712 (R.I. 1999)]

A Question of Ethics and Social Responsibility

10–10. Three-year-old Randy Welch, the son of Steve and Teresa Griffith, climbed up to a shelf and obtained a disposable butane cigarette lighter. Randy then used the lighter to ignite a flame, which set fire to his pajama top. Welch and his parents sued the lighter's manufacturer, Scripto-Tokai Corp., for damages, alleging that the lighter was defective and unreasonably dangerous because it was not child resistant. In view of this factual background, consider the following questions. [*Welch v. Scripto-Tokai Corp.*, 651 N.E.2d 810 (Ind.App. 1995)]

1. One of the questions raised in this case was whether the risks attending the lighter were sufficiently "open and obvious" that the manufacturer did not need to warn of those risks. If you were the judge, how would you decide this issue? Explain your reasoning.

2. If a product is not dangerous to an extent beyond that contemplated by the ordinary consumer, should the manufacturer nonetheless be held liable if it could have made the product safer? Explain.

3. How can a court decide what kinds of risks should be open and obvious for the ordinary consumer?

For Critical Analysis

10–11. The United States has the strictest product liability laws in the world today. Why do you think many other countries, particularly developing countries, are more lax with respect to holding manufacturers liable for product defects?

Interacting with the Internet

■ For updated links to resources available on the Web, as well as a variety of other materials, visit this text's Web site at

http://leet.westbuslaw.com

■ For information on the *Restatements of the Law*, including the *Restatement (Second) of Torts* and the *Restatement (Third) of Torts: Products Liability*, go to the Web site of the American Law Institute at

http://www.ali.org

■ The law firm of Horvitz & Levy offers a review of recent judicial decisions in the area of product liability at

http://www.horvitzlevy.com/ yirtoc4b.html

■ For information on product liability suits against tobacco companies and recent settlements, go to

http://www.usatoday.com/news/ smoke/smoke00.htm

■ A discussion of the "demise of privity" with respect to product liability in leading cases decided by the New York Court of Appeals can be found at the following Web page within the site offered by the *New York Law Journal:*

**http://www.nylj.com/links/
150sterk.html**

■ Law Journal EXTRA! has articles on current cases and issues in the area of product liability, as well as proposed legislation, at

**http://www.ljx.com/practice/
productliability/index.html**

Online Legal Research Exercises

Go to **http://leet.
westbuslaw.com,** the Web site that accompanies this text. Select "Interactive Study Center," and then click on "Chapter 10." There you will find the following Internet research exercise that you can perform to learn more about product liability litigation:

Activity 10–1: Product Liability Litigation

Before the Test

Go to **http://leet.westbuslaw.
com,** the Web site that accompanies this text. Select "Interactive Quizzes." You will find a number of interactive questions relating to this chapter.

Intellectual Property and Cyberlaw

contents

chapter objectives

After reading this chapter, you should be able to:

1. Summarize the laws protecting trademarks, patents, and copyrights.

2. Describe how trade secrets are protected by the law.

3. Discuss what is meant by the term *virtual property*.

4. Indicate what legal protection exists for trademarks, copyrights, and other intellectual property existing in digital form.

5. Give examples of how technological developments are affecting the laws governing intellectual property.

O f significant concern to businesspersons is the need to protect their rights in intellectual property. **Intellectual property** is any property resulting from intellectual, creative processes—the products of an individual's mind. Although it is an abstract term for an abstract concept, intellectual property is nonetheless wholly familiar to virtually everyone. The information contained in books and computer files is intellectual property. The software you use, the movies you see, and the music you listen to are all forms of intellectual property. In fact, in today's information age, it should come as no surprise that the value of the world's intellectual property now exceeds the value of physical property, such as machines and houses.

In this chapter, we first examine the protection given to intellectual property rights under trademark, patent, copyright, and other laws. We then look at how technology affects business practices and, for this reason, can affect business law. Cyberspace, the Internet, and the World Wide Web represent the latest in technological developments. In general, the law is attempting to catch up with, to paraphrase the quotation alongside, these profoundly different capabilities that we have not had before.

> "The Internet, by virtue of its ability to mesh what will be hundreds of millions of people together, . . . is . . . a profoundly different capability that by and large human beings have not had before."
>
> Tony Rutkowski, 1943–
> (Executive director of the Internet Society, 1994–1996)

Intellectual Property
Property resulting from intellectual, creative processes.

Intellectual Property Protection

The need to protect creative works was voiced by the framers of the U.S. Constitution over two hundred years ago: Article I, Section 8, of the Constitution authorized Congress "[t]o promote the Progress of Science and useful Arts, by securing for limited Times to Authors and Inventors the exclusive Right to their respective Writings and Discoveries." Laws protecting patents, trademarks, and copyrights are explicitly designed to protect and reward inventive and artistic creativity.

An understanding of intellectual property law is important because intellectual property has taken on increasing significance, not only in the United States but globally as well. Today, ownership rights in intangible intellectual property are more important to the prosperity of many U.S. companies than are their tangible assets. Protecting these assets in today's online world has proved particularly challenging, as you will read later in this chapter.

Trademarks and Related Property

A **trademark** is a distinctive mark, motto, device, or emblem that a manufacturer stamps, prints, or otherwise affixes to the goods it produces so that they may be identified on the market and their origin vouched for. At common law, the person who used a symbol or mark to identify a business or product was protected in the use of that trademark. Clearly, if one used the trademark of another, it would lead consumers to believe that one's goods were made by the other. The law seeks to avoid this kind of confusion. In the following famous case concerning Coca-Cola, the defendants argued that the Coca-Cola trademark was entitled to no protection under the law, because the term did not accurately represent the product.

Trademark A distinctive mark, motto, device, or emblem that a manufacturer stamps, prints, or otherwise affixes to the goods it produces so that they may be identified on the market and their origins made known. Once a trademark is established (under the common law or through registration), the owner is entitled to its exclusive use.

Case 11.1 ● The Coca-Cola Co. v. Koke Co. of America

Supreme Court of the United States, 1920.
254 U.S. 143,
41 S.Ct. 113,
65 L.Ed. 189.
http://www.findlaw.com/
casecode/supreme.html[a]

Company Profile   *John Pemberton, an Atlanta pharmacist, invented a caramel-colored, carbonated soft drink in 1886. His bookkeeper, Frank Robinson, named the beverage Coca-Cola after two of the ingredients, coca leaves and kola nuts. Asa Candler bought the Coca-Cola Company in 1891, and within seven years, he made the soft drink available in all of the United States, as well as in parts of Canada and Mexico. Candler continued to sell Coke aggressively and to open up new markets, reaching Europe before 1910. In doing so, however, he attracted numerous competitors, some of whom tried to capitalize directly on the Coke name.*

Background and Facts   The Coca-Cola Company brought an action in a federal district court to enjoin other beverage companies from using the words "Koke" and "Dope" for the defendants' products. The defendants contended that the Coca-Cola trademark was a fraudulent representation and that Coca-Cola was therefore not entitled to any help from the courts. By use of the Coca-Cola name, the defendants alleged, the Coca-Cola Company represented that the beverage contained cocaine (from coca leaves). The district court granted the injunction, but the federal appellate court reversed. The Coca-Cola Company appealed to the United States Supreme Court.

---

a. This is the "U.S. Supreme Court Opinions" page within the Web site of the "Findlaw Internet Legal Resources" database. This page provides several options for accessing an opinion. Because you know the citation for this case, you can go to the "Citation Search" box, type in the appropriate volume and page numbers for the *United States Reports* ("254" and "143," respectively, for the *Coca-Cola* case), and click on "Get It."

In the Words of the Court . . .
Mr. Justice HOLMES delivered the opinion of the court.

* * * *

* * * Before 1900 the beginning of [Coca-Cola's] good will was more or less helped by the presence of cocaine, a drug that, like alcohol or caffein or opium, may be described as a deadly poison or as a valuable item of the pharmacopœa according to the rhetorical purposes in view. * * * [A]fter the Food and Drug Act of June 30, 1906, if not earlier, long before this suit was brought, it was eliminated from the plaintiff's compound. * * *

* * * Since 1900 the sales have increased at a very great rate corresponding to a like increase in advertising. The name now characterizes a beverage to be had at almost any soda fountain. It means a single thing coming from a single source, and well known to the community. It hardly would be too much to say that the drink characterizes the name as much as the name the drink. In other words Coca-Cola probably means to most persons the plaintiff's familiar product to be had everywhere rather than a compound of particular substances. * * * [B]efore this suit was brought the plaintiff had advertised to the public that it must not expect and would not find cocaine, and had eliminated everything tending to suggest cocaine effects except the name and the picture of the leaves and nuts, which probably conveyed little or nothing to most who saw it. It appears to us that it would be going too far to deny the plaintiff relief against a palpable fraud because possibly here and there an ignorant person might call for the drink with the hope for incipient cocaine intoxication. The plaintiff's position must be judged by the facts as they were when the suit was begun, not by the facts of a different condition and an earlier time.

Case 11.1 Continued

Decision and Remedy The United States Supreme Court upheld the district court's injunction. The competing beverage companies were enjoined from calling their products "Koke." The Court did not prevent them, however, from calling their products "Dope."

For Critical Analysis—Social Consideration *How can a court determine when a particular nickname for a branded product has entered into common use?*

STATUTORY PROTECTION OF TRADEMARKS Statutory protection of trademarks and related property is provided at the federal level by the Lanham Trade-Mark Act of 1946.[1] The Lanham Act was enacted in part to protect manufacturers from losing business to rival companies that used confusingly similar trademarks. The Lanham Act incorporates the common law of trademarks and provides remedies for owners of trademarks who wish to enforce their claims in federal court. Many states also have trademark statutes.

In 1995, Congress amended the Lanham Act by passing the Federal Trademark Dilution Act,[2] which extended the protection available to trademark owners by creating a federal cause of action for trademark *dilution.* Until the passage of this amendment, federal trademark law only prohibited the unauthorized use of the same mark on competing—or on noncompeting but "related"—goods or services when such use would likely confuse consumers as to the origin of those goods and services. Trademark dilution laws, which about half of the states have also enacted, protect "distinctive" or "famous" trademarks (such as Jergens, McDonald's, RCA, and Macintosh) from certain unauthorized uses of the marks *regardless* of a showing of competition or a likelihood of confusion.

A famous mark may be diluted not only by the use of an *identical* mark but also by the use of a *similar* mark. • **Example 11.1** A case was brought by Ringling Bros.-Barnum & Bailey, Combined Shows, Inc., against the state of Utah. Ringling Bros. claimed that Utah's use of the slogan "The Greatest Snow on Earth"—to attract visitors to the state's recreational and scenic resorts—diluted the distinctiveness of the circus's famous trademark, "The Greatest Show on Earth." Utah moved to dismiss the suit, arguing that the 1995 provisions only protect owners of famous trademarks against the unauthorized use of identical marks. A federal court disagreed and refused to grant Utah's motion to dismiss the case.[3] •

TRADEMARK REGISTRATION Trademarks may be registered with the state or with the federal government. To register for protection under federal trademark law, a person must file an application with the U.S. Patent and Trademark Office in Washington, D.C. Under current law, a mark can be registered (1) if it is currently in commerce or (2) if the applicant intends to put the mark into commerce within six months.

Under extenuating circumstances, the six-month period can be extended by thirty months, giving the applicant a total of three years from the date of

> "The protection of trademarks is the law's recognition of the psychological function of symbols. If it is true that we live by symbols, it is no less true that we purchase goods by them."
>
> Felix Frankfurter, 1882–1965
> (Associate Justice of the United States Supreme Court, 1939–1962)

---

1. 15 U.S.C. Sections 1051–1128.
2. 15 U.S.C. Section 1125.
3. *Ringling Bros.-Barnum & Bailey, Combined Shows, Inc. v. Utah Division of Travel Development,* 935 F.Supp. 736 (E.D.Va. 1996).

notice of trademark approval to make use of the mark and file the required use statement. Registration is postponed until actual use of the mark. Nonetheless, during this waiting period, any applicant can legally protect his or her trademark against a third party who previously has neither used the mark nor filed an application for it. Registration is renewable between the fifth and sixth years after the initial registration and every ten years thereafter (every twenty years for trademarks registered before 1990).

TRADEMARK INFRINGEMENT Registration of a trademark with the U.S. Patent and Trademark Office gives notice on a nationwide basis that the trademark belongs exclusively to the registrant. The registrant is also allowed to use the symbol ® to indicate that the mark has been registered. Whenever that trademark is copied to a substantial degree or used in its entirety by another, intentionally or unintentionally, the trademark has been *infringed* (used without authorization). When a trademark has been infringed, the owner of the mark has a cause of action against the infringer. A person need not have registered a trademark in order to sue for trademark infringement, but registration does furnish proof of the date of inception of the trademark's use.

DISTINCTIVENESS OF MARK The Lanham Act states, "No trademark by which the goods of the applicant may be distinguished from the goods of others shall be refused registration."[4] Only those trademarks that are deemed sufficiently distinctive from all competing trademarks will be protected, however. The trademarks must be sufficiently distinct to enable consumers to identify the manufacturer of the goods easily and to differentiate among competing products.

Strong Marks. Fanciful, arbitrary, or suggestive trademarks are generally considered to be the most distinctive (strongest) trademarks, because they are normally taken from outside the context of the particular product and thus provide the best means of distinguishing one product from another.

  • **Example 11.2** Fanciful trademarks include invented words, such as "Xerox" for one manufacturer's copiers and "Kodak" for another company's photographic products. Arbitrary trademarks include actual words that have no literal connection to the product, such as "English Leather" used as a name for an after-shave lotion (and not for leather processed in England). Suggestive trademarks are those that suggest something about a product without describing the product directly. For example, "Dairy Queen" suggests an association between its products and milk, but it does not directly describe ice cream.•

Secondary Meaning. Descriptive terms, geographical terms, and personal names are not inherently distinctive and do not receive protection under the law until they acquire a secondary meaning. A secondary meaning may arise when customers begin to associate a specific term or phrase, such as "London Fog," with specific trademarked items (coats with "London Fog" labels). Whether a secondary meaning becomes attached to a term or name usually depends on how extensively the product is advertised, the market for the product, the number of sales, and other factors. Once a secondary meaning is attached to a term or name, a trademark is considered distinctive and is protected.

A billboard and theater marquee in New York City. Why are trademarks protected by the law?

---

4. 15 U.S.C. Section 1052.

Even a shade of *color* can qualify for trademark protection, once customers associate the color with the product.[5]

Generic Terms. Generic terms, such as *bicycle* or *computer,* receive no protection, even if they acquire secondary meanings. A particularly thorny problem arises when a trademark acquires generic use. For example, *aspirin* and *thermos* were originally trademarked products, but today the words are used generically. Other examples are *escalator, trampoline, raisin bran, dry ice, lanolin, linoleum, nylon,* and *corn flakes.* Even so, the courts will not allow another firm to use those marks in such a way as to deceive a potential consumer. In the following case, the issue before the court was whether the phrase "You Have Mail" is a generic term.

---

5. *Qualitex Co. v. Jacobson Products Co.,* 514 U.S. 159, 115 S.Ct. 1300, 131 L.Ed.2d 248 (1995).

Case 11.2 ● America Online, Inc. v. AT&T Corp.

United States District Court,
Eastern District of Virginia, 1999.
64 F.Supp.2d 549.
**http://zeus.bna.com/e-law/
cases/aolatt.html[a]**

Background and Facts In the late 1960s and early 1970s, AT&T Corporation developed UNIX, a computer operating system facilitating communications over the Internet. When a user connects to UNIX,

if the user has e-mail, the system displays a phrase something like "You Have Mail." In the 1980s, America Online, Inc. (AOL), the world's largest Internet service provider, started using "YOU HAVE MAIL" in its e-mail notification service for its members. AT&T provides Internet access to subscribers through its WorldNet Service. Since 1998, when a member visits the WorldNet home page, a "You Have Mail!" notification window pops up. AOL filed a suit in a federal district court against AT&T, alleging in part trademark infringement of the phrase "YOU HAVE MAIL," which AOL claimed to own. AT&T filed a motion for summary judgment, asking the court to rule that the term was generic.

---

a. This is a page in the library of documents at the "Electronic Commerce & Law Report" Web site maintained by the Bureau of National Affairs, Inc.

In the Words of the Court . . .
HILTON, J. [Judge]

* * * *

* * * [A] plaintiff who is seeking to establish a valid trademark must show that the primary significance of the term in the minds of the consuming public is not the product but the producer. * * * [T]he following evidence [may] be used to determine the primary significance of a mark: (1) competitors' use of the mark, (2) plaintiff's use of the mark, (3) dictionary definitions, (4) media usage, (5) testimony of persons in the trade, and (6) consumer surveys.

* * * *

* * * Under the primary significance test, the "mail" component of YOU HAVE MAIL means "e-mail."

First, the Court notes that even AOL uses the words "mail" and "e-mail" interchangeably. For example, in its * * * complaint AOL repeatedly uses the word "mail" as referring to "e-mail." * * *

Next, it is undisputed that numerous competitors of AOL use "mail" as a synonym for "e-mail." * * *

(Continued)

Case 11.2 Continued

Regarding media usage and testimony of persons involved in the trade, [there are] numerous examples of the books printed to describe the e-mail notification features used by both UNIX and AOL. All of the authors, without fail, use "mail" and "e-mail" interchangeably. * * *

Last, the Court would note that * * * consumer surveys [are used] as a means of determining whether the primary significance of a mark is generic. However, when determining whether a mark is generic, the Court is not to consider whether the mark has acquired any secondary meaning, because generic marks with secondary meaning are still not entitled to protection. * * *

* * * *

The primary significance of the phrase YOU HAVE MAIL indicates to the public-at-large what the service is, not where it came from. * * * Further, this holding does not rest on considering solely the "mail" component of the YOU HAVE MAIL. * * * The "you" and the "have" of YOU HAVE MAIL (either separately or together) do not carry with them any especial significance which would change the primary significance of the mark as previously stated. Since the "you," "have," and "mail" of YOU HAVE MAIL are all used for their everyday, common meaning, the phrase as a whole is generic * * * .

Decision and Remedy The court granted a summary judgment in favor of AT&T. The court ruled that "You have mail" is a generic expression and therefore cannot be owned by AOL.

For Critical Analysis—Social Consideration *Particular shapes, sounds, colors, and even scents that have acquired secondary meanings have qualified for trademark protection. Yet, as the court noted in this case, generic marks will not be protected as trademarks even if they have acquired secondary meanings. Can you see any reason for this principle of trademark law?*

Service Mark A mark used in the sale or the advertising of services, such as to distinguish the services of one person from the services of others. Titles, character names, and other distinctive features of radio and television programs may be registered as service marks.

SERVICE, CERTIFICATION, AND COLLECTIVE MARKS A **service mark** is similar to a trademark but is used to distinguish the services of one person or company from those of another. For example, each airline has a particular mark or symbol associated with its name. Titles and character names used in radio and television are frequently registered as service marks.

Other marks protected by law include certification marks and collective marks. A *certification mark* is used by one or more persons other than the owner to certify the region, materials, mode of manufacture, quality, or accuracy of the owner's goods or services. When used by members of a cooperative, association, or other organization, it is referred to as a *collective mark*.

• **Example 11.3** Certification marks include such marks as "Good Housekeeping Seal of Approval" and "UL Tested." Collective marks appear at the ends of the credits of movies to indicate the various associations and organizations that participated in the making of the movies. The union marks found on the tags of certain products are also collective marks.•

Trade Name A term that is used to indicate part or all of a business's name and that is directly related to the business's reputation and goodwill. Trade names are protected under the common law (and under trademark law, if the name is the same as the firm's trademarked property).

TRADE NAMES Trademarks apply to *products*. The term **trade name** is used to indicate part or all of a business's name, whether the business is a sole proprietorship, a partnership, or a corporation. Generally, a trade name is directly related to a business and its goodwill. Trade names may be protected as trademarks if the trade name is the same as the company's trademarked product—for example, Coca-Cola. Unless also used as a trademark or service mark, a trade name cannot be registered with the federal government. Trade names are protected under the common law, however. As with trademarks, words must be unusual or fancifully used if they are to be protected as trade names. The word *Safeway,* for example, was held by the courts to be sufficiently fanciful to obtain protection as a trade name for a food-store chain.[6]

A "UL" certification mark. How does a certification mark differ from a trademark?

TRADE DRESS   The term **trade dress** refers to the image and overall appearance of a business. For example, the distinctive decor, menu, layout, and style of service of a particular restaurant may be regarded as the restaurant's trade dress. Similarly, if a golf course is distinguished from other golf courses by prominent features, those features may be considered the golf course's trade dress. Basically, trade dress is subject to the same protection as trademarks. In cases involving trade dress infringement, as in trademark infringement cases, a major consideration is whether consumers are likely to be confused by the allegedly infringing use.

Trade Dress The image and overall appearance of a business—for example, the distinctive decor, menu, layout, and style of service of a particular restaurant. Basically, trade dress is subject to the same protection as trademarks.

Patents

A **patent** is a grant from the government that gives an inventor the exclusive right to make, use, and sell an invention for a period of twenty years from the date of filing the application for a patent. Patents for a fourteen-year period are given for designs, as opposed to inventions. For either a regular patent or a design patent, the applicant must demonstrate to the satisfaction of the U.S. Patent and Trademark Office that the invention, discovery, process, or design is genuine, novel, useful, and not obvious in light of current technology. A patent holder gives notice to all that an article or design is patented by placing on it the word *Patent* or *Pat.* plus the patent number. In contrast to patent law in other countries, in the United States patent protection is given to the first person to invent a product or process, even though someone else may have been the first to file for a patent on that product or process.

Patent A government grant that gives an inventor the exclusive right or privilege to make, use, or sell his or her invention for a limited time period.

At one time, it was difficult for developers and manufacturers of software to obtain patent protection because many software products simply automate procedures that can be performed manually. In other words, the computer programs do not meet the "novel" and "not obvious" requirements previously mentioned. Also, the basis for software is often a mathematical equation or formula, which is not patentable. In 1981, the United States Supreme Court held that it is possible, however, to obtain a patent for a *process* that incorporates a computer program—providing, of course, that the process itself is patentable.[7] Subsequently, many patents have been issued for software-related inventions.

> **"The patent system . . . added the fuel of interest to the fire of genius."**
>
> Abraham Lincoln, 1809–1865 (Sixteenth president of the United States, 1861–1865)

If a firm makes, uses, or sells another's patented design, product, or process without the patent owner's permission, it commits the tort of patent infringement. Patent infringement may exist even though the patent owner has not put the patented product in commerce. Patent infringement may also occur even though not all features or parts of an invention are copied. (With respect to a

---

6. *Safeway Stores v. Suburban Foods,* 130 F.Supp. 249 (E.D.Va. 1955).
7. *Diamond v. Diehr,* 450 U.S. 175, 101 S.Ct. 1048, 67 L.Ed.2d 155 (1981).

patented process, however, all steps or their equivalent must be copied for infringement to exist.)

Often, litigation for patent infringement is so costly that the patent holder will instead offer to sell to the infringer a license to use the patented design, product, or process. (Licensing will be discussed later in this chapter.) Indeed, in many cases the costs of detection, prosecution, and monitoring are so high that patents are valueless to their owners; the owners cannot afford to protect them.

Copyrights

Copyright The exclusive right of "authors" to publish, print, or sell an intellectual production for a statutory period of time. A copyright has the same monopolistic nature as a patent or trademark, but it differs in that it applies exclusively to works of art, literature, and other works of authorship (including computer programs).

A **copyright** is an intangible property right granted by federal statute to the author or originator of certain literary or artistic productions. Currently, copyrights are governed by the Copyright Act of 1976,[8] as amended. Works created after January 1, 1978, are automatically given statutory copyright protection for the life of the author plus 70 years. For copyrights owned by publishing houses, the copyright expires 95 years from the date of publication or 120 years from the date of creation, whichever is first. For works by more than one author, the copyright expires 70 years after the death of the last surviving author.[9]

Copyrights can be registered with the U.S. Copyright Office in Washington, D.C. A copyright owner no longer needs to place a © or *Copr.* or *Copyright* on the work, however, to have the work protected against infringement. Chances are that if somebody created it, somebody owns it.

WHAT IS PROTECTED EXPRESSION? Works that are copyrightable include books, records, films, artworks, architectural plans, menus, music videos, product packaging, and computer software. To obtain protection under the Copyright Act, a work must be original and fall into one of the following categories: (1) literary works; (2) musical works; (3) dramatic works; (4) pantomimes and choreographic works; (5) pictorial, graphic, and sculptural works; (6) films and other audiovisual works; and (7) sound recordings. To be protected, a work must be "fixed in a durable medium" from which it can be perceived, reproduced, or communicated. Protection is automatic. Registration is not required.

Be Careful If a creative work does not fall into a certain category, it may not be copyrighted, but it may be protected by other intellectual property law.

Section 102 of the Copyright Act specifically excludes copyright protection for any "idea, procedure, process, system, method of operation, concept, principle, or discovery, regardless of the form in which it is described, explained, illustrated, or embodied." Note that it is not possible to copyright an idea. The underlying ideas embodied in a work may be freely used by others. What is copyrightable is the particular way in which an idea is expressed. Whenever an idea and an expression are inseparable, the expression cannot be copyrighted. Generally, anything that is not an original expression will not qualify for copyright protection. Facts widely known to the public are not copyrightable. Page numbers are not copyrightable, because they follow a sequence known to everyone. Mathematical calculations are not copyrightable.

Compilations of facts, however, are copyrightable. Section 103 of the Copyright Act defines a compilation as "a work formed by the collection and assembling of preexisting materials of data that are selected, coordinated, or

---

8. 17 U.S.C. Sections 101 *et seq.*
9. These time periods reflect the extensions set forth in the Sonny Bono Copyright Term Extension Act of 1998.

arranged in such a way that the resulting work as a whole constitutes an original work of authorship." The key requirement in the copyrightability of a compilation is originality. • **Example 11.4** The White Pages of a telephone directory do not qualify for copyright protection when the information that makes up the directory (names, addresses, and telephone numbers) is not selected, coordinated, or arranged in an original way.[10] In one case, even the Yellow Pages of a telephone directory did not qualify for copyright protection.[11]•

COPYRIGHT PROTECTION FOR SOFTWARE In 1980, Congress passed the Computer Software Copyright Act, which amended the Copyright Act of 1976 to include computer programs in the list of creative works protected by federal copyright law. The 1980 statute, which classifies computer programs as "literary works," defines a computer program as a "set of statements or instructions to be used directly or indirectly in a computer in order to bring about a certain result."

Because of the unique nature of computer programs, the courts have had many problems in applying and interpreting the 1980 act. In a series of cases decided in the 1980s, the courts held that copyright protection extended not only to those parts of a computer program that can be read by humans, such as the "high-level" language of a source code, but also to the binary-language object code of a computer program, which is readable only by the computer.[12]

---

10. *Feist Publications, Inc. v. Rural Telephone Service Co.*, 499 U.S. 340, 111 S.Ct. 1282, 113 L.Ed.2d 358 (1991).
11. *Bellsouth Advertising & Publishing Corp. v. Donnelley Information Publishing, Inc.*, 999 F.2d 1436 (11th Cir. 1993).
12. See *Stern Electronics, Inc. v. Kaufman*, 669 F.2d 852 (2d Cir. 1982); and *Apple Computer, Inc. v. Franklin Computer Corp.*, 714 F.2d 1240 (3d Cir. 1983).

Ethical Issue 11.1

Should copyright protection extend to "reimported" goods?

Cases involving claims of copyright infringement can sometimes involve questions of fairness. One such question that reached the United States Supreme Court involved L'anza Research International, Inc., a company that sells hair-care products. L'anza sells its products in the United States only to distributors who agree to resell the products in certain geographic areas to authorized retailers. L'anza also sells its products in foreign markets but for lower prices—because it does little advertising abroad. At one point, an American firm purchased L'anza hair products abroad from a L'anza distributor, "reimported" the goods into the United States, and sold them at discount prices to unauthorized retailers. L'anza claimed that this activity infringed on its exclusive rights under the Copyright Act to reproduce and distribute the copyrighted material (the labels on the products) in the United States. According to the United States Supreme Court, however, no infringement occurred. The Court stated that under the "first-sale" doctrine, which is codified in the Copyright Act, the purchaser of copyrighted material is entitled, without the permission of the copyright owner, to sell or otherwise dispose of the purchased copyrighted materials, imported or not.[a]

---

a. *Quality King Distributors, Inc. v. L'anza Research International, Inc.*, 523 U.S. 135, 118 S.Ct. 1125, 140 L.Ed.2d 254 (1998).

Additionally, such elements as the overall structure, sequence, and organization of a program were deemed copyrightable.[13]

By the early 1990s, the issue had evolved into whether the "look and feel"—the general appearance, command structure, video images, menus, windows, and other screen displays—of computer programs should also be protected by copyright. Although the courts have disagreed on this issue, the tendency has been not to extend copyright protection to look-and-feel aspects of computer programs. • **Example 11.5** In 1995 the Court of Appeals for the First Circuit held that Lotus Development Corporation's menu command hierarchy for its Lotus 1-2-3 spreadsheet is not protectable under the Copyright Act. The court deemed that the menu command hierarchy is a "method of operation," and Section 102 of the Copyright Act specifically excludes methods of operation from copyright protection.[14] The decision was affirmed by the United States Supreme Court in 1996.[15] •

COPYRIGHT INFRINGEMENT Whenever the form or expression of an idea is copied, an infringement of copyright occurs. The reproduction does not have to be exactly the same as the original, nor does it have to reproduce the original in its entirety.

Penalties or remedies can be imposed on those who infringe copyrights. These range from actual damages (damages based on the actual harm caused to the copyright holder by the infringement) or statutory damages (damages provided for under the Copyright Act, not to exceed $150,000) to criminal proceedings for willful violations (which may result in fines and/or imprisonment).

An exception to liability for copyright infringement is made under the "fair use" doctrine. In certain circumstances, a person or organization can reproduce copyrighted material without paying royalties (fees paid to the copyright holder for the privilege of reproducing the copyrighted material). Section 107 of the Copyright Act provides as follows:

> [T]he fair use of a copyrighted work, including such use by reproduction in copies or phonorecords or by any other means specified by [Section 106 of the Copyright Act,] for purposes such as criticism, comment, news reporting, teaching (including multiple copies for classroom use), scholarship, or research, is not an infringement of copyright. In determining whether the use made of a work in any particular case is a fair use the factors to be considered shall include—
>
> (1) the purpose and character of the use, including whether such use is of a commercial nature or is for nonprofit educational purposes;
> (2) the nature of the copyrighted work;
> (3) the amount and substantiality of the portion used in relation to the copyrighted work as a whole; and
> (4) the effect of the use upon the potential market for or value of the copyrighted work.

Because these guidelines are very broad, the courts determine whether a particular use is fair on a case-by-case basis. Thus, anyone reproducing copyrighted material may be subject to a violation.

The following case indicates what must be proved to win a case involving charges of copyright infringement of a musical work.

---

13. *Whelan Associates, Inc. v. Jaslow Dental Laboratory, Inc.,* 797 F.2d 1222 (3d Cir. 1986).
14. *Lotus Development Corp. v. Borland International, Inc.,* 49 F.3d 807 (1st Cir. 1995).
15. *Lotus Development Corp. v. Borland International, Inc.,* 517 U.S. 843, 116 S.Ct. 804, 113 L.Ed.2d 610 (1996).

Case 11.3 ● Repp v. Webber

United States Court of Appeals,
Second Circuit, 1997.
132 F.3d 882.
http://www.tourolaw.edu/
2ndCircuit/December97/ᵃ

Historical and Cultural Setting *Musical works fall within the category of works of authorship that can be protected by copyright. A protected musical work can consist of lyrics or music alone, or of both lyrics and music, as in a song. A musical work can exist in a number of different forms, including a tape, a compact disk, and sheet music. To determine whether a copyright of a musical work has been infringed, an expert might dissect the works into musical phrases and compare those phrases to other works by the same, or other, composers. Pitch and rhythm—the elements of a melody—might also be dissected and compared. Harmony—the chordal elements that support the melody—can also be an important element in comparing pop compositions.*

---

a. This is the "Decisions for December 1997" page within the collection of opinions of the U.S. Court of Appeals for the Second Circuit. Scroll down the list of cases to the entry for the *Repp* case. Click on the case name to read the court's opinion.

Background and Facts Over a period of thirty years, Ray Repp wrote and published more than 120 musical compositions, including the song "Till You," which was registered with the U.S. Copyright Office in 1978. Repp included "Till You" on his album "Benedicamus" and in two books of sheet music, and performed the song in over two hundred concerts. Andrew Lloyd Webber, the composer of such musicals as *Cats* and *Evita,* wrote the musical *Phantom of the Opera* in 1983 and 1984. Claiming that "Phantom Song," one of the songs in *Phantom of the Opera,* infringed on the copyright of "Till You," Repp and others filed a suit in a federal district court against Lloyd Webber and others. Lloyd Webber responded that he never heard of Repp or "Till You" and that "Phantom Song" was an "independent creation." Musical experts offered conflicting testimony about the similarity of the songs' melodies, harmonics, and phrases. Despite this conflict, the court stated that "the two songs do not share a striking similarity" and issued a summary judgment for Lloyd Webber. The court added that Repp failed to show "Phantom Song" was not created independently. Repp appealed to the U.S. Court of Appeals for the Second Circuit.

In the Words of the Court . . .
MINER, Circuit Judge:

* * * *

While there was little, if any, evidence demonstrating access, there was considerable evidence that "Phantom Song" is so strikingly similar to "Till You" as to preclude the possibility of independent creation and to allow access to be inferred without direct proof. * * * Two highly qualified experts * * * gave unequivocal opinions based on musicological analyses. * * *
* * * The issue of "striking similarity," by virtue of the supported opinions of the experts * * * was shown to be a genuine issue of material fact. Access to the music of Repp being an essential element of his case, it cannot be said that there is an absence of evidence to support proof of that element through the inference generated by the striking similarity of the two pieces.

* * * *

* * * The plaintiffs here have established a *prima facie* case of access through striking similarity * * * . Whether the evidence of independent creation here is sufficient to rebut the *prima facie* case established in this action is a question for the factfinder * * * .

Decision and Remedy The U.S. Court of Appeals reversed the decision of the lower court and remanded the case. Because the issues of "striking similarity" and "independent creation" were disputed, there was a genuine controversy about the material facts and summary judgment was not appropriate.

For Critical Analysis—Cultural Consideration *Considering that there are a limited number of musical notes and a limited number of works into which those notes can be composed, should the fact that infringement might be "subconscious" affect liability in a copyright suit?*

Trade Secrets

Some business processes and information that are not or cannot be patented, copyrighted, or trademarked are nevertheless protected against appropriation by a competitor as trade secrets. **Trade secrets** consist of customer lists, plans, research and development, pricing information, marketing techniques, production techniques, and generally anything that makes an individual company unique and that would have value to a competitor.

Trade Secrets Information or processes that give a business an advantage over competitors who do not know the information or processes.

Until recently, virtually all law with respect to trade secrets was common law. In an effort to reduce the unpredictability of the common law with respect to trade secrets, a model act, the Uniform Trade Secrets Act, was presented to the states in 1979 for adoption. Parts of it have been adopted in over twenty states. Typically, a state that has adopted parts of the act has adopted only those parts that encompass its own existing common law. In 1996, Congress passed the Economic Espionage Act, which made the theft of trade secrets a federal crime. We examined the provisions and significance of this act in Chapter 8, in the context of criminal law.

Unlike copyright and trademark protection, protection of trade secrets extends both to ideas and to their expression. (For this reason, and because a trade secret involves no registration or filing requirements, trade secret protection may be well suited for software.) Of course, the secret formula, method, or other information must be disclosed to some persons, particularly to key employees. Businesses generally attempt to protect their trade secrets by having all employees who use the process or information agree in their contracts, or in confidentiality agreements, never to divulge it.

International Protection

For many years, the United States has been a party to various international agreements relating to intellectual property rights. For example, the Paris Convention of 1883, to which about ninety countries are signatory, allows parties in one country to file for patent and trademark protection in any of the other member countries. Other international agreements include the Berne Convention and the TRIPS agreement, discussed next.

Currently, the laws of many countries as well as international laws are being updated to reflect changes in technology and the expansion of the Internet. Copyright holders and other owners of intellectual property generally agree that changes in the law are needed to stop the increasing international piracy of their property. We will look at some of these developments later in this chapter, in the context of international protection for intellectual property rights in cyberspace.

THE BERNE CONVENTION   Under the Berne Convention of 1886, an international copyright agreement, if an American writes a book, his or her copyright in the book must be recognized by every country that has signed the convention. Also, if a citizen of a country that has not signed the convention first publishes a book in a country that has signed, all other countries that have signed the convention must recognize that author's copyright. Copyright notice is not needed to gain protection under the Berne Convention for works published after March 1, 1989.

These and other international agreements have given some protection to intellectual property on a worldwide level. None of them, however, has been as significant and far reaching in scope as the agreement on Trade-Related Aspects of Intellectual Property Rights, or, more simply, TRIPS.

THE TRIPS AGREEMENT   The TRIPS agreement was signed by representatives from over one hundred nations in 1994. The agreement established, for the first time, standards for the international protection of intellectual property rights, including patents, trademarks, and copyrights for movies, computer programs, books, and music.

Prior to the agreement, one of the difficulties faced by U.S. sellers of intellectual property in the international market was either the lack of protection of intellectual property rights under other countries' laws or the lack of enforcement of those laws that do exist. To address this problem, the TRIPS agreement provides that each member country must include in its domestic laws broad intellectual property rights and effective remedies (including civil and criminal penalties) for violations of those rights.

Generally, the TRIPS agreement provides that each member nation must not discriminate (in terms of the administration, regulation, or adjudication of intellectual property rights) against foreign owners of such rights. In other words, a member nation cannot give its own nationals (citizens) favorable treatment without offering the same treatment to nationals of all member countries. For example, if a U.S. software manufacturer brings a suit for the infringement of intellectual property rights under a member nation's national laws, the U.S. manufacturer is entitled to receive the same treatment as a domestic manufacturer. Each member nation must also ensure that legal procedures are available for parties who wish to bring actions for infringement of intellectual property rights. Additionally, in a related document, a mechanism was established for settling disputes among member nations.

Particular provisions of the TRIPS agreement refer to patent, trademark, and copyright protection for intellectual property. The agreement specifically provides copyright protection for computer programs by stating that compilations of data, databases, or other materials are "intellectual creations" and that they are to be protected as copyrightable works. Other provisions relate to trade secrets and the rental of computer programs and cinematographic works.

Virtual Property

The legal issues relating to **virtual property**—property in cyberspace—are essentially legal questions involving intellectual property. As discussed earlier in this chapter, intellectual property consists of trademarks, patents, copyrights, and trade secrets. Legal protection for these forms of property makes it possible to market goods and services profitably, which provides an incentive to market competitive goods and services.

In the context of cyberspace, a fundamental issue has to do with the degree of legal protection that should be given to virtual property. If the protection is inadequate, the incentive to make new works available online will be reduced. If the protection is too strict, the free flow and fair use of data will be impaired.

Virtual Property Property that, in the context of cyberspace, is conceptual, as opposed to physical. Intellectual property that exists on the Internet is virtual property.

Cyber Marks

Many legal issues relating to **cyber marks** concern the rights of trademark owners to use their marks in domain names, or Internet addresses. We have already discussed, in Chapter 5, how disputes relating to domain names are being resolved and the important role of the Internet Corporation for Assigned Names and Numbers (ICANN) in this process. Here we look further at issues concerning trademarks in cyberspace and how these issues are being addressed

Cyber Mark A trademark in cyberspace.

by the courts or through new laws. One concern has to do with what is called linking and framing. (For a discussion of this topic, see this chapter's *Inside the Legal Environment* feature.) Other issues relate to cybersquatting, a matter we touched on briefly in Chapter 5; meta tags; trademark dilution on the Web; and the use of licensing as a way to avoid liability for infringing on another's intellectual property rights.

ANTICYBERSQUATTING LEGISLATION   One of the early questions concerning cyber marks had to do with cybersquatting. **Cybersquatting** occurs when a person registers for a domain name that is the same as, or confusingly similar to, the trademark of another and then offers to sell the domain name back to the trademark owner. During the 1990s, cybersquatting became a contentious issue and led to much litigation. Often in controversy in these cases was whether cybersquatting constituted a commercial use of the mark so as to violate federal trademark law. Additionally, it was not always easy to separate

Cybersquatting The act of registering a domain name that is the same as, or confusingly similar to, the trademark of another with the intention of selling (at a profit) the domain name to the trademark owner.

Inside the Legal Environment

Linking and Framing Issues

When a user clicks on an icon, or highlighted or underlined text, that is programmed to be a hypertext link, the user is immediately taken to a new online location. The link may lead to another point within the same site or to a different, unrelated site somewhere else in cyberspace.

Sometimes, a site owner may ask the permission of other owners to link to their sites, but this is not normally done. Linking by underlining the name of a linked site is legal and does not require permission. Linking is considered one of the primary factors in the success of Internet commerce, and is part of the revolution of the new technology. Site owners are less agreeable to *framing,* however.

Framing Others' Web Pages

If a linking site is a framing site, the pages of the linked site will appear in a window of the original site. With frames, a single site can let users view several sites simultaneously. Using linking and framing technology, any site owner can divert traffic from another site. This may be desired because search engines base their results on the number of hits (visits to a site). More hits can mean more advertising revenue and more sales. An owner may even appropriate a competitor's content and hide it, so that an unsuspecting user is transported to the appropriator's site even though he

or she cannot see the appropriated material. This is a violation of trademark law (and copyright law).

Avoiding Liability for Trademark Infringement

Although the law is not settled on the issue, framing has given rise to lawsuits alleging trademark violation. For example, in one case Ticketmaster Corporation sued Microsoft Corporation in a federal district court, alleging that Microsoft Network's unauthorized links to interior pages of Ticketmaster's site constituted trademark infringement and unfair competition. Ticketmaster argued that its Web site is the same as a trademark and that it should be allowed to control the way in which others use it. Because the case was settled by the parties in 1999, we do not know how the court might have ruled.

The issue will likely come up again, however, and to be on the safe side, owners of linking sites should take several precautions. Consent should be obtained if a link falsely implies an affiliation between the sites, if a link uses the linked site's logo or trademark, if an imaged link is used, if the link is "deep" (to internal pages), or if a frame modifies or distorts the linked site. Also, consent should be obtained if the linked site requests or requires it, or if the link diverts advertising revenue from the linked site. Finally, a linking site should include a disclaimer.

For Critical Analysis: *Can you think of any reasons why a Web site owner would object to having the contents of his or her site, which are already available to anyone using the Internet, framed by another site?*

cybersquatting from legitimate business activity. Although no clear rules emerged from this litigation, many courts held that cybersquatting violated trademark law.[16]

In 1999, Congress addressed this issue by passing the Anticybersquatting Consumer Reform Act (ACRA), which amended the Lanham Act—the federal law protecting trademarks, as discussed earlier in this chapter. The ACRA makes it illegal for a person to "register, traffic in, or use" a domain name (a) if the name is identical or confusingly similar to the trademark of another and (b) if the one registering, trafficking in, or using the domain name has a "bad faith intent" to profit from that trademark. The act does not define what constitutes bad faith. Instead, it lists several factors that courts can consider in deciding whether bad faith exists. Some of these factors are the trademark rights of the other person, the intent to divert consumers in a way that could harm the goodwill represented by the trademark, whether there is an offer to transfer or sell the domain name to the trademark owner, and whether there is an intent to use the domain name to offer goods and services.

The ACRA applies to all domain name registrations, even domain names registered before the passage of the act. Successful plaintiffs in suits brought under the act can collect actual damages and profits, or elect to receive statutory damages of from $1,000 to $100,000. In fact, immediately after the act's passage, a number of trademark owners filed suits against cybersquatters to recover damages.

META TAGS   Search engines compile their results by looking through a Web site's key words field. **Meta tags** are words that are inserted in this field to increase a site's appearance in search engine results, even if the site has nothing to do with the inserted words. Using this same technique, one site may appropriate the key words of other sites with more frequent hits, so that the appropriating site appears in the same search engine results as the more popular site. One use of meta tags was at issue in the following case.

> **Meta Tags** Words inserted into a Web site's key words field to increase the site's appearance in search engine results.

---

16. See, for example, *Panavision International, L.P. v. Toeppen,* 141 F.3d 1316 (9th Cir. 1998).

Case 11.4 ● Playboy Enterprises, Inc. v. Welles

United States District Court,
Southern District of California, 1998.
7 F.Supp.2d 1098.
http://www.Loundy.com/
CASES/ Playboy_v_Wells.html[a]

Company Profile *Playboy Enterprises, Inc. (PEI), is an international publishing and entertainment company. Since 1953, PEI has published* Playboy *magazine, a popular magazine with approximately ten million readers each month. PEI also publishes numerous specialty magazines and other publications. In addition, PEI produces television programming for cable and satellite transmission, and sells and licenses other*

goods and services. PEI bestows on its models, who appear in the magazine, such titles as "Playmate of the Month" and "Playmate of the Year." PEI encourages its models to identify themselves and to use their titles for their self-promotion and the promotion of its magazines and other goods and services.

Background and Facts Playboy Enterprises, Inc. (PEI), maintains Web sites to promote *Playboy* magazine and PEI models. PEI's trademarks include the terms "Playboy," "Playmate," and "Playmate of the Year." Terri Welles is a self-employed model and spokesperson, who was featured as the "Playmate of the Year" in June 1981. Welles maintains a Web site

---

a. This is a page within the E-LAW site of David J. Loundy, an attorney and author.

(Continued)

Case 11.4 Continued

titled "Terri Welles—Playmate of the Year 1981." As meta tags, Welles's site uses the terms "Playboy" and "Playmate," among others. PEI asked Welles to stop using these terms, but she refused. PEI filed a suit in a federal district court against Welles, asking the court to order her to, among other things, stop using those terms as meta tags. PEI argued, in part, that this constituted trademark infringement under the Lanham Act (discussed earlier in this chapter). Welles responded in part that her use of the terms is a "fair use," because she was and is the "Playmate of the Year 1981."

In the Words of the Court . . .
GRAHAM, District Judge.

* * * *

In a case where the mark is used only to describe the goods or services of [a] party, or their geographic origin, trademark law recognizes a "fair use" defense. * * *

* * * *

It is clear that defendant is selling Terri Welles and only Terri Welles on the website. There is no overt attempt to confuse the websurfer into believing that her site is a Playboy-related website. In this case, then, defendant's use of the term Playmate of the Year 1981 is descriptive of and used fairly and in good faith only to describe [herself]. * * *

With respect to the meta tags, the court finds there to be no trademark infringement where defendant has used plaintiff's trademarks in good faith to index the content of her website. * * * Much like the subject index of a card catalog, the meta tags give the websurfer using a search engine a clearer indication of the content of a website. The use of the term Playboy is not an infringement because it references not only her identity as a "Playboy Playmate of the Year 1981," but it may also reference the legitimate editorial uses of the term Playboy contained in the text of defendant's website.

Decision and Remedy The court held that a party can use another's trademarks as meta tags when those marks describe the party who uses them. The court ruled that Welles was entitled to the "fair use" of the "Playboy" and "Playmate" marks as meta tags.

For Critical Analysis—Technological Consideration *Why would PEI encourage its models to use its marks outside cyberspace but attempt to block such uses within cyberspace?*

DILUTION ON THE WEB As discussed earlier in this chapter, trademark *dilution* occurs when a trademark is used, without authorization, in a way that diminishes the distinctive quality of the mark. Unlike trademark infringement, a dilution cause of action does not require proof that consumers are likely to be confused by a connection between the unauthorized use and the mark. For this reason, the products involved do not have to be similar. In the first case alleging dilution on the Web, a court precluded the use of "candyland.com" as the URL for an adult site, in a suit by the maker of the "Candyland" children's game and owner of the "Candyland" mark.[17]

A dilution case does require, however, that a mark be famous when the dilution occurs. • **Example 11.6** Gateway 2000 has been making personal com-

---

17. *Hasbro, Inc. v. Internet Entertainment Group, Ltd.,* 1996 WL 84853 (W.D. Wash. 1996).

puters since 1985 and owns the mark "Gateway 2000." In 1988, Gateway.com, Inc., an entirely different company, began to use "gateway.com" as part of its URL and registered it as a domain name in 1990. Gateway 2000 later filed a suit to block the use of "gateway" on the ground of dilution. The court refused to grant the request, concluding that Gateway 2000 could not prove that its name was famous at the time when Gateway.com chose "gateway" as a domain name.•

In another interesting case, a court issued an injunction on the ground that spamming under another's logo is trademark dilution.[18] In that case, Hotmail, Inc., provided e-mail services and worked to dissociate itself from spam. Van$ Money Pie, Inc., and others spammed thousands of e-mail customers, using the free e-mail service Hotmail as a return address. The court ordered the defendants to stop.

LICENSING   One of the ways to make use of another's mark (or another's copyright, patent, or trade secret), while avoiding litigation, is to obtain a *license* to do so. A license in this context is essentially an agreement to permit the use of a mark for certain purposes. A *licensee* (the party obtaining the license) might be allowed to use the mark of the *licensor* (the party issuing the license) as part of the name of its company, or as part of its domain name, without otherwise using the mark on any products or services.

A licensee must not break the terms of the license, however, or litigation could ensue and liability may result. • **Example 11.7** In the first case involving a trademark license in cyberspace, the licensee took advantage of its licensor's increasingly famous mark to make its Web site look more like the licensor's. Alleging a violation of the licensing agreement, the licensor sued. The court granted the licensor's motion for a preliminary injunction, holding that the licensee likely breached the license and infringed the mark.[19]•

In 1999, the National Conference of Commissioners on Uniform State Laws approved the Uniform Computer Information Transactions Act (UCITA) and submitted it to the states for adoption. The act was drafted to address problems unique to electronic contracting and to the purchase and sale (licensing) of computer information, such as software. The UCITA and some of its major provisions will be discussed in further detail in Chapter 14, in the context of e-contracts.

Patents Online

There are four noteworthy aspects to patents and the new technology. First is the rapidly increasing number of patents that the U.S. Patent and Trademark Office (USPTO) has granted in recent years. Software patents number in the thousands, with more than ten thousand applications pending. Software technology has progressed quickly. This points to another important feature of the new technology that relates to patents.

Software developers use combinations of previous software to create new products and processes. This practice has led to uncertainty and controversy about the ownership and the use of patent rights to the hybrid products. One way to prevent legal problems in this regard is for a software developer or maker to obtain licenses for others' products and to issue licenses for its own.

---

18. *Hotmail Corp. v. Van$ Money Pie, Inc.*, 1998 WL 388389 (N.D.Cal. 1998).
19. *Digital Equipment Corp. v. AltaVista Technology, Inc.*, 960 F.Supp. 456 (D.Mass. 1997).

The third aspect to patents related to the new technology concerns one of the most important reasons that a patent is granted. A developer obtains a patent to prevent others from patenting the same product or process. When more than one party is developing the same product or process, the first party to obtain a patent is the party who gets the protection. Even before a patent is obtained, however, the disclosure of a product or process can block others from obtaining a patent for it. For this reason, those who reveal their inventions to the public are rewarded. It is a practice in the software industry to keep technology secret, but this is risky. A developer could lose all rights to a product by keeping it secret.

Finally, a significant development relating to patents is the availability online of the world's patent databases. The USPTO provides at its Web site searchable databases covering U.S. patents granted since 1976, as well as AIDS-related patents issued by U.S., Japanese, and European patent offices. The European Patent Office maintains at its Web site databases covering all patent documents in sixty-five nations and the legal status of patents in twenty-two of those countries.

Copyrights in Digital Information

Copyright law is probably the most important form of intellectual property protection on the Internet. This is because much of the material on the Internet consists of works of authorship (including multimedia presentations, software, and database information). These works are the traditional focus of copyright law. Copyright law is also important because the nature of the Internet requires that data be "copied" to be transferred online. Copies are a significant part of the traditional controversies arising in this area of the law.

DOES OLD COPYRIGHT LAW COVER WORKS IN NEW ELECTRONIC FORMS?
Remember from the discussion of copyright law earlier in this chapter that copyright law is concerned chiefly with the creation, distribution, and sale of protected works of authorship. When Congress drafted the principal U.S. law governing copyrights, the Copyright Act of 1976, cyberspace did not exist for most of us. The threat to copyright owners was not posed by computer technology but by unauthorized tangible copies of works and the sale of rights to movies, television, and other media.

Some of the issues that were unimagined when the Copyright Act was drafted have posed thorny questions for the courts. For example, to sell a copy of a work, permission of the copyright holder is necessary. Because of the nature of cyberspace, however, one of the early controversies was determining at what point an intangible, electronic "copy" of a work has been made. The courts have held that loading a file or program into a computer's random access memory, or RAM, constitutes the making of a "copy" for purposes of copyright law.[20] RAM is a portion of a computer's memory into which a file, for example, is loaded so that it can be accessed (read or written over). (For another example of how new technology is challenging traditional copyright laws, see this chapter's *Legal E-nvironment* feature on page 310.)

Others rights, including those relating to the revision of "collective works" such as magazines, were acknowledged thirty years ago but were considered

---

20. *MAI Systems Corp. v. Peak Computer, Inc.*, 991 F.2d 511 (9th Cir. 1993).

to have only limited economic value. Today, technology has made some of those rights vastly more significant. Does the old law apply to these rights? That was one of the questions in the following case.

Case 11.5 ● Tasini v. New York Times Co.

United States District Court,
Southern District of New York, 1997.
972 F.Supp. 804.
http://www.ljextra.com/
copyright/ tasini.html[a]

Historical and Technological Setting   *In the early 1980s, the New York Times Company and other publishers of periodicals began to sell the contents of their publications to e-publishers, including Lexis/Nexis, a division of Reed Elsevier, Inc. Lexis/Nexis, for example, has carried online the articles appearing in the* New York Times *since 1983. UMI Company has distributed* The New York Times OnDisc, *a text-based CD-ROM, since 1992, and the*

New York Times Magazine *and* Book Review *have been available on an image-based CD-ROM since 1990.*

Background and Facts   Magazines and newspapers, including the *New York Times,* buy and publish articles written by freelance writers. Besides circulating hard copies of their periodicals, these publishers sell the contents to e-publishers for inclusion in online and other electronic databases. Jonathan Tasini and other freelance writers filed a suit in a federal district court against the New York Times Company and other publishers, including the e-publishers, contending that the e-publication of the articles violated the Copyright Act. The publishers responded, among other things, that the Copyright Act gave them a right to produce "revisions" of their publications. The writers argued that the Copyright Act did not cover electronic "revisions." The publishers filed a motion for summary judgment.

---

a. This opinion is reproduced in a Law Journal Extra! database, in a section titled "Copyright." This site is owned by American Lawyer Media, Inc.

In the Words of the Court . . .
GRAHAM, District Judge.

* * * *

* * * [T]o the extent that the electronic reproductions qualify as revisions under [the Copyright Act] the defendant publishers were entitled to authorize the electronic defendants to create those revisions.

* * * *

* * * If the disputed periodicals manifest an original selection or arrangement of materials, and if that originality is preserved electronically, then the electronic reproductions can be deemed permissible revisions of the publisher defendants' collective works. * * *

* * * *

One of the defining original aspects of the publisher defendants' periodicals is the selection of articles included in those works. * * *

* * * *

* * * By retaining the publisher defendants' original selection of articles, * * * the electronic defendants have managed to retain one of the few defining original elements of the publishers' collective works. * * * For the purposes of [the Copyright Act] then, defendants have succeeded at creating * * * revision[s] of those collective works.

Decision and Remedy   The court held that publishers can put the contents of their periodicals into e-databases and onto CD-ROMs without securing the permission of the writers whose contributions are

(Continued)

included in the periodicals. The court granted the publishers' motion for summary judgment.

For Critical Analysis—Political Consideration *When technology creates a situation in which* *rights such as those in this case are more valuable than originally anticipated, should the law be changed to redistribute the economic benefit of those rights?*

RECENT DEVELOPMENTS IN COPYRIGHT LAW In 1996, the United States signed the World Intellectual Property Organization (WIPO) Copyright Treaty, a special agreement under the Berne Convention, discussed earlier in this chapter. Special provisions of the WIPO treaty relate to rights in digital data. The treaty strengthens some rights for copyright owners, in terms of their applica-

---

Legal *e*-nvironment

Code-Cracking Software for DVDs Online— The Courts Speak

Digital versatile disks (DVDs) promise to give a boost to the at-home movie rental and purchase industry. DVDs provide numerous advantages over traditional videocassettes. For one thing, they are more compact. They also offer superior audio and video quality. Additionally, they provide for numerous enhancements, such as directors' commentaries, separate foreign language audio tracks, and various foreign language subtitles. Not surprisingly, the owners of motion picture copyrights have a vested interest in preventing renters and owners of DVDs from making the contents of those DVDs available on the Internet. All DVDs include an encryption system created to protect against the unauthorized copying of the contents of the DVDs.

Cracking the Code

Almost as soon as encryption technology was used to safeguard the contents of DVDs, the code was cracked by a group of hackers, including nineteen-year-old Norwegian Jon Johansen. His decryption program, called DeCCS, was quickly made available on the Internet. One such site was 2600.com, owned by Ed Corly. Almost immediately after DeCCS was posted, a group of movie companies, including Disney and Twentieth Century-Fox, filed suit.

Violation of the Digital Millennium Copyright Act

In what was seen as a victory for the motion picture industry, U.S. District Court Judge Lewis A. Kaplan ruled that DeCCS violated the Digital Millennium Copyright Act of 1998.[a] As discussed elsewhere in the chapter, this act essentially prohibits individuals from breaking encryption programs put in place to protect digital versions of intellectual property such as movies, music, and the like. After all, reasoned the court, since the posting of DeCCS, along with a separate video-compression program known as Divx, the pirating of movies has become increasingly common on the Internet.

The defendants argued that software programs designed to break encryption schemes were simply a form of constitutionally protected speech. The court, however, rejected the free speech argument. "Computer code is not purely expressive any more than the assassination of a political figure is purely a political statement. . . . The Constitution, after all, is a framework for building a just and democratic society. It is not a suicide pact," stated Judge Kaplan.

For Critical Analysis: *Will this decision have any practical effect, given that literally thousands of copies of DeCCS already existed on the Internet before the decision was made?*

a. *Universal City Studios, Inc. v. Reimerdes*, 111 F.Supp.2d 294 (S.D.N.Y. 2000).

tion in cyberspace, but leaves other questions unresolved. For example, the treaty does not make clear what, for purposes of international law, constitutes the making of a "copy" in electronic form. The United States implemented the the terms of the WIPO treaty in the Digital Millennium Copyright Act of 1998, which is the subject of the *Landmark in the Legal Environment* on page 312.

Trade Secrets in Cyberspace

The nature of the new technology—the versatility of e-mail in particular—undercuts a business firm's ability to protect its confidential information, including trade secrets (trade secrets are defined and discussed in more detail earlier in this chapter).[21] For example, a dishonest employee could transmit trade secrets in a company's computer to anyone via an e-mail connection on the Internet. "Anyone" could be a thief, a competitor, or a future employer. If e-mail is not an option, the employee might walk out with the information on a computer disk. Even honest employees can make mistakes, sending confidential data to the wrong e-mail address—a competitor, for example, instead of a client—or losing a disk on a business trip.

• **Example 11.8** An illustration of what a departing employee might do is provided by a criminal case that involved two competing software developers, Borland International, Inc., and Symantec. Eugene Wang, a Borland vice president, expressed dissatisfaction with his job and quit. Other Borland officers reviewed Wang's e-mail files and found messages to Gordon Eubanks,

---

21. Note that in one case, it was indicated that customers' e-mail addresses may constitute trade secrets. See *T-N-T Motorsports, Inc. v. Hennessey Motorsports, Inc.,* 965 S.W.2d 18 (Tex.App.—Hous. [1 Dist.] 1998), rehearing overruled (1998), petition dismissed (1998).

International Perspective

Should Copyright Laws Be Uniform around the Globe?

One of the main problems for the international online community is that copyright protection varies among jurisdictions. For example, in the United States, for U.S. authors, there is no recognition of what are called *moral rights.* Moral rights include the rights of an author to proclaim or disclaim authorship, and to object to any change to the author's work that would injure his or her reputation. These rights are considered to be personal to the author, and they cannot be taken away or abridged. Other countries, such as France, recognize and enforce these rights. In Great Britain, an author of a copyrighted work is entitled to be identified as the author. This is called a *paternity right.*

International copyright treaties and agreements have, of course, helped to create uniformity among nations with respect to the protection given to copyrighted works. A current challenge in the international legal environment is how to protect copyrighted works in digital form. Although the WIPO Copyright Treaty and the Digital Millennium Copyright Act of 1998 (discussed elsewhere in this chapter) represent significant steps toward establishing new principles for copyright protection in an electronic age, several copyright issues arising in cyberspace remain unsettled—as you will read shortly.

For Critical Analysis: *Should there be a different copyright law solely for cyberspace? If so, what rights should it include?*

Landmark in the Legal Environment

The Digital Millennium Copyright Act of 1998

The United States leads the world in the production of creative products, including books, films, videos, recordings, and software. In fact, the creative industries are more important to the U.S. economy than the more traditional product industries are. The value of the export of U.S. creative products, for example, surpasses that of every other U.S. industry. Creative industries are growing at nearly three times the rate of the economy as a whole.

Technology, particularly the Internet, offers new outlets for these products. It also makes them easier to steal. Copyrighted works can be pirated and distributed around the world quickly and efficiently. To curb this crime, the World Intellectual Property Organization (WIPO) enacted two treaties in 1996 to upgrade global standards of copyright protection, particularly for the Internet.

In 1998, Congress implemented the provisions of these treaties to update U.S. copyright law. Besides standing as a beacon to the rest of the world, because of the leading position of the United States in the creative industries, this action is a landmark step in the protection of copyright. Among other things, the new law—the Digital Millennium Copyright Act of 1998—created civil and criminal penalties for anyone who circumvents encryption software or other technological antipiracy protection. Also prohibited are the manufacture, import, sale, or distribution of devices or services for circumvention.

There are exceptions to fit the needs of libraries, scientists, universities, and others. In general, the new law does not restrict the "fair use" of circumvention for educational and other noncommercial purposes. For example, circumvention is allowed to test computer security, to conduct encryption research, to protect personal privacy, or to allow parents to monitor their children's journeys over the Internet. The exceptions are to be reconsidered every three years.

An Internet service provider (ISP) is not liable for any copyright infringement by its customer if the ISP is unaware of the subscriber's violation. An ISP may be held liable only after learning of the violation and failing to take action to shut the subscriber down. A copyright holder has to act promptly, however, by pursuing a claim in court, or the subscriber has the right to be restored to online access.

For Critical Analysis: *How will the Digital Millennium Copyright Act of 1998 spur the growth of commerce online?*

Symantec's president and chief executive officer. Believing that the messages contained trade secrets and other confidential information, Borland filed a civil suit to recover damages and also notified the police. After an investigation, criminal charges, including the theft of trade secrets, were filed against both Wang and Eubanks.[22]●

---

22. *People v. Eubanks,* 14 Cal.4th 580, 14 Cal.4th 1282D, 927 P.2d 310, 59 Cal.Rptr.2d 200 (1996), as modified on denial of rehearing (1997). The charges were dismissed after Borland paid a substantial part of the cost of the criminal investigation. The California Supreme Court felt that Borland's payment made it unlikely that the defendants would receive fair treatment.

Key Terms

copyright   298
cyber mark   303
cybersquatting   304
intellectual property   291

meta tags   305
patent   297
service mark   296
trade dress   297

trade name   296
trade secret   302
trademark   291
virtual property   303

Chapter Summary • Intellectual Property and Cyberlaw

Intellectual Property Protection
(See pages 291–303.)

1. **Trademark infringement and infringement of related property**—Occurs when one uses the protected trademark, service mark, trade name, or trade dress of another without permission when marketing goods or services.

2. **Patent infringement**—Occurs when one uses or sells another's patented design, product, or process without the patent owner's permission. Computer software may be patented.

3. **Copyright infringement**—Occurs whenever the form or expression of an idea is copied without the permission of the copyright holder. An exception applies if the copying is deemed a "fair use." The Computer Software Copyright Act of 1980 specifically includes software among the kinds of intellectual property covered by copyright law.

4. **Trade secrets**—Customer lists, plans, research and development, pricing information, and so on are protected under the common law and, in some states, under statutory law against misappropriation by competitors.

5. **International protection**—International protection for intellectual property exists under various international agreements. A landmark agreement is the 1994 agreement on Trade-Related Aspects of Intellectual Property Rights (TRIPS), which provides for enforcement procedures in all countries signatory to the agreement.

Virtual Property
(See pages 303–312.)

1. **Cyber marks**—Trademark infringement may occur in cyberspace if (1) another site's key words are used improperly as meta tags; (2) the quality of another's mark is diluted by improper use; (3) another's mark is used without a license; or (4) a licensing agreement is broken. Trademark infringement can also occur with certain uses of hypertext links and framing technology.

2. **Patents**—Patent infringement of a cyberspace product or process may occur if a user, including a software developer, fails to obtain a license to use the item.

3. **Copyrights**—Under U.S. copyright law, loading a computer program or data into the RAM of a computer is making a "copy." (International law does not clearly resolve this issue.) The Digital Millennium Copyright Act of 1998 created civil and criminal penalties for anyone who circumvents encryption software or other technological antipiracy protection.

4. **Trade secrets**—Communicating trade secrets via new technology without authorization may be a violation of criminal and civil laws.

For Review

1. What is intellectual property? How does the law protect intellectual property?

2. What is a trade secret? How are trade secrets protected by law?

3. What is virtual property?

4. What legal protection is there for intellectual property existing in digital form?

5. Generally, how has technology affected intellectual property rights?

Questions and Case Problems

11–1. Copyright Infringement. In which of the following situations would a court likely hold Maruta liable for copyright infringement?

(a) At the library, Maruta photocopies ten pages from a scholarly journal relating to a topic on which she is writing a term paper.

(b) Maruta makes leather handbags and sells them in her small leather shop. She advertises her handbags as "Vutton handbags," hoping that customers might mistakenly assume that they were made by Vuitton, the well-known maker of high-quality luggage and handbags.

(c) Maruta owns a video store. She purchases the latest videos from various video manufacturers but buys only one copy of each video. Then, using blank videotapes, she makes copies to rent or sell to her customers.

(d) Maruta teaches Latin American history at a small university. She has a videocassette recorder (VCR) and frequently tapes television programs relating to Latin America. She then takes the videos to her classroom so that her students can watch them.

11–2. Patent Infringement. John and Andrew Doney invented a hard-bearing device for balancing rotors. Although they registered their invention with the U.S. Patent and Trademark Office, it was never used as an automobile wheel balancer. Some time later, Exetron Corp. produced an automobile wheel balancer that used a hard-bearing device with a support plate similar to that of the Doneys. Given the fact that the Doneys had not used their device for automobile wheel balancing, does Exetron's use of a similar hard-bearing device infringe on the Doneys' patent?

11–3. Copyright Infringement. Max plots a new Batman adventure and carefully and skillfully imitates the art of DC Comics to create an authentic-looking Batman comic. Max is not affiliated with the owners of the copyright to Batman. Can Max publish the comic without infringing on the owners' copyright?

11–4. Copyright Infringement. James Smith, the owner of Michigan Document Services, Inc. (MDS), a commercial copyshop, concluded that it was unnecessary to obtain the copyright owners' permission to reproduce copyrighted materials in course packs. Smith publicized his conclusion, claiming that professors would not have to worry about any delay in production at his shop. MDS then compiled, bound, and sold course packs to students at the University of Michigan without obtaining the permission of copyright owners. Princeton University Press and two other publishers filed a suit in a federal district court against MDS, alleging copyright infringement.

MDS claimed that its course packs were covered under the fair use doctrine. Were they? Explain. [*Princeton University Press v. Michigan Document Services, Inc.*, 99 F.3d 1381 (6th Cir. 1996)]

11–5. Trademarks. Sara Lee Corp. manufactures pantyhose under the L'eggs trademark. Originally, L'eggs were sold in egg-shaped packaging, a design that Sara Lee continues to use with its product. Sara Lee's only nationwide competitor in the same pantyhose markets is Kayser-Roth Corp. When Kayser-Roth learned of Sara Lee's plan to introduce L'eggs Everyday, a new line of hosiery, Kayser-Roth responded by simultaneously introducing a new product, Leg Looks. Sara Lee filed a complaint in a federal district court against Kayser-Roth, asserting that the name Leg Looks infringed on the L'eggs mark. Does Kayser-Roth's Leg Looks infringe on Sara Lee's L'eggs? Why or why not? [*Sara Lee Corp. v. Kayser-Roth Corp.*, 81 F.3d 455 (4th Cir. 1996)]

11–6. Trademark Infringement. Elvis Presley Enterprises, Inc. (EPE), owns all of the trademarks of the Elvis Presley estate. None of these marks is registered for use in the restaurant business. Barry Capece registered "The Velvet Elvis" as a service mark for a restaurant and tavern with the U.S. Patent and Trademark Office. Capece opened a nightclub called "The Velvet Elvis" with a menu, décor, advertising, and promotional events that evoked Elvis Presley and his music. EPE filed a suit in a federal district court against Capece and others, claiming, among other things, that "The Velvet Elvis" service mark infringed on EPE's trademarks. During the trial, witnesses testified that they thought the bar was associated with Elvis Presley. Should Capece be ordered to stop using "The Velvet Elvis" mark? Why or why not? [*Elvis Presley Enterprises, Inc. v. Capece*, 141 F.3d 188 (5th Cir. 1998)]

11–7. Cyber Marks. Playboy Enterprises, Inc. (PEI), owns the rights to the cyber marks "Playboy," "Playboy magazine," and "Playmate." Without authorization, Calvin Designer Label used the terms as meta tags for its Web sites on the Internet. As tags, the terms were invisible to viewers (in black type on a black background), but they caused the Web sites to be returned at the top of the list of a search engine query for "Playboy" or "Playmate." PEI filed a suit in a federal district court against Calvin Designer Label, alleging, among other things, trademark infringement. Should the court order the defendants to stop using the terms as tags? Why or why not? [*Playboy Enterprises, Inc. v. Calvin Designer Label*, 985 F.Supp. 1220 (N.D.Cal. 1997)]

11–8. Copyrights. Webbworld operates a Web site called Neptics, Inc. The site accepts downloads of certain images from third parties and makes these images available to any user who accesses the site. Before being allowed to view the images, however, the user must pay a subscription fee of $11.95 per month. Over a period of several months, images were available that were originally created by or for Playboy Enterprises, Inc. (PEI). The images were displayed at Neptics's site without PEI's permission. PEI filed a suit in a federal district court against Webbworld, alleging copyright infringement. Webbworld argued in part that it should not be held liable because, like an Internet service provider that provides access to the Internet, it did not create or control the content of the information available to its subscribers. Do you agree with Webbworld? Why or why not? [*Playboy Enterprises, Inc. v. Webbworld,* 968 F.Supp. 1171 (N.D.Tex. 1997)]

11–9. Trademark Infringement. A&H Sportswear Co., a swimsuit maker, obtained a trademark for its MIRACLESUIT in 1992. The MIRACLESUIT design makes the wearer appear slimmer. The MIRACLESUIT, which was widely advertised and discussed in the media, was also sold for a brief time in the Victoria's Secret (VS) catalogue, which is published by Victoria's Secret Catalogue, Inc. In 1993, Victoria's Secret Stores, Inc., began selling a cleavage-enhancing bra, which was named the MIRACLE BRA and for which a trademark was obtained. The next year, the MIRACLE BRA swimwear debuted in the VS catalogue and stores. A&H filed a suit in a federal district court against VS Stores and VS Catalogue, alleging in part that the MIRACLE BRA mark, when applied to swimwear, infringed on the MIRACLESUIT mark. A&H argued that there was a "possibility of confusion" between the marks. The VS entities contended that the appropriate standard was "likelihood of confusion" and that in this case, there was no likelihood of confusion. In whose favor will the court rule, and why? [*A&H Sportswear, Inc. v. Victoria's Secret Stores, Inc.,* 166 F.3d 197 (3d Cir. 1999)]

A Question of Ethics and Social Responsibility

11–10. Storm Impact, Inc., produces software, including the games TaskMaker and MacSki. To market upgraded versions of the games, Storm distributed them as shareware with locks built into the programs. A user could sample the unlocked portions at no charge and then buy a key, in the form of a floppy disk and registration number, to use the whole program. A legend expressly encouraged users to give unaltered copies to others but prohibited users from charging others for the shareware. Software of the Month Club (SOMC) provides collections of new shareware to its members for a $24.95 per month fee. When Storm's games were included in one of SOMC's collections, Storm filed a suit in a federal district court against SOMC, alleging, among other things, copyright infringement. SOMC argued that its copying and distribution of the games constituted a "fair use." The court held that SOMC had infringed Storm's copyrights and awarded Storm $20,000 in damages. [*Storm Impact, Inc. v. Software of the Month Club,* 13 F.Supp.2d 782 (N.D.Ill. 1998)]

1. SOMC claimed that by endorsing and distributing shareware, it was performing a service for the creators, much like a book reviewer does for a book. Do you agree? Why or why not? How might SOMC have avoided this suit? (To fully answer these questions, you may need to review the "fair use" doctrine discussed in this chapter.)

2. Should the fact that SOMC was charging for something that was otherwise free on the Internet affect the outcome in this suit? Should Storm's restriction on charging for its shareware affect the result? Why or why not? What are the implications of the holding in this case for other shareware distributors?

For Critical Analysis

11–11. Can the distribution of copyrighted materials via the Internet ever be effectively regulated by copyright laws? Should it?

Interacting with the Internet

■ For updated links to resources available on the Web, as well as a variety of other materials, visit this text's Web site at

http://leet.westbuslaw.com

■ You can find answers to frequently asked questions (FAQs) about trademark and patent law—and links to registration forms, statutes, international patent and trademark offices, and numerous other related materials—at the Web site of the U.S. Patent and Trademark Office. Go to

http://www.uspto.gov

■ To access the federal database of registered trademarks directly, go to

www.uspto.gov/tmdb/index.html

■ To perform patent searches and to access information on the patenting process, go to

http://www.bustpatents.com

■ You can also access information on patent law at the following Internet site:

http://www.patents.com

■ For information on copyrights, go to the U.S. Copyright Office at

lcweb.loc.gov/copyright

■ You can find extensive information on copyright law—including United States Supreme Court decisions in this area and the texts of the Berne Convention and other international treaties on copyright issues—at the Web site of the Legal Information Institute at Cornell University's School of Law. Go to

**http://www.law.cornell.edu/topics/
copyright.html**

■ An online magazine that deals, in part, with intellectual property issues is *Law Technology Product News*. The URL for this publication is

http://www.ljextra.com/ltpn

■ The Cyberspace Law Institute (CLI) offers articles and information on such topics as copyright infringement, privacy, trade secrets, and trademarks. To access the CLI's Web site, go to

http://www.cli.org

Online Legal Research Exercises

Go to **http://leet.
westbuslaw.com**, the Web site that accompanies this text. Select "Interactive Study Center," and then click on "Chapter 11." There you will find the following Internet research exercise that you can perform to learn more about intellectual property rights:

Activity 11–1: Gray-Market Goods

Before the Test

Go to **http://leet.
westbuslaw.com**, the Web site that accompanies this text. Select "Interactive Quizzes." You will find a number of interactive questions relating to this chapter.

Contract Formation

chapter objectives

After reading this chapter, you should be able to:

1. Define the term *contract,* and discuss the function of contracts in our society.

2. Identify the types of contracts that are subject to Article 2 of the Uniform Commercial Code.

3. Summarize each of the four basic requirements for a valid contract.

4. Explain the contractual rights and obligations of minors.

5. Give some examples of how third parties may acquire rights in contracts.

A s Roscoe Pound—an eminent jurist—observed in the quotation alongside, "keeping promises" is important to a stable social order. Contract law deals with, among other things, the formation and keeping of promises.

Like other types of law, contract law reflects our social values, interests, and expectations at a given point in time. It shows, for example, what kinds of promises our society thinks should be legally binding. It shows what excuses our society accepts for breaking such promises. Additionally, it shows what promises are considered to be contrary to public policy and therefore legally void. If a promise goes against the interests of society as a whole, it will be invalid. Also, if it was made by a child or a mentally incompetent person, or on the basis of false information, a question will arise as to whether the promise should be enforced. Resolving such questions is the essence of contract law. In business law and the legal environment of business, questions and disputes concerning contracts arise daily.

The Law Governing Contracts

Although aspects of contract law vary from state to state, much of it is based on the common law.

The Common Law of Contracts

In 1932, the American Law Institute compiled the *Restatement of the Law of Contracts*. This work is a nonstatutory, authoritative exposition of the present law on the subject of contracts and is presently in its second edition (although a third edition is in the process of being drafted). Throughout the following chapters on contracts, we will refer to the second edition of the *Restatement of the Law of Contracts* as simply the *Restatement (Second) of Contracts*.

Contracts for the Sale of Goods

Sales Contract A contract for the sale of goods under which the ownership of goods is transferred from a seller to a buyer for a price.

The Uniform Commercial Code (UCC), which governs **sales contracts**, or contracts for the sale of goods, and lease contracts, occasionally departs from common law contract rules. Generally, the different treatment of contracts falling under the UCC stems from the general policy of encouraging commerce. Some of the ways in which the UCC changes common law contract rules are discussed in this chapter and in Chapter 13.

To facilitate commercial transactions, Article 2 modifies some of the common law contract requirements that are discussed in this chapter. To the extent that it has not been modified by the UCC, however, the common law of contracts also applies to sales contracts. For example, the common law requirements for a valid contract—agreement (offer and acceptance), consideration, capacity, and legality—that we discuss in this chapter are applicable to sales contracts as well. In general, the rule is that whenever there is a conflict between a common law contract rule and the UCC, the UCC controls. In other words, when a UCC provision addresses a certain issue, the UCC governs; when the UCC is silent, the common law governs.

In regard to Article 2, you should keep in mind two things. First, Article 2 deals with the sale of *goods*; it does not deal with real property (real estate), services, or intangible property such as stocks and bonds. Thus, if the subject matter of a dispute is goods, the UCC governs. If it is real estate or services, the common law applies. The relationship between general contract law and the law governing sales of goods is illustrated in Exhibit 12–1. Second, in some cases, the rules may vary quite a bit, depending on whether the buyer or the seller is a *merchant*. Because of its importance in the legal environment of sales transactions, the full text of Article 2 of the UCC is included at the end of this text as Appendix D.

The Function of Contracts

Contract law assures the parties to private agreements that the promises they make will be enforceable. Clearly, many promises are kept because of a moral obligation to do so or because keeping a promise is in the mutual self-interest of the parties involved, not because the **promisor** (the person making the promise) or the **promisee** (the person to whom the promise is made) is conscious of the rules of contract law. Nevertheless, the rules of contract law are often followed in business agreements to avoid potential problems.

A **contract** is an agreement that can be enforced in court. It is formed by parties who agree to perform or to refrain from performing some act now or in the future. Every contract involves at least two parties. The **offeror** is the party making the offer. The **offeree** is the party to whom the offer is made. The offeror always promises to do or not to do something and thus is also a promisor. Generally, contract disputes arise when there is a promise of future performance. If the contractual promise is not fulfilled, the party who made it is subject to the sanctions of a court (see Chapter 13). That party may be required to pay money damages for failing to perform; in limited instances, the party may be required to perform the promised act.

Promisor A person who makes a promise.

Promisee A person to whom a promise is made.

Contract An agreement that can be enforced in court; formed by two or more parties who agree to perform or to refrain from performing some act now or in the future.

Offeror A person who makes an offer.

Offeree A person to whom an offer is made.

Types of Contracts

There are numerous types of contracts. The categories into which contracts are placed involve legal distinctions as to formation, enforceability, or performance. The best method of explaining each type of contract is to compare one type with another.

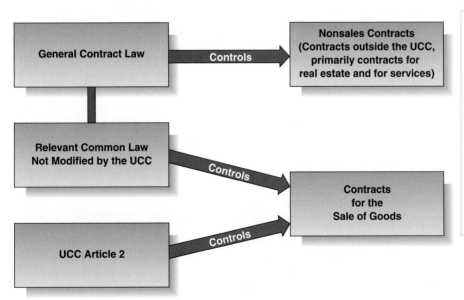

General Contract Law — Controls → **Nonsales Contracts (Contracts outside the UCC, primarily contracts for real estate and for services)**

Relevant Common Law Not Modified by the UCC — Controls →

UCC Article 2 — Controls →

Contracts for the Sale of Goods

Exhibit 12–1 Law Governing Contracts
This exhibit graphically illustrates the relationship between general contract law and the law governing contracts for the sale of goods. Sales contracts are not governed exclusively by Article 2 of the Uniform Commercial Code but also by general contract law whenever it is relevant and has not been modified by the UCC.

Is it possible to enter into a contract over the phone? If so, what would make such a contract a bilateral contract rather than a unilateral contract?

Bilateral versus Unilateral Contracts

Whether a contract is classified as *unilateral* or *bilateral* depends on what the offeree must do to accept the offer and to bind the offeror to a contract.

Bilateral Contract A type of contract that arises when a promise is given in exchange for a return promise.

If to accept the offer the offeree must only *promise* to perform, the contract is a **bilateral contract**. Hence, a bilateral contract is a "promise for a promise." An example of a bilateral contract is a contract in which one person agrees to buy another person's automobile for a specified price. No performance, such as the payment of money or delivery of goods, need take place for a bilateral contract to be formed. The contract comes into existence at the moment the promises are exchanged.

Unilateral Contract A contract that results when an offer can only be accepted by the offeree's performance.

If the offer is phrased so that the offeree can accept only by completing the contract performance, the contract is a **unilateral contract**. Hence, a unilateral contract is a "promise for an act." • **Example 12.1** Joe says to Celia, "If you walk across the Brooklyn Bridge, I'll give you $10." Joe promises to pay only if Celia walks the entire span of the bridge. Only on Celia's complete crossing does she fully accept Joe's offer to pay $10. If she chooses not to undertake the walk, there are no legal consequences.• Contests, lotteries, and other competitions in which prizes are awarded are also examples of offers for unilateral contracts. If a person complies with the rules of the contest—such as by submitting the right lottery number at the right place and time—a unilateral contract is formed, binding the organization offering the prize to a contract to perform as promised in the offer.

Express versus Implied Contracts

Express Contract A contract in which the terms of the agreement are fully and explicitly stated in words, oral or written.

An **express contract** is one in which the terms of the agreement are fully and explicitly stated in words, oral or written. A signed lease for an apartment or a house is an express written contract. • **Example 12.2** If a classmate calls you on the phone and agrees to buy your textbooks from last semester for $50, an express oral contract has been made.•

An **implied-in-fact contract,** or an implied contract, differs from an express contract in that the *conduct* of the parties, rather than their words, creates and defines at least some of the terms of the contract. • Example 12.3 Suppose that you need an accountant to fill out your tax return this year. You look through the Yellow Pages and find an accounting firm located in your neighborhood. You drop by the firm's office, explain your problem to an accountant, and learn what fees will be charged. The next day you return, giving the receptionist all of the necessary information and documents, such as canceled checks, W-2 forms, and so on. You say nothing expressly to the receptionist; rather, you walk out the door. In this situation, you have entered into an implied-in-fact contract to pay the accountant the usual and reasonable fees for the accounting services. The contract is implied by your conduct. The accountant expects to be paid for completing your tax return. By bringing in the records the accountant will need to do the work, you have implied an intent to pay for the services.•

An important issue facing employers today is whether promises made in employment manuals, such as "employees will not be terminated without good cause," constitute implied-in-fact contracts. This issue is explored in this chapter's *Inside the Legal Environment* feature on the next page.

Quasi Contracts—Contracts Implied in Law

Quasi contracts, or contracts *implied in law,* are wholly different from actual contracts. Express contracts and implied-in-fact contracts are actual, or true, contracts. Quasi contracts, as the term suggests, are not true contracts. They do not arise from any agreement, express or implied, between the parties themselves. Rather, quasi contracts are fictional contracts imposed on parties by courts in the interests of fairness and justice. Quasi contracts are therefore equitable, rather than contractual, in nature. Usually, quasi contracts are imposed to avoid the *unjust enrichment* of one party at the expense of another.

Implied-in-Fact Contract A contract formed in whole or in part from the conduct of the parties (as opposed to an express contract).

> **"Outward actions are a clue to hidden secrets."**
>
> (Legal maxim)

> **Be Aware** An implied-in-fact contract is as legally binding as an express contract.

Quasi Contract A fictional contract imposed on parties by a court in the interests of fairness and justice; usually, quasi contracts are imposed to avoid the unjust enrichment of one party at the expense of another.

What determines whether a contract for accounting, tax preparation, or any other service is an express contract or an implied-in-fact contract?

Inside the Legal Environment

Employment Manuals and Implied Contracts

It is a common practice today for large companies or other organizations to create and distribute to their employees an employment manual, or handbook, setting forth the conditions of employment. Yet when drafting and distributing such manuals to employees, business owners and managers must consider the following question: Do statements made in an employee handbook constitute "promises" in an implied-in-fact employment contract? Increasingly, the courts are holding that they do. For example, if an employment handbook states that employees will only be fired for "good cause," the employer may be held to that "promise."[a]

The At-Will Employment Doctrine and Implied-in-Fact Contracts

This is possible even if, under state law, employment is "at will." Under the employment-at-will doctrine (see Chapter 17), employers may hire and fire employees at will, with or without cause. The at-will doctrine will not apply, however, if the terms of employment are subject to a contract between the employer and the employee. If a court holds that an implied employment contract exists, on the basis of promises made in an employment manual, the employer will be bound by the contract and liable for damages for breaching the contract. Generally, the key consideration in determining whether an employment manual creates an implied contractual obligation is the reasonable expectation of employees.[b]

What Employers Can Do to Avoid Liability

Generally, to avoid being contractually bound by terms in an employment manual, employers should avoid making definite statements (such as "Employees will only be terminated for good cause") that would cause employees to reasonably believe that those statements are contractual promises. Managers should also inform employees, when initially giving them the handbook or discussing its contents with them, that it is not intended as a contract. A conspicuous written disclaimer to this effect could also be included in the employment manual. The disclaimer might read as follows: "This policy manual describes the basic personnel policies and practices of our Company. You should understand that the manual does not modify our Company's 'at-will' employment doctrine or provide employees with any kind of contractual rights."

For Critical Analysis: *Why would any person accept employment with a firm without a written contract?*

a. See, for example, *Pepe v. Rival Co.*, 85 F.Supp.2d 349 (D.N.J. 1999).

b. *Doll v. Port Authority Trans-Hudson Corp.*, 92 F.Supp.2d 416 (D.N.J. 2000).

> **Remember** Quasi contract is an equitable concept, but most courts can apply the doctrine, because in most states, courts of law and equity have merged.

● **Example 12.4** Suppose that a vacationing doctor is driving down the highway and comes upon Emerson, who is lying unconscious on the side of the road. The doctor renders medical aid that saves Emerson's life. Although the injured, unconscious Emerson did not solicit the medical aid and was not aware that the aid had been rendered, Emerson received a valuable benefit, and the requirements for a quasi contract were fulfilled. In such a situation, the law normally will impose a quasi contract, and Emerson will have to pay the doctor for the reasonable value of the medical services rendered.●

Executed versus Executory Contracts

Executed Contract A contract that has been completely performed by both parties.

Executory Contract A contract that has not as yet been fully performed.

Contracts are also classified according to their state of performance. A contract that has been fully performed on both sides is called an **executed contract**. A contract that has not been fully performed on either side is called an **executory contract**. If one party has fully performed but the other has not, the contract is said to be executed on the one side and executory on the other, but the contract is still classified as executory.

Ethical Issue 12.1

Why should contracts be implied in law?

Quasi contracts, or contracts implied in law, arise to establish justice and fairness. The term *quasi contract* is misleading, because a quasi contract is not really a contract at all. It does not arise from any agreement between two individuals. Rather, a court imposes a quasi contract on the parties when justice so requires to prevent unjust enrichment. The doctrine of unjust enrichment is based on the theory that individuals should not be allowed to profit or enrich themselves inequitably at the expense of others. This belief is fundamental in our society and is clearly inspired by ethical considerations.

● **Example 12.5** Assume that you agree to buy ten tons of coal from the Western Coal Company. Further assume that Western has delivered the coal to your steel mill, where it is now being burned. At this point, the contract is an executory contract—it is executed on the part of Western and executory on your part. After you pay Western for the coal, the contract will be executed on both sides.●

> **"A legal fiction is always consistent with equity."**
>
> (Legal maxim)

Valid, Void, Voidable, and Unenforceable Contracts

A **valid contract** has the elements necessary for contract formation. Those elements consist of (1) an agreement (offer and an acceptance) (2) supported by legally sufficient consideration (3) for a legal purpose and (4) made by parties who have the legal capacity to enter into the contract. We will discuss each of these elements in this chapter.

Valid Contract A contract that results when elements necessary for contract formation (agreement, consideration, legal purpose, and contractual capacity) are present.

A **void contract** is no contract at all. The terms *void* and *contract* are contradictory. A void contract produces no legal obligations on the part of any of the parties. ● **Example 12.6** A contract can be void because one of the parties was adjudged by a court to be legally insane (and thus lacked the legal capacity to enter into a contract) or because the purpose of the contract was illegal.●

Void Contract A contract having no legal force or binding effect.

A **voidable contract** is a *valid* contract but one that can be avoided at the option of one or both of the parties. The party having the option can elect either to avoid any duty to perform or to *ratify* (make valid) the contract. If the contract is avoided, both parties are released from it. If it is ratified, both parties must fully perform their respective legal obligations.

Voidable Contract A contract that may be legally avoided (canceled, or annulled) at the option of one of the parties.

As a general rule, contracts made by minors are voidable at the option of the minor. Contracts entered into under fraudulent conditions are voidable at the option of the defrauded party. In addition, contracts entered into under legally defined duress or undue influence are voidable.

An **unenforceable contract** is one that cannot be enforced because of certain legal defenses against it. It is not unenforceable because a party failed to satisfy a legal requirement of the contract; rather, it is a valid contract rendered unenforceable by some statute or law. ● **Example 12.7** Certain contracts must be in writing, and if they are not, they will not be enforceable except in certain exceptional circumstances.●

Unenforceable Contract A valid contract rendered unenforceable by some statute or law.

Requirements of a Contract

The four requirements that constitute what are known as the elements of a contract are (1) agreement, (2) consideration, (3) capacity, and (4) legality. We discuss the element of agreement first.

Agreement

Agreement A meeting of two or more minds in regard to the terms of a contract; usually broken down into two events—an offer by one party to form a contract, and an acceptance of the offer by the person to whom the offer is made.

An essential element for contract formation is **agreement**—the parties must agree on the terms of the contract. Ordinarily, agreement is evidenced by two events: an *offer* and an *acceptance*. One party offers a certain bargain to another party, who then accepts that bargain.

In determining whether a contract has been formed, the element of intent is of prime importance, as will be discussed shortly. In contract law, intent is determined by what is referred to as the *objective theory of contracts,* not by the personal or subjective intent, or belief, of a party. The theory is that a party's intention to enter into a contract is judged by outward, objective facts as interpreted by a reasonable person, rather than by the party's own secret, subjective intentions. Objective facts include (1) what the party said when entering into the contract,[1] (2) how the party acted or appeared, and (3) the circumstances surrounding the transaction. As discussed earlier, in the section on express versus implied contracts, intent to form a contract may be manifested not only in words, oral or written, but also by conduct.

Offer A promise or commitment to perform or refrain from performing some specified act in the future.

REQUIREMENTS OF THE OFFER An **offer** is a promise or commitment to perform or refrain from performing some specified act in the future. Three elements are necessary for an offer to be effective:

1. There must be a *serious, objective intention* by the offeror.

---

1. As Judge Learned Hand once said, a court will give words their usual meaning even if "it were proved by twenty bishops that they intended something else." *Hotchkiss v. National City Bank of New York,* 200 F. 287 (2d Cir. 1911), aff'd 231 U.S. 50, 34 S.Ct. 20, 58 L.Ed. 115 (1913). (The term *aff'd* is an abbreviation for *affirmed;* an appellate court can affirm a lower court's judgment, decree, or order, thereby declaring that it is valid and must stand as rendered.)

International Perspective

How Intent to Form a Contract Is Measured in Other Countries

U.S. courts routinely adhere to the objective theory of contracts. Courts in some nations, however, give more weight to subjective intentions. Under French law, for example, when there is a conflict between an objective interpretation and a subjective interpretation of a contract, the French civil law code prefers the subjective construction. Other nations that have civil law codes take this same approach. French courts, nonetheless, will look to writings and other objective evidence to determine a party's subjective intent. In operation, the difference between the French and U.S. approaches is therefore perhaps not as significant as it may seem at first blush.

For Critical Analysis: *What problems may arise when a court attempts to look at the subjective basis of a contract?*

2. The terms of the offer must be reasonably *certain*, or *definite*, so that the parties and the court can ascertain the terms of the contract.
3. The offer must be communicated to the offeree.

Once an effective offer has been made, the offeree has the power to accept the offer. If the offeree accepts, the offer is translated into an agreement (and into a contract, if other essential elements are present).

Intention. The first requirement for an effective offer to exist is a serious, objective intention on the part of the offeror. Intent is not determined by the *subjective* intentions, beliefs, or assumptions of the offeror. Rather, it is determined by what a reasonable person in the offeree's position would conclude the offeror's words and actions meant. Offers made in obvious anger, jest, or undue excitement do not meet the serious-and-objective-intent test. Because these offers are not effective, an offeree's acceptance does not create an agreement.

An expression of opinion is not an offer or a promise. It does not evidence an intention to enter into a binding agreement. • **Example 12.8** In *Hawkins v. McGee,*[2] Hawkins took his son to McGee, a doctor, and asked McGee to operate on the son's hand. McGee said that the boy would be in the hospital three or four days and that the hand would *probably* heal a few days later. The son's hand did not heal for a month, but nonetheless the father did not win a suit for breach of contract. The court held that McGee did not make an offer to heal the son's hand in three or four days. He merely expressed an opinion as to when the hand would heal.•

Similarly, a *statement of intention* is not an offer. • **Example 12.9** If Ari says "I *plan* to sell my stock in Novation, Inc., for $150 per share," a contract is not created if John "accepts" and tenders the $150 per share for the stock. Ari has merely expressed his intention to enter into a future contract for the sale of the stock. If John accepts and tenders the $150 per share, no contract is formed, because a reasonable person would conclude that Ari was only *thinking about* selling his stock, not promising to sell it.•

Preliminary negotiations must also be distinguished from an offer. A request or invitation to negotiate is not an offer; it only expresses a willingness to discuss the possibility of entering into a contract. Examples are statements such as "Will you sell Forest Acres?" and "I wouldn't sell my car for less than $1,000." A reasonable person in the offeree's position would not conclude that such a statement evidenced an intention to enter into a binding obligation. Likewise, when the government and private firms need to have construction work done, contractors are invited to submit bids. The *invitation* to submit bids is not an offer, and a contractor does not bind the government or private firm by submitting a bid. (The bids that the contractors submit are offers, however, and the government or private firm can bind the contractor by accepting the bid.) In general, advertisements, mail-order catalogues, price lists, and circular letters (meant for the general public) are treated not as offers to contract but as invitations to negotiate.[3]

Lucy v. Zehmer, presented next, is a classic case in the area of contractual agreement. The case involves a business transaction in which boasts, brags,

A worker takes apart machinery. If the worker makes a design modification that the manufacturer incorporates into later models of the machine, without a contract, should the worker be compensated?

Be Careful An opinion is not an offer and not a contract term. Goods or services can be "perfect" in one party's opinion and "poor" in another's.

---

2. 84 N.H. 114, 146 A. 641 (1929).
3. *Restatement (Second) of Contracts,* Section 26, Comment b.

and dares "after a few drinks" resulted in a contract to sell certain property. The sellers claimed that the offer had been made in jest and that, in any event, the contract was voidable at their option because they were intoxicated when the offer was made and thus lacked contractual capacity (discussed later in this chapter). The court, however, looked to the words and actions of the parties—not their secret intentions—to determine whether a contract had been formed.

Case 12.1 ● Lucy v. Zehmer

Supreme Court of Appeals of Virginia, 1954.
196 Va. 493,
84 S.E.2d 516.

Background and Facts Lucy and Zehmer had known each other for fifteen or twenty years. For some time, Lucy had been wanting to buy Zehmer's farm. Zehmer had always told Lucy that he was not interested in selling. One night, Lucy stopped in to visit with the Zehmers at a restaurant they operated. Lucy said to Zehmer, "I bet you wouldn't take $50,000 for that place." Zehmer replied, "Yes, I would, too; you wouldn't give fifty." Throughout the evening, the conversation returned to the sale of the farm. At the same time, the parties were drinking whiskey. Eventually, Zehmer wrote up an agreement, on the back of a restaurant check, for the sale of the farm, and he asked his wife to sign it—which she did. When Lucy brought an action in a Virginia state court to enforce the agreement, Zehmer argued that he had been "high as a Georgia pine" at the time and that the offer had been made in jest: "two doggoned drunks bluffing to see who could talk the biggest and say the most." Lucy claimed that he had not been intoxicated and did not think Zehmer had been, either, given the way Zehmer handled the transaction. The trial court ruled in favor of the Zehmers, and Lucy appealed.

In the Words of the Court . . .
BUCHANAN, J. [Justice] delivered the opinion of the court.

* * * *

The appearance of the contract, the fact that it was under discussion for forty minutes or more before it was signed; Lucy's objection to the first draft because it was written in the singular, and he wanted Mrs. Zehmer to sign it also; the rewriting to meet that objection and the signing by Mrs. Zehmer; the discussion of what was to be included in the sale, the provision for the examination of the title, the completeness of the instrument that was executed, the taking possession of it by Lucy with no request or suggestion by either of the defendants that he give it back, are facts which furnish persuasive evidence that the execution of the contract was a serious business transaction rather than a casual, jesting matter as defendants now contend.

* * * *

In the field of contracts, as generally elsewhere, *"We must look to the outward expression of a person as manifesting his intention rather than to his secret and unexpressed intention. 'The law imputes to a person an intention corresponding to the reasonable meaning of his words and acts.'"* [Emphasis added.]

Decision and Remedy The Supreme Court of Virginia determined that the writing was an enforceable contract and reversed the ruling of the lower court. The Zehmers were required by court order to carry through with the sale of the farm to the Lucys.

For Critical Analysis—Cultural Consideration *How does the court's decision in this case relate to the objective theory of contracts?*

Definiteness. The second requirement for an effective offer involves the definiteness of its terms. An offer must have reasonably definite terms so that a court can determine if a breach has occurred and give an appropriate remedy.[4]
• Example 12.10 You offer to sell "some" of your textbooks to a friend, and the friend accepts your offer. No contract was formed by your friend's acceptance because the term *some* is too indefinite.•

An offer may invite an acceptance to be worded in such specific terms that the contract is made definite. • Example 12.11 Suppose that Marcus Business Machines contacts your corporation and offers to sell "from one to ten MacCool copying machines for $1,600 each; state number desired in acceptance." Your corporation agrees to buy two copiers. Because the quantity is specified in the acceptance, the terms are definite, and the contract is enforceable.•

For contracts for the sale of goods, Article 2 of the UCC relaxes considerably the common law requirement of definiteness of terms. Section 2–204 of the UCC provides that a contract will not fail for indefiniteness even if one or more terms are left open as long as the parties intended to make a contract and there is a reasonably certain basis for the court to grant an appropriate remedy. A seller and buyer of goods can thus create an enforceable contract even if several terms, including terms relating to price, payment, and delivery, are left unspecified. For example, if the price term is left open, Article 2 provides that the price will be "a reasonable price at the time of delivery" [UCC 2–305(1)]. If the payment term is left open, Article 2 states that "payment is due at the time and place at which the buyer is to receive the goods" [UCC 2–310(a)]. Under Article 2, the only term that normally must be specified is the quantity term; otherwise, the court will have no basis for determining a remedy.

Communication. A third requirement for an effective offer is communication, resulting in the offeree's knowledge of the offer. • Example 12.12 Suppose that Tolson advertises a reward for the return of her lost cat. Dirlik, not knowing of the reward, finds the cat and returns it to Tolson. Ordinarily, Dirlik cannot recover the reward, because an essential element of a reward contract is that the one who claims the reward must have known it was offered. A few states would allow recovery of the reward, but not on contract principles—Dirlik would be allowed to recover on the basis that it would be unfair to deny him the reward just because he did not know about it.•

TERMINATION OF THE OFFER The communication of an effective offer to an offeree gives the offeree the power to transform the offer into a binding, legal obligation (a contract) by an acceptance. This power of acceptance, however, does not continue forever. It can be terminated by *action of the parties* or by *operation of law.*

Termination by Action of the Parties. An offer can be terminated by the action of the parties in any of three ways: by revocation, by rejection, or by counteroffer. The offeror's act of withdrawing an offer is referred to as **revocation.** Unless an offer is irrevocable, the offeror usually can revoke the offer (even if he or she has promised to keep the offer open), as long as the revocation is communicated to the offeree before the offeree accepts. Revocation may be accomplished by express repudiation of the offer (for example, with a statement such

> "[Contracts] must not be the sports of an idle hour, mere matters of pleasantry and badinage, never intended by the parties to have any serious effect whatever."
>
> William Stowell, 1745–1836
> (English jurist)

Revocation In contract law, the withdrawal of an offer by an offeror; unless the offer is irrevocable, it can be revoked at any time prior to acceptance without liability.

---

4. *Restatement (Second) of Contracts,* Section 33.

> **Be Careful** The way in which a response to an offer is phrased can determine whether the offer is accepted or rejected.

Counteroffer An offeree's response to an offer in which the offeree rejects the original offer and at the same time makes a new offer.

Mirror Image Rule A common law rule that requires, for a valid contractual agreement, that the terms of the offeree's acceptance adhere exactly to the terms of the offeror's offer.

as "I withdraw my previous offer of October 17") or by performance of acts inconsistent with the existence of the offer, which are made known to the offeree.

The offer may be rejected by the offeree, in which case the offer is terminated. A rejection is ordinarily accomplished by words or by conduct evidencing an intent not to accept the offer. As with revocation, rejection of an offer is effective only when it is actually received by the offeror or the offeror's agent. A **counteroffer** is a rejection of the original offer and the simultaneous making of a new offer. • **Example 12.13** Suppose that Burke offers to sell his home to Lang for $170,000. Lang responds, "Your price is too high. I'll offer to purchase your house for $165,000." Lang's response is termed a counteroffer because it rejects Burke's offer to sell at $170,000 and creates a new offer by Lang to purchase the home at a price of $165,000.•

At common law, the **mirror image rule** requires that the offeree's acceptance match the offeror's offer exactly. In other words, the terms of the acceptance must "mirror" those of the offer. If the acceptance materially changes or adds to the terms of the original offer, it will be considered not an acceptance but a counteroffer—which, of course, need not be accepted. The original offeror can, however, accept the terms of the counteroffer and create a valid contract. The mirror image rule has been greatly modified in regard to contracts for the sale of goods. Section 2–207 of the UCC provides, with some exceptions, that a contract is formed if the offeree makes a definite expression of acceptance (such as signing the form in the appropriate location), even though the terms of the acceptance modify or add to the terms of the original offer.

Termination by Operation of Law. The offeree's power to transform an offer into a binding, legal obligation can be terminated by operation of the law if any of four conditions occur. First, an offer terminates automatically by law when the period of time specified in the offer has passed. • **Example 12.14** Jane offers to sell her boat to Jonah if he accepts within twenty days. Jonah must accept within the twenty-day period, or the offer will lapse (terminate).• If no time for acceptance is specified in the offer, the offer terminates at the end of a *reasonable* period of time. A reasonable period of time is determined by the subject matter of the contract, business and market conditions, and other relevant circumstances. An offer to sell farm produce, for example, will terminate sooner than an offer to sell farm equipment, because farm produce is perishable and subject to greater fluctuations in market value.

Second, an offer is automatically terminated if the specific subject matter of the offer is destroyed before the offer is accepted. For example, if Bekins offers to sell his cow to Yatsen, but the cow dies before Yatsen can accept, the offer is automatically terminated. Third, an offeree's power of acceptance is terminated when the offeror or offeree dies or is deprived of legal capacity to enter into the proposed contract, unless the offer is irrevocable.[5] Finally, a statute or court decision that makes an offer illegal will automatically terminate the offer. • **Example 12.15** If Acme Finance Corporation offers to lend Jack $20,000 at 15 percent annually, and a state statute is enacted prohibiting loans at interest rates greater than 12 percent before Jack can accept, the offer

---

5. *Restatement (Second) of Contracts,* Section 48. If the offer is irrevocable, it is not terminated when the offeror dies. Also, if the offer is such that it can be accepted by the performance of a series of acts, and those acts began before the offeror died, the offeree's power of acceptance is not terminated.

is automatically terminated. (If the statute is enacted after Jack accepts the offer, a valid contract is formed, but the contract may still be unenforceable.)•

ACCEPTANCE An **acceptance** is a voluntary act by the offeree that shows assent, or agreement, to the terms of an offer. The offeree's act may consist of words or conduct. Generally, a third person cannot substitute for the offeree and effectively accept the offer. After all, the identity of the offeree is as much a condition of a bargaining offer as any other term contained therein. Thus, except in special circumstances, only the person to whom the offer is made or that person's agent can accept the offer and create a binding contract. For example, Lottie makes an offer to Paul. Paul is not interested, but Paul's friend José accepts the offer. No contract is formed.

Unequivocal Acceptance. To exercise the power of acceptance effectively, the offeree must accept unequivocally. This is the *mirror image rule* previously discussed. If the acceptance is subject to new conditions or if the terms of the acceptance materially change the original offer, the acceptance may be deemed a counteroffer that implicitly rejects the original offer.

Certain terms, when added to an acceptance, will not qualify the acceptance sufficiently to constitute rejection of the offer. • **Example 12.16** Suppose that in response to a person offering to sell a painting by a well-known artist, the offeree replies, "I accept; please send a written contract." The offeree is requesting a written contract but is not making it a condition for acceptance. Therefore, the acceptance is effective without the written contract. If the offeree replies, "I accept if you send a written contract," however, the acceptance is expressly conditioned on the request for a writing, and the statement is not an acceptance but a counteroffer. (Notice how important each word is!)•

As noted earlier, in regard to sales contracts, the UCC provides that an acceptance may still be valid even if some terms are added. The new terms are simply treated as proposals for additions to the contract, or become part of the contract [UCC 2–207(2)].

Communication of Acceptance. Whether the offeror must be notified of the acceptance depends on the nature of the contract. In a bilateral contract, communication of acceptance is necessary, because acceptance is in the form of a promise (not performance), and the contract is formed when the promise is made (rather than when the act is performed). The offeree must communicate the acceptance to the offeror. Communication of acceptance is not necessary, however, if the offer dispenses with the requirement. Also, if the offer can be accepted by silence, no communication is necessary. Note that under the UCC, an order or other offer to buy goods that are to be promptly shipped may be treated as an offer and can be accepted by a promise to ship or by actual shipment [UCC 2–206 (1)(b)].

Because in a unilateral contract the full performance of some act is called for, acceptance is usually evident, and notification is therefore unnecessary. Exceptions do exist, however. When the offeror requests notice of acceptance or has no adequate means of determining whether the requested act has been performed, or when the law requires such notice of acceptance, then notice is necessary.

Mode and Timeliness of Acceptance. The general rule is that acceptance in a bilateral contract is timely if it is effected within the duration of the offer.

Acceptance A voluntary act by the offeree that shows assent, or agreement, to the terms of an offer; may consist of words or conduct.

Don't Forget When an offer is rejected, it is terminated.

If an offeror expressly authorizes acceptance of his or her offer by first-class mail or express delivery, can the offeree accept by a faster means, such as a fax?

Problems arise, however, when the parties involved are not dealing face to face. In such cases, the offeree may use an authorized mode of communication. Acceptance takes effect, thus completing formation of the contract, at the time the offeree sends the communication via the mode expressly or impliedly authorized by the offeror. This is the so-called **mailbox rule,** also called the "deposited acceptance rule," which the majority of courts uphold. Under this rule, if the authorized mode of communication is the mail, then an acceptance becomes valid when it is dispatched—not when it is received by the offeror.

Consideration

In every legal system, some promises will be enforced, and some promises will not be enforced. The simple fact that a party has made a promise, then, does not mean the promise is enforceable. Under the common law, a primary basis for the enforcement of promises is consideration.

ELEMENTS OF CONSIDERATION **Consideration** is usually defined as the value given in return for a promise. Often, consideration is broken down into two parts: (1) something of *legally sufficient value* must be given in exchange for the promise, and (2) there must be a *bargained-for* exchange.

Legal Value. The "something of legally sufficient value" may consist of (1) a promise to do something that one has no prior legal duty to do (to pay money on receipt of certain goods, for example), (2) the performance of an action that one is otherwise not obligated to undertake (such as providing accounting services), or (3) the refraining from an action that one has a legal right to undertake. Generally, to be legally sufficient, consideration must be either *detrimental to the promisee* or *beneficial to the promisor.* Note that legal detriment is not the same as economic, or actual, detriment (such as suffering economic losses). Legal detriment is simply the assumption of a legal obligation that one was not otherwise required to assume.

What if, in return for a promise to pay, a person forbears to pursue harmful habits, such as the use of tobacco and alcohol? Does such forbearance represent a legal detriment to the promisee and thus create consideration for the contract, or does it in fact benefit the promisee and thus *not* create consideration for the contract? This was the issue before the court in *Hamer v. Sidway,* a classic case concerning consideration, which we present in this chapter's *Landmark in the Legal Environment.*

Bargained-for Exchange. The second element of consideration is that it must provide the basis for the bargain struck between the contracting parties. The consideration given by the promisor must induce the promisee to incur a legal detriment either now or in the future, and the detriment incurred must induce the promisor to make the promise. This element of bargained-for exchange distinguishes contracts from gifts.

ADEQUACY OF CONSIDERATION As mentioned, consideration involves the requirement that consideration be something of value in the eyes of the law. Adequacy of consideration involves "how much" consideration is given. Essentially, adequacy of consideration concerns the fairness of the bargain. On the surface, fairness would appear to be an issue when the values of items exchanged are unequal. In general, however, courts do not question the adequacy

---

Mailbox Rule A rule providing that an acceptance of an offer becomes effective on dispatch (on being placed in a mailbox), if mail is, expressly or impliedly, an authorized means of communication of acceptance to the offeror.

Consideration Generally, the value given in return for a promise. The consideration, which must be present to make the contract legally binding, must result in a detriment to the promisee (something of legally sufficient value and bargained for) or a benefit to the promisor.

"It is the essence of a consideration, that, by the terms of the agreement, it is given and accepted as the motive or inducement of the promise."

Oliver Wendell Holmes, Jr., 1841–1935 (Associate justice of the United States Supreme Court, 1902–1932)

Landmark in the Legal Environment

Hamer v. Sidway (1891)

In *Hamer v. Sidway*,[a] the issue before the court arose from a contract created in 1869 between William Story, Sr., and his nephew, William Story II. The uncle promised his nephew that if the nephew refrained from drinking alcohol, using tobacco, and playing billiards and cards for money until he reached the age of twenty-one, the uncle would pay him $5,000. The nephew, who indulged occasionally in all of these "vices," agreed to refrain from them and did so for the next six years. Following his twenty-first birthday in 1875, the nephew wrote to his uncle that he had performed his part of the bargain and was thus entitled to the promised $5,000. A few days later, the uncle wrote the nephew a letter stating, "[Y]ou shall have the five thousand dollars, as I promised you." The uncle said that the money was in the bank, and that the nephew could "consider this money on interest."

The nephew left the money in the care of his uncle, who held it for the next twelve years. When the uncle died in 1887, however, the executor of the uncle's estate refused to pay the $5,000 claim brought by Hamer, a third party to whom the promise had been *assigned*. (The law allows parties to assign, or transfer, rights in contracts to third parties.) The executor, Sidway, contended that the contract was invalid because there was insufficient consideration to support it. He argued that neither a benefit to the promisor (the uncle) nor a detriment to the promisee (the nephew) existed in this case. The uncle had received nothing, and the nephew had actually benefited by fulfilling the uncle's wishes. Therefore, no contract existed.

Although a lower court upheld Sidway's position, the New York Court of Appeals reversed and ruled in favor of the plaintiff, Hamer. "The promisee used tobacco, occasionally drank liquor, and he had a legal right to do so," the court stated. "That right he abandoned for a period of years upon the strength of the promise of the testator [one who makes a will] that for such forbearance he would give him $5,000. We need not speculate on the effort which may have been required to give up the use of those stimulants. It is sufficient that he restricted his lawful freedom of action within certain prescribed limits upon the faith of his uncle's agreement."

For Critical Analysis: *How might one argue that this contract also benefited the promisor (Story, Sr.)?*

a. 124 N.Y. 538, 27 N.E. 256 (1891).

---

of consideration if the consideration is legally sufficient. Under the doctrine of freedom of contract, parties are usually free to bargain as they wish. If people could sue merely because they had entered into an unwise contract, the courts would be overloaded with frivolous suits.

In extreme cases, however, a court of law may look to the amount or value (the adequacy) of the consideration, because apparently inadequate consideration can indicate that fraud, duress, or undue influence was involved or that a gift was made (if a father "sells" a $100,000 house to his daughter for only $1, for example). Additionally, in cases in which the consideration is grossly inadequate, the courts may declare the contract unenforceable on the ground that it is unconscionable[6]—that is, generally speaking, it is so one sided under the circumstances as to be overly unfair. (Unconscionability will be discussed later in this chapter.)

> **Be Aware** A consumer's signature on a contract does not always guarantee that the contract will be enforced. Ultimately, the terms must be fair.

CONTRACTS THAT LACK CONSIDERATION Sometimes, one of the parties (or both parties) to a contract may think that the parties have exchanged consideration when in fact they have not. Here we look at some situations in which the parties' promises or actions do not qualify as contractual consideration.

---

6. Pronounced un-*kon*-shun-uh-bul.

Preexisting Duty.   Under most circumstances, a promise to do what one already has a legal duty to do does not constitute legally sufficient consideration, because no legal detriment is incurred.[7] The preexisting legal duty may be imposed by law or may arise out of a previous contract. A sheriff, for example, cannot collect a reward for information leading to the capture of a criminal if the sheriff already has a legal duty to capture the criminal. Likewise, if a party is already bound by contract to perform a certain duty, that duty (the consideration given in the contract) cannot serve as consideration for a second contract.

● **Example 12.17** Suppose that Bauman-Bache, Inc., begins construction on a seven-story office building and after three months demands an extra $75,000 on its contract. If the extra $75,000 is not paid, it will stop working. The owner of the land, having no one else to complete construction, agrees to pay the extra $75,000. The agreement is not enforceable, because it is not supported by legally sufficient consideration; Bauman-Bache had a preexisting contractual duty to complete the building. ●

The rule regarding preexisting duty is meant to prevent extortion and the so-called holdup game. What happens, though, when an honest contractor, who has contracted with a landowner to build a house, runs into extraordinary difficulties that were totally unforeseen at the time the contract was formed? In the interests of fairness and equity, the courts sometimes allow exceptions to the preexisting duty rule. In the example just mentioned, if the landowner agrees to pay extra compensation to the contractor for overcoming the unforeseen difficulties (such as having to use dynamite and special equipment to remove an unexpected rock formation in order to build a basement), the court may refrain from applying the preexisting duty rule and enforce the agreement. When the "unforeseen difficulties" that give rise to a contract modification are the types of risks ordinarily assumed in business, however, the courts will usually assert the preexisting duty rule.

Article 2 of the UCC significantly modifies the preexisting duty rule with respect to sales contracts. Under Article 2, any agreement modifying a contract needs no consideration to be binding [UCC 2–209(1)].

Past Consideration.   Promises made in return for actions or events that have already taken place are unenforceable. These promises lack consideration in that the element of bargained-for exchange is missing. In short, you can bargain for something to take place now or in the future but not for something that has already taken place. Therefore, **past consideration** is no consideration.

Past Consideration An act done before the contract is made, which ordinarily, by itself, cannot be consideration for a later promise to pay for the act.

● **Example 12.18** Suppose that Elsie, a real estate agent, does her friend Judy a favor by selling Judy's house and not charging any commission. Later, Judy says to Elsie, "In return for your generous act, I will pay you $3,000." This promise is made in return for past consideration and is thus unenforceable; in effect, Judy is stating her intention to give Elsie a gift. ●

Illusory Promises.   If the terms of the contract express such uncertainty of performance that the promisor has not definitely promised to do anything, the promise is said to be *illusory*—without consideration and unenforceable.
● **Example 12.19** The president of Tuscan Corporation says to his employees, "All of you have worked hard, and if profits continue to remain high, a 10 per-

---

7. See *Foakes v. Beer,* 9 App.Cas. 605 (1884).

cent bonus at the end of the year will be given—if management thinks it is warranted." This is an *illusory promise,* or no promise at all, because performance depends solely on the discretion of the president (the management). There is no bargained-for consideration. The statement declares merely that management may or may not do something in the future. •

PROMISES ENFORCEABLE WITHOUT CONSIDERATION—PROMISSORY ESTOPPEL Sometimes individuals rely on promises, and such reliance may form a basis for contract rights and duties. Under the doctrine of **promissory estoppel** (also called *detrimental reliance*), a person who has reasonably relied on the promise of another can often hope to obtain some measure of recovery. When the doctrine of promissory estoppel is applied, the promisor (the offeror) is *estopped* (barred, or impeded) from revoking the promise. For the doctrine of promissory estoppel to be applied, the following elements are required:

Promissory Estoppel A doctrine that applies when a promisor makes a clear and definite promise on which the promisee justifiably relies; such a promise is binding if justice will be better served by the enforcement of the promise.

1. There must be a clear and definite promise.
2. The promisee must justifiably rely on the promise.
3. The reliance normally must be of a substantial and definite character.
4. Justice will be better served by the enforcement of the promise.

• **Example 12.20** Your uncle tells you, "I'll pay you $150 a week so you won't have to work anymore." In reliance on your uncle's promise, you quit your job, but your uncle refuses to pay you. Under the doctrine of promissory estoppel, you may be able to enforce such a promise.[8] Now your uncle makes a promise to give you $10,000 with which to buy a car. If you buy the car and he does not pay you, you may once again be able to enforce the promise under this doctrine. •

> "To break an oral agreement which is not legally binding is morally wrong."
>
> The Talmud,
> *Bava Metzi'a*

---

8. *Ricketts v. Scothorn,* 57 Neb. 51, 77 N.W. 365 (1898).

Ethical Issue 12.2

Should social promises be enforced under the doctrine of promissory estoppel?

Suppose that a bride-to-be spends thousands of dollars preparing for a wedding, only to be stranded by the groom at the altar. In such a case, is the groom's promise of marriage enforceable? In other words, because of the detrimental reliance, would a court impose a contractual relationship on the parties so that the bride-to-be could collect damages for breach of a "contract"? A number of plaintiffs over the years have tried to collect damages in similar cases, but to no avail. Recently, for example, a college freshman whose boyfriend broke their prom date sued the boyfriend for the cost of her unused prom dress. A Minnesota state court, however, dismissed the case, suggesting that "[w]hether the defendant has a social or moral duty to help the plaintiff with her prom costs is a question for the likes of Emily Post or Miss Manners, not for courts of this state." As discussed earlier, contract law reflects society's decisions on what promises will be enforced and what promises will not. Clearly, society has determined that social agreements such as those just mentioned do not fall into the category of promises that should be enforceable.[a]

---

a. *The National Law Journal,* June 22, 1998, p. A23.

In the following case, an individual sought to recover damages under the doctrine of promissory estoppel from a prospective employer that reneged on its promise of employment.

Case 12.2 ● Goff-Hamel v. Obstetricians & Gynecologists, P.C.

Supreme Court of Nebraska, 1999.
256 Neb. 19, 588 N.W.2d 798.
http://www.findlaw.com/
11stategov/ne/neca.html[a]

Background and Facts Julie Goff-Hamel worked for Hastings Family Planning. After eleven years, Goff-Hamel was earning $24,000, plus benefits: six weeks' paid maternity leave, six weeks' vacation, twelve paid holidays, twelve sick days, educational reimbursement, and medical and dental insurance. In July 1993, representatives of Obstetricians & Gynecologists, P.C.,[b] (Obstetricians)—including part owner Dr. George Adam and personnel consultant Larry Draper—asked Goff-Hamel to work for Obstetricians. Adam told Goff-Hamel that the position was full-time, at a salary of $10 per hour, and included two weeks'

paid vacation, three or four paid holidays, uniforms, and an educational stipend. A retirement plan would start after the end of the second year, retroactive to the end of the first year. The job did not include health insurance. Goff-Hamel agreed to start in October and gave notice to Hastings in August. She was given uniforms for her new job and a copy of her work schedule. The day before she was scheduled to start, Draper told her that she need not report to work and that Janel Foote, the wife of Dr. Terry Foote, a part owner, opposed her hiring. Goff-Hamel filed a suit in a Nebraska state court against Obstetricians, seeking damages in part on the basis of detrimental reliance. The court concluded that because she was to be employed at will,[c] her employment could be terminated at any time—which included before she began working—and issued a summary judgment in favor of Obstetricians. Goff-Hamel appealed to the Nebraska Supreme Court.

a. On this page, below "Supreme Court Opinions," click on "1999." On that page, click on "January." Scroll down to the case name, and click on "4-19990129" to access the opinion.
b. *P.C.* is an abbreviation for "professional corporation," which is a special form for a business entity. Corporations are discussed in more detail in Chapter 16.

c. As mentioned earlier in this chapter, *employment at will* is an employment relationship that either party may terminate at any time for any reason. Employment at will is explained in more detail in Chapter 17.

In the Words of the Court . . .
WRIGHT, J. [Justice]

* * * *

Other jurisdictions which have addressed the question of whether a cause of action for promissory estoppel can be stated in the context of a prospective at-will employee are split on the issue. Some have held that an employee can recover damages incurred as a result of resigning from the former at-will employment in reliance on a promise of other at-will employment. They have determined that when a prospective employer knows or should know that a promise of employment will induce an employee to leave his or her current job, such employer shall be liable for the reliant's damages. * * * [T]hey have concluded that the employee would have continued to work in his or her prior employment if it were not for the offer by the prospective employer. Although damages have not been allowed for wages lost from the prospective at-will employment, damages have been allowed based upon wages from the prior employment and other damages incurred in reliance on the job offer.

In contrast, other jurisdictions have held as a matter of law that a prospective employee cannot recover damages incurred in reliance on an unfulfilled promise of at-will employment, concluding that reliance on a

Case 12.2 Continued

promise consisting solely of at-will employment is unreasonable as a matter of law because the employee should know that the promised employment could be terminated by the employer at any time for any reason without liability. These courts have stated that an anomalous result occurs when recovery is allowed for an employee who has not begun work, when the same employee's job could be terminated without liability 1 day after beginning work.

* * * *

* * * [W]e conclude under the facts of this case that promissory estoppel can be asserted in connection with the offer of at-will employment and that the trial court erred in granting Obstetricians summary judgment. *A cause of action for promissory estoppel is based upon a promise which the promisor should reasonably expect to induce action or forbearance on the part of the promisee [and] which does in fact induce such action or forbearance.* * * * [Emphasis added.]

* * * *

The facts are not disputed that Obstetricians offered Goff-Hamel employment. Apparently, at the direction of the spouse of one of the owners, Obstetricians refused to honor its promise of employment. It is also undisputed that Goff-Hamel relied upon Obstetricians' promise of employment to her detriment in that she terminated her employment of 11 years. Therefore, under the facts of this case, the trial court should have granted summary judgment in favor of Goff-Hamel on the issue of liability.

Decision and Remedy The Supreme Court of Nebraska reversed the judgment of the trial court. The state supreme court held that promissory estoppel can be asserted in connection with an offer of at-will employment. The court remanded the case for a determination of the amount of damages to which Goff-Hamel was entitled.

For Critical Analysis—Economic Consideration *If you were a judge in the trial court to which this case was remanded, what factors would you consider in determining the amount of damages that should be awarded to Goff-Hamel?*

Capacity

The third element required for the formation of a contract (after agreement and consideration) is **contractual capacity**—the legal ability to enter into a contractual relationship. Courts generally presume the existence of contractual capacity, but there are some situations in which capacity is lacking or may be questionable. A person *adjudged by a court* to be mentally incompetent, for example, cannot form a legally binding contract with another party. In other situations, a party may have the capacity to enter into a valid contract but also have the right to avoid liability under it. For example, minors usually are not legally bound by contracts.

Contractual Capacity The threshold mental capacity required by the law for a party who enters into a contract to be bound by that contract.

MINORS Today, in virtually all states, the *age of majority* (when a person is no longer a minor) for contractual purposes is eighteen years for both sexes.[9]

---

9. The age of majority may still be twenty-one for other purposes, such as the purchase and consumption of alcohol. The word *infant* is usually used synonymously with the word *minor*.

In addition, some states provide for the termination of minority on marriage. Subject to certain exceptions, the contracts entered into by a minor are voidable at the option of that minor.

The general rule is that a minor can enter into any contract an adult can, provided that the contract is not one prohibited by law for minors (for example, the sale of alcoholic beverages). Although minors have the right to avoid their contracts, there are exceptions.

Disaffirmance. For a minor to exercise the option to avoid a contract, he or she need only manifest an intention not to be bound by it. The minor "avoids" the contract by disaffirming it. The technical definition of **disaffirmance** is the legal avoidance, or setting aside, of a contractual obligation. Words or conduct may serve to express this intent. The contract can ordinarily be disaffirmed at any time during minority or for a reasonable time after the minor comes of age. In some states, however, when there is a contract for the sale of land by a minor, the minor cannot disaffirm the contract until he or she reaches the age of majority. When a minor disaffirms a contract, all property that he or she has transferred to the adult as consideration can be recovered, even if it is then in the possession of a third party.[10]

Note that an adult who enters into a contract with a minor cannot avoid his or her contractual duties on the ground that the minor can do so. Unless the minor exercises the option to disaffirm the contract, the adult party normally is bound by it.

Minor's Obligations on Disaffirmance. All state laws permit minors to disaffirm contracts (with certain exceptions—to be discussed shortly), including executed contracts. States differ, however, on the extent of a minor's obligations on disaffirmance. Courts in a majority of states hold that the minor need only return the goods (or other consideration) subject to the contract, provided the goods are in the minor's possession or control. ● **Example 12.21** Suppose that Jim Garrison, a seventeen-year-old, purchases a computer from Radio Shack. While transporting the computer to his home, Garrison, through no fault of his own, is involved in a car accident. As a result of the accident, the plastic casing of the computer is broken. The next day, he returns the computer to Radio Shack and disaffirms the contract. Under the majority view, this return fulfills Garrison's duty even though the computer is now damaged. ●

A minor who enters into a contract for necessaries may disaffirm the contract but remains liable for the reasonable value of the goods. **Necessaries** are basic needs, such as food, clothing, shelter, and medical services, at a level of value required to maintain the minor's standard of living or financial and social status. Thus, what will be considered a necessary for one person may be a luxury for another.

Generally, to qualify as a contract for necessaries, (1) the item contracted for must be necessary to the minor's existence, (2) the value of the necessary item may be up to a level required to maintain the minor's standard of living or financial and social status, and (3) the minor must not be under the care of a parent or guardian who is required to supply this item. Unless these three criteria are met, the minor can disaffirm the contract *without* being liable for the reasonable value of the goods used.

Disaffirmance The legal avoidance, or setting aside, of a contractual obligation.

Necessaries Necessities required for life, such as food, shelter, clothing, and medical attention; may include whatever is believed to be necessary to maintain a person's standard of living or financial and social status.

Be Aware A minor's station in life (financial and social status, lifestyle, and so on) is important in determining whether an item is a necessary or a luxury. For example, clothing is a necessary, but if a minor from a low-income family contracts for the purchase of a $2,000 coat, a court may deem the coat a luxury. In this situation, the contract would not be for "necessaries."

---

10. Section 2–403(1) of the UCC allows an exception if the third party is a "good faith purchaser for value."

Two young men discuss the sale of a car. When a minor disaffirms a contract, such as a contract to buy a car, most states require the minor to return only whatever consideration he or she received, if it is within his or her control. Why do some states require more?

Ratification. In contract law, **ratification** is the act of accepting and giving legal force to an obligation that previously was not enforceable. A minor who has reached the age of majority can ratify a contract expressly or impliedly.

Express ratification occurs when the minor expressly states, orally or in writing, that he or she intends to be bound by the contract. Implied ratification exists when the conduct of the minor is inconsistent with disaffirmance (as when the minor enjoys the benefits of the contract) or when the minor fails to disaffirm an executed (fully performed) contract within a reasonable time after reaching the age of majority. If the contract is still executory (not yet performed or only partially performed), however, failure to disaffirm the contract will not necessarily imply ratification.

Generally, the courts base their determination on whether the minor, after reaching the age of majority, has had ample opportunity to consider the nature of the contractual obligations he or she entered into as a minor and the extent to which the adult party to the contract has performed.

INTOXICATED PERSONS Another situation in which contractual capacity becomes an issue is when a contract is formed by a person who claims to have been intoxicated at the time the contract was made. The general rule is that if a person who is sufficiently intoxicated to lack mental capacity enters into a contract, the contract is voidable at the option of the intoxicated person. This is true even if the intoxication was purely voluntary. For the contract to be voidable, it must be proved that the intoxicated person's reason and judgment were impaired to the extent that he or she did not comprehend the legal consequences of entering into the contract. If the person was intoxicated but understood these legal consequences, the contract is enforceable.

Simply because the terms of the contract are foolish or are obviously favorable to the other party does not mean the contract is voidable (unless the other party fraudulently induced the person to become intoxicated). Problems often arise in determining whether a party was sufficiently intoxicated to avoid legal duties. Generally, contract avoidance on the ground of intoxication is rarely permitted.

Ratification The act of accepting and giving legal force to an obligation that previously was not enforceable.

Be Careful A contract will almost always be enforced if both parties knew what they were signing.

MENTALLY INCOMPETENT PERSONS If a person has been adjudged mentally incompetent by a court of law and a guardian has been appointed, any contract made by the mentally incompetent person is *void*—no contract exists. Only the guardian can enter into a binding contract on behalf of the mentally incompetent person.

If a mentally incompetent person not previously so adjudged by a court enters into a contract, the contract may be *voidable* if the person does not know he or she is entering into the contract or lacks the mental capacity to comprehend its nature, purpose, and consequences. A contract entered into by a mentally incompetent person (but not previously so adjudged by a court) may also be deemed valid and enforceable if the contract was formed during a lucid interval. For such a contract to be valid, it must be shown that the person was able to comprehend the nature, purpose, and consequences of the contract *at the time the contract was formed.*

Legality

To this point, we have discussed three of the requirements for a valid contract to exist—agreement, consideration, and contractual capacity. Now we examine a fourth—legality. For a contract to be valid and enforceable, it must be formed for a legal purpose. A contract to do something that is prohibited by federal or state statutory law is illegal and, as such, void from the outset and thus unenforceable. Additionally, a contract to commit a tortious act or to commit an action that is contrary to public policy is illegal and unenforceable.

CONTRACTS CONTRARY TO STATUTE Statutes sometimes prescribe the terms of contracts. In some instances, the laws are specific, even providing for the inclusion of certain clauses and their wording. Other statutes prohibit certain contracts on the basis of their subject matter, the time at which they are entered into, or the status of the contracting parties. We examine here several ways in which contracts may be contrary to a statute and thus illegal.

Usury. Virtually every state has a statute that sets the maximum rate of interest that can be charged for different types of transactions, including ordinary loans. A lender who makes a loan at an interest rate above the lawful maximum commits **usury**. The maximum rate of interest varies from state to state.

Usury Charging an illegal rate of interest.

Gambling. In general, gambling contracts are illegal and thus void. All states have statutes that regulate gambling—defined as any scheme that involves the distribution of property by chance among persons who have paid valuable consideration for the opportunity (chance) to receive the property.[11] Gambling is the creation of risk for the purpose of assuming it. In some states, certain forms of gambling, such as casino gambling or horse racing, are legal. Many states also have legalized state-operated lotteries, as well as lotteries (such as bingo) arranged for charitable purposes. A number of states also allow gambling on Indian reservations.

One of the challenges facing the states today is how to enforce gambling laws in an online environment. For a discussion of this topic, see this chapter's *Legal E-nvironment* feature.

---

11. See *Wishing Well Club v. Akron*, 66 Ohio Law Abs. 406, 112 N.E.2d 41 (1951).

Legal *e*-nvironment

Online Gambling Operations

At one time, few states permitted gambling in any form. Even by 1976, only thirteen states had lotteries, two states had approved off-track wagering, and there were no casinos outside Nevada. Today, in contrast, thirty-seven states have lotteries, twenty-eight states have casinos, and twenty-two states allow off-track betting.[a] Moreover, the advent of the Internet has given Americans unprecedented access to gambling facilities.

Jurisdictional Challenges

As noted in Chapter 5, jurisdictional issues become complicated in cases involving Internet transactions. Certainly, this is true with respect to online gambling. For example, in those states that do not allow casino gambling or off-track betting, what can a state government do if residents of the state place bets online? After all, states have no constitutional authority to regulate activities that occur in other states. Complicating the problem is the fact that many Internet gambling sites are located outside the United States in countries in which Internet gambling is legal, and no state government has jurisdiction over activities that take place in other countries.

Of course, as you learned in Chapter 3, under certain conditions a state court can exercise jurisdiction over an out-of-state party that has a threshold level of contacts ("minimum contacts") with the state. A number of courts have shown a willingness to exercise jurisdiction over gambling sites located out of state—or even out of the country—based on the assumption that Internet advertising of gambling sites constitutes minimum contacts.[b]

Where Does the Gambling Occur?

Another threshold issue in regulating online gambling has to do with determining where the physical act of placing a bet on the Internet occurs. Is it where the gambler is located or where the gambling site is based? For example, suppose that a resident of New York places bets via the Internet at a gambling site located in Antigua. Is the actual act of "gambling" taking place in New York or in Antigua? According to a New York trial court, the act of entering a bet and transmitting information from New York to Antigua via the Internet was adequate to constitute gambling activity within New York.[c] How the majority of courts will decide this question, however, is not yet clear.

Collecting Credit-Card Gambling Debts

Many states have laws that bar the collection of illegal gambling debts. Given that nearly 90 percent of Internet gambling is accomplished through the use of credit cards, these laws may have significant implications for credit-card companies, banks, and other issuers of credit cards. Specifically, will credit-card issuers be able to collect debts from cardholders who use their cards to obtain funds for online gambling?

In a series of class-action cases against credit-card companies that are currently before the federal courts, the plaintiffs have alleged that they should not have to pay credit-card debts that they incurred for gambling purposes. Clearly, the courts' decisions in these cases will have important consequences for the online gambling industry. In the meantime, opponents of Internet gambling are pressuring Congress to pass legislation that would prohibit the use of the Internet for gambling purposes. Additionally, four states—Illinois, Louisiana, Nevada, and Texas—already have specifically banned Internet gambling.

For Critical Analysis: *Should credit-card companies be held responsible for the gambling losses of their cardholders? Why or why not?*

a. Rachel A. Volberg *et al.,* "From Back Room to Living Room: Changing Attitudes toward Gambling," *Public Perspective,* August/September 1999, p. 9.

b. See, for example, *Minnesota v. Granite Gate Resorts, Inc.,* 568 N.W.2d 715 (Minn.App. 1997); aff'd., 576 N.W.2d 747 (Minn. 1998); and *Thompson v. Handa-Lopez, Inc.,* 998 F.Supp. 738 (W.D.Tex. 1998).

c. *People v. World Interactive Gaming Corp.,* No. 404428/98 (N.Y.Sup.Ct. July 29, 1999); unpublished opinion.

Sabbath (Sunday) Laws. Statutes called Sabbath (Sunday) laws prohibit the formation or performance of certain contracts on a Sunday. Under the common law, such contracts are legal in the absence of this statutory prohibition.

Under some state and local laws, all contracts entered into on a Sunday are illegal. Laws in other states or municipalities prohibit only the sale of certain types of merchandise, such as alcoholic beverages, on a Sunday.

Blue laws State or local laws that prohibit the performance of certain types of commercial activities on Sunday.

These laws, which date back to colonial times, are often called **blue laws.** Blue laws get their name from the blue paper on which New Haven, Connecticut, printed its new town ordinance in 1781. The ordinance prohibited all work on Sunday and required all shops to close on the "Lord's Day." A number of states and municipalities enacted laws forbidding the carrying on of "all secular labor and business on the Lord's Day." Exceptions to Sunday laws permit contracts for necessities (such as food) and works of charity. A fully performed (executed) contract that was entered into on a Sunday normally cannot be rescinded (canceled).

Recall Under the First Amendment, the government cannot promote or place a significant burden on religion.

Sunday laws are often not enforced, and some of these laws have been held to be unconstitutional on the ground that they are contrary to the freedom of religion. Nonetheless, as a precaution, business owners contemplating doing business in a particular locality should check to see if any Sunday statutes or ordinances will affect their business activities.

Licensing Statutes. All states require that members of certain professions obtain licenses allowing them to practice. Physicians, lawyers, real estate brokers, architects, electricians, and stockbrokers are but a few of the people who must be licensed. Some licenses are obtained only after extensive schooling and examinations, which indicate to the public that a special skill has been acquired. Others require only that the particular person be of good moral character.

Generally, business licenses provide a means of regulating and taxing certain businesses and protecting the public against actions that could threaten the general welfare. For example, in nearly all states, a stockbroker must be licensed and must file a bond with the state to protect the public from fraudulent transactions in stock. Similarly, a plumber must be licensed and bonded to protect the public against incompetent plumbers and to protect the public

Adults gamble at a casino in Las Vegas, where casino gambling is legal. Would this same activity be illegal if it were conducted online? If so, could it be prevented? How?

health. Only persons or businesses possessing the qualifications and complying with the conditions required by statute are entitled to licenses. Typically, for example, an owner of a saloon or tavern is required to sell food as a condition of obtaining a license to sell liquor for consumption on the premises.

When a person enters into a contract with an unlicensed individual, the contract may still be enforceable, depending on the nature of the licensing statute. Some states expressly provide that the lack of a license in certain occupations bars the enforcement of work-related contracts. If the statute does not expressly state this, one must look to the underlying purpose of the licensing requirements for a particular occupation. If the purpose is to protect the public from unauthorized practitioners, a contract involving an unlicensed individual is illegal and unenforceable. If, however, the underlying purpose of the statute is to raise government revenues, a contract with an unlicensed practitioner is enforceable—although the unlicensed person is usually fined.

CONTRACTS CONTRARY TO PUBLIC POLICY Although contracts involve private parties, some are not enforceable because of the negative impact they would have on society. These contracts are said to be *contrary to public policy.* Examples include a contract to commit an immoral act (such as a surrogate-parenting contract, which several courts and state statutes equate with "baby selling") and a contract that prohibits marriage. • **Example 12.22** Suppose that Everett offers a young man $500 if he refrains from marrying Everett's daughter. If the young man accepts, no contract is formed (the contract is void) because it is contrary to public policy. Thus, if the man marries Everett's daughter, Everett cannot sue him for breach of contract.• Business contracts that may be contrary to public policy include contracts in restraint of trade and unconscionable contracts or clauses.

Contracts in Restraint of Trade. Contracts in restraint of trade (anticompetitive agreements) usually adversely affect the public, which favors competition in the economy. Typically, such contracts also violate one or more federal or state statutes.[12] An exception is recognized when the restraint is reasonable and it is *ancillary* to (is a subsidiary part of) a contract, such as a contract for the sale of a business or an employment contract. Many such exceptions involve a type of restraint called a *covenant not to compete,* or a restrictive covenant.

Covenants not to compete are often contained in contracts concerning the sale of an ongoing business. A covenant not to compete is created when a seller agrees not to open a new store in a certain geographical area surrounding the old store. Such an agreement, when it is ancillary to a sales contract and reasonable in terms of time and geographic area, enables the seller to sell, and the purchaser to buy, the "goodwill" and "reputation" of an ongoing business. If, for example, a well-known merchant sells his or her store and opens a competing business a block away, many of the merchant's customers will likely do business at the new store. This renders valueless the good name and reputation sold to the other merchant for a price. If a covenant not to compete was not ancillary to a sales agreement, however, it would be void, because it unreasonably restrains trade and is contrary to public policy.

Agreements not to compete can also be contained in employment contracts. It is common for many people in middle-level and upper-level management

> "Public policy is in its nature so uncertain and fluctuating, varying with the habits of the day, . . . that it is difficult to determine its limits with any degree of exactness."
>
> Joseph Story, 1779–1845
> (Associate Justice of the United States Supreme Court, 1811–1845)

12. Such as the Sherman Antitrust Act, the Clayton Act, and the Federal Trade Commission Act (see Chapter 23).

positions to agree not to work for competitors or not to start a competing business for a specified period of time after terminating employment. Such agreements are generally legal so long as the specified period of time is not excessive in duration and the geographical restriction is reasonable. Basically, the restriction on competition must be reasonable—that is, not any greater than necessary to protect a legitimate business interest. The following case illustrates this point.

Case 12.3 ● Brunswick Floors, Inc. v. Guest

Court of Appeals of Georgia, 1998.
506 S.E.2d 670.

Historical and Social Setting

The value of a business depends on the goodwill between key employees and customers. To enhance this value, a business will invest its key employees with training, experience, customer lists, trade secrets, and other valuable information. It can be devastating when a key employee quits, or is fired, and goes into business to compete with his or her former employer. A covenant not to compete can protect goodwill, and other assets, by at least prohibiting an employee from stealing customers. A covenant not to compete is enforceable if its provisions are reasonable, if it is part of a valid contract, and if it is related to the protection of a legitimate interest. As much as a business might wish, however, legitimate interests do not include preventing competition.

Background and Facts Brian Guest was a floor covering installer for Brunswick Floors, Inc. Guest signed a covenant not to compete that prohibited him for two years after termination of employment from engaging in the floor covering business in virtually any way, within an eighty-mile radius of Brunswick's location. After Guest quit Brunswick, he went to work as an independent flooring contractor. Brunswick filed a suit in a Georgia state court against Guest based on the covenant not to compete. The court ruled in part that the covenant unduly restricted Guest's right to earn a living. Brunswick appealed.

In the Words of the Court . . .
RUFFIN, Judge.

* * * *

* * * [A]n employer is permitted to include in * * * a covenant [not to compete] the territory in which the employee has in fact performed work, thus protecting itself from the unfair appropriation of good will and information acquired in the course of that work. In contrast, [a] restriction relating to the area in which the employer does business is generally unenforceable due to overbreadth, unless the employer can show a legitimate business interest that will be protected by such an expansive geographic description.

In this case, the covenant restricts Guest from working within an 80 mile radius of Brunswick Floors' location * * * . The 80 mile radius relates to the area in which the employer, Brunswick Floors, and not the employee, Guest, did business. * * *

[Robert] Blake [the president of Brunswick] testified that "if our employees start * * * working for our competitors, then certainly our market share would face, you know, diminishing status." Avoidance of competition, however, is not a legitimate business interest.

Brunswick Floors contends the training and money expended on Guest legitimizes their interest. * * * Here, Guest's minimal training does not outweigh the substantial harm imposed by prohibiting him from installing carpet in an 80 mile radius. Thus, we find this to be an overbroad territorial limitation.

Case 12.3 Continued

> We also find the scope of activity prohibited in the non-compete provision
> is overbroad. * * * This imposes a greater limitation on the employee than
> is necessary because [Guest] is prohibited from being an officer or director
> or owning stock in other companies, activities which are very different from
> [his] work as [a floor covering installer].

Decision and Remedy The Court of Appeals of Georgia held that a covenant not to compete is unenforceable if it bars an employee from engaging in the employer's business in virtually any way within the area in which the employer does business. The court affirmed the decision of the lower court.

For Critical Analysis—Technological Consideration *Should these same limits apply to employers who do business only on the Internet?*

Unconscionable Contracts or Clauses. Ordinarily, a court does not look at the fairness or equity of a contract; in other words, it does not inquire into the adequacy of consideration. Persons are assumed to be reasonably intelligent, and the court does not come to their aid just because they have made unwise or foolish bargains. In certain circumstances, however, bargains are so oppressive that the courts relieve innocent parties of part or all of their duties. Such a bargain is called an **unconscionable contract** (or **unconscionable clause**). Both the Uniform Commercial Code (UCC) and the Uniform Consumer Credit Code (UCCC) embody the unconscionability concept—the former with regard to the sale of goods and the latter with regard to consumer loans and the waiver of rights.[13] The concept is now applied to common law contracts as well.

Contracts entered into because of one party's vastly superior bargaining power may be deemed unconscionable. These situations usually involve an **adhesion contract,** which is a contract drafted by the dominant party and then presented to the other—the adhering party—on a "take it or leave it" basis.[14]

Exculpatory Clauses. Often closely related to the concept of unconscionability are **exculpatory clauses,** defined as clauses that release a party from liability in the event of monetary or physical injury, *no matter who is at fault.* Indeed, some courts refer to such clauses in terms of unconscionability. • Example 12.23 Suppose that Madison Manufacturing Company hires a laborer and has him sign a contract containing the following clause:

> Said employee hereby agrees with employer, in consideration of such employment, that he will take upon himself all risks incident to his position and will in no case hold the company liable for any injury or damage he may sustain, in his person or otherwise, by accidents or injuries in the factory, or which may result from defective machinery or carelessness or misconduct of himself or any other employee in service of the employer.

Unconscionable Contract (or Unconscionable Clause) A contract or clause that is void on the basis of public policy because one party, as a result of his or her disproportionate bargaining power, is forced to accept terms that are unfairly burdensome and that unfairly benefit the dominating party.

Adhesion Contract A standard-form contract, such as that between a large retailer and a consumer, in which the stronger party dictates the terms.

Exculpatory Clause A clause that releases the contractual party from liability in the event of a monetary or physical injury, no matter who is at fault.

---

13. See, for example, UCC Sections 2–302 and 2–719 (and UCCC Sections 5.108 and 1.107).
14. See, for example, *Henningsen v. Bloomfield Motors, Inc.,* 32 N.J. 358, 161 A.2d 69 (1960).

This contract provision attempts to remove Madison's potential liability for injuries occurring to the employee, and it would usually be held contrary to public policy.[15]

Generally, an exculpatory clause will not be enforced if the party seeking its enforcement is involved in a business that is important to the public interest. These businesses include public utilities, common carriers, and banks. Because of the essential nature of these services, the companies offering them have an advantage in bargaining strength and could insist that anyone contracting for their services agree not to hold them liable. This would tend to relax their carefulness and increase the number of injuries. Imagine the results, for example, if all exculpatory clauses in contracts between airlines and their passengers were enforced.

Exculpatory clauses may be enforced, however, when the parties seeking their enforcement are not involved in businesses considered important to the public interest. These businesses have included health clubs, amusement parks, horse-rental concessions, golf-cart concessions, and skydiving organizations. Because these services are not essential, the firms offering them are sometimes considered to have no relative advantage in bargaining strength, and anyone contracting for their services is considered to do so voluntarily.

THE EFFECT OF ILLEGALITY In general, an illegal contract is void: the contract is deemed never to have existed, and the courts will not aid either party. In most illegal contracts, both parties are considered to be equally at fault—*in pari delicto*. The general rule is that neither party to an illegal bargain can sue for breach and neither can recover for performance rendered. There are some exceptions to this rule, however, which we look at here.

Justifiable Ignorance of the Facts. When one of the parties to a contract is relatively innocent (has no knowledge or any reason to know that the contract is illegal), that party can often obtain restitution or recovery of benefits conferred in a partially executed contract. The courts do not enforce the contract but do allow the parties to return to their original positions. It is also possible for an innocent party who has fully performed under the contract to enforce the contract against the guilty party.

• **Example 12.24** A trucking company contracts with Gillespie to carry goods to a specific destination for a normal fee of $500. The trucker delivers the goods and later finds out that the contents of the shipped crates were illegal. Although the law specifies that the shipment, use, and sale of the goods were illegal, the trucker, being an innocent party, can still legally collect the $500 from Gillespie.•

Members of Protected Classes. When a statute protects a certain class of people, a member of that class can enforce an illegal contract even though the other party cannot. For example, there are statutes that prohibit certain employees (such as flight attendants) from working more than a specified number of hours per month. These employees thus constitute a class protected by statute. An employee who is required to work more than the maximum can recover for those extra hours of service.

---

15. For a case with similar facts, see *Little Rock & Fort Smith Railway Co. v. Eubanks,* 48 Ark. 460, 3 S.W. 808 (1887). In such a case, the exculpatory clause may also be illegal on the basis of a violation of a state workers' compensation law.

Fraud, Duress, or Undue Influence. Whenever a plaintiff has been induced to enter into an illegal bargain as a result of fraud, duress, or undue influence, he or she can either enforce the contract or recover for its value.

Third Party Rights

A valid contract—that is, a contract that meets the four requirements for a valid contract just discussed—creates certain rights and duties. If one party fails to fulfill a contractual promise, the other party is entitled to a remedy, a topic examined in Chapter 13. Because a contract is a private agreement between the parties who have entered into it, it is fitting that these parties alone should have rights and liabilities under the contract. This concept is referred to as *privity of contract,* and it establishes the basic principle that third parties have no rights in contracts to which they are not parties.

There are two important exceptions to the rule of privity of contract. One exception allows a party to a contract to transfer the rights arising from the contract to another or to free himself or herself from the duties of a contract by having another person perform them. Legally, the first of these actions is referred to as an *assignment of rights* and the second, as a *delegation of duties.* A second exception to the rule of privity of contract involves a *third party beneficiary* contract. Here, the rights of a third party against the promisor arise from the original contract, as the parties to the original contract normally make it with the intent to benefit the third party.

Assignments

In a bilateral (mutual) contract, the two parties have corresponding rights and duties. One party has a right to require the other to perform some task, and the other has a duty to perform it. The transfer of *rights* to a third person is known as an **assignment**. When rights under a contract are assigned unconditionally, the rights of the *assignor* (the party making the assignment) are extinguished.[16] The third party (the *assignee,* or party receiving the assignment) has a right to demand performance from the other original party to the contract (the *obligor*). The assignee takes only those rights that the assignor originally had.

Assignment The act of transferring to another all or part of one's rights arising under a contract.

As a general rule, all rights can be assigned. Exceptions are made, however, in special circumstances. If a statute expressly prohibits assignment, the particular right in question cannot be assigned. When a contract is *personal* in nature, the rights under the contract cannot be assigned unless all that remains is a money payment.[17] A right cannot be assigned if assignment will materially increase or alter the risk or duties of the obligor.[18] If a contract stipulates that the right cannot be assigned, then *ordinarily* it cannot be assigned.

There are several exceptions to the fourth restriction. These exceptions are as follows:

1. A contract cannot prevent an assignment of the right to receive money. This exception exists to encourage the free flow of money and credit in modern business settings.

---

16. *Restatement (Second) of Contracts,* Section 317.
17. *Restatement (Second) of Contracts,* Sections 317 and 318.
18. See UCC 2–210(2).

2. The assignment of rights in real estate often cannot be prohibited, because such a prohibition is contrary to public policy. Prohibitions of this kind are called restraints against **alienation** (transfer of land ownership).

3. The assignment of *negotiable instruments* (checks and certain other items) cannot be prohibited.

4. In a contract for the sale of goods, the right to receive damages for breach of contract or for payment of an account owed may be assigned even though the sales contract prohibits such assignment.[19]

In the following case, the central issue was whether a covenant not to compete contained in an employment contract could be assigned.

---

19. See UCC 2–210(2).

Case 12.4 ● Reynolds and Reynolds Co. v. Hardee

United States District Court,
Eastern District of Virginia, 1996.
932 F.Supp. 149.

Background and Facts Thomas Hardee worked for Jordan Graphics, Inc., as a sales representative under an employment contract that included a covenant not to compete. Reynolds and Reynolds Company contracted to buy most of Jordan's assets. On the day of the sale, Jordan terminated Hardee's employment. Reynolds offered Hardee a new contract that contained a more restrictive covenant not to compete. Hardee rejected the offer and began selling in competition with Reynolds. Reynolds filed a suit in a federal district court against Hardee, seeking, among other things, to enforce the covenant not to compete that was in the contract between Hardee and Jordan. Hardee filed a motion to dismiss the case, asserting that Reynolds was not an assignee of that contract and could not enforce it.

In the Words of the Court . . .
REBECCA BEACH SMITH, District Judge.

* * * *

* * * [C]ontracts for personal services are not assignable, unless both parties agree to the assignment. Defendant's [Hardee's] Employment Agreement with Jordan [was] clearly a contract for personal services, based on trust and confidence. Defendant's position involved direct sales to clients; he acted as Jordan's agent in its dealings with customers. A person in such a position must necessarily obtain the trust and confidence of his or her employer. Defendant also placed considerable trust in Jordan by even agreeing to the non-compete clause, namely trusting that Jordan would not fire him and then invoke the covenant not to compete.

* * * *

* * * Without question, an employment contract of the sort involved in this case is not assignable * * * .

Decision and Remedy The court found that Reynolds was not an assignee of the contract between Hardee and Jordan and thus could not enforce it. The court dismissed this part of Reynolds's claim.

For Critical Analysis—Social Consideration *What interests must a court balance when deciding whether a covenant not to compete is assignable?*

Delegations

Just as a party can transfer rights to a third party through an assignment, a party can also transfer duties. Duties are not assigned, however; they are *delegated*. Normally, a **delegation of duties** does not relieve the party making the delegation (the *delegator*) of the obligation to perform in the event that the party to whom the duty has been delegated (the *delegatee*) fails to perform. No special form is required to create a valid delegation of duties. As long as the delegator expresses an intention to make the delegation, it is effective; the delegator need not even use the word *delegate*.

As a general rule, any duty can be delegated. There are, however, some exceptions to this rule. Delegation is prohibited in the following circumstances:

1. When performance depends on the *personal* skill or talents of the obligor.
2. When special trust has been placed in the obligor.
3. When performance by a third party will vary materially from that expected by the obligee (the one to whom performance is owed) under the contract.
4. When the contract expressly prohibits delegation.

If a delegation of duties is enforceable, the *obligee* (the one to whom performance is owed) must accept performance from the delegatee (the one to whom the duties are delegated). The obligee can legally refuse performance from the delegatee only if the duty is one that cannot be delegated. A valid delegation of duties does not relieve the delegator of obligations under the contract.[20] Thus, if the delegatee fails to perform, the delegator is still liable to the obligee.

> **Delegation of Duties** The act of transferring to another all or part of one's duties arising under a contract.

> **Compare** In an assignment, the assignor's original contract rights are extinguished after assignment. In a delegation, the delegator remains liable for performance under the contract if the delegatee fails to perform.

Third Party Beneficiaries

To have contractual rights, a person normally must be a party to the contract. In other words, privity of contract must exist. As mentioned earlier in this chapter, an exception to the doctrine of privity exists when the original parties to the contract intend at the time of contracting that the contract performance directly benefit a third person. In this situation, the third person becomes a **third party beneficiary** of the contract. As an **intended beneficiary** of the contract, the third party has legal rights and can sue the promisor directly for breach of the contract.

The benefit that an **incidental beneficiary** receives from a contract between two parties is unintentional. Therefore, an incidental beneficiary cannot enforce a contract to which he or she is not a party. • **Example 12.25** Ed contracts with Ona to build a recreational facility on Ona's land. Once the facility is constructed, it will greatly enhance the property values in the neighborhood. If Ed subsequently refuses to build the facility, Tandy, Ona's neighbor, cannot enforce the contract against Ed.•

> **Third Party Beneficiary** One for whose benefit a promise is made in a contract but who is not a party to the contract.

> **Intended Beneficiary** A third party for whose benefit a contract is formed; an intended beneficiary can sue the promisor if such a contract is breached.

> **Incidental Beneficiary** A third party who incidentally benefits from a contract but whose benefit was not the reason the contract was formed; an incidental beneficiary has no rights in a contract and cannot sue to have the contract enforced.

---

20. *Crane Ice Cream Co. v. Terminal Freezing & Heating Co.*, 147 Md. 588, 128 A. 280 (1925).

Key Terms

(Continued)

Key Terms

Chapter Summary • Contract Formation

The Law Governing Contracts (See pages 318–319.)	1. **Common law**—Governs many aspects of contract law. In applying the common law to contracts, courts often are guided by the *Restatement (Second) of Contracts*, which is a nonstatutory, authoritative exposition of the common law of contracts.
	2. **Article 2 of the Uniform Commercial Code (UCC)**—Modifies the common law for contracts for the sale of goods (sales contracts). If the common law has not been modified by Article 2, then the common law governs; when the common law has been modified by Article 2, then Article 2 governs.
The Function of Contracts (See page 319.)	Contract law establishes what kinds of promises will be legally binding and supplies procedures for enforcing legally binding promises, or agreements.
Types of Contracts (See pages 319–323.)	1. **Bilateral**—A promise for a promise.
	2. **Unilateral**—A promise for an act (acceptance is the completed—or substantial—performance of the act).
	3. **Express**—Formed by words (oral, written, or a combination).
	4. **Implied in fact**—Formed by the conduct of the parties.
	5. **Quasi contract (contract implied in law)**—Imposed by law to prevent unjust enrichment.
	6. **Executed**—A fully performed contract.
	7. **Executory**—A contract not yet fully performed.
	8. **Valid**—The contract has the necessary contractual elements of offer and acceptance, consideration, parties with legal capacity, and having been made for a legal purpose.
	9. **Void**—No contract exists, or there is a contract without legal obligations.
	10. **Voidable**—One party has the option of avoiding or enforcing the contractual obligation.
	11. **Unenforceable**—A contract exists, but it cannot be enforced because of a legal defense.

Chapter Summary • Contract Formation

AGREEMENT

Requirements of the Offer (See pages 324–327.)	1. **Intent**—There must be a serious, objective intention by the offeror to become bound by the offer. Nonoffer situations include (a) expressions of opinion; (b) statements of intention; (c) preliminary negotiations; and (d) generally, advertisements, catalogues, and circulars.
	2. **Definiteness**—The terms of the offer must be sufficiently definite to be ascertainable by the parties or by a court.
	3. **Communication**—The offer must be communicated to the offeree.
Termination of the Offer (See pages 327–329.)	1. **By action of the parties**—An offer can be revoked or rejected at any time before acceptance without liability. A counteroffer is a rejection of the original offer and the making of a new offer.
	2. **By operation of law**—An offer can terminate by (a) lapse of time, (b) destruction of the specific subject matter of the offer, (c) death or incompetence of the parties, or (d) supervening illegality.
Acceptance (See pages 329–330.)	1. Can be made only by the offeree or the offeree's agent.
	2. Must be unequivocal. Under the common law (mirror image rule), if new terms or conditions are added to the acceptance, it will be considered a counteroffer.

CONSIDERATION

Elements of Consideration (See page 330.)	Consideration is broken down into two parts: (1) something of *legally sufficient value* must be given in exchange for the promise, and (2) there must be a *bargained-for exchange*. To be legally sufficient, consideration must involve a legal detriment to the promisee, a legal benefit to the promisor, or both. One incurs a legal detriment by doing (or refraining from doing) something that one had no prior legal duty to do (or to refrain from doing).
Adequacy of Consideration (See pages 330–331.)	Adequacy of consideration relates to "how much" consideration is given and whether a fair bargain was reached. Courts will inquire into the adequacy of consideration (if the consideration is legally sufficient) only when fraud, undue influence, duress, a gift, or unconscionability may be involved.
Contracts That Lack Consideration (See pages 331–333.)	Consideration is lacking in the following situations:
	1. **Preexisting duty**—Consideration is not legally sufficient if one is either by law or by contract under a preexisting duty to perform the action being offered as consideration for a new contract.
	2. **Past consideration**—Actions or events that have already taken place do not constitute legally sufficient consideration.
	3. **Illusory promises**—When the nature or extent of performance is too uncertain, the promise is rendered illusory (without consideration and unenforceable).
Promissory Estoppel (See pages 333–335.)	When a promisor reasonably expects a promise to induce definite and substantial action or forbearance by the promisee, and the promisee does act in reliance on the promise, the promise is binding if injustice can be avoided only by enforcement of the promise.

(Continued)

Chapter Summary • Contract Formation, *Continued*

CAPACITY

Minors
(See pages 335–337.)

Contracts with minors are voidable at the option of the minor. When disaffirming executed contracts, the minor has a duty to return received goods if they are still in the minor's control or (in some states) to pay their reasonable value.

Intoxicated Persons
(See page 337.)

1. A contract entered into by an intoxicated person is voidable at the option of the intoxicated person if the person was sufficiently intoxicated to lack mental capacity, even if the intoxication was voluntary.

2. A contract with an intoxicated person is enforceable if, despite being intoxicated, the person understood the legal consequences of entering into the contract.

Mentally Incompetent Persons
(See page 338.)

1. A contract made by a person adjudged by a court to be mentally incompetent is void.

2. A contract made by a mentally incompetent person not adjudged by a court to be mentally incompetent is voidable at the option of the mentally incompetent person.

LEGALITY

Contracts Contrary to Statute
(See pages 338–341.)

1. **Usury**—Occurs when a lender makes a loan at an interest rate above the lawful maximum. The maximum rate of interest varies from state to state.

2. **Gambling**—Gambling contracts that contravene (go against) state statutes are deemed illegal and thus void.

3. **Sabbath (Sunday) laws**—Laws prohibiting the formation or the performance of certain contracts on Sunday. Such laws vary widely from state to state, and many states do not enforce them.

4. **Licensing statutes**—Contracts entered into by persons who do not have a license, when one is required by statute, will not be enforceable *unless* the underlying purpose of the statute is to raise government revenues (and not to protect the public from unauthorized practitioners).

Contracts Contrary to Public Policy
(See pages 341–344.)

1. **Contracts in restraint of trade**—Contracts to reduce or restrain free competition are illegal. An exception is a *covenant not to compete*. It is usually enforced by the courts if the terms are ancillary to a contract (such as a contract for the sale of a business or an employment contract) and are reasonable as to time and area of restraint.

2. **Unconscionable contracts and clauses**—When a contract or contract clause is so unfair that it is oppressive to one party, it can be deemed unconscionable; as such, it is illegal and cannot be enforced.

3. **Exculpatory clauses**—An exculpatory clause is a clause that releases a party from liability in the event of monetary or physical injury, no matter who is at fault. In certain situations, exculpatory clauses may be contrary to public policy and thus unenforceable.

THIRD PARTY RIGHTS

Assignment
(See pages 345–346.)

1. An assignment is the transfer of rights under a contract to a third party. The party assigning the rights is the *assignor*, and the party to whom the rights are assigned

Chapter Summary • Contract Formation

Assignment— continued	is the *assignee*. The assignee has a right to demand performance from the other original party to the contract. 2. Generally, all rights can be assigned, except in the following circumstances: **a.** When assignment is expressly prohibited by statute (for example, workers' compensation benefits).
Delegation (See page 347.)	A delegation is the transfer of duties under a contract to a third party (the delegatee), who then assumes the obligation of performing the contractual duties previously held by the one making the delegation (the delegator). A valid delegation of duties does not relieve the delegator of obligations under the contract. If the delegatee fails to perform, the delegator is still liable to the obligee.
Third Party Beneficiaries (See page 347.)	A third party beneficiary contract is one made for the purpose of benefiting a third party. 1. **Intended beneficiary**—One for whose benefit a contract is created. When the promisor (the one making the contractual promise that benefits a third party) fails to perform as promised, the third party can sue the promisor directly. 2. **Incidental beneficiary**—A third party who indirectly (incidentally) benefits from a contract but for whose benefit the contract was not specifically intended. Incidental beneficiaries have no rights to the benefits received and cannot sue to have the contract enforced.

For Review

1. What is the difference between a void contract and a voidable contract?

2. What are the four basic elements necessary to the formation of a valid contract?

3. What elements are necessary for an effective offer? What are some examples of nonoffers?

4. What is consideration? What is required for consideration to be legally sufficient?

5. Generally, a minor can disaffirm any contract. What are some exceptions to this rule?

Questions and Case Problems

12–1. Express versus Implied Contracts. Suppose that McDougal, a local businessperson, is a good friend of Krunch, the owner of a local candy store. Every day on his lunch hour McDougal goes into Krunch's candy store and spends about five minutes looking at the candy. After examining Krunch's candy and talking with Krunch, McDougal usually buys one or two candy bars. One afternoon, McDougal goes into Krunch's candy shop, looks at the candy, and picks up a $1 candy bar. Seeing that Krunch is very busy, he waves the candy bar at Krunch without saying a word and walks out. Is there a contract? If so, classify it within the categories presented in this chapter.

12–2. Contract Classification. Jennifer says to her neighbor, Gordon, "On completion of mowing my lawn, I'll pay you $25." Gordon orally accepts her offer. Is there a contract? Is Jennifer's offer intended to create a bilateral or a unilateral contract? What is the legal significance of the distinction?

12–3. Consideration. Ben hired Lewis to drive his racing car in a race. Tuan, a friend of Lewis, promised to pay Lewis $3,000 if he won the race. Lewis won the race, but Tuan refused to pay the $3,000. Tuan contended that no legally binding contract had been formed, because he had received no consideration from Lewis for his promise to pay the $3,000. Lewis sued Tuan for breach of contract, arguing that winning the race was the consideration given in exchange for Tuan's promise to pay the $3,000. What rule of law discussed in this chapter supports Tuan's claim? Explain.

12–4. Acceptance. On Saturday, Arthur mailed Tanya an offer to sell his car to her for $2,000. On Monday, having changed his mind and not having heard from Tanya, Arthur sent her a letter revoking his offer. On Wednesday, before she had received Arthur's letter of revocation, Tanya mailed a letter of acceptance to Arthur. When Tanya demanded that Arthur sell his car to her as promised, Arthur claimed that no contract existed because he had revoked his offer prior to Tanya's acceptance. Is Arthur correct? Explain.

12–5. Contracts by Minors. Kalen is a seventeen-year-old minor who has just graduated from high school. He is attending a university two hundred miles from home and has contracted to rent an apartment near the university for one year at $500 per month. He is working at a convenience store to earn enough money to be self-supporting. After living in the apartment and paying monthly rent for four months, a dispute arises between him and the landlord. Kalen, still a minor, moves out and returns the key to the landlord. The landlord wants to hold Kalen liable for the balance of the payments due under the lease. Discuss fully Kalen's liability in this situation.

12–6. Offers versus Nonoffers. The Olivers were planning to sell some of their ranch land and mentioned this fact to Southworth, a neighbor. Southworth expressed interest in purchasing the property and later notified the Olivers that he had the money available to buy it. The Olivers told Southworth they would let him know shortly about the details concerning the sale. The Olivers later sent a letter to Southworth—and (unknown to Southworth) to several other neighbors—giving information about the sale, including the price, the location of the property, and the amount of acreage involved. When Southworth received the letter, he sent a letter to the Olivers "accepting" their offer. The Olivers stated that the information letter had not been intended as an "offer" but merely as a starting point for negotiations. Southworth brought suit against the Olivers to enforce the "contract." Did a contract exist? Why or why not? Explain fully. [*Southworth v. Oliver,* 284 Or. 361, 587 P.2d 994 (1978)]

12–7. Gambling Contracts. No law prohibits citizens in a state that does not sponsor a state-operated lottery from purchasing lottery tickets in a state that does have such a lottery. Because Georgia did not have a state-operated lottery, Talley and several other Georgia resi-

dents allegedly agreed to purchase a ticket in a lottery sponsored by Kentucky and to share the proceeds if they won. They did win, but apparently Talley had difficulty collecting his share of the proceeds. In Talley's suit to obtain his share of the funds, a Georgia trial court held that the "gambling contract" was unenforceable because it was contrary to Georgia's public policy. On appeal, how should the court rule on this issue? Discuss. [*Talley v. Mathis,* 265 Ga. 179, 453 S.E.2d 704 (1995)]

12–8. Preexisting Duty. New England Rock Services, Inc., agreed to work as a subcontractor on a sewer project on which Empire Paving, Inc., was the general contractor. For drilling and blasting a certain amount of rock, Rock Services was to be paid $29 per cubic yard or on a time-and-materials basis, whichever was less. From the beginning, Rock Services experienced problems. The primary obstacle was a heavy concentration of water, which, according to the custom in the industry, Empire should have controlled but did not. Rock Services was compelled to use more costly and time-consuming methods than anticipated, and it was unable to complete the work on time. The subcontractor asked Empire to pay for the rest of the project on a time-and-materials basis. Empire signed a modification of the original agreement. On completion of the work, Empire refused to pay Rock Services the balance due under the modification. Rock Services filed a suit in a Connecticut state court against Empire. Empire claimed that the modification lacked consideration and was thus not valid and enforceable. Is Empire right? Why or why not? [*New England Rock Services, Inc. v. Empire Paving, Inc.,* 53 Conn.App. 771, 731 A.2d 784 (1999)]

12–9. Contracts by Minors. Sergei Samsonov is a Russian and one of the top hockey players in the world. When Samsonov was seventeen years old, he signed a contract to play hockey for two seasons with the Central Sports Army Club, a Russian club known by the abbreviation CSKA. Before the start of the second season, Samsonov learned that because of a dispute between CSKA coaches, he would not be playing in Russia's premier hockey league. Samsonov hired Athletes and Artists, Inc. (A&A), an American sports agency, to make a deal with a U.S. hockey team. Samsonov signed a contract to play for the Detroit Vipers (whose corporate name was, at the time, Arena Associates, Inc.). Neither A&A nor Arena knew about the CSKA contract. CSKA filed a suit in a federal district court against Arena and others, alleging, among other things, wrongful interference with a contractual relationship. What effect will Samsonov's age have on the outcome of this suit? [*Central Sports Army Club v. Arena Associates, Inc.,* 952 F.Supp. 181 (S.D.N.Y. 1997)]

12–10. Third Party Beneficiary. John Castle and Leonard Harlan, who headed Castle Harlan, Inc., an investment firm, entered into an agreement with the federal government to buy Western Empire Federal Savings and Loan. Under the agreement, Castle Harlan was to invest a nominal amount in the bank and arrange for others to invest much more, in exchange for, among other things, a promise that for two years, Western Empire would not be subject to certain restrictions in federal regulations. The government's enforcement of other regulations against Western Empire led to its going out of business. Castle, Harlan, and the other investors filed a suit in the U.S. Court of Federal Claims against the government, alleging breach of contract. The government filed a motion to dismiss all of the plaintiffs except Castle and Harlan, on the ground that the others did not sign the contract between the government and Castle and Harlan. Is the government correct? Should the court dismiss the claims brought by the other investors? Why or why not? [*Castle v. United States*, 42 Fed.Cl. 859 (1999)]

A Question of Ethics and Social Responsibility

12–11. Bath Iron Works (BIW) offered a job to Thomas Devine, contingent on Devine's passing a drug test. The testing was conducted by NorDx, a subcontractor of Roche Biomedical Laboratories. When NorDx found that Devine's urinalysis showed the presence of opiates, a result confirmed by Roche, BIW refused to offer Devine permanent employment. Devine claimed that the ingestion of poppy seeds can lead to a positive result and that he tested positive for opiates only because of his daily consumption of poppy seed muffins. In Devine's

suit against Roche, Devine argued, among other things, that he was a third party beneficiary of the contract between his employer (BIW) and NorDx (Roche). Given this factual background, consider the following questions. [*Devine v. Roche Biomedical Laboratories*, 659 A.2d 868 (Me. 1995)]

1. Is Devine an intended third party beneficiary of the BIW-NorDx contract? In deciding this issue, should the court focus on the nature of the promises made in the contract itself or on the consequences of the contract for Devine, a third party?
2. Should employees whose job security and reputation have suffered as a result of false test results be allowed to sue the drug-testing labs for the tort of negligence? In such situations, do drug-testing labs have a duty to the employees to exercise reasonable care in conducting the tests?

For Critical Analysis

12–12. Review the list of basic requirements for contract formation given at the beginning of this chapter. In view of those requirements, analyze the relationship entered into when a student enrolls in a college or university. Has a contract been formed? If so, is it a bilateral contract or a unilateral contract? Discuss.

Interacting with the Internet

Online Legal Research Exercises

Go to **http://leet. westbuslaw.com**, the Web site that accompanies this text. Select "Interactive Study Center," and then click on "Chapter 12." There you will find the following Internet research exercises that you can perform to learn more about contracts:

Activity 12–1: Minors and the Law
Activity 12–2: Promissory Estoppel

Before the Test

Go to **http://leet. westbuslaw.com**, the Web site that accompanies this text. Select "Interactive Quizzes." You will find a number of interactive questions relating to this chapter.

Contract Defenses, Discharge, and Remedies

chapter objectives

After reading this chapter, you should be able to:

1. Describe the circumstances in which an otherwise valid contract may be unenforceable.

2. Summarize the ways in which contractual obligations can be discharged.

3. Define the different types of damages that may be obtainable on the breach of a contract.

4. Indicate the usual measure of damages for breach of various types of contracts.

5. List the equitable remedies that may be granted by courts, and indicate when they will be granted.

contents

Breach of Contract The failure, without legal excuse, of a promisor to perform the obligations of a contract.

A s the Athenian political leader Solon instructed centuries ago, a contract will not be broken so long as "it is to the advantage of both" parties not to break it. Normally, the reason a person enters into a contract with another is to secure an advantage, and parties usually perform their contractual obligations to enjoy the advantages gained through contracts. Sometimes, however, a party may decide that he or she does not want to, or cannot, perform as promised. When this happens, the party might claim that the contract should not be enforced because he or she did not genuinely assent to its terms. If the contract was oral, the party may assert that even though the contract may be valid (meet all of the requirements for a valid contract specified in Chapter 12), it is nonetheless unenforceable because the contract is one that is required by law to be in writing. Essentially, these types of claims are defenses to contract enforceability—a topic we examine in the opening pages of this chapter.

Alternatively, when it is no longer advantageous for a party to fulfill his or her contractual obligations, the contract may be breached. A **breach of contract** occurs when a party fails to perform part or all of the required duties under a contract. Once a party fails to perform or performs inadequately, the other party—the nonbreaching party—can choose one or more of several remedies. As discussed in Chapter 1, courts distinguish between *remedies at law* and *remedies in equity,* or equitable remedies. Today, the remedy at law is normally money damages. Equitable remedies include rescission and restitution, specific performance, and reformation.

Bear in mind that parties usually fulfill their contractual promises, and thus *discharge* their obligations under the contract. In this chapter, after discussing the defenses to contract formation or enforceability, we look at the ways in which contracts can be discharged. We then examine the remedies available to nonbreaching parties when contracts are breached.

Defenses to Contract Enforceability

A contract has been entered into by two parties, each with full legal capacity and for a legal purpose. The contract is also supported by consideration. Nonetheless, the contract may be unenforceable if the parties have not genuinely assented to the terms. Lack of genuine assent is a defense to the enforcement of a contract.

A contract that is otherwise valid may also be unenforceable if it is not in the proper form. For example, if a contract is required by law to be in writing, and there is no written evidence of the contract, it may not be enforceable.

Genuineness of Assent

Genuineness of assent may be lacking because of mistake, misrepresentation, undue influence, or duress. Generally, a party who demonstrates that he or she did not genuinely assent to the terms of a contract can choose either to carry out the contract or to rescind (cancel) it, and thus avoid the entire transaction.

MISTAKES Generally, courts distinguish between *mistakes as to judgment of market value or conditions* and *mistakes as to fact.* Only the latter normally have legal significance.

• **Example 13.1** Suppose that Jud Wheeler contracts to buy ten acres of land because he believes that he can resell the land at a profit to Bart. Can Jud escape his contractual obligations if it later turns out that he was mistaken? Not likely. Jud's overestimation of the value of the land or of Bart's interest in it is an ordinary risk of business for which a court will not normally provide relief. Now suppose that Jud purchases a painting of a landscape from Roth's Gallery. Both Jud and Roth believe that the painting is by the artist Van Gogh. Jud later discovers that the painting is a very clever fake. Because neither Jud nor Roth was aware of this fact when they made their deal, Jud can rescind the contract and recover the purchase price of the painting.•

Mistakes occur in two forms—*unilateral* and *bilateral (mutual)*. A unilateral mistake is made by only one of the contracting parties; a mutual mistake is made by both.

Unilateral Mistakes. A unilateral mistake involves some *material fact*—that is, a fact important to the subject matter of the contract. In general, a unilateral mistake does not afford the mistaken party any right to relief from the contract. In other words, the contract normally is enforceable.[1] • **Example 13.2** Ellen intends to sell her motor home for $17,500. When she learns that Chin is interested in buying a used motor home, she faxes him an offer to sell her vehicle to him, but when typing the fax, she mistakenly keys in the price of $15,700. Chin writes back, accepting Ellen's offer. Even though Ellen intended to sell her motor home for $17,500, she has made a unilateral mistake and is bound by contract to sell the vehicle to Chin for $15,700.•

> **Be Careful** What a party to a contract knows or should know can determine whether the contract is enforceable.

Mutual Mistakes. When both parties are mistaken about the same material fact, the contract can be rescinded by either party.[2] Note that, as with unilateral mistakes, the mistake must be about a *material fact* (one that is important and central to the contract). If, instead, a mutual mistake concerns the later market value or quality of the object of the contract, the contract normally can be enforced by either party. This rule is based on the theory that both parties assume certain risks when they enter into a contract. Without this rule, almost any party who did not receive what he or she considered a fair bargain could argue bilateral mistake. In essence, this would make adequacy of consideration a factor in determining whether a contract existed, and as discussed previously, the courts normally do not inquire into the adequacy of the consideration.

A word or term in a contract may be subject to more than one reasonable interpretation. In that situation, if the parties to the contract attach materially different meanings to the term, their mutual misunderstanding may allow the contract to be rescinded, or canceled. The following classic case on mutual misunderstanding involved a ship named *Peerless* that was to sail from Bombay with certain cotton goods on board. More than one ship named *Peerless* sailed from Bombay that winter, however.

> **"Mistakes are the inevitable lot of mankind."**
>
> Sir George Jessel, 1824–1883
> (English jurist)

---

1. *The Restatement (Second) of Contracts,* Section 153, liberalizes the general rule to take into account the modern trend of allowing avoidance in some circumstances even though only one party has been mistaken.
2. *Restatement (Second) of Contracts,* Section 152.

Case 13.1 ● Raffles v. Wichelhaus

Court of Exchequer, England, 1864.
159 Eng.Rep. 375.

Historical and Political Setting *Before the Civil War, the states in the southern United States were largely agricultural. By the mid-nineteenth century, the staple of this agricultural area had become cotton. Cotton was important to the economy of the South and to the economy of the European textile industry, which by 1860 was booming. In the 1860s, when the southern states seceded from the United States to form the Confederate States, the United States announced a blockade of southern ports. The states of the Confederacy knew that cotton was important to the European economy, and they were confident that Europe would exert pressure on the United States to lift the blockade. Instead, to obtain cotton, European merchants turned to other sources, including India.*

Background and Facts Wichelhaus purchased a shipment of cotton from Raffles to arrive on a ship called the *Peerless* from Bombay, India. Wichelhaus meant a ship called the *Peerless* sailing from Bombay in October; Raffles meant another ship called the *Peerless* sailing from Bombay in December. When the goods arrived on the December *Peerless*, Raffles delivered them to Wichelhaus. By that time, however, Wichelhaus was no longer willing to accept them.

In the Words of the Court . . .
PER CURIAM [by the whole court].

* * * *

There is nothing on the face of the contract to show that any particular ship called the "Peerless" was meant; but the moment it appears that two ships called the "Peerless" were about to sail from Bombay there is a latent ambiguity * * * . That being so, there was no consensus * * * , and therefore no binding contract.

Decision and Remedy The judgment was for the defendant, Wichelhaus. The court held that no mutual assent existed, because each party attached a materially different meaning to an essential term of the written contract—that is, a mutual mistake of fact had occurred.

For Critical Analysis—Social Consideration *What policy considerations underlie the general rule that contracts involving mutual mistakes of fact may be rescinded, whereas contracts involving unilateral mistakes of fact may not be?*

> "It was beautiful and simple as all truly great swindles are."
>
> O. Henry, 1862–1910
> (American author)

FRAUDULENT MISREPRESENTATION Although fraud is a tort, the presence of fraud also affects the genuineness of the innocent party's consent to a contract. When an innocent party consents to a contract induced by fraud, the contract usually can be avoided, because he or she has not *voluntarily* consented to the terms.[3] Normally, the innocent party can either rescind (cancel) the contract and be restored to his or her original position or enforce the contract and seek damages for injuries resulting from the fraud.

Typically, there are three elements of fraud:

1. A misrepresentation of a material fact must occur.
2. There must be an intent to deceive.
3. The innocent party must justifiably rely on the misrepresentation.

Additionally, to collect damages, a party must have been injured as a result of the misrepresentation.

---

3. *Restatement (Second) of Contracts*, Sections 163 and 164.

Ordinarily, neither party to a contract has a duty to come forward and disclose facts, and a contract normally will not be set aside because certain pertinent information has not been volunteered. Generally, however, if a *serious* defect or a *serious* potential problem is known to the seller but cannot reasonably be suspected to be known by the buyer, the seller may have a duty to speak.

One of the challenging problems facing the states and the federal government today is how to curb online fraud. For a discussion of this issue, see this chapter's *Legal E-nvironment* feature.

> **Remember** To collect damages in almost any lawsuit, there must be some sort of injury.

INNOCENT MISREPRESENTATION As mentioned in Chapter 9, misrepresentation may also be innocently made. If a person makes a statement that he or she believes to be true but that actually misrepresents material facts, *innocent misrepresentation,* not fraud, has occurred. In this situation, the aggrieved party can rescind (cancel) the contract but usually cannot seek damages.
● **Example 13.3** Parris tells Roberta that a tract of land contains 250 acres. Parris does not know that the tract contains only 215 acres and is thus mistaken. Roberta is induced by the statement to form a contract to purchase the land. Even though the misrepresentation is innocent, Roberta can avoid the contract if the misrepresentation is material.●

Legal *e*-nvironment

Online Fraud

The expanding world of e-commerce has created many benefits for Americans. It has also led to some challenging problems, including fraud conducted via the Internet. In the past few years, a number of federal agencies have been tackling this problem.

One of these agencies is the Federal Trade Commission (FTC). The FTC is an administrative agency established by Congress in 1914 to enforce laws prohibiting unfair and deceptive trade practices, including deceptive advertising. For years, the FTC has fought deceptive advertising in printed materials and in radio and television broadcasts. Since the late 1990s, it has spent a considerable portion of its resources on fighting deceptive advertising on the Internet. The FTC has moved particularly quickly on commercial Internet fraud schemes. It has even provided "hot links" on Web sites that it has targeted. A hot link takes the user to the FTC's own Web site, on which the complaint, restraining order, and other documents in the case can be read and downloaded.

Another agency fighting online fraud and false advertising is the Securities and Exchange Commission (SEC). The SEC has initiated actions against dozens of entities that have perpetrated online investment scams. One fraudulent scheme involved twenty thousand investors, who lost in all more than $3 million. Some cases have concerned false claims about the earnings potential of home-business programs, such as the claim that one could "earn $4,000 or more each month." Others have related to claims for "guaranteed credit repair."

The Department of Transportation (DOT), as well as the Food and Drug Administration (FDA), have also brought actions against purported online violators of advertising and disclosure laws. The DOT fined Virgin Airlines for failing to disclose the true price of a flight that it advertised on the Web. The FDA has not yet brought any actions against apparent online violators of regulations governing drug advertising, however. One issue that the FDA has yet to resolve is the distinction between advertising and labeling. Also, the Consumer Product Safety Commission (CPSC) has created what it calls a one-stop Web site at which it provides information that allows consumers to avoid the most obvious fraud problems on the Web and elsewhere.

For Critical Analysis: *Given the seemingly infinite number of Web sites, are government agency "watchdogs" fighting a losing battle in trying to control fraud and deceptive advertising on the Internet?*

> **Contrast** Even when there is no undue influence, a minor can avoid a contract.

UNDUE INFLUENCE Undue influence arises from relationships in which one party can greatly influence another party, thus overcoming that party's free will. Minors and elderly people, for example, are often under the influence of guardians. If a guardian induces a young or elderly *ward* (a person placed by a court under the care of a guardian) to enter into a contract that benefits the guardian, the guardian may have exerted undue influence.

Undue influence can arise from a number of confidential relationships or relationships founded on trust, including attorney-client, physician-patient, guardian-ward, parent-child, husband-wife, and trustee-beneficiary relationships. The essential feature of undue influence is that the party being taken advantage of does not, in reality, exercise free will in entering into a contract. A contract entered into under excessive or undue influence lacks genuine assent and is therefore voidable.[4]

DURESS Assent to the terms of a contract is not genuine if one of the parties is *forced* into the agreement. Forcing a party to enter into a contract because of the fear created by threats is legally defined as *duress*.[5] In addition, blackmail or extortion to induce consent to a contract constitutes duress. Duress is both a defense to the enforcement of a contract and a ground for rescission, or cancellation, of a contract. Therefore, a party who signs a contract under duress can choose to carry out the contract or to avoid the entire transaction. (The wronged party usually has this choice in cases in which assent is not real or genuine.)

The Statute of Frauds—Requirement of a Writing

A commonly used defense to the enforceability of an oral contract is that it is required to be in writing. Today, almost every state has a statute that stipulates what types of contracts must be in writing or at least evidenced by a legally sufficient memorandum. In this text, we refer to such statutes as the **Statute of Frauds.** The primary purpose of the statute is to ensure that there is reliable evidence of the existence and terms of certain classes of contracts deemed historically to be important or complex.

> **Statute of Frauds** A state statute under which certain types of contracts must be in writing to be enforceable.

CONTRACTS INVOLVING TRANSFERS OF INTERESTS IN LAND Land is real property, which includes not only land but all physical objects that are permanently attached to the soil, such as buildings, plants, trees, and the soil itself. Under the Statute of Frauds, a contract involving the transfer of an interest in land, to be enforceable, must be evidenced by a writing.[6] ● **Example 13.4** If Carol contracts orally to sell Seaside Shelter to Axel but later decides not to sell, Axel cannot enforce the contract. Similarly, if Axel refuses to close the deal, Carol cannot force Axel to pay for the land by bringing a lawsuit. The Statute of Frauds is a *defense* to the enforcement of this type of oral contract.●

A contract for the sale of land ordinarily involves the entire interest in the real property, including buildings, growing crops, vegetation, minerals, timber, and anything else affixed to the land. Therefore, a *fixture* (personal property so affixed or so used as to become a part of the realty) is treated as real property.

---

4. *Restatement (Second) of Contracts,* Section 177.
5. *Restatement (Second) of Contracts,* Sections 174 and 175.
6. In some states, the contract will be enforced, however, if each party admits to the existence of the oral contract in court or admits to its existence during discovery before trial (see Chapter 3).

The Statute of Frauds requires written contracts not just for the sale of land but also for the transfer of other interests in land, such as mortgages and long-term leases.

THE ONE-YEAR RULE Contracts that cannot, *by their own terms,* be performed within one year from the day after the contract is formed must be in writing to be enforceable. Because disputes over such contracts are unlikely to occur until some time after the contracts are made, resolution of these disputes is difficult unless the contract terms have been put in writing. The one-year period begins to run *the day after the contract is made.* Exhibit 13–1 illustrates the one-year rule.

The test for determining whether an oral contract is enforceable under the one-year rule of the statute is not whether the agreement is *likely* to be performed within one year from the date of contract formation but whether performance within a year is *possible.* When performance of a contract is objectively impossible during the one-year period, the oral contract will be unenforceable.

Example 13.5 Suppose that Bankers Life orally contracts to loan $40,000 to Janet Lawrence "as long as Lawrence and Associates operates its financial consulting firm in Omaha, Nebraska." The contract does not fall within the Statute of Frauds—that is, no writing is required—because Lawrence and Associates could go out of business in one year or less. In this event, the contract would be fully performed within one year.

COLLATERAL PROMISES A **collateral promise,** or secondary promise, is one that is ancillary (subsidiary) to a principal transaction or primary contractual relationship. In other words, a collateral promise is one made by a third party to assume the debts or obligations of a primary party to a contract if that party does not perform. Any collateral promise of this nature falls under the Statute of Frauds and therefore must be in writing to be enforceable.

There is an exception. An oral promise to answer for the debt of another is covered by the Statute of Frauds *unless* the guarantor's main purpose in accepting secondary liability is to secure a personal benefit. Under the "main purpose" rule, this type of contract need not be in writing.[7] The assumption is that a court can infer from the circumstances of a case whether the "leading objective" of the promisor was to secure a personal benefit and thus, in effect, to answer for his or her own debt.

> **Collateral Promise** A secondary promise that is ancillary (subsidiary) to a principal transaction or primary contractual relationship, such as a promise made by one person to pay the debts of another if the latter fails to perform. A collateral promise normally must be in writing to be enforceable.

---

7. *Restatement (Second) of Contracts,* Section 116.

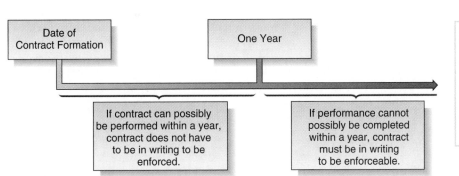

Exhibit 13–1
The One-Year Rule
A contract falls under the Statute of Frauds (must be in writing to be enforceable) if it cannot possibly be performed within one year from the day after it was formed.

PROMISES MADE IN CONSIDERATION OF MARRIAGE   A unilateral promise to pay a sum of money or to give property in consideration of a promise to marry must be in writing. If Mr. Baumann promises to pay Joe Villard $10,000 if Villard promises to marry Baumann's daughter, the promise must be in writing. The same rule applies to **prenuptial agreements**—agreements made before marriage (also called *antenuptial agreements*) that define each partner's ownership rights in the other partner's property. For example, a prospective wife may wish to limit the amount her prospective husband could obtain if the marriage ended in divorce. Prenuptial agreements made in consideration of marriage must be in writing to be enforceable.

Prenuptial Agreement An agreement made before marriage that defines each partner's ownership rights in the other partner's property. Prenuptial agreements must be in writing to be enforceable.

CONTRACTS FOR THE SALE OF GOODS   The Uniform Commercial Code (UCC) contains several Statute of Frauds provisions that require written evidence of a contract. Section 2–201 contains the major provision, which generally requires a writing or memorandum for the sale of goods priced at $500 or more. A writing that will satisfy the UCC requirement need only state the quantity term; other terms agreed on need not be stated "accurately" in the writing, as long as they adequately reflect both parties' intentions. The contract will not be enforceable, however, for any quantity greater than that set forth in the writing. In addition, the writing must be signed by the person against whom enforcement is sought. Beyond these two requirements, the writing need not designate the buyer or the seller, the terms of payment, or the price.

EXCEPTIONS TO THE STATUTE OF FRAUDS   Exceptions to the applicability of the Statute of Frauds are made in certain situations. We describe those situations here.

Partial Performance.   In cases involving contracts relating to the transfer of interests in land, if the purchaser has paid part of the price, taken possession, and made permanent improvements to the property, and if the parties cannot

---

International Perspective

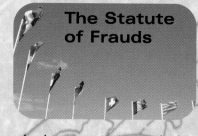

The Statute of Frauds

As you will read later in this chapter, the United Nations Convention on Contracts for the International Sale of Goods (CISG) provides rules that govern international sales contracts between countries that have ratified the convention, or agreement. Article 11 of the CISG does not incorporate any Statute of Frauds provisions. Rather, it states that a "contract for sale need not be concluded in or evidenced by writing and is not subject to any other requirements as to form."

Article 11 accords with the legal customs of most nations, in which contracts no longer need to meet certain formal or writing requirements to be enforceable. Ironically, even England, the nation that created the original Statute of Frauds in 1677, has repealed all of it except the provisions relating to collateral promises and to transfers of interests in land. Many other countries that once had such statutes have also repealed all or parts of them. Civil law countries, such as France, never have required certain types of contracts to be in writing.

For Critical Analysis: *If there were no Statute of Frauds and if a dispute arose concerning an oral agreement, how would the parties substantiate their respective positions?*

be returned to their status quo prior to the contract, a court may grant *specific performance* (performance of the contract according to its precise terms). Whether the courts will enforce an oral contract for an interest in land when partial performance has taken place is usually determined by the degree of injury that would be suffered if the court chose *not* to enforce the oral contract. In some states, mere reliance on certain types of oral contracts is enough to remove them from the Statute of Frauds.

Under the UCC, an oral contract is enforceable to the extent that a seller accepts payment or a buyer accepts delivery of the goods [UCC 2–201(3)(c)]. • **Example 13.6** If Ajax Corporation ordered by telephone twenty crates of bleach from Cloney, Inc., and repudiated the contract after ten crates had been delivered and accepted, Cloney could enforce the contract to the extent of the ten crates accepted by Ajax.•

Admissions. In some states, if a party against whom enforcement of an oral contract is sought "admits" in pleadings, testimony, or otherwise in court proceedings that a contract for sale was made, the contract will be enforceable.[8] A contract subject to the UCC will be enforceable, but only to the extent of the quantity admitted [UCC 2–201(3)(b)]. Thus, in Example 13.6, if the president of Ajax Corporation admits under oath that an oral agreement was made with Cloney, Inc., for twenty crates of bleach, the agreement will be enforceable to that extent.

Promissory Estoppel. In some states, an oral contract that would otherwise be unenforceable under the Statute of Frauds may be enforced under the doctrine of promissory estoppel, or detrimental reliance. If a promisor makes a promise on which the promisee justifiably relies to his or her detriment, a court may *estop* (prevent) the promisor from denying that a contract exists. Section 139 of the *Restatement (Second) of Contracts* provides that in these circumstances, an oral promise can be enforceable notwithstanding the Statute of Frauds if the reliance was foreseeable to the person making the promise and if injustice can be avoided only by enforcing the promise.

Special Exceptions under the UCC. Special exceptions to the applicability of the Statute of Frauds apply to sales contracts. Oral contracts for customized goods may be enforced in certain circumstances. Oral contracts *between merchants* that have been confirmed in writing may also be enforceable.

The Parol Evidence Rule

A written contract is ordinarily assumed to be the complete embodiment of the parties' agreement. This assumption underlies the **parol evidence rule,** which prohibits the introduction at trial of evidence of the parties' prior negotiations, prior agreements, or contemporaneous oral agreements if that evidence contradicts or varies the terms of written contracts. Because of the rigidity of the parol evidence rule, however, courts make several exceptions:

1. Evidence of a *subsequent modification* of a written contract can be introduced in court. Keep in mind that the oral modifications may not be

Parol Evidence Rule A substantive rule of contracts, as well as a procedural rule of evidence, under which a court will not receive into evidence the parties' prior negotiations, prior agreements, or contemporaneous oral agreements if that evidence contradicts or varies the terms of the parties' written contract.

---

8. *Restatement (Second) of Contracts*, Section 133.

enforceable if they come under the Statute of Frauds—for example, if they increase the price of the goods for sale to $500 or more or increase the term for performance to more than one year. Also, oral modifications will not be enforceable if the original contract provides that any modification must be in writing.

2. Oral evidence can be introduced in all cases to show that the contract was voidable or void (for example, induced by mistake, fraud, or misrepresentation).

3. When the terms of a written contract are ambiguous, evidence is admissible to show the meaning of the terms.

4. Evidence is admissible when the written contract is incomplete in that it lacks one or more of the essential terms. The courts allow evidence to "fill in the gaps" in the contract.

5. Under the UCC, evidence can be introduced to explain or supplement a written contract by showing a prior dealing, course of performance, or usage of trade. When buyers and sellers deal with each other over extended periods of time, certain customary practices develop. These practices are often overlooked in the writing of the contract, so courts allow the introduction of evidence to show how the parties have acted in the past. Usage of trade—practices and customs generally followed in a particular industry—also can shed light on the meaning of certain contract provisions, and thus evidence of trade usage may be admissible.

6. The parol evidence rule does not apply if the existence of the entire written contract is subject to an orally agreed-on condition. Proof of the condition does not alter or modify the written terms but affects the *enforceability* of the written contract. • **Example 13.7** Jelek agrees to purchase Armand's car for $4,000, but only if Jelek's mechanic, Frank, inspects the car and approves of the purchase. Armand agrees to this condition, but because he is leaving town for the weekend and Jelek wants to use the car (if he buys it) before Armand returns, Jelek drafts a contract of sale, and they both sign it. Frank, the mechanic, does not approve of the purchase, and when Jelek does not buy the car, Armand sues him, alleging that he breached the contract. In this case, Jelek's oral agreement did not alter or modify the terms of the written agreement but concerned whether or not the contract existed at all. •

7. When an *obvious* or *gross* clerical (or typographic) error exists that clearly would not represent the agreement of the parties, parol evidence is admissible to correct the error. • **Example 13.8** Sharon agrees to lease 1,000 square feet of office space at the current monthly rate of $3 per square foot from Stone Enterprises. The signed written lease provides for a monthly lease payment of $300 rather than the $3,000 agreed to by the parties. Because the error is obvious, Stone Enterprises would be allowed to admit parol evidence to correct the mistake. •

Contract Discharge

As mentioned earlier, normally parties perform their contractual duties. Indeed, the most common way to **discharge**, or terminate, one's contractual duties is by the **performance** of those duties. The duty to perform under a contract may be *conditioned* on the occurrence or nonoccurrence of a certain event, or the duty may be *absolute*. In addition to performance, there are numerous

Discharge The termination of an obligation. In contract law, discharge occurs when the parties have fully performed their contractual obligations or when events, conduct of the parties, or operation of the law releases the parties from performance.

Performance In contract law, the fulfillment of one's duties arising under a contract with another; the normal way of discharging one's contractual obligations.

other ways in which a contract can be discharged, including discharge by agreement of the parties and discharge based on impossibility of performance.

Discharge by Performance

The contract comes to an end when both parties fulfill their respective duties by performance of the acts they have promised. Performance can also be accomplished by tender. **Tender** is an unconditional offer to perform by a person who is ready, willing, and able to do so. Therefore, a seller who places goods at the disposal of a buyer has tendered delivery and can demand payment according to the terms of the agreement. A buyer who offers to pay for goods has tendered payment and can demand delivery of the goods. Once performance has been tendered, the party making the tender has done everything possible to carry out the terms of the contract. If the other party then refuses to perform, the party making the tender can consider the duty discharged and sue for breach of contract.

Tender An unconditional offer to perform an obligation by a person who is ready, willing, and able to do so.

COMPLETE VERSUS SUBSTANTIAL PERFORMANCE Normally, conditions expressly stated in the contract must fully occur in all aspects for *complete performance* (strict performance) of the contract to occur. Any deviation breaches the contract and discharges the other party's obligations to perform. Although in most contracts the parties fully discharge their obligations by complete performance, sometimes a party fails to fulfill all of the duties or completes the duties in a manner contrary to the terms of the contract. The issue then arises as to whether the performance was nonetheless sufficiently substantial to discharge the contractual obligations.

To qualify as *substantial performance*, the performance must not vary greatly from the performance promised in the contract, and it must create substantially the same benefits as those promised in the contract. If performance is substantial, the other party's duty to perform remains absolute (less damages, if any, for the minor deviations).[9]

PERFORMANCE TO THE SATISFACTION OF ANOTHER When the subject matter of the contract is personal, a contract to be performed to the satisfaction of one of the parties is conditioned, and performance must actually satisfy that party. • Example 13.9 Contracts for portraits, works of art, and tailoring are considered personal. Therefore, only the personal satisfaction of the party fulfills the condition—unless a jury finds the party is expressing dissatisfaction only to avoid payment or otherwise is not acting in good faith.•

MATERIAL BREACH OF CONTRACT When a breach of contract is *material*[10]—that is, when performance is not deemed substantial—the nonbreaching party is excused from the performance of contractual duties and has a cause of action to sue for damages caused by the breach. If the breach is *minor* (not material), the nonbreaching party's duty to perform can sometimes be suspended until the breach is remedied, but the duty is not entirely excused. Once the minor breach is cured, the nonbreaching party must resume performance of the contractual obligations undertaken.

"The law is not exact upon the subject, but leaves it open to a good man's judgment."

Hugo Grotius, 1583–1645
(Dutch jurist, political leader, and theologian)

---

9. For a classic case on substantial performance, see *Jacobs & Young, Inc. v. Kent*, 230 N.Y. 239, 129 N.E. 889 (1921).
10. *Restatement (Second) of Contracts*, Section 241.

A breach entitles the nonbreaching party to sue for damages, but only a material breach discharges the nonbreaching party from the contract. The policy underlying these rules is that contracts should go forward when only minor problems occur, but contracts should be terminated if major problems arise.[11]

Does preventing an employee from working constitute a breach of contract if the employer continues to pay her salary? That was the issue in the following case.

---

11. See UCC 2–612, which provides that an installment contract for the sale of goods is breached only when one or more nonconforming installments *substantially impairs* the value of the *whole* contract.

Case 13.2 ● Van Steenhouse v. Jacor Broadcasting of Colorado, Inc.

Supreme Court of Colorado, 1998.
958 P.2d 464.

Historical and Social Setting

The nature of television and radio broadcasting has changed dramatically in the 1990s. Unlike previous decades, the most popular shows in the media today are news programs and talk shows. Also unlike previous decades, competition has proliferated with the expansion of cable and satellite television and the development of the World Wide Web. As a consequence, broadcasters are constantly looking to increase the sizes of their audiences by adding or dropping programs based on their popularity at the moment.

Background and Facts Jacor Broadcasting of Colorado, Inc., owns and operates Newsradio 85 KOA.

In June 1991, Andrea Van Steenhouse signed a three-year agreement to perform as a radio talk-show host for KOA. She was to receive a base salary and a performance bonus, depending on how many people tuned into her show. In January 1994, Jacor replaced her show with Rush Limbaugh's program. Jacor paid Van Steenhouse her base salary for the rest of the term of their agreement but did not employ her as a talk-show host. Van Steenhouse filed a suit in a Colorado state court against Jacor and others, claiming, among other things, breach of contract. The court ruled that Jacor materially breached the contract and awarded Van Steenhouse an amount representing the bonus she could have received if she had not been taken off the air. The state intermediate appellate court affirmed the judgment. Jacor appealed to the Supreme Court of Colorado.

In the Words of the Court . . .
Chief Justice VOLLACK delivered the Opinion of the Court.

* * * *

Ordinarily, an employment agreement does not obligate an employer to furnish work for an employee. However, such an obligation may be inferred depending on the circumstances under which the agreement for employment is made or the nature of the employment. In particular, an obligation to furnish work arises if the employee materially benefits from performing the duties described in the agreement * * * . [W]hen an employer fails to furnish the kind of work specified in an employment agreement, the employee has a cause of action for breach of contract.

* * * *

* * * [I]n this case * * * Jacor breached the Agreement by depriving Van Steenhouse of the opportunity to perform as a talk show host on KOA. * * * As a result, Van Steenhouse lost the opportunity to build and maintain her professional marketability. In addition, Van Steenhouse lost the opportunity to earn a 1994 performance bonus.

Jacor deprived Van Steenhouse of these benefits by refusing to broadcast her show [as] specified by the clear terms of the Agreement. Accordingly, we hold that Van Steenhouse stated a valid claim for breach of contract.

Case 13.2 Continued

Decision and Remedy The Supreme Court of Colorado held that an employee's claim for breach of contract can be based solely on an employer's failure to provide an opportunity to work. The court affirmed this part of the lower court's decision.

For Critical Analysis—Social Consideration *If courts routinely held that only performance could discharge employment contracts, how would this affect employment relations?*

ANTICIPATORY REPUDIATION OF A CONTRACT Before either party to a contract has a duty to perform, one of the parties may refuse to perform his or her contractual obligations. This is called **anticipatory repudiation**.[12] When anticipatory repudiation occurs, it is treated as a material breach of contract, and the nonbreaching party is permitted to bring an action for damages immediately, even though the scheduled time for performance under the contract may still be in the future.[13] Until the nonbreaching party treats this early repudiation as a breach, however, the breaching party can retract his or her anticipatory repudiation by proper notice and restore the parties to their original obligations.

Anticipatory Repudiation
An assertion or action by a party indicating that he or she will not perform an obligation that the party is contractually obligated to perform at a future time.

There are two reasons for treating an anticipatory repudiation as a present, material breach. First, the nonbreaching party should not be required to remain ready and willing to perform when the other party has already repudiated the contract. Second, the nonbreaching party should have the opportunity to seek a similar contract elsewhere and should have the duty to do so to minimize his or her loss.

Quite often, an anticipatory repudiation occurs when a sharp fluctuation in market prices creates a situation in which performance of the contract would be extremely unfavorable to one of the parties. ● **Example 13.10** Shasta Manufacturing Company contracts to manufacture and sell 100,000 personal computers to New Age, Inc., a computer retailer with 500 outlet stores. Delivery is to be made eight months from the date of the contract. One month later, three suppliers of computer parts raise their prices to Shasta. Because of these higher prices, Shasta stands to lose $500,000 if it sells the computers to New Age at the contract price. Shasta writes to New Age, informing New Age that it cannot deliver the 100,000 computers at the agreed-on contract price. Even though you might sympathize with Shasta, its letter is an anticipatory repudiation of the contract, allowing New Age the option of treating the repudiation as a material breach and proceeding immediately to pursue remedies, even though the actual contract delivery date is still seven months away.● [14]

Remember The risks that prices will fluctuate and values will change are ordinary business risks for which the law does not provide relief.

"Agreement makes law."

(Legal maxim)

PERFORMANCE OF A SALES CONTRACT In the performance of a sales contract, the basic obligation of the seller is to transfer and deliver conforming goods. The basic obligation of the buyer is to accept and pay for conforming goods in accordance with the contract [UCC 2–301]. Overall performance

---

12. *Restatement (Second) of Contracts*, Section 253, and UCC 2–610.
13. The doctrine of anticipatory repudiation first arose in the landmark case of *Hochster v. De La Tour*, 2 Ellis and Blackburn Reports 678 (1853), when the English court recognized the delay and expense inherent in a rule requiring a nonbreaching party to wait until the time of performance before suing on an anticipatory repudiation.
14. Another illustration can be found in *Reliance Cooperage Corp. v. Treat*, 195 F.2d 977 (8th Cir. 1952).

of a sales contract is controlled by the agreement between the parties. When the contract is unclear and disputes arise, the courts look to the UCC.

Discharge by Agreement

Any contract can be discharged by the agreement of the parties. The agreement can be contained in the original contract, or the parties can form a new contract for the express purpose of discharging the original contract.

Rescission A remedy whereby a contract is canceled and the parties are returned to the positions they occupied before the contract was made; may be effected through the mutual consent of the parties, by their conduct, or by court decree.

DISCHARGE BY RESCISSION   **Rescission** is the process in which the parties cancel the contract and are returned to the positions they occupied prior to the contract's formation. For *mutual rescission* to take place, the parties must make another agreement that also satisfies the legal requirements for a contract—there must be an *offer,* an *acceptance,* and *consideration.* Ordinarily, if the parties agree to rescind the original contract, their promises *not* to perform those acts promised in the original contract will be legal consideration for the second contract.

Mutual rescission can occur in this manner when the original contract is executory on both sides (that is, neither party has completed performance). The agreement to rescind an executory contract is generally enforceable, even if it is made orally and even if the original agreement was in writing.[15] When one party has fully performed, however, an agreement to rescind the original contract is not usually enforceable. Because the performing party has received no consideration for the promise to call off the original bargain, additional consideration is necessary. Under UCC 2–209(1), however, no consideration is needed to modify a contract for a sale of goods.

Novation The substitution, by agreement, of a new contract for an old one, with the rights under the old one being terminated. Typically, there is a substitution of a new person who is responsible for the contract and the removal of the original party's rights and duties under the contract.

DISCHARGE BY NOVATION   The process of **novation** substitutes a third party for one of the original parties. Essentially, the parties to the original contract and one or more new parties all get together and agree to the substitution. The requirements of a novation are as follows:

1. The existence of a previous, valid obligation.
2. Agreement by all of the parties to a new contract.
3. The extinguishing of the old obligation (discharge of the prior party).
4. A new, valid contract.

DISCHARGE BY ACCORD AND SATISFACTION   In an *accord and satisfaction,* the parties agree to accept performance different from the performance originally promised. An *accord* is defined as an executory contract (one that has not yet been performed) to perform some act in order to satisfy an existing contractual duty that is not yet discharged.[16] A *satisfaction* is the performance of the accord agreement. An *accord* and its *satisfaction* discharge the original contractual obligation.

When Performance Is Impossible

Impossibility of Performance A doctrine under which a party to a contract is relieved of his or her duty to perform when performance becomes impossible or totally impracticable (through no fault of either party).

After a contract has been made, performance may become impossible in an objective sense. This is known as **impossibility of performance** and may discharge a contract.[17] *Objective impossibility* ("It can't be done") must be distinguished from *subjective impossibility* ("I'm sorry, I simply can't do it"). Examples of subjective impossibility include contracts in which goods cannot

---

15. Agreements to rescind contracts involving transfers of realty, however, must be evidenced by a writing. Another exception has to do with the sale of goods under the UCC, when the sales contract requires written rescission.
16. *Restatement (Second) of Contracts,* Section 281.
17. *Restatement (Second) of Contracts,* Section 261.

be delivered on time because of a freight car shortage[18] and contracts in which money cannot be paid on time because the bank is closed.[19] In effect, the non-performing party is saying, "It is impossible for *me* to perform," not "It is impossible for *anyone* to perform." Accordingly, such excuses do not discharge a contract, and the nonperforming party is normally held in breach of contract.

COMMERCIAL IMPRACTICABILITY The discharge of contractual obligations based on impossibility of performance may occur when performance becomes *commercially impracticable*—that is, much more difficult or expensive than anticipated. In such situations, courts may excuse parties from their performance obligations under the doctrine of *commercial impracticability*. For example, in one case, a court held that a contract could be discharged because a party would have to pay ten times more than the original estimate to excavate a certain amount of gravel.[20]

TEMPORARY IMPOSSIBILITY An occurrence or event that makes performance temporarily impossible operates to *suspend* performance until the impossibility ceases. Then, ordinarily, the parties must perform the contract as originally planned. If, however, the lapse of time and the change in circumstances surrounding the contract make it substantially more burdensome for the parties to perform the promised acts, the contract is discharged.

The leading case on the subject, *Autry v. Republic Productions,*[21] involved an actor who was drafted into the army in 1942. Being drafted rendered the actor's contract temporarily impossible to perform, and it was suspended until the end of the war. When the actor got out of the army, the value of the dollar had so changed that performance of the contract would have been substantially burdensome to him. Therefore, the contract was discharged.

> **"Law is a practical matter."**
>
> Roscoe Pound, 1870–1964
> (American jurist)

---

18. *Minneapolis v. Republic Creosoting Co.,* 161 Minn. 178, 201 N.W. 414 (1924).
19. *Ingham Lumber Co. v. Ingersoll & Co.,* 93 Ark. 447, 125 S.W. 139 (1910).
20. *Mineral Park Land Co. v. Howard,* 172 Cal. 289, 156 P. 458 (1916).
21. 30 Cal.2d 144, 180 P.2d 888 (1947).

Ethical Issue 13.1

Should the courts allow the defense of impossibility of performance to be used more often?

The doctrine of impossibility is applied only when the parties could not have reasonably foreseen, at the time the contract was formed, the event or events that rendered performance impossible. In some cases, it would seem that the courts go too far in holding that certain events or conditions should have been foreseen by the parties, thus precluding parties from avoiding contractual obligations under the doctrine of impossibility of performance. Yet even though the courts rarely excuse parties from performance under the doctrine of impossibility, they allow parties to raise this defense more often than they once did. Indeed, until the latter part of the nineteenth century courts were reluctant to discharge a contract even when it appeared that performance was literally impossible. Generally, the courts must balance the freedom of parties to contract as they will (and assume the risks involved) against the injustice that may result when certain contractual obligations are enforced. If the courts allowed parties to raise impossibility of performance as a defense to contractual obligations more often, freedom of contract would suffer.

> **Remember** The terms of a contract must be sufficiently definite for a court to determine the amount of damages to award.

Damages

A breach of contract entitles the nonbreaching party to sue for money damages. As you read in Chapter 9, damages are designed to compensate a party for harm suffered as a result of another's wrongful act. In the context of contract law, damages are designed to compensate the nonbreaching party for the loss of the bargain. Often, courts say that innocent parties are to be placed in the position they would have occupied had the contract been fully performed.[22]

Types of Damages

There are basically four kinds of damages: compensatory, consequential, punitive, and nominal damages.

COMPENSATORY DAMAGES As discussed in Chapter 9, *compensatory damages* compensate an injured party for injuries or damages actually sustained by that party. The nonbreaching party must prove that the actual damages arose directly from the loss of the bargain caused by the breach of contract. The amount of compensatory damages is the difference between the value of the breaching party's promised performance under the contract and the value of his or her actual performance. This amount is reduced by any loss that the injured party has avoided, however.

● **Example 13.11** Suppose that you contract with Marinot Industries to perform certain personal services exclusively for Marinot during August for a payment of $3,500. Marinot cancels the contract and is in breach. You are able to find another job during August but can only earn $1,000. You normally can sue Marinot for breach and recover $2,500 as compensatory damages. You may also recover from Marinot the amount you spent to find the other job. ● Expenses or costs that are caused directly by a breach of contract—such as those incurred to obtain performance from another source—are *incidental damages*.

The measurement of compensatory damages varies by type of contract. Certain types of contracts deserve special mention—contracts for the sale of goods, contracts for the sale of land, and construction contracts.

Sale of Goods. In a contract for the sale of goods, the usual measure of compensatory damages is an amount equal to the difference between the contract price and the market price.[23] ● **Example 13.12** Suppose that MediQuick Laboratories contracts with Cal Computer Industries to purchase ten Model X-15 computer workstations for $8,000 each. If Cal Computer fails to deliver the ten workstations, and the current market price of the workstations is $8,150, MediQuick's measure of damages is $1,500 (10 × $150). ● In cases in which the buyer breaches and the seller has not yet produced the goods, compensatory damages normally equal the lost profits on the sale, not the difference between the contract price and the market price.

Sale of Land. The measure of damages in a contract for the sale of land is ordinarily the same as it is for contracts involving the sale of goods—that is, the difference between the contract price and the market price of the land. The majority of states follow this rule regardless of whether it is the buyer or the seller who breaches the contract.

---

22. *Restatement (Second) of Contracts*, Section 347; and UCC 1–106(1).
23. That is, the difference between the contract price and the market price at the time and place at which the goods were to be delivered or tendered. See UCC 2–708 and 2–713.

PARTY IN BREACH	TIME OF BREACH	MEASUREMENT OF DAMAGES
Owner	Before construction begins	Profits (contract price less cost of materials and labor)
Owner	After construction begins	Profits plus costs incurred up to time of breach
Owner	After construction is completed	Contract price
Contractor	Before construction is completed	Generally, all costs incurred by owner to complete construction

Exhibit 13–2
Measurement of Damages—Breach of Construction Contracts

A minority of states, however, follow a different rule when the seller breaches the contract and the breach is not deliberate. An example of a non-deliberate breach of a contract to sell land occurs when a previously unknown easement (a right of use over the property of another) is discovered and renders title to the land unmarketable. (In real property law, *title* means the right to own property or the evidence of that right.) In such a situation, these states allow the prospective purchaser to recover any down payment plus any expenses incurred (such as fees for title searches or attorneys). This minority rule effectively places a purchaser in the position that he or she occupied prior to the contract of sale.

Construction Contracts. With construction contracts, the measure of damages often varies depending on which party breaches and at what stage the breach occurs. See Exhibit 13–2 for illustrations. In the following case, the issue centers on the proper measure of damages in a breached construction contract.

Case 13.3 Shadow Lakes, Inc. v. Cudlipp Construction and Development Co.

District Court of Appeal of Florida, Second District, 1995.
658 So.2d 116.

Historical and Economic Setting *In the last half of the twentieth century, the housing industry has experienced extraordinary growth. Since 1960, nearly sixty million units (including single-family houses, apartments, and mobile homes) have been built—twenty million more than in the previous forty years. Since 1920, however, the population has increased by only about 150 million. In other words, between 1920 and 1995, a new unit was built for every one and a half persons. Much of this growth has occurred in Florida, which is now the fourth most populous state.*

Background and Facts Cudlipp Construction and Development Company agreed to build up to 375 houses for Shadow Lakes, Inc., near Tampa, Florida. Under the contract, the parties were bound to complete fourteen of the houses, but either party had the right to terminate the agreement with regard to future houses if prices could not be mutually agreed on by the parties. For each house, Shadow Lakes agreed to pay a fixed price, which included the costs of construction and a fee for Cudlipp's services. The contract indicated that the fee covered "off-site and on-site supervision, office overhead and general support," as well as Cudlipp's profit—which, according to Cudlipp's testimony at trial—was to be $10,000 per house. Problems

(Continued)

Case 13.3 Continued

developed between the parties after Cudlipp had begun to construct eight houses. Cudlipp filed a suit in a Florida state court against Shadow Lakes, alleging, among other things, breach of contract. The damages Cudlipp sought included lost profits of $3,670,000 ($10,000 for 367 houses—375 houses less the 8 houses already under construction). The jury awarded Cudlipp $3,670,000 in lost profits, and Shadow Lakes appealed.

In the Words of the Court . . .
QUINCE, Judge.

* * * *

* * * Whether or not the parties would have come to a meeting of the minds regarding other houses beyond the original fourteen is pure speculation and conjecture. Not only did the parties have to agree on price, but the acreage needed for the project had to be purchased by Shadow Lakes.

* * * [T]he total amount of profit to be realized on each home is * * * speculative. Although Mr. Cudlipp initially stated the $10,000 for each house was to be pure profit, he later acknowledged certain overhead and other expenses should be subtracted from that figure. The contract itself indicated the figure included off-site and on-site supervision, office overhead and general support. Moreover, Mr. Cudlipp stated * * * that the $10,000 figure also included possible upgrades to the houses by the ultimate purchasers.

Decision and Remedy The District Court of Appeal of Florida reversed the award and remanded for a new trial on the amount.

For Critical Analysis—Economic Consideration *What might be an appropriate measure of* *damages if in fact a contractor was realizing no profit, or was even actually losing money, on a contract?*

What factors influence the measure of damages on the breach of a construction contract?

CONSEQUENTIAL DAMAGES Foreseeable damages that result from a party's breach of contract are referred to as **consequential damages,** or *special damages*. Consequential damages differ from compensatory damages in that they are caused by special circumstances beyond the contract itself. When a seller does not deliver goods, *knowing* that a buyer is planning to resell those goods immediately, consequential damages are awarded for the loss of profits from the planned resale. • **Example 13.13** Gilmore contracts to have a specific item shipped to her—one that she desperately needs to repair her printing press. In contracting with the shipper, Gilmore tells him that she must receive the item by Monday or she will not be able to print her paper and will lose $750. If the shipper is late, Gilmore normally can recover the consequential damages caused by the delay (that is, the $750 in losses).•

For a nonbreaching party to recover consequential damages, the breaching party must know (or have reason to know) that special circumstances will cause the nonbreaching party to suffer an additional loss. This rule was enunciated in *Hadley v. Baxendale,* a case decided in England in 1854 and presented in this chapter's *Landmark in the Legal Environment*. Today, the rule still applies.

> **Consequential Damages**
> Special damages that compensate for a loss that is not direct or immediate (for example, lost profits). The special damages must have been reasonably foreseeable at the time the breach or injury occurred in order for the plaintiff to collect them.

> **Note** A seller who does not wish to take on the risk of consequential damages can limit the buyer's remedies.

Landmark in the Legal Environment

Hadley v. Baxendale (1854)

A landmark case in establishing the rule that notice of special ("consequential") circumstances must be given if consequential damages are to be recovered is *Hadley v. Baxendale,*[a] decided in 1854. This case involved a broken crankshaft used in a flour mill run by the Hadley family in Gloucester, England. The crankshaft attached to the steam engine in the mill broke, and the shaft had to be sent to a foundry located in Greenwich so that a new shaft could be made to fit the other parts of the engine. The Hadleys hired Baxendale, a common carrier, to transport the shaft from Gloucester to Greenwich. Baxendale received payment in advance and promised to deliver the shaft the following day. It was not delivered for several days, however. As a consequence, the mill was closed during those days because the Hadleys had no extra crankshaft on hand to use. The Hadleys sued Baxendale to recover the profits they lost during that time. Baxendale contended that the loss of profits was "too remote."

In the mid-1800s, it was normal for large mills, such as that run by the Hadleys, to have more than one crankshaft in case the main one broke and had to be repaired, as it did in this case. Also, in those days it was common knowledge that flour mills did indeed have spares. It is against this background that the parties argued their respective positions on whether the damages resulting from loss of profits while the crankshaft was out for repair were "too remote" to be recoverable.

The crucial issue before the court was whether the Hadleys had informed the carrier, Baxendale, of the special circumstances surrounding the crankshaft's repair, particularly of the fact that the mill would have to shut down while the crankshaft was being repaired. If Baxendale had been notified of this circumstance at the time the contract was formed, then the remedy for breaching the contract would have been the amount of damages that would reasonably follow from the breach—including the Hadleys' lost profits. In the court's opinion, however, the only circumstances communicated by the Hadleys to Baxendale at the time the contract was made were that the item to be transported was a broken crankshaft of a mill and that the Hadleys were the owners and operators of that mill. The court concluded that these circumstances did not reasonably indicate that the mill would have to stop operations if the delivery of the crankshaft was delayed.

For Critical Analysis: *If it had not been the custom in the mid-1800s for mills to have extra crankshafts on hand, how would this circumstance have affected the court's ruling?*

a. 9 Exch. 341, 156 Eng.Rep. 145 (1854).

When damages are awarded, compensation is given only for those injuries that the defendant *could reasonably have foreseen* as a probable result of the usual course of events following a breach. If the injury complained of is outside the usual and foreseeable course of events, the plaintiff must show specifically that the defendant had reason to know the facts and foresee the injury.

PUNITIVE DAMAGES   Recall from Chapter 9 that *punitive damages* are designed to punish a wrongdoer and set an example to deter similar conduct in the future. Punitive damages, which are also referred to as *exemplary damages,* are generally not recoverable in an action for breach of contract. Such damages have no legitimate place in contract law because they are, in essence, penalties, and a breach of contract is not unlawful in a criminal sense. A contract is simply a civil relationship between the parties. The law may compensate one party for the loss of the bargain—no more and no less.

In a few situations, a person's actions can cause both a breach of contract and a tort. For example, the parties can establish by contract a certain reasonable standard or duty of care. Failure to live up to that standard is a breach of contract, and the act itself may constitute negligence. An intentional tort (such as fraud) may also be tied to a breach of contract. In such a situation, it is possible for the nonbreaching party to recover punitive damages for the tort in addition to compensatory and consequential damages for the breach of contract.

NOMINAL DAMAGES   Damages that are awarded to an innocent party when only a technical injury is involved and no actual damage (no financial loss) has been suffered are called **nominal damages**. Nominal damage awards are often small, such as one dollar, but they do establish that the defendant acted wrongfully.

 • **Example 13.14**   Suppose that Parrott contracts to buy potatoes at fifty cents a pound from Lentz. Lentz breaches the contract and does not deliver the potatoes. Meanwhile, the price of potatoes falls. Parrott is able to buy them in the open market at half the price he agreed to pay Lentz. Parrott is clearly better off because of Lentz's breach. Thus, in a suit for breach of contract, Parrott may be awarded only nominal damages for the technical injury he sustained, as no monetary loss was involved. • Most lawsuits for nominal damages are brought as a matter of principle under the theory that a breach has occurred and some damages must be imposed regardless of actual loss.

Mitigation of Damages

In most situations, when a breach of contract occurs, the injured party is held to a duty to mitigate, or reduce, the damages that he or she suffers. Under this doctrine of **mitigation of damages,** the required action depends on the nature of the situation. For example, in the majority of states, wrongfully terminated employees have a duty to mitigate damages suffered by their employers' breach. The damages they will be awarded are their salaries less the incomes they would have received in similar jobs obtained by reasonable means. It is the employer's burden to prove the existence of such jobs and to prove that the employee could have been hired. An employee is, of course, under no duty to take a job that is not of the same type and rank. This is illustrated in the following case. (For another illustration of the concept of mitigation of damages, see this chapter's *Inside the Legal Environment* feature on page 376.)

> "The duty to keep a contract at common law means a prediction that you must pay damages if you do not keep it—and nothing else."
>
> Oliver Wendell Holmes, Jr., 1841–1935
> (Associate justice of the United States Supreme Court, 1902–1932)

Nominal Damages A small monetary award (often one dollar) granted to a plaintiff when no actual damage was suffered.

Mitigation of Damages A rule requiring a plaintiff to have done whatever was reasonable to minimize the damages caused by the defendant.

Case 13.4 ● Parker v. Twentieth Century-Fox Film Corp.

Supreme Court of California, 1970.
3 Cal.3d 176,
474 P.2d 689,
89 Cal.Rptr. 737.

Company Profile *Daryl Zanuck and Joseph Schenk formed the Twentieth Century Company in 1933 to make movies. Two years later, they merged with the Fox Film Company, which had been founded by William Fox, and became Twentieth Century-Fox Film Corporation. Today, Twentieth Century-Fox produces movies and television shows as part of the News Corporation Limited, which is headquartered in Australia. The News Corporation also has interests in the production and distribution of newspapers, magazines, books, television programs, and films in Great Britain, Hong Kong, New Zealand, and other countries.*

Background and Facts Twentieth Century-Fox Film Corporation planned to produce a musical, *Bloomer*

Girl, and contracted with Shirley MacLaine Parker to play the leading female role. According to the contract, Fox was to pay Parker $53,571.42 per week for fourteen weeks, for a total of $750,000. Fox later decided not to produce *Bloomer Girl* and tried to substitute another contract for the existing contract. Under the terms of this second contract, Parker would play the leading role in a Western movie for the same amount of money guaranteed by the first contract. Fox gave Parker one week in which to accept the new contract. Parker filed a suit in a California state court against Fox to recover the amount of compensation guaranteed in the first contract because, she maintained, the two roles were not at all equivalent. The *Bloomer Girl* production was a musical, to be filmed in California, and it could not be compared with a "western-type" production that Fox tentatively planned to produce in Australia. When the trial court held for Parker, Fox appealed. Ultimately, the California Supreme Court reviewed the case.

In the Words of the Court . . .
BURKE, Justice.

* * * *

The general rule is that the measure of recovery by a wrongfully discharged employee is the amount of salary agreed upon for the period of service, less the amount which the employer affirmatively proves the employee has earned or with reasonable effort might have earned from other employment. However, before projected earnings from other employment opportunities not sought or accepted by the discharged employee can be applied in mitigation, the employer must show that the other employment was comparable, or substantially similar, to that of which the employee has been deprived * * * .

* * * *

* * * The mere circumstance that *Bloomer Girl* was to be a musical review calling upon plaintiff's talents as a dancer as well as an actress, and was to be produced in the City of Los Angeles, whereas *Big Country* was a straight dramatic role in a "Western Type" story taking place in an opal mine in Australia, demonstrates the difference in kind between the two employments; the female lead as a dramatic actress in a western style motion picture can by no stretch of imagination be considered the equivalent of or substantially similar to the lead in a song-and-dance production.

Decision and Remedy The Supreme Court of California affirmed the trial court's ruling. Parker could not be required to accept Fox's offer of the western-movie contract to mitigate the damages she incurred as a result of the breach of contract.

For Critical Analysis—International Consideration *Many legal systems, including that of France, have no clear requirement that damages must be mitigated. Can justice be better served by requiring that damages be mitigated? If so, how?*

Inside the Legal Environment

Even Victims of Employment Discrimination Must Try to Mitigate Damages

American employees are protected in their employment under a variety of laws, such as Title VII of the Civil Rights Act of 1964, the Age Discrimination in Employment Act of 1967, and the Americans with Disabilities Act of 1990. Employees who are fired in violation of one of these acts typically are awarded damages to compensate the employee for lost wages. In some cases of intentional discrimination against employees, punitive damages may be awarded as well. There is a presumption, nonetheless, that even a person who has been wrongfully terminated must attempt to mitigate damages by seeking alternative, comparable employment. The U.S. Court of Appeals for the Second Circuit confirmed this principle in the case of *Greenway v. Buffalo Hilton Hotel.*[a]

That case was brought by Danny Greenway against his former employer, the Buffalo Hilton Hotel. Earlier, when Greenway was hired by the hotel to be a bartender, he did not reveal to his employer that he had tested positive for HIV, the virus that causes AIDS. Five years later, when he took a disability leave, he informed his employer that he was HIV positive. He returned to work but was disciplined on numerous occasions and was ultimately fired.

---

a. 143 F.3d 47 (1998).

At trial, Greenway succeeded in convincing the court that he was fired in violation of the Americans with Disabilities Act (ADA) of 1990, and the jury awarded him $1.4 million. That amount included compensatory damages for back pay, front pay (lost future wages), and future medical costs (for health insurance, medication, and the like) that would have been covered by Hilton's group insurance policy had Greenway not been fired. The amount also included $1 million in punitive damages. Following the trial, the trial court judge reduced the punitive damages award to $200,000 and modified other damages, reducing the total amount awarded to approximately $771,000.

On appeal, the Second Circuit upheld the trial jury's finding that the hotel had violated the ADA but held that Greenway was not entitled to receive damages for front pay, future health insurance premiums, or future medication costs. Why? Because Greenway had failed to mitigate his damages by seeking other permanent employment. Greenway worked for six months at a temporary agency. After that, he made no effort whatsoever to find suitable employment as a bartender. The court noted that under a number of case precedents, victims of employment discrimination have been required to mitigate their damages.[b]

For Critical Analysis: *If the wrongfully discharged employee does seek employment but fails to find any, why does the burden then fall on the former employer to prove that suitable employment was nonetheless available?*

---

b. Among other cases, the court cited *Ford Motor Company v. EEOC,* 458 U.S. 219, 102 S.Ct. 3057, 73 L.Ed.2d 721 (1982); and *Dailey v. Société Générale,* 108 F.3d 451 (2d Cir. 1997).

Liquidated Damages versus Penalties

Liquidated Damages An amount, stipulated in the contract, that the parties to a contract believe to be a reasonable estimation of the damages that will occur in the event of a breach.

A **liquidated damages** provision in a contract specifies that a certain amount of money is to be paid in the event of a future default or breach of contract. (*Liquidated* means determined, settled, or fixed.) Liquidated damages differ from penalties. A **penalty** specifies a certain amount to be paid in the event of a default or breach of contract and is designed to penalize the breaching party. Liquidated damages provisions normally are enforceable; penalty provisions are not. This is also the rule under the Uniform Commercial Code [UCC 2–718(1)].

Penalty A sum inserted into a contract, not as a measure of compensation for its breach but rather as punishment for a default. The agreement as to the amount will not be enforced, and recovery will be limited to actual damages.

To determine whether a particular provision is for liquidated damages or for a penalty, the court must answer two questions: First, at the time the contract was formed, was it difficult to estimate the potential damages that would be incurred if the contract was not performed on time? Second, was the amount set as damages a reasonable estimate of those potential damages and not excessive?[24] If the answers to both questions are yes, the provision will be enforced. If either answer is no, the provision will normally not be enforced. In a construction contract, it is difficult to estimate the amount of damages that might be caused by a delay in completing construction, so liquidated damages clauses are often used.

Equitable Remedies

When the remedy at law (money damages) is inadequate, a court may grant a remedy in equity, or equitable remedy, such as one of the remedies discussed here.

Rescission and Restitution

When fraud, mistake, duress, or failure of consideration is present, rescission is available. The failure of one party to perform under a contract entitles the other party to rescind (cancel, or undo) the contract.[25] The rescinding party must give prompt notice to the breaching party. Furthermore, both parties must make **restitution** to each other by returning goods, property, or money previously conveyed.[26] If the goods or property can be restored *in specie*—that is, if they can be returned—they must be. If the goods or property have been consumed, restitution must be made in an equivalent amount of money. Essentially, restitution refers to the recapture of a benefit conferred on the defendant through which the defendant has been unjustly enriched.

Restitution An equitable remedy under which a person is restored to his or her original position prior to loss or injury, or placed in the position he or she would have been in had the breach not occurred.

---

24. *Restatement (Second) of Contracts*, Section 356(1).
25. The rescission discussed here refers to *unilateral* rescission, in which only one party wants to undo the contract. In *mutual* rescission, both parties agree to undo the contract. Mutual rescission discharges the contract; unilateral rescission is generally available as a remedy for breach of contract.
26. *Restatement (Second) of Contracts*, Section 370.

Ethical Issue 13.2

Should disproportionately high "late fees" on monthly bills be considered "penalties"?

Nearly every service provider has to deal with the issue of late payments from its subscribers. One way that some companies have dealt with this problem is to charge a "late fee." But what if the late fee is significantly higher than the actual loss incurred by a company due to a late payment? In this situation, can customers sue the company under the common law rules governing liquidated damages versus penalties? At least one court has answered that question in the affirmative. The case involved a subscriber contract between a cable TV company in Baltimore, Maryland, and its customers. The contract provided that whenever a payment was late, the customer would be charged $5. In fact, the cable company lost, on average, only 38 cents when someone paid his or her bill late. In a class-action suit against the company, the customers alleged that late fees constitute a form of liquidated damages but that "grossly excessive" fees constitute penalties. A Maryland state trial court agreed, concluding that the "cable company's late fee is exorbitant, bears no reasonable relation to the real cost of handling and collecting the late payment, and constitutes a tool of profit for the collection of additional revenues." The court ordered the company to pay $5.4 million in damages.[a]

---

a. *Burch v. United Cable Television of Baltimore Limited Partnership*, Baltimore City (Maryland) Circuit Court, September 16, 1997, as cited in *Lawyers Weekly USA*, October 20, 1997, pp. 9–10.

● **Example 13.15** Andrea pays $10,000 to Miles in return for Miles's promise to design a house for her. The next day Miles calls Andrea and tells her that he has taken a position with a large architectural firm in another state and cannot design the house. Andrea decides to hire another architect that afternoon. Andrea can get restitution of $10,000, because she conferred an unjust benefit of $10,000 on Miles. ●

Specific Performance

Specific Performance An equitable remedy requiring *exactly* the performance that was specified in a contract; usually granted only when money damages would be an inadequate remedy and the subject matter of the contract is unique (for example, real property).

The equitable remedy of **specific performance** calls for the performance of the act promised in the contract. This remedy is often attractive to a non-breaching party, because it provides the exact bargain promised in the contract. It also avoids some of the problems inherent in a suit for money damages. First, the nonbreaching party need not worry about collecting the judgment.[27] Second, the nonbreaching party need not look around for another contract. Third, the actual performance may be more valuable than the money damages. Although the equitable remedy of specific performance is often preferable to other remedies, normally it is not granted unless the party's legal remedy (money damages) is inadequate.[28]

For example, contracts for the sale of goods that are readily available on the market rarely qualify for specific performance. Money damages ordinarily are adequate in such situations, because substantially identical goods can be bought or sold in the market. If the goods are unique, however, a court of equity will decree specific performance. For example, paintings, sculptures, and rare books and coins are often unique, and money damages will not enable a buyer to obtain substantially identical substitutes in the market. The same principle applies to contracts relating to sales of land or interests in land, because each parcel of land is unique by legal description.

Courts normally refuse to grant specific performance of contracts for personal services. Sometimes the remedy at law may be adequate if substantially identical services are available from other persons (as with lawn-mowing services). Even for individually tailored personal-service contracts, courts are very hesitant to order specific performance by a party, because public policy strongly discourages involuntary servitude.[29] Moreover, the courts do not want to monitor a personal-service contract. For example, if you contract with a brain surgeon to perform brain surgery on you and the surgeon refuses to perform, the court would not compel (and you certainly would not want) the surgeon to perform under these circumstances. There is no way the court can assure meaningful performance in such a situation.[30]

> **"Specific performance is a remedy of grace and not a matter of right, and the test of whether or not it should be granted depends on the particular circumstances of each case."**
>
> George Bushnell, 1887–1965
> (American jurist)

---

27. Courts dispose of cases, after trials, by entering judgments. A judgment may order the losing party to pay money damages to the winning party. Collection of judgments, however, poses problems—such as when the judgment debtor is insolvent (cannot pay his or her bills when they become due) or has only a small net worth, or when the debtor's assets cannot be seized, under exemption laws, by a creditor to satisfy a debt (see Chapter 15).
28. *Restatement (Second) of Contracts,* Section 359.
29. The Thirteenth Amendment to the U.S. Constitution prohibits involuntary servitude, but negative injunctions (that is, prohibiting rather than ordering certain conduct) are possible. Thus, you may not be able to compel a person to perform under a personal-service contract, but you may be able to restrain that person from engaging in similar contracts with others for a period of time.
30. Similarly, courts often refuse to order specific performance of construction contracts, because courts are not set up to operate as construction supervisors or engineers.

A collection of antique coins and other artifacts. When is specific performance the appropriate remedy for a breach of contract?

Reformation

When the parties have imperfectly expressed their agreement in writing, the equitable remedy of *reformation* allows the contract to be rewritten to reflect the parties' true intentions. This remedy applies most often when fraud or mutual mistake (for example, a clerical error) has occurred. If Keshan contracts to buy a certain piece of equipment from Shelley but the written contract refers to a different piece of equipment, a mutual mistake has occurred. Accordingly, a court could reform the contract so that the writing conforms to the parties' original intention as to which piece of equipment is being sold.

Two other examples deserve mention. The first involves two parties who have made a binding oral contract. They further agree to reduce the oral contract to writing, but in doing so, they make an error in stating the terms. Universally, the courts allow into evidence the correct terms of the oral contract, thereby reforming the written contract.

The second example has to do with written covenants not to compete. As discussed in Chapter 12, if a covenant not to compete is for a valid and legitimate purpose (such as the sale of a business), but the area or time restraints of the covenant are unreasonable, some courts reform the restraints by making them reasonable and enforce the entire contract as reformed. Other courts throw the entire restrictive covenant out as illegal.

Recovery Based on Quasi Contract

Recall from Chapter 12 that a quasi contract is not a true contract but a fictional contract that is imposed on the parties to obtain justice and prevent unjust enrichment. Hence, a quasi contract becomes an equitable basis for relief. Generally, when one party confers a benefit on another, justice requires that the party receiving the benefit pay a reasonable value for it so as not to be unjustly enriched at the other party's expense.

Don't Forget The function of a quasi contract is to impose a legal obligation on parties who made no actual promises.

Quasi-contractual recovery is useful when one party has *partially* performed under a contract that is unenforceable. It can be an alternative to suing for damages, and it allows the party to recover the reasonable value of the partial performance. For quasi-contractual recovery to occur, the party seeking recovery must show the following:

1. A benefit was conferred on the other party.
2. The party conferring the benefit did so with the expectation of being paid.
3. The party seeking recovery did not act as a volunteer in conferring the benefit.
4. Retaining the benefit without paying for it would result in an unjust enrichment of the party receiving the benefit.

Example 13.16 Suppose that Ericson contracts to build two oil derricks for Petro Industries. The derricks are to be built over a period of three years, but the parties do not create a written contract. Enforcement of the contract will therefore be barred by the one-year rule of the Statute of Frauds, discussed earlier in this chapter. Ericson completes one derrick, and then Petro Industries informs him that it will not pay for the derrick. Ericson can sue in quasi contract because (1) a benefit (one oil derrick) has been conferred on Petro Industries; (2) Ericson conferred the benefit (built the derrick) expecting to be paid; (3) Ericson did not volunteer to build the derrick but built it under an unenforceable oral contract; and (4) allowing Petro Industries to retain the derrick without paying would enrich the company unjustly. Therefore, Ericson should be able to recover the reasonable value of the oil derrick (under the theory of *quantum meruit*[31]—"as much as he deserves"). The reasonable value is ordinarily equal to the fair market value.

Election of Remedies

> **Be Aware** Which remedy a plaintiff elects depends on the subject of the contract, the defenses of the breaching party, the advantages that might be gained in terms of tactics against the defendant, and what the plaintiff can prove with respect to the remedy sought.

In many cases, a nonbreaching party has several remedies available. Because the remedies may be inconsistent with one another, the common law of contracts requires the party to choose which remedy to pursue. This is called *election of remedies*. The purpose of the doctrine of election of remedies is to prevent double recovery. **Example 13.17** Suppose that Jefferson agrees to sell his land to Adams. Then Jefferson changes his mind and repudiates the contract. Adams can sue for compensatory damages or for specific performance. If she receives damages as a result of the breach, she should not also be granted specific performance of the sales contract, because that would mean she would end up with both the land and damages, which would be unfair. In effect, she would recover twice for the same breach of contract. The doctrine of election of remedies requires Adams to choose the remedy she wants, and it eliminates any possibility of double recovery.

Unfortunately, the doctrine has been applied in a rigid and technical manner, leading to some harsh results. **Example 13.18** In a Wisconsin case, a man named Carpenter was fraudulently induced to buy a piece of land for $100. He spent $140 moving onto the land and then discovered the fraud. Instead of suing for damages, Carpenter sued to rescind the contract. The court denied recovery of the $140 because the seller, Mason, had not received

---

31. Pronounced *kwahn*-tuhm *mehr*-oo-wuht.

the $140 and was therefore not required to reimburse Carpenter for his moving expenses. So Carpenter suffered a net loss of $140 on the transaction. If Carpenter had sued for damages, he could have recovered the $100 purchase price and the $140.[32] Because of the harsh results of the doctrine of election of remedies, the Uniform Commercial Code expressly rejects it. Remedies under the UCC are essentially *cumulative* in nature, as will be discussed next.

Remedies for a Breach of a Sales Contract

Sometimes circumstances make it difficult for a person to carry out the performance promised in a contract, in which case the contract may be breached. When breach occurs, the aggrieved party looks for remedies. These remedies range from retaining the goods to requiring the breaching party's performance under the contract. The general purpose of these remedies is to put the aggrieved party "in as good a position as if the other party had fully performed." As just mentioned, remedies under the Uniform Commercial Code (UCC) are *cumulative* in nature. In other words, an innocent party to a breached sales or lease contract is not limited to one, exclusive remedy. (Of course, a party still may not recover twice for the same harm.)

Remedies of the Seller

A buyer breaches a sales contract by any of the following actions: (1) wrongfully rejecting tender of the goods; (2) wrongfully revoking acceptance of the goods; (3) failing to make payment on or before delivery of the goods; or (4) repudiating the contract. On the buyer's breach, the seller is afforded several distinct remedies under the UCC. These include the right to stop or withhold delivery of the goods and the right to recover damages or to recover the purchase price of the goods.

Remedies of the Buyer

A seller breaches a sales contract by failing to deliver conforming goods or repudiating the contract prior to delivery. On the breach, the buyer has a choice of several remedies under the UCC. These remedies include the right to reject nonconforming or improperly delivered goods; to *cover* (that is, to buy the goods elsewhere and recover from the seller the extra cost of obtaining the substitute goods); to recover damages; and, in certain circumstances, to obtain specific performance of the contract.

Provisions Limiting Remedies

A contract may include provisions stating that no damages can be recovered for certain types of breaches or that damages must be limited to a maximum amount. The contract may also provide that the only remedy for breach is replacement, repair, or refund of the purchase price. Provisions stating that no damages can be recovered are called *exculpatory clauses* (see Chapter 12). Provisions that affect the availability of certain remedies are called *limitation-of-liability clauses*.

> **Recall** Exculpatory clauses are often held unconscionable, depending on the relative bargaining positions of the parties and the importance to the public interest of the business seeking to enforce the clause.

Whether these contract provisions and clauses will be enforced depends on the type of breach that is excused by the provision. For example, a provision

---

32. See *Carpenter v. Mason*, 181 Wis. 114, 193 N.W. 973 (1923).

International currency. The values of different types of currencies fluctuate. What other variables should a party consider when entering into an international sales contract?

excluding liability for fraudulent or intentional injury will not be enforced. Likewise, a clause excluding liability for illegal acts or violations of law will not be enforced. A clause excluding liability for negligence may be enforced in some cases. When an exculpatory clause for negligence is contained in a contract made between parties who have roughly equal bargaining positions, the clause usually will be enforced.

The UCC provides that in a contract for the sale of goods, remedies can be limited.

Contracts for the International Sale of Goods

International sales contracts between firms or individuals located in different countries are governed by the 1980 United Nations Convention on Contracts for the International Sale of Goods (CISG)—if the countries of the parties to the contract have ratified the CISG (and if the parties have not agreed that some other law will govern their contract). As of 2000, fifty-eight countries had ratified or acceded to the CISG, including the United States, Canada, Mexico, some Central and South American countries, and most of the European nations. Essentially, the CISG is to international sales contracts what Article 2 of the UCC is to domestic sales contracts.

Businesspersons must take special care when drafting international sales contracts to avoid problems caused by distance, including language differences and varying national laws. The fold-out exhibit contained within this chapter, which shows an actual international sales contract used by Starbucks Coffee Company, illustrates many of the special terms and clauses that are typically contained in international contracts for the sale of goods. Annotations in the exhibit explain the meaning and significance of specific clauses in the contract. (See Chapter 25 for a discussion of other laws that frame global business transactions.)

Key Terms

Chapter Summary • Contract Defenses, Discharge, and Remedies

DEFENSES TO CONTRACT ENFORCEABILITY

Genuineness of Assent (See pages 356–360.)	1. Mistakes—
	
	   a. Unilateral—Generally, the mistaken party is bound by the contract.
	
	   b. Bilateral—When both parties are mistaken about the same material fact, such as identity, either party can avoid the contract. If the mistake concerns value or quality, either party can enforce the contract.

Chapter Summary • Contract Defenses, Discharge, and Remedies

Genuineness of Assent—continued	2. **Fraudulent or innocent misrepresentation**—When fraud occurs, usually the innocent party can enforce or avoid the contract. For damages, the innocent party must suffer an injury. When innocent misrepresentation occurs, the contract may be rescinded (canceled) but damages are not available.
	3. **Undue influence**—Undue influence arises from special relationships, such as fiduciary or confidential relationships, in which one party's free will has been overcome by the undue influence exerted by the other party. Usually, the contract is voidable.
	4. **Duress**—Duress is defined as forcing a party to enter a contract under the fear of a threat—for example, the threat of violence or serious economic loss. The party forced to enter the contract can rescind the contract.
The Statute of Frauds and the Parol Evidence Rule (See pages 360–364.)	1. **Statute of Frauds**—The following types of contracts fall under the Statute of Frauds and must be in writing or evidenced by a legally sufficient memorandum to be enforceable: (1) contracts involving transfers of interests in land, (2) contracts the terms of which cannot be performed within one year, (3) collateral promises, (4) promises made in consideration of marriage, and (5) contracts for the sale of goods priced at $500 or more. Exceptions include partial performance, admissions, and promissory estoppel.
	2. **Parol evidence rule**—A rule that prohibits the introduction at trial of evidence of the parties' prior negotiations, prior agreements, or contemporaneous oral agreements if that evidence contradicts or varies the terms of written contracts. Because of the rigidity of the parol evidence rule, however, courts make several exceptions.

WAYS TO DISCHARGE A CONTRACT

Performance (See pages 365–368.)	A contract may be discharged by complete (strict) or by substantial performance. In some cases, performance must be to the satisfaction of another. Totally inadequate performance constitutes a material breach of contract. An anticipatory repudiation of a contract allows the other party to sue immediately for breach of contract.
Agreement (See page 368.)	Parties may agree to discharge their contractual obligations in several ways:
	1. **By rescission**—The parties mutually agree to rescind (cancel) the contract.
	2. **By novation**—A new party is substituted for one of the primary parties to a contract.
	3. **By accord and satisfaction**—The parties agree to render performance different from that originally agreed on.
Objective Impossibility of Performance (See pages 368–369.)	Parties' obligations under contracts may be discharged by objective impossibility of performance or commercial impracticability of performance.

THE COMMON REMEDIES AVAILABLE TO THE NONBREACHING PARTY

Damages (See pages 370–377.)	The legal remedy of damages is designed to compensate the nonbreaching party for the loss of the bargain. By awarding money damages, the court tries to place the parties in the positions that they would have occupied had the contract been fully

(Continued)

Chapter Summary • **Contract Defenses, Discharge, and Remedies,** *Continued*

Damages—continued

performed. The nonbreaching party frequently has a duty to mitigate (lessen or reduce) the damages incurred as a result of the contract's breach. There are five broad categories of damages:

1. **Compensatory damages**—Damages that compensate the nonbreaching party for injuries actually sustained and proved to have arisen directly from the loss of the bargain resulting from the breach of contract.

    a. In breached contracts for the sale of goods, the usual measure of compensatory damages is an amount equal to the difference between the contract price and the market price.

    b. In breached contracts for the sale of land, the measure of damages is ordinarily the same as in contracts for the sale of goods.

    c. In breached construction contracts, the measure of damages depends on which party breaches and at what stage of construction the breach occurs.

2. **Consequential damages**—Damages resulting from special circumstances beyond the contract itself; the damages flow only from the consequences of a breach. For a party to recover consequential damages, the damages must be the foreseeable result of a breach of contract, and the breaching party must have known at the time the contract was formed that special circumstances existed and that the nonbreaching party would incur additional loss on breach of the contract. Also called *special damages*.

3. **Punitive damages**—Damages awarded to punish the breaching party. Usually not awarded in an action for breach of contract unless a tort is involved.

4. **Nominal damages**—Damages small in amount (such as one dollar) that are awarded when a breach has occurred but no actual damages have been suffered. Awarded only to establish that the defendant acted wrongfully.

5. **Liquidated damages**—Damages that may be specified in a contract as the amount to be paid to the nonbreaching party in the event the contract is later breached. Clauses providing for liquidated damages are enforced if the damages were difficult to estimate at the time the contract was formed and if the amount stipulated is reasonable. If construed to be a penalty, the clause will not be enforced.

Equitable Remedies
(See pages 377–380.)

1. **Rescission and restitution**—A remedy whereby a contract is canceled and the parties are restored to the original positions that they occupied prior to the transaction. Available when fraud, a mistake, duress, or failure of consideration is present. The rescinding party must give prompt notice of the rescission to the breaching party. When a contract is rescinded, both parties must make restitution to each other by returning the goods, property, or money previously conveyed. Restitution prevents the unjust enrichment of the defendant.

2. **Specific performance**—An equitable remedy calling for the performance of the act promised in the contract. Specific performance is only available in special situations—such as those involving contracts for the sale of unique goods or land—and when monetary damages would be an inadequate remedy. Specific performance is not available as a remedy in breached contracts for personal services.

3. **Reformation**—An equitable remedy allowing a contract to be "reformed," or rewritten, to reflect the parties' true intentions. Available when an agreement is imperfectly expressed in writing.

Chapter Summary • Contract Defenses, Discharge, and Remedies

Equitable Remedies—continued	**4. Recovery based on quasi contract**—An equitable theory imposed by the courts to obtain justice and prevent unjust enrichment in a situation in which no enforceable contract exists. The party seeking recovery must show that a benefit was conferred on the other party, the party conferring the benefit did so with the expectation of being paid, the benefit was not volunteered, and retaining the benefit without paying for it would result in the unjust enrichment of the party receiving the benefit.

CONTRACT DOCTRINES RELATING TO REMEDIES

Election of Remedies (See pages 380–381.)	A common law doctrine under which a nonbreaching party must choose one remedy from those available. This doctrine prevents double recovery.
Remedies for Breach of a Sales Contract (See page 381.)	When the buyer breaches a contract for the sale of goods, the seller may stop or withhold delivery of the goods, or recover damages or the purchase price of the goods. When the seller breaches a sales contract, the buyer may reject the goods, recover damages, obtain specific performance, or cover (buy replacement goods) and obtain from the seller the extra cost of the cover.
Provisions Limiting Remedies (See pages 381–382.)	A contract may provide that no damages (or only a limited amount of damages) can be recovered in the event the contract is breached. Clauses excluding liability for fraudulent or intentional injury or for illegal acts cannot be enforced. Clauses excluding liability for negligence may be enforced if both parties hold roughly equal bargaining power. Under the UCC, in contracts for the sale of goods, remedies may be limited.
Contracts for the International Sale of Goods (See page 382.)	International sales contracts are governed by the United Nations Convention on Contracts for the International Sale of Goods (CISG)—if the countries of the parties to the contract have ratified the CISG (and if the parties have not agreed that some other law will govern their contract). Essentially, the CISG is to international sales contracts what Article 2 of the UCC is to domestic sales contracts.

For Review

1. What defenses can be raised against the enforceability of an otherwise valid contract?

2. What contracts must be in writing to be enforceable?

3. How are most contracts discharged?

4. What is the difference between compensatory damages and consequential damages? What are nominal damages, and when might they be awarded by a court?

5. Under what circumstances will the remedy of rescission and restitution be available? When might specific performance be granted as a remedy?

Questions and Case Problems

13–1. Liquidated Damages. Carnack contracts to sell his house and lot to Willard for $100,000. The terms of the contract call for Willard to pay 10 percent of the purchase price as a deposit toward the purchase price, or as a down payment. The terms further stipulate that should the buyer breach the contract, the deposit will be retained by Carnack as liquidated damages. Willard pays the deposit, but because her expected financing of the $90,000 balance falls through, she breaches the contract. Two weeks later Carnack sells the house and lot to Balkova for $105,000. Willard demands her $10,000 back, but Carnack refuses, claiming that Willard's breach and the contract terms entitle him to keep the deposit. Discuss who is correct.

13–2. Election of Remedies. Perez contracts to buy a new Oldsmobile from Central City Motors, paying $2,000 down and agreeing to make twenty-four monthly payments of $350 each. He takes the car home and, after making one payment, learns that his Oldsmobile has a Chevrolet engine in it rather than the famous Olds Super V-8 engine. Central City never informed Perez of this fact. Perez immediately notifies Central City of his dissatisfaction and returns the car to Central City. Central City accepts the car and returns to Perez the $2,000 down payment plus the one $350 payment. Two weeks later Perez, without a car and feeling angry, files a suit against Central City, seeking damages for breach of warranty and fraud. Discuss the effect of Perez's actions.

13–3. Specific Performance. In which of the following situations might a court grant specific performance as a remedy for the breach of contract?

(a) Tarrington contracts to sell her house and lot to Rainier. Then, on finding another buyer willing to pay a higher purchase price, she refuses to deed the property to Rainier.

(b) Marita contracts to sing and dance in Horace's nightclub for one month, beginning June 1. She then refuses to perform.

(c) Juan contracts to purchase a rare coin from Edmund, who is breaking up his coin collection. At the last minute, Edmund decides to keep his coin collection intact and refuses to deliver the coin to Juan.

(d) There are three shareholders of Astro Computer Corp.: Coase, who owns 48 percent of the stock; De Valle, who owns 48 percent; and Cary, who owns 4 percent. Cary contracts to sell his 4 percent to De Valle but later refuses to transfer the shares to him.

13–4. Measure of Damages. Johnson contracted to lease a house to Fox for $700 a month, beginning October 1. Fox stipulated in the contract that before

he moved in, the interior of the house had to be completely repainted. On September 9, Johnson hired Keever to do the required painting for $1,000. He told Keever that the painting had to be finished by October 1 but did not explain why. On September 28, Keever quit for no reason, having completed approximately 80 percent of the work. Johnson then paid Sam $300 to finish the painting, but Sam did not finish until October 4. Fox, when the painting had not been completed as stipulated in his contract with Johnson, leased another home. Johnson found another tenant who would lease the property at $700 a month, beginning October 15. Johnson then sued Keever for breach of contract, claiming damages of $650. This amount included the $300 Johnson paid Sam to finish the painting and $350 for rent for the first half of October, which Johnson had lost as a result of Keever's breach. Johnson had not yet paid Keever anything for Keever's work. Can Johnson collect the $650 from Keever? Explain.

13–5. Measure of Damages. Ben owns and operates a famous candy store. He makes most of the candy sold in the store, and business is particularly heavy during the Christmas season. Ben contracts with Sweet, Inc., to purchase ten thousand pounds of sugar, to be delivered on or before November 15. Ben informs Sweet that this particular order is to be used for the Christmas season business. Because of production problems, the sugar is not tendered to Ben until December 10, at which time Ben refuses the order because it is so late. Ben has been unable to purchase the quantity of sugar needed to meet the Christmas orders and has had to turn down numerous regular customers, some of whom have indicated that they will purchase candy elsewhere in the future. The sugar that Ben has been able to purchase has cost him ten cents per pound above Sweet's price. Ben sues Sweet for breach of contract, claiming as damages the higher price paid for the sugar from others, lost profits from this year's lost Christmas sales, future lost profits from customers who have indicated that they will discontinue doing business with him, and punitive damages for failure to meet the contracted-for delivery date. Sweet claims Ben is limited to compensatory damages only. Discuss who is correct, and why.

13–6. Limitation of Liability. Westinghouse Electric Corp. entered into a contract with New Jersey Electric to manufacture and install a turbine generator for producing electricity. The contract price was over $10 million. The parties engaged in three years of negotiations and bargaining before they agreed on a suitable contract. The ultimate contract provided, among other things, that Westinghouse would not be liable for any injuries to the property belonging to the utility or to its customers or employees. Westinghouse warranted only that it would repair any defects in workmanship and materials appearing within one year of installation. After installation, part of New Jersey Electric's plant was damaged, and several of its employees were injured because of a defect in the turbine. New Jersey Electric sued Westinghouse, claiming that Westinghouse was liable for the damages because the exculpatory provisions in the contract were unconscionable. What was the result? [*Royal Indemnity Co. v. Westinghouse Electric Corp.*, 385 F.Supp. 520 (S.D.N.Y. 1974)]

13–7. Fraudulent Misrepresentation. In 1987, United Parcel Service Co. and United Parcel Service of America, Inc. (together known as "UPS"), decided to change its parcel delivery business from relying on contract carriers to establishing its own airline. During the transition, which took sixteen months, UPS hired 811 pilots. At the time, UPS expressed a desire to hire pilots who remained throughout that period with its contract carriers, which included Orion Air. A UPS representative met with more than fifty Orion pilots and made promises of future employment. John Rickert, a captain with Orion, was one of the pilots. Orion ceased operation after the UPS transition, and UPS did not hire Rickert, who obtained employment about six months later as a second officer with American Airlines, but at a lower salary. Rickert filed a suit in a Kentucky state court against UPS, claiming, in part, fraud based on the promises made by the UPS representative. UPS filed a motion for a directed verdict. What are the elements for a cause of action based on fraudulent misrepresentation? In whose favor should the court rule in this case, and why? [*United Parcel Service, Inc. v. Rickert*, 996 S.W.2d 464 (Ky. 1999)]

13–8. Performance. Steven McPheters, a house builder and developer, hired Terry Tentinger, who did business as New Horizon Construction, to do some touching up and repainting on one of McPheters's new houses. Tentinger worked two days, billed McPheters $420 (a three-man crew for fourteen hours at $30 per hour), and offered to return to the house to remedy any defects in his workmanship at no cost. McPheters objected to the number of hours on the bill—although he did not express dissatisfaction with the work—and offered Tentinger $250. Tentinger refused to accept this amount and filed a suit in an Idaho state court to collect the full amount. McPheters filed a counterclaim, alleging that Tentinger failed to perform the job in a workmanlike manner, resulting in $2,500 in damages, which it would cost $500 to repair. Tentinger's witnesses testified that although some touch-up work needed to be done, the job had been performed in a workmanlike manner. McPheters presented testimony indicating that the workmanship was so defective as to render it commercially unreasonable. On what basis could the court rule in Tentinger's favor? Explain fully. [*Tentinger v. McPheters*, 132 Idaho 620, 977 P.2d 234 (Idaho App. 1999)]

13–9. Rescission. Jeffrey Stambovsky was a resident of New York City. While looking at houses in the village of Nyack, New York, Stambovsky came across a riverfront Victorian house that he liked. He purchased it, only to discover later that the house had a local reputation for being haunted. The seller, Helen Ackley, had promoted this reputation herself by reporting to the *Reader's Digest* in 1977 and to the local press in 1982 that the house was haunted. By 1989, the house was included in a five-home walking tour of Nyack because of the purported presence of ghosts in the house. There was even a newspaper article describing it as "a riverfront Victorian (with ghost)." Stambovsky brought an action to rescind the contract, contending that the house's reputation for being haunted impaired the value of the property. What will the court decide? Discuss fully. [*Stambovsky v. Ackley*, 169 A.D.2d 254, 572 N.Y.S.2d 672 (1991)]

13–10. Damages. In December 1992, Beys Specialty Contracting, Inc., contracted with New York City's Metropolitan Transportation Authority (MTA) for construction work. Beys subcontracted with Hudson Iron Works, Inc., to perform some of the work for $175,000. Under the terms of the subcontract, within seven days after the MTA approved Hudson's work and paid Beys, Beys would pay Hudson. The MTA had not yet approved any of Hudson's work when Beys submitted to the MTA invoices dated May 20 and June 21, 1993. Without proof that the MTA had paid Beys on those invoices, Hudson submitted to Beys an invoice dated September 10, claiming that the May 20 and June 21 invoices incorporated its work. Beys refused to pay, Hudson stopped working, and Beys paid another contractor $25,083 more to complete the job than if Hudson had completed its subcontract. Hudson filed a suit in a New York state court to collect on its invoice. Beys filed a counterclaim for the additional money spent to complete Hudson's job. In whose favor should the court rule, and why? What might be the measure of damages, if any? [*Hudson Iron Works, Inc. v. Beys Specialty Contracting, Inc.*, 691 N.Y.S.2d 132 (N.Y.A.D., 2 Dept. 1999)]

A Question of Ethics and Social Responsibility

13–11. Bobby Murray Chevrolet, Inc., contracted to supply 1,200 school bus chassis to local school boards. The contract stated that "products of any manufacturer may be offered," but Bobby Murray submitted its orders exclusively to General Motors Corp. (GMC). When a shortage in automatic transmissions occurred, GMC informed the dealer that it could not fill the orders. Bobby Murray told the school boards, which then bought the chassis from another dealer. The boards sued Bobby Murray for breach of contract. The dealer responded that its obligation to perform was excused under the doctrine of commercial impracticability, in part because of GMC's failure to fill its orders. Given these facts, answer the following questions. [*Alamance County Board of Education v. Bobby Murray Chevrolet, Inc.*, 121 N.C.App. 222, 465 S.E.2d 306 (1996)]

1. How will the court likely decide this issue? What factors will the court consider in making its decision? Discuss fully.
2. If the decision were yours to make, would you excuse Bobby Murray from its performance obligations in these circumstances? Would your decision be any different if Bobby Murray had specified in its contract that GMC would be the exclusive source of supply instead of stating that "products of any manufacturer may be offered"?
3. Generally, how does the doctrine of commercial impracticability attempt to balance the rights of both parties to a contract?

Case Briefing Assignment

13–12. Examine Case A.4 [*Potter v. Oster*, 426 N.W.2d 148 (Iowa 1988)] in Appendix A. The case has been excerpted there in great detail. Review and then brief the case, making sure that you include answers to the following questions in your brief.

1. Why was Oster appealing the trial court's decision?
2. Why did Oster assert that allowing the remedy of rescission and restitution in this case would lead to an inequitable result?
3. According to the court, what three requirements must be met before rescission will be granted?
4. Did the Potters meet these three requirements, and if so, why?
5. What reasons did the court give for its conclusion that remedies at law were inadequate in this case?
6. Why are remedies at law presumed to be inadequate for breach of real estate contracts?

For Critical Analysis

13–13. Review the discussion of the doctrine of election of remedies in this chapter. What are some of the advantages and disadvantages of this doctrine?

Interacting with the Internet

■ For updated links to resources available on the Web, as well as a variety of other materials, visit this text's Web site at

http://leet.westbuslaw.com

■ Law Guru can lead you to other sources of law relating to contract performance and discharge. Go to

http://www.lawguru.com/ lawlinks.html

■ The following sites offer information on contract law, including breach of contract and remedies:

http://www.nolo.com/Chunkcm/ CM9.html

http://www.law.cornell.edu/topics/ contracts.html

Online Legal Research Exercises

Go to **http://leet. westbuslaw.com**, the Web site that accompanies this text. Select "Interactive Study Center," and then click on "Chapter 13." There you will find the following Internet research exercises that you can perform to learn more about aspects of contract law:

Activity 13–1: The Statute of Frauds
Activity 13–2: Fraudulent Misrepresentation

Before the Test

Go to **http://leet. westbuslaw.com**, the Web site that accompanies this text. Select "Interactive Quizzes." You will find a number of interactive questions relating to this chapter.

E-Contracts

chapter objectives

After reading this chapter, you should be able to:

1. Discuss whether shrink-wrap and click-on agreements are enforceable.

2. Describe the nature and function of electronic agents and some of the legal issues raised by such agents.

3. Summarize the background and general coverage of the Uniform Computer Information Transactions Act (UCITA).

4. Define what constitutes an e-signature and the legal validity of such signatures.

5. State some of the major provisions of the Uniform Electronic Transactions Act (UETA).

"The law of toasters, televisions, and chain saws is not appropriate for contracts involving online databases, artificial intelligence systems, software, multimedia, and Internet trade in information."

Prefatory Note
Uniform Computer Information
Transactions Act

E-Contract A contract entered into in e-commerce.

Shrink-Wrap Agreement An agreement the terms of which are expressed inside a box in which goods are packaged. Sometimes called a *shrink-wrap license.*

Contract law forms the basis for most commercial activity. This is as true for business in the computer industry, and in cyberspace in particular, as it is for business in general. E-commerce is a growing part of this commercial activity, and it is estimated that business-to-business (B2B) transactions will soon exceed $1 trillion annually.

The question is whether doing business in cyberspace creates any special contract problems or calls for any other changes in the law as it has traditionally been applied to contracts. Of course, the overriding goal should be to facilitate e-commerce.

Many observers argue that the development of cyberspace is revolutionary and that new legal theories, and new law, are needed to govern **e-contracts**, or contracts entered into in e-commerce. To date, most courts have applied traditional common law principles to cases arising in the e-environment. New laws have been drafted, however, to apply in situations in which old laws have sometimes been thought inadequate.[1] This chapter considers some of the circumstances that exist in the computer industry and in e-commerce and some of the new laws that apply in those situations.

Shrink-Wrap Agreements

In the business world generally, the terms of a contract are frequently negotiated at the beginning of a business deal, before either party has started to perform. Sometimes, however, the parties start to perform before they have agreed on the contract's terms.

In the computer industry, this occurs in the form of a **shrink-wrap agreement** (or *shrink-wrap license,* as it is sometimes called)—an agreement the terms of which are expressed inside a box in which the goods are packaged. (The term *shrink-wrap* refers to the plastic that covers the box.) Usually, the party who opens the box is informed that he or she agrees to the terms by keeping whatever is in the box.

In most cases, this agreement is not between a retailer and a buyer, but between the manufacturer of the hardware or software and the ultimate buyer-user of the product. The terms generally concern warranties, remedies, and other issues associated with the use of the product.

Enforceable Contract Terms

In many cases, the courts have enforced the terms of shrink-wrap agreements the same as the terms of other contracts. • **Example 14.1** In an early case on this issue, a software producer sued some of its users who had downloaded telephone listings stored in the software and made the listings available on the Internet. A central question in the case was whether shrink-wrapped licenses were enforceable. Significantly, the Court of Appeals for the Seventh Circuit held that they were. The court stated that "shrink-wrapped licenses are enforceable unless their terms are objectionable on grounds applicable to contracts in general."[2] • Sometimes, the courts have reasoned that by including

---

1. In the session of Congress in 2000, for example, more than four hundred bills were introduced that contained the word *Internet.* Only a few of these were enacted, however, and most of those did not have much legal effect.
2. *ProCD, Inc. v. Zeidenberg,* 86 F.3d 1447 (7th Cir. 1996).

the terms with the product, the seller proposed a contract that the buyer could accept by using the product after having had an opportunity to read the terms.

Also, it seems practical from a business's point of view to enclose a full statement of the legal terms of a sale with the product rather than to read the statement over the phone, for example, when a buyer calls in an order for the product.

The issue in the following case was whether the court should enforce a clause in a shrink-wrap license under the Uniform Commercial Code (UCC). The specific question in the case was whether the limitation on liability in the clause was enforceable against a buyer of the software.

Case 14.1 ● M. A. Mortenson Co. v. Timberline Software Corp.

Washington Supreme Court, 2000.
140 Wash.2d 568,
998 P.2d 305.
http://www.findlaw.com/
11stategov/wa/waca.html[a]

Background and Facts Beginning in 1990, M. A. Mortenson Company, a nationwide construction contractor, bought software from Timberline Software Corporation. The software analyzed construction project requirements and bid information from subcontractors, and found the lowest-cost combination of subcontractors to do the work. The software was distributed subject to a license set forth on the outside of each disk's pouch and the inside cover of the instruction

manuals. The first screen that appeared each time the program was used also referred to the license, which included a limitation on Timberline's liability arising from the use of the software. When Mortenson upgraded its computer system in 1993, it bought Timberline's upgraded software, *Precision Bid Analysis*. This software required the use of special "protection device" hardware. After Mortenson used *Precision* to prepare a bid, it was discovered that the bid was $1.95 million less than it should have been. The software had a bug. Timberline was already aware of the problem and had provided a newer version of *Precision* to some of its other customers. Mortenson filed a suit in a Washington state court against Timberline, alleging that the software was defective. Mortenson asserted that the shrink-wrap limitation on Timberline's liability was not part of the parties' contract. Timberline filed a motion for summary judgment, which the court granted. A state intermediate appellate court affirmed the order. Mortenson appealed to the Washington Supreme Court.

---

a. This Web site is maintained by FindLaw. This page contains links to recent opinions of the Washington state courts. In the "Supreme Court" section, click on "2000." When the page opens, scroll to "May. 04, 2000" and the name of the case, and click on "67796–4" to access the opinion.

In the Words of the Court . . .
JOHNSON, J. [Justice]

* * * *

[UCC 2–204] states:

(1) A contract for sale of goods may be made in any manner sufficient to show agreement, including conduct by both parties which recognizes the existence of such a contract.

* * * *

* * * We * * * hold under [UCC 2–204] the terms of the license were part of the contract between Mortenson and Timberline, and Mortenson's use of the software constituted its assent to the agreement, including the license terms.

The terms of Timberline's license were either set forth explicitly or referenced in numerous locations. The terms were included within the

(Continued)

Case 14.1 Continued

shrinkwrap packaging of each copy of *Precision Bid Analysis;* they were present in the manuals accompanying the software; they were included with the protection devices for the software, without which the software could not be used. The fact the software was licensed was also noted on the introductory screen each time the software was used. Even accepting Mortenson's contention it never saw the terms of the license, as we must do on summary judgment, *it was not necessary for Mortenson to actually read the agreement in order to be bound by it.* [Emphasis added.]

Furthermore, [UCC 1–201(3)] defines an "agreement" as "the bargain of the parties in fact as found in their language or by implication from other circumstances including course of dealing or usage of trade or course of performance * * * ." Mortenson and Timberline had a course of dealing; Mortenson had purchased licensed software from Timberline for years prior to its upgrade to *Precision Bid Analysis.* All Timberline software, including the prior version of *Bid Analysis* used by Mortenson since at least 1990, is distributed under license. Moreover, extensive testimony and exhibits before the trial court demonstrate an unquestioned use of such license agreements throughout the software industry. Although Mortenson questioned the relevance of this evidence, there is no evidence in the record to contradict it. * * *

As the license was part of the contract between Mortenson and Timberline, its terms are enforceable unless objectionable on grounds applicable to contracts in general.

Decision and Remedy The Washington Supreme Court affirmed the decision of the lower court. The shrink-wrap license that accompanied Timberline's software was enforceable, and its limitation on Timberline's liability caused by use of the software was valid. The parties had dealt with each other for years, and the terms of the license, which was sim- ilar to those used throughout the software industry, were set forth in several locations.

For Critical Analysis—Ethical Consideration *Is it fair to hold that a person can be bound by an agreement that he or she has not read? Why or why not?*

Proposals for Additional Terms

Not all of the terms presented in shrink-wrap agreements have been enforced.[3] One important consideration is whether the parties form their contract before or after the seller communicates the terms of the shrink-wrap agreement to the buyer. If a court finds that the buyer learned of the shrink-wrap terms *after* the parties entered into a contract, the court might conclude that those terms were proposals for additional terms, which were not part of the contract unless the buyer expressly agreed to them.

In the following case, the court was asked to decide, among other things, whether to enforce an arbitration clause that was part of a set of "Standard Terms and Conditions" included in every box of every computer the defendant sold.

---

3. See, for example, *Step-Saver Data Systems, Inc. v. Wyse Technology,* 939 F.2d 91 (3d Cir. 1991).

Case 14.2 ● Klocek v. Gateway, Inc.

United States District Court,
District of Kansas, 2000.
104 F.Supp.2d 1332.

Background and Facts Whenever it sells a computer, Gateway, Inc., includes a copy of its "Standard Terms and Conditions Agreement" in the box that contains the power cables and instruction manuals. At the top of the first page, in a printed box and in emphasized type, is the following: "NOTE TO THE CUSTOMER: * * * By keeping your Gateway 2000 computer system beyond five (5) days after the date of delivery, you accept these Terms and Conditions." This document is four pages long and contains sixteen numbered paragraphs. Paragraph 10 states, "dispute resolution. Any dispute or controversy arising out of or relating to this Agreement or its interpretation shall be settled exclusively and finally by arbitration." William Klocek bought a Gateway computer. Dissatisfied when it proved to be incompatible with his other computer equipment, he filed a suit in a federal district court against Gateway and others, alleging in part breach of contract. Gateway filed a motion to dismiss, asserting that Klocek was required to submit his claims to arbitration under Gateway's "Standard Terms." Klocek argued that these terms were not part of the contract for the purchase of the computer.

In the Words of the Court . . .
VRATIL, District Judge.

* * * *

* * * [UCC 2–207] provides:

Additional terms in acceptance or confirmation. (1) A definite and seasonable [timely] expression of acceptance or a written confirmation which is sent within a reasonable time operates as an acceptance even though it states terms additional to or different from those offered or agreed upon, unless acceptance is expressly made conditional on assent to the additional or different terms.

(2) The additional terms are to be construed as proposals for addition to the contract [if the contract is not between merchants].

* * * *

Under [UCC] 2–207, [Gateway's] Standard Terms constitute either an expression of acceptance or written confirmation. As an expression of acceptance, the Standard Terms would constitute a counter-offer only if Gateway expressly made its acceptance conditional on plaintiff's [Klocek's] assent to the additional or different terms. The conditional nature of the acceptance must be clearly expressed in a manner sufficient to notify the offeror [Klocek] that the offeree [Gateway] is unwilling to proceed with the transaction unless the additional or different terms are included in the contract. Gateway provides no evidence that at the time of the sales transaction, it informed plaintiff that the transaction was conditioned on plaintiff's acceptance of the Standard Terms. Moreover, the mere fact that Gateway shipped the goods with the terms attached did not communicate to plaintiff any unwillingness to proceed without plaintiff's agreement to the Standard Terms.

Because plaintiff is not a merchant, additional or different terms contained in the Standard Terms did not become part of the parties' agreement unless plaintiff expressly agreed to them. Gateway argues that plaintiff demonstrated acceptance of the arbitration provision by keeping the computer more than five days after the date of delivery. Although the Standard Terms purport to work that result, Gateway has not presented evidence that plaintiff expressly

(Continued)

Case 14.2 Continued

agreed to those Standard Terms. Gateway states only that it enclosed the Standard Terms inside the computer box for plaintiff to read afterwards. It provides no evidence that it informed plaintiff of the five-day review-and-return period as a condition of the sales transaction, or that the parties contemplated additional terms to the agreement. * * * Thus, * * * the Court overrules Gateway's motion to dismiss.

Decision and Remedy The court denied Gateway's motion to dismiss. The court reasoned that it would enforce the arbitration provision in Gateway's "Standard Terms" if they were part of the contract for the sale of the computer. The court concluded that those terms were not part of the contract, because Gateway did not show, as required under UCC 2–207, that it told Klocek its acceptance of the deal was conditioned on his agreeing to those terms or that he agreed to them.[a]

For Critical Analysis—Technological Consideration *Note how the court in this case applied UCC provisions to a shrink-wrap contract. Can you think of some other ways in which the courts are applying traditional laws to business practices that did not exist when the UCC was drafted?*

_____

a. Klocek's complaint was later dismissed on the ground that his claim did not satisfy the court's amount-in-controversy requirement for diversity jurisdiction. See *Klocek v. Gateway, Inc.,* 104 F.Supp.2d 1332 (D.Kan. 2000).

Click-On Agreements

Click-On Agreement This occurs when a buyer, completing a transaction on a computer, is required to indicate his or her assent to be bound by the terms of an offer by clicking on a button that says, for example, "I agree." Sometimes referred to as a *click-on license* or a *click-wrap agreement.*

A **click-on agreement** (or *click-on license* or *click-wrap agreement,* as it is sometimes called) occurs when a buyer, completing a transaction on a computer, is required to indicate his or her assent to be bound by the terms of an offer by clicking on a button that says, for example, "I agree." The terms may be contained on a Web site through which the buyer is obtaining goods or services, or they may appear on a computer screen when software is loaded. • **Example 14.2** Suppose that you want to install some antivirus software on your computer. You purchase a CD-ROM containing the software from the manufacturer and start the installation process. Before you can actually install it, however, a licensing agreement pops up on the screen. The agreement lists what you may and may not do with respect to the software, what warranties and damages disclaimers are being made by the manufacturer, and so on. At the top of the agreement, in all capital letters, is a statement that the software will be licensed to you "only upon the condition that you accept all of the terms contained in this license agreement." Only if you click on "Accept" can you proceed to install the software.•

Exhibit 14–1 contains the language of a click-on disclaimer that accompanies software made and marketed by Adobe Systems, Inc.

Click-on agreements can be an important part of doing business online. E-commerce may involve businesses selling goods and services to consumers in business-to-consumer, or B2C, transactions. An increasing percentage of the deals transacted in cyberspace, however, involve business-to-business (B2B) transactions. For more information about this aspect of e-commerce, see this chapter's *Legal E-nvironment* feature on page 398.

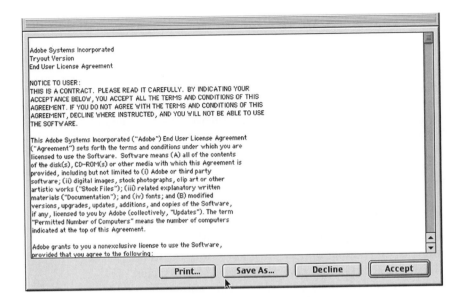

Exhibit 14–1
A Click-On
Disclaimer

Under the Uniform Commercial Code (UCC), parties can make a contract for a sale of goods "in any manner sufficient to show agreement, including conduct by both parties which recognizes the existence of a contract."[4] The *Restatement (Second) of Contracts* states that parties may agree to a contract "by written or spoken words or by other action or by failure to act."[5] With these provisions in mind, it seems that a binding contract can be created over the Internet by clicking on an "I agree" button.

The following case was the first one to involve the enforceability of a click-on agreement. The court was asked to decide, among other things, whether the defendants had breached certain "Terms of Service" that were posted on a Web site and accompanied by an "I agree" button, which the defendants had clicked.

---

4. UCC 2–204.
5. *Restatement (Second) of Contracts*, Section 19.

Case 14.3 ● Hotmail Corp. v. Van$ Money Pie, Inc.

United States District Court,
Northern District of California, 1998.
47 U.S.P.Q.2d 1020.[a]

Background and Facts Hotmail Corporation provides free e-mail service to more than eighty million subscribers. To obtain the service, at Hotmail's Web site a prospective subscriber clicks on an "I accept" button to agree to Hotmail's "Terms of Service." These terms prohibit a subscriber from using

the service to send spam.[b] All of the millions of daily e-mail messages that subscribers send and receive automatically display Hotmail's domain name "hotmail.com" and its signature statement, "Get Your Private, Free Email at **http://www.hotmail. com**." In 1997, Van$ Money Pie, Inc., and others began using Hotmail's service to send spam peddling pornography, bulk e-mailing software, "get-rich-quick" schemes, and other items. Hotmail was soon inundated

---

a. This reporter is the *United States Patent Quarterly, Second Series*, which is published by the Bureau of National Affairs, Inc., in Washington, D.C.

b. *Spam* is unsolicited commercial bulk e-mail similar to "junk" mail sent through the U.S. Postal Service.

(Continued)

Case 14.3 Continued

with hundreds of thousands of misdirected responses to the spam, including complaints from subscribers and returned e-mail that had been sent to nonexistent or incorrect addresses. This took up a substantial amount of Hotmail's computer capacity, threatened to adversely affect subscribers in sending and receiving e-mail, and resulted in significant costs to Hotmail in terms of increased personnel to sort and respond to the complaints. Hotmail filed a suit in a federal district court against the spammers, alleging, among other things, breach of contract and fraud. Hotmail asked the court to enjoin the defendants' use of Hotmail's service before the trial.

In the Words of the Court . . .
WARE, J. [Judge]

* * * *

Breach of Contract
* * * The evidence supports a finding that plaintiff will likely prevail on its breach of contract claim and that there are at least serious questions going to the merits of this claim in that plaintiff has presented evidence of the following: that defendants obtained a number of Hotmail mailboxes and access to Hotmail's services; that in so doing defendants agreed to abide by Hotmail's Terms of Service which prohibit using a Hotmail account for purposes of sending spam and/or pornography; that defendants breached their contract with Hotmail by using Hotmail's services to facilitate sending spam and/or pornography; that Hotmail complied with the conditions of the contract except those from which its performance was excused; and that if defendants are not enjoined they will continue to create such accounts in violation of the Terms of Service.

Fraud and Misrepresentation
* * * The cause of action for fraud includes willfully deceiving another with intent to induce him to alter his position to his injury or risk by asserting, as a fact, that which is not true, by one who has no reasonable ground for believing it to be true; or by suppressing a fact, by one who is bound to disclose it, or who gives information of other facts which are likely to mislead for want of communication of that fact; or by making a promise without any intention of performing it.
* * * The evidence supports a finding that plaintiff will likely prevail on its fraud and misrepresentation claim and that there are at least serious questions going to the merits of this claim in that plaintiff has presented evidence of the following: that defendants fraudulently obtained a number of Hotmail accounts, promising to abide by the Terms of Service without any intention of doing so and suppressing the fact that such accounts were created for the purpose of facilitating a spamming operation, and that defendants' fraud and misrepresentation caused Hotmail to allow defendants to create and use Hotmail's accounts to Hotmail's injury. In addition, the evidence supports a finding that defendants' falsification of e-mails to make it appear that such messages and the responses thereto were authorized to be transmitted via Hotmail's computers and stored on Hotmail's computer system—when defendants knew that sending such spam was unauthorized by Hotmail—constitutes fraud and misrepresentation, and that Hotmail relied on such misrepresentations to allow the e-mails to be transmitted over Hotmail's services and to take up storage space on Hotmail's computers, to Hotmail's injury.

Case 14.3 Continued

Decision and Remedy The court concluded that Hotmail was entitled to a preliminary injunction on several grounds, including the likelihood that Hotmail would prevail on its claims for breach of contract and fraud. In reaching this conclusion, the court recognized Hotmail's online service agreement, with its click-on acceptance button, to be an enforceable contract.

For Critical Analysis—Social Consideration *In your opinion, are most consumers fully aware of the legal consequences of clicking an "I agree" box on a Web site?*

E-Signatures

As discussed in Chapter 13, in many cases a contract, to be enforced, requires the signature of the party against whom enforcement is sought. A significant issue in the context of e-commerce has to do with how electronic signatures, or **e-signatures,** can be created and verified on e-contracts.

Before the days when most people could write, they signed documents with an "X." Then came the handwritten signature, followed by typed signatures, printed signatures, and, most recently, digital signatures that are transmitted electronically. Throughout the evolution of signature technology, debates over what constitutes a valid signature have occurred, and with good reason—without some consensus on what constitutes a valid signature, little business or legal work could be accomplished.

> **Recall** The Statute of Frauds requires that a contract for the sale of goods priced at $500 or more must be in writing to be enforceable.

> **E-Signature** An electronic sound, symbol, or process attached to or logically associated with a record and executed or adopted by a person with the intent to sign the record, according to the Uniform Electronic Transactions Act.

E-Signature Technologies

Today, there are numerous technologies that allow electronic documents to be signed. These include digital signatures and alternative technologies.

The most prevalent e-signature technology is the *asymmetric cryptosystem,* which creates a digital signature using two different (asymmetric) cryptographic "keys." In such a system, a person attaches a digital signature to a document using a private key, or code. The key has a publicly available counterpart. Anyone can use it with the appropriate software to verify that the digital signature was made using the private key. A **cybernotary,** or legally recognized certification authority, issues the key pair, identifies the owner of the keys, and certifies the validity of the public key. The cybernotary also serves as a repository for public keys. Cybernotaries already are available, but they do not operate within any existing legal framework because they are so new.

> **Cybernotary** A legally recognized certification authority that issues the keys for digital signatures, identifies their owners, certifies their validity, and serves as a repository for public keys.

Another type of signature technology, known as *signature dynamics,* involves capturing a sender's signature using a stylus and an electronic digitizer pad. A computer program takes the signature's measurements, the sender's identity, the time and date of the signature, and the identity of the hardware. This information is then placed in an encrypted *biometric token* attached to the document being transmitted. To verify the authenticity of the signature, the recipient of the document compares the measurements of the signature with the measurements in the token. When this type of e-signature is used, it is not necessary to have a third party verify the signatory's identity.

Other forms of e-signature have been—or are now being—developed as well. For example, some e-signatures use "smart cards." A smart card is a credit-card–size device that is embedded with code and other data. As with

Legal *e*-nvironment

The Burgeoning Business-to-Business Online Marketplace

The concept of an auction has been around for thousands of years. The most famous auction site on the Internet—eBay—has been around for only several years. Initially, eBay online auctions consisted of individuals selling items to other individuals, called consumer-to-consumer, or C2C, transactions. Eventually, merchants began selling overstocks and other items directly to consumers through the eBay auction site and on many other similar sites that were created, such as Yahoo Auction. These types of online auction transactions have been labeled business-to-consumer, or B2C, transactions.

Enter the B2B Market

It wasn't long before the power of the Internet to reduce the cost of doing business became apparent. The result has been the advent of numerous business-to-business (B2B) online sites. These have taken on many forms. Some are simply a collection of supplier sites linked together with powerful software. They enable a business that wishes to purchase, for example, paper supplies to search a B2B sales site to find the lowest price among a variety of competing businesses that sell paper supplies.

More generally, though, online B2B sites have created a giant marketplace for the exchange of goods and services, the likes of which has never been seen. One of the largest is Covisint. This Internet marketplace is jointly owned by five large automakers: General Motors, Ford, DaimlerChrysler, Renault, and Nissan Motors. Covisint's online joint venturers also include two information technology companies, Commerce One and Oracle. The five automakers plan to eventually funnel their combined annual spending of over $300 billion through this single Internet portal. Automobile manufacturer suppliers might add another $500 billion. The goal, of course, is to achieve significant cost savings. This Internet site features procurement, online quoting, and collaborative product design. It is estimated that the automobile makers using Covisint will reduce costs by up to 5 percent—which translates into millions of dollars per year for each company. This site offers auctions, catalogues, and expansion of supply-change management.

Similar sites exist in virtually every industry now. Boeing Company has created a B2B exchange for the aerospace industry. Its participants include Lockheed Martin Corporation, Raytheon Company, and BAE Systems, all three of which are Boeing's largest competitors. In the wood-products industry, Weyerhaeuser has created an exchange that includes its competitors, International Paper and Georgia-Pacific Corporation.

Potential Government Concerns

When competitors get together, governments get worried. Consequently, regulatory agencies in the United States, Germany, and elsewhere have been examining carefully the functions of large electronic B2B exchanges that are funded and supported by competitors in a single industry. It took months before the Federal Trade Commission (FTC) decided, in late 2000, to give regulatory approval to the automakers that established Covisint. The FTC indicated that it wanted to make sure that automakers were not simply collaborating to form an illegal cartel whose sole aim was to fix prices and harm competing suppliers. Undoubtedly, the FTC will examine B2B Web sites in the areas of health care, steel manufacturing, agriculture, and aerospace—to name only a few. (For additional issues concerning antitrust and cyberspace, see Chapter 23.)

For Critical Analysis: *Traditional methods used to procure goods have been via mail, fax, and phone. Does procurement online via B2B create any new legal issues?*

credit and debit cards, this smart card can be inserted into computers to transfer information. Unlike those other cards, however, a smart card could be used to establish a person's identity as validly as a signature on a piece of paper. In addition, technological innovations now under way will allow an e-signature to be evidenced by an image of one's retina, fingerprint, or face that is scanned by a computer and then matched to a numeric code. The scanned image and the numeric code are then filed with security companies that maintain files on an accessible server that can be used to authenticate a transaction.

State Laws Governing E-Signatures

Most states have laws governing e-signatures. The problem is that the state e-signature laws are not uniform. • **Example 14.3** Some states—California is a notable example—provide that many types of documents cannot be signed with e-signatures, while other states are more permissive in this respect. Additionally, some states recognize the validity of only digital signatures, while others permit other types of e-signatures.•

In an attempt to create more uniformity among the states, the National Conference of Commissioners on Uniform State Laws promulgated the Uniform Electronic Transactions Act (UETA) in 1999. The UETA defines an *e-signature* as "an electronic sound, symbol, or process attached to or logically associated with a record and executed or adopted by a person with the intent to sign the record."[6] A **record** is "information that is inscribed on a tangible medium or that is stored in an electronic or other medium and is retrievable in perceivable form."[7]

This definition of *e-signature* includes encrypted digital signatures, names (intended as signatures) at the ends of e-mail, and a click on a Web page if the click includes the identification of the person. The UETA also states, among other things, that a signature may not be denied legal effect or enforceability solely because it is in electronic form. (Other aspects of the UETA are discussed later in this chapter.)

> **Be Aware** A uniform act does not become law in a state until adopted as law by that state's legislature.

> **Record** Information that is inscribed in either a tangible medium or stored in an electronic or other medium and that is retrievable, according to the Uniform Electronic Transactions Act. The Uniform Computer Information Transaction Act uses *record* instead of *writing*.

Federal Law on E-Signatures and E-Documents

In 2000, Congress enacted the Electronic Signatures in Global and National Commerce Act (E-SIGN Act) to provide that no contract, record, or signature may be "denied legal effect" solely because it is in an electronic form. In other words, under this law, an electronic signature is as valid as a signature on paper, and an electronic document can be as enforceable as a paper one.

For an electronic signature to be enforceable, the contracting parties must have agreed to use electronic signatures. For an electronic document to be valid, it must be in a form that can be retained and accurately reproduced.

Contracts and documents that are exempt include court papers, divorce decrees, evictions, foreclosures, health-insurance terminations, prenuptial agreements, and wills. Also, the only agreements governed by the Uniform Commercial Code (UCC) that fall under this law are those covered by Articles 2 and 2A, and UCC 1–107 and 1–206.

Despite the limitations, the E-SIGN Act expands enormously the possibilities for contracting online. • **Example 14.4** From a remote location, a businessperson might open an account with a financial institution, obtain a mortgage or other loan, and buy insurance, over the Internet. Payments and transfers of funds could be done entirely online. This can avoid the time and costs associated with producing, delivering, signing, and returning paper documents.• (See this chapter's *Inside the Legal Environment* on the next page for a further discussion of the E-SIGN Act and its implications for e-commerce.)

---

6. UETA 102(8).
7. UETA 102(15).

Inside the Legal Environment

E-Signatures: What Lies Ahead?

Many have heralded the Electronic Signatures in Global and National Commerce Act (E-SIGN Act), which became effective October 1, 2000, as the single most important piece of technology legislation ever enacted. According to one observer, "Not since notarized written signatures replaced wax and signet rings has history seen such a fundamental change in contract law."[a] Perhaps to underscore the act's historic significance, President Clinton signed the act into law in Philadelphia, the city in which the U.S. Constitution was drafted over 224 years ago—and signed with quill pens (in contrast to the digital signature used by President Clinton).

As discussed on the previous page, the act provided that electronic signatures, or e-signatures, are legally valid and enforceable. Although a contract signed electronically may be invalid or unenforceable for other reasons, it cannot be deemed unenforceable merely because an electronic signature or electronic record was used in its formation.

Who Will Benefit from E-SIGN?

Today, business-to-consumer (B2C) transactions make up a large part of Internet e-commerce traffic. Some predict that as a result of the E-SIGN Act, consumers will readily turn to the Internet to purchase even more items than they currently do, including homes, groceries, online novels, and the like. Yet until the online industry comes up with a system of obtaining and protecting digital signatures, and convincing consumers that they are safe and secure, consumers will be wary of using them.

Others believe that the real beneficiaries will be parties engaged in business-to-business (B2B) transactions, which can easily involve substantial sums and complicated agreements to be performed over time. By giving legal effect to e-signatures, the E-SIGN Act increased the acceptability of e-contracts and, because of the time and cost savings e-contracts generate, they will likely become much more widely used in the B2B marketplace.

What the Act Did Not Do

What the act did *not* do is provide any standard for authenticating e-signatures or include solutions to other problems associated with e-contracting. How will the technology be managed? What kind of signature verification process will be required? If encryption "keys" are used, how will they be generated? Where can you get one? Will there be digital notaries? What if a hacker or other technologically sophisticated person "steals" one's signature and "forges" electronic documents with it? Basically, the act left these and other questions to be decided by the parties to e-commerce contracts, the technology industry, and the states.

There is another problem. An element common to all valid signatures is that they evidence an *intent to be bound* by the document that is being signed. Section 1–201(39) of the Uniform Commercial Code, for example, provides that a signature may include "any symbol executed or adopted by a party with present intention to authenticate a writing." Thus, any symbol, including an *X*, a person's initials, or even a thumbprint, can suffice as a signature—but *only* if the symbol is used with the intention of authenticating the writing. Section 106(5) of the E-SIGN Act emphasizes the intent factor by defining an electronic signature as any "electronic sound, symbol, or process, attached to or logically associated with a contract or other record and executed or adopted by a person with the intent to sign the record." Yet how can intent be measured in the electronic-contracting environment? How do you know if an online party even has contractual capacity? Again, this question is left up to the parties and the states to decide.

A major goal of the E-SIGN Act was to encourage e-commerce through the use of electronic signatures. Yet the act itself does not accomplish this goal. More sigificant will be how quickly the states and the marketplace adopt uniform standards for authenticating e-signatures, because this technology is the key to the expansion of e-commerce.

For Critical Analysis: *At the time the E-SIGN Act was passed, twenty-two states already had enacted some form of electronic-transactions laws, and another twenty-four states had addressed e-commerce contracts in some way. Why, then, did Congress and the president decide that federal legislation was necessary?*

---

a. Mark Ballard, "E-SIGN a Nudge, Not Revolution," *The National Law Journal*, September 25, 2000, p. B1.

E-Agents

As you will learn in Chapter 17, an *agency* relationship is one in which one party (called the *agent*) agrees to represent or act for the other (called the *principal*). An electronic agent, or **e-agent**, is not a person but a semi-autonomous computer program that is capable of executing specific tasks.[8] Examples of e-agents in e-commerce include software that can search through many databases and retrieve only relevant information for the user.

Some e-agents are used to make purchases on the Internet. An Internet user might employ one of the following e-agents to search the Web for a particular book: PriceScan, MX Bookfinder, and Bestbookbuys. Any one of these e-agents will scour the Web for the lowest price for that particular book title. Once found, the e-agent usually offers links to the appropriate Web sites. Other shopping e-agents locate other specific products in online catalogues and actually negotiate product acquisition, as well as delivery.

> **E-Agent** A computer program, or electronic or other automated means used to independently initiate an action or to respond to electronic messages or performances without review by an individual, according to the Uniform Computer Information Transactions Act.

How Much Authority?

An important aspect of agency law is the scope of an agent's authority to act on behalf of his or her principal. Under traditional agency law, contracts formed by an agent normally are legally binding on the principal *if* the principal authorized the agent, either expressly or impliedly, to form the contracts. One of the controversies involving e-agents concerns the extent of an e-agent's authority to act on behalf of its principal. Consider a not-too-uncommon example.

● **Example 14.5** Software that an e-agent might find for its principal will undoubtedly involve a click-on agreement. E-agents searching the Internet may run into a variety of such click-on agreements, which contain different terms and conditions. If the e-agent ignores the terms and conditions of a licensing agreement outlined in the click-on setting, is the principal bound by the agreement? Conversely, a click-on agreement may exempt a third party from liability resulting from an underlying product or service. Is the principal bound by this term? With respect to human agents, the courts occasionally have found that an agent could not agree to such a term without explicit authority. ●

Possible Solutions

To avoid problems created by the use of e-agents, some online stores have blocked e-agents from accessing pricing information. Other online stores are developing click-on agreements that can be understood by a computer and that are therefore more conspicuous for e-agents.

The Uniform Computer Information Transactions Act (UCITA), a proposed law issued in 1999 and discussed in detail in the next section, specifically addresses the issue of e-agents. Section 107(d) of the act provides that any individual or company that uses an e-agent "is bound by the operations of the electronic agent, even if no individual was aware of or reviewed the agent's operations or the results of the operations." The liability of individuals and

---

8. The Uniform Computer Information Transactions Act (UCITA), discussed later in this chapter, defines an *e-agent* as "a computer program, electronic or other automated means used to independently initiate an action or to respond to electronic messages or performances without review by an individual" [UCITA 102(a)(28)].

companies for the acts of e-agents, however, is qualified by Section 206(a) of the UCITA, which states that "a court may grant appropriate relief if the operations resulted from fraud, electronic mistake, or the like."

The Uniform Computer Information Transactions Act

Among the proposed new laws that go beyond the existing law is the Uniform Computer Information Transactions Act (UCITA). The UCITA is a draft of legislation suggested to the states by the National Conference of Commissioners on Uniform State Laws (NCCUSL) and the American Law Institute (ALI). These organizations have initiated many of the most significant laws that apply to traditional commerce, including the Uniform Commercial Code (UCC).

The UCITA's History

In the early 1990s, with the continued development of the software industry, it became apparent that Article 2 of the Uniform Commercial Code (UCC), which deals with the sale of goods (tangible property), could not be applied to most transactions involving software.

There are two basic reasons for this. First, software is not a "good" (tangible property)—it is electronic information (intangible property). Second, the "sale" of software generally involves a license (right to use) rather than a sale (passage of title from the seller to the purchaser). The producer of the software either directly contracted with the licensee (user) or employed a distribution system—for example, authorizing retailers to distribute (sell) copies of its software to customers (end users). Because neither transaction involved the sale of goods, new rules needed to be established.

During the next eight years, the development of these new rules by a drafting committee of the NCCUSL were widely discussed and debated in a variety of forums. Controversy surrounded the proposed drafts, which probably received more comment from more groups than any other proposed uniform act.

PROPOSED UCC ARTICLE 2B   Initially, the drafters tried to modify Article 2 of the UCC to incorporate the licensing of goods with the sale of goods. In 1995, the NCCUSL decided that a separate article to be titled "Article 2B—Licenses" was needed. The drafting committee consisted of representatives of the NCCUSL and the ALI, members of the American Bar Association, and Professor Raymond T. Nimmer (University of Houston Law Center), who served as committee reporter. The first drafts issued by this committee covered the licensing of *all* information. A number of powerful industry groups, including broadcast groups, music associations, and print publishers, objected to this broad inclusion. As a result, the drafting committee narrowed the scope of Article 2B to the licensing of computer information only and retained coverage of electronic contracting.

A final proposed draft of Article 2B was published early in 1999. The ALI, which has approved and supported passage of all of the other articles of the UCC, rejected Article 2B. In April 1999, the NCCUSL and the ALI issued a press release stating that the draft would no longer be a proposed addition (Article 2B) to the UCC but would be submitted as a separate uniform act entitled the Uniform Computer Information Transactions Act (UCITA).

RECOMMENDATION TO THE STATES   The NCCUSL, by removing the draft as a part of the UCC, could proceed on its own to recommend to the states that they enact the UCITA—ALI approval was not required. In July 1999, the delegates of the NCCUSL approved the draft, by a vote of forty-three to six, for submission to the states for adoption.

For more information about the current status of the UCITA, and to learn more about other uniform laws proposed by the NCCUSL, see the discussion of the NCCUSL's Web site later in this chapter.

OPPOSITION AND AMENDMENTS   The UCITA, as it was proposed in 1999, met opposition from a number of industry associations, state insurance commissions, and consumer groups. In fact, the industry associations indicated that they would strongly oppose state adoptions. These industry associations included the Motion Picture Association of America, Magazine Publishers of America, the Newspaper Association of America, the National Cable Television Association, the National Association of Broadcasters, the Recording Industry Association of America, and various groups in the telecommunications industry. Perhaps this opposition contributed substantially to the fact that there were only two state adoptions in 1999.

Because of this disapproval and the concerns of these groups, plus the need for clarity concerning whether transactions involving the relationships between an insured and the insurer were excluded, the NCCUSL worked out a package of amendments for passage in August 2000. The amendments basically excluded from the UCITA the business activities of the members of the industry organizations just mentioned. On passage of the amendments, the associations agreed formally in writing to withdraw their opposition to the individual states' enactment of the UCITA. Various consumer groups continue to oppose the UCITA, however, as you will learn in *Ethical Issue 14.1* later in this chapter on page 409.

The UCITA's Coverage and Content

The UCITA establishes a comprehensive set of rules covering contracts involving computer information. **Computer information** is "information in electronic form obtained from or through use of a computer, or that is in digital or equivalent form capable of being processed by a computer."[9]

Under this definition, the act covers contracts to license or purchase software, contracts to create a computer program, contracts for computer games, contracts for online access to databases, contracts to distribute information on the Internet, "diskettes" that contain computer programs, online books, and other similar contracts.

Computer Information
Information in electronic form obtained from or through use of a computer, or that is in digital or an equivalent form capable of being processed by a computer.

THE UCITA MAY APPLY TO ONLY PART OF A TRANSACTION   The UCITA does not apply generally to the sale of goods even if software is embedded in or used in the production of the goods (except a computer). Examples include television sets, stereos, books, and automobiles. It also does not apply to traditional movies, records, or cable. These industries are, for the most part, specifically excluded.

When a transaction includes computer information as defined in the act and subject matter other than computer information, the UCITA generally provides

---

9. UCITA 102(10).

that if the primary subject matter deals with computer and information rights, the act applies to the entire transaction. If this is not the primary subject matter, then the act applies only to the part "of the transaction involving computer information, informational rights in it and creation or modification of it."

PARTIES CAN "OPT OUT"   As with most other uniform acts that apply to business, the UCITA allows the parties to waive or vary the provisions of the act by a contract. The parties may even agree to "opt out" of the act and, for contracts not covered by the act, to "opt in." In other words, the UCITA expressly recognizes the freedom to contract and supports the idea that this is a basic principle of contract law.

Default Rules Under the Uniform Computer Information Transaction Act, rules that apply only in the absence of an agreement between contracting parties to the contrary.

The UCITA stresses the parties' agreement (similar to the emphasis in UCC Article 2), and the act's provisions apply in the absence of an agreement.[10] These provisions are called **default rules**. As with other uniform statutes, rules relating to good faith, diligence, public policy, unconscionability, and related principles cannot be varied or deleted by agreement.

RIGHTS AND RESTRICTIONS   The licensing of information is the primary method used for transferring computer information in business today. A license contract involves a transfer of computer information, such as software, from a seller (the licensor) to a buyer (the licensee). The licensee is given certain rights to use and control the computer information during the license period. Title does not pass, and quite often the license places restrictions on the licensee's use of, and rights to copy and control, the computer information. Many of the sections of the UCITA deal with the rights and restrictions that can be imposed on the parties in the license.

FROM CONTRACT FORMATION TO CONTRACT REMEDIES   The UCITA, which consists of nine "parts," covers everything from the formation of a contract to remedies for breach of contract. To give you an idea of the extent of the act's coverage, we list the titles of the parts and subparts of the act in Exhibit 14–2.

Highlights OF THE UCITA

The UCITA resembles UCC Article 2. Both acts have similar general provisions, including definitions (approximately sixty-six) and formal requirements (such as a Statute of Frauds, which, in the case of the UCITA, requires a written memorandum when a contract calls for a payment of $5,000 or more). Other comparable provisions include rules for offer and acceptance, unconscionable contracts or terms, parol evidence, and other principles.[11]

The UCITA goes further, however, with provisions covering the contracting parties' choice of law and choice of forum, the UCITA's relationship to federal law and other state laws, and many others.[12] These provisions make the UCITA more comprehensive in scope than UCC Article 2.

Described in the next sections are some of the UCITA's highlights. As you will note, most of them address situations that arise due to the unique nature of licensing computer information.

---

10. UCITA 113.
11. See, for example, UCITA 111.
12. See, for example, UCITA 109 and 110.

Exhibit 14–2 The UCITA—Titles of Parts and Subparts

UNIFORM COMPUTER INFORMATION TRANSACTIONS ACT	
PART I **GENERAL PROVISIONS** [SUBPART A. SHORT TITLE AND DEFINITIONS] [SUBPART B. GENERAL SCOPE AND TERMS] **PART 2** **FORMATION AND TERMS** [SUBPART A. FORMATION OF CONTRACT] [SUBPART B. TERMS OF RECORDS] [SUBPART C. ELECTRONIC CONTRACTS: GENERALLY] **PART 3** **CONSTRUCTION** [SUBPART A. GENERAL] [SUBPART B. INTERPRETATION] **PART 4** **WARRANTIES** **PART 5** **TRANSFER OF INTERESTS AND RIGHTS** [SUBPART A. OWNERSHIP AND TRANSFERS] [SUBPART B. FINANCING ARRANGEMENTS]	**PART 6** **PERFORMANCE** [SUBPART A. GENERAL] [SUBPART B. PERFORMANCE IN DELIVERY OF COPIES] [SUBPART C. SPECIAL TYPES OF CONTRACTS] [SUBPART D. LOSS AND IMPOSSIBILITY] [SUBPART E. TERMINATION] **PART 7** **BREACH OF CONTRACT** [SUBPART A. GENERAL] [SUBPART B. DEFECTIVE COPIES] [SUBPART C. REPUDIATION AND ASSURANCES] **PART 8** **REMEDIES** [SUBPART A. GENERAL] [SUBPART B. DAMAGES] [SUBPART C. REMEDIES RELATED TO PERFORMANCE] **PART 9** **MISCELLANEOUS PROVISIONS**

MASS-MARKET LICENSES Basically, a *mass-market* transaction is either (1) a consumer contract or (2) a transaction in which the computer information is directed to the general public and the end-user licensee acquires the information in a retail transaction.

A **mass-market license** is an electronic form contract that is usually presented with a package of computer information purchased. These licenses are commonly passed on by having the license contract shrink-wrapped or, in the case of an online transaction, click-wrapped with the computer information (when a certain link is clicked on).

Mass-Market License An e-contract that is presented with a package of computer information in the form of a *click-on license* or a *shrink-wrap license*.

These licenses are different from negotiated licenses in that mass-market licenses are automatically enforceable, as long as the terms are readily available and the licensee has had an opportunity to review the license terms.

If the licensee does not want the computer information for any reason, the UCITA allows the licensee to return the computer information for a refund and recover any reasonable expenses incurred in making the removal and return of the computer information. The UCITA provides that these rights of return and entitlement to reasonable expenses cannot be waived or disclaimed by the licensor.

WARRANTIES The UCITA provides for basically the same warranties as provided for in UCC Article 2. Thus, the licensor's affirmations of fact or promises concerning the computer information (as a basis for the bargain) constitute express warranties.[13] Implied warranties are also provided for by the act (and can be disclaimed, as under UCC Article 2).[14] The UCITA's implied warranties of merchantability and fitness are closely tailored to the information content and the "compatibility of the computer systems."[15]

AUTHENTICATION AND ATTRIBUTION Before the emergence of electronic contracting, parties generally knew each other, and many contracts contained the signatures of the parties. Today, we deal with electronic signatures, or e-signatures. We want to be sure that the "person" sending the electronic message is in fact the person whose electronic message is being transmitted. For this reason, like the revisions of other statutes, the UCITA's rules were revised to provide for the authentication of e-signatures.

Authenticate To sign a record, or with the intent to sign a record, to execute, or to adopt an electronic sound, symbol, or the like to link with the record. See *record*.

To **authenticate** means to sign a record, or with the intent to sign a record, to execute, or to adopt an electronic sound, symbol, or the like to link with the record. As noted earlier in this chapter, a record is information that is inscribed in either a tangible medium or stored in an electronic or other medium and that is retrievable. The UCITA uses the word *record* instead of *writing*.

To ensure that the person sending the electronic computer information is the same person whose e-signature accompanies the information, the UCITA has a procedure, referred to as the *attribution procedure,* that sets forth steps for identifying a person that sends an electronic communication. These steps, which can be specified by the contracting parties, can be simple or complex as long as they are commercially reasonable.

Attribution procedures can also have an effect on liability for errors in the message content. If the attribution procedure is in place to detect errors, the party who conforms to the procedure is not bound by the error. Consumers who make unintended errors are not bound as long as the consumer notifies the other party promptly, returns the computer information received, and has not benefited from its use.

Under the UCITA, as under previous law, there is no requirement that all of the terms in a contract actually must have been read by all of the parties to be effective. For example, clicking on a link that states to do so is to agree to certain terms can be enough. The following case illustrates a court's evaluation of the validity of a clause in a click-on agreement.

---

13. UCITA 402.
14. UCITA 401.
15. UCITA 403 and 405.

Case 14.4 ● Caspi v. Microsoft Network, LLC[a]

New Jersey Superior Court,
Appellate Division, 1999.
323 N.J.Super. 118,
732 A.2d 528.
**http://lawlibrary.rutgers.edu/
search.shtml**[b]

b. This Web site is maintained by Rutgers University School of Law—Camden. This page contains links to recent opinions of the New Jersey state courts. In the "Additional Information:" row, click on "Search by party name." When that page opens, in the first column, click the "Appellate Division" box. In the second column, in the "First Name" box, enter "Caspi," and click on "Submit Form." When the results appear, click on the appropriate link to access the opinion.

a. *LLC* is an abbreviation for limited liability company, a hybrid form of business enterprise that offers the limited liability of a corporation and the tax advantages of a partnership. See Chapter 16.

Case 14.4 Continued

Background and Facts Microsoft Network, LLC (MSN), is an online computer service. Before becoming an MSN member, a prospective subscriber is prompted by MSN software to view multiple computer screens of information, including a membership agreement that contains a forum-selection clause.[c] This clause calls for any claims against MSN to be litigated in the state of Washington. MSN's membership agreement appears on the computer screen in a scrollable window next to blocks providing the choices "I Agree" and "I Don't Agree." Prospective members have the option to click "I Agree" or "I Don't Agree" at any point while scrolling through the agreement. Registration proceeds only after the potential sub-scriber has the opportunity to view, and assents to, the membership agreement. No charges are incurred until a subscriber clicks on "I Agree." Steven Caspi was a subscriber. Alleging that MSN rolled over his membership into a more expensive plan without notice,[d] Caspi filed a suit in a New Jersey state court against MSN. Other subscribers, claiming to represent 1.5 million members, joined the suit. MSN filed a motion to dismiss on the ground that the forum-selection clause called for the suit to be heard in the state of Washington. The court granted the motion. The plaintiffs appealed to a state intermediate appellate court, arguing that they did not have adequate notice of the clause and therefore it was not part of their contracts.

In the Words of the Court . . .
KESTIN, J.A.D. [Judge, Appellate Division]

* * * *

The scenario presented here is different [from a case in which a forum-selection clause appeared in the fine print on the back of a cruise ticket] because of the medium used, electronic versus printed; but, in any sense that matters, there is no significant distinction. The plaintiffs in [the other case] could have perused all the fine-print provisions of their travel contract if they wished before accepting the terms by purchasing their cruise ticket. The plaintiffs in this case were free to scroll through the various computer screens that presented the terms of their contracts before clicking their agreement.

Also, it seems clear that there was nothing extraordinary about the size or placement of the forum selection clause text. By every indication we have, the clause was presented in exactly the same format as most other provisions of the contract. It was the first item in the last paragraph of the electronic document. We note that a few paragraphs in the contract were presented in upper case typeface, presumably for emphasis, but most provisions, including the forum selection clause, were presented in lower case typeface. We discern nothing about the style or mode of presentation, or the placement of the provision, that can be taken as a basis for concluding that the forum selection clause was proffered unfairly, or with a design to conceal or deemphasize its provisions. *To conclude that plaintiffs are not bound by that clause would be equivalent to holding that they were bound by no other clause either, since all provisions were identically presented.* Plaintiffs must be taken to have known that they were entering into a contract; and no good purpose, consonant [in agreement or accord] with the dictates of reasonable reliability in commerce, would be served by permitting them to disavow particular provisions or the contracts as a whole. [Emphasis added.]

---

c. A *forum-selection clause* in a contract designates the court, the jurisdiction, or the dispute-resolution entity to decide any disputes arising under the contract.

d. This is known as *unilateral negative option billing,* a practice at one time condemned by the attorneys general of twenty-one states, including the attorney general of New Jersey, with regard to an MSN competitor, America Online, Inc.

(Continued)

Case 14.4 Continued

The issue of reasonable notice regarding a forum selection clause is a question of law for the court to determine. We agree with the trial court that, in the absence of a better showing than has been made, plaintiffs must be seen to have had adequate notice of the forum selection clause.

Decision and Remedy The state intermediate appellate court affirmed the decision of the lower court. The forum-selection clause contained in the click-on subscriber agreement was valid and enforceable, because it was presented in the same format as most of the rest of the agreement and potential subscribers had sufficient opportunity to view it.

For Critical Analysis—Economic Consideration *Many attorneys advise their business clients that it is especially important, when forming e-contracts, to include forum-selection clauses. Would including such a clause be more important when forming an e-contract than when forming a traditional, printed contract?*

Access Contract A contract to obtain by electronic means access to, or information from, another person's information processing system, or the equivalent of such access, according to the Uniform Computer Information Transactions Act.

ACCESS CONTRACTS The UCITA defines an **access contract** as "a contract to obtain by electronic means access to, or information from an information processing system of another person, or the equivalent of such access." This is important for most of us, if for no other reason than our ability to use the Internet. The UCITA, however, has special rules governing available times and manner of access.

SUPPORT AND SERVICE CONTRACTS TO CORRECT PERFORMANCE PROBLEMS The UCITA covers licensor support and service contracts, but no licensor is required to provide such support and service. Computer software support contracts are common, and once made, the licensor is obligated to comply with the express terms of the support contract or, if the contract is silent on an issue, to do what is reasonable in light of ordinary business standards.

ELECTRONIC SELF-HELP The UCITA allows the licensor to cancel, repossess, prevent continued use, and take similar actions on a licensee's breach of a license. The act permits the licensor to undertake "electronic self-help" to enforce the licensor's rights through electronic means.

Outside the UCITA, "self-help" refers to the right of a lessor, for example, under Article 2A of the UCC, which deals with the lease of goods, to repossess a leased computer if the lessee fails to make payments according to the terms of the lease. A lender may have this same right under Article 9, which covers secured transactions (transactions in which collateral is given as security for a loan) if a borrower fails to make payments on a loan secured by a computer.

In a transaction governed by the UCITA, electronic self-help includes the right of a software licensor to install a "turn-off" function in the software so that if the licensee violates the terms of the license, the software can be disabled from a distance. This right is most important to a small firm that licenses its software to a much larger company. Electronic self-help may be the licensor's only practical remedy if the license is breached.

There are some limitations on this right.[16] For example, the amendments to the UCITA passed in August 2000 prohibit electronic self-help in mass-market transactions. In addition, the remedy is not available unless the parties agree

---

16. See UCITA 816.

to permit electronic self-help. The licensor must give notice of the intent to use the self-help remedy at least fifteen days before doing so, along with full disclosure of the nature of the breach and information to enable the licensee to cure the breach or to communicate with the licensor concerning the situation.

A licensor is entitled on a licensee's breach to incidental and consequential damages. Of course, a licensor must attempt to mitigate those damages, but electronic self-help cannot be used if the licensor "has reason to know that its use will result in substantial injury or harm to the public health or safety or grave harm to the public interest affecting third persons involved in the dispute."

These limitations on the use of electronic self-help cannot be waived or varied by contract.

> **Remember** *Incidental damages* that result from the breach of a contract include all reasonable expenses incurred because of the breach. *Consequential damages* compensate for an indirect loss that was reasonably foreseeable at the time of the breach, such as a loss of profits.

The Uniform Electronic Transactions Act

As mentioned earlier in this chapter, another uniform law proposed by the National Conference of Commissioners on Uniform State Laws (NCCUSL) concerning e-commerce is the Uniform Electronic Transactions Act (UETA). The goal of the UETA is not to create rules for electronic transactions—for example, the act does not require digital signatures—but to support the enforcement of e-contracts.

The Validity of E-Contracts

Under the UETA, contracts entered into online, as well as other electronic documents, are presumed valid. In other words, a contract is not unenforceable simply because it is in an electronic form. The UETA does not apply to transactions governed by the UCC or the UCITA, or to wills or testamentary trusts.

The UETA and the UCITA Compared

The UETA and the UCITA have many similarities. The drafters of the laws attempted to make them consistent. Both proposals provide for such items as the following:

Ethical Issue 14.1

Does the UCITA favor the software industry over consumers?

Some consumer groups argue that the UCITA favors the software industry and will have harsh effects for consumers. One of the initial concerns of these groups was the licensor's right of electronic self-help under the act. As already mentioned, this concern was addressed by the August 2000 amendments, which prohibited the use electronic self-help with respect to mass-market transactions. Notwithstanding these amendments, a number of consumer advocates continue to oppose the UCITA. Among other things, they object to the automatic enforceability of licensing agreements, including shrink-wrap or click-on agreements, which can easily go unread by consumers. To be sure, consumers often do not take the time to read the "fine print" even in printed documents. Consumer groups who object to the enforceability of licensing agreements claim that this problem is even more prevalent with shrink-wrap and click-on agreements. (Consumers also face other problems in the e-commerce environment—for a discussion of some of these problems, see the *Legal E-nvironment* feature in Chapter 20.)

- The equivalency of records and writings.
- The validity of e-signatures.
- The formation of contracts by e-agents.
- The formation of contracts between an e-agent and a natural person.
- The attribution of an electronic act to a person if it can be proved that the act was done by the person or his or her agent.
- A provision that parties do not need to participate in e-commerce to make binding contracts.

These two uniform laws also have differences. Those differences include the following:

- The UETA supports all electronic transactions, but it does not create rules for them. The UCITA concerns only contracts that involve computer information, but for those contracts, the UCITA imposes rules.
- The UETA does not apply unless contracting parties agree to use e-commerce in their transactions. The UCITA applies to any agreement that falls within its scope.

In sum, the chief difference between the UETA and the UCITA is that the UCITA addresses e-commerce issues that the UETA does not. Those issues, and how the UCITA deals with them, were discussed in the previous sections.

The NCCUSL's Web Site

The text of the law has always been available to the public in published form. The law has never been as accessible, however, as it is now on the Internet. This means that businesspersons can be better informed about their legal rights and responsibilities today than they could even ten years ago.

One important cyberspace connection to the text of the law is the Web site of the National Conference of Commissioners on Uniform State Laws (NCCUSL). To make this connection, log on to the site at **http://www.nccusl.org**.

Site Map

The site is divided into ten sections. On one page, the NCCUSL provides information about itself ("About Us"), including its history, rules, and bylaws. On another page, the NCCUSL details the projects that it is currently working on ("Drafting Projects Underway"). "Topics under Discussion" lists subjects that the organization has assigned to its committees to review as subjects for draft legislation. The site also contains links to the NCCUSL's press releases ("Newsroom") and "What's New."

Most informative are the updates on the jurisdictions that have introduced and adopted the NCCUSL's proposed laws ("Legislative Status and Information on Uniform Acts"). This page includes, for each proposed act, a "Legislative Fact Sheet," a "Summary," and a selection of "Questions and Answers." The other sections at this site are "Meetings," "Links," "Contact Us," and "Site Map."

The UCITA and UETA Links

As of this writing, only two states—Maryland and Virginia—had adopted the UCITA. It had been introduced, however, in at least six other jurisdictions—

Delaware, Hawaii, Illinois, New Jersey, Alabama, and the District of Columbia—although no action was expected for the remainder of these states' legislative sessions. Twenty-nine states had enacted, or considered enacting, the UETA.

The NCCUSL's Web site includes an update of this short list of the states that have adopted the UCITA and the UETA or considered them for adoption. The site also contains summaries of the acts and "Question and Answer" sections concerning these proposed laws.

To access the NCCUSL's most recent information about the UCITA, select "Legislative Status and Information on Uniform Acts," and then click on the box entitled "By Subject Matter." Then select "Business Laws," scroll down to "Computer Information Transactions," and click on the type of information you desire. To find similar information about the UETA, follow the same steps, but in "Business Laws," scroll down to "Electronic Transactions," and click on the appropriate link.

To read one of the drafts of the UCITA or the UETA, however, you will need to go off this site through a link to a different site that the NCCUSL maintains with the University of Pennsylvania Law School at **http://www.law.upenn. edu/bll/ulc/ulc_frame.htm**. This site also contains the drafts of many of the other uniform laws that the NCCUSL has issued, including the UCC.

Key Terms

access contract 408	cybernotary 397	e-signature 397
authenticate 406	default rules 404	mass-market license 405
click-on agreement 394	e-agent 401	record 399
computer information 403	e-contract 390	shrink-wrap agreement 390

Chapter Summary • E-Contracts

Shrink-Wrap Agreements (See pages 390–394.)	1. **Definition**—An agreement whose terms are expressed inside a box in which the goods are packaged. The party who opens the box is informed that, by keeping the goods in the box, he or she agrees to the terms of the shrink-wrap agreement.
	2. **Enforceability**—The courts have often enforced shrink-wrap agreements, even if the purchaser-user of the goods did not read the terms of the agreement. A court may deem a shrink-wrap agreement unenforceable, however, if the buyer learns of the shrink-wrap terms *after* the parties entered into the agreement.
Click-On Agreements (See pages 394–397.)	1. **Definition**—An agreement created when a buyer, completing a transaction on a computer, is required to indicate his or her assent to be bound by the terms of an offer by clicking on a button that says, for example, "I agree." The terms of the agreement may appear on the Web site through which the buyer is obtaining goods or services, or they may appear on a computer screen when software is loaded.
	2. **Enforceability**—The courts have enforced click-on agreements, holding that by clicking "I agree," the offeree has indicated acceptance by conduct.

(Continued)

Chapter Summary • E-Contracts, *Continued*

E-Signatures
(See pages 397–400.)

1. **Definition**—The Uniform Electronic Transactions Act (UETA) defines the term *e-signature* as an electronic sound, symbol, or process attached to or logically associated with a record and executed or adopted by a person with the intent to sign the record.

2. **E-signature technologies**—Include the *asymmetric cryptosystem* (which creates a digital signature using two different cryptographic "keys"—a private key and its publicly available counterpart); *signature dynamics* (which involves capturing a sender's signature using a stylus and an electronic digitizer pad); a *smart card* (a credit-card-size device that is embedded with code and other data); and, probably in the near future, scanned images of retinas, fingerprints, or other physical characteristics linked to numeric codes.

3. **State laws governing e-signatures**—Although most states have laws governing e-signatures, these laws are not uniform. Two recently promulgated uniform acts—the UETA and the Uniform Computer Information Transactions Act (UCITA)—provide for the validity of e-signatures and may ultimately create more uniformity among the states in this respect.

4. **Federal law on e-signatures and e-documents**—The Electronic Signatures in Global and National Commerce Act (E-SIGN Act) of 2000 gave validity to e-signatures by providing that no contract, record, or signature may be "denied legal effect" solely because it is in an electronic form.

E-Agents
(See pages 401–402.)

1. **Definition**—An e-agent, or electronic agent, is a semiautonomous computer program that is capable of executing specific tasks, such as software that can search through databases and retrieve only relevant information for the agent's principal.

2. **Scope of authority**—Under agency law, a principal normally is not bound by a contract formed by an agent who lacks the authority to form that contract. One of the problems posed by e-agents is the extent to which the e-agent is authorized to form e-contracts through, for example, click-on agreements. The Uniform Computer Information Transactions Act (UCITA) addresses this problem by including specific provisions relating to e-agents.

The Uniform Computer Information Transactions Act (UCITA)
(See pages 402–409.)

1. **Definition**—A uniform act submitted to the states for adoption by the National Conference of Commissioners on Uniform State Laws (NCCUSL).

2. **Purpose**—To govern transactions involving the licensing of intangible property, such as computer information, which are not covered by Article 2 of the Uniform Commercial Code (UCC), because Article 2 deals with the sale of goods, defined as the passage of title to tangible goods from a seller to a buyer.

3. **Coverage and content**—The act applies to contracts involving computer information, such as contracts to license or purchase software. *Computer information* is defined as "information in electronic form obtained from or through use of a computer, or that is in digital or equivalent form capable of being processed by a computer." As with most other uniform acts that apply to business, the UCITA allows the parties to waive or vary its provisions by contract or even agree to "opt out" or "opt in" to UCITA provisions. The UCITA covers all aspects of e-contracts involving computer information, from contract formation to contract remedies.

Chapter Summary • E-Contracts

The Uniform Electronic Transactions Act (UETA) (See pages 409–410.)	1. **Definition**—A uniform act submitted to the states for adoption by the NCCUSL.
	2. **Purpose**—To create rules to support the enforcement of e-contracts. Under the UETA, contracts entered into online, as well as other documents, are presumed valid. The UETA does not apply to transactions governed by the UCC or the UCITA.
	3. **The UETA and the UCITA compared**—The chief difference between the UETA and the UCITA is that the latter addresses e-commerce issues that the UETA does not. For example, the UETA does not apply unless contracting parties agree to use e-commerce in their transactions, while the UCITA applies to any agreement that falls within its scope.

For Review

1. When is a shrink-wrap agreement or a click-on agreement enforceable?
2. For the purposes of the UCITA, what is computer information?
3. What important, general legal principle does the UCITA recognize?
4. What is a mass-market license?
5. State some of the similarities and differences between the UCITA and the UETA.

Questions and Case Problems

14–1. Click-On Agreements. Paul is a financial analyst for King Investments, Inc., a brokerage firm. Paul uses the Internet to investigate the background and activities of companies that might be good investments for King's customers. While visiting the Web site of Business Research, Inc., Paul sees on his screen a message that reads, "Welcome to businessresearch.com. By visiting our site, you have been entered as a subscriber to our e-publication, *Companies Unlimited*. This publication will be sent to you daily at a cost of $7.50 per week. An invoice will be included with *Companies Unlimited* every four weeks. You may cancel your subscription at any time." Has Paul entered into an enforceable contract to pay for *Companies Unlimited*? Why or why not? (To answer this question fully, you might want to review the elements of a contract discussed in Chapter 12.)

14–2. Click-On Agreements. Anne is a reporter for the *Daily Business Journal*, a print publication consulted by investors and other businesspersons. Anne often uses the Internet to perform research for the articles that she writes for the publication. While visiting the Web site of Cyberspace Investments Corporation, Anne reads a pop-up window that states, "Our business newsletter, *E-Commerce Weekly*, is available at a one-year subscription rate of $5 per issue. To subscribe, enter your e-mail address below and click 'SUBSCRIBE.' By subscribing, you agree to the terms of the subscriber's agreement. To read this agreement, click 'AGREEMENT.' " Anne enters her e-mail address, but does not click on "AGREEMENT" to read the terms. Has Anne entered into an enforceable contract to pay for *E-Commerce Weekly*? Explain.

14–3. E-Agents. Alpha Business Products, Inc., sells software on its Web site through an online ordering system, an e-agent. Through this system, Beth, a purchasing agent for Medical Insurance Company, orders an upgrade for Medical's word-processing software. Before completing the order, Beth enters, in a "Comments" box, the following: "We will accept this upgrade if we are satisfied with the software after ten days' trial use." Do Alpha and Medical have a contract under the UCITA? Do they have a contract under the UETA? Discuss.

14–4. Attribution. Frank, an employee for Lloyd & Wright Architects, orders drafting supplies from Precision Supplies, Inc., through Precision's Web site. On the order page at the site, Frank is asked to type in his name, company name, e-mail address, phone number, and a credit-card or Precision account number. Precision's Web site asks Frank to check this information before clicking "SUBMIT," at which time the order will be accepted and the supplies will be shipped. For purposes of the UCITA, what part of this transaction could be considered an attribution procedure? Is there an enforceable contract between Lloyd & Wright and Precision, under the UCITA, even though there is nothing in writing? Explain.

14–5. Remedies. Mary enters into a licensing agreement with Scientific Research Corporation to obtain certain data for Chemical Engineering, Inc. The agreement requires an initial registration fee and a monthly subscription fee for the data, which is owned by, and available only from, Scientific Research. Chemical Engineering pays the initial fee and the first month's subscription charge, but Scientific Research refuses to provide Chemical Engineering with access to the data. Chemical Engineering files a suit against Scientific Research. How might the court rule, and why? If the court rules in Chemical Engineering's favor, what remedies are available?

14–6. Shrink-Wrap Terms. Over the phone, Rich and Enza Hill ordered a computer from Gateway 2000, Inc. Inside the box were the computer and a list of contract terms, which provided that the terms governed the transaction unless the customers returned the computer within thirty days. Among those terms was a clause that required any claims to be submitted to arbitration. The Hills kept the computer for more than thirty days before complaining to Gateway about the computer's components and its performance. When the matter was not resolved to their satisfaction, the Hills filed a suit in a federal district court against Gateway, arguing, among other things, that the computer was defective. Gateway asked the court to enforce the arbitration clause. The Hills claimed that this term was not part of the contract to buy the computer because the list on which it appeared had been in the box after the computer was delivered. Is the term a part of the contract? Why or why not? [*Hill v. Gateway 2000, Inc.,* 105 F.3d 1147 (7th Cir. 1997)]

14–7. License Agreement. Management Computer Controls, Inc. (known as "MC 2"), is a Tennessee corporation in the business of selling software. Charles Perry Construction, Inc., is a Florida corporation. Perry entered into two contracts with MC 2 to buy software designed to perform estimating and accounting functions for construction firms. Each contract was printed on a standard order form containing a paragraph that referred to a license agreement. The license agreement included a choice-of-forum and choice-of-law provision: "Agreement is to be interpreted and construed according to the laws of the State of Tennessee. Any action, either by you or MC 2, arising out of this Agreement shall be initiated and prosecuted in the Court of Shelby County, Tennessee, and nowhere else." Each of the software packages arrived with the license agreement affixed to the outside of the box. Additionally, the boxes were sealed with an orange sticker bearing the following warning: "By opening this packet, you indicate your acceptance of the MC 2 license agreement." Alleging that the software was not suitable for use with Windows NT (Microsoft's network operating system), Perry filed a suit against MC 2 in a Florida state court. MC 2 filed a motion to dismiss the complaint on the ground that the suit should be heard in Tennessee. How should the court rule? Why? [*Management Computer Controls, Inc. v. Charles Perry Construction, Inc.,* 743 So.2d 627 (Fla.App. 1 Dist. 1999)]

A Question of Ethics and Social Responsibility

14–8. Bob is a sales representative for Central Computer Company. Bob occasionally uses the Internet to obtain information about his customers and to look for new sales leads. While visiting the Web site of Marketing World, Inc., Bob is presented with an on-screen message that offers, "To improve your ability to make deals, read our monthly online magazine, *Sales Genius,* available at a subscription rate of $15 a month. To subscribe, fill in your name, company name, and e-mail address below, and click "YES!.' By clicking 'YES!,' you agree to the terms of the subscription contract. To read this contract, click 'TERMS.'" Among those terms is a clause that allows Marketing World to charge interest for subscription bills not paid within a certain time. Bob clicks "Yes!" to subscribe to the online magazine. Although Bob has not paid his subscription bills on time over a period of several months, he refuses to pay the interest that Marketing World claims he owes for the late payments. Bob claims that he is not obligated to pay interest because he never read or agreed to the "terms" of the contract.

(a) Is it fair that Bob should have to pay interest on the bills, given that he did not agree to do so when he clicked "YES!" and subscribed to the online magazine? Should Marketing World have made it impossible for a user to subscribe online without even opening the "TERMS" page? From an ethical perspective, what obligations do online merchants have with respect to their customers, who may not realize the importance of contract terms that need not be accessed before clicking "I agree" or "I accept" on a Web site?

(b) Suppose that Marketing World sues Bob for the interest. How would a court likely rule in this case? Why?

For Critical Analysis

14–9. Some people and organizations have begun to look with a more critical eye at the communications revolution brought about by the Internet and the rapid expansion of e-commerce. One such organization, the Turning Point Project (at **http://www.turnpoint.org**), contends that while this development may "empower" corporations, it will not similarly empower individuals—whose privacy and human connection with others will only be diminished. Analyze this argument.

Interacting with the Internet

■ For updated links to resources available on the Web, as well as a variety of other materials, visit this text's Web site at
http://leet.westbuslaw.com

■ For information on PriceScan, go to
http://www.pricescan.com

■ SelectSurf includes links to shopping e-agents at
http://www.selectsurf.com/shopping/compare

■ For a comprehensive review of the UCITA, go to
http://www.ucitaonline.com

■ The UETA is online at
http://www.law.upenn.edu/bll/ulc/uecicta/uetast84.htm

Online Legal Research Exercises

Go to **http://leet.westbuslaw.com**, the Web site that accompanies this text. Select "Interactive Study Center," and then click on "Chapter 14." There you will find the following Internet research exercise that you can perform to learn more about electronic contracts:

Activity 14–1: E-Contracts

Before the Test

Go to **http://leet.westbuslaw.com**, the Web site that accompanies this text. Select "Interactive Quizzes." You will find a number of interactive questions relating to this chapter.

Creditors' Rights and Bankruptcy

chapter objectives

After reading this chapter, you should be able to:

1. Summarize the various remedies available to creditors, and indicate how and when creditors use these remedies to collect debts.

2. Differentiate between suretyship and guaranty arrangements.

3. Outline the typical steps in a bankruptcy proceeding.

4. Describe what property constitutes a debtor's estate in a bankruptcy proceeding and what property is exempt.

5. Compare and contrast the types of relief available under Chapter 7, Chapter 11, Chapter 12, and Chapter 13 of the Bankruptcy Code.

merica's font of practical wisdom, Benjamin Franklin, observed a truth known to all debtors—that creditors do observe "set days and times" and will expect to recover their money at the agreed-on times. Historically, debtors and their families have been subjected to punishment, including involuntary servitude and imprisonment, for their inability to pay debts. The modern legal system, however, has moved away from a punishment philosophy in dealing with debtors. In fact, many observers say that it has moved too far in the other direction, to the detriment of creditors.

Normally, creditors have no problem collecting the debts owed to them. When disputes arise over the amount owed, however, or when the debtor simply cannot or will not pay, what happens? What remedies are available to creditors when debtors default? In the first part of this chapter, we focus on other laws that assist the debtor and creditor in resolving their disputes without the debtor's having to resort to bankruptcy. The second part of this chapter discusses bankruptcy as a last resort in resolving debtor-creditor problems.

Laws Assisting Creditors

Both the common law and statutory laws create various rights and remedies for creditors. We discuss here some of these rights and remedies.

Liens

A *lien* is an encumbrance on (claim against) property to satisfy a debt or protect a claim for the payment of a debt. Creditors' liens include mechanic's, artisan's, innkeeper's, and judicial liens.

MECHANIC'S LIEN   When a person contracts to provide labor, services, or materials for the purpose of making improvements or repairs on real property (land and things attached to the land, such as buildings and trees—see Chapter 22) but does not immediately pay for the improvements, the creditor can file a **mechanic's lien** on the property. This creates a special type of debtor-creditor relationship in which the real estate itself becomes security for the debt.

•**Example 15.1** A painter agrees to paint a house for a homeowner for an agreed-on price to cover labor and materials. If the homeowner refuses to pay for the work or pays only a portion of the charges, the painter can file a mechanic's lien against the property. The painter is the lienholder, and the real property is encumbered (burdened) with a mechanic's lien for the amount owed. If the homeowner does not pay the lien, the property can be sold to satisfy the debt. Notice of the foreclosure (the process by which the creditor deprives the debtor of his or her property) and sale must be given to the debtor in advance, however.•

Note that state law governs mechanic's liens. The time period within which a mechanic's lien must be filed is usually within 60 to 120 days from the last date labor or materials were provided.

ARTISAN'S LIEN   An **artisan's lien** is a security device created at common law through which a creditor can recover payment from a debtor for labor and materials furnished in the repair or improvement of personal property.

Painters finish the trim on a house. If the homeowner does not pay for the work, what can the painters do to collect what they are owed?

Mechanic's Lien A statutory lien on the real property of another, created to ensure payment for work performed and materials furnished in the repair or improvement of real property, such as a building.

Artisan's Lien A possessory lien given to a person who has made improvements and added value to another person's personal property as security for payment for services performed.

● **Example 15.2** If Cindy leaves her diamond ring at the jeweler's to be repaired and fails to pay for the repairs when they are completed, unless otherwise agreed the jeweler has a lien on Cindy's ring for the amount of the bill and normally can sell the ring in satisfaction of the lien.●

In contrast to a mechanic's lien, an artisan's lien is possessory. The lienholder ordinarily must have retained possession of the property and have expressly or impliedly agreed to provide the services on a cash, not a credit, basis. When this occurs, the lien remains in existence as long as the lienholder maintains possession, and the lien is terminated once possession is voluntarily surrendered—unless the surrender is only temporary. If it is a temporary surrender, there must be an agreement that the property will be returned to the lienholder. Even with such an agreement, if a third party obtains rights in that property while it is out of the possession of the lienholder, the lien is lost. In a few situations, if state law so permits, a lienholder can protect a lien and surrender possession at the same time by recording notice of the lien in accordance with state lien and recording statutes.

Most statutes permit the holder of an artisan's lien to foreclose and sell the property subject to the lien to satisfy payment of the debt. As with the mechanic's lien, the holder of an artisan's lien is required to give notice to the owner of the property prior to foreclosure and sale. The sale proceeds are used to pay the debt and the costs of the legal proceedings, and the surplus, if any, is paid to the former owner.

Innkeeper's Lien A possessory lien placed on the luggage of hotel guests for hotel charges that remain unpaid.

INNKEEPER'S LIEN An **innkeeper's lien** is another possessory security device created at common law. An innkeeper's lien is placed on the baggage of guests for the agreed-on hotel charges that remain unpaid. If no express agreement has been made concerning the amount of those charges, then the lien will be for the reasonable value of the accommodations furnished. The innkeeper's lien is terminated either by the guest's payment of the hotel charges or by the innkeeper's surrender of the baggage to the guest, unless the surrender is temporary. Additionally, the lien is terminated by the innkeeper's foreclosure and sale of the property.

JUDICIAL LIENS When a debt is past due, a creditor can bring a legal action against the debtor to collect the debt. If a creditor is successful in the action, the court awards the creditor a judgment against the debtor (usually for the amount of the debt plus any interest and legal costs incurred in obtaining the judgment). Frequently, however, the creditor is unable to collect the awarded amount.

To ensure that a judgment in the creditor's favor will be collectible, creditors are permitted to request that certain nonexempt property of the debtor be seized to satisfy the debt. (As will be discussed later in this chapter, under state or federal statutes, certain property is exempt from seizure by creditors.) If the court orders the debtor's property to be seized prior to a judgment in the creditor's favor, the court's order is referred to as a *writ of attachment*. If the court orders the debtor's property to be seized following a judgment in the creditor's favor, the court's order is referred to as a *writ of execution*.

Attachment In the context of judicial liens, a court-ordered seizure and taking into custody of property prior to the securing of a judgment for a past-due debt.

Attachment. In the context of judicial liens, **attachment** is a court-ordered seizure and taking into custody of property prior to the securing of a judgment for a past-due debt. Attachment rights are created by state statutes. Attachment is a *prejudgment* remedy, because it occurs either at the time of default or immediately after the commencement of a lawsuit and before the entry of a final judgment. By statute, the restrictions and requirements for a creditor to attach before judgment are specific and limited. The due process clause of the Fourteenth Amendment to the Constitution limits the courts' power to authorize seizure of a debtor's property without notice to the debtor or a hearing on the facts.

To use attachment as a remedy, the creditor must have an enforceable right to payment of the debt under law, and the creditor must follow certain procedures. Otherwise, the creditor can be liable for damages for wrongful attachment. He or she must file with the court an *affidavit* (a written or printed statement, made under oath or sworn to) stating that the debtor is in default and stating the statutory grounds under which attachment is sought. The creditor must also post a bond to cover at least court costs, the value of the loss of use of the good(s) suffered by the debtor, and the value of the property attached. When the court is satisfied that all the requirements have been met, it issues a **writ of attachment,** which directs the sheriff or other officer to seize nonexempt property. If the creditor prevails at trial, the seized property can be sold to satisfy the judgment.

Writ of Execution. If the debtor will not or cannot pay the judgment, the creditor is entitled to go back to the court and obtain a court order, directing the sheriff to seize (levy) and sell any of the debtor's nonexempt real or personal property that is within the court's geographical jurisdiction (usually the county in which the courthouse is located). This order is called a **writ of execution**. The proceeds of the sale are used to pay off the judgment, accrued interest, and the costs of the sale. Any excess is paid to the debtor. The debtor can pay the judgment and redeem the nonexempt property any time before the sale takes place. (Because of exemption laws and bankruptcy laws, however, many judgments are virtually uncollectible.)

Garnishment

Garnishment occurs when a creditor is permitted to collect a debt by seizing property of the debtor that is being held by a third party. Property held by a third party that is owed to the debtor may include the debtor's savings or checking-account funds held by a bank or wages held by an employer. Typically, a garnishment judgment is served on a debtor's employer so that part of the debtor's usual paycheck will be paid to the creditor. As a result of a garnishment proceeding, the court orders the debtor's employer to turn over a portion of the debtor's wages to pay the debt.

The legal proceeding for a garnishment action is governed by state law, and garnishment operates differently from state to state. According to the laws in some states, the creditor needs to obtain only one order of garnishment, which will then continuously apply to the debtor's weekly wages until the entire debt is paid. In other states, the creditor must go back to court for a separate order of garnishment for each pay period. Garnishment is usually a postjudgment remedy, but it can be a prejudgment remedy with a proper hearing by a court.

Both federal laws and state laws limit the amount of money that can be garnished from a debtor's weekly take-home pay.[1] Federal law provides a framework to protect debtors from suffering unduly when paying judgment debts.[2]

Writ of Attachment A court's order, prior to a trial to collect a debt, directing the sheriff or other officer to seize nonexempt property of the debtor; if the creditor prevails at trial, the seized property can be sold to satisfy the judgment.

Writ of Execution A court's order, after a judgment has been entered against the debtor, directing the sheriff to seize (levy) and sell any of the debtor's nonexempt real or personal property. The proceeds of the sale are used to pay off the judgment, accrued interest, and costs of the sale; any surplus is paid to the debtor.

Garnishment A legal process used by a creditor to collect a debt by seizing property of the debtor (such as wages) that is being held by a third party (such as the debtor's employer).

---

1. Some states (for example, Texas) do not permit garnishment of wages by private parties except under a child-support order.
2. For example, the federal Consumer Credit Protection Act of 1968, 15 U.S.C. Sections 1601–1693r, provides that a debtor can retain either 75 percent of the disposable earnings per week or the sum equivalent to thirty hours of work paid at federal minimum wage rates, whichever is greater.

State laws also provide dollar exemptions, and these amounts are often larger than those provided by federal law. Under federal law, garnishment of an employee's wages for any one indebtedness cannot be a ground for dismissal of an employee.

Creditors' Composition Agreements

Creditors may contract with the debtor for discharge of the debtor's liquidated debts (debts that are definite, or fixed, in amount) on payment of a sum less than that owed. These agreements are called **creditors' composition agreements,** or simply *composition agreements,* and are usually held to be enforceable.

Mortgage Foreclosure

Mortgage holders have the right to foreclose on mortgaged property in the event of a debtor's default. The usual method of foreclosure is by judicial sale of the property, although the statutory methods of foreclosure vary from state to state. If the proceeds of the foreclosure sale are more than sufficient to cover both the costs of the foreclosure and the mortgaged debt, the debtor receives any surplus. If the sale proceeds are insufficient to cover the foreclosure costs and the mortgaged debt, however, the **mortgagee** (the creditor-lender) can seek to recover the difference from the **mortgagor** (the debtor) by obtaining a deficiency judgment representing the difference between the mortgaged debt and the amount actually received from the proceeds of the foreclosure sale.

The mortgagee obtains a deficiency judgment in a separate legal action that he or she pursues subsequent to the foreclosure action. The deficiency judgment entitles the mortgagee to recover the amount of the deficiency from other nonexempt property owned by the debtor.

Suretyship and Guaranty

When a third person promises to pay a debt owed by another in the event the debtor does not pay, either a *suretyship* or a *guaranty* relationship is created. Suretyship and guaranty have a long history under the common law and provide creditors with the right to seek payment from the third party if the primary debtor defaults on his or her obligations. Exhibit 15–1 illustrates the relationship between a suretyship or guaranty party and the creditor.

SURETY A contract of **strict suretyship** is a promise made by a third person (the **surety**) to be primarily liable to a creditor, but by agreement with the principal debtor (co-debtor) can seek full reimbursement from the co-debtor if the surety pays the debt. It is an express contract between the surety (the third party) and the creditor, and it need not be in writing to be enforceable. The surety is primarily liable for the debt of the principal debtor. The creditor need not exhaust all legal remedies against the principal debtor before holding the surety responsible for payment. The creditor can demand payment from the surety from the moment the debt is due.

Example 15.3 Robert Delmar wants to borrow money from the bank to buy a used car. Because Robert is still in college, the bank will not lend him the funds unless his father, Joseph Delmar, who has dealt with the bank before, will cosign the note (add his signature to the note, thereby becoming a surety and thus jointly liable for payment of the debt). When Joseph Delmar cosigns the note, he becomes primarily liable to the bank. By agreement between Robert

---

Creditors' Composition Agreement An agreement formed between a debtor and his or her creditors in which the creditors agree to accept a lesser sum than that owed by the debtor in full satisfaction of the debt.

Mortgagee Under a mortgage agreement, the creditor who takes a security interest in the debtor's real property.

Mortgagor Under a mortgage agreement, the debtor who gives the creditor a security interest in the debtor's real property in return for a mortgage loan.

Strict Suretyship An express contract in which a third party to a debtor-creditor relationship (the surety) promises to be primarily responsible for the debtor's obligation. The surety has a right to be reimbursed by the co-debtor.

Surety A person, such as a cosigner on a note, who agrees to be primarily responsible for the debt of another.

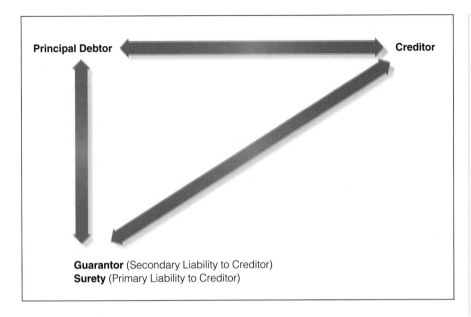

Principal Debtor

Creditor

Guarantor (Secondary Liability to Creditor)
Surety (Primary Liability to Creditor)

Exhibit 15-1
Suretyship and Guaranty Parties
In a suretyship or guaranty arrangement, a third party promises to be responsible for a debtor's obligations. A third party who agrees to be *primarily* liable for the debt (that is, liable even if the principal debtor does not default) is known as a surety; a third party who agrees to be *secondarily* liable for the debt (that is, liable only if the principal debtor defaults) is known as a guarantor. Normally a promise of guaranty (a collateral, or secondary, promise) must be in writing to be enforceable.

and Joseph, if Joseph pays the debt, then he, as the surety, will be entitled to be reimbursed by Robert. On the note's due date, the bank has the option of seeking payment from either Robert or Joseph Delmar, or both jointly.●

GUARANTY A guaranty contract is similar to a suretyship contract in that it includes a promise to answer for the debt or default of another. With a guaranty arrangement, the **guarantor**—the third person making the guaranty—is *secondarily* liable. The guarantor can be required to pay the obligation *only after the principal debtor defaults,* and default usually takes place only after the creditor has made an attempt to collect from the debtor.

● **Example 15.4** A small corporation, BX Enterprises, needs to borrow money to meet its payroll. The bank is skeptical about the creditworthiness of BX and requires Dawson, its president, who is a wealthy businessperson and the owner of 70 percent of BX Enterprises, to sign an agreement making himself personally liable for payment if BX does not pay off the loan. As a guarantor of the loan, Dawson cannot be held liable until BX Enterprises is in default.●

The Statute of Frauds requires that a guaranty contract between the guarantor and the creditor must be in writing to be enforceable unless the *main purpose* exception applies. This exception provides that if the main purpose of the guaranty agreement is to benefit the guarantor, then the contract need not be in writing to be enforceable.

DEFENSES OF THE SURETY AND THE GUARANTOR The defenses of the surety and the guarantor are basically the same. Therefore, the following discussion applies to both, although it refers only to the surety.

Certain actions will release the surety from the obligation. For example, any binding material modification in the terms of the original contract made between the principal debtor and the creditor—including a binding agreement to extend the time for making payment—without first obtaining the consent of the surety will discharge a gratuitous surety completely and a compensated

Guarantor A person who agrees to satisfy the debt of another (the debtor) only after the principal debtor defaults; a guarantor's liability is thus secondary.

surety to the extent that the surety suffers a loss. (An example of a gratuitous surety is a father who agrees to assume responsibility for his daughter's obligation; an example of a compensated surety is a venture capitalist who will profit from a loan made to the principal debtor.)

Naturally, if the principal obligation is paid by the debtor or by another person on behalf of the debtor, the surety is discharged from the obligation. Similarly, if valid tender of payment is made, and the creditor rejects it with knowledge of the surety's existence, then the surety is released from any obligation on the debt.

Generally, the surety can use any defenses available to a principal debtor to avoid liability on the obligation to the creditor. Defenses available to the principal debtor that the surety *cannot* use include the principal debtor's incapacity or bankruptcy and the statute of limitations. The ability of the surety to assert any defenses the debtor may have against the creditor is the most important concept in suretyship, because most of the defenses available to the surety are also those of the debtor.

Obviously, a surety may also have his or her own defenses—for example, incapacity or bankruptcy. If the creditor fraudulently induced the surety to guarantee the debt of the debtor, the surety can assert fraud as a defense. In most states, the creditor has a legal duty to inform the surety, prior to the formation of the suretyship contract, of material facts known by the creditor that would substantially increase the surety's risk. Failure to do so is presumed to constitute fraud and makes the suretyship obligation voidable. In addition, if a creditor surrenders the collateral to the debtor or impairs the collateral while knowing of the surety and without the surety's consent, the surety is released to the extent of any loss suffered from the creditor's actions. The primary reason for this requirement is to protect the surety who agreed to become obligated only because the debtor's collateral was in the possession of the creditor.

RIGHTS OF THE SURETY AND THE GUARANTOR The rights of the surety and the guarantor are basically the same. Therefore, again, the following discussion applies to both.

When the surety pays the debt owed to the creditor, the surety is entitled to certain rights. First, the surety has the legal **right of subrogation**. Simply stated, this means that any right the creditor had against the debtor now becomes the right of the surety. Included are creditor rights in bankruptcy, rights to collateral possessed by the creditor, and rights to judgments secured by the creditor. In short, the surety now stands in the shoes of the creditor and may pursue any remedies that were available to the creditor against the debtor.

Second, the surety has the **right of reimbursement** from the debtor. Basically, the surety is entitled to receive from the debtor all outlays made on behalf of the suretyship arrangement. Such outlays can include expenses incurred as well as the actual amount of the debt paid to the creditor.

Third, in the case of **co-sureties** (two or more sureties on the same obligation owed by the debtor), a surety who pays more than his or her proportionate share on a debtor's default is entitled to recover from the co-sureties the amount paid above the surety's obligation. This is the **right of contribution**. Generally, a co-surety's liability either is determined by agreement or, in the absence of agreement between the co-sureties, can be specified in, or inferred from, the suretyship contract itself.

Right of Subrogation The right of a person to stand in the place of (be substituted for) another, giving the substituted party the same legal rights that the original party had.

Right of Reimbursement The legal right of a person to be restored, repaid, or indemnified for costs, expenses, or losses incurred or expended on behalf of another.

Co-Surety A joint surety; a person who assumes liability jointly with another surety for the payment of an obligation.

Right of Contribution The right of a co-surety who pays more than his or her proportionate share on a debtor's default to recover the excess paid from other co-sureties.

• **Example 15.5** Assume that two co-sureties are obligated under a suretyship contract to guarantee the debt of a debtor. Together, the sureties' maximum liability is $25,000. As specified in the suretyship contract, surety A's maximum liability is $15,000, and surety B's is $10,000. The debtor owes $10,000 and is in default. Surety A pays the creditor the entire $10,000. In the absence of any agreement between the two co-sureties, it is implied that the right of contribution is based on the ratio of maximum liability. Thus, surety A can recover $4,000 from surety B ($10,000/$25,000 × $10,000 = $4,000).•

Laws Assisting Debtors

The law protects debtors as well as creditors. Certain property of the debtor, for example, is exempt from creditors' actions. Probably the most familiar of these exemptions is the homestead exemption. Each state permits the debtor to retain the family home, either in its entirety or up to a specified dollar amount, free from the claims of judgment creditors or trustees in bankruptcy. The purpose of the **homestead exemption** is to ensure that the debtor will retain some form of shelter.

Homestead Exemption A law permitting a debtor to retain the family home, either in its entirety or up to a specified dollar amount, free from the claims of unsecured creditors or trustees in bankruptcy.

• **Example 15.6** Suppose that Van Cleave owes Acosta $40,000. The debt is the subject of a lawsuit, and the court awards Acosta a judgment of $40,000 against Van Cleave. Van Cleave's home is valued at $50,000, and the state exemption on homesteads is $25,000. There are no outstanding mortgages or other liens. To satisfy the judgment debt, Van Cleave's family home is sold at public auction for $45,000. The proceeds of the sale are distributed as follows:

1. Van Cleave is given $25,000 as his homestead exemption.
2. Acosta is paid $20,000 toward the judgment debt, leaving a $20,000 deficiency judgment that can be satisfied from any other nonexempt property (personal or real) that Van Cleave may have.•

A notice announces the auction of a house. If the sale is to pay a debt, should the creditor be paid in full before the debtor receives any proceeds?

State exemption statutes usually include both real and personal property. Personal property that is most often exempt from satisfaction of judgment debts includes the following:

1. Household furniture up to a specified dollar amount.
2. Clothing and certain personal possessions, such as family pictures or a Bible.
3. A vehicle (or vehicles) for transportation (up to a specified dollar amount).
4. Certain classified animals, usually livestock but including pets.
5. Equipment that the debtor uses in a business or trade, such as tools or professional instruments, up to a specified dollar amount.

Consumer protection statutes (see Chapter 20) also protect debtors' rights. Of course, bankruptcy laws, which are discussed in the next section, are designed specifically to assist debtors in need of relief from their debts.

Bankruptcy and Reorganization

At one time, debtors who could not pay their debts as they came due faced harsh consequences, including imprisonment and involuntary servitude. Today, in contrast, debtors have numerous rights. Some of these rights have already been mentioned. We now look at another significant right of debtors: the right to petition for bankruptcy relief under federal law.

Bankruptcy law in the United States has two goals—to protect a debtor by giving him or her a fresh start, free from creditors' claims; and to ensure equitable treatment to creditors who are competing for a debtor's assets. Bankruptcy law is federal law, but state laws on secured transactions, liens, judgments, and exemptions also play a role in federal bankruptcy proceedings.

Current bankruptcy law is based on the Bankruptcy Reform Act of 1978, as amended. In this chapter, we refer to this act, as amended, as the Bankruptcy Code (or, more simply, the Code). This chapter's *Landmark in the Legal Environment* traces the historical evolution of bankruptcy law and the importance of the 1978 Bankruptcy Reform Act.

> "How often have I been able to trace bankruptcies and insolvencies to some lawsuit, . . . the costs of which have mounted up to large sums."
>
> Henry Peter Brougham, 1778–1868
> (English politician)

Recall Congress regulates the jurisdiction of the federal courts, within the limits set by the Constitution. Congress can expand or reduce the number of federal courts at any time.

Bankruptcy Courts

Bankruptcy proceedings are held in federal bankruptcy courts. A bankruptcy court's primary function is to hold *core proceedings*[3] dealing with the procedures required to administer the estate of the debtor in bankruptcy. Bankruptcy courts are under the authority of U.S. district courts (see the chart showing the federal court system in Exhibit 3–2 in Chapter 3), and rulings from bankruptcy courts can be appealed to the district courts. Fundamentally, a bankruptcy court fulfills the role of an administrative court for the district court concerning matters in bankruptcy. A bankruptcy court can conduct a jury trial if the appropriate district court has authorized it and if the parties to the bankruptcy consent to a jury trial.

---

3. Core proceedings are procedural functions, such as allowance of claims, decisions on preferences, automatic-stay proceedings, confirmation of bankruptcy plans, discharge of debts, and so on. These terms and procedures are defined and discussed in the following sections of this chapter.

Landmark in the Legal Environment

The Bankruptcy Reform Act of 1978

Article I, Section 8, of the U.S. Constitution gives Congress the power to establish "uniform Laws on the subject of Bankruptcies throughout the United States." Congress exercised this power in 1800, when the first bankruptcy law was enacted as a result of the business crisis created by restraints imposed on American trade by the British and French. In 1803, the law was repealed, and during the rest of the century—always in response to some crisis—Congress periodically enacted (and later repealed) other bankruptcy legislation. The National Bankruptcy Act of 1898, however, was not repealed, and since that time the United States has had ongoing federal statutory laws concerning bankruptcy. The 1898 act allowed only for *liquidation* in bankruptcy proceedings (which occurs when the debtor's assets are sold and the proceeds are distributed to creditors). Some relief through reorganization was first allowed by amendments to the 1898 act in the 1930s.

Modern bankruptcy law is based on the Bankruptcy Reform Act of 1978, which repealed the 1898 act and represented a major overhaul of federal bankruptcy law. The 1978 act attempted to remedy previous abuses of bankruptcy law and introduced more clarity into bankruptcy procedures. A major organizational change in the 1978 act was the establishment of a new system of bankruptcy courts, in which each federal judicial district would have an adjunct bankruptcy court with exclusive jurisdiction over bankruptcy cases. The act also specified that, in contrast to the lifetime terms of judges in other federal courts, bankruptcy court judges would have a fourteen-year term.

The 1978 act, referred to now simply as the Bankruptcy Code, has been amended several times since its passage. Amendments to the Code have created additional bankruptcy judgeships, placed bankruptcy court judges under the authority of the U.S. district courts, extended the bankruptcy trustee system nationally, granted more power to bankruptcy trustees in the handling of bankruptcy matters, and added a new chapter to the Bankruptcy Code (Chapter 12) to aid financially troubled farmers. The most significant amendments to the Bankruptcy Code were made by the Bankruptcy Reform Act of 1994. Among the many important changes of the 1994 act was the creation of a "fast-track" procedure for small-business debtors (those not involved in owning or managing real estate and with debts of less than $2 million) under Chapter 11 of the Code.

The 1978 act, which generally made it easier for debtors to obtain bankruptcy relief, has been criticized for making it too easy for debtors to discharge their debts in bankruptcy. Since 1980, the number of bankruptcy filings per year have climbed from less than 300,000 to over 1.4 million. This steep rise in the number of personal bankruptcy filings, which has continued even when the economy is booming, has caused Congress to again consider far-reaching bankruptcy reform measures. Bills currently before Congress would, among other things, make it more difficult to discharge certain debts in bankruptcy.

For Critical Analysis: *The Code no longer refers to persons who file for bankruptcy as "bankrupts" but simply as "debtors." What does this change in terminology signify, if anything?*

Types of Bankruptcy Relief

The Bankruptcy Code, which is contained in Title 11 of the U.S. Code (U.S.C.), is divided into a series of "chapters." Chapters 1, 3, and 5 of the Code include general definitional provisions and provisions governing case administration and procedures, creditors, the debtor, and the estate. These three chapters of the Code apply generally to all types of bankruptcies. The next five chapters set forth the different types of relief that debtors may seek. Chapter 7 provides for **liquidation** proceedings (the selling of all nonexempt assets and the distribution of the proceeds to the debtor's creditors). Chapter 9 governs the adjustment of the debts of municipalities. Chapter 11 governs

Liquidation The sale of all of the nonexempt assets of a debtor and the distribution of the proceeds to the debtor's creditors. Chapter 7 of the Bankruptcy Code provides for liquidation bankruptcy proceedings.

reorganizations. Chapter 12 (for family farmers) and Chapter 13 (for individuals) provide for adjustment of the debts of parties with regular income.[4]

In the following pages, we deal first with liquidation proceedings under Chapter 7 of the Code. We then examine the procedures required to obtain relief under Chapter 11, Chapter 12, and Chapter 13 of the Bankruptcy Code.

Chapter 7—Liquidation

Liquidation is the most familiar type of bankruptcy proceeding and is often referred to as an *ordinary,* or *straight, bankruptcy.* Put simply, debtors in straight bankruptcies state their debts and turn their assets over to trustees. The trustees sell the nonexempt assets and distribute the proceeds to creditors. With certain exceptions, the remaining debts are then **discharged** (extinguished), and the debtors are relieved of the obligation to pay the debts.

Any "person"—defined as including individuals, partnerships, and corporations—may be a debtor under Chapter 7. Railroads, insurance companies, banks, savings and loan associations, investment companies licensed by the Small Business Administration, and credit unions *cannot* be Chapter 7 debtors, however. Other chapters of the Code or other federal or state statutes apply to them. A husband and wife may file jointly for bankruptcy under a single petition.

Discharge In bankruptcy proceedings, the extinction of the debtor's dischargeable debts.

Filing the Petition

A straight bankruptcy may be commenced by the filing of either a voluntary or an involuntary **petition in bankruptcy**—the document that is filed with a bankruptcy court to initiate bankruptcy proceedings.

VOLUNTARY BANKRUPTCY A voluntary petition is brought by the debtor, who files official forms designated for that purpose in the bankruptcy court. A **consumer-debtor** (defined as an individual whose debts were incurred primarily for personal or family reasons) who has selected Chapter 7 must state in the petition, at the time of filing, that he or she understands the relief available under other chapters and has chosen to proceed under Chapter 7. If the consumer-debtor is represented by an attorney, the attorney must file an affidavit stating that he or she has informed the debtor of the relief available under each chapter. Any debtor who is liable on a claim held by a creditor can file a voluntary petition. The debtor does not even have to be insolvent to do so.[5] The voluntary petition contains the following schedules:

Petition in Bankruptcy The document that is filed with a bankruptcy court to initiate bankruptcy proceedings. The official forms required for a petition in bankruptcy must be completed accurately, sworn to under oath, and signed by the debtor.

Consumer-Debtor An individual whose debts are primarily for purchases made for personal or household use.

1. A list of both secured and unsecured creditors, their addresses, and the amount of debt owed to each.
2. A statement of the financial affairs of the debtor.
3. A list of all property owned by the debtor, including property claimed by the debtor to be exempt.
4. A listing of current income and expenses.

---

4. There are no Chapters 2, 4, 6, 8, or 10 in Title 11. Such "gaps" are not uncommon in the U.S.C. This is because chapter numbers (or other subdivisional unit numbers) are sometimes reserved for future use when a statute is enacted. (A gap may also appear if a law has been repealed.)
5. The inability to pay debts as they become due is known as *equitable* insolvency. A *balance-sheet* insolvency, which exists when a debtor's liabilities exceed assets, is not the test. Thus, it is possible for debtors to petition voluntarily for bankruptcy even though their assets far exceed their liabilities. This situation may occur when a debtor's cash-flow problems become severe.

The official forms must be completed accurately, sworn to under oath, and signed by the debtor. To conceal assets or knowingly supply false information on these schedules is a crime under the bankruptcy laws. If the voluntary petition for bankruptcy is found to be proper, the filing of the petition will itself constitute an order for relief. An **order for relief** relieves the debtor of the immediate obligation to pay the debts listed in the petition. Once a consumer-debtor's voluntary petition has been filed, the clerk of the court (or person directed) must give the trustee and creditors mailed notice of the order for relief not more than twenty days after the entry of the order.

As mentioned previously, debtors do not have to be insolvent to file for voluntary bankruptcy. Debtors do not have unfettered access to Chapter 7 bankruptcy proceedings, however. Section 707(b) of the Bankruptcy Code allows a bankruptcy court to dismiss a petition for relief under Chapter 7 if the granting of relief would constitute "substantial abuse" of Chapter 7.

• **Example 15.7** Howard Rock, a consumer-debtor, petitions for Chapter 7 relief. The court might determine, after evaluating Rock's schedule listing current income and expenses, that Rock would be able to pay his creditors a reasonable amount from future income. In this situation, the court might conclude that it would be a substantial abuse of Chapter 7 to allow Rock to have his or her debts completely discharged. The court might dismiss Rock's Chapter 7 petition after a hearing and encourage Rock to file a repayment plan under Chapter 13 of the Code, if that would result in a substantial improvement in the creditors' receipt of payments.• In the following case, the court had to decide whether granting a Chapter 7 discharge to the debtor would constitute substantial abuse.

Order for Relief A court's grant of assistance to a complainant. In bankruptcy proceedings, the order relieves the debtor of the immediate obligation to pay the debts listed in the bankruptcy petition.

Case 15.1 ● Matter of Blair

United States Bankruptcy Court, Northern District of Alabama, Eastern Division, 1995. 180 Bankr. 656.

Historical and Political Setting
In the early 1980s, retailers and consumer lenders complained to Congress of an increasing number of Chapter 7 discharges being granted to debtors who creditors felt could actually afford to pay their debts. In response, Congress enacted the substantial abuse provision. The provision illustrates the tension between two principles underlying bankruptcy law: to give debtors the opportunity for a fresh start and to help creditors thwart the abuse of consumer credit. An indication of this tension is the fact that Congress did not define "substantial abuse" but left the task to the courts.

Background and Facts James Blair, Jr., owed primarily consumer debts of less than $7,000, and his income exceeded his living expenses by more than $200 a month. When he filed a petition for relief under Chapter 7, the court concluded that if he were to file a repayment plan under Chapter 13, his debts would be paid off in forty months. The bankruptcy administrator filed a motion to dismiss Blair's petition.

In the Words of the Court . . .
JAMES S. SLEDGE, Bankruptcy Judge.

* * * *

* * * [T]he substantial abuse determination must be made on a case by case basis, in light of the totality of the circumstances. * * * [F]actors [that] should be considered * * * [include:] (1) Whether the bankruptcy petition was filed because of sudden illness, calamity, disability, or unemployment; (2) Whether the debtor incurred cash advances and made consumer

(Continued)

Case 15.1 Continued

purchases far in excess of his ability to pay; (3) Whether the debtor's proposed family budget is excessive or unreasonable; (4) Whether the debtor's schedules and statement of current income and expenses reasonably and accurately reflect the true financial condition; and (5) Whether the petition was filed in good faith.

* * * *

* * * [T]his Court concludes that granting this debtor relief under Chapter 7 would be a substantial abuse of the provisions of the chapter as well as perverting the purpose of the Bankruptcy Code: to give a fresh start to the honest but unfortunate debtor.

Decision and Remedy The court dismissed Blair's petition.

For Critical Analysis—Economic Consideration *The court also stated that granting Blair re-* *lief under Chapter 7 would be "perverting the purpose of the Bankruptcy Code." What did the court mean by this statement?*

A store advertises a court-ordered bankruptcy sale. On what basis might a court enter an order for relief in an involuntary bankruptcy proceeding initiated by the store's creditors?

INVOLUNTARY BANKRUPTCY An involuntary bankruptcy occurs when the debtor's creditors force the debtor into bankruptcy proceedings. An involuntary case cannot be commenced against a farmer[6] or a charitable institution (or those entities not eligible for Chapter 7 relief, mentioned earlier), however. For an involuntary action to be filed against debtors, the following requirements must be met: If the debtor has twelve or more creditors, three or more of those creditors having unsecured claims totaling at least $10,775 must join in the petition. If a debtor has fewer than twelve creditors, one or more creditors having a claim of $10,775 may file.

If the debtor challenges the involuntary petition, a hearing will be held, and the debtor's challenge will fail if the bankruptcy court finds either of the following:

1. That the debtor is generally not paying debts as they become due.
2. That a general receiver, custodian, or assignee took possession of, or was appointed to take charge of, substantially all of the debtor's property within 120 days before the filing of the petition.

If the court allows the bankruptcy to proceed, the debtor will be required to supply the same information in the bankruptcy schedules as in a voluntary bankruptcy.

An involuntary petition should not be used as an everyday debt-collection device, and the Code provides penalties for the filing of frivolous (unjustified) petitions against debtors. Judgment may be granted against the petitioning creditors for the costs and attorneys' fees incurred by the debtor in defending against an involuntary petition that is dismissed by the court. If the petition is filed in bad faith, damages can be awarded for injury to the debtor's reputation. Punitive damages may also be awarded.

---

6. *Farmers* are defined as persons who receive more than 80 percent of their gross income from farming operations, such as tilling the soil; dairy farming; ranching; or the production or raising of crops, poultry, or livestock. Corporations and partnerships, as well as individuals, can be farmers.

Automatic Stay

The filing of a petition, either voluntary or involuntary, operates as an **automatic stay** on (suspension of) virtually all litigation and other action by creditors against the debtor or the debtor's property. In other words, once a petition is filed, creditors cannot commence or continue most legal actions against the debtor to recover claims or to repossess property in the hands of the debtor. A secured creditor, however, may petition the bankruptcy court for relief from the automatic stay in certain circumstances, such as when a creditor seeks "adequate protection" against the possible loss or deterioration of the secured property. The automatic stay also does not apply to paternity, alimony, or family maintenance and support debts.

A creditor's failure to abide by an automatic stay imposed by the filing of a petition can be costly. If a creditor *knowingly* violates the automatic-stay provision (a willful violation), any party injured is entitled to recover actual damages, costs, and attorneys' fees and may also be entitled to recover punitive damages.

Automatic Stay In bankruptcy proceedings, the suspension of virtually all litigation and other action by creditors against the debtor or the debtor's property; the stay is effective the moment the debtor files a petition in bankruptcy.

Creditors' Meeting and Claims

Within a reasonable time after the order of relief is granted (not less than ten days or more than thirty days), the bankruptcy court must call a meeting of the creditors listed in the schedules filed by the debtor. The bankruptcy judge does not attend this meeting. The debtor must attend this meeting (unless excused by the court) and submit to an examination under oath. Failure to appear or making false statements under oath may result in the debtor's being denied a discharge of bankruptcy. At the meeting, the trustee ensures that the debtor is advised of the potential consequences of bankruptcy and of his or her ability to file under a different chapter.

In a bankruptcy case in which the debtor has no assets (called a "no-asset" case), creditors are notified of the debtor's petition for bankruptcy but are instructed not to file a claim. In such a situation, the creditors will receive no payment, and most, if not all, of the debtor's debts will be discharged.

If there are sufficient assets to be distributed to creditors, however, each creditor must normally file a *proof of claim* with the bankruptcy court clerk within ninety days of the creditors' meeting to be entitled to receive a portion of the debtor's estate. The proof of claim lists the creditor's name and address, as well as the amount that the creditor asserts is owed to the creditor by the debtor. If a creditor fails to file a proof of claim, the bankruptcy court or trustee may file the proof of claim on the creditor's behalf but is not obligated to do so. If a claim is for a disputed amount, the bankruptcy court will set the value of the claim.

Creditors' claims are automatically allowed unless contested by the trustee, the debtor, or another creditor. The Code, however, does not allow claims for breach of employment contracts or real estate leases for terms longer than one year. These claims are limited to one year's wages or rent, despite the remaining length of either contract in breach.

Be Aware In most cases, creditors' meetings take only five or ten minutes. But a debtor who lies, commits bribery, conceals assets, uses a false name, or makes false claims is subject to a $5,000 fine and up to five years in prison.

Property of the Estate

On the commencement of a liquidation proceeding under Chapter 7, an **estate in property** is created. The estate consists of all the debtor's legal and equitable interests in property presently held, wherever located, together with

Estate in Property In bankruptcy proceedings, all of the debtor's legal and equitable interests in property presently held, wherever located, together with certain jointly owned property, property transferred in transactions voidable by the trustee, proceeds and profits from the property of the estate, and certain property interests to which the debtor becomes entitled within 180 days after filing for bankruptcy.

certain jointly owned property, property transferred in transactions voidable by the trustee, proceeds and profits from the property of the estate, and certain after-acquired property. Interests in certain property—such as gifts, inheritances, property settlements (resulting from divorce), or life insurance death proceeds—to which the debtor becomes *entitled within 180 days after filing* may also become part of the estate. Thus, the filing of a bankruptcy petition generally fixes a dividing line: property acquired prior to the filing becomes property of the estate, and property acquired after the filing, except as just noted, remains the debtor's.

The issue in the following case was whether payments made under a covenant not to compete should be included in a debtor's estate. The covenant was entered into *before* the petition was filed, but the payments were due *after* the filing.

Case 15.2 ● In re Andrews

United States Court of Appeals,
Fourth Circuit, 1996.
80 F.3d 906.
http://www.law.emory.edu/
4circuit[a]

Company Profile *John Andrews worked in the ready-mix concrete business most of his life. In 1974, he and various partners formed a ready-mix concrete company in Herndon, Virginia. The company, which ultimately came to be known as AMAX Corporation, grew to be successful, with annual sales of approximately $30 million. By expanding the customer contacts he developed at AMAX, in 1980 Andrews formed*

a. This Web page, which is part of a Web site maintained by Emory University School of Law, provides access to published opinions of the U.S. Court of Appeals for the Fourth Circuit. Click on "1996" and then on the "April" link. When that page opens, scroll down the list of cases to *Andrews v. Riggs National Bank of Washington*. Click on the case name to access this opinion.

a real estate development company, which participated in joint ventures with builders and developers. In 1989, the owners of AMAX began negotiations with Tarmac Acquisition, Inc., for the purchase of AMAX. Experts valued the assets at about $9 million. AMAX's customer list, which represented the goodwill of the company, was valued at an additional $1 million.

Background and Facts Tarmac Acquisition, Inc., bought AMAX Corporation, a ready-mix concrete company. As part of the deal, the AMAX owners, including John Andrews, signed agreements not to compete with Tarmac. Andrews was to receive $1 million, payable in quarterly installments over a five-year period. Three years later, Andrews filed a bankruptcy petition. He asked the federal bankruptcy court not to include, in the property of his estate (which would ultimately be distributed to creditors), any future installments. The court refused, and a federal district court affirmed this decision. Andrews appealed to the U.S. Court of Appeals for the Fourth Circuit.

In the Words of the Court . . .
ELLIS, District Judge:

* * * *

* * * Pre-petition assets, like the NCA [noncompetition agreement] payments, are those assets rooted in the debtor's pre-petition activities, including any proceeds that may flow from those assets in the future. These assets belong to the estate and ultimately to the creditors. Post-petition assets are those that result from the debtor's post-petition activities and are his to keep free and clear of the bankruptcy proceeding.

* * * *

Seen in this light, the NCA payments due Andrews fall clearly on the pre-bankruptcy or "past" side of the bright line. These payments are plainly rooted in, and grow out of, Andrews's pre-petition activities. * * * [B]ut for

Case 15.2 Continued

> the [AMAX] sale, there would have been no NCA and no quarterly payments to Andrews. * * * Given this close connection between the NCA and the pre-petition sale of the debtor's share in the concrete business, we are persuaded that the payments were well rooted in the pre-bankruptcy past. * * * [T]hey should be included in Andrews's estate.

Decision and Remedy The U.S. Court of Appeals for the Fourth Circuit affirmed the lower court's decision.

For Critical Analysis—Ethical Consideration *How can you reconcile the court's decision with the rule that certain property interests to which the debtor becomes entitled within 180 days after filing a bankruptcy petition are a part of the debtor's estate?*

Exempted Property

Any individual debtor is entitled to exempt certain property from the property of the estate. The Bankruptcy Code establishes a federal exemption scheme under which the following property is exempt:[7]

1. Up to $16,150 in equity in the debtor's residence and burial plot (the homestead exemption).
2. Interest in a motor vehicle up to $2,575.
3. Interest in household goods and furnishings, wearing apparel, appliances, books, animals, crops, and musical instruments up to $425 in a particular item but limited to $8,625 in total.
4. Interest in jewelry up to $1,750.
5. Any other property worth up to $850, plus any unused part of the $16,150 homestead exemption up to an amount of $8,075.
6. Interest in any tools of the debtor's trade, up to $1,625.
7. Certain life insurance contracts owned by the debtor.
8. Certain interests in accrued dividends or interests under life insurance contracts owned by the debtor.
9. Professionally prescribed health aids.
10. The right to receive Social Security and certain welfare benefits, alimony and support payments, and certain pension benefits.
11. The right to receive certain personal injury and other awards, up to $16,150.

Individual states have the power to pass legislation precluding debtors in their states from using the federal exemptions. At least thirty-four states have done this. In those states, debtors may use only state (not federal) exemptions. In the rest of the states, an individual debtor (or husband and wife who file jointly) may choose between the exemptions provided under state law and the federal exemptions. State laws may provide significantly greater protection for debtors than federal law. For example, Florida and Texas traditionally have provided for generous exemptions for homeowners. State laws may also define the property coming within an exemption differently than the federal law.

---

7. The dollar amounts stated in the Bankruptcy Code were adjusted automatically on April 1, 1998, and will be adjusted every three years thereafter based on changes in the Consumer Price Index.

The Trustee's Role

Promptly after the order for relief has been entered, an interim, or provisional, trustee is appointed by the **U.S. trustee** (a government official who performs certain administrative tasks that a bankruptcy judge would otherwise have to perform). The interim trustee administers the debtor's estate until the first meeting of creditors, at which time either a permanent trustee is elected or the interim trustee becomes the permanent trustee. Trustees are entitled to compensation for services rendered, plus reimbursement for expenses.

The basic duty of the trustee is to collect the debtor's available estate and reduce it to money for distribution, preserving the interests of both the debtor and unsecured creditors. In other words, the trustee is accountable for administering the debtor's estate. To enable the trustee to accomplish this duty, the Code gives him or her certain powers, stated in both general and specific terms. (For a discussion of the nature of assets in e-bankruptcies, as well as online sales of assets during bankruptcy proceedings, see this chapter's feature, *Legal E-nvironment: E-Bankruptcies*.)

TRUSTEE'S POWERS The trustee has the power to require persons holding the debtor's property at the time the petition is filed to deliver the property to the trustee. To enable the trustee to implement this power, the Code provides that the trustee occupies a position equivalent in rights to that of certain other parties. For example, in some situations, the trustee has the same rights as creditors and can obtain a judicial lien or levy execution on the debtor's property. This means that a trustee has priority over an unperfected secured party to the debtor's property. The trustee also has rights equivalent to those of the debtor.

In addition, the trustee has the power to avoid (cancel) certain types of transactions—including those transactions that the debtor could otherwise rightfully avoid, *preferences,* certain statutory *liens,* and *fraudulent transfers* by the debtor. Avoidance powers must be exercised within two years of the order for relief (the period runs even if a trustee has not been appointed). These powers of the trustee are discussed in more detail in the following subsections.

VOIDABLE RIGHTS A trustee steps into the shoes of the debtor. Thus, any reason that a debtor can use to obtain the return of his or her property can be used by the trustee as well. These grounds (for recovery) include fraud, duress, incapacity, and mutual mistake.

• **Example 15.8** Rob sells his boat to Inga. Inga gives Rob a check, knowing that there are insufficient funds in her bank account to cover the check. Inga has committed fraud. Rob has the right to avoid that transfer and recover the boat from Inga. If Rob has filed for bankruptcy, once an order for relief has been entered for Rob, the trustee can exercise the same right to recover the boat from Inga. If the trustee does not take action, Rob is still able to enforce that right.[8] •

PREFERENCES A debtor is not permitted to transfer property or to make a payment that favors—or gives a **preference** to—one creditor over others. The trustee is allowed to recover payments made both voluntarily and involuntarily to one creditor in preference over another.

---

8. In a Chapter 11 reorganization (to be discussed later), the debtor usually continues to operate the business and has the same avoiding powers as a trustee in a Chapter 7 liquidation. In repayment plans under Chapters 12 and 13 (also to be discussed later), a trustee must be appointed.

Legal *e*-nvironment

E-Bankrupcies

Anyone who starts a new business knows the chilling fact: out of one hundred businesses that are founded, ten will prosper in the long run. Internet companies are certainly no different. In the late 1990s, they could do no wrong and their stock market valuation soared. By 2000, though, the bloodbath started as investors realized that many of them would never turn a profit. After that time, the number of "dot.com" bankruptcies increased. Many struggling Internet companies were unable to obtain additional financing from venture capitalists. They were unable to float initial public offerings or secondary offerings. Consequently, many companies—even big ones—were bought up by stronger entities, often at bargain-basement prices.

Others simply shut their doors and went into Chapter 11 reorganization or Chapter 7 liquidation. One of the most spectacular was Boo.com, an international clothing Web site. Private investors put in more than $150 million. In 2000, the company closed its doors and sold its assets for less than a million dollars. APBNews.com, a crime-story Web site, went into Chapter 11 and was bought for less than a million dollars—this after private investors had put up almost $40 million during the previous eighteen months.

Using the Internet to Sell Off the Assets of Bankrupt Internet Companies

At the end of the twentieth century, a milestone occurred—the bankruptcy court in Boston conducted its first online auction of assets. Not many months later, some of those online asset auctions included assets of bankrupt Internet companies. It is a strange irony indeed—the court system utilizing the engine of the dot.com revolution as the instrument for liquidating and reorganizing financially troubled Internet companies!

Bankruptcy trustees are increasingly using Internet auctions. According to Lawrence Freedman, vice president of the National Association of Bankruptcy Trustees, "This is the hottest, fastest-growing, most innovative area of bankruptcy liquidation in 50 years."[a]

Clearly, online auctions for the sale of bankrupts' estates enlarge the market. The most common items that Chapter 7 trustees put up for bid on the Internet are office equipment, automobiles, commercial real estate, jewelry, promissory notes, judgments, and partnership interests. In fact, many items that have been abandoned by Chapter 7 trustees can now be auctioned on the Internet, such as vacation time-shares and interests in condominiums.

There are already a number of auction sites catering specifically to bankruptcy estates. Even the National Association of Bankruptcy Trustees (NABT) posts items for sale on its Web site (at **http://www.nabt.com/cfdocs/upcome.cfm**). One way of finding a ready audience for the merchandise is to put up the auction site directly on the bankrupt company's own Web site. This was done, for example, with an outdoor-clothing catalogue company, Atlantic Rancher. Trustees who have used online auctions claim that they receive higher bids because of the wider exposure available online, as compared to traditional offerings. Such online auctions are not free; however, neither are conventional auctions for bankruptcy estates. Fair Market, Inc. (at **http://www.fairmarket.com**), for example, charges 10 percent of the auction proceeds. Bid4Assets.com (at **http://bid4assets.com**) charges 6 to 8 percent.

New Territory for Bankruptcy Judges

The growth of online auctions utilized by Chapter 7 trustees has not been explosive, nonetheless. Trustees who are used to doing things one way are slow to convert to new methods. More important, any type of sale has to be approved by the bankruptcy court. Internet auctions are relatively new territory for most bankruptcy judges. For example, there is an issue related to notice to the creditors. Do all creditors truly have the ability and knowledge to search for online auctions? In addition, there are different rules in different jurisdictions. In order for auction companies to be paid, they would have to satisfy these different requirements. Some jurisdictions, for example, require an auctioneer to post a bond. Other jurisdictions demand postsale confirmation by the court, which would certainly have a chilling effect on online purchasing.

Another issue concerns objections from debtors, creditors, or disappointed bidders. Any objection to an online sale may require a hearing on whether the sale was conducted in a proper manner or whether the buyer was a bona fide purchaser. A potential online buyer living in a distant jurisdiction may not want to risk having to attend a hearing after making an online purchase.

For Critical Analysis: *Why don't Chapter 7 trustees simply place the bankruptcy estate's assets for sale on eBay?*

---

a. *Lawyers Weekly USA,* September 20, 2000, p. 1.

To have made a preferential payment that can be recovered, an *insolvent* debtor generally must have transferred property, for a *preexisting* debt, during the *ninety days* prior to the filing of the petition in bankruptcy. The transfer must give the creditor more than the creditor would have received as a result of the bankruptcy proceedings. The trustee does not have to prove insolvency, as the Code provides that the debtor is presumed to be insolvent during this ninety-day period.

Sometimes the creditor receiving the preference is an insider—an individual, a partner, a partnership, or an officer or a director of a corporation (or a relative of one of these) who has a close relationship with the debtor. If this is the case, the avoidance power of the trustee is extended to transfers made within *one year* before filing; however, the *presumption* of insolvency is confined to the ninety-day period. Therefore, the trustee must prove that the debtor was insolvent at the time of an earlier transfer.

Not all transfers are preferences. To be a preference, the transfer must be made for something other than current consideration. Therefore, it is generally assumed by most courts that payment for services rendered within ten to fifteen days prior to the payment of the current consideration is not a preference. If a creditor receives payment in the ordinary course of business, such as payment of last month's telephone bill, the payment cannot be recovered by the trustee in bankruptcy. To be recoverable, a preference must be a transfer for an antecedent (preexisting) debt, such as a year-old printing bill. In addition, the Code permits a consumer-debtor to transfer any property to a creditor up to a total value of $600, without the transfer's constituting a preference. Also, payments of certain other debts, including alimony and child support, are not preferences. If a preferred creditor has sold the property to an innocent third party, the trustee cannot recover the property from the innocent party.

> **Note** What the trustee does with property recovered as a preference, in most cases, is to sell it and distribute the proceeds to the debtor's creditors.

LIENS ON DEBTOR'S PROPERTY   The trustee is permitted to avoid the fixing of certain statutory liens, such as a mechanic's lien, on property of the debtor. Liens that first become effective on the date that the bankruptcy petition was filed are also voidable by the trustee.

FRAUDULENT TRANSFERS   The trustee may avoid fraudulent transfers or obligations if they were made within one year of the filing of the petition or if they were made with actual intent to hinder, delay, or defraud a creditor. Transfers made for less than a reasonably equivalent consideration are also voidable if the debtor thereby became insolvent, was left engaged in business with an unreasonably small amount of capital, or intended to incur debts that would be beyond his or her ability to pay. When a fraudulent transfer is made outside the Code's one-year limit, creditors may seek alternative relief under state laws. State laws often allow creditors to recover for transfers made up to three years prior to the filing of a petition.

Property Distribution

Creditors are either secured or unsecured. A *secured* creditor has a security interest in collateral that secures the debt. An *unsecured* creditor does not have any security interest.

SECURED CREDITORS   The Code provides that a consumer-debtor, within thirty days of the filing of a Chapter 7 petition or before the date of the first meeting of the creditors (whichever is first), must file with the clerk a statement of intention with respect to the secured collateral. The statement must indicate whether the debtor will retain the collateral or surrender it to the secured party. Additionally, if applicable, the debtor must specify whether the collateral will be claimed as exempt property and whether the debtor intends to redeem the property or reaffirm the debt secured by the collateral. The trustee is obligated to enforce the debtor's statement within forty-five days after the statement is filed.

If the collateral is surrendered to the perfected secured party, the secured creditor can enforce the security interest either by accepting the property in full satisfaction of the debt or by foreclosing on the collateral and using the proceeds to pay off the debt. Thus, the secured party has priority over unsecured parties to the proceeds from the disposition of the secured collateral. Indeed, the Code provides that if the value of the secured collateral exceeds the secured party's claim, the secured party also has priority to the proceeds in an amount that will cover reasonable fees (including attorneys' fees, if provided for in the security agreement) and costs incurred because of the debtor's default. Any excess over this amount is used by the trustee to satisfy the claims of unsecured creditors. Should the secured collateral be insufficient to cover the secured debt owed, the secured creditor becomes an unsecured creditor for the remainder of the debt.

UNSECURED CREDITORS Bankruptcy law establishes an order or priority for classes of debts owed to *unsecured* creditors, and they are paid in the order of their priority. Each class of debt must be fully paid before the next class is entitled to any of the proceeds—if there are sufficient funds to pay the entire class. If not, the proceeds are distributed *proportionately* to each creditor in the class, and all classes lower in priority on the list receive nothing. The order of priority among classes of unsecured creditors is as follows:

1. Administrative expenses—including court costs, trustee fees, and bankruptcy attorneys' fees.
2. In an involuntary bankruptcy, expenses incurred by the debtor in the ordinary course of business from the date of the filing of the petition up to the appointment of the trustee or the issuance by the court of an order for relief.
3. Unpaid wages, salaries, and commissions earned within ninety days of the filing of the petition, limited to $4,300 per claimant. Any claim in excess of $4,300 is treated as a claim of a general creditor (listed as number 9 below).
4. Unsecured claims for contributions to be made to employee benefit plans, limited to services performed during 180 days prior to the filing of the bankruptcy petition and $4,300 per employee.
5. Claims by farmers and fishers, up to $4,300, against debtor operators of grain storage or fish storage or processing facilities.
6. Consumer deposits of up to $1,950 given to the debtor before the petition was filed in connection with the purchase, lease, or rental of property or the purchase of services that were not received or provided. Any claim in excess of $1,950 is treated as a claim of a general creditor (listed as number 9 below).
7. Paternity, alimony, maintenance, and support debts.
8. Certain taxes and penalties due to government units, such as income and property taxes.
9. Claims of general creditors.

If any amount remains after the priority classes of creditors have been satisfied, it is turned over to the debtor.

Discharge

From the debtor's point of view, the purpose of a liquidation proceeding is to obtain a fresh start through the discharge of debts.[9] Certain debts, however, are not dischargeable in a liquidation proceeding. Also, certain debtors may not qualify—because of their conduct—to have all debts discharged in bankruptcy.

> **Be Aware** Often, a discharge in bankruptcy—even under Chapter 7—does not free a debtor of *all* of his or her debts.

EXCEPTIONS TO DISCHARGE Claims that are not dischargeable under Chapter 7 of the Bankruptcy Code include the following:

1. Claims for back taxes accruing within three years prior to bankruptcy.
2. Claims for amounts borrowed by the debtor to pay federal taxes.
3. Claims against property or funds obtained by the debtor under false pretenses or by false representations.
4. Claims by creditors who were not notified of the bankruptcy; these claims did not appear on the schedules the debtor was required to file.
5. Claims based on fraud or misuse of funds by the debtor while he or she was acting in a fiduciary capacity or claims involving the debtor's embezzlement or larceny. (See this chapter's *Inside the Legal Environment* for a further discussion of exceptions to discharge based on fraud.)
6. Alimony, child support, and (with certain exceptions) property settlements.
7. Claims based on willful or malicious conduct by the debtor toward another or the property of another.

---

9. Discharges are granted under Chapter 7 only to *individuals*, not to corporations or partnerships. The latter may use Chapter 11, or they may terminate their existence under state law.

Ethical Issue 15.1

Should punitive damages for fraud be dischargeable in bankruptcy?

As stated earlier, claims based on fraud are not dischargeable in bankruptcy. Often, a claim based on fraud consists of damages that were awarded to the creditor by a court in a lawsuit against the debtor for fraud. A question that sometimes comes before the courts is whether punitive damages, as well as actual damages, should be nondischargeable. How this question is answered depends on how a court interprets the language of the Bankruptcy Code with respect to fraud-based claims. Section 523(a)(2)(A) of the Code denies discharge in bankruptcy for "any debt . . . for money,

property, services, or an extension, renewal, or refinancing of credit, to the extent obtained by . . . false pretenses, a false representation, or actual fraud."

To resolve conflicting interpretations of this provision by the lower courts, the United States Supreme Court recently addressed the issue. In making its decision, the Court emphasized that the Bankruptcy Code "has long prohibited debtors from discharging liabilities incurred on account of their fraud, embodying a basic policy animating the Code of affording relief only to an 'honest but unfortunate debtor.'" According to the high court, when read in the historical context of bankruptcy law and other provisions of the current Bankruptcy Code, the relevant provision of the Code should be interpreted to mean that punitive damages for fraud are nondischargeable.[a]

---

a. *Cohen v. De La Cruz*, 523 U.S. 213, 118 S.Ct. 1212, 140 L.Ed.2d 341 (1998).

Inside the Legal Environment

Credit-Card Fraud—The Intent Factor

Today, it is relatively easy to obtain credit cards. It is also relatively easy, as many consumers have learned, to go heavily into debt by using credit cards. Indeed, sometimes consumers have taken advances on their credit cards even though they were aware that they probably would not be able to meet their credit-card payments. At issue in a number of bankruptcy cases is whether debtors who run up credit-card bills, knowing that they lack the ability to pay them, have engaged in fraud. How the courts decide this issue is important for both debtors and creditors because if such activity amounts to fraud, then the debt will not be dischargeable in bankruptcy.

Fraud, of course, requires intent. So a central question in bankruptcy cases dealing with this issue is whether a debtor's inability to pay a debt equates to fraud. In the past, many lower courts held that it did. This assumption seems to be changing, however. Consider a case that came before the Sixth Circuit Court of Appeals. In that case, Benethel Rembert, a woman who took $11,600 in cash advances on her credit cards to finance her gambling habit, was allowed to discharge the debt in bankruptcy. Rembert testified that she had hoped to repay the debt out of her gambling winnings, even though she realized that there was no reasonable expectation of being able to do this. Nonetheless, said the court, there was no fraud, because the debtor *intended* to repay the debt. According to the court, "To measure a debtor's intention to repay by her ability to do so, without more, would be contrary to one of the main reasons consumers use credit cards: because they often lack the ability to pay in full at the time they desire credit."

In determining a debtor's subjective intent, stated the court, it is necessary to look at the "totality of the circumstances." In Rembert's case, no evidence was presented to the bankruptcy court that indicated that Rembert used the credit cards without intending to repay the credit-card companies. Furthermore, Rembert had previously taken out a second mortgage on her home in the amount of $28,000 and used almost all of that amount to pay credit-card bills. She continued to make payments on her credit-card debts whenever she could. According to the court, "These facts indicate that Rembert subjectively intended to repay her debts. The fact that Rembert later admitted that it probably was not reasonable to believe that she would win enough money to repay the [debts] does not indicate a subjective intent not to repay her debts in this case."[a]

In making its determination, the court cited a previous case decided by the U.S. Court of Appeals for the Ninth Circuit, the only other federal appellate court to address this issue. That court had concluded that the "hopeless state of a debtor's financial condition should never become a substitute for an actual finding of bad faith."[b]

These rulings, while they may be good news for debtors, are not so for creditors. According to attorney Robert Markoff of Chicago, "Creditors are faced with a real uphill battle. If the debtor says she intended to pay, you're pretty much stuck."[c] (Note that a provision in a bankruptcy reform bill pending in Congress at the time of this writing addresses this problem by stating that any debt incurred by the use of a credit card within ninety days before a bankruptcy petition is filed would be nondischargeable.)

For Critical Analysis: *What steps might creditors take to protect themselves against such problems?*

a. *In re Rembert*, 141 F.3d 277 (6th Cir. 1998).
b. *In re Anastas*, 94 F.3d 1280 (9th Cir. 1996).
c. As quoted in Jake Halpern, "Credit Cards Easier to Discharge," *Lawyers Weekly USA*, May 4, 1998, p. 19.

8. Certain government fines and penalties.
9. Certain student loans, unless payment of the loans imposes an undue hardship on the debtor and the debtor's dependents.
10. Consumer debts of more than $1,075 for luxury goods or services owed to a single creditor incurred within sixty days of the order for relief. This denial of discharge is a rebuttable presumption (that is, the denial may be challenged by the debtor), however, and any debts reasonably incurred to support the debtor or dependents are not classified as luxuries.

11. Cash advances totaling more than $1,075 that are extensions of open-end consumer credit obtained by the debtor within sixty days of the order for relief. A denial of discharge of these debts is also a rebuttable presumption.

12. Judgments or consent decrees against a debtor as a result of the debtor's operation of a motor vehicle while intoxicated.

In the following case, the debtor sought to have her student loans discharged in bankruptcy. The question before the court was whether payment of the loan would constitute an "undue hardship" for the debtor.

Case 15.3 ● In re Baker

United States Bankruptcy Court,
Eastern District of Tennessee, 1981.
10 Bankr. 870.

Historical and Social Setting

In 1980, about 53 percent of married women in the United States were working, compared with about 41 percent ten years earlier. More than 60 percent of wives who were separated from their husbands worked outside the home in 1980, compared with about 52 percent in 1970; for divorced women, the figures were about 74 percent and 72 percent, respectively. On average, however, in 1980, women earned only 62 cents for every dollar that men earned. In American families, husbands averaged nearly $21,000 in earnings and wives, $8,600. At the same time, of mothers who were entitled to child support, less than 75 percent actually received any payments. Of mothers living below the poverty line, more than 60 percent received nothing at all.

Background and Facts Mary Lou Baker attended three different institutions of higher learning. At these three schools, she received educational loans totaling $6,635. After graduation, she was employed, but her monthly take-home pay was less than $650. Monthly expenses for herself and her three children were approximately $925. Her husband had left town and provided no child or other financial support. She received no public aid and had no other income. In January 1981, just prior to this action, Baker's church paid her gas bill so that she and her children could have heat in their home. One child had reading difficulty, and another required expensive shoes. Baker had not been well and had been unable to pay her medical bills. She filed for bankruptcy. In her petition, she sought a discharge of her educational loans based on the hardship provision.

In the Words of the Court . . .
Ralph H. KELLEY, Bankruptcy Judge.

* * * *

* * * The restriction [against discharge of student loans] was designed to remedy an abuse by students who, immediately upon graduation, would file bankruptcy to secure a discharge of educational loans. These students often had no other indebtedness and could easily pay their debts from future wages.

* * * *

The court concludes that under the circumstances of this case, requiring the debtor to repay the debts * * * would impose upon her and her dependents an undue hardship. In passing [the restriction against discharge of student loans], Congress intended to correct an abuse. It did not intend to deprive those who have truly fallen on hard times of the "fresh start" policy of the new Bankruptcy Code.

Decision and Remedy The debtor's student loans were discharged. Given the fact that she had "truly fallen on hard times," Baker should be allowed to have her debts discharged in bankruptcy to avoid undue hardship.

For Critical Analysis—Economic Consideration *Why does the Bankruptcy Code generally prohibit the discharge of student loans, such as those obtained through government-guaranteed educational loan programs?*

OBJECTIONS TO DISCHARGE In addition to the exceptions to discharge previously listed, the following circumstances (relating to the debtor's conduct and not the debt) will cause a discharge to be denied:

1. The debtor's concealment or destruction of property with the intent to hinder, delay, or defraud a creditor.
2. The debtor's fraudulent concealment or destruction of financial records.
3. The debtor's discharge in bankruptcy within six years of the filing of the petition.[10]

When a discharge is denied under these circumstances, the assets of the debtor are still distributed to the creditors, but the debtor remains liable for the unpaid portions of all claims.

EFFECT OF DISCHARGE The primary effect of a discharge is to void, or set aside, any judgment on a discharged debt and prohibit any action to collect a discharged debt. A discharge does not affect the liability of a co-debtor.

REVOCATION OF DISCHARGE The Code provides that a debtor's discharge may be revoked. On petition by the trustee or a creditor, the bankruptcy court may, within one year, revoke the discharge decree if it is discovered that the debtor was fraudulent or dishonest during the bankruptcy proceedings. The revocation renders the discharge void, allowing creditors not satisfied by the distribution of the debtor's estate to proceed with their claims against the debtor.

REAFFIRMATION OF DEBT A debtor may voluntarily agree to pay off a debt—for example, a debt owed to a family member, close friend, or any creditor—notwithstanding the fact that the debt could be discharged in bankruptcy. An agreement to pay a debt dischargeable in bankruptcy is referred to as a *reaffirmation agreement*.

To be enforceable, reaffirmation agreements must be made before a debtor is granted a discharge, and they must be filed with the court. If the debtor is represented by an attorney, court approval is not required if the attorney files a declaration or affidavit stating that (1) the debtor has been fully informed of the consequences of the agreement (and a default under the agreement), (2) the agreement is made voluntarily, and (3) the agreement does not impose undue hardship on the debtor or the debtor's family. If the debtor is not represented by an attorney, court approval is required, and the agreement will be approved only if the court finds that the agreement will result in no undue hardship to the debtor and is in the best interest of the debtor.

The agreement must contain a clear and conspicuous statement advising the debtor that reaffirmation is not required. The debtor can rescind, or cancel, the agreement at any time prior to discharge or within sixty days of filing the agreement, *whichever is later*. This rescission period must be stated clearly and conspicuously in the reaffirmation agreement.

Chapter 11—Reorganization

The type of bankruptcy proceeding used most commonly by a corporate debtor is the Chapter 11 *reorganization*. In a reorganization, the creditors and

> "**Debt rolls a man over and over, binding him hand and foot, and letting him hang upon the fatal mesh until the long-legged interest devours him.**"
>
> Henry Ward Beecher, 1813–1887 (American clergyman, writer, and abolitionist)

---

10. A discharge under Chapter 13 of the Code within six years of the filing of the petition does not bar a subsequent Chapter 7 discharge when a good faith Chapter 13 plan paid at least 70 percent of all allowed unsecured claims and was the debtor's "best effort."

the debtor formulate a plan under which the debtor pays a portion of his or her debts and the rest of the debts are discharged. The debtor is allowed to continue in business. Although this type of bankruptcy is commonly a corporate reorganization, any debtor (except a stockbroker or a commodities broker) who is eligible for Chapter 7 relief is eligible for relief under Chapter 11.[11] Railroads are also eligible.

The same principles that govern the filing of a liquidation petition apply to reorganization proceedings. The case may be brought either voluntarily or involuntarily. The same principles govern the entry of the order for relief. The automatic-stay provision is also applicable in reorganizations.

In some instances, creditors may prefer private, negotiated debt-adjustment agreements, also known as **workouts,** to bankruptcy proceedings. Often these out-of-court workouts are much more flexible and thus more conducive to a speedy settlement. Speed is critical, because delay is one of the most costly elements in any bankruptcy proceeding. Another advantage of workouts is that they avoid the various administrative costs of bankruptcy proceedings.

A bankruptcy court, after notice and a hearing, may dismiss or suspend all proceedings in a case at any time if dismissal or suspension would better serve the interests of the creditors. The Code also allows a court, after notice and a hearing, to dismiss a case under reorganization "for cause." Cause includes the absence of a reasonable likelihood of rehabilitation, the inability to effect a plan, and an unreasonable delay by the debtor that is prejudicial to (may harm the interests of) creditors.[12] A debtor need not be insolvent to be entitled to Chapter 11 protection.[13]

> **Workout** An out-of-court agreement between a debtor and his or her creditors in which the parties work out a payment plan or schedule under which the debtor's debts can be discharged.

Debtor in Possession

On entry of the order for relief, the debtor generally continues to operate his or her business as a **debtor in possession (DIP).** The court, however, may appoint a trustee (often referred to as a *receiver*) to operate the debtor's business if gross mismanagement of the business is shown or if appointing a trustee is in the best interests of the estate.

The DIP's role is similar to that of a trustee in a liquidation. The DIP is entitled to avoid preferential payments made to creditors and fraudulent transfers of assets that occurred prior to the filing of the Chapter 11 petition. The DIP has the power to decide whether to cancel or assume obligations under executory contracts (contracts that have not yet been performed) that were made prior to the petition.

> **Debtor in Possession (DIP)** In Chapter 11 bankruptcy proceedings, a debtor who is allowed to continue in possession of the property (the business) and to continue business operations.

Creditors' Committees

As soon as practicable after the entry of the order for relief, a creditors' committee of unsecured creditors is appointed. The committee may consult with the trustee or the DIP concerning the administration of the case or the formulation of the reorganization plan. Additional creditors' committees may be appointed to represent special interest creditors. Orders affecting the estate generally will not be made without either the consent of the committee or a hearing in which the judge evaluates the position of the committee.

---

11. *Toibb v. Radloff,* 501 U.S. 157, 111 S.Ct. 2197, 115 L.Ed.2d 145 (1991).
12. See 11 U.S.C. Section 1112(b).
13. *In re Johns-Manville Corp.,* 36 Bankr. 727 (S.D.N.Y. 1984).

Ethical Issue 15.2

Should those who "bankrupt" a firm be allowed to continue to manage the firm as debtors in possession?

Chapter 11 reorganizations have become the target of substantial criticism. One of the arguments against Chapter 11 is that it allows the very managers who "bankrupted" a firm to continue to manage the firm as debtors in possession while the firm is in Chapter 11 proceedings. According to some critics, the main beneficiaries of Chapter 11 corporate reorganizations are not the shareholder-owners of the corporations but attorneys and current management. Basically, these critics argue that reorganizations do not preserve companies' assets, because large firms must pay millions of dollars for attorneys and accountants during the reorganization process, which can take years to complete.

Businesses with debts of less than $2 million that do not own or manage real estate can avoid creditors' committees. In these cases, bankruptcy judges may enter orders without a committee's consent.

The Reorganization Plan

A reorganization plan to rehabilitate the debtor is a plan to conserve and administer the debtor's assets in the hope of an eventual return to successful operation and solvency. The plan must be fair and equitable and must do the following:

1. Designate classes of claims and interests.
2. Specify the treatment to be afforded the classes. (The plan must provide the same treatment for each claim in a particular class.)
3. Provide an adequate means for execution.

FILING THE PLAN Only the debtor may file a plan within the first 120 days after the date of the bankruptcy court's order for relief. If the debtor does not meet the 120-day deadline, however, or if the debtor fails to obtain the required creditor consent (see below) within 180 days, any party may propose a plan. The plan need not provide for full repayment to unsecured creditors. Instead, unsecured creditors may receive a percentage of each dollar owed to them by the debtor. If a small-business debtor chooses to avoid creditors' committees, the time for the debtor's filing is shortened to 100 days, and any other party's plan must be filed within 160 days.

ACCEPTANCE AND CONFIRMATION OF THE PLAN Once the plan has been developed, it is submitted to each class of creditors for acceptance. Each class must accept the plan unless the class is not adversely affected by the plan. A class has accepted the plan when a majority of the creditors, representing two-thirds of the amount of the total claim, vote to approve it. Even when all classes of claims accept the plan, the court may refuse to confirm it if it is not "in the best interests of the creditors." A spouse or child of the debtor can block the plan if it does not provide for payment of his or her maintenance, alimony, or support claims in cash.

Cram-Down Provision A provision of the Bankruptcy Code that allows a court to confirm a debtor's Chapter 11 reorganization plan even though only one class of creditors has accepted it. To exercise the court's right under this provision, the court must demonstrate that the plan does not discriminate unfairly against any creditors and is fair and equitable.

Remember A secured debt is a debt in which a security interest in personal property or fixtures assures payment of the obligation.

Even if only one class of claims has accepted the plan, the court may still confirm the plan under the Code's so-called **cram-down provision**. In other words, the court may confirm the plan over the objections of a class of creditors. Before the court can exercise this right of cram-down confirmation, it must be demonstrated that the plan "does not discriminate unfairly" against any creditors and that the plan is "fair and equitable."

The plan is binding on confirmation. The debtor is given a reorganization discharge from all claims not protected under the plan. This discharge does not apply to any claims that would be denied discharge under liquidation.

Chapter 13—Repayment Plan

Chapter 13 of the Bankruptcy Code provides for the "Adjustment of Debts of an Individual with Regular Income." Individuals (not partnerships or corporations) with regular income who owe fixed unsecured debts of less than $269,250 or fixed secured debts of less than $807,750 may take advantage of bankruptcy repayment plans. This includes salaried employees; individual proprietors; and individuals who live on welfare, Social Security, fixed pensions, or investment income. Many sole proprietors have a choice of filing under either Chapter 11 or Chapter 13. There are several advantages to repayment plans. One advantage is that they are less expensive and less complicated than reorganization proceedings or liquidation proceedings.

A Chapter 13 repayment plan can be initiated only by the filing of a voluntary petition by the debtor. Certain liquidation and reorganization cases may be converted to Chapter 13 with the consent of the debtor. A Chapter 13 repayment plan may be converted to a Chapter 7 liquidation at the request of either the debtor or, under certain circumstances, a creditor. A Chapter 13 repayment plan also may be converted to a Chapter 11 reorganization after a hearing. On the filing of a petition under Chapter 13, a trustee must be appointed. The automatic stay previously discussed also takes effect. Although the stay applies to all or part of a consumer debt, it does not apply to any business debt incurred by the debtor.

The Repayment Plan

Shortly after the petition is filed, the debtor must file a repayment plan. This plan may provide either for payment of all obligations in full or for payment of a lesser amount. A plan of rehabilitation by repayment provides for the turnover to the trustee of such future earnings or income of the debtor as is necessary for execution of the plan. The time for payment under the plan may not exceed three years unless the court approves an extension. The term, with extension, may not exceed five years.

The Code requires the debtor to make "timely" payments, and the trustee is required to ensure that the debtor commences these payments. The debtor must begin making payments under the proposed plan within thirty days after the plan has been filed with the court. If the plan has not been confirmed, the trustee is instructed to retain the payments until the plan is confirmed and then distribute them accordingly. If the plan is denied, the trustee will return the payments to the debtor less any costs. Failure of the debtor to make timely payments or to begin payments within the thirty-day period will allow the court to convert the repayment plan to a liquidation bankruptcy or to dismiss the petition.

CONFIRMATION OF THE PLAN After the plan is filed, the court holds a confirmation hearing, at which interested parties may object to the plan. The court will confirm a plan with respect to each claim of a secured creditor under any of the following circumstances:

1. If the secured creditors have accepted the plan.
2. If the plan provides that creditors retain their claims against the debtor's property and if the value of the property to be distributed to the creditors under the plan is not less than the secured portion of their claims.
3. If the debtor surrenders the property securing the claim to the creditors.

OBJECTION TO THE PLAN Unsecured creditors do not have a vote to confirm a repayment plan, but they can object to it. The court can approve a plan over the objection of the trustee or any unsecured creditor only in either of the following situations:

1. When the value of the property to be distributed under the plan is at least equal to the amount of the claims.
2. When all the debtor's projected disposable income to be received during the three-year plan period will be applied to making payments. Disposable income is all income received less amounts needed to support the debtor and dependents and/or amounts needed to meet ordinary expenses to continue the operation of a business.

As emphasized by the decision in the following case, the timing of creditors' objections to a Chapter 13 plan is critical.

Case 15.4 ● In re Andersen

United States Bankruptcy Appellate Panel,[a] Tenth Circuit, 1998.
215 Bankr. 792.
http://www.utb.uscourts.gov/bap/cron-dir.html[b]

Historical and Social Setting *Resolving disputes as to the dischargeability of student loans has been a thorny issue for the courts. The Bankruptcy Code appears to require an all-or-nothing finding— that is, the entire amount of a student loan is either dischargeable or not. Most courts have agreed.[c] Frequently, a debtor may be able to pay part, but not all, of a loan, or may be able to pay the loan in full in*

the future when he or she is gainfully employed. In light of these variables, some courts allow more creative repayment plans, stating that only part of a debt is dischargeable or that repayment terms may be modified by the court. Permitting debtors to use Chapter 13 to resolve a dispute about the dischargeability of a student loan can encourage the parties to find other inventive ways to compromise.

Background and Facts Doreen Andersen had student loan obligations to a number of educational loan guaranty agencies and lending banks. She filed a Chapter 13 plan that contained the following information:

> All timely filed and allowed unsecured claims, including the claims of Higher Education Assistance Foundation [HEAF] and [other] government guaranteed education loans, shall be paid ten percent (10%) of each claim, and the balance of each claim shall be discharged. * * *

a. A bankruptcy appellate panel, with the consent of the parties, has jurisdiction to hear appeals from final judgments, orders, and decrees of bankruptcy judges.

b. This is the Web site for the U.S. Bankruptcy Court for the District of Utah. When the page opens, scroll down the list to the *Andersen* case (number 39), and click on the link to open it.

c. See, for example, *In re Shankwiler,* 208 Bankr. 701 (Bankr.C.D.Cal. 1997); and *In re Rivers,* 213 Bankr. 616 (Bankr.S.D.Ga. 1997).

(Continued)

Case 15.4 Continued

[E]xcepting the aforementioned education loans from discharge will impose an undue hardship on the debtor and the debtor's dependents. Confirmation of debtor's plan shall constitute a finding to that effect and that said debt is dischargeable.

The lenders filed an objection to the treatment of their claims. Because the objection was untimely, how-ever, the court denied it and confirmed the plan. Three years later, after Andersen fulfilled the plan, the court entered a discharge. When the lenders attempted to collect the balance of the loans, Andersen filed a suit in a bankruptcy court against them. The court held that the debts had not been discharged. Andersen appealed.

In the Words of the Court . . .
MATHESON, Bankruptcy Judge.

* * * *

* * * The plan process, whether in a Chapter 11 or 12 or 13, is essentially consensual. It is carried on through a bargaining process. The Code allows a great deal of flexibility in devising the terms of these plans. It is important to remember that Chapter 13 imposes very few mandatory requirements as to the contents of a plan. Congress intended for debtors to have flexibility in dealing with their creditors. A plan that is filed and served is simply an offer to the creditors, one that may be deemed to have been accepted if the creditor does not object.

* * * [Andersen's] plan specifically stated the treatment to be accorded the [student] loans. No argument has been made that [the lenders were] not properly served with the plan and with notice, or that [they] lacked the opportunity either to object or to have a meaningful hearing. Indeed, [they] did respond and filed an objection, thereby indicating that [they] understood that the plan intended to grant relief affecting [their] interests. However, the objection was not timely filed and was denied for that reason, leading to confirmation of the plan. * * *

* * * *

* * * [Andersen's] plan does not purport to make a nondischargeable debt dischargeable. The plan, instead, resolved a potential controversy about whether payment of the student [loans] would result in an undue hardship to the debtor. Confirmation of the plan constituted a finding to that effect, thereby rendering the [loans] dischargeable. Thus the ultimate order of discharge properly discharged the balance of the student loan obligation.

Decision and Remedy The bankruptcy appellate panel held that confirmation of the plan constituted a determination that payment of the student loans, beyond what was provided for in the plan, would be an undue hardship for the debtor and made the loans dischargeable. The panel reversed the decision of the lower court and remanded the case for fur-ther proceedings, including the entry of a judgment that the unpaid student loans were discharged.

For Critical Analysis—Economic Consideration *How might the lenders have avoided the outcome in this case?*

MODIFICATION OF THE PLAN   Prior to the completion of payments, the plan may be modified at the request of the debtor, the trustee, or an unsecured creditor. If any interested party has an objection to the modification, the court must hold a hearing to determine approval or disapproval of the modified plan.

Discharge

After the completion of all payments, the court grants a discharge of all debts provided for by the repayment plan. Except for allowed claims not provided for by the plan, certain long-term debts provided for by the plan, and claims for alimony and child support, all other debts are dischargeable. A discharge of debts under a Chapter 13 repayment plan is sometimes referred to as a "superdischarge." One of the reasons for this is that the law allows a Chapter 13 discharge to include fraudulently incurred debt and claims resulting from malicious or willful injury. Therefore, a discharge under Chapter 13 may be much more beneficial to some debtors than a liquidation discharge under Chapter 7 might be.

Even if the debtor does not complete the plan, a hardship discharge may be granted if failure to complete the plan was due to circumstances beyond the debtor's control and if the value of the property distributed under the plan was greater than creditors would have received in a liquidation proceeding. A discharge can be revoked within one year if it was obtained by fraud.

Chapter 12—Family-Farmer Plan

The Bankruptcy Code defines a *family farmer* as one whose gross income is at least 50 percent farm dependent and whose debts are at least 80 percent farm related. The total debt must not exceed $1.5 million. A partnership or closely held corporation that is at least 50 percent owned by the farm family can also take advantage of Chapter 12.

The procedure for filing a family-farmer bankruptcy plan is very similar to the procedure for filing a repayment plan under Chapter 13. The farmer-debtor must file a plan not later than ninety days after the order for relief. The filing of the petition acts as an automatic stay against creditors' actions against the estate.

The content of a family-farmer plan is basically the same as that of a Chapter 13 repayment plan. The plan can be modified by the farmer-debtor but, except for cause, must be confirmed or denied within forty-five days of the filing of the plan.

Court confirmation of the plan is the same as for a repayment plan. In summary, the plan must provide for payment of secured debts at the value of the collateral. If the secured debt exceeds the value of the collateral, the remaining debt is unsecured. For unsecured debtors, the plan must be confirmed if either the value of the property to be distributed under the plan equals the amount of the claim or the plan provides that all of the farmer-debtor's disposable income to be received in a three-year period (or longer, by court approval) will be applied to making payments. Completion of payments under the plan discharges all debts provided for by the plan.

A farmer who has already filed a reorganization or repayment plan may convert the plan to a family-farmer plan. The farmer-debtor may also convert a family-farmer plan to a liquidation plan.

Key Terms

Chapter Summary • Creditors' Rights and Bankruptcy

REMEDIES AVAILABLE TO CREDITORS

Liens
(See pages 417–419.)
	1. **Mechanic's lien**—A nonpossessory, filed lien on an owner's real estate for labor, services, or materials furnished to or made on the realty.
	
	2. **Artisan's lien**—A possessory lien on an owner's personal property for labor performed or value added.
	
	3. **Innkeeper's lien**—A possessory lien on a hotel guest's baggage for hotel charges that remain unpaid.
	
	4. **Judicial liens**—
	
	   a. **Attachment**—A court-ordered seizure of property prior to a court's final determination of the creditor's rights to the property. Attachment is available only on the creditor's posting of a bond and in strict compliance with the applicable state statutes.
	
	   b. **Writ of execution**—A court order directing the sheriff to seize (levy) and sell a debtor's nonexempt real or personal property to satisfy a court's judgment in the creditor's favor.

Garnishment (See pages 419–420.)	A collection remedy that allows the creditor to attach a debtor's money (such as wages owed or bank accounts) and property that are held by a third person.
Creditors' Composition Agreement (See page 420.)	A contract between a debtor and his or her creditors by which the debtor's debts are discharged by payment of a sum less than the sum that is actually owed.
Mortgage Foreclosure (See page 420.)	On the debtor's default, the entire mortgage debt is due and payable, allowing the creditor to foreclose on the realty by selling it to satisfy the debt.
Suretyship or Guaranty (See pages 420–423.)	Under contract, a third person agrees to be primarily or secondarily liable for the debt owed by the principal debtor. A creditor can turn to this third person for satisfaction of the debt.

Chapter Summary • Creditors' Rights and Bankruptcy

LAWS ASSISTING DEBTORS

Exemptions
(See pages 423–424.)
	Numerous laws, including consumer protection statutes, assist debtors. Additionally, state laws exempt certain types of real and personal property from levy of execution or attachment.
	
	1. **Real property**—Each state permits a debtor to retain the family home, either in its entirety or up to a specified dollar amount, free from the claims of judgment creditors or trustees in bankruptcy (homestead exemption).
	
	2. **Personal property**—Personal property that is most often exempt from satisfaction of judgment debts includes the following:
	
	   a. Household furniture up to a specified dollar amount.
	
	   b. Clothing and certain personal possessions.
	
	   c. Transportation vehicles up to a specified dollar amount.
	
	   d. Certain classified animals, such as livestock and pets.
	
	   e. Equipment used in a business or trade up to a specified dollar amount.

BANKRUPTCY—A COMPARISON OF CHAPTERS 7, 11, 12, AND 13

Issue	Chapter 7	Chapter 11	Chapters 12 and 13
Purpose	Liquidation.	Reorganization.	Adjustment.
Who Can Petition	Debtor (voluntary) or creditors (involuntary).	Debtor (voluntary) or creditors (involuntary).	Debtor (voluntary) only.
Who Can Be a Debtor	Any "person" (including partnerships and corporations) except railroads, insurance companies, banks, savings and loan institutions, investment companies licensed by the Small Business Administration, and credit unions. Farmers and charitable institutions cannot be involuntarily petitioned.	Any debtor eligible for Chapter 7 relief; railroads are also eligible.	**Chapter 12**—Any family farmer (one whose gross income is at least 50 percent farm dependent and whose debts are at least 80 percent farm related) or any partnership or closely held corporation at least 50 percent owned by a farm family, when total debt does not exceed $1.5 million. **Chapter 13**—Any individual (not partnerships or corporations) with regular income who owes fixed unsecured debts of less than $269,250 or fixed secured debts of less than $807,750.
Procedure Leading to Discharge	Nonexempt property is sold with proceeds to be distributed (in order) to priority groups. Dischargeable debts are terminated.	Plan is submitted; if it is approved and followed, the remaining debts are discharged.	Plan is submitted and must be approved if the debtor turns over disposable income for a three-year period; if the plan is followed, debts are discharged.

(Continued)

Chapter Summary • Creditors' Rights and Bankruptcy, *Continued*

Issue	Chapter 7	Chapter 11	Chapters 12 and 13
Advantages	On liquidation and distribution, most debts are discharged, and the debtor has an opportunity for a fresh start.	Debtor continues in business. Creditors can either accept the plan, or it can be "crammed down" on them. The plan allows for the reorganization and liquidation of debts over the plan period.	Debtor continues in business or possession of assets. If the plan is approved, most debts are discharged after a three-year period.

For Review

1. What is a prejudgment attachment? What is a writ of execution? How does a creditor use these remedies?

2. What is garnishment? When might a creditor undertake a garnishment proceeding?

3. In a bankruptcy proceeding, what constitutes the debtor's estate in property? What property is exempt from the estate under federal bankruptcy law?

4. What is the difference between an exception to discharge and an objection to discharge?

5. In a Chapter 11 reorganization, what is the role of the debtor in possession?

Questions and Case Problems

15–1. Creditors' Remedies. In what circumstances would a creditor resort to each of the following remedies when trying to collect on a debt?

(a) Mechanic's lien.
(b) Artisan's lien.
(c) Innkeeper's lien.
(d) Writ of attachment.
(e) Writ of execution.
(f) Garnishment.

15–2. Rights of the Surety. Meredith, a farmer, borrowed $5,000 from Farmer's Bank and gave the bank $4,000 in bearer bonds to hold as collateral for the loan. Meredith's neighbor, Peterson, who had known Meredith for years, signed as a surety on the note. Because of a drought, Meredith's harvest that year was only a fraction of what it normally was, and he was forced to default on his payments to Farmer's Bank. The bank did not immediately sell the bonds but instead requested $5,000 from Peterson. Peterson paid the $5,000 and then demanded that the bank give him the $4,000 in securities. Can Peterson enforce this demand? Explain.

15–3. Rights of the Guarantor. Sabrina is a student at Sunnyside University. In need of funds to pay for tuition and books, she attempts to secure a short-term loan from University Bank. The bank agrees to make a loan if Sabrina will have someone financially responsible guarantee the loan payments. Abigail, a well-known businessperson and a friend of Sabrina's family, calls the bank and agrees to pay the loan if Sabrina cannot. Because of Abigail's reputation, the bank makes the loan. Sabrina makes several payments on the loan, but because of illness she is not able to work for one month. She requests that University Bank extend the loan for three months. The bank agrees and raises the interest rate for the extended period. Abigail has not been notified of the extension (and therefore has not consented to it). One month later, Sabrina drops out of school. All attempts to collect from Sabrina have failed. University Bank wants to hold Abigail liable. Will the bank succeed? Explain.

15–4. Distribution of Property. Runyan voluntarily petitions for bankruptcy. He has three major claims against his estate. One is by Calvin, a friend who holds Runyan's negotiable promissory note for $2,500; one is by Kohak, an employee who is owed three months' back wages of $4,500; and one is by the First Bank of Sunny Acres on an unsecured loan of $5,000. In addition, Martinez, an accountant retained by the trustee, is owed $500, and property taxes of $1,000 are owed to Micanopa County. Runyan's nonexempt property has been liquidated, with the proceeds totaling $5,000. Discuss fully what amount each party will receive, and why.

15–5. Creditors' Remedies. Orkin owns a relatively old home valued at $45,000. He notices that the bathtubs and fixtures in both bathrooms are leaking and need to be replaced. He contracts with Pike to replace the bathtubs and fixtures. Pike replaces them and submits her bill of $4,000 to Orkin. Because of financial difficulties, Orkin does not pay the bill. Orkin's only asset is his home, which under state law is exempt up to $40,000 as a homestead. Discuss fully Pike's remedies in this situation.

15–6. Dismissal of Chapter 7 Case. Ellis and Bonnie Jarrell filed a Chapter 7 petition. The reason for filing was not a calamity, sudden illness, disability, or unemployment—both Jarrells were employed. Their petition was full of inaccuracies that understated their income and overstated their obligations. For example, they declared as an expense a monthly contribution to an investment plan. The truth was that they had monthly income of $3,197.45 and expenses of $2,159.44. They were attempting to discharge a total of $15,391.64 in unsecured debts. Most of these were credit-card debts, at least half of which had been taken as cash advances. Should the court dismiss the petition? If so, why? Discuss. [*In re Jarrell,* 189 Bankr. 374 (M.D.N.C. 1995)]

15–7. Artisan's Lien. Air Ruidoso, Ltd., operated a commuter airline and air charter service between Ruidoso, New Mexico, and airports in Albuquerque and El Paso. Executive Aviation Center, Inc., provided services for airlines at the Albuquerque International Airport. When Air Ruidoso failed to pay more than $10,000 that it owed for fuel, oil, and oxygen, Executive Aviation took possession of Air Ruidoso's plane. Executive Aviation claimed that it had a lien on the plane and filed a suit in a New Mexico state court to foreclose. Do supplies such as fuel, oil, and oxygen qualify as "materials" for the purpose of creating an artisan's lien? Why or why not? [*Air Ruidoso, Ltd. v. Executive Aviation Center, Inc.,* 122 N.M. 71, 920 P.2d 1025 (1996)]

15–8. Automatic Stay. David Sisco had about $600 in an account in Tinker Federal Credit Union. Sisco owed DPW Employees Credit Union a little more than $1,100. To collect on the debt, DPW obtained a garnishment judgment and served it on Tinker. The next day, Sisco filed a bankruptcy petition. Tinker then told DPW that, because of the bankruptcy filing, it could not pay the garnishment. DPW objected, and Tinker asked an Oklahoma state court to resolve the issue. What effect, if any, does Sisco's bankruptcy filing have on DPW's garnishment action? [*DPW Employees Credit Union v. Tinker Federal Credit Union,* 925 P.2d 93 (Okla.App.4th 1996)]

15–9. Voidable Preference. The Securities and Exchange Commission (SEC) filed a suit in a federal district court against First Jersey Securities, Inc., and others, alleging fraud in First Jersey's sale of securities (stock). The court ordered the defendants to turn over to the SEC $75 million in illegal profits. This order made the SEC the largest unsecured creditor of First Jersey. First Jersey filed a voluntary petition in a federal bankruptcy court to declare bankruptcy under Chapter 11. On the same day, the debtor transferred 200,001 shares of stock to its law firm, Robinson, St. John, & Wayne (RSW), in payment for services in the SEC suit and the bankruptcy petition. The stock represented essentially all of the debtor's assets. RSW did not find a buyer for the stock for more than two months. The SEC objected to the transfer, contending that it was a voidable preference, and asked that RSW be disqualified from representing the debtor. RSW responded that the transfer was made in the ordinary course of business. Also, asserted RSW, the transfer was not in payment of an "antecedent debt," because the firm had not presented First Jersey with a bill for its services and therefore the debt was not yet past due. Was the stock transfer a voidable preference? Should the court disqualify RSW? Why or why not? [*In re First Jersey Securities, Inc.,* 180 F.3d 504 (3d Cir. 1999)]

A Question of Ethics and Social Responsibility

15–10. In September 1986, Edward and Debora Davenport pleaded guilty in a Pennsylvania court to welfare fraud and were sentenced to probation for one year. As a condition of their probation, the Davenports were ordered to make monthly restitution payments to the county probation department, which would forward the payments to the Pennsylvania Department of Public Welfare, the victim of the Davenports' fraud. In May 1987, the Davenports filed a petition for Chapter 13 relief and listed the restitution payments among their debts. The bankruptcy court held that the restitution obligation was a dischargeable debt. Ultimately, the United States Supreme Court reviewed the case. The Court noted that under the Bankruptcy Code, a debt is defined as a liability on a claim, and a claim is defined as a right to payment. Because the restitution obligations clearly constituted a right to payment, the Court held that the obligations were dischargeable in bankruptcy. [*Pennsylvania Department of Public Welfare v. Davenport,* 495 U.S. 552, 110 S.Ct. 2126, 109 L.Ed.2d 588 (1990)]

1. Critics of this decision contend that the Court adhered to the letter, but not the spirit, of bankruptcy law in arriving at its conclusion. In what way, if any, did the Court not abide by the "spirit" of bankruptcy law?

2. Do you think that Chapter 13 plans, which allow nearly all types of debts to be discharged, tip the scales of justice too far in favor of debtors?

Case Briefing Assignment

15–11. Examine Case A.5 [*Hawley v. Cement Industries, Inc.*, 51 F.3d 246 (11th Cir. 1995)] in Appendix A. The case has been excerpted there in great detail. Review and then brief the case, making sure that you include answers to the following questions in your brief.

1. How did the case originate, and who are the parties?
2. What was the central issue to be decided?
3. What law governs the issue?
4. How did the lower court decide the case?
5. What was the appellate court's decision on the matter?

For Critical Analysis

15–12. Has the Bankruptcy Code made it too easy for debtors to avoid their obligations by filing for bankruptcy? What are the implications of the increased number of bankruptcy filings for future potential debtors who seek to obtain credit?

Interacting with the Internet

■ For updated links to resources available on the Web, as well as a variety of other materials, visit this text's Web site at

http://leet.westbuslaw.com

■ The Legal Information Institute at Cornell University offers a collection of law materials concerning debtor-creditor relationships at

http://www.law.cornell.edu/ topics/debtor_creditor.html

■ For an example of one state's (South Dakota's) laws on garnishment, go to

http://www.state.sd.us/state/legis/ lrc/statutes/21/18/211800h.htm

■ The U.S. Bankruptcy Code is online at

http://www.law.cornell.edu:80/ uscode/11

■ You can find links to an extensive number of bankruptcy resources on the Internet by accessing the Bankruptcy Lawfinder at

http://www.agin.com/lawfind

■ Another good resource for bankruptcy information is the American Bankruptcy Institute (ABI) at

http://www.abiworld.org

Online Legal Research Exercises

Go to **http://leet. westbuslaw.com**, the Web site that accompanies this text. Select "Interactive Study Center," and then click on "Chapter 15." There you will find the following Internet research exercises that you can perform to learn more about bankruptcy and its alternatives:

Activity 15–1: Debtor-Creditor Relations
Activity 15–2: Bankruptcy

Before the Test

Go to **http://leet. westbuslaw.com**, the Web site that accompanies this text. Select "Interactive Quizzes." You will find a number of interactive questions relating to this chapter.

Business Organizations

chapter objectives

After reading this chapter, you should be able to:

1. Identify and describe the three major traditional forms of business organization.

2. Summarize the advantages and disadvantages of doing business as a partnership and as a corporation, respectively.

3. Specify how the limited liability company and the limited liability partnership address needs that are not met by traditional forms of business.

4. Define the term *franchise,* and indicate how a franchising relationship arises.

5. Describe the roles of corporate directors, officers, and shareholders.

"[E]veryone thirsteth after gaine."

Sir Edward Coke, 1552–1634
(English jurist and politician)

Entrepreneur One who initiates and assumes the financial risks of a new enterprise and undertakes to provide or control its management.

Many Americans would agree with Sir Edward Coke that most people, at least, "thirsteth after gaine." Certainly, an entrepreneur's primary motive for undertaking a business enterprise is to make profits. An **entrepreneur** is by definition one who initiates and *assumes the financial risks* of a new enterprise and undertakes to provide or control its management.

One of the questions faced by any entrepreneur who wishes to start up a business is what form of business organization he or she should choose for the business endeavor. (Another question faced by entrepreneurs is how to locate potential investors in the enterprise. How investors can be located online is discussed in this chapter's *Legal E-nvironment* feature.) In this chapter, we first examine the basic features of the three major traditional business forms—sole proprietorships, partnerships, and corporations. We then look at two relatively new, but significant, business forms: the limited liability company, or LLC, and limited liability partnership, or LLP. The LLC is rapidly becoming an attractive alternative to the traditional corporate form. The LLP is a variation of the LLC. We also discuss private franchises. In the final pages of the chapter, we look at the roles, rights, and duties of corporate directors, officers, and shareholders, and at some of the ways in which conflicts among these corporate participants are resolved.

Major Traditional Business Forms

Traditionally, entrepreneurs have used three major forms to structure their business enterprises: the sole proprietorship, the partnership, and the corporation.

Sole Proprietorships

Sole Proprietorship The simplest form of business, in which the owner is the business; the owner reports business income on his or her personal income tax return and is legally responsible for all debts and obligations incurred by the business.

The simplest form of business is a **sole proprietorship**. In this form, the owner is the business; thus, anyone who does business without creating a sep-

A manager checks a shipment of the products that his firm sells. Could this be a sole proprietorship?

Legal *e*-nvironment

Locating Potential Investors

Technology via the Internet has allowed promoters and others to access, easily and inexpensively, a large number of potential investors. Today, there are several online "matching services." These services specialize in matching potential investors with companies or future companies that are seeking investors. A corporate promoter or a small company seeking capital investment can pay a fee to one of these service companies, which then includes a description of the company in a list that it makes available to investors—also for a fee.

Matching services are not new. For decades, a number of enterprises have provided such services by using computerized databases to match business firms' investment needs with potential investors. What is new is that several of these service providers are now online, and many of them have significantly expanded the geographic scope of their operations.

Online Listings

For example, the American Venture Capital Exchange, or AVCE (at **http://www.avce.com**), lists hundreds of companies that seek financing. Some of these companies are just starting up, while others are existing firms that wish to expand their businesses. For each company listed, AVCE provides a summary of its business plan for potential investors to review. Potential investors can then contact the companies in which they are interested.

A similar service is offered by the National Finance Company (at **http://www.natlfinance.com/company.htm**). The company's "Computer Capital Matching" service is designed to match those seeking financing to expand or start up a business with potential investors. Garage.com (at **http://www.garage.com**) provides a list of start-up companies and summaries of their business plans in the "Garage" area of its site and a list of potential investors in the "Heaven" area. Potential investors who are interested in one of the listed start-up companies may contact those companies directly.

Hundreds of other Web sites offer useful information and contacts for entrepreneurs and venture capitalists. To begin a search for this type of information, go to any major search engine and search for "venture capital."

Industry-Specific Matching Services

A number of companies specialize in matching entrepreneurs in specific industries with potential investors. For example, Capital Access Network (at **http://neturn.com/can/finance4tek.html**) offers matching services for "techpreneurs"—persons seeking capital for high-tech ventures. Also, some companies include listings of companies or start-ups not only in the United States but in other countries as well. For example, AVCE's listings include companies or start-ups in Canada, Europe, Russia, Mexico, South America, Asia, and Australia. Other companies restrict their services to firms within a certain region, such as the Pacific Northwest in the United States.

For Critical Analysis: *What factors would a venture capitalist be likely to consider when deciding whether to invest in a start-up company?*

---

arate business organization has a sole proprietorship. Sole proprietorships constitute over two-thirds of all American businesses. They are also usually small enterprises—about 1 percent of the sole proprietorships existing in the United States have revenues that exceed $1 million per year. Sole proprietors can own and manage any type of business from an informal, home-office undertaking to a large restaurant or construction firm.

A major advantage of the sole proprietorship is that the proprietor receives all of the profits (because he or she assumes all of the risk). In addition, it is often easier and less costly to start a sole proprietorship than to start any other kind of business, as few legal forms are involved. This type of business organization also entails more flexibility than does a partnership or a corporation. The sole proprietor is free to make any decision he or she wishes to concerning the business—whom to hire, when to take a vacation, what kind of business to pursue, and so on. A sole proprietor pays only personal income taxes on

What are the advantages of operating a bakery as a sole proprietorship?

profits, which are reported as personal income on the proprietor's personal income tax form. Sole proprietors are also allowed to establish certain tax-exempt retirement accounts such as Keogh plans.[1]

The major disadvantage of the sole proprietorship is that, as sole owner, the proprietor alone bears the burden of any losses or liabilities incurred by the business enterprise. In other words, the sole proprietor has unlimited liability, or legal responsibility, for all obligations incurred in doing business. This unlimited liability is a major factor to be considered in choosing a business form. Another disadvantage is that the proprietor's opportunity to raise capital is limited to personal funds and the funds of those who are willing to make loans. The sole proprietorship also has the disadvantage of lacking continuity on the death of the proprietor. When the owner dies, so does the business—it is automatically dissolved. If the business is transferred to family members or other heirs, a new proprietorship is created.

Partnerships

Traditionally, partnerships have been classified as either general partnerships or limited partnerships. The two forms of partnership differ considerably in regard to legal requirements and the rights and liabilities of partners. We look here at the basic characteristics of each of these forms.

Partnership An agreement by two or more persons to carry on, as co-owners, a business for profit.

GENERAL PARTNERSHIPS A general partnership, or **partnership**, arises from an agreement, express or implied, between two or more persons to carry on a business for profit. Partners are co-owners of a business and have joint control over its operation and the right to share in its profits. No particular form of partnership agreement is necessary for the creation of a partnership, but for practical reasons, the agreement should be in writing. Basically, the partners may agree to almost any terms when establishing the partnership so long as they are not illegal or contrary to public policy.

A partnership is a legal entity only for limited purposes, such as the partnership name and title of ownership and property. A key advantage of the partnership is that the firm itself does not pay federal income taxes, although the firm must file an information return with the Internal Revenue Service (IRS). A partner's profit from the partnership (whether distributed or not) is taxed as individual income to the individual partner. The main disadvantage of the partnership is that the partners are subject to personal liability for partnership obligations. In other words, if the partnership cannot pay its debts, the personal assets of the partners are subject to creditors' claims.

Limited Partnership A partnership consisting of one or more general partners (who manage the business and are liable to the full extent of their personal assets for debts of the partnership) and of one or more limited partners (who contribute only assets and are liable only up to the amount contributed by them).

General Partner In a limited partnership, a partner who assumes responsibility for the management of the partnership and liability for all partnership debts.

Limited Partner In a limited partnership, a partner who contributes capital to the partnership but has no right to participate in the management and operation of the business. The limited partner assumes no liability for partnership debts beyond the capital contributed.

LIMITED PARTNERSHIPS A special and quite popular form of partnership is the **limited partnership**, which consists of at least one general partner and one or more limited partners. A limited partnership is a creature of statute, because it does not come into existence until a *certificate of partnership* is filed with the appropriate state office. A **general partner** assumes responsibility for the management of the partnership and liability for all partnership debts. A **limited partner** has no right to participate in the general management or operation of the partnership and assumes no liability for partnership

---

1. A *Keogh plan* is a retirement program designed for self-employed persons through which a certain percentage of their income can be contributed tax free to the plan, and principal and interest earnings will not be taxed until funds are withdrawn from the plan.

debts beyond the amount of capital he or she has contributed. Thus, one of the major benefits of becoming a limited partner is this limitation on liability, both with respect to lawsuits brought against the partnership and the amount of money placed at risk.

Corporations

A third and very widely used type of business organizational form is the **corporation.** Corporations are owned by *shareholders*—those who have purchased ownership shares in the business. A *board of directors,* elected by the shareholders, manages the business. The board of directors normally employs *officers* to oversee day-to-day operations.

The corporation, like the limited partnership, is a creature of statute. The corporation's existence as a legal entity, which can be perpetual, depends generally on state law.

One of the key advantages of the corporate form of business is that the liability of its owners (shareholders) is limited to their investments. The shareholders usually are not personally liable for the obligations of the corporation. Another advantage is that a corporation can raise capital by selling shares of corporate stock to investors. A key disadvantage of the corporate form is that any distributed corporate income is taxed twice. The corporate entity pays taxes on the firm's income, and when income is distributed to shareholders, the shareholders again pay taxes on that income.

S CORPORATIONS Some small corporations are able to avoid this double-taxation feature of the corporation by electing to be treated, for tax purposes, as an **S corporation.** Subchapter S of the Internal Revenue Code allows qualifying corporations to be taxed in a way similar to the way a partnership is taxed. In other words, an S corporation is not taxed at the corporate level. As in a partnership, the income is taxed only once—when it is distributed to the shareholder-owners, who pay personal income taxes on their respective shares of the profits.

QUALIFICATION REQUIREMENTS FOR S CORPORATIONS Among the numerous requirements for S corporation status, the following are the most important:

1. The corporation must be a domestic corporation.
2. The corporation must not be a member of an affiliated group of corporations.
3. The shareholders of the corporation must be individuals, estates, or certain trusts. Partnerships and nonqualifying trusts cannot be shareholders. Corporations can be shareholders under certain circumstances.
4. The corporation must have seventy-five or fewer shareholders.
5. The corporation must have only one class of stock, although not all shareholders need have the same voting rights.
6. No shareholder of the corporation may be a nonresident alien.

Limited Liability Companies

The two most common forms of business organization selected by two or more persons entering into business together are the partnership and the corporation. As already explained, each form has distinct advantages and

Corporation A legal entity formed in compliance with statutory requirements. The entity is distinct from its shareholder-owners.

S Corporation A close business corporation that has met certain requirements as set out by the Internal Revenue Code and thus qualifies for special income-tax treatment. Essentially, an S corporation is taxed the same as a partnership, but its owners enjoy the privilege of limited liability.

"The art of taxation consists in so plucking the goose as to obtain the largest amount of feathers with the smallest possible amount of hissing."

Jean Baptiste Colbert, 1619–1683 (French politician and financial reformer)

disadvantages. For partnerships, the advantage is that partnership income is taxed only once (all income is "passed through" the partnership entity to the partners themselves, who are taxed only as individuals); the disadvantage is the personal liability of the partners. For corporations, the advantage is the limited liability of shareholders; the disadvantage is the double taxation of corporate income. For many entrepreneurs and investors, the ideal business form would combine the tax advantages of the partnership form of business with the limited liability of the corporate enterprise.

The limited partnership and the S corporation partially address these needs. The limited liability of limited partners, however, is conditional: limited liability exists only so long as the limited partner does *not* participate in management. The problem with S corporations is that only small corporations (those with seventy-five or fewer shareholders) may acquire S corporation status. Furthermore, with few exceptions, only *individuals* may be shareholders in an S corporation; partnerships and corporations normally cannot be shareholders. Finally, no nonresident alien can be a shareholder in an S corporation. This means that if, say, a European investor wanted to purchase shares in an S corporation, it would not be permissible.

Since 1977, an increasing number of states have authorized a new form of business organization called the **limited liability company (LLC)**. The LLC is a hybrid form of business enterprise that offers the limited liability of the corporation but the tax advantages of a partnership. The origins and characteristics of this increasingly significant form of business organization are discussed in this chapter's *Landmark in the Legal Environment*.

> **Contrast** A partnership must have at least two partners. In many states, an LLC can be created with only one shareholder-member.

> **Limited Liability Company (LLC)** A hybrid form of business enterprise that offers the limited liability of the coporation but the tax advantages of a partnership.

Landmark in the Legal Environment

Limited Liability Company (LLC) Statutes

In 1977, Wyoming became the first state to pass legislation authorizing the creation of a limited liability company (LLC). Although LLCs emerged in the United States only in 1977, they have been in existence for over a century in other areas, including several European and South American nations. For example, the South American *limitada* is a form of business organization that operates more or less as a partnership but provides limited liability for the owners.

In the United States, after Wyoming's adoption of an LLC statute, it still was not known how the Internal Revenue Service (IRS) would treat the LLC for tax purposes. In 1988, however, the IRS ruled that Wyoming LLCs would be taxed as partnerships instead of as corporations, providing that certain requirements were met. Prior to this ruling, only one other state—Florida, in 1982—had authorized LLCs. The 1988 ruling en-

couraged other states to enact LLC statutes, and in less than a decade, all states had done so.

New IRS rules that went into effect on January 1, 1997, encouraged even more widespread use of LLCs in the business world. These rules provide that any unincorporated business will automatically be taxed as a partnership unless it indicates otherwise on the tax form. The exceptions involve publicly traded companies, companies formed under a state incorporation statute, and certain foreign-owned companies. If a business chooses to be taxed as a corporation, it can indicate this choice by checking a box on the IRS form.

Part of the impetus behind creating LLCs in this country is that foreign investors are allowed to become LLC members. Generally, in an era increasingly characterized by global business efforts and investments, the LLC offers U.S. firms and potential investors from other countries flexibility and opportunities greater than those available through partnerships or corporations.

For Critical Analysis: *Given the fact that the tax and liability characteristics of partnerships and corporations have long been in existence, why is it that LLC statutes have emerged only relatively recently?*

Formation of an LLC

Like the corporation, an LLC must be formed and operated in compliance with state law. About one-fourth of the states specifically require LLCs to have at least two owners, called **members.** In the rest of the states, although some LLC statutes are silent on this issue, one-member LLCs are usually permitted.

To form an LLC, **articles of organization** must be filed with a central state agency—usually the secretary of state's office. Typically, the articles are required to set forth such information as the name of the business, its principal address, the name and address of a registered agent, the names of the owners, and information on how the LLC will be managed. The business's name must include the words "Limited Liability Company" or the initials "LLC." In addition to filing the articles of organization, a few states require that a notice of the intention to form an LLC be published in a local newspaper.

Member The term used to designate a person who has an ownership interest in a limited liability company.

Articles of Organization The document filed with a designated state official by which a limited liability company is formed.

Advantages and Disadvantages of LLCs

A key advantage of the LLC is that the liability of members is limited to the amount of their investments. Another significant advantage is that an LLC with two or more members can choose whether to be taxed as a partnership or a corporation. Unless the LLC indicates that it wishes to be taxed as a corporation, it is automatically taxed as a partnership by the Internal Revenue Service (IRS). This means that the LLC as an entity pays no taxes; rather, as in a partnership, profits are "passed through" the LLC and paid personally by the members. If LLC members want to reinvest profits in the business, however, rather than distribute the profits to members, they may prefer to be taxed as a corporation if corporate income tax rates are lower than personal tax rates. Part of the attractiveness of the LLC for businesspersons is this flexibility with respect to taxation options. For federal income tax purposes, one-member LLCs are automatically taxed as sole proprietorships unless they indicate that they wish to be taxed as corporations. Still another advantage of the LLC for businesspersons is the flexibility it offers in terms of business operations and management—as will be discussed shortly.

Remember A uniform law is a "model" law. It does not become the law of any state until the state legislature adopts it, either in part or in its entirety.

The disadvantages of the LLC are relatively few. Some of the initial disadvantages with respect to uncertainties over how LLCs would be taxed no longer exist. The only remaining disadvantage of the LLC is that state statutes are not yet uniform. In an attempt to promote some uniformity among the states in respect to LLC statutes, the National Conference of Commissioners on Uniform State Laws drafted a Uniform Limited Liability Company Act for submission to the states to consider for adoption. Until all of the states have adopted the uniform law, however, an LLC in one state will have to check the rules in the other states in which the firm does business to ensure that it retains its limited liability.

The LLC Operating Agreement

The LLC is also a flexible business entity in another important way. In an LLC, the members themselves can decide how to operate the various aspects of the business by forming an **operating agreement.** Operating agreements typically contain provisions relating to management, decision-making procedures, how profits will be divided, the transfer of membership interests, whether the LLC will be dissolved on the death or departure of a member, and other important issues.

Operating Agreement In a limited liability company, an agreement in which the members set forth the details of how the business will be managed and operated. State statutes typically give the members wide latitude in deciding for themselves the rules that will govern their organization.

Operating agreements need not be in writing, and indeed they need not even be formed for an LLC to exist. Generally, though, LLC members should protect their interests by forming a written operating agreement. As with any business arrangement, disputes may arise over any number of issues. If there is no agreement covering the topic being disputed, such as how profits will be divided, the state LLC statute will govern the outcome. For example, most LLC statutes provide that if the members have not specified how profits will be divided among the members, they will be divided equally. Generally, with respect to issues not covered by an operating agreement or by an LLC statute, the principles of partnership law are applied.

Limited Liability Partnerships

Limited Liability Partnership (LLP) A business organizational form that is similar to the LLC but that is designed more for professionals who normally do business as partners in a partnership. The LLP is a pass-through entity for tax purposes, like the general partnership, but it limits the personal liability of the partners.

The **limited liability partnership (LLP)** is similar to the LLC. The difference between an LLP and an LLC is that the LLP is designed more for professionals who normally do business as partners in a partnership. The major advantage of the LLP is that it allows a partnership to continue as a pass-through entity for tax purposes but limits the personal liability of the partners.

The first state to enact an LLP statute was Texas, in 1991. Other states quickly followed suit, and by 1997, virtually all of the states had enacted LLP statutes. Like LLCs, LLPs must be formed and operated in compliance with state statutes. The appropriate form must be filed with a central state agency, usually the secretary of state's office, and the business's name must include either "Limited Liability Partnership" or "LLP."

In most states, it is relatively easy to convert a traditional partnership into an LLP because the firm's basic organizational structure remains the same. Additionally, all of the statutory and common law rules governing partnerships still apply (apart from those modified by the LLP statute). Normally, LLP statutes are simply amendments to a state's already existing partnership law.

The LLP is especially attractive for two categories of businesses: professional services and family businesses. Professional service firms include law firms and accounting firms. Family limited liability partnerships are basically business organizations in which all of the partners are related. Generally, the LLP allows professionals to avoid personal liability for the malpractice of other partners. Although LLP statutes vary from state to state, generally each state statute limits in some way the liability of partners. For example, Delaware law protects each innocent partner from the "debts and obligations of the partnership arising from negligence, wrongful acts, or misconduct." In North Carolina, Texas, and Washington, D.C., the statutes protect innocent partners from obligations arising from "errors, omissions, negligence, incompetence, or malfeasance." Partners in an LLP are liable for their own wrongful acts, however, as well as the wrongful acts of those whom they supervise.

Major Business Forms Compared

When deciding which form of business organization would be most appropriate, businesspersons normally take several factors into consideration. These factors include ease of creation, the liability of the owners, tax considerations, and the need for capital. Each major form of business organization offers distinct advantages and disadvantages with respect to these and other factors. Exhibit 16–1 on pages 460 and 461 summarizes the essential advantages and disadvantages of each of the forms of business organization discussed in this chapter.

Private Franchises

Times have changed dramatically since Ray Kroc, the late founder of McDonald's, launched the franchising boom more than thirty-five years ago. Today, over a third of all retail sales and an increasing part of the total annual national output of the United States are generated by private franchises.

A **franchise** is defined as any arrangement in which the owner of a trademark, a trade name, or a copyright licenses others to use the trademark, trade name, or copyright in the selling of goods or services. A **franchisee** (a purchaser of a franchise) is generally legally independent of the **franchisor** (the seller of the franchise). At the same time, the franchise is economically dependent on the franchisor's integrated business system. In other words, a franchisee can operate as an independent businessperson but still obtain the advantages of a regional or national organization. Well-known franchises include McDonald's, KFC, and Burger King.

Types of Franchises

Because the franchising industry is so extensive (at least sixty-five types of distinct businesses sell franchises), it is difficult to summarize the many types of franchises that now exist. Generally, though, the majority of franchises fall into one of the following three classifications: distributorships, chain-style business operations, or manufacturing or processing-plant arrangements. We briefly describe these types of franchises here.

DISTRIBUTORSHIP   A *distributorship* arises when a manufacturing concern (franchisor) licenses a dealer (franchisee) to sell its product. Often, a distributorship covers an exclusive territory. An example of this type of franchise is an automobile dealership.

CHAIN-STYLE BUSINESS OPERATION   A *chain-style business operation* exists when a franchise operates under a franchisor's trade name and is identified as a member of a select group of dealers that engages in the franchisor's business. Often, the franchisor requires that the franchisee maintain certain standards of operation. In addition, sometimes the franchisee is obligated to deal exclusively with the franchisor to obtain materials and supplies. Examples of this type of franchise are McDonald's and most other fast-food chains.

MANUFACTURING OR PROCESSING-PLANT ARRANGEMENT   A *manufacturing or processing-plant arrangement* exists when the franchisor transmits to the franchisee the essential ingredients or formula to make a particular product. The franchisee then markets the product either at wholesale or at retail in accordance with the franchisor's standards. Examples of this type of franchise are Coca-Cola and other soft-drink bottling companies.

Laws Governing Franchising

Because a franchise relationship is primarily a contractual relationship, it is governed by contract law. If the franchise exists primarily for the sale of

Franchise Any arrangement in which the owner of a trademark, trade name, or copyright licenses another to use that trademark, trade name, or copyright, under specified conditions or limitations, in the selling of goods and services.

Franchisee One receiving a license to use another's (the franchisor's) trademark, trade name, or copyright in the sale of goods and services.

Franchisor One licensing another (the franchisee) to use his or her trademark, trade name, or copyright in the sale of goods or services.

Exhibit 16–1 Major Business Forms Compared

CHARACTERISTIC	SOLE PROPRIETORSHIP	PARTNERSHIP	CORPORATION
Method of Creation	Created at will by owner.	Created by agreement of the parties.	Charter issued by state—created by statutory authorization.
Legal Position	Not a separate entity; owner is the business.	Not a separate legal entity in many states.	Always a legal entity separate and distinct from its owners—a legal fiction for the purposes of owning property and being a party to litigation.
Liability	Unlimited liability.	Unlimited liability.	Limited liability of shareholders—shareholders are not liable for the debts of the corporation.
Duration	Determined by owner; automatically dissolved on owner's death.	Terminated by agreement of the partners, by the death of one or more of the partners, by withdrawal of a partner, by bankruptcy, and so on.	Can have perpetual existence.
Transferability of Interest	Interest can be transferred, but individual's proprietorship then ends.	Although partnership interest can be assigned, assignee does not have full rights of a partner.	Shares of stock can be transferred.
Management	Completely at owner's discretion.	Each general partner has a direct and equal voice in management unless expressly agreed otherwise in the partnership agreement.	Shareholders elect directors, who set policy and appoint officers.
Taxation	Owner pays personal taxes on business income.	Each partner pays *pro rata* share of income taxes on net profits, whether or not they are distributed.	Double taxation—corporation pays income tax on net profits, with no deduction for dividends, and shareholders pay income tax on disbursed dividends they receive.
Organizational Fees, Annual License Fees, and Annual Reports	None.	None.	All required.
Transaction of Business in Other States	Generally no limitation.	Generally no limitation.[a]	Normally must qualify to do business and obtain certificate of authority.

a. A few states have enacted statutes requiring that foreign partnerships qualify to do business there.

Exhibit 16-1 Major Business Forms Compared—Continued

CHARACTERISTIC	LIMITED PARTNERSHIP	LIMITED LIABILITY COMPANY	LIMITED LIABILITY PARTNERSHIP
Method of Creation	Created by agreement to carry on a business for a profit. At least one party must be a general partner and the other(s) limited partner(s). Certificate of limited partnership is filed. Charter must be issued by the state.	Created by an agreement of the owner-members of the company. Articles of organization are filed. Charter must be issued by the state.	Created by agreement of the partners. Certificate of a limited liability partnership is filed. Charter must be issued by the state.
Legal Position	Treated as a legal entity.	Treated as a legal entity.	Generally, treated same as a general partnership.
Liability	Unlimited liability of all general partners; limited partners are liable only to the extent of capital contributions.	Member-owners' liability is limited to the amount of capital contributions or investment.	Varies from state to state but usually limits liability of a partner for certain acts committed by other partners.
Duration	By agreement in certificate, or by termination of the last general partner (withdrawal, death, and so on) or last limited partner.	Unless a single-member LLC, can have perpetual existence (same as a corporation).	Terminated by agreement of partners, by death or withdrawal of a partner, or by law (such as bankruptcy).
Transferability of Interest	Interest can be assigned (same as general partnership), but if assignee becomes a member with consent of other partners, certificate must be amended.	Member interests are freely transferable.	Interest can be assigned (same as in a general partnership).
Management	General partners have equal voice or by agreement. Limited partners may not retain limited liability if they actively participate in management.	Member-owners can fully participate in management, or management is selected by member-owners who manage on behalf of the members.	Same as a general partnership.
Taxation	Generally taxed as a partnership.	LLC is not taxed, and members are taxed personally on profits "passed through" the LLC.	Same as a general partnership.
Organizational Fees, Annual License Fees, and Annual Reports	Organizational fee required; usually not others.	Organizational fee required; others vary with states.	Organizational fee required (such as a set amount per partner); usually not others.
Transaction of Business in Other States	Generally, no limitations.	Generally, no limitation but may vary depending on state.	Generally, no limitation, but state laws vary as to formation and limitation of liability.

Keep in Mind Because a franchise involves the licensing of a trademark, a trade name, or a copyright, the law governing intellectual property may apply in some cases.

products manufactured by the franchisor, the law governing sales contracts as expressed in Article 2 of the Uniform Commercial Code applies (see Chapter 12). Additionally, the federal government and most states have enacted laws governing certain aspects of franchising. Generally, these laws are designed to protect prospective franchisees from dishonest franchisors and to prohibit franchisors from terminating franchises without good cause.

FEDERAL REGULATION OF FRANCHISING Automobile dealership franchisees are protected from automobile manufacturers' bad faith termination of their franchises by the Automobile Dealers' Franchise Act[2]—also known as the Automobile Dealers' Day in Court Act—of 1965. If a manufacturer-franchisor terminates a franchise because of a dealer-franchisee's failure to comply with unreasonable demands (for example, failure to attain an unrealistically high sales quota), the manufacturer may be liable for damages.

Another federal statute is the Petroleum Marketing Practices Act (PMPA)[3] of 1979, which prescribes the grounds and conditions under which a franchisor may terminate or decline to renew a gasoline station franchise. Federal antitrust laws (discussed in Chapter 23), which prohibit certain types of anticompetitive agreements, may also apply in certain circumstances.

In 1979, the Federal Trade Commission (FTC) issued regulations that require franchisors to disclose material facts necessary to a prospective franchisee's making an informed decision concerning the purchase of a franchise.

STATE REGULATION OF FRANCHISING State legislation tends to be similar to federal statutes and the FTC regulations. For example, to protect fran-

---

2. 15 U.S.C. Sections 1221 *et seq.*
3. 15 U.S.C. Sections 2801 *et seq.*

Ethical Issue 16.1

Why does the law protect franchisees?

A franchising relationship is based on a contract, and contract law thus applies. Why, then, has the government deemed it necessary to enact laws to protect franchisees from the consequences of contracts into which they have voluntarily entered? One reason is that a franchisee often relies heavily on information about the business provided by the franchisor when deciding to purchase a franchise. Disclosure laws, such as the FTC rules and disclosure requirements under state statutes, help to ensure that prospective franchisees have accurate information when deciding whether to enter into a franchise contract.

Another reason is that many franchise contracts are essentially adhesion contracts—in the sense that the purchaser of a franchise often has little bargaining power relative to the franchisor and little say in the contract provisions. Additionally, franchise contracts are typically lengthy documents, consisting of perhaps fifty pages (McDonald's eleven-page contract is an exception). A franchisee who is relatively inexperienced in business may not realize the economic and legal consequences of particular clauses in the contract or of the absence of certain clauses—such as a clause granting the franchisee exclusive rights to sell the franchisor's products in a particular territory.

For Critical Analysis: *Are lengthy franchise contracts necessarily disadvantageous to franchisees? Explain.*

chisees, a state law might require the disclosure of information that is material to making an informed decision regarding the purchase of a franchise. This could include such information as the actual costs of operation, recurring expenses, and profits earned, along with facts substantiating these figures. State deceptive trade practices acts may also prohibit certain types of actions on the part of franchisors.

In response to the need for a uniform franchise law, the National Conference of Commissioners on Uniform State Laws drafted a model law that standardizes the various state franchise regulations. Because the uniform law represents a compromise of so many diverse interests, it has met with little success in being adopted as law by the various states.

> **Remember** Unfair contracts between a party with a great amount of bargaining power and another with little power are generally not enforced. This is part of the freedom from contract.

The Franchise Contract

The franchise relationship is defined by a contract between the franchisor and the franchisee. The franchise contract specifies the terms and conditions of the franchise and spells out the rights and duties of the franchisor and the franchisee. If either party fails to perform the contractual duties, that party may be subject to a lawsuit for breach of contract. Generally, the statutory law and case law governing franchising tend to emphasize the importance of good faith and fair dealing in franchise relationships.

Because each type of franchise relationship has its own characteristics, it is difficult to describe the broad range of details a franchising contract may include. We now look at some of the major issues that typically are addressed in a franchise contract.

PAYMENT FOR THE FRANCHISE   The franchisee ordinarily pays an initial fee or lump-sum price for the franchise license (the privilege of being granted a franchise). This fee is separate from the various products that the franchisee purchases from or through the franchisor. In some industries, the franchisor relies heavily on the initial sale of the franchise for realizing a profit. In other industries, the continued dealing between the parties brings profit to both. In most situations, the franchisor will receive a stated percentage of the annual sales or annual volume of business done by the franchisee. The franchise agreement may also require the franchisee to pay a percentage of advertising costs and certain administrative expenses.

BUSINESS PREMISES   The franchise agreement may specify whether the premises for the business must be leased or purchased outright. In some cases, construction of a building is necessary to meet the terms of the agreement. The agreement usually will specify whether the franchisor supplies equipment and furnishings for the premises or whether this is the responsibility of the franchisee.

LOCATION OF THE FRANCHISE   Typically, the franchisor will determine the territory to be served. Some franchise contracts will give the franchisee exclusive rights, or "territorial rights," to a certain geographical area. Other franchise contracts, while they define the territory allotted to a particular franchise, either specifically state that the franchise is nonexclusive or are silent on the issue of territorial rights.

Many franchise cases involve disputes over territorial rights, and this is one area of franchising in which the implied covenant of good faith and fair dealing often comes into play. ● **Example 16.1** Suppose that a franchisee is not given exclusive territorial rights in the franchise contract, or the contract is silent on the issue. If the franchisor allows a competing franchise to be established nearby, the franchisee may suffer a significant loss in profits. In this situation, a court may hold that the franchisor's actions breached an implied covenant of good faith and fair dealing. ●

In the following case, the franchisee did not have any exclusive territorial rights under the franchise contract. When the franchisor built a competing operation nearby, the franchisee sued the franchisor. At issue in the case was whether the franchisor had breached an implied covenant of good faith and fair dealing.

Case 16.1 ● Camp Creek Hospitality Inns, Inc. v. Sheraton Franchise Corp.

United States Court of Appeals, Eleventh Circuit, 1998.
139 F.3d 1396.
http://www.findlaw.com/ casecode/courts/11th.html[a]

Historical and Economic Setting *Before 1950, travel was often slow, at best. By the end of the 1950s, airlines had established regular routes between American and European cities, and the travel industry began to change dramatically. Thirty years later, the federal government relaxed the tight control it maintained over U.S. air routes. Over the next decade, travel became even more common, frequent weekend trips replaced the standard two-week family vacation, and business travelers filled more than half of the hotel rooms in the United States. Despite these trends, the hotel industry suffered losses in the late 1980s and the early 1990s.*

a. This Web site is maintained by FindLaw. This page contains links to recent opinions of the U.S. Court of Appeals for the Eleventh Circuit. In the "1998" row, click on the "April" link. When the results appear, click on the *Camp Creek* case name to access the opinion.

Background and Facts In 1990, Camp Creek Hospitality Inns, Inc., entered into a contract with Sheraton Franchise Corporation (a subsidiary of ITT Sheraton Corporation) to operate a Sheraton Inn franchise west of the Atlanta airport. Because another franchisee, the Sheraton Hotel Atlanta Airport, already served that market, Sheraton named Camp Creek's facility "Sheraton Inn Hartsfield-West, Atlanta Airport." Three years later, ITT Sheraton bought a Hyatt hotel in the vicinity of the Atlanta airport and gave it the name "Sheraton Gateway Hotel, Atlanta Airport." The presence of three Sheraton properties in the same market caused some customer confusion. Also, the Inn and the Gateway competed for the same customers, which caused the Inn to suffer a decrease in the growth of its business. Camp Creek filed a suit in a federal district court against Sheraton and others, alleging in part that by establishing the Gateway, ITT Sheraton denied Camp Creek the fruits of its contract in breach of the implied covenant of good faith and fair dealing. The court issued a summary judgment in favor of the defendants. Camp Creek appealed to the U.S. Court of Appeals for the Eleventh Circuit.

In the Words of the Court . . .
BIRCH, Circuit Judge:

* * * *

* * * [T]he contract, as executed, says nothing about whether or where Sheraton could establish a competing hotel. * * * Camp Creek had no contractual right to expect the Sheraton Franchise to refrain from licensing the Sheraton name to additional franchises beyond the site of the Inn. By the express terms of the contract, therefore, Sheraton could have authorized a competing franchise directly across the street from the Inn, and Camp Creek would have little recourse.

Case 16.1 Continued

Sheraton, however, did not establish such a franchise in this case; instead, it purchased and operated the Gateway on its own behalf. * * *

As a result, we must determine whether the implied covenant of good faith and fair dealing permits the Sheraton to establish its own hotel in the same vicinity as the Inn. * * *

* * * Sheraton emphasizes that the Inn has been more profitable every year since the Gateway opened. Camp Creek, however, * * * describe[d] a number of trends present in the market for hotel rooms in the Atlanta area, both before and after Sheraton began operating the Gateway, and present[ed] credible theories and measures of damages attributable to the additional intra-brand competition associated with the Gateway's entry to the market. We hold that Camp Creek's evidence is sufficient to withstand Sheraton's motion for summary judgment on this claim.

Decision and Remedy The U.S. Court of Appeals for the Eleventh Circuit held that unless a franchise contract expressly provides otherwise, it could violate the implied covenant of good faith and fair dealing for a franchisor to compete against a franchisee in the same market for the same customers. The court reversed the judgment of the lower court and remanded the case for trial.

For Critical Analysis—Economic Consideration *Why would a franchisor compete directly with its franchisee?*

BUSINESS ORGANIZATION OF THE FRANCHISEE The business organization of the franchisee is of great concern to the franchisor. Depending on the terms of the franchise agreement, the franchisor may specify particular requirements for the form and capital structure of the business. The franchise agreement may also provide that standards of operation—relating to such aspects of the business as sales quotas, quality, and record keeping—be met by the franchisee. Furthermore, a franchisor may wish to retain stringent control over the training of personnel involved in the operation and over administrative aspects of the business.

QUALITY CONTROL BY THE FRANCHISOR Although the day-to-day operation of the franchise business is normally left up to the franchisee, the franchise agreement may provide for the amount of supervision and control agreed on by the parties. When the franchise is a service operation, such as a motel, the contract often provides that the franchisor will establish certain standards for the facility. Typically, the contract will provide that the franchisor is permitted to make periodic inspections to ensure that the standards are being maintained in order to protect the franchise's name and reputation.

> **Recall** Under the doctrine of *respondeat superior,* an employer may be liable for the torts of his or her employees if they occur within the scope of employment, without regard to the personal fault of the employer.

As a general rule, the validity of a provision permitting the franchisor to establish and enforce certain quality standards is unquestioned. Because the franchisor has a legitimate interest in maintaining the quality of the product or service to protect its name and reputation, it can exercise greater control in this area than would otherwise be tolerated. Increasingly, however, franchisors are finding that if they exercise too much control over the operations of their franchisees, they may incur liability under agency theory for the acts of their franchisees' employees—as the following case illustrates. (A franchisee may even be held to be an employee of the franchisor—see this chapter's *Inside the Legal Environment* on page 467 for a discussion of this topic.)

Case 16.2 ● Miller v. D. F. Zee's, Inc.

United States District Court,
District of Oregon, 1998.
31 F.Supp.2d 792.

Company Profile *Based in South
Carolina, Flagstar Corporation franchised or
owned Denny's restaurants, as well as the Carrows,
Coco's, El Pollo Loco, Hardee's, and Quincy's Family
Steakhouse chains. In the early 1990s, Denny's was the
defendant in two civil rights class-action suits brought
by African American customers who claimed that some
restaurants refused to seat or serve them. Denny's paid
more than $54 million to settle those suits and re-
sponded "quickly, decisively, and sincerely" to, among
other things, hire and promote more minorities.*[a] *In the
mid-1990s, Flagstar declared bankruptcy, sold the
Hardee's and Quincy's chains, and renamed itself
Advantica Restaurant Group, Inc. By the late 1990s,
Advantica's annual sales approached $3 billion, with
about 2 percent annual growth.*

———
a. Anne Faircloth, "Guess Who's Coming to Denny's,"
Fortune, August 3, 1998.

Background and Facts D. F. Zee's, Inc., owns
a Denny's restaurant in Tualatin, Oregon. Under the
franchise agreement, Zee's agreed to train and supervise employees in accordance with Denny's Operations
and Food Service Standards Manuals. Denny's regularly sent inspectors to assess compliance and reserved
the right to terminate the franchise for noncompliance.
The Denny's logo was displayed throughout the restaurant, and there was no indication that its owners were
other than "Denny's." Christine Miller worked as a
server at the restaurant. After several incidents of sexually inappropriate comments and conduct by her co-
workers, Miller complained to Stanley Templeton, the
manager. When her complaints were unavailing, Miller
contacted the manager of another Denny's restaurant,
who referred her to the district franchise manager for
Denny's, who referred the complaint to Zee's.
Templeton resigned, but the harassment continued.
Finally, Miller and three other employees filed a suit in
a federal district court against Zee's, Denny's, and others. Denny's filed a motion for summary judgment,
contending in part that a franchisor cannot be held liable for harassment by franchise employees.

In the Words of the Court . . .
AIKEN, J.

* * * *

Here, Denny's is responsible for acts of harassment by employees at the
Tualatin Denny's because employees of the Tualatin Denny's are agents of
[Denny's].

* * * [A]n agency results from the manifestation of consent by one
person to another so that the other will act on his or her behalf and
"subject" to his or her control, and consent by the other to so act. *An
agency relationship may be evidenced by an express agreement between the
parties, or it may be implied from the circumstances and conduct of the
parties.* The principal's consent and "right to control" are the essential
elements of an agency relationship. * * * [Emphasis added.]

* * * *

Here, * * * the franchise agreement requires adherence to
comprehensive, detailed [Franchise Operations and Food Service Standards]
manuals for the operation of the restaurant. * * *
Here, * * * defendants enforce the use of these methods by regularly
sending inspectors into the restaurant to assess compliance and by its
retained power to cancel the agreement.

Further, the Franchise Operations Manual provides that the defendants
had the right to control their franchisees in the precise parts of the
franchisee's business that allegedly resulted in plaintiffs' injuries—training
and discipline of employees.

Case 16.2 Continued

Decision and Remedy The court denied Denny's motion for summary judgment. The court held that a franchisor may be held vicariously liable under an agency theory for intentional acts of discrimination by the employees of a franchisee.

For Critical Analysis—Ethical Consideration *Should a franchisor be allowed to control the operation of its franchisee without liability for the franchisee's conduct?*

Inside the Legal Environment

Is It a Franchise . . . or Not?

A series of court decisions in the late 1990s has put businesspersons on notice that what will or will not be deemed a franchise may not always be determined by private contracts.

Franchisees May Be Deemed Employees

Some courts have held that franchisees are, in fact, employees. For example, in one case a franchisee of West Sanitation Services, Inc., a commercial sanitation company, was deemed to be an employee of the company even though he was designated as a franchisee in a franchise contract with the company.

The franchisee, Glenroy Francis, began working for West in 1986 as an employee. As an employee, he serviced commercial customers in a certain area. In 1987, West initiated a franchise program, in which some of its service employees, including Francis, became franchisees. When West later terminated its franchising arrangement with Francis for cause, Francis applied for unemployment insurance benefits.

The state labor department, after investigating Francis's working relationship with West, decided that an employment relationship existed because of the degree of direction and control exercised by West over Francis's work schedule and activities. The department ruled that Francis, as a former "employee," was entitled to unemployment benefits. The department further ruled that West was liable for unemployment insurance contributions, based on the amount West had paid to Francis and the other franchisees.

Ultimately, a New York appellate court upheld the labor department's ruling, concluding that "the franchise agreement vested West with substantial control over claimant's activities."[a]

In another case, the National Labor Relations Board ruled that some five hundred drivers for a New York company that provided limousine services should be considered as employees for labor law purposes, despite their franchise contracts with the company. Again, the decision was based on the extensive control exercised by the company over the drivers' activities.[b]

De Facto Franchises

In yet other cases, courts have gone in the opposite direction—they have found franchising relationships to exist even though the parties had *not* formed franchise contracts. In a number of states, if a business arrangement meets the definition of a franchising relationship under state law, it may be held to be a *de facto* franchise in that state. These cases typically arise because one of the parties wants to take advantage of a state franchising statute that offers certain protections to franchisees that would not be available under other types of contractual arrangements. For example, in one case a Mitsubishi subsidiary terminated its relationship with one of its distributors. The distributor sued for wrongful termination under the state franchising law and received $1.5 million in damages.[c]

For Critical Analysis: *Under what common law concept is the degree of control over a worker's activities a significant factor in determining employee status?*

---

a. *West Sanitation Services, Inc. v. Francis,* 1998 WL 11023 (N.Y.Sup.Ct.App.Div. 1998).

b. *In re Elite Limousine Plus, Inc.,* 324 NLRB No. 182 (November 6, 1997).

c. *To-Am Equipment Co. v. Mitsubishi Caterpillar Forklift America, Inc.,* 953 F.Supp. 987 (N.D.Ill. 1997).

PRICING ARRANGEMENTS   Franchises provide the franchisor with an outlet for the firm's goods and services. Depending on the nature of the business, the franchisor may require the franchisee to purchase certain supplies from the franchisor at an established price.[4] A franchisor who sets the prices at which the franchisee will resell the goods may violate state or federal antitrust laws, or both, however.

TERMINATION OF THE FRANCHISE   The duration of the franchise is a matter to be determined between the parties. Generally, a franchise will start out for a short period, such as a year, so that the franchisee and the franchisor can determine whether they want to stay in business with one another. Usually, the franchise agreement will specify that termination must be "for cause," such as death or disability of the franchisee, insolvency of the franchisee, breach of the franchise agreement, or failure to meet specified sales quotas. Most franchise contracts provide that notice of termination must be given. If no set time for termination is specified, then a reasonable time, with notice, will be implied. A franchisee must be given reasonable time to wind up the business—that is, to do the accounting and return the copyright or trademark or any other property of the franchisor.

Because a franchisor's termination of a franchise often has adverse consequences for the franchisee, much franchise litigation involves claims of wrongful termination. Generally, the termination provisions of contracts are more favorable to the franchisor. This means that the franchisee, who normally invests a substantial amount of time and funds in the franchise operation to make it successful, may receive little or nothing for the business on termination. The franchisor owns the trademark and hence the business.

It is in this area that statutory law and case law become important. The federal and state laws discussed earlier attempt, among other things, to protect franchisees from the arbitrary or unfair termination of their franchises by the franchisors. Generally, both statutory and case law emphasize the importance of good faith and fair dealing in terminating a franchise relationship.

In determining whether a franchisor has acted in good faith when terminating a franchise agreement, the courts generally try to balance the rights of both parties. If a court perceives that a franchisor has arbitrarily or unfairly terminated a franchise, the franchisee will be provided with a remedy for wrongful termination. If a franchisor's decision to terminate a franchise was made in the normal course of the franchisor's business operations, however, and reasonable notice of termination was given to the franchisee, normally a court would not consider such a termination wrongful.

The Nature of the Corporation

The corporation is a creature of statute. Its existence depends generally on state law. Each state has its own body of corporate law, and these laws are not entirely uniform. The Model Business Corporation Act (MBCA) is a codification of modern corporation law that has been influential in the drafting and

> "A corporation is an artificial being, invisible, intangible, and existing only in contemplation of law."
>
> John Marshall, 1755–1835
> (Chief justice of the United States
> Supreme Court, 1801–1835)

4. Although a franchisor can require franchisees to purchase supplies from it, requiring a franchisee to purchase exclusively from the franchisor may violate federal antitrust laws (see Chapter 23). For two landmark cases in these areas, see *United States v. Arnold, Schwinn & Co.*, 388 U.S. 365, 87 S.Ct. 1956, 18 L.Ed.2d (1967); and *Fortner Enterprises, Inc. v. U.S. Steel Corp.*, 394 U.S. 495, 89 S.Ct. 1252, 22 L.Ed.2d 495 (1969).

revision of state corporation statutes. Today, the majority of state statutes are guided by the revised version of the MBCA, known as the Revised Model Business Corporation Act (RMBCA).

A *corporation* can consist of one or more *natural* persons (as opposed to the artificial "person" of the corporation) identified under a common name. The primary document needed to incorporate (that is, form the corporation according to state law) is the **articles of incorporation,** which include such information about the corporation as its functions and the structure of its organization. As soon as a corporation is formed, an organizational meeting is held to adopt **bylaws** (rules for managing the firm) and to elect a board of directors.

The corporation substitutes itself for its shareholders in conducting corporate business and in incurring liability, yet its authority to act and the liability for its actions are separate and apart from the individuals who own it. (In certain limited situations, the "corporate veil" can be pierced; that is, liability for the corporation's obligations can be extended to shareholders, a topic to be discussed later in this chapter.)

Articles of Incorporation The document filed with the appropriate governmental agency, usually the secretary of state, when a business is incorporated; state statutes usually prescribe what kind of information must be contained in the articles of incorporation.

Bylaws A set of governing rules adopted by a corporation or other association.

Corporate Personnel

Responsibility for the overall management of the corporation is entrusted to a *board of directors,* which is elected by the shareholders. The board of directors hires *corporate officers* and other employees to run the daily business operations of the corporation.

When an individual purchases a share of stock in a corporation, that person becomes a *shareholder* and an owner of the corporation. Unlike the members in a partnership, the body of shareholders can change constantly without affecting the continued existence of the corporation. A shareholder can sue the corporation, and the corporation can sue a shareholder. Additionally, under certain circumstances, a shareholder can sue on behalf of a corporation.

Corporate Taxation

Corporate profits are taxed by state and federal governments. Corporations can do one of two things with corporate profits—retain them or pass them on to shareholders in the form of **dividends**. The corporation receives no tax deduction for dividends distributed to shareholders. Dividends are again taxable (except when they represent distributions of capital) as ordinary income to the shareholder receiving them. This double-taxation feature of the corporation is one of its major disadvantages.

Profits not distributed are retained by the corporation. These **retained earnings,** if invested properly, will yield higher corporate profits in the future and thus normally cause the price of the company's stock to rise. Individual shareholders can then reap the benefits of these retained earnings in the capital gains they receive when they sell their shares.

The consequences of a failure to pay corporate taxes can be severe. The state may dissolve a corporation for this reason. Alternatively, corporate status may be suspended until the taxes are paid.

Dividend A distribution to corporate shareholders of corporate profits or income, disbursed in proportion to the number of shares held.

Retained Earnings The portion of a corporation's profits that has not been paid out as dividends to shareholders.

Constitutional Rights of Corporations

A corporation is recognized under state and federal law as a "person," and it enjoys many of the same rights and privileges that U.S. citizens enjoy. The Bill of Rights guarantees a person, as a citizen, certain protections, and corporations are considered persons in most instances. Accordingly, a corporation has the same right as a natural person to equal protection of the laws under the Fourteenth Amendment. It has the right of access to the courts as an entity that can sue or be sued. It also has the right of due process before denial of life, liberty, or property, as well as freedom from unreasonable searches and seizures and from double jeopardy.

Under the First Amendment, corporations are entitled to freedom of speech. As we pointed out in Chapter 6, however, commercial speech (such as advertising) and political speech (such as contributions to political causes or candidates) receive significantly less protection than noncommercial speech.

Only the corporation's individual officers and employees possess the Fifth Amendment right against self-incrimination.[5] Additionally, the privileges and immunities clause of the Constitution (Article IV, Section 2) does not protect corporations.[6] This clause requires each state to treat citizens of other states equally with respect to access to courts, travel rights, and so forth.

Torts and Criminal Acts

A corporation is liable for the torts committed by its agents or officers within the course and scope of their employment. This principle applies to a corporation exactly as it applies to the ordinary agency relationships discussed in Chapter 17. It follows the doctrine of *respondeat superior.*

As you learned in Chapter 8, under modern criminal law, a corporation can sometimes be held liable for the criminal acts of its agents and employees, provided the punishment is one that can be applied to the corporation. Corporate criminal prosecutions were at one time relatively rare, but in the past decade they have increased significantly in number. Obviously, corporations cannot be imprisoned, but they can be fined. Of course, corporate directors and officers can be imprisoned, and in recent years, many have faced criminal penalties for their own actions or for the actions of employees under their supervision.

Classification of Corporations

The classification of a corporation depends on its purpose, ownership characteristics, and location. A corporation is referred to as a **domestic corporation** by its home state (the state in which it incorporates). A corporation formed in one state but doing business in another is referred to in that other state as a **foreign corporation**. A corporation formed in another country—say, Mexico—but doing business in the United States is referred to in the United States as an **alien corporation**.

A corporation does not have an automatic right to do business in a state other than its state of incorporation. It normally must obtain a *certificate of authority* in any state in which it plans to do business. Once the certificate has been issued, the powers conferred on a corporation by its home state generally can be exercised in the other state.

---

5. *In re Grand Jury No. 86-3 (Will Roberts Corp.),* 816 F.2d 569 (11th Cir. 1987).
6. *W. C. M. Window Co. v. Bernardi,* 730 F.2d 486 (7th Cir. 1984).

"Did you expect a corporation to have a conscience, when it has no soul to be damned and no body to be kicked?"

Edward Thurlow, 1731–1806
(English jurist)

Domestic Corporation In a given state, a corporation that does business in, and is organized under the law of, that state.

Foreign Corporation In a given state, a corporation that does business in the state without being incorporated therein.

Alien Corporation A designation in the United States for a corporation formed in another country but doing business in the United States.

BMW automobiles are inspected at a plant in the United States. BMW is classified as an alien corporation. What is the difference between an alien corporation and a foreign corporation?

Corporate Management—Shareholders

The acquisition of a share of stock makes a person an owner and shareholder in a corporation. Shareholders thus own the corporation. Although they have no legal title to corporate property, such as buildings and equipment, they do have an *equitable* (ownership) interest in the firm.

As a general rule, shareholders have no responsibility for the daily management of the corporation, although they are ultimately responsible for choosing the board of directors, which does have such control. Ordinarily, corporate officers and other employees owe no direct duty to individual shareholders. Their duty is to the corporation as a whole. A director, however, is in a fiduciary relationship to the corporation and therefore serves the interests of the shareholders. Generally, there is no legal relationship between shareholders and creditors of the corporation. Shareholders can, in fact, be creditors of the corporation and thus have the same rights of recovery against the corporation as any other creditor.

> **Be Aware** Shareholders are not normally agents of their corporation.

In this section, we look at the powers and voting rights of shareholders, which are generally established in the articles of incorporation and under the state's general incorporation law.

Shareholders' Powers

Shareholders must approve fundamental corporate changes before the changes can be effected. Hence, shareholders are empowered to amend the articles of incorporation (charter) and bylaws, approve a merger or the dissolution of the corporation, and approve the sale of all or substantially all of the corporation's assets. Some of these powers are subject to prior board approval.

Directors are elected to (and removed from) the board of directors by a vote of the shareholders. The first board of directors is either named in the articles of incorporation or chosen by the incorporators to serve until the first shareholders' meeting. From that time on, the selection and retention of directors are exclusively shareholder functions.

Directors usually serve their full terms; if they are unsatisfactory, they are simply not reelected. Shareholders have the inherent power, however, to remove a director from office *for cause* (breach of duty or misconduct) by a majority vote.[7] Some state statutes (and some corporate charters) even permit removal of directors *without cause* by the vote of a majority of the holders of outstanding shares entitled to vote.

Shareholders' Meetings

Shareholders' meetings must occur at least annually, and additional, special meetings can be called as needed to take care of urgent matters. Because it is usually not practical for owners of only a few shares of stock of publicly traded corporations to attend shareholders' meetings, such stockholders normally give third parties written authorization to vote their shares at the meeting. This authorization is called a **proxy** (from the Latin *procurare,* "to manage, take care of"). Proxies are often solicited by management, but any person can solicit proxies to concentrate voting power.

Proxy In corporation law, a written agreement between a stockholder and another under which the stockholder authorizes the other to vote the stockholder's shares in a certain manner.

SHAREHOLDER VOTING For shareholders to act during a meeting, a quorum must be present. Generally, a quorum exists when shareholders holding more than 50 percent of the outstanding shares are present. Corporate business matters are presented in the form of *resolutions,* which shareholders vote to approve or disapprove. Some state statutes have set forth specific voting requirements, and corporations' articles or bylaws must abide by these statutory requirements. Some states provide that the unanimous written consent of shareholders is a permissible alternative to holding a shareholders' meeting. Once a quorum is present, a majority vote of the shares represented at the meeting is usually required to pass resolutions.

Be Careful Once a quorum is present, a vote can be taken even if some shareholders leave without casting their votes.

At times, a greater-than-majority vote will be required either by a statute or by the corporate charter. Extraordinary corporate matters, such as a merger, consolidation, or dissolution of the corporation, require a higher percentage of the representatives of all corporate shares entitled to vote, not just a majority of those present at that particular meeting.

CUMULATIVE VOTING Most states permit or even require shareholders to elect directors by cumulative voting, a method of voting designed to allow minority shareholders representation on the board of directors.[8] When cumulative voting is allowed or required, the number of members of the board to be elected is multiplied by the total number of voting shares. The result equals the number of votes a shareholder has, and this total can be cast for one or more nominees for director. All nominees stand for election at the same time. When cumulative voting is not required either by statute or under the articles, the entire board can be elected by a simple majority of shares at a shareholders' meeting.

• **Example 16.2** Suppose that a corporation has 10,000 shares issued and outstanding. One group of shareholders (the minority shareholders) holds

---

7. A director can often demand court review of removal for cause.
8. See, for example, California Corporate Code Section 708. Under RMBCA 7.28, however, no cumulative voting rights exist unless the articles of corporation so provide.

only 3,000 shares, and the other group of shareholders (the majority shareholders) holds the other 7,000 shares. Three members of the board are to be elected. The majority shareholders' nominees are Acevedo, Barkley, and Craycik. The minority shareholders' nominee is Drake. Can Drake be elected by the minority shareholders?

If cumulative voting is allowed, the answer is yes. The minority shareholders have 9,000 votes among them (the number of directors to be elected times the number of shares held by the minority shareholders equals 3 times 3,000, which equals 9,000 votes). All of these votes can be cast to elect Drake. The majority shareholders have 21,000 votes (3 times 7,000 equals 21,000 votes), but these votes have to be distributed among their three nominees. The principle of cumulative voting is that no matter how the majority shareholders cast their 21,000 votes, they will not be able to elect all three directors if the minority shareholders cast all of their 9,000 votes for Drake, as illustrated in Exhibit 16–2.●

Corporate Management—Directors

A corporation typically is governed by a board of directors. Subject to statutory limitations, the number of directors is set forth in the corporation's articles or bylaws.

Election of Directors

The first board of directors is normally appointed by the incorporators on the creation of the corporation, or directors are named by the corporation itself in the articles. The first board serves until the first annual shareholders' meeting. Subsequent directors are elected by a majority vote of the shareholders.

The term of office for a director is usually one year—from annual meeting to annual meeting. Longer and staggered terms are permissible under most state statutes. A common practice is to elect one-third of the board members each year for a three-year term. In this way, there is greater management continuity.

Directors' Qualifications and Compensation

Few legal requirements exist concerning directors' qualifications. Only a handful of states impose minimum age and residency requirements. A director is sometimes a shareholder, but this is not a necessary qualification—unless, of course, statutory provisions or corporate articles or bylaws require ownership.

Ballot	Majority Shareholders' Votes			Minority Shareholders' Votes	Directors Elected
	Acevedo	Barkley	Craycik	Drake	
1	10,000	10,000	1,000	9,000	Acevedo/Barkley/Drake
2	9,001	9,000	2,999	9,000	Acevedo/Barkley/Drake
3	6,000	7,000	8,000	9,000	Barkley/Craycik/Drake

Exhibit 16–2
Results of Cumulative Voting
This exhibit illustrates how cumulative voting gives minority shareholders a greater chance of electing a director of their choice. By casting all of their 9,000 votes for one candidate (Drake), the minority shareholders will succeed in electing Drake to the board of directors.

Compensation for directors is ordinarily specified in the corporate articles or bylaws. Because directors have a fiduciary relationship to the shareholders and to the corporation, an express agreement or provision for compensation often is necessary for them to receive money from the funds that they control and for which they have responsibilities.

Board of Directors' Meetings

The board of directors conducts business by holding formal meetings with recorded minutes. The date on which regular meetings are held is usually established in the articles or bylaws or by board resolution, and no further notice is customarily required. Special meetings can be called, with notice sent to all directors.

Quorum The number of members of a decision-making body that must be present before business may be transacted.

Quorum requirements can vary among jurisdictions. (A **quorum** is the minimum number of members of a body of officials or other group that must be present in order for business to be validly transacted.) Many states leave the decision as to quorum requirements to the corporate articles or bylaws. In the absence of specific state statutes, most states provide that a quorum is a majority of the number of directors authorized in the articles or bylaws. Voting is done in person (unlike voting at shareholders' meetings, which can be done by proxy, as discussed earlier in this chapter).[9] The rule is one vote per director. Ordinary matters generally require a simple majority vote; certain extraordinary issues may require a greater-than-majority vote.

Directors' Management Responsibilities

Directors have responsibility for all policymaking decisions necessary to the management of corporate affairs. Just as shareholders cannot act individually to bind the corporation, the directors must act as a body in carrying out routine corporate business. One director has one vote, and generally the majority rules. The general areas of responsibility of the board of directors include the following:

1. Declaration and payment of corporate dividends to shareholders.
2. Authorization for major corporate policy decisions—for example, the initiation of proceedings for the sale or lease of corporate assets outside the regular course of business, the determination of new product lines, and the overseeing of major contract negotiations and major management-labor negotiations.
3. Appointment, supervision, and removal of corporate officers and other managerial employees and the determination of their compensation.
4. Financial decisions, such as the issuance of authorized shares and bonds.

The board of directors can delegate some of its functions to an executive committee or to corporate officers. In doing so, the board is not relieved of its overall responsibility for directing the affairs of the corporation, but corporate officers and managerial personnel are empowered to make decisions relating to ordinary, daily corporate affairs within well-defined guidelines.

---

9. Except in Louisiana, which allows a director to vote by proxy under certain circumstances. Some states, such as Michigan and Texas, and Section 8.20 of the RMBCA permit telephone conferences for board of directors' meetings.

Role of Officers and Directors

A director occupies a position of responsibility unlike that of other corporate personnel. Directors are sometimes inappropriately characterized as *agents* because they act on behalf of the corporation. No *individual* director, however, can act as an agent to bind the corporation; and as a group, directors collectively control the corporation in a way that no agent is able to control a principal. Directors are often incorrectly characterized as *trustees* because they occupy positions of trust and control over the corporation. Unlike trustees, however, they do not own or hold title to property for the use and benefit of others.

The officers and other executive employees are hired by the board of directors or, in rare instances, by the shareholders. In addition to carrying out the duties articulated in the bylaws, corporate and managerial officers act as agents of the corporation, and the ordinary rules of agency (discussed in Chapter 17) normally apply to their employment. The qualifications required of officers and executive employees are determined at the discretion of the corporation and are included in the articles or bylaws. In most states, a person can hold more than one office and can be both an officer and a director of the corporation.

Directors and officers have *fiduciary duties* to the corporation, because their relationship with the corporation and its shareholders is one of trust and confidence. The fiduciary duties of the directors and officers include the duty of care and the duty of loyalty. The duty of care requires directors and officers to be honest and use prudent business judgment in the conduct of corporate affairs. Directors and officers must carry out their responsibilities in an informed, businesslike manner. The duty of loyalty requires the subordination of the self-interest of the directors and officers to the interest of the corporation. In general, it prohibits directors and officers from using corporate funds or confidential corporate information for personal advantage. Directors and

Contrast Shareholders own a corporation and directors make policy decisions, but officers who run the daily business of the corporation often have significant decision-making power.

"It is not the crook in modern business that we fear but the honest man who does not know what he is doing."

Owen D. Young, 1874–1962
(American corporate executive and public official)

Corporate executives discuss the business of their firm. How do the rights and duties of corporate officers differ from those of corporate directors?

officers can be held liable to the corporation and to the shareholders for breach of either of these duties.

A breach of the duty of loyalty occurs when an officer or director, for his or her personal gain, takes advantage of a business opportunity that is financially within the corporation's reach, is in line with the firm's business, is to the firm's practical advantage, and is one in which the corporation has an interest. Whether buying certain corporate property constituted the violation of two directors' fiduciary duties to their corporation was at issue in the following case.

Case 16.3 ● Stokes v. Bruno

Court of Appeal of Louisiana,
Third Circuit, 1998.
720 So.2d 388.

Historical and Social Setting *A nonstock corporation is a corporation the ownership of which is not recognized by stock but by a membership charter or agreement. Membership might be created according to a particular attribute, such as the ownership of land within the corporation's geographic reach. A corporation organized for other than a profit-making purpose is a nonprofit corporation. No part of the income of a nonprofit corporation is distributable to the directors, officers, or members. An example of a nonstock, nonprofit corporation might be a homeowner's association that is organized in a corporate form.*

Background and Facts Point Cotile Parks Association, Inc. (PCPA), is a nonstock, nonprofit cor-

poration the members of which are limited to owners of lots or building sites within the Point Cotile Subdivision. The board of directors, including Gerald Bruno and Michael Wright, adopted resolutions that effectively granted Bruno and Wright the authority to sell certain "common ground" on PCPA's behalf. The board designated lots and set prices, based on professional appraisals. Six years later, when some of the lots had not sold for their original prices, Bruno and Wright sold to themselves, and to Bruno's wife, 5.45 acres of the "common ground." The sale included lots with timber that had not been previously offered for sale. On their own appraisal, Bruno and Wright set the price for the acreage lower than the board had set for the individual lots. When the board learned of the sale, Craig Stokes and other PCPA members filed a suit in a Louisiana state court against Bruno and Wright. The court declared the sale *ultra vires* and void. Bruno appealed.

In the Words of the Court . . .
DECUIR, Judge.

* * * *

* * * This apparently was a clear case of self-dealing. * * * [Bruno] should have a duty to disclose to the Corporation several items. First that the sale consummated was the whole tract, not just the first lots as had been offered in prior sales. * * * Next he had a duty to disclose to the Corporation the potential for sales of timber, as well as the fact that the revised values he was negotiating with himself on behalf of the Corporation were based on his own determinations and no outside source. Once he took the position of evaluator of the land, he would be barred by fiduciary duty from consummating the sale without disclosing the reduction in price, offering an opportunity for other [PCPA] members to purchase, or [from making] an effort to market the entire tract of land, as opposed to just the front lots. * * * Mr. Bruno and Mr. Wright owed a fiduciary [duty] to the Corporation to maximize the return and the mere fact that a portion of the property had not sold at the original requested prices did not give them the unilateral authorization to add more land, reduce the price and then purchase themselves without disclosure.

Case 16.3 Continued

Decision and Remedy The state intermediate appellate court affirmed the lower court's judgment. The sale of PCPA property under these circumstances was a breach of Bruno and Wright's fiduciary duty to the corporation. The appellate court ordered a rescission of the sale.

For Critical Analysis—Ethical Consideration *Under what circumstances might a sale by a director of corporate property to himself or herself be justified?*

Conflicts of Interest

The duty of loyalty also requires officers and directors to disclose fully to the board of directors any possible conflict of interest that might occur in conducting corporate transactions. The various state statutes contain different standards, but a contract will generally *not* be voidable if it was fair and reasonable to the corporation at the time it was made, if there was a full disclosure of the interest of the officers or directors involved in the transaction, and if the contract was approved by a majority of the disinterested directors or shareholders.

• **Example 16.3** Southwood Corporation needs more office space. Lambert Alden, one of its five directors, owns the building adjoining the corporation's main office building. He negotiates a lease with Southwood for the space, making a full disclosure to Southwood and the other four board directors. The lease arrangement is fair and reasonable, and it is unanimously approved by the corporation's board of directors. In this situation, Alden has not breached his duty of loyalty to the corporation, and the contract is thus valid. The rule is one of reason. If it were otherwise, directors would be prevented from ever giving financial assistance to the corporations they serve.•

Ethical Issue 16.2

What happens to the duty of loyalty when a director sits on the boards of two corporations?

Corporate directors often have many business affiliations, and they may even sit on the board of more than one corporation. (Of course, directors generally are precluded from sitting on the boards of directors of competing companies.) The duty of loyalty can become cloudy when corporate directors sit on the board of more than one corporation. Because of the potential for abuse in transactions negotiated between corporations whose boards have some members in common, courts tend to scrutinize such actions closely.

For example, suppose that four individuals own a total of 70 percent of the shares of Company A and 100 percent of the shares of Company B. All four of these shareholders sit on the boards of directors of both corporations. Company A decides to purchase all of Company B's stock for $6 million, when in fact it is worth only $3 million. The shareholder-directors of both firms have not breached their duty to Company B, because the $6 million price is beneficial to that company. A court would likely hold that the directors breached their duty to the other shareholders of Company A (who owned the remaining 30 percent of Company A's shares), however, because these other shareholders had nothing to gain by the transaction and much to lose by Company A's purchase of Company B at an inflated price.[a]

a. See, for example, *Gries Sports Enterprises, Inc. v. Cleveland Browns Football Co.,* 26 Ohio St.3d 15, 496 N.E.2d 959 (1986).

"**All business proceeds on beliefs, or judgments of probabilities, and not on certainties.**"

Charles Eliot, 1834–1936
(American educator and editor)

Business Judgment Rule
A rule that immunizes corporate management from liability for actions that result in corporate losses or damages if the actions are undertaken in good faith, and are within both the power of the corporation and the authority of management to make.

The Business Judgment Rule

Directors and officers are expected to exercise due care and to use their best judgment in guiding corporate management, but they are not insurers of business success. Honest mistakes of judgment and poor business decisions on their part do not make them liable to the corporation for resulting damages. This is the **business judgment rule**. The rule generally immunizes directors and officers from liability for the consequences of a decision that is within managerial authority, as long as the decision complies with management's fiduciary duties and as long as acting on the decision is within the powers of the corporation. Consequently, if there is a reasonable basis for a business decision, it is unlikely that the court will interfere with that decision, even if the corporation suffers as a result.

To benefit from the rule, directors and officers must act in good faith, in what they consider to be the best interests of the corporation, and with the care that an ordinarily prudent person in a similar position would exercise in similar circumstances. This requires an informed decision, with a rational basis, and with no conflict between the decision maker's personal interest and the interest of the corporation. To be informed the director or officer must do what is necessary to become informed: attend presentations, ask for information from those who have it, read reports, review other written materials such as contracts—in other words, carefully study a situation and its alternatives.

To be free of conflicting interests, the director must not engage in self-dealing. • **Example 16.4** A director should not oppose a *tender offer* (an offer to purchase shares in the company made by another company directly to the shareholders) that is in the corporation's best interest simply because its acceptance may cost the director her or his position. Similarly, a director should not accept a tender offer with only a moment's consideration based solely on the market price of the corporation's shares.•

Rights and Duties of Officers and Managers

The rights of corporate officers and other high-level managers are defined by employment contracts, because these persons are employees of the company. Corporate officers normally can be removed by the board of directors at any time with or without cause and regardless of the terms of the employment contracts—although in so doing, the corporation may be liable for breach of contract. The duties of corporate officers are the same as those of directors, because both groups are involved in decision making and are in similar positions of control. Hence, officers are viewed as having the same fiduciary duties of care and loyalty in their conduct of corporate affairs as directors have.

Rights of Shareholders

Shareholders possess numerous rights. A significant right—the right to vote their shares—has already been discussed. We now look at some additional rights of shareholders.

Stock Certificates

Stock Certificate A certificate issued by a corporation evidencing the ownership of a specified number of shares in the corporation.

A **stock certificate** is a certificate issued by a corporation that evidences ownership of a specified number of shares in the corporation. Stock is intangible personal property, and the ownership right exists independently of the certificate itself. A stock certificate may be lost or destroyed, but ownership is not destroyed with it. A new certificate can be issued to replace one that has been lost or destroyed.[10] Notice of shareholders' meetings, dividends, and operational and financial reports are all distributed according to the recorded ownership listed in the corporation's books, not on the basis of possession of the certificate.

Preemptive Rights

A **preemptive right** is a common law concept under which a preference is given to shareholders over all other purchasers to subscribe to or purchase shares of a *new issue* of stock in proportion to the percentage of total shares they already hold. This allows each shareholder to maintain his or her portion of control, voting power, or financial interest in the corporation. Most statutes either (1) grant preemptive rights but allow them to be negated in the corporation's articles or (2) deny preemptive rights except to the extent that they are granted in the articles. The result is that the articles of incorporation determine the existence and scope of preemptive rights. Generally, preemptive rights apply only to additional, newly issued stock sold for cash, and the preemptive rights must be exercised within a specified time period (usually thirty days).

Preemptive Rights Rights held by shareholders that entitle them to purchase newly issued shares of a corporation's stock, equal in percentage to shares presently held, before the stock is offered to any outside buyers. Preemptive rights enable shareholders to maintain their proportionate ownership and voice in the corporation.

Dividends

As mentioned earlier in this chapter, a *dividend* is a distribution of corporate profits or income ordered by the directors and paid to the shareholders in proportion to their respective shares in the corporation. Dividends can be paid in cash, property, stock of the corporation that is paying the dividends, or stock of other corporations.[11]

State laws vary, but each state determines the general circumstances and legal requirements under which dividends are paid. State laws also control the sources of revenue to be used; only certain funds are legally available for paying dividends.

ILLEGAL DIVIDENDS A dividend paid while the corporation is insolvent is automatically an illegal dividend, and shareholders may be liable for returning the payment to the corporation or its creditors. Furthermore, as just discussed, dividends are generally required by statute to be distributed only from certain authorized corporate accounts. Sometimes dividends are improperly paid from an unauthorized account, or their payment causes the corporation to become insolvent. Generally, in such cases, shareholders must return illegal dividends only if they knew that the dividends were illegal when they received them. Whenever dividends are illegal or improper, the board of directors can be held personally liable for the amount of the payment. When directors can show that a shareholder knew that a dividend was illegal when it was received, however, the directors are entitled to reimbursement from the shareholder.

---

10. For a lost or destroyed certificate to be reissued, a shareholder normally must furnish an indemnity bond to protect the corporation against potential loss should the original certificate reappear at some future time in the hands of a bona fide purchaser [UCC 8–302, 8–405(2)].
11. Technically, dividends paid in stock are not dividends. They maintain each shareholder's proportional interest in the corporation. On one occasion, a distillery declared and paid a "dividend" in bonded whiskey.

DIRECTORS' FAILURE TO DECLARE A DIVIDEND   When directors fail to declare a dividend, shareholders can ask a court to compel the directors to meet and to declare a dividend. For the shareholders to succeed, they must show that the directors have acted so unreasonably in withholding the dividend that the directors' conduct is an abuse of their discretion.

Often, large money reserves are accumulated for a bona fide purpose, such as expansion, research, or other legitimate corporate goals. The mere fact that sufficient corporate earnings or surplus is available to pay a dividend is not enough to compel directors to distribute funds that, in the board's opinion, should not be paid. The courts are circumspect about interfering with corporate operations and will not compel directors to declare dividends unless abuse of discretion is clearly shown. In the following classic case, the shareholders brought a court action to compel Ford Motor Company to declare a dividend.

Case 16.4 ● Dodge v. Ford Motor Co.

Supreme Court of Michigan, 1919.
204 Mich. 459,
170 N.W. 668.

Historical and Social Setting

Corporations are owned by shareholders but run by directors and officers. Practical and ethical problems are inevitable. Directors are supposed to act in the best interests of the corporation, which is presumed to be the same as the best interests of the shareholders. Directors and shareholders may have different views about the corporation's best interests, however. Directors who look toward long-term growth and future profitability may want to reinvest profits in the firm. Shareholders may be more interested in receiving those profits as current dividends.

Background and Facts   Henry Ford was the president and major shareholder of Ford Motor Company. In the company's early years, business expanded rapidly, and in addition to regular quarterly dividends, special dividends were often paid. By 1916, surplus above capital was still $111,960,907. That year, however, Henry Ford declared that the company would no longer pay special dividends but would put back into the business all the earnings of the company above the regular dividend of 5 percent. According to the court, Ford stated as follows: "My ambition is to employ still more men, to spread the benefits of this industrial system to the greatest possible number, to help them build up their lives and their homes. To do this, we are putting the greatest share of our profits back into the business." The minority shareholders, who owned 10 percent of the stock, filed a lawsuit in a Michigan state court against Ford and others to force the declaration of a dividend. The court ordered the Ford directors to declare a dividend, and the plaintiffs appealed.

In the Words of the Court . . .
OSTRANDER, Chief Justice.

 *   *   *   *

 *   *   * Courts of equity will not interfere in the management of the directors unless it is clearly made to appear that they are guilty of fraud or misappropriation of the corporate funds, or refuse to declare a dividend when the corporation has a surplus of net profits which it can, without detriment to its business, divide among its stockholders, and when a refusal to do so would amount to such an abuse of discretion as would constitute a fraud, or breach of that good faith which they are bound to exercise towards the stockholders.

 *   *   *   *

Defendants say, and it is true, that a considerable cash balance must be at all times carried by such a concern [as Ford]. But * * * there was a large daily, weekly, monthly, receipt of cash. The output was practically

Case 16.4 Continued

continuous and was continuously, and within a few days, turned into cash. Moreover, the contemplated expenditures were not to be immediately made. * * * So that, without going further, it would appear that, accepting and approving the plan of the directors, it was their duty to distribute * * * a very large sum of money to stockholders.

Decision and Remedy The Supreme Court of Michigan ordered the Ford Motor Company to declare a dividend. The court held that, in view of the firm's large capital surplus, to withhold a dividend would violate the directors' duty to the shareholders.

For Critical Analysis—Social Consideration *Generally, how can a court determine when directors should pay dividends?*

Inspection Rights

Shareholders in a corporation enjoy both common law and statutory inspection rights.[12] The shareholder's right of inspection is limited, however, to the inspection and copying of corporate books and records for a *proper purpose,* provided the request is made in advance. The shareholder can inspect in person, or an attorney, agent, accountant, or other type of assistant can do so.

Transfer of Shares

Stock certificates generally are negotiable and freely transferable by indorsement and delivery. Transfer of stock in closely held corporations, however, usually is restricted by the bylaws, by a restriction stamped on the stock certificate, or by a shareholder agreement. The existence of any restrictions on transferability must always be noted on the face of the stock certificate, and these restrictions must be reasonable.

Sometimes, corporations or their shareholders restrict transferability by reserving the option to purchase any shares offered for resale by a shareholder. This **right of first refusal** remains with the corporation or the shareholders for only a specified time or a reasonable time. Variations on the purchase option are possible. For example, a shareholder might be required to offer the shares to other shareholders first or to the corporation first.

Right of First Refusal The right to purchase personal or real property—such as corporate shares or real estate—before the property is offered for sale to others.

When shares are transferred, a new entry is made in the corporate stock book to indicate the new owner. Until the corporation is notified and the entry is complete, the current record owner has the right to be notified of (and attend) shareholders' meetings, the right to vote the shares, the right to receive dividends, and all other shareholder rights.

Shareholder's Derivative Suit

When those in control of a corporation—the corporate directors—fail to sue in the corporate name to redress a wrong suffered by the corporation, shareholders are permitted to do so "derivatively" in what is known as a **shareholder's derivative suit.** Some wrong must have been done to the corporation, and

Shareholder's Derivative Suit A suit brought by a shareholder to enforce a corporate cause of action against a third person.

---

12. See, for example, *Schwartzman v. Schwartzman Packing Co.,* 99 N.M. 436, 659 P.2d 888 (1983).

before a derivative suit can be brought, the shareholders must first state their complaint to the board of directors. Only if the directors fail to solve the problem or take appropriate action can the derivative suit go forward.

The right of shareholders to bring a derivative action is especially important when the wrong suffered by the corporation results from the actions of corporate directors or officers. This is because the directors and officers would probably want to prevent any action against themselves.

The shareholder's derivative suit is singular in that those suing are not pursuing rights or benefits for themselves personally but are acting as guardians of the corporate entity. Therefore, any damages recovered by the suit normally go into the corporation's treasury, not to the shareholders personally.

Liability of Shareholders

One of the hallmarks of the corporate organization is that shareholders are not personally liable for the debts of the corporation. If the corporation fails, shareholders can lose their investments, but that is generally the limit of their liability. In certain instances of fraud, undercapitalization, or careless observance of corporate formalities, a court will pierce the corporate veil (disregard the corporate entity) and hold the shareholders individually liable. These situations are the exception, however, not the rule. Although they are rare, certain other instances arise where a shareholder can be personally liable. One relates to illegal dividends, which were discussed previously. Two others relate to *stock subscriptions* and *watered stock*, which we discuss here.

Sometimes stock-subscription agreements—written contracts by which one agrees to buy capital stock of a corporation—exist prior to incorporation. Normally, these agreements are treated as continuing offers and are irrevocable (for up to six months under RMBCA 6.20). Once the corporation has been formed, it can sell shares to shareholder investors. In either situation, once the subscription agreement or stock offer is accepted, a binding contract is formed. Any refusal to pay constitutes a breach resulting in the personal liability of the shareholder.

International Perspective

Derivative Actions in Other Nations

In the United States, during the 1980s and the early 1990s, there was a dramatic increase in the number of shareholder suits brought against directors and officers for alleged breaches of duties. Today, most of the claims brought against directors and officers are those alleged in shareholders' derivative suits. Other nations, however, are more restrictive in regard to the use of such suits. In Germany, for example, there is no provision for derivative litigation, and a corporation's duty to its employees is just as significant as its duty to the shareholder-owners of the company. The United Kingdom has no statute authorizing derivative actions, which are permitted only to challenge directors' actions that the shareholders could not legally ratify. Japan authorizes derivative actions but also permits a company to bring a suit against the shareholder-plaintiff for damages if the action is unsuccessful.

For Critical Analysis: *Do corporations benefit from shareholders' derivative suits? If so, how?*

Shares of stock can be paid for by property or by services rendered instead of cash. They cannot be purchased with promissory notes, however. The general rule is that for **par-value shares** (shares that have a specific face value, or formal cash-in value, written on them, such as one penny or one dollar), the corporation must receive a value at least equal to the par-value amount. For **no-par shares** (shares that have no face value—no specific amount printed on their face), the corporation must receive the value of the shares as determined by the board or the shareholders when the stock was issued. When the corporation issues shares for less than these stated values, the shares are referred to as **watered stock**.[13] Usually, the shareholder who receives watered stock must pay the difference to the corporation (the shareholder is personally liable). In some states, the shareholder who receives watered stock may be liable to creditors of the corporation for unpaid corporate debts.

Par-Value Shares Corporate shares that have a specific face value, or formal cash-in value, written on them, such as one dollar.

No-Par Shares Corporate shares that have no face value— that is, no specific dollar amount is printed on their face.

Watered Stock Shares of stock issued by a corporation for which the corporation receives, as payment, less than the stated value of the shares.

Duties of Majority Shareholders

In some cases, a majority shareholder is regarded as having a fiduciary duty to the corporation and to the minority shareholders. This occurs when a single shareholder (or a few shareholders acting in concert) owns a sufficient number of shares to exercise *de facto* control over the corporation. In these situations, majority shareholders owe a fiduciary duty to the minority shareholders when they sell their shares, because such a sale would be, in fact, a transfer of control of the corporation.

---

13. The phrase *watered stock* was originally used to describe cattle that—kept thirsty during a long drive—were allowed to drink large quantities of water just prior to their sale. The increased weight of the "watered stock" allowed the seller to reap a higher profit.

Key Terms

alien corporation   470
articles of incorporation   469
articles of organization   457
business judgment rule   478
bylaws   469
corporation   455
dividend   469
domestic corporation   470
entrepreneur   452
foreign corporation   470
franchise   459
franchisee   459

franchisor   459
general partner   454
limited liability company
   (LLC)   456
limited liability partnership
   (LLP)   458
limited partner   454
limited partnership   454
member   457
no-par share   483
operating agreement   457
par-value share   483

partnership   454
preemptive right   479
proxy   472
quorum   474
retained earnings   469
right of first refusal   481
S corporation   455
shareholder's derivative suit   481
sole proprietorship   452
stock certificate   478
watered stock   483

Chapter Summary • Business Organizations

Major Traditional Business Forms
(See pages 452–455.)

1. **Sole proprietorships**—The simplest form of business; used by anyone who does business without creating an organization. The owner is the business. The owner pays personal income taxes on all profits and is personally liable for all business debts.

(Continued)

Chapter Summary • Business Organizations, *Continued*

Major Traditional Business Forms —continued	**2. Partnerships—** a. **General partnerships**—Created by agreement of the parties; not treated as an entity except for limited purposes. Partners have unlimited liability for partnership debts, and each partner normally has an equal voice in management. Income is "passed through" the partnership to the individual partners, who pay personal taxes on the income. b. **Limited partnerships**—Must be formed in compliance with statutory requirements. A limited partnership consists of one or more general partners, who have unlimited liability for partnership losses, and one or more limited partners, who are liable only to the extent of their contributions. Only general partners can participate in management. **3. Corporations**—A corporation is formed in compliance with statutory requirements, is a legal entity separate and distinct from its owners, and can have perpetual existence. The shareholder-owners elect directors, who set policy and hire officers to run the day-to-day business of the corporation. Shareholders normally are not personally liable for the debts of the corporation. The corporation pays income tax on net profits; shareholders pay income tax on disbursed dividends.
Limited Liability Companies (LLCs) (See pages 455–458.)	**1. Formation**—Articles of organization must be filed with the appropriate state office—usually the office of the secretary of state—setting forth the name of the business, its principal address, the names of the owners (called *members*), and other relevant information. **2. Advantages and disadvantages of the LLC**—Advantages of the LLC include limited liability, the option to be taxed as a partnership or as a corporation, and flexibility in deciding how the business will be managed and operated. **3. Operating agreement**—When an LLC is formed, the members decide, in an operating agreement, how the business will be managed and what rules will apply to the organization.
Limited Liability Partnerships (LLPs) (See page 458.)	**1. Formation**—Articles must be filed with the appropriate state agency, usually the secretary of state's office. Typically, an LLP is formed by professionals who work together as partners in a partnership. Under most state LLP statutes, it is relatively easy to convert a traditional partnership into an LLP. **2. Liability of partners**—LLP statutes vary, but generally they allow professionals to avoid personal liability for the malpractice of other partners. Partners in an LLP continue to be liable for their own wrongful acts and for the wrongful acts of those whom they supervise.
Private Franchises (See pages 459–468.)	**1. Types of franchises—** a. Distributorship (for example, automobile dealerships). b. Chain-style operation (for example, fast-food chains). c. Manufacturing/processing-plant arrangement (for example, soft-drink bottling companies, such as Coca-Cola). **2. Laws governing franchising**—Franchises are governed by contract law, occasionally by agency law, and by federal and state statutory and regulatory laws.

Chapter Summary • Business Organizations

Private Franchises —continued	**3. The franchise contract—**
	a. Ordinarily requires the franchisee (purchaser) to pay a price for the franchise license.
	b. Specifies the territory to be served by the franchisee's firm.
	c. May require the franchisee to purchase certain supplies from the franchisor at an established price.
	d. May require the franchisee to abide by certain standards of quality relating to the product or service offered but cannot set retail resale prices.
	e. Usually provides for the date and/or conditions of termination of the franchise arrangement. Both federal and state statutes attempt to protect certain franchisees from franchisors who unfairly or arbitrarily terminate franchises.
The Nature of the Corporation (See pages 468–470.)	The corporation is a legal entity distinct from its owners. Formal statutory requirements, which vary somewhat from state to state, must be followed in forming a corporation. The corporation can have perpetual existence or be chartered for a specific period of time.
	1. Corporate personnel—The shareholders own the corporation. They elect a board of directors to govern the corporation. The board of directors hires corporate officers and other employees to run the daily business of the firm.
	2. Corporate taxation—The corporation pays income tax on net profits; shareholders pay income tax on the disbursed dividends that they receive from the corporation (double-taxation feature).
	3. Torts and criminal acts—The corporation is liable for the torts committed by its agents or officers within the course and scope of their employment (under the doctrine of *respondeat superior*). In some circumstances, a corporation can be held liable (and be fined) for the criminal acts of its agents and employees. In certain situations, corporate officers may be held personally liable for corporate crimes.
Classification of Corporations (See page 470.)	A corporation is referred to as a *domestic corporation* within its home state (the state in which it incorporates). A corporation is referred to as a *foreign corporation* by any state that is not its home state. A corporation is referred to as an *alien corporation* if it originates in another country but does business in the United States.
Directors and Officers (See pages 473–478.)	**1. Election of directors**—The first board of directors is usually appointed by the incorporators; thereafter, directors are elected by the shareholders. Directors usually serve a one-year term, although longer and staggered terms are permitted under most state statutes.
	2. Directors' qualifications and compensation—Few qualifications are required; a director can be a shareholder but is not required to be. Compensation is usually specified in the corporate articles or bylaws.
	3. Board of directors' meetings—The board of directors conducts business by holding formal meetings with recorded minutes. The date of regular meetings is usually established in the corporate articles or bylaws; special meetings can be called, with notice sent to all directors. Quorum requirements vary from state to state; usually, a quorum is the majority of the corporate directors. Voting must usually be done in person, and in ordinary matters only a majority vote is required. *(Continued)*

Chapter Summary • Business Organizations, *Continued*

Directors and Officers—continued	**4. Directors' management responsibilities**—Directors are responsible for declaring and paying corporate dividends to shareholders; authorizing major corporate decisions; appointing, supervising, and removing corporate officers and other managerial employees; determining employees' compensation; making financial decisions necessary to the management of corporate affairs; and issuing authorized shares and bonds. Directors may delegate some of their responsibilities to executive committees and corporate officers and executives.

5. Duties—Directors are obligated to act in good faith, to use prudent business judgment in the conduct of corporate affairs, and to act in the corporation's best interests. Directors have a fiduciary duty to subordinate their own interests to those of the corporation in matters relating to the corporation. If a director fails to exercise these duties, he or she can be answerable to the corporation and to the shareholders for breaching the duties.

6. Business judgment rule—This rule immunizes a director from liability for a corporate decision as long as the decision was within the powers of the corporation and the authority of the director to make and was an informed, reasonable, and loyal decision.

Shareholders
(See pages 471–473 and 478–483.)

1. Shareholders' meetings—Shareholders' meetings must occur at least annually; special meetings can be called when necessary. Notice of the date, time, and place of the meeting (and its purpose, if it is specially called) must be sent to shareholders. Shareholders may vote by proxy (authorizing someone else to vote their shares) and may submit proposals to be included in the company's proxy materials sent to shareholders before meetings.

2. Shareholder voting—Shareholder voting requirements and procedures are as follows:

a. A minimum number of shareholders (a quorum—generally, more than 50 percent of shares held) must be present at a meeting for business to be conducted; resolutions are passed (usually) by simple majority vote.

b. Cumulative voting may or may not be required or permitted. Cumulative voting gives minority shareholders a better chance to be represented on the board of directors.

c. A shareholder may appoint a proxy (substitute) to vote his or her shares.

3. Shareholders' rights—Shareholders have numerous rights, which may include the following:

a. The right to a stock certificate and preemptive rights.

b. The right to obtain a dividend (at the discretion of the directors).

c. Voting rights.

d. The right to inspect the corporate records.

e. The right to sue on behalf of the corporation (bring a shareholder's derivative suit) when the directors fail to do so.

4. Shareholders' liability—Shareholders may be liable for the retention of illegal dividends, for breach of a stock-subscription agreement, and for the value of watered stock.

5. Duties of majority shareholders—In certain situations, majority shareholders may be regarded as having a fiduciary duty to minority shareholders and will be liable if that duty is breached.

For Review

1. Which form of business organization is the simplest?

2. What are some advantages and disadvantages of doing business as a partnership or corporation, respectively?

3. How do limited liablility companies and limited liability partnerships differ from traditional corporations and partnerships?

4. What is a franchise? What are the most common types of franchises?

5. What are the duties of the directors and officers of a corporation? If a group of shareholders perceives that the corporation has suffered a wrong and the directors refuse to take action, can the shareholders compel the directors to act? If so, how?

Questions and Case Problems

16–1. Forms of Business Organization. In each of the following situations, determine whether Georgio's Fashions is a sole proprietorship, a partnership, a limited partnership, or a corporation.

(a) Georgio's defaults on a payment to supplier Dee Creations. Dee sues Georgio's and each of the owners of Georgio's personally for payment of the debt.

(b) Georgio's raises $200,000 through the sale of shares of its stock.

(c) At tax time, Georgio's files a tax return with the IRS and pays taxes on the firm's net profits.

(d) Georgio's is owned by three persons, two of whom are not allowed to participate in the firm's management.

16–2. Choice of Business Form. Jorge, Marta, and Jocelyn are college graduates, and Jorge has come up with an idea for a new product that he believes could make the three of them very rich. His idea is to manufacture soft-drink dispensers for home use and market them to consumers throughout the Midwest. Jorge's personal experience qualifies him to be both first-line supervisor and general manager of the new firm. Marta is a born salesperson. Jocelyn has little interest in sales or management but would like to invest a large sum of money that she has inherited from her aunt. What factors should Jorge, Marta, and Jocelyn consider in deciding which form of business organization to adopt?

16–3. Rights of Shareholders. Dmitri has acquired one share of common stock of a multimillion-dollar corporation with over 500,000 shareholders. Dmitri's ownership is so small that he is questioning what his rights are as a shareholder. For example, he wants to know whether this one share entitles him to attend and vote at shareholders' meetings, inspect the corporate books, and receive periodic dividends. Discuss Dmitri's rights in these matters.

16–4. Duties of Directors. Overland Corp. is negotiating with Wharton Construction Co. for the reno-

vation of Overland's corporate headquarters. Wharton, the owner of Wharton Construction, is also one of the five members of the board of directors of Overland. The contract terms are standard for this type of contract. Wharton has previously informed two of the other Overland directors of his interest in the construction company. Overland's board approves the contract on a three-to-two vote, with Wharton voting with the majority. Discuss whether this contract is binding on the corporation.

16–5. Rights of Shareholders. Jacob Schachter and Herbert Kulik, the founders of Ketek Electric Corp., each owned 50 percent of the corporation's shares and served as the corporation's only officers. Arnold Glenn, as trustee, and Kulik brought a shareholder's derivative suit in a New York state court against Schachter, alleging that Schachter had diverted Ketek assets and opportunities to Hoteltron Systems, Inc., a corporation wholly owned by Schachter. The trial court held for Glenn and Kulik, and it awarded damages to Kulik, not to Ketek. On appeal, the appellate court ruled that the damages should be awarded to the injured corporation, Ketek, rather than to the innocent shareholder, Kulik. Kulik appealed to the state supreme court, arguing that awarding damages to the corporation was inequitable because Schachter, as a shareholder of Ketek, would ultimately share in the proceeds of the award. How should the state supreme court rule, and why? [*Glenn v. Hoteltron Systems, Inc.,* 74 N.Y.2d 386, 547 N.E.2d 71, 547 N.Y.S.2 816 (1989)]

16–6. The Franchise Contract. Kubis & Perszyk Associates, Inc., was in business as Entre Computer. As a franchise, Entre sold, among other products, computer systems marketed by Sun Microsystems, Inc. Entre's agreement with Sun included a forum-selection clause that provided that any suit between the parties had to be filed in a California court. When Sun terminated its relationship with Entre, Entre filed a suit in a New Jersey state court. Sun asked the court to dismiss the suit on the basis of the forum-selection clause. Entre argued that the clause violated state franchise law, which invalidated such clauses in auto dealership franchises. On what basis might the court extend this law to cover Entre's franchise? Discuss. [*Kubis & Perszyk Associates, Inc. v. Sun Microsystems, Inc.,* 146 N.J. 176, 680 A.2d 618 (1996)]

16–7. Franchise Termination. C. B. Management Co. operated McDonald's restaurants in Cleveland, Ohio, under a franchise agreement with McDonald's Corp. The agreement required C. B. to make monthly payments of, among other things, certain percentages of the gross sales to McDonald's. If any payment was more than thirty days late, McDonald's had the right to terminate the franchise. The agreement stated, "No waiver by [McDonald's] of any breach . . . shall constitute a waiver of any subsequent breach." McDonald's sometimes accepted C. B.'s late payments, but when C. B. defaulted on the payments in July 1997 McDonald's gave notice of thirty days to comply or surrender possession of the restaurants. C. B. missed the deadline. McDonald's demanded that C. B. vacate the restaurants. C. B. refused. McDonald's filed a suit in a federal district court against C. B., alleging violations of the franchise agreement. C. B. counterclaimed in part that McDonald's had breached the implied covenant of good faith and fair dealing. McDonald's filed a motion to dismiss C. B.'s counterclaim. On what did C. B. base its claim? Will the court agree? Why or why not? [*McDonald's Corp. v. C. B. Management Co.,* 13 F.Supp.2d 705 (N.D.Ill. 1998)]

16–8. Duty of Loyalty. Mackinac Cellular Corp. offered to sell Robert Broz a license to operate a cellular phone system in Michigan. Broz was a director of Cellular Information Systems, Inc. (CIS). CIS, as a result of bankruptcy proceedings, was in the process of selling its cellular holdings. Broz did not formally present the opportunity to the CIS board, but he told some of the firm's officers and directors, who replied that CIS was not interested. At the time, PriCellular, Inc., a firm that was interested in the Michigan license, was attempting to buy CIS. Without telling PriCellular, Broz bought the license himself. After PriCellular took over CIS, the company filed a suit in a Delaware state court against Broz, alleging that he had usurped a corporate opportunity. For what reasons might a court decide that Broz had done nothing wrong? Discuss. [*Broz v. Cellular Information Systems, Inc.,* 673 A.2d 148 (Del. 1996)]

16–9. Business Judgment Rule. The board of directors of Baltimore Gas and Electric Company (BGE) recommended a merger with Potomac Electric Power Company (PEPCO). After full disclosure, the BGE shareholders approved the merger. On the ground that each BGE director stood a chance of being named to the new company's board, Janice Wittman, a BGE share-

holder, filed a suit in a Maryland state court against the directors, alleging, among other things, that they were prohibited from deciding whether to recommend the merger. Did the directors breach their duty of care by voting in favor of the merger? How should the court rule? Discuss. [*Wittman v. Crooke,* 120 Md.App. 369, 707 A.2d 422 (1998)]

16–10. Business Judgment Rule. Charles Pace and Maria Fuentez were shareholders of Houston Industries, Inc. (HII), and employees of Houston Lighting & Power, a subsidiary of HII, when they lost their jobs because of a company-wide reduction in its work force. Pace, as a shareholder, three times wrote to HII, demanding that the board of directors terminate certain HII directors and officers, and file a suit to recover damages for breach of fiduciary duty. Three times, the directors referred the charges to board committees and an outside law firm, which found that the facts did not support the charges. The board also received input from federal regulatory authorities about the facts behind some of the charges. The board notified Pace that it would refuse his demands. In response, Pace and Fuentez filed a shareholder's derivative suit against Don Jordan and the other HII directors, contending that the board's investigation was inadequate. The defendants moved for summary judgment, arguing that the suit was barred by the business judgment rule. How should the court rule? Why? [*Pace v. Jordan,* 999 S.W.2d 615 (Tex.App.—Houston [1 Dist.] 1999)]

A Question of Ethics and Social Responsibility

16–11. McQuade was the manager of the New York Giants baseball team. McQuade and John McGraw purchased shares in the National Exhibition Co., the corporation that owned the Giants, from Charles Stoneham, who owned a majority of National Exhibition's stock. As part of the transaction, each of the three agreed to use his best efforts to ensure that the others continued as directors and officers of the organization. Stoneham and McGraw, however, subsequently failed to use their best efforts to ensure that McQuade continued as the treasurer and a director of the corporation, and McQuade sued to compel specific performance of the agreement. A court reviewing the matter noted that McQuade had been "shabbily" treated by the others but refused to grant specific performance on the ground that the agreement was void because it interfered with the duty of the others as directors to do what was best for all the shareholders. Although shareholders may join to elect corporate directors, they may not join to limit the directors' discretion in managing the business affairs of an organization; the directors must retain their independent judgment. Consider the implications of the case, and address the following questions. [*McQuade v. Stoneham,* 263 N.Y. 323, 189 N.E. 234 (1934)]

1. Given that even the court sympathized with McQuade, was it ethical to put the business judgment of the directors ahead of an otherwise valid promise they had made?
2. Are there practical considerations that support the court's decision? How can directors perform the tasks dictated to them if their judgment is constrained by earlier agreements with some of the shareholders?
3. Can you think of any circumstances in which it would be fair to the shareholders, as a group, to interfere with the directors' business judgment by holding some of the directors to a similar prior agreement with some or all of the other directors?

Case Briefing Assignment

16–12. Examine Case A.6 [*Maschmeier v. Southside Press, Ltd.,* 435 N.W.2d 377 (Iowa App. 1989)] in Appendix A. The case has been excerpted there in great detail. Review and then brief the case, making sure that you include answers to the following questions in your brief.

1. What was the primary reason for this lawsuit?

2. What restriction did the corporate bylaws place on the transfer of corporate shares? On transfer, how was the price of shares to be determined?
3. How did the majority shareholders (the parents) effectively "freeze out" or "squeeze out" the minority shareholders (the sons)?
4. Why was it necessary for the court to determine the fair value of shares, as the shareholders had agreed in the bylaws on a method for accomplishing this?
5. Why was it necessary to establish that the majority shareholders had acted oppressively toward the minority shareholders or wasted corporate assets before the court could fashion its particular remedy in this case?

For Critical Analysis

16–13. As indicated in this chapter, the law permits individuals to exercise the option of organizing their business enterprises in many different forms. What policy interests are served by granting entrepreneurs these options? Would it be better if the law required that everyone organize his or her business in the same form? Discuss.

Interacting with the Internet

■ For updated links to resources available on the Web, as well as a variety of other materials, visit this text's Web site at

http://leet.westbuslaw.com

■ The Web site of the law firm of Reinhart et al. provides extensive information about business organizations. The URL for this site is

http://www.rbvdnr.com

■ To learn how the U.S. Small Business Administration assists in forming, financing, and operating businesses, go to

http://www.sbaonline.sba.gov

■ For information on the FTC regulations on franchising, as well as state laws regulating franchising, go to

http://www.ftc.gov/bcp/franchise/ netfran.htm

■ A good source of information on the purchase and sale of franchises is Franchising.org, which is online at

http://www.franchising.org

■ One of the best sources on the Web for information on corporations, including their directors, is the EDGAR database of the Securities and Exchange Commission (SEC) at

http://ww.sec.gov/edgarhp.htm

■ Cornell University's Legal Information Institute has links to state corporation statutes at

http://fatty.law.cornell.edu/topics/ state_statutes.html

Online Legal Research Exercises

Go to http://leet. westbuslaw.com, the Web site that accompanies this text. Select "Interactive Study Center," and then click on "Chapter 16." There you will find the following Internet research exercises that you can perform to learn more about business organizations:

Activity 16–1: Limited Liability Companies
Activity 16–2: Franchises

Before the Test

Go to http://leet. westbuslaw.com, the Web site that accompanies this text. Select "Interactive Quizzes." You will find a number of interactive questions relating to this chapter.

Unit III Cumulative Hypothetical Problem

Samuel Polson has an idea for a new software application. Polson hires an assistant and invests a considerable amount of his own time and money developing the application. To develop other software, and to manufacture and market his applications, Polson needs capital.

1. Polson borrows $5,000 from his friend, Michael Brant. Polson promises to repay Brant the $5,000 in three weeks. Brant, in urgent need of money, borrows $5,000 from his friend Mary Viva and assigns his rights to the $5,000 Polson owes him to Viva in return for the loan. Viva notifies Polson of the assignment. Polson pays Brant the $5,000 on the date stipulated in their contract. Brant refuses to give the money to Viva, and Viva sues Polson. Is Polson obligated to pay Viva $5,000 also? Discuss.

2. Polson learns that a competitor, Trivan, Inc., has already filed for a patent on a nearly identical program and has manufactured and sold the software to some customers. Polson learns from a reliable source that Trivan paid Polson's assistant a substantial sum of money to obtain a copy of the program. What legal recourse does Polson have against Trivan? Discuss fully.

3. While Polson is developing his idea and founding his business, he has no income. He continues to have living expenses, however, as well as payments due on his mortgage, various credit-card debts, and some loans that he took out to pay for his son's college tuition. As his business begins to make money. Polson files for Chapter 7 liquidation to be rid of his personal debts entirely, even though he believes he could probably pay them off over a four-year period if he scrimped and used every cent available to pay his creditors. Are all of Polson's personal debts dischargeable under Chapter 7, including the debts incurred for his son's education? Given the fact that Polson could foreseeably pay off his debts over a four-year period, will the court allow Polson to obtain relief under Chapter 7? Why or why not?

4. Polson is the sole owner of the business and pays no business income taxes. What is the form of Polson's business organization? What other options, in terms of business organizational forms, does Polson have? What are the advantages and disadvantages of each option? If Polson decides to incorporate the business under the name Polson Software, Inc., what steps will he need to take to do so?

The Employment Environment

Employment Relationships

chapter objectives

After reading this chapter, you should be able to:

1. Distinguish between employees and independent contractors.

2. Outline the ways in which an agency relationship can arise.

3. Specify the duties that agents and principals owe to each other and describe the liability of the principal and the agent with respect to third parties.

4. Describe the major laws relating to health and safety in the workplace.

5. Summarize the laws governing the rights of employees with respect to pension plans, family and medical leave, and privacy.

Employment relationships are agency relationships. Indeed, one of the most common, important, and pervasive legal relationships is that of **agency**. In an agency relationship between two parties, one of the parties, called the *agent,* agrees to represent or act for the other, called the *principal.* The principal has the right to control the agent's conduct in matters entrusted to the agent, and the agent must exercise his or her powers "for the benefit of the principal only," as Justice Joseph Story indicated in the quotation alongside. By using agents, a principal can conduct multiple business operations simultaneously in various locations. Thus, for example, contracts that bind the principal, such as a corporation or other business firm, can be made at different places with different persons at the same time. Because agency relationships permeate the business world, an understanding of the law of agency is crucial to understanding the legal environment of business.

Also important to the framework of the legal environment of business are employment statutes. For most of this century, the relationship of employer and employee has been the subject of federal and state legislation. Many of these statutes are discussed in the last part of this chapter.

> "[It] is a universal principle in the law of agency, that the powers of the agent are to be exercised for the benefit of the principal only, and not of the agent or of third parties."
>
> Joseph Story, 1779–1845
> (Associate justice of the United States Supreme Court, 1811–1844)

Agency Relationships

Section 1(1) of the *Restatement (Second) of Agency*[1] defines *agency* as "the fiduciary relation which results from the manifestation of consent by one person to another that the other shall act in his behalf and subject to his control, and consent by the other so to act." In other words, in a principal-agent relationship, the parties have agreed that the agent will act on *behalf and instead of* the principal in negotiating and transacting business with third persons. The term **fiduciary** is at the heart of agency law. When used as an adjective, as in "fiduciary relationship," it means that the relationship involves trust and confidence.

Agency relationships commonly exist between employers and employees. Agency relationships may sometimes also exist between employers and independent contractors who are hired to perform special tasks or services.

Agency A relationship between two parties in which one party (the agent) agrees to represent or act for the other (the principal).

Fiduciary As a noun, a person having a duty created by his or her undertaking to act primarily for another's benefit in matters connected with the undertaking. As an adjective, a relationship founded on trust and confidence.

Employer-Employee Relationships

Normally, all employees who deal with third parties are deemed to be agents.
• **Example 17.1** A salesperson in a department store is an agent of the store's owner (the principal) and acts on the owner's behalf. Any sale of goods made by the salesperson to a customer is binding on the principal. Similarly, most representations of fact made by the salesperson with respect to the goods sold are binding on the principal.•

Because employees who deal with third parties are normally deemed agents of their employers, agency law and employment law overlap considerably. Agency relationships, though, as will become apparent, can exist outside an employee-employer relationship and thus have a broader reach than employment laws do. Additionally, bear in mind that agency law is based on the common law. In the employment realm, many common law doctrines have been

---

1. The *Restatement (Second) of Agency* is an authoritative summary of the law of agency and is often referred to by jurists in their decisions and opinions.

displaced by statutory law and government regulations governing employment relationships.

Employment laws (state and federal) apply only to the employer-employee relationship. Statutes governing Social Security, withholding taxes, workers' compensation, unemployment compensation, workplace safety, employment discrimination, and the like are applicable only if there is employer-employee status. *These laws do not apply to the independent contractor.*

Employer–Independent Contractor Relationships

Independent contractors are not employees, because by definition, those who hire them have no control over the details of their physical performance. Section 2 of the *Restatement (Second) of Agency* defines an **independent contractor** as follows:

Independent Contractor
One who works for, and receives payment from, an employer but whose working conditions and methods are not controlled by the employer. An independent contractor is not an employee but may be an agent.

> [An independent contractor is] a person who contracts with another to do something for him but who is not controlled by the other nor subject to the other's right to control with respect to his physical conduct in the performance of the undertaking. He may or may not be an agent.

Building contractors and subcontractors are independent contractors, and a property owner does not control the acts of either of these professionals. Truck drivers who own their equipment and hire themselves out on a per-job basis are independent contractors, but truck drivers who drive company trucks on a regular basis are usually employees.

The relationship between a person or firm and an independent contractor may or may not involve an agency relationship. • **Example 17.2** An owner of real estate who hires a real estate broker to negotiate a sale of his or her property not only has contracted with an independent contractor (the real estate broker) but also has established an agency relationship for the specific purpose of assisting in the sale of the property. •

Criteria for Determining Employee Status

A question the courts frequently face in determining liability under agency law is whether a person hired by another to do a job is an employee or an independent contractor. Because employers are normally held liable as principals for the actions taken by their employee-agents within the scope of employment (as will be discussed later in this chapter), the court's decision as to employee versus independent-contractor status can be significant for the parties. In making this determination, courts often consider the following questions:

1. How much control can the employer exercise over the details of the work? (If an employer can exercise considerable control over the details of the work, this would indicate employee status.)
2. Is the worker engaged in an occupation or business distinct from that of the employer? (If not, this would indicate employee status.)
3. Is the work usually done under the employer's direction or by a specialist without supervision? (If the work is usually done under the employer's direction, this would indicate employee status.)
4. Does the employer supply the tools at the place of work? (If so, this would indicate employee status.)
5. For how long is the person employed? (If the person is employed for a long period of time, this would indicate employee status.)

6. What is the method of payment—by time period or at the completion of the job? (Payment by time period, such as once every two weeks or once a month, would indicate employee status.)

7. What degree of skill is required of the worker? (If little skill is required, this may indicate employee status.)

Often, the criteria for determining employee status are established by a statute or administrative agency regulation. The Internal Revenue Service (IRS), for example, establishes its own criteria for determining whether a worker is an independent contractor or an employee. In the past, these criteria consisted of a list of twenty factors. In 1996, however, these twenty factors were abolished in favor of rules that essentially encourage IRS examiners to look more closely at just one of the factors—the degree of control the business exercises over the worker.

The IRS tends to scrutinize closely a firm's classification of a worker as an independent contractor rather than an employee, because independent contractors can avoid certain tax liabilities by taking advantage of business organizational forms available to small businesses. Regardless of the firm's classification of a worker's status as an independent contractor, if the IRS decides that the worker should be classified as an employee, then the employer will be responsible for paying any applicable Social Security, withholding, and unemployment taxes.

Sometimes, it is advantageous to have employee status—to take advantage of laws protecting employees, for example. At other times, it may be advantageous to have independent-contractor status—for tax purposes, for example. The following case involves a dispute over ownership rights in a computer program. The outcome of the case hinged on whether the creator of the program, at the time it was created, was an employee or an independent contractor.

Case 17.1 ● Graham v. James

United States Court of Appeals, Second Circuit, 1998.
144 F.3d 229.
http://www.findlaw.com/ casecode/courts/2nd.html[a]

Historical and Social Setting *Under the Copyright Act of 1976, any copyrighted work created by an employee within the scope of his or her employment at the request of the employer is a "work for hire," and the employer owns the copyright to the work. When an employer hires an independent contractor—a freelance artist, writer, or computer programmer, for example—the contractor owns the copyright unless the parties agree in writing that the work is a "work for hire" and the work falls into one* of nine specific categories, including audiovisual and other works.

Background and Facts Richard Graham marketed CD-ROM disks containing compilations of shareware, freeware, and public domain software.[b] With five to ten thousand programs per disk, Graham needed a file-retrieval program to allow users to access the software on the disks. Larry James agreed to create the program in exchange for, among other things, credit on the final product. James built into the final version of the program a notice attributing authorship and copyright to himself. Graham removed the notice, claiming that the program was a work for hire and the copyright was his. Graham used the program on

---

a. This is part of the FindLaw Web site. This is a page with links to some of the opinions of the U.S. Court of Appeals for the Second Circuit. In the "1998" row, click on "May." When that page opens, scroll down the list of cases to the *Graham* case and click on the link to access it.

b. *Shareware* is software released to the public to sample, with the understanding that anyone using it will register with the author and pay a fee. *Freeware* is software available for free use. *Public domain software* is software unprotected by copyright.

(Continued)

Case 17.1 Continued

several subsequent releases. James sold the program to another CD-ROM publisher. Graham filed a suit in a federal district court against James, alleging, among other things, copyright infringement. The court ruled that James was an independent contractor and that he owned the copyright. Graham appealed the ruling.

In the Words of the Court . . .
JACOBS, Circuit Judge.

* * * *

The Copyright Act provides, *inter alia* [among other things], that "a work prepared by an employee within the scope of his or her employment" is a work for hire. "[T]he employer or other person for whom the work [for hire] was prepared is considered the author" and the employer owns the copyright * * * .

* * * *

* * * [In determining whether a hired party is an employee, the important factors are:] (i) the hiring party's right to control the manner and means of creation; (ii) the skill required; (iii) the provision of employee benefits; (iv) the tax treatment of the hired party; and (v) whether the hiring party had the right to assign additional projects to the hired party. * * *

We are persuaded by the district court's conclusion that James was an independent contractor. Almost all of the * * * factors line up in favor of that conclusion: James is a skilled computer programmer, he was paid no benefits, no payroll taxes were withheld, and his engagement by Graham was project-by-project. The only * * * factor arguably favoring Graham is his general control over the work; but the district court has found, plausibly, that Graham's participation in the development of the [file-retrieval program] was minimal and that his instructions to James were very general.

Decision and Remedy The U.S. Court of Appeals for the Second Circuit affirmed the lower court's judgment on this issue. The court agreed that James owned the copyright because he was an independent contractor when he developed the program.

For Critical Analysis—Economic Consideration *What are some other advantages of being an independent contractor? What might be some disadvantages?*

Agency Formation

Agency relationships normally are consensual; that is, they come about by voluntary consent and agreement between the parties. Generally, the agreement need not be in writing,[2] and consideration is not required. A principal must have contractual capacity, however. A person who cannot legally enter into contracts directly is not allowed to do so indirectly through an agent.

An agency relationship can be created for any legal purpose. An agency relationship that is created for an illegal purpose or that is contrary to public policy is unenforceable. • **Example 17.3** Suppose that Sharp (as principal) con-

---

2. There are two main exceptions to the statement that agency agreements need not be in writing: (1) Whenever agency authority empowers the agent to enter into a contract that the Statute of Frauds requires to be in writing, then the agent's authority from the principal must likewise be in writing. (2) A power of attorney, which confers authority to an agent, must be in writing.

tracts with Blesh (as agent) to sell illegal narcotics. This agency relationship is unenforceable, because selling illegal narcotics is a felony and is contrary to public policy.● It is also illegal for medical doctors and other licensed professionals to employ unlicensed agents to perform professional actions.

Generally, there are four ways in which an agency relationship can arise: by agreement of the parties, by ratification, by estoppel, and by operation of law. We look here at each of these possibilities.

Agency by Agreement

Because an agency relationship is, by definition, normally consensual, ordinarily it must be based on an express or implied agreement that the agent will act for the principal and the principal agrees to have the agent so act. An agency agreement can take the form of an express written or oral contract. An agency agreement can also be implied by conduct. ● **Example 17.4** A hotel allows only Boris Koontz to park cars, but Boris has no employment contract there. The hotel's manager tells Boris when to work, as well as where and how to park the cars. The hotel's conduct amounts to a manifestation of its willingness to have Boris park its customers' cars, and Boris can infer from the hotel's conduct that he has authority to act as a parking valet. It can be inferred that Boris is an agent for the hotel, his purpose being to provide valet parking services for hotel guests.●

Agency by Ratification

On occasion, a person who is in fact not an agent (or who is an agent acting outside the scope of his or her authority) may make a contract on behalf of another (a principal). If the principal approves or affirms that contract by word or by action, an agency relationship is created by **ratification**. Ratification is a question of intent, and intent can be expressed by either words or conduct.

Ratification The act of accepting and giving legal force to an obligation that previously was not enforceable.

Agency by Estoppel

When a principal causes a third person to reasonably believe that another person is his or her agent, and the third person deals with the supposed agent, the principal is "estopped to deny" the agency relationship. In such a situation, the principal's actions create the *appearance* of an agency that does not in fact exist.
● **Example 17.5** Suppose that Andrew accompanies Charles, a seed sales representative, to call on a customer, Steve, the proprietor of the General Seed Store. Andrew has done independent sales work but has never signed an employment agreement with Charles. Charles boasts to Steve that he wishes he had three more assistants "just like Andrew." Steve has reason to believe from Charles's statements that Andrew is an agent for Charles. Steve then places seed orders with Andrew. If Charles does not correct the impression that Andrew is an agent, Charles will be bound to fill the orders just as if Andrew were really Charles's agent. Charles's representation to Steve created the impression that Andrew was Charles's agent and had authority to solicit orders.●

The acts or declarations of a purported *agent* in and of themselves do not create an agency by estoppel. Rather, it is the deeds or statements of the *principal* that create an agency by estoppel. ● **Example 17.6** Suppose that Olivia walks into Dru's Dress Boutique and claims to be a sales agent for an exclusive Paris dress designer, Pierre Dumont. Dru has never had business relations

A proprietor reviews the inventory in her clothing store. Under what circumstances might a clothing importer be considered to act as an agent for the store?

with Pierre Dumont. Based on Olivia's claim, however, Dru gives Olivia an order and prepays 15 percent of the sales price. Olivia is not an agent, and the dresses are never delivered. Dru cannot hold Pierre Dumont liable. Olivia's acts and declarations alone do not create an agency by estoppel.●

The court in the following case considered whether an agency existed by estoppel between the owner of a jewelry cart in a mall and the seller of "The Only Completely Safe, Sterile Ear Piercing Method."

Case 17.2 ● Williams v. Inverness Corp.

Supreme Judicial Court of Maine, 1995.
664 A.2d 1244.

Company Profile *Inverness Corporation is the world's largest maker of body-piercing equipment. Sam Mann founded Inverness in 1975 with a design for piercing equipment that was more sterile and less threatening than the products then in use. The first year's sales to-taled more than $750,000. Today, the company makes disposable ear-piercing kits, skin-care products, hair-removal waxes, electrolysis kits, and jewelry dips. Based in Fair Lawn, New Jersey, Inverness sells its products in fifty-two countries.*

Background and Facts The Inverness Corporation markets the Inverness Ear Piercing System, which includes a training course, an "eye-catching assortment of selling aids" such as counter displays, and release forms that tout the system as "The Only Completely Safe, Sterile Ear Piercing Method." Margaret Barrera, the owner of a jewelry cart in a mall, bought the system, took the course, and set up the displays. Seventeen-year-old Angela Williams paid Barrera to pierce Williams's ear. The ear became infected, which led to complications. Williams's mother filed a suit on Angela's behalf in a Maine state court against Inverness and Barrera, claiming in part that Inverness was liable on a theory of agency by estoppel. When the court issued a judgment in Williams's favor, Inverness appealed to Maine's highest court.

In the Words of the Court . . .
DANA, Justice.

* * * *

* * * There are critical pieces of evidence in the record that can fairly be interpreted as leading to an inference that Inverness did hold Barrera out as its agent. Most important, a jury reasonably could infer that Inverness knew, or should have known, that Barrera distributed Inverness's release forms * * * .

* * * A jury reasonably could infer * * * that Inverness knew, or should have known, that Barrera was using the Inverness Ear Piercing System, that she displayed Inverness's "eye-catching assortment of selling aids," and that she used Inverness's training program.

Finally, there was evidence that Angela believed that Barrera was Inverness's agent, that Angela relied on Inverness's manifestations of agency, and that Angela's reliance on Barrera's care and skill was justifiable. * * * The release form and display promote the Inverness Ear Piercing System as "The Only Completely Safe, Sterile Ear Piercing Method."

Decision and Remedy The Supreme Judicial Court of Maine affirmed the lower court's judgment.

For Critical Analysis—Social Consideration *What are the policy reasons for holding a firm liable on a theory of agency by estoppel?*

Agency by Operation of Law

There are other situations in which the courts will find an agency relationship in the absence of a formal agreement. This may occur in family relationships. For example, suppose one spouse purchases certain basic necessaries and charges them to the other spouse's charge account. The courts will often rule that the latter is liable for payment for the necessaries, either because of a social policy of promoting the general welfare of the spouse or because of a legal duty to supply necessaries to family members.

Agency by operation of law may also occur in emergency situations, when the agent's failure to act outside the scope of his or her authority would cause the principal substantial loss. If the agent is unable to contact the principal, the courts will often grant this emergency power. For example, a railroad engineer may contract on behalf of his or her employer for medical care for an injured motorist hit by the train.

Duties of Agents and Principals

The principal-agent relationship gives rise to duties that govern both parties' conduct. As discussed previously, an agency relationship is *fiduciary*—one of trust. In a fiduciary relationship, each party owes the other the duty to act with the utmost good faith. In general, for every duty of the principal, the agent has a corresponding right, and vice versa.

When one party to the agency relationship violates his or her duty to the other party, the remedies available to the nonbreaching party arise out of contract and tort law. These remedies include monetary damages, termination of the agency relationship, injunction, and required accountings.

> "I am 'in a fiduciary position'—which is always a d_____ uncomfortable position."
>
> Frederic W. Maitland, 1850–1906
> (English jurist and historian)

Agent's Duties to the Principal

Generally, the agent owes the principal five duties—performance, notification, loyalty, obedience, and accounting.

PERFORMANCE   An implied condition in every agency contract is the agent's agreement to use reasonable diligence and skill in performing the work. When an agent fails to perform his or her duties entirely, liability for breach of contract normally will result. The degree of skill or care required of an agent is usually that expected of a reasonable person under similar circumstances. Generally, this is interpreted to mean ordinary care. An agent may, however, have represented himself or herself as possessing special skills (such as those that an accountant or attorney possesses). In these situations, the agent is expected to exercise the skill or skills claimed. Failure to do so constitutes a breach of the agent's duty.

> **Be Aware** An agent's disclosure of confidential information could constitute the business tort of misappropriation of trade secrets.

NOTIFICATION   There is a maxim in agency law that notice to the agent is notice to the principal. An agent is thus required to notify the principal of all matters that come to his or her attention concerning the subject matter of the agency. This is the duty of notification. The law assumes that the principal knows of any information acquired by the agent that is relevant to the agency—regardless of whether the agent actually passes on this information to the principal.

A real estate agent stands by a "For Sale" sign. If this agent knows a buyer who is willing to pay more than the asking price for this property, what duty would the agent breach if he bought the property and then sold it at a profit to the buyer?

LOYALTY   Loyalty is one of the most fundamental duties in a fiduciary relationship. Basically stated, the agent has the duty to act solely for the benefit of his or her principal and not in the interest of the agent or a third party. For example, an agent cannot represent two principals in the same transaction unless both know of the dual capacity and consent to it. The duty of loyalty also means that any information or knowledge acquired through the agency relationship is considered confidential. It would be a breach of loyalty to disclose such information either during the agency relationship or after its termination. Typical examples of confidential information are trade secrets and customer lists compiled by the principal. In short, the agent's loyalty must be undivided. The agent's actions must be strictly for the benefit of the principal and must not result in any secret profit for the agent.

• **Example 17.7** Suppose that Ryder contracts with Alton, a real estate agent, to sell Ryder's property. Alton knows that he can find a buyer who will pay substantially more for the property than Ryder is asking. If Alton secretly purchased Ryder's property, however, and then sold it at a profit to another buyer, Alton would breach his duty of loyalty as Ryder's agent. Alton has a duty to act in Ryder's best interests and can only become the purchaser in this situation with Ryder's knowledge and approval.•

OBEDIENCE   When an agent is acting on behalf of the principal, a duty is imposed on that agent to follow all lawful and clearly stated instructions of the principal. Any deviation from such instructions is a violation of this duty. During emergency situations, however, when the principal cannot be consulted, the agent may deviate from such instructions without violating this duty. Whenever instructions are not clearly stated, the agent can fulfill the duty of obedience by acting in good faith and in a manner reasonable under the circumstances.

ACCOUNTING   Unless an agent and a principal agree otherwise, the agent has the duty to keep and make available to the principal an account of all property and money received and paid out on behalf of the principal. This includes gifts from third persons in connection with the agency. For example, a

---

Ethical Issue 17.1

What happens when the duty of loyalty conflicts with other duties?

The duty of loyalty to one's employer-principal is a fundamental ethical duty that has been written into law. The duty is rooted in the principle that a person cannot serve two masters at the same time. In an agency relationship, the agent's loyalty must be undivided. There are times, however, when the ethical duty of loyalty may come into conflict with another duty, such

as one's duty to society. For example, suppose that one's principal-employer is involved in an illegal activity. Or suppose that this employer is aware that a company product is dangerous but refuses to acknowledge consumer complaints or even act on its own studies showing that the product is defective. In either of these situations, must an agent-employee of the firm keep silent, out of loyalty to his or her employer? Or should the agent-employee disregard the duty of loyalty in these situations and "blow the whistle" on the employer's actions (by reporting them to a government official, for example, or to the press)?

Some scholars have argued that many of the greatest evils in the past twenty-five years have been accomplished in the name of "duty" to the principal.

gift from a customer to a salesperson for prompt deliveries made by the salesperson's firm, in the absence of a company policy to the contrary, belongs to the firm. The agent has a duty to maintain separate accounts for the principal's funds and for the agent's personal funds, and no intermingling of these accounts is allowed.

Principal's Duties to the Agent

The principal also owes certain duties to the agent. These duties relate to compensation, reimbursement and indemnification, cooperation, and safe working conditions.

COMPENSATION In general, when a principal requests certain services from an agent, the agent reasonably expects payment. The principal therefore has a duty to pay the agent for services rendered. For example, when an accountant or an attorney is asked to act as an agent, an agreement to compensate the agent for such service is implied. The principal also has a duty to pay that compensation in a timely manner. Except in a gratuitous agency relationship, in which an agent does not act for money, the principal must pay the agreed-on value for an agent's services. If no amount has been expressly agreed on, then the principal owes the agent the customary compensation for such services.

REIMBURSEMENT AND INDEMNIFICATION Whenever an agent disburses sums of money to fulfill the request of the principal or to pay for necessary expenses in the course of a reasonable performance of his or her agency duties, the principal has the duty to reimburse the agent for these payments. Agents cannot recover for expenses incurred by their own misconduct or negligence, however.

Subject to the terms of the agency agreement, the principal has the duty to compensate, or *indemnify*, an agent for liabilities incurred because of authorized and lawful acts and transactions. For example, if the principal fails to perform a contract formed by the agent with a third party and the third party then sues the agent, the principal is obligated to compensate the agent for any costs incurred in defending against the lawsuit. Additionally, the principal must indemnify (pay) the agent for the value of benefits that the agent confers on the principal. The amount of indemnification is usually specified in the agency contract. If it is not, the courts will look to the nature of the business and the type of loss to determine the amount.

> **Remember** An agent who signs a negotiable instrument on behalf of a principal may be personally liable on the instrument. Liability depends in part on whether the identity of the principal is disclosed and whether the parties intend the agent to be bound.

COOPERATION A principal has a duty to cooperate with the agent and to assist the agent in the agent's performance of his or her duties. The principal must do nothing to prevent such performance. ● **Example 17.8** Suppose that Akers (the principal) grants Johnson (the agent) an exclusive territory within which Johnson may sell Akers's products, thus creating an exclusive agency. In this situation, Akers cannot compete with Johnson within that territory—or appoint or allow another agent to so compete—because this would violate the exclusive agency. If Akers did so, he would be exposed to liability for Johnson's lost sales or profits.●

SAFE WORKING CONDITIONS The common law requires the principal to provide safe working premises, equipment, and conditions for all agents and employees. The principal has a duty to inspect working conditions and to warn agents and employees about any unsafe areas. When the agency is one of employment, the employer's liability and the safety standards with which the employer must comply normally are covered by federal and state statutes and regulations.

Agent's Authority

An agent's authority to act can be either *actual* (express or implied) or *apparent. Express authority* is authority declared in clear, direct, and definite terms. Express authority can be given orally or in writing. *Implied authority* can be (1) conferred by custom, (2) inferred from the position the agent occupies, or (3) inferred as being reasonably necessary to carry out express authority. • **Example 17.9** Mueller is employed by Al's Supermarket to manage one of its stores. Al's has not expressly stated that Mueller has authority to contract with third persons. In this situation, however, authority to manage a business implies authority to do what is reasonably required (as is customary or can be inferred from a manager's position) to operate the business. Reasonably required actions include creating contracts to hire employees, to buy merchandise and equipment, and to arrange for advertising the products sold in the store.•

Actual authority arises from what the principal manifests *to the agent. Apparent authority,* in contrast, exists when the principal, by either words or actions, causes a *third party* reasonably to believe that an agent has authority to act, even though the agent has no express or implied authority. If the third party changes his or her position in reliance on the principal's representations, the principal may be *estopped* from denying that the agent had authority. Note that here, in contrast to agency formation by estoppel, the issue has to do with the apparent authority of an *agent,* not the apparent authority of a person who is in fact not an agent.

Liability in Agency Relationships

Frequently, the issue arises as to which party, the principal or the agent, should be held liable for the contracts formed by the agent or for the torts or crimes committed by the agent. We look here at these aspects of agency law.

Liability for Contracts

An important consideration in determining liability for a contract formed by an agent is whether the third party knew the identity of the principal at the time the contract was made. The *Restatement (Second) of Agency,* Section 4, classifies principals as disclosed, partially disclosed, or undisclosed.

A principal whose identity is known to the third party at the time the agent makes the contract is a **disclosed principal.** For example, if an agent signs a contract with a third party for office supplies and indicates his or her status as purchasing agent for the owner of an office supply store, the principal—the store's owner—is fully disclosed. The identity of a **partially disclosed principal** is not known by the third party, but the third party knows that the agent is or may be acting for a principal at the time the contract is made. • **Example 17.10** Sarah has contracted with a real estate agent to sell certain property. She wishes to keep her identity a secret, but the agent can make it perfectly clear to a purchaser of the real estate that the agent is acting in an

---

> "The law is not a series of calculating machines where definitions and answers come tumbling out when the right levers are pushed."
>
> William O. Douglas, 1898–1980
> (Associate justice of the United States Supreme Court, 1939–1975)

Be Aware An agent who exceeds his or her authority to enter into a contract that the principal does not ratify may be liable to the third party on the ground of misrepresentation.

Disclosed Principal A principal whose identity is known to a third party at the time the agent makes a contract with the third party.

Partially Disclosed Principal A principal whose identity is unknown by a third person, but the third person knows that the agent is or may be acting for a principal at the time the agent and the third person form a contract.

agency capacity for a principal. In this situation, Sarah is a partially disclosed principal.•

A disclosed or partially disclosed principal is liable to a third party for a contract made by an agent who is acting within the scope of his or her authority. Ordinarily, if the principal is disclosed or partially disclosed, the agent has no contractual liability if the principal or the third party does not perform the contract. If the agent *exceeds* the scope of his or her authority and the principal fails to ratify (affirm) the unauthorized contract, however, the third party cannot hold the principal liable for nonperformance. In such situations, the agent is generally liable unless the third party knew of the agent's lack of authority.

The identity of an **undisclosed principal** is totally unknown to the third party. Furthermore, the third party has no knowledge that the agent is acting in an agency capacity at the time the contract is made. When neither the fact of agency nor the identity of the principal is disclosed, a third party is deemed to be dealing with the agent personally, and the agent is liable as a party to the contract. If an agent has acted within the scope of his or her authority, the undisclosed principal is also liable as a party to the contract, just as if the principal had been fully disclosed at the time the contract was made. Conversely, with some exceptions, the undisclosed principal can hold the third party to the contract.

Undisclosed Principal A principal whose identity is unknown by a third person, and the third person has no knowledge that the agent is acting for a principal at the time the agent and the third person form a contract.

Liability for Torts and Crimes

Obviously, an agent is liable for his or her own torts and crimes. Whether the principal can also be held liable depends on several factors. A principal may be liable for an agent's torts under the doctrine of **respondeat superior,**[3] a Latin term meaning "let the master respond." This doctrine, which is discussed in the *Landmark in the Legal Environment* on page 504, is similar to the theory of strict liability discussed in Chapter 10. The doctrine imposes vicarious (indirect) liability on the employer without regard to the personal fault of the employer for torts committed by an employee in the course or scope of employment.

Respondeat Superior In Latin, "Let the master respond." A doctrine under which a principal or an employer is held liable for the wrongful acts committed by agents or employees while acting within the course and scope of their agency or employment.

The key to determining whether a principal may be liable for the torts of the agent under the doctrine of *respondeat superior* is whether the torts are committed within the scope of the agency or employment. The *Restatement (Second) of Agency,* Section 229, indicates the factors that courts will consider in determining whether or not a particular act occurred within the course and scope of employment. These factors are as follows:

1. Whether the act was authorized by the employer.
2. The time, place, and purpose of the act.
3. Whether the act was one commonly performed by employees on behalf of their employers.
4. The extent to which the employer's interest was advanced by the act.
5. The extent to which the private interests of the employee were involved.
6. Whether the employer furnished the means or instrumentality (for example, a truck or a machine) by which the injury was inflicted.
7. Whether the employer had reason to know that the employee would do the act in question and whether the employee had ever done it before.
8. Whether the act involved the commission of a serious crime.

A truck lies on its side following an accident. If the driver had stopped at a bar during working hours and become inebriated, and this accident was caused by the driver's inebriated state, who would be held responsible for the damage?

---

3. Pronounced ree-*spahn*-dee-uht soo-*peer*-ee-your.

Landmark in the Legal Environment

The Doctrine of *Respondeat Superior*

The idea that a master (employer) must respond to third persons for losses negligently caused by the master's servant (employee) first appeared in Lord Holt's opinion in *Jones v. Hart* (1698).[a] By the early nineteenth century, this maxim had been adopted by most courts and was referred to as the doctrine of *respondeat superior.*

The vicarious (indirect) liability of the master for the acts of the servant has been supported primarily by two theories. The first theory rests on the issue of *control,* or *fault:* the master has control over the acts of the servant and is thus responsible for injuries arising out of such service. The second theory is economic in nature: because the master takes the benefits or profits of the servant's service, he or she should also suffer the losses; moreover, the master is better able than the servant to absorb such losses.

The *control* theory is clearly recognized in the *Restatement (Second) of Agency,* in which the master is defined as "a principal who employs an agent to perform service in his affairs and who controls, or has

the right to control, the physical conduct of the other in the performance of the service." Accordingly, a servant is defined as "an agent employed by a master to perform service in his affairs whose physical conduct in his performance of the service is controlled, or is subject to control, by the master."

There are limitations on the master's liability for the acts of the servant, however. An employer (master) is only responsible for the wrongful conduct of an employee (servant) that occurs in "the scope of employment." The criteria used by the courts in determining whether an employee is acting within the scope of employment are set forth in the *Restatement (Second) of Agency* and will be discussed shortly. Generally, the act must be of a kind the servant was employed to do; must have occurred within "authorized time and space limits"; and must have been "activated, at least in part, by a purpose to serve the master."

The courts have accepted the doctrine of *respondeat superior* for nearly two centuries. This theory of vicarious liability is laden with practical implications in all situations in which a principal-agent (master-servant, employer-employee) relationship exists. The small-town grocer with one clerk and the multinational corporation with thousands of employees are equally subject to the doctrinal demand of "let the master respond."

For Critical Analysis: *How does the doctrine of* respondeat superior *relate to the doctrine of strict product liability?*

a. K.B. 642, 90 Eng. Reprint 1255 (1698).

> **Note** An agent-employee going to or from work or meals is not usually considered to be within the scope of employment. An agent-employee whose job requires travel, however, is considered to be within the scope of employment for the entire trip, including the return.

A principal is exposed to tort liability whenever a third person sustains a loss due to the agent's misrepresentation. The principal's liability depends on whether or not the agent was actually or apparently authorized to make representations and whether such representations were made within the scope of the agency. The principal is always directly responsible for an agent's misrepresentation made within the scope of the agent's authority, whether the misrepresentation was made fraudulently or simply by the agent's mistake or oversight.

LIABILITY FOR INDEPENDENT CONTRACTOR'S TORTS   Generally, the principal is not liable for physical harm caused to a third person by the negligent act of an independent contractor in the performance of the contract. This is because the employer does not have the *right to control* the details of an independent contractor's performance. Exceptions to this rule are made in certain situations, however, as when exceptionally hazardous activities are involved. Examples of such activities include blasting operations, the transportation of highly volatile chemicals, or the use of poisonous gases. In these situations, a principal cannot be shielded from liability merely by using an independent contractor. Strict liability is imposed on the principal as a matter of law and, in some states, by statute. (For a discussion of other exceptions to the general rule, see this chapter's *Inside the Legal Environment* on page 506.)

International Perspective

Islamic Law and *Respondeat Superior*

The doctrine of *respondeat superior* is well established in the legal systems of the United States and most Western countries. Middle Eastern countries, however, do not employ the principle. Islamic law, codified in the *Shari'a*, holds to a strict principle that responsibility for human actions lies with the individual and cannot be vicariously extended to others. This principle and other concepts of Islamic law are based on the sayings of Mohammed, the seventh-century prophet and founder of Islam.

For Critical Analysis: *How would American society be affected if employers could not be held vicariously liable for their employees' torts?*

LIABILITY FOR AGENT'S CRIMES An agent is liable for his or her own crimes. A principal or employer is not liable for an agent's crime even if the crime was committed within the scope of authority or employment—unless the principal participated by conspiracy or other action. In some jurisdictions, under specific statutes, a principal may be liable for an agent's violation, in the course and scope of employment, of regulations, such as those governing sanitation, prices, weights, and the sale of liquor.

Wage-Hour Laws

In the 1930s, Congress enacted several laws regulating the wages and working hours of employees. In 1931, Congress passed the Davis-Bacon Act,[4] which requires the payment of "prevailing wages" to employees of contractors and subcontractors working on government construction projects. In 1936, the Walsh-Healey Act[5] was passed. This act requires that a minimum wage, as well as overtime pay of time and a half, be paid to employees of manufacturers or suppliers entering into contracts with agencies of the federal government.

In 1938, Congress passed the Fair Labor Standards Act[6] (FLSA). This act extended wage-hour requirements to cover all employers engaged in interstate commerce or engaged in the production of goods for interstate commerce, plus selected types of businesses. We examine here the FLSA's provisions in regard to child labor, maximum hours, and minimum wages.

Child Labor

The FLSA prohibits oppressive child labor. Children under fourteen years of age are allowed to do certain types of work, such as deliver newspapers, work for their parents, and work in the entertainment and (with some exceptions) agricultural areas. Children who are fourteen or fifteen years of age are allowed to work, but not in hazardous occupations. Most states require persons under sixteen years of age to obtain work permits. There are also numerous restrictions on how many hours per day and per week they can work.
● **Example 17.11** Children in this age group cannot work during school hours, for more than three hours on a school day (or eight hours on a nonschool day),

Children take a break from their work in a coal mine in the early twentieth century. What restrictions do employers face in employing children today?

---

4. 40 U.S.C. Sections 276a–276a-5.
5. 41 U.S.C. Sections 35–45.
6. 29 U.S.C. Sections 201–260.

Inside the Legal Environment

Torts by Independent Contractors

As discussed elsewhere, as a general rule an employer of an independent contractor is not liable for the torts committed by the independent contractor. As one court pointed out, however, this rule is so riddled with exceptions that the "exceptions . . . have practically subsumed the rule."[a] Exceptions to the general rule come in many forms. For example, suppose that you own or manage a retail business. You have hired an independent contractor to maintain your parking lot in a safe condition for your customers. If the contractor fails to do so and a customer is injured as a result, who will be liable for the customer's injuries, your firm or the independent contractor?

A Case Example

Consider a similar case that came before the supreme court of New Hampshire. In that case, a woman sued a shopping mall owner to recover for injuries she sustained when she fell while walking on a snow-covered sidewalk at the entryway to the mall. The mall owner asserted that it was not liable for the injuries because the entryway was maintained by an independent con-

tractor. Although the mall owner prevailed at trial, the New Hampshire supreme court reversed the trial court's ruling. In support of its decision, the court cited Section 425 of the *Restatement (Second) of Torts,* which provides that an owner or tenant of business premises who employs an independent contractor "to maintain in [a] safe condition land which he holds open to the entry of the public as his place of business" is subject to liability for injuries caused by the contractor's "negligent failure to maintain the land in reasonably safe condition." According to the court, the duty owned by owners or possessors of business premises to those whom they invite onto those premises simply cannot be delegated to others.[b]

Have the Exceptions Become the Rule?

Business owners and managers should realize that they may be held liable for the actions of their independent contractors despite the "general rule" to the contrary. Even the *Restatement (Second) of Torts,* in Comment b to Section 409, states that the exceptions to the rule "are so numerous, and they have so far eroded the 'general rule,' that is can now be said to be 'general' only in the sense that it is applied where no good reason is found for departing from it."

For Critical Analysis: *What policy interest is furthered by imposing liability on employers for the torts of their independent contractors?*

---

a. *Rowley v. City of Baltimore,* 305 Md. 456, 505 A.2d 494 (1986).

b. *Valenti v. Net Properties Management, Inc.,* 142 N.H. 633, 710 A.2d 399 (1998).

---

for more than eighteen hours during a school week (or forty hours during a nonschool week), or before 7 A.M. or after 7 P.M. (9 P.M. during the summer).

Persons between the ages of sixteen and eighteen do not face such restrictions on working times and hours, but they cannot be employed in hazardous jobs or in jobs detrimental to their health and well-being. Persons over the age of eighteen are not affected by any of the above-mentioned restrictions.

Hours and Wages

Under the FLSA, any employee who agrees to work more than forty hours per week must be paid no less than one and a half times his or her regular pay for all hours over forty. Note that the FLSA overtime provisions only apply after an employee has worked more than forty hours per *week.* Thus, employees who work for ten hours a day, four days per week, are not entitled to overtime pay because they do not work more than forty hours a week.

Certain employees are exempt from the overtime provisions of the act. Exempt employees fall into four categories: executives, administrative employees, professional employees, and outside salespersons. Generally, to fall into one of these categories, an employee must earn more than a specified amount of income per week and devote a certain percentage of work time to the performance of specific types of duties, as determined by the FLSA. To qualify as an outside salesperson, the employee must regularly engage in sales work away from the office and spend no more than 20 percent of work time per week performing duties other than sales.

The FLSA provides that a **minimum wage** of a specified amount (currently, $5.15 per hour) must be paid to employees in covered industries. Congress periodically revises such minimum wages. Under the FLSA, the term *wages* includes the reasonable cost of the employer in furnishing employees with board, lodging, and other facilities if they are customarily furnished by that employer.

Minimum Wage The lowest wage, either by government regulation or union contract, that an employer may pay an hourly worker.

Worker Health and Safety

Under the common law, employees injured on the job had to rely on tort law or contract law theories in suits they brought against their employers. Additionally, workers had some recourse under the common law governing agency relationships, which imposes a duty on a principal-employer to provide a safe workplace for his or her agent-employee. Today, numerous state and federal statutes protect employees and their families from the risk of accidental injury, death, or disease resulting from their employment. This section discusses the primary federal statute governing health and safety in the workplace, along with state workers' compensation acts.

The Occupational Safety and Health Act

At the federal level, the primary legislation for employee health and safety protection is the Occupational Safety and Health Act of 1970.[7] Congress passed this act in an attempt to ensure safe and healthful working conditions for practically every employee in the country. The act provides for specific standards that employers must meet, plus a general duty to keep workplaces safe.

ENFORCEMENT AGENCIES   Three federal agencies develop and enforce the standards set by the Occupational Safety and Health Act. The Occupational Safety and Health Administration (OSHA) is part of the Department of Labor and has the authority to promulgate standards, make inspections, and enforce the act. OSHA has safety standards governing many workplace details, such as the structural stability of ladders and the requirements for railings. OSHA also establishes standards that protect employees against exposure to substances that may be harmful to their health.

The National Institute for Occupational Safety and Health is part of the Department of Health and Human Services. Its main duty is to conduct research on safety and health problems and to recommend standards for OSHA to adopt. Finally, the Occupational Safety and Health Review Commission is an independent agency set up to handle appeals from actions taken by OSHA administrators.

PROCEDURES AND VIOLATIONS   OSHA compliance officers may enter and inspect facilities of any establishment covered by the Occupational Safety and

---

7. 29 U.S.C. Sections 553, 651–678.

Health Act.[8] Employees may also file complaints of violations. Under the act, an employer cannot discharge an employee who files a complaint or who, in good faith, refuses to work in a high-risk area if bodily harm or death might result.

Employers with eleven or more employees are required to keep occupational injury and illness records for each employee. Each record must be made available for inspection when requested by an OSHA inspector. Whenever a work-related injury or disease occurs, employers must make reports directly to OSHA. Whenever an employee is killed in a work-related accident or when five or more employees are hospitalized in one accident, the employer must notify the Department of Labor within forty-eight hours. If the company fails to do so, it will be fined. Following the accident, a complete inspection of the premises is mandatory.

Criminal penalties for willful violation of the Occupational Safety and Health Act are limited. Employers may be prosecuted under state laws, however. In other words, the act does not preempt state and local criminal laws.[9] In the following case, an employer argued that it should not be penalized by OSHA for violating a regulation of which the employer was ignorant.

8. In the past, warrantless inspections were conducted. In 1978, however, the United States Supreme Court held that warrantless inspections violated the warrant clause of the Fourth Amendment to the Constitution. See *Marshall v. Barlow's, Inc.*, 436 U.S. 307, 98 S.Ct. 1816, 56 L.Ed.2d 305 (1978). 9. *Pedraza v. Shell Oil Co.*, 942 F.2d 48 (1st Cir. 1991); cert. denied, *Shell Oil Co. v. Pedraza*, 502 U.S. 1082, 112 S.Ct. 993, 117 L.Ed.2d 154 (1992).

Case 17.3 ● Valdak Corp. v. Occupational Safety and Health Review Commission

United States Court of Appeals, Eighth Circuit, 1996.
73 F.3d 1466.
http://ls.wustl.edu/8th.cir/opinions.html[a]

Historical and Social Setting *Since the Occupational Safety and Health Act was enacted in 1970, the rates of deaths and injuries in the workplace have been cut in half. In 1970, for example, eighteen of every one hundred thousand workers were killed on the job. In 1996, the rate was eight per one hundred thousand. To prevent accidental injuries and deaths,*

a. This Web site is maintained by Washington University School of Law in St. Louis, Missouri. This page contains links to some of the opinions of the U.S. Court of Appeals for the Eighth Circuit. Click on the "Party Name" link. In the "Search string" box, type "Valdak" and click "Begin Search." When the results appear, click on the case number to access the opinion.

employers often impose safety measures. Such measures are particularly important when an employer's work force is young and inexperienced, as in many restaurants, retail establishments, and car washes.

Background and Facts The Valdak Corporation operates a car wash that uses an industrial dryer to spin-dry towels. The dryer was equipped with a device that was supposed to keep it locked while it spun, but the device often did not work. An employee reached into the dryer while it was spinning, and his arm was cut off above the elbow. OSHA cited Valdak for, among other things, a willful violation of a machine-guarding regulation and assessed a $28,000 penalty. Valdak appealed to the Occupational Safety and Health Review Commission, which upheld the penalty. Valdak appealed to the U.S. Court of Appeals for the Eighth Circuit, arguing in part that it did not know about the specific regulation.

In the Words of the Court . . .
JOHN R. GIBSON, Circuit Judge.

* * * *

Valdak's claimed ignorance of the OSHA standard does not negate a finding of willfulness. Willfulness can be proved by "plain indifference" to

Case 17.3 Continued

the [Occupational Safety and Health Act's] requirements. Plain indifference to the machine guarding requirement is amply demonstrated by the facts that the dryer was equipped with an interlocking device, the interlocking device did not work, and Valdak continued to use the dryer with the broken interlock device. * * *

Decision and Remedy The U.S. Court of Appeals for the Eighth Circuit upheld the agency's finding.

For Critical Analysis—Ethical Consideration *For what policy reasons might an employer set up a formal safety program or issue a written safety manual?*

Workers' Compensation

State **workers' compensation laws** establish an administrative procedure for compensating workers injured on the job. Instead of suing, an injured worker files a claim with the administrative agency or board that administers the local workers' compensation claims.

Most workers' compensation statutes are similar. No state covers all employees. Typically excluded are domestic workers, agricultural workers, temporary employees, and employees of common carriers (companies that provide transportation services to the public). Typically, the statutes cover minors. Usually, the statutes allow employers to purchase insurance from a private insurer or a state fund to pay workers' compensation benefits in the event of a claim. Most states also allow employers to be self-insured—that is, employers who show an ability to pay claims do not need to buy insurance.

In general, the right to recover benefits is predicated wholly on the existence of an employment relationship and the fact that the injury was *accidental* and *occurred on the job or in the course of employment,* regardless of fault. Intentionally inflicted self-injury, for example, would not be considered accidental and hence would not be covered. If an injury occurred while an employee was commuting to or from work, it would not usually be considered to have occurred on the job or in the course of employment and hence would not be covered.

An employee must notify his or her employer promptly (usually within thirty days) of an injury. Generally, an employee also must file a workers' compensation claim with the appropriate state agency or board within a certain period (sixty days to two years) from the time the injury is first noticed, rather than from the time of the accident.

An employee's acceptance of workers' compensation benefits bars the employee from suing for injuries caused by the employer's negligence. By barring lawsuits for negligence, workers' compensation laws also bar employers from raising common law defenses to negligence, such as contributory negligence, assumption of risk, or injury caused by a "fellow servant" (another employee). A worker may sue an employer who *intentionally* injures the worker, however.

The court in the following case considered whether an employee's injury in an automobile accident arose out of and in the course of employment for purposes of workers' compensation.

Workers' Compensation Laws State statutes establishing an administrative procedure for compensating workers' injuries that arise out of—or in the course of—their employment, regardless of fault.

Case 17.4 ● Rogers v. Pacesetter Corp.

Missouri Court of Appeals,
Eastern District,
Division 4, 1998.
972 S.W.2d 540.
http://www.osca.state.mo.us/
courts/pubopinions.nsf[a]

Company Profile *Pacesetter Corporation, which has been in the home-improvement business since 1962, calls itself "America's Leading Home Improvement Company!" Pacesetter sells a range of building supplies, including cabinet refacing, doors, siding, windows, and patio awnings and covers. The company designs, manufactures, finances the purchase of, installs, guarantees, and services its products, which are advertised as durable and energy efficient.*

---

a. This Web site is maintained by the Missouri Office of State Courts Administrator. This page contains links to some of the opinions of the Missouri state courts. Click on "Eastern District." When that page opens, click on "Search." In the "Search for the following word(s)" box, type "Pacesetter." From the results, click on the *Rogers* case name to access the opinion.

Background and Facts Sean Rogers was a manager for Pacesetter Corporation. He worked at the Pacesetter offices from 9:00 A.M. to 9:00 P.M. Mondays through Fridays and 10:00 A.M. to 4:00 P.M. Saturdays. He also worked at home, drafting ads and conducting performance reviews, because he did not have enough time to do all of his work at the office. At the invitation of Rogers's supervisor, Rogers and the supervisor met at the River Port Club, a bar, to discuss a promotion. It was a Monday, when Rogers normally conducted performance reviews at home, which he planned to do after leaving the bar. While driving home, Rogers was injured in an automobile accident. He filed a claim for workers' compensation with the Missouri Division of Workers' Compensation. After a hearing, the administrative law judge awarded Rogers temporary compensation for a permanent partial disability. Pacesetter appealed to the Missouri Labor and Industrial Relations Commission, which reversed the award. Rogers appealed to a Missouri state court.

In the Words of the Court . . .
ROBERT G. DOWD, Jr., Presiding Judge.

* * * *

An employee's injuries arise out of his employment if they are a natural and reasonable incident thereof, and they are in the course of employment if the accident occurs within the period of employment at a place where the employee may reasonably be fulfilling the duties of employment. * * *

* * * *

* * * [C]ompensation for injuries while traveling home may be proper * * * when it can genuinely * * * be said that the home has become part of the employment premises. * * * *[A]n employee demonstrates this by showing a clear business use of the home at the end of the specific journey during which the accident occurred.* [Emphasis added.]

* * * *

* * * Here, Claimant [Rogers] regularly worked twelve hours, Monday through Friday, and six hours each Saturday. Claimant also regularly did work for his employer at home * * * . The night of the accident was a Monday and it was Claimant's practice to do performance reviews * * * on Monday evenings in order that on Tuesday mornings he could discuss [the employees'] performance with them. Claimant testified it was necessary to conduct these performance reviews at home because * * * "there was insufficient time to perform [his duties] during regular office hours." Moreover, * * * the work performed at home by Claimant was an integral part of the conduct of his employer's business, and not only a convenience to Claimant. Clearly a benefit accrued to employer by Claimant conducting these performance reviews at home. We conclude that * * * Claimant demonstrated that the demands of his employment created the expectation that work needed to be done at home for the benefit of his employer.

Case 17.4 Continued

Decision and Remedy   The court reversed the decision of the commission and remanded the case for the entry of an award of compensation. The court held that Rogers's injury arose out of and in the course of employment for purposes of workers' compensation.

For Critical Analysis—Social Consideration   *Should workers' compensation be denied to a worker who is injured off the employer's premises, regardless of the reason the worker is off the premises?*

Income Security

Federal and state governments participate in insurance programs designed to protect employees and their families by covering the financial impact of retirement, disability, death, hospitalization, and unemployment. The key federal law on this subject is the Social Security Act of 1935.[10]

Social Security and Medicare

The Social Security Act provides for old age (retirement), survivors, and disability insurance. The act is therefore often referred to as OASDI. Both employers and employees must "contribute" under the Federal Insurance Contributions Act (FICA)[11] to help pay for the employees' loss of income on retirement. The basis for the employee's and the employer's contribution is the employee's annual wage base—the maximum amount of the employee's wages that are subject to the tax. The employer withholds the employee's FICA contribution from the employee's wages and then matches this contribution. (In 2001, employers were required to withhold 6.2 percent of each employee's wages, up to a maximum wage base of $80,400, and to match this contribution.)

Retired workers are then eligible to receive monthly payments from the Social Security Administration, which administers the Social Security Act. Social Security benefits are fixed by statute but increase automatically with increases in the cost of living.

Medicare, a health-insurance program, is administered by the Social Security Administration for people sixty-five years of age and older and for some under the age of sixty-five who are disabled. It has two parts, one pertaining to hospital costs and the other to nonhospital medical costs, such as visits to doctors' offices. People who have Medicare hospital insurance can also obtain additional federal medical insurance if they pay small monthly premiums, which increase as the cost of medical care increases. As with Social Security contributions, both the employer and the employee contribute to Medicare. Currently, 2.9 percent of the amount of *all* wages and salaries paid to employees goes toward financing Medicare. Unlike Social Security contributions, there is no cap on the amount of wages subject to the Medicare tax.

> **Be Aware** Social Security currently covers almost all jobs in the United States. Nine out of ten workers contribute to this protection for themselves and their families.

Private Pension Plans

There has been significant legislation to regulate employee retirement plans set up by employers to supplement Social Security benefits. The major federal act covering these retirement plans is the Employee Retirement Income Security Act (ERISA) of 1974.[12] This act empowers the Labor Management Services Administration of the Department of Labor to enforce its provisions governing

---

10. 42 U.S.C. Sections 301–1397e.
11. 26 U.S.C. Sections 3101–3125.
12. 29 U.S.C. Sections 1001 *et seq.*

employers who have private pension funds for their employees. ERISA does not require an employer to establish a pension plan. When a plan exists, however, ERISA establishes standards for its management.

Vesting The creation of an absolute or unconditional right or power.

A key provision of ERISA concerns vesting. **Vesting** gives an employee a legal right to receive pension benefits at some future date when he or she stops working. Before ERISA was enacted, some employees who had worked for companies for as long as thirty years received no pension benefits when their employment terminated, because those benefits had not vested. ERISA establishes complex vesting rules. Generally, however, all employee contributions to pension plans vest immediately, and employee rights to employer pension-plan contributions vest after five years of employment.

In an attempt to prevent mismanagement of pension funds, ERISA has established rules on how they must be invested. Pension managers must be cautious in their investments and refrain from investing more than 10 percent of the fund in securities of the employer. ERISA also contains detailed record-keeping and reporting requirements.

Unemployment Insurance

The United States has a system of unemployment insurance in which employers pay into a fund, the proceeds of which are paid out to qualified unemployed workers. The Federal Unemployment Tax Act (FUTA) of 1935[13] created a state-administered system that provides unemployment compensation to eligible individuals. The FUTA and state laws require employers that fall under the provisions of the act to pay unemployment taxes at regular intervals.

COBRA

Federal legislation also addresses the issue of health insurance for workers whose jobs have been terminated—and who are thus no longer eligible for group health-insurance plans. The Consolidated Omnibus Budget Reconciliation Act (COBRA) of 1985[14] prohibits the elimination of a worker's medical, optical, or dental insurance coverage on the voluntary or involuntary termination of the worker's employment. Employers, with some exceptions, must comply with COBRA if they employ twenty or more workers and provide a benefit plan to those workers. They must inform an employee of COBRA's provisions when a group health plan is established and if that worker faces termination or a reduction of hours that would affect his or her eligibility for coverage under the plan.

The employer is relieved of the responsibility to provide benefit coverage if it completely eliminates its group benefit plan. An employer is also relieved of responsibility when the worker becomes eligible for Medicare, becomes covered under a spouse's health plan, becomes insured under a different plan (with a new employer, for example), or fails to pay the premium. An employer that does not comply with COBRA risks substantial penalties, such as a tax of up to 10 percent of the annual cost of the group plan or $500,000, whichever is less.[15]

Family and Medical Leave

In 1993, Congress passed the Family and Medical Leave Act (FMLA)[16] to allow employees to take time off work for family or medical reasons. A ma-

---

13. 26 U.S.C. Sections 3301–3310.
14. 29 U.S.C. Sections 1161–1169.
15. Proposed health-care legislation may supersede COBRA.
16. 29 U.S.C. Sections 2601, 2611–2619, 2651–2654.

jority of the states also have legislation allowing for a leave from employment for family or medical reasons, and many employers maintain private family-leave plans for their workers.

The FMLA requires employers who have fifty or more employees to provide employees with up to twelve weeks of unpaid family or medical leave during any twelve-month period. During the employee's leave, the employer must continue the worker's health-care coverage and guarantee employment in the same position or a comparable position when the employee returns to work. An important exception to the FMLA, however, allows the employer to avoid reinstatement of a *key employee*—defined as an employee whose pay falls within the top 10 percent of the firm's work force. Additionally, the act does not apply to employees who have worked less than one year or less than twenty-five hours a week during the previous twelve months.

Generally, an employee may take family leave when he or she wishes to care for a newborn baby, an adopted child, or a foster child.[17] An employee may take medical leave when the employee or the employee's spouse, child, or parent has a "serious health condition" requiring care. For most absences, the employee must demonstrate that the health condition requires continued treatment by a health-care provider and includes a period of incapacity of more than three days. Under regulations issued by the Department of Labor (DOL) in 1995, however, employees suffering from certain chronic health conditions, such as asthma or diabetes, may take FMLA leave for their own incapacities that require absences of less than three days.

Employers who violate the FMLA may be held liable for damages to compensate employees for unpaid wages (or salary), lost benefits, denied compensation, and actual monetary losses (such as the cost of providing for care) up to an amount equivalent to the employee's wages for twelve weeks. The employer may also be required to reinstate an employee in his or her job or grant a promotion that had been denied. A successful plaintiff is also entitled to

---

17. The foster care must be state sanctioned before such an arrangement falls within the coverage of the FMLA.

Ethical Issue 17.2

Should the coverage of the FMLA be broadened?

Now that the Family and Medical Leave Act (FMLA) has been in effect for some years, members of Congress and others are taking stock. For employees who face major illnesses or family emergencies, the FMLA has meant that they can take care of these problems without losing their jobs. Some employers even claim that they have benefited by the act. According to a study conducted by the Families and Work Institute, about 84 percent of employers regard the act has having had a positive impact on their workplaces, and nearly 25 percent of employers grant even more leave than the FMLA requires with respect to pregnancy leave.[a] Supporters of the FMLA have concluded that a problem with the act is that it does not go far enough. As it is, the act applies only to employers with fifty or more employees. This means that more than half of the work force in the private sector does not fall under the protection of the act. Congress is currently considering legislation that would broaden coverage of the law to cover employers with twenty-five or more employees and to provide leave for school-related purposes.

---

a. "Five Years after Its Passage, FMLA Remains a Hot Issue," *BNA's Corporate Counsel Weekly,* September 16, 1998, p. 8.

court costs; attorneys' fees; and in cases involving bad faith on the part of the employer, double damages.

Employee Privacy Rights

Recall from Chapter 6 that there is no provision in the U.S. Constitution that guarantees a right to privacy. A personal right to privacy, however, has been inferred from other constitutional guarantees provided by the First, Third, Fourth, Fifth, and Ninth Amendments to the Constitution. In the last two decades, concerns about the privacy rights of employees have arisen in response to the sometimes invasive tactics used by employers in their efforts to monitor and screen workers. Drug tests and other practices have increasingly been subject to challenge as violations of employee privacy rights.

In the interests of public safety and to reduce unnecessary costs, many of today's employers, including the government, require their employees to submit to drug testing. State laws relating to the privacy rights of private-sector employees vary from state to state. Some state constitutions may prohibit private employers from testing for drugs, and state statutes may restrict drug testing by private employers in any number of ways. A collective bargaining agreement may also provide protection against drug testing. In some instances, employees have brought an action against the employer for the tort of invasion of privacy (discussed in Chapter 9).

Constitutional limitations apply to the testing of government employees. The Fourth Amendment provides that individuals have the right to be "secure in their persons" against "unreasonable searches and seizures" conducted by government agents. Drug tests have been held constitutional, however, when there was a reasonable basis for suspecting government employees of using drugs. Additionally, when drug use in a particular government job could threaten public safety, testing has been upheld. • **Example 17.12** A Department of Transportation rule that requires employees engaged in oil and gas pipeline operations to submit to random drug testing was upheld, even though the rule did not require that before being tested the individual must have been suspected of drug use.[18] The court held that the government's interest in promoting public safety in the pipeline industry outweighed the employees' privacy interests.•

A number of employers also test their workers for acquired immune deficiency syndrome (AIDS). Some state laws restrict AIDS testing, and federal statutes offer some protection to employees or job applicants who have AIDS or have tested positive for the AIDS virus. The federal Americans with Disabilities Act of 1990 (discussed in Chapter 18), for example, prohibits discrimination against persons with disabilities and the term *disability* has been broadly defined to include those individuals with diseases such as AIDS. The law also requires employers to reasonably accommodate the needs of persons with disabilities. As a rule, although the law may not prohibit AIDS testing, it may prohibit the discharge of employees based on the results of those tests.

A particularly troublesome privacy issue concerns employers' monitoring of their employees' computer files, voice mail, e-mail, or other electronic communications. For a discussion of this topic, see this chapter's *Legal E-nvironment* feature.

---

18. *Electrical Workers Local 1245 v. Skinner,* 913 F.2d 1454 (9th Cir. 1990).

Legal *e*-nvironment

Electronic Monitoring in the Workplace

In today's workplace, employees' use of electronic communications systems may subject employers to liability on many fronts. One risk is that e-mail could be used to harass employees. Another risk is that employees could reproduce, without authorization, copyright-protected materials on the Internet. Still another risk is that confidential information contained in e-mail or voice mail messages could fall into the hands of an outside party. Finally, personal use of the Internet by employees cuts into their work time.

In an attempt to shield themselves from liability and to increase worker productivity, some companies monitor their employees' electronic communications. According to the American Management Association, more than 45 percent of U.S. corporations engage in some intrusive employee monitoring practices. These practices may include monitoring employees' e-mail, voice mail, and telephone exchanges; recording employees' computer keystrokes, tracking employees' Internet use; and video-recording employees' job performance.[a] Tracking employees' Internet use is made easy by a variety of specially designed software products that are currently available on the market.

Clearly, employers need to protect themselves from liability for their employees' online activities. At the same time, employees expect to have a certain zone of privacy in the workplace, and some claim that employers have gone too far in their monitoring practices.

Laws Governing Electronic Monitoring

Generally, there is little specific government regulation of monitoring activities, although electronic monitoring by employers may violate the Electronic Communications Privacy Act (ECPA) of 1986.[b] This act amended existing federal wiretapping law to cover electronic forms of communications, such as communications via cellular telephones or e-mail. The ECPA prohibits the intentional interception of any wire or electronic communication or the intentional disclosure or use of the information obtained by the interception.

The act excludes from coverage, however, any electronic communications through devices that are "furnished to the subscriber or user by a provider of wire or electronic communication service" and that are being used by the subscriber or user, or by the provider of the service, "in the ordinary course of its business." Another exception to the ECPA allows employers to avoid liability under the act if employees *consent* to having their electronic communications intercepted by the employer. Thus, an employer may be able to avoid what laws do exist by simply informing employees that they are subject to monitoring. Then, if employees challenge the monitoring practice, the employer can raise the defense of consent by claiming that the employees consented to the monitoring.[c] Generally, in cases challenging employee monitoring practices, the courts have sided with the employers, concluding that the employers' actions are based on legitimate concerns.

Alternative Approaches

Many companies are finding that the benefits of electronic monitoring may not be worth the costs—a major cost being employee resentment of monitoring practices. An alternative being pursued by a growing number of companies, particularly in the high-tech industry, is to allow their employees to use their own discretion with respect to Internet use. Hewlett-Packard, for example, does not monitor employees' Internet use or block access to any Web sites.

Some observers claim that this "hands-off" approach with respect to employee use of the Internet is a sensible one. For one thing, some highly qualified job candidates may not want to work for a company that monitors their Internet use. For another, there is no evidence that Internet monitoring has increased worker productivity. Finally, how can an employer monitor Internet use while its employees are traveling or working at home—as more and more employees are doing?

For Critical Analysis: *Should an employee have a reasonable expectation of privacy when using his or her employer's computer system to send personal e-mail messages? Why or why not?*

a. "Don't Expect Privacy in the Workplace," *International Herald Tribune,* January 16–17, 1999, p. 4.
b. 18 U.S.C. Sections 2510–2521.

c. In some cases, even a verbal announcement to employees that their electronic communications would be monitored was sufficient to justify the use of the consent defense. See, for example, *Griffin v. City of Milwaukee,* 74 F.3d 824 (7th Cir. 1996).

Key Terms

agency 493	minimum wage 507	undisclosed principal 503
disclosed principal 502	partially disclosed principal 502	vesting 512
fiduciary 493	ratification 497	workers' compensation laws 509
independent contractor 494	*respondeat superior* 503	

Chapter Summary • Employment Relationships

Agency Relationships
(See pages 493–496.)

In a *principal-agent* relationship, an agent acts on behalf of and instead of the principal in dealing with third parties. An employee who deals with third parties is normally an agent. An independent contractor is not an employee, and the employer has no control over the details of physical performance. The independent contractor is not usually an agent.

Agency Formation
(See pages 496–499.)

1. **By agreement**—Through express consent (oral or written) or implied by conduct.

2. **By ratification**—The principal, either by act or agreement, ratifies the conduct of an agent who acted outside the scope of authority or the conduct of a person who is in fact not an agent.

3. **By estoppel**—When the principal causes a third person to believe that another person is his or her agent, and the third person deals with the supposed agent in reasonable reliance on the agency's existence, the principal is "estopped to deny" the agency relationship.

4. **By operation of law**—Based on a social duty (such as the need to support family members) or created in emergency situations when the agent is unable to contact the principal.

Duties of Agents and Principals
(See pages 499–502.)

1. Duties of the agent—

   a. **Performance**—The agent must use reasonable diligence and skill in performing his or her duties or use the special skills that the agent has represented to the principal that the agent possesses.

   b. **Notification**—The agent is required to notify the principal of all matters that come to his or her attention concerning the subject matter of the agency.

   c. **Loyalty**—The agent has a duty to act solely for the benefit of his or her principal and not in the interest of the agent or a third party.

   d. **Obedience**—The agent must follow all lawful and clearly stated instructions of the principal.

   e. **Accounting**—The agent has a duty to make available to the principal records of all property and money received and paid out on behalf of the principal.

2. Duties of the principal—

   a. **Compensation**—Except in a gratuitous agency relationship, the principal must pay the agreed-on value (or reasonable value) for an agent's services.

   b. **Reimbursement and indemnification**—The principal must reimburse the agent for all sums of money disbursed at the request of the principal and for all sums of money the agent disburses for necessary expenses in the course of reasonable performance of his or her agency duties.

Chapter Summary • Employment Relationships

Duties of Agents and Principals— continued	**c. Cooperation**—A principal must cooperate with and assist an agent in performing his or her duties. **d. Safe working conditions**—A principal must provide safe working conditions for the agent-employee.
Agent's Authority (See page 502.)	**1. Actual authority**—can be either express or implied. *Express authority* can be oral or in writing. Authorization must be in writing if the agent is to execute a contract that must be in writing. *Implied authority* is authority that is customarily associated with the position of the agent or authority that is deemed necessary for the agent to carry out expressly authorized tasks. **2. Apparent authority**—Exists when the principal, by word or action, causes a third party reasonably to believe that an agent has authority to act, even though the agent has no express or implied authority.
Liability in Agency Relationships (See pages 502–505.)	**1. Liability for contracts**—If the principal's identity is disclosed or partially disclosed at the time the agent forms a contract with a third party, the principal is liable to the third party under the contract if the agent acted within the scope of his or her authority. If the principal's identity is undisclosed at the time of contract formation, the agent is personally liable to the third party, but if the agent acted within the scope of authority, the principal is also bound by the contract. **2. Liability for agent's torts**—Under the doctrine of *respondeat superior,* the principal is liable for any harm caused to another through the agent's torts if the agent was acting within the scope of his or her employment at the time the harmful act occurred. The principal is also liable for an agent's misrepresentation, whether made knowingly or by mistake. **3. Liability for independent contractor's torts**—A principal is not liable for harm caused by an independent contractor's negligence, unless hazardous activities are involved (in which situation the principal is strictly liable for any resulting harm) or other exceptions apply. **4. Liability for agent's crimes**—An agent is responsible for his or her own crimes, even if the crimes were committed while the agent was acting within the scope of authority or employment. A principal will be liable for an agent's crime only if the principal participated by conspiracy or other action or (in some jurisdictions) if the agent violated certain government regulations in the course of employment.
Wage-Hour Laws (See pages 505–507.)	**1. Davis-Bacon Act (1931)**—Requires the payment of "prevailing wages" to employees of contractors and subcontractors working on federal government construction projects. **2. Walsh-Healey Act (1936)**—Requires that a minimum wage and overtime pay be paid to employees of firms that contract with federal agencies. **3. Fair Labor Standards Act (1938)**—Extended wage-hour requirements to cover all employers whose activities affect interstate commerce plus certain businesses. The act has specific requirements in regard to child labor, maximum hours, and minimum wages.

(Continued)

Chapter Summary • Employment Relationships, *Continued*

Worker Health and Safety
(See pages 507–511.)

1. The Occupational Safety and Health Act of 1970 requires employers to meet specific safety and health standards that are established and enforced by the Occupational Safety and Health Administration (OSHA).

2. State workers' compensation laws establish an administrative procedure for compensating workers who are injured in accidents that occur on the job, regardless of fault.

Income Security
(See pages 511–512.)

1. **Social Security and Medicare**—The Social Security Act of 1935 provides for old age (retirement), survivors, and disability insurance. Both employers and employees must make contributions under the Federal Insurance Contributions Act (FICA) to help pay for the employees' loss of income on retirement. The Social Security Administration administers Medicare, a health-insurance program for older or disabled persons.

2. **Private pension plans**—The federal Employee Retirement Income Security Act (ERISA) of 1974 establishes standards for the management of employer-provided pension plans.

3. **Unemployment insurance**—The Federal Unemployment Tax Act of 1935 created a system that provides unemployment compensation to eligible individuals. Covered employers are taxed to help cover the costs of unemployment compensation.

COBRA
(See page 512.)

The Consolidated Omnibus Budget Reconciliation Act (COBRA) of 1985 requires employers to give employees, on termination of employment, the option of continuing their medical, optical, or dental insurance coverage for a certain period.

Family and Medical Leave
(See pages 512–514.)

The Family and Medical Leave Act (FMLA) of 1993 requires employers with fifty or more employees to provide their employees (except for key employees) with up to twelve weeks of unpaid family or medical leave during any twelve-month period for the following reasons:

1. **Family leave**—May be taken to care for a newborn baby, an adopted child, or a foster child.

2. **Medical leave**—May be taken when the employee or the employee's spouse, child, or parent has a serious health condition requiring care.

Employee Privacy Rights
(See pages 514–515.)

A right to privacy has been inferred from guarantees provided by the First, Third, Fourth, Fifth, and Ninth Amendments to the U.S. Constitution. State laws may also provide for privacy rights. Employer practices that are often challenged by employees as invasive of their privacy rights include drug testing, AIDS testing, and performance monitoring.

For Review

1. How do agency relationships arise? What duties do principals and agents owe to each other?

2. What criteria are generally used in determining whether a worker is an employee or an independent contractor?

3. In what circumstances will principals *not* be liable to third parties under contracts formed by an agent? Is the principal liable for an agent's torts?

4. What federal statutes govern wages and worker health and safety in the workplace? What is the purpose of workers' compensation laws?

5. How does the government provide for workers' income security? What are some issues relating to employees' privacy rights?

Questions and Case Problems

17–1. Agency Formation. Pete Gaffrey is a well-known, wealthy financier living in the city of Takima. Alan Winter, Gaffrey's friend, tells Til Borge that he (Winter) is Gaffrey's agent for the purchase of rare coins. Winter even shows Borge a local newspaper clipping mentioning Gaffrey's interest in coin collecting. Borge, knowing of Winter's friendship with Gaffrey, contracts with Winter to sell to Gaffrey a rare coin valued at $25,000. Winter takes the coin and disappears with it. On the date of contract payment, Borge seeks to collect from Gaffrey, claiming that Winter's agency made Gaffrey liable. Gaffrey does not deny that Winter was a friend, but he claims that Winter was never his agent. Discuss fully whether an agency was in existence at the time the contract for the rare coin was made.

17–2. Agent's Duties to Principal. Iliana is a traveling sales agent. Iliana not only solicits orders but also delivers the goods and collects payments from her customers. Iliana places all payments in her private checking account and at the end of each month draws sufficient cash from her bank to cover the payments made. Giberson Corp., Iliana's employer, is totally unaware of this procedure. Because of a slowdown in the economy, Giberson tells all its sales personnel to offer 20 percent discounts on orders. Iliana solicits orders, but she offers only 15 percent discounts, pocketing the extra 5 percent paid by customers. Iliana has not lost any orders by this practice, and she is rated as one of Giberson's top salespersons. Giberson now learns of Iliana's actions. Discuss fully Giberson's rights in this matter.

17–3. Health and Safety Regulations. Denton and Carlo were employed at an appliance plant. Their job required them to do occasional maintenance work while standing on a wire mesh twenty feet above the plant floor. Other employees had fallen through the mesh, one of whom had been killed by the fall. When Denton and Carlo were asked by their supervisor to do work that would likely require them to walk on the mesh, they refused due to their fear of bodily harm or death. Because of their refusal to do the requested work, the two employees were fired from their jobs. Was their discharge wrongful? If so, under what federal employment law? To what federal agency or department should they turn for assistance?

17–4. Workers' Compensation. Galvin Strang worked for a tractor company in one of its factories. Near his work station there was a conveyor belt that ran through a large industrial oven. Sometimes, the workers would use the oven to heat their meals. Thirty-inch-high flasks containing molds were fixed at regular intervals on the conveyor and were transported into the oven. Strang had to walk between the flasks to get to his work station.

One day, the conveyor was not moving, and Strang used the oven to cook a frozen pot pie. As he was removing the pot pie from the oven, the conveyor came on. One of the flasks struck Strang and seriously injured him. Strang sought recovery under the state workers' compensation law. Should he recover? Why or why not?

17–5. Respondeat Superior. Richard Lanno worked for Thermal Equipment Corp. as a project engineer. Lanno was allowed to keep a company van and tools at his home because he routinely drove to work sites directly from his home and because he was often needed for unanticipated business trips during his off hours. The arrangement had been made for the convenience of Thermal Equipment, even though Lanno's managers permitted him to make personal use of the van. Lanno was involved in a collision with Lazar while driving the van home from work one day. At the time of the accident, Lanno had taken a detour in order to stop at a store—he had intended to purchase a few items and then go home. Lazar sued Thermal Equipment, claiming that Lanno had acted within the scope of his employment. Discuss whether Lazar was able to recover from Thermal Equipment. Can employees act on behalf of their employers and themselves at the same time? Discuss. [*Lazar v. Thermal Equipment Corp.*, 148 Cal.App.3d 458, 195 Cal.Rptr. 890 (1983)]

17–6. Employee versus Independent Contractor. Stephen Hemmerling was a driver for the Happy Cab Co. Hemmerling paid certain fixed expenses and abided by a variety of rules relating to the use of the cab, the hours that could be worked, the solicitation of fares, and so on. Rates were set by the state. Happy Cab did not withhold taxes from Hemmerling's pay. While driving a cab, Hemmerling was injured in an accident and filed a claim against Happy Cab in a Nebraska state court for workers' compensation benefits. Such benefits are not available to independent contractors. On what basis might the court hold that Hemmerling is an employee? Explain. [*Hemmerling v. Happy Cab Co.*, 247 Neb. 919, 530 N.W.2d 916 (1995)]

17–7. Workers' Compensation. Linda Burnett Kidwell, employed as a state traffic officer by the California Highway Patrol (CHP), suffered an injury at home, off duty, while practicing the standing long jump. The jump is part of a required test during the CHP's annual physical performance program fitness test. Kidwell filed a claim for workers' compensation benefits. The CHP and the California workers' compensation appeals board denied her claim. Kidwell appealed to a state appellate court. What is the requirement for granting a workers' compensation claim? Should Kidwell's claim be granted? [*Kidwell v. Workers' Compensation Appeals*

Board, 33 Cal.App.4th 1130, 39 Cal.Rptr.2d 540 (1995)]

17-8. Undisclosed Principal. John Dunning was the sole officer of the R. B. Dunning Company and was responsible for the management and operation of the business. When the company rented a warehouse from Samuel and Ruth Saliba, Dunning did not say that he was acting for the firm. The parties did not have a written lease. Business faltered, and the firm stopped paying rent. Eventually, it went bankrupt and vacated the property. The Salibas filed a suit in a Maine state court against Dunning personally, seeking to recover the unpaid rent. Dunning claimed the debt belonged to the company because he had only been acting as its agent. Who is liable for the rent, and why? [*Estate of Saliba v. Dunning,* 682 A.2d 224 (Me. 1996)]

17-9. Hours and Wages. Richard Ackerman was an advance sales representative and account manager for Coca-Cola Enterprises, Inc. His primary responsibility was to sell Coca-Cola products to grocery stores, convenience stores, and other sales outlets. Coca-Cola also employed merchandisers, who did not sell Coca-Cola products but performed tasks associated with their distribution and promotion, including restocking shelves, filling vending machines, and setting up displays. The account managers, who serviced the smaller accounts themselves, regularly worked between fifty-five and seventy-two hours each week. Coca-Cola paid them a salary, bonuses, and commissions, but it did not pay them—unlike the merchandisers—additional compensation for the overtime. Ackerman and the other account managers filed a suit in a federal district court against Coca-Cola, alleging that they were entitled to overtime compensation. Coca-Cola responded that because of an exemption under the Fair Labor Standards Act, it was not required to pay them overtime. Is Coca-Cola correct? Explain. [*Ackerman v. Coca-Cola Enterprises, Inc.,* 179 F.3d 1260 (10th Cir. 1999)]

A Question of Ethics and Social Responsibility

17-10. Keith Cline worked for Wal-Mart Stores, Inc., as a night maintenance supervisor. When he suffered a recurrence of a brain tumor, he took a leave from work, which was covered by the Family Medical and Leave Act of 1993 and authorized by his employer. When he returned to work, his employer refused to allow him to continue his supervisory job and demoted him to the status of a regular maintenance worker. A few weeks later, the company fired him, ostensibly because he "stole" company time by clocking in thirteen minutes early for a company meeting. Cline sued Wal-Mart, alleging, among other things, that Wal-Mart had violated the FMLA by refusing to return him to his prior position when he returned to work. In view of these facts, answer the following questions. [*Cline v. Wal-Mart Stores, Inc.,* 144 F.3d 294 (4th Cir. 1998)]

(a) Did Wal-Mart violate the FMLA by refusing to return Cline to his prior position when he returned to work?

(b) From an ethical perspective, the FMLA has been viewed as a choice on the part of society to shift to the employer family burdens caused by changing economic and social needs. What "changing" needs does the act meet? In other words, why did Congress feel that workers should have the right to family and medical leave in 1993, but not in 1983, or 1973, or earlier?

(c) "Congress should amend the FMLA, which currently applies to employers with fifty or more employees, so that it applies to employers with twenty-five or more employees." Do you agree with this statement? Why or why not?

For Critical Analysis

17-11. When a worker is injured on the job, normally the sole remedy is provided through state workers' compensation statutes, regardless of fault or the employer's negligence. On average, recoveries under these statutes are less than half what recoveries in tort lawsuits would be. In view of the law's increasing concern with compensating injured parties, why are these statutes retained? What policy considerations underlie their retention?

 Interacting with the Internet

■ For updated links to resources available on the Web, as well as a variety of other materials, visit this text's Web site at

http://leet.westbuslaw.com

■ An excellent source for information on agency law, including court cases involving agency concepts, is the Legal Information Institute (LII) at Cornell University. You can access the LII's Web page on this topic at

http://www.law.cornell.edu/topics/ agency.html

■ The 'Lectric Law Library's Lawcopedia contains a summary of agency laws at

http://www.lectlaw.com/d-a.htm

Scroll down through the A's and select the link to Agent for useful information on this area of the law.

■ An outstanding Web site for information on employee benefits, including the full text of the FMLA, COBRA, other relevant statutes and case law, and current articles, is BenefitsLink. Go to

http://www.benefitslink.com/ columns.shtml

■ The American Federation of Labor-Congress of Industrial Organizations (AFL-CIO) provides links to a broad variety of labor-related resources at

http://www.aflcio.org

■ The Occupational Safety and Health Administration (OSHA) offers information related to workplace health and safety at

http://www.osha.gov

■ The Bureau of Labor Statistics provides a wide variety of data on employment, including data on employment compensation, working conditions, and productivity. Go to

http://stats.bls.gov/blshome.html

■ The National Labor Relations Board is online at the following URL:

http://www.nlrb.gov

 Online Legal Research Exercises

Go to **http://leet.west buslaw.com**, the Web site that accompanies this text. Select "Interactive Study Center," and then click on "Chapter 17." There you will find the following Internet research exercises that you can perform to learn more about employment laws and issues:

Activity 17–1: Employees or Independent Contractors?
Activity 17–2: Workplace Monitoring and Surveillance

 Before the Test

Go to **http://leet.west buslaw.com**, the Web site that accompanies this text. Select "Interactive Quizzes." You will find a number of interactive questions relating to this chapter.

chapter 18

Equal Employment Opportunities

contents

chapter objectives

After reading this chapter, you should be able to:

1. Indicate what types of discrimination are prohibited by federal laws.

2. List and describe the three major federal statutes that prohibit employment discrimination.

3. Distinguish between disparate-treatment discrimination and disparate-impact discrimination.

4. Summarize the remedies available to victims of employment discrimination.

5. Discuss how employers can defend against claims of employment discrimination.

During the early 1960s we, as a nation, focused our attention on the civil rights of all Americans, including our rights under the Fourteenth Amendment to the equal protection of the laws. Out of this movement to end racial and other forms of discrimination grew a body of law protecting workers against discrimination in the workplace. This protective legislation further eroded the employment-at-will doctrine. In the past several decades, judicial decisions, administrative agency actions, and legislation have restricted the ability of employers, as well as unions, to discriminate against workers on the basis of race, color, religion, national origin, gender, age, or disability. A class of persons defined by one or more of these criteria is known as a **protected class**.

Several federal statutes prohibit discrimination in the employment context against members of protected classes. The most important statute is Title VII of the Civil Rights Act of 1964.[1] Title VII prohibits discrimination on the basis of race, color, religion, national origin, and gender at any stage of employment. Discrimination on the basis of age and disability are prohibited by the Age Discrimination in Employment Act of 1967[2] and the Americans with Disabilities Act of 1990,[3] respectively.

The focus of this chapter is on the kinds of discrimination prohibited by these federal statutes. Note, however, that discrimination against employees on the basis of any of the above-mentioned criteria may also violate state human rights statutes or other state laws or public policies prohibiting discrimination.

> **"Nor shall any State . . . deny to any person within its jurisdiction the equal protection of the laws."**
>
> The Fourteenth Amendment to the U.S. Constitution

Protected Class A group of persons protected by specific laws because of the group's defining characteristics. Under laws prohibiting employment discrimination, these characteristics include race, color, religion, national origin, gender, age, or disability.

Title VII of the Civil Rights Act of 1964

Title VII of the Civil Rights Act of 1964 and its amendments prohibit **employment discrimination** against employees, applicants, and union members on the basis of race, color, national origin, religion, or gender at any stage of employment. Title VII applies to employers with fifteen or more employees, labor unions with fifteen or more members, labor unions that operate hiring halls (to which members go regularly to be rationed jobs as they become available), employment agencies, and state and local governing units or agencies. A special section of the act prohibits discrimination in most federal government employment.

Compliance with Title VII is monitored by the Equal Employment Opportunity Commission (EEOC). A victim of alleged discrimination, before bringing a suit against the employer, must first file a claim with the EEOC. The EEOC may investigate the dispute and attempt to obtain the parties' voluntary consent to an out-of-court settlement. If voluntary agreement cannot be reached, the EEOC may then file a suit against the employer on the employee's behalf. If the EEOC decides not to investigate the claim, the victim may bring his or her own lawsuit against the employer.

The EEOC does not investigate every claim of employment discrimination, regardless of the merits of the claim. In accordance with its 1996 "National Enforcement Plan," the EEOC investigates only "priority cases." The plan contains a list of the types of cases that the EEOC wants to investigate and take to litigation and those that it does not. Generally, priority cases are cases

Employment Discrimination Treating employees or job applicants unequally on the basis of race, color, national origin, religion, gender, age, or disability; prohibited by federal statutes.

---

1. 42 U.S.C. Sections 2000e–2000e-17.
2. 29 U.S.C. Sections 621–634.
3. 42 U.S.C. Sections 12102–12118.

that affect many workers, cases involving retaliatory discharge (firing an employee in retaliation for submitting a claim to the EEOC), and cases involving types of discrimination that are of particular concern to the EEOC.

Types of Discrimination

Title VII prohibits both intentional and unintentional discrimination. Intentional discrimination by an employer against an employee is known as **disparate-treatment discrimination**. Because intent may sometimes be difficult to prove, courts have established certain procedures for resolving disparate-treatment cases. Suppose that a woman applies for employment with a construction firm and is rejected. If she sues on the basis of disparate-treatment discrimination in hiring, she must show that (1) she is a member of a protected class, (2) she applied and was qualified for the job in question, (3) she was rejected by the employer, and (4) the employer continued to seek applicants for the position or filled the position with a person not in a protected class.

> **Disparate-Treatment Discrimination** A form of employment discrimination that results when an employer intentionally discriminates against employees who are members of protected classes.

If the woman can meet these relatively easy requirements, she makes out a **prima facie case** of illegal discrimination. Making out a *prima facie* case of discrimination means that the plaintiff has met her initial burden of proof and will win in the absence of a legally acceptable employer defense (defenses to claims of employment discrimination will be discussed later in this chapter). The burden then shifts to the employer-defendant, who must articulate a legal reason for not hiring the plaintiff. To prevail, the plaintiff must then show that the employer's reason is a *pretext* (not the true reason) and that discriminatory intent actually motivated the employer's decision.

> *Prima Facie* Case A case in which the plaintiff has produced sufficient evidence of his or her conclusion that the case can go to a jury; a case in which the evidence compels the plaintiff's conclusion if the defendant produces no affirmative defense or evidence to disprove it.

Employers often find it necessary to use interviews and testing procedures to choose from among a large number of applicants for job openings. Minimum educational requirements are also common. Employer practices, such as those involving educational requirements, may have an unintended discriminatory impact on a protected class. **Disparate-impact discrimination** occurs when, as a result of educational or other job requirements or hiring procedures, an employer's work force does not reflect the percentage of nonwhites, women, or members of other protected classes that characterizes qualified individuals in the local labor market. If a person challenging an employment practice having a discriminatory effect can show a connection between the practice and the disparity, he or she makes out a *prima facie* case, and no evidence of discriminatory intent needs to be shown. Disparate-impact discrimination can also occur when an educational or other job requirement or hiring procedure excludes members of a protected class from an employer's work force at a substantially higher rate than nonmembers, regardless of the racial balance in the employer's work force.

> **Disparate-Impact Discrimination** A form of employment discrimination that results from certain employer practices or procedures that, although not discriminatory on their face, have a discriminatory effect.

Discrimination Based on Race, Color, and National Origin

If a company's standards or policies for selecting or promoting employees have the effect of discriminating against employees or job applicants on the basis of race, color, or national origin, they are illegal—unless they have a substantial, demonstrable relationship to realistic qualifications for the job in question. Discrimination against these protected classes in regard to employment conditions and benefits is also illegal. In the following case, the court had to decide whether an employer's decision to promote one employee over another constituted race-based discrimination.

Case 18.1 ● McCullough v. Real Foods, Inc.

United States Court of Appeals,
Eighth Circuit, 1998.
140 F.3d 1123.
http://www.ca8.courts/gov/
index.html[a]

Historical and Technological Setting

In grocery stores, cash registers have been replaced with scanning systems that automatically register prices, compute totals, and keep running inventories to help a grocery store maintain its stock. Some stores provide hand-held scanners to customers so that the customers can record their purchases as they shop. Many retailers use electronic benefit transfer systems to process food stamps and other forms of government welfare. Magnetic readers read e-cards to automatically deduct discounts and print out coupons based on purchases. These technological innovations contrast sharply with human attitudes, which sometimes seem slow to change.

a. This Web site contains links to opinions of the U.S. Court of Appeals for the Eighth Circuit. Click on the "Party Name" link. In the "Search string" box, type "Real Foods" and click "Begin Search." When the results appear, click on the case number to access the opinion.

Background and Facts

In 1992, Cynthia McCullough, an African American woman with a college degree in urban affairs, began working at a deli in Chubb's Finer Foods (Real Foods, Inc.), a grocery store owned and managed by Ron Meredith. More than a year later, Meredith hired Kathy Craven, a white woman, to work at the deli. Craven had no prior deli experience, only a sixth-grade education, and poor reading and math skills. For example, Craven could not calculate prices or read recipes. McCullough and Craven were the only deli employees. Three months after Craven's arrival, Meredith appointed her "deli manager." Meredith later said that he did not promote McCullough because he "understood" that she would not work past 3:00 P.M., that she felt she was overeducated for the position, that she spoke of quitting, and that she would not accept a managerial job for the salary he was willing to pay. Denying all of what Meredith "understood," McCullough filed a suit in a federal district court against Real Foods, alleging discrimination on the basis of race. The court granted a summary judgment in favor of Real Foods, and McCullough appealed to the U.S. Court of Appeals for the Eighth Circuit.

In the Words of the Court . . .
HANSEN, Circuit Judge.

* * * *

* * * McCullough had 15 months more hands-on experience working in the deli than did Craven, * * * [and] McCullough's objective educational qualifications greatly exceeded those of Craven. * * * [W]hen McCullough's education and experience are contrasted with Craven's poor reading, writing, and math skills—as evidenced by her inability to read recipes or calculate prices—a reasonable inference arises that Meredith promoted a substantially less qualified white woman over a substantially better qualified black woman. We believe it is common business practice to pick the best qualified candidate for promotion. When that is not done, a reasonable inference arises that the employment decision was based on something other than the relative qualifications of the applicants.

Critical to our analysis in this case is the extremely subjective nature of the employer's stated promotion criteria. * * * [S]ubjective criteria for promotions are particularly easy for an employer to invent in an effort to sabotage a plaintiff's *prima facie* case and mask discrimination. * * *

* * * [W]hen the employer's asserted nondiscriminatory reasons are essentially checkmated by McCullough's denials that she ever made the statements the employer advances as its nondiscriminatory reasons, the failure to promote the objectively better qualified black woman raises a reasonable, nonspeculative inference that the decision to promote the less qualified white woman was based on an impermissible consideration—in this case race.

(Continued)

Case 18.1 Continued

Decision and Remedy The U.S. Court of Appeals for the Eighth Circuit reversed the lower court's judgment and remanded the case for trial. The court held McCullough raised an inference that Real Foods's articulated reasons for promoting Craven were a pretext and that the real reason was illegal discriminatory intent.

For Critical Analysis—Social Consideration *When applying Title VII in cases such as McCullough's, do you think that courts are acting as "super-personnel departments" reviewing the wisdom or fairness of the business judgments made by employers?*

Discrimination Based on Religion

Title VII of the Civil Rights Act of 1964 also prohibits government employers, private employers, and unions from discriminating against persons because of their religion. An employer must "reasonably accommodate" the religious practices of its employees, unless to do so would cause undue hardship to the employer's business. For example, if an employee's religion prohibits him or her from working on a certain day of the week or at a certain type of job, the employer must make a reasonable attempt to accommodate these religious requirements. Employers must reasonably accommodate an employee's religious belief even if the belief is not based on the tenets or dogma of a particular church, sect, or denomination. The only requirement is that the belief be sincerely held by the employee.[4]

> "A sign that says 'men only' looks very different on a bathroom door than a courthouse door."
>
> Thurgood Marshall, 1908–1993
> (Associate justice of the United States Supreme Court, 1967–1991)

Discrimination Based on Gender

Under Title VII, as well as other federal acts, employers are forbidden to discriminate against employees on the basis of gender. Employers are prohibited from classifying jobs as male or female and from advertising in help-wanted columns that are designated male or female unless the employer can prove that the gender of the applicant is essential to the job. Furthermore, employers cannot have separate male and female seniority lists.

Generally, to succeed in a suit for gender discrimination, a plaintiff must demonstrate that gender was a determining factor in the employer's decision to hire, fire, or promote him or her. Typically, this involves looking at all of the surrounding circumstances.

The Pregnancy Discrimination Act of 1978,[5] which amended Title VII, expanded the definition of gender discrimination to include discrimination based on pregnancy. Women affected by pregnancy, childbirth, or related medical conditions must be treated—for all employment-related purposes, including the receipt of benefits under employee benefit programs—the same as other persons not so affected but similar in ability to work.

In the following case, the plaintiff charged the defendant with gender discrimination. The plaintiff made out a *prima facie* case, and the defendant presented a nondiscriminatory reason as a defense. Was the defendant's reason a pretext covering a discriminatory motive? That was the question before the court.

---

4. *Frazee v. Illinois Department of Employment Security,* 489 U.S. 829, 109 S.Ct. 1514, 103 L.Ed.2d 914 (1989).
5. 42 U.S.C. Section 2000e(k).

Case 18.2 ● Carey v. Mount Desert Island Hospital

United States Court of Appeals,
First Circuit, 1998.
156 F.3d 31.
http://www.law.emory.edu/
1circuit/aug98[a]

Company Profile *Mount Desert Island Hospital (MDI) is a forty-nine-bed facility in Bar Harbor, Maine, with a medical staff that specializes in family practice, general surgery, internal medicine, ophthalmology, pathology, and radiology. A consulting staff includes practitioners of other medical specialties. MDI also operates an occupational health service, community health education, and affiliated health centers: Community Health Center in Southwest Harbor; Family Health Center, Women's Health Center, Breast Center, and High Street Health Center in Bar Harbor; and Northeast Harbor Clinic, open seasonally in Northeast Harbor. MDI is licensed by the state of Maine and fully accredited by the Joint Commission on Accreditation of Healthcare Organizations.*

a. This Web site is maintained by Emory University School of Law in Atlanta, Georgia. This page contains links to opinions of the U.S. Court of Appeals for the First Circuit decided in August 1998. Click on the *Carey* case name to access the opinion.

Background and Facts Michael Carey was a vice president in charge of the finance department for Mount Desert Island Hospital (MDI). When the position of chief executive officer (CEO) opened up, Carey applied, and his application was endorsed by Dan Hobbs, the acting CEO. At the time, an audit of the finance department revealed some deficiencies, but the auditor concluded that the department was "already attacking the problem." MDI's board offered the CEO post to Leslie Hawkins, a woman, who accepted. Less than a year later, Hawkins terminated Carey, giving as reasons the problems cited in the audit and "lack of confidence" in Carey. Carey filed a suit in a federal district court against MDI for gender discrimination in violation of Title VII and other laws. Evidence introduced during the trial included a statement by one female executive that "we have different standards for men and women," with regard to discipline and termination; and a statement by another female executive that "it's about time that we get a woman for this [CEO] position." The court awarded Carey more than $300,000 in damages. MDI appealed to the U.S. Court of Appeals for the First Circuit.

In the Words of the Court . . .
COFFIN, Senior Circuit Judge.

* * * *

* * * [T]his was a case with much to say on either side, involving the always difficult question of probing the wellsprings of human motivation. * * *
* * * *

In a case such as this, where a plaintiff must rely on circumstantial as opposed to direct evidence of gender discrimination, the evidence will necessarily be composed of bits and pieces, which may or may not point to an atmosphere of gender discrimination. While an employer should not find itself in jeopardy by reason of occasional stray remarks by ordinary employees, circumstantial evidence of a discriminatory atmosphere at a plaintiff's place of employment is relevant to the question of motive in considering a discrimination claim * * *.
* * * *

* * * [Based on the record, we] hold that there was sufficient evidence to support a finding that deficiencies in Carey's handling of financial controls were not the real reason for his discharge but instead covered an action stemming from gender discrimination.

Decision and Remedy The U.S. Court of Appeals for the First Circuit affirmed the lower court's judgment. The court held that that there was sufficient evidence to support a finding that the reason for Carey's discharge was gender discrimination.

For Critical Analysis—Cultural Consideration *Is it possible for jurors and judges to overcome their own prejudices in deciding cases in which gender plays a key role?*

Sexual Harassment

Title VII also protects employees against **sexual harassment** in the workplace. Sexual harassment has often been classified as either *quid pro quo* harassment or hostile-environment harassment. *Quid pro quo* is a Latin phrase that is often translated to mean "something in exchange for something else." *Quid pro quo* harassment occurs when job opportunities, promotions, salary increases, and so on are given in return for sexual favors. According to the United States Supreme Court, hostile-environment harassment occurs when "the workplace is permeated with discriminatory intimidation, ridicule, and insult, that is sufficiently severe or pervasive to alter the conditions of the victim's employment and create an abusive working environment."[6]

Generally, the courts apply this Supreme Court guideline on a case-by-case basis. Some courts have held that just one incident of sexually offensive conduct—such as a sexist remark by a co-worker or a photo on an employer's desk of his bikini-clad wife—can create a hostile environment.[7] At least one court has held that a worker may recover damages under Title VII because *other* persons were harassed sexually in the workplace.[8] According to some employment specialists, employers should assume that hostile-environment harassment has occurred if an employee claims that it has. (See this chapter's *Legal E-nvironment* feature for a discussion of how e-mail and online communications may create a hostile environment.)

Realize that hostile-environment harassment extends beyond gender. Subjecting employees to insults or offensive actions based on the employees' race, color, religion, national origin, age, or disability may also be deemed by the courts as a form of hostile-environment harassment.

HARASSMENT BY SUPERVISORS AND CO-WORKERS What if an employee is harassed by a manager or supervisor of a large firm, and the firm itself (the "employer") is not aware of the harassment? Should the employer be held liable for the harassment nonetheless? For some time, the courts were in disagreement on this issue. Typically, employers were held liable for Title VII violations by the firm's managerial or supervisory personnel in *quid pro quo* harassment cases regardless of whether the employer knew about the harassment. In hostile-environment cases, the majority of courts tended to hold employers liable only if the employer knew or should have known of the harassment and failed to take prompt remedial action. In 1998, the Supreme Court addressed this issue and set forth some significant guidelines (see this chapter's *Inside the Legal Environment* on page 531 for details).

Often, employees alleging harassment complain that the actions of co-workers, not supervisors, are responsible for creating a hostile working environment. In such cases, the employee still has a cause of action against the employer. Normally, though, the employer will be held liable only if it knew, or should have known, about the harassment and failed to take immediate remedial action.

HARASSMENT BY NONEMPLOYEES Employers may also be liable for harassment by *nonemployees* in certain circumstances. • **Example 18.1** If a restaurant owner or manager knows that a certain customer repeatedly harasses a

---

6. *Harris v. Forklift Systems,* 510 U.S. 17, 114 S.Ct. 367, 126 L.Ed.2d 295 (1993).
7. For other examples, see *Radtke v. Everett,* 442 Mich. 368, 501 N.W.2d 155 (1993); and *Nadeau v. Rainbow Rugs, Inc.,* 675 A.2d 973 (Me. 1996).
8. *Leibovitz v. New York City Transit Authority,* 4 F.Supp.2d 144 (E.D.N.Y. 1998).

Legal *e*-nvironment

Workplace Harassment in an Online World

The trend is clear—the Internet has created avenues to enhance worker efficiency, but at the same time there is now a greater chance that employers will be held liable for certain bulletin board postings or e-mail communications. These may be private postings or open postings on electronic bulletin boards.

Publicly Accessible Electronic Bulletin Boards

Consider the New Jersey Supreme Court's decision in *Blakey v. Continental Airlines.*[a] Pilots employed by Continental Airlines maintain an online computer bulletin board called the "Crew Members Forum." The company approved this bulletin board because it allowed pilots and crew members to learn about their schedules and flight assignments. When certain male pilots posted derogatory comments about Tammy S. Blakey, the first female captain to fly an Airbus A300 aircraft, she sued Continental, alleging that the comments on the bulletin board constituted sexual harassment.

The court concluded that the company's electronic bulletin board was related to the workplace environment and beneficial to Continental. Thus, the Court held that there were grounds for employer liability based on sexual harassment in the workplace. While the Court did not expect Continental to monitor the private communications of its employees, it did expect the company to take action once it received notice of workplace harassment on this company-approved electronic bulletin board.

Private E-Mails May Create Liability, Too

Racial jokes, ethnic slurs, or other comments contained in e-mail may also be the basis for a claim of hostile-environment harassment or other forms of discrimination. In one case, for example, Chevron Corporation had to pay $2.2 million to four female employees who maintained that they had been sexually harassed by e-mail messages.[b] A number of companies monitor their employees' use of the Internet, including their e-mail, in an attempt to increase worker productivity as well as to minimize the risk of lawsuits for harassment. Decisions such as those against Chevron will only increase this trend.

Trade-Offs Are Involved

Generally, employers who want to avoid online harassment in the workplace seem to be caught between the proverbial "rock and a hard place." On the one hand, if they do not take effective steps to curb such harassment, they may face liability for violating Title VII. On the other hand, if they monitor their employees' communications, they may face liability under other laws—for invading their employees' privacy, for example. Additionally, there are constitutional rights to be considered. As one federal appellate court noted, "Where pure expression is involved, Title VII steers into the territory of the First Amendment . . . [W]hen Title VII is applied to sexual-harassment claims based solely on verbal insults or pictorial or literary matter, the statute imposes content-based . . . restrictions on speech.[c] In another case, an Oregon court held that religious speech that unintentionally creates a hostile environment is constitutionally protected.[d]

For Critical Analysis: *Can you think of any ways, other than those mentioned above, in which Internet use in the workplace might create a hostile environment?*

b. Tamar Lewin, "Chevron Settles Sexual Harassment Charges," *The New York Times,* February 21, 1995, p. A14. See also *Owens v. Morgan Stanley & Co.,* 1997 WL 793004 (S.D.N.Y. 1997).
c. *DeAngelis v. El Paso Municipal Police Officers Association,* 51 F.3d 591 (5th Cir. 1995).
d. *Meltebeke v. B.O.L.I.,* 903 P.2d 351 (Ore. 1995).

a. 164 N.J. 38, 751 A.2d 538 (2000).

waitress and permits the harassment to continue, the restaurant owner may be liable under Title VII even though the customer is not an employee of the restaurant. The issue turns on the control that the employer exerts over a non-employee. In one case, an owner of a Pizza Hut franchise was held liable for the harassment of a waitress by two male customers because no steps were taken to prevent the harassment.[9] •

9. *Lockard v. Pizza Hut, Inc.,* 162 F.3d 1062 (10th Cir. 1998).

International Perspective

Sexual Harassment in Other Nations

The problem of sexual harassment in the workplace is not confined to the United States. Indeed, it is a worldwide problem for women workers. In Egypt, Turkey, Argentina, Brazil, and many other countries, there is no legal protection against any form of employment discrimination. Even in those countries that do have laws prohibiting discriminatory employment practices, including gender-based discrimination, those laws often do not specifically include sexual harassment as a discriminatory practice. Several countries have attempted to remedy this omission by passing new laws or amending others to specifically prohibit sexual harassment in the workplace. Japan, for example, has amended its Equal Employment Opportunity Law to include a provision making sexual harassment illegal. The revised law went into effect in 1999. In 1998, Thailand passed its first sexual-harassment law.

The European Union, which some years ago outlawed gender-based discrimination, is considering a proposal that would specifically identify sexual harassment as a form of discrimination. In the meantime, old traditions die hard. Women's support groups throughout Europe contend that corporations in European countries tend to view sexual harassment with "quiet tolerance." They contrast this attitude with that of most U.S. corporations, which have implemented specific procedures to deal with harassment claims.

For Critical Analysis: *Why do you think U.S. corporations are more aggressive than European companies in taking steps to prevent sexual harassment in the workplace?*

SAME-GENDER HARASSMENT The courts have also had to address the issue of whether men who are harassed by other men, or women who are harassed by other women, are also protected by laws that prohibit gender-based discrimination in the workplace. For example, what if the male president of a firm demands sexual favors from a male employee? Does this action qualify as sexual harassment? For some time, the courts were widely split on this issue. In 1998, in *Oncale v. Sundowner Offshore Services, Inc.,*[10] the Supreme Court resolved the issue by holding that Title VII protection extended to situations in which individuals are harassed by members of the same sex.

Remedies under Title VII

Employer liability under Title VII may be extensive. If the plaintiff successfully proves that unlawful discrimination occurred, he or she may be awarded reinstatement, back pay, retroactive promotions, and damages. Prior to the Civil Rights Act of 1991, damages were not available under Title VII. Plaintiffs alleging racial discrimination therefore often brought actions under 42 U.S.C. Section 1981. Section 1981, which was enacted as part of the Civil Rights Act of 1866, prohibits discrimination on the basis of race or ethnicity in the formation or enforcement of contracts. The 1991 Civil Rights Act allowed compensatory damages to be awarded in cases brought under other employment laws, such as Title VII, thus significantly broadening the rights of victims of employment discrimination.

Under the 1991 act, compensatory damages are available only in cases of intentional discrimination. The statute also stipulates that compensatory dam-

---

10. 523 U.S. 75, 118 S.Ct. 998, 140 L.Ed.2d 207 (1998).

Inside the Legal Environment

Supreme Court Guidelines on Liability for Sexual Harassment

In 1998, in two separate cases, the United States Supreme Court issued some significant guidelines relating to the liability of employers for their supervisors' harassment of employees in the workplace.

In one case, *Faragher v. City of Boca Raton,*[a] the issue was whether the employer could be held liable for a supervisor's harassment of employees even though the employer was unaware of the behavior. The case was brought by Beth Faragher, who, while working as a lifeguard for the city of Boca Raton, Florida, had allegedly been sexually harassed by male supervisors. When Faragher complained to a supervising captain about the harassment, the captain said that there was nothing he could do about it. When the case reached the Supreme Court, the Court ruled that the city could be held liable in these circumstances even though it was unaware of the behavior. The Court reached this conclusion primarily because, although the city had a written policy against sexual harassment, the policy had not been distributed to city employees. Additionally, the city had not established any procedures that could be followed by employees who felt that they were victims of sexual harassment.

In the other case, *Burlington Industries, Inc. v. Ellerth,*[b] the Court focused on whether a company could be held liable for the harassment of an employee by one of its vice presidents even though the employee suffered no adverse job consequences. The case was brought by Kimberly Ellerth, who claimed that she had been subjected to offensive sexual advances by a company vice president when she worked for Burlington Industries, Inc. Ellerth never complained to Burlington's human resources department about the behavior, and her refusal to accommodate the vice president's sexual wishes never caused her to be fired or demoted—in fact, she was promoted before leaving the company and bringing her harassment suit. Burlington argued that before it could be held liable, Ellerth would have to prove that she was fired or demoted because she did not submit to the vice president's sexual advances. The Supreme Court ruled that an employer could be liable for sexual harassment even if the employee did not suffer any adverse job consequences.

These two cases established some common-sense guidelines on liability for workplace harassment that will be helpful to employers and employees alike. On the one hand, employees benefit by the ruling that employers may be held liable for their supervisors' harassment even though they were unaware of the actions and even though the employees suffered no adverse job consequences. On the other hand, the Court made it clear in both decisions that employers have an affirmative defense against liability for their supervisors' harassment of employees if they can show that (1) they have taken "reasonable care to prevent and correct promptly any sexually harassing behavior" (by establishing effective harassment policies and complaint procedures, for example), and (2) the employee suing for harassment failed to follow these policies and procedures.

For Critical Analysis: *The Court indicated at one point that an employer's potential liability for sexual harassment in the workplace might be considered just one of the "costs of doing business." Is it fair to impose such a burden on businesses? Would it be fair not to do so?*

a. 524 U.S. 725, 118 S.Ct. 2275, 141 L.Ed.2d 662 (1998).
b. 524 U.S. 742, 118 S.Ct. 2257, 141 L.Ed.2d 633 (1998).

ages shall not include back pay, interest on back pay, or other relief already available under Title VII. Punitive damages may be recovered against a private employer only if the employer acted with malice or reckless indifference to an individual's rights. The sum of the amount of compensatory and punitive damages is limited by the statute to specific amounts against specific employers—ranging from $50,000 against employers with one hundred or fewer employees to $300,000 against employers with more than five hundred employees.

Ethical Issue 18.1

Should employees be deprived of statutory remedies because of arbitration clauses in their contracts?

An ongoing issue in employment relationships concerns arbitration clauses in employment contracts. On the one hand, public policy, as expressed in the Federal Arbitration Act of 1925 and various state statutes, favors arbitration or some other method of alternative dispute resolution in the settlement of employment disputes. Remember from Chapter 4 that the Supreme Court, in *Gilmer v. Interstate/Johnson Lane Corp.,*[a] held that arbitration agreements will be enforced even though an employee claims protection under a specific federal statute governing employees. In *Gilmer*, the relevant statute was the Age Discrimination in Employment Act (ADEA) of 1967. On the other hand, critics of this policy (and of the Supreme Court's decision in *Gilmer*) claim that all employees, even those who sign contracts containing arbitration clauses, should be allowed to pursue remedies for employment discrimination provided by Title VII, the ADEA, and the Americans with Disabilities Act of 1990. Some recent court decisions indicate a similar concern. For a further discussion of this significant issue in the employment context, refer back to the *Inside the Legal Environment* feature in Chapter 4.

---

a. 500 U.S. 20, 111 S.Ct. 1647, 114 L.Ed.2d 26 (1991).

Equal Pay Act of 1963

The Equal Pay Act of 1963 was enacted as an amendment to the Fair Labor Standards Act of 1938. Basically, the act prohibits gender-based discrimination in the wages paid for equal work on jobs when their performance requires equal skill, effort, and responsibility under similar conditions. It is job content rather than job description that controls in all cases. To determine whether the Equal Pay Act has been violated, a court will thus look to the primary duties of the two jobs. The jobs of a barber and a beautician, for example, are considered essentially "equal." So, too, are those of a tailor and a seamstress. For the equal pay requirements to apply, the act requires that male and female employees must work at the same establishment.

A wage differential for equal work is justified if it is shown to be because of (1) seniority, (2) merit, (3) a system that pays according to quality or quantity of production, or (4) any factor other than gender. Small differences in job content, however, do not justify higher pay for one gender.

Discrimination Based on Age

Age discrimination is potentially the most widespread form of discrimination, because anyone—regardless of race, color, national origin, or gender—could be a victim at some point in life. The Age Discrimination in Employment Act (ADEA) of 1967, as amended, prohibits employment discrimination on the basis of age against individuals forty years of age or older. An amendment to the act prohibits mandatory retirement for nonmanagerial workers. For the act to apply, an employer must have twenty or more employees.

The burden-shifting procedure under the ADEA is similar to that under Title VII. If a plaintiff can establish that he or she (1) was a member of the pro-

Remember The Fourteenth Amendment prohibits any state from denying any person "the equal protection of the laws." This prohibition applies to the federal government through the due process clause of the Fifth Amendment.

tected age group, (2) was qualified for the position from which he or she was discharged, and (3) was discharged under circumstances that give rise to an inference of discrimination, the plaintiff has established a *prima facie* case of unlawful age discrimination. The burden then shifts to the employer, who must articulate a legitimate (nondiscriminatory) reason for the employment decision. If the plaintiff can prove that the employer's reason is only a pretext and that the plaintiff's age was a determining factor in the employer's decision, the employer will be held liable under the ADEA.

Numerous cases of alleged age discrimination have been brought against employers who, to cut costs, replaced older, higher-salaried employees with younger, lower-salaried workers. Companies generally defend a decision to discharge an older worker by asserting that the worker could no longer perform his or her duties or that the worker's skills were no longer needed. The employee must prove that the discharge was motivated, at least in part, by age bias. Proof that qualified older employees are generally discharged before younger employees or that co-workers continually made unflattering age-related comments about the discharged worker may be enough.

In the past, courts had sometimes held that to establish a *prima facie* case of age discrimination, the plaintiff must also prove that he or she was replaced by a person outside the protected class—that is, by a person under the age of forty years. In 1996, however, in *O'Connor v. Consolidated Coin Caterers Corp.*,[11] the United States Supreme Court held that a cause of action for age discrimination under the ADEA does not require the replacement worker to be outside the protected class. Rather, the issue in all ADEA cases turns on whether age discrimination has, in fact, occurred, regardless of the age of the replacement worker. In the following case, the court had to decide whether there was sufficient evidence to support a jury's finding of discrimination on the basis of age.

---

11. 517 U.S. 308, 116 S.Ct 1307, 134 L.Ed.2d 433 (1996).

Case 18.3 ● Rhodes v. Guiberson Oil Tools

United States Court of Appeals, Fifth Circuit, 1996. 75 F.3d 989.

Historical and Economic Setting *Exploring and drilling for oil can be an expensive operation; drills, pipes, pumps, testing and measuring equipment, trucks, tankers, helicopters, and a variety of services are utilized. Suppliers of these products and services depend entirely on the activities of oil companies in the field. If no one is drilling for oil, the suppliers are out of business. In 1986, the oil industry was in the throes of a severe economic downturn.*

Background and Facts Calvin Rhodes sold oil field equipment for Guiberson Oil Tools. When he was discharged in 1986 at age fifty-six, he was told that the discharge was part of a reduction in the work force (RIF), and that he would be considered for reemployment. Within six weeks, Guiberson hired a forty-two-year-old person to do the same job. Rhodes filed a suit in a federal district court against Guiberson under the Age Discrimination in Employment Act. At the trial, Guiberson officials testified that they had not told Rhodes the truth about why they discharged him and that they had intended to replace him. Guiberson offered as a defense Rhodes's "poor work performance" but did not present any company sales records or goals. Rhodes countered with customers' testimony about his expertise and diligence. The jury found that Rhodes was discharged because of his age. Guiberson appealed to the U.S. Court of Appeals for the Fifth Circuit.

(Continued)

Case 18.3 Continued

In the Words of the Court . . .
W. EUGENE DAVIS and DUHE, Circuit Judges:

* * * *

Based on this evidence, the jury was entitled to find that the reasons given for Rhodes' discharge were pretexts for age discrimination. The jury was entitled to find that Guiberson's stated reason for discharging Rhodes—RIF—was false. Additionally, the reason for discharge that Guiberson Oil proffered in court * * * was countered with evidence from which the jury could have found that Rhodes was an excellent salesman who met Guiberson Oil's legitimate productivity expectations. * * * [A] reasonable jury could have found that Guiberson Oil discriminated against Rhodes on the basis of his age.

Decision and Remedy The U.S. Court of Appeals for the Fifth Circuit affirmed the jury's finding.

For Critical Analysis—Ethical Consideration *If age is not the sole reason for an adverse em-ployment decision, how significant a factor do you think it should be to support a finding of discrimination?*

Discrimination Based on Disability

The Americans with Disabilities Act (ADA) of 1990 is designed to eliminate discriminatory employment practices that prevent otherwise qualified workers with disabilities from fully participating in the national labor force. Prior to 1990, the major federal law providing protection to those with disabilities was the Rehabilitation Act of 1973. That act covered only federal government employees and those employed under federally funded programs. The ADA extends federal protection against disability-based discrimination to all workplaces with fifteen or more workers. Basically, the ADA requires that employers "reasonably accommodate" the needs of persons with disabilities unless to do so would cause the employer to suffer an "undue hardship."

To prevail on a claim under the ADA, a plaintiff must show that he or she (1) has a disability, (2) is otherwise qualified for the employment in question, and (3) was excluded from the employment solely because of the disability. As in Title VII cases, a claim alleging violation of the ADA may be commenced only after the plaintiff has pursued the claim through the EEOC. Plaintiffs may sue for many of the same remedies available under Title VII. They may seek reinstatement, back pay, a limited amount of compensatory and punitive damages (for intentional discrimination), and certain other forms of relief. Repeat violators may be ordered to pay fines of up to $100,000.

What Is a Disability?

The ADA is broadly drafted to define persons with disabilities as persons with a physical or mental impairment that "substantially limits" their everyday activities. More specifically, the ADA defines *disability* as "(1) a physical or mental impairment that substantially limits one or more of the major life activities of such individuals; (2) a record of such impairment; or (3) being regarded as having such an impairment."

Co-workers discuss business matters. Which workers with disabilities are protected from employment discrimination by the Americans with Disabilities Act?

Generally, the determination of whether an individual has a disability as defined by the ADA is made on a case-by-case basis. Unlike plaintiffs in cases brought under Title VII or the ADEA, who clearly either are or are not members of the classes protected by those acts, a plaintiff suing under the ADA must *prove* that he or she has a disability—and thus falls under the protection of the ADA. Meeting this first requirement for a case of disability-based discrimination is sometimes difficult.

Health conditions that have been considered disabilities under federal law include blindness, alcoholism, heart disease, cancer, muscular dystrophy, cerebral palsy, paraplegia, diabetes, acquired immune deficiency syndrome (AIDS), and morbid obesity (defined as existing when an individual's weight is two times that of the normal person).[12] The ADA excludes from coverage certain conditions, such as kleptomania.

One issue that frequently arises in ADA cases is whether a person whose disability is controlled by medication still qualifies for protection under the ADA. For example, a federal appellate court recently reviewed a case involving a person who suffers from high blood pressure but functions "normally" when the problem is controlled by medication. According to the court, in these circumstances the person could not be considered "disabled."[13] Generally, however, the courts are divided on this issue.

For some time, the courts were split on another issue: Should a person who is infected with the human immunodeficiency virus (HIV) but who has no symptoms of AIDS come under the protection of the ADA as a person with a disability? In 1998, the Supreme Court resolved this issue by holding that an HIV infection is a disability even if the infection has not yet progressed to the symptomatic phase.[14]

One issue that frequently arises in ADA cases is whether a person whose impairment is mitigated by medication or a corrective device qualifies for protection under the ADA. That issue arose in the following case, which was appealed to the United States Supreme Court by two pilots whose severe myopia could be corrected with glasses or contact lenses.

---

12. *Cook v. Rhode Island Department of Mental Health,* 10 F.3d 17 (1st Cir. 1993).
13. *Murphy v. United Parcel Service, Inc.,* 141 F.3d 1185 (10th Cir. 1998).
14. *Bragdon v. Abbott,* 524 U.S. 624, 118 S.Ct. 2196, 141 L.Ed.2d 540 (1998).

Case 18.4 ● Sutton v. United Airlines, Inc.

Supreme Court of the United States, 1999.
527 U.S. 471,
119 S.Ct. 2139,
144 L.Ed.2d 450.
http://supct.law.cornell.edu/
supct/supct.1999a.html[a]

Background and Facts Karen and Kimberly Sutton are twin sisters, both of whom have severe myopia. Each woman's uncorrected visual acuity is

---

a. This page includes an alphabetical list of the 1999 decisions of the United States Supreme Court. Scroll down the list of cases to the *Sutton* case, and click on the case name to access the opinion.

20/200 or worse in her right eye and 20/400 or worse in her left eye, but with the use of corrective lenses, such as glasses or contact lenses, each has vision that is 20/20 or better. In other words, without corrective lenses, neither individual can see well enough to do such things as drive a vehicle, watch television, or shop, but with corrective measures, each functions identically to individuals without a similar impairment. In 1992, the Suttons applied to United Airlines, Inc. (UA), for employment as commercial airline pilots. They met UA's age, education, experience, and Federal Aviation Administration certification qualifications,

(Continued)

Case 18.4 Continued

and were invited to flight simulator tests and interviews. Because the Suttons did not meet UA's minimum vision requirement, which was uncorrected visual acuity of 20/100 or better, the interviews were terminated, and neither pilot was offered a position. The Suttons filed a suit in a federal district court against UA, alleging discrimination under the Americans with Disabilities Act (ADA). The Suttons asserted in part that due to their severe myopia, they have a substantially limiting impairment and are thus disabled. The court disagreed and dismissed their complaint, and the U.S. Court of Appeals for the Tenth Circuit affirmed this judgment. The Suttons appealed to the United States Supreme Court.

In the Words of the Court . . .
Justice O'CONNOR delivered the opinion of the Court.

* * * *

 * * * The Act defines a "disability" as "a physical or mental impairment that substantially limits one or more of the major life activities" of an individual. Because the phrase "substantially limits" appears in the Act in the present indicative verb form, we think the language is properly read as requiring that a person be presently—not potentially or hypothetically—substantially limited in order to demonstrate a disability. A "disability" exists only where an impairment "substantially limits" a major life activity, not where it "might," "could," or "would" be substantially limiting if mitigating measures were not taken. A person whose physical or mental impairment is corrected by medication or other measures does not have an impairment that presently "substantially limits" a major life activity. To be sure, a *person whose physical or mental impairment is corrected by mitigating measures still has an impairment, but if the impairment is corrected it does not "substantially limi[t]" a major life activity.* [Emphasis added.]

* * * *

 * * * The use of a corrective device does not, by itself, relieve one's disability. Rather, one has a disability under [the Act] if, notwithstanding the use of a corrective device, that individual is substantially limited in a major life activity. For example, individuals who use prosthetic limbs or wheelchairs may be mobile and capable of functioning in society but still be disabled because of a substantial limitation on their ability to walk or run. The same may be true of individuals who take medicine to lessen the symptoms of an impairment so that they can function but nevertheless remain substantially limited. * * * The use or nonuse of a corrective device does not determine whether an individual is disabled; that determination depends on whether the limitations an individual with an impairment actually faces are in fact substantially limiting.

Applying this reading of the Act to the case at hand, we conclude that the Court of Appeals correctly resolved the issue of disability in respondent's favor. * * * [P]etitioners allege that with corrective measures, their visual acuity is 20/20, and that they "function identically to individuals without a similar impairment." In addition, petitioners concede that they "do not argue that the use of corrective lenses in itself demonstrates a substantially limiting impairment." Accordingly, because we decide that *disability under the Act is to be determined with reference to corrective measures,* we agree with the courts below that petitioners have not stated a claim that they are substantially limited in any major life activity. [Emphasis added.]

Case 18.4 Continued

Decision and Remedy The United States Supreme Court affirmed the decision of the lower court. The Supreme Court held that a person is not disabled (substantially limited in any major life activity) under the ADA if he or she has a condition that can be corrected with medication, or one, such as poor vision, that can be rectified with corrective devices, such as glasses.

For Critical Analysis—Political Consideration *When the ADA of 1990 went into effect, the* *courts were faced with the challenge of interpreting the act's provisions—for example, determining when an individual in a specific case qualified as a person with a disability. Over time, a body of case law has been created so that today, there is less uncertainty as to how the act will be applied. One could thus argue that, at least to some extent, the courts have "written" the ADA. Should Congress pay more attention to details when it drafts legislation? Is it appropriate for the courts to assume such "lawmaking" responsibilities?*

Reasonable Accommodation

The ADA does not require that *unqualified* applicants with disabilities be hired or retained. Therefore, employers are not obligated to accommodate the needs of job applicants or employees with disabilities who are not otherwise qualified for the work. If a job applicant or an employee with a disability, with reasonable accommodation, can perform essential job functions, however, then the employer must make the accommodation. Required modifications may include installing ramps for a wheelchair, establishing more flexible working hours, creating or modifying job assignments, and creating or improving training materials and procedures.

Generally, employers should give primary consideration to employees' preferences in deciding what accommodations should be made. What happens if a job applicant or employee does not indicate to the employer how his or her

---

Ethical Issue 18.2

Who should decide when a person with disabilities is "otherwise qualified" for a particular job?

A significant issue concerning the ADA has to do with the determination of whether a person with disabilities is "otherwise qualified" for a particular job. Consider just one example: Should a freight company or airline be required to hire job candidates with monocular vision—persons who are blind in one eye? According to some federal courts, the answer to this question is yes. For example, in one case, a federal appellate court held that a truck driver who was blind in one eye was "disabled" and thus could sue an employer who refused to hire him under the ADA.[a] In another case, a federal appellate court held that a pilot with vision in only one eye was entitled to sue Aloha Islandair, a passenger airline, for refusing to hire him.[b]

These are just two of several examples of situations in which courts have held that employers can be liable for failing to accommodate employees with visual impairments. Such cases raise the question of whether such decisions should be left up to the employer, who may face substantial liability in the event of an accident, or to the courts, who are charged with the responsibility of upholding the mandates of the ADA.

a. *Kirkingburg v. Albertson's, Inc.,* 143 F.3d 1228 (9th Cir. 1998).
b. *Aloha Islandair, Inc. v. Tseu,* 128 F.3d 1301 (9th Cir. 1998).

disability can be accommodated so that the employee can perform essential job functions? In this situation, the employer may avoid liability for failing to hire or retain the individual on the ground that the applicant or employee has failed to meet the "otherwise qualified" requirement.[15]

Employers who do not accommodate the needs of persons with disabilities must demonstrate that the accommodations will cause "undue hardship." Generally, the law offers no uniform standards for identifying what is an undue hardship other than the imposition of a "significant difficulty or expense" on the employer.

Usually, the courts decide whether an accommodation constitutes an undue hardship on a case-by-case basis. In one case, the court decided that paying for a parking space near the office for an employee with a disability was not an undue hardship.[16] In another case, the court held that accommodating the request of an employee with diabetes for indefinite leave until his disease was under control would create an undue hardship for the employer, because the employer would not know when the employee was returning to work. The court stated that reasonable accommodation under the ADA means accommodation so that the employee can perform the job now or "in the immediate future" rather than at some unspecified distant time.[17]

We now look at some specific requirements of the ADA in regard to the extent to which employers must reasonably accommodate the needs of employees with disabilities.

<table>
<tr><td>**Don't Forget**
Preemployment screening procedures must be applied carefully in regard to all job applicants.</td></tr>
</table>

JOB APPLICATIONS AND PREEMPLOYMENT PHYSICAL EXAMS   Employers must modify their job-application process so that those with disabilities can compete for jobs with those who do not have disabilities. • **Example 18.2** A job announcement that only has a phone number would discriminate against potential job applicants with hearing impairments. Thus, the job announcement must also provide an address.•

Employers are restricted in the kinds of questions they may ask on job-application forms and during preemployment interviews. Furthermore, they cannot require persons with disabilities to submit to physical examinations until after an offer of employment has been made and then only if such exams are required of all other applicants. Employers can condition an offer of employment on the employee's successfully passing a medical examination, but disqualifications must result from the discovery of problems that render the applicant unable to perform the job for which he or she is to be hired.

DANGEROUS WORKERS   Employers are not required to hire or retain workers who, because of their disabilities, pose a "direct threat to the health or safety" of their co-workers or the public. This danger must be substantial and immediate; it cannot be speculative. In the wake of the AIDS epidemic, many employers are concerned about hiring or continuing to employ a worker who has AIDS under the assumption that the worker might pose a direct threat to the health or safety of others in the workplace. Courts have generally held, however, that AIDS is not so contagious as to disqualify employees in most

---

15. See, for example, *Beck v. University of Wisconsin Board of Regents*, 75 F.3d 1130 (7th Cir. 1996); and *White v. York International Corp.*, 45 F.3d 357 (10th Cir. 1995).
16. See *Lyons v. Legal Aid Society*, 68 F.3d 1512 (2d Cir. 1995).
17. *Myers v. Hase*, 50 F.3d 278 (4th Cir. 1995).

jobs. Therefore, employers must reasonably accommodate job applicants or employees who have AIDS or who test positive for the human immunodeficiency virus (HIV), the virus that causes AIDS.

HEALTH-INSURANCE PLANS   Workers with disabilities must be given equal access to any health insurance provided to other employees. Employers can exclude from coverage preexisting health conditions and certain types of diagnostic or surgical procedures, however. An employer can also put a limit, or cap, on health-care payments in its particular group-health policy—as long as such caps are "applied equally to all insured employees" and do not "discriminate on the basis of disability." Whenever a group health-care plan makes a disability-based distinction in its benefits, the plan violates the ADA. The employer must then be able to justify the distinction by proving one of the following:

1. That limiting coverage of certain ailments is required to keep the plan financially sound.
2. That coverage of certain ailments would cause a significant increase in premium payments or their equivalent such that the plan would be unappealing to a significant number of workers.
3. That the disparate treatment is justified by the risks and costs associated with a particular disability.

A discussion occurs at a meeting of Alcoholics Anonymous. Should employers be allowed to discriminate against persons suffering from alcoholism?

THE ADA AND SUBSTANCE ABUSERS   Drug addiction is a disability under the ADA, because drug addiction is a substantially limiting impairment. Those who are currently using illegal drugs are not protected by the act. The ADA only protects persons with *former* drug addictions—those who have completed a supervised drug-rehabilitation program or who are currently in a supervised rehabilitation program. Individuals who have used drugs casually in the past are not protected under the act. They are not considered addicts and therefore do not have a disability (addiction).

People recovering from alcoholism are protected by the ADA. Employers cannot legally discriminate against employees simply because they are suffering from alcoholism and must treat them in the same way as they treat other employees. In other words, an employee suffering from alcoholism cannot be disciplined any differently than anyone else simply because he or she was drinking the night before and came to work late. Of course, employers have the right to prohibit the use of alcohol in the workplace and can require that employees not be under the influence of alcohol while working. Employers can also fire or refuse to hire a person suffering from alcoholism if he or she poses a substantial risk of harm to either himself or herself or to others and the risk cannot be reduced by reasonable accommodation.

Defenses to Employment Discrimination

The first line of defense for an employer charged with employment discrimination is, of course, to assert that the plaintiff has failed to meet his or her initial burden of proof—proving that discrimination in fact occurred.

Once a plaintiff succeeds in proving that discrimination occurred, then the burden shifts to the employer to justify the discriminatory practice. Often, employers attempt to justify the discrimination by claiming that it was a result of a business necessity, a bona fide occupational qualification, or a seniority system. As mentioned in this chapter's *Inside the Legal Environment,* in some cases an effective antiharassment policy and prompt remedial action when harassment occurs also may shield employers from liability under Title VII for sexual harassment.

Business Necessity

Business Necessity A defense to allegations of employment discrimination in which the employer demonstrates that an employment practice that discriminates against members of a protected class is related to job performance.

An employer may defend against a claim of disparate-impact discrimination by asserting that a practice that has a discriminatory effect is a **business necessity.** • Example 18.3 If requiring a high school diploma is shown to have a discriminatory effect, an employer might argue that a high school education is required for workers to perform the job at a required level of competence. If the employer can demonstrate to the court's satisfaction that there exists a definite connection between a high school education and job performance, then the employer will succeed in this business necessity defense.•

Bona Fide Occupational Qualification

Bona Fide Occupational Qualification (BFOQ) Identifiable characteristics reasonably necessary to the normal operation of a particular business. These characteristics can include gender, national origin, and religion, but not race.

Another defense applies when discrimination against a protected class is essential to a job—that is, when a particular trait is a **bona fide occupational qualification (BFOQ).** For example, a men's fashion magazine might legitimately hire only male models. Similarly, the Federal Aviation Administration can legitimately impose age limits for airline pilots. Race, however, can never be a BFOQ. Generally, courts have restricted the BFOQ defense to instances in which the employee's gender is essential to the job. In 1991, the United States Supreme Court held that even a fetal-protection policy that was adopted to protect the unborn children of female employees from the harmful effects of exposure to lead was an unacceptable BFOQ.[18]

Seniority Systems

Seniority System In regard to employment relationships, a system in which those who have worked longest for the company are first in line for promotions, salary increases, and other benefits; they are also the last to be laid off if the work force must be reduced.

An employer with a history of discrimination may have no members of protected classes in upper-level positions. Even if the employer now seeks to be unbiased, it may face a lawsuit seeking an order that minorities be promoted ahead of schedule to compensate for past discrimination. If no present intent to discriminate is shown, and promotions or other job benefits are distributed according to a fair **seniority system** (in which workers with more years of service are promoted first, or laid off last), however, the employer has a good defense against the suit.

After-Acquired Evidence Is No Defense

In some situations, employers have attempted to avoid liability for employment discrimination on the basis of "after-acquired evidence" of an employee's misconduct. • Example 18.4 Suppose that an employer fires a worker, and the employee sues the employer for employment discrimination. During pretrial investigation, the employer learns that the employee made material misrepresentations on his or her employment application—misrepresentations that, had the employer known about them, would have served as a ground to fire the individual.•

---

18. *United Auto Workers v. Johnson Controls, Inc.,* 113 U.S. 158, 111 S.Ct. 1196, 113 L.Ed.2d 158 (1991).

Can such after-acquired evidence be used as a defense? The United States Supreme Court addressed this question in *McKennon v. Banner Publishing Co.*,[19] a case decided in 1995. The Court stated that both Title VII and the ADEA share a common purpose: "the elimination of discrimination in the workplace." The Court held that allowing employers to avoid liability for discrimination on the basis of after-acquired evidence did "not accord" with this purpose. After-acquired evidence of wrongdoing should not operate, "in every instance, to bar all relief for an earlier violation of the Act." Since this decision, the courts have generally held that after-acquired evidence cannot be used to shield employers from liability for employment discrimination, although it may be a factor in determining the amount of damages awarded to plaintiffs.

Affirmative Action

Federal statutes and regulations providing for equal opportunity in the workplace were designed to reduce or eliminate discriminatory practices with respect to hiring, retaining, and promoting employees. **Affirmative action** programs go a step further and attempt to "make up" for past patterns of discrimination by giving members of protected classes preferential treatment in hiring or promotion.

Affirmative Action Job-hiring policies that give special consideration to members of protected classes in an effort to overcome present effects of past discrimination.

Affirmative action programs have caused much controversy, particularly when they result in what is frequently called "reverse discrimination"—discrimination against "majority" workers, such as white males (or discrimination against other minority groups that may not be given preferential treatment under a particular affirmative action program). At issue is whether affirmative action programs, because of their inherently discriminatory nature, violate the equal protection clause of the Fourteenth Amendment to the Constitution.

The *Bakke* Case

An early case addressing this issue, *Regents of the University of California v. Bakke*,[20] involved an affirmative action program implemented by the University of California at Davis. Allan Bakke, who had been turned down for medical school at the Davis campus, sued the university for reverse discrimination after he discovered that his academic record was better than those of some of the minority applicants who had been admitted to the program.

The United States Supreme Court held that affirmative action programs were subject to "intermediate scrutiny." Recall from the discussion of the equal protection clause in Chapter 2 that any law or action evaluated under a standard of intermediate scrutiny, to be constitutionally valid, must be substantially related to important government objectives. Applying this standard, the Court held that the university could give favorable weight to minority applicants as part of a plan to increase minority enrollment so as to achieve a more culturally diverse student body. The Court stated, however, that the use of a quota system, in which a certain number of places is explicitly reserved for minority applicants, violated the equal protection clause of the Fourteenth Amendment.

---

19. 573 U.S. 352, 115 S.Ct. 879, 130 L.Ed.2d 852 (1995).
20. 438 U.S. 265, 98 S.Ct. 2733, 57 L.Ed.2d 750 (1978).

The *Adarand* Case and Subsequent Developments

Although the *Bakke* case and later court decisions alleviated the harshness of the quota system, today's courts are going even further in questioning the constitutional validity of affirmative action programs. In 1995, in its landmark decision in *Adarand Constructors, Inc. v. Peña*,[21] the United States Supreme Court held that any federal, state, or local affirmative action program that uses racial or ethnic classifications as the basis for making decisions is subject to strict scrutiny by the courts.

In effect, the Court's opinion in *Adarand* means that an affirmative action program is constitutional only if it attempts to remedy past discrimination and does not make use of quotas or preferences. Furthermore, once such a program has succeeded in the goal of remedying past discrimination, it must be changed or dropped. Since then, other federal courts have followed the Supreme Court's lead by declaring affirmative action programs invalid unless they attempt to remedy past or current discrimination.[22]

The Court of Appeals for the Fifth Circuit went even further than the Supreme Court in its 1996 decision in *Hopwood v. State of Texas*.[23] In that case, two white law school applicants sued the University of Texas School of Law in Austin, alleging that they were denied admission because of the school's affirmative action program. The program allowed admitting officials to take racial and other factors into consideration when determining which students would be admitted. The Court of Appeals for the Fifth Circuit held that the program violated the equal protection clause because it discriminated in favor of minority applicants. In its decision, the court directly challenged the *Bakke* decision by stating that the use of race even as a means of achieving diversity on college campuses "undercuts the Fourteenth Amendment." The United States Supreme Court declined to hear the case, thus letting the lower court's decision stand.

Additionally, California and Washington, by voter initiatives in 1996 and 1998, respectively, ended state-sponsored affirmative action in those states. Similar movements are currently under way in other states as well, such as Florida.

State Laws Prohibiting Discrimination

Although the focus of this chapter is on federal legislation, most states also have statutes that prohibit employment discrimination. Generally, the kinds of discrimination prohibited under federal legislation are also prohibited by state laws. In addition, state statutes often provide protection for certain individuals who are not protected under federal laws. For example, a New Jersey appellate court has held that anyone over the age of eighteen was entitled to sue for age discrimination under the state law, which specified no threshold age limit.[24] Furthermore, state laws prohibiting discrimination may apply to firms with fewer employees than the threshold number required under federal statutes, thus offering protection to a greater number of workers. Finally, state laws may provide for additional damages, such as damages for emotional distress, that are not provided for under federal statutes.

21. 575 U.S. 200, 115 S.Ct. 2097, 132 L.Ed.2d 158 (1995).
22. See, for example, *Taxman v. Board of Education of the Township of Piscataway*, 91 F.3d 1547 (3d Cir. 1996); and *Schurr v. Resorts International Hotel, Inc.*, 196 F.3d 486 (3d Cir. 1999).
23. 84 F.3d 720 (5th Cir. 1996).
24. *Bergen Commercial Bank v. Sisler*, 307 N.J.Super. 333, 704 A.2d 1017 (1998).

Key Terms

affirmative action   541

bona fide occupational qualification
    (BFOQ)   540

business necessity   540

disparate-impact
    discrimination   524

disparate-treatment
    discrimination   524

employment discrimination   523

prima facie case   524

protected class   523

seniority system   540

sexual harassment   528

Chapter Summary • Equal Employment Opportunities

Title VII of the Civil Rights Act of 1964 (See pages 523–531.)	Title VII prohibits employment discrimination based on race, color, national origin, religion, or gender. 1. **Procedures**—Employees must file a claim with the Equal Employment Opportunity Commission (EEOC). The EEOC may sue the employer on the employee's behalf; if not, the employee may sue the employer directly. 2. **Types of discrimination**—Title VII prohibits both intentional (disparate-treatment) and unintentional (disparate-impact) discrimination. Disparate-impact discrimination occurs when an employer's practice, such as hiring only persons with a certain level of education, has the effect of discriminating against a class of persons protected by Title VII. 3. **Remedies for discrimination under Title VII**—If a plaintiff proves that unlawful discrimination occurred, he or she may be awarded reinstatement, back pay, and retroactive promotions. Damages (both compensatory and punitive) may be awarded for intentional discrimination.
Discrimination Based on Age (See pages 532–534.)	The Age Discrimination in Employment Act (ADEA) of 1967 prohibits employment discrimination on the basis of age against individuals forty years of age or older. Procedures for bringing a case under the ADEA are similar to those for bringing a case under Title VII.
Discrimination Based on Disability (See pages 534–539.)	The Americans with Disabilities Act (ADA) of 1990 prohibits employment discrimination against persons with disabilities who are otherwise qualified to perform the essential functions of the jobs for which they apply. 1. **Procedures and remedies**—To prevail on a claim under the ADA, the plaintiff must show that he or she has a disability, is otherwise qualified for the employment in question, and was excluded from the employment solely because of the disability. Procedures under the ADA are similar to those required in Title VII cases; remedies are also similar to those under Title VII. 2. **Definition of disability**—The ADA defines the term *disability* as a physical or mental impairment that substantially limits one or more major life activities; a record of such impairment; or being regarded as having such an impairment. 3. **Reasonable accommodation**—Employers are required to reasonably accommodate the needs of persons with disabilities. Reasonable accommodations may include altering job-application procedures, modifying the physical work environment, and permitting more flexible work schedules.

(Continued)

Chapter Summary • Equal Employment Opportunities, *Continued*

Discrimination Based on Disability— continued	Employers are not required to accommodate the needs of all workers with disabilities. For example, employers need not accommodate workers who pose a definite threat to health and safety in the workplace or those who are not otherwise qualified for their jobs.
Defenses to Employment Discrimination (See pages 539–541.)	If a plaintiff proves that employment discrimination occurred, employers may avoid liability by successfully asserting certain defenses. Employers may assert that the discrimination was required for reasons of business necessity, to meet a bona fide occupational qualification, or to maintain a legitimate seniority system. Evidence of prior employee misconduct acquired after the employee has been fired is not a defense to discrimination.
Affirmative Action (See pages 541–542.)	Affirmative action programs attempt to "make up" for past patterns of discrimination by giving members of protected classes preferential treatment in hiring or promotion. Increasingly, such programs are being strictly scrutinized by the courts, and state-sponsored affirmative action has been banned in California.
State Laws Prohibiting Discrimination (See page 542.)	Generally, the kinds of discrimination prohibited by federal statutes are also prohibited by state laws. State laws may provide for more extensive protection and remedies than federal laws.

For Review

1. Generally, what kind of conduct is prohibited by Title VII of the Civil Rights Act of 1964, as amended?

2. What is the difference between disparate-treatment discrimination and disparate-impact discrimination?

3. What remedies are available under Title VII of the 1964 Civil Rights Act, as amended?

4. What federal acts prohibit discrimination based on age and discrimination based on disability?

5. Name and discuss three defenses to claims of employment discrimination.

Questions and Case Problems

18–1. Title VII Violations. Discuss fully whether any of the following actions would constitute a violation of Title VII of the 1964 Civil Rights Act, as amended:

(a) Tennington, Inc., is a consulting firm and has ten employees. These employees travel on consulting jobs in seven states. Tennington has an employment record of hiring only white males.

(b) Novo Films, Inc., is making a film about Africa and needs to employ approximately one hundred extras for this picture. Novo advertises in all major newspapers in southern California for the hiring of these extras. The ad states that only African Americans need apply.

18–2. Discrimination Based on Age. Tavo Jones had worked since 1974 for Westshore Resort, where he maintained golf carts. During the first decade, he received positive job evaluations and numerous merit pay raises. He was promoted to the position of supervisor of golf-cart maintenance at three courses. Then a new employee, Ben Olery, was placed in charge of the golf courses. He demoted Jones, who was over the age of forty, to running only one of the three cart facilities, and he froze Jones's salary indefinitely. Olery also demoted five other men over the age of forty. Another cart facility was placed under the supervision of Blake Blair. Later, the cart facilities for the three courses were again consolidated, but Blair—not Jones—was put in charge. At the time, Jones was still in his forties, and Blair was in his twenties. Jones overheard Blair say that "we are going to have to do away with these . . . old and senile" men. Jones quit and sued Westshore for employment discrimination. Should he prevail? Explain.

18–3. Discrimination Based on Gender.
Beginning in June 1966, Corning Glass Works started to open up jobs on the night shift to women. The previously separate male and female seniority lists were consolidated, and the women became eligible to exercise their seniority on the same basis as men and to bid for higher-paid night inspection jobs as vacancies occurred. On January 20, 1969, however, a new collective bargaining agreement went into effect; it established a new job evaluation system for setting wage rates. This agreement abolished (for the future) separate base wages for night-shift and day-shift inspectors and imposed a uniform base wage for inspectors that exceeded the wage rate previously in effect for the night shift. The agreement, though, did allow for a higher "red circle" rate for employees hired prior to January 20, 1969, when they were working as inspectors on the night shift. This "red circle" wage served essentially to perpetuate the differential in base wages between day and night inspectors. Had Corning violated Title VII of the Civil Rights Act of 1964? Discuss. [*Corning Glass Works v. Brennan,* 417 U.S. 188, 94 S.Ct. 2223, 41 L.Ed.2d 1 (1974)]

18–4. Defenses to Employment Discrimination. Dorothea O'Driscoll had worked as a quality control inspector for Hercules, Inc., for six years when her employment was terminated in 1986. O'Driscoll, who was over forty years of age, sued Hercules for age discrimination in violation of the Age Discrimination in Employment Act of 1967. While preparing for trial, Hercules learned that O'Driscoll had made several misrepresentations when she applied for the job. Among other things, she misrepresented her age, did not disclose a previous employer, falsely represented that she had never applied for work with Hercules before, and falsely stated that she had completed two quarters of study at a technical college. Additionally, on her application for group insurance coverage, she misrepresented the age of her son, who would otherwise have been ineligible for coverage as her dependent. Hercules defended against O'Driscoll's claim of age discrimination by stating that had it known of this misconduct, it would have terminated her employment anyway. What should the court decide? Discuss fully. [*O'Driscoll v. Hercules, Inc.,* 12 F.3d 176 (10th Cir. 1994)]

18–5. Discrimination Based on National Origin. Phanna Xieng was sent by the Cambodian government to the United States in 1974 for "advanced military training." When the Cambodian government fell in 1975, Xieng remained in the United States and eventu-

ally was employed by Peoples National Bank of Washington in 1979. In performance appraisals from 1980 through 1985, Xieng was rated by his supervisors as "capable of dealing effectively with customers" and qualified for promotion, although in each appraisal it was noted that Xieng might improve his communication skills to maximize his possibilities for future advancement. Xieng sought job promotions on numerous occasions but was never promoted. In 1986, he filed a complaint against the bank, alleging employment discrimination based on national origin. The employer argued that its refusal to promote Xieng because of his accent or communication skills did not amount to discrimination based on national origin. Is it possible to separate discrimination based on an employee's accent and communication skills from discrimination based on national origin? How should the court rule on this issue? [*Xieng v. Peoples National Bank of Washington,* 120 Wash.2d 512, 844 P.2d 389 (1993)]

18–6. Disparate-Impact Discrimination.
Local 1066 of the Steamship Clerks Union accepted only new members who were sponsored by existing members. All of the existing members were white. During a six-year period, the local admitted thirty new members, all of whom were relatives of present members and also white. The Equal Employment Opportunity Commission filed a suit in a federal district court against the union, alleging that this practice constituted disparate-impact discrimination under Title VII. The union argued that it was only continuing a family tradition. What does each party have to prove to win its case? Should the union be required to change its practice? [*EEOC v. Steamship Clerks Union, Local 1066,* 48 F.3d 594 (1st Cir. 1995)]

18–7. Discrimination Based on Disability.
When the University of Maryland Medical System Corp. learned that one of its surgeons was HIV positive, the university offered him transfers to positions that did not involve surgery. The surgeon refused, and the university terminated him. The surgeon filed a suit in a federal district court against the university, alleging in part a violation of the Americans with Disabilities Act. The surgeon claimed that he was "otherwise qualified" for his former position. What does he have to prove to win his case? Should he be reinstated? [*Doe v. University of Maryland Medical System Corp.,* 50 F.3d 1261 (4th Cir. 1995)]

18–8. Discrimination Based on Race.
Theodore Rosenblatt, a white attorney, worked for the law firm of Bivona & Cohen, P.C. When Bivona & Cohen terminated Rosenblatt's employment, he filed a suit in a federal district court against the firm. Rosenblatt claimed that he had been discharged because he was married to an African American and that a discharge for such a reason violated Title VII and other laws. The firm filed a motion for summary judgment, arguing that he was alleging discrimination against his wife, not himself, and

thus did not have standing to sue under Title VII for racial discrimination. Should the court grant or deny the motion? Explain. [*Rosenblatt v. Bivona & Cohen, P.C.,* 946 F.Supp. 298 (S.D.N.Y. 1996)]

18-9. Religious Discrimination. Mary Tiano, a devout Roman Catholic, worked for Dillard Department Stores, Inc. (Dillard's), in Phoenix, Arizona. Dillard's considered Tiano a productive employee because her sales exceeded $200,000 a year. At the time, the store gave its managers the discretion to grant unpaid leave to employees but prohibited vacations or leave during the holiday season—October through December. Tiano felt that she had a "calling" to go on a "pilgrimage" in October 1988 to Medjugorje, Yugoslavia, where some persons claimed to have had visions of the Virgin Mary. The Catholic Church had not designated the site an official pilgrimage site, the visions were not expected to be stronger in October, and tours were available at other times. The store managers denied Tiano's request for leave, but she had a nonrefundable ticket and left anyway. Dillard's terminated her employment. For a year, Tiano searched for a new job and did not attain the level of her Dillard's salary for four years. She filed a suit in a federal district court against Dillard's, alleging religious discrimination in violation of Title VII. Can Tiano establish a *prima facie* case of religious discrimination? Explain. [*Tiano v. Dillard Department Stores, Inc.,* 139 F.3d 679 (9th Cir. 1998)]

18-10. Discrimination Based on Disability. Vaughn Murphy was first diagnosed with hypertension (high blood pressure) when he was ten years old. Unmedicated, his blood pressure is approximately 250/160. With medication, however, he can function normally and engage in the same activities as anyone else. In 1994, United Parcel Service, Inc. (UPS), hired Murphy to be a mechanic, a position that required him to drive commercial motor vehicles. To get the job, Murphy had to meet a U.S. Department of Transportation (DOT) regulation that a driver have "no current clinical diagnosis of high blood pressure likely to interfere with his/her ability to operate a commercial vehicle safely." At the time, Murphy's blood pressure was measured at 186/124, but he was erroneously certified and started work. Within a month, the error was discovered and he was fired. Murphy obtained another mechanic's job—one that did not require DOT certification—and filed a suit in a federal district court against UPS, claiming discrimination under the Americans with Disabilities Act. UPS filed a motion

for summary judgment. Should the court grant UPS's motion? Explain. [*Murphy v. United Parcel Service, Inc.,* 527 U.S. 516, 119 S.Ct. 2133, 144 L.Ed.2d 484 (1999)]

A Question of Ethics and Social Responsibility

18-11. Luz Long and three other Hispanic employees (the plaintiffs) worked as bank tellers for the Culmore branch of the First Union Corp. of Virginia. The plaintiffs often conversed with one another in Spanish, their native language. In 1992, the Culmore branch manager adopted an "English-only" policy, which required all employees to speak English during working hours unless they had to speak another language to assist customers. The plaintiffs refused to cooperate with the new policy and were eventually fired. In a suit against the bank, the plaintiffs alleged that the English-only policy discriminated against them on the basis of their national origin. The court granted the bank's motion for summary judgment, concluding that "[t]here is nothing in Title VII which . . . provides that an employee has a right to speak his or her native tongue while on the job." [*Long v. First Union Corp. of Virginia,* 894 F.Supp. 933 (E.D.Va. 1995)]

1. The bank argued that the policy was implemented in response to complaints made by fellow employees that the Spanish-speaking employees were creating a hostile environment by speaking Spanish among themselves in the presence of other employees. From an ethical perspective, is this a sufficient reason to institute an English-only policy?
2. Is it ever ethically justifiable for employers to deny bilingual employees the opportunity to speak their native language while on the job?
3. Might there be situations in which English-only policies are necessary to promote worker health and safety?
4. Generally, what are the pros and cons of English-only policies in the workplace?

For Critical Analysis

18-12. Why has the federal government limited the application of the statutes discussed in this chapter only to firms with a specified number of employees, such as fifteen or twenty? Should these laws apply to all employers, regardless of size?

Interacting with the Internet

■ For updated links to resources available on the Web, as well as a variety of other materials, visit this text's Web site at

http://leet.westbuslaw.com

■ The law firm of Arent Fox posts articles on current issues in the area of employment law, including sexual harassment, on its Web site at

http://www.arentfox.com

■ An abundance of helpful information on disability-based discrimination, including the text of the

Americans with Disabilities Act of 1990, can be found at the following Web site:

http://janweb.icdi.wvu.edu/kinder

■ An excellent source for information on various forms of employment discrimination is the Equal Employment Opportunity Commission's Web site at

http://www.eeoc.gov

Online Legal Research Exercises

Go to **http://leet.west buslaw.com**, the Web site that accompanies this text. Select "Interactive Study Center," and then click on "Chapter 18." There you will find the following Internet research exercises that you can perform to learn more about laws prohibiting employment discrimination:

Activity 18–1: Americans with Disabilities
Activity 18–2: Equal Employment Opportunity

Before the Test

Go to **http://leet.west buslaw.com**, the Web site that accompanies this text. Select "Interactive Quizzes." You will find a number of interactive questions relating to this chapter.

Labor-Management Relations

contents

chapter objectives

After reading this chapter, you should be able to:

1. Describe the process behind union elections and collective bargaining.

2. Explain which strikes are legal and which strikes are illegal.

3. List unfair employer practices.

4. Identify unfair employee practices.

5. Define the rights of nonunion employees.

Through the first half of the nineteenth century, most Americans were self-employed, often in agriculture. For those who were employed by others, the employers generally set the terms of employment. The nature of employment changed with the growth of the industrial revolution, which had begun about 1760. Fewer Americans were self-employed. Terms of employment were sometimes set through bargaining between employees and employers. Most industrial enterprises were in their infancies, however, and to encourage their development, the government gave employers considerable freedom to hire, fire, and determine other employment standards in response to changing conditions in the marketplace.

With increasing industrialization, the size of workplaces and the number of workplace hazards increased. Workers came to believe that to counter the power and freedom of their employers and to protect themselves, they needed to organize into unions. Employers discouraged—sometimes forcibly—collective activities such as unions. In support of unionization, Congress enacted such legislation as the Railway Labor Act of 1926.[1] These laws were often restricted to particular industries. Beginning in 1932, Congress enacted a number of statutes that increased employees' rights in general. As the opening quotation indicates, at the heart of these rights is the right to join unions and engage in collective bargaining with management to negotiate working conditions, salaries, and benefits for a group of workers.

This chapter describes the development of labor law and legal recognition of the right to form unions. The laws that govern the management-union relationship are set forth in historical perspective. Then we discuss the process of unionizing a company, the collective bargaining required of a unionized employer, the "industrial war" of strikes and lockouts that may result if bargaining fails, and the labor practices that are considered unfair under federal law.

Federal Labor Law

Federal labor laws governing union-employer relations have developed considerably since the first law was enacted in 1932. Initially, the laws were concerned with protecting the rights and interests of workers. Subsequent legislation placed some restraints on unions and granted rights to employers. This section summarizes the four major federal labor law statutes.

Norris-LaGuardia Act

Congress protected peaceful strikes, picketing, and boycotts in 1932 in the Norris-LaGuardia Act.[2] The statute restricted federal courts in their power to issue injunctions against unions engaged in peaceful strikes. The act also provided that contracts limiting an employee's right to join a union are unlawful. Such contracts are known as **yellow dog contracts**. (In the early part of the twentieth century, "yellow dog" meant "coward.") In effect, this act declared a national policy permitting employees to organize.

In the following case, a union threatened to picket an employer unless the employer agreed to subcontract work only to subcontractors who employed the union's members. The court had to decide whether, under the Norris-LaGuardia Act, it could issue an injunction to restrain the union from picketing.

---

1. 45 U.S.C. Sections 151–188.
2. 29 U.S.C. Sections 101–115.

"Experience has proved that protection by law of the right of employees to organize and bargain collectively . . . promotes the flow of commerce."

National Labor Relations Act of 1935, Section 1

Yellow Dog Contract An agreement under which an employee promises his or her employer, as a condition of employment, not to join a union.

An employer's rules. How do federal labor laws influence the adoption of such rules?

Case 19.1 ● Burlington Northern Santa Fe Railway Co. v. International Brotherhood of Teamsters Local 174

United States Court of Appeals,
Ninth Circuit, 2000.
203 F.3d 703.
http://www.ca9.uscourts.gov[a]

Background and Facts Burlington Northern and Santa Fe Railway Company operates a hub in Seattle, Washington. Burlington terminated a subcontract with Eagle Systems, Inc., for loading and unloading services at the Seattle hub and transferred the work to another subcontractor, Parsec, Inc. As a consequence, fifty-three Eagle employees lost their jobs. International Brotherhood of Teamsters Local 174 represented the Eagle employees who lost their jobs, as well as the employees of other subcontractors who worked under subcontracts with Burlington.

Local 174 did not represent the Parsec employees, however. The union was afraid that Burlington's use of other subcontractors who did not employ Local 174's members would cause "substantial economic costs and personal hardship." The union asked Burlington to persuade Parsec to hire the former Eagle employees. Burlington refused. Local 174 asked Burlington to agree not to subcontract in the future any loading and unloading services to any subcontractor whose employees were not represented by Local 174. The union threatened to picket in support of this demand. Burlington filed a suit in a federal district court against Local 174, alleging violations of federal labor law, among other things, and seeking an injunction. The court granted the injunction, restraining Local 174 from "[c]alling, ordering, authorizing, encouraging, inducing, approving, continuing, starting, suffering, permitting or carrying out any strike, picket or work stoppage" at Burlington's facilities. The union appealed to the U.S. Court of Appeals for the Ninth Circuit.

a. In the left column, click on "Opinions." On the page, click on "2000." In the expanded list, click on "February." In that list, scroll to the name of the case ("BURLINGTON NORTHERN V IBET") and click on it to access the opinion.

In the Words of the Court . . .
PREGERSON, Circuit Judge.

* * * *

The Norris-LaGuardia Act deprives federal courts of jurisdiction to issue an injunction to restrain peaceful picketing in "any case involving or growing out of any labor dispute." Norris-LaGuardia defines the term "labor dispute" as

> any controversy concerning terms or conditions of employment, or concerning the association or representation of persons in negotiating, fixing, maintaining, changing, or seeking to arrange terms or conditions of employment, regardless of whether or not the disputants stand in the proximate relation of employer and employee.

We hold that a dispute between a union and a client company (here, Burlington Northern) over whether the client company's subcontractors must employ that union's members is a Norris-LaGuardia labor dispute. Thus, * * * the district court had no power to enjoin Local 174 from picketing Burlington Northern.

* * * *

* * * *The [United States] Supreme Court has consistently characterized Norris-LaGuardia's definition of "labor dispute" as "broad."* Equally expansive is the test that the Supreme Court fashioned for determining whether a particular controversy is a labor dispute. Simply, "the employer-employee relationship [must be at] the matrix of the controversy." [Emphasis added.]

It is clear that "the matrix" of Local 174's dispute with Burlington Northern is "the employer-employee relationship." Members of Local 174 lost their jobs because Burlington Northern transferred their work to a

Case 19.1 Continued

subcontractor who did not rehire them and who signed a collective bargaining agreement with a different union. Local 174 feared that Burlington Northern would terminate other subcontracts under which its members worked, leading to more job losses and causing wages and working conditions to deteriorate. Local 174 asked Burlington Northern to guarantee that this process would not occur, but Burlington Northern refused. In short, this dispute is about who will perform work at Burlington Northern's Seattle hub, which union will represent the employees of Burlington Northern's subcontractors, and what will be the terms of their employment.

Decision and Remedy The U.S. Court of Appeals for the Ninth Circuit vacated the lower court's order and remanded with instructions to dismiss the case. The court could not issue an injunction to block Local 174's picketing because the disagreement between Burlington and Local 174 was a "labor dispute" within the meaning of the Norris-LaGuardia Act. Under that act, a federal court cannot issue an injunc-

tion to block peaceful picketing that is part of a labor dispute.

For Critical Analysis—Social Consideration *Generally, how would the relationship between labor and management be affected if unions did not have the right to picket?*

National Labor Relations Act

The National Labor Relations Act of 1935 (NLRA),[3] also called the Wagner Act, established the right of employees to form unions, the right of those unions to engage in collective bargaining (negotiate contracts for their members), and the right to strike. The act also created the National Labor Relations Board (NLRB) to oversee union elections and to prevent employers from engaging in unfair labor union activities and unfair labor practices. Details of the NLRA are provided in this chapter's *Landmark in the Legal Environment* on page 553.

To be protected under the NLRA, an individual must be an "employee," as that term is defined in the statute.[4] Courts have long held that job applicants fall within the definition (otherwise, the NLRA's ban on discrimination in regard to hiring would mean nothing). In the following case, the United States Supreme Court considered whether an individual can be a company's "employee" if, at the same time, a union pays the individual to organize the company.

---

3. 29 U.S.C. Sections 151–169.
4. 29 U.S.C. Section 152(3).

Case 19.2 ● NLRB v. Town & Country Electric, Inc.

Supreme Court of the United States, 1995
516 U.S. 85,
116 S.Ct. 450, 133 L.Ed.2d 371.
http://www.findlaw.com/ casecode/supreme.html[a]

---

a. This Web site is maintained by FindLaw. This page contains links to opinions of the United States Supreme Court. In the "Party Name Search" box, type "Town & Country Electric" and click "Search." When the results appear, click on the case name to access the opinion.

Historical and Social Setting *Over the last two decades, the percentage of private-sector workers who are union members has declined. Perhaps this is due, at least in part, to a popular belief that unions represent only a level of interference between a company's making profits and the workers' getting paid. In the public sector, however, unions are becoming more popular and are growing in force. Unions themselves are consolidating and still attempting to organize workers.*

(Continued)

Case 19.2 Continued

Background and Facts Town & Country Electric, Inc., advertised for job applicants but refused to interview ten of eleven applicants who were members of a union, the International Brotherhood of Electrical Workers. The applicants were union "salts"—persons paid by the union to apply for a job with a company and then, when hired, to unionize the company (in this case, Town & Country's work force). The applicants filed a complaint with the National Labor Relations Board (NLRB), alleging that the company had committed an unfair labor practice by discriminating against the applicants on the basis of union membership. The issue turned on whether job applicants paid by a union to organize a company could be considered employees under the National Labor Relations Act (NLRA). The NLRB determined that the applicants were employees and ruled in their favor. Town & Country appealed, and the U.S. Court of Appeals for the Eighth Circuit reversed. The applicants appealed to the United States Supreme Court.

In the Words of the Court . . .
Justice BREYER delivered the opinion of the Court.

* * * *

* * * [T]he Board's decision is consistent with the broad language of the [NLRA] * * *. The ordinary dictionary definition of "employee" includes any "person who works for another in return for financial or other compensation." The phrasing of the [NLRA] seems to reiterate the breadth of the ordinary dictionary definition, for it says "[t]he term 'employee' shall include any employee." * * *

For another thing, the Board's broad, literal interpretation of the word "employee" is consistent with several of the [NLRA's] purposes, such as protecting "the right of employees to organize for mutual aid without employer interference" * * *.

Decision and Remedy The United States Supreme Court reversed the decision of the appellate court and remanded the case. The Court held that the applicants were employees and thus could not be discriminated against.

For Critical Analysis—Social Consideration *How would the relationship between labor and management be affected if job applicants did not have rights under the NLRA?*

Labor-Management Relations Act

Closed Shop A firm that requires union membership by its workers as a condition of employment. The closed shop was made illegal by the Labor-Management Relations Act of 1947.

Union Shop A place of employment in which all workers, once employed, must become union members within a specified period of time as a condition of their continued employment.

Right-to-Work Law A state law providing that employees are not to be required to join a union as a condition of obtaining or retaining employment.

The Labor-Management Relations Act of 1947 (LMRA, or the Taft-Hartley Act)[5] was passed to proscribe certain union practices. The Taft-Hartley Act contained provisions protecting employers as well as employees. The act was bitterly opposed by organized labor groups. It provided a detailed list of unfair labor activities that unions as well as management were now forbidden to practice. In addition, the law gave the president the authority to intervene in labor disputes and delay strikes that would "imperil the national health or safety."

An important provision of the LMRA concerned the **closed shop**—a firm that requires union membership of its workers as a condition of obtaining employment. Closed shops were made illegal under the Taft-Hartley Act. The act preserved the legality of the **union shop,** which does not require membership as a prerequisite for employment but can, and usually does, require that workers join the recognized union after a specified amount of time on the job. The act also allowed individual states to pass their own **right-to-work laws**—laws making it illegal for union membership to be required for *continued* employment in any establishment. Thus, union shops are technically illegal in states with right-to-work laws.

---

5. 29 U.S.C. Sections 141, 504.

Labor-Management Reporting and Disclosure Act

The Labor-Management Reporting and Disclosure Act of 1959 (the Landrum-Griffin Act)[6] established an employee bill of rights, as well as reporting requirements for union activities to prevent corruption. The Landrum-Griffin Act strictly regulated internal union business procedures.

---

6. 29 U.S.C. Sections 153, 1111.

Landmark in the Legal Environment

The National Labor Relations Act (1935)

The National Labor Relations Act of 1935 is often referred to as the Wagner Act because it was sponsored by Senator Robert Wagner. (Appendix E presents excerpts from the National Labor Relations Act.) During the 1930s, Wagner sponsored several pieces of legislation, particularly in the field of labor law. Until the early 1930s, employers had been free to establish the terms and conditions of employment. Collective activities by employees, such as participation in unions, were discouraged by employers. In 1934, when Wagner introduced the bill subsequently enacted as the National Labor Relations Act (NLRA), he saw it as a vehicle through which the disparate balance of power between employers and employees could be corrected.

Section 1 of the NLRA justifies the act under the commerce clause of the Constitution. Section 1 states that unequal bargaining power between employees and employers leads to economic instability, and refusals of employers to bargain collectively lead to strikes. These disturbances impede the flow of interstate commerce. It is declared to be the policy of the United States, under the authority given to the federal government under the commerce clause, to ensure the free flow of commerce by encouraging collective bargaining and unionization.

Purposes of the NLRA

The pervading purpose of the NLRA was to protect interstate commerce by securing for employees the rights established by Section 7 of the act: to organize, to bargain collectively through representatives of their own choosing, and to engage in concerted activities for that and other purposes. In Section 8, the act specifically defined a number of employer practices as unfair to labor:

1. Interference with the efforts of employees to form, join, or assist labor organizations or to engage in concerted activities for their mutual aid or protection [Section 8(a)(1)].
2. Domination of a labor organization or contribution of financial or other support to it [Section 8(a)(2)].
3. Discrimination in the hiring or awarding of tenure to employees because of union affiliation [Section 8(a)(3)].
4. Discrimination against employees for filing charges under the act or giving testimony under the act [Section 8(a)(4)].
5. Refusal to bargain collectively with the duly designated representative of the employees [Section 8(a)(5)].

Another purpose of the act was to promote fair and just settlements of disputes by peaceful processes and to avoid industrial warfare. The act created the National Labor Relations Board (NLRB) to oversee elections and to prevent employers from engaging in unfair and illegal union activities and unfair labor practices. The board was granted investigatory powers and was authorized to issue and serve complaints against employers in response to employee charges of unfair labor practices. The board was further empowered to issue cease-and-desist orders—which could be enforced by a federal court of appeals if necessary—when violations were found.

Criticisms of the Act

Employers viewed the Wagner Act as a drastic piece of legislation, and the bill elicited a great deal of opposition. Those who opposed the act claimed that it did not come under the commerce clause of the U.S. Constitution and therefore Congress had no power to act. Those who were willing to admit that it did fall under the commerce clause claimed that it created an undue burden, which therefore rendered it unconstitutional. The constitutionality of the act was tested in 1937 in *National Labor Relations Board v. Jones & Laughlin Steel Corp.*[a] In its decision, the United States Supreme Court held that the act and its application were constitutionally valid.

---

a. 301 U.S. 1, 57 S.Ct. 615, 81 L.Ed. 893 (1937).

Union elections, for example, are regulated by the Landrum-Griffin Act, which requires that regularly scheduled elections of officers occur and that secret ballots be used. Ex-convicts and Communists are prohibited from holding union office. Moreover, union officials are made accountable for union property and funds. Members have the right to attend and to participate in union meetings, to nominate officers, and to vote in most union proceedings.

Coverage and Procedures

Coverage of the federal labor laws is broad and extends to all employers whose business activity either involves or affects interstate commerce. Some workers are specifically excluded from these laws. Railroads and airlines are not covered by the NLRA but are covered by a separate act, the Railway Labor Act, which closely parallels the NLRA. Other types of workers, such as agricultural workers and domestic servants, are excluded from the NLRA and have no coverage under separate legislation.

When a union or employee believes that the employer has violated federal labor law (or vice versa), the union or employee files a charge with a regional office of the NLRB. The form for an employee to use to file an unfair labor practice charge against an employer is shown in Exhibit 19–1. The charge is investigated, and if it is found worthy, the regional director files a complaint. An administrative law judge (ALJ) initially hears the complaint and rules on it (see Chapter 7). The board reviews the ALJ's findings and decision. If the NLRB finds a violation, it may issue remedial orders (including requiring rehiring of discharged workers). The NLRB decision may be appealed to a U.S. court of appeals.

The Decision to Form or Select a Union

The key starting point for labor relations law is the decision by a company's employees to form a union, which is usually referred to in the law as their bargaining representative. Many workplaces have no union, and workers bargain individually with the employer. If the workers decide that they want the added power of collective union representation, they must follow certain steps to have a union certified. Usually, the employer will fight these efforts to unionize.

Preliminary Organizing

Suppose that a national union, such as the American Federation of Labor and Congress of Industrial Organizations (AFL–CIO), wants to organize workers who produce semiconductor chips. The union would visit a manufacturing plant of a company—SemiCo in this example. If some SemiCo workers are interested in joining the union, they must begin organizing. An essential part of the process is to decide exactly which workers will be covered in the planned union. Will all manufacturing workers be covered or just those engaged in a single step in the manufacturing process?

The first step in forming a union is to get the relevant workers to sign **authorization cards**. These cards usually state that the worker desires to have a certain union, such as the AFL–CIO, represent the work force. If those in favor of the union can obtain authorization cards from a majority of workers, they may present the cards to the employer and ask the employer, SemiCo, to recognize the union formally. SemiCo is not required to do so, however.

Authorization Card A card signed by an employee that gives a union permission to act on his or her behalf in negotiations with management once a majority of the employees has signed such cards.

Exhibit 19–1 Unfair Labor Practice Complaint Form

FORM EXEMPT UNDER 44 U.S.C. 3512

FORM NLRB-501 (8-83)	UNITED STATES OF AMERICA NATIONAL LABOR RELATIONS BOARD **CHARGE AGAINST EMPLOYER**	**DO NOT WRITE IN THIS SPACE**

Case	Date Filed

INSTRUCTIONS: File an original and 4 copies of this charge with NLRB Regional Director for the region in which the alleged unfair labor practice occurred or is occurring.

1. EMPLOYER AGAINST WHOM CHARGE IS BROUGHT

a. Name of Employer	b. Number of workers employed

c. Address (*street, city, state, ZIP code*)	d. Employer Representative	e. Telephone No.

f. Type of Establishment (*factory, mine, wholesaler, etc.*)	g. Identify principal product or service

h. The above-named employer has engaged in and is engaging in unfair labor practices within the meaning of section 8(a). subsections (1) and (list subsections) _____ of the National Labor Relations Act. and these unfair labor practices are unfair practices affecting commerce within the meaning of the Act.

2. Basis of the Charge (*be specific as to facts, names, addresses, plants involved, dates, places, etc.*)

By the above and other acts, the above-named employer has interfered with, restrained, and coerced employees in the exercise of the rights guaranteed in Section 7 of the Act.

3. Full name of party filing charge (*if labor organization, give full name, including local name and number*)

4a. Address (*street and number, city, state, and ZIP code*)	4b. Telephone No.

5. Full name of national or international labor organization of which it is an affiliate or constituent unit (*to be filled in when charge is filed by a labor organization*)

6. DECLARATION

I declare that I have read the above charge and that the statements are true to the best of my knowledge and belief.

By _____   _____
(*signature of representative or person making charge*)   (*title if any*)

Address _____   _____   _____
                                                          (*Telephone No.*)   (*date*)

WILLFUL FALSE STATEMENTS ON THIS CHARGE CAN BE PUNISHED BY FINE AND IMPRISONMENT (U.S. CODE, TITLE 18, SECTION 1001)

More frequently, authorization cards are obtained to justify an election among workers for unionization. If SemiCo refuses to recognize the union based on authorization cards, an election is necessary to determine whether unionization has majority support among the workers. After the unionizers obtain authorization cards from at least 30 percent of the workers to be represented, the unionizers present these cards to the NLRB regional office with a petition for an election.

This 30 percent support is generally considered a sufficient showing of interest to justify an election on union representation. Union backers are not required to employ authorization cards but generally must have some evidence that at least 30 percent of the relevant work force supports a union or an election on unionization.

Appropriate Bargaining Unit

The NLRB considers the employees' petition as a basis for calling an election. In addition to a sufficient showing of interest in unionization, the proposed union must represent an **appropriate bargaining unit**.

Appropriate Bargaining Unit A designation based on job duties, skill levels, and so on, of the proper entity that should be covered by a collective bargaining agreement.

Not every group of workers can form together into a single union. One key requirement of an appropriate bargaining unit is a *mutuality of interest* among all the workers to be represented. Groups of workers with significantly conflicting interests may not be represented in a single union.

JOB SIMILARITY   One factor in determining the mutuality of interest is the *similarity of the jobs* of all the workers to be unionized. The NLRB considers factors such as similar levels of skill and qualifications, similar levels of wages and benefits, and similar working conditions. If represented workers have vastly different working conditions, they are unlikely to have the mutuality of interest necessary to bargain as a single unit with their employer.

One issue of job similarity has involved companies that employ both general industrial workers and craft workers (those with specialized skills, such as electricians). On many occasions, the NLRB has found that industrial and craft workers should be represented by different unions, although this is not an absolute rule.

WORK-SITE PROXIMITY   A second important factor in determining the appropriate bargaining unit is *geographical*. If workers at only a single manufacturing plant are to be unionized, the geographical factor is not a problem. Even if the workers desire to join a national union, such as the AFL–CIO, they can join together in a single "local" division of that union. Geographical disparity may become a problem if a union is attempting to join workers at many different manufacturing sites together into a single union.

NONMANAGEMENT EMPLOYEES   A third factor to be considered is the rule against unionization of *management* employees. The labor laws differentiate between labor and management and preclude members of management from being part of a union. There is no clear-cut definition of management, but supervisors are considered management and may not be included in worker unions. A supervisor is an individual who has the discretionary authority, as a representative of the employer, to make decisions such as hiring, suspending, promoting, firing, or disciplining other workers.[7] Professional employees, in-

---

7. *Waldau v. Merit Systems Protection Board*, 19 F.3d 1395 (Fed.Cir. 1994).

cluding legal and medical personnel, may be considered labor rather than management.

Moving toward Certification

A union, then, becomes certified through a procedure that begins with petitioning the NLRB. The proposed union must present authorization cards or other evidence showing an employee interest level of at least 30 percent. The organization must also show that the proposed union represents an appropriate bargaining unit. If the workers are under the NLRA's jurisdiction and if no other union has been certified within the past twelve months for these workers, the NLRB will schedule an election.

Union Election

Labor law provides for an election to determine whether employees choose to be represented by a union and, if so, which union. The NLRB supervises this election, ensuring secret voting and voter eligibility. The election is usually held about a month after the NLRB orders the vote (although it may be much longer, if management disputes the composition of an appropriate bargaining unit). If the election is a fair one, and if the proposed union receives majority support, the board certifies the union as the bargaining representative. Otherwise, the board will not certify the union.

Sometimes, a plant with an existing union may attempt to *decertify* the union (de-unionize). Although this action may be encouraged by management, it must be conducted by the employees. This action also requires a petition to the NLRB, with a showing of 30 percent employee support and no certification within the past year. The NLRB may grant this petition and call for a decertification election.

Union Election Campaign

Union organizers may campaign among workers to solicit votes for unionization. Considerable litigation has arisen over the rights of workers and outside union supporters to conduct such campaigns.

The employer retains great control over any activities, including unionization campaigns, that take place on company property and company time. Employers may lawfully use this authority to limit the campaign activities of union supporters. • Example 19.1 Management may prohibit all solicitations and distribution of pamphlets on company property as long as it has a legitimate business reason for doing so (such as to ensure safety or to prevent interference with business). The employer may also reasonably limit the places where solicitation occurs (for example, limit it to the lunchroom), limit the times during which solicitation can take place, and prohibit all outsiders from access to the workplace. All these actions are lawful.•

Suppose that a union seeks to organize clerks at a department store. Courts have found that an employer can prohibit all solicitation in areas of the store open to the public. Union campaign activities in these circumstances could seriously interfere with the store's business.

There are some legal restrictions on management regulation of union solicitation. The key restriction is the *nondiscrimination* rule. An employer may prohibit all solicitation during work time or in certain places but may not selectively prohibit union solicitation during work time. If the employer permits political candidates to campaign on the employer's premises, for example, it also must permit union solicitation.[8]

Workers have a right to some reasonable opportunity to campaign. • **Example 19.2** The United States Supreme Court held that employees have a right to distribute a pro-union newsletter in nonworking areas on the employer's property during nonworking time. In this case, management had the burden to show some material harm from this action and could not do so.[9] •

Management Election Campaign

Management may also campaign among its workers against the union (or for decertification of an existing union). Campaign tactics, however, are carefully monitored and regulated by the NLRB. Otherwise, the economic power of management might allow coercion of the workers.

Management still has many advantages in the campaign. For example, management is allowed to call all workers together during work time and make a speech against unionization. Management need not give the union supporters an equal opportunity for rebuttal. The NLRB does restrict what management may say in such a speech, however.

NO THREATS In campaigning against the union, the employer may not make threats of reprisals if employees vote to unionize. • **Example 19.3** A supervisor may not state, "If the union wins, you'll all be fired." This would be a threat. Even if an employer says, "Our competitor's plant in town unionized, and half the workers lost their jobs," the NLRB might consider this to be a veiled threat and therefore unfair. •

An interesting controversy arose over a film that employers showed during union campaigns, *And Women Must Weep*. This film was prepared to help employers fight unionization efforts. The film dramatizes union misconduct during a strike, including vandalism, bomb threats, and attacks on neutral individuals such as a minister and an infant, who is shot and killed. Although this film is arguably inaccurate, courts have found it legal. One court wrote that "the film is a one-sided brief against unionism, devoid of significant rational content perhaps, but nevertheless not reasonably to be construed as threatening retaliation or force."[10]

"LABORATORY CONDITIONS" Obviously, union election campaigns are not like national political campaigns, in which a political party can make almost any claim. The NLRB tries to maintain "laboratory conditions" for a fair election that is unaffected by pressure. In establishing such conditions, the board considers the totality of circumstances in the campaign. The NLRB is especially strict about promises (or threats) made by the employer at the last minute, immediately before the election, because the union lacks an opportunity to respond effectively to these last-minute statements.

There is even a specific rule that prohibits an employer from making any election speech on company time, to massed assemblies of workers, within

---

8. *Nonemployee* union organizers do not have the right to trespass on an employer's property to organize employees, however. See *Lechmere, Inc. v. NLRB,* 502 U.S. 527, 112 S.Ct. 841, 117 L.Ed.2d 79 (1992).

9. *Eastex, Inc. v. NLRB,* 437 U.S. 556, 98 S.Ct. 2505, 57 L.Ed.2d 428 (1978).

10. *Luxuray of New York v. NLRB,* 447 F.2d 112 (2d Cir. 1971).

twenty-four hours of the time for voting. Such last-minute speeches are permitted only if employees attend voluntarily and on their own time.[11]

The employer is also prohibited from taking actions that might intimidate its workers. Employers may not undertake certain types of surveillance of workers or even create the impression of observing workers to identify union sympathizers. Management also is limited in its ability to question individual workers about their positions on unionization. These actions are deemed to contain implicit threats.

NLRB OPTIONS   If the employer issues threats or engages in other unfair labor practices and then wins the election, the NLRB may invalidate the results. The NLRB may certify the union, even though it lost the election, and direct the employer to recognize the union as the employees' exclusive bargaining representative. Or the NLRB may ask a court to order a new election.

Collective Bargaining

If a fair election is held and the union wins, the NLRB will certify the union as the *exclusive bargaining representative* of the workers polled. Unions may provide a variety of services to their members, but the central legal right of a union is to serve as the sole representative of the group of workers in bargaining with the employer over the workers' rights.

The concept of bargaining is at the heart of the federal labor laws. When a union is officially recognized, it may make a demand to bargain with the employer. The union then sits at the table opposite the representatives of management to negotiate contracts for its workers. The terms of employment that result from the negotiations apply to all workers in the bargaining unit, even those who do not choose to belong to the union. This process is known as **collective bargaining.** Such bargaining is like most other business negotiations, and each side uses its economic power to pressure or persuade the other side to grant concessions.

Bargaining is a somewhat vague term. Bargaining does not mean that either side must give in on demands or even that the sides must always compromise.

Collective Bargaining The process by which labor and management negotiate the terms and conditions of employment, including working hours and workplace conditions.

---

11. Political party–like electioneering on behalf of a union, on the day of a union election, however, has been held acceptable and does not invalidate the election. See *Overnite Transportation Co. v. NLRB,* 104 F.3d 109 (7th Cir. 1997).

International Perspective

Union Rights in Great Britain

A British union that has been recognized by an employer for collective bargaining purposes has certain rights. These rights include the right to receive information related to collective bargaining issues, the right to time off, the right to appoint a representative to handle safety matters, and the right to be consulted before an employer relocates its place of business.

For Critical Analysis: *Do you think employees have rights that should apply in all countries around the world under all circumstances?*

It does mean that a demand must be taken seriously and considered as part of a package to be negotiated. Most important, both sides must bargain in "good faith."

Subjects of Bargaining

A common issue in collective bargaining concerns the subjects over which the parties can bargain. The law makes certain subjects mandatory for collective bargaining. These topics cannot be "taken off the table" unilaterally but must be discussed and bargained over.

TERMS AND CONDITIONS OF EMPLOYMENT The NLRA provides that employers may bargain with workers over wages, hours of work, and other terms and conditions of employment. These are broad terms that cover many employment issues. Suppose that a union wants a contract provision granting all workers four weeks of paid vacation. The company need not give in to this demand but must at least consider it and bargain over it.

Many other employment issues are also considered appropriate subjects for collective bargaining. These include safety rules, insurance coverage, pension and other employee benefit plans, procedures for employee discipline, and procedures for employee grievances against the company. The Supreme Court has held that an employer must bargain even over the price of food sold in the company cafeteria.[12]

A few subjects are illegal in collective bargaining. Management need not bargain over a provision that would be illegal if included in a contract. Thus, if a union presents a demand for **featherbedding** (the hiring of unnecessary excess workers) or for an unlawful closed shop, management need not respond to these demands.

CLOSING OR RELOCATING A PLANT Management need not bargain with a union over the decision to close a particular facility. Similarly, management need not bargain over a decision to relocate a plant if the move involves a basic change in the nature of the employer's operation.[13] Management may choose to bargain over such decisions, however, to obtain concessions on other bargaining subjects.

Management must bargain over the economic consequences of such decisions. Thus, issues such as **severance pay** (compensation for the termination of employment) in the event of a plant shutdown are appropriate for collective bargaining. Also, if a relocation does *not* involve a basic change in the nature of an operation, management must bargain over the decision unless it can show (1) that the work performed at the new location varies significantly from the work performed at the former plant; (2) that the work performed at the former plant is to be discontinued entirely and not moved to the new location; (3) that the move involves a change in the scope and direction of the enterprise; (4) that labor costs were not a factor in the decision; or (5) that even if labor costs were a factor, the union could not have offered concessions that would have changed the decision to relocate.

> "I see an America where the workers are really free and through their great unions . . . can take their proper place in the council tables with the owners and managers of business."
>
> Franklin D. Roosevelt, 1882–1945
> (Thirty-second president of the United States, 1932–1945)

Featherbedding A requirement that more workers be employed to do a particular job than are actually needed.

Severance Pay Funds in excess of normal wages or salaries paid to an employee on termination of his or her employment with a company.

---

12. *Ford Motor Co. v. NLRB*, 441 U.S. 488, 99 S.Ct. 1842, 60 L.Ed.2d 420 (1979).
13. *Dubuque Packing Co.*, 303 N.L.R.B. No. 386 (1991).

Good Faith Bargaining

Parties engaged in collective bargaining often claim that the other side is not bargaining in good faith, as required by labor law. Although good faith is a matter of subjective intent, a party's actions are used to evaluate the finding of good or bad faith in bargaining.

Obviously, the employer must be willing to meet with union representatives. Excessive delaying tactics may be proof of bad faith, as is insistence on obviously unreasonable contract terms. Suppose that a company makes a single overall contract offer on a "take it or leave it" basis and refuses to consider modifications of individual terms. This also is considered bad faith in bargaining.

While bargaining is going on, management may not make unilateral changes in important working conditions, such as wages or hours of employment. These changes must be bargained over. Once bargaining reaches an impasse, management may make such unilateral changes. The law also includes an exception permitting unilateral changes in cases of business necessity.

A series of decisions have found other actions to constitute bad faith in bargaining, including the following:

- Engaging in a campaign among workers to undermine the union.
- Constantly shifting positions on disputed contract terms.
- Sending bargainers who lack authority to commit the company to a contract.

If an employer (or a union) refuses to bargain in good faith without justification, it has committed an unfair labor practice, and the other party may petition the NLRB for an order requiring good faith bargaining. Except in extreme cases, the NLRB does not have authority to require a party to accede to any specific contract terms. The NLRB may require a party to reimburse the other side for its litigation expenses.

A party to collective bargaining may be excused from bargaining when the other party refuses to bargain. The following case illustrates this situation.

Case 19.3 ● Stroehmann Bakeries, Inc. v. NLRB

United States Court of Appeals,
Second Circuit, 1996.
95 F.3d 218.
http://www.findlaw.com/
casecode/courts/2nd.html[a]

Background and Facts Stroehmann Bakeries, Inc., operated a distribution center for its baked goods in Syracuse, New York, where employees—known as shippers—loaded the goods onto local delivery trucks. The shippers were represented by a union. When their collective bargaining agreement expired, Stroehmann

proposed eliminating their positions. In subsequent negotiations, the company admitted that it could obtain the capital to keep the Syracuse center open and proposed cutting only half of the positions. The union asked Stroehmann for extensive financial information, including lists of customers and sales accounts, accounts payable journals, supplier invoices, production reports, employee compensation, and employee pension plans. The company refused to comply with the request and, when the union did not return to the negotiations, declared that bargaining was at an impasse. Ten days later, Stroehmann eliminated the shippers' jobs. The National Labor Relations Board ordered the company to reinstate the shippers. Stroehmann asked the U.S. Court of Appeals for the Second Circuit to deny enforcement of the order.

(Continued)

---

a. This page contains links to opinions of the U.S. Court of Appeals for the Second Circuit. In the "Browsing" section, in the "1996" row, click on "Sept." When that page opens, scroll down the list of cases to the *Stroehmann* case and click on the case name to access the opinion.

Case 19.3 Continued

In the Words of the Court . . .
WINTER, Circuit Judge.

* * * *

Once Stroehmann conceded that it had access to capital sufficient to continue the Syracuse shipping unit, the Union's need for financial information to bargain intelligently was virtually non-existent. * * * Stroehmann did not enter the negotiations with a closed mind but rather offered proposals in response to the Union's request for ways to save jobs. It was the Union that refused to bargain after it made a request for financial information [that was denied].

The comprehensive and detailed information requested by the Union had virtually no relevance to the issues at stake in bargaining * * * . We conclude, therefore, that Stroehmann was under no obligation to respond to the voluminous requests for information submitted by the Union.

Because Stroehmann's refusal to furnish the information was permissible, it was entitled to declare an impasse when the Union refused to return to the bargaining table. The unilateral decision to close the shipping unit was, therefore, lawful.

Decision and Remedy The U.S. Court of Appeals for the Second Circuit denied enforcement of the NLRB's order. The company acted within its rights in eliminating the shippers' jobs.

For Critical Analysis—Political Consideration *Why might a union (or an employee) make "voluminous requests for information" and refuse to bargain if the requests are not met?*

Strikes

The law does not require parties to reach a contract agreement in collective bargaining. Even when parties have bargained in good faith, they may be unable to reach a final agreement. When extensive collective bargaining has been conducted and the parties still cannot agree, an impasse has been reached.

When bargaining has reached an impasse, the union may call a strike against the employer to pressure it into making concessions. A strike occurs when the unionized workers leave their jobs and refuse to work. The workers also typically picket the plant, standing outside the facility with signs that complain of management's unfairness. (Additionally, they might organize a *cyber demonstration*, as discussed in this chapter's *Legal E-nvironment* feature.)

A strike is an extreme action. Striking workers lose their right to be paid. Management loses production and may lose customers, whose orders cannot be filled. Labor law regulates the circumstances and conduct of strikes. Most strikes are "economic strikes," which are initiated because the union wants a better contract. A union may also strike when the employer has engaged in unfair labor practices.

The right to strike is guaranteed by the NLRA, within limits, and strike activities, such as picketing, are protected by the free speech guarantee of the First Amendment to the Constitution. Nonworkers have a right to participate in picketing an employer. The NLRA also gives workers the right to refuse to cross a picket line of fellow workers who are engaged in a lawful strike. Not all strikes are lawful, however.

Legal *e*-nvironment

Cyber Picketing and Cyber Demonstrations

The Internet has affected virtually every economic activity. Not surprisingly, the Internet has become a powerful tool for organizing labor activities, such as picketing and demonstrations, and promoting union goals.

International Cyber Demonstrations

Today, with the simple click of a mouse, members in various unions throughout the world can be notified of a multinational company's allegedly unfair labor practice—and the union members can respond as easily. One of the first cyber demonstrations occurred in the mid-1990s when Bridgestone-Firestone Tire was facing a strike. After Bridgestone-Firestone had fired and replaced 2,300 striking employees, the International Federation of Chemical Workers Unions (IFCWU) decided it needed to do something. So it sent out a message via the Internet to all of its members throughout the world. The message requested members to inundate Bridgestone-Firestone management with e-mail protesting what had happened. The federation also had its members send e-mail messages to management personnel at automobile tire resale outlets, as well as at the banks and other corporations that did business with Bridgestone-Firestone, informing these groups of Bridgestone-Firestone's actions.

Prior to the mid-1990s, campaigns such as the one against Bridgestone-Firestone normally were conducted using faxes. The difference between the two types of campaigns is remarkable. According to Vic Thorpe, the general secretary of the IFCWU, at the time the demonstration against Bridgestone-Firestone was being organized, to send one fax to 150 unions associated with the federation required several hours and a huge phone bill.[a] In contrast, to send e-mail messages around the globe is nearly instantaneous and costs virtually nothing.

Enlisting Support from Other Groups

When unions want to put pressure on a particular employer, they can also engage consumers and others in their fight. This can be done through individual e-mail messages, as well as through specially created Web pages. An example occurred in 1997 when dockers were on strike in Liverpool, England. They created their own Web home page, which they claimed was useful in fighting against media indifference to their cause. Their Web site declared, "The world is our picket line!" The dockers were effective at linking their Web site to various search engines, such as Yahoo, WebCrawler, Excite, and Lycos. They linked themselves to discussion forums in numerous sites dealing with union activities. One result was a sympathy cyber strike against Drake International, one of the two companies providing replacement workers for the striking Liverpool dockers. This cyber strike was organized by Canadian union members.

For Critical Analysis: *With respect to labor-management relations, does the Internet offer similar advantages to employers as well?*

---

a. *Libération*, April 25, 1997, Multimedia Section, p. ii.

Illegal Strikes

An otherwise lawful strike may become illegal because of the conduct of the strikers. Violent strikes (including the threat of violence) are illegal. The use of violence against management employees or substitute workers is illegal. Certain forms of "massed picketing" are also illegal. If the strikers form a barrier and deny management or other nonunion workers access to the plant, the strike is illegal. Similarly, "sit-down" strikes, in which employees simply stay in the plant without working, are illegal.

SECONDARY BOYCOTTS A strike directed against someone other than the strikers' employer, such as the companies that sell materials to the employer, is a **secondary boycott**. Suppose that the unionized workers of SemiCo (our hypothetical semiconductor company) go out on strike. To increase their

Secondary Boycott A union's refusal to work for, purchase from, or handle the products of a secondary employer, with whom the union has no dispute, for the purpose of forcing that employer to stop doing business with the primary employer, with whom the union has a labor dispute.

Striking workers picket to publicize their labor dispute. Why is the right to strike important to unions?

economic leverage, the workers picket the leading suppliers and customers of SemiCo in an attempt to hurt the company's business. SemiCo is considered the primary employer, and its suppliers and customers are considered secondary employers. Picketing of the suppliers or customers is a secondary boycott, which was made illegal by the Taft-Hartley Act.

Common Situs Picketing. A controversy may arise in a strike when both the primary employer and a secondary employer occupy the same job site. In this case, it may be difficult to distinguish between lawful picketing of the primary employer and an unlawful strike against a secondary employer. The law permits a union to picket a site occupied by both primary and secondary employers, an act called **common situs picketing**. If evidence indicates that the strike is directed against the secondary employer, however, it may become illegal. • **Example 19.4** If a union sends a threatening letter to the secondary employer about the strike, that fact may show that the picketing includes an illegal secondary boycott.•

Common Situs Picketing
The illegal picketing of a primary employer's site by workers who are involved in a labor dispute with a secondary employer.

Hot-Cargo Agreements. In what is called a **hot-cargo agreement**, employers voluntarily agree with unions not to handle, use, or deal in non-union-produced goods of other employers. This particular type of secondary boycott was *not* made illegal by the Taft-Hartley Act, because that act only prevented unions from inducing *employees* to strike or otherwise act to force employers not to handle these goods. The Landrum-Griffin Act addressed this problem:

Hot-Cargo Agreement An agreement in which employers voluntarily agree with unions not to handle, use, or deal in non-union-produced goods of other employers; a type of secondary boycott explicitly prohibited by the Labor-Management Reporting and Disclosure Act of 1959.

> It shall be [an] unfair labor practice for any labor organization and any employer to enter into any contract or any agreement . . . whereby such employer . . . agrees to refrain from handling, using, selling, transporting or otherwise dealing in any of the products of any other employer, or to cease doing business with any other person.

Hot-cargo agreements are therefore illegal. Parties injured by an illegal hot-cargo agreement or other secondary boycott may sue the union for damages.

A union may legally urge consumer boycotts of the primary employer, even at the site of a secondary employer. • **Example 19.5** Suppose that a union is on strike against SemiCo, which manufactures semiconductors that are bought by Intellect, Inc., a distributor of electronic components. Intellect sells SemiCo's semiconductors to computer manufacturers. The striking workers can urge the manufacturers not to buy SemiCo's products. The workers cannot urge a total boycott of Intellect, as that would constitute a secondary boycott.•

WILDCAT STRIKES A **wildcat strike** occurs when a minority group of workers, perhaps dissatisfied with a union's representation, calls its own strike. The union is the exclusive bargaining representative of a group of workers, and only the union can call a strike. A wildcat strike, unauthorized by the certified union, is illegal.

> **Wildcat Strike** A strike that is not authorized by the union that ordinarily represents the striking employees.

  • **Example 19.6** In one case, several concrete workers left their jobs because it was raining and went on "strike." The court found the strike illegal because it was not preceded by a demand on the employer for action and because the employer had made shelter available for the workers and paid them for waiting time.•

STRIKES THAT THREATEN NATIONAL HEALTH OR SAFETY The law also places some restrictions on strikes that threaten national health or safety. The law does not prohibit such strikes, nor does it require the settlement of labor disputes that threaten the national welfare. The Taft-Hartley Act simply provides time to encourage the settlement of these disputes, called the "cooling-off period."

One of the most controversial aspects of the Taft-Hartley Act was the establishment of this **eighty-day cooling-off period**—a provision allowing federal courts to issue injunctions against strikes that would create a national emergency. The president of the United States can obtain a court injunction that will last for eighty days, and presidents have occasionally used this provision. During these eighty days, the president and other government officials can work with the employer and the union to produce a settlement and avoid a strike that may cause a national emergency.

> **Eighty-Day Cooling-Off Period** A provision of the Taft-Hartley Act that allows federal courts to issue injunctions against strikes that might create a national emergency.

STRIKES THAT CONTRAVENE NO-STRIKE CLAUSES A strike may also be illegal if it contravenes a **no-strike clause**. The previous collective bargaining agreement between a union and an employer may have contained a clause in which the union agreed not to strike (a no-strike clause). The law permits the employer to enforce this no-strike clause and obtain an injunction against the strike in some circumstances.

> **No-Strike Clause** Provision in a collective bargaining agreement that states the employees will not strike for any reason and labor disputes will be resolved by arbitration.

The Supreme Court held that a no-strike clause could be enforced with an injunction if the contract contained a clause providing for arbitration of unresolved disputes.[14] The Court held that the arbitration clause was an effective substitute for the right to strike. In the absence of an applicable arbitration provision, however, an employer cannot enjoin (forbid) a strike, even if the contract contains a no-strike clause.

Replacement Workers

Suppose that SemiCo's workers go out on strike. SemiCo is not required to shut down its operations but may find substitute workers to replace the

---

14. *Boys Markets, Inc. v. Retail Clerks Local 770*, 398 U.S. 235, 90 S.Ct. 1583, 26 L.Ed.2d 199 (1970).

strikers, if possible. These substitute workers are often called "scabs" by union supporters. An employer may even give the replacement workers permanent positions with the company.

In the 1930s and 1940s, strikes were powerful in part because employers often had difficulty finding trained replacements to keep their businesses running during strikes. Since the illegal air traffic controller strike in 1981, when President Ronald Reagan successfully hired replacement workers, employers have increasingly used this strategy, with considerable success. • **Example 19.7** Even the National Football League (NFL), when struck by the players in 1987, found replacements to play for the NFL teams. Although some scoffed at the ability of the replacement players, the tactic was largely successful for management, as the strike was called off after only three weeks.• An employer can even use an employment agency to recruit replacement workers.[15]

Rights of Strikers after the Strike

An important issue concerns the rights of strikers after the strike ends. In a typical economic strike over working conditions, the strikers have no right to return to their jobs. If satisfactory replacement workers have been found, the strikers may find themselves out of work. The law does prohibit the employer from discriminating against former strikers. Even if the employer fires all the strikers and retains all the replacement workers, former strikers must be rehired to fill any new vacancies. Former strikers who are rehired retain their seniority rights.

Different rules apply when a union strikes because the employer has engaged in unfair labor practices. If an employer is discriminating against a union's workers, they may go out on an unfair labor practice strike. Furthermore, an economic strike may become an unfair labor practice strike if the employer refuses to bargain in good faith. In the case of an unfair labor practice strike, the employer may still hire replacements but must give the strikers back their jobs once the strike is over. An employer may, however, refuse to rehire unfair labor practice strikers if the strike was deemed unlawful or if there is simply no longer any work for them to do.

Lockouts

Lockout The closing of a plant to employees by an employer to gain leverage in collective bargaining negotiations.

Lockouts are the employer's counterpart to the worker's right to strike. A **lockout** occurs when the employer shuts down to prevent employees from working. Lockouts are usually used when the employer believes that a strike is imminent.

Lockouts may be a legal employer response. • **Example 19.8** In the leading Supreme Court case on this issue, a union and an employer had reached a stalemate in collective bargaining. The employer feared that the union would delay a strike until the busy season and thereby cause the employer to suffer more greatly from the strike. The employer called a lockout before the busy season to deny the union this leverage, and the Supreme Court held that this action was legal.[16]•

---

15. *Professional Staff Nurses Association v. Dimensions Health Corp.*, 110 Md.App. 270, 677 A.2d 87 (1996).
16. *American Ship Building Co. v. NLRB*, 380 U.S. 300, 85 S.Ct. 955, 13 L.Ed.2d 855 (1965).

Some lockouts are illegal, however. An employer may not use its lockout weapon as a tool to break the union and pressure employees into decertification. Consequently, an employer must show some economic justification for instituting a lockout.

Unfair Labor Practices

The preceding sections have discussed unfair labor practices in the significant acts of union elections, collective bargaining, and strikes. Many unfair labor practices may occur within the normal working relationship as well. The most significant of these practices are discussed below. Exhibit 19–2 lists the basic unfair labor practices.

Employer's Refusal to Recognize the Union and to Negotiate

As noted above, once a union has been certified as the exclusive representative of a bargaining unit, an employer must recognize and bargain in good faith with the union over issues affecting all employees who are within the bargaining unit. Failure to do so is an unfair labor practice. Because the National Labor Relations Act embraces a policy of majority rule, certification of the union as the bargaining unit's representative binds *all* of the employees in that bargaining unit. Thus, the union must fairly represent all the members of the bargaining unit.[17]

PRESUMPTION OF EMPLOYEE SUPPORT   Certification does not mean that a union will continue indefinitely as the exclusive representative of the bargaining unit. If the union loses the majority support of those it represents, an employer is not obligated to continue recognition of, or negotiation with, the union. As a practical matter, a newly elected representative needs time to establish itself among the workers and to begin to formulate and implement its programs. Therefore, as a matter of labor policy, a union is immune from attack by employers and from repudiation by the employees for a period of one

---

17. Thus, when an employee has a grievance against the employer, the union cannot arbitrarily ignore it or handle it perfunctorily, although a union does not have to pursue all employee grievances to arbitration. See *Vaca v. Sipes*, 386 U.S. 171, 87 S.Ct. 903, 17 L.Ed.2d 842 (1967).

Exhibit 19–2 Basic Unfair Labor Practices

Employers *It is unfair to . . .*	**Unions** *It is unfair to . . .*
1. Refuse to recognize a union and refuse to bargain in good faith.	1. Refuse to bargain in good faith.
2. Interfere with, restrain, or coerce employees in their efforts to form a union and bargain collectively.	2. Picket to coerce unionization without the majority's support of the employees.
3. Dominate a union.	3. Demand the hiring of unnecessary excess workers.
4. Discriminate against union workers.	4. Discriminate against nonunion workers.
5. Agree to participate in a secondary boycott.	5. Agree to participate in a secondary boycott.
6. Punish employees for engaging in concerted activity.	6. Engage in an illegal strike.
	7. Charge excessive membership fees.

year after certification. During this period, it is *presumed* that the union enjoys majority support among the employees; the employer cannot refuse to deal with the union as the employees' exclusive representative, even if the employees prefer not to be represented by that union.

Beyond the one-year period, the presumption of majority support continues, but it is *rebuttable*. An employer may rebut (refute) the presumption with objective evidence that a majority of employees do not wish to be represented by the union. If the evidence is sufficient to support a *good faith* belief that the union no longer enjoys majority support among the employees, the employer may refuse to continue to recognize and negotiate with the union.[18]

QUESTIONS OF MAJORITY SUPPORT   A delicate question arises during a strike in which an employer hires replacement workers. Specifically, should it be *assumed* that the replacement workers do not support the union? If they do not, and if as a result the union no longer has majority support, the employer need not continue negotiating with the union.

Another question arises when two companies merge or consolidate, when one company buys the assets or stock of another, or when, under any other circumstances, one employer steps into the shoes of another. Is a collective bargaining agreement between a union and a predecessor employer binding on the union and the successor employer? This was the issue in the following case.

---

18. An employer cannot agree to a collective bargaining agreement and later refuse to abide by it, however, on the ground of a good faith belief that the union did not have majority support when the agreement was negotiated. See *Auciello Iron Works, Inc. v. NLRB,* 517 U.S. 781, 116 S.Ct. 1754, 135 L.Ed.2d 64 (1996).

Case 19.4 ● Canteen Corp. v. NLRB

United States Court of Appeals, Seventh Circuit, 1997.
103 F.3d 1355.
http://www.ca7.uscourts.gov[a]

Background and Facts   The food service employees at the Medical College of Wisconsin were represented by the Hotel Employees and Restaurant Employees Union. When Canteen Corporation took over the food service, it agreed to negotiate a new contract with the union. Meanwhile, without informing the union, Canteen told the employees that their wages would be cut 20 to 25 percent. The employees resigned. Canteen then recruited employees from other sources and refused to negotiate with the union on the ground that it no longer represented the employees. The union filed an unfair labor practice charge with the National Labor Relations Board (NLRB). The NLRB ordered Canteen to reinstate the employees at their previous wage rates until a new contract could be negotiated. Canteen asked the U.S. Court of Appeals for the Seventh Circuit to review the order.

---

a. This page provides access to some of the opinions of the U.S. Court of Appeals for the Seventh Circuit, which maintains this Web site. In the left column, click on "Judicial Opinions." When that page opens, in the box under "Last Name or Corporation," enter "Canteen," select "Begins," and click "Search for Person." From the results, click on docket number "95-2736" next to the case name to access the opinion.

In the Words of the Court . . .
RIPPLE, Circuit Judge.

* * * *

* * * A new employer must consult with the union when it is clear that the employer intends to hire the employees of its predecessor as the initial workforce. * * *

Case 19.4 Continued

* * * *

* * * The totality of Canteen's conduct demonstrated that it was perfectly clear that Canteen planned to retain the predecessor employees.

* * *

* * * Canteen's intention to retain the * * * employees was backed by an expectation so strong that it neglected to take serious steps to recruit from other sources until it was informed that they had rejected job offers. * * * Canteen intended from the outset to hire all of the predecessor employees and did not mention in [its] discussions [with the union] the possibility of any other changes in its initial terms and conditions of employment.

Decision and Remedy The U.S. Court of Appeals for the Seventh Circuit ordered that the NLRB's order be enforced. The employer was required to reinstate the employees at their previous wage rates until a new contract could be negotiated.

For Critical Analysis—Social Consideration *Why should an employer be forced to honor a collective bargaining agreement between a union and the employer's predecessor?*

Employer's Interference in Union Activities

The NLRA declares it to be an unfair labor practice for an employer to interfere with, restrain, or coerce employees in the exercise of their rights to form a union and bargain collectively. Unlawful employer interference may take a variety of forms.

Courts have found it an unfair labor practice for an employer to make threats that may interfere with an employee's decision to join a union. Even asking employees about their views on the union may be considered coercive. Employees responding to such questioning must be able to remain anonymous and must receive assurances against employer reprisals. Employers also may not prohibit certain forms of union activity in the workplace. If an employee has a grievance with the company, the employer cannot prevent the union's participation in support of the employee, for example.

If an employer has unlawfully interfered with the operation of a union, the NLRB or a reviewing court may issue a cease-and-desist order halting the practice. The company typically is required to post the order on a bulletin board and renounce its past unlawful conduct.

Employer's Domination of Union

In the early days of unionization, employers fought back by forming employer-sponsored unions to represent employees. These "company unions" were seldom more than the puppets of management. The NLRA outlawed company unions and any other form of employer domination of workers' unions.

A number of acts are considered unfair labor practices under the law against employer domination. For example, an employer can have no say in which employees belong to the union or which employees serve as union officers. Nor may supervisors or other management personnel participate in union meetings.

Company actions that support a union may be considered improper potential domination. For this reason, a company cannot give union workers pay for time spent on union activities, because this is considered undue support for the union. The company may not provide financial aid to a union and may not solicit workers to join a union.

Employer's Discrimination against Union Employees

The NLRA prohibits employers from discriminating against workers because they are union officers or are otherwise associated with a union. When workers must be laid off, the company cannot consider union participation as a criterion for deciding whom to fire.

The provisions prohibiting discrimination also apply to hiring decisions. • **Example 19.9** Suppose that certain employees of SemiCo are represented by a union, but the company is attempting to weaken the union's strength. The company is prohibited from requiring potential new hires to guarantee that they will not join the union.•

Discriminatory punishment of union members or officers can be difficult to prove. The company will claim to have good reasons for its action. The NLRB has specified a series of factors to be considered in determining whether an action had an unlawful, discriminatory motivation. These include giving inconsistent reasons for the action, applying rules inconsistently and more strictly against union members, failing to give an expected warning prior to discharge or other discipline, and acting contrary to worker seniority.

• **Example 19.10** In one case, an employer, Wright Line, fired an employee, Bernard Lamoureux, for knowingly altering time reports and payroll records. Lamoureux conceded that he had not worked the precise hours he reported on his time card but claimed that he had worked an equivalent number of hours at other times. Lamoureux had been a leading union advocate. The NLRB found that the company had shown particular dislike for Lamoureux because it considered him to be the "union kingpin" in the company. In addition, the company had never before discharged a worker for this type of violation. The NLRB found that this was sufficient evidence of discrimination to shift the burden of proof to the company to demonstrate that it had not had a discriminatory motive. The company could not meet this burden, and the discharge was held unlawful.[19]•

The decision to close a facility cannot be made with a discriminatory motive. If a company has several facilities and only one is unionized, the company cannot shut down the union plant simply because of the union. The company could shut down the union plant if it were demonstrably less efficient than the other facilities, however.

Union's Unfair Labor Practices

Certain union activities are declared to be unfair labor practices by the Taft-Hartley Act. Secondary boycotts, discussed above, are one such union unfair labor practice.

COERCION   Another significant union unfair labor practice is coercion or restraint on an employee's decision to participate in or refrain from participating in union activities. Obviously, it is unlawful for a union to threaten an employee or a family with violence for failure to join the union. The law's pro-

---

19. *Wright Line, a Division of Wright Line, Inc.*, 251 N.L.R.B. No. 150 (1980).

hibition includes economic coercion as well. Suppose that a union official declares, "We have a lot of power here; you had better join the union, or you may lose your job." This threat is an unfair labor practice.

The NLRA provides unions with the authority to regulate their own internal affairs, which includes disciplining union members. This discipline cannot be used in an improperly coercive fashion, however. ● **Example 19.11** Suppose a disaffected union member feels that the union is no longer providing proper representation for employees and starts a campaign to decertify the union. The union may expel the employee from membership but may not fine or otherwise discipline the worker.●

DISCRIMINATION Another significant union unfair labor practice is discrimination. A union may not discriminate against workers because they refuse to join. This provision also prohibits a union from using its influence to cause an employer to discriminate against workers who refuse to join the union. A union cannot force an employer to deny promotions to workers who fail to join the union.

OTHER UNFAIR PRACTICES Other union unfair labor practices include featherbedding, participation in picketing to coerce unionization without majority employee support, and refusal to engage in good faith bargaining with employer representatives.

Unions are allowed to bargain for certain "union security clauses" in contracts. Although closed shops are illegal, a union can bargain for a provision that requires workers to contribute to the union within thirty days after they are hired. This is typically called an agency shop, or union shop, clause.

The union shop clause can compel workers to begin paying dues to the certified union but cannot require the worker to "join" the union. Dues payment can be required to prevent workers from taking the benefits of union bargaining without contributing to the union's efforts. The clause cannot require workers to contribute their efforts to the union, however, or to go out on strike.

Even a requirement of dues payment has its limits. Excessive initiation fees or dues may be illegal. Unions often use their revenues to contribute to causes or to lobby politicians. A nonunion employee subject to a union shop clause who must pay dues cannot be required to contribute to this sort of union expenditure.[20]

Rights of Nonunion Employees

Most of labor law involves the formation of unions and associated rights. Even nonunion employees have some similar rights, however. Most workers do not belong to unions, so this issue is significant. The NLRA protects concerted employee action, for example, and does not limit its protection to certified unions.

Concerted Activity

Data from the NLRB indicate that growing numbers of nonunion employees are challenging employer barriers to their **concerted action**. Protected

Concerted Action Action by employees, such as a strike or picketing, with the purpose of furthering their bargaining demands or other mutual interests.

---

20. *Communication Workers of America v. Beck,* 487 U.S. 735, 108 S.Ct. 2641, 101 L.Ed.2d 634 (1988).

concerted action is that taken by employees for their mutual benefit regarding wages, hours, or terms and conditions of employment.

Even an action by a single employee may be protected concerted activity, if that action is taken for the benefit of other employees and if the employee has at least discussed the action with other approving workers. If only a single worker engages in a protest or walkout, the employer will not be liable for an unfair labor practice if it fires the worker unless the employer is aware that this protest or walkout is concerted activity taken with the assent of other workers. Sometimes the mutual interest of other workers should be obvious to the employer, however.

Safety

A common circumstance for nonunion activity is concern over workplace safety. The Labor-Management Relations Act authorizes an employee to walk off the job if he or she has a good faith belief that the working conditions are abnormally dangerous. The employer cannot lawfully discharge the employee under these conditions.

● **Example 19.12** Suppose that Knight Company operates a plant building mobile homes. A large ventilation fan at the plant blows dust and abrasive materials into the faces of workers. The workers have complained, but Knight Company has done nothing. The workers finally refuse to work until the fan is modified, and Knight fires them. The NLRB will find that the walkout is a protected activity and can command Knight to rehire the workers with back pay.●

To be protected under federal labor law, a safety walkout must be *concerted* activity. If a single worker walks out over a safety complaint, other workers must be affected by the safety issue for the walkout to be protected under the LMRA.

Employee Committees

Personnel specialists note that worker problems are often attributable to a lack of communication between labor and management. In a nonunion work force, a company may wish to create some institution to communicate with workers and act together with them to improve workplace conditions.

Employee Committee
Committee created by an employer and composed of representatives of management and nonunion employees to act together to improve workplace conditions.

This institution, generally called an **employee committee,** is composed of representatives from both management and labor. The committee meets periodically and has some authority to create rules. The committee gives employees a forum to voice their dissatisfaction with certain conditions and gives management a conduit to inform workers fully of policy decisions.

The creation of an employee committee may be entirely motivated by good intentions on the company's part and may serve the interests of workers as well as management. Nevertheless, employee committees are fraught with potential problems under federal labor laws, and management must be aware of these difficulties.

The central problem with employee committees is that they may become the functional equivalent of unions dominated by management, in violation of the NLRA. Thus, these committees cannot perform union functions. ● **Example 19.13** The employee representatives on such a committee should not present a package of proposals on wages and terms of employment, because this is the role of a union negotiating committee.●

In the following case, a union complained that an employer had committed an unfair labor practice by maintaining an employee committee.

Case 19.5 ● In re Simmons Industries, Inc.

National Labor Relations Board, 1996.
321 N.L.R.B. No. 32.

Historical and Social Setting *In the 1930s and 1940s, after Congress enacted the first laws protecting unions, union membership as a percentage of the work force grew rapidly, until about a third of all workers belonged to unions. As the size of the work force continued to grow, however, the number of workers belonging to unions did not increase proportionately. By the mid-1990s, union members made up only about 15 percent of the work force. Unions, which have sometimes been frustrated by employees' reluctance to organize, often blame unsuccessful attempts to unionize a particular employer's work force on the employer.*

Background and Facts Simmons Industries, Inc., operated chicken processing plants. One of

Simmons's customers was Kentucky Fried Chicken (KFC). To satisfy KFC's concerns with quality, Simmons formed at each plant a total quality management (TQM) committee. Simmons appointed managers and employees from a cross section of the plants to serve on the committees and set the committees' agendas, which included such topics as employee bonuses and absences. Later, the United Food and Commercial Workers Union attempted unsuccessfully to organize the employees. The union filed a complaint with the National Labor Relations Board (NLRB), alleging that Simmons had committed unfair labor practices by, among other things, maintaining a TQM committee at its plant in Jay, Oklahoma. The union argued that the committee was a "labor organization" dominated by management in violation of the National Labor Relations Act (NLRA).

In the Words of the NLRB . . .
DECISION AND ORDER

* * * *

* * * [T]he concept of "labor organization" * * * includes very loose, informal, unstructured, and irregular meeting groups. Such a loose organization will meet the [NLRA] definition if: (1) employees participate, (2) the organization exists, at least in part, for the purpose of dealing with employers, and (3) these dealings concern conditions of work or concern other statutory subjects such as grievances, labor disputes, wages, rates of pay, or hours of employment.

* * * *

* * * [E]mployee members [of the TQM committee] were representative of each * * * grouping of employees. * * * [T]he Committee discussed and made proposals solicited by [Simmons] with respect to the formulation and implementation of an incentive bonus pay program, clearly a mandatory bargaining subject. [Simmons] accepted some of the committee's proposals and guided itself by others in formulating the bonus plan. * * * Furthermore, the * * * Committee continued * * * to discuss and make proposals with respect to employee discipline, attendance and punctuality problems and employee courtesy breaks. On recommendations based in large part on employee member complaints, the plant manager issued a set of rules that clearly affected these conditions of employment and mandatory bargaining subjects. Thus the * * * Committee * * * effectively constituted a representational employee committee, in effect a labor organization, which was unlawfully dominated, interfered with in operation and administration, and rendered unlawful assistance to by [Simmons] in violation of [the NLRA].

Decision and Remedy The NLRB ordered Simmons to, among other things, "[i]mmediately disestablish and cease giving assistance or any other support" to its TQM committee.[a]

For Critical Analysis—Technological Consideration *How might an employer give employees a forum to voice their dissatisfaction with certain conditions without forming an illegal employee committee?*

---

a. This decision was an application of the principle declared in the leading case in this area, *Electromation, Inc.,* 309 N.L.R.B. 990 (1992).

Key Terms

appropriate bargaining unit 556	eighty-day cooling-off period 565	right-to-work law 552
authorization card 554	employee committee 572	secondary boycott 563
closed shop 552	featherbedding 560	severance pay 560
collective bargaining 559	hot-cargo agreement 564	union shop 552
common situs picketing 564	lockout 566	wildcat strike 565
concerted action 571	no-strike clause 565	yellow dog contract 549

Chapter Summary • Labor-Management Relations

Federal Labor Law
(See pages 549–554.)

1. **Norris-LaGuardia Act of 1932**—Extended legal protection to peaceful strikes, picketing, and boycotts. Restricted the power of the courts to issue injunctions against unions engaged in peaceful strikes.

2. **National Labor Relations Act of 1935 (Wagner Act)**—Established the rights of employees to engage in collective bargaining and to strike. Created the National Labor Relations Board (NLRB) to oversee union elections and prevent employers from engaging in unfair labor practices (such as refusing to recognize and negotiate with a certified union or interfering in union activities).

3. **Labor-Management Relations Act of 1947 (Taft-Hartley Act)**—Extended to employers protections already enjoyed by employees. Provided a list of activities prohibited to unions (secondary boycotts, use of coercion or discrimination to influence employees' decisions to participate or refrain from union activities) and allowed employers to propagandize against unions before any NLRB election. Prohibited closed shops (which require that all workers belong to a union as a condition of employment), allowed states to pass right-to-work laws, and provided for an eighty-day cooling-off period.

4. **Labor-Management Reporting and Disclosure Act of 1959 (Landrum-Griffin Act)**—Regulated internal union business procedures and union elections. Imposed restrictions on the types of persons who may serve as union officers and outlawed hot-cargo agreements.

Union Organizing
(See pages 554–559.)

1. **Authorization cards**—Before beginning an organizing effort, a union will attempt to assess worker support for unionization by obtaining signed authorization cards from the employees. It can then ask the employer to recognize the union, or it can submit the cards with a petition to the National Labor Relations Board.

2. **Appropriate bargaining unit**—In determining whether workers constitute an appropriate bargaining unit, the NLRB will consider whether the skills, tasks, and jobs of the workers are sufficiently similar so that they can all be adequately served by a single negotiating position.

3. **Union election campaign**—The NLRB is charged with monitoring union elections. During an election campaign, an employer may legally limit union activities as long as it can offer legitimate business justifications for those limitations. In regulating the union's presence on the business premises, the employer must treat the union in the same way it would treat any other entity having on-site contact with its workers. The NLRB is particularly sensitive to any threats in an employer's communications to workers, such as declarations that a union victory will result in the closing of the plant. The NLRB will also closely monitor sudden policy changes regarding compensation, hours, or working conditions that the employer makes before the election.

Chapter Summary • Labor-Management Relations

Union Organizing—continued	**4. Union certification**—Certification by the NLRB means that the union is the exclusive representative of a bargaining unit and that the employer must recognize the union and bargain in good faith with it over issues affecting all employees who are within the bargaining unit.
Collective Bargaining (See pages 559–562.)	Once a union is elected, its representatives will engage in collective bargaining with the employer. Topics such as wages, hours of work, and other conditions of employment are discussed during collective bargaining sessions. Some demands, such as a demand for featherbedding or for a closed shop, are illegal. If the parties reach an impasse, the union may call a strike against the employer to bring additional economic pressure to bear. This is one way in which the union can offset management's superior bargaining power.
Strikes and Lockouts (See pages 562–567.)	**1. Right to strike**—The right to strike is protected by the U.S. Constitution. During a strike, an employer is no longer obligated to pay union members, and union members are no longer required to show up for work.
	2. Secondary boycott—Strikers are not permitted to engage in a secondary boycott by picketing the suppliers of an employer. Similarly, striking employees are not permitted to coerce the employer's customers into agreeing not to do business with it.
	3. Wildcat strike—A wildcat strike occurs when a small group of union members engages in a strike against the employer without the permission of the union.
	4. Replacement workers—An employer may hire permanent replacement employees in the event of an economic strike. If the strike is called by the union to protest the employer's unwillingness to engage in good faith negotiations, then the employer must rehire the striking workers after the strike is settled, even if it has since replaced them with other workers.
	5. Lockouts—Employers may respond to threatened employee strikes by shutting down the plant altogether to prevent employees from working. Lockouts are used when the employer believes a strike is imminent.
Unfair Labor Practices (See pages 567–571.)	**1.** An employer's refusal to recognize or negotiate with the union, interference in union activities, domination of the union, and discrimination against union employees.
	2. A union's coercive actions against employees, discrimination against nonunion members, featherbedding, and other practices.
Rights of Nonunion Employees (See pages 571–573.)	The National Labor Relations Act protects concerted action on the part of nonunion employees. Protected concerted action includes walkouts and other activities regarding wages, hours, workplace safety, or other terms or conditions of employment.

For Review

1. What federal statutes govern labor unions and collective bargaining?
2. How does the way in which a union election is conducted protect the rights of employees and employers?
3. What type of strikes are illegal?
4. What activities are prohibited as unfair employer practices?
5. What are the rights of nonunion employees?

Questions and Case Problems

19–1. Preliminary Organizing. A group of employees at the Briarwood Furniture Company's manufacturing plant were interested in joining a union. A representative of the American Federation of Labor and Congress of Industrial Organizations (AFL–CIO) told the group that her union was prepared to represent the workers and suggested that the group members begin organizing by obtaining authorization cards from their fellow employees. After obtaining 252 authorization cards from among Briarwood's 500 nonmanagement employees, the organizers requested that the company recognize the AFL–CIO as the official representative of the employees. The company refused. Has the company violated federal labor laws? What should the organizers do?

19–2. Appropriate Bargaining Unit. The Briarwood Furniture Company, discussed in the preceding problem, employs 400 unskilled workers and 100 skilled workers in its plant. The unskilled workers operate the industrial machinery used in processing Briarwood's line of standardized plastic office furniture. The skilled workers, who work in an entirely separate part of the plant, are experienced artisans who craft Briarwood's line of expensive wood furniture products. Do you see any problems with a single union's representing all the workers at the Briarwood plant? Explain. Would your answers to Problem 19–1 change if you knew that 51 of the authorization cards had been signed by the skilled workers, with the remainder signed by the unskilled workers?

19–3. Unfair Labor Practices. Suppose that Consolidated Stores is undergoing a unionization campaign. Prior to the election, management says that the union is unnecessary to protect workers. Management also provides bonuses and wage increases to the workers during this period. The employees reject the union. Union organizers protest that the wage increases during the election campaign unfairly prejudiced the vote. Should these wage increases be regarded as an unfair labor practice? Discuss.

19–4. Unfair Labor Practices. SimpCo was engaged in ongoing negotiations over a new labor contract with the union representing the company's employees. As the deadline for expiration of the old labor contract drew near, several employees who were active in union activities were disciplined for being late to work. The union claimed that other employees had not been dealt with as harshly and that the company was discriminating on the basis of union activity. When the negotiations failed to prove fruitful and the old contract expired, the union called a strike. The company claimed the action was an economic strike to press the union's demands for higher wages. The union contended the action was an unfair labor practice strike because of the alleged discrimination. What importance does the distinction have for the striking workers and the company?

19–5. Appropriate Bargaining Unit. Westvaco operated plants that manufactured printed folding cartons, and its production and maintenance employees were represented by a union. The company hired four new technicians to work at the facility. The union argued that the technicians should be part of the unionized work force. Westvaco disputed this argument, claiming that the technicians, because of their greater skills, were not properly part of the same bargaining unit as the existing production and maintenance employees—the technicians had previously been put through an extensive and specialized training course that lasted about four months. The National Labor Relations Board agreed with the union and added the new technicians to the bargaining unit. Westvaco appealed to the court. How should the court rule? Explain fully. [*Westvaco, Virginia, Folding Box Division v. NLRB,* 795 F.2d 1171 (4th Cir. 1986)]

19–6. Secondary Boycotts. For many years, grapefruit was shipped to Japan from Fort Pierce and Port Canaveral, Florida. In 1990, Coastal Stevedoring Co. in Fort Pierce and Port Canaveral Stevedoring, Ltd., in Port Canaveral—nonunion firms—were engaged in a labor dispute with the International Longshoremen's Association (ILA). The ILA asked the National Council of Dockworkers' Unions of Japan to prevent Japanese shippers from using nonunion stevedores in Florida, and the council warned Japanese firms that their workers would not unload fruit loaded in the United States by nonunion labor. The threat caused all citrus shipments from Florida to Japan to go through Tampa, where they were loaded by stevedores represented by the ILA. Coastal, Canaveral, and others complained to the National Labor Relations Board (NLRB), alleging that the ILA's request of the Japanese unions was an illegal secondary boycott. How should the NLRB rule? [*International Longshoremen's Association, AFL–CIO,* 313 N.L.R.B. No. 53 (1993)]

19–7. Unfair Labor Practices. The Teamsters Union represented twenty-seven employees of Curtin Matheson Scientific, Inc. When a collective bargaining agreement between the union and the company expired, the company made an offer for a new agreement, which the union rejected. The company locked out the twenty-seven employees, and the union began an economic strike. The company hired replacement workers. When the union ended its strike and offered to accept the company's earlier offer, the company refused. The company also refused to bargain further, asserting doubt that the union was supported by a majority of the employees. The union sought help from the National Labor Relations Board (NLRB), which refused to presume that the replacement workers did not support the union. On the company's appeal, a court overturned the NLRB's ruling. The union appealed to the United States Supreme Court. How should the Court rule? [*NLRB v. Curtin Matheson Scientific, Inc.,* 494 U.S. 775, 110 S.Ct. 1542, 108 L.Ed.2d 801 (1990)]

19–8. Good Faith Bargaining. American Commercial Barge Line Co. was an affiliation made up of a number of barge and towing companies. The Seafarers International Union of North America (SIU) represented workers for Inland Tugs (IT), a separate corporate division of American Commercial Barge Line. When SIU and IT began negotiating a new collective bargaining agreement, SIU demanded that the bargaining unit include all the employees of American Commercial Barge Line. SIU also demanded that any contract include a pledge by other American Commercial Barge Line companies to continue their contributions to SIU funds, which provided for union activities. Unable to agree on these issues, the parties continued to meet for several years. Meanwhile, on the basis of an employee poll, IT changed its system of calculating wages. SIU filed a complaint with the NLRB, claiming that these changes were an unfair labor practice. IT responded that SIU was not bargaining in good faith. How should the NLRB rule? Explain. [*Inland Tugs, A Division of American Commercial Barge Line Co. v. NLRB,* 918 F.2d 1299 (7th Cir. 1990)]

19–9. Union Recognition. The International Association of Machinists and Aerospace Workers was certified as the exclusive representative of a unit of employees of F & A Food Sales, Inc. The employees were associated with F & A's trucking operations. The parties negotiated a collective bargaining agreement (CBA) that recognized the union as the employees' representative and reserved F & A's right to subcontract work as the company deemed necessary. Five months after negotiating the CBA, F & A subcontracted the services performed by the unit to Ryder Dedicated Logistics, Inc. Ryder operated from the same facility, used the same trucks, and employed substantially the same employees as had F & A. The union did not represent the workers while Ryder employed them. Seventeen months later, Ryder terminated the subcontract, and F & A resumed its own trucking operations with the same facility, the same trucks, and many of the same employees. The union asserted its right to represent the employees under the CBA. F & A refused to recognize the union. The union filed a charge of unfair labor practice with the NLRB. Is the CBA still in effect? Is the union still the representative of this unit of employees? Explain. [*National Labor Relations Board v. F & A Food Sales, Inc.,* 202 F.3d 1258 (10th Cir. 2000)]

A Question of Ethics and Social Responsibility

19–10. Salvatore Monte was president of Kenrich Petrochemicals, Inc. Helen Chizmar had been Kenrich's office manager since 1963. Among the staff that Chizmar supervised were her sister, daughter, and daughter-in-law. In 1987, Chizmar's relatives and four other staff members designated the Oil, Chemical, and Atomic Workers International Union as their bargaining representative. Chizmar was not involved, but when Monte was notified that his office was unionizing, he told Chizmar that someone else could do her job for "$20,000 less" and fired her. He told another employee that one of his reasons for firing Chizmar was that he "was not going to put up with any union bullsh—." During negotiations with the union, Monte said that he planned to "get rid of the whole family." Chizmar's family complained to the National Labor Relations Board (NLRB) that the firing was an unfair labor practice. The NLRB agreed and ordered that Chizmar be reinstated with back pay. Kenrich appealed. In view of these facts, consider the following questions. [*Kenrich Petrochemicals, Inc. v. NLRB,* 907 F.2d 400 (3d Cir. 1990)]

1. The National Labor Relations Act does not protect supervisors who engage in union activities. Should the appellate court affirm the NLRB's order nonetheless?
2. If the appellate court does not affirm the NLRB's order, what message will be sent to the supervisors and employees of Kenrich?
3. Is there anything Kenrich could (legally) do to avoid the unionization of its employees? Would it be ethical to counter the wishes of the employees to unionize?

For Critical Analysis

19–11. Although the law continues to evolve in response to changes in the workplace and in society, no significant labor legislation has been passed since the 1950s, and labor law issues have declined in importance in recent years. Why is this?

Interacting with the Internet

■ For updated links to resources available on the Web, as well as a variety of other materials, visit this text's Web site at

http://leet.westbuslaw.com

The Web sites on the next page offer information relevant to the topics covered in this chapter.

■ The American Federation of Labor–Congress of Industrial Organizations (AFL–CIO) provides links to a broad variety of labor-related resources at

http://www.aflcio.org

■ The National Labor Relations Board is online at the following URL:

http://www.nlrb.gov

Online Legal Research Exercises

Go to **http://leet.westbus law.com**, the Web site that accompanies this text. Select "Interactive Study Center," and then click on "Chapter 19." There you will find the following Internet research exercise that you can perform to learn more about labor law:

Activity 19–1: The National Labor Relations Board

Before the Test

Go to **http://leet.west buslaw.com**, the Web site that accompanies this text. Select "Interactive Quizzes." You will find a number of interactive questions relating to this chapter.

Unit IV Cumulative Hypothetical Problem

Falwell Motors, Inc., is a large corporation that manufactures automobile batteries.

1. One of Falwell's salespersons, Loren, puts in long hours every week. He spends most of his time away from the office generating sales. Less than 10 percent of his work time is devoted to other duties. Usually, he receives a substantial bonus at the end of each year from his employer, and Loren now relies on this supplement to his annual salary and commission. One year, the employer does not give any of its employees year-end bonuses. Loren calculates the number of hours he had worked during the year beyond the required forty hours a week. Then he tells Falwell's president that if he is not paid for these overtime hours, he will sue the company for the overtime pay he has "earned." Falwell's president tells Loren that Falwell is not obligated to pay Loren overtime because Loren is a salesperson. What federal statute governs this dispute? Under this statute, is Falwell required to pay Loren for the "overtime hours"? Why or why not?

2. One day Barry, one of the salespersons, anxious to make a sale, intentionally quotes a price to a customer that is $500 lower than Falwell has authorized for that particular product. The customer purchases the product at the quoted price. When Falwell learns of the deal, it claims that it is not legally bound to the sales contract because it did not authorize Barry to sell the product at that price. Is Falwell bound by the contract? Discuss fully.

3. One day Gina, a Falwell employee, suffered a serious burn when she accidentally spilled some acid on her hand. The accident occurred because another employee, who was suspected of using illegal drugs, carelessly bumped into her. The hand required a series of skin grafting operations before it healed sufficiently to allow Gina to return to work. Gina wants to obtain compensation for her lost wages and medical expenses. Can she do so? If so, how?

4. After Gina's injury, Falwell decides to conduct random drug tests on all of its employees. Several employees claim that the testing violates their privacy rights. If the dispute is litigated, what factors will the court consider in deciding whether the random drug testing is legally permissible?

5. Aretha, a Falwell employee, is disgusted by the sexually offensive behavior of several male employees. She has complained to her supervisor on several occasions about the offensive behavior, but the supervisor merely laughs at her concerns. Aretha decides to bring a legal action against the company for sexual harassment. Does Aretha's complaint concern *quid pro quo* harassment or hostile-environment harassment? What federal statute protects employees from sexual harassment? What remedies are available under that statute? What procedures must Aretha follow in pursuing her legal action?

The Regulatory Environment

Consumer Protection

contents

chapter objectives

After reading this chapter, you should be able to:

1. Summarize the major consumer protection laws.

2. Indicate some specific ways in which consumers are protected against deceptive advertising and sales practices.

3. Explain how the government protects consumers who are involved in credit transactions.

4. List and describe the major statutes that protect consumer health and safety.

5. Identify state consumer protection laws.

The "public interest" referred to by Justice William O. Douglas in the quotation alongside was evident during the 1960s and 1970s in what has come to be known as the consumer movement. Some have labeled the 1960s and 1970s "the age of the consumer," because so much legislation was passed to protect consumers against purportedly unfair practices and unsafe products of sellers. Since the 1980s, the impetus driving the consumer movement has lessened, to a great extent because so many of its goals have been achieved.

All statutes, agency rules, and common law judicial decisions that serve to protect the interest of consumers are classified as **consumer law.** Consumer transactions take a variety of forms but broadly include those that involve an exchange of value for the purpose of acquiring goods, services, land, or credit for personal or family use.

Traditionally, in disputes involving consumers, it was assumed that the freedom to contract carried with it the obligation to live by the deal made. Therefore, the watchword in most such transactions was *caveat emptor*—"let the buyer beware." Over time, this attitude has changed considerably. Today, myriad federal and state laws protect consumers from unfair trade practices, unsafe products, discriminatory or unreasonable credit requirements, and other problems related to consumer transactions. Nearly every agency and department of the federal government has an office of consumer affairs, and most states have one or more such offices to assist consumers. Also, typically the attorney general's office assists consumers at the state level.

Because of the wide variation among state consumer protection laws, our primary focus in this chapter is on federal legislation—specifically, on legislation governing advertising practices, labeling and packaging, sales, health protection, product safety, and credit protection. Realize, though, that state laws often provide more sweeping and significant protections for the consumer than do federal laws. State consumer protection laws are discussed later in this chapter.

Deceptive Advertising

One of the earliest—and still one of the most important—federal consumer protection laws was the Federal Trade Commission Act of 1914.[1] The act created the Federal Trade Commission (FTC) to carry out the broadly stated goal of preventing unfair and deceptive trade practices, including deceptive advertising.[2]

Deceptive Advertising Defined

Advertising will be deemed deceptive if a consumer would be misled by the advertising claim. Vague generalities and obvious exaggerations are permissible. These claims are known as *puffing*. When a claim takes on the appearance of literal authenticity, however, it may create problems. Advertising that would *appear* to be based on factual evidence but that in fact is not will be deemed deceptive. A classic example is provided by a 1944 case in which the claim that a skin cream would restore youthful qualities to aged skin was deemed deceptive.[3]

> **"Subject to specific constitutional limitations, when the legislature has spoken, the public interest has been declared in terms well nigh conclusive."**
>
> William O. Douglas, 1898–1980
> (Associate justice of the United States
> Supreme Court, 1939–1975)

Consumer Law The body of statutes, agency rules, and judicial decisions protecting consumers of goods and services from dangerous manufacturing techniques, mislabeling, unfair credit practices, deceptive advertising, and so on.

An ad for a "diet pill." What determines whether such ads are deceptive?

---

1. 15 U.S.C. Sections 41–58.
2. 15 U.S.C. Section 45.
3. *Charles of the Ritz Distributing Corp. v. Federal Trade Commission,* 143 F.2d 676 (2d Cir. 1944).

Some advertisements contain "half-truths," meaning that the presented information is true but incomplete, and it leads consumers to a false conclusion. ● **Example 20.1** The makers of Campbell's soups advertised that "most" Campbell's soups were low in fat and cholesterol and thus were helpful in fighting heart disease. What the ad did not say was that Campbell's soups are high in sodium, and high-sodium diets may increase the risk of heart disease. The FTC ruled that Campbell's claims were thus deceptive. ● Advertising that contains an endorsement by a celebrity may be deemed deceptive if the celebrity actually makes no use of the product.

Bait-and-Switch Advertising

Bait-and-Switch Advertising Advertising a product at a very attractive price (the "bait") and then informing the consumer, once he or she is in the store, that the advertised product is either not available or is of poor quality; the customer is then urged to purchase ("switched" to) a more expensive item.

The FTC has promulgated specific rules to govern advertising techniques. One of the most important rules is contained in the FTC's "Guides Against Bait Advertising,"[4] issued in 1968. The rule seeks to prevent **bait-and-switch advertising**—that is, advertising a very low price for a particular item that will likely be unavailable to the consumer, who will then be encouraged to purchase a more expensive item. The low price is the "bait" to lure the consumer into the store. The salesperson is instructed to "switch" the consumer to a different, more expensive item. Under the FTC guidelines, bait-and-switch advertising occurs if the seller refuses to show the advertised item, fails to have in stock a reasonable quantity of the item, fails to promise to deliver the advertised item within a reasonable time, or discourages employees from selling the item.

FTC Actions against Deceptive Advertising

Cease-and-Desist Order An administrative or judicial order prohibiting a person or business firm from conducting activities that an agency or court has deemed illegal.

Counteradvertising New advertising that is undertaken pursuant to a Federal Trade Commission order for the purpose of correcting earlier false claims that were made about a product.

Multiple Product Order An order issued by the Federal Trade Commission to a firm that has engaged in deceptive advertising by which the firm is required to cease and desist from false advertising not only in regard to the product that was the subject of the action but also in regard to all the firm's other products.

The FTC receives complaints from many sources, including competitors of alleged violators, consumers, consumer organizations, trade associations, Better Business Bureaus, government organizations, and state and local officials. If enough consumers complain and the complaints are widespread, the FTC will investigate the problem and perhaps take action. If, after its investigations, the FTC believes that a given advertisement is unfair or deceptive, it drafts a formal complaint, which is sent to the alleged offender. The company may agree to settle the complaint without further proceedings.

If the company does not agree to settle the complaint, the FTC can conduct a hearing in which the company can present its defense. As discussed in Chapter 7, a hearing conducted by an administrative agency is held before an administrative law judge instead of a federal district court judge. If the FTC succeeds in proving that an advertisement is unfair or deceptive, it usually issues a **cease-and-desist order** requiring that the challenged advertising be stopped. It might also impose a sanction known as **counteradvertising,** or corrective advertising, by requiring the company to advertise anew—in print, on radio, and on television—to inform the public about the earlier misinformation. The FTC may institute **multiple product orders,** which require a firm to cease and desist from false advertising not only in regard to the product that was the subject of the action but also in regard to all of the firm's other products.

● **Example 20.2** Novartis Corporation, in its advertising for one of its products, "Doan's Pills," claimed that the pills were particularly effective in reliev-

---

4. 16 C.F.R. Part 238.

ing back pain and that they contained an active ingredient not found in other over-the-counter analgesics. The FTC concluded that while each claim was literally true, in combination the claims implied that the pills were superior to other analgesics in relieving back pain because of their special ingredient—an assertion that was not true. The FTC ordered that Novartis had to include in future advertisements a disclaimer stating that "there is no evidence that Doan's is more effective than other pain relievers for back pain." The corrective advertising was to "continue for one year and until [Novartis] has expended on Doan's advertising a sum equal to the average spent annually during the eight years of the challenged [advertising] campaign."[5]●

Is it false or misleading to advertise a product as effective when its only effectiveness results from users' belief that it works? The court addressed this issue in the following case.

---

5. *Novartis Corp. v. Federal Trade Commission*, 223 F.3d 783 (D.C.Cir. 2000).

Case 20.1 ● Federal Trade Commission v. Pantron I Corp.

United States Court of Appeals, Ninth Circuit, 1994.
33 F.3d 1088.

Historical and Social Setting

Hair has been part of people's self-image since primitive men and women first adorned it with clay, trophies, and badges. Sometimes, an abundance of hair is interpreted as characteristic of virility. At other times, a bald pate is seen as indicating masculinity. Regardless of how it is viewed, male-pattern baldness (the loss of hair from the upper scalp) results from an individual's genetic background and hormone levels. There is no "cure," and even hair transplants may have no lasting effect.

Background and Facts Pantron I Corporation sold the Helsinki Formula as a "cure" for baldness. Pantron claimed that the product reduced hair loss and promoted hair growth. The Federal Trade Commission filed a suit in a federal district court against Pantron and its owner, Hal Lederman, alleging that these claims constituted an unfair or deceptive trade practice. The court concluded in part that the product had a "placebo effect"—that is, that it worked when its users believed it would. The court issued an order that, among other things, allowed Pantron to continue claiming its product "works some of the time for a lot of people." The FTC appealed this order.

In the Words of the Court . . .
REINHARDT, Circuit Judge.

* * * *

* * * Where, as here, a product's effectiveness arises solely as a result of the placebo effect, a representation that the product is effective constitutes a false advertisement even though some consumers may experience positive results. In such circumstances, the efficacy claim is misleading because the [product] is not inherently effective, its results being attributable to the psychosomatic effect produced by * * * advertising * * * .

* * * Under the evidence in the record before us, it appears that massaging vegetable oil on one's head would likely produce the same positive results as using the Helsinki Formula. * * * [A] court should not allow a seller to rely on such a placebo effect in supporting a claim of effectiveness * * * . [W]ere we to hold otherwise, advertisers would be encouraged to foist unsubstantiated claims on an unsuspecting public in the hope that consumers would believe the ads and the claims would be self-fulfilling.

(Continued)

Case 20.1 Continued

Decision and Remedy The U.S. Court of Appeals for the Ninth Circuit reversed this part of the lower court's order and remanded the case. Pantron could not continue to claim that its product "works some of the time for a lot of people."

For Critical Analysis—Political Consideration *What other government agencies might have taken action against Pantron and the Helsinki Formula, which is classified as a drug and sold through the mail?*

Telemarketing and Electronic Advertising

The pervasive use of the telephone to market goods and services to homes and businesses led to the passage in 1991 of the Telephone Consumer Protection Act (TCPA).[6] The act prohibits telephone solicitation using an automatic telephone dialing system or a prerecorded voice. Most states also have laws regulating telephone solicitation.[7]

Not surprisingly, the widespread use of fax machines has led to the use of faxes as a tool for direct marketing. Advertising by fax is less expensive than mailing a letter, and faxes normally receive greater attention than "junk mail." At the same time, unsolicited fax messages tie up the recipient's fax machine and impose a cost on the recipient, who must pay for fax paper, toner, and other supplies. The TCPA also makes it illegal to transmit ads via fax without first obtaining the recipient's permission.

The act is enforced by the Federal Communications Commission and also provides for a private right of action. Consumers can recover any actual monetary loss resulting from a violation of the act or receive $500 in damages for each violation, whichever is greater. If a court finds that a defendant willfully or knowingly violated the act, the court has the discretion to treble the damages awarded.

The Telemarketing and Consumer Fraud and Abuse Prevention Act[8] of 1994 directed the FTC to establish rules governing telemarketing and to bring actions against fraudulent telemarketers. The FTC's Telemarketing Sales Rule[9] of 1995 requires telemarketers, before making a sales pitch, to inform recipients that the call is a sales call and to identify the seller's name and the product being sold. The rule makes it illegal for telemarketers to misrepresent information (including facts about their goods or services, earnings potential, profitability, the risk attending an investment, or the nature of a prize). Additionally, telemarketers must inform the people they call of the total cost of the goods being sold, any restrictions on obtaining or using them, and whether a sale will be considered to be final and nonrefundable.

A major challenge in today's legal environment has to do with the advertising of products and services over the Internet. Recall from the *Legal E-nvironment* feature in Chapter 13 that one of these challenges is how to detect and prevent online fraudulent schemes. Another issue is whether the federal government should regulate junk e-mail, or "spam"—as discussed in the *Ethical Issue* on the following page.

---

6. 47 U.S.C. Sections 227 *et seq.*
7. For a discussion of the constitutionality of the TCPA, which some plaintiffs have alleged goes too far in restricting free speech, see *Moser v. FCC*, 46 F.3d 970 (9th Cir. 1995); *cert. denied*, 515 U.S. 1161, 115 S.Ct. 2615, 132 L.Ed.2d 857 (1995).
8. 15 U.S.C. Sections 6101–6108.
9. 16 C.F.R. Sections 310.1–310.8.

Ethical Issue 20.1

Should the federal government regulate "spam"?

A recurring problem for Internet users is the receipt of junk e-mail, or spam. Spam typically consists of a product ad sent to all of the users on an e-mailing list or all of the members of a newsgroup. Spam can waste user time, network bandwidth (the amount of data that can be transmitted within a certain time), and computer storage capacity. For these and other reasons, some states have passed laws specifically dealing with spam. For example, in California an unsolicited e-mail ad must state in its subject line that it is an ad ("ADV"). The ad must also include a toll-free tele-phone number or return e-mail address through which the recipient can contact the sender to request that no more ads be e-mailed.[a]

California law also provides that an Internet service provider (ISP) can bring a suit in a California state court against a spammer who violates the ISP's policy that prohibits or restricts unsolicited e-mail ads. A court can award damages of up to $25,000 per day.[b] Additionally, some courts have concluded that spamming is a form of trespass (a tort discussed in Chapter 9).[c] Should the federal government enact legislation to regulate spam? Although several proposals addressing spamming problems have been considered at the federal level, to date no legislation has been enacted.

---

a. Ca. Bus. & Prof. Code Section 17538.4.
b. Ca. Bus. & Prof. Code Section 17538.45.
c. See, for example, *CompuServe, Inc. v. Cyber Promotions, Inc.*, 962 F.Supp. 1015 (S.D.Ohio 1997).

Labeling and Packaging Laws

In addition to broadly restricting advertising, a number of federal and state laws deal specifically with the information given on labels and packages. The restrictions are designed to provide accurate information about the product and to warn about possible dangers from its use or misuse. In general, labels must be accurate. That is, they must use words that are understood by the ordinary consumer. For example, a box of cereal cannot be labeled "giant" if it would exaggerate the amount of cereal contained in the box. In some instances, labels must specify the raw materials used in the product, such as the percentage of cotton, nylon, or other fibers used in a garment. In other instances, the products must carry a warning. Cigarette packages and advertising, for example, must include one of several warnings about the health hazards associated with smoking.[10]

Federal laws regulating the labeling and packaging of products include the Wool Products Labeling Act of 1939,[11] the Fur Products Labeling Act of 1951,[12] the Flammable Fabrics Act of 1953,[13] the Fair Packaging and Labeling Act of 1966,[14] the Smokeless Tobacco Health Education Act of 1986,[15] and the Nutrition Labeling and Education Act of 1990.[16] The Smokeless Tobacco Health Education Act, for example, requires that producers, packagers, and importers of smokeless tobacco label their product with one of several warnings

---

10. 15 U.S.C. Sections 1331 *et seq.*
11. 15 U.S.C. Section 68.
12. 15 U.S.C. Section 69.
13. 15 U.S.C. Section 1191.
14. 15 U.S.C. Sections 1451–1461.
15. 15 U.S.C. Sections 4401–4408.
16. 21 U.S.C. Section 343-1.

about the health hazards associated with the use of smokeless tobacco; the warnings are similar to those contained on other tobacco product packages.

The Fair Packaging and Labeling Act requires that products carry labels that identify the product; the net quantity of the contents, as well as the quantity of servings, if the number of servings is stated; the manufacturer; and the packager or distributor. The act also authorizes requirements concerning words used to describe packages, terms that are associated with savings claims, information disclosures for ingredients in nonfood products, and standards for the partial filling of packages. Food products must bear labels detailing nutritional content, including how much fat a product contains and what kind of fat it is. These restrictions are enforced by the Department of Health and Human Services, as well as the Federal Trade Commission. The Nutrition Labeling and Education Act of 1990 requires standard nutrition facts (including fat content) on food labels; regulates the use of such terms as *fresh* and *low-fat*; and, subject to the federal Food and Drug Administration's approval, authorizes certain health claims.

Sales

Many of the laws that protect consumers concern the disclosure of certain terms in sales transactions and provide rules governing the various forms of sales, such as door-to-door sales, mail-order sales, referral sales, and the unsolicited receipt of merchandise. Much of the federal regulation of sales is conducted by the FTC under its regulatory authority to curb unfair trade practices. Other federal agencies, however, are involved to various degrees. For example, the Federal Reserve Board of Governors has issued **Regulation Z**,[17] which governs credit provisions associated with sales contracts. Many states have also enacted laws governing consumer sales transactions. Moreover, states have provided a number of consumer protection provisions through the adoption of the Uniform Commercial Code and, in those states that have adopted it, the Uniform Consumer Credit Code.

Increasingly, consumers are purchasing goods and services via the Internet from online merchants. E-commerce is clearly here to stay, but what are some of the consequences of e-contracts and e-commerce for consumers? We explore this topic in this chapter's *Legal E-nvironment: E-Contracts and Consumer Welfare.*

> **Regulation Z** A set of rules promulgated by the Federal Reserve Board to implement the provisions of the Truth-in-Lending Act.

17. 12 C.F.R. Sections 226.1–226.30.

Legal *e*-nvironment

E-Contracts and Consumer Welfare

As you read in Chapter 14, the 1999 federal legislation validating e-signatures means that contracts that are formed and signed electronically now have the force of law. Additionally, the National Conference of Commissioners on Uniform State Laws has recently promulgated a uniform act (the Uniform Computer Information Transactions Act) that, if widely adopted, will provide uniform principles for e-contracts throughout the states. Clearly, these developments are a boon for e-commerce.

E-commerce in general creates actual and potential savings for most consumers. These savings may be monetary or may simply be a savings in time—the time not wasted by leaving one's house to purchase an item.

Legal *e*-nvironment

While there are many advantages to e-commerce, consumers continue to be plagued by problems stemming from contracts formed online. Recall from Chapter 13 that online fraud is a growing problem. Additional difficulties, while they may not constitute fraud, also exist.

Late Deliveries

Most e-retailing sites do 40 to 60 percent of their business in the ten weeks before Christmas. The closer it is to Christmas, the greater the number of orders. Consequently, the pressure to deliver in time for Christmas is great. After the first truly significant e-commerce Christmas selling season in 1999, irate consumers throughout the country raised their collective voice against several dozen online selling sites for failing to deliver orders on time.

In July 2000, the Federal Trade Commission (FTC) reached a settlement with seven online retailers. The FTC complaint alleged that the following companies had violated their agreements with consumers: Toysrus.com, Inc.; Macys.com, Inc.; KBkids.com, LLC; CDNow, Inc.; Patriot Computer Corp.; Original Honey Baked Ham Company; and MinidisNow.com. The FTC found that these online merchants failed to ship Christmas gifts on time and simultaneously failed to notify their customers of these delays. As a result, the companies were ordered to pay fines ranging from $20,000 to $350,000. The FTC stated that the steep fines would serve as a warning to other online retailers that they would be held liable for violating delivery rules if they repeated this type of behavior the following Christmas. Toysrus.com decided to reduce the probability of such an event reoccurring by forming an alliance with Amazon.com to launch a joint site. This alliance allows Amazon to help Toysrus.com handle traffic and avoid Christmas delivery delays.

The Problem of Hidden Costs

The FTC has also taken action against certain sites because they failed to fully disclose the terms of attractive offers that turned out to have hidden costs. For example, several online retailers, including Buy.com and Value America, Inc., advertised "free" and "low-cost" computers to online shoppers. What these companies failed to disclose, however, was that there were numerous hidden costs associated with such purported bargains. Individuals would obtain the free or low-cost computers only after they agreed to a three-year Internet service subscription. Moreover, the Internet subscription services offered were often ones that charged an hourly rate or required long-distance telephone charges because the affiliated Internet service provider had no local access numbers.

The Issue of Fine Print

When someone talks about "reading the fine print," he or she is usually referring to contractual terms printed on an agreement. In cyberspace, e-contracts often contain the same amount of fine print—but there is a difference: while it may be difficult to read the fine print on a printed page, it is often even more difficult to read it on a computer screen, particularly if that screen is not very large. Not surprisingly, most people do not read the fine print in e-contracts. Clicking on "I agree" while engaging in online e-commerce may not be done with full knowledge of to what type of e-contract one is actually agreeing. So far, there has been little regulatory work in this area.

Short-Term versus Long-Term Contracts

Most e-contracts currently involve short-term agreements, such as for the sale and delivery of goods. But what if electronic contracts become routinely used for long-term agreements, such as mortgages or insurance agreements? A long-term contract signed and stored on a computer may not be accessible in the long run without upgrading one's software and perhaps hardware. Typically, during the life of a long-term loan contract, such as an automobile loan or a mortgage, the loan will be purchased by two or more banks. How does the borrower continue to communicate with the ultimate owner of that loan contract?

In addition, what if a borrower's hard disk crashes, leaving the borrower without the original contract? At a minimum, all significant contracts, whether they are short term or long term, should be copied onto a removable storage source, such as a Zip disk or similar storage device.

For Critical Analysis: *Is there truly any difference between problems with fine print in paper contracts and those in electronic contracts?*

Door-to-Door Sales

Door-to-door sales are singled out for special treatment in the laws of most states, in part because of the nature of the sales transaction. Repeat purchases are not as likely as they are in stores, and thus the seller has less incentive to cultivate the goodwill of the purchaser. Furthermore, the seller is unlikely to present alternative products and their prices. Thus, a number of states have passed "cooling-off" laws that permit the buyers of goods sold door-to-door to cancel their contracts within a specified period of time, usually two to three days after the sale.

An FTC regulation also requires sellers to give consumers three days to cancel any door-to-door sale. Because this rule applies in addition to the relevant state statutes, consumers are given the most favorable benefits of the FTC rule and their own state statutes. In addition, the FTC rule requires that consumers be notified of this right in a different language if the oral negotiations for the sale were in that language.

Telephone and Mail-Order Sales

Sales made by either telephone or mail order are the greatest source of complaints to the nation's Better Business Bureaus. Many mail-order firms are far removed from most of their buyers, thus making it more burdensome for buyers to bring complaints against them. To a certain extent, consumers are protected under federal laws prohibiting mail fraud and under state consumer protection laws that parallel and supplement the federal laws.

The FTC Mail or Telephone Order Merchandise Rule of 1993, which amended the FTC Mail-Order Rule of 1975,[18] provides specific protections for consumers who purchase goods via phone lines or through the mails. The 1993 rule extended the 1975 rule to include sales in which orders are transmitted by computer, fax machine, or some similar means involving telephone lines. Among other things, the rule requires mail-order merchants to ship orders within the time promised in their catalogues or advertisements, to notify consumers when orders cannot be shipped on time, and to issue a refund within a specified period of time when a consumer cancels an order.

In addition, the Postal Reorganization Act of 1970[19] provides that *unsolicited* merchandise sent by U.S. mail may be retained, used, discarded, or disposed of in any manner deemed appropriate, without the recipient's incurring any obligation to the sender.

FTC Regulation of Specific Industries

Over the last decade, the FTC has begun to target certain sales practices on an industry-wide basis. Two examples involve the used-car business and the funeral-home trade. In 1984, the FTC enacted the Used Motor Vehicle Regulation Rule,[20] which is more commonly known as the used-car rule. This rule requires used-car dealers to affix a buyer's guide label to all cars sold on their lots. The label must disclose the following information: (1) the car's warranty or a statement that the car is being sold "as is," (2) information regarding any service contract or promises being made by the dealer, and (3) a suggestion that the purchaser obtain both an inspection of the car and a written statement of any promises made by the dealer.

In 1984, the FTC also enacted rules requiring that funeral homes provide customers with itemized prices of all charges incurred for a funeral.[21] In addi-

> **Don't Forget** A seller's puffery—his or her opinion about the goods—is not a legally binding warranty or promise.

---

18. 16 C.F.R. Sections 435.1–435.2.
19. 39 U.S.C. Section 3009.
20. 16 C.F.R. Sections 455.1–455.5.
21. 16 C.F.R. Section 453.2.

tion, the regulations prohibit funeral homes from requiring specific embalming procedures or specific types of caskets for bodies that are to be cremated.

Real Estate Sales

Various federal and state laws apply to consumer transactions involving real estate. These laws are designed to prevent fraud and to provide buyers with certain types of information. In some cases, these protections mirror those provided in non–real estate sales. The disclosure requirements of the Truth-in-Lending Act apply to a number of real estate transactions, as will be discussed shortly.

INTERSTATE LAND SALES FULL DISCLOSURE ACT The Interstate Land Sales Full Disclosure Act[22] was passed by Congress in 1968, and it is administered by the Department of Housing and Urban Development (HUD). The purpose of the act is to ensure disclosure of certain information to consumers so that they can make reasoned decisions about land purchases. The act is similar to the Securities Act of 1933 in both purpose and design. The act requires anyone proposing to sell or lease one hundred or more lots of unimproved land, if the sale or lease is to be part of a common promotional plan, to file an initial statement of record with HUD's Office of Interstate Land Sales Registration.

The act only applies if the promotional plan can be deemed part of interstate commerce. As in cases involving securities, this is generally an easy requirement to meet. • **Example 20.3** Even strictly local sales might be considered interstate commerce if transacted in part over the phone; although the calls might be local, the phone lines traverse state boundaries. For the same reason, use of the mail system is likely to ensure that a promotional plan is in the stream of interstate commerce.•

Once the initial statement is filed, it must be approved by HUD before the developer can begin to offer the land for sale or lease. The act also provides purchasers with a private right of action for the land promoter's fraud, misrepresentation, or noncompliance with pertinent provisions of the act. Criminal penalties are provided under the act, and HUD is given certain rights with regard to inspections, injunctions, and prosecution of offenses. Three provisions of the act give purchasers rights of rescission (cancellation).

REAL ESTATE SETTLEMENT PROCEDURES ACT For many individuals, purchasing a home involves a bewildering array of procedures and requirements. Settlement (finalizing a real estate transaction) may require title insurance, attorneys' fees, appraisal fees, taxes, insurance, and brokers' fees. To aid home buyers, federal legislation requires specific disclosures regarding settlement procedures. The 1976 revisions of the Real Estate Settlement Procedures Act of 1974[23] make the following stipulations:

1. Within three business days after a person applies for a mortgage loan, the lender must send a booklet prepared by HUD that explains the settlement procedures, describes the costs to the potential buyer, and outlines the applicant's legal rights.

---

22. 15 U.S.C. Sections 1701–1720.
23. 12 U.S.C. Sections 2601–2617.

2. Within the three-day period, the lender must give an estimate of most of the settlement costs.
3. The lender must clearly identify individuals or firms that the applicant is required to use for legal or other services, including title search and insurance.
4. If the loan is approved, the lender must provide a truth-in-lending statement that shows the annual percentage rate on the mortgage loan.
5. Lenders, title insurers, and others involved in the transaction cannot pay kickbacks for business referred to them.

Credit Protection

Because of the extensive use of credit by American consumers, credit protection has become an especially important area regulated by consumer protection legislation. One of the most significant statutes regulating the credit and credit-card industry is Title I of the Consumer Credit Protection Act (CCPA),[24] which was passed by Congress in 1968 and is commonly referred to as the Truth-in-Lending Act (TILA).

The Truth-in-Lending Act

The TILA is basically a *disclosure law*. It is administered by the Federal Reserve Board and requires sellers and lenders to disclose credit terms or loan terms so that individuals can shop around for the best financing arrangements. TILA requirements apply only to persons who, in the ordinary course of business, lend money, sell on credit, or arrange for the extension of credit. Thus, sales or loans made between two consumers do not come under the protection of the act. Additionally, only debtors who are *natural* persons (as opposed to the artificial "person" of the corporation) are protected by this law; other legal entities are not.

The disclosure requirements are contained in Regulation Z, which, as mentioned earlier in this chapter, was promulgated by the Federal Reserve Board. If the contracting parties are subject to the TILA, the requirements of Regulation Z apply to any transaction involving an installment sales contract in which payment is to be made in more than four installments. Transactions subject to Regulation Z typically include installment loans, retail and installment sales, car loans, home-improvement loans, and certain real estate loans if the amount of financing is less than $25,000.

Under the provisions of the TILA, all of the terms of a credit instrument must be clearly and conspicuously disclosed. The TILA provides for contract rescission (cancellation) if a creditor fails to follow *exactly* the procedures required by the act.[25] TILA requirements are strictly enforced.

In the following case, a consumer sued a lender, alleging TILA violations. The lender claimed that the consumer was not entitled to relief because she had lied on her credit application.

> **Note** The Federal Reserve Board is part of the Federal Reserve System, which influences the lending and investing activities of commercial banks and the cost and availability of credit.

---

24. 15 U.S.C. Sections 1601–1693r.
25. Note, however, that amendments to the TILA enacted in 1995 prevent borrowers from rescinding loans for minor clerical errors in closing documents [15 U.S.C. Sections 1605, 1631, 1635, 1640, and 1641].

Case 20.2 ● Purtle v. Eldridge Auto Sales, Inc.

United States Court of Appeals,
Sixth Circuit, 1996.
91 F.3d 797.

Background and Facts Renee Purtle bought a 1986 Chevrolet Blazer from Eldridge Auto Sales, Inc. To finance the purchase through Eldridge, Purtle filled out a credit application on which she misrepresented her employment status. Based on the misrepresentation, Eldridge extended credit. In the credit contract, Eldridge did not disclose the finance charge, the annual percentage rate, or the total sales price or use the term *amount financed,* as the TILA and its regulations require. Purtle defaulted on the loan, and Eldridge repossesed the vehicle. Purtle filed a suit in a federal district court against Eldridge, alleging violations of the TILA. The court awarded Purtle $1,000 in damages, plus attorneys' fees and costs. Eldridge appealed, arguing in part that Purtle was not entitled to damages because she had committed fraud on her credit application.

In the Words of the Court . . .
FORESTER, District Judge.

* * * *

* * * [T]he TILA imposes mandatory disclosure requirements on those who extend credit to consumers. * * * In the event that a creditor fails to disclose any of the credit terms required under the TILA and its regulations, a consumer may bring a civil action against the creditor. If a violation is proven, the consumer may recover twice the amount of the finance charge (but not less than $100.00 nor more than $1,000.00). The purpose of the statutory recovery is "to encourage lawsuits by individual consumers as a means of enforcing creditor compliance with the Act." The TILA also permits recovery of reasonable attorney's fees and costs. * * *

* * * *

* * * [O]nce a court finds a violation of the TILA, no matter how technical, the court has no discretion as to the imposition of civil liability.

* * * Based on the unambiguous statutory language, it is clear that * * * the district court appropriately awarded Purtle the statutory penalty set out above.

Decision and Remedy The U.S. Court of Appeals for the Sixth Circuit affirmed the lower court's award. The lender was required to pay damages based on its violation of the TILA, despite the borrower's fraud.

For Critical Analysis—Social Consideration *Do you think that the greatest number of consumers are protected by strict enforcement of consumer laws?*

EQUAL CREDIT OPPORTUNITY In 1974, the Equal Credit Opportunity Act (ECOA)[26] was enacted as an amendment to the TILA. The ECOA prohibits the denial of credit solely on the basis of race, religion, national origin, color, gender, marital status, or age. The act also prohibits credit discrimination on the basis of whether an individual receives certain forms of income, such as public-assistance benefits. Under the ECOA, a creditor may not require the signature of an applicant's spouse, other than as a joint applicant, on a credit instrument if the applicant qualifies under the creditor's standards of creditworthiness for the amount and terms of the credit request.

---

26. 15 U.S.C. Section 1691–1691f.

Ethical Issue 20.2

Is it fair for consumers who take unfair advantage of the TILA to obtain remedies under the act?

In some cases, consumers have taken unfair advantage of the TILA's requirements to avoid genuine obligations that they voluntarily assumed. For example, under the TILA, borrowers are allowed three business days to rescind, without penalty, a consumer loan that uses their principal dwelling as security. The lender must state specifically the last day on which the borrower can rescind the agreement. If the lender fails to do so, the borrower can rescind the loan within three years after it was made. This is true even if the lender inadvertently (unintentionally) failed to comply with the TILA's requirements.

Is it fair to hold creditors liable for TILA violations regardless of whether the violations were intentional or unintentional? According to the courts, the answer to this question is yes. The courts reason that, overall, consumers will benefit from strict compliance requirements, even though some consumers may abuse the act. In essence, the TILA is a "strict liability" statute (this is generally true of most consumer protection statutes). In other words, intention normally is irrelevant in determining whether a consumer protection statute has been violated.

For Critical Analysis: *In your opinion, should the courts give more weight to the circumstances surrounding a transaction and the intent factor in deciding cases involving alleged TILA violations? Why or why not?*

Creditors are permitted to request any information from a credit applicant except that which would be used for the type of discrimination covered in the act or its amendments. In the following case, the issue concerned whether a creditor violated the ECOA by requiring the signature of an applicant's spouse on a loan guaranty.

Case 20.3 ● Federal Deposit Insurance Corp. v. Medmark, Inc.

United States District Court,
District of Kansas, 1995.
897 F.Supp. 511.

Background and Facts Bruce Shalberg was a director of Medmark, Inc., a small medical equipment supply company. As a condition of a loan to Medmark, the Merchants Bank asked Shalberg—whom the bank found to be independently creditworthy—to sign a guaranty of repayment. Later, for another loan, the bank required Shalberg's wife, Mary—who had nothing to do with Medmark—to sign the guaranty. When the bank failed, the Federal Deposit Insurance Corporation (FDIC) took over its assets. The FDIC filed a suit in a federal district court against Medmark and the Shalbergs to recover the amount of the loans. Mary Shalberg filed a motion for summary judgment, contending that the bank, in requiring her to sign the guaranty, had violated the Equal Credit Opportunity Act (ECOA).

In the Words of the Court . . .
VRATIL, District Judge.

* * * *

[A regulation issued under the ECOA] specifically provides that a creditor may not require the signature of an applicant's spouse if the applicant qualifies under the creditor's standards of creditworthiness for the amount and terms of the credit requested. The FDIC argues that the Bank "obviously" did not believe Mr. Shalberg to be independently creditworthy

Case 20.3 Continued

* * * . [But the] record contains no evidence that Mr. Shalberg was not creditworthy, in his own right, in the Bank's eyes. Summary judgment in favor of Mrs. Shalberg is therefore appropriate.

Decision and Remedy The federal district court issued a summary judgment in favor of Mary Shalberg, relieving her from any obligation on the loans. The creditor violated the ECOA by requiring Shalberg's signature on the loan guaranty.

For Critical Analysis—Political Consideration *Why does the ECOA prohibit lenders from requiring a spouse's signature on a credit application if the applicant independently qualifies for the credit?*

CREDIT-CARD RULES The TILA also contains provisions regarding credit cards. One provision limits the liability of a cardholder to $50 per card for unauthorized charges made before the creditor is notified that the card has been lost. Another provision prohibits a credit-card company from billing a consumer for any unauthorized charges if the credit card was improperly issued by the company. • **Example 20.4** If a consumer receives an unsolicited credit card in the mail and the card is later stolen and used by the thief to make purchases, the consumer to whom the card was sent will not be liable for the unauthorized charges.•

> **Compare** The Electronic Fund Transfer Act also limits, under certain circumstances, the liability of a consumer to $50 for unauthorized transfers made before the issuer of an access card is notified that the card is lost.

Further provisions of the act concern billing disputes related to credit-card purchases. If a debtor thinks that an error has occurred in billing or wishes to withhold payment for a faulty product purchased by credit card, the act outlines specific procedures for both the consumer and the credit-card company to follow in settling the dispute.

A mounting concern today has to do with identity theft—for example, the use of another's personal identifying information to fraudulently obtain credit cards or other types of credit. For a discussion of this topic, see this chapter's *Inside the Legal Environment* on the next page.

CONSUMER LEASES The Consumer Leasing Act (CLA) of 1988[27] amended the TILA to provide protection for consumers who lease automobiles and other goods. The CLA applies to those who lease or arrange to lease consumer goods in the ordinary course of their business. The act only applies if the goods are priced at $25,000 or less and if the lease term exceeds four months. The CLA and its implementing regulation, Regulation M,[28] require lessors to disclose in writing all of the material terms of the lease.

The Fair Credit Reporting Act

In 1970, to protect consumers against inaccurate credit reporting, Congress enacted the Fair Credit Reporting Act (FCRA).[29] The act provides that consumer credit reporting agencies may issue credit reports to users only for specified purposes, including the extension of credit, the issuance of insurance

---

27. 15 U.S.C. Sections 1667–1667e.
28. 12 C.F.R. Part 213.
29. 15 U.S.C. Sections 1681–1681t.

Inside the Legal Environment

The Growing Problem of Identity Theft

"Someone used my Social Security number to get credit in my name. This has caused a lot of problems. I have been turned down for jobs, credit, and refinancing offers." "Someone is using my name and Social Security number to open credit-card accounts. All the accounts are in collections." "Someone applied for a credit card in [my elderly parents'] name and charged nearly $20,000. . . . The [collection] agency doesn't believe Mom and Dad didn't authorize the account. What can we do to stop the debt collector?" These are just a few of the more than one thousand complaints of "identity theft" (ID theft) that the Federal Trade Commission (FTC) receives each month.

Complaints of ID theft are not new, of course. What is new is the rapidly growing number of such complaints—according to the FTC, such complaints tripled in just a six-month period during 2000. Certainly, the widespread use of the Internet for e-commerce and other transactions since the 1990s has made it much easier than it was in the past to obtain personal information about others, including their Social Security numbers, information on their driver's licenses, credit-card numbers, and the like.

Common Forms of ID Theft

The most common form of ID theft reported by consumers is the use of another's personal identifying information, such as his or her Social Security number, to fraudulently obtain a credit card. Nationwide, approximately 54 percent of complaints received by the FTC involve credit-card fraud. Approximately 28 percent of complaints concern communications services—the use of one's personal information by another to open up telephone, cellular, or other utility services. About 17 percent of the complaints involve bank fraud—unauthorized access to checking or savings accounts. Other complaints include those alleging that personal identifying information has been used by ID thieves to obtain loans, driver's licenses, or other documents or benefits.

What the Government Is Doing

In 1999, because of the rising number of complaints about ID theft, the FTC established the Identity Theft Data Clearinghouse to receive and process consumer complaints. Since then, the clearinghouse has created a database containing information gleaned from consumer complaints about how ID theft is occurring and, when possible, by whom. The clearinghouse also refers, when appropriate, certain claims for prosecution. According to the FTC, this database, which can be accessed by law enforcement and appropriate regulatory offices, will help officials to learn about common schemes and perpetrators involved in ID theft and to take appropriate action.

The FTC has also established an ID theft hotline (at 1-877-IDTHEFT) that consumers can use to report ID theft problems. Additionally, the FTC has created a special Web site (at **http://www.consumer. gov/idtheft**) dealing solely with the issue of ID theft. The site contains extensive information on the issue, including what steps you can take to prevent becoming a victim of ID theft and what to do if you do become a victim.

Congress is also currently considering a bill designed to prevent ID theft. If passed, the bill would provide consumers with access to information that could reveal when someone else was using their identities. For example, the bill would require credit-card issuers to advise their customers whenever a change of address is requested on a credit account. The bill would also provide for free annual credit reports to consumers.

For Critical Analysis: *"ID theft is a natural consequence of living in an electronic age and there is little that government can do to effectively control it." Analyze this statement.*

policies, compliance with a court order, and compliance with a consumer's request for a copy of his or her own credit report. The act further provides that any time a consumer is denied credit or insurance on the basis of the consumer's credit report, or is charged more than others ordinarily would be for credit or insurance, the consumer must be notified of that fact and of the name and address of the credit reporting agency that issued the credit report.

Under the act, consumers may request the source of any information being given out by a credit agency, as well as the identity of anyone who has received an agency's report. Consumers are also permitted to have access to the information contained about them in a credit reporting agency's files. If a consumer discovers that a credit reporting agency's files contain inaccurate information about the consumer's credit standing, the agency, on the consumer's written request, must investigate the matter and delete any unverifiable or erroneous information within a reasonable period of time.

An agency that fails to comply with the act is liable for actual damages, plus additional damages not to exceed $1,000 and attorneys' fees.[30] Damages are also available against anyone who uses a credit report for an improper purpose, as well as banks, credit-card companies, and other businesses that report information to credit agencies and do not respond adequately to customer complaints.

The following case illustrates the liability exposure of companies that maintain credit reports and ratings.

---

30. 15 U.S.C. Section 1681n.

Case 20.4 ● Guimond v. Trans Union Credit Information Co.

United States Court of Appeals,
Ninth Circuit, 1995.
45 F.3d 1329.

Historical and Economic Setting *A credit report reflects a consumer's bill-paying history. It lists the consumer's creditors and whether he or she has made payments on time. Inaccurate information can keep an individual from obtaining credit, because lenders rely on credit reports when deciding whether to extend credit. The major credit reporting agencies include the Trans Union Credit Information Company.*

Background and Facts Renie Guimond learned of inaccuracies that Trans Union Credit Information Company had in its file on her. She notified Trans Union, which told her the file would be corrected; however, it was not corrected for a year. Guimond filed a suit in a federal district court against Trans Union, in part to recover damages under the Fair Credit Reporting Act (FCRA) for the company's failure to correct the information more quickly. Trans Union countered that Guimond had no claim, because she had not been denied credit before the information was corrected. The court ruled in favor of Trans Union, and Guimond appealed.

In the Words of the Court . . .
FONG, District Judge:

* * * *

[The FCRA] states: Whenever a consumer reporting agency prepares a consumer report it shall follow reasonable procedures to assure maximum possible accuracy of the information * * * .

* * * *

Liability * * * is predicated on the reasonableness of the credit reporting agency's procedures * * * .

* * * [T]he focus should not have been on Guimond's damage claims. Rather the inquiry should have centered on whether Trans Union's procedures for preparing Guimond's file contained reasonable procedures to prevent inaccuracies. Guimond has made out a *prima facie* case under [the FCRA] by showing that there were inaccuracies in her credit report. The district court was then required to consider whether Trans Union was liable

(Continued)

Case 20.4 Continued

under [the FCRA] before it determined that Guimond had suffered no recoverable damages.

Decision and Remedy The U.S. Court of Appeals for the Ninth Circuit reversed this part of the lower court's ruling and remanded the case for trial. The agency could be held liable if its procedures to assure the accuracy of its information were not reasonable.

For Critical Analysis—Social Consideration *How do the policies underlying the FCRA support the court's interpretation of the statute in Guimond's case?*

Fair Debt Collection Practices Act

In 1977, Congress enacted the Fair Debt Collection Practices Act (FDCPA)[31] in an attempt to curb what were perceived to be abuses by collection agencies. The act applies only to specialized debt-collection agencies that regularly attempt to collect debts on behalf of someone else, usually for a percentage of the amount owed. Creditors attempting to collect debts are not covered by the act unless, by misrepresenting themselves, they cause debtors to believe they are collection agencies. The act explicitly prohibits a collection agency from using any of the following tactics:

1. Contacting the debtor at the debtor's place of employment if the debtor's employer objects.
2. Contacting the debtor during inconvenient or unusual times (for example, calling the debtor at three o'clock in the morning) or at any time if the debtor is being represented by an attorney.
3. Contacting third parties other than the debtor's parents, spouse, or financial adviser about payment of a debt unless a court authorizes such action.
4. Using harassment or intimidation (for example, using abusive language or threatening violence) or employing false or misleading information (for example, posing as a police officer).
5. Communicating with the debtor at any time after receiving notice that the debtor is refusing to pay the debt, except to advise the debtor of further action to be taken by the collection agency.

Validation Notice An initial notice to a debtor from a collection agency informing the debtor that he or she has thirty days to challenge the debt and request verification.

The FDCPA also requires a collection agency to include a **validation notice** whenever it initially contacts a debtor for payment of a debt or within five days of that initial contact. The notice must state that the debtor has thirty days within which to dispute the debt and to request a written verification of the debt from the collection agency. The debtor's request for debt validation must be in writing.

The enforcement of the FDCPA is primarily the responsibility of the Federal Trade Commission. The act provides that a debt collector that fails to comply with the act is liable for actual damages, plus additional damages not to exceed $1,000[32] and attorneys' fees.

---

31. 15 U.S.C. Section 1692.
32. According to the U.S. Court of Appeals for the Sixth Circuit, the $1,000 limit on damages applies to each lawsuit, not to each violation. See *Wright v. Finance Service of Norwalk, Inc.,* 22 F.3d 647 (6th Cir. 1994).

Cases brought under the FDCPA often raise questions as to who qualifies as a debt collector or debt-collecting agency subject to the act. ● **Example 20.5** For several years it was not clear whether attorneys who attempted to collect debts owed to their clients were subject to the FDCPA's provisions. In 1995, the United States Supreme Court addressed this issue to resolve conflicting opinions in the lower courts. The Court held that an attorney who regularly tries to obtain payment of consumer debts through legal proceedings meets the FDCPA's definition of "debt collector."[33] ●

Another question that sometimes arises in the context of FDCPA litigation has to do with what, exactly, constitutes a "debt." In the following case, the court considered whether a dishonored check constituted a "debt" within the meaning of the FDCPA.

---

33. *Heintz v. Jenkins,* 514 U.S. 291, 115 S.Ct. 1489, 131 L.Ed.2d 395 (1995).

Case 20.5 ● Snow v. Jesse L. Riddle, P.C.

United States Court of Appeals,
Tenth Circuit, 1998.
143 F.3d 1350.
http://www.washlaw.edu/
ca10/caselist/caselist.htm[a]

Historical and Social Setting *The FDCPA defines debt as "any obligatory or alleged obligation of a consumer to pay money arising out of a transaction in which the money, property, insurance, or services which are the subject of the transaction are primarily for personal, family, or household purposes, whether or not such obligation has been reduced to judgment."[b] At one time, it was generally held that the type of transaction giving rise to a debt, within this definition, is the same type of transaction that is dealt with in all other parts of the Consumer Credit Protection Act: a transaction that involves an offer or extension of*

credit to a consumer. By the time the U.S. Court of Appeals for the Tenth Circuit decided this case, however, this view had changed.

Background and Facts At a Circle-K store, Alan Snow paid for merchandise with his personal check in the amount of $23.12. Circle-K deposited the check at its bank, but the check was dishonored because of insufficient funds. Circle-K sent the returned check to its attorney, Jesse L. Riddle, P.C., for collection. In a letter to Snow, Riddle wrote that "the check amount, along with a service fee of $15, must be paid within seven (7) days of this notice. If it is not paid, . . . [a] suit [will] be filed." Snow paid the check and then filed a suit in a federal district court against Riddle. Snow alleged in part that Riddle's letter violated the FDCPA because it did not contain a "validation notice." Riddle filed a motion to dismiss on the ground that the FDCPA does not cover a dishonored check because it is not an "offer or extension of credit." The court granted the motion, and Snow appealed to the U.S. Court of Appeals for the Tenth Circuit.

---

a. This Web site is maintained by the Washburn University School of Law. This page contains links to opinions of the U.S. Court of Appeals for the Tenth Circuit. Scroll down the list of cases and click on the *Snow* case name to access the opinion.
b. 15 U.S.C. Section 1692a(5).

In the Words of the Court . . .
McWILLIAMS, Senior Circuit Judge.

* * * *

[The FDCPA] provides as follows:
* * * Abusive debt collection practices contribute to the number of personal bankruptcies, to marital instability, to the loss of jobs, and to invasions of individual privacy. * * * It is the purpose of [the FDCPA] to eliminate abusive debt collection practices by debt collectors * * * .
* * * *

(Continued)

Case 20.5 Continued

* * * [A] payment obligation arising from a dishonored check create[s] a "debt" triggering the protections of the [FDCPA].* * * [A]n offer or extension of credit is not required for a payment obligation to constitute a "debt" under the [FDCPA]. * * *

* * * *

* * * Under the "plain meaning" test, it would seem to us that a "debt" is created where one obtains goods and gives a dishonored check in return therefor.

Decision and Remedy The U.S. Court of Appeals for the Tenth Circuit reversed the decision of the lower court and remanded the case. The appellate court held that a dishonored check constitutes a debt within the meaning of the FDCPA.

For Critical Analysis—Political Consideration *Should those who write bad checks to pay for consumer goods or services be protected by the FDCPA?*

Garnishment of Wages

Despite the increasing number of protections afforded debtors, creditors are not without means of securing payment on debts. One of these is the right to garnish a debtor's wages after the debt has gone uncollected for a prolonged period. Recall from Chapter 15 that *garnishment* is the legal procedure by which a creditor may collect on a debt by directly attaching, or seizing, a portion of the debtor's assets (such as wages) that are in the possession of a third party (such as an employer).

State law provides the basis for a process of garnishment, but the law varies among the states as to how easily garnishment can be obtained. Indeed, a few states, such as Texas, prohibit garnishment of wages altogether except for child support. In addition, constitutional due process and federal legislation under the TILA provide further protections against abuse.[34] In general, the debtor is entitled to notice and an opportunity to be heard in a process of garnishment. Moreover, wages cannot be garnished beyond 25 percent of the debtor's after-tax earnings, and the garnishment must leave the debtor with at least a specified minimum income.

Consumer Health and Safety

Laws discussed earlier regarding the labeling and packaging of products go a long way toward promoting consumer health and safety. But there is a significant distinction between regulating the information dispensed about a product and regulating the content of the product. The classic example is tobacco products. Tobacco products have not been altered by regulation or banned outright despite their obvious hazards. What has been regulated are the warnings that producers are required to give consumers about the hazards of tobacco.[35] This section focuses on laws that regulate the actual products made available to consumers.

---

34. 15 U.S.C. Sections 1671–1677.
35. We are ignoring recent civil litigation concerning the liability of tobacco product manufacturers for injuries that arise from the use of tobacco.

The Federal Food, Drug and Cosmetic Act

The first federal legislation regulating food and drugs was enacted in 1906 as the Pure Food and Drugs Act. That law, as amended in 1938, exists presently as the Federal Food, Drug and Cosmetic Act (FFDCA).[36] The act protects consumers against adulterated and misbranded foods and drugs. More recent amendments have added substantive and procedural requirements to the act. In its present form, the act establishes food standards, specifies safe levels of potentially hazardous food additives, and sets classifications of food and food advertising.

Most of these statutory requirements are monitored and enforced by the Food and Drug Administration (FDA). Under an extensive set of procedures established by the FDA, drugs must be shown to be effective as well as safe before they may be marketed to the public, and the use of some food additives suspected of being carcinogenic is prohibited. A 1976 amendment to the FFDCA[37] authorizes the FDA to regulate medical devices, such as pacemakers and other health devices and equipment, and to withdraw from the market any such device that is mislabeled.

> **Be Aware** The Food and Drug Administration is authorized to obtain, among other things, orders for the recall and seizure of certain products.

The Consumer Product Safety Act

Consumer product safety legislation began in 1953 with enactment of the Flammable Fabrics Act, which prohibits the sale of highly flammable clothing or materials. Over the next two decades, Congress enacted legislation regarding the design or composition of specific classes of products. Then, in 1972, Congress, by enacting the Consumer Product Safety Act,[38] created a comprehensive scheme of regulation over matters of consumer safety. The act also established far-reaching authority over consumer safety under the Consumer Product Safety Commission (CPSC).

The CPSC conducts research on the safety of individual products, and it maintains a clearinghouse of information on the risks associated with various consumer products. The Consumer Product Safety Act authorizes the CPSC to set standards for consumer products and to ban the manufacture and sale of any product that it deems to be potentially hazardous to consumers. The CPSC also has authority to remove from the market any products it believes to be imminently hazardous and to require manufacturers to report on any products already sold or intended for sale if the products have proved to be hazardous. The CPSC also has authority to administer other product safety legislation, such as the Child Protection and Toy Safety Act of 1969[39] and the Federal Hazardous Substances Act of 1960.[40]

The CPSC's authority is sufficiently broad to allow it to ban any product that it believes poses an "unreasonable risk" to consumers. Some of the products that the CPSC has banned include various types of fireworks, cribs, and toys, as well as many products containing asbestos or vinyl chloride.

State Consumer Protection Laws

Thus far, our primary focus has been on federal legislation. As mentioned, however, state laws often provide more sweeping and significant protections

---

36. 21 U.S.C. Sections 301–393.
37. 21 U.S.C. Sections 352(o), 360(j), 360(k), and 360c–360k.
38. 15 U.S.C. Sections 2051–2083.
39. This act consists of amendments to 15 U.S.C. Sections 1261, 1262, and 1274.
40. 15 U.S.C. Sections 1261–1277.

for the consumer than do federal laws. The warranty and unconscionability provisions of the Uniform Commercial Code (discussed in Chapters 12 and 13) offer important protections for consumers against unfair practices on the part of sellers and lessors. The Magnuson-Moss Warranty Act of 1975[41] supplements the UCC provisions in cases involving both a consumer transaction of at least $10 and an express written warranty.

Far less widely adopted than the UCC is the Uniform Consumer Credit Code (UCCC). The UCCC has provisions concerning truth in lending, maximum credit ceilings, door-to-door sales, fine-print clauses, and other practices affecting consumer transactions.

Virtually all states have specific consumer protection acts, often titled "deceptive trade practices acts." Although state consumer protection statutes vary widely in their provisions, a common thread runs through most of them. Typically, state consumer protection laws are directed at deceptive trade practices, such as a seller's providing false or misleading information to consumers. As just mentioned, some of the legislation provides broad protection for consumers. A prime example is the Texas Deceptive Trade Practices Act of 1973, which forbids a seller from selling to a buyer anything that the buyer does not need or cannot afford.

---

41. 15 U.S.C. Sections 2301–2312.

Key Terms

bait-and-switch advertising 582	counteradvertising 582	Regulation Z 586
cease-and-desist order 582	multiple product orders 582	validation notice 596
consumer law 581		

Chapter Summary • Consumer Protection

Deceptive Advertising (See pages 581–584.)	1. **Definition of deceptive advertising**—Generally, an advertising claim will be deemed deceptive if it would mislead a reasonable consumer.
	
	2. **Bait-and-switch advertising**—Advertising a lower-priced product (the "bait") when the intention is not to sell the advertised product but to lure consumers into the store and convince them to buy a higher-priced product (the "switch") is prohibited by the FTC.
	
	3. **FTC actions against deceptive advertising**—
	
	  a. Cease-and-desist orders—Requiring the advertiser to stop the challenged advertising.
	
	  b. Counteradvertising—Requiring the advertiser to advertise to correct the earlier misinformation.

Telemarketing and Electronic Advertising (See pages 584–585.)	The Telephone Consumer Protection Act of 1991 prohibits telephone solicitation using an automatic telephone dialing system or a prerecorded voice, as well as the transmission of advertising materials via fax without first obtaining the recipient's permission to do so.

Chapter Summary • Consumer Protection

Labeling and Packaging (See pages 585–586.)	Manufacturers must comply with labeling or packaging requirements for their specific products. In general, all labels must be accurate and not misleading.

Sales
(See pages 586–590.)

1. **Door-to-door sales**—The FTC requires all door-to-door sellers to give consumers three days (a "cooling-off" period) to cancel any sale. States also provide for similar protection.

2. **Telephone and mail-order sales**—Federal and state statutes and regulations govern certain practices of sellers who solicit over the telephone or through the mails and prohibit the use of the mails to defraud individuals.

3. **Regulations affecting specific industries**—The FTC has regulations that apply to specific industries, such as the used-car business and funeral homes.

4. **Real estate sales**—Various federal and state laws apply to consumer transactions involving real estate.

Credit Protection
(See pages 590–598.)

1. **Consumer Credit Protection Act, Title I (Truth-in-Lending Act, or TILA)**—A disclosure law that requires sellers and lenders to disclose credit terms or loan terms in certain transactions, including retail and installment sales and loans, car loans, home-improvement loans, and certain real estate loans. Additionally, the TILA provides for the following:

   a. **Equal credit opportunity**—Creditors are prohibited from discriminating on the basis of race, religion, marital status, gender, and so on.

   b. **Credit-card protection**—Credit-card users may withhold payment for a faulty product sold, or for an error in billing, until the dispute is resolved; liability of cardholders for unauthorized charges is limited to $50, providing notice requirements are met; consumers are not liable for unauthorized charges made on unsolicited credit cards.

   c. **Consumer leases**—The Consumer Leasing Act (CLA) of 1988 protects consumers who lease automobiles and other goods priced at $25,000 or less if the lease term exceeds four months.

2. **Fair Credit Reporting Act**—Entitles consumers to request verification of the accuracy of a credit report and to have unverified information removed from their files.

3. **Fair Debt Collection Practices Act**—Prohibits debt collectors from using unfair debt-collection practices, such as contacting the debtor at his or her place of employment if the employer objects or at unreasonable times, contacting third parties about the debt, harassing the debtor, and so on.

Consumer Health and Safety Protection
(See pages 598–599.)

1. **Food and drugs**—The Federal Food, Drug and Cosmetic Act of 1938, as amended, protects consumers against adulterated and misbranded foods and drugs. The act establishes food standards, specifies safe levels of potentially hazardous food additives, and sets classifications of food and food advertising.

2. **Consumer product safety**—The Consumer Product Safety Act of 1972 seeks to protect consumers from risk of injury from hazardous products. The Consumer Product Safety Commission has the power to remove products that are deemed imminently hazardous from the market and to ban the manufacture and sale of hazardous products.

(Continued)

Chapter Summary • Consumer Protection, *Continued*

State Consumer Protection Laws (See pages 599–600.)	State laws often provide for greater consumer protection against deceptive trade practices than do federal laws. In addition, the warranty and unconscionability provisions of the Uniform Commercial Code protect consumers against sellers' deceptive practices. The Uniform Consumer Credit Code, which has not been widely adopted by the states, provides credit protection for consumers.

For Review

1. When will advertising be deemed deceptive?
2. How does the Federal Food, Drug and Cosmetic Act protect consumers?
3. What are the major federal statutes providing for consumer protection in credit transactions?
4. How does the Consumer Product Safety Act protect consumers?
5. What are the major state statutes that protect consumers?

Questions and Case Problems

20–1. Unsolicited Merchandise. Andrew, a California resident, received a flyer in the U.S. mail announcing a new line of regional cookbooks distributed by the Every-Kind Cookbook Co. Andrew was not interested and threw the flyer away. Two days later, Andrew received in the mail an introductory cookbook entitled *Lower Mongolian Regional Cookbook,* as announced in the flyer, on a "trial basis" from Every-Kind. Andrew was not interested but did not go to the trouble to return the cookbook. Every-Kind demanded payment of $20.95 for the *Lower Mongolian Regional Cookbook.* Discuss whether Andrew can be required to pay for the cookbook.

20–2. Consumer Protection. Fireside Rocking Chair Co. advertised in the newspaper a special sale price of $159 on machine-caned rocking chairs. In the advertisement was a drawing of a natural-wood rocking chair with a caned back and seat. The average person would not be able to tell from the drawing whether the rocking chair was machine caned or hand caned. Hand-caned rocking chairs sold for $259. Lowell and Celia Gudmundson went to Fireside because they had seen the ad for the machine-caned rocking chair and were very interested in purchasing one. The Gudmundsons arrived on the morning the sale began. Fireside's agent said the only machine-caned rocking chairs he had were painted lime green and were priced at $159. He immediately turned the Gudmundsons' atten-

tion to the hand-caned rocking chairs, praising their quality and pointing out that for the extra $100, the hand-caned chairs were surely a good value. The Gudmundsons, preferring the natural-wood machine-caned rocking chair for $159 as pictured in the advertisement, said they would like to order one. The Fireside agent said he could not order a natural-wood, machine-caned rocking chair. Discuss fully whether Fireside has violated any consumer protection laws.

20–3. Door-to-Door Sales. On June 28, a sales representative for Renowned Books called on the Gonchars at their home. After a very persuasive sales pitch on the part of the sales agent, the Gonchars agreed in writing to purchase a twenty-volume set of historical encyclopedias from Renowned Books for a total of $299. An initial down payment of $35 was required, with the remainder of the price to be paid in monthly payments over a one-year period. Two days later the Gonchars, having second thoughts, contacted the book company and stated that they had decided to rescind the contract. Renowned Books said this would be impossible. Has Renowned Books violated any consumer law by not allowing the Gonchars to rescind their contract? Explain.

20–4. Truth in Lending. Michael and Patricia Jensen purchased a new 1989 Ford Tempo from Ray Kim Ford, Inc. The Jensens signed a retail installment contract that provided for an estimated trade-in value of $800 for their old car. When the traded-in car turned out to be worth $1,388.08, Ray Kim prepared a second retail installment contract without the Jensens' knowledge. The second contract, although it credited the increased trade-in value of the car, compensated for this credit by increasing the interest rate, increasing the sales price of the car, and making other adjustments so that the second contract basically called for future cash payments by the Jensens of about the same amount as the first contract. In effect, the second contract gave the Jensens almost no benefit for the increased value of their traded-in car. The Jensens made payments under the contract until they noticed the minor difference in monthly payments, asked for a copy of the contract, and realized that it was not the contract that they had signed. The Jensens sued Ray Kim, alleging that the second contract was a forgery and that Ray Kim had violated the Truth-in-Lending Act (TILA) by not disclosing to them the credit terms of the second contract. Has Ray Kim violated the TILA? If the Jensens choose to adopt the terms of the second contract, despite the forgery, has the act been violated? Discuss fully. [*Jensen v. Ray Kim Ford, Inc.,* 920 F.2d 3 (7th Cir. 1990)]

20–5. Deceptive Advertising. Thompson Medical Co. marketed a new cream called Aspercreme that was supposed to help arthritis victims and others suffering from minor aches. Aspercreme contained no aspirin. Thompson's television advertisements stated that the product provided "the strong relief of aspirin right where you hurt" and showed the announcer holding up aspirin tablets as well as a tube of Aspercreme. The Federal Trade Commission held that the advertisements were misleading, because they led consumers to believe that Aspercreme contained aspirin. Thompson Medical Co. appealed this decision and argued that the advertisements never actually stated that the product contained aspirin. How should the court rule? Discuss. [*Thompson Medical Co. v. Federal Trade Commission,* 791 F.2d 189 (D.C. Cir. 1986)]

20–6. Deceptive Advertising. Dennis and Janice Geiger saw an advertisement in a newspaper for a Kimball Whitney spinet piano on sale for $699 at the McCormick Piano & Organ Co. Because the style of the piano drawn in the advertisement matched their furniture, the Geigers were particularly interested in the Kimball. When they went to McCormick Piano & Organ, however, they learned that the drawing closely resembled another, more expensive Crest piano and that the Kimball spinet looked quite different from the piano sketched in the drawing. The salesperson told the Geigers that she was unable to order a spinet piano of the style they requested. When the Geigers asked for the names of other customers who had purchased the advertised pianos, the

salesperson became extremely upset and said she would not, under any circumstances, sell the Geigers a piano. The Geigers then brought suit against the piano store, alleging that the store had engaged in deceptive advertising in violation of Indiana law. Was the McCormick Piano & Organ Co. guilty of deceptive advertising? Explain. [*McCormick Piano & Organ Co. v. Geiger,* 412 N.E.2d 842 (Ind.App. 1980)]

20–7. Equal Credit Opportunity. The Riggs National Bank of Washington, D.C., lent more than $11 million to Samuel Linch and Albert Randolph. To obtain the loan, Linch and Randolph provided personal financial statements. Linch's statement included substantial assets that he owned jointly with his wife, Marcia. As a condition of the loan, Riggs required that Marcia, as well as Samuel and Albert, sign a personal guaranty for repayment. When the borrowers defaulted, Riggs filed a suit in a federal district court to recover its money, based on the personal guaranties. The court ruled against the borrowers, who appealed. On what basis might the borrowers argue that Riggs violated the Equal Credit Opportunity Act? [*Riggs National Bank of Washington, D.C. v. Linch,* 36 F.3d 370 (4th Cir. 1994)]

20–8. Fair Debt Collection. A condominium association, Rancho Santa Margarita Recreation and Landscape Corp., attempted unsuccessfully to collect an assessment fee from Andrew Ladick. The association referred the matter to the Law Offices of Gerald J. Van Gemert. Van Gemert sent Ladick a letter demanding payment of the fee. The letter did not include a "validation notice," as required by the Fair Debt Collection Practices Act (FDCPA), nor did it disclose that Van Gemert was attempting to collect a debt and that any information obtained would be used for that purpose. Ladick filed a suit in a federal district court against Van Gemert and his office, alleging violations of the FDCPA. Van Gemert filed a motion for summary judgment on the ground that the assessment was not a "debt," as defined by the FDCPA, in part because there was no "transaction," as required by the FDCPA definition, out of which Ladick's obligation arose. Will the court agree with Van Gemert? Why or why not? [*Ladick v. Van Gemert,* 146 F.3d 1205 (10th Cir. 1998)]

20–9. Fair Debt Collection. Gloria Mahon incurred a bill of $279.70 for medical services rendered by Dr. Larry Bowen. For more than two years, Bowen sent monthly billing statements to the Mahons at their home address (where they had lived for forty-five years). Getting no response, Bowen assigned the collection of their account to Credit Bureau of Placer County, Inc. Credit Bureau uses computerized collection tracking and filing software, known as Columbia Ultimate Business Systems (CUBS). CUBS automatically generates standardized collection notices and acts as an electronic filing system for each account, recording all collection activities, including which notices are sent to whom and on what date. Credit Bureau employees monitor the activity, routinely noting whether an envelope is returned undelivered. Credit Bureau mailed three CUBS–generated notices to the Mahons. According to Credit Bureau's records, the notices were not returned and the Mahons did not respond. Credit Bureau reported the Mahons' account as delinquent. The Mahons filed a suit in a federal district court against Credit Bureau, alleging in part that the agency had failed to send a validation notice, as required by the Fair Debt Collection Practices Act. Credit Bureau filed a motion for summary judgment. Should a notice be considered sent only if a debtor acknowledges its receipt? Why or why not? [*Mahon v. Credit Bureau of Placer County, Inc.,* 171 F.3d 1197 (9th Cir. 1999)]

A Question of Ethics and Social Responsibility

20–10. On July 16, 1982, the Semars signed a loan contract with Platte Valley Federal Savings & Loan Association, offering a second mortgage on their home as collateral. Under the Truth-in-Lending Act (TILA), borrowers are allowed three business days to rescind, without penalty, a consumer loan that uses their principal dwelling as security. The TILA requires lenders in such situations to state specifically the last date on which the borrower can rescind the loan agreement, and if they fail to include this date, the borrower may rescind the loan within three years after it was made. Platte Valley's form omitted the exact expiration date of the three-day period, although it stated that the rescission right expired three business days after July 16. The Semars ceased making monthly payments on the loan in

September 1983 and sent a Notice of Rescission to Platte Valley on February 15, 1984. The Semars claimed that Platte Valley had violated the TILA by failing to specify in the loan contract the exact date of the expiration of the three-day rescission period. Because of this violation, the Semars maintained they had three years in which to rescind the contract. Although the court found the Semars to be "unsympathetic plaintiffs," it nevertheless held that rescission was appropriate for the technical violation of the TILA. [*Semar v. Platte Valley Federal Savings & Loan Association,* 791 F.2d 699 (9th Cir. 1986)]

1. Do you think that the court, by adhering so strictly to the letter of the law, violated the spirit of the law?
2. When deciding issues involving alleged violations of consumer protection legislation, such as the TILA, should courts balance the equities of the cases? That is, should the ethical (or unethical) behavior of the parties to a particular transaction be taken into consideration?
3. How might you justify, on ethical grounds, the court's decision in this case?

For Critical Analysis

20–11. In some cases, the federal government has named corporate officers as defendants in prosecutions for violations of the Federal Food, Drug and Cosmetic Act. The liability of these officers does not depend on their knowledge of, or personal participation in, a criminal act. On what, then, does their liability depend? With the answer to the previous question in mind, what might a manager plead in his or her defense to avoid liability?

Interacting with the Internet

Online Legal Research Exercises

Go to http://leet. westbuslaw.com, the Web site that accompanies this text. Select "Interactive Study Center," and then click on "Chapter 20." There you will find the following Internet research exercise that you can perform to learn more about consumer law:

Activity 20–1: Consumer Law

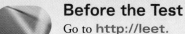

Before the Test

Go to http://leet. westbuslaw.com, the Web site that accompanies this text. Select "Interactive Quizzes." You will find a number of interactive questions relating to this chapter.

chapter
21

Protecting the Environment

contents

chapter objectives

After reading this chapter, you should be able to:

1. Identify common law actions available against polluters.

2. Describe the National Environmental Policy Act.

3. Explain how the government regulates air and water pollution.

4. List and describe the major statutes that regulate toxic chemicals.

5. Identify the purpose and functions of Superfund.

We now turn to a discussion of the various ways in which businesses are regulated by the government in the interest of protecting the environment. Concern over the degradation of the environment has increased over time in response to the environmental effects of population growth, urbanization, and industrialization. Society's generation of waste threatens not only the quality of the environment but also—as indicated by the connection made in the quotation alongside—the quality of human life. Environmental protection is not without a price, however. For many businesses, the costs of complying with environmental regulations are high, and for some they are too high. There is constant tension between the desirability of increasing profits and productivity and the need to attain higher quality in the environment.

Environmental law—all law pertaining to environmental protection—is not new. Indeed, the federal government began to regulate some activities, such as those involving the pollution of navigable waterways, in the late 1800s. In the last few decades, however, the body of environmental law has expanded substantially as government has attempted to control industrial waste and to protect certain natural resources and endangered species. (In recent years, various nongovernmental organizations, including "corporate watch" groups, have also pressured corporations to be more sensitive to the need to protect the environment. See this chapter's *Legal E-nvironment* on the next page for a discussion of some of the tactics used by these groups.)

In this chapter, we first discuss the common law actions that can be brought against business firms and individuals for damages caused by polluting activities. The remainder of the chapter examines the various statutes and regulations that have been created to protect the environment.

> **"Man, however much he may like to pretend the contrary, is part of nature."**
>
> Rachel Carson, 1907–1964
> (American writer and conservationist)

Environmental Law The body of statutory, regulatory, and common law relating to the protection of the environment.

Common Law Actions

Common law remedies against environmental pollution originated centuries ago in England. Those responsible for operations that created dirt, smoke, noxious odors, noise, or toxic substances were sometimes held liable under common law theories of nuisance or negligence. Today, injured individuals continue to rely on the common law to obtain damages and injunctions against business polluters. (Statutory remedies are also available, a topic that we treat later.)

Nuisance

Under the common law doctrine of **nuisance,** persons may be held liable if they use their property in a manner that unreasonably interferes with others' rights to use or enjoy their own property. In these situations, it is common for courts to balance the equities between the harm caused by the pollution and the costs of stopping it.

Courts have often denied injunctive relief on the ground that the hardships to be imposed on the polluter and on the community are greater than the hardships to be suffered by the plaintiff. ● **Example 21.1** A factory that causes neighboring landowners to suffer from smoke, dirt, and vibrations may be left in operation if it is the core of a local economy. The injured parties may be awarded only money damages. These damages may include compensation for the decreased value of their property that results from the factory's operation. ●

Nuisance A common law doctrine under which persons may be held liable for using their property in a manner that unreasonably interferes with others' rights to use or enjoy their own property.

Legal *e*-nvironment

Online Environmental Activism

Environmental activism is not new. Indeed, since the 1960s, various environmental groups have promoted corporate environmental accountability through such tactics as boycotts, negative publicity, and the like. Since the 1990s, however, environmental activists have acquired a new weapon in their struggle to protect the environment: the Internet. As mentioned in the *Legal E-nvironment* feature in Chapter 2, the Internet allows various corporate watch groups, including environmental groups, to organize campaigns against targeted corporations with relative ease and at low (or no) cost. Indeed, there are now Web sites that give training courses in how to become a "virtual activist" (see, for example, Net Action's Web site at **http://www.netaction.org**).

Online environmental groups use a variety of tactics in their efforts to promote corporate environmental responsibility and accountability, including those discussed here.

Exposing "Greenwash"

One tactic used by several online environmental groups is to post articles on the Web exposing "greenwash." As defined by Corporate Watch (at **http://www.corpwatch.org**), *greenwash* occurs whenever "socially and environmentally destructive corporations" attempt "to preserve and expand their markets by posing as friends of the environment and leaders in the struggle to eradicate poverty." Each year, Corporate Watch doles out greenwash awards to companies that do the best job of promoting their "green" images, even though, in Corporate Watch's opinion, their actions are not environmentally friendly.

Another Web site (at **http://www.earthday2000.org**), which calls itself the Consumer Clearinghouse for the Environmental Decade, issues "Don't Be Fooled" awards to the top ten "greenwashers." On its Web site, Earth Day 2000 juxtaposes each company's attempts to build a favorable image through advertising with the company's actual practices with respect to the environment.

Calls for Action

Nearly all online environmental activist groups urge visitors to their sites to take some kind of action—by sending an e-mail message to a targeted company, for example, or by boycotting certain products that the groups believe are environmentally destructive. Consider EarthLink's Web site (at **http://www.earthlink.net**). This site lists products—including pesticides, genetically engineered foods, and pharmaceutical products—that should be boycotted because they are allegedly harmful to the environment or unsafe for human consumption.

For Critical Analysis: *Online criticism of corporate behavior is well and good, say some, because it helps to promote corporate social responsibility and accountability. Yet suppose that an online group makes misleading or untrue statements about a company. Is there anything the firm can do to counter the misinformation?*

> **"A nuisance may be merely a right thing in the wrong place, like a pig in the parlor instead of the barnyard."**
>
> George Sutherland, 1862–1942
> (American jurist)

A property owner may be given relief from pollution in situations in which he or she can identify a distinct harm separate from that affecting the general public. This harm is referred to as a "private" nuisance. Under the common law, citizens were denied standing (access to the courts—see Chapter 3) unless they suffered a harm distinct from the harm suffered by the public at large. Some states still require this. Therefore, a group of citizens who wished to stop a new development that would cause significant water pollution was denied access to the courts on the ground that the harm to them did not differ from the harm to the general public.[1] A public authority (such as a state's attorney general) can sue to abate a "public" nuisance.

---

1. *Save the Bay Committee, Inc. v. Mayor of City of Savannah,* 227 Ga. 436, 181 S.E.2d 351 (1971).

In the following case, landowners sued their neighbor, the operator of a gravel pit, under the common law doctrine of nuisance. The landowners contended that the operator's excavation in the gravel pit resulted in the drying up of a spring running under their property.

Case 21.1 ● Maddocks v. Giles

Supreme Judicial Court of Maine, 1996. 686 A.2d 1069.

Background and Facts Sewall and Janice Maddocks owned property next to a gravel pit owned and operated by Elbridge Giles, doing business as E. A. Giles & Son. Below the surface of the Maddockses' property was a subterranean spring that produced large quantities of high-quality water. Giles's excavation in the gravel pit caused the spring to dry up. The Maddockses filed a suit against Giles in a Maine state court, seeking damages on the ground that the excavation was a nuisance because the excavation caused a disruption of the flow of the spring. The court dismissed the complaint, and the Maddockses appealed to the state's highest court, the Supreme Judicial Court of Maine.

In the Words of the Court . . .
GLASSMAN, Justice.

* * * *

Although we recognize the general principle that a property owner may use his land as he pleases for all lawful purposes, there is a long standing limitation of this rule preventing a landowner from drastically altering the flow of a watercourse. * * * A watercourse cannot be stopped up or diverted to the injury of other[s]. There is a public or natural [right] in such a stream, belonging to all persons whose lands are benefitted by it. * * * Application of these principles to the facts of this case leads us to conclude that the trial court erred when it dismissed the Maddockses' complaint.

The complaint alleges that Giles' excavation activities created a nuisance that caused a disruption of the flow of a subterranean spring from aquifers beneath Giles' property into the Maddockses' property. * * * [W]e conclude that the complaint sufficiently alleges a nuisance by the disruption of a watercourse * * * .

Decision and Remedy The Supreme Judicial Court of Maine vacated (set aside) the lower court's dismissal of the Maddockses' complaint. Disruption of the flow of a subterranean spring may constitute a nuisance. The case could proceed to trial.

For Critical Analysis—Economic Consideration *What are the competing considerations in pollution cases that might operate to allow pollution to continue?*

Negligence and Strict Liability

An injured party may sue a business polluter in tort under the negligence and strict liability theories discussed in Chapters 9 and 10. The basis for a negligence action is a business's alleged failure to use reasonable care toward a party whose injury was foreseeable and, of course, caused by the lack of reasonable care. For example, employees might sue an employer whose failure to use proper pollution controls contaminated the air, causing the employees to suffer respiratory illnesses. A developing area of tort law involves **toxic torts**—actions against toxic polluters.

Toxic Tort Failure to use or to clean up properly toxic chemicals that cause harm to a person or society.

Businesses that engage in ultrahazardous activities—such as the transportation of radioactive materials—are strictly liable for whatever injuries the activities cause. In a strict liability action, the injured party does not need to prove that the business failed to exercise reasonable care.

Federal Regulation

Congress has passed a number of statutes to control the impact of human activities on the environment. Exhibit 21–1 lists and summarizes the major federal environmental statutes discussed in this chapter. Some of these statutes were passed in an attempt to improve the quality of air and water. Some of them specifically regulate toxic chemicals—including pesticides, herbicides, and hazardous wastes. Some are concerned with radiation.

Environmental Regulatory Agencies

Much of the body of federal law governing business activities consists of the regulations issued and enforced by administrative agencies. The most well known of the agencies regulating environmental law is, of course, the Environmental Protection Agency (EPA), which was created in 1970 to coordinate federal environmental responsibilities. Other federal agencies with authority for regulating specific environmental matters include the Department of the Interior, the Department of Defense, the Department of Labor, the Food and Drug Administration, and the Nuclear Regulatory Commission. These regulatory agencies—and all other agencies of the federal government—must take environmental factors into consideration when making significant decisions.

Most federal environmental laws provide that citizens can sue to enforce environmental regulations if government agencies fail to do so—or if agencies go too far in their enforcement actions. Typically, a threshold hurdle in such suits is meeting the requirements for standing to sue—a topic discussed in this chapter's *Inside the Legal Environment* on page 612.

Assessment of the Impact of Agency Actions on the Environment

The National Environmental Policy Act (NEPA) of 1969[2] requires that for every major federal action that significantly affects the quality of the environment, an **environmental impact statement (EIS)** must be prepared. An action qualifies as "major" if it involves a substantial commitment of resources (monetary or otherwise). An action is "federal" if a federal agency has the power to control it. Construction by a private developer of a ski resort on federal land, for example, may require an EIS.[3] Building or operating a nuclear plant, which requires a federal permit,[4] or constructing a dam as part of a federal project would require an EIS.[5] If an agency decides that an EIS is unnecessary, it must issue a statement supporting this conclusion.

Environmental Impact Statement (EIS) A statement required by the National Environmental Policy Act for any major federal action that will significantly affect the quality of the environment. The statement must analyze the action's impact on the environment and explore alternative actions that might be taken.

2. 42 U.S.C. Sections 4321–4370d.
3. *Robertson v. Methow Valley Citizens' Council,* 490 U.S. 332, 109 S.Ct. 1835, 104 L.Ed.2d 351 (1989).
4. *Calvert Cliffs Coordinating Committee v. Atomic Energy Commission,* 449 F.2d 1109 (D.C. Cir. 1971).
5. *Marsh v. Oregon Natural Resources Council,* 490 U.S. 360, 109 S.Ct. 1851, 104 L.Ed.2d 377 (1989).

Exhibit 21–1 Federal Environmental Statutes

POPULAR NAME	PURPOSE	STATUTE REFERENCE
Rivers and Harbors Appropriations Act (1899)	To prohibit ships and manufacturers from discharging and depositing refuse in navigable waterways.	33 U.S.C. Sections 401–418.
Federal Insecticide, Fungicide, and Rodenticide Act (FIFRA) (1947)	To control the use of pesticides and herbicides.	7 U.S.C. Sections 136–136y.
Federal Water Pollution Control Act (FWPCA) (1948)	To eliminate the discharge of pollutants from major sources into navigable waters.	33 U.S.C. Sections 1251–1387.
Atomic Energy Act (1954)	To eliminate environmental harm from the private nuclear industry.	42 U.S.C. Sections 2011 to 2297g-4.
Clean Air Act (1963)	To control air pollution from mobile and stationary sources.	42 U.S.C. Sections 7401–7671q.
National Environmental Policy Act (NEPA) (1969)	To limit environmental harm from federal government activities.	42 U.S.C. Sections 4321–4370d.
Marine Protection, Research, and Sanctuaries Act (Ocean Dumping Act) of 1972	To regulate the transporting and dumping of material into ocean waters.	16 U.S.C. Sections 1401–1445.
Noise Control Act (1972)	To regulate noise pollution from transportation and nontransportation sources.	42 U.S.C. Sections 4901–4918.
Endangered Species Act (1973)	To protect species that are threatened with extinction.	16 U.S.C. Sections 1531–1544.
Safe Drinking Water Act (1974)	To regulate pollutants in public drinking water systems.	42 U.S.C. Sections 300f to 300j-25.
Resource Conservation and Recovery Act (RCRA) (1976)	To establish standards for hazardous waste disposal.	42 U.S.C. Sections 6901–6986.
Toxic Substances Control Act (1976)	To regulate toxic chemicals and chemical compounds.	15 U.S.C. Sections 2601–2692.
Comprehensive Environmental Response, Compensation, and Liability Act (CERCLA) (Superfund) (1980)	To regulate the clean-up of hazardous waste–disposal sites.	42 U.S.C. Sections 9601–9675.
Low Level Radioactive Waste Policy Act (1980)	To assign to the states responsibility for nuclear power plants' low-level radioactive waste.	42 U.S.C. Sections 2021b–2021j.
Nuclear Waste Policy Act (1982)	To provide for the designation of a permanent radioactive waste–disposal site.	42 U.S.C. Sections 10101–10270.
Oil Pollution Act (1990)	To establish liability for the clean-up of nagivable waters after oil-spill disasters.	33 U.S.C. Sections 2701–2761.

Inside the Legal Environment

Can Citizens Sue the Government for "Overregulating" the Environment?

There is a constant tension between the two policy goals of economic productivity and environmental protection. This tension was highlighted in a case brought by two Oregon ranchers—Brad Bennett and Mario Giordano—and two Oregon irrigation districts (collectively, the Bennett group) against the Fish and Wildlife Service (FWS) and the secretary of the Department of the Interior.

The case originated after the FWS proposed that the minimum water levels in two reservoirs be increased to protect two endangered species of fish. If the proposal were implemented, less water could be drawn from the reservoirs for irrigation and other purposes, which would have a serious economic impact on the ranchers' businesses. In a citizens' suit against the FWS, the Bennett group claimed that the agency neglected to use the best available scientific and commercial data in making its decision, as required under the Endangered Species Act (ESA) of 1973; nor did the FWS take into account the economic impact of its water-level recommendations.

The Standing-to-Sue Issue

At issue in the case, which ultimately reached the United States Supreme Court, was whether the ranchers had standing to sue under the ESA. The question was significant because the Bennett group was not seeking to protect the environment but to protect their economic interests. Both a federal district court and a federal appellate court held that the group did not

have standing to sue because its claim did not fall within the "zone of interests" protected by the ESA, which was to protect species. The zone-of-interests test has long been applied by the federal courts in determining whether a party has standing to sue under a specific law. Basically, to have standing under this test, a plaintiff must show that the interest that he or she seeks to protect is the kind of interest protected by that specific law.

The Supreme Court, however, unanimously reversed the appellate court's decision. In applying the zone-of-interests test, the Court looked to the citizen-suit language of the ESA, which gives "any person" the right to sue. According to the Court, this language was expansive enough to include the economic interests of the Bennett group.

Looking at the Overall Purpose of Legislation

The Court held that in determining whether a party has standing, the courts must look not to the overall purpose of an act but to the particular provision of an act on which the party based his or her complaint. In this case, the Bennett group alleged that the FWS failed to abide by a specific ESA provision that requires an agency to use the "best scientific and commercial data available." The Court noted that while this provision "no doubt serves to advance the ESA's overall goal of species preservation, we think it readily apparent that another objective (if not indeed the primary one) is to avoid needless economic dislocation produced by agency officials zealously but unintelligently pursuing their environmental objectives."[a]

For Critical Analysis: *What are some implications of this decision for other businesses whose economic interests are harmed by environmental laws?*

a. *Bennett v. Spear*, 520 U.S. 154, 117 S.Ct. 1154, 137 L.Ed.2d 281 (1997).

An EIS must analyze (1) the impact on the environment that the action will have, (2) any adverse effects on the environment and alternative actions that might be taken, and (3) irreversible effects the action might generate. EISs have become instruments for private citizens, consumer interest groups, businesses, and others to challenge federal agency actions on the basis that the actions improperly threaten the environment.

Other federal laws also require that environmental values be considered in agency decision making. Among the most important of these laws are those that have been enacted to protect fish and wildlife. Under the Fish and Wildlife

International Perspective

Standards for Environmental Management

Today's business managers can no longer afford to ignore the effect of their decisions on the environment. This is true not only in the United States but in other countries around the globe as well.

To guide companies in their attempts to be environmentally responsible, the Geneva-based International Organization for Standardization has created fourteen thousand universally applicable standards for the development of environmental management systems. The standards are the outgrowth of the nine thousand quality management and quality assurance standards pub-

lished by the organization in 1987. The nine thousand standards achieved wide acceptance in the United States, Europe, and Asia.

The standards are not regulatory in nature and do not impose any restrictions on polluting activities. Rather, they offer a variety of management tools and devices to help companies perform their environmental obligations. Essentially, the standards set forth a series of recommendations on how a company can establish an effective and totally integrated environmental management system. The standards reflect the commercial reality that firms doing business internationally, because they are subject to different national environmental laws, need a consistent set of environmental standards to guide them.

For Critical Analysis: *Why don't the standards impose restrictions on polluting activities?*

Coordination Act of 1958,[6] federal agencies proposing to approve the impounding or diversion of the waters of a stream must consult with the Fish and Wildlife Service with a view to preventing the loss of fish and wildlife resources. Also important is the Endangered Species Act of 1973.[7] Under this act, all federal agencies are required to take steps to ensure that their actions "do not jeopardize the continued existence of endangered species" or the habitat of an endangered species. An action may jeopardize the continued existence of a species if it sets in motion a chain of events that reduces the chances that the species will survive.

Air Pollution

Federal involvement with air pollution goes back to the 1950s, when Congress authorized funds for air-pollution research. In 1963, the federal government passed the Clean Air Act,[8] which focused on multistate air pollution and provided assistance to states. Various amendments, particularly in 1970, 1977, and 1990, strengthened the government's authority to regulate the quality of air. These laws provide the basis for issuing regulations to control pollution coming primarily from mobile sources (such as automobiles) and stationary sources (such as electric utilities and industrial plants).

Mobile Sources

Regulations governing air pollution from automobiles and other mobile sources specify pollution standards and time schedules for meeting these

---

6. 16 U.S.C. Sections 661–666c.
7. 16 U.S.C. Sections 1531–1544.
8. 42 U.S.C. Sections 7401–7671q.

Who suffers the harm when automobiles pollute? Who pays the price to reduce automobile pollution? Who should pay?

standards. For example, under the 1990 amendments to the Clean Air Act, automobile manufacturers must cut new automobiles' exhaust emission of nitrogen oxide by 60 percent and emission of other pollutants by 35 percent. By 1998, all new automobiles had to meet this standard. Regulations that will go into effect beginning with 2004 model cars call for cutting nitrogen oxide tailpipe emissions by nearly 10 percent by 2007. For the first time, sport utility vehicles and light trucks were also required to meet the same emission standards as automobiles.

Service stations are also subject to environmental regulations. The 1990 amendments require service stations to sell gasoline with a higher oxygen content in forty-one cities that experience carbon monoxide pollution in the winter. Service stations are required to sell even cleaner burning gasoline in Los Angeles and another eight of the most polluted urban areas.

The EPA attempts to update pollution-control standards when new scientific information becomes available. In light of evidence that very small particles (2.5 microns, or millionths of a meter) of soot affect our health as significantly as larger particles, the EPA issued new particulate standards for motor vehicle exhaust systems and other sources of pollution. The EPA also increased the acceptable standard for ozone, which is formed when sunlight combines with pollutants from cars and other sources. Ozone is the basic ingredient of smog. The EPA's particulate standards and the acceptable standard for ozone are being challenged in the courts.[9] Meanwhile, the old standards are in force.

---

9. See, for example, *American Trucking Associations v. Environmental Protection Agency,* 175 F.3d 1027 (D.C.Cir. 1999), modified on rehearing, 195 F.3d 4 (D.C.Cir. 1999); and *American Petroleum Institute v. U.S. Environmental Protection Agency,* 198 F.3d 275 (D.C.Cir. 2000).

Stationary Sources

The Clean Air Act authorizes the EPA to establish air-quality standards for stationary sources (such as manufacturing plants) but recognizes that the primary responsibility for preventing and controlling air pollution rests with state and local governments. The EPA sets primary and secondary levels of ambient standards—that is, the maximum levels of certain pollutants—and the states formulate plans to achieve those standards. The plans are to provide for the attainment of primary standards within three years and secondary standards within a reasonable time. For economic, political, and technological reasons, however, the deadlines are often subject to change.

Different standards apply to sources of pollution in clean areas and those in polluted areas. Different standards also apply to existing sources of pollution and major new sources. Major new sources include existing sources modified by a change in a method of operation that increases emissions. Performance standards for major sources require use of the *maximum achievable control technology,* or MACT, to reduce emissions from the combustion of fossil fuels (coal and oil). As mentioned, the EPA issues guidelines as to what equipment meets this standard.

Under the 1990 amendments to the Clean Air Act, 110 of the oldest coal-burning power plants in the United States must cut their emissions by 40 percent by the year 2001 to reduce acid rain. Utilities were granted "credits" to emit certain amounts of sulfur dioxide, and those that emit less than the allowed amounts can sell their credits to other polluters. Controls on other factories and businesses are intended to reduce ground-level ozone pollution in ninety-six cities to healthful levels by 2005 (except Los Angeles, which has until 2010). Industrial emissions of 189 hazardous air pollutants must be reduced by 90 percent by 2000. By 2002, the production of chlorofluorocarbons (such as Freon), carbon tetrachloride, and methyl chloroform—used in air conditioning, refrigeration, and insulation and linked to depletion of the ozone layer—must stop.

Hazardous Air Pollutants

Hazardous air pollutants are those likely to cause an increase in mortality or in serious irreversible or incapacitating illness. As noted, there are 189 of these pollutants, including asbestos, benzene, beryllium, cadmium, mercury, and vinyl chloride. These pollutants may cause cancer as well as neurological and reproductive damage. They are emitted from stationary sources by a variety of business activities, including smelting, dry cleaning, house painting, and commercial baking. Instead of establishing specific emissions standards for each hazardous air pollutant, the 1990 amendments to the Clean Air Act require industry to use pollution-control equipment that represents the maximum achievable control technology, or MACT, to limit emissions. As mentioned, the EPA issues guidelines as to what equipment meets this standard.

In 1996, the EPA issued a rule to regulate hazardous air pollutants emitted by landfills. The rule requires landfills constructed after May 30, 1991, that emit more than a specified amount of pollutants to install landfill gas collection and control systems. The rule also requires the states to impose the same requirements on landfills constructed before May 30, 1991, if they accepted waste after November 8, 1987.[10]

---

10. 40 C.F.R. Sections 60.750–759.

Violations of the Clean Air Act

For violations of emission limits under the Clean Air Act, the EPA can assess civil penalties of up to $25,000 per day. Additional fines of up to $5,000 per day can be assessed for other violations, such as failing to maintain the required records. To penalize those for whom it is more cost effective to violate the act than to comply with it, the EPA is authorized to obtain a penalty equal to the violator's economic benefits from noncompliance. Persons who provide information about violators may be paid up to $10,000. Private citizens can also sue violators.

Those who knowingly violate the act may be subject to criminal penalties, including fines of up to $1 million and imprisonment for up to two years (for false statements or failures to report violations). Corporate officers are among those who may be subject to these penalties.

Water Pollution

"Among the treasures of our land is water—fast becoming our most valuable, most prized, most critical resource."

Dwight D. Eisenhower, 1890–1969
(Thirty-fourth president of the United States, 1953–1961)

Federal regulations governing the pollution of water can be traced back to the Rivers and Harbors Appropriations Act of 1899.[11] These regulations prohibited ships and manufacturers from discharging or depositing refuse in navigable waterways.

Navigable Waters

Once limited to waters actually used for navigation, the term *navigable waters* is today interpreted to include coastal and freshwater wetlands (how the EPA defines wetlands will be discussed shortly), as well as intrastate lakes and streams used by interstate travelers and industries. In 1948, Congress passed the Federal Water Pollution Control Act (FWPCA),[12] but its regulatory system and enforcement proved inadequate. In 1972, amendments to the FWPCA—known as the Clean Water Act—established the following goals: (1) make waters safe for swimming, (2) protect fish and wildlife, and (3) eliminate the discharge of pollutants into the water. The amendments required that municipal and industrial polluters apply for permits before discharging wastes into navigable waters.

They also set forth specific time schedules, which were extended by amendment in 1977 and by the Water Quality Act of 1987.[13] Under these schedules, the EPA establishes limitations for discharges of types of pollutants based on the technology available for controlling them. Regulations, for the most part, specify that the *best available control technology,* or BACT, be installed. The EPA issues guidelines as to what equipment meets this standard, which essentially requires the most effective pollution-control equipment available. New sources must install BACT equipment before beginning operations. Existing sources are subject to timetables for installation of BACT equipment. These sources must immediately install equipment that utilizes the *best practical control technology,* or BPCT. The EPA also issues guidelines as to what equipment meets this standard.

---

11. 33 U.S.C. Sections 401–418.
12. 33 U.S.C. Sections 1251–1387.
13. This act amended 33 U.S.C. Section 1251.

A scientist tests water from an industrial source that has been cleaned of pollutants. How "clean" should such water be before it is released into the environment?

WETLANDS The Clean Water Act prohibits the filling or dredging of **wetlands** unless a permit is obtained from the Army Corps of Engineers. The EPA defines wetlands as "those areas that are inundated or saturated by surface or ground water at a frequency and duration sufficient to support, and that under normal circumstances do support, a prevalence of vegetation typically adapted for life in saturated soil conditions." In recent years, federal regulatory policy in regard to wetlands has elicited substantial controversy because of the broad interpretation of what constitutes a wetland subject to the regulatory authority of the federal government. The following case is illustrative.

Wetlands Areas of land designated by government agencies (such as the Army Corps of Engineers or the Environmental Protection Agency) as protected areas that support wildlife and that therefore cannot be filled in or dredged by private contractors or parties.

Case 21.2 ● Hoffman Homes, Inc. v. Administrator, United States Environmental Protection Agency

United States Court of Appeals, Seventh Circuit, 1993. 999 F.2d 256.

Company Profile *Sam and Jack Hoffman started F&S Construction in 1947. Over the next few years, the company—renamed the Hoffman Group—built thousands of low-priced houses throughout the United States, becoming the nation's third largest builder by 1955. Norman Hassinger, a residential marketing expert, became president of the Hoffman Group in 1982 and gradually took over the firm. In 1987, the Hoffman Group became the Hassinger Companies. Hassinger created Hoffman Homes, Inc., as a home-building subsidiary.*

Background and Facts Hoffman Homes, Inc., in preparation for the construction of a housing subdivision, filled and graded a 0.8-acre, bowl-shaped depression ("Area A"). Before Hoffman filled Area A, rainwater periodically collected there. The EPA issued an order stating that Hoffman had filled wetlands without a permit in violation of the Clean Water Act and ordered Hoffman to, among other things, cease its filling activities and pay a fine of $50,000 for violating the act. Hoffman protested that the EPA had no regulatory authority over Area A because the area in no way affected interstate commerce. The EPA stated that it had authority to regulate discharges of fill materials into intrastate wetlands that have a "minimal, potential effect" on interstate commerce and that Area A had such an effect because migratory birds could potentially use the area. Hoffman appealed the decision to the Seventh Circuit Court of Appeals.

(Continued)

Case 21.2 Continued

In the Words of the Court . . .
HARLINGTON WOOD, Senior Circuit Judge.

* * * *

* * * It is true, of course, that migratory birds can alight most anywhere. As [a witness] testified, he has seen mallards in parking lot puddles. The ALJ [administrative law judge of the EPA], however, was in the unique position to view the evidence, to hear the testimony, and to judge the credibility of the witnesses. He concluded that the evidence did not support the conclusion that Area A had characteristics whose use by and value to migratory birds is well established. We agree. The migratory birds are better judges of what is suitable for their welfare than are we [or anyone at the EPA]. Having avoided Area A the migratory birds have thus spoken and submitted their own evidence. We see no need to argue with them. No justification whatsoever is seen from the evidence to interfere with private ownership based on what appears to be no more than a well intentioned effort in these particular factual circumstances to expand government control beyond reasonable or practical limits. After April showers not every temporary wet spot necessarily becomes subject to government control.

Decision and Remedy The court, holding that Area A was not subject to regulation under the Clean Water Act, vacated the EPA's order requiring Hoffman Homes to pay a $50,000 administrative penalty for the filling of Area A.

For Critical Analysis *In evaluating cases concerning wetlands, does it matter that the EPA, and not Congress, defines specifically what constitutes a "wetland"?*

VIOLATIONS OF THE CLEAN WATER ACT Under the Clean Water Act, violators are subject to a variety of civil and criminal penalties. Civil penalties for each violation range from a maximum of $10,000 per day, and not more than $25,000 per violation, to as much as $25,000 per day. Criminal penalties range from a fine of $2,500 per day and imprisonment for up to one year to a fine of $1 million and fifteen years' imprisonment. Injunctive relief and damages can also be imposed. The polluting party can be required to clean up the pollution or pay for the cost of doing so. Criminal penalties apply only if a violation was intentional.

Drinking Water

Another statute governing water pollution is the Safe Drinking Water Act.[14] Passed in 1974, this act requires the EPA to set maximum levels for pollutants in public water systems. Operators of public water supply systems must come as close as possible to meeting the EPA's standards by using the best available technology that is economically and scientifically feasible. The EPA is particularly concerned with contamination from underground sources. Pesticides and wastes leaked from landfills or disposed of in underground injection wells are among the more than two hundred pollutants known to exist in groundwater

---

14. 42 U.S.C. Sections 300f to 300j-25.

used for drinking in at least thirty-four states. Many of these substances are associated with cancer and damage to the central nervous system, liver, and kidneys.

The act was amended in 1996 to give the EPA greater flexibility in setting regulatory standards governing drinking water. Prior to the 1996 amendments, the EPA had to set standards for twenty-five different drinking water contaminants every three years, which it had largely failed to do. Under the 1996 amendments, the EPA can move at whatever rate it deems necessary to control contaminants that are of greatest concern to the public health. The 1996 amendments also imposed new requirements on suppliers of drinking water. Each supplier must send to every household it supplies with water an annual statement describing the source of its water, the level of any contaminants contained in the water, and any possible health concerns associated with the contaminants.

Ocean Dumping

The Marine Protection, Research, and Sanctuaries Act of 1972[15] (known popularly as the Ocean Dumping Act) regulates the transportation and dumping of material into ocean waters. (The term *material* is synonymous with the term *pollutant* as used in the Federal Water Pollution Control Act.) The Ocean Dumping Act prohibits entirely the ocean dumping of radiological, chemical, and biological warfare agents and high-level radioactive waste. The act establishes a permit program for transporting and dumping other materials. There are specific exemptions—materials subject to the permit provisions of other pollution legislation, wastes from structures regulated by other laws (for example, offshore oil exploration and drilling platforms), sewage, and other wastes. The Ocean Dumping Act also authorizes the designation of marine sanctuaries for "preserving or restoring such areas for their conservation, recreational, ecological, or esthetic values."

Each violation of any provision or permit may result in a civil penalty of not more than $50,000 or revocation or suspension of the permit. A knowing violation is a criminal offense that may result in a $50,000 fine, imprisonment for not more than a year, or both. An injunction may also be imposed.

Oil Pollution

The Oil Pollution Act of 1990[16] provides that any onshore or offshore oil facility, oil shipper, vessel owner, or vessel operator that discharges oil into navigable waters or onto an adjoining shore may be liable for clean-up costs, as well as damages. The act created a $1 billion oil clean-up and economic compensation fund and decreed that by the year 2011, oil tankers using U.S. ports must be double hulled to limit the severity of accidental spills.

Under the act, damage to natural resources, private property, and the local economy, including the increased cost of providing public services, is compensable. The act provides for civil penalties of $1,000 per barrel spilled or $25,000 for each day of the violation. The party held responsible for the clean-up costs can bring a civil suit for contribution from other potentially liable parties.

---

15. 16 U.S.C. Sections 1401–1445.
16. 33 U.S.C. Sections 2701–2761.

Noise Pollution

Regulations concerning noise pollution include the Noise Control Act of 1972.[17] This act requires the EPA to establish noise emission standards (maximum noise levels below which no harmful effects occur from interference with speech or other activity)—for example, for railroad noise emissions. The standards must be achievable by the best available technology, and they must be economically within reason.

The act prohibits, among other things, distributing products manufactured in violation of the noise emission standards and tampering with noise control devices. Either of these activities can result in an injunction or whatever other remedy "is necessary to protect the public health and welfare." Illegal product distribution can also result in a fine and imprisonment. Violations of provisions of the Noise Control Act can result in penalties of not more than $50,000 per day and imprisonment for not more than two years.

Toxic Chemicals

Originally, most environmental clean-up efforts were directed toward reducing smog and making water safe for fishing and swimming. Over time, however, control of toxic chemicals has become an important part of environmental law.

Pesticides and Herbicides

The first toxic chemical problem to receive widespread public attention was that posed by pesticides and herbicides. Using these chemicals to kill insects and weeds has increased agricultural productivity, but their residue remains in the environment. In some instances, accumulations of this residue have killed animals, and scientists have identified potential long-term effects that are detrimental to people.

FEDERAL INSECTICIDE, FUNGICIDE, AND RODENTICIDE ACT (FIFRA) The federal statute regulating pesticides and herbicides is the Federal Insecticide, Fungicide, and Rodenticide Act (FIFRA) of 1947.[18] Under FIFRA, pesticides and herbicides must be (1) registered before they can be sold, (2) certified and used only for approved applications, and (3) used in limited quantities when applied to food crops. If a substance is identified as harmful, the EPA can cancel its registration after a hearing. If the harm is imminent, the EPA can suspend registration pending the hearing. The EPA, or state officers or employees, may also inspect factories in which these chemicals are manufactured.

Under 1996 amendments to the Federal Food, Drug and Cosmetic Act, for a pesticide to remain on the market, there must be a "reasonable certainty of no harm" to people from exposure to the pesticide.[19] This means that there must be no more than a one-in-a-million risk to people of developing cancer from exposure in any way, including eating food that contains residues from the pesticide. Pesticide residues are in nearly all fruits and vegetables and processed foods. Under the 1996 amendments, the EPA must distribute to grocery stores brochures on high-risk pesticides that are in food, and the stores must display these brochures for consumers.

> "All property in this country is held under the implied obligation that the owner's use of it shall not be injurious to the community."
>
> John Harlan, 1899–1971
> (Associate justice of the United States Supreme Court, 1955–1971)

---

17. 42 U.S.C. Sections 4901–4918.
18. 7 U.S.C. Sections 136–136y.
19. 21 U.S.C. Section 346a.

VIOLATIONS OF FIFRA It is a violation of FIFRA to sell a pesticide or herbicide that is unregistered, a pesticide or herbicide with a registration that has been canceled or suspended, or a pesticide or herbicide with a false or misleading label. For example, it is an offense to sell a substance that is adulterated (that has a chemical strength different from the concentration declared on the label). It is also an offense to destroy or deface any labeling required under the act. The act's labeling requirements include directions for the use of the pesticide or herbicide, warnings to protect human health and the environment, a statement of treatment in the case of poisoning, and a list of the ingredients.

A private party can petition the EPA to suspend or cancel the registration of a pesticide or herbicide. If the EPA fails to act, the private party can petition a federal court to review the EPA's failure. Penalties for registrants and producers for violating FIFRA include imprisonment for up to one year and a fine of no more than $50,000. Penalties for commercial dealers include imprisonment for up to one year and a fine of no more than $25,000. Farmers and other private users of pesticides or herbicides who violate the act are subject to a $1,000 fine and imprisonment for up to thirty days.

Toxic Substances

The first comprehensive law covering toxic substances was the Toxic Substances Control Act of 1976.[20] The act was passed to regulate chemicals and chemical compounds that are known to be toxic—such as asbestos and polychlorinated biphenyls, popularly known as PCBs—and to institute investigation of any possible harmful effects from new chemical compounds. The regulations authorize the EPA to require that manufacturers, processors, and other organizations planning to use chemicals first determine their effects on human health and the environment. The EPA can regulate substances that may pose an imminent hazard or an unreasonable risk of injury to health or the environment. The EPA may require special labeling, limit the use of a substance, set production quotas, or prohibit the use of a substance altogether.

Hazardous Wastes

Some industrial, agricultural, and household wastes pose more serious threats than others. If not properly disposed of, these toxic chemicals may present a substantial danger to human health and the environment. If released into the environment, they may contaminate public drinking water resources.

RESOURCE CONSERVATION AND RECOVERY ACT In 1976, Congress passed the Resource Conservation and Recovery Act (RCRA)[21] in reaction to an ever-increasing concern with the effects of hazardous waste materials on the environment. The RCRA required the EPA to establish regulations to monitor and control hazardous waste disposal and to determine which forms of solid waste should be considered hazardous and thus subject to regulation. The act authorized the EPA to promulgate various technical requirements for some types of facilities for storage and treatment of hazardous waste. The act also requires all producers of hazardous waste materials to label and package properly any hazardous waste to be transported.

> **Be Careful** Under the Resource Conservation and Recovery Act, anyone who generates, treats, stores, or transports hazardous waste must obtain a permit.

---

20. 15 U.S.C. Sections 2601–2692.
21. 42 U.S.C. Sections 6901–6986.

The RCRA was amended in 1984 and 1986 to decrease the use of land containment in the disposal of hazardous waste and to require compliance with the act by some generators of hazardous waste—such as those generating less than 1,000 kilograms (2,200 pounds) a month—that had previously been excluded from regulation under the RCRA.

Under the RCRA, a company may be assessed a civil penalty based on the seriousness of the violation, the probability of harm, and the extent to which the violation deviates from RCRA requirements. The assessment may be up to $25,000 for each violation. Criminal penalties include fines up to $50,000 for each day of violation, imprisonment for up to two years (in most instances), or both. Criminal fines and the time of imprisonment can be doubled for certain repeat offenders.

SUPERFUND In 1980, Congress passed the Comprehensive Environmental Response, Compensation, and Liability Act (CERCLA),[22] commonly known as Superfund. The basic purpose of Superfund is to regulate the clean-up of disposal sites in which hazardous waste is leaking into the environment. A special federal fund was created for that purpose. Because of its impact on the business community, the act is presented as this chapter's *Landmark in the Legal Environment*.

Potentially Responsible Party (PRP) A party liable under the Comprehensive Environmental Response, Compensation, and Liability Act (CERCLA). Any person who generated the hazardous waste, transported the hazardous waste, owned or operated a waste site at the time of disposal, or currently owns or operates a site may be responsible for some or all of the clean-up costs involved in removing the hazardous chemicals.

Potentially Responsible Parties under Superfund. Superfund provides that when a release or a threatened release of hazardous chemicals from a site occurs, the EPA can clean up the site and recover the cost of the clean-up from the following persons: (1) the person who generated the wastes disposed of at the site, (2) the person who transported the wastes to the site, (3) the person who owned or operated the site at the time of the disposal, or (4) the current owner or operator. A person falling within one of these categories is referred to as a **potentially responsible party (PRP).**

---

22. 42 U.S.C. Sections 9601–9675.

Ethical Issue 21.1

Who should be a potentially responsible party under Superfund?

Deciding who qualifies as a potentially responsible party (PRP) under Superfund is not always easy; nor are the results of such decisions always necessarily fair. In some cases, courts have even "pierced the corporate veil" to hold corporate shareholder-officers personally liable because of the degree of control they exercised over their corporations. Should parent companies be liable for their subsidiaries' polluting activities? One argument in favor of imposing liability on parent companies is, of course, that parent companies may have "deeper pockets" than their subsidiaries—that is, they can better afford to pay the clean-up costs. In 1998, the United States Supreme Court resolved a split among the lower courts on this issue by holding that a parent company can be liable as a PRP under Superfund only if it was directly involved in running the polluting facility.[a] Decisions as to who qualifies as a PRP have important ramifications, because liability under Superfund can be extensive.

---

a. *United States v. Best Foods*, 524 U.S. 51, 118 S.Ct. 1876, 141 L.Ed.2d 43 (1998).

Landmark in the Legal Environment

Superfund

The origins of the Comprehensive Environmental Response, Compensation, and Liability Act (CERCLA) of 1980, which is commonly referred to as Superfund, can be traced to drafts that the Environmental Protection Agency (EPA) started to circulate in 1978. EPA officials emphasized the political necessity of new legislation by pointing to what they thought were "ticking time bombs"—dump sites around the country that were ready to explode and injure the public with toxic fumes.

The popular press also gave prominence to hazardous waste dump sites at the time. The New York Love Canal disaster began to make the headlines in 1978 after residents in the area complained about health problems, contaminated sludge oozing into their basements, and chemical "volcanoes" erupting in their yards as a result of Hooker Chemical's dumping of approximately 21,000 tons of chemicals into the canal from 1942 to 1953. The Love Canal situation made the national news virtually every day from the middle of May to the middle of June in 1980.

The basic purpose of CERCLA, which was amended in 1986 by the Superfund Amendments and Reauthorization Act, is to regulate the clean-up of leaking hazardous waste–disposal sites. The act has four primary elements:

- It established an information-gathering and analysis system that allows federal and state governments to characterize chemical dump sites and to develop priorities for appropriate action.
- It authorized the EPA to respond to hazardous substance emergencies and to clean up leaking sites directly through contractors or through co-

A warning to trespassers is posted at a hazardous waste site. Who should pay the cost of cleaning up the site?

operative agreements with the states if the persons responsible for the problem fail to clean up the site.

- It created a Hazardous Substance Response Trust Fund (Superfund) to pay for the clean-up of hazardous sites. Monies for the fund are obtained through taxes on certain businesses, including those processing or producing petroleum and chemical feed stock.
- It allowed the government to recover the cost of clean-up from the persons who were (even remotely) responsible for hazardous substance releases.

For Critical Analysis: *Must all of the contamination be removed from a hazardous waste site to ensure that it no longer poses any threat of harm to life? Would some lesser amount satisfy a reasonable degree of environmental quality?*

Joint and Several Liability under Superfund. Liability under Superfund is usually joint and several—that is, a person who generated only a fraction of the hazardous waste disposed of at the site may nevertheless be liable for all of the clean-up costs. CERCLA authorizes a party who has incurred clean-up costs to bring a "contribution action" against any other person who is liable or potentially liable for a percentage of the costs. The following case involved a challenge to a court's allocation of clean-up costs among PRPs.

Case 21.3 ● Browning-Ferris Industries of Illinois, Inc. v. Ter Maat

United States Court of Appeals, Seventh Circuit, 1999. 195 F.3d 953.

http://www.ca7.uscourts.gov[a]

Background and Facts In 1971, the owners of a landfill leased it to a company that later became Browning-Ferris Industries of Illinois, Inc., which operated it until the fall of 1975. During that time, the operator illegally dumped at the site a large quantity of particularly toxic wastes from an auto plant run by Chrysler Corporation. Between the fall of 1975 and 1988, M.I.G. Investments, Inc., and AAA Disposal Systems, Inc., operated the landfill. Richard Ter Maat was the president and principal shareholder of M.I.G. and AAA. In June 1988, after

a. In the left-hand column, click on "Judicial Opinions." On that page, in the "Last Name or Corporation" section, click on "Begins," enter "Browning-Ferris" in the box, and click on "Search for Person." When the result appears, click on the docket number for the case to access the opinion.

AAA was sold and Ter Maat moved to Florida, M.I.G. abandoned the landfill without covering it properly. Two years later, the EPA ordered that the site be cleaned up. Browning-Ferris, and other companies that shared responsibility for the pollution at the site, agreed to clean it up. Browning-Ferris and the others then filed a suit in a federal district court against Ter Maat, M.I.G., and AAA under CERCLA to recover the costs. The court ruled, among other things, that 45 percent of the costs was allocable to the owners of the landfill and the generators of the toxic wastes dumped in it, 22 percent was the responsibility of Browning-Ferris, and the other 33 percent was the responsibility of M.I.G. and AAA. The plaintiffs appealed to the U.S. Court of Appeals for the Seventh Circuit. Browning-Ferris claimed in part that too much of the liability for the pollution at the site had been allocated to it relative to M.I.G. and AAA. Browning-Ferris argued that the costs should be allocated according to the volume of wastes for which each party was responsible.

In the Words of the Court . . .
POSNER, Chief Judge.

* * * *

The * * * question * * * is whether the court must find a causal relation between a party's pollution and the actual cost of cleaning up the site. To answer this question we have to distinguish between a necessary condition (or "but-for cause") and a sufficient condition. If event A is a necessary condition of event B, this means that, without A, B will not occur. If A is a sufficient condition of B, this means that, if A occurs, B will occur. If A is that the murder weapon was loaded and B is the murder, then A is a necessary condition. If A is shooting a person through the heart and B is the death of the shooting victim, then A is a sufficient condition of B but not a necessary condition, because a wound to another part of the victim's body might have been fatal as well.

This distinction may sometimes be important in the pollution context. It is easy to imagine a case in which, had X not polluted a site, no clean-up costs would have been incurred; X's pollution would be a necessary condition of those costs and it would be natural to think that he should pay at least a part of them. But suppose that even if X had not polluted the site, it would have to be cleaned up—and at the same cost—because of the amount of pollution by Y. * * * Then X's pollution would not be a necessary condition of the clean up, or of any of the costs incurred in the clean up. But that should not necessarily let X off the hook. For suppose that though if X had not polluted the site at all there still would have been enough pollution from Y to require a clean up, if Y had not polluted the site X's pollution would have been sufficient to require the clean up. In that case, the conduct of X and the conduct of Y would each be a sufficient but not a necessary condition of the clean up, and it would be entirely arbitrary to let

Case 21.3 Continued

either (or, even worse, both) off the hook on this basis. So far as appears, this is such a case; Browning-Ferris's pollution was serious enough (if indeed it dumped a large quantity of Chrysler's particularly toxic wastes) to require that the site be cleaned up, but the other pollution at the site was also enough. If Browning-Ferris's conduct was thus a sufficient though not a necessary condition of the clean up, it is not inequitable to make it contribute substantially to the cost.

* * * [N]o principle of law, logic, or common sense required the court to allocate [the] total costs among the polluters on the basis of the volume of wastes alone. Not only do wastes differ in their toxicity, harm to the environment, and costs of cleaning up, and so relative volume is not a reliable guide to the marginal costs imposed by each polluter; but polluters differ in the blameworthiness of the decisions or omissions that led to the pollution, and blameworthiness is relevant to an equitable allocation of joint costs.

Decision and Remedy The U.S. Court of Appeals for the Seventh Circuit held that the allocation of 22 percent of the clean-up costs to Browning-Ferris had been fair. There were a number of factors to consider, and the lower court had not abused its discretion in deciding that those factors warranted this allocation. The court remanded the case for the determination of other issues.

For Critical Analysis—Ethical Consideration *Can you think of a fairer system for cleaning up leaking hazardous waste sites than the system provided for by CERCLA?*

Radiation

Nuclear power plants are built and operated by private industry. The nuclear industry is regulated almost exclusively by the federal government under the Atomic Energy Act of 1954.[23] The Nuclear Regulatory Commission (NRC) is the federal agency responsible for regulating the private nuclear industry. The NRC reviews the plans for each proposed nuclear plant and issues a construction permit only after preparing an environmental impact statement that considers the impact of an accidental release of radiation. After construction, the NRC licenses the plant's operation.

The Environmental Protection Agency sets standards for radioactivity in the overall environment and for the disposal of some radioactive waste. Low-level radioactive waste generated by private facilities is the responsibility of each state under the Low Level Radioactive Waste Policy Act of 1980.[24] The NRC regulates the use and disposal of other nuclear materials and radioactive waste. Some radioactive waste is buried, burned, or dumped in the ocean. Currently, however, most of it is stored at the plants in which it is produced. Under the Nuclear Waste Policy Act of 1982,[25] the government is looking for a permanent disposal site.

---

23. 42 U.S.C. Sections 2011 to 2297g-4.
24. 42 U.S.C. Sections 2021b–2021j.
25. 42 U.S.C. Sections 10101–10270.

A common law theory may serve as the basis for liability for harms caused by radiation. For example, in one case, the court held that the party creating a radiation hazard is strictly liable in tort for its clean-up and any damages.[26] Liability for injury resulting from radiation may also arise under one of the statutes discussed elsewhere in this chapter. For example, the release of radioactive materials into the environment may violate the Clean Water Act, the RCRA, or the CERCLA.[27]

State and Local Regulation

Many states regulate the degree to which the environment may be polluted. Thus, for example, even when state zoning laws permit a business's proposed development, the proposal may have to be altered to change the development's impact on the environment. State laws may restrict a business's discharge of chemicals into the air or water or regulate its disposal of toxic wastes. States may also regulate the disposal or recycling of other wastes, including glass, metal, and plastic containers and paper. Additionally, states may restrict the emissions from motor vehicles.

City, county, and other local governments control some aspects of the environment. For instance, local zoning laws control some land use. These laws may be designed to inhibit or direct the growth of cities and suburbs or to protect the natural environment. Other aspects of the environment may be subject to local regulation for other reasons. Methods of waste and garbage removal and disposal, for example, can have a substantial impact on a community. The appearance of buildings and other structures, including advertising signs and billboards, may affect traffic safety, property values, or local aesthetics. Noise generated by a business or its customers may be annoying, disruptive, or damaging to its neighbors. The location and condition of parks, streets, and other public uses of land subject to local control affect the environment and can also affect business.

---

26. *T&E Industries, Inc. v. Safety Light Corp.*, 123 N.J. 371, 587 A.2d 1249 (1991).
27. See, for example, *Ohio v. Department of Energy*, 904 F.2d 1058 (6th Cir. 1990).

Key Terms

environmental impact statement (EIS) 610	nuisance 607	toxic tort 609
environmental law 607	potentially responsible party (PRP) 622	wetlands 617

Chapter Summary • Protecting the Environment

Common Law Actions (See pages 607–610.)	1. **Nuisance**—A common law doctrine under which actions against pollution-causing activities may be brought. An action is permissible only if an individual suffers a harm separate and distinct from that of the general public. 2. **Negligence and strict liability**—Parties may recover damages for injuries sustained as a result of pollution-causing activities of a firm if it can be demonstrated that the harm was a foreseeable result of the firm's failure to exercise reasonable care (negligence); businesses engaging in ultrahazardous activities are liable for whatever injuries the activities cause, regardless of whether the firms exercise reasonable care.
Federal Regulation (See pages 610–626.)	The National Environmental Policy Act of 1969 imposes environmental responsibilities on all federal agencies and requires for every major federal action the preparation of an environmental impact statement (EIS). An EIS must analyze the action's impact on the environment, its adverse effects and possible alternatives, and its irreversible effects on environmental quality. The Environmental Protection Agency was created in 1970 to coordinate federal environmental programs; it administers most federal environmental policies and statutes. Important areas regulated by the federal government include the following: 1. **Air pollution**—Regulated under the authority of the Clean Air Act of 1963 and its amendments, particularly those of 1970, 1977, and 1990. 2. **Water pollution**—Regulated under the authority of the Rivers and Harbors Appropriations Act of 1899, as amended, and the Federal Water Pollution Control Act of 1948, as amended by the Clean Water Act of 1972. 3. **Noise pollution**—Regulated by the Noise Control Act of 1972. 4. **Toxic chemicals**—Pesticides and herbicides, toxic substances, and hazardous waste are regulated under the authority of the Federal Insecticide, Fungicide, and Rodenticide Act of 1947, the Toxic Substances Control Act of 1976, and the Resource Conservation and Recovery Act of 1976, respectively. The Comprehensive Environmental Response, Compensation, and Liability Act (CERCLA) of 1980, as amended, regulates the clean-up of hazardous waste–disposal sites. 5. **Radiation**—The private nuclear industry is regulated under the Atomic Energy Act of 1954. Low-level radioactive waste generated by private facilities is the responsibility of each state under the Low Level Radioactive Waste Policy Act of 1980. Under the Nuclear Waste Policy Act of 1982, the government is looking for a permanent disposal site for nuclear materials and radioactive waste.
State and Local Regulation (See page 626.)	Activities affecting the environment are controlled at the local and state levels through regulations relating to land use, the disposal and recycling of garbage and waste, and pollution-causing activities in general.

For Review

1. Under what common law theories may polluters be held liable?

2. What is an environmental impact statement, and who must file one?

3. What does the Environmental Protection Agency do?

4. What major federal statutes regulate air and water pollution?

5. What is Superfund? To what categories of persons does liability under Superfund extend?

Questions and Case Problems

21-1. Clean Air Act. The Environmental Protection Agency (EPA) has set ambient standards for several pollutants, including sulfur dioxide, specifying the maximum concentration allowable in the outdoor air. One way to meet these standards is to reduce emissions. Companies discovered, however, that they could also meet the standards at less cost by building very high smokestacks. When emitted from such high stacks, pollutants were more widely dispersed and remained below the concentration level specified by the ambient standards. Environmental groups claimed that the Clean Air Act was designed to reduce pollution, not to disperse it, and argued that industry should not be allowed to rely on tall stacks. Are the environmental groups correct, or should industry be allowed to use the less expensive dispersal method? Discuss.

21-2. Clean Air Act. Some scientific knowledge indicates that there is no safe level of exposure to a cancer-causing agent. In theory, even one molecule of such a substance has the potential for causing cancer. Section 112 of the Clean Air Act requires that all cancer-causing substances be regulated to ensure a margin of safety. Some environmental groups have argued that all emissions of such substances must be eliminated in order for such a margin of safety to be reached. A total elimination would likely shut down many major U.S. industries. Should the Environmental Protection Agency totally eliminate all emissions of cancer-causing chemicals? Discuss.

21-3. Environmental Laws. Moonbay is a real estate development corporation that primarily develops retirement communities. Farmtex owns a number of feedlots in Sunny Valley. Moonbay purchased twenty thousand acres of farmland in the same area and began building and selling retirement homes on this acreage. In the meantime, Farmtex continued to expand its feedlot business, and eventually only five hundred feet separated the two operations. Because of the odor and flies from the feedlots, Moonbay found it difficult to sell the homes in its development. Moonbay wants to enjoin Farmtex from operating its feedlots in the vicinity of the retirement home development. Discuss under what theory Moonbay would file this action. Discuss fully whether Farmtex has violated any federal environmental laws.

21-4. Environmental Laws. Fruitade, Inc., is a processor of a soft drink called Freshen Up. Fruitade uses returnable bottles, as well as a special acid to clean its bottles for further beverage processing. The acid is diluted by water and then allowed to pass into a navigable stream. Fruitade crushes its broken bottles and throws the crushed glass into the stream. Discuss fully any environmental laws that Fruitade has violated.

21-5. Pesticide Regulation. The Environmental Protection Agency (EPA) canceled the registration of the pesticide Diazinon for use on golf courses and sod farms because of concern about the effects of Diazinon on birds. The Federal Insecticide, Fungicide, and Rodenticide Act authorizes cancellation of the registration of products that "generally cause unreasonable adverse effects on the environment." The statute further defines "unreasonable adverse effects on the environment" to mean "any unreasonable risk to man or the environment, taking into account the . . . costs and benefits." Thus, in determining whether a pesticide should continue to be used, one must balance the risks and benefits of the use of the pesticide. Does this mean that the pesticide must be found to kill birds more often than not before its use can be prohibited? [*CIBA-Geigy Corp. v. Environmental Protection Agency,* 874 F.2d 277 (5th Cir. 1989)]

21-6. Common Law Nuisance. Taylor Bay Protective Association is a nonprofit corporation established for the purpose of restoring and improving the water quality of Taylor Bay. Local water districts began operating a flood control project in the area. As part of the project, a pumping station was developed. Testimony at trial revealed that the pumps were operated contrary to the instructions provided in the operation and maintenance manual. The pumps acted as vacuums, sucking up increased amounts of silt and depositing the silt in Taylor Bay. Thus, the project resulted in sedimentation and turbidity problems in the downstream watercourse of Taylor Bay. The association sued the local water districts, alleging that the pumping operations created a nuisance. Do the pumping operations qualify as a common law nuisance? Who should be responsible for the clean-up costs? Discuss both questions fully. [*Taylor Bay Protective Association v. Environmental Protection Agency,* 884 F.2d 1073 (8th Cir. 1989)]

21-7. Water Pollution. The Environmental Protection Agency (EPA) promulgated water-pollution discharge limits for several mining industries. These standards authorized variances exempting mining operations from coverage by the standards if the operations could show that they used special processes or facilities that made the standards inapplicable. Cost was not a consideration in granting the variances. An industry trade association sued, claiming that the EPA should consider costs in granting variances, and the Fourth Circuit Court of Appeals agreed. Discuss whether the United States Supreme Court should overturn this decision or affirm it and let costs be considered in the granting of variances under the Clean Water Act. [*Environmental Protection Agency v. National Crushed Stone Association,* 449 U.S. 64, 101 S.Ct. 295, 66 L.Ed.2d 268 (1980)]

21-8. Superfund. During the 1970s, a number of chemical companies disposed of their wastes at a facility maintained by South Carolina Recycling and Disposal, Inc. Hazardous chemical wastes were stored rather haphazardly; some leaked into the ground, and fires occurred on several occasions. Eventually, the Environmental Protection Agency (EPA) conducted clean-up operations under Superfund and sued companies that had used the site for the costs of the clean-up. Five of the defendant companies claimed that they should not be liable for the clean-up costs because there was no evidence that their waste materials had contributed in any way to the leakage problem or to any other hazard posed by the site. The EPA asserted that causation was not required for the companies' liability, only evidence that the companies had sent waste to the site. Will the EPA succeed in its claim? Discuss. [*United States v. South Carolina Recycling and Disposal, Inc.,* 653 F.Supp. 984 (D.S.C. 1986)]

21-9. Common Law Nuisance. In 1987, John and Jean Zarlenga purchased a new home in Bloomingdale, Illinois. Bloomingdale Partners (BP) then built an eight-story apartment complex across the street from the Zarlenga home. Each of the 168 apartments had an air conditioner weighing about nine hundred pounds. Over sixty air conditioners were on the side of the complex that faced the Zarlenga home. The Zarlengas testified that the noise from these air conditioners during the summer was a "loud rumbling sound" that was "continuous and monotonous." The machines disrupted their sleep. Jean Zarlenga suffered from headaches and irritability. In her testimony, she stated, "It's made my life miserable. I cannot use my deck. I cannot have company over . . . I can't open my windows in my bedroom. I toss and turn all night." The Zarlengas sued BP for creating a nuisance, claiming that the apartment complex substantially interfered with the use and enjoyment of their home. The Zarlengas sought damages from BP for the devaluation of their home caused by the noise and for their suffering. How should the court decide this case? Discuss fully. [*In re Bloomingdale Partners,* 160 Bankr. 101 (N.D.Ill. 1993)]

21-10. Clean Water Act. Attique Ahmad owned the Spin-N-Market, a convenience store and gas station. The gas pumps were fed by underground tanks, one of which had a leak at its top that allowed water to enter. Ahmad emptied the tank by pumping its contents into a storm drain and a sewer system. Through the storm drain, gasoline flowed into a creek, forcing the city to clean the water. Through the sewer system, gasoline flowed into a sewage treatment plant, forcing the city to evacuate the plant and two nearby schools. Ahmad was charged with discharging a pollutant without a permit, which is a criminal violation of the Clean Water Act. The act provides that a person who "knowingly violates" the act commits a felony. Ahmad claimed that he had believed he was discharging only water. Did Ahmad commit a felony? Why or why not? Discuss fully. [*U.S. v. Ahmad,* 101 F.3d 386 (5th Cir. 1996)]

A Question of Ethics and Social Responsibility

21-11. The Endangered Species Act of 1973 makes it unlawful for any person to "take" endangered or threatened species. The act defines take to mean to "harass, harm, pursue," "wound," or "kill." The secretary of the interior (Bruce Babbitt) issued a regulation that further defined harm to include "significant habitat modification or degradation where it actually kills or injures wildlife." A group of businesses and individuals involved in the timber industry brought an action against the secretary of the interior and others. The group complained that the application of the "harm" regulation to the red-cockaded woodpecker and the northern spotted owl had injured the group economically, because it prevented logging operations (habitat modification) in Pacific Northwest forests containing these species. The group challenged the regulation's validity, contending that Congress did not intend the word *take* to include habitat modification. The case ultimately reached the United States Supreme Court, which held that the secretary had reasonably construed Congress's intent when he defined harm to include habitat modification. [*Babbitt v. Sweet Home Chapter of Communities for a Great Oregon,* 515 U.S. 687, 115 S.Ct. 2407, 132 L.Ed.2d 597 (1995)]

1. Traditionally, the term *take* has been used to refer to the capture or killing of wildlife, usually for private gain. Is the secretary's regulation prohibiting habitat modification consistent with this definition?
2. One of the issues in this case was whether Congress intended to protect existing generations of species or future generations. How do the terms *take* and *habitat* modification relate to this issue?
3. Three dissenting Supreme Court justices contended that construing the act as prohibiting habitat modification "imposes unfairness to the point of financial ruin—not just upon the rich, but upon the simplest farmer who finds his land conscripted to national zoological use." Should private parties be required to bear the burden of preserving habitats for wildlife?
4. Generally, should the economic welfare of private parties be taken into consideration when environmental statutes and regulations are created and applied?

For Critical Analysis

21-12. It has been estimated that for every dollar spent cleaning up hazardous waste sites, administrative agencies spend seven dollars in overhead. Can you think of any way to trim the administrative costs associated with the clean-up of contaminated sites?

Interacting with the Internet

■ For updated links to resources available on the Web, as well as a variety of other materials, visit this text's Web site at

http://leet.westbuslaw.com

■ The Virtual Law Library of the Indiana University School of Law provides numerous links to online environmental law sources. Go to

http://www.law.indiana.edu

■ For information on the standards, guidelines, and regulations of the Environmental Protection Agency, go to

http://www.epa.gov

Online Legal Research Exercises

Go to **http://leet. westbuslaw.com**, the Web site that accompanies this text. Select "Interactive Study Center," and then click on "Chapter 21." There you will find the following Internet research exercise that you can perform to learn more about environmental law:

Activity 21–1: Nuisance Law

Before the Test

Go to **http://leet. westbuslaw.com**, the Web site accompanying this text. Select "Interactive Quizzes." You will find a number of interactive questions relating to this chapter.

Land-Use Control and Real Property

chapter objectives

After reading this chapter, you should be able to:

1. Distinguish among different types of possessory ownership interests in real property.

2. Identify three types of nonpossessory interests in real property.

3. Discuss how ownership interests in real property can be transferred.

4. Indicate what a leasehold estate is and how a landlord-tenant relationship comes into existence.

5. Outline the rights of property owners concerning the use of their property.

> **"The right of property is the most sacred of all the rights of citizenship."**
>
> Jean-Jacques Rousseau, 1712–1778
> (French writer and philosopher)

From earliest times, property has provided a means for survival. Primitive peoples lived off the fruits of the land, eating the vegetation and wildlife. Later, as the wildlife was domesticated and the vegetation cultivated, property provided pasturage and farmland. In the twelfth and thirteenth centuries, the power of feudal lords was determined by the amount of land that they held; the more land they held, the more powerful they were. After the age of feudalism passed, property continued to be an indicator of family wealth and social position. In the Western world, the protection of an individual's right to his or her property has become, in the words of Jean-Jacques Rousseau, one of the "most sacred of all the rights of citizenship."

In this chapter, we first examine closely the nature of real property. We then look at the various ways in which real property can be owned and at how ownership rights in real property are transferred from one person to another. We also include a discussion of leased property and landlord-tenant relationships. The chapter concludes with a discussion of how the use of land is controlled.

The Nature of Real Property

Real property consists of land and the buildings, plants, and trees that it contains. Real property also includes subsurface and air rights, as well as personal property that has become permanently attached to real property. Whereas personal property is movable, real property—also called *real estate* or *realty*—is immovable.

Land

Land includes the soil on the surface of the earth and the natural or artificial structures that are attached to it. It further includes all the waters contained on or under the surface and much, but not necessarily all, of the airspace above it. The exterior boundaries of land extend down to the center of the earth and up to the farthest reaches of the atmosphere (subject to certain qualifications).

Air and Subsurface Rights

The owner of real property has relatively exclusive rights to the airspace above the land, as well as to the soil and minerals underneath it.

AIR RIGHTS Early cases involving air rights dealt with matters such as the right to run a telephone wire across a person's property when the wire did not touch any of the property[1] and whether a bullet shot over a person's land constituted trespass.[2] Today, disputes concerning air rights may involve the right of commercial and private planes to fly over property and the right of individuals and governments to seed clouds and produce rain artificially. Flights over private land do not normally violate the property owners' rights unless the flights are low and frequent enough to cause a direct interference with the enjoyment and use of the land.[3] Leaning walls or buildings and projecting eave spouts or roofs may also violate the air rights of an adjoining property owner.

1. *Butler v. Frontier Telephone Co.*, 186 N.Y. 486, 79 N.E. 716 (1906).
2. *Herrin v. Sutherland*, 74 Mont. 587, 241 P. 328 (1925). Shooting over a person's land constitutes trespass.
3. *United States v. Causby*, 328 U.S. 256, 66 S.Ct. 1062, 90 L.Ed. 1206 (1946).

A plane flies low over a residential area. Are the property owners' rights violated by such a low-flying plane?

SUBSURFACE RIGHTS In many states, the owner of the surface of a piece of land is not the owner of the subsurface, and hence the land ownership may be separated. Subsurface rights can be extremely valuable, as these rights include the ownership of minerals and, in most states, oil and natural gas. Water rights are also extremely valuable, especially in the West. When the ownership is separated into surface and subsurface rights, each owner can pass title to what he or she owns without the consent of the other owner. Each owner has the right to use the land owned, and in some cases a conflict arises between a surface owner's use and the subsurface owner's need to extract minerals, oil, and natural gas. When this occurs, one party's interest may become subservient to the other party's interest, either by statute or case decision.

> **Be Aware** If, during an excavation, a subsurface owner causes the land to subside, he or she may be liable to the owner of the surface.

Significant limitations on either air rights or subsurface rights normally have to be indicated on the deed transferring title at the time of purchase. (Deeds and the types of warranties they contain are discussed later in this chapter.)

Plant Life and Vegetation

Plant life, both natural and cultivated, is also considered to be real property. In many instances, the natural vegetation, such as trees, adds greatly to the value of the realty. When a parcel of land is sold and the land has growing crops on it, the sale includes the crops, unless otherwise specified in the sales contract. When crops are sold by themselves, however, they are considered to be personal property or goods. Consequently, the sale of crops is a sale of goods, and therefore it is governed by the Uniform Commercial Code rather than by real property law.[4]

Fixtures

Certain personal property can become so closely associated with the real property to which it is attached that the law views it as real property. Such property

---

4. See UCC 2–107(2).

Fixture A thing that was once personal property but that has become attached to real property in such a way that it takes on the characteristics of real property and becomes part of that real property.

is known as a **fixture**—a thing *affixed* to realty, meaning it is attached to it by roots; embedded in it; permanently situated on it; or permanently attached by means of cement, plaster, bolts, nails, or screws. The fixture can be physically attached to real property, be attached to another fixture, or even be without any actual physical attachment to the land (such as a statue). As long as the owner intends the property to be a fixture, normally it will be a fixture.

Fixtures are included in the sale of land if the sales contract does not provide otherwise. The sale of a house includes the land and the house and the garage on the land, as well as the cabinets, plumbing, and windows. Because these are permanently affixed to the property, they are considered to be a part of it. Unless otherwise agreed, however, the curtains and throw rugs are not included. Items such as drapes and window-unit air conditioners are difficult to classify. Thus, a contract for the sale of a house or commercial realty should indicate which items of this sort are included in the sale. At issue in the following case was whether telephone poles, wires, and other communications equipment qualified as fixtures.

Case 22.1 ● New England Telephone and Telegraph Co. v. City of Franklin

Supreme Court of New Hampshire, 1996.
685 A.2d 913.
**http://www.state.nh.us/
courts/supreme/opinions/
9611/netel.htm**[a]

Historical and Technological Setting
Although telephone poles, wires, and underground conduits often have an expected life of at least forty years, the equipment is installed with its removal and relocation in mind. As a result, removal is normally not complicated or time consuming, and it does not harm the underlying real property or change its usefulness. In obtaining a state license, a property owner's consent, or an easement to install telecommunications equipment, the installer typically insists on maintaining ownership of it and refuses any requests to make it a permanent

a. This page contains the opinion in this case. This opinion is part of a database on a Web site maintained by the New Hampshire state library for the New Hampshire state government.

part of the real property. In fact, telecommunications office equipment is also usually portable and designed to permit easy removal and relocation. Technology changes quickly, and telecommunications companies want to be able to adapt.

Background and Facts To obtain revenue, cities and towns tax the owners of real property within their jurisdictions. The tax is based on an assessment of the value of the property. New England Telephone and Telegraph Company (NETT) and other telephone companies filed a lawsuit in a New Hampshire state court against the City of Franklin and other municipalities, challenging the cities' property assessments. NETT and the other plaintiffs objected to the inclusion in their assessments of communications equipment, including telephone poles, wires, and central office equipment. They argued that the equipment was personal property and therefore should not have been taxed. The court granted the telephone companies' motion for summary judgment, and the cities appealed.

In the Words of the Court . . .
HORTON, Justice.

* * * *

* * * [W]hether an item of property is properly classified as either personalty or a fixture turns on several factors, including: the item's nature and use; the intent of the party making the annexation; the degree and extent to which the item is specially adapted to the realty; the degree and extent of the item's annexation to the realty; and the relationship between

Case 22.1 Continued

the realty's owner and the person claiming the item. The central factors are the nature of the article and its use, as connected with the use of the underlying land, because these factors provide the basis for ascertaining the intent of the party who affixes or annexes the item in question.

In this case, the items of communications equipment did not constitute fixtures. * * * The poles, wires, and central office equipment, though placed in the ground or bolted to the buildings, were readily removable and transportable without affecting the utility of the underlying land, the buildings, or the equipment itself. * * * In addition, the very nature of telephone poles and wires, as well as their use by the [telephone companies] in connection with integrated telecommunications systems, belies the proposition that the equipment became a permanent and essential part of the underlying realty so as to pass by conveyance with it.

Decision and Remedy The Supreme Court of New Hampshire affirmed the trial court's decision. The telephone poles, wires, and central equipment were not fixtures and thus not subject to taxation by the cities as real property.

For Critical Analysis—Social Consideration *Intent is an important factor in determining whether an item is a fixture, yet how can a court objectively decide whether someone did or did not intend an item to be a fixture?*

Ownership of Real Property

> "Few . . . men own their property. The property owns them."
>
> Robert G. Ingersoll, 1833–1899
> (American politician and lecturer)

Ownership of property is an abstract concept that cannot exist independently of the legal system. No one can actually possess or *hold* a piece of land, the air above it, the earth below it, and all the water contained on it. The legal system therefore recognizes certain rights and duties that constitute ownership interests in real property.

Property ownership is often viewed as a bundle of rights. One who possesses the entire bundle of rights is said to hold the property in *fee simple,* which is the most complete form of ownership. When only some of the rights in the bundle are transferred to another person, the effect is to limit the ownership rights of both the one transferring the rights and the one receiving them.

Ownership in Fee Simple

The most common type of property ownership today is the fee simple. Generally, the term *fee simple* is used to designate a **fee simple absolute,** in which the owner has the greatest possible aggregation of rights, privileges, and power. The fee simple is limited absolutely to a person and his or her heirs and is assigned forever without limitation or condition. The rights that accompany a fee simple include the right to use the land for whatever purpose the owner sees fit, subject to laws that prevent the owner from unreasonably interfering with another person's land and subject to applicable zoning laws. Furthermore, the owner has the rights of *exclusive* possession and use of the property. A fee simple is potentially infinite in duration and can be disposed of by deed or by will (by selling or giving away). When there is no will, the fee simple passes to the owner's legal heirs.

Fee Simple Absolute An ownership interest in land in which the owner has the greatest possible aggregation of rights, privileges, and power. Ownership in fee simple absolute is limited absolutely to a person and his or her heirs.

Conveyance The transfer of a title to land from one person to another by deed; a document (such as a deed) by which an interest in land is transferred from one person to another.

Fee Simple Defeasible An ownership interest in real property that can be taken away (by the prior grantor) on the occurrence or nonoccurrence of a specified event.

Life Estate An interest in land that exists only for the duration of the life of some person, usually the holder of the estate.

Future Interest An interest in real property that is not at present possessory but will or may become possessory in the future.

Reversionary Interest A future interest in property retained by the original owner.

Ownership in fee simple may become limited whenever a **conveyance**, or transfer of real property, is made to another party *conditionally*. When this occurs, the fee simple is known as a **fee simple defeasible** (the word *defeasible* means capable of being terminated or annulled). • **Example 22.1** A conveyance "to A and his heirs as long as the land is used for charitable purposes" creates a fee simple defeasible, because ownership of the property is conditioned on the land's being used for charitable purposes. The original owner retains a *partial* ownership interest, because if the specified condition does not occur (if the land ceases to be used for charitable purposes), then the land reverts, or returns, to the original owner. If the original owner is not living at the time, the land passes to his or her heirs.•

Life Estates

A **life estate** is an estate that lasts for the life of some specified individual. A conveyance "to A for his life" creates a life estate.[5] In a life estate, the life tenant has fewer rights of ownership than the holder of a fee simple defeasible, because the rights necessarily cease to exist on the life tenant's death.

The life tenant has the right to use the land, provided that he or she commits no waste (injury to the land). In other words, the life tenant cannot injure the land in a manner that would adversely affect its value. The life tenant can use the land to harvest crops or, if mines and oil wells are already on the land, can extract minerals and oil from it, but the life tenant cannot exploit the land by creating new wells or mines. The life tenant is entitled to any rents or royalties generated by the realty and has the right to mortgage the life estate and create liens, easements, and leases; but none can extend beyond the life of the tenant. In addition, with few exceptions, the owner of a life estate has an exclusive right to possession during his or her life.

Along with these rights, the life tenant also has some duties—to keep the property in repair and to pay property taxes. In short, the owner of the life estate has the same rights as a fee simple owner except that he or she must maintain the value of the property during his or her tenancy, less the decrease in value resulting from the normal use of the property allowed by the life tenancy.

Future Interests

When an owner in fee simple absolute conveys the estate conditionally to another (such as with a fee simple defeasible) or for a limited period of time (such as with a life estate), the original owner still retains an interest in the land. The owner retains the right to repossess ownership of the land if the conditions of the fee simple defeasible are not met or when the life of the life-estate holder ends. The interest in the property that the owner retains (or transfers to another) is called a **future interest**, because if it arises, it will only arise in the future.

If the owner retains ownership of the future interest, then the future interest is described as a **reversionary interest**, because the property will revert to the original owner if the condition specified in a fee simple defeasible fails or when a life tenant dies. If, however, the owner of the future interest transfers ownership rights in that future interest to another, the future interest is de-

---

5. A less common type of life estate is created by the conveyance "to A for the life of B." This is known as an estate *pur autre vie,* or an estate for the duration of the life of another.

scribed as a **remainder.** For example, a conveyance "to A for life, then to B" creates a life estate for A and a remainder (future interest) for B. An **executory interest** is a type of future interest very similar to a remainder, the difference being that an executory interest does not take effect immediately on the expiration of another interest, such as a life estate. For example, a conveyance "to A and his (or her) heirs, as long as the premises are used for charitable purposes, and if not so used for charitable purposes, then to B" creates an executory interest in the property for B.

Nonpossessory Interests

In contrast to the types of property interests just described, some interests in land do not include any rights to possess the property. These interests are thus known as *nonpossessory interests*. Three forms of nonpossessory interests are easements, profits, and licenses.

An **easement** is the right of a person to make limited use of another person's real property without taking anything from the property. An easement, for example, can be the right to travel over another's property. In contrast, a **profit**[6] is the right to go onto land in possession of another and take away some part of the land itself or some product of the land. If Akmed, the owner of Sandy View, gives Carmen the right to go there and remove all the sand and gravel that she needs for her cement business, Carmen has a profit.

A **license** is the revocable right of a person to come onto another person's land. It is a personal privilege that arises from the consent of the owner of the land and that can be revoked by the owner. A ticket to attend a movie at a theater is an example of a license. • **Example 22.2** Assume that a Broadway theater owner issues to Carla a ticket to see a play. If Carla is refused entry into the theater because she is improperly dressed, she has no right to force her way into the theater. The ticket is only a revocable license, not a conveyance of an interest in property. •

Transfer of Ownership

Ownership of real property can pass from one person to another in a number of ways. Commonly, ownership interests in land are transferred by sale, in which case the terms of the transfer are specified in a real estate sales contract. When real property is sold or transferred as a gift, title to the property is conveyed by means of a **deed**—the instrument of conveyance of real property. We look here at transfers of real property by deed, as well as some other ways in which ownership rights in real property can be transferred.

Deeds

A valid deed must contain the following elements:

1. The names of the buyer (grantee) and seller (grantor).
2. Words evidencing an intent to convey the property (for example, "I hereby bargain, sell, grant, or give").
3. A legally sufficient description of the land.
4. The grantor's (and, sometimes, the spouse's) signature.

Remainder A future interest in property held by a person other than the original owner.

Executory Interest A future interest, held by a person other than the grantor, that begins after the termination of the preceding estate.

Easement A nonpossessory right to use another's property in a manner established by either express or implied agreement.

Profit In real property law, the right to enter on and remove things from the property of another (for example, the right to enter onto a person's land and remove sand and gravel therefrom).

License A revocable right or privilege of a person to come on another person's land.

Deed A document by which title to property (usually real property) is passed.

---

6. The term *profit,* as used here, does not refer to the "profits" made by a business firm. Rather, it means a gain or an advantage.

Additionally, to be valid, a deed must be delivered to the person to whom the property is being conveyed or to his or her agent.

WARRANTY DEEDS Different types of deeds provide different degrees of protection against defects of title. A **warranty deed** warrants the greatest number of things and thus provides the greatest protection for the buyer, or grantee. In most states, special language is required to make a deed a general warranty deed; normally, the deed must include a written promise to protect the buyer against all claims of ownership of the property. A sample warranty deed is shown in Exhibit 22–1. Warranty deeds commonly include a number of *covenants,* or promises, that the grantor makes to the grantee.

A *covenant of seisin*[7] and a *covenant of the right to convey* warrant that the seller has title to the estate that the deed describes and the power to convey the estate, respectively. The covenant of seisin specifically assures the buyer that the grantor has the property in the purported quantity and quality.

A *covenant against encumbrances* is a covenant that the property being sold or conveyed is not subject to any outstanding rights or interests that will diminish the value of the land, except as explicitly stated. Examples of common encumbrances include mortgages, liens, profits, easements, and private deed restrictions on the use of the land.

A *covenant of quiet enjoyment* guarantees that the buyer will not be disturbed in his or her possession of the land by the seller or any third persons. • **Example 22.3** Assume that Julio sells a two-acre lot and office building by warranty deed. Subsequently, a third person shows better title than Julio had and proceeds to evict the buyer. Here, the covenant of quiet enjoyment has been breached, and the buyer can sue to recover the purchase price of the land plus any other damages incurred as a result of the eviction.•

QUITCLAIM DEEDS A **quitclaim deed** offers the least amount of protection against defects in the title. Basically, a quitclaim deed conveys to the grantee whatever interest the grantor had; so if the grantor had no interest, then the grantee receives no interest. Quitclaim deeds are often used when the seller, or grantor, is uncertain as to the extent of his or her rights in the property.

RECORDING STATUTES Every jurisdiction has **recording statutes,** which allow deeds to be recorded. Recording a deed gives notice to the public that a certain person is now the owner of a particular parcel of real estate. Thus, prospective buyers can check the public records to see whether there have been earlier transactions creating interests or rights in specific parcels of real property. Placing everyone on notice as to the identity of the true owner is intended to prevent the previous owners from fraudulently conveying the land to other purchasers. Deeds are recorded in the county in which the property is located. Many state statutes require that the grantor sign the deed in the presence of two witnesses before it can be recorded.

Will or Inheritance

Property that is transferred on an owner's death is passed either by will or by state inheritance laws. If the owner of land dies with a will, the land passes in

Warranty Deed A deed in which the grantor assures (warrants to) the grantee that the grantor has title to the property conveyed in the deed, that there are no encumbrances on the property other than what the grantor has represented, and that the grantee will enjoy quiet possession of the property; a deed that provides the greatest amount of protection for the grantee.

Quitclaim Deed A deed intended to pass any title, interest, or claim that the grantor may have in the property but not warranting that such title is valid. A quitclaim deed offers the least amount of protection against defects in the title.

Recording Statutes Statutes that allow deeds, mortgages, and other real property transactions to be recorded so as to provide notice to future purchasers or creditors of an existing claim on the property.

---

7. Pronounced *see*-zuhn.

Exhibit 22-1   A Sample Warranty Deed

Date: May 31, 2002

Grantor: GAYLORD A. JENTZ AND WIFE, JOANN H. JENTZ

Grantor's Mailing Address (including county):
4106 North Loop Drive
Austin, Travis County, Texas

Grantee: DAVID F. FRIEND AND WIFE, JOAN E. FRIEND AS JOINT TENANTS
WITH RIGHT OF SURVIVORSHIP

Grantee's Mailing Address (including county):
5929 Fuller Drive
Austin, Travis County, Texas

Consideration:
For and in consideration of the sum of Ten and No/100 Dollars ($10.00) and other
valuable consideration to the undersigned paid by the grantees herein named, the
receipt of which is hereby acknowledged, and for which no lien is retained, either
express or implied.

Property (including any improvements):
Lot 23, Block "A", Northwest Hills, Green Acres Addition, Phase 4, Travis County,
Texas, according to the map or plat of record in volume 22, pages 331-336 of the
Plat Records of Travis County, Texas.

Reservations from and Exceptions to Conveyance and Warranty:

This conveyance with its warranty is expressly made subject to the following:

Easements and restrictions of record in Volume 7863, Page 53, Volume 8430,
Page 35, Volume 8133, Page 152 of the Real Property Record of Travis County,
Texas; Volume 22, Pages 335-339, of the Plat Records of Travis County, Texas;
and to any other restrictions and easements affecting said property which are
of record in Travis County, Texas.

Grantor, for the consideration and subject to the reservations from and exceptions to conveyance and warranty,
grants, sells, and conveys to Grantee the property, together with all and singular the rights and appurtenances thereto in
any wise belonging, to have and hold it to Grantee, Grantee s heirs, executors, administrators, successors, or assigns
forever. Grantor binds Grantor and Grantor s heirs, executors, administrators, and successors to warrant and forever
defend all and singular the property to Grantee and Grantee s heirs, executors, administrators, successors, and assigns
against every person whomsoever lawfully claiming or to claim the same or any part thereof, except as to the reservations
from and exceptions to conveyance and warranty.

When the context requires, singular nouns and pronouns include the plural.

BY: _Gaylord A. Jentz_
Gaylord A. Jentz

BY: _John H. Jentz_
JoAnn H. Jentz

(Acknowledgment)

STATE OF TEXAS
COUNTY OF TRAVIS

This instrument was acknowledged before me on the   31st day of May,   2002
by Gaylord A. and JoAnn H. Jentz

Rosemary Potter
Notary Public.State of Texas
Notary s name (printed): Rosemary Potter

Notary Seal

Notary s commission expires: 1/31/2004

accordance with the terms of the will. If the owner dies without a will, state inheritance statutes prescribe how and to whom the property will pass.

Adverse Possession

Adverse Possession The acquisition of title to real property by occupying it openly, without the consent of the owner, for a period of time specified by a state statute. The occupation must be actual, open, notorious, exclusive, and in opposition to all others, including the owner.

Adverse possession is a means of obtaining title to land without delivery of a deed. Essentially, when one person possesses the property of another for a certain statutory period of time (three to thirty years, with ten years being most common), that person, called the *adverse possessor,* acquires title to the land and cannot be removed from it by the original owner. The adverse possessor is vested with a perfect title just as if there had been a conveyance by deed.

For property to be held adversely, four elements must be satisfied:

1. Possession must be actual and exclusive; that is, the possessor must take sole physical occupancy of the property.
2. The possession must be open, visible, and notorious, not secret or clandestine. The possessor must occupy the land for all the world to see.
3. Possession must be continuous and peaceable for the required period of time. This requirement means that the possessor must not be interrupted in the occupancy by the true owner or by the courts.
4. Possession must be hostile and adverse. In other words, the possessor must claim the property as against the whole world. He or she cannot be living on the property with the permission of the owner.

Leasehold Estates

Lease In real property law, a contract by which the owner of real property (the landlord, or lessor) grants to a person (the tenant, or lessee) an exclusive right to use and possess the property, usually for a specified period of time, in return for rent or some other form of payment.

Often, real property is used by those who do not own it. A **lease** is a contract by which the owner of real property (the landlord, or lessor) grants to a person (the tenant, or lessee) an exclusive right to use and possess the property, usually for a specified period of time, in return for rent or some other form of

---

Ethical Issue 22.1

What public policies underlie the doctrine of adverse possession?

There are a number of public-policy reasons for the adverse possession doctrine. One reason is that it furthers society's interest in resolving boundary disputes in as fair a manner as possible. For example, suppose that a couple mistakenly assumes that they own a certain strip of land by their driveway. They plant grass and shrubs in the area, and maintain the property over the years. The shrubs contribute to the beauty of their lot and to the value of the property. Some thirty years later, their neighbors have a survey taken, and the results show that the strip of property actually belongs to them. In this situation, the couple could claim that they owned the property by adverse possession, and a court would likely agree.[a]

The doctrine of adverse possession thus helps to determine ownership rights when title to property is in question. The doctrine also furthers the policies of rewarding possessors for putting land to productive use, keeping land in the stream of commerce, and not rewarding owners who sit on their rights too long.

---

a. In a case with similar facts, a Pennsylvania court held that the party that had maintained the strip of land for over thirty years acquired title to the land by adverse possession. See *Klos v. Molenda,* 355 Pa.Super. 399, 513 A.2d 490 (1986).

Undeveloped seashore stretches into the distance. Should the government be permitted to take such property from private citizens for public use?

payment. Property in the possession of a tenant is referred to as a **leasehold estate.**

The respective rights and duties of the landlord and tenant that arise under a lease agreement will be discussed shortly. Here we look at the types of leasehold estates, or tenancies, that can be created when real property is leased.

Leasehold Estate An estate in realty held by a tenant under a lease. In every leasehold estate, the tenant has a qualified right to possess and/or use the land.

Tenancy for Years

A **tenancy for years** is created by an express contract by which property is leased for a specified period of time, such as a day, a month, a year, or a period of years. For example, signing a one-year lease to occupy an apartment creates a tenancy for years. At the end of the period specified in the lease, the lease ends (without notice), and possession of the apartment returns to the lessor. If the tenant dies during the period of the lease, the lease interest passes to the tenant's heirs as personal property. Often, leases include renewal or extension provisions.

Tenancy for Years A type of tenancy under which property is leased for a specified period of time, such as a month, a year, or a period of years.

Periodic Tenancy

A **periodic tenancy** is created by a lease that does not specify how long it is to last but does specify that rent is to be paid at certain intervals. This type of tenancy is automatically renewed for another rental period unless properly terminated. For example, a periodic tenancy is created by a lease that states, "Rent is due on the tenth day of every month." This provision creates a tenancy from month to month. This type of tenancy can also extend from week to week or from year to year.

Under the common law, to terminate a periodic tenancy, the landlord or tenant must give at least one period's notice to the other party. If the tenancy extends from month to month, for example, one month's notice must be given prior to the last month's rent payment. State statutes may require a different period for notice of termination in a periodic tenancy, however.

Periodic Tenancy A lease interest in land for an indefinite period involving payment of rent at fixed intervals, such as week to week, month to month, or year to year.

Tenancy at Will

Tenancy at Will A type of tenancy under which either party can terminate the tenancy without notice; usually arises when a tenant who has been under a tenancy for years retains possession, with the landlord's consent, after the tenancy for years has terminated.

Suppose that a landlord rents an apartment to a tenant "for as long as both agree." In such a situation, the tenant receives a leasehold estate known as a **tenancy at will.** Under the common law, either party can terminate the tenancy without notice (that is, "at will"). This type of estate usually arises when a tenant who has been under a tenancy for years retains possession after the termination date of that tenancy with the landlord's consent. Before the tenancy has been converted into a periodic tenancy (by the periodic payment of rent), it is a tenancy at will, terminable by either party without notice. Once the tenancy is treated as a periodic tenancy, termination notice must conform to the one already discussed for that type of tenancy. The death of either party or the voluntary commission of waste by the tenant will terminate a tenancy at will.

Tenancy at Sufferance

Tenancy at Sufferance A type of tenancy under which one who, after rightfully being in possession of leased premises, continues (wrongfully) to occupy the property after the lease has been terminated. The tenant has no rights to possess the property and occupies it only because the person entitled to evict the tenant has not done so.

The mere possession of land without right is called a **tenancy at sufferance.** It is not a true tenancy. A tenancy at sufferance is not an estate, because it is created when a tenant *wrongfully* retains possession of property. Whenever a tenancy for years, periodic tenancy, or tenancy at will ends and the tenant continues to retain possession of the premises without the owner's permission, a tenancy at sufferance is created. When a tenancy at sufferance arises, the owner can immediately evict the tenant.

Landlord-Tenant Relationships

In the past several decades, landlord-tenant relationships have become much more complex than they were before, as has the law governing them. Generally, the law has come to apply contract doctrines, such as those providing for implied warranties and unconscionability, to the landlord-tenant relationship. Increasingly, landlord-tenant relationships have become subject to specific state and local statutes and ordinances as well. In 1972, in an effort to create more uniformity in the law governing landlord-tenant relationships, the National Conference of Commissioners on Uniform State Laws issued the Uniform Residential Landlord and Tenant Act (URLTA). We look now at how a landlord-tenant relationship is created and at the respective rights and duties of landlords and tenants.

Creating the Landlord-Tenant Relationship

A landlord-tenant relationship is established by a lease contract. As mentioned, a lease contract arises when a property owner (landlord) agrees to give another party (the tenant) the exclusive right to possess the property—usually for a price and for a specified term. (For some examples of how Internet companies are redefining leasing requirements, see this chapter's *Legal E-nvironment* feature.)

FORM OF THE LEASE A lease contract may be oral or written. Under the common law, an oral lease is valid. As with most oral contracts, however, a party who seeks to enforce an oral lease may have difficulty proving its existence. In most states, statutes mandate that leases be in writing for some tenancies (such as those exceeding one year). To ensure the validity of a lease agreement, it should therefore be in writing and do the following:

Legal *e*-nvironment

Leasing Requirements in a Cyber Age

Traditionally, entrepreneurs who sought to lease premises for their businesses were interested primarily in one thing—location. A warehouser, for example, would want to lease a building easily accessible by carriers, such as trucks. A retailer would want to lease premises that were easily accessible by prospective customers and that offered a reasonable amount of safety for these "business invitees." A professional would want to lease space in a conveniently located office building. Details of the leasing agreement—such as which party would pay for utilities, repairs, and the like—were important, of course, but location was usually a primary factor in the decision to lease specific premises. In today's world of e-commerce, however, Internet companies are redefining leasing needs—needs that must be addressed in lease contracts.

Access to Telecommunications Services

Foremost among the needs of any company selling its products or services online is access to high-capacity fiber-optic cable and phone lines. Thus, access to telecommunications services, not location, is often the primary consideration in deciding where to lease property. In fact, access requirements often lead Internet start-up companies to lease premises in areas that in other respects would be unfavorable. For example, the best access to telecommunications systems is often in downtown areas that are near central phone company distribution centers, not in the newer areas of a city.

Flexibility, Added Security, and Financing

Physical access needs also differ for online companies because they often operate on a 24/7 (twenty-four-hour-a day, seven-days-a-week) basis. This means that the tenant must have access to the premises at any hour of the day during every day of the week, and parking must also be available on the same basis. Because employees may be coming and going during the middle of the night, extra security guards may be required to escort employees to and from their cars.

A relatively new development involves using equity ownership in a new Internet company as a bargaining tool when negotiating lease terms. For example, a start-up company may offer to transfer company stock, or stock options (see Chapter 24), to the landlord in return for a reduced rent.

For Critical Analysis: *If you were a landlord, what factors would you consider when deciding whether to accept stock in a new Internet company in return for a reduced rental payment?*

---

1. Express an intent to establish the relationship.
2. Provide for the transfer of the property's possession to the tenant at the beginning of the term.
3. Provide for the landlord's reversionary interest, which entitles the property owner to retake possession at the end of the term.
4. Describe the property—for example, give its street address.
5. Indicate the length of the term, the amount of the rent, and how and when it is to be paid.

LEGAL REQUIREMENTS State or local law often dictates permissible lease terms. For example, a statute or ordinance might prohibit the leasing of a structure that is in a certain physical condition or is not in compliance with local building codes. Similarly, a statute may prohibit the leasing of property for a particular purpose. For instance, a state law might prohibit gambling houses. Thus, if a landlord and tenant intend that the leased premises be used only to house an illegal betting operation, their lease is unenforceable.

A property owner cannot legally discriminate against prospective tenants on the basis of race, color, national origin, religion, gender, or disability. Similarly, a tenant cannot legally promise to do something counter to laws prohibiting discrimination. A tenant, for example, cannot legally promise to

> **Note** Sound business practice dictates that a lease for commercial property should be written carefully and should clearly define the parties' rights and obligations.

do business only with members of a particular race. The public policy underlying these prohibitions is to treat all people equally. In the following case, a rental housing applicant claimed that her rental application had been denied because of her live-in boyfriend's race.

Case 22.2 ● Osborn v. Kellogg

Court of Appeals of Nebraska, 1996.
4 Neb.App. 594,
547 N.W.2d 504.

Historical and Environmental
Setting *Since its founding as the village of Lancaster in 1859, Lincoln has grown to become the second largest city in Nebraska. Lincoln is the state capital and the home of the University of Nebraska. With a population of more than 200,000, Lincoln is often included on lists of the best cities in the United States in which to live. In the early 1990s, the average monthly apartment rental ranged from $275 to $500 and the average monthly house rental was between $350 and $700. The average cost of a house in the city was $75,000 to $100,000. Unemployment was less than 3 percent, and the typical wage for a manufacturing job was between $5 and $15 per hour.*

Background and Facts Kristi Kellogg, her daughter Mindy, and her boyfriend James Greene attempted to lease half of a house. The house was owned by Keith Osborn and Pam Lyman, and managed, as rental property, by Keith's mother, Barbara Osborn. Kellogg was white. Greene was African American. The owners refused to rent to them, claiming, among other things, that three people were too many, Greene's income was too low, and Greene had not provided credit references. They later rented half of the house to the Li family, which had five members, and the other half to the Suggett family, which numbered three. Both the Li family and the Suggett family had less income than Kellogg and Greene. Kellogg had provided extensive credit references, but the Lis and the Suggetts had provided none. Kellogg filed a complaint with the Nebraska Equal Opportunity Commission (NEOC) against the Osborns and Lyman. The NEOC concluded that the defendants had discriminated against Kellogg in violation of state fair housing laws. A Nebraska state trial court adopted the NEOC's conclusion. The defendants appealed to an intermediate state appellate court.

In the Words of the Court . . .
WARREN, District Judge * * *

* * * *

* * * While Kellogg is not a member of a racial minority, we note that she qualifies as * * * a person who claims to have been injured by a discriminatory housing practice. It is undisputed that Greene is a member of a racial minority. The evidence further shows that Kellogg applied for and was qualified to rent the house from the Osborns, as evidenced by the rental applications of the Lis and the Suggetts; that her application was rejected, which is undisputed; and that the housing opportunity remained available, which is also undisputed. * * *

* * * *

The NEOC hearing examiner found that Kellogg proved by a preponderance of the evidence that the Osborns' seemingly legitimate reasons for rejecting Kellogg were, in fact, a pretext for intentional discrimination. * * * [W]e conclude that competent evidence supports the NEOC hearing examiner's factual findings.

Decision and Remedy The intermediate state appellate court affirmed the judgment of the lower court. The Osborns and Lyman had discriminated against Kellogg in violation of fair housing laws.

For Critical Analysis—Ethical Consideration *What if the Osborns and Lyman discriminated against Kellogg not because her boyfriend was African American but because they disapproved of cohabitation by unmarried couples? Should this form of discrimination be permissible?*

Rights and Duties

The rights and duties of landlords and tenants generally pertain to four broad areas of concern—the possession, use, and maintenance of leased property and, of course, rent.

POSSESSION Possession involves both the obligation of the landlord to deliver possession to the tenant at the beginning of the lease term and the right of the tenant to obtain possession and retain it until the lease expires.

The covenant of quiet enjoyment mentioned previously also applies to leased premises. Under this covenant, the landlord promises that during the lease term, neither the landlord nor anyone having a superior title to the property will disturb the tenant's use and enjoyment of the property. This covenant forms the essence of the landlord-tenant relationship, and if it is breached, the tenant can terminate the lease and sue for damages.

If the landlord deprives the tenant of the tenant's possession of the leased property or interferes with the tenant's use or enjoyment of it, an eviction occurs. An **eviction** occurs, for example, when the landlord changes the lock and refuses to give the tenant a new key. A **constructive eviction** occurs when the landlord wrongfully performs or fails to perform any of the undertakings the lease requires, thereby making the tenant's further use and enjoyment of the property exceedingly difficult or impossible. Examples of constructive eviction include a landlord's failure to provide heat in the winter, light, or other essential utilities.

> **Eviction** A landlord's act of depriving a tenant of possession of the leased premises.
>
> **Constructive Eviction** A form of eviction that occurs when a landlord fails to perform adequately any of the undertakings (such as providing heat in the winter) required by the lease, thereby making the tenant's further use and enjoyment of the property exceedingly difficult or impossible.

USE AND MAINTENANCE OF THE PREMISES If the parties do not limit by agreement the uses to which the property may be put, the tenant may make any use of it, as long as the use is legal and reasonably relates to the purpose for which the property is adapted or ordinarily used and does not injure the landlord's interest.

The tenant is responsible for any damages to the premises that he or she causes, intentionally or negligently, and the tenant may be held liable for the cost of returning the property to the physical condition it was in at the lease's inception. Unless the parties have agreed otherwise, the tenant is not responsible for ordinary wear and tear and the property's consequent depreciation in value.

Usually, the landlord must comply with state statutes and city ordinances that delineate specific standards for the construction and maintenance of buildings. Typically, these codes contain structural requirements common to the construction, wiring, and plumbing of residential and commercial buildings. In some jurisdictions, landlords of residential property are required by statute to maintain the premises in good repair.

IMPLIED WARRANTY OF HABITABILITY The **implied warranty of habitability** requires a landlord who leases residential property to deliver the premises to the tenant in a habitable condition—that is, in a condition that is safe and suitable for people to live in—at the beginning of a lease term and to maintain them in that condition for the lease's duration. Some state legislatures have enacted this warranty into law. In other jurisdictions, courts have based the warranty on the existence of a landlord's statutory duty to keep leased premises in good repair, or they have simply applied it as a matter of public policy.

> **Implied Warranty of Habitability** An implied promise by a landlord that rented residential premises are fit for human habitation—that is, in a condition that is safe and suitable for people to live in.

Generally, this warranty applies to major, or *substantial,* physical defects that the landlord knows or should know about and has had a reasonable time to repair—for example, a large hole in the roof. An unattractive or annoying feature, such as a crack in the wall, may be unpleasant, but unless the crack is a structural defect or affects the residence's heating capabilities, it is probably not sufficiently substantial to make the place uninhabitable.

At issue in the following case was whether the lack of a smoke detector constituted a violation of a statutory requirement that rental property be "in reasonable repair and fit for human habitation."

Case 22.3 ● Schiernbeck v. Davis

United States Court of Appeals, Eighth Circuit, 1998.
143 F.3d 434.
http://laws.findlaw.com/8th[a]

Historical and Technological Setting   *Different smoke detectors come with a variety of capabilities. Some can detect flames with little smoke and can detect even "smokeless" fires. Other devices include strobe lights for alerting the hearing impaired, fixtures for lighting darkened areas, "hush" buttons for nuisance alarms, and buttons for testing the functions. A basic, battery-operated smoke detector, with an alarm only, can cost as little as $6. Some states require the installation of smoke detectors on property*

offered for rent. A missing smoke detector in residential rental property is a violation of some local building codes. Not every jurisdiction requires their use, however.

Background and Facts   Linda Schiernbeck rented a house from Clark and Rosa Davis. A month after moving into the house, Schiernbeck noticed a discolored circular area where, she determined, a smoke detector had previously been attached to the wall. Schiernbeck later claimed that she told Clark Davis about the missing detector. Davis did not remember the conversation. He admitted, however, that he gave Schiernbeck a detector, which she denied. At any rate, when a fire in the house severely injured Schiernbeck, she filed a suit in a federal district court against the Davises, alleging negligence and breach of contract for failing to provide a detector. The Davises filed a motion for summary judgment, arguing that they had no duty to install a detector in a rental house. The court ruled in the Davises' favor, and Schiernbeck appealed to the U.S. Court of Appeals for the Eighth Circuit.

---

a. This Web site is maintained by FindLaw. This page provides access to some of the opinions of the U.S. Court of Appeals for the Eighth Circuit. In the "Search" box, type "97-3431" and click "Search" to access the *Schiernbeck* opinion.

In the Words of the Court . . .
WATERS, District Judge.

* * * *

* * * South Dakota Codified Laws Section 43-32-8 requires that the lessor keep the leased premises "in reasonable repair and fit for human habitation * * * ." We do not believe that equipping the leased premises with a smoke detector constitutes keeping the premises in "reasonable repair." * * * [T]he accepted dictionary definition [of "repair" is:] "To restore to a sound or good state after decay, injury, dilapidation, or partial destruction." Schiernbeck cites an additional part of the dictionary's definition which states * * * "to supply * * * that which is lost or destroyed" to include replacing a missing smoke detector in the definition of repair. We conclude, however, that when reading the entire definition, the term "repair" does not encompass replacing a missing smoke detector.

* * * *

In addition, we do not believe that the Davises were required to replace the smoke detector in order to make the rental house "fit for human habitation." * * * Clearly, unstable stairs create a place that is unfit for

Case 22.3 Continued

> human habitation, as does a lack of running water, heat, or electricity. We do not believe, however, that a lessor * * * is required to equip his or her residential premises with smoke detectors, fire extinguishers, carbon monoxide detectors, etc. in order to make the leased premises "fit for human habitation."

Decision and Remedy The U.S. Court of Appeals for the Eighth Circuit held that a landlord's statutory duty to keep rental premises "in reasonable repair and fit for human habitation" does not include installing a smoke detector. The court affirmed the lower court's judgment.

For Critical Analysis—Ethical Consideration *What is a landlord's ethical duty with respect to keeping rental premises "fit for human habitation"?*

RENT *Rent* is the tenant's payment to the landlord for the tenant's occupancy or use of the landlord's real property. Generally, the tenant must pay the rent even if he or she refuses to occupy the property or moves out, as long as the refusal or the move is unjustifiable and the lease is in force.

Under the common law, destruction by fire or flood of a building leased by a tenant did not relieve the tenant of the obligation to pay rent and did not permit the termination of the lease. Today, however, state statutes have altered the common law rule. If the building burns down, apartment dwellers in most states are not continuously liable to the landlord for the payment of rent.

In some situations, such as when a landlord breaches the implied warranty of habitability, a tenant is allowed to withhold rent as a remedy. When rent withholding is authorized under a statute (sometimes referred to as a "rent-strike" statute), the tenant must usually put the amount withheld into an *escrow account.* This account is held in the name of the depositor (in this case, the tenant) and an *escrow agent* (in this case, usually the court or a government agency), and the funds are returnable to the depositor if the third person (in this case, the landlord) fails to fulfill the escrow condition. Generally, the tenant may withhold an amount equal to the amount by which the defect rendering the premises unlivable reduces the property's rental value. How much that is may be determined in different ways, and the tenant who withholds more than is legally permissible is liable to the landlord for the excessive amount withheld.

> **Note** Options that may be available to a tenant on a landlord's breach of the implied warranty of habitability include repairing the defect and deducting the amount from the rent, canceling the lease, and suing for damages.

Transferring Rights to Leased Property

Either the landlord or the tenant may wish to transfer his or her rights to the leased property during the term of the lease.

TRANSFERRING THE LANDLORD'S INTEREST Just as any other real property owner can sell, give away, or otherwise transfer his or her property, so can a landlord—who is, of course, the leased property's owner. If complete title to the leased property is transferred, the tenant becomes the tenant of the new owner. The new owner may collect subsequent rent but must abide by the terms of the existing lease agreement.

TRANSFERRING THE TENANT'S INTEREST The tenant's transfer of his or her entire interest in the leased property to a third person is an *assignment of* *the lease.* A lease assignment is an agreement to transfer all rights, title, and interest in the lease to the assignee. It is a complete transfer. Many leases require that the assignment have the landlord's written consent, and an assignment that lacks consent can be avoided (nullified) by the landlord. A landlord who knowingly accepts rent from the assignee, however, will be held to have waived the requirement. An assignment does not terminate a tenant's liabilities under a lease agreement, however, because the tenant may assign rights but not duties. Thus, even though the assignee of the lease is required to pay rent, the original tenant is not released from the contractual obligation to pay the rent if the assignee fails to do so.

Sublease A lease executed by the lessee of real estate to a third person, conveying the same interest that the lessee enjoys but for a shorter term than that held by the lessee.

The tenant's transfer of all or part of the premises for a period shorter than the lease term is a **sublease.** The same restrictions that apply to an assignment of the tenant's interest in leased property apply to a sublease. • **Example 22.4** A student named Derek leases an apartment for a two-year period. Although Derek had planned on attending summer school, he is offered a job in Europe for the summer months and accepts. Because he does not wish to pay three months' rent for an unoccupied apartment, Derek subleases the apartment to Singleton, who becomes a sublessee. (Derek may have to obtain his landlord's consent for this sublease if the lease requires it.) Singleton is bound by the same terms of the lease as Derek, but as in a lease assignment, Derek remains liable for the obligations under the lease if Singleton fails to fulfill them.•

Land-Use Control

Property owners—even those who possess the entire bundle of rights set out earlier in this chapter—cannot do with their property whatever they wish. The rights of every property owner are subject to certain conditions and limitations.

There are three sources of land-use control. First, the law of torts (see Chapter 9) places on the owners of land obligations to protect the interests of individuals who come on the land and the interests of the owners of nearby land. Second, landowners may agree with others to restrict or limit the use of their property. Such agreements may "run with the land" when ownership is transferred to others. Thus, one who acquires real property with actual or *constructive* (imputed by law) notice of a restriction may be bound by an earlier, voluntary agreement to which he or she was not a party.

Third, controls are imposed by the government. Land use is subject to regulation by the state within whose political boundaries the land is located. Most states authorize control over land use through various planning boards and zoning authorities at a city or county level. The federal government does not engage in land-use control under normal circumstances, except with respect to federally owned land.[8] The federal government does influence state and local regulation, however, through the allocation of federal funds. Stipulations on land use may be a condition to the states' receiving such funds.

Sources of Public Control

The states' power to control the use of land through legislation is derived from their *police power* and the doctrine of *eminent domain.* Under their police

---

8. Federal (and state) laws concerning environmental matters such as air and water quality, the protection of endangered species, and the preservation of natural wetlands are also a source of land-use control. Some of these laws were discussed in Chapter 21.

power, state governments enact legislation that promotes the health, safety, and welfare of their citizens. This legislation includes land-use controls. The power of **eminent domain** is the government's authority to take private property for public use or purpose without the owner's consent. Typically, this is accomplished through a judicial proceeding to obtain title to the land.

Eminent Domain The power of a government to take land for public use from private citizens for just compensation.

Police Power

As an exercise of its police power,[9] a state can regulate the use of land within its jurisdiction. A few states control land use at the state level. Hawaii, for instance, employs a statewide land-use classification scheme. Some states have a land-permit process that operates in conjunction with local control. Florida, for example, uses such a scheme in certain areas of "critical environmental concern" to permit or prohibit development on the basis of available roads, sewers, and so on. Vermont also utilizes a statewide land-permit scheme.

Usually, however, a state authorizes its city or county governments to regulate the use of land within their local jurisdictions. A state confers this power through *enabling legislation*. Enabling legislation normally requires local governments to devise *general plans* before imposing other land-use controls. Enabling acts also typically authorize local bodies to enact *zoning laws* to regulate the use of land and the types of and specifications for structures. Local planning boards may regulate the development of subdivisions, in which private developers subdivide tracts of land and construct commercial or residential units for resale to others. Local governments may also enact growth-management ordinances to control development in their jurisdictions.

GOVERNMENT PLANS Most states require that land-use laws follow a local government's general plan. A **general plan** is a comprehensive, long-term scheme dealing with the physical development, and in some cases redevelopment, of a city or community. It addresses such concerns as types of housing, protection of natural resources, provision of public facilities and transportation, and other issues related to land use. A plan indicates the direction of growth in a community and the contributions that private developers must make toward providing such public facilities as roads. If a proposed use is not authorized by the general plan, the plan may be amended to permit the use. (A plan may also be amended to preclude a proposed use.)

General Plan A comprehensive document that local jurisdictions are often required by state law to devise and implement as a precursor to specific land-use regulations.

Even when a proposed use complies with a general plan, it may not be allowed. Most jurisdictions have requirements in addition to those in the general plan. These requirements are then included in specific plans—also called special, area, or community plans. Specific plans typically pertain to only a portion of a jurisdiction's area. For example, a specific plan may concern a downtown area subject to redevelopment efforts, an area with special environmental concerns, or an area with increased public transportation needs arising from population growth.

ZONING LAWS In addition to complying with a general plan and any specific plans, a particular land use must comply with zoning laws. The term **zoning** refers to the dividing of an area into districts to which specific land-use

Zoning The division of a city by legislative regulation into districts and the application in each district of regulations having to do with structural and architectural designs of buildings and prescribing the use to which buildings within designated districts may be put.

---

9. As pointed out in Chapter 6, the police power of a state encompasses the right to regulate private activities to protect or promote the public order, health, safety, morals, and general welfare.

regulations apply. A typical zoning law consists of a zoning map and a zoning ordinance. The zoning map indicates the characteristics of each parcel of land within an area and divides that area into districts. The zoning ordinance specifies the restrictions on land use within those districts.

Zoning ordinances generally include two types of restrictions. One type pertains to the kind of land use—such as commercial versus residential—to which property within a particular district may be put. The second type dictates the engineering features and architectural design of structures built within that district.

Use Restrictions. Districts are typically zoned for residential, commercial, industrial, or agricultural use. Each district may be further subdivided for degree or intensity of use. For example, a residential district may be subdivided to permit a certain number of apartment buildings and a certain number of units in each building. Commercial and industrial districts are often zoned to permit *heavy* or *light* activity. Heavy activity might include the operation of large factories. Light activity might include the operation of professional office buildings or small retail shops. Zoning that specifies the use to which property may be put is referred to as **use zoning.**

Use Zoning Zoning classifications within a particular municipality that may be distinguished based on the uses to which the land is to be put.

Structural Restrictions. Restrictions known as *bulk regulations* cover such details as minimum floor-space requirements and minimum lot-size restrictions. For example, a particular district's minimum floor-space requirements might specify that a one-story building contain a minimum of 1,240 square feet of floor space, and minimum lot-size restrictions might specify that each single-family dwelling be built on a lot that is at least one acre in size. Referred to collectively as **bulk zoning,** these regulations also dictate *setback* (the distance between a building and a street, sidewalk, or other boundary) and the height of buildings, with different requirements for buildings in different areas.

Bulk Zoning Zoning regulations that restrict the amount of structural coverage on a particular parcel of land.

Restrictions related to structure may also be concerned with such matters as architectural control, the overall appearance of a community, and the preservation of historic buildings. An ordinance may require that all proposed construction be approved by a design review board composed of local architects. A community may restrict the size and placement of outdoor advertising, such as billboards and business signs. A property owner may be prohibited from tearing down or remodeling a historic landmark or building. In challenges against these types of restrictions, the courts have generally upheld the regulations.[10]

Zoning Variance The granting of permission by a municipality or other public board to a landowner to use his or her property in a way that does not strictly conform with the zoning regulations so as to avoid causing the landowner undue hardship.

Variances. A **zoning variance** allows property to be used or structures to be built in some way that varies from the restrictions of a zoning ordinance. ● **Example 22.5** A variance may exempt property from a use restriction to allow, for example, a bakery shop in a residential area. Or a variance may exempt a building from a height restriction so that, for example, a two-story house can be built in a district in which houses are otherwise limited to one floor. ● Some jurisdictions do not permit variances from use restrictions.

Variances are normally granted by local adjustment boards. In general, a property owner must meet three criteria to obtain a variance:

---

10. See, for example, *Penn Central Transportation Co. v. New York City,* 438 U.S. 104, 98 S.Ct. 2646, 57 L.Ed.2d 631 (1978).

1. The owner must find it impossible to realize a reasonable return on the land as currently zoned.
2. The adverse effect of the zoning ordinance must be particular to the party seeking the variance and not have a similar effect on other owners in the same zone.
3. Granting the variance must not substantially alter the essential character of the zoned area.

Perhaps the most important of these criteria is whether the variance would substantially alter the character of the area. Courts are more lenient about the other requirements when reviewing decisions of adjustment boards. As the following case illustrates, courts also tend to defer to the discretion of such boards unless there has been a clear abuse of authority.

Case 22.4 ● Allegheny West Civic Council, Inc. v. Zoning Board of Adjustment of the City of Pittsburgh

Supreme Court of Pennsylvania, 1997.
689 A.2d 225.

Background and Facts Irwin Associates, Inc., contracted to sell, for $431,500, a vacant lot in an area in Pittsburgh, Pennsylvania, zoned for residential use. The deal collapsed when it was learned that the lot was contaminated with petroleum hydrocarbon and benzene in excess of state and federal guidelines. Estimated clean-up costs were $2.5 million to $3 million, with addi-

tional annual monitoring costs of $10,000 to $20,000. Irwin asked the Pittsburgh Zoning Board of Adjustment for a variance to use the property as a parking lot. Allegheny West Civic Council wanted residential housing in the area and opposed Irwin's request. The board concluded that Irwin's proposed use would not be detrimental to the neighborhood and granted the variance. Allegheny West appealed to a Pennsylvania state court, which affirmed the board's decision. Ultimately, the case was appealed to the state supreme court.

In the Words of the Court . . .
NIGRO, Justice.

* * * *

Irwin Associates' environmental consultant testified that the contamination exceeded state and federal guidelines and that a building on the property may be a health hazard because vapors could accumulate inside. Its real estate financing expert testified that it was unlikely that a financial institution would lend money for a construction project on the property because it would expose itself to potential liability for [clean-up] costs. Irwin Associates' president testified that the relatively small size of the lot precluded other permitted uses not involving improvements. The environmental consultant estimated that the [clean-up] cost would be $2.5 [million] to $3 million and annual monitoring costs would be $10,000 to $20,000. There is thus substantial evidence that Irwin Associates cannot use the property for a permitted purpose or can only conform it for a permitted purpose at a prohibitive cost. Furthermore, * * * there is evidence that the property is now without value as zoned. The local property assessment board assigned the property a fair market value of zero.

The Zoning Board did not abuse its discretion * * * in granting the variance.

(Continued)

Case 22.4 Continued

Decision and Remedy The Supreme Court of Pennsylvania affirmed the board's decision to grant the variance. The variant use would not harm the character of the neighborhood, and denying the variance would create unnecessary hardship for the property owner.

For Critical Analysis—Economic Consideration *What might have happened to neighboring property values if the variance had not been granted?*

SUBDIVISION REGULATIONS   When subdividing a parcel of land into smaller plots, a private developer must comply not only with local zoning ordinances but also with local subdivision regulations. Subdivision regulations are different from zoning ordinances, although they may be administered by the same local agencies that oversee the zoning process. In the design of a subdivision, the local authorities may demand, for example, the allocation of space for a public park or school or may require a developer to construct streets to accommodate a specific level of traffic.

GROWTH-MANAGEMENT ORDINANCES   To prevent population growth from racing ahead of the community's ability to provide necessary public services, local authorities may enact a growth-management ordinance to limit, for example, the number of residential building permits. A property owner may thus be precluded from constructing a residential building on his or her property even if the area is zoned for the use and the proposed structure complies with all other requirements. A growth-management ordinance may prohibit the issuance of residential building permits for a specific period of time, until the occurrence of a specific event (such as a decline in the total number of residents in the community), or on the basis of the availability of necessary public services (such as the capacity for drainage in the area or the proximity of hospitals and police stations).

LIMITATIONS ON THE EXERCISE OF POLICE POWER   The government's exercise of its police power to regulate the use of land is limited in at least three ways. Two of these limitations arise under the Fourteenth Amendment to the Constitution. The third limitation arises under the Fifth Amendment and requires that, under certain circumstances, the government must compensate an owner who is deprived of the use of his or her property.

Due Process and Equal Protection.   A government cannot regulate the use of land in a way that violates either the due process clause or the equal protection clause of the Fourteenth Amendment. A government may be deemed to violate the due process clause if it acts arbitrarily or unreasonably. Thus, there must be a *rational basis* for classifications that are imposed on property. Any classification that is reasonably related to the health or general welfare of the public is deemed to have a rational basis.

Under the equal protection clause, land-use controls cannot be discriminatory. A zoning ordinance is discriminatory if it affects one parcel of land in a way in which it does not affect surrounding parcels and if there is no rational basis for the difference. For example, classifying a single parcel in a way that does not accord with a general plan is discriminatory. Similarly, a zoning ordinance cannot be racially discriminatory. • **Example 22.6** A community may not zone itself to exclude all low-income housing if the intention is to exclude minorities. •

The following case involved a challenge to a zoning ordinance on the ground that it did not relate to any legitimate governmental health, safety, or welfare concerns.

Case 22.5 ● Shemo v. Mayfield Heights

Supreme Court
of Ohio, 2000.
88 Ohio St.3d 7,
722 N.E.2d 1018.
**http://www.lawyersweekly.
com/ohsc.htm**ᵃ

Background and Facts Michael Shemo and Larry Goldberg owned an undeveloped 22.6-acre parcel of land in Mayfield Heights, Ohio. Residential properties were to the west of the parcel. Commercial properties, including a Best Buy store, a Budgetel Motel, and a Bob Evans restaurant, bordered the property to the south. High-tension power lines and Interstate 271, with high-intensity lighting, ran along

---

a. This Web site is maintained by Lawyers Weekly, Inc., a publisher of legal newspapers for practicing attorneys. In the "2000 Opinions" section, click on "February." When the page opens, scroll to the name of the case and click on it to access the opinion.

the eastern edge of the property. A shopping center was on the other side of the highway. The property was zoned "U-1" for single-family homes when the Mayfield Heights City Council enacted an ordinance to rezone the property "U-2-A" for cluster single-family homes. Shemo and Goldberg filed a suit in an Ohio state court against the city to invalidate the ordinance and have the property rezoned "U-4" to permit retail and warehouse use. They proposed to widen and replace the commercial driveway and install a traffic light to improve the traffic flow. They also proposed to limit access from their property to the residential streets to emergency vehicles. The court declared the ordinance unconstitutional, in part on the ground that it did not substantially advance a legitimate health, safety, or welfare concern of the city. The city appealed to a state intermediate appellate court, which remanded the case for reconsideration. Shemo and Goldberg appealed to the Ohio Supreme Court.

In the Words of the Court . . .
FRANCIS E. SWEENEY, SR., J. [Judge]

* * * *

The city argued that the zoning ordinance advances three legitimate governmental health, safety, and welfare concerns: (1) it will maintain the residential character of the neighborhood, (2) it will maintain a balanced mix of uses in the city, and (3) it will not exacerbate traffic congestion * * * .

* * * *

* * * [T]he city presented the testimony of some current residents who are opposed to the commercial development of the property because there will likely be increased traffic in their neighborhood. While we do not mean to minimize the concerns of these residents and, in fact, sympathize with their plight, we cannot ignore the fact that their homes are adjacent to high-density commercial property, which carries with it a heavy volume of traffic. * * * We reject the city's argument that the U-2-A zoning is necessary to maintain the residential character of the neighborhood.

We also reject the city's argument that the U-2-A zoning classification is necessary to advance the legitimate governmental interests of maintaining a balanced mix of uses in the city * * * . Since the area contains both residential and commercial properties, there already exists a balanced mix of uses in the city. * * *

(Continued)

Case 22.5 Continued

Nor did the trial court err in rejecting the city's argument that decreasing traffic congestion is a legitimate governmental concern. Although the U-4 zoning classification would increase traffic in the area, one of appellants' expert witnesses testified that the impact of the increased traffic would not be severe. * * * [A]ppellants have proposed to widen and replace the current driveway at their expense and to have a traffic light installed to improve the flow of traffic in the area and to alleviate current safety concerns. Appellants have also proposed to limit direct access from their property to the residential streets to cases of emergency only. * * *

* * * *

Since appellants have shown that the city lacks any legitimate governmental health, safety, and welfare concerns in support of the U-2-A zoning classification, we find that the trial court was correct in declaring the U-2-A zoning ordinance unconstitutional.

Decision and Remedy The Ohio Supreme Court reversed the judgment of the state intermediate appellate court and reinstated the trial court's judgment declaring the zoning ordinance unconstitutional. Shemo and Goldberg showed that the city did not have any legitimate governmental health, safety, or welfare concerns to support the ordinance.

For Critical Analysis—Ethical Consideration *To what extent do you think that Shemo and Goldberg's proposals—to replace and widen the commercial driveway, install a traffic light, and limit access to the residential streets to emergency vehicles—affected the outcome of this case?*

> "[A] strong public desire to improve the public condition is not enough to warrant achieving the desire by a shorter cut than . . . paying for the change."
>
> Oliver Wendell Holmes, Jr.,
> 1841–1935
> (Associate justice of the United States
> Supreme Court, 1902–1932)

JUST COMPENSATION Under the Fifth Amendment, private property may not be taken for a public purpose without the payment of just compensation.[11] If government restrictions on a landowner's property rights are overly burdensome, the regulation may be deemed a taking. A taking occurs when a regulation denies an owner the ability to use his or her property for any reasonable income-producing or private purpose for which it is suited. This requires the government to pay the owner.

• **Example 22.7** Suppose that Perez purchases a large tract of land with the intent to subdivide and develop it into residential properties. At the time of the purchase, there are no zoning laws restricting use of the land. After Perez has taken significant steps to develop the property, the county attempts to zone the tract "public parkland only." If this prohibits Perez from developing any of the land, it will be deemed a taking. If the county does not fairly compensate Perez, the regulation will be held unconstitutional and void.•

The distinction between an ordinance that merely restricts land use and an outright taking is crucial. A restriction is simply an exercise of the state's police power; even though it limits a property owner's land use, the owner generally need not be compensated for the limitation. An ordinance that completely deprives an owner of use or benefit of property, or an outright governmental taking of property, however, must be compensated.

The United States Supreme Court has held that restrictions do not constitute a taking of an owner's property if they "substantially advance legitimate

---

11. Although the Fifth Amendment pertains to actions taken by the federal government, the Fourteenth Amendment has been interpreted as extending this limitation to state actions.

A view of the ocean from a public park. If this had once been private property, why would the government have been prohibited from taking it for public use without paying the owner?

state interests" and do not "den[y] an owner economically viable use of his land."[12] It is not clear, however, exactly what constitutes a "legitimate state interest" or when particular restrictions "substantially advance" that interest. Furthermore, the term "economically viable use" has not yet been clearly defined. One of the issues discussed in this chapter's *Inside the Legal Environment* on the next page is whether the focus should be on the value of the land or the use to which it could be put.

Eminent Domain

As noted above, governments have an inherent power to take property for public use or purpose without the consent of the owner. This is the power of eminent domain, and it is very important in the public control of land use.

Every property owner holds his or her interest in land subject to a superior interest. Just as in medieval England the king was the ultimate landowner, so in the United States the government retains an ultimate ownership right in all land. This right, known as eminent domain, is sometimes referred to as the *condemnation power* of the government to take land for public use. It gives to the government a right to acquire possession of real property in the manner directed by the Constitution and the laws of the state whenever the public interest requires it. Property may not be taken for private benefit, but only for public use.

• **Example 22.8** When a new public highway is to be built, the government must decide where to build it and how much land to condemn. After the government determines that a particular parcel of land is necessary for public use, it brings a judicial proceeding to obtain title to the land.•

---

12. *Agins v. Tiburon*, 447 U.S. 255, 100 S.Ct. 2138, 65 L.Ed. 2d 106 (1980).

Inside the Legal Environment

Land-Use Regulations and the Takings Clause

Environmental regulations and other legislation to control land use are prevalent throughout the United States. Generally, these laws reflect the public's interest in preserving natural resources and habitats and in allowing the public to have access to and enjoy limited natural resources, such as coastal areas. Although few would disagree with the rationale underlying these laws, the owners of the private property directly affected by the laws often feel that they should be compensated for the limitation imposed on their right to do as they wish with their land.

The Takings Issue

Several cases have been brought by private-property owners who allege that regulations limiting their control over their own land essentially constitute a taking of private property in the public interest. Therefore, the property owners should receive the just compensation guaranteed under the Fifth Amendment.

For example, in one case the owners of ocean-front property in Monterey, California, applied to the city of Monterey several times for a permit to build a residential development. Del Monte Dunes at Monterey, Limited, bought the property and continued to seek a permit. Each time, the city denied the use of more of the property, until no part remained available for any use that would be inconsistent with leaving the property in its natural state. The city justified its actions by stating that it was seeking to protect various forms of wildlife that inhabit the coastal sand dunes, particularly the endangered Smith's blue butterfly. This butterfly, which is unique to the region and is nearly extinct, lays its eggs on the branches of a type of buckwheat plant that is native to the region's dunes.

Del Monte finally sold the property to the city and filed suit against the city in a federal district court. Del Monte claimed that the restrictions on use amounted to an unconstitutional taking without the "just compensation" required by the Fifth Amendment. The jury agreed and awarded Del Monte nearly $1.45 million in damages. The city appealed, but it fared no better in the federal appellate court, which affirmed the jury's award.[a]

Should Juries Decide When a Taking Occurs?

An interesting aspect of this case is the city's claim that the issue of whether a taking had occurred should never have gone before a jury. Traditionally, lawsuits involving the power of eminent domain—such as when a local government takes private property to create a road—have been heard by judges. The city argued that this case should also have been decided by a judge, as land-use cases usually are. For one thing, a judge is more knowledgeable than lay jurors are about the land-use regulations at issue and the legal theory of regulatory takings. For another, if such actions were to be decided by jurors, who are more likely than judges to be sympathetic to the plaintiffs, more and more citizens would bring suits challenging zoning laws. The federal appellate court held that jury trials may be demanded at every step along the way.

This procedural question was ultimately decided by the United States Supreme Court, when it reviewed the case. The Supreme Court held that because the issue of "whether a landowner has been deprived of all economically viable use of his property is a predominantly factual question," it was a question for a jury to decide. Thus, the high court affirmed the appellate court's decision in favor of Del Monte Dunes.[b]

For Critical Analysis: *"When a government body, such as a city or state government, imposes limitations on private landowners' rights in order to preserve environmental resources and habitats for endangered species, the private landowners should be compensated for such a 'taking' of their property."* Do you agree with this contention? Why, or why not?

a. *Del Monte Dunes at Monterey, Ltd. v. City of Monterey,* 95 F.3d 1422 (9th Cir. 1996).
b. *City of Monterey v. Del Monte Dunes at Monterey, Ltd.,* 526 U.S. 687, 119 S.Ct. 1624, 143 L.Ed.2d 882 (1999).

Under the Fifth Amendment, although the government may take land for public use, it must pay fair and just compensation for it. Thus, in the previous highway example, after the proceeding to obtain title to the land, there is a second proceeding in which the court determines the *fair value* of the land. Fair value is usually approximately equal to market value.

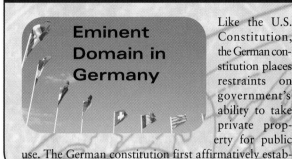

International Perspective

Eminent Domain in Germany

Like the U.S. Constitution, the German constitution places restraints on government's ability to take private property for public use. The German constitution first affirmatively estab-lishes the right of the government to take private property for public use and then requires some pay-ment to the landowner for the property that is taken. The German constitution also states that private-property owners have a duty to use their property for the public good.

For Critical Analysis: *Why might a govern-ment choose not to pay its citizens for property that is taken?*

Key Terms

adverse possession   640
bulk zoning   650
constructive eviction   645
conveyance   636
deed   637
easement   637
eminent domain   649
eviction   645
executory interest   637
fee simple absolute   635
fee simple defeasible   636
fixture   634

future interest   636
general plan   649
implied warranty of
    habitability   645
lease   640
leasehold estate   641
license   637
life estate   636
periodic tenancy   641
profit   637
quitclaim deed   638
recording statute   638

remainder   637
reversionary interest   636
sublease   648
tenancy at sufferance   642
tenancy at will   642
tenancy for years   641
use zoning   650
warranty deed   638
zoning   649
zoning variance   650

Chapter Summary • Land-Use Control and Real Property

The Nature of Real Property (See pages 632–635.)	Real property (also called real estate or realty) is immovable. It includes land, subsurface and air rights, plant life and vegetation, and fixtures.
Ownership of Real Property (See pages 635–637.)	1. **Fee simple absolute**—The most complete form of ownership. 2. **Fee simple defeasible**—Ownership in fee simple that can end if a specified event or condition occurs. 3. **Life estate**—An estate that lasts for the life of a specified individual; ownership rights in a life estate are subject to the rights of the future-interest holder. 4. **Future interest**—A residuary interest not granted by the grantor in conveying an estate to another for life, for a specified period of time, or on the condition that a specific event does or does not occur. The grantor may retain the residuary interest (which is then called a reversionary interest) or transfer ownership rights in the future interest to another (the interest is then referred to as a remainder).

(Continued)

Chapter Summary • Land-Use Control and Real Property, *Continued*

Ownership of Real Property— continued	5. **Nonpossessory interest**—An interest that involves the right to use real property but not to possess it. Easements, profits, and licenses are nonpossessory interests.

Transfer of Ownership (See pages 637–640.)	1. **By deed**—When real property is sold or transferred as a gift, title to the property is conveyed by means of a deed. A deed must meet specific legal requirements. A *warranty deed* warrants the most extensive protection against defects of title. A *quitclaim deed* conveys to the grantee whatever interest the grantor had; it warrants less than any other deed. A deed may be recorded in the manner prescribed by *recording statutes* in the appropriate jurisdiction to give third parties notice of the owner's interest.
	2. **By will or inheritance**—If the owner dies after having made a valid will, the land passes as specified in the will. If the owner dies without having made a will, the heirs inherit according to state inheritance statutes.
	3. **By adverse possession**—When a person possesses the property of another for a statutory period of time (three to thirty years, with ten years being the most common), that person acquires title to the property, provided the possession is actual and exclusive, open and visible, continuous and peaceable, and hostile and adverse (without the permission of the owner).

Leasehold Estates (See pages 640–642.)	A leasehold estate is an interest in real property that is held only for a limited period of time, as specified in the lease agreement. Types of tenancies relating to leased property include the following:
	1. **Tenancy for years**—Tenancy for a period of time stated by express contract.
	2. **Periodic tenancy**—Tenancy for a period determined by the frequency of rent payments; automatically renewed unless proper notice is given.
	3. **Tenancy at will**—Tenancy for as long as both parties agree; no notice of termination is required.
	4. **Tenancy at sufferance**—Possession of land without legal right.

Landlord-Tenant Relationships (See pages 642–648.)	1. **Lease agreement**—The landlord-tenant relationship is created by a lease agreement. State or local laws may dictate whether the lease must be in writing and what lease terms are permissible.
	2. **Rights and duties**—The rights and duties that arise under a lease agreement generally pertain to the following areas:
	a. **Possession**—The tenant has an exclusive right to possess the leased premises, which must be available to the tenant at the agreed-on time. Under the covenant of quiet enjoyment, the landlord promises that during the lease term neither the landlord nor anyone having superior title to the property will disturb the tenant's use and enjoyment of the property.
	b. **Use and maintenance of the premises**—Unless the parties agree otherwise, the tenant may make any legal use of the property. The tenant is responsible for any damage that he or she causes. The landlord must comply with laws that set specific standards for the maintenance of real property. The implied warranty

Chapter Summary • Land-Use Control and Real Property

Landlord-Tenant Relationships— continued	of habitability requires that a landlord furnish and maintain residential premises in a habitable condition (that is, in a condition safe and suitable for human life).
	c. Rent—The tenant must pay the rent as long as the lease is in force, unless the tenant justifiably refuses to occupy the property or withholds the rent because of the landlord's failure to maintain the premises properly.
	3. **Transferring rights to leased property—**
	a. If the landlord transfers complete title to the leased property, the tenant becomes the tenant of the new owner. The new owner may then collect the rent but must abide by the existing lease.
	b. Generally, tenants may assign their rights (but not their duties) under a lease contract to a third person. Tenants may also sublease leased property to a third person, but the original tenant is not relieved of any obligations to the landlord under the lease. In either case, the landlord's consent may be required.
Land-Use Control— Private Control (See page 648.)	1. **The law of torts**—Owners are obligated to protect the interests of those who come on the land and those who own nearby land.
	2. **Private agreements**—Owners may agree with others to limit the use of their property.
Land-Use Control— Government Police Power (See pages 649–655.)	1. **Government plans**—Most states require that local land-use laws follow a general plan.
	2. **Zoning laws**—Laws that divide an area into districts to which specific land-use regulations apply. Districts may be zoned for residential, commercial, industrial, or agricultural use. Within all districts there may be minimum lot-size requirements, structural restrictions, and other bulk zoning regulations. A variance allows for the use of property in ways that vary from the restrictions.
	3. **Subdivision regulations**—Laws directing the dedication of specific plots of land to specific uses within a subdivision.
	4. **Growth-management ordinances**—Limits on, for example, the number of residential building permits.
	5. **Limits on the police power:**
	a. Due process and equal protection—Land-use controls cannot be arbitrary, unreasonable, or discriminatory.
	b. Just compensation—Private property taken for a public purpose requires payment of just compensation. "Taking" for a public purpose includes enacting overly burdensome regulations.
Land-Use Control—Eminent Domain (See pages 655–656.)	1. **Condemnation power**—Governments have the inherent power to take property for public use without the consent of the owner.
	2. **Limits on the power of eminent domain**—Private property taken for a public purpose requires payment of just compensation.

For Review

1. What can a person who holds property in fee simple absolute do with the property? Can a person who holds property as a life estate do the same?

2. What are the requirements for acquiring property by adverse possession?

3. What is a leasehold estate? What types of leasehold estates, or tenancies, can be created when real property is leased?

4. What are the respective duties of the landlord and tenant concerning the use and maintenance of leased property? Is the tenant responsible for all damages that he or she causes, intentionally or negligently?

5. What limitations may be imposed on the rights of property owners?

Questions and Case Problems

22–1. Tenant's Rights and Responsibilities. You are a student in college and plan to attend classes for nine months. You sign a twelve-month lease for an apartment. Discuss fully each of the following situations.

(a) You have a summer job in another town and wish to assign the balance of your lease (three months) to a fellow student who will be attending summer school. Can you do so?

(b) You are graduating in May. The lease will have three months remaining. Can you terminate the lease without liability by giving a thirty-day notice to the landlord?

22–2. Property Ownership. Antonio is the owner of a lakeside house and lot. He deeds the house and lot "to my wife, Angela, for life, then to my son, Charles." Given these facts, answer the following questions:

(a) Does Antonio have any ownership interest in the lakeside house after making these transfers? Explain.

(b) What is Angela's interest called? Is there any limitation on her rights to use the property as she wishes?

(c) What is Charles's interest called? Why?

22–3. Property Ownership. Lorenz was a wanderer twenty-two years ago. At that time, he decided to settle down on an unoccupied, three-acre parcel of land that he did not own. People in the area indicated to him that they had no idea who owned the property. Lorenz built a house on the land, got married, and raised three children while living there. He fenced in the land, placed a gate with a sign above it that read "Lorenz's Homestead," and had trespassers removed. Lorenz is now confronted by Joe Reese, who has a deed in his name as owner of the property. Reese, claiming ownership of the land, orders Lorenz and his family off the property. Discuss who has the better "title" to the property.

22–4. Deeds. Wiley and Gemma are neighbors. Wiley's lot is extremely large, and his present and future use of it will not involve the entire area. Gemma wants to build a single-car garage and driveway along the present lot boundary. Because of ordinances requiring buildings to be set back fifteen feet from an adjoining property line, and because of the placement of her existing structures, Gemma cannot build the garage. Gemma contracts to purchase ten feet of Wiley's property along their boundary line for $3,000. Wiley is willing to sell but will give Gemma only a quitclaim deed, whereas Gemma wants a warranty deed. Discuss the differences between these deeds as they would affect the rights of the parties if the title to this ten feet of land later proved to be defective.

22–5. Subdivision Regulations. Suppose that as a condition of a developer's receiving approval for constructing a new residential community, the local authorities insist that the developer dedicate, or set aside, land for a new hospital. The hospital would serve not only the proposed residential community but also the rest of the city. If the developer challenges the condition in court, under what standard might the court invalidate the condition?

22–6. The Lease Contract. Christine Callis formed a lease agreement with Colonial Properties, Inc., to lease property in a shopping center in Montgomery, Alabama. Callis later alleged that before signing the lease agreement, she had told a representative of Colonial that she wanted to locate in a shopping center that would attract a wealthy clientele, and the representative had assured her that no discount stores would be allowed to lease space in the shopping center. The written lease agreement, which Callis signed, contained a clause stating that "[n]o representation, inducement, understanding or anything of any nature whatsoever made, stated or represented on Landlord's behalf, either orally or in writing (except this Lease), has induced Tenant to enter into this lease." The lease also stipulated that Callis would not conduct any type of business commonly called a discount store, surplus store, or other similar business. Later, Colonial did, in fact, lease space to discount stores, and Callis sued Colonial for breach of the lease contract. Will Callis succeed in her claim? Discuss fully. [*Callis v. Colonial Properties, Inc.,* 597 So.2d 660 (Ala. 1991)]

22–7. Taking. Richard and Jaquelyn Jackson owned property in a residential subdivision near an airport operated by the Metropolitan Knoxville Airport Authority in Blount County, Tennessee. The Airport Authority considered extending a runway near the subdivision and undertook a study that found that the noise, vibration, and pollution from aircraft using the extension would render the Jacksons' property incompatible with residential use. The airport built the extension, bringing about the predicted results, and the Jacksons filed a suit against the Airport Authority, alleging a taking of their property. The Airport Authority responded that there was no taking because there were no direct flights over the Jacksons' property. In whose favor will the court rule, and why? [*Jackson v. Metropolitan Knoxville Airport Authority,* 922 S.W.2d 860 (Tenn. 1996)]

22–8. Limitations on Police Power. John and Florence Dolan owned the A-Boy West Hardware store in downtown Tigard, Oregon. Wanting to expand the store and its parking lot, the Dolans applied to the city for a permit. Under the local zoning regulations, the city could attach conditions to downtown development to provide for projected public needs. The city told the Dolans that they could expand if they would dedicate a portion of their property for the improvement of a storm drainage system and dedicate an additional strip of land as a pedestrian and bicycle path. The dedication would involve about 10 percent of the Dolans' property. The Dolans sought a variance, which the city denied, and the Dolans appealed. The city claimed that there was a sufficient connection between the expansion of the store and the dedication requirements, because the expansion would increase traffic to the area and would also increase storm runoff. The Dolans conceded that there would be increases but contended that the increases would not be enough to justify taking 10 percent of their property. The Dolans claimed that the city's condition was an uncompensated taking of their property in violation of the Fifth Amendment. How should the court rule? Discuss fully. [*Dolan v. City of Tigard,* 512 U.S. 374, 114 S.Ct. 2309, 129 L.Ed.2d 304 (1994)]

22–9. Warranty of Habitability. Three-year-old Nkenge Lynch fell from the window of her third-floor apartment and suffered serious and permanent injuries. There were no window stops or guards on the window. The use of window stops, even if installed, is optional with the tenant. Stanley James owned the apartment building. Zsa Zsa Kinsey, Nkenge's mother, filed a suit on Nkenge's behalf in a Massachusetts state court against James, alleging in part a breach of an implied warranty of habitability. The plaintiff did not argue that the absence of stops or guards made the apartment unfit for human habitation but that their absence "endangered and materially impaired her health and safety," and therefore the failure to install them was a breach of warranty. Should the court rule that the absence of window stops breached a warranty of habitability? Should the court mandate that landlords provide window guards? Why or why not? [*Lynch v. James,* 44 Mass.App.Ct. 448, 692 N.E.2d 81 (1998)]

22–10. Eminent Domain. The state of Indiana, through its department of transportation, planned to improve U.S. Highway 41 in Parke County, Indiana. To accomplish the improvement, Indiana sought to obtain from Thomas Collom approximately half an acre of his property abutting the east side of the highway and offered him $4,495 for it. When Collom refused to sell, the state filed a suit in an Indiana state court against Collom to obtain the property. Collom denied that his half acre was necessary for the improvement that the state wanted to make to the highway. He asserted that the state did not need his land because the highway would curve west, away from his property, and no drainage ditch was necessary given the existing water flow in the area. The state argued that this was not an appropriate response because a determination of the need for a taking was the responsibility of the state, not the owner of the property that the state was trying to take. In whose favor should the court rule, and why? [*State of Indiana v. Collom,* 720 N.E.2d 737 (Ind.App. 1999)]

A Question of Ethics and Social Responsibility

22–11. John and Terry Hoffius own property in Jackson, Michigan, which they rent. Kristal McCready and Keith Kerr responded to the Hoffiuses' ad about the property. The Hoffiuses refused to rent to McCready and Kerr, however, when they learned that the two were single and intended to live together. John Hoffius told all prospective tenants that unmarried cohabitation violated his religious beliefs. McCready and others filed a suit in a Michigan state court against the Hoffiuses. They alleged in part that the Hoffiuses' actions violated the plaintiffs' civil rights under a state law that prohibits discrimination on the basis of "marital status." The Hoffiuses responded in part that forcing them to rent to unmarried couples in violation of the Hoffiuses' religious beliefs would be unconstitutional. [*McCready v. Hoffius,* 586 N.W.2d 723 (Mich. 1998)]

1. Was it the plaintiffs' "marital status" or their conduct to which the defendants objected? Did the defendants violate the plaintiffs' civil rights? Explain.

2. Should a court, in the interest of preventing discrimination in housing, compel a landlord to violate his or her conscience? In other words, whose rights should prevail in this case? Why?

3. Is there an objective rule that determines when civil rights or religious freedom, or any two similarly important principles, should prevail? If so, what is it? If not, should there be?

For Critical Analysis

22–12. Real property law dates back hundreds of years. What changes have occurred in society, including business and technological changes, that have affected the development and application of real property law? (Hint: Was airspace an issue three hundred years ago?)

Interacting with the Internet

■ For updated links to resources available on the Web, as well as a variety of other materials, visit this text's Web site at

http://leet.westbuslaw.com

■ Homes and Communities is a Web site offered by the U.S. Department of Housing and Urban Development. Information of interest to both

consumers and businesses is available at this site, which can be accessed at

http://www.hud.gov

■ Information on the buying and financing of homes, as well as the full text of the Real Estate Settlement Procedures Act, is online at

http://www.hud.gov/fha

Online Legal Research Exercises

Go to **http://leet. westbuslaw.com**, the Web site that accompanies this text. Select "Interactive Study Center," and then click on "Chapter 22." There you will find the following Internet research exercise that you can perform to learn more about laws governing real property:

Activity 22–1: Real Estate Law

Before the Test

Go to **http://leet. westbuslaw.com**, the Web site that accompanies this text. Select "Interactive Quizzes." You will find a number of interactive questions relating to this chapter.

Promoting Competition

23

chapter objectives

After reading this chapter, you should be able to:

1. Explain the purpose of antitrust laws and identify the major federal antitrust statutes.

2. Summarize the types of activities prohibited by Sections 1 and 2 of the Sherman Act, respectively.

3. Indicate why the Clayton Act was passed and summarize the types of activities prohibited by this act.

4. Describe how the antitrust laws are enforced.

5. Name several exemptions from the antitrust laws.

contents

Antitrust Laws Laws protecting commerce from unlawful restraints.

Today's antitrust laws are the direct descendants of common law actions intended to limit *restraints on trade* (agreements between firms that have the effect of reducing competition in the marketplace). Such actions date to the fifteenth century in England. In America, concern over monopolistic practices arose following the Civil War with the growth of large corporate enterprises and their attempts to reduce or eliminate competition. To thwart competition, they legally tied themselves together in *trusts,* legal entities in which trustees hold title to property for the benefit of others. The most powerful of these trusts, the Standard Oil trust, is examined in this chapter's *Landmark in the Legal Environment.*

Many states attempted to control such monopolistic behavior by enacting statutes outlawing the use of trusts. That is why all of the laws that regulate economic competition today are referred to as **antitrust laws.** At the national level, Congress passed the Sherman Antitrust Act in 1890. In 1914, Congress passed the Clayton Act and the Federal Trade Commission Act to further curb anticompetitive or unfair business practices. Since their passage, the 1914 acts have been amended by Congress to broaden and strengthen their coverage.

This chapter examines these major antitrust statutes, focusing particularly on the Sherman Act and the Clayton Act, as amended, and the types of activities prohibited by those acts. Remember in reading this chapter that the basis of antitrust legislation is the desire to foster competition. Antitrust legislation was initially created—and continues to be enforced—because of our belief that competition leads to lower prices, generates more product information, and results in a better distribution of wealth between consumers and producers. As Oliver Wendell Holmes, Jr., indicated in the opening quotation, free competition is worth more to our society than the cost we pay for it. The cost is, of course, government regulation of business behavior.

The Sherman Antitrust Act

In 1890, Congress passed "An Act to Protect Trade and Commerce against Unlawful Restraints and Monopolies"—commonly known as the Sherman Antitrust Act or, more simply, as the Sherman Act. The Sherman Act was and remains one of the government's most powerful weapons in the struggle to maintain a competitive economy.

Major Provisions of the Sherman Act

Sections 1 and 2 contain the main provisions of the Sherman Act:

> **1:** Every contract, combination in the form of trust or otherwise, or conspiracy, in restraint of trade or commerce among the several States, or with foreign nations, is hereby declared to be illegal [and is a felony punishable by fine and/or imprisonment].
>
> **2:** Every person who shall monopolize, or attempt to monopolize, or combine or conspire with any other person or persons, to monopolize any part of the trade or commerce among the several States, or with foreign nations, shall be deemed guilty of a felony [and is similarly punishable].

These two sections of the Sherman Act are quite different. Violation of Section 1 requires two or more persons, as a person cannot contract or combine or conspire alone. Thus, the essence of the illegal activity is the *act of joining together.* Section 2 applies both to several people who have joined together and

Landmark in the Legal Environment

The Sherman Antitrust Act of 1890

The author of the Sherman Antitrust Act of 1890, Senator John Sherman, was the brother of the famed Civil War general and a recognized financial authority. Sherman had been concerned for years with the diminishing competition within American industry. This concern led him to introduce into Congress in 1888, in 1889, and again in 1890 bills designed to destroy the large combinations of capital that were, he felt, creating a lack of balance within the nation's economy. He told Congress that the Sherman Act "does not announce a new principle of law, but applies old and well-recognized principles of the common law."[a]

The common law regarding trade regulation was not always consistent. Certainly it was not very familiar to the legislators of the Fifty-first Congress of the United States. The public concern over large business integrations and trusts was familiar, however. By 1890, the Standard Oil trust had become the foremost petroleum manufacturing and marketing combination in the United States. Streamlined, integrated, and cen-

trally and efficiently controlled, its monopoly over the industry could not be disputed. Standard Oil controlled 90 percent of the U.S. market for refined petroleum products, and small manufacturers were incapable of competing with such an industrial leviathan.

The increasing consolidation occurring in American industry, and particularly the Standard Oil trust, did not escape the attention of the American public. In March 1881, Henry Demarest Lloyd, a young journalist from Chicago, published an article in the *Atlantic Monthly* entitled "The Story of a Great Monopoly," which discussed the success of the Standard Oil Company. The article brought to the public's attention for the first time the fact that the petroleum industry in America was dominated by one firm—Standard Oil. Lloyd's article, which was so popular that the issue was reprinted six times, marked the beginning of the American public's growing awareness of, and concern over, the growth of monopolies, a concern that eventually prompted Congress to pass the Sherman Act in 1890.

In the pages that follow, we look closely at the major provisions of this act. Generally, the act prohibits business combinations and conspiracies that restrain trade and commerce, as well as certain monopolistic practices.

For Critical Analysis: *Is monopoly power (the ability to control a particular market) necessarily harmful to society's interests?*

a. 21 Congressional Record 2456 (1890).

---

to individual persons, because it specifies "[e]very person who . . . ." Thus, unilateral conduct can result in a violation of Section 2.

The cases brought to court under Section 1 of the Sherman Act differ from those brought under Section 2. Section 1 cases are often concerned with finding an agreement (written or oral) that leads to a restraint of trade. Section 2 cases deal with the structure of a monopoly that already exists in the marketplace. The term **monopoly** is generally used to describe a market in which there is a single or a limited number of sellers. Whereas Section 1 focuses on agreements that are restrictive—that is, agreements that have a wrongful purpose—Section 2 looks at the so-called misuse of **monopoly power** in the marketplace. Monopoly power exists when a firm has an extremely great amount of **market power**—the power to affect the market price of its product. We return to a discussion of these two sections of the Sherman Act after we look at the act's jurisdictional requirements.

Jurisdictional Requirements

Because Congress can regulate only interstate commerce, the Sherman Act applies only to restraints that affect interstate commerce. As discussed in Chapter 3, courts have construed the meaning of *interstate commerce*

Monopoly A term generally used to describe a market in which there is a single seller or a limited number of sellers.

Monopoly Power The ability of a monopoly to dictate what takes place in a given market.

Market Power The power of a firm to control the market price of its product. A monopoly has the greatest degree of market power.

broadly, bringing even local activities within the regulatory power of the national government. In regard to the Sherman Act, courts have generally held that any activity that substantially affects interstate commerce is covered by the act. The Sherman Act also extends to nationals abroad who are engaged in activities that have an effect on U.S. foreign commerce. (The extraterritorial application of U.S. antitrust laws will be discussed in this chapter's *International Perspective* on page 681 as well as in Chapter 25.)

Section 1 of the Sherman Act

The underlying assumption of Section 1 of the Sherman Act is that society's welfare is harmed if rival firms are permitted to join in an agreement that consolidates their market power or otherwise restrains competition. The types of trade restraints that Section 1 of the Sherman Act prohibits generally fall into two broad categories: *horizontal restraints* and *vertical restraints*. Some restraints are so blatantly and substantially anticompetitive that they are deemed **per se violations**—illegal *per se* (on their face, or inherently)—under Section 1. Other agreements, however, even though they result in enhanced market power, do not *unreasonably* restrain trade. Under what is called the **rule of reason**, anticompetitive agreements that allegedly violate Section 1 of the Sherman Act are analyzed with the view that they may, in fact, constitute reasonable restraints on trade.

Per Se Violations versus the Rule of Reason

The need for a rule-of-reason analysis of some agreements in restraint of trade is obvious—if the rule of reason had not been developed, virtually any business agreement could conceivably be held to violate the Sherman Act. Justice Louis Brandeis effectively phrased this sentiment in *Chicago Board of Trade v. United States,* a case decided in 1918:

> Every agreement concerning trade, every regulation of trade, restrains. To bind, to restrain, is of their very essence. The true test of legality is whether the restraint imposed is such as merely regulates and perhaps thereby promotes competition or whether it is such as may suppress or even destroy competition.[1]

When analyzing an alleged Section 1 violation under the rule of reason, a court will consider several factors. These factors include the purpose of the agreement, the parties' power to implement the agreement to achieve that purpose, and the effect or potential effect of the agreement on competition. Yet another factor that a court might consider is whether the parties could have relied on less restrictive means to achieve their purpose.

The dividing line between agreements that constitute *per se* violations and agreements that should be judged under a rule of reason is seldom clear. Moreover, in some cases, the United States Supreme Court has stated that it is applying a *per se* rule, and yet a careful reading of the Court's analysis suggests that the Court is weighing benefits against harms under a rule of reason. Perhaps the most that can be said with certainty is that although the distinction between the two rules seems clear in theory, in the actual application of antitrust laws, the distinction has not always been so clear.

---

1. 246 U.S. 231, 38 S.Ct. 242, 62 L.Ed. 683 (1918).

Per Se Violation A type of anticompetitive agreement—such as a horizontal price-fixing agreement—that is considered to be so injurious to the public that there is no need to determine whether it actually injures market competition; rather, it is in itself (*per se*) a violation of the Sherman Act.

Rule of Reason A test by which a court balances the positive effects (such as economic efficiency) of an agreement against its potentially anticompetitive effects. In antitrust litigation, many practices are analyzed under the rule of reason.

Section 1—Horizontal Restraints

The term **horizontal restraint** is encountered frequently in antitrust law. A horizontal restraint is any agreement that in some way restrains competition between rival firms competing in the same market. In the following subsections, we look at several types of horizontal restraints.

Horizontal Restraint Any agreement that in some way restrains competition between rival firms competing in the same market.

PRICE FIXING Any agreement among competitors to fix prices constitutes a *per se* violation of Section 1. Perhaps the definitive case regarding **price-fixing agreements** remains the 1940 case of *United States v. Socony-Vacuum Oil Co.*[2] In that case, a group of independent oil producers in Texas and Louisiana were caught between falling demand due to the Great Depression of the 1930s and increasing supply from newly discovered oil fields in the region. In response to these conditions, a group of the major refining companies agreed to buy "distress" gasoline (excess supplies) from the independents so as to dispose of it in an "orderly manner." Although there was no explicit agreement as to price, it was clear that the purpose of the agreement was to limit the supply of gasoline on the market and thereby raise prices.

Price-Fixing Agreement An agreement between competitors in which the competitors agree to fix the prices of products or services at a certain level.

The United States Supreme Court recognized the dangerous effects that such an agreement could have on open and free competition. The Court held that the asserted reasonableness of a price-fixing agreement is never a defense; any agreement that restricts output or artificially fixes price is a *per se* violation of Section 1. The rationale of the *per se* rule was best stated in what is now the most famous portion of the Court's opinion—footnote 59. In that footnote, Justice William O. Douglas compared a freely functioning price system to a body's central nervous system, condemning price-fixing agreements as threats to "the central nervous system of the economy."

GROUP BOYCOTTS A **group boycott** is an agreement by two or more sellers to boycott, or refuse to deal with, a particular person or firm. Such group boycotts have been held to constitute *per se* violations of Section 1 of the Sherman Act. Section 1 has been violated if it can be demonstrated that the boycott or joint refusal to deal was undertaken with the intention of eliminating competition or preventing entry into a given market. Some boycotts, such as group boycotts against a supplier for political reasons, may be protected under the First Amendment right to freedom of expression, however.

Group Boycott The refusal to deal with a particular person or firm by a group of competitors; prohibited by the Sherman Act.

HORIZONTAL MARKET DIVISION It is a *per se* violation of Section 1 of the Sherman Act for competitors to divide up territories or customers. • **Example 23.1** Manufacturers A, B, and C compete against each other in the states of Kansas, Nebraska, and Iowa. By agreement, A sells products only in Kansas; B sells only in Nebraska; and C sells only in Iowa. This concerted action not only reduces marketing costs but also allows all three (assuming there is no other competition) to raise the price of the goods sold in their respective states. The same violation would take place if A, B, and C simply agreed that A would sell only to institutional purchasers (such as school districts, universities, state agencies and departments, and municipalities) in all three states, B only to wholesalers, and C only to retailers.•

---

2. 310 U.S. 150, 60 S.Ct. 811, 84 L.Ed.2d 1129 (1940).

In the following case, after a partnership's dissolution, the former partners agreed to restrict future advertising to certain geographical regions. At issue was whether the agreement constituted a *per se* violation of Section 1 of the Sherman Act.

Case 23.1 ● Blackburn v. Sweeney

United States Court of Appeals,
Seventh Circuit, 1995.
53 F.3d 825.

Historical and Social Setting

Disagreements over the allocation of funds often lead to the breakup of partnerships and other business associations. Perhaps the most common mistake of partners—including lawyers who practice law together—is failing to adopt the common-sense approach of putting their partnership agreement in writing when business begins. It is the wrong time to attempt to come to an agreement after relations have become hostile, especially if the partnership has already dissolved.

Background and Facts Thomas Blackburn, Raymond Green, Charles Sweeney, and Daniel Pfeiffer practiced law together as partners, relying on advertising to attract clients. When they came to a disagreement over the use of partnership funds, they split into separate partnerships—Blackburn and Green, and Sweeney and Pfeiffer. After the split, they negotiated and signed an agreement that restricted, for an indefinite time, the geographical area within which each partnership could advertise. Less than a year later, the Blackburn firm filed a suit in a federal district court against the Sweeney firm, alleging in part that the restriction on advertising was a *per se* violation of the Sherman Act. The court ruled in favor of Sweeney, and Blackburn appealed.

In the Words of the Court . . .
CUMMINGS, Circuit Judge.

* * * *

* * * The purpose of the advertising Agreement was, as testified to by defendant Sweeney, to "really trade markets * * * . We, in effect, said that'll be your market." Both parties in this case * * * rely heavily on advertising as their primary source of clients. * * * [T]he reciprocal Agreement to limit advertising to different geographical regions was intended to be, and sufficiently approximates an agreement to allocate markets so that the *per se* rule of illegality applies.

Decision and Remedy The U.S. Court of Appeals for the Seventh Circuit reversed the ruling of the lower court and remanded the case for the entry of a judgment in favor of the Blackburn firm.

For Critical Analysis—Ethical Consideration *Why didn't the court see the agreement to limit advertising as a reasonable covenant not to compete?*

TRADE ASSOCIATIONS Businesses in the same general industry or profession frequently organize trade associations to pursue common interests. A trade association's activities may include facilitating exchanges of information, representing members' business interests before governmental bodies, conducting advertising campaigns, and setting regulatory standards to govern the industry or profession.

Generally, the rule of reason is applied to many of these horizontal actions. If a court finds that a trade association practice or agreement that restrains trade is sufficiently beneficial both to the association and to the public, it may deem the restraint reasonable. Other trade association agreements may have such substantially anticompetitive effects that the court will consider them to be in violation of Section 1 of the Sherman Act. • **Example 23.2** In *National Society of Professional Engineers v. United States,*[3] it was held that the society's code of ethics—which prohibited members from discussing prices with a potential customer until after the customer had chosen an engineer—was a Section 1 violation. The United States Supreme Court found that this ban on competitive bidding was "nothing less than a frontal assault on the basic policy of the Sherman Act."•

JOINT VENTURES   Joint ventures undertaken by competitors are also subject to antitrust laws. A *joint venture* is an undertaking by two or more individuals or firms for a specific purpose. If a joint venture does not involve price fixing or market divisions, the agreement will be analyzed under the rule of reason. Whether the venture will then be upheld under Section 1 depends on an overall assessment of the purposes of the venture, a strict analysis of the potential benefits relative to the likely harms, and—in some cases—an assessment of whether there are less restrictive alternatives for achieving the same goals.[4]

Section 1—Vertical Restraints

A **vertical restraint** of trade is one that results from an agreement between firms at different levels in the manufacturing and distribution process. In contrast to horizontal relationships, which occur at the same level of operation, vertical relationships encompass the entire chain of production: the purchase of inventory, basic manufacturing, distribution to wholesalers, and eventual sale of a product at the retail level. For some products, these distinct phases may be carried out by different firms. If a single firm carries out two or more of the different functional phases involved in bringing a product to the final consumer, the firm is considered to be a **vertically integrated firm.**

Even though firms operating at different functional levels are not in direct competition with one another, they are in competition with other firms. Thus, agreements between firms standing in a vertical relationship do significantly affect competition.

> **Vertical Restraint** Any restraint on trade created by agreements between firms at different levels in the manufacturing and distribution process.

> **Vertically Integrated Firm** A firm that carries out two or more functional phases (manufacture, distribution, retailing, and so on) of a product.

TERRITORIAL OR CUSTOMER RESTRICTIONS   In arranging for the distribution of its product, a manufacturing firm often wishes to insulate dealers from direct competition with other dealers selling the product. To this end, it may institute territorial restrictions, or it may attempt to prohibit wholesalers or retailers from reselling the product to certain classes of buyers, such as competing retailers. There may be legitimate, procompetitive reasons for imposing such territorial or customer restrictions. • **Example 23.3** A computer manufacturer may wish to prevent a dealer from cutting costs and undercutting rivals by providing computers without promotion or customer service, while relying on nearby dealers to provide these services. This is an illustration of the "free rider" problem.•

Vertical territorial and customer restrictions are judged under a rule of reason. In *United States v. Arnold, Schwinn & Co.,*[5] a case decided in 1967, the

---

3. 453 U.S. 679, 98 S.Ct. 1355, 55 L.Ed.2d 637 (1978).
4. See, for example, *United States v. Morgan,* 118 F.Supp. 621 (S.D.N.Y. 1953). This case is often cited as a classic example of how to judge joint ventures under the rule of reason.
5. 388 U.S. 365, 87 S.Ct. 1856, 18 L.Ed.2d 1249 (1967).

A retail store displays a well-known designer's clothing. Is an agreement between the manufacturer and an independent retailer to sell the clothing at a certain price considered a violation of the Sherman Act?

Supreme Court had held that vertical territorial and customer restrictions were *per se* violations of Section 1 of the Sherman Act. Ten years later, however, in *Continental T.V., Inc. v. GTE Sylvania, Inc.,*[6] the Court overturned the *Schwinn* decision and held that such vertical restrictions should be judged under the rule of reason. The *Continental* case marked a definite shift from rigid characterization of these kinds of vertical restraints to a more flexible, economic analysis of the restraints under the rule of reason.

RESALE PRICE MAINTENANCE AGREEMENTS An agreement between a manufacturer and a distributor or retailer in which the manufacturer specifies what the retail prices of its products must be is referred to as a **resale price maintenance agreement.** This type of agreement may violate Section 1 of the Sherman Act.

Resale Price Maintenance Agreement An agreement between a manufacturer and a retailer in which the manufacturer specifies what the retail price of its products must be.

In a 1968 case, *Albrecht v. Herald Co.,*[7] the United States Supreme Court held that these vertical price-fixing agreements constituted *per se* violations of Section 1 of the Sherman Act. In the following case, which involved an agreement that set a maximum price for the resale of products supplied by a wholesaler to a dealer, the Supreme Court reevaluated its approach in *Albrecht*. At issue was whether such price-fixing arrangements should continue to be deemed *per se* violations of Section 1 of the Sherman Act or whether the rule of reason should be applied.

6. 433 U.S. 36, 97 S.Ct. 2549, 53 L.Ed.2d 568 (1977).
7. 390 U.S. 145, 88 S.Ct. 869, 19 L.Ed.2d 998 (1968).

Case 23.2 ● State Oil Co. v. Khan

Supreme Court of the United States, 1997.
522 U.S. 3,
118 S.Ct. 275,
139 L.Ed.2d 199.
**http://www.findlaw.com/
casecode/supreme.html**[a]

a. This page, which is part of a Web site maintained by FindLaw, contains links to opinions of the United States Supreme Court. In the "Party Name Search" box, type "Khan" and click "Search." When the results appear, click on the case name to access the opinion.

Case 23.2 Continued

Historical and Social Setting *For more than thirty years, it was illegal for a supplier and a distributor to set the price that the distributor could charge its customers. It did not matter whether the price was intended to be the maximum or the minimum price. Such vertical price-fixing agreements were held to be* per se *violations in the same category as horizontal price-fixing agreements (agreements between competitors).*[b] *The decision of the United States Supreme Court that established this rule was much criticized by other courts and by many commentators. There are circumstances, the critics contended, when vertical maximum price fixing can be procompetitive.*

_____
b. *Albrecht v. Herald Co.,* 390 U.S. 145, 88 S.Ct. 869, 19 L.Ed.2d 998 (1968).

Background and Facts Barkat Khan leased a gas station under a contract with State Oil Company, which also agreed to supply gas to Khan for resale. Under the contract, State Oil would set a suggested retail price and sell gas to Khan for 3.25 cents per gallon less than that price. Khan could sell the gas at a higher price, but he would then be required to pay State Oil the difference (which would equal the entire profit Khan realized from raising the price). Khan failed to pay some of the rent due under the lease, and State Oil terminated the contract. Khan filed a suit in a federal district court against State Oil, alleging, among other things, price fixing in violation of the Sherman Act. The U.S. Court of Appeals for the Seventh Circuit reversed this judgment, and State Oil appealed to the United States Supreme Court.

In the Words of the Court . . .
Justice O'CONNOR delivered the opinion of the Court.

* * * *

* * * Our analysis is * * * guided by our general view that the primary purpose of the antitrust laws is to protect interbrand competition. * * * [C]ondemnation of practices resulting in lower prices to consumers is especially costly because cutting prices in order to increase business often is the very essence of competition.

* * * [W]e find it difficult to maintain that vertically-imposed maximum prices could harm consumers or competition to the extent necessary to justify their *per se* invalidation. * * *

* * * *

* * * [T]he *per se* rule * * * could in fact exacerbate problems related to the unrestrained exercise of market power by monopolist-dealers. Indeed, both courts and antitrust scholars have noted that [the *per se*] rule may actually harm consumers and manufacturers. * * *

* * * *

* * * [V]ertical maximum price fixing, like the majority of commercial arrangements subject to the antitrust laws, should be evaluated under the rule of reason. In our view, rule-of-reason analysis can effectively identify those situations in which vertical maximum price fixing amounts to anticompetitive conduct.

Decision and Remedy The United States Supreme Court vacated the decision of the appellate court and remanded the case. The Supreme Court held that vertical price fixing is not a *per se* violation of the Sherman Act but should be evaluated under the rule of reason.

For Critical Analysis—Economic Consideration *Should all "commercial arrangements subject to the antitrust laws" be evaluated under the rule of reason?*

REFUSALS TO DEAL As discussed previously, joint refusals to deal (group boycotts) are subject to close scrutiny under Section 1 of the Sherman Act. A single manufacturer acting unilaterally, however, is generally free to deal, or not to deal, with whomever it wishes. In vertical arrangements, even though a manufacturer cannot set retail prices for its products, it can refuse to deal with retailers or dealers that cut prices to levels substantially below the manufacturer's suggested retail prices. In *United States v. Colgate & Co.*,[8] for example, the United States Supreme Court held that a manufacturer's advance announcement that it would not sell to price cutters was not a violation of the Sherman Act.

There are instances, however, in which a unilateral refusal to deal will violate antitrust laws. These instances involve offenses proscribed under Section 2 of the Sherman Act and occur only if (1) the firm refusing to deal has—or is likely to acquire—monopoly power and (2) the refusal is likely to have an anticompetitive effect on a particular market.

Section 2 of the Sherman Act

Section 1 of the Sherman Act proscribes certain concerted, or joint, activities that restrain trade. In contrast, Section 2 condemns "every person who shall monopolize, or attempt to monopolize." There are two distinct types of behavior that are subject to sanction under Section 2: *monopolization* and *attempts to monopolize*. A tactic that may be involved in either offense is **predatory pricing**. Predatory pricing involves an attempt by one firm to drive its competitors from the market by selling its product at prices substantially *below* the normal costs of production; once the competitors are eliminated, the firm will attempt to recapture its losses and go on to earn very high profits by driving prices up far above their competitive levels.

Monopolization

In *United States v. Grinnell Corp.*,[9] the United States Supreme Court defined the offense of **monopolization** as involving the following two elements: "(1) the possession of monopoly power in the relevant market and (2) the willful acquisition or maintenance of the power as distinguished from growth or development as a consequence of a superior product, business acumen, or historic accident." A violation of Section 2 requires that both these elements—monopoly power and an intent to monopolize—be established.

MONOPOLY POWER The Sherman Act does not define *monopoly*. In economic parlance, monopoly refers to control by a single entity. It is well established in antitrust law, however, that a firm may be a monopolist even though it is not the sole seller in a market. Additionally, size alone does not determine whether a firm is a monopoly. For example, a "mom and pop" grocery located in an isolated desert town is a monopolist if it is the only grocery serving that particular market. Size in relation to the market is what matters, because monopoly involves the power to affect prices and output. *Monopoly power*, as mentioned earlier in this chapter, exists when a firm has an extremely great

Predatory Pricing The pricing of a product below cost with the intent to drive competitors out of the market.

Monopolization The possession of monopoly power in the relevant market and the willful acquisition or maintenance of the power, as distinguished from growth or development as a consequence of a superior product, business acumen, or historic accident.

"A rule of such a nature as to bring all trade or traffic into the hands of one company, or one person, and to exclude all others, is illegal."

Sir Edward Coke, 1552–1634
(British jurist and legal scholar)

---

8. 250 U.S. 300, 39 S.Ct. 465, 63 L.Ed. 992 (1919).
9. 384 U.S. 563, 86 S.Ct. 1698, 16 L.Ed.2d 778 (1966).

amount of market power. If a firm has sufficient market power to control prices and exclude competition, that firm has monopoly power.

As difficult as it is to define market power precisely, it is even more difficult to measure it. Courts often use the so-called **market-share test**[10]—a firm's percentage share of the "relevant market"—in determining the extent of the firm's market power. A firm may be considered to have monopoly power if its share of the relevant market is 70 percent or more. This is merely a rule of thumb, however; it is not a binding principle of law. In some cases, a smaller share may be held to constitute monopoly power.[11]

The relevant market consists of two elements: (1) a relevant product market and (2) a relevant geographical market. What should the relevant product market include? No doubt, it must include all products that, although produced by different firms, have identical attributes, such as sugar. Products that are not identical, however, may sometimes be substituted for one another. Coffee may be substituted for tea, for example. In defining the relevant product market, the key issue is the degree of interchangeability between products. If one product is a sufficient substitute for another, the two products are considered to be part of the same product market.

The second component of the relevant market is the geographical boundaries of the market. For products that are sold nationwide, the geographical boundaries of the market encompass the entire United States. If a producer and its competitors sell in only a limited area (one in which customers have no access to other sources of the product), then the geographical market is limited to that area. A national firm may thus compete in several distinct areas and have monopoly power in one area but not in another.

THE INTENT REQUIREMENT Monopoly power, in and of itself, does not constitute the offense of monopolization under Section 2 of the Sherman Act. The offense also requires an *intent* to monopolize. A dominant market share may be the result of business acumen or the development of a superior product. It may simply be the result of historical accident. In these situations, the acquisition of monopoly power is not an antitrust violation. Indeed, it would be contrary to society's interest to condemn every firm that acquired a position of power because it was well managed, efficient, and marketed a product desired by consumers.

If, however, a firm possesses market power as a result of carrying out some purposeful act to acquire or maintain that power through anticompetitive means, then it is in violation of Section 2. In most monopolization cases, intent may be inferred from evidence that the firm had monopoly power and engaged in anticompetitive behavior.

Attempts to Monopolize

Section 2 also prohibits **attempted monopolization** of a market. Any action challenged as an attempt to monopolize must have been specifically intended

> **Market-Share Test** The primary measure of monopoly power. A firm's market share is the percentage of a market that the firm controls.

> **Keep in Mind** Section 2 of the Sherman Act essentially condemns the act of monopolizing, not the possession of monopoly power.

> **Attempted Monopolization** Any actions by a firm to eliminate competition and gain monopoly power.

---

10. Other measures of market power have been devised, but the market-share test is the most widely used.
11. This standard was first articulated by Judge Learned Hand in *United States v. Aluminum Co. of America*, 148 F.2d 416 (2d Cir. 1945). A 90 percent share was held to be clear evidence of monopoly power. Anything less than 64 percent, said Judge Hand, made monopoly power doubtful, and anything less than 30 percent was clearly not monopoly power.

to exclude competitors and garner monopoly power. In addition, the attempt must have had a "dangerous" probability of success—only *serious* threats of monopolization are condemned as violations. The probability cannot be dangerous unless the alleged offender possesses some degree of market power. (See this chapter's *Legal E-nvironment* feature for a discussion of the widely publicized case brought against Microsoft Corporation for alleged violations of antitrust laws, including monopolization and attempted monopolization.)

The Clayton Act

In 1914, Congress attempted to strengthen federal antitrust laws by enacting the Clayton Act. The Clayton Act was aimed at specific anticompetitive or monopolistic practices that the Sherman Act did not cover. The substantive provisions of the act deal with four distinct forms of business behavior, which are declared illegal but not criminal. With regard to each of the four provisions, the act's prohibitions are qualified by the general condition that the behavior is illegal only if it substantially tends to lessen competition or tends to create monopoly power. The major offenses under the Clayton Act are set out in Sections 2, 3, 7, and 8 of the act.

Section 2—Price Discrimination

Price Discrimination Setting prices in such a way that two competing buyers pay two different prices for an identical product or service.

Section 2 of the Clayton Act prohibits **price discrimination**, which occurs when a seller charges different prices to competitive buyers for identical goods. Because businesses frequently circumvented Section 2 of the act, Congress strengthened this section by amending it with the passage of the Robinson-Patman Act in 1936.

As amended, Section 2 prohibits price discrimination that cannot be justified by differences in production costs, transportation costs, or cost differences due to other reasons. To violate Section 2, the seller must be engaged in interstate commerce, and the effect of the price discrimination must be to substantially lessen competition or create a competitive injury. Under Section 2, as amended, a seller is prohibited from reducing a price to one buyer below the price charged to that buyer's competitor. (Even offering goods to different customers at the same price but with different delivery arrangements may violate Section 2 in some circumstances—see, for example, the case discussed in this chapter's *Inside the Legal Environment* on page 676.)

An exception is made if the seller can justify the price reduction by demonstrating that he or she charged the lower price temporarily and in good faith to meet another seller's equally low price to the buyer's competitor. To be predatory, a seller's pricing policies must also include a reasonable prospect of the seller's recouping its losses.[12]

Section 3—Exclusionary Practices

Under Section 3 of the Clayton Act, sellers or lessors cannot sell or lease goods "on the condition, agreement or understanding that the . . . purchaser or lessee thereof shall not use or deal in the goods . . . of a competitor or

---

12. See, for example, *Brooke Group, Ltd. v. Brown & Williamson Tobacco Corp.*, 509 U.S. 209, 113 S.Ct. 2578, 125 L.Ed.2d 168 (1993), in which the Supreme Court held that a seller's price-cutting policies could not be predatory "[g]iven the market's realities"—the size of the seller's market share, the expanding output by other sellers, plus other factors.

Legal *e*-nvironment

The Application of Antitrust Law against Microsoft Corporation

The largest and most well-known computer company in the world is Microsoft. Founded more than twenty-five years ago by a dropout from Harvard, Bill Gates, and some of his friends, Microsoft eventually came to dominate the computer operating systems for PCs throughout the world. Indeed, some versions of Microsoft's operating system are installed on more than 90 percent of the personal computers in the world. Because of this dominance, Microsoft was an obvious candidate for antitrust scrutiny.

The Case against Microsoft

In "findings of fact" issued in late 1999, U.S. district court judge Thomas Jackson declared that Microsoft held monopoly power in the relevant market and that it had used its dominant position in the operating-system and browser markets to thwart competition from other companies.[a] The judge then referred the case for mediation. When mediation attempts failed, Judge Jackson issued his "finding of law"—his ruling in the case—in April 2000.[b]

The judge held that Microsoft was a monopoly and that it had "maintained its monopoly by anticompetitive means and attempted to monopolize the Web browser market." Microsoft had illegally used its power to keep an "oppressive thumb" on competitors and stifle innovation, hurting consumers in the process. Judge Jackson reasoned that because there are so many current applications made specifically for Microsoft's operating systems, there can be no commercially viable potential competitor. Why? Because the cost of creating alternative applications for a new competing operating system would be too high. While Judge Jackson maintained that there are currently 70,000 software applications for Windows, critics of his decision did not find any source for this statement.

Rather, his critics pointed out that a potential competitor need create only less than 2 percent of that number to offer a viable alternative to Windows.[c]

The government did not prove every allegation, however. According to Judge Jackson, the government had failed to prove that Microsoft's exclusive marketing arrangements with other firms constituted unlawful exclusive dealing under federal antitrust law.

The Browser Wars Revisited

The impetus for bringing the antitrust suit against Microsoft started with the so-called browser wars between Explorer and Navigator. The Justice Department first tried to stop Microsoft from giving away Explorer free as part of the Windows 98 version of its operating system. During the trial, though, events occurred that some critics argued should have stopped the trial. First, while Netscape lost market share soon after Microsoft entered the browser war, during the two years of the trial Navigator users increased from 15 million to more than 35 million. Second, during the trial, America Online paid more than $10 billion to purchase Netscape.

The Final Judgment—Break It Up

Judge Jackson's final ruling was to break Microsoft up into an applications company and an operating system company. The goal of the government is to set the stage for a newly created Microsoft applications company to develop application suites for alternative operating systems. For example, this company might create its well-known Office Suite (word processing, spreadsheets, and so on) for the Linex operating system.

Microsoft's future is still uncertain, however. The case is now on appeal and may be tied up in the appellate process for years.

For Critical Analysis: *Antitrust actions are typically brought against a company that has restricted output and thereby raised prices to consumers. In the Microsoft case, even the government admitted that the price of the Windows operating system and virtually all applications associated with it have fallen rather dramatically over time. Where, then, does one see the negative results for consumers of Microsoft's purported monopoly power?*

---

a. *United States v. Microsoft Corp.*, 65 F.Supp.2d 1 (D.D.C. 1999).
b. *United States v. Microsoft*, 87 F.Supp.2d 30 (D.D.C. 2000).

c. See, for example, S.J. Liebowitz and S.E. Margolis, *Winners, Losers, and Microsoft: Competition and Antitrust in High Technology* (Oakland, Calif.: Independent Institute, 1999).

Inside the Legal Environment

A Closer Look at the "Price" in Price Discrimination

Suppose that a seller charges two customers the same price for a specific product but provides free delivery services to one customer but not the other. Is this a form of price discrimination? Jack and Bob Bell thought so when they faced a similar situation. The Bell brothers purchased feed from Fur Breeders Agricultural Cooperative for use in their fur-breeding business. The price they paid was the same as that paid by every other member. The cooperative, however, offered free delivery services to all of its members except the Bells, who had to pick up the feed.

The Bells sued the cooperative in a federal district court, alleging that the cooperative's actions constituted price discrimination in violation of the Robinson-Patman Act, which amended Section 2 of the Clayton Act. The Bells argued that the added costs they had to incur in picking up the feed effectively raised the "price" they paid for the feed relative to the other members. According to the Bells, the fur-breeding industry is an intensively competitive one in which it is difficult to make significant profits. Because of the cooperative's actions, the Bells were at a com-petitive disadvantage. They claimed that the cost over time of picking up their feed caused them to reap lower profits relative to their competitors.

The cooperative made a motion to dismiss the case on the ground that all members were charged the same "price," and therefore there could be no "price" dis-crimination. Furthermore, claimed the cooperative, even if the different treatment with respect to delivery services amounted to price discrimination, the Bells had not proved that this different treatment caused their lower profits.

The court refused to dismiss the case, holding that the Bells had stated a valid claim of price discrimination in violation of the Robinson-Patman Act. To the court, it seemed "obvious" that a plaintiff's "competitive op-portunities may be harmed when it is forced to incur $16,000 to $17,000 in costs each year to pick up feed that its competitors have delivered at no cost. This is clearly the type of competitive injury the Robinson-Patman Act was designed to discourage and prevent."[a]

For Critical Analysis: *Suppose that a business offered free delivery services to customers within a certain geographical area but not to customers located outside that area. Would this practice constitute price discrimination?*

a. *Bell v. Fur Breeders Agricultural Cooperative,* 3 F.Supp.2d 1241 (D.Utah 1998).

competitors of the seller." In effect, this section prohibits two types of vertical agreements involving exclusionary practices—exclusive-dealing contracts and tying arrangements.

EXCLUSIVE-DEALING CONTRACTS A contract under which a seller forbids a buyer to purchase products from the seller's competitors is called an **exclusive-dealing contract.** A seller is prohibited from making an exclusive-dealing contract under Section 3 if the effect of the contract is "to substantially lessen competition or tend to create a monopoly."

● **Example 23.4** In *Standard Oil Co. of California v. United States,*[13] a lead-ing case decided by the United States Supreme Court in 1949, the then-largest gasoline seller in the nation made exclusive-dealing contracts with independ-ent stations in seven western states. The contracts involved 16 percent of all retail outlets, whose sales were approximately 7 percent of all retail sales in that market. The Court noted that the market was substantially concentrated because the seven largest gasoline suppliers all used exclusive-dealing contracts

Exclusive-Dealing Contract An agreement under which a seller forbids a buyer to purchase products from the seller's competitors.

13. 37 U.S. 293, 69 S.Ct. 1051, 93 L.Ed. 1371 (1949).

with their independent retailers and together controlled 65 percent of the market. Looking at market conditions after the arrangements were instituted, the Court found that market shares were extremely stable, and entry into the market was apparently restricted. Thus, the Court held that Section 3 of the Clayton Act had been violated, because competition was "foreclosed in a substantial share" of the relevant market.●

TYING ARRANGEMENTS When a seller conditions the sale of a product (the tying product) on the buyer's agreement to purchase another product (the tied product) produced or distributed by the same seller, a **tying arrangement,** or *tie-in sales agreement,* results. The legality of a tie-in agreement depends on many factors, particularly the purpose of the agreement and the agreement's likely effect on competition in the relevant markets (the market for the tying product and the market for the tied product).

● **Example 23.5** In 1936, the United States Supreme Court held that International Business Machines and Remington Rand had violated Section 3 of the Clayton Act by requiring the purchase of their own machine cards (the tied product) as a condition to the leasing of their tabulation machines (the tying product). Because only these two firms sold completely automated tabulation machines, the Court concluded that each possessed market power sufficient to "substantially lessen competition" through the tying arrangements.[14]●

Section 3 of the Clayton Act has been held to apply only to commodities, not to services. Tying arrangements, however, also can be considered agreements that restrain trade in violation of Section 1 of the Sherman Act. Thus, those cases involving tying arrangements of services have been brought under Section 1 of the Sherman Act. Traditionally, the courts have held tying arrangements brought under the Sherman Act to be illegal *per se.* In recent years, however, courts have shown a willingness to look at factors that are important in a rule-of-reason analysis.

What if a tying arrangement affects only one customer? Can the arrangement nonetheless violate Section 1 of the Sherman Act? The following case addressed this issue.

> **Tying Arrangement** An agreement between a buyer and a seller in which the buyer of a specific product or service becomes obligated to purchase additional products or services from the seller.

> **"Combinations are no less unlawful because they have not as yet resulted in restraint."**
>
> Hugo L. Black, 1886–1971
> (Associate Justice of the United States Supreme Court, 1937–1971)

---

14. *International Business Machines Corp. v. United States,* 298 U.S. 131, 56 S.Ct. 701, 80 L.Ed. 1085 (1936).

Case 23.3 ● Datagate, Inc. v. Hewlett-Packard Co.

United States Court of Appeals,
Ninth Circuit, 1995.
60 F.3d 1421.
http://www.findlaw.com/
casecode/courts/9th.html[a]

Historical and Technological Setting
Military investment in the 1940s fueled the growth of

the electronics industry. Computers made at this time weighed several tons and required the space of a warehouse to store operating components. With the advent of smaller components in the 1960s, computers and other technological equipment became more compact. The Hewlett-Packard Company (HP) produced the first hand-held scientific calculator in 1972. In the decades since then, the growth of the electronics and computer industries has seemed unstoppable. Today, HP makes a variety of electronic products, including computer hardware and software.

a. This page, which is part of a Web site maintained by FindLaw, contains links to recent opinions of the U.S. Court of Appeals for the Ninth Circuit. In the "Browsing" section, click on the "1995" link. When that page opens, scroll down the list of cases to the *Datagate* case and click on the case name to access the opinion.

(Continued)

Case 23.3 Continued

Background and Facts Datagate, Inc., provided repair service for computer hardware made by the Hewlett-Packard Company (HP). HP offered the same service. HP also offered support for those who used its software, but the company refused to provide software support to those who did not buy its hardware service. Datagate filed a suit in a federal district court against HP, claiming in part that HP's practice constituted an illegal tying arrangement. The arrangement had been imposed on only one HP customer, Rockwell International, but the Rockwell hardware service contract was worth $100,000 per year. The court held that one customer was not enough and entered a judgment in favor of HP. Datagate appealed.

In the Words of the Court . . .
BEEZER, Circuit Judge:

* * * *

[One of the] elements [that] must be satisfied to establish that a tying arrangement is illegal *per se* [is that] the tying arrangement affects a not insubstantial volume of commerce. * * *

* * * *

* * * The * * * requirement can be satisfied by the foreclosure of a single purchaser, so long as the purchaser represents a "not insubstantial" dollar-volume of sales.

* * * *

* * * [T]he Rockwell hardware service contract at issue was worth approximately $100,000 per year. * * *

This amount is sufficient.

Decision and Remedy The U.S. Court of Appeals for the Ninth Circuit reversed the decision of the lower court and remanded the case for trial.

For Critical Analysis—Economic Consideration *Did Rockwell International have an alternative to the tying arrangement required by HP?*

Section 7—Mergers

Under Section 7 of the Clayton Act, a person or business organization cannot hold stock and/or assets in another entity "where the effect . . . may be to substantially lessen competition." Section 7 is the statutory authority for preventing mergers or acquisitions that could result in monopoly power or a substantial lessening of competition in the marketplace. Section 7 applies to three specific types of mergers: horizontal mergers, vertical mergers, and conglomerate mergers. We discuss each type of merger in the following subsections.

Market Concentration The percentage of a particular firm's market sales in a relevant market area.

A crucial consideration in most merger cases is the **market concentration** of a product or business. Determining market concentration involves allocating percentage market shares among the various companies in the relevant market. When a small number of companies share a larger part of the market, the market is concentrated. For example, if the four largest grocery stores in Chicago accounted for 80 percent of all retail food sales, the market clearly would be concentrated in those four firms. Competition, however, is not necessarily diminished solely as a result of market concentration, and other factors will be considered in determining whether a merger will violate Section 7. One factor of particular importance in evaluating the effects of a merger is whether the merger will make it more difficult for potential competitors to enter the relevant market.

HORIZONTAL MERGERS Mergers between firms that compete with each other in the same market are called **horizontal mergers**. If a horizontal merger creates an entity with anything other than a small percentage market share, the merger will be presumed illegal. This is because of the United States Supreme Court's interpretation that Congress, in amending Section 7 of the Clayton Act in 1950, intended to prevent mergers that increase market concentration.[15] Three other factors that the courts also consider in analyzing the legality of a horizontal merger are overall concentration of the relevant product market, the relevant market's history of tending toward concentration, and whether the apparent design of the merger is to establish market power or to restrict competition.

The Federal Trade Commission (FTC) and the Department of Justice (DOJ) have established guidelines indicating which mergers will be challenged. Under the guidelines, the first factor to be considered in determining whether a merger will be challenged is the degree of concentration in the relevant market.

In determining market concentration, the FTC and DOJ employ what is known as the **Herfindahl-Hirschman Index (HHI)**. The HHI is the sum of the squares of the percentage market shares of the firms in the relevant market. For example, if there are four firms with shares of 30 percent, 30 percent, 20 percent, and 20 percent, respectively, then the HHI equals 2,600 ($30^2 + 30^2 + 20^2 + 20^2 = 2,600$).

If the premerger HHI is less than 1,000, then the market is unconcentrated, and the merger will not likely be challenged. If the premerger HHI is between 1,000 and 1,800, the industry is moderately concentrated, and the merger will be challenged only if it increases the HHI by 100 points or more. If the premerger HHI is greater than 1,800, the market is highly concentrated. In a highly concentrated market, a merger that produces an increase in the HHI between 50 and 100 points raises significant competitive concerns. Mergers that produce an increase in the HHI of more than 100 points in a highly concentrated market are deemed likely to enhance the market power of the surviving corporation. Thus, any attempted merger by the above four firms would be challenged by the FTC or the DOJ.

The FTC and the DOJ will also look at a number of other factors, including the ease of entry into the relevant market, economic efficiency, the financial condition of the merging firms, the nature and price of the product or products involved, and so on. If a firm is a leading one—having at least a 35 percent share and twice that of the next leading firm—any merger with a firm having as little as a 1 percent share will probably be challenged.

VERTICAL MERGERS A **vertical merger** occurs when a company at one stage of production acquires a company at a higher or lower stage of production. An example of a vertical merger is a company merging with one of its suppliers or retailers. Courts in the past have almost exclusively focused on "foreclosure" in assessing vertical mergers. Foreclosure occurs because competitors of the merging firms lose opportunities to either sell or buy products from the merging firms.

• **Example 23.6** In *United States v. E. I. du Pont de Nemours & Co.,*[16] du Pont was challenged for acquiring a considerable amount of General Motors

Horizontal Merger A merger between two firms that are competing in the same marketplace.

Herfindahl-Hirschman Index (HHI) An index of market power used to calculate whether a merger of two businesses will result in sufficient monopoly power to violate antitrust laws.

Vertical Merger The acquisition by a company at one level in a marketing chain of a company at a higher or lower level in the chain (such as a company merging with one of its suppliers or retailers).

15. *Brown Shoe v. United States,* 370 U.S. 294, 82 S.Ct. 1502, 8 L.Ed.2d 510 (1962).
16. 353 U.S. 586, 77 S.Ct. 872, 1 L.Ed.2d 1057 (1957).

(GM) stock. In holding that the transaction was illegal, the United States Supreme Court noted that stock acquisition would enable du Pont to prevent other sellers of fabrics and finishes from selling to GM, which then accounted for 50 percent of all auto fabric and finishes purchases.■

Today, whether a vertical merger will be deemed illegal generally depends on several factors, including market concentration, barriers to entry into the market, and the apparent intent of the merging parties. Mergers that do not prevent competitors of either of the merging firms from competing in a segment of the market will not be condemned as "foreclosing" competition and are legal.

Conglomerate Merger A merger between firms that do not compete with each other because they are in different markets (as opposed to horizontal and vertical mergers).

CONGLOMERATE MERGERS There are three general types of **conglomerate mergers:** market-extension, product-extension, and diversification mergers. A market-extension merger occurs when a firm seeks to sell its product in a new market by merging with a firm already established in that market. A product-extension merger occurs when a firm seeks to add a closely related product to its existing line by merging with a firm already producing that product. For example, a manufacturer might seek to extend its line of household products to include floor wax by acquiring a leading manufacturer of floor wax. Diversification occurs when a firm merges with another firm that offers a product or service wholly unrelated to the first firm's existing activities. An example of a diversification merger is an automobile manufacturer's acquisition of a motel chain.

Although in a conglomerate merger no firm is removed from the marketplace, conglomerate mergers can be challenged under Section 7 of the Clayton Act. In deciding whether the act has been violated, the courts usually evaluate (1) whether the merger will allow the acquiring firm to shift assets and revenue to the acquired firm to potentially drive out businesses who compete with the acquired firm, and (2) whether the merger creates a barrier, keeping other firms from entering the relevant market.

Section 8—Interlocking Directorates

Contrast Section 5 of the Federal Trade Commission Act is broader than the other antitrust laws. It covers virtually all anticompetitive behavior, including conduct that does not violate either the Sherman Act or the Clayton Act.

Section 8 of the Clayton Act deals with *interlocking directorates*—that is, the practice of having individuals serve as directors on the boards of two or more competing companies simultaneously. Specifically, no person may be a director in two or more competing corporations at the same time if either of the corporations has capital, surplus, or undivided profits aggregating more than $16,732,000 or competitive sales of $1,673,200 or more. The threshold amounts are adjusted each year by the Federal Trade Commission (FTC). (The amounts given here are those announced by the FTC in 2000.)

The Federal Trade Commission Act

The Federal Trade Commission Act was enacted in 1914, the same year the Clayton Act was written into law. Section 5 is the sole substantive provision of the act. It provides, in part, as follows: "Unfair methods of competition in or affecting commerce, and unfair or deceptive acts or practices in or affecting commerce are hereby declared illegal." Section 5 condemns all forms of anticompetitive behavior that are not covered under other federal antitrust laws. The act also created the Federal Trade Commission to implement the act's provisions.

Enforcement of Antitrust Laws

The federal agencies that enforce the federal antitrust laws are the U.S. Department of Justice (DOJ) and the Federal Trade Commission (FTC). The DOJ can prosecute violations of the Sherman Act as either criminal or civil violations. Violations of the Clayton Act are not crimes, and the DOJ can enforce that statute only through civil proceedings. The various remedies that the DOJ has asked the courts to impose include **divestiture** (making a company give up one or more of its operating functions) and dissolution. The DOJ might force a group of meat packers, for example, to divest itself of control or ownership of butcher shops.

Divestiture The act of selling one or more of a company's parts, such as a subsidiary or plant; often mandated by the courts in merger or monopolization cases.

The FTC also enforces the Clayton Act (but not the Sherman Act) and has sole authority to enforce violations of Section 5 of the Federal Trade Commission Act. FTC actions are effected through administrative orders, but if a firm violates an FTC order, the FTC can seek court sanctions for the violation.

A private party can sue for treble damages and attorneys' fees under Section 4 of the Clayton Act if the party is injured as a result of a violation of any of the federal antitrust laws, except Section 5 of the Federal Trade Commission Act. In some instances, private parties may also seek injunctive relief to prevent antitrust violations. The courts have determined that the ability to sue depends on the directness of the injury suffered by the would-be plaintiff. Thus, a person wishing to sue under the Sherman Act must prove (1) that the antitrust violation either caused or was a substantial factor in causing the injury that was suffered and (2) that the unlawful actions of the accused party affected business activities of the plaintiff that were protected by the antitrust laws.

International Perspective

The Extraterritorial Application of Antitrust Laws

As mentioned earlier in this chapter, the reach of U.S. antitrust laws extends beyond the territorial borders of the United States. The U.S. government (the DOJ or the FTC) and private parties may bring an action against a foreign party that has violated Section 1 of the Sherman Act. The FTC Act may also be applied to foreign trade. Foreign mergers, if Section 7 of the Clayton Act applies, may also be brought within the jurisdiction of U.S. courts. Before U.S. courts will exercise jurisdiction and apply antitrust laws to actions occurring in other countries, however, normally it must be shown that the alleged violation had a substantial effect on U.S. commerce. (See Chapter 25 for a further discussion of the extraterritorial application of U.S. antitrust laws.)

In the past, companies usually only had to be concerned with U.S. antitrust laws. Today, however, many countries have adopted antitrust laws. The European Union has antitrust provisions that are broadly analogous to Sections 1 and 2 of the Sherman Act, as well as laws governing mergers. Japanese antitrust laws prohibit unfair trade practices, monopolization, and restrictions that unreasonably restrain trade. Several southeastern nations, including Vietnam, Indonesia, and Malaysia, have either enacted anticompetitive statutes or are in the process of considering them for adoption. Argentina, Peru, Brazil, Chile, and several other Latin American countries have adopted modern antitrust laws as well. Most of the antitrust laws apply extraterritorially, as U.S. antitrust laws do. This means that a U.S. company may be subject to another nation's antitrust laws if the company's conduct has a substantial affect on that nation's commerce.

For Critical Analysis: *Do antitrust laws place too great a burden on commerce in the global marketplace?*

In recent years, more than 90 percent of all antitrust actions have been brought by private plaintiffs. One reason for this is, of course, that successful plaintiffs may recover three times the damages that they have suffered as a result of the violation. Such recoveries by private plaintiffs for antitrust violations have been rationalized as encouraging people to act as "private attorneys general" who will vigorously pursue antitrust violators on their own initiative.

Exemptions from Antitrust Laws

There are many legislative and constitutional limitations on antitrust enforcement. Most statutory and judicially created exemptions to the antitrust laws apply to the following areas or activities:

1. *Labor.* Section 6 of the Clayton Act generally permits labor unions to organize and bargain without violating antitrust laws. Section 20 of the Clayton Act specifies that strikes and other labor activities are not violations of any law of the United States. A union can lose its exemption, however, if it combines with a nonlabor group rather than acting simply in its own self-interest.

2. *Agricultural associations and fisheries.* Section 6 of the Clayton Act (along with the Capper-Volstead Act of 1922) exempts agricultural cooperatives from the antitrust laws. The Fisheries Cooperative Marketing Act of 1976 exempts from antitrust legislation individuals in the fishing industry who collectively catch, produce, and prepare for market their products. Both exemptions allow members of such co-ops to combine and set prices for a particular product, but they do not allow them to engage in exclusionary practices or restraints of trade directed at competitors.

3. *Insurance.* The McCarran-Ferguson Act of 1945 exempts the insurance business from the antitrust laws whenever state regulation exists. This exemption does not cover boycotts, coercion, or intimidation on the part of insurance companies.

4. *Foreign trade.* Under the provisions of the 1918 Webb-Pomerene Act, American exporters may engage in cooperative activity to compete with similar foreign associations. This type of cooperative activity may not, however, restrain trade within the United States or injure other American exporters. The Export Trading Company Act of 1982 broadened the Webb-Pomerene Act by permitting the Department of Justice to certify properly qualified export trading companies. Any activity within the scope described by the certificate is exempt from public prosecution under the antitrust laws.

5. *Professional baseball.* In 1922, the United States Supreme Court held that professional baseball was not within the reach of federal antitrust laws because it did not involve "interstate commerce."[17] Some of the effects of this decision, however, were modified by the Curt Flood Act of 1998. (See the *Ethical Issue* on the next page for a further discussion of the baseball exemption.)

6. *Oil marketing.* The 1935 Interstate Oil Compact allows states to determine quotas on oil that will be marketed in interstate commerce.

7. *Cooperative research and production.* Cooperative research among small business firms is exempt under the Small Business Administration Act of

---

17. *Federal Baseball Club of Baltimore, Inc. v. National League of Professional Baseball Clubs,* 259 U.S. 200, 42 S.Ct. 465, 66 L.Ed. 898 (1922).

1958, as amended. Research or production of a product, process, or service by joint ventures consisting of competitors is exempt under special federal legislation, including the National Cooperative Research Act of 1984 and the National Cooperative Production Amendments of 1993.

8. *Joint efforts by businesspersons to obtain legislative or executive action.* This is often referred to as the Noerr-Pennington doctrine.[18] For example, video producers might jointly lobby Congress to change the copyright laws, or a video-rental company might sue another video-rental firm, without being held liable for attempting to restrain trade. Though selfish rather than purely public-minded conduct is permitted, there is an exception: an action will not be protected if it is clear that the action is "objectively baseless in the sense that no reasonable [person] could reasonably expect success on the merits" and it is an attempt to make anticompetitive use of government processes.[19]

9. *Other exemptions.* Other activities exempt from antitrust laws include activities approved by the president in furtherance of the defense of our nation (under the Defense Production Act of 1950, as amended); state actions, when the state policy is clearly articulated and the policy is actively supervised by the state;[20] and activities of regulated industries (such as the communication and banking industries) when federal commissions, boards, or agencies (such as the Federal Communications Commission and the Federal Maritime Commission) have primary regulatory authority.

> **Note** State actions include the regulation of public utilities, the rates of which may be set by the states in which they do business.

---

18. See *United Mine Workers of America v. Pennington*, 381 U.S. 657, 89 S.Ct. 1585, 14 L.Ed.2d 626 (1965); and *Eastern Railroad Presidents Conference v. Noerr Motor Freight, Inc.*, 365 U.S. 127, 81 S.Ct. 523, 5 L.Ed.2d 464 (1961).
19. *Professional Real Estate Investors Inc. v. Columbia Pictures Industries, Inc.*, 508 U.S. 49, 113 S.Ct. 1920, 123 L.Ed.2d 611 (1993).
20. See *Parker v. Brown*, 347 U.S. 341, 63 S.Ct. 307, 87 L.Ed. 315 (1943).

Ethical Issue 23.1

Should the baseball exemption from antitrust laws be completely abolished?

The fact that until recently, baseball remained totally exempt from antitrust laws not only seemed unfair to many but also defied logic: Why was an exemption made for baseball but not for other professional sports? The answer to this perfectly reasonable question has always been the same: baseball was exempt because the United States Supreme Court, in 1922, said that it was. The Court held that baseball was a sport played only locally by local players. Because the activity purportedly did not involve interstate commerce, it did not meet the requirement for federal jurisdiction. The exemption was challenged in the early 1970s, but the Supreme Court ruled that it was up to Congress, not the Court, to overturn the exemption. In 1998, Congress did address the issue and passed the Curt Flood Act—named for the St. Louis Cardinals' star outfielder who challenged the exemption in the early 1970s.

Essentially, the act allows players the option of suing team owners for anticompetitive practices if, for example, the owners collude to "blacklist" players, hold down players' salaries, or force players to play for specific teams. Although the act's sponsors, including Senator Orrin Hatch of Utah, claim that the statute brings the rule of antitrust law to baseball, in fact the act did not overturn the 1922 Supreme Court decision but only limited some of the effects of baseball's exempt status. Baseball is still not subject to antitrust laws to the extent that football, basketball, and other professional sports are. Critics of the act claim that the exemption should be completely abolished because it simply makes no sense to continue to treat a $2-billion-a-year enterprise as a "local" activity.

Key Terms

antitrust law   664
attempted monopolization   673
conglomerate merger   680
divestiture   681
exclusive-dealing contract   676
group boycott   667
Herfindahl-Hirschman Index
    (HHI)   679
horizontal merger   679

horizontal restraint   667
market concentration   678
market power   665
market-share test   673
monopolization   672
monopoly   665
monopoly power   665
per se violation   666
predatory pricing   672

price discrimination   674
price-fixing agreement   667
resale price maintenance
    agreement   670
rule of reason   666
tying arrangement   677
vertical merger   679
vertical restraint   669
vertically integrated firm   669

Chapter Summary • Promoting Competition

Sherman Antitrust Act (1890) (See pages 664–674.)	1. **Major provisions—** a. **Section 1**—Prohibits contracts, combinations, and conspiracies in restraint of trade. (1) Horizontal restraints subject to Section 1 include price-fixing agreements, group boycotts (joint refusals to deal), horizontal market division, trade association agreements, and joint ventures. (2) Vertical restraints subject to Section 1 include resale price maintenance agreements, territorial or customer restrictions, and refusals to deal. b. **Section 2**—Prohibits monopolies and attempts to monopolize. 2. **Jurisdictional requirements**—The Sherman Act applies only to activities that have a significant impact on interstate commerce. 3. **Interpretative rules—** a. *Per se* rule—Applied to restraints on trade that are so inherently anticompetitive that they cannot be justified and are deemed illegal as a matter of law. b. Rule of reason—Applied when an anticompetitive agreement may be justified by legitimate benefits. Under the rule of reason, the lawfulness of a trade restraint will be determined by the purpose and effects of the restraint.
Clayton Act (1914) (See pages 674–680.)	The major provisions are as follows: 1. **Section 2**—As amended in 1936 by the Robinson-Patman Act, prohibits price discrimination that substantially lessens competition and prohibits a seller engaged in interstate commerce from selling to two or more buyers goods of similar grade and quality at different prices when the result is a substantial lessening of competition or the creation of a competitive injury. 2. **Section 3**—Prohibits exclusionary practices, such as exclusive-dealing contracts and tying arrangements, when the effect may be to substantially lessen competition. 3. **Section 7**—Prohibits mergers when the effect may be to substantially lessen competition or to tend to create a monopoly. a. Horizontal mergers—The acquisition by merger or consolidation of a competing firm engaged in the same relevant market. Will be unlawful only if a

Chapter Summary • Promoting Competition

Clayton Act (1914)
—continued
	merger results in the merging firms' holding a disproportionate share of the market, resulting in a substantial lessening of competition, and if the merger does not enhance consumer welfare by increasing efficiency of production or marketing.
	
	   b. Vertical mergers—The acquisition by a seller of one of its buyers or vice versa. Will be unlawful if the merger prevents competitors of either merging firm from competing in a segment of the market that otherwise would be open to them, resulting in a substantial lessening of competition.
	
	   c. Conglomerate mergers—The acquisition of a noncompeting business.
	
	4. Section 8—Prohibits interlocking directorates.

Federal Trade Commission Act (1914) (See page 680.)	Prohibits unfair methods of competition; established and defined the powers of the Federal Trade Commission.
Enforcement of Antitrust Laws (See pages 681–682.)	Antitrust laws are enforced by the Department of Justice, by the Federal Trade Commission, and in some cases by private parties, who may be awarded treble damages and attorneys' fees.
Exemptions from Antitrust Laws (See pages 682–683.)	**1. Labor unions** (under Section 6 of the Clayton Act of 1914). **2. Agricultural associations and fisheries** (under Section 6 of the Clayton Act of 1914, the Capper-Volstead Act of 1922, and the Fisheries Cooperative Marketing Act of 1976). **3. Insurance**—when state regulation exists (under the McCarran-Ferguson Act of 1945). **4. Export trading companies** (under the Webb-Pomerene Act of 1918 and the Export Trading Company Act of 1982). **5. Professional baseball** (by a 1922 judicial decision), although modified by a 1998 federal statute. **6. Oil marketing** (under the Interstate Oil Compact of 1935). **7. Cooperative research and production** (under various acts, including the Small Business Administration Act of 1958, as amended, the National Cooperative Research Act of 1984, and the National Cooperative Production Amendments of 1993). **8. Joint efforts by businesspersons to obtain legislative or executive action** (under the Noerr-Pennington doctrine). **9.** Other activities, including certain national defense actions, state actions, and actions of certain regulated industries.

For Review

1. What is a monopoly? What is market power? How do these concepts relate to each other?

2. What type of activity is prohibited by Section 1 of the Sherman Act? What type of activity is prohibited by Section 2 of the Sherman Act?

(Continued)

3. What are the four major provisions of the Clayton Act, and what types of activities do these provisions prohibit?

4. What agencies of the federal government enforce the federal antitrust laws?

5. Name four activities that are exempt from the antitrust laws.

Questions and Case Problems

23–1. Sherman Act. An agreement that is blatantly and substantially anticompetitive is deemed a *per se* violation of Section 1 of the Sherman Act. Under what rule is an agreement analyzed if it appears to be anticompetitive but is not a *per se* violation? In making this analysis, what factors will a court consider?

23–2. Antitrust Laws. Allitron, Inc., and Donovan, Ltd., are interstate competitors selling similar appliances, principally in the states of Indiana, Kentucky, Illinois, and Ohio. Allitron and Donovan agree that Allitron will no longer sell in Ohio and Indiana and that Donovan will no longer sell in Kentucky and Illinois. Have Allitron and Donovan violated any antitrust laws? If so, which law? Explain.

23–3. Antitrust Laws. The partnership of Alvaredo and Parish is engaged in the oil-wellhead service industry in the states of New Mexico and Colorado. The firm presently has about 40 percent of the market for this service. Webb Corp. competes with the Alvaredo-Parish partnership in the same state area. Webb has approximately 35 percent of the market. Alvaredo and Parish acquire the stock and assets of the Webb Corp. Do the antitrust laws prohibit the type of action undertaken by Alvaredo and Parish? Discuss fully.

23–4. Horizontal Restraints. Jorge's Appliance Corp. was a new retail seller of appliances in Sunrise City. Because of its innovative sales techniques and financing, Jorge's caused a substantial loss of sales from the appliance department of No-Glow Department Store, a large chain store with a great deal of buying power. No-Glow told a number of appliance manufacturers that if they continued to sell to Jorge's, No-Glow would discontinue its large volume of purchases from them. The manufacturers immediately stopped selling appliances to Jorge's. Jorge's filed suit against No-Glow and the manufacturers, claiming that their actions constituted an antitrust violation. No-Glow and the manufacturers were able to prove that Jorge's was a small retailer with a small portion of the market. They claimed that because the relevant market was not substantially affected, they were not guilty of restraint of trade. Discuss fully whether there was an antitrust violation.

23–5. Exclusionary Practices. Instant Foto Corp. is a manufacturer of photography film. At the present time, Instant Foto has approximately 50 percent of the market. Instant Foto advertises that the purchase price for Instant Foto film includes photo processing by Instant Foto Corp. Instant Foto claims that its film processing is specially designed to improve the quality of photos taken with Instant Foto film. Is Instant Foto's combination of film purchase and film processing an antitrust violation? Explain.

23–6. Sherman Act, Section 1. Harcourt Brace Jovanovich Legal and Professional Publications (HBJ), the nation's largest provider of bar review materials and lecture services, began offering a Georgia bar review course in 1976. It was in direct, and often intense, competition with BRG of Georgia, Inc., the other main provider of bar review courses in Georgia, from 1977 to 1979. In early 1980, HBJ and BRG entered into an agreement that gave BRG the exclusive right to market HBJ's materials in Georgia and to use its trade name, Bar/Bri. The parties agreed that HBJ would not compete with BRG in Georgia and that BRG would not compete with HBJ outside of Georgia. Immediately after the 1980 agreement, the price of BRG's course was increased from $150 to over $400. Jay Palmer, a former law student, brought an action against the two firms, alleging that the 1980 agreement violated Section 1 of the Sherman Act. What will the court decide? Discuss fully. [*Palmer v. BRG of Georgia, Inc.,* 498 U.S. 46, 111 S.Ct. 401, 112 L.Ed.2d 349 (1990)]

23–7. Tying Arrangements. Eastman Kodak Co. has about a 20 percent share of the highly competitive market for high-volume photocopiers and microfilm equipment and controls nearly the entire market for replacement parts for its equipment (which are not interchangeable with parts for other manufacturers' equipment). Prior to 1985, Kodak sold replacement parts for its equipment without significant restrictions. As a result, a number of independent service organizations (ISOs) purchased Kodak parts to use when repairing and servicing Kodak copiers. In 1985, Kodak changed its policy to prevent the ISOs from competing with Kodak's own service organizations. It ceased selling parts to ISOs and refused to sell replacement parts to its customers unless they agreed not to have their equipment serviced by ISOs. In 1987, Image Technical Services, Inc., and seventeen other ISOs sued Kodak, alleging that Kodak's policy was a tying arrangement in violation of Section 1 of the Sherman Act. Assuming that Kodak does not have market power in the market for photocopying and microfilm equipment, does Kodak's restrictive policy constitute an illegal tying arrangement? Does it violate antitrust laws in any way? Discuss fully. [*Eastman Kodak Co. v. Image Technical Services, Inc.,* 504 U.S. 451, 112 S.Ct. 2072, 119 L.Ed.2d 265 (1992)]

23–8. Clayton Act, Section 2. Stelwagon Manufacturing Co. agreed with Tarmac Roofing Systems, Inc., to promote and develop a market for Tarmac's products in the Philadelphia area. In return, Tarmac promised not to sell its products to other area distributors. In 1991, Stelwagon learned that Tarmac had been selling its products to Stelwagon's competitors—the Standard Roofing Co. and the Celotex Corp.—at substantially lower prices. Stelwagon filed a suit against Tarmac in a federal district court. What is the principal factor in determining whether Tarmac violated Section 2 of the Clayton Act, as amended? Did Tarmac violate the act? [*Stelwagon Manufacturing Co. v. Tarmac Roofing Systems, Inc.,* 63 F.3d 1267 (3d Cir. 1995)]

23–9. Antitrust Laws. Great Western Directories, Inc. (GW), is an independent publisher of telephone directory Yellow Pages. GW buys information for its listings from Southwestern Bell Telephone Co. (SBT). Southwestern Bell Corp. owns SBT and Southwestern Bell Yellow Pages (SBYP), which publishes a directory in competition with GW. In June 1988, in some markets, SBT raised the price for its listing information, and SBYP lowered the price for advertising in its Yellow Pages. GW feared that these companies would do the same thing in other local markets, and it would then be too expensive to compete in those markets. Because of this fear, GW left one market and declined to compete in another. Consequently, SBYP had a monopoly in those markets. GW and another independent publisher filed a suit in a federal district court against Southwestern Bell Corp. What antitrust law, if any, did Southwestern Bell Corp. violate? Should the independent companies be entitled to damages? [*Great Western Directories, Inc. v. Southwestern Bell Telephone Co.,* 74 F.3d 613 (5th Cir. 1996)]

23–10. Restraint of Trade. The National Collegiate Athletic Association (NCAA) coordinates the intercollegiate athletic programs of its members by issuing rules and setting standards governing, among other things, the coaching staffs. The NCAA set up a "Cost Reduction Committee" to consider ways to cut the costs of intercollegiate athletics while maintaining competition. The committee included financial aid personnel, intercollegiate athletic administrators, college presidents, university faculty members, and a university chancellor. It was felt that "only a collaborative effort could reduce costs

while maintaining a level playing field." The committee proposed a rule to restrict the annual compensation of certain coaches to $16,000. The NCAA adopted the rule. Basketball coaches affected by the rule filed a suit in a federal district court against the NCAA, alleging a violation of Section 1 of the Sherman Antitrust Act. Is the rule a *per se* violation of the Sherman Act, or should it be evaluated under the rule of reason? If it is subject to the rule of reason, is it an illegal restraint of trade? Discuss fully. [*Law v. National Collegiate Athletic Association,* 134 F.3d 1010 (10th Cir. 1998)]

A Question of Ethics and Social Responsibility

23–11. A group of lawyers in the District of Columbia regularly acted as court-appointed attorneys for indigent defendants in District of Columbia criminal cases. At a meeting of the Superior Court Trial Lawyers Association (SCTLA), the attorneys agreed to stop providing this representation until the district increased their compensation. Their subsequent boycott had a severe impact on the district's criminal justice system, and the District of Columbia gave in to the lawyers' demands for higher pay. After the lawyers had returned to work, the Federal Trade Commission filed a complaint against the SCTLA and four of its officers and, after an investigation, ruled that the SCTLA's activities constituted an illegal group boycott in violation of antitrust laws. [*Federal Trade Commission v. Superior Court Trial Lawyers Association,* 493 U.S. 411, 110 S.Ct. 768, 107 L.Ed.2d 851 (1990)]

1. The SCTLA obviously was aware of the negative impact its decision would have on the district's criminal justice system. Given this fact, do you think the lawyers behaved ethically?

2. On appeal, the SCTLA claimed that its boycott was undertaken to publicize the fact that the attorneys were underpaid and that the boycott thus constituted an expression protected by the First Amendment. Do you agree with this argument?

3. Labor unions have the right to strike when negotiations between labor and management fail to result in agreement. Is it fair to prohibit members of the SCTLA from "striking" against their employer, the District of Columbia, simply because the SCTLA is a professional organization and not a labor union?

For Critical Analysis

23–12. Critics of antitrust law claim that in the long run, competitive market forces will eliminate private monopolies unless they are fostered by government regulation. Do you agree with these critics? Why or why not?

Interacting with the Internet

■ For updated links to resources available on the Web, as well as a variety of other materials, visit this text's Web site at

http://leet.westbuslaw.com

■ The Federal Trade Commission offers an abundance of information on antitrust law, including "A Plain English Guide to Antitrust Laws," at

http://www.ftc.gov/ftc/antitrust.htm

■ The Tech Law Journal presents "news, records, and analysis of legislation, litigation, and regulation affecting the computer and Internet industry" in the area of antitrust law at

http://www.techlawjournal.com/atr/default.htm

■ You can access the Antitrust Division of the U.S. Department of Justice online at

http://www.usdoj.gov

■ To see the American Bar Association's Web page on antitrust law, go to

http://www.abanet.org/antitrust

Online Legal Research Exercises

Go to **http://leet.westbuslaw.com**, the Web site that accompanies this text. Select "Interactive Study Center," and then click on "Chapter 23." There you will find the following Internet research exercise that you can perform to learn more about the application of antitrust laws to vertical restraints:

Activity 23–1: Vertical Restraints and the Rule of Reason

Before the Test

Go to **http://leet.westbuslaw.com**, the Web site that accompanies this text. Select "Interactive Quizzes." You will find a number of interactive questions relating to this chapter.

Investor Protection

chapter objectives

After reading this chapter, you should be able to:

1. Define what is meant by the term *securities*.

2. Describe the purpose and provisions of the Securities Act of 1933.

3. Explain the purpose and provisions of the Securities Exchange Act of 1934.

4. Identify federal laws that specifically regulate investment companies.

5. Point out some of the features of state securities laws.

> **"It shall be unlawful for any person in the offer or sale of any security . . . to engage in any transaction, practice, or course of business which operates or would operate as a fraud or deceit upon the purchaser."**
>
> Securities Act of 1933, Section 17

Security Generally, a stock certificate, bond, note, debenture, warrant, or other document given as evidence of an ownership interest in a corporation or as a promise of repayment by a corporation.

After the stock market crash of 1929, many members of Congress argued in favor of regulating securities markets. Basically, legislation for such regulation was enacted to provide investors with more information to help them make buying and selling decisions about **securities**—generally defined as any documents evidencing corporate ownership (stock) or debts (bonds)—and to prohibit deceptive, unfair, and manipulative practices. Today, the sale and transfer of securities are heavily regulated by federal and state statutes and by government agencies.

This chapter will discuss the nature of federal securities regulations and their effects on the business world. First, though, it is necessary to understand the paramount role played by the Securities and Exchange Commission (SEC) in the regulation of federal securities laws. Because of its importance in this area, we examine the origin and functions of the SEC in the *Landmark in the Legal Environment* below.

Securities Act of 1933

The Securities Act of 1933[1] was designed to prohibit various forms of fraud and to stabilize the securities industry by requiring that all relevant information concerning the issuance of securities be made available to the investing public. Essentially, the purpose of this act is to require disclosure.

---

1. 15 U.S.C. Sections 77–77aa.

Landmark in the Legal Environment

The Securities and Exchange Commission

In 1931, the Senate passed a resolution calling for an extensive investigation of securities trading. The investigation led, ultimately, to the passage by Congress of the Securities Act of 1933, which is also known as the *truth-in-securities* bill. In the following year, Congress passed the Securities Exchange Act. This 1934 act created the Securities and Exchange Commission as an independent regulatory agency whose function was to administer the 1933 and 1934 acts. Its major responsibilities in this respect are as follows:

1. Requiring disclosure of facts concerning offerings of securities listed on national securities exchanges and of certain securities traded over the counter (OTC).

2. Regulating the trade in securities on the thirteen national and regional securities exchanges and in the over-the-counter markets.
3. Investigating securities fraud.
4. Regulating the activities of securities brokers, dealers, and investment advisers and requiring their registration.
5. Supervising the activities of mutual funds.
6. Recommending administrative sanctions, injunctive remedies, and criminal prosecution against those who violate securities laws. (The SEC can bring enforcement actions for civil violations of federal securities laws. The Fraud Section of the Criminal Division of the Department of Justice prosecutes criminal violations.)

Since its creation, the SEC's regulatory functions have gradually been increased by legislation granting it authority in different areas. We look at the expanding powers of the SEC later in the chapter.

For Critical Analysis: *What is the source of the national government's authority to regulate the securities industry?*

What Is a Security?

Section 2(1) of the Securities Act states that securities include the following:

> [A]ny note, stock, treasury stock, bond, debenture, evidence of indebtedness, certificate of interest or participation in any profit-sharing agreement, collateral-trust certificate, preorganization certificate or subscription, transferable share, investment contract, voting-trust certificate, certificate of deposit for a security, fractional undivided interest in oil, gas, or other mineral rights, or, in general, any interest or instrument commonly known as a "security," or any certificate of interest or participation in, temporary or interim certificate for, receipt for, guarantee of, or warrant or right to subscribe to or purchase, any of the foregoing.[2]

Generally, the courts have interpreted the Securities Act's definition of what constitutes a security[3] to mean that a security exists in any transaction in which a person (1) invests (2) in a common enterprise (3) reasonably expecting profits (4) derived *primarily* or *substantially* from others' managerial or entrepreneurial efforts.[4]

For our purposes, it is probably most convenient to think of securities in their most common forms—stocks and bonds issued by corporations. Bear in mind, however, that securities can take many forms and have been held to include whiskey, cosmetics, worms, beavers, boats, vacuum cleaners, muskrats, and cemetery lots, as well as investment contracts in condominiums, franchises, limited partnerships, oil or gas or other mineral rights, and farm animals accompanied by care agreements.

Registration Statement

Section 5 of the Securities Act of 1933 broadly provides that if a security does not qualify for an exemption, that security must be *registered* before it is offered to the public either through the mails or through any facility of interstate commerce, including securities exchanges. Issuing corporations must file a *registration statement* with the SEC. Investors must be provided with a prospectus that describes the security being sold, the issuing corporation, and the investment or risk attaching to the security. In principle, the registration statement and the prospectus supply sufficient information to enable unsophisticated investors to evaluate the financial risk involved.

CONTENTS OF THE REGISTRATION STATEMENT The registration statement must include the following:

1. A description of the significant provisions of the security offered for sale, including the relationship between that security and the other capital securities of the registrant. Also, the corporation must disclose how it intends to use the proceeds of the sale.
2. A description of the registrant's properties and business.
3. A description of the management of the registrant and its security holdings; remuneration; and other benefits, including pensions and stock options. Any interests of directors or officers in any material transactions with the corporation must be disclosed.

Note Congress intended the federal securities laws to protect the public from unethical business practices.

> "Spending and investing differ only in degree, depending on the length of time elapsing between the expenditure and the enjoyment."
>
> Irving Fisher, 1867–1947
> (U.S. economist)

Don't Forget The purpose of the Securities Act of 1933 is disclosure—the SEC does not consider whether a security is worth the investment.

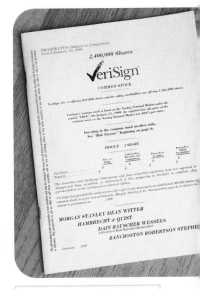

A registration statement discusses a security that is being offered to the public. What are the major contents of a registration statement?

---

2. 15 U.S.C. Section 77b(1). Amendments in 1982 added stock options.
3. See 15 U.S.C. Section 77b(a)(1).
4. *SEC v. W. J. Howey Co.*, 328 U.S. 293, 66 S.Ct. 1100, 90 L.Ed. 1244 (1946).

4. A financial statement certified by an independent public accounting firm.
5. A description of pending lawsuits.

OTHER REQUIREMENTS   Before filing the registration statement and the prospectus with the SEC, the corporation is allowed to obtain an *underwriter*—a company that agrees to purchase the new issue of securities for resale to the public. There is a twenty-day waiting period (which can be accelerated by the SEC) after registration before the sale can take place. During this period, oral offers between interested investors and the issuing corporation concerning the purchase and sale of the proposed securities may take place, and very limited written advertising is allowed. At this time, the so-called **red herring** prospectus may be distributed. It gets its name from the red legend printed across it stating that the registration has been filed but has not become effective.

After the waiting period, the registered securities can be legally bought and sold. Written advertising is allowed in the form of a **tombstone ad,** so named because historically the format resembles a tombstone. Such ads simply tell the investor where and how to obtain a prospectus. Normally, any other type of advertising is prohibited.

Exempt Securities

A number of specific securities are exempt from the registration requirements of the Securities Act of 1933. These securities—which can also generally be resold without being registered—include the following:[5]

1. All bank securities sold prior to July 27, 1933.
2. Commercial paper, if the maturity date does not exceed nine months.
3. Securities of charitable organizations.
4. Securities resulting from a corporate reorganization issued for exchange with the issuer's existing security holders and certificates issued by trustees, receivers, or debtors in possession under the bankruptcy laws (bankruptcy was discussed in Chapter 15).
5. Securities issued exclusively for exchange with the issuer's existing security holders, provided no commission is paid (for example, stock dividends and stock splits).
6. Securities issued to finance the acquisition of railroad equipment.
7. Any insurance, endowment, or annuity contract issued by a state-regulated insurance company.
8. Government-issued securities.
9. Securities issued by banks, savings and loan associations, farmers' cooperatives, and similar institutions subject to supervision by governmental authorities.
10. In consideration of the "small amount involved,"[6] an issuer's offer of up to $5 million in securities in any twelve-month period.

For the last exemption, under Regulation A,[7] the issuer must file with the SEC a notice of the issue and an offering circular, which must also be provided to investors before the sale. This is a much simpler and less expensive process than the procedures associated with full registration. Companies are allowed

Red Herring   A preliminary prospectus that can be distributed to potential investors after the registration statement (for a securities offering) has been filed with the Securities and Exchange Commission. The name derives from the red legend printed across the prospectus stating that the registration has been filed but has not become effective.

Tombstone Ad   An advertisement, historically in a format resembling a tombstone, of a securities offering. The ad informs potential investors of where and how they may obtain a prospectus.

Be Aware   The issuer of an exempt security does not have to disclose the same information that other issuers do.

---

5. 15 U.S.C. Section 77c.
6. 15 U.S.C. Section 77c(b).
7. 17 C.F.R. Sections 230.251–230.263.

to "test the waters" for potential interest before preparing the offering circular. To test the waters means to determine potential interest without actually selling any securities or requiring any commitment on the part of those who are interested. Small-business issuers (companies with less than $25 million in annual revenues and less than $25 million in outstanding voting stock) can also use an integrated registration and reporting system that uses simpler forms than the full registration system.

Exhibit 24–1 summarizes the securities and transactions (discussed next) that are exempt from the registration requirements under the Securities Act of 1933 and SEC regulations.

Exempt Transactions

An issuer of securities that are not exempt under one of the ten categories listed in the previous subsection can avoid the high cost and complicated procedures associated with registration by taking advantage of certain transaction exemptions. An offering may qualify for more than one exemption. These exemptions are very broad, and thus many sales occur without registration.

Exhibit 24–1   Exemptions under the 1933 Securities Act

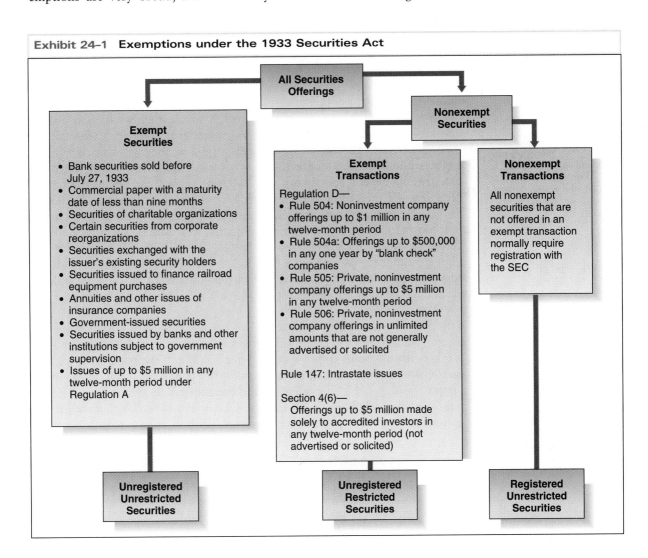

Because there is some overlap in the coverage of the exemptions, an offering may qualify for more than one.

SMALL OFFERINGS—REGULATION D The SEC's Regulation D contains four separate exemptions from registration requirements for limited offers (offers that either involve a small amount of money or are made in a limited manner). Regulation D provides that any of these offerings made during any twelve-month period are exempt from the registration requirements.

Rule 504. Noninvestment company offerings up to $1 million in any one year are exempt. In contrast to investment companies (discussed later in this chapter), noninvestment companies are firms that are not engaged primarily in the business of investing or trading in securities.

Rule 504a. Offerings up to $500,000 in any one year by so-called blank check companies—companies with no specific business plans except to locate and acquire presently unknown businesses or opportunities—are exempt if no general solicitation or advertising is used; the SEC is notified of the sales; and precaution is taken against nonexempt, unregistered resales.[8] The limits on advertising and unregistered resales do not apply if the offering is made solely in states that provide for registration and disclosure and the securities are sold in compliance with those provisions.[9]

Rule 505. Private, noninvestment company offerings up to $5 million in any twelve-month period are exempt, regardless of the number of **accredited investors** (banks, insurance companies, investment companies, the issuer's executive officers and directors, and persons whose income or net worth exceeds certain limits), so long as there are no more than thirty-five unaccredited investors; no general solicitation or advertising is used; the SEC is notified of the sales; and precaution is taken against nonexempt, unregistered resales. If the sale involves any unaccredited investors, *all* investors must be given material information about the offering company, its business, and the securities before the sale. Unlike Rule 506 (discussed next), Rule 505 includes no requirement that the issuer believe each unaccredited investor "has such knowledge and experience in financial and business matters that he is capable of evaluating the merits and the risks of the prospective investment."[10]

Rule 506. Private offerings in unlimited amounts that are not generally solicited or advertised are exempt if the SEC is notified of the sales; precaution is taken against nonexempt, unregistered resales; and the issuer believes that each unaccredited investor has sufficient knowledge or experience in financial matters to be capable of evaluating the investment's merits and risks. There may be no more than thirty-five unaccredited investors, although there may be an unlimited number of accredited investors. If there are *any* unaccredited in-

---

8. Precautions to be taken against nonexempt, unregistered resales include asking the investor whether he or she is buying the securities for others; before the sale, disclosing to each purchaser in writing that the securities are unregistered and thus cannot be resold, except in an exempt transaction, without first being registered; and indicating on the certificates that the securities are unregistered and restricted.
9. 17 C.F.R. Section 230.504a.
10. 17 C.F.R. Section 230.505.

vestors, the issuer must provide to *all* purchasers material information about itself, its business, and the securities before the sale.[11]

This exemption is perhaps most important to those firms that want to raise funds through the sale of securities without registering them. It is often referred to as the *private placement* exemption, because it exempts "transactions not involving any public offering."[12] This provision applies to private offerings to a limited number of persons who are sufficiently sophisticated and in a sufficiently strong bargaining position to be able to assume the risk of the investment (and who thus have no need for federal registration protection), as well as to private offerings to similarly situated institutional investors.

SMALL OFFERINGS—SECTION 4(6)   Under Section 4(6) of the Securities Act of 1933, an offer made *solely* to accredited investors is exempt if its amount is not more than $5 million. Any number of accredited investors may participate, but no unaccredited investors may do so. No general solicitation or advertising may be used; the SEC must be notified of all sales; and precaution must be taken against nonexempt, unregistered resales. Precaution is necessary because these are *restricted* securities and may be resold only by registration or in an exempt transaction.[13] (The securities purchased and sold by most people who deal in stock are called, in contrast, *unrestricted* securities.)

INTRASTATE ISSUES—RULE 147   Also exempt are intrastate transactions involving purely local offerings.[14] This exemption applies to most offerings that are restricted to residents of the state in which the issuing company is organized and doing business. For nine months after the last sale, virtually no resales may be made to nonresidents, and precautions must be taken against this possibility. These offerings remain subject to applicable laws in the state of issue.

RESALES   Most securities can be resold without registration (although some resales may be subject to restrictions, which are discussed above in connection with specific exemptions). The Securities Act of 1933 provides exemptions for resales by most persons other than issuers or underwriters. The average investor who sells shares of stock does not have to file a registration statement with the SEC. Resales of restricted securities acquired under Rule 504a, Rule 505, Rule 506, or Section 4(6), however, trigger the registration requirements unless the party selling them complies with Rule 144 or Rule 144A. These rules are sometimes referred to as "safe harbors."

Rule 144.   Rule 144 exempts restricted securities from registration on resale if there is adequate current public information about the issuer, the person selling the securities has owned them for at least two years, they are sold in certain limited amounts in unsolicited brokers' transactions, and the SEC is given notice of the resale.[15] "Adequate current public information" consists of the reports that certain companies are required to file under the Securities Exchange Act of 1934. A person who has owned the securities for at least

11. 17 C.F.R. Section 230.506.
12. 15 U.S.C. Section 77d(2).
13. 15 U.S.C. Section 77d(6).
14. 15 U.S.C. Section 77c(a)(11); 17 C.F.R. Section 230.147.
15. 17 C.F.R. Section 230.144.

three years is subject to none of these requirements, unless the person is an affiliate. An *affiliate* is one who controls, is controlled by, or is in common control with the issuer. Sales of *nonrestricted* securities by an affiliate are also subject to the requirements for an exemption under Rule 144 (except that the affiliate need not have owned the securities for at least two years).

Rule 144A.   Securities that at the time of issue are not of the same class as securities listed on a national securities exchange or quoted in a U.S. automated interdealer quotation system may be resold under Rule 144A.[16] They may be sold only to a qualified institutional buyer (an institution, such as an insurance company, an investment company, or a bank, that owns and invests at least $100 million in securities). The seller must take reasonable steps to ensure that the buyer knows that the seller is relying on the exemption under Rule 144A. A sample restricted stock certificate is shown in Exhibit 24–2.

> **Contrast** Securities do not have to be held for two years to be exempt from registration on a resale under Rule 144A, as they do under Rule 144.

---

16. 17 C.F.R. Section 230.144A.

Exhibit 24–2   A Sample Restricted Stock Certificate

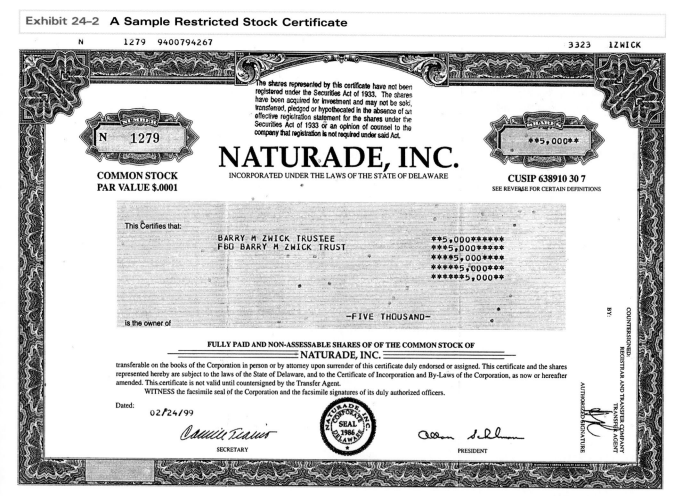

Violations of the 1933 Act

As mentioned, the SEC has the power to investigate and bring civil enforcement actions against companies that violate federal securities laws, including the Securities Act of 1933. Criminal violations are prosecuted by the Department of Justice. Violators may be penalized by fines up to $10,000, imprisonment for up to five years, or both. Private parties may also bring suits against those who violate federal securities laws. Those who purchase securities and suffer harm as a result of false or omitted statements, or other violations, may bring a suit in a federal court to recover their losses and other damages.

Securities Exchange Act of 1934

The Securities Exchange Act of 1934 provides for the regulation and registration of securities exchanges; brokers; dealers; and national securities associations, such as the National Association of Securities Dealers (NASD). The SEC regulates the markets in which securities are traded by maintaining a continuous disclosure system for all corporations with securities on the securities exchanges and for those companies that have assets in excess of $10 million and five hundred or more shareholders. These corporations are referred to as Section 12 companies, because they are required to register their securities under Section 12 of the 1934 act.

The act regulates proxy solicitation for voting (discussed in Chapter 16) and allows the SEC to engage in market surveillance to regulate undesirable market practices such as fraud, market manipulation, and misrepresentation.

Section 10(b), SEC Rule 10b-5, and Insider Trading

Section 10(b) is one of the most important sections of the Securities Exchange Act of 1934. This section proscribes the use of "any manipulative or deceptive device or contrivance in contravention of such rules and regulations as the [SEC] may prescribe." Among the rules that the SEC has promulgated pursuant to the 1934 act is **SEC Rule 10b-5,** which prohibits the commission of fraud in connection with the purchase or sale of any security.

One of the most important purposes of Section 10(b) and SEC Rule 10b-5 relates to so-called **insider trading.** Because of their positions, corporate directors and officers often obtain advance inside information that can affect the future market value of the corporate stock. Obviously, their positions can give them a trading advantage over the general public and shareholders. The 1934 Securities Exchange Act defines inside information and extends liability to officers and directors for taking advantage of such information in their personal transactions when they know that it is unavailable to the persons with whom they are dealing.

Section 10(b) of the 1934 act and SEC Rule 10b-5 cover not only corporate officers, directors, and majority shareholders but also any persons having access to or receiving information of a nonpublic nature on which trading is based.

In the following classic case, a shareholder alleged that a corporate officer and a corporate director had breached their fiduciary duties by trading corporate shares on the basis of nonpublic information.

SEC Rule 10b-5 A rule of the Securities and Exchange Commission that makes it unlawful, in connection with the purchase or sale of any security, to make any untrue statement of a material fact or to omit a material fact if such omission causes the statement to be misleading.

Insider Trading The purchase or sale of securities on the basis of information that has not been made available to the public.

Case 24.1 ● Diamond v. Oreamuno

Court of Appeals of New York, 1969.
24 N.Y.2d 494,
248 N.E.2d 910,
301 N.Y.S.2d 78.

Historical and Ethical Setting

Officers and directors owe fiduciary duties to their corporation and its shareholders with respect to corporate business and property. Shares in the corporation are private property, however, and trading in those shares is not usually a corporate transaction. Thus, at common law a century ago, directors and officers were considered to owe no fiduciary duties when they traded in the shares of their corporations. Directors or officers with inside information could trade with impunity without disclosing the information (as long as they avoided outright fraud). Today, in contrast, the law holds that officers and directors owe a fiduciary duty to their corporation not to engage in the trading of shares in the corporation on the basis of inside information.

Background and Facts The defendants in this case were the chairman of the board (Oreamuno) and president (Gonzalez) of Management Assistance, Inc. (MAI), a corporation that bought and leased computers, with maintenance services being provided by IBM. The defendants learned that IBM was going to increase its maintenance prices dramatically, to such an extent that MAI's profits would be cut by 75 percent per month. Just before the IBM maintenance price increase was announced, the defendants sold their MAI stock for $28 per share. After IBM publicly announced its price increase, MAI stock fell to $11 per share. A shareholder of the corporation (Diamond) brought a shareholder's derivative lawsuit in a New York state court on behalf of MAI to recover the profits the defendants had made by selling their shares at the higher price. The trial court granted the defendants' motion to dismiss, and Diamond appealed.

In the Words of the Court . . .
FULD, Chief Judge.

* * * *

Accepting the truth of the complaint's allegations, there is no question but that the defendants were guilty of withholding material information from the purchasers of the shares and, indeed, the defendants acknowledge that the facts asserted constitute a violation of rule 10b-5. * * * Of course, any individual purchaser, who could prove an injury as a result of a rule 10b-5 violation can bring his own action for rescission but we have not been referred to a single case in which such an action has been successfully prosecuted where the public sale of securities is involved. The reason for this is that sales of securities, whether through a stock exchange or over-the-counter, are characteristically anonymous transactions, usually handled through brokers, and the matching of the ultimate buyer with the ultimate seller presents virtually insurmountable obstacles. * * *

In view of the practical difficulties inherent in an action under the Federal law, the desirability of creating an effective common-law remedy is manifest. * * * There is ample room in a situation such as is here presented for a "private Attorney General" to come forward and enforce proper behavior on the part of corporate officials through the medium of the derivative action brought in the name of the corporation. Only by sanctioning such a cause of action will there be any effective method to prevent the type of abuse of corporate office complained of in this case.

Decision and Remedy The court of appeals held that when corporate fiduciaries have breached their duty to the corporation by the use of nonpublic information, a shareholder may bring a derivative action for any profit resulting from the breach of duty.

For Critical Analysis—Economic Consideration *What is the difference between a suit brought by an individual investor-shareholder and a shareholder's derivative suit? (HINT: Review the discussion of the shareholder's derivative suit in Chapter 16.)*

DISCLOSURE UNDER SEC RULE 10b-5 Any material omission or misrepresentation of material facts in connection with the purchase or sale of a security may violate not only Section 11 of the Securities Act of 1933 but also the antifraud provisions of Section 10(b) and SEC Rule 10b-5 of the 1934 act. The key to liability (which can be civil or criminal) under Section 10(b) and SEC Rule 10b-5 is whether the insider's information is *material*. The following are some examples of material facts calling for a disclosure under the rule:

1. A new ore discovery.
2. Fraudulent trading in the company stock by a broker-dealer.
3. A dividend change (whether up or down).
4. A contract for the sale of corporate assets.
5. A new discovery (process or product).
6. A significant change in the firm's financial condition.

Ironically, one of the effects of SEC Rule 10b-5 was to deter the disclosure of material information. • **Example 24.1** A company announces that its projected earnings in a certain time period will be X amount. It turns out that the forecast is wrong. The earnings are in fact much lower, and the price of the company's stock is affected—negatively. The shareholders then bring a class-action suit against the company, alleging that the directors violated SEC Rule 10b-5 by disclosing misleading financial information.• (Online disclosures can create similar problems—see this chapter's *Legal E-nvironment* feature on page 701 for details.)

In an attempt to rectify this problem and promote disclosure, Congress passed the Private Securities Litigation Reform Act of 1995. Among other things, the act provides a "safe harbor" for publicly held companies that make forward-looking statements, such as financial forecasts. Those who make such statements are protected against liability for securities fraud as long as the statements are accompanied by "meaningful cautionary statements identifying important factors that could cause actual results to differ materially from those in the forward-looking statement."[17]

The following is one of the landmark cases interpreting SEC Rule 10b-5. The SEC sued Texas Gulf Sulphur Company for issuing a misleading press release. The release underestimated the magnitude and the value of a mineral discovery. The SEC also sued several of Texas Gulf Sulphur's directors, officers, and employees under SEC Rule 10b-5 for purchasing large amounts of the corporate stock prior to the announcement of the corporation's rich ore discovery.

> **"There are three kinds of lies: lies, damned lies, and statistics."**
>
> Benjamin Disraeli, 1804–1881
> (British prime minister, 1868, 1874–1880)

---

17. 15 U.S.C. Sections 77z-2, 78u-5.

Case 24.2 ● SEC v. Texas Gulf Sulphur Co.

United States Court of Appeals,
Second Circuit, 1968.
401 F.2d 833.

Historical and Environmental Setting *No court has ever held that every buyer or seller is entitled to all of the information relating to all of the circumstances in every stock transaction. By the mid-1950s, however, significant understatement of the value of the assets of a company had been held to be materially misleading.[a] In 1957, the Texas Gulf Sulphur Company (TGS) began exploring for minerals in eastern Canada. In March 1959, aerial geophysical surveys were conducted over more than fifteen thousand square miles of the area. The operations*

---

a. *Speed v. Transamerica* Corp., 99 F.Supp. 808 (D.Del. 1951).

(Continued)

Case 24.2 Continued

revealed numerous and extraordinary variations in the conductivity of the rock, which indicated a remarkable concentration of commercially exploitable minerals. One site of such variations was near Timmins, Ontario. On October 29 and 30, 1963, a ground survey of the site near Timmins indicated a need to drill for further evaluation.

Background and Facts The Texas Gulf Sulphur Company drilled a hole on November 12, 1963, that appeared to yield a core with an exceedingly high mineral content. TGS kept secret the results of the core sample. Officers and employees of the company made substantial purchases of TGS's stock or accepted stock options after learning of the ore discovery, even though further drilling was necessary to establish whether there was enough ore to be mined commer-

cially. On April 11, 1964, an unauthorized report of the mineral find appeared in the newspapers. On the following day, April 12, TGS issued a press release that played down the discovery and stated that it was too early to tell whether the ore finding would be a significant one. Later on, TGS announced a strike of at least twenty-five million tons of ore, substantially driving up the price of TGS stock. The SEC brought suit in a federal district court against the officers and employees of TGS for violating the insider-trading prohibition of SEC Rule 10b-5. The officers and employees argued that the prohibition did not apply. They reasoned that the information on which they had traded was not material, as the mine had not been commercially proved. The court held that most of the defendants had not violated SEC Rule 10b-5, and the SEC appealed.

In the Words of the Court . . .
WATERMAN, Circuit Judge.

* * * *

* * * [W]hether facts are material within Rule 10b-5 when the facts relate to a particular event and are undisclosed by those persons who are knowledgeable thereof will depend at any given time upon a balancing of both the indicated probability that the event will occur and the anticipated magnitude of the event in light of the totality of the company activity. Here, * * * knowledge of the possibility, which surely was more than marginal, of the existence of a mine of the vast magnitude indicated by the remarkably rich drill core located rather close to the surface (suggesting mineability by the less expensive openpit method) within the confines of a large anomaly (suggesting an extensive region of mineralization) might well have affected the price of TGS stock and would certainly have been an important fact to a reasonable * * * investor in deciding whether he should buy, sell, or hold. After all, this first drill core was "unusually good and * * * excited the interest and speculation of those who knew about it."

* * * *

* * * [A] major factor in determining whether the * * * discovery was a material fact is the importance attached to the drilling results by those who knew about it. * * * [T]he timing by those who knew of it of their stock purchases and their purchases of *short-term* calls [rights to buy shares at a specified price within a specified time period]—purchases in some cases by individuals who had never before purchased calls or even TGS stock—virtually compels the inference that the insiders were influenced by the drilling results.

* * * *

We hold, therefore, that all transactions in TGS stock or calls by individuals apprised of the drilling results * * * were made in violation of Rule 10b-5.

Decision and Remedy The U.S. Court of Appeals for the Second Circuit ruled in favor of the SEC. All of the trading by insiders who knew of the mineral find violated Rule 10b-5.

For Critical Analsis—Economic Consideration *Who is hurt by insider trading?*

Legal *e*-nvironment

Online Securities Offerings and Disclosures

We have emphasized elsewhere in this text how technological advances have affected business practices, as well as the law governing those practices. Not surprisingly, technology is also affecting practices in the securities industry—and securities law. Corporations are using the Internet to communicate information to the Securities and Exchange Commission (SEC), shareholders, potential investors, and others. Indeed, the SEC has changed or modified a number of its rules to encourage online filings of securities documents, including prospectuses.

Investors, in turn, can now use the Internet to access information that can help them make informed decisions. At the SEC's Web site (at **http://www.sec.gov**), for example, investors and others can view new SEC rules, recent announcements, enforcement actions, and the EDGAR (Electronic Data Gathering, Analysis, and Retrieval) database. This database includes initial public offerings, proxy statements, annual corporate reports, registration statements, and other documents that have been filed with the SEC. EDGAR also provides public access to information regarding securities trading suspensions and current class-action suits for securities fraud.

Online Securities Offerings

In 1996, when the SEC allowed Spring Street Brewing Company to trade its shares via its Web site without registering as a broker-dealer, many people looked to the Internet as the stock market of tomorrow. It appears, however, that we are going to have to wait a few more years for that to take place. Although many other companies have taken advantage of the SEC's "green light" and offered stock directly to the public over the Internet, there have been no great success stories so far. No doubt, this will soon change as more and more established firms begin to use the Internet to publish prospectuses.

To date, offerings by small, nonpublic companies have been limited in scope, mainly because of regulatory restraints. To a large extent, any company wishing to make an initial public offering (IPO) of securities over the Internet has to comply with filing requirements dictated by federal and state law. Such filings are costly and time consuming. Typically, only those companies that are exempt from registration requirements have gone to the Internet to raise capital. Another problem relates to the lack of secondary markets for IPO shares sold directly on the Internet.

Online Disclosures

Virtually all major companies today have Web sites on which they post a variety of information, including forward-looking statements, press releases, and the like. If any of this information is misleading, a firm may face liability under securities laws for violating the SEC's disclosure requirements.

For example, suppose that a company posts a press release on its Web site stating that its earnings for 2001 were $300 million and that the company expects to double those earnings in 2002. In June of 2002, the company learns that its 2001 earnings were, in fact, only $200 million and that the earnings could not possibly climb to $600 million in 2002. Further suppose that the company does not remove the former statement, which is now misleading, from its Web site. In this situation, the company would face potential liability for violating the disclosure requirements of the Securities Exchange Act of 1934.

A company also may face potential liability for misleading reports by securities analysts and magazine articles that are hyperlinked to the company's Web site. Even though the information may have been accurate when it was published, a viewer might reasonably rely on the information after it becomes outdated—and the company, by hyperlinking the materials to its Web page, could be held liable for violating SEC disclosure requirements.

For Critical Analysis: *The SEC has initiated enforcement actions against issuers of securities, holding them responsible for false or misleading information disseminated online through third party analyst reports, even though the issuer did not participate in preparing the information. Is this fair?*

APPLICABILITY OF SEC RULE 10b-5 SEC Rule 10b-5 applies in virtually all cases concerning the trading of securities, whether on organized exchanges, in over-the-counter markets, or in private transactions. The rule covers notes, bonds, certificates of interest and participation in any profit-sharing agreement, agreements to form a corporation, and joint-venture agreements; in short, it covers just about any form of security. It is immaterial whether a firm has securities registered under the 1933 act for the 1934 act to apply.

Although SEC Rule 10b-5 is applicable only when the requisites of federal jurisdiction—such as the use of the mails, of stock exchange facilities, or of any instrumentality of interstate commerce—are present, virtually no commercial transaction can be completed without such contact. In addition, the states have corporate securities laws, many of which include provisions similar to SEC Rule 10b-5.

OUTSIDERS AND SEC RULE 10b-5   The traditional insider-trading case involves true insiders—corporate officers, directors, and majority shareholders who have access to (and trade on) inside information. Increasingly, liability under Section 10(b) of the 1934 act and SEC Rule 10b-5 has been extended to include certain "outsiders"—those persons who trade on inside information acquired indirectly. Two theories have been developed under which outsiders may be held liable for insider trading: the *tipper/tippee theory* and the *misappropriation theory*.

Tipper/Tippee Theory.   Anyone who acquires inside information as a result of a corporate insider's breach of his or her fiduciary duty can be liable under SEC Rule 10b-5. This liability extends to **tippees** (those who receive "tips" from insiders) and even remote tippees (tippees of tippees).

The key to liability under this theory is that the inside information be obtained as a result of someone's breach of a fiduciary duty to the corporation whose shares are involved in the trading. Unless there is a breach of a duty not to disclose inside information, the disclosure was in exchange for personal benefit, and the tippee knows of this breach (or should know of it) and benefits from it, there is no liability under this theory.[18] Is the offering of a tip as

> **Tippee**   A person who receives inside information.

---

18. See, for example, *Chiarella v. United States,* 445 U.S. 222, 100 S.Ct. 1108, 63 L.Ed.2d 348 (1980); and *Dirks v. SEC,* 463 U.S. 646, 103 S.Ct. 3255, 77 L.Ed.2d 911 (1983).

Ethical Issue 24.1

Should insider trading be legal?

SEC Rule 10b-5 has broad applicability. As will be discussed shortly, the rule covers not only corporate insiders but even "outsiders"—those who receive and trade on tips received from insiders. Investigating and prosecuting violations of SEC Rule 10b-5 is costly, both for the government and for those accused of insider trading. Some people doubt that such extensive regulation is necessary and even contend that insider trading should be legal. Would there

be any benefit from the legalization of insider trading? To evaluate this question, review the facts in *SEC v. Texas Gulf Sulphur* Co. (Case 24.2 in this chapter).

If insider trading were legal, the discovery of the ore sample would probably have caused many more company insiders to purchase stock. Consequently, the price of Texas Gulf's stock would have increased fairly quickly. These increases presumably would have attracted the attention of outside investors, who would have learned sooner that something positive had happened to the company and would thus have had the opportunity to purchase the stock. The higher demand for the stock would have more quickly translated into higher prices for the stock and hence, perhaps, a more efficient capital market.

a gift of profits to someone with whom the insider has a close relationship enough to infer that the insider realized a personal benefit? That was an issue in the following case.

Case 24.3 ● SEC v. Warde

United States Court of Appeals, Second Circuit, 1998.
151 F.3d 42.
http://www.tourolaw.edu/
2ndcircuit/July98ª

Historical and Social Setting *In 1983, the United States Supreme Court considered a case involving alleged insider trading by a financial analyst named Raymond Dirks. In that case, the Court held that for a recipient of material, nonpublic information to be liable for insider trading, the person who disclosed the information must benefit from the disclosure.*[b] *In subsequent cases, the Securities and Exchange Commission (SEC) often found it difficult to prove that the tipper benefited from passing on inside information.*

Background and Facts Edward Downe was a close friend of Fred Sullivan, chairman of Kidde, Inc.

a. This page provides access to opinions of the U.S. Court of Appeals for the Second Circuit decided in July 1998. Scroll down the list of cases to the *Warde* case and click on the link to access the opinion.
b. *Dirks v. SEC,* 463 U.S. 646, 103 S.Ct. 3255, 77 L.Ed.2d 911 (1983).

At Sullivan's request, Downe became a director of Kidde. Thomas Warde was a good friend of Downe. In June 1987, Sullivan learned that Kidde was the target of a takeover attempt by Hanson Trust PLC, a British firm. After negotiations, the Kidde board announced in August that it would merge with Hanson. The price of Kidde stock increased, and warrants for the shares, which had been priced at $1 in June, went to $26.50.[c] Between learning about the takeover attempt in June and the merger in August, Downe and Warde bought and sold warrants several times, earning very large profits. The SEC filed a suit in a federal district court against Warde and others, alleging insider trading in violation, in part, of Section 10(b). Warde contended that his purchases were based on market savvy, rumor, and public information. The jury found him liable. The court ordered him to pay more than $3 million in penalties and interest. Warde appealed to the U.S. Court of Appeals for the Second Circuit.

c. A *warrant* is an agreement to buy stock at a certain price before a certain date. If, before the warrant is exercised, the price goes up, the buyer profits. If the price never exceeds the level in the warrant, the warrant is worthless.

In the Words of the Court . . .
LEVAL, Circuit Judge:

* * * *

To affirm Warde's liability as a tippee * * * , we must find sufficient evidence to permit a reasonable finding that * * * Downe benefitted by the disclosure to Warde. * * *

* * * *

* * * [In *Dirks v. SEC,* 463 U.S. 646, 103 S.Ct. 3255, 77 L.Ed.2d 911 (1983), the United States] Supreme Court * * * made plain that to prove a Section 10(b) violation, the SEC need not show that the tipper expected or received a specific or tangible benefit in exchange for the tip. Rather, the "benefit" element of Section 10(b) is satisfied when the tipper "intend[s] to benefit the * * * recipient" or "makes a gift of confidential information to a trading relative or friend."

Under this standard, Downe clearly benefitted from Warde's inside trades. Warde's trades "resemble[d] trading by the insider himself followed by a gift of the profits to the recipient." The close friendship between Downe and Warde suggests that Downe's tip was "inten[ded] to benefit" Warde, and therefore allows a jury finding that Downe's tip breached a duty under Section 10(b).

(Continued)

Case 24.3 Continued

Decision and Remedy The U.S. Court of Appeals for the Second Circuit affirmed the lower court's decision, concluding that the SEC presented sufficient evidence to support every element necessary to hold Warde liable. Warde was ordered to pay the fines, with interest.

For Critical Analysis—Social Consideration *How does the decision in this case make it easier for the SEC to win in other insider-trading cases?*

Misappropriation Theory. Liability for insider trading may also be established under the misappropriation theory. This theory holds that if an individual wrongfully obtains (misappropriates) inside information and trades on it for his or her personal gain, then the individual should be held liable because, in essence, the individual stole information rightfully belonging to another.

The misappropriation theory has been controversial because it significantly extends the reach of SEC Rule 10b-5 to outsiders who would not ordinarily be deemed fiduciaries of the corporations in whose stock they trade. In the following case, the United States Supreme Court addressed the issue of whether liability under Rule 10b-5 can be based on the misappropriation theory.

Case 24.4 ● United States v. O'Hagan

Supreme Court of the United States, 1997.
521 U.S. 642,
117 S.Ct. 2199,
138 L.Ed.2d 724.
**http://supct.law.cornell.
edu/supct**[a]

Company Profile *The law firm of Dorsey & Whitney LLP (Limited Liability Partnership) was founded in 1912. Today, Dorsey & Whitney is one of the forty largest law firms in the United States, with more than five hundred lawyers and seven hundred support staff. The firm is based in Minneapolis, Minnesota, with offices in a dozen other U.S. cities and in London, Brussels, and Hong Kong. The firm's attorneys have included Harry Blackmun, a former United States Supreme Court justice, and Walter Mondale, a former vice president of the United States and ambassador to Japan. The firm is organized into two large groups,*

each of which is broken down into smaller "practice" groups. These smaller groups include "Mergers & Acquisitions," the members of which, according to the firm's Web site at **www.dorseylaw.com**, *"have extensive experience in all types of mergers and acquisitions work."*

Background and Facts James O'Hagan was a partner in the law firm of Dorsey & Whitney. Grand Metropolitan PLC (Grand Met), a United Kingdom firm, hired Dorsey & Whitney to assist in a takeover of the Pillsbury Company. Before Grand Met made its tender offer, O'Hagan bought shares of Pillsbury stock. When the tender offer was announced, the price of Pillsbury stock increased by more than 35 percent. O'Hagan sold his shares for a profit of over $4 million. The Securities and Exchange Commission (SEC) prosecuted O'Hagan for, among other things, securities fraud in violation of Rule 10b-5 under the misappropriation theory. The SEC contended that O'Hagan breached his fiduciary duties to his law firm and to Grand Met. When O'Hagan was convicted, he appealed to the U.S. Court of Appeals for the Eighth Circuit, which reversed the convictions. The SEC appealed to the United States Supreme Court.

a. This page provides access to some of the published opinions of the United States Supreme Court. In the right-hand column, in the "Arrayed by party name" list, in the "1997" row, click on "2nd party." When that page opens, find the *O'Hagan* case name and click on the link. From that page, click on the appropriate link to access the Court's opinion.

In the Words of the Court . . .
JUSTICE GINSBURG delivered the opinion of the Court.

* * * *

Case 24.4 Continued

> * * * [M]isappropriation * * * satisfies [Section] 10(b)'s requirement that chargeable conduct involve a "deceptive device or contrivance" used "in connection with" the purchase or sale of securities. * * * [M]isappropriators * * * deal in deception. A fiduciary who pretends loyalty to the principal while secretly converting the principal's information for personal gain dupes or defrauds the principal.
>
> * * * *
>
> * * * [T]he fiduciary's fraud is consummated * * * when, without disclosure to his principal, he uses the information to purchase or sell securities. * * *
>
> * * * *
>
> * * * An investor's informational disadvantage *vis-à-vis* a misappropriator with material, nonpublic information stems from contrivance, not luck; it is a disadvantage that cannot be overcome with research or skill.

Decision and Remedy The United States Supreme Court held that liability under Rule 10b-5 can be based on the misappropriation theory, reversed the judgment, and remanded the case.

For Critical Analysis—Ethical Consideration *If a nonlawyer employee of Dorsey & Whitney, such as a paralegal, learned about the tender offer and traded profitably on the inside information, could the employee be held liable under the misappropriation theory? Why or why not?*

Insider Reporting and Trading—Section 16(b)

Officers, directors, and certain large stockholders[19] of Section 12 corporations (corporations that are required to register their securities under Section 12 of the 1934 act) must file reports with the SEC concerning their ownership and trading of the corporations' securities.[20] To discourage such insiders from using nonpublic information about their companies for their personal benefit in the stock market, Section 16(b) of the 1934 act provides for the recapture by the corporation of all profits realized by an insider on any purchase and sale or sale and purchase of the corporation's stock within any six-month period.[21] It is irrelevant whether the insider actually uses inside information; all such short-swing profits must be returned to the corporation.

Section 16(b) applies not only to stock but to warrants, options, and securities convertible into stock. In addition, the courts have fashioned complex rules for determining profits. Corporate insiders are wise to seek specialized counsel prior to trading in the corporation's stock. Exhibit 24–3 on the next page compares the effects of SEC Rule 10b-5 and Section 16(b).

---

19. Those stockholders owning 10 percent of the class of equity securities registered under Section 12 of the 1934 act.
20. 15 U.S.C. Section 78*l*.
21. When a decline is predicted in the market for a particular stock, one can realize profits by "selling short"—selling at a high price and repurchasing later at a lower price to cover the "short sale."

Exhibit 24–3
Comparison of Coverage, Application, and Liabilities under SEC Rule 10b-5 and Section 16(b)

AREAS OF COMPARISON	SEC RULE 10b-5	SECTION 16(b)
What is the subject matter of the transaction?	Any security (does not have to be registered).	Any security (does not have to be registered).
What transactions are covered?	Purchase or sale.	Short-swing purchase and sale or short-swing sale and purchase.
Who is subject to liability?	Virtually anyone with inside information under a duty to disclose—including officers, directors, controlling stockholders, and tippees.	Officers, directors, and certain 10 percent stockholders.
Is omission or misrepresentation necessary for liability?	Yes.	No.
Are there any exempt transactions?	No.	Yes, there are a variety of exemptions.
Is direct dealing with the party necessary?	No.	No.
Who may bring an action?	A person transacting with an insider, the SEC, or a purchaser or seller damaged by a wrongful act.	A corporation or a shareholder by derivative action.

Proxy Statements

Section 14(a) of the Securities Exchange Act of 1934 regulates the solicitation of proxies from shareholders of Section 12 companies. The SEC regulates the content of proxy statements. A proxy statement is a statement that is sent to shareholders by corporate officials who are requesting authority to vote on behalf of the shareholders in a particular election on specified issues. Whoever solicits a proxy must fully and accurately disclose in the proxy statement all of the facts that are pertinent to the matter on which the shareholders are to vote. SEC Rule 14a-9 is similar to the antifraud provisions of SEC Rule 10b-5. Remedies for violation are extensive; they range from injunctions that prevent a vote from being taken to monetary damages.

Violations of the 1934 Act

Violations of Section 10(b) of the Securities Exchange Act of 1934 and SEC Rule 10b-5 include insider trading. This is a criminal offense, with criminal penalties. Violators of these laws may also be subject to civil liability. For any sanctions to be imposed, however, there must be *scienter*—the violator must have had an intent to defraud or knowledge of his or her misconduct. *Scienter* can be proved by showing that a defendant made false statements or wrong-fully failed to disclose material facts. (For a further discussion of *scienter* and liability for insider trading, see this chapter's *Inside the Legal Environment*.)

Violations of Section 16(b) include the sale by insiders of stock acquired less than six months before the sale. These violations are subject to civil sanctions. Liability under Section 16(b) is strict liability. *Scienter* is not required.

CRIMINAL PENALTIES For violations of Section 10(b) and Rule 10b-5, an individual may be fined up to $1 million, imprisoned for up to ten years, or both. A partnership or a corporation may be fined up to $2.5 million.

Inside the Legal Environment

Insider Trading: The Use-Possession Debate

An emerging issue in insider-trading cases has to do with the *scienter* requirement for insider-trading liability. As discussed elsewhere, *scienter* requires an intent to defraud or to deceive another. The question is this: Does the mere *possession* of inside information while trading in securities establish an intent to defraud, or must the trader actually *use* the inside information for intent to be established?

On one side of this possession-use debate are the government and the SEC, which have adopted the position that the intent to defraud can be inferred when a person trades in securities while in the possession of inside information. This position was bolstered by a 1993 case decided by the U.S. Court of Appeals for the Second Circuit, *United States v. Teicher*.[a] In that case, the court suggested that proof of the possession of inside information is "sufficient to sustain an insider-trading prosecution and that the government need not affirmatively prove that the investor used the information in formulating his trade." Among other things, the court noted that inside information has a subtle, and perhaps unconscious effect, on traders: "Unlike a loaded weapon which may stand ready but unused, material information cannot lay idle in the human brain."

On the other side of the debate are those who maintain that for liability for insider trading to be established, the government must show that the trading was actually based on the information. In *United States v. Smith*,[b] one of the few court decisions to squarely address this issue, the U.S. Court of Appeals for the Ninth Circuit came down firmly on the "use" side of the debate. The court noted that the Supreme Court, in its *O'Hagan* decision (see Case 24.4) as well as in earlier decisions,[c] stressed that a violation of Rule 10b-5 requires an intent to deceive or defraud investors. In the opinion of the Ninth Circuit, the SEC's "possession" standard was inconsistent with the Supreme Court's position because the standard was too broad—it extended beyond situations involving actual fraud. "For instance," said the court, "an investor who has a preexisting plan to trade, and who carries through with that plan after coming into possession of material nonpublic information, does not intend to defraud or deceive; he simply intends to implement his pre-possession financial strategy."

The Ninth Circuit stated that it did "not take lightly" the SEC's argument that a "use" requirement poses difficulties of proof. The court, however, concluded that the difficulties were not insurmountable and that various types of circumstantial evidence might be used to demonstrate use. "Suppose, for instance, that an individual who has never before invested comes into possession of material nonpublic information and the very next day invests a significant sum of money." The court was "confident that the government would have little trouble demonstrating 'use' in such a situation, or in other situations in which unique trading patterns or unusually large trading quantities suggest that an investor had used inside information."

For Critical Analysis: *Does anyone who unwittingly acquires inside information face a legal risk?*

a. 987 F.2d 112 (2d Cir. 1993).

b. 155 F.3d 1051 (9th Cir. 1998).

c. See, for example, *Dirks v. SEC*, 463 U.S. 646, 103 S.Ct. 3255, 77 L.Ed.2d 911 (1983).

CIVIL SANCTIONS Both the SEC and private parties can bring actions to seek civil sanctions against violators of the 1934 act.

The Insider Trading Sanctions Act of 1984 permits the SEC to bring suit in a federal district court against anyone violating or aiding in a violation of the 1934 act or SEC rules by purchasing or selling a security while in the possession of material nonpublic information.[22] The violation must occur on or through the facilities of a national securities exchange or from or through a broker or dealer. Transactions pursuant to a public offering by an issuer of securities are excepted. The court may assess as a penalty as much as triple the profits gained or the loss avoided by the guilty party. Profit or loss is defined as "the difference between the purchase or sale price of the security and the value of that security as measured by the trading price of the security at a reasonable period of time after public dissemination of the nonpublic information."[23]

The Insider Trading and Securities Fraud Enforcement Act of 1988 enlarged the class of persons who may be subject to civil liability for insider-trading violations. This act also gave the SEC authority to award **bounty payments** (rewards given by government officials for acts beneficial to the state) to persons providing information leading to the prosecution of insider-trading violations.[24]

Bounty Payment A reward (payment) given to a person or persons who perform a certain service—such as informing legal authorities of illegal actions.

Private parties may also sue violators of Section 10(b) and Rule 10b-5. A private party may obtain rescission of a contract to buy securities or damages to the extent of the violator's illegal profits. Those found liable have a right to seek contribution from those who share responsibility for the violations, including accountants, attorneys, and corporations.[25] For violations of Section 16(b), a corporation can bring an action to recover the short-swing profits.

The Expanded Powers of the SEC

From the time of its creation until the present, the SEC's regulatory functions have gradually been increased by legislation granting it authority in different areas. In the last decade, for example, Congress has passed several acts that have significantly expanded the SEC's powers.

To further curb securities fraud, the Securities Enforcement Remedies and Penny Stock Reform Act[26] of 1990 amended existing securities laws to expand greatly the types of securities violation cases that SEC administrative law judges can hear and the SEC's enforcement options. The act also provides that courts can bar persons who have engaged in securities fraud from serving as officers and directors of publicly held corporations.

The 1990 Securities Acts Amendments[27] authorized the SEC to seek sanctions against those who violate foreign securities laws. These amendments increase the ability of the SEC to cooperate in international securities law enforcement. Under the Market Reform Act of 1990,[28] the SEC can suspend

---

22. 15 U.S.C. Section 78u(d)(2)(A).
23. 15 U.S.C. Section 78u(d)(2)(C).
24. 15 U.S.C. Section 78u-1.
25. Note that a private cause of action under Section 10(b) and SEC Rule 10b-5 cannot be brought against accountants, attorneys, and others who "aid and abet" violations of the act. Only the SEC can bring actions against so-called aiders and abettors. See *SEC v. Fehn*, 97 F.3d 1276 (9th Cir. 1996).
26. 15 U.S.C. Section 77g.
27. 15 U.S.C. Section 78a.
28. 15 U.S.C. Section 78i(h).

trading in securities in the event that the prices rise and fall excessively in a short period of time.

The National Securities Markets Improvement Act of 1996 expanded the power of the SEC to exempt persons, securities, and transactions from the requirements of the securities laws.[29] (This part of the act is also known as the Capital Markets Efficiency Act.) The act also limited the authority of the states to regulate certain securities transactions, as well as certain investment advisory firms.[30]

Currently, both Congress and the SEC are in the process of making fundamental changes in the regulatory framework applying to securities transactions. Over the years, as more and more SEC rules were issued, the body of regulations governing securities transactions became increasingly cumbersome and complex. Congress and the SEC are eliminating some rules, revising others, and generally attempting to streamline the regulatory process to make it more efficient and more relevant to today's securities trading practices. The SEC is also making it easy for the public to access information on securities law and trading by posting such information on its Web site.

The Regulation of Investment Companies

Investment companies, and mutual funds in particular, grew rapidly after World War II. **Investment companies** act on behalf of many smaller shareholders by buying a large portfolio of securities and professionally managing that portfolio. A **mutual fund** is a specific type of investment company that continually buys or sells to investors shares of ownership in a portfolio. Such companies are regulated by the Investment Company Act of 1940,[31] which provides for SEC regulation of their activities. The act was expanded by the 1970 amendments to the Investment Company Act. Further minor changes were made in the Securities Act Amendments of 1975 and in later years.

The 1940 act requires that every investment company register with the SEC and imposes restrictions on the activities of these companies and persons connected with them. For the purposes of the act, an investment company is defined as any entity that (1) is engaged primarily "in the business of investing, reinvesting, or trading in securities" or (2) is engaged in such business and has more than 40 percent of its assets in investment securities. Excluded from coverage by the act are banks, insurance companies, savings and loan associations, finance companies, oil and gas drilling firms, charitable foundations, tax-exempt pension funds, and other special types of institutions, such as closely held corporations.

All investment companies must register with the SEC by filing a notification of registration. Each year, registered investment companies must file reports with the SEC. To safeguard company assets, all securities must be held in the custody of a bank or stock exchange member, and that bank or stock exchange member must follow strict procedures established by the SEC.

No dividends may be paid from any source other than accumulated, undistributed net income. Furthermore, there are some restrictions on investment activities. For example, investment companies are not allowed to purchase securities on the margin (pay only part of the total price, borrowing the rest), sell short (sell shares not yet owned), or participate in joint trading accounts.

Investment Company A company that acts on behalf of many smaller shareholders/owners by buying a large portfolio of securities and professionally managing that portfolio.

Mutual Fund A specific type of investment company that continually buys or sells to investors shares of ownership in a portfolio.

---

29. 15 U.S.C. Sections 77z-3, 78mm.
30. 15 U.S.C. Section 80b-3a.
31. 15 U.S.C. Sections 80a-1 to 64.

State Securities Laws

Today, all states have their own corporate securities laws, or "blue sky laws," that regulate the offer and sale of securities within individual state borders.[32] (The phrase *blue sky laws* dates to a 1917 decision by the United States Supreme Court in which the Court declared that the purpose of such laws was to prevent "speculative schemes which have no more basis than so many feet of 'blue sky.' ")[33] Article 8 of the Uniform Commercial Code, which has been adopted by all of the states, also imposes various requirements relating to the purchase and sale of securities. State securities laws apply only to intrastate transactions. Since the adoption of the 1933 and 1934 federal securities acts, the state and federal governments have regulated securities concurrently. Issuers must comply with both federal and state securities laws, and exemptions from federal law are not exemptions from state laws.

There are differences in philosophy among state statutes, but certain features are common to all state blue sky laws. Typically, state laws have disclosure requirements and antifraud provisions, many of which are patterned after Section 10(b) of the Securities Exchange Act of 1934 and SEC Rule 10b-5. State laws also provide for the registration or qualification of securities offered or issued for sale within the state and impose disclosure requirements. Unless an applicable exemption from registration is found, issuers must register or qualify their stock with the appropriate state official, often called a *corporations commissioner.* Additionally, most state securities laws regulate securities brokers and dealers. The Uniform Securities Act, which has been adopted in part by several states, was drafted to be acceptable to states with differing regulatory philosophies.

---

32. These laws are catalogued and annotated in the *Blue Sky Law Reports,* a loose-leaf service provided by CCH, Inc.
33. *Hall v. Geiger-Jones Co.,* 242 U.S. 539, 37 S.Ct. 217, 61 L.Ed. 480 (1917).

Key Terms

accredited investor 694	mutual fund 709	tippee 702
bounty payment 708	red herring 692	tombstone ad 692
insider trading 697	SEC Rule 10b-5 697	
investment company 709	security 690	

Chapter Summary • Investor Protection

The Securities Act of 1933
(See pages 690–697.)

Prohibits fraud and stabilizes the securities industry by requiring disclosure of all essential information relating to the issuance of stocks to the investing public.

1. **Registration requirements**—Securities, unless exempt, must be registered with the SEC before being offered to the public through the mails or any facility of interstate commerce (including securities exchanges). The *registration statement* must include detailed financial information about the issuing corporation; the intended use of the proceeds of the securities being issued; and certain disclosures, such as interests of directors or officers and pending lawsuits.

Chapter Summary • Investor Protection

The Securities Act of 1933 —continued	2. **Prospectus**—A *prospectus* must be provided to investors, describing the security being sold, the issuing corporation, and the risk attaching to the security.
	3. **Exemptions**—The SEC has exempted certain offerings from the requirements of the Securities Act of 1933. Exemptions may be determined on the basis of the size of the issue, whether the offering is private or public, and whether advertising is involved. Exemptions are summarized in Exhibit 24–1.
The Securities Exchange Act of 1934 (See pages 697–708.)	Provides for the regulation and registration of securities exchanges, brokers, dealers, and national securities associations (such as the NASD). Maintains a continuous disclosure system for all corporations with securities on the securities exchanges and for those companies that have assets in excess of $5 million and five hundred or more shareholders (Section 12 companies).
	1. **SEC Rule 10b-5 [under Section 10(b) of the 1934 act]**—
	a. Applies to insider trading by corporate officers, directors, majority shareholders, and any persons receiving information not available to the public who base their trading on this information.
	b. Liability for violation can be civil or criminal.
	c. May be violated by failing to disclose "material facts" that must be disclosed under this rule.
	d. Applies in virtually all cases concerning the trading of securities—a firm does not have to have its securities registered under the 1933 act for the 1934 act to apply.
	e. Liability may be based on the tipper-tippee or misappropriation theory.
	f. Applies only when the requisites of federal jurisdiction (such as use of the mails, stock exchange facilities, or any facility of interstate commerce) are present.
	2. **Insider trading [under Section 16(b) of the 1934 act]**—To prevent corporate officers and directors from taking advantage of inside information (information not available to the investing public), the 1934 act requires officers, directors, and shareholders owning 10 percent or more of the issued stock of a corporation to turn over to the corporation all short-term profits (called short-swing profits) realized from the purchase and sale or sale and purchase of corporate stock within any six-month period.
	3. **Proxies [under Section 14(a) of the 1934 act]**—The SEC regulates the content of proxy statements sent to shareholders by corporate managers of Section 12 companies who are requesting authority to vote on behalf of the shareholders in a particular election on specified issues. Section 14(a) is essentially a disclosure law, with provisions similar to the antifraud provisions of SEC Rule 10b-5.
Regulation of Investment Companies (See page 709.)	The Investment Company Act of 1940 provides for SEC regulation of investment company activities. It was altered and expanded by the amendments of 1970 and 1975.
State Securities Laws (See page 710.)	All states have corporate securities laws (*blue sky laws*) that regulate the offer and sale of securities within state borders; designed to prevent "speculative schemes which have no more basis than so many feet of 'blue sky.'" States regulate securities concurrently with the federal government.

For Review

1. What is the essential purpose of the Securities Act of 1933? What is the essential purpose of the Securities Exchange Act of 1934?

2. What is a registration statement? What must a registration statement include? What is a prospectus?

3. Basically, what constitutes a security under the Securities Act of 1933?

4. What is SEC Rule 10b-5? What is the key to liability under this rule? To what kinds of transactions does SEC Rule 10b-5 apply?

5. Discuss two theories under which "outsiders" can be held liable for violating SEC Rule 10b-5.

Questions and Case Problems

24–1. Registration Requirements. Langley Brothers, Inc., a corporation incorporated and doing business in Kansas, decides to sell no-par common stock worth $1 million to the public. The stock will be sold only within the state of Kansas. Joseph Langley, the chairman of the board, says the offering need not be registered with the SEC. His brother, Harry, disagrees. Who is right? Explain.

24–2. Registration Requirements. Huron Corp. had 300,000 common shares outstanding. The owners of these outstanding shares lived in several different states. Huron decided to split the 300,000 shares two for one. Will Huron Corp. have to file a registration statement and prospectus on the 300,000 new shares to be issued as a result of the split? Explain.

24–3. Definition of a Security. The W. J. Howey Co. (Howey) owned large tracts of citrus acreage in Lake County, Florida. For several years, it planted about five hundred acres annually, keeping half of the groves itself and offering the other half to the public to help finance additional development. Howey-in-the-Hills Service, Inc., was a service company engaged in cultivating and developing these groves, including the harvesting and marketing of the crops. Each prospective customer was offered both a land sales contract and a service contract, after being told that it was not feasible to invest in a grove unless service arrangements were made. Of the acreage sold by Howey, 85 percent was sold with a service contract with Howey-in-the-Hills Service. Howey did not register with the SEC or meet the other administrative requirements that issuers of securities must fulfill. The SEC sued to enjoin Howey from continuing to offer the land sales and service contracts. Howey responded that no SEC violation existed, because no securities had been issued. Evaluate the definition of a security given in this chapter, and then determine which party should prevail in court, Howey or the SEC. [*SEC v. W. J. Howey Co.*, 328 U.S. 293, 66 S.Ct. 1100, 90 L.Ed. 1244 (1946)]

24–4. Definition of a Security. U.S. News & World Report, Inc., set up a profit-sharing plan in 1962 that allotted to certain employees specially issued stock known as bonus or anniversary stock. The stock was given to the employees for past services and could not be traded or sold to anyone other than the corporate issuer, U.S. News. This special stock was issued only to employees and for no other purpose than as bonuses. Because there was no market for the stock, U.S. News hired an independent appraiser to estimate the fair value of the stock so that the employees could redeem the shares. Charles Foltz and several other employees held stock through this plan and sought to redeem the shares with U.S. News, but Foltz disputed the value set by the appraisers. Foltz sued U.S. News for violation of securities regulations. What defense would allow U.S. News to resist successfully Foltz's claim? [*Foltz v. U.S. News & World Report, Inc.*, 627 F.Supp. 1143 (D.D.C. 1986)]

24–5. Short-Swing Profits. Emerson Electric Co. purchased 13.2 percent of Dodge Manufacturing Co.'s stock in an unsuccessful takeover attempt in June 1967. Less than six months later, when Dodge merged with Reliance Electric Co., Emerson decided to sell its shares. To avoid being subject to the short-swing profit restrictions of Section 16(b) of the Securities Exchange Act of 1934, Emerson decided on a two-step selling plan. First, it sold off sufficient shares to reduce its holdings to 9.96 percent [owners with less than 10 percent are exempt from Section 16(b)], and then it sold the remaining stock—all within a six-month period. Emerson in this way succeeded in avoiding Section 16(b) requirements. Reliance demanded that Emerson return the profits made on both sales. Emerson sought a declaratory judgment from the court that it was not liable, arguing that because at the time of the second sale it had not owned 10 percent of Dodge stock, Section 16(b) did not apply. Does Section 16(b) of the Securities Exchange Act of 1934 apply to Emerson's transactions, and is Emerson liable to Reliance for its profits? Discuss fully. [*Reliance Electric Co. v. Emerson Electric Co.,* 404 U.S. 418, 92 S.Ct. 596, 30 L.E.2d 575 (1972)]

24–6. SEC Rule 10b-5. In early 1985, FMC Corp. made plans to buy some of its own stock as part of a restructuring of its balance statement. Unknown to FMC management, the brokerage firm FMC employed—Goldman, Sachs & Co.—disclosed information on the stock purchase that found its way to Ivan Boesky. FMC was one of the seven major corporations in whose stock Boesky allegedly traded using inside information. Boesky made purchases of FMC's stock between February 18 and February 21, 1986, and between March 12 and April 4, 1986. Boesky's purchases amounted to a substantial portion of the total volume of FMC stock traded during these periods. The price of FMC stock increased from $71.25 on February 20, 1986, to $97.00 on April 25, 1986. As a result, FMC paid substantially more for the repurchase of its own stock than anticipated. When FMC discovered Boesky's knowledge of its recapitalization plan, FMC sued Boesky for the excess price it had paid—approximately $220 million. Discuss whether FMC should recover under Section 10(b) of the Securities Exchange Act and SEC Rule 10b-5. [*In re Ivan F. Boesky Securities Litigation,* 36 F.3d 255 (2d Cir. 1994)]

24–7. SEC Rule 10b-5. Louis Ferraro was the chairman and president of Anacomp, Inc. In June 1988, Ferraro told his good friend Michael Maio that Anacomp was negotiating a tender offer for stock in Xidex Corp. Maio passed on the information to Patricia Ladavac, a friend of both Ferraro and Maio. Maio and Ladavac immediately purchased shares in Xidex stock. On the day that the tender offer was announced—an announcement that caused the price of Xidex shares to increase—Maio and Ladavac sold their Xidex stock and made substantial profits (Maio made $211,000 from the transactions, and Ladavac gained $78,750). The SEC brought an action against the three individuals, alleging that they had violated, among other laws, SEC Rule 10b-5. Maio and Ladavac claimed that they had done nothing illegal. They argued that they had no fiduciary duty either to Anacomp or to Xidex, and therefore had no duty to disclose or abstain from trading in the stock of those corporations. Had Maio and Ladavac violated SEC Rule 10b-5? Discuss fully. [*SEC v. Maio,* 51 F.3d 623 (7th Cir. 1995)]

24–8. Section 10(b). Joseph Jett worked for Kidder, Peabody & Co., a financial services firm owned by General Electric Co. (GE). Over a three-year period, Jett allegedly engaged in a scheme to generate false profits at Kidder, Peabody to increase his performance-based bonuses. When the scheme was discovered, Daniel Chill and other GE shareholders who had bought stock in the previous year filed a suit in a federal district court against GE. The shareholders alleged that GE had engaged in securities fraud in violation of Section 10(b). They claimed

that GE's interest in justifying its investment in Kidder, Peabody gave GE "a motive to willfully blind itself to facts casting doubt on Kidder's purported profitability." On what basis might the court dismiss the shareholders' complaint? Discuss fully. [*Chill v. General Electric Co.,* 101 F.3d 263 (2d Cir. 1996)]

24–9. SEC Rule 10b-5. Grand Metropolitan PLC (Grand Met) planned to make a tender offer as part of an attempted takeover of the Pillsbury Company. Grand Met hired Robert Falbo, an independent contractor, to complete electrical work as part of security renovations to its offices to prevent leaks of information concerning the planned tender offer. Falbo was given a master key to access the executive offices. When an executive secretary told Falbo that a takeover was brewing, he used his key to access the offices and eavesdrop on conversations to learn that Pillsbury was the target. Falbo bought thousands of shares of Pillsbury stock for less than $40 per share. Within two months, Grand Met made an offer for all outstanding Pillsbury stock at $60 per share and ultimately paid up to $66 per share. Falbo made over $165,000 in profits. The Securities and Exchange Commission (SEC) filed a suit in a federal district court against Falbo and others for alleged violations of, among other things, SEC Rule 10b-5. Under what theory might Falbo be liable? Do the circumstances of this case meet all of the requirements for liability under that theory? Explain. [*SEC v. Falbo,* 14 F.Supp.2d 508 (S.D.N.Y. 1998)]

24–10. Definition of a Security. In 1997, Scott and Sabrina Levine formed Friendly Power Co. (FPC) and Friendly Power Franchise Co. (FPC-Franchise). FPC obtained a license to operate as a utility company in California. FPC granted FPC-Franchise the right to pay commissions to "operators" who converted residential customers to FPC. Each operator paid for a "franchise"—a geographic area, determined by such factors as the number of households and competition from other utilities. In exchange for 50 percent of FPC's net profits on sales to residential customers in its territory, each franchise was required to maintain a 5 percent market share of power customers in that territory. Franchises were sold to telemarketing firms, which solicited customers. The telemarketers sold interests in each franchise to between fifty and ninety-four "partners," each of whom invested money. FPC began supplying electricity to its customers in May 1998. Less than three months later, the Securities and Exchange Commission (SEC) filed a suit in a federal district court against the Levines and others, alleging that the "franchises" were unregistered securities offered for sale to the public in violation of the Securities Act of 1933. What is the definition of a security? Should the court rule in favor of the SEC? Why or why not? [*SEC v. Friendly Power Co., LLC,* 49 F.Supp.2d 1363 (S.D.Fla. 1999)]

A Question of Ethics and Social Responsibility

24–11. Susan Waldbaum was a niece of the president and controlling shareholder of Waldbaum, Inc. Susan's mother (the president's sister) told Susan that the company was going to be sold at a favorable price and that a tender offer was soon to be made. She told Susan not to tell anyone except her husband, Keith Loeb, about the sale. (Loeb did not work for the company and was never brought into the family's inner circle, in which family members discussed confidential business information.) The next day, Susan told her husband of the sale and cautioned him not to tell anyone, because "it could possibly ruin the sale." The day after he learned of the sale, Loeb told Robert Chestman, his broker, about the sale, and Chestman purchased shares of the company for both Loeb and himself. Chestman was later convicted by a jury of, among other things, trading on misappropri-

ated inside information in violation of SEC Rule 10b-5. [*United States v. Chestman,* 947 F.2d 551 (2d Cir. 1991)]

1. On appeal, the central question was whether Chestman had acquired the inside information about the tender offer as a result of an insider's breach of a fiduciary duty. Could Loeb—the "tipper" in this case—be considered an insider?
2. If Loeb was not an insider, did he owe any fiduciary (legal) duty to his wife or his wife's family to keep the information confidential? Would it be fair of the court to impose such a legal duty on Loeb?

For Critical Analysis

24–12. Do you think that the tipper/tippee and misappropriation theories extend liability under SEC Rule 10b-5 too far? Why or why not?

Interacting with the Internet

■ For updated links to resources available on the Web, as well as a variety of other materials, visit this text's Web site at

http://leet.westbuslaw.com

■ To access the SEC's EDGAR database, go to

http://www.sec.gov/edgarhp.htm

■ The Center for Corporate Law at the University of Cincinnati College of Law examines all of the acts discussed in this chapter. Go to

http://www.law.uc.edu/CCL

■ To find the Securities Act of 1933, go to

http://www.law.uc.edu/CCL/33Act/index.html

■ To examine the Securities Exchange Act of 1934, go to

http://www.law.uc.edu/CCL/34Act/index.html

■ For information on investor protection and securities fraud, including answers to frequently asked questions on the topic of securities fraud, go to

http://www.securieslaw.com

Online Legal Research Exercises

Go to **http://leet.westbuslaw.com**, the Web site that accompanies this text. Select "Interactive Study Center," and then click on "Chapter 24." There you will find the following Internet research exercise that you can perform to learn more about the SEC:

Activity 24–1: The SEC's Role

Before the Test

Go to **http://leet.westbuslaw.com**, the Web site that accompanies this text. Select "Interactive Quizzes." You will find a number of interactive questions relating to this chapter.

Unit V **Cumulative Hypothetical Problem**

Falwell Motors, Inc., is a large corporation that manufactures automobile batteries.

1. The Federal Trade Commission (FTC) learns that one of the retail stores that sells Falwell's batteries engages in deceptive advertising practices. What actions can the FTC take against the retailer?

2. For years, Falwell has shipped the toxic waste created by its manufacturing process to a waste-disposal site in the next county. The waste site has become contaminated by leakage from toxic waste containers delivered to the site by other manufacturers. Can Falwell be held liable for clean-up costs, even though its containers were not the ones that leaked? If so, what is the extent of its liability?

3. Falwell faces stiff competition from Alchem, Inc., another battery manufacturer. To acquire control over Alchem, Falwell makes a tender offer to Alchem's shareholders. If Falwell succeeds in its attempt and Alchem is merged into Falwell, will the merger violate any antitrust laws? Suppose the merger falls through. The vice president of Falwell's battery division and the president of Alchem agree to divide up the market between them, so they will not have to compete for customers. In this agreement legal? Explain.

4. One of Falwell's employees learns that Falwell is contemplating a takeover of a rival. The employee tells her husband about the possibility. The husband calls their broker, who purchases shares in the target corporation for the employee and her husband, as well as for himself. Has the employee violated any securities law? Has her husband? Has the broker? Explain.

The International Environment

The Regulation of International Transactions

chapter objectives

After reading this chapter, you should be able to:

1. Identify and discuss some basic principles and doctrines that frame international business transactions.

2. Describe some ways in which U.S. businesspersons do business internationally.

3. Explain how parties to international contracts protect against various risks through contractual clauses and letters of credit.

4. Discuss how specific types of international business activities are regulated by governments.

5. Give examples of the extraterritorial application of certain U.S. laws.

Since ancient times, independent peoples and nations have traded their goods and wares with one another. In other words, international business transactions are not unique to the modern world, because people have always found that they can benefit from exchanging goods with others, as suggested by President Woodrow Wilson's statement in the opening quotation. What is new in our time is that, particularly since World War II, business has become increasingly *multinational*. It is not uncommon, for example, for a U.S. corporation to have investments or manufacturing plants in a foreign country, or for a foreign corporation to have operations within the United States.

Transacting business on an international level is considerably different from transacting business within the boundaries of just one nation. Buyers and sellers face far greater risks in the international marketplace than they do in a domestic context because the laws governing these transactions are more complex and uncertain. For example, the Uniform Commercial Code will govern many disputes that arise between U.S. buyers and sellers of goods unless they have provided otherwise in their contracts. What happens, however, if a U.S. buyer breaches a contract formed with a British seller? What law will govern the dispute—British or American? What if an investor owns substantial assets in a developing nation and the government of that nation decides to nationalize—assert its ownership over—the property? What recourse does the investor have against the actions of a foreign government? Questions such as these, which normally do not arise in a domestic context, can become critical in international business dealings.

Because the exchange of goods, services, and ideas on a global level is now a common activity, the student of business law should be familiar with the laws pertaining to international business transactions. In this chapter, we first examine the legal context of international business transactions. We then look at some selected areas relating to business activities in a global context, including international sales contracts, civil dispute resolution, letters of credit, and investment protection. We conclude the chapter with a discussion of the application of certain U.S. laws in a transnational setting.

> "Our interests are those of the open door—a door of friendship and mutual advantage. This is the only door we care to enter."
>
> Woodrow Wilson, 1856–1924
> (Twenty-eighth president of the United States, 1913–1921)

International Principles and Doctrines

Recall from our discussion in Chapter 1 that *international law* is a body of written and unwritten laws that are observed by otherwise independent nations and that govern the acts of individuals as well as states. The major sources of international law include international customs, treaties between nations, and international organizations and conferences. *National law*—consisting of the laws of particular nations (see Chapter 1)—also plays an important role in the international legal landscape. In this section, we look at some legal principles and doctrines that have evolved over time and that the courts of various nations have employed—to a greater or lesser extent—to resolve or reduce conflicts that involve a foreign element. The three important legal principles and doctrines discussed in the following sections are based primarily on courtesy and respect and are applied in the interests of maintaining harmonious relations among nations.

The Principle of Comity

Under what is known as the principle of **comity,** one nation will defer and give effect to the laws and judicial decrees of another country, as long as those laws

Comity A deference by which one nation gives effect to the laws and judicial decrees of another nation. This recognition is based primarily on respect.

and judicial decrees are consistent with the law and public policy of the accommodating nation. This recognition is based primarily on courtesy and respect.

● **Example 25.1** Assume that a Swedish seller and an American buyer have formed a contract, which the buyer breaches. The seller sues the buyer in a Swedish court, which awards damages. The buyer's assets, however, are in the United States and cannot be reached unless the judgment is enforced by a U.S. court of law. In this situation, if it is determined that the procedures and laws applied in the Swedish court were consistent with U.S. national law and policy, a court in the United States will likely defer to (and enforce) the foreign court's judgment.●

The Act of State Doctrine

Act of State Doctrine A doctrine that provides that the judicial branch of one country will not examine the validity of public acts committed by a recognized foreign government within its own territory.

The **act of state doctrine** is a judicially created doctrine that provides that the judicial branch of one country will not examine the validity of public acts committed by a recognized foreign government within its own territory. This doctrine is premised on the theory that the judicial branch should not "pass upon the validity of foreign acts when to do so would vex the harmony of our international relations with that foreign nation."[1]

Expropriation The seizure by a government of privately owned business or personal property for a proper public purpose and with just compensation.

Confiscation A government's taking of privately owned business or personal property without a proper public purpose or an award of just compensation.

The act of state doctrine can have important consequences for individuals and firms doing business with, and investing in, other countries. For example, this doctrine is frequently employed in cases involving expropriation or confiscation. **Expropriation** occurs when a government seizes a privately owned business or privately owned goods for a proper public purpose and awards just compensation. When a government seizes private property for an illegal purpose or without just compensation, the taking is referred to as a **confiscation**. The line between these two forms of taking is sometimes blurred because of differing interpretations of what is illegal and what constitutes just compensation.

● **Example 25.2** Tim Flaherty, an American businessperson, owns a mine in Brazil. The government of Brazil seizes the mine for public use and claims that the profits that Tim has realized from the mine in preceding years constitute just compensation. Tim disagrees, but the act of state doctrine may prevent Tim's recovery in a U.S. court of law.●

When applicable, both the act of state doctrine and the doctrine of sovereign immunity (to be discussed next) tend to immunize foreign nations from the jurisdiction of U.S. courts. What this means is that firms or individuals who own property overseas often have little legal protection against government actions in the countries in which they operate.

The Doctrine of Sovereign Immunity

Sovereign Immunity A doctrine that immunizes foreign nations from the jurisdiction of U.S. courts when certain conditions are satisfied.

Under certain conditions, the doctrine of **sovereign immunity** immunizes (protects) foreign nations from the jurisdiction of the U.S. courts. In 1976, Congress codified this rule in the Foreign Sovereign Immunities Act (FSIA). The FSIA exclusively governs the circumstances in which an action may be brought in the United States against a foreign nation, including attempts to attach a foreign nation's property.

Section 1605 of the FSIA sets forth the major exceptions to the jurisdictional immunity of a foreign state or country. A foreign state is not immune from the jurisdiction of the courts of the United States when the state has

---

1. *Libra Bank, Ltd. v. Banco Nacional de Costa Rica, S.A.*, 570 F.Supp. 870 (S.D.N.Y. 1983).

"waived its immunity either explicitly or by implication" or when the action is "based upon a commercial activity carried on in the United States by the foreign state."[2]

Issues frequently arise as to what entities fall within the category of a foreign state. The question of what is a commercial activity has also been the subject of dispute. Under Section 1603 of the FSIA, a *foreign state* is defined to include both a political subdivision of a foreign state and an instrumentality of a foreign state. A *commercial activity* is broadly defined under Section 1603 to mean a commercial activity that is carried out by a foreign state within the United States. The act, however, does not define the particulars of what constitutes a commercial activity. Rather, it is left up to the courts to decide whether a particular activity is governmental or commercial in nature. (See this chapter's *Inside the Legal Environment* feature on page 723 for a further discussion of this issue.)

In the following case, a foreign government claimed immunity from the jurisdiction of U.S. courts on the basis of sovereign immunity. The issue turned on whether the actions of the foreign government were commercial activities.

---

2. 28 U.S.C. Section 1605(a)(1), (2).

Case 25.1 ● Holden v. Canadian Consulate

United States Court of Appeals,
Ninth Circuit, 1996.
92 F.3d 918.

Historical and International Setting *In the early 1990s, the initiating of diplomatic services in more than twenty new countries, mostly in Eastern Europe, and governmental budget cuts forced many nations to reorganize their diplomatic offices. The governments of Australia and Sweden, for example, closed their consulates in Chicago. Similarly, actions by the Canadian government forced Canada's External Affairs Department to close its San Francisco consulate, an office that had been open for almost fifty years. The operations of the Canadian consul in San Francisco were transferred to Los Angeles. Canada continues to maintain its embassy in Washington, D.C., and consulates in eleven other U.S. cities.*

Background and Facts Canada closed its consulate in San Francisco and laid off many employees, including Arlene Holden, who had worked for thirteen years as one of the consulate's commercial officers. In place of the consulate, Canada opened a small office staffed with only one commercial officer—Mark Ritchie, a man younger and less experienced than Holden. Holden filed a suit in a U.S. district court against the consulate, alleging, among other things, discrimination. The consulate asked the court to dismiss the suit based on sovereign immunity under the Foreign Sovereign Immunities Act (FSIA). The court concluded that the consulate's employment of Holden was a "commercial activity." The consulate appealed.

In the Words of the Court . . .
LEAVY, Circuit Judge:

* * * *

* * * [T]he [FSIA's] legislative history * * * provides a useful framework for analyzing [commercial activity.] The * * * House Report states, " * * * * [A] government's * * * employment or engagement of laborers, clerical staff or public relations or marketing agents * * * would be among those [activities] included within the definition [of commercial activity]."

* * * *

(Continued)

Case 25.1 Continued

The district court examined the nature of Holden's work to determine if she was a civil servant, and found that she was not. * * * Holden did not compete for any examination prior to being hired, was not entitled to tenure, was not provided the same benefits as foreign service officers and did not receive any civil service protections from the Canadian government. * * *
* * * *

Although Holden * * * was a part of the Consulate's staff, her work was not that of a diplomat. As the district court found, Holden's activities were primarily promoting and marketing and she was not involved in any policy making and was not privy to any governmental policy deliberations. She did not engage in any lobbying activity or legislative work for Canada, and she could not speak for the government. * * * Furthermore, as an American, she was not allowed in the Consulate unless in the company of a foreign service officer.

Her employment is more analogous to a marketing agent. * * * The nature of Holden's work, promotion of products, is regularly done by private persons. As such, her employment was a commercial activity, and thus the Consulate is not entitled to sovereign immunity under the FSIA.

Decision and Remedy   The U.S. Court of Appeals for the Ninth Circuit affirmed the lower court's ruling. The appellate court denied the consulate sovereign immunity on the ground that the consulate's employment of Holden was a commercial activity.

For Critical Analysis—Political Consideration   *Does the "commercial activities" exception to the FSIA conflict with the act of state doctrine?*

Doing Business Internationally

Export   To sell products to buyers located in other countries.

A U.S. domestic firm can engage in international business transactions in a number of ways. The simplest way to engage in international business transactions is to seek out foreign markets for domestically produced products or services. In other words, U.S. firms can look abroad for **export** markets for their goods and services.

Alternatively, a U.S. firm can establish foreign production facilities so as to be closer to the foreign market or markets in which its products are sold. The advantages may include lower labor costs, fewer government regulations, and lower taxes and trade barriers. A domestic firm can obtain revenues through the licensing of technology to an existing foreign company. Yet another way to expand abroad is by selling franchises to overseas entities. The presence of McDonald's, Burger King, and KFC franchises throughout the world attests to the popularity of franchising.

> "Commerce is the great equalizer. We exchange ideas when we exchange fabrics."
>
> R. G. Ingersoll, 1833–1899
> (American lawyer and orator)

Exporting

The initial foray into international business by most U.S. companies is through exporting. Exporting can take two forms: direct exporting and indirect exporting. In *direct exporting,* a U.S. company signs a sales contract with a foreign purchaser that provides for the conditions of shipment and payment for the

Inside the Legal Environment

What Is a "Commercial Activity"?

Unlike the economy of the United States, which is primarily controlled by private interests, the economies of many other countries, particularly developing nations, are often extensively controlled by government. This means that if a U.S. plaintiff sues a business or institution that is controlled by a foreign government, the foreign defendant may assert the defense of sovereign immunity under the Foreign Sovereign Immunities Act (FSIA) of 1976. In this situation, a U.S. court cannot exercise jurisdiction over the dispute unless the plaintiff can prove, among other things, that the defendant's actions constituted a "commercial activity." What, however, is a "commercial activity"?

Although the FSIA does not define this phrase with any precision, the United States Supreme Court has provided some guidance on the issue. For example, in *Saudi Arabia v. Nelson,*[a] the Court addressed the question of whether the Saudi Arabian government's allegedly wrongful arrest, imprisonment, and torture of an American employee of a Saudi hospital constituted a commercial activity. The court concluded that it did not, holding that a state engages in commercial activity "where it exercises 'only those powers that can also be exercised by private citizens,' as distinct from those 'powers peculiar to sovereigns.'" The Court held that the alleged tortious actions of the Saudi government against the American employee were "sovereign" in character, and thus the Saudi government was immune from liability under the FSIA.

In 1995, the District of Columbia Court of Appeals applied this distinction between activities of a "sovereign character" and a "commercial character" in *Janini v. Kuwait University.*[b] The plaintiffs in the case were an American citizen, George Janini, and other former professors and employees of Kuwait University (KU). The plaintiffs were terminated from their positions when the government of Kuwait, following Iraq's invasion of Kuwait in August 1990, issued a decree stating, among other things, that "contracts concluded between the Government and those non-Kuwaiti workers who worked for it . . . shall be considered automatically abrogated because of the impossibility of enforcement due to the Iraqi invasion."

The plaintiffs sued KU in a U.S. court, alleging that their termination breached their employment contracts, which required nine months' notice before termination. The plaintiffs sought back pay and other benefits to which they were entitled under their contracts. The question before the court was whether terminating the professors' positions constituted a commercial activity. The court held that it did. The court concluded that "there is nothing 'peculiarly sovereign' about unilaterally terminating an employment contract. Private parties often repudiate contracts in everyday commerce and may be held liable therefor. That the termination here may have been accomplished by a formal decree of abrogation does not affect its commercial nature."

For Critical Analysis: *In addition to finding that a government-controlled foreign defendant has engaged in a commercial activity, what other requirement must be met before a U.S. court can exercise jurisdiction over the defendant?*

a. 507 U.S. 349, 113 S.Ct. 1471, 123 L.Ed.2d 47 (1993).

b. 43 F.3d 1534, 310 U.S.App.D.C. 109 (D.C. Cir. 1995).

goods. (How payments are made in international transactions is discussed later in this chapter.) If business develops sufficiently in foreign countries, a U.S. corporation may develop a specialized marketing organization that, for example, sells directly to consumers in that country. Such *indirect exporting* can be undertaken by the appointment of a foreign agent or a foreign distributor.

FOREIGN AGENT   When a U.S. firm desires a limited involvement in an international market, it will typically establish an *agency relationship* with a foreign firm. In an agency relationship (discussed in Chapter 17), one person (the agent) agrees to act on behalf of another (the principal). The foreign agent is thereby empowered to enter into contracts in the agent's country on behalf of the U.S. principal.

FOREIGN DISTRIBUTOR   When a substantial market exists in a foreign country, a U.S. firm may wish to appoint a distributor located in that country. The U.S. firm and the distributor enter into a **distribution agreement,** which is a contract between the seller and the distributor setting out the terms and conditions of the distributorship—for example, price, currency of payment, availability of supplies, and method of payment. The terms and conditions primarily involve contract law. Disputes concerning distribution agreements may involve jurisdictional or other issues (discussed in detail later in this chapter). In addition, some **exclusive distributorships**—in which distributors agree to distribute only the sellers' goods—have raised antitrust problems.

Distribution Agreement A contract between a seller and a distributor of the seller's products setting out the terms and conditions of the distributorship.

Exclusive Distributorship A distributorship in which the seller and distributor of the seller's products agree that the distributor has the exclusive right to distribute the seller's products in a certain geographic area.

Manufacturing Abroad

An alternative to direct or indirect exporting is the establishment of foreign manufacturing facilities. Typically, U.S. firms want to establish manufacturing plants abroad if they believe that by doing so they will reduce costs—particularly for labor, shipping, and raw materials—and thereby be able to compete more effectively in foreign markets. Apple Computer, IBM, General Motors, and Ford are some of the many U.S. companies that have established manufacturing facilities abroad. Foreign firms have done the same in the United States. Sony, Nissan, and other Japanese manufacturers have established U.S. plants to avoid import duties that the U.S. Congress may impose on Japanese products entering this country.

There are several ways in which an American firm can manufacture goods in other countries. They include licensing and franchising, as well as investing in a wholly owned subsidiary or a joint venture.

Technology Licensing Allowing another to use and profit from intellectual property (patents, copyrights, trademarks, innovative products or processes, and so on) for consideration. In the context of international business transactions, technology licensing is sometimes an attractive alternative to the establishment of foreign production facilities.

LICENSING   It is possible for U.S. firms to license their technologies to foreign manufacturers. **Technology licensing** may involve a process innovation that lowers the cost of production, or it may involve a product innovation that generates a superior product. Technology licensing may be an attractive alternative to establishing foreign production facilities, particularly if the process or product innovation has been patented, because the patent protects—at least to some extent—against the possibility that the innovation might be pirated. Like any licensing agreement, a licensing agreement with a foreign-based firm calls for a payment of royalties on some basis—such as so many cents per unit produced or a certain percentage of profits from units sold in a particular geographical territory.

In some circumstances, even in the absence of a patent, a firm may be able to license the "know-how" associated with a particular manufacturing process—for example, a plant design or a secret formula. The foreign firm that agrees to sign the licensing agreement further agrees to keep the know-how confidential and to pay royalties. For example, the Coca-Cola Bottling Company licenses firms worldwide to use (and keep confidential) its secret formula for the syrup used in that soft drink, in return for a percentage of the income gained from the sale of Coca-Cola by those firms.

The licensing of technology benefits all parties to the transaction. Those who receive the license can take advantage of an established reputation for quality, and the firm that grants the license receives income from the foreign sales of the firm's products, as well as establishing a worldwide reputation. Additionally, once a firm's trademark is known worldwide, the demand for other products manufactured or sold by that firm may increase—obviously an important consideration.

FRANCHISING   Franchising is a well-known form of licensing. Recall from Chapter 16 that a franchise can be defined as an arrangement in which the owner of a trademark, trade name, or copyright (the franchisor) licenses another (the franchisee) to use the trademark, trade name, or copyright—under certain conditions or limitations—in the selling of goods or services in exchange for a fee, usually based on a percentage of gross or net sales. Examples of international franchises include McDonald's, the Coca-Cola Bottling Company, Holiday Inn, Avis, and Hertz.

INVESTING IN A WHOLLY OWNED SUBSIDIARY OR A JOINT VENTURE   One way to expand into a foreign market is to establish a wholly owned subsidiary firm in a foreign country. The European subsidiary would likely take the form of the *société anonyme* (S.A.), which is similar to a U.S. corporation. In German-speaking nations, it would be called an *Aktiengesellschaft* (A.G.). When a wholly owned subsidiary is established, the parent company, which remains in the United States, retains complete ownership of all the facilities in the foreign country, as well as complete authority and control over all phases of the operation.

The expansion of a U.S. firm into international markets can also take the form of a joint venture. In a joint venture, the U.S. company owns only part of the operation; the rest is owned either by local owners in the foreign country or by another foreign entity. In a joint venture, all of the firms involved share responsibilities, as well as profits and liabilities.

Commercial Contracts in an International Setting

Like all commercial contracts, an international contract should be in writing. For an example of an actual international sales contract, refer back to the foldout contract in Chapter 13.

Language and legal differences among nations can create special problems for parties to international contracts when disputes arise. It is possible to avoid these problems by including in a contract special provisions designating the official language of the contract, the legal forum (court or place) in which disputes under the contract will be settled, and the substantive law that will be applied in settling any disputes. Parties to international contracts should also indicate in their contracts what acts or events will excuse the parties from performance under the contract and whether disputes under the contract will be arbitrated or litigated.

With the growth of e-commerce, an emerging concern is how to protect consumers in international business-to-consumer contracts. For recent developments in this area, see this chapter's *Legal E-nvironment* feature on page 726.

> **Recall** The interpretation of the words in a contract can be the basis for a dispute even when both parties communicate in the same language.

Choice of Language

A deal struck between a U.S. company and a company in another country normally involves two languages. The complex contractual terms involved may not be understood by one party in the other party's language. Typically, many

Legal *e*-nvironment

Protecting Consumers Worldwide

Assume that Arlington Ranch Supplies in Texas places an online order for specially prepared leather from Asia Leather Suppliers in Singapore. This is a cross-border transaction conducted via the Internet. What happens if Arlington makes payment for the goods, but Asia Leather never ships the goods? What happens if Asia Leather ships the goods, but they are defective? In the consumer arena, individuals are engaging in similar types of transactions every day—and face similar types of potential problems.

The number of cross-border online transactions is growing and will continue to grow for years to come. Protecting consumers and businesses alike has been the goal of numerous organizations around the world. The most prominent has been the Organization of Economic Cooperation and Development (OECD).

E-Commerce Consumer Guidelines Issued by the OECD

For several years, representatives of the largest countries in the world have met to discuss guidelines for consumer protection in e-commerce. The final version of *Guidelines for Consumer Protection in the Context of Electronic Commerce* was issued on December 9, 1999.[a] Many of the guidelines resemble those already issued by the U.S. Federal Trade Commission. The key elements outlined in this document require e-businesses to:

- Comply with representations made online.
- Not use the Internet to hide their identities or to avoid compliance with consumer protection standards.

a. These guidelines are online at **www.OECD.org/ dsti/sti/it/consumer/prod/guidelines.htm**.

- Implement procedures to prevent consumers from receiving unsolicited e-mail (spam).
- Take special care in advertising to children.
- Consider the various regulatory characteristics of those markets that they target.
- Indicate the location of service of legal process.
- Delineate the conditions of purchase.
- Provide information on after-sales service.
- Provide information on refund, return, exchange, or cancellation policies.

The *Guidelines* also suggest that business-to-consumer activities online should be carried out in accordance with the OECD's privacy guidelines. The OECD's privacy guidelines, which relate to the privacy of personal data flowing across national borders and the privacy of data accessible by global networks, have already been widely adopted as international standards.

The Question of Jurisdiction Still Remains

Cross-border e-commerce activities create the potential for jurisdictional questions. What happens when there is a dispute involving parties in different countries that resulted from an online contract? While no definitive recommendation was given in the *Guidelines*, the document recommends the development of alternative dispute-resolution (ADR) systems. Such systems would require the cooperation of consumer groups, businesses, and governments.

Governments, in particular, would have to harmonize the interests of business and consumer groups to make such cross-border ADR systems work. Consumer groups have at all times advocated adopting the jurisdiction of the consumer as the government of jurisdiction. The creators of the *Guidelines* chose not to include this recommendation.

For Critical Analysis: *Under what circumstances will the* Guidelines *have the force of law in the United States (or in other countries)?*

---

phrases in one language are not readily translatable into another. To make sure that no disputes arise out of this language problem, an international sales contract should have a **choice-of-language clause** designating the official language by which the contract will be interpreted in the event of disagreement.

Choice of Forum

When several countries are involved, litigation may be sought in courts in different nations. There are no universally accepted rules regarding the jurisdiction

Choice-of-Language Clause A clause in a contract designating the official language by which the contract will be interpreted in the event of a future disagreement over the contract's terms.

International Perspective

Language Requirements in France

In 1995, France implemented a law making the use of the French language mandatory in certain legal documents. Documents relating to securities offerings, such as prospectuses, for example, must be written in French. So must instruction manuals and warranties for goods and services offered for sale in France. Additionally, all agreements entered into with French state or local authorities, with entities controlled by state or local authorities, and with private entities carrying out a public service (such as providing utilities) must be written in French. The law has posed problems for some businesspersons because certain legal terms or phrases in documents governed by, say, U.S. or English law have no equivalent terms or phrases in the French legal system.

For Critical Analysis: *How might language differences affect the meaning of certain terms or phrases in an international contract?*

---

of a particular court over subject matter or parties to a dispute. Consequently, parties to an international transaction should always include in the contract a **forum-selection clause** indicating what court, jurisdiction, or tribunal will decide any disputes arising under the contract. It is especially important to indicate specifically what court will have jurisdiction. The forum does not necessarily have to be within the geographical boundaries of either of the parties' nations.

Forum-Selection Clause A provision in a contract designating the court, jurisdiction, or tribunal that will decide any disputes arising under the contract.

Choice of Law

A contractual provision designating the applicable law—such as the law of Germany or England or California—is called a **choice-of-law clause**. Every international contract typically includes a choice-of-law clause. At common law (and in European civil law systems), parties are allowed to choose the law that will govern their contractual relationship provided that the law chosen is the law of a jurisdiction that has a substantial relationship to the parties and to the international business transaction.

Choice-of-Law Clause A clause in a contract designating the law (such as the law of a particular state or nation) that will govern the contract.

Under Section 1–105 of the Uniform Commercial Code, parties may choose the law that will govern the contract as long as the choice is "reasonable." Article 6 of the United Nations Convention on Contracts for the International Sale of Goods (discussed in Chapter 13), however, imposes no limitation on the parties in their choice of what law will govern the contract. The 1986 Hague Convention on the Law Applicable to Contracts for the International Sale of Goods—often referred to as the Choice-of-Law Convention—allows unlimited autonomy in the choice of law. The Hague Convention indicates that whenever a choice of law is not specified in a contract, the governing law is that of the country in which the *seller's* place of business is located.

Force Majeure Clause

Every contract, particularly those involving international transactions, should have a ***force majeure* clause**. *Force majeure* is a French term meaning "impossible or irresistible force"—which sometimes is loosely identified as "an act of God." In international business contracts, *force majeure* clauses commonly stipulate that in addition to acts of God, a number of other eventualities (such as governmental orders or regulations, embargoes, or shortages of materials) may excuse a party from liability for nonperformance.

***Force Majeure* Clause** A provision in a contract stipulating that certain unforeseen events—such as war, political upheavals, acts of God, or other events—will excuse a party from liability for nonperformance of contractual obligations.

Civil Dispute Resolution

International contracts frequently include arbitration clauses. By means of such clauses, the parties agree in advance to be bound by the decision of a specified third party in the event of a dispute, as discussed in Chapter 4. The third party may be a neutral entity (such as the International Chamber of Commerce), a panel of individuals representing both parties' interests, or some other group or organization. (For an example of an arbitration clause in an international contract, refer to the fold-out exhibit in Chapter 13.) The United Nations Convention on the Recognition and Enforcement of Foreign Arbitral Awards (often referred to as the New York Convention) assists in the enforcement of arbitration clauses, as do provisions in specific treaties between nations. The New York Convention has been implemented in nearly one hundred countries, including the United States.

If no arbitration clause is contained in the sales contract, litigation may occur. If forum-selection and choice-of-law clauses are included in the contract, the lawsuit will be heard by a court in the forum specified and decided according to that forum's law. If no forum and choice of law have been specified, however, legal proceedings will be more complex and attended by much more uncertainty. For example, litigation may take place in two or more countries, with each country applying its own choice-of-law rules to determine which substantive law will be applied to the particular transactions.

Even if a plaintiff wins a favorable judgment in a lawsuit litigated in the plaintiff's country, there is no way to predict whether the court's judgment will be enforced by judicial bodies in the defendant's country. As discussed earlier in this chapter, under the principle of comity, the judgment may be enforced in the defendant's country, particularly if the defendant's country is the United States and the foreign court's decision is consistent with U.S. national law and policy. Other nations, however, may not be as accommodating as the United States in this respect. Difficulties with enforcing judgments against defendants located in foreign countries is one of the reasons for the increasing interest in—and use of—online dispute-resolution procedures (see Chapter 5).

Making Payment on International Transactions

Currency differences among nations and the geographical distance among parties to international sales contracts add a degree of complexity to international sales that does not exist within the domestic market. Because international contracts involve greater financial risks, special care should be taken in drafting these contracts to specify both the currency in which payment is to be made and the method of payment.

Monetary Systems

While it is true that our national currency, the U.S. dollar, is one of the primary forms of international currency, any U.S. firm undertaking business transactions abroad must be prepared to deal with one or more other currencies. After all, just as a U.S. firm wants to be paid in U.S. dollars for goods and services sold abroad, so, too, does a Japanese firm want to be paid in Japanese yen for goods and services sold outside Japan. Both firms therefore must rely on the convertibility of currencies.

FOREIGN EXCHANGE MARKETS Currencies are convertible when they can be freely exchanged one for the other at some specified market rate in a

International Perspective

Arbitration versus Litigation

One of the reasons many businesspersons find it advantageous to include arbitration clauses in their international contracts is because arbitration awards are usually easier to enforce than court judgments. As mentioned, the New York Convention provides for the enforcement of arbitration awards in those countries that have signed the convention. Enforcement of court judgments, though, normally depends on the principle of comity and bilateral agreements providing for such enforcement. How the principle of comity is applied, however, varies from one nation to another, and many countries have not agreed, in bilateral agreements, to enforce judgments rendered in U.S. courts. Furthermore, even in the United States a court might not enforce a foreign court's judgment if that judgment conflicts with U.S. laws or policies. For example, in one case the Court of Appeals of Maryland, that state's highest court, refused to enforce the judgment of a British court in a libel case. The Maryland court pointed out that the judgment was contrary to the public policy of Maryland and the United States generally, which "favors a much broader and more protective freedom of the press than [has] ever been provided for under English law."[a]

For Critical Analysis: *What might be some other advantages of arbitration in the context of international transactions? Are there any disadvantages?*

a. *Telnikoff v. Matusevitch,* 159 F.3d 636 (D.C. Cir. 1998).

---

foreign exchange market. Foreign exchange markets are a worldwide system for the buying and selling of foreign currencies. At any point in time, the foreign exchange rate is set by the forces of supply and demand in unrestricted foreign exchange markets. The foreign exchange rate is simply the price of a unit of one country's currency in terms of another country's currency. For example, if today's exchange rate is one hundred Japanese yen for one dollar, that means that anybody with one hundred yen can obtain one dollar, and vice versa.

Foreign Exchange Market A worldwide system in which foreign currencies are bought and sold.

CORRESPONDENT BANKING Frequently, a U.S. company can deal directly with its domestic bank, which will take care of the international funds-transfer problem. Commercial banks sometimes have **correspondent banks** in other countries. Correspondent banking is a major means of transferring funds internationally.

● **Example 25.3** Suppose that a customer of Citibank wishes to pay a bill in French francs to a company in Paris. Citibank can draw a bank check payable in francs on its account in Crédit Lyonnais, a Paris correspondent bank, and then send it to the French company to which its customer owes the funds. Alternatively, Citibank's customer can request a wire transfer of the funds to the French company. Citibank instructs Crédit Lyonnais by wire to pay the necessary amount in French francs.●

Correspondent Bank A bank in which another bank has an account (and vice versa) for the purpose of facilitating fund transfers.

The Clearinghouse Interbank Payment System (CHIPS) handles about 90 percent of both national and international interbank transfers of U.S. funds. In addition, the Society for Worldwide International Financial Telecommunications (SWIFT) is a communication system that provides banks with messages concerning transactions.

Letters of Credit

Because buyers and sellers engaged in international business transactions are often separated by thousands of miles, special precautions are frequently taken to ensure performance under the contract. Sellers want to avoid delivering goods for

Letter of Credit A written instrument, usually issued by a bank on behalf of a customer or other person, in which the issuer promises to honor drafts or other demands for payment by third persons in accordance with the terms of the instrument.

which they might not be paid. Buyers desire the assurance that sellers will not be paid until there is evidence that the goods have been shipped. Thus, **letters of credit** are frequently used to facilitate international business transactions.

In a simple letter-of-credit transaction, the issuer (a bank) agrees to issue a letter of credit and to ascertain whether the *beneficiary* (seller) performs certain acts. In return, the *account party* (buyer) promises to reimburse the issuer for the amount paid to the beneficiary. There may also be an *advising bank* that transmits information, and a *paying bank* may be involved to expedite payment under the letter of credit. Exhibit 25–1 summarizes the "life cycle" of a letter of credit.

Under a letter of credit, the issuer is bound to pay the beneficiary (seller) when the beneficiary has complied with the terms and conditions of the letter of credit. The beneficiary looks to the issuer, not to the account party (buyer), when it presents the documents required by the letter of credit. Typically, the letter of credit will require that the beneficiary deliver to the issuing bank a *bill of lading* to prove that shipment has been made. Letters of credit assure beneficiaries (sellers) of payment while at the same time assuring account parties (buyers) that payment will not be made until the beneficiaries have complied with the terms and conditions of the letter of credit.

Don't Forget A letter of credit is independent of the underlying contract between the buyer and the seller.

THE VALUE OF A LETTER OF CREDIT The basic principle behind letters of credit is that payment is made against the documents presented by the beneficiary and not against the facts that the documents purport to reflect. Thus, in a letter-of-credit transaction, the issuer does not police the underlying contract; a letter of credit is independent of the underlying contract between the buyer and the seller. Eliminating the need for banks (issuers) to inquire into whether or not actual conditions have been satisfied greatly reduces the costs of letters of credit. Moreover, the use of a letter of credit protects both buyers and sellers.

Exhibit 25–1 The "Life Cycle" of a Letter of Credit

Although the letter of credit appears quite complex at first, it is not difficult to understand. This cycle merely involves the exchange of documents (and money) through intermediaries. The following steps depict the letter-of-credit procurement cycle.

Step 1: The buyer and seller agree on the terms of sale. The sales contract dictates that a letter of credit is to be used to finance the transaction.

Step 2: The buyer completes an application for a letter of credit and forwards it to his or her bank, which will issue the letter of credit.

Step 3: The issuing (buyer's) bank then forwards the letter of credit to a correspondent bank in the seller's country.

Step 4: The correspondent's bank relays the letter of credit to the seller.

Step 5: Having received assurance of payment, the seller makes the necessary shipping arrangements.

Step 6: The seller prepares the documents required under the letter of credit and delivers them to the correspondent bank.

Step 7: The correspondent bank examines the documents. If it finds them in order, it sends them to the issuing bank and pays the seller in accordance with the terms of the letter of credit.

Step 8: The issuing bank, having received the documents, examines them. If they are in order, the issuing bank will charge the buyer's account and send the documents on to the buyer or his or her customs broker. The issuing bank also will reimburse the correspondent bank.

Step 9: The buyer or broker receives the documents and picks up the merchandise from the shipper (carrier).

Source: National Association of Purchasing Management.

COMPLIANCE WITH A LETTER OF CREDIT In a letter-of-credit transaction, generally at least three separate and distinct contracts are involved: the contract between the account party (buyer) and the beneficiary (seller); the contract between the issuer (bank) and the account party (buyer); and finally, the letter of credit itself, which involves the issuer (bank) and the beneficiary (seller). These contracts are separate and distinct, and the issuer's obligations under the letter of credit do not concern the underlying contract between the buyer and the seller. Rather, it is the issuer's duty to ascertain whether the documents presented by the beneficiary (seller) comply with the terms of the letter of credit.

If the documents presented by the beneficiary comply with the terms of the letter of credit, the issuer (bank) must honor the letter of credit. Sometimes, however, it is difficult to determine exactly what a letter of credit requires. Moreover, the courts are divided as to whether *strict* or *substantial* compliance with the terms of the letter of credit is required. Traditionally, courts required strict compliance with the terms of a letter of credit, but in recent years, some courts have moved to a standard of *reasonable* compliance.

If the issuing bank refuses to pay the seller (beneficiary) even though the seller has complied with all the requirements of the letter of credit, the seller can bring an action to enforce payment. In the international context, the fact that the issuing bank may be thousands of miles distant from the seller's business location can pose difficulties for the seller—as the following case illustrates.

Case 25.2 ● Pacific Reliant Industries, Inc. v. Amerika Samoa Bank

United States Court of Appeals,
Ninth Circuit, 1990.
901 F.2d 735.
196 Va. 493,
84 S.E.2d 516.

Historical and Social Setting *Samoa, which was originally inhabited by Polynesians, is a group of islands 2,610 miles south of Hawaii. In 1899, the islands were divided into Western Samoa and American Samoa by the Treaty of Berlin, which was signed by Great Britain, Germany, and the United States. Thus, the United States acquired American Samoa. In 1960, American Samoa adopted a constitution, which it revised in 1967, but it remains a non–self-governing, unincorporated territory of the United States. Its currency is the U.S. dollar, its languages are Samoan and English, and it is administered by the U.S. Department of the Interior. The population of American Samoa is less than fifty thousand.*

Background and Facts Pacific Reliant Industries, Inc., an Oregon company, sold building materials to Paradise Development Company, a company located in American Samoa. Pacific was reluctant to make several large deliveries, totaling more than $1 million in value, without some protection against non-

payment. Accordingly, representatives from Pacific, Paradise, and Amerika Samoa Bank (ASB) met in American Samoa on two occasions to discuss the supply contract and a letter of credit. Following these negotiations, ASB issued a letter of credit in favor of Pacific on Paradise's account. Later, alleging that ASB had wrongfully dishonored the letter of credit, Pacific brought suit in the U.S. district court for the district of Oregon against ASB to recover payment. The court dismissed the suit for lack of personal jurisdiction, holding that ASB lacked sufficient "minimum contacts" (see Chapter 3) with the state of Oregon to subject it to a lawsuit in that state.[a] Pacific appealed, contending that this case was not typical of other letter-of-credit cases because ASB had participated in forming the underlying contract, had had personal contact with the beneficiary (Pacific), and had known that Pacific would not extend credit or ship goods from Oregon without the letter of credit.

---

a. State law governs some cases that may be brought in a federal court because the parties to the case are citizens of different states or are aliens. In such a case, the federal court normally applies the law of the state in which the court is located.

(Continued)

Case 25.2 Continued

In the Words of the Court . . .
CANBY, Circuit Judge:

*   *   *   *

Here, both the negotiations for the underlying contract and the letter of credit occurred in American Samoa. * * * ASB did not initiate the transactions between itself, Paradise, or Pacific. Nor did ASB take any significant actions in Oregon. ASB did not invoke the benefits and protections of Oregon law and could not reasonably have expected to be haled into court there. We conclude that ASB's conduct as an issuing bank of a letter of credit does not subject it to suit in Oregon * * * .

Decision and Remedy The U.S Court of Appeals for the Ninth Circuit affirmed the lower court's ruling. Pacific could not bring suit against ASB in Oregon.

For Critical Analysis—Political Consideration *If a court could exercise jurisdiction over a* nonresident corporation that did not have minimum contacts with the jurisdiction in which the suit was brought, what might result?

Regulation of Specific Business Activities

Doing business abroad can affect the economies, foreign policy, domestic politics, and other national interests of the countries involved. For this reason, nations impose laws to restrict or facilitate international business. Controls may also be imposed by international agreement. We discuss here how different types of international activities are regulated.

Investing

Investing in foreign nations involves a risk that the foreign government may take possession of the investment property. Expropriation, as already mentioned, occurs when property is taken and the owner is paid just compensation for what is taken. This does not violate generally observed principles of international law. Confiscation occurs when property is taken and no (or inadequate) compensation is paid. International legal principles are violated when property is confiscated. Few remedies are available for confiscation of property by a foreign government. Claims are often resolved by lump-sum settlements after negotiations between the United States and the taking nation.

To counter the deterrent effect that the possibility of confiscation may have on potential investors, many countries guarantee that foreign investors will be compensated if their property is taken. A guaranty can take the form of national constitutional or statutory laws or provisions in international treaties. As further protection for foreign investments, some countries provide insurance for their citizens' investments abroad.

Note Most countries restrict exports for the same reasons: to protect national security, to protect foreign policy, to prevent the spread of nuclear weapons, and to preserve scarce commodities.

Export Restrictions and Incentives

The U.S. Constitution provides in Article I, Section 9, that "No Tax or Duty shall be laid on Articles exported from any State." Thus, Congress cannot impose any export taxes. Congress can, however, use a variety of other devices to control exports. Congress may set export quotas on various items, such as grain being sold abroad. Under the Export Administration Act of 1979,[3] restrictions can be imposed on the flow of technologically advanced products and technical data.

Devices to stimulate exports and thereby aid domestic businesses include export incentives and subsidies. The Revenue Act of 1971,[4] for example, gave tax benefits to firms marketing their products overseas through certain foreign sales corporations, exempting income produced by the exports. Under the Export Trading Company Act of 1982,[5] U.S. banks are encouraged to invest in export trading companies. An export trading company consists of exporting firms joined to export a line of goods. The Export-Import Bank of the United States provides financial assistance, which consists primarily of credit guaranties given to commercial banks that in turn loan funds to U.S. exporting companies.

Import Restrictions

All nations have restrictions on imports, and the United States is no exception. Restrictions include strict prohibitions, quotas, and tariffs. Under the Trading with the Enemy Act of 1917,[6] for example, no goods may be imported from nations that have been designated enemies of the United States. Other laws prohibit the importation of illegal drugs, books that urge insurrection against the United States, and agricultural products that pose dangers to domestic crops or animals.

QUOTAS AND TARIFFS   Quotas are limits on the amounts of goods that can be imported. Tariffs are taxes on imports. A tariff is usually a percentage of the value of the import, but it can be a flat rate per unit (for example, per barrel of oil). Tariffs raise the prices of goods, which causes some consumers to purchase less expensive, domestically manufactured goods.

DUMPING   The United States has specific laws directed at what it sees as unfair international trade practices. **Dumping,** for example, is the sale of imported goods at "less than fair value." "Fair value" is usually determined by the price of those goods in the exporting country. Foreign firms that engage in dumping in the United States hope to undersell U.S. businesses to obtain a larger share of the U.S. market. To prevent this, an extra tariff—known as an antidumping duty—may be assessed on the imports.

MINIMIZING TRADE BARRIERS   Restrictions on imports are also known as trade barriers. The elimination of trade barriers is sometimes seen as essential to the world's economic well-being. Most of the world's leading trade nations are members of the World Trade Organization (WTO), which was established in 1995. To minimize trade barriers among nations, each member country of the WTO is required to grant **most-favored-nation status** to other member countries. This means each member is obligated to treat other members at least as well as it treats that country that receives its most favorable treatment with regard to imports or exports.

> "The notion dies hard that in some sort of way exports are patriotic but imports are immoral."
>
> Lord Harlech (David Ormsley Gore), 1918–1985 (English writer)

Dumping The selling of goods in a foreign country at a price below the price charged for the same goods in the domestic market.

Most-Favored-Nation Status A status granted in an international treaty by a provision stating that the citizens of the contracting nations may enjoy the privileges accorded by either party to citizens of the most favored nations. Generally, most-favored-nation clauses are designed to establish equality of international treatment.

---

3. 50 U.S.C. Sections 2401–2420.
4. 26 U.S.C. Sections 991–994.
5. 15 U.S.C. Sections 4001, 4003.
6. 12 U.S.C. Section 95a.

Various regional trade agreements, or associations, also help to minimize trade barriers between nations. The European Union (EU), for example, attempts to minimize or remove barriers to trade among European member countries. The EU is the result of negotiations undertaken by European nations since the 1950s. Currently, the EU is a single integrated European trading unit made up of fifteen European nations. Another important regional trade agreement is the North American Free Trade Agreement (NAFTA). NAFTA, which became effective on January 1, 1994, created a regional trading unit consisting of Mexico, the United States, and Canada. The primary goal of NAFTA is to eliminate tariffs among these three countries on substantially all goods over a period of fifteen to twenty years.

Bribing Foreign Officials

Giving cash or in-kind benefits to foreign government officials to obtain business contracts and other favors is often considered normal practice. To reduce such bribery by representatives of U.S. corporations, Congress enacted the Foreign Corrupt Practices Act (FCPA) in 1977.[7] This act and its implications for American businesspersons engaged in international business transactions were discussed in detail in the *Landmark in the Legal Environment* in Chapter 2.

U.S. Laws in a Global Context

The internationalization of business raises questions of the extraterritorial effect of a nation's laws—that is, the effect of the country's laws outside the country. To what extent do U.S. domestic laws affect other nations' businesses? To what extent are U.S. businesses affected by domestic laws when doing business abroad? The following subsections discuss these questions in the context of U.S. antitrust law. We also look at the extraterritorial application of U.S. laws prohibiting employment discrimination.

U.S. Antitrust Laws

U.S. antitrust laws (discussed in Chapter 23) have a wide application. They may *subject* persons in foreign nations to their provisions, as well as *protect* foreign consumers and competitors from violations committed by U.S. citizens. Consequently, *foreign persons,* a term that by definition includes foreign governments, may sue under U.S. antitrust laws in U.S. courts.

Section 1 of the Sherman Act provides for the extraterritorial effect of the U.S. antitrust laws. The United States is a major proponent of free competition in the global economy, and thus any conspiracy that has a *substantial effect* on U.S. commerce is within the reach of the Sherman Act. The violation may even occur outside the United States, and foreign governments as well as persons can be sued for violations of U.S. antitrust laws.

Before U.S. courts will exercise jurisdiction and apply antitrust laws, it must be shown that the alleged violation had a substantial effect on U.S. commerce. U.S. jurisdiction is automatically invoked, however, when a *per se* violation occurs. A *per se* violation may consist of resale price fixing and tying, or tie-in, contracts. ● **Example 25.4** If a domestic firm joins a foreign cartel to control the production, price, or distribution of goods, and this cartel has a

---

7. 15 U.S.C. Sections 78m–78ff.

substantial restraining effect on U.S. commerce, a *per se* violation may exist. Hence, both the domestic firm and the foreign cartel may be sued for violation of the U.S. antitrust laws. Likewise, if foreign firms doing business in the United States enter into a price-fixing or other anticompetitive agreement to control a portion of U.S. markets, a *per se* violation may exist.●

In the following case, the court considered whether a *criminal* prosecution under the Sherman Act could be based on price-fixing activities that took place entirely outside the United States but had a substantial effect in this country.

Case 25.3 ● United States v. Nippon Paper Industries Co.

United States Court of Appeals,
First Circuit, 1997.
109 F.3d 1.

Company Profile *In 1993, two Japanese paper companies merged to form Nippon Paper Industries Company. Nippon makes paper and paper products, operating tree plantations and lumber mills in Australia and Chile. In thirteen other countries, Nippon engages in import and export activities in the chemicals, cosmetics, food, and pharmaceuticals industries. Paper production, however, accounts for about three-quarters of the company's sales. In the late 1980s and early 1990s, one of Nippon's predecessors sold thermal fax paper for use in fax machines and medical printing equipment. In 1990, North American thermal fax paper sales by Japanese firms accounted for $120 million, of which $6 million went to Nippon's predecessor.*

Background and Facts A federal grand jury issued a criminal indictment against Nippon Paper Industries Company (NPI) and others, charging the defendants with agreeing to fix the price of thermal fax paper throughout North America. The indictment alleged that the meetings to reach the agreement had occurred entirely in Japan but that the defendants had sold the paper through subsidiaries in the United States at above-normal prices. The indictment stated that these activities had had a substantial adverse effect on commerce in the United States and had unreasonably restrained trade in violation of Section 1 of the Sherman Act. NPI filed a motion to dismiss the indictment. The court granted the motion, declaring that a criminal antitrust prosecution could not be based on wholly extraterritorial conduct. The government appealed.

In the Words of the Court . . .
SELYA, Circuit Judge.

* * * *

* * * [C]ivil antitrust actions predicated on wholly foreign conduct which has an intended and substantial effect in the United States come within Section One's jurisdictional reach. * * *

* * * *

* * * [I]n both criminal and civil cases, the claim that Section One applies extraterritorially is based on the same language in the same section of the same statute * * * .

* * * It is a fundamental interpretive principle that identical words or terms used in different parts of the same act are intended to have the same meaning. * * * It follows, therefore, that if the language upon which the indictment rests were the same as the language upon which civil liability rests but appeared in a different section of the Sherman Act, or in a different part of the same section, we would * * * construe the two iterations [statements] of the language identically. Where, as here, the tie binds more tightly—that is, the text under consideration is not merely a duplicate appearing somewhere else in the statute, but is the original phrase in the original setting—* * * the case for reading the language in a [consistent] manner * * * is irresistible.

(Continued)

Case 25.3 Continued

Decision and Remedy   The U.S. Court of Appeals for the First Circuit reversed the decision of the lower court. The criminal indictment under the Sherman Act would not be dismissed simply because the actions on which it was based occurred outside the United States.

For Critical Analysis—Economic Consideration   *Why should the United States apply its antitrust laws to business firms owned by citizens or the government of another nation?*

Discrimination Laws

As explained in Chapter 18, there are laws in the United States prohibiting discrimination on the basis of race, color, national origin, religion, gender, age, and disability. These laws, as they affect employment relationships, generally apply extraterritorially. Since 1984, for example, the Age Discrimination in Employment Act (ADEA) of 1967 has covered U.S. employees working abroad for U.S. employers. The Americans with Disabilities Act of 1990, which requires employers to accommodate the needs of workers with disabilities, also applies to U.S. nationals working abroad for U.S. firms.

For some time, it was uncertain whether the major U.S. law regulating discriminatory practices in the workplace, Title VII of the Civil Rights Act of 1964, applied extraterritorially. The Civil Rights Act of 1991 addressed this issue. The act provides that Title VII applies extraterritorially to all U.S. employees working for U.S. employers abroad. Generally, U.S. employers must abide by U.S. discrimination laws unless to do so would violate the laws of the country in which their workplaces are located. This "foreign laws exception" allows employers to avoid being subjected to conflicting laws.

Key Terms

act of state doctrine 720	distribution agreement 724	foreign exchange market 729
choice-of-language clause 726	dumping 733	forum-selection clause 727
choice-of-law clause 727	exclusive distributorship 724	letter of credit 730
comity 719	export 722	most-favored-nation status 733
confiscation 720	expropriation 720	sovereign immunity 720
correspondent bank 729	*force majeure* clause 727	technology licensing 724

Chapter Summary • The Regulation of International Transactions

International Principles and Doctrines
(See pages 719–722.)

1. **The principle of comity**—Under this principle, nations give effect to the laws and judicial decrees of other nations for reasons of courtesy and international harmony.

2. **The act of state doctrine**—A doctrine under which American courts avoid passing judgment on the validity of public acts committed by a recognized foreign government within its own territory.

(Continued)

Chapter Summary • The Regulation of International Transactions

International Principles and Doctrines —continued	3. **The doctrine of sovereign immunity**—When certain conditions are satisfied, foreign nations are immune from U.S. jurisdiction under the Foreign Sovereign Immunities Act of 1976. Exceptions are made (a) when the foreign state has "waived its immunity either explicitly or by implication" or (b) when the action is "based upon a commercial activity carried on in the United States by the foreign state."
Doing Business Internationally (See pages 722–725.)	Ways in which U.S. domestic firms engage in international business transactions include (a) exporting, which may involve foreign agents or distributors, and (b) manufacturing abroad through licensing arrangements, franchising operations, wholly owned subsidiaries, or joint ventures.
Commercial Contracts in an International Setting (See pages 725–728.)	Choice-of-language, forum-selection, and choice-of-law clauses are often included in international business contracts to reduce the uncertainties associated with interpreting the language of the agreement and dealing with legal differences. *Force majeure* clauses are included in most domestic and international contracts. They commonly stipulate that certain events, such as floods, fire, accidents, labor strikes, and shortages, may excuse a party from liability for nonperformance of the contract. Arbitration clauses are also frequently found in international contracts.
Making Payment on International Transactions (See pages 728–732.)	1. **Currency conversion**—Because nations have different monetary systems, payment on international contracts requires currency conversion at a rate specified in a foreign exchange market. 2. **Correspondent banking**—Correspondent banks facilitate the transfer of funds from a buyer in one country to a seller in another. 3. **Letters of credit**—Letters of credit facilitate international transactions by ensuring payment to sellers and ensuring to buyers that payment will not be made until the sellers have complied with the terms of the letters of credit. Typically, compliance occurs when a bill of lading is delivered to the issuing bank.
Regulation of Specific Business Activities (See pages 732–734.)	In the interests of their economies, foreign policies, domestic policies, or other national priorities, nations impose laws that restrict or facilitate international business. Such laws regulate foreign investments; exporting and importing activities; and in the United States, the bribery of foreign officials to obtain favorable contracts. The General Agreement on Tariffs and Trade (now the World Trade Organization) attempts to minimize trade barriers among nations, as do regional trade agreements, including the European Union and the North American Free Trade Agreement.
U.S. Laws in a Global Context (See pages 734–736.)	1. **Antitrust laws**—U.S. antitrust laws may be applied beyond the borders of the United States. Any conspiracy that has a substantial effect on commerce within the United States may be subject to the Sherman Act, even if the violation occurs outside the United States. 2. **Discrimination laws**—The major U.S. laws prohibiting employment discrimination, including Title VII of the Civil Rights Act of 1964, the Age Discrimination in Employment Act of 1967, and the Americans with Disabilities Act of 1990, cover U.S. employees working abroad for U.S. firms—*unless* to apply the U.S. laws would violate the laws of the host country.

For Review

1. What is the principle of comity, and why do courts deciding disputes involving a foreign law or judicial decree apply this principle?

2. What is the act of state doctrine? In what circumstances is this doctrine applied?

3. A foreign nation is not immune from the jurisdiction of U.S. courts if the nation waives its immunity. Under the Foreign Sovereign Immunities Act of 1976, on what other basis might a foreign state be considered subject to the jurisdiction of U.S. courts?

4. In what circumstances will U.S. antitrust laws be applied extraterritorially?

5. Do U.S. laws prohibiting employment discrimination apply in all circumstances to U.S. employees working for U.S. employers abroad?

Questions and Case Problems

25–1. Letters of Credit. James Reynolds entered into an agreement to purchase dental supplies from Tooth-Tech, Inc. Reynolds also secured a letter of credit from Central Bank to pay for the supplies. Tooth-Tech placed sixty crates of dental supplies on board a steamship and received in return the invoices required under the letter of credit. The purchaser, Reynolds, subsequently learned that Tooth-Tech, Inc., had filled the sixty crates with rubbish, not dental supplies. Given the fact that an issuer's obligation under a letter of credit is independent of the underlying contract between the buyer and the seller, would the issuer be required to pay the seller in this situation? Explain.

25–2. Letters of Credit. The Swiss Credit Bank issued a letter of credit in favor of Antex Industries to cover the sale of 92,000 electronic integrated circuits manufactured by Electronic Arrays. The letter of credit specified that the chips would be transported to Tokyo by ship. Antex shipped the circuits by air. Payment on the letter of credit was dishonored because the shipment by air did not fulfill the precise terms of the letter of credit. Should a court compel payment? Explain. [*Board of Trade of San Francisco v. Swiss Credit Bank*, 728 F.2d 1241 (9th Cir. 1984)]

25–3. Act of State Doctrine. Sabbatino, an American, contracted with a Cuban corporation that was largely owned by U.S. residents to buy Cuban sugar. When the Cuban government expropriated the corporation's property and rights in retaliation against a U.S. reduction of the Cuban sugar quota, Sabbatino entered into a new contract to make payment for the sugar to Banco Nacional de Cuba, a government-owned Cuban bank. Sabbatino refused to make the promised payment, and Banco subsequently filed an action in a U.S. district court seeking to recover payment for the sugar. The issue was whether the act of state doctrine should apply when a foreign state violates international law. (If the doctrine were

applied, the Cuban government's action would be presumed valid, and thus Banco's claim would be legitimate.) Should the act of state doctrine be applied in these circumstances? Discuss. [*Banco Nacional de Cuba v. Sabbatino*, 376 U.S. 398, 84 S.Ct. 923, 11 L.Ed.2d 804 (1964)]

25–4. Antitrust Claims. Billy Lamb and Carmon Willis (the plaintiffs) were tobacco growers in Kentucky. Phillip Morris, Inc., and B.A.T. Industries, PLC, routinely purchased tobacco not only from Kentucky but also from producers in several foreign countries. In 1982, subsidiaries of Phillip Morris and B.A.T. (the defendants) entered into an agreement with La Fundación Del Niño (the Children's Foundation) of Caracas, Venezuela, headed by the wife of the president of Venezuela. The agreement provided that the two subsidiaries would donate a total of approximately $12.5 million to the Children's Foundation, and in exchange, the subsidiaries would obtain price controls on Venezuelan tobacco, elimination of controls on retail cigarette prices in Venezuela, tax deductions for the donations, and assurances that existing tax rates applicable to tobacco companies would not be increased. The plaintiffs brought an action, alleging that the Venezuelan arrangement was an inducement designed to restrain trade in violation of U.S. antitrust laws. Such an arrangement, the plaintiffs contended, would result in the artificial depression of tobacco prices to the detriment of domestic tobacco growers, while ensuring lucrative retail prices for tobacco products sold abroad. The trial court held that the plaintiffs' claim was barred by the act of state doctrine. What will result on appeal? Discuss. [*Lamb v. Phillip Morris, Inc.*, 915 F.2d 1024 (6th Cir. 1990)]

25–5. Sovereign Immunity. The Bank of Jamaica, which is wholly owned by the government of Jamaica, contracted with Chisholm & Co. in January 1981 for Chisholm to arrange for lines of credit from various U.S. banks and to obtain $50 million in credit insurance from the Export-Import Bank of the United States. This Chisholm successfully did, but subsequently the Bank of Jamaica refused the deals arranged by Chisholm, and the bank refused to pay Chisholm for its services. Chisholm sued the bank in a federal district court for breach of an implied contract. The bank moved to dismiss the case, claiming, among other things, that it was immune from the jurisdiction of U.S. courts under the doctrine of sovereign immunity. What factors will the court consider in deciding whether the bank is immune from the jurisdiction of U.S. courts under the doctrine of sovereign immunity? Will the court agree? Discuss fully. [*Chisholm & Co. v. Bank of Jamaica*, 643 F.Supp. 1393 (S.D.Fla. 1986)]

25–6. Forum-Selection Clauses. Royal Bed and Spring Co., a Puerto Rican distributor of furniture products, entered into an exclusive distributorship agreement with Famossul Industria e Comercio de Moveis Ltda., a Brazilian manufacturer of furniture products. Under the terms of the contract, Royal Bed was to distribute in Puerto Rico the furniture products manufactured by Famossul in Brazil. The contract contained choice-of-forum and choice-of-law clauses, which designated the judicial district of Curitiba, State of Paraná, Brazil, as the judicial forum and the Brazilian Civil Code as the law to be applied in the event of any dispute. Famossul terminated the exclusive distributorship and suspended the shipment of goods without just cause. Under Puerto Rican law, forum-selection clauses providing for foreign venues are not enforced as a matter of public policy. In what jurisdiction should Royal Bed bring suit? Discuss fully. [*Royal Bed and Spring Co. v. Famossul Industria e Comercio de Moveis Ltda.*, 906 F.2d 45 (5th Cir. 1990)]

25–7. Discrimination Claims. Radio Free Europe and Radio Liberty (RFE/RL), a U.S. corporation doing business in Germany, employs more than three hundred U.S. citizens at its principal place of business in Munich, Germany. The concept of mandatory retirement is deeply embedded in German labor policy, and a contract formed in 1982 between RFE/RL and a German labor union contained a clause that required workers to be retired when they reach the age of sixty-five. When William Mahoney and other American employees (the plaintiffs) reached the age of sixty-five, RFE/RL terminated their employment as required under its contract with the labor union. The plaintiffs sued RFE/RL for discriminating against them on the basis of age, in violation of the Age Discrimination in Employment Act of 1967. Will the plaintiffs succeed in their suit? Discuss fully. [*Mahoney v. RFE/RL, Inc.*, 47 F.3d 447 (D.C. Cir. 1995)]

25–8. Sovereign Immunity. Reed International Trading Corp., a New York corporation, agreed to sell down jackets to Alink, a Russian business. Alink referred Reed to the Bank for Foreign and Economic Affairs of the Russian Federation for payment and gave Reed a letter of credit payable in New York. When Reed tried to collect, the bank refused to pay. Reed (and others) filed a suit in a federal district court against the bank (and others). The bank qualified as a "sovereign" under the Foreign Sovereign Immunities Act and thus claimed in part that it was immune from suit in U.S. courts. On what basis might the court hold that the bank was not immune? Explain. [*Reed International Trading Corp. v. Donau Bank, A.G.*, 866 F.Supp. 750 (S.D.N.Y. 1994)]

25–9. Sovereign Immunity. Nuovo Pignone, Inc., is an Italian company that designs and manufactures turbine systems. Nuovo sold a turbine system to Cabinda Gulf Oil Co. (CABGOC). The system was manufactured, tested, and inspected in Italy, then sent to Louisiana for mounting on a platform by CABGOC's contractor. Nuovo sent a representative to consult on the mounting. The platform went to a CABGOC site off the coast of West Africa. Marcus Pere, an instrument technician at the site, was killed when a turbine within the system exploded. Pere's widow filed a suit in a U.S. federal district court against Nuovo and others. Nuovo claimed sovereign immunity on the ground that its majority shareholder at the time of the explosion was Ente Nazionale Idrocaburi, which was created by the government of Italy to lead its oil and gas exploration and development. Is Nuovo exempt from suit under the doctrine of sovereign immunity? Is it subject to suit under the "commercial activity" exception? Why or why not? [*Pere v. Nuovo Pignone, Inc.*, 150 F.3d 477 (5th Cir. 1998)]

25–10. Dumping. In response to a petition filed on behalf of the U.S. pineapple industry, the U.S. Commerce Department initiated an investigation of canned pineapple fruit imported from Thailand. The investigation concerned Thai producers of the canned fruit, including The Thai Pineapple Public Co. The Thai producers also turned out products, such as pineapple juice and juice concentrate, outside the scope of the investigation. These products use separate parts of the same fresh pineapple, and so they share raw material costs. The Commerce Department had to calculate the Thai producers' cost of production, for the purpose of determining fair value and antidumping duties, and in so doing, had to allocate a portion of the shared fruit costs to the canned fruit. These allocations were based on the producers' own financial records, which were consistent with Thai generally accepted accounting principles. The result was a determination that more than 90 percent of the canned fruit sales were below the cost of production. The producers filed a suit in the U.S. Court of International Trade against the federal government, challenging this allocation. The producers argued that their records did not reflect actual production costs, which instead should be based on the weight of fresh fruit used to make the products. Did the Commerce Department act reasonably in determining the cost of production? Why or why not? [*The Thai Pineapple Public Co. v. United States*, 187 F.3d 1362 (Fed.Cir. 1999)]

A Question of Ethics and Social Responsibility

25–11. Ronald Riley, an American citizen, and Council of Lloyd's, a British insurance corporation with its principal place of business in London, entered into an agreement in 1980 that allowed Riley to underwrite insurance through Lloyd's. The agreement provided that if any dispute arose between Lloyd's and Riley, the courts of England would have exclusive jurisdiction, and the laws of England would apply. Over the next decade, some of the parties insured under policies that Riley underwrote experienced large losses, for which they filed claims. Instead of paying his share of the claims, Riley filed a lawsuit in a U.S. district court against Lloyd's and its managers and directors (all British citizens or entities), seeking, among other things, rescission of the 1980 agreement. Riley alleged that the defendants had violated the Securities Act of 1933, the Securities Exchange Act of 1934, and Rule 10b-5. The defendants asked the court to enforce the forum-selection clause in the agreement. Riley argued that if the clause was enforced, he would be deprived of his rights under the U.S. securities laws. The court held that the parties were to resolve their dispute in England. [*Riley v. Kingsley Underwriting Agencies, Ltd.,* 969 F.2d 953 (10th Cir. 1992)]

1. Did the court's decision fairly balance the rights of the parties? How would you argue in support of the court's decision in this case? How would you argue against it?
2. Should the fact that an international transaction may be subject to laws and remedies different from or less favorable than those of the United States be a valid basis for denying enforcement of forum-selection and choice-of-law clauses?
3. All parties to this litigation other than Riley were British. Should this fact be considered by the court in deciding this case?

Case Briefing Assignment

25–12. Examine Case A.7 [*Trans-Orient Marine Corp. v. Star Trading & Marine, Inc.,* 731 F.Supp. 619 (S.D.N.Y. 1990)] in Appendix A. The case has been excerpted there in great detail. Review and then brief the case, making sure that you include answers to the following questions in your brief.

1. What specific circumstances led to this lawsuit?
2. What was the central international legal issue addressed by the court?
3. How did the court distinguish a "succession of state" from a "succession of government," and what was the effect of the distinction on executory contracts of the state?
4. What "seminal decision" on this issue was referred to by the court? On what other cases did the court rely in its reasoning?

For Critical Analysis

25–13. Business cartels and monopolies that are legal in some countries may engage in practices that violate U.S. antitrust laws. In view of this fact, what are some of the implications of applying U.S. antitrust laws extraterritorially?

Interacting with the Internet

■ For updated links to resources available on the Web, as well as a variety of other materials, visit this text's Web site at

http://leet.westbuslaw.com

■ The University of Arizona College of Law has an online collection of various resources relating to international law. You can access this collection by going to

http://www.law.arizona.edu/
library/Internet/legal_links.html

■ The Library of Congress's Global Legal Information Network has information on the national laws of more than thirty-five countries, as well as a comprehensive Guide to Law Online. You can access this site at

http://lcweb2.loc.gov/glin/
lawhome.html

Online Legal Research Exercises

Go to **http://leet.west buslaw.com**, the Web site that accompanies this text. Select "Interactive Study Center," and then click on "Chapter 25." There you will find the following Internet research exercises that you can perform to learn more about international organizations and trade:

Activity 25–1: The World Trade Organization
Activity 25–2: Overseas Business Opportunities

Before the Test

Go to **http://leet.west buslaw.com**, the Web site that accompanies this text. Select "Interactive Quizzes." You will find a number of interactive questions relating to this chapter.

Unit VI Cumulative Hypothetical Problem

Macrotech, Inc., makes an innovative computer chip on which the firm obtains a patent and markets under the trademarked brand name "Flash."

1. Macrotech wants to sell the Flash chip to Nitron, Ltd., in Pacifica, a foreign country. Macrotech is concerned, however, that after an initial purchase, Nitron will duplicate the chip, pirate it, and sell the pirated version to computer manufacturers in Pacifica. To avoid this situation, Macrotech could establish its own manufacturing facility in Pacifica, but it does not want to do this. How can Macrotech, without establishing a manufacturing facility in Pacifica, protect against Flash being pirated by Nitron?

2. A representative of Pixel, S.A., in Raretania, a foreign country, contacts Macrotech, says that Pixel may be interested in buying a quantity of the Flash chips, and asks for a demonstration and a list of prices. Before Pixel makes a buy, Macrotech learns that there is a proposal in Congress to tax certain exports, including products such as Flash. Macrotech also learns of a proposal to impose restrictions on the export of Flash and similar products. Which of these proposals is most likely to be implemented, and why? If Congress wanted to stimulate, rather than restrict, the export of Flash, what steps might it take to do so?

3. Quaro Corp. and Selecta Corp., which are manufacturers in Techuan, a foreign country, make products that compete with the Flash chip. When Quaro and Selecta products seem to flood the U.S. market at low prices, Macrotech believes that its competitors have conspired to fix their prices. Can Macrotech file a suit against Quaro and Selecta in a U.S. court? If Quaro thought Macrotech was conspiring with other firms against it, could Quaro file a suit against Macrotech in a U.S. court? What could the U.S. government do if it found that Quaro and Selecta were selling their products in U.S. markets at "less than fair value"?

appendix A

Briefing Cases and Analyzing Case Problems

How to Brief a Case

To fully understand the law with respect to business, you need to be able to read and understand court decisions. To make this task easier, you can use a method of case analysis that is called *briefing*. There is a fairly standard procedure that you can follow when you "brief" any court case. You must first read the case opinion carefully. When you feel you understand the case, you can prepare a brief of it.

Although the format of the brief may vary, typically it will present the essentials of the case under headings such as those listed below.

1. **Citation.** Give the full citation for the case, including the name of the case, the date it was decided, and the court that decided it.
2. **Facts.** Briefly indicate (a) the reasons for the lawsuit; (b) the identity and arguments of the plaintiff(s) and defendant(s), respectively; and (c) the lower court's decision—if appropriate.
3. **Issue.** Concisely phrase, in the form of a question, the essential issue before the court. (If more than one issue is involved, you may have two—or even more—questions here.)
4. **Decision.** Indicate here—with a "yes" or "no," if possible—the court's answer to the question (or questions) in the *Issue* section above.
5. **Reason.** Summarize as briefly as possible the reasons given by the court for its decision (or decisions) and the case or statutory law relied on by the court in arriving at its decision.

When you prepare your brief, be sure that you include all of the important facts. The basic format is illustrated below in the briefed version of the sample court case that was presented in the appendix to Chapter 1 in Exhibit 1A–3. We have also annotated the briefed version to indicate the kind of information that is contained in each section.

Briefed Sample Court Case

FEDERAL EXPRESS CORP. v.
FEDERAL ESPRESSO, INC.
United States Court of Appeals,
Second Circuit, 2000.
201 F.3d 168.

Facts In 1997, Federal Express sued a small company called Federal Espresso and its owners, John Dobbs, Anna Dobbs, and David J. Ruston (collectively, the defendants). The defendants operated two coffee shops called Federal Espresso in Syracuse, New York. Federal Express asserted that the defendants, by using the name Federal Espresso, had infringed on its trademark and diluted the distinctive quality of its famous mark. Federal Express sought a preliminary injunction against the defendants' continued use of the Federal Espresso name for their business. The district court denied the motion, concluding that Federal Express had failed to demonstrate any likelihood of confusion between the two products and hence did not show that it was likely to succeed on the merits of those claims. Federal Express appealed.

Issue Was there a likelihood of confusion sufficient to allow Federal Express to succeed on the merits of its trademark claims, thus warranting a preliminary injunction?

Decision No. The appellate court affirmed the lower court's decision.

Reason The appellate court stated that because coffee and overnight delivery service were dissimilar products, there would be little likelihood of confusion. The court also emphasized that while Federal Express is "a vast organization, operating in 210 countries, employing 140,000 persons, and grossing more than $11 billion annually," the defendants were merely three individuals who operated two stores in Syracuse, New York. Given the dissimilar products and the small extent of overlap among customers of Federal Express and Federal Espresso, Federal Express was unlikely to succeed on the merits of its trademark claims, and thus a preliminary injunction against Federal Espresso was not warranted.

Review of Sample Court Case

Here we provide a review of the briefed version to indicate the kind of information that is contained in each section.

Citation The name of the case is *Federal Express Corp. v. Federal Espresso, Inc.* The plaintiff is Federal Express Corp., and the defendant is Federal Espresso, Inc. The case was decided by the United States Court of Appeals for the Second Circuit in 2000. The citation indicates that the case can be found in Volume 201 of West's *Federal Reporter, Third Series,* on page 168.

Facts The *Facts* section identifies the parties to the lawsuit—the plaintiff and the defendants—and describes the events leading up to the lawsuit and its appeal. Because this is an appeal to a federal appellate court—the United States Court of Appeals for the Second Circuit— the lower (district) court's opinion is included as part of the history of the case.

Issue The *Issue* section presents the central issue (or issues) to be decided by the court. In this case, the issue before the United States Court of Appeals for the Second Circuit is whether the trial court erred in refusing to grant Federal Express's motion for a preliminary injunction against Federal Espresso's continued use of its business name. Because this question turns on whether Federal Express had a cause of action for trademark infringement, including dilution, the real question on appeal was whether there was a likelihood of confusion between the products of the two companies sufficient to allow Federal Express to succeed on the merits of its trademark claims, thus warranting a preliminary injunction.

Decision The *Decision* section, as the term indicates, contains the court's decision on the issue or issues before it. The decision reflects the opinion of the majority of the judges or justices hearing the case. Decisions by appellate courts are frequently phrased in reference to the lower court's decision. That is, the appellate court may "affirm" the lower court's decision or "reverse" it. In this particular case, the federal appellate court affirmed the lower (district) court's decision.

Reason The *Reason* section indicates what relevant laws and judicial principles were applied in forming the particular conclusion arrived at in the case at bar (before the court). In this case, the relevant law consisted of judicial principles that have been established over time to indicate when a "likelihood of confusion" between trademarks may exist.

How to Analyze Case Problems

In addition to learning how to brief cases, students of business law also find it helpful to know how to analyze case problems. Part of the study of business law usually involves analyzing case problems, such as those included in this text at the end of each chapter.

For each case problem in this book, we provide the relevant background and facts of the lawsuit and the issue before the court. When you are assigned one of these problems, your job will be to determine how the court should decide the issue and why. In other words, you will need to engage in legal analysis and reasoning. Here we offer some suggestions on how to make this task less daunting. We begin by presenting a sample problem:

> While Janet Lawson, a famous pianist, was shopping in Quality Market, she slipped and fell on a wet floor in one of the aisles. The floor had recently been mopped by one of the store's employees, but there were no signs warning customers that the floor in that area was wet. As a result of the fall, Lawson injured her right arm and was unable to perform piano concerts for the next six months. Had she been able to perform the scheduled concerts, she would have earned approximately $60,000 over that period of time. Lawson sued Quality Market for this amount, plus another $10,000 in medical expenses. She claimed that the store's failure to warn customers of the wet floor constituted negligence and therefore the market was liable for her injuries. Will the court agree with Lawson? Discuss.

Understand the Facts

This may sound obvious, but before you can analyze or apply the relevant law to a specific set of facts, you must clearly understand those facts. In other words, you should read through the case problem carefully and more than once, if necessary, to make sure you understand the identity of the plaintiff(s) and defendant(s) in the case and the progression of events that led to the lawsuit.

In the sample case just given, the identity of the parties is fairly obvious. Janet Lawson is the one bringing the suit; therefore, she is the plaintiff. Quality Market, against whom she is bringing the suit, is the defendant. Some of the case problems you work on may have multiple plaintiffs or defendants. Often, it is helpful to use abbreviations for the parties. To indicate a reference to a plaintiff, for example, the pi symbol—π—is often used, and a defendant is denoted by a delta—Δ—a triangle.

The events leading to the lawsuit are also fairly straightforward. Lawson slipped and fell on a wet floor, and she contends that Quality Market should be liable for her injuries because it was negligent in not posting a sign warning customers of the wet floor.

When you are working on case problems, realize that the facts should be accepted as they are given. For example, in our sample problem, it should be accepted that the floor was wet and that there was no sign. In other words, avoid making conjectures, such as "Maybe the floor wasn't too wet," or "Maybe an employee was getting a sign to put up," or "Maybe someone stole the sign."

Questioning the facts as they are presented only adds confusion to your analysis.

Legal Analysis and Reasoning

Once you understand the facts given in the case problem, you can begin to analyze the case. The IRAC method is a helpful tool to use in the legal analysis and reasoning process. IRAC is an acronym for Issue, Rule, Application, Conclusion. Applying this method to our sample problem would involve the following steps:

1. First, you need to decide what legal **issue** is involved in the case. In our sample case, the basic issue is whether Quality Market's failure to warn customers of the wet floor constituted negligence. As discussed in Chapter 9, negligence is a *tort*—a civil wrong. In a tort lawsuit, the plaintiff seeks to be compensated for another's wrongful act. A defendant will be deemed negligent if he or she breached a duty of care owed to the plaintiff and the breach of that duty caused the plaintiff to suffer harm.

2. Once you have identified the issue, the next step is to determine what **rule of law** applies to the issue. To make this determination, you will want to review carefully the text of the chapter in which the problem appears to find the relevant rule of law. Our sample case involves the tort of negligence, covered in Chapter 9. The applicable rule of law is the tort law principle that business owners owe a duty to exercise reasonable care to protect their customers ("business invitees"). Reasonable care, in this context, includes either removing—or warning customers of—*foreseeable* risks about which the owner *knew* or *should have known*. Business owners need not warn customers of "open and obvious" risks, however. If a business owner breaches this duty of care (fails to exercise the appropriate degree of care toward customers), and the breach of duty causes a customer to be injured, the business owner will be liable to the customer for the customer's injuries.

3. The next—and usually the most difficult—step in analyzing case problems is the **application** of the relevant rule of law to the specific facts of the case you are studying. In our sample problem, applying the tort law principle just discussed presents few difficulties. An employee of the store had mopped the floor in the aisle where Lawson slipped and fell, but no sign was present indicating that the floor was wet. That a customer might fall on a wet floor is clearly a foreseeable risk. Therefore, the failure to warn customers about the wet floor was a breach of the duty of care owed by the business owner to the store's customers.

4. Once you have completed step 3 in the IRAC method, you should be ready to draw your **conclusion.** In our sample case, Quality Market is liable to Lawson for her injuries, because the market's breach of its duty of care caused Lawson's injuries.

The fact patterns in the case problems presented in this text are not always as simple as those presented in our sample problem. Often, for example, there may be more than one plaintiff or defendant. There also may be more than one issue involved in a case and more than one applicable rule of law. Furthermore, in some case problems the facts may indicate that the general rule of law should not apply. For example, suppose a store employee advised Lawson not to walk on the floor in the aisle because it was wet, but Lawson decided to walk on it anyway. This fact could alter the outcome of the case because the store could then raise the defense of assumption of risk (see Chapter 9). Nonetheless, a careful review of the chapter should always provide you with the knowledge you need to analyze the problem thoroughly and arrive at accurate conclusions.

Selected Cases for Briefing

In the remaining pages of this appendix, we present excerpts from the court opinions referred to in *Case Briefing Assignments.* Court opinions can run from a few pages to hundreds of pages in length. For reasons of space, only the essential parts of the opinions are presented in the cases that follow. A series of three asterisks indicates that a portion of the text—other than citations and footnotes—has been omitted. Four asterisks indicate the omission of at least one paragraph.

Case A.1   *Reference: Problem 4–11*

RODRIGUEZ de QUIJAS v.
SHEARSON/AMERICAN EXPRESS, INC.
United States Supreme Court, 1989.
490 U.S. 477,
109 S.Ct. 1917,
104 L.Ed.2d 526.

KENNEDY, Justice.

The question here is whether a predispute agreement to arbitrate claims under the Securities Act of 1933 is un-enforceable, requiring resolution of the claims only in a judicial forum.

I

Petitioners are individuals who invested about $400,000 in securities. They signed a standard customer agreement with the broker, which included a clause stating that the parties agreed to settle any controversies "relating to [the] accounts" through binding arbitration that complies with specified procedures. The agreement to arbitrate these controversies is unqualified, unless it is found to be unenforceable under federal or state law. * * * The investments turned sour, and petitioners eventually sued respondent and its broker-agent in charge of the accounts, alleging that their money was lost in unauthorized and fraudulent transactions. In their complaint they pleaded various violations of federal and state law, including claims under § 12(2) of the Securities Act of 1933, * * * and claims under three sections of the Securities Exchange Act of 1934.

The District Court ordered all the claims to be submitted to arbitration except for those raised under § 12(2) of the Securities Act. It held that the latter claims must proceed in the court action under our clear holding on the point in *Wilko v. Swan,* 346 U.S. 427, 74 S.Ct. 182, 98 L.Ed. 168 (1953). The District Court reaffirmed its ruling upon reconsideration, and also entered a default judgment against the broker, who is no longer in the case. The Court of Appeals reversed, concluding that the arbitration agreement is enforceable because this Court's subsequent decisions have reduced Wilko to "obsolescence." * * *

II

The Wilko case, decided in 1953, required the Court to determine whether an agreement to arbitrate future controversies constitutes a binding stipulation "to waive compliance with any provision" of the Securities Act, which is nullified by § 14 of the Act. * * * The Court considered the language, purposes, and legislative history of the Securities Act, and concluded that the agreement to arbitrate was void under § 14. But the decision was a difficult one in view of the competing legislative policy embodied in the Arbitration Act, which the Court described as "not easily reconcilable," and which strongly favors the enforcement of agreements to arbitrate as a means of securing "prompt, economical and adequate solution of controversies." * * *

It has been recognized that Wilko was not obviously correct, for "the language prohibiting waiver of 'compliance with any provision of this title' could easily have been read to relate to substantive provisions of the Act without including the remedy provisions." * * * The Court did not read the language this way in Wilko, however, and gave two reasons. First, the Court rejected the argument that "arbitration is merely a form of trial to be used in lieu of a trial at law." * * * The Court found instead that § 14 does not permit waiver of "the right to select the judicial forum" in favor of arbitration, * * * because "arbitration lacks the certainty of a suit at law under the Act to enforce [the buyer's] rights," * * *. Second, the Court concluded that the Securities Act was intended to protect buyers of securities, who often do not deal at arm's length and on equal terms with sellers, by offering them "a wider choice of courts and venue" than is enjoyed by participants in other business transactions,

making "the right to select the judicial forum" a particularly valuable feature of the Securities Act. * * *

* * * The shift in the Court's views on arbitration away from those adopted in Wilko is shown by the flat statement in [a prior case]: "By agreeing to arbitrate a statutory claim, a party does not forgo the substantive rights afforded by the statute; it only submits to their resolution in an arbitral, rather than a judicial, forum." * * * To the extent that Wilko rested on suspicion of arbitration as a method of weakening the protections afforded in the substantive law to would-be complainants, it has fallen far out of step with our current strong endorsement of the federal statutes favoring this method of resolving disputes.

Once the outmoded presumption of disfavoring arbitration proceedings is set to one side, it becomes clear that the right to select the judicial forum and the wider choice of courts are not such essential features of the Securities Act that § 14 is properly construed to bar any waiver of these provisions. Nor are they so critical that they cannot be waived under the rationale that the Securities Act was intended to place buyers of securities on an equal footing with sellers. Wilko identified two different kinds of provisions in the Securities Act that would advance this objective. Some are substantive, such as placing on the seller the burden of proving lack of *scienter* when a buyer alleges fraud. * * * Others are procedural. The specific procedural improvements highlighted in Wilko are the statute's broad venue provisions in the federal courts; the existence of nationwide service of process in the federal courts; the extinction of the amount-in-controversy requirement that had applied to fraud suits when they were brought in federal courts under diversity jurisdiction rather than as a federal cause of action; and the grant of concurrent jurisdiction in the state and federal courts without possibility of removal.

There is no sound basis for construing the prohibition in § 14 on waiving "compliance with any provision" of the Securities Act to apply to these procedural provisions. Although the first three measures do facilitate suits by buyers of securities, the grant of concurrent jurisdiction constitutes explicit authorization for complainants to waive those protections by filing suit in state court without possibility of removal to federal court. These measures, moreover, are present in other federal statutes which have not been interpreted to prohibit enforcement of predispute agreements to arbitrate. * * * [T]he party opposing arbitration carries the burden of showing that Congress intended in a separate statute to preclude a waiver of judicial remedies, or that such a waiver of judicial remedies inherently conflicts with the underlying purposes of that other statute. * * * But as Justice Frankfurter said in dissent in Wilko, so it is true in this case: "There is nothing in the record before us, nor in the facts of which we can take judicial notice, to indicate that the arbitral system . . . would not afford the plaintiff the rights to which he is entitled." * * *

The language quoted above from § 2 of the Arbitration Act also allows the courts to give relief where the party opposing arbitration presents "well-supported claims that the agreement to arbitrate resulted from the sort of fraud or overwhelming economic power that would provide grounds 'for the revocation of any contract.'" * * * This avenue of relief is in harmony with the Securities Act's concern to protect buyers of securities by removing "the disadvantages under which buyers labor" in their dealings with sellers. * * *

III

We now conclude that Wilko was incorrectly decided and is inconsistent with the prevailing uniform construction of other federal statutes governing arbitration agreements in the setting of business transactions. Although we are normally and properly reluctant to overturn our decisions construing statutes, we have done so to achieve a uniform interpretation of similar statutory language

* * * and to correct a seriously erroneous interpretation of statutory language that would undermine congressional policy as expressed in other legislation, * * * Both purposes would be served here by overruling the Wilko decision. In this case, for example, petitioners' claims under the 1934 Act were subjected to arbitration, while their claim under the 1933 Act was not permitted to go to arbitration, but was required to proceed in court. That result makes little sense for similar claims, based on similar facts, which are supposed to arise within a single federal regulatory scheme. In addition, the inconsistency * * * undermines the essential rationale for a harmonious construction of the two statutes, which is to discourage litigants from manipulating their allegations merely to cast their claims under one of the securities laws rather than another. For all of these reasons, therefore, we overrule the decision in Wilko.

The judgment of the Court of Appeals is AFFIRMED.

Case A.2   *Reference: Problem 6–12*

AUSTIN v. BERRYMAN
United States Court of Appeals,
Fourth Circuit, 1989.
878 F.2d 786.

MURNAGHAN, Circuit Judge:

We have before us for *en banc* [by the whole court] reconsideration an appeal taken from an action successfully brought by Barbara Austin in the United States District Court for the Western District of Virginia against the Virginia Employment Commission, challenging a denial of unemployment compensation benefits. * * * In brief, Austin charged, *inter alia* [among other things], that the denial of her claim for unemployment benefits, based on a Virginia statute specifically precluding such benefits for any individual who voluntarily quits work to join his or her spouse in a new location, was an unconstitutional infringement upon the incidents of marriage protected by the Fourteenth Amendment and an unconstitutional burden on her First Amendment right to the free exercise of her religion. Her religion happened to command that she follow her spouse wherever he might go and the sincerity of her religious belief was not questioned. The district court found in Austin's favor and awarded injunctive relief and retroactive benefits.

On appeal, Judge Sprouse, writing for a panel majority, found that the denial of benefits did not implicate Austin's Fourteenth Amendment rights, but that it did unconstitutionally burden Austin's right to the free exercise of her religion. The panel also found, however, that any award of retroactive benefits was barred by the Eleventh

Amendment. One panel member concurred with the panel majority as to the Fourteenth and Eleventh Amendment issues, but dissented as to the existence of a free exercise violation. The panel opinion now, of course, has been vacated by a grant of rehearing *en banc*.

After careful consideration of the additional arguments proffered by both sides, the Court, *en banc*, is convinced that the panel majority correctly concluded that denying Austin unemployment benefits did not infringe upon fundamental marital rights protected by the Fourteenth Amendment. To this extent, we adopt the majority panel opinion. We also find, however, that the denial of benefits did not unconstitutionally burden Austin's First Amendment right to the free exercise of her religion. We are persuaded that the views expressed on the First Amendment, free exercise of religion claim in the opinion dissenting in part from the panel majority are correct, and we hereby adopt that opinion as that of the *en banc* court. As we find that Austin is not entitled to any relief, we need not address whether the Eleventh Amendment bars an award of retroactive benefits.

The decisive consideration, as we see it, is that the proximate cause of Austin's unemployment is geographic distance, not her religious beliefs. There is no conflict between the circumstances of work and Austin's religious precepts. Austin's religious beliefs do not "require" her "to refrain from the work in question." Austin is unable to work simply because she is now too far removed from her employer to make it practical. In striking contrast, if one, for genuine religious beliefs, moves to a new residence in order to continue to live with a spouse, and that residence is not geographically so removed as to preclude regular attendance at the worksite, no unemployment, and hence no unemployment benefits, will arise. That amounts to proof that extent of geographical non-propinquity, not religious belief, led to Austin's disqualification for unemployment benefits.

Austin voluntarily decided to quit her job and join her spouse in a new geographic location 150 miles away. Virginia has stated that every individual who follows such a course, no matter what the reason, religious or non-religious, is disqualified for unemployment benefits.

To craft judicially a statutory exception only for those individuals who profess Austin's religious convictions, particularly in the absence of a direct conflict between a given employment practice and a religious belief, would, in our view, result in a subsidy to members of a particular religious belief, impermissible under the Establishment Clause.

Accordingly, the judgment of the district court is REVERSED.

Case A.3   *Reference: Problem 9–12*

BURLINGHAM v. MINTZ
Supreme Court of Montana, 1995.
891 P.2d 527.

HUNT, Justice.
* * * *

On March 21, 1990, Candance Burlingham visited Dr. Mintz for a check-up and teeth cleaning. Dr. Mintz determined that she needed further treatment. Dr. Mintz also determined that Candance suffered from temporomandibular joint (TMJ) pain. On April 20, 1990, Candance returned to Dr. Mintz for treatment of her upper left rear molar. After applying a local anesthetic, Dr. Mintz noted that Candance had difficulty keeping her mouth open. To help keep her mouth open, Dr. Mintz placed a bite block between Candance's jaws. A bite block is a rubber coated tapered device with a serrated surface to keep it in place. The bite block was left in for approximately 45 minutes to one hour while Dr. Mintz completed the work. Later that day Candance began to suffer severe TMJ pain which did not abate. Dr. Mintz filled several more of Candance's teeth over the next few months, although he was hindered by her TMJ pain. In October 1990, Dr. Mintz referred Candance to a * * * specialist [in Kalispell, Montana,] who attempted, without success, to relieve Candance's pain. Eventually, Candance underwent restorative arthroscopic surgery in Spokane, Washington, to alleviate her TMJ pain.

On September 18, 1992, appellants filed suit alleging that Dr. Mintz's negligence caused Candance's TMJ injury. Appellants' first standard of care expert, Dr. James McGivney, was deposed on June 11, 1993. On August 12, 1993, appellants filed a motion asking the District Court to qualify Dr. McGivney as an expert [a person whose professional training or experience qualifies him or her to testify on a particular subject]. * * *

On February 8, 1994, the District Court denied appellants' motion[,] finding that Dr. McGivney, a suburban St. Louis dentist, was not familiar with the standards of practice or medical facilities available in Eureka, Montana, in a similar locality in Montana, or a similar locality anywhere in the country. The District Court

granted appellants until the end of February to find another expert.
* * * *

On June 7, 1994, respondent filed a motion for summary judgment, arguing that appellants were not able to present expert testimony to meet their burden of proof to establish * * * a violation by respondent of his standard of care. The District Court granted respondent's motion. Appellants appeal from the order granting summary judgment.
* * * *

The District Court concluded that appellants' proposed experts had no idea of the standards of practice in Eureka, Montana, in a similar locality in Montana, or in a similar place anywhere else in the country. A review of the testimony of respondent's and appellants' standard of care experts reveals little, if any, contradictory testimony as to the applicable standard of care for a dentist treating a patient suffering from TMJ pain in Eureka, Montana, or any other community in the country. Respondent's first standard of care expert testified that, with the exception of limited specialties, the same standard of care that applies to dentists in San Francisco and Kalispell, applies to dentists in Eureka. He agreed that the standard of care required in the diagnosis of and the treatment decisions regarding TMJ pain would be the same in San Francisco, Kalispell, and Eureka. Respondent's second standard of care expert testified that in non-emergency situations the standard of care for dentists in Eureka is the same as the non-emergency standard of care anywhere else in the United States.
* * * *

We conclude that appellants' standard of care experts were familiar with the applicable non-emergency standard of care for dentists in Eureka if, by either direct or indirect knowledge, they were familiar with the applicable non-emergency standard of care for dentists in their communities, regardless of size or location. As a result, we hold that the District Court erred by excluding appellants' standard of care experts.
* * * *

* * * We reverse the summary judgment and remand this case to the District Court for further proceedings.

Case A.4

Reference: Problem 13–12

POTTER v. OSTER
Supreme Court of Iowa, 1988.
426 N.W.2d 148.

NEUMAN, Justice.

This is a suit in equity brought by the plaintiffs to re-scind an installment land contract based on the seller's inability to convey title. The question on appeal is whether, in an era of declining land values, returning the parties to the status quo works an inequitable result. We think not. Accordingly, we affirm the district court judgment for rescission and restitution.

The facts are largely undisputed. Because the case was tried in equity, our review is *de novo*. We give weight to the findings of the trial court, particularly where the credibility of witnesses is concerned, but we are not bound thereby.

The parties, though sharing a common interest in agribusiness, present a study in contrasts. We think the disparity in their background and experience is notable insofar as it bears on the equities of the transaction in issue. Plaintiff Charles Potter is a farm laborer and his wife, Sue, is a homemaker and substitute teacher. They have lived all their lives within a few miles of the real estate in question. Defendant Merrill Oster is an agricultural journalist and recognized specialist in land investment strategies. He owns Oster Communications, a multimillion dollar publishing concern devoted to furnishing farmers the latest in commodity market analysis and advice on an array of farm issues.

In May 1978, Oster contracted with Florence Stark to purchase her 160-acre farm in Howard County, Iowa, for $260,000 on a ten-year contract at seven percent interest. Oster then sold the homestead and nine acres to Charles and Sue Potter for $70,000. Potters paid $18,850 down and executed a ten-year installment contract for the balance at 8.5% interest. Oster then executed a contract with Robert Bishop for the sale of the remaining 151 acres as part of a package deal that included the sale of seventeen farms for a sum exceeding $5.9 million.

These back-to-back contracts collapsed like dominoes in March 1985 when Bishop failed to pay Oster and Oster failed to pay Stark the installments due on their respective contracts. Stark commenced forfeiture proceedings [proceedings to retake the property because Oster failed to perform a legal obligation—payment under the contract—and thus forfeited his right to the land]. Potters had paid every installment when due under their contract with Oster and had included Stark as a joint payee [one of two or more payees—persons to whom checks or notes are payable] with Oster on their March 1, 1985, payment. But they were financially unable to exercise their right to advance the sums due on the entire 160 acres in order to preserve their interest in the nine acres and

homestead. As a result, their interest in the real estate was forfeited along with Oster's and Bishop's and they were forced to move from their home in August 1985.

Potters then sued Oster to rescind their contract with him, claiming restitution damages for all consideration paid. * * *

Trial testimony * * * revealed that the market value of the property had decreased markedly since its purchase. Expert appraisers valued the homestead and nine acres between $27,500 and $35,000. Oster himself placed a $28,000 value on the property; Potter $39,000. Evidence was also received placing the reasonable rental value of the property at $150 per month, or a total of $10,800 for the six-year Potter occupancy.

The district court concluded the Potters were entitled to rescission of the contract and return of the consideration paid including principal and interest, cost of improvements, closing expenses, and taxes for a total of $65,169.37. From this the court deducted $10,800 for six years' rental, bringing the final judgment to $54,369.37.

On appeal, Oster challenges the judgment. * * * [H]e claims Potters had an adequate remedy at law for damages which should have been measured by the actual economic loss sustained * * * .

* * * *

Rescission is a restitutionary remedy which attempts to restore the parties to their positions at the time the contract was executed. The remedy calls for a return of the land to the seller, with the buyer given judgment for payments made under the contract plus the value of improvements, less reasonable rental value for the period during which the buyer was in possession. The remedy has long been available in Iowa to buyers under land contracts when the seller has no title to convey.

Rescission is considered an extraordinary remedy, however, and is ordinarily not available to a litigant as a matter of right but only when, in the discretion of the court, it is necessary to obtain equity. Our cases have established three requirements that must be met before rescission will be granted. First, the injured party must not be in default. Second, the breach must be substantial and go to the heart of the contract. Third, remedies at law must be inadequate.

The first two tests are easily met in the present case. Potters are entirely without fault in this transaction. They tendered their 1985 installment payment to Oster before the forfeiture, and no additional payments were due until 1986. On the question of materiality, Oster's loss of equitable title [ownership rights protected in equity] to the homestead by forfeiture caused not only substantial, but total breach of his obligation to insure peaceful possession [an implied promise made by a landowner, when selling or renting land, that the buyer or tenant will not be evicted or disturbed by the landowner or a person having a lien or superior title] and convey marketable title under the Oster-Potter contract.

Only the third test—the inadequacy of damages at law—is contested by Oster on appeal. * * *

Restoring the status quo is the goal of the restitutionary remedy of rescission. Here, the district court accomplished the goal by awarding Potters a sum representing all they had paid under the contract rendered worthless by Oster's default. Oster contends that in an era of declining land values, such a remedy goes beyond achieving the status quo and results in a windfall to the Potters. Unwilling to disgorge the benefits he has received under the unfulfilled contract, Oster would have the court shift the "entrepreneurial risk" [the risk assumed by one who initiates, and provides or controls the management of, a business enterprise] of market loss to the Potters by limiting their recovery to the difference between the property's market value at breach ($35,000) and the contract balance ($27,900). In other words, Oster claims the court should have awarded * * * damages. * * *

* * * *

* * * [L]egal remedies are considered inadequate when the damages cannot be measured with sufficient certainty. Contrary to Oster's assertion that Potters' compensation should be limited to the difference between the property's fair market value and contract balance at time of breach, * * * damages are correctly calculated as the difference between contract price and market value at the time for performance. Since the time of performance in this case would have been March 1990, the market value of the homestead and acreage cannot be predicted with any certainty, thus rendering such a formulation inadequate.

Most importantly, the fair market value of the homestead at the time of forfeiture is an incorrect measure of the benefit Potters lost. It fails to account for the special value Potters placed on the property's location and residential features that uniquely suited their family. For precisely this reason, remedies at law are presumed inadequate for breach of a real estate contract. Oster has failed to overcome that presumption here. His characterization of the transaction as a mere market loss for Potters, compensable by a sum which would enable them to make a nominal down payment on an equivalent homestead, has no legal or factual support in this record.

* * *

* * * *

In summary, we find no error in the trial court's conclusion that Potters were entitled to rescission of the contract and return of all benefits allowed thereunder, less the value of reasonable rental for the period of occupancy * * *.

AFFIRMED.

Case A.5   *Reference: Problem 15–11*

HAWLEY v. CEMENT INDUSTRIES, INC.
United States Court of Appeals, Eleventh Circuit, 1995.
51 F.3d 246.

PER CURIAM:

* * * *

In September 1990, Appellant Phillip E. Hawley ("Appellant") filed a Chapter 7 bankruptcy petition, claiming less than $20,000 in assets. In a signed statement dated June 15, 1989, Appellant listed his total assets at $13,822,477, total liabilities at $1,876,814, and total net worth at $11,945,663. Later in 1990, one of Appellant's creditors, Cement Industries, Inc. ("Appellee"), filed an adversary proceeding pursuant to 11 U.S.C. s 727(a)(5), urging the court to deny Appellant's discharge based on his failure to satisfactorily explain the loss of his assets between the filings of his financial statement and his bankruptcy petition.

Section 727(a)(5) of the Bankruptcy Code provides as follows: * * * ["](a) the court shall grant the debtor a discharge, unless— * * * the debtor has failed to explain satisfactorily, before determination of denial of discharge under this paragraph, any loss of assets or deficiency of assets to meet the debtor's liabilities.["]

* * * *

The bankruptcy court denied Appellant's discharge, observing that the Appellant, a "sophisticated and experienced businessman," had been unable to present documentation to explain the discrepancy between the value of his assets as listed in 1989 and the value he had listed in his bankruptcy petition in 1990. The court found a "complete lack of documentation to support the Debtor's loss of assets" and determined that "when examining the totality of the circumstances, this Court finds a pattern which leads this Court to conclude that the Debtor has not satisfactorily explained the loss or diminution of his assets."

The Appellant appealed to the district court. The district court affirmed and adopted the opinion of the bankruptcy court "as fully as if copied verbatim." The district court dismissed the appeal and Appellant then appealed to this Court * * *.

* * * *

* * * Appellant argues that Appellee failed to carry its burden in showing that Appellant's explanations for the loss of his assets were unsatisfactory. In its [Section] 727(a)(5) action, Appellee had the initial burden of proving its objection to Appellant's discharge. Appellee sustained this burden by showing the vast discrepancies

between Appellant's 1989 financial statement and his 1990 Chapter 7 schedules. Once the party objecting to the discharge establishes the basis for its objection, the burden then shifts to the debtor "to explain satisfactorily the loss." "To be satisfactory, 'an explanation' must convince the judge." "Vague and indefinite explanations of losses that are based on estimates uncorroborated by documentation are unsatisfactory." Obviously, Appellant's explanations did not "convince the judge." The bank-ruptcy judge clearly found Appellant's testimony and complete lack of documentation unconvincing. Upon review of the record, we find that the bankruptcy judge did not clearly err in finding that Appellant's explanation of his loss of more than $13 million in assets over the course of fifteen months was too vague and indefinite to be "satisfactory." Therefore, the judgment of the district court is AFFIRMED.

Case A.6

Reference: Problem 16–12

MASCHMEIER v. SOUTHSIDE PRESS, LTD.
Court of Appeals of Iowa, 1989.
435 N.W.2d 377.

HABHAB, Judge.

Defendant Kenneth E. Maschmeier and Charlotte A. Maschmeier created a corporation, Southside Press, Ltd., that did business at 1220 Second Avenue North in Council Bluffs. This building is owned by Kenneth and Charlotte and was leased by them to the corporation.

Kenneth and Charlotte are the majority shareholders, with each having 1300 shares. They are the only officers and directors of the corporation.

They gifted to their two sons [Marty and Larry] each 1200 shares of stock. All the parties were employed by Southside Press until the summer of 1985 when, because of family disagreements, Marty and Larry were terminated as employees. * * *

The parents on August 2, 1985, created a new corporation, Southside Press of the Midlands, Ltd. They are its only officers and directors. As individuals they terminated the lease of their building * * * with Southside and leased the same premises to Midlands. In addition, Kenneth, as president of Southside, entered into a lease with himself as president of Midlands whereby the printing equipment and two of the vehicles were leased to Midlands for $22,372 per year for five years, with an option to buy such assets at the end of the lease term at their fair market value but not to exceed $20,000. In addition, the inventory and two other vehicles owned by Southside were sold by it to Midlands. Notwithstanding the fact that a substantial part of the assets of Southside had been disposed of, the parents still received an annual salary from it of more than $20,000.

After Marty and Larry's employment with Southside had terminated, each obtained employment with other printing companies in the same metropolitan area. The family disagreement continued. All stockholders were employed by companies that were competitive to Southside. Ultimately, the parents, as majority shareholders, offered to buy the sons' shares of stock for $20 per share. Their sons felt that this amount was inadequate. Thus, this lawsuit.

In 1985, Southside Press had gross sales of more than $600,000. The trial court found that in 1985 the corporate assets had a fair market value of $160,745. Shareholders' equity was found to be $236,502.92, and divided by the number of shares equals $47.30 per share. The court found that the majority shareholders had been abusive and oppressive to the minority shareholders by wasting the corporate assets and leaving Southside Press only a shell of a corporation. The court ordered the majority shareholders to pay $47.30 per share to the sons, or $56,760 to each son, plus interest at the maximum legal rate from the date of the filing of the petition.

* * * *

* * * [D]efendants state that the shares were valued at $20 pursuant to the corporate bylaws and should be enforced as an agreement of the shareholders. * * *

* * * *

Whenever a situation exists which is contrary to the principles of equity and which can be redressed within the scope of judicial action, a court of equity will devise a remedy to meet the situation though no similar relief has been granted before. The district court has the power to liquidate a corporation under [Iowa Code] section 496A.94(1). This statute also allows the district court to fashion other equitable relief.

It is contended that, in order for the trial court to have properly invoked the powers under section 496A.94(1), it had to find either the majority shareholders were oppressive in their conduct towards the minority shareholders, or that the majority shareholders misapplied or wasted corporate assets.

* * * The alleged oppressive conduct by those in control of a close corporation must be analyzed in terms of "fiduciary duties" owed by majority shareholders to the minority shareholders and "reasonable expectations" held by minority shareholders in committing capital and labor to the particular enterprise, in light of the predicament in which minority shareholders in a close corporation can be placed by a "freeze-out" situation.

* * * The trial court found * * * here [that] the majority shareholders attempted to "freeze out" or "squeeze out" the minority shareholders by terminating their employment and not permitting them to participate in the business.

* * * *

We concur with the trial court's findings that the majority shareholders acted oppressively toward the minority shareholders and wasted corporate assets. In this respect, we further determine that the trial court properly invoked Iowa Code section 496A.94 when it fashioned the remedy requiring the majority shareholders to purchase the shares of the minority.

But that does not resolve the problem[.] * * * The appellant challenges the method fashioned by the trial court in fixing the value of the stock and payment thereof by asserting it should be governed by the bylaws.

The articles of incorporation of Southside vested in the directors of the corporation the "authority to make provisions in the Bylaws of the corporation restricting the transfer of shares of this corporation." This the board of directors did when they adopted the following bylaw that relates to restrictions on the transferability of stock. * * *

* * * *

Section 3 [of the corporate bylaws] is a restriction on stock transfer. If a shareholder intends to sell his stock, he must first offer it to the corporation at a price "agreed upon by the shareholders at each annual meeting." The shareholders must agree on the value of the stock and if they are unable to do so, each has a right to select an appraiser and the appraisers shall appoint another and in this instance the five appraisers are to act as a Board of Appraisers to value the stock.

* * * Since none of the shareholders requested appraisers, we deem this, as the trial court did, to be a waiver. We concur with this statement from the trial court's ruling: "All parties have left the Court with the burden of evaluating the corporate stock."

* * * *

We agree with the defendants that a contractual formula price is enforceable even if the formula price is less than its fair market value. But here the parties were unable to agree to a price, i.e., at the last meeting of the stockholders. Thus the trial court was called upon to do so.

Courts have generally held that no one factor governs the valuation of shares; but that all factors, such as market value, asset value, future earning prospects, should be considered. In this case, the parties relied rather heavily on what is referred to in the record as book value (shareholders' equity) in arriving at stock value. The trial court likewise used shareholder equity but adjusted that amount by the present day fair market value of corporate assets.

* * * *

We determine that under the circumstances here the valuation per share as fixed by the trial court and the method it employed in arriving at value is fair and reasonable. However, we further conclude that the amount Larry and Marty are to receive must be reduced by the total amount of loans made to them as they appear on the corporate books.

* * * *

We affirm and modify.

Case A.7

Reference: Problem 25–11

TRANS-ORIENT MARINE CORP. v. STAR TRADING & MARINE, INC.
United States District Court,
Southern District of New York, 1990.
731 F.Supp. 619.

WILLIAM C. CONNER, District Judge:

Defendant Republic of the Sudan moves this Court to dismiss the complaint for failure to state a claim or for summary judgment. It claims that the new Republic of the Sudan, as successor state, is not liable for the alleged breach of a five-year exclusive agency contract entered into by the prior sovereign state of Sudan. Defendant further asserts that a fundamental change in circumstances relieves it of any prior contractual obligations.

FACTS

Plaintiff's cause of action for breach of contract arises from an alleged five-year exclusive agency agreement to represent the Sudan in the United States P.L. 480 program [an agricultural trade development and assistance program]. The alleged October 14, 1983 agreement was effective from October 1, 1984 through September 30, 1989. In April 1985, a military coup deposed the then head of state, declaring a state of emergency and suspending the constitution. A twelve-month transitional military regime followed, which was then replaced by a civilian coalition government. The name of the state was changed from the Sudan to the Republic of Sudan. In June 1989, there was another military coup in which the present military regime overthrew the former civilian administration and suspended the constitution. Both parties agree that the Republic of the Sudan is a foreign sovereign state.

On January 3 and 4, 1985, the then Sudanese government sent letters advising plaintiff that a new agent, CIDCO, had been appointed to handle the contracts under P.L. 480 and that CIDCO would select the shipping agent. This alleged termination of the then-executory contract did not provide the one-year termination notice required under the original contract. Since January 1985, the Sudan has awarded CIDCO a continuing series of contracts to handle the wheat and wheat flour transportation under P.L. 480, in alleged violation of plaintiff's exclusive agency contract. No additional facts are relevant to the present motion.

DISCUSSION

The present Sudanese government asserts that it is not liable for the contractual obligations of the prior sovereign, pointing to the two military coups of 1985 and 1989 to sustain its position that both the 1985 military regime and the present administration are successor states and that there has been a fundamental change in circumstances. Plaintiff contends that neither the 1985 regime nor the present regime is a successor state but that they represent mere changes in government which do not relieve the present regime from the prior government's contractual obligations. Plaintiff further argues that even if either regime is a successor state, they have ratified the prior government's contract. For the following reasons, summary judgment is denied.

Whether a new administration may terminate the executory portions of its predecessor's contracts is based on the succession of state theory. International law sharply distinguishes the succession of state, which may create a discontinuity of statehood, from a succession of government, which leaves statehood unaffected. It is generally accepted that a change in government, regime or ideology has no effect on that state's international rights and obligations because the state continues to exist despite the change. * * *

However, where one sovereign succeeds another, and a new state is created, the rights and obligations of the successor state are affected. The rule with regard to contracts with private foreign individuals involves a balancing of competing interests. While the successor state is permitted to terminate existing contracts originally executed by the former sovereign and the private party, the successor state is liable to that party only for any amount due him as of the date of the change of sovereignty. But if the contract is totally executory, the successor state is released from the contract.

The Restatement of Foreign Relations Law describes a successor state to include: a state that wholly absorbs another state, that takes over part of the territory of another state, that becomes independent of another state of which it had formed a part, or that arises because of the dismemberment of the state of which it had been a part.

Careful study of defendant's submission reveals that the state of Sudan has not (1) wholly absorbed or been wholly absorbed by another state; (2) partly taken over or been partly taken over by another state; (3) become independent from another state of which it had formed a part; or (4) arisen out of dismemberment of a state of which it had been a part since the date of plaintiff's contract. Under the Restatement's definition, the state of Sudan has remained the same entity since its independ-

ence in 1956. Defendant's own exhibit in support of its motion substantiates that only a change in government was effected by the two military coups * * *.

Accordingly, the only changes in the Sudan since its independence in 1956 have been in the government, with seven distinct successive administrations. But there has been only one state.

Defendant unpersuasively emphasizes various aspects of the relevant transitions to reflect the creation of a new state: that the transitions resulted by way of military coups as opposed to routine, constitutional processes, the re-naming of the nation, the suspension of the constitution, the closing of the borders and the declaration of a state of emergency. Treatises, as well as applicable case law, demonstrate that such features do not effect a succession of state. * * *

Furthermore, the Restatement's comparative chart in a Recognition of States section illustrates that a change in government by armed force or fraud, as well as institution of another regime following a civil war, leaves "no question of the existence of the state." It offers as contemporary examples of mere changes in government: Pinochet's 1973 ouster of Allende in Chile, Franco's 1936–39 takeover of Spain, and the Communist revolution in China.

The seminal decision on the distinction between a succession of state versus a change in government is the U. S. Supreme Court decision in *The Sapphire*. In *The Sapphire*, the Supreme Court considered whether a lawsuit begun by the French Emperor, Napoleon III, was abated by the overthrow of the Emperor during the course of litigation. In holding that the action was not extinguished, the Supreme Court stated that, "on the [Emperor's] deposition the sovereignty does not change, but merely the person or persons in whom it resides. . . . A change in such representative works no change in the national sovereignty or its rights."

* * * *

* * * In *United States v. National City Bank of New York*, the district court held the post-revolutionary State of Russia liable on the treasury notes of the pre-revolutionary state. Similarly, in *Jackson v. People's Republic of China*, the district court determined that the People's Republic, as successor government to the Imperial Chinese Government, was successor to its obligations, specifically, payment of principal due on the prior government-issued bonds. The law is clear that the obligations of a state are unaffected by a mere change in government. It is of no consequence that the Sudan allegedly breached an executory contract. The distinction between executed and executory contracts only applies where there has been a succession of state. The military coups of 1985 and 1989 did not effect a succession of state of the Sudan but merely changed the state's governing body, leaving the state's obligations undisturbed.

Defendant's alternative claim that a fundamental change of circumstances has occurred since October, 1983 relieving it of any prior contractual obligations is unsubstantiated. Defendant presents no explanation as to what "circumstances constituted an essential basis of the consent of the parties to be bound by the agreement" or what changes have "radically transform[ed] the extent of obligations still to be performed under the agreement." Having failed to demonstrate a fundamental change in circumstances, the present government is therefore contractually obligated to plaintiff under the October 14, 1983 five-year extension of agency contract if its predecessor indeed breached that agreement.

CONCLUSION

For the reasons discussed above, summary judgment is denied.

SO ORDERED.

The Constitution
of the United States

PREAMBLE

We the People of the United States, in Order to form a more perfect Union, establish Justice, insure domestic Tranquility, provide for the common defence, promote the general Welfare, and secure the Blessings of Liberty to ourselves and our Posterity, do ordain and establish this Constitution for the United States of America.

ARTICLE I

Section 1. All legislative Powers herein granted shall be vested in a Congress of the United States, which shall consist of a Senate and House of Representatives.

Section 2. The House of Representatives shall be composed of Members chosen every second Year by the People of the several States, and the Electors in each State shall have the Qualifications requisite for Electors of the most numerous Branch of the State Legislature.

No Person shall be a Representative who shall not have attained to the Age of twenty five Years, and been seven Years a Citizen of the United States, and who shall not, when elected, be an Inhabitant of that State in which he shall be chosen.

Representatives and direct Taxes shall be apportioned among the several States which may be included within this Union, according to their respective Numbers, which shall be determined by adding to the whole Number of free Persons, including those bound to Service for a Term of Years, and excluding Indians not taxed, three fifths of all other Persons. The actual Enumeration shall be made within three Years after the first Meeting of the Congress of the United States, and within every subsequent Term of ten Years, in such Manner as they shall by Law direct. The Number of Representatives shall not exceed one for every thirty Thousand, but each State shall have at Least one Representative; and until such enumeration shall be made, the State of New Hampshire shall be entitled to chuse three, Massachusetts eight, Rhode Island and Providence Plantations one, Connecticut five, New York six, New Jersey four, Pennsylvania eight, Delaware one, Maryland six, Virginia ten, North Carolina five, South Carolina five, and Georgia three.

When vacancies happen in the Representation from any State, the Executive Authority thereof shall issue Writs of Election to fill such Vacancies.

The House of Representatives shall chuse their Speaker and other Officers; and shall have the sole Power of Impeachment.

Section 3. The Senate of the United States shall be composed of two Senators from each State, chosen by the Legislature thereof, for six Years; and each Senator shall have one Vote.

Immediately after they shall be assembled in Consequence of the first Election, they shall be divided as equally as may be into three Classes. The Seats of the Senators of the first Class shall be vacated at the Expiration of the second Year, of the second Class at the Expiration of the fourth Year, and of the third Class at the Expiration of the sixth Year, so that one third may be chosen every second Year; and if Vacancies happen by Resignation, or otherwise, during the Recess of the Legislature of any State, the Executive thereof may make temporary Appointments until the next Meeting of the Legislature, which shall then fill such Vacancies.

No Person shall be a Senator who shall not have attained to the Age of thirty Years, and been nine Years a Citizen of the United States, and who shall not, when elected, be an Inhabitant of that State for which he shall be chosen.

The Vice President of the United States shall be President of the Senate, but shall have no Vote, unless they be equally divided.

The Senate shall chuse their other Officers, and also a President pro tempore, in the Absence of the Vice President, or when he shall exercise the Office of President of the United States.

The Senate shall have the sole Power to try all Impeachments. When sitting for that Purpose, they shall be on Oath or Affirmation. When the President of the United States is tried, the Chief Justice shall preside: And no Person shall be convicted without the Concurrence of two thirds of the Members present.

Judgment in Cases of Impeachment shall not extend further than to removal from Office, and disqualification to hold and enjoy any Office of honor, Trust, or Profit under the United States: but the Party convicted shall nevertheless be liable and subject to Indictment, Trial, Judgment, and Punishment, according to Law.

Section 4. The Times, Places and Manner of holding Elections for Senators and Representatives, shall be prescribed in each State by the Legislature thereof; but the Congress may at any time by Law make or alter such Regulations, except as to the Places of chusing Senators.

The Congress shall assemble at least once in every Year, and such Meeting shall be on the first Monday in

December, unless they shall by Law appoint a different Day.

Section 5. Each House shall be the Judge of the Elections, Returns, and Qualifications of its own Members, and a Majority of each shall constitute a Quorum to do Business; but a smaller Number may adjourn from day to day, and may be authorized to compel the Attendance of absent Members, in such Manner, and under such Penalties as each House may provide.

Each House may determine the Rules of its Proceedings, punish its Members for disorderly Behavior, and, with the Concurrence of two thirds, expel a Member.

Each House shall keep a Journal of its Proceedings, and from time to time publish the same, excepting such Parts as may in their Judgment require Secrecy; and the Yeas and Nays of the Members of either House on any question shall, at the Desire of one fifth of those Present, be entered on the Journal.

Neither House, during the Session of Congress, shall, without the Consent of the other, adjourn for more than three days, nor to any other Place than that in which the two Houses shall be sitting.

Section 6. The Senators and Representatives shall receive a Compensation for their Services, to be ascertained by Law, and paid out of the Treasury of the United States. They shall in all Cases, except Treason, Felony and Breach of the Peace, be privileged from Arrest during their Attendance at the Session of their respective Houses, and in going to and returning from the same; and for any Speech or Debate in either House, they shall not be questioned in any other Place.

No Senator or Representative shall, during the Time for which he was elected, be appointed to any civil Office under the Authority of the United States, which shall have been created, or the Emoluments whereof shall have been increased during such time; and no Person holding any Office under the United States, shall be a Member of either House during his Continuance in Office.

Section 7. All Bills for raising Revenue shall originate in the House of Representatives; but the Senate may propose or concur with Amendments as on other Bills.

Every Bill which shall have passed the House of Representatives and the Senate, shall, before it become a Law, be presented to the President of the United States; If he approve he shall sign it, but if not he shall return it, with his Objections to the House in which it shall have originated, who shall enter the Objections at large on their Journal, and proceed to reconsider it. If after such Reconsideration two thirds of that House shall agree to pass the Bill, it shall be sent together with the Objections, to the other House, by which it shall likewise be reconsidered, and if approved by two thirds of that House, it shall become a Law. But in all such Cases the Votes of both Houses shall be determined by Yeas and Nays, and the Names of the Persons voting for and against the Bill shall be entered on the Journal of each House respectively. If any Bill shall not be returned by the President within ten Days (Sundays excepted) after it shall have been presented to him, the Same shall be a Law, in like Manner as if he had signed it, unless the Congress by

their Adjournment prevent its Return in which Case it shall not be a Law.

Every Order, Resolution, or Vote, to which the Concurrence of the Senate and House of Representatives may be necessary (except on a question of Adjournment) shall be presented to the President of the United States; and before the Same shall take Effect, shall be approved by him, or being disapproved by him, shall be repassed by two thirds of the Senate and House of Representatives, according to the Rules and Limitations prescribed in the Case of a Bill.

Section 8. The Congress shall have Power To lay and collect Taxes, Duties, Imposts and Excises, to pay the Debts and provide for the common Defence and general Welfare of the United States; but all Duties, Imposts and Excises shall be uniform throughout the United States;

To borrow Money on the credit of the United States;

To regulate Commerce with foreign Nations, and among the several States, and with the Indian Tribes;

To establish an uniform Rule of Naturalization, and uniform Laws on the subject of Bankruptcies throughout the United States;

To coin Money, regulate the Value thereof, and of foreign Coin, and fix the Standard of Weights and Measures;

To provide for the Punishment of counterfeiting the Securities and current Coin of the United States;

To establish Post Offices and post Roads;

To promote the Progress of Science and useful Arts, by securing for limited Times to Authors and Inventors the exclusive Right to their respective Writings and Discoveries;

To constitute Tribunals inferior to the supreme Court;

To define and punish Piracies and Felonies committed on the high Seas, and Offenses against the Law of Nations;

To declare War, grant Letters of Marque and Reprisal, and make Rules concerning Captures on Land and Water;

To raise and support Armies, but no Appropriation of Money to that Use shall be for a longer Term than two Years;

To provide and maintain a Navy;

To make Rules for the Government and Regulation of the land and naval Forces;

To provide for calling forth the Militia to execute the Laws of the Union, suppress Insurrections and repel Invasions;

To provide for organizing, arming, and disciplining, the Militia, and for governing such Part of them as may be employed in the Service of the United States, reserving to the States respectively, the Appointment of the Officers, and the Authority of training the Militia according to the discipline prescribed by Congress;

To exercise exclusive Legislation in all Cases whatsoever, over such District (not exceeding ten Miles square) as may, by Cession of particular States, and the Acceptance of Congress, become the Seat of the Government of the United States, and to exercise like Authority over all Places purchased by the Consent of the Legislature of the State in which the Same shall be, for the Erection of Forts, Magazines, Arsenals, dock-Yards, and other needful Buildings;—And

To make all Laws which shall be necessary and proper for carrying into Execution the foregoing Powers, and all other Powers vested by this Constitution in the Government of the United States, or in any Department or Officer thereof.

Section 9. The Migration or Importation of such Persons as any of the States now existing shall think proper to admit, shall not be prohibited by the Congress prior to the Year one thousand eight hundred and eight, but a Tax or duty may be imposed on such Importation, not exceeding ten dollars for each Person.

The privilege of the Writ of Habeas Corpus shall not be suspended, unless when in Cases of Rebellion or Invasion the public Safety may require it.

No Bill of Attainder or ex post facto Law shall be passed.

No Capitation, or other direct, Tax shall be laid, unless in Proportion to the Census or Enumeration herein before directed to be taken.

No Tax or Duty shall be laid on Articles exported from any State.

No Preference shall be given by any Regulation of Commerce or Revenue to the Ports of one State over those of another: nor shall Vessels bound to, or from, one State be obliged to enter, clear, or pay Duties in another.

No Money shall be drawn from the Treasury, but in Consequence of Appropriations made by Law; and a regular Statement and Account of the Receipts and Expenditures of all public Money shall be published from time to time.

No Title of Nobility shall be granted by the United States: And no Person holding any Office of Profit or Trust under them, shall, without the Consent of the Congress, accept of any present, Emolument, Office, or Title, of any kind whatever, from any King, Prince, or foreign State.

Section 10. No State shall enter into any Treaty, Alliance, or Confederation; grant Letters of Marque and Reprisal; coin Money; emit Bills of Credit; make any Thing but gold and silver Coin a Tender in Payment of Debts; pass any Bill of Attainder, ex post facto Law, or Law impairing the Obligation of Contracts, or grant any Title of Nobility.

No State shall, without the Consent of the Congress, lay any Imposts or Duties on Imports or Exports, except what may be absolutely necessary for executing its inspection Laws: and the net Produce of all Duties and Imposts, laid by any State on Imports or Exports, shall be for the Use of the Treasury of the United States; and all such Laws shall be subject to the Revision and Controul of the Congress.

No State shall, without the Consent of Congress, lay any Duty of Tonnage, keep Troops, or Ships of War in time of Peace, enter into any Agreement or Compact with another State, or with a foreign Power, or engage in War, unless actually invaded, or in such imminent Danger as will not admit of delay.

Article II

Section 1. The executive Power shall be vested in a President of the United States of America. He shall hold his Office during the Term of four Years, and, together with the Vice President, chosen for the same Term, be elected, as follows:

Each State shall appoint, in such Manner as the Legislature thereof may direct, a Number of Electors, equal to the whole Number of Senators and Representatives to which the State may be entitled in the Congress; but no Senator or Representative, or Person holding an Office of Trust or Profit under the United States, shall be appointed an Elector.

The Electors shall meet in their respective States, and vote by Ballot for two Persons, of whom one at least shall not be an Inhabitant of the same State with themselves. And they shall make a List of all the Persons voted for, and of the Number of Votes for each; which List they shall sign and certify, and transmit sealed to the Seat of the Government of the United States, directed to the President of the Senate. The President of the Senate shall, in the Presence of the Senate and House of Representatives, open all the Certificates, and the Votes shall then be counted. The Person having the greatest Number of Votes shall be the President, if such Number be a Majority of the whole Number of Electors appointed; and if there be more than one who have such Majority, and have an equal Number of Votes, then the House of Representatives shall immediately chuse by Ballot one of them for President; and if no Person have a Majority, then from the five highest on the List the said House shall in like Manner chuse the President. But in chusing the President, the Votes shall be taken by States, the Representation from each State having one Vote; A quorum for this Purpose shall consist of a Member or Members from two thirds of the States, and a Majority of all the States shall be necessary to a Choice. In every Case, after the Choice of the President, the Person having the greater Number of Votes of the Electors shall be the Vice President. But if there should remain two or more who have equal Votes, the Senate shall chuse from them by Ballot the Vice President.

The Congress may determine the Time of chusing the Electors, and the Day on which they shall give their Votes; which Day shall be the same throughout the United States.

No person except a natural born Citizen, or a Citizen of the United States, at the time of the Adoption of this Constitution, shall be eligible to the Office of President; neither shall any Person be eligible to that Office who shall not have attained to the Age of thirty five Years, and been fourteen Years a Resident within the United States.

In Case of the Removal of the President from Office, or of his Death, Resignation or Inability to discharge the Powers and Duties of the said Office, the same shall devolve on the Vice President, and the Congress may by Law provide for the Case of Removal, Death, Resignation or Inability, both of the President and Vice President, declaring what Officer shall then act as President, and such Officer shall act accordingly, until the Disability be removed, or a President shall be elected.

The President shall, at stated Times, receive for his Services, a Compensation, which shall neither be increased nor diminished during the Period for which he shall have been elected, and he shall not receive within that Period any other Emolument from the United States, or any of them.

Before he enter on the Execution of his Office, he shall take the following Oath or Affirmation: "I do solemnly swear (or affirm) that I will faithfully execute the Office of President of the United States, and will to the best of my Ability, preserve, protect and defend the Constitution of the United States."

Section 2. The President shall be Commander in Chief of the Army and Navy of the United States, and of the Militia of the several States, when called into the actual Service of the United States; he may require the Opinion, in writing, of the principal Officer in each of the executive Departments, upon any Subject relating to the Duties of their respective Offices, and he shall have Power to grant Reprieves and Pardons for Offenses against the United States, except in Cases of Impeachment.

He shall have Power, by and with the Advice and Consent of the Senate to make Treaties, provided two thirds of the Senators present concur; and he shall nominate, and by and with the Advice and Consent of the Senate, shall appoint Ambassadors, other public Ministers and Consuls, Judges of the supreme Court, and all other Officers of the United States, whose Appointments are not herein otherwise provided for, and which shall be established by Law; but the Congress may by Law vest the Appointment of such inferior Officers, as they think proper, in the President alone, in the Courts of Law, or in the Heads of Departments.

The President shall have Power to fill up all Vacancies that may happen during the Recess of the Senate, by granting Commissions which shall expire at the End of their next Session.

Section 3. He shall from time to time give to the Congress Information of the State of the Union, and recommend to their Consideration such Measures as he shall judge necessary and expedient; he may, on extraordinary Occasions, convene both Houses, or either of them, and in Case of Disagreement between them, with Respect to the Time of Adjournment, he may adjourn them to such Time as he shall think proper; he shall receive Ambassadors and other public Ministers; he shall take Care that the Laws be faithfully executed, and shall Commission all the Officers of the United States.

Section 4. The President, Vice President and all civil Officers of the United States, shall be removed from Office on Impeachment for, and Conviction of, Treason, Bribery, or other high Crimes and Misdemeanors.

ARTICLE III

Section 1. The judicial Power of the United States, shall be vested in one supreme Court, and in such inferior Courts as the Congress may from time to time ordain and establish. The Judges, both of the supreme and inferior Courts, shall hold their Offices during good Behaviour, and shall, at stated Times, receive for their Services a Compensation, which shall not be diminished during their Continuance in Office.

Section 2. The judicial Power shall extend to all Cases, in Law and Equity, arising under this Constitution, the Laws of the United States, and Treaties made, or which shall be made, under their Authority;—to all Cases affecting Ambassadors, other public Ministers and Consuls;—to all Cases of admiralty and maritime Jurisdiction;—to Controversies to which the United States shall be a Party;—to Controversies between two or more States;—between a State and Citizens of another State;—between Citizens of different States;—between Citizens of the same State claiming Lands under Grants of different States, and between a State, or the Citizens thereof, and foreign States, Citizens or Subjects.

In all Cases affecting Ambassadors, other public Ministers and Consuls, and those in which a State shall be a Party, the supreme Court shall have original Jurisdiction. In all the other Cases before mentioned, the supreme Court shall have appellate Jurisdiction, both as to Law and Fact, with such Exceptions, and under such Regulations as the Congress shall make.

The Trial of all Crimes, except in Cases of Impeachment, shall be by Jury; and such Trial shall be held in the State where the said Crimes shall have been committed; but when not committed within any State, the Trial shall be at such Place or Places as the Congress may by Law have directed.

Section 3. Treason against the United States, shall consist only in levying War against them, or, in adhering to their Enemies, giving them Aid and Comfort. No Person shall be convicted of Treason unless on the Testimony of two Witnesses to the same overt Act, or on Confession in open Court.

The Congress shall have Power to declare the Punishment of Treason, but no Attainder of Treason shall work Corruption of Blood, or Forfeiture except during the Life of the Person attainted.

ARTICLE IV

Section 1. Full Faith and Credit shall be given in each State to the public Acts, Records, and judicial Proceedings of every other State. And the Congress may by general Laws prescribe the Manner in which such Acts, Records and Proceedings shall be proved, and the Effect thereof.

Section 2. The Citizens of each State shall be entitled to all Privileges and Immunities of Citizens in the several States.

A Person charged in any State with Treason, Felony, or other Crime, who shall flee from Justice, and be found in another State, shall on Demand of the executive Authority of the State from which he fled, be delivered up, to be removed to the State having Jurisdiction of the Crime.

No Person held to Service or Labour in one State, under the Laws thereof, escaping into another, shall, in Consequence of any Law or Regulation therein, be discharged from such Service or Labour, but shall be delivered up on Claim of the Party to whom such Service or Labour may be due.

Section 3. New States may be admitted by the Congress into this Union; but no new State shall be formed or erected within the Jurisdiction of any other State; nor any State be formed by the Junction of two or more States, or Parts of States, without the Consent of the Legislatures of the States concerned as well as of the Congress.

The Congress shall have Power to dispose of and make all needful Rules and Regulations respecting the Territory or other Property belonging to the United States; and nothing in this Constitution shall be so construed as to Prejudice any Claims of the United States, or of any particular State.

Section 4. The United States shall guarantee to every State in this Union a Republican Form of Government, and shall protect each of them against Invasion; and on Application of the Legislature, or of the Executive (when the Legislature cannot be convened) against domestic Violence.

ARTICLE V

The Congress, whenever two thirds of both Houses shall deem it necessary, shall propose Amendments to this Constitution, or, on the Application of the Legislatures of two thirds of the several States, shall call a Convention for proposing Amendments, which, in either Case, shall be valid to all Intents and Purposes, as part of this Constitution, when ratified by the Legislatures of three fourths of the several States, or by Conventions in three fourths thereof, as the one or the other Mode of Ratification may be proposed by the Congress; Provided that no Amendment which may be made prior to the Year One thousand eight hundred and eight shall in any Manner affect the first and fourth Clauses in the Ninth Section of the first Article; and that no State, without its Consent, shall be deprived of its equal Suffrage in the Senate.

ARTICLE VI

All Debts contracted and Engagements entered into, before the Adoption of this Constitution shall be as valid against the United States under this Constitution, as under the Confederation.

This Constitution, and the Laws of the United States which shall be made in Pursuance thereof; and all Treaties made, or which shall be made, under the Authority of the United States, shall be the supreme Law of the Land; and the Judges in every State shall be bound thereby, any Thing in the Constitution or Laws of any State to the Contrary notwithstanding.

The Senators and Representatives before mentioned, and the Members of the several State Legislatures, and all executive and judicial Officers, both of the United States and of the several States, shall be bound by Oath or Affirmation, to support this Constitution; but no religious Test shall ever be required as a Qualification to any Office or public Trust under the United States.

ARTICLE VII

The Ratification of the Conventions of nine States shall be sufficient for the Establishment of this Constitution between the States so ratifying the Same.

AMENDMENT I [1791]

Congress shall make no law respecting an establishment of religion, or prohibiting the free exercise thereof; or abridging the freedom of speech, or of the press; or the right of the people peaceably to assembly, and to petition the Government for a redress of grievances.

AMENDMENT II [1791]

A well regulated Militia, being necessary to the security of a free State, the right of the people to keep and bear Arms, shall not be infringed.

AMENDMENT III [1791]

No Soldier shall, in time of peace be quartered in any house, without the consent of the Owner, nor in time of war, but in a manner to be prescribed by law.

AMENDMENT IV [1791]

The right of the people to be secure in their persons, houses, papers, and effects, against unreasonable searches and seizures, shall not be violated, and no Warrants shall issue, but upon probable cause, supported by Oath or affirmation, and particularly describing the place to be searched, and the persons or things to be seized.

AMENDMENT V [1791]

No person shall be held to answer for a capital, or otherwise infamous crime, unless on a presentment or indictment of a Grand Jury, except in cases arising in the land or naval forces, or in the Militia, when in actual service in time of War or public danger; nor shall any person be subject for the same offence to be twice put in jeopardy of life or limb; nor shall be compelled in any criminal case to be a witness against himself, nor be deprived of life, liberty, or property, without due process of law; nor shall private property be taken for public use, without just compensation.

AMENDMENT VI [1791]

In all criminal prosecutions, the accused shall enjoy the right to a speedy and public trial, by an impartial jury of the State and district wherein the crime shall have been committed, which district shall have been previously ascertained by law, and to be informed of the nature and cause of the accusation; to be confronted with the witnesses against him; to have compulsory process for obtaining witnesses in his favor, and to have the Assistance of Counsel for his defence.

AMENDMENT VII [1791]

In Suits at common law, where the value in controversy shall exceed twenty dollars, the right of trial by jury shall be preserved, and no fact tried by jury, shall be otherwise re-examined in any Court of the United States, than according to the rules of the common law.

AMENDMENT VIII [1791]

Excessive bail shall not be required, nor excessive fines imposed, nor cruel and unusual punishments inflicted.

AMENDMENT IX [1791]

The enumeration in the Constitution, of certain rights, shall not be construed to deny or disparage others retained by the people.

AMENDMENT X [1791]

The powers not delegated to the United States by the Constitution, nor prohibited by it to the States, are reserved to the States respectively, or to the people.

AMENDMENT XI [1798]

The Judicial power of the United States shall not be construed to extend to any suit in law or equity, commenced or prosecuted against one of the United States by Citizens of another State, or by Citizens or Subjects of any Foreign State.

AMENDMENT XII [1804]

The Electors shall meet in their respective states, and vote by ballot for President and Vice-President, one of whom, at least, shall not be an inhabitant of the same state with themselves; they shall name in their ballots the person voted for as President, and in distinct ballots the person voted for as Vice-President, and they shall make distinct lists of all persons voted for as President, and of all persons voted for as Vice-President, and of the number of votes for each, which lists they shall sign and certify, and transmit sealed to the seat of the government of the United States, directed to the President of the Senate;—The President of the Senate shall, in the presence of the Senate and House of Representatives, open all the certificates and the votes shall then be counted;—The person having the greatest number of votes for President, shall be the President, if such number be a majority of the whole number of Electors appointed; and if no person have such majority, then from the persons having the highest numbers not exceeding three on the list of those voted for as President, the House of Representatives shall choose immediately, by ballot, the President. But in choosing the President, the votes shall be taken by states, the representation from each state having one vote; a quorum for this purpose shall consist of a member or members from two-thirds of the states, and a majority of all states shall be necessary to a choice. And if the House of Representatives shall not choose a President whenever the right of choice shall devolve upon them, before the fourth day of March next following, then the Vice-President shall act as President, as in the case of the death or other constitutional disability of the President.—The person having the greatest number of votes as Vice-President, shall be the Vice-President, if such number be a majority of the whole number of Electors appointed, and if no person have a majority, then from the two highest numbers on the list, the Senate shall choose the Vice-President; a quorum for the purpose shall consist of two-thirds of the whole number of Senators, and a majority of the whole number shall be necessary to a choice. But no person constitutionally ineligible to the office of President shall be eligible to that of Vice-President of the United States.

AMENDMENT XIII [1865]

Section 1. Neither slavery nor involuntary servitude, except as a punishment for crime whereof the party shall have been duly convicted, shall exist within the United States, or any place subject to their jurisdiction.

Section 2. Congress shall have power to enforce this article by appropriate legislation.

AMENDMENT XIV [1868]

Section 1. All persons born or naturalized in the United States, and subject to the jurisdiction thereof, are citizens of the United States and of the State wherein they reside. No State shall make or enforce any law which shall abridge the privileges or immunities of citizens of the United States; nor shall any State deprive any person of life, liberty, or property, without due process of law; nor deny to any person within its jurisdiction the equal protection of the laws.

Section 2. Representatives shall be apportioned among the several States according to their respective numbers, counting the whole number of persons in each State, excluding Indians not taxed. But when the right to vote at any election for the choice of electors for President and Vice President of the United States, Representatives in Congress, the Executive and Judicial officers of a State, or the members of the Legislature thereof, is denied to any of the male inhabitants of such State, being twenty-one years of age, and citizens of the United States, or in any way abridged, except for participation in rebellion, or other crime, the basis of representation therein shall be reduced in the proportion which the number of such male citizens shall bear to the whole number of male citizens twenty-one years of age in such State.

Section 3. No person shall be a Senator or Representative in Congress, or elector of President and Vice President, or hold any office, civil or military, under the United States, or under any State, who having previously taken an oath, as a member of Congress, or as an officer of the United States, or as a member of any State legislature, or as an executive or judicial officer of any State, to support the Constitution of the United States, shall have engaged in insurrection or rebellion against the same, or given aid or comfort to the enemies thereof. But Congress may by a vote of two-thirds of each House, remove such disability.

Section 4. The validity of the public debt of the United States, authorized by law, including debts incurred for payment of pensions and bounties for services in suppressing insurrection or rebellion, shall not be questioned. But neither the United States nor any State shall assume or pay any debt or obligation incurred in aid of insurrection or rebellion against the United States, or any claim for the loss or emancipation of any slave; but all such debts, obligations and claims shall be held illegal and void.

Section 5. The Congress shall have power to enforce, by appropriate legislation, the provisions of this article.

AMENDMENT XV [1870]

Section 1. The right of citizens of the United States to vote shall not be denied or abridged by the United States or by any State on account of race, color, or previous condition of servitude.

Section 2. The Congress shall have power to enforce this article by appropriate legislation.

AMENDMENT XVI [1913]

The Congress shall have power to lay and collect taxes on incomes, from whatever source derived, without apportionment among the several States, and without regard to any census or enumeration.

AMENDMENT XVII [1913]

Section 1. The Senate of the United States shall be composed of two Senators from each State, elected by the people thereof, for six years; and each Senator shall have one vote. The electors in each State shall have the qualifications requisite for electors of the most numerous branch of the State legislatures.

Section 2. When vacancies happen in the representation of any State in the Senate, the executive authority of such State shall issue writs of election to fill such vacancies: Provided, That the legislature of any State may empower the executive thereof to make temporary appointments until the people fill the vacancies by election as the legislature may direct.

Section 3. This amendment shall not be so construed as to affect the election or term of any Senator chosen before it becomes valid as part of the Constitution.

AMENDMENT XVIII [1919]

Section 1. After one year from the ratification of this article the manufacture, sale, or transportation of intoxicating liquors within, the importation thereof into, or the exportation thereof from the United States and all territory subject to the jurisdiction thereof for beverage purposes is hereby prohibited.

Section 2. The Congress and the several States shall have concurrent power to enforce this article by appropriate legislation.

Section 3. This article shall be inoperative unless it shall have been ratified as an amendment to the Constitution by the legislatures of the several States, as provided in the Constitution, within seven years from the date of the submission hereof to the States by the Congress.

AMENDMENT XIX [1920]

Section 1. The right of citizens of the United States to vote shall not be denied or abridged by the United States or by any State on account of sex.

Section 2. Congress shall have power to enforce this article by appropriate legislation.

AMENDMENT XX [1933]

Section 1. The terms of the President and Vice President shall end at noon on the 20th day of January, and the terms of Senators and Representatives at noon on the 3d day of January, of the years in which such terms would have ended if this article had not been ratified; and the terms of their successors shall then begin.

Section 2. The Congress shall assemble at least once in every year, and such meeting shall begin at noon on the 3d day of January, unless they shall by law appoint a different day.

Section 3. If, at the time fixed for the beginning of the term of the President, the President elect shall have died, the Vice President elect shall become President. If the President shall not have been chosen before the time fixed for the beginning of his term, or if the President elect shall have failed to qualify, then the Vice President elect shall act as President until a President shall have qualified; and the Congress may by law provide for the case wherein neither a President elect nor a Vice President elect shall have qualified, declaring who shall then act as President, or the manner in which one who is to act shall be selected, and such person shall act accordingly until a President or Vice President shall have qualified.

Section 4. The Congress may by law provide for the case of the death of any of the persons from whom the House of Representatives may choose a President whenever the right of choice shall have devolved upon them, and for the case of the death of any of the persons from whom the Senate may choose a Vice President whenever the right of choice shall have devolved upon them.

Section 5. Sections 1 and 2 shall take effect on the 15th day of October following the ratification of this article.

Section 6. This article shall be inoperative unless it shall have been ratified as an amendment to the Constitution by the legislatures of three-fourths of the several States within seven years from the date of its submission.

AMENDMENT XXI [1933]

Section 1. The eighteenth article of amendment to the Constitution of the United States is hereby repealed.

Section 2. The transportation or importation into any State, Territory, or possession of the United States for delivery or use therein of intoxicating liquors, in violation of the laws thereof, is hereby prohibited.

Section 3. This article shall be inoperative unless it shall have been ratified as an amendment to the Constitution by conventions in the several States, as provided in the Constitution, within seven years from the date of the submission hereof to the States by the Congress.

AMENDMENT XXII [1951]

Section 1. No person shall be elected to the office of the President more than twice, and no person who has held the office of President, or acted as President, for more than two years of a term to which some other person was elected President shall be elected to the office of President more than once. But this Article shall not apply to any person holding the office of President when this Article was proposed by the Congress, and shall not prevent any person who may be holding the office of President, or acting as President, during the term within which this Article becomes operative from holding the office of President or acting as President during the remainder of such term.

Section 2. This article shall be inoperative unless it shall have been ratified as an amendment to the Constitution by the legislatures of three-fourths of the several States within seven years from the date of its submission to the States by the Congress.

Amendment XXIII [1961]

Section 1. The District constituting the seat of Government of the United States shall appoint in such manner as the Congress may direct:

A number of electors of President and Vice President equal to the whole number of Senators and Representatives in Congress to which the District would be entitled if it were a State, but in no event more than the least populous state; they shall be in addition to those appointed by the states, but they shall be considered, for the purposes of the election of President and Vice President, to be electors appointed by a state; and they shall meet in the District and perform such duties as provided by the twelfth article of amendment.

Section 2. The Congress shall have power to enforce this article by appropriate legislation.

Amendment XXIV [1964]

Section 1. The right of citizens of the United States to vote in any primary or other election for President or Vice President, for electors for President or Vice President, or for Senator or Representative in Congress, shall not be denied or abridged by the United States, or any State by reason of failure to pay any poll tax or other tax.

Section 2. The Congress shall have power to enforce this article by appropriate legislation.

Amendment XXV [1967]

Section 1. In case of the removal of the President from office or of his death or resignation, the Vice President shall become President.

Section 2. Whenever there is a vacancy in the office of the Vice President, the President shall nominate a Vice President who shall take office upon confirmation by a majority vote of both Houses of Congress.

Section 3. Whenever the President transmits to the President pro tempore of the Senate and the Speaker of the House of Representatives his written declaration that he is unable to discharge the powers and duties of his office, and until he transmits to them a written declaration to the contrary, such powers and duties shall be discharged by the Vice President as Acting President.

Section 4. Whenever the Vice President and a majority of either the principal officers of the executive departments or of such other body as Congress may by law provide, transmit to the President pro tempore of the Senate and the Speaker of the House of Representatives their written declaration that the President is unable to discharge the powers and duties of his office, the Vice President shall immediately assume the powers and duties of the office as Acting President.

Thereafter, when the President transmits to the President pro tempore of the Senate and the Speaker of the House of Representatives his written declaration that no inability exists, he shall resume the powers and duties of his office unless the Vice President and a majority of either the principal officers of the executive department or of such other body as Congress may by law provide, transmit within four days to the President pro tempore of the Senate and the Speaker of the House of Representatives their written declaration that the President is unable to discharge the powers and duties of his office. Thereupon Congress shall decide the issue, assembling within forty-eight hours for that purpose if not in session. If the Congress, within twenty-one days after receipt of the latter written declaration, or, if Congress is not in session, within twenty-one days after Congress is required to assemble, determines by two-thirds vote of both Houses that the President is unable to discharge the powers and duties of his office, the Vice President shall continue to discharge the same as Acting President; otherwise, the President shall resume the powers and duties of his office.

Amendment XXVI [1971]

Section 1. The right of citizens of the United States, who are eighteen years of age or older, to vote shall not be denied or abridged by the United States or by any State on account of age.

Section 2. The Congress shall have power to enforce this article by appropriate legislation.

Amendment XXVII [1992]

No law, varying the compensation for the services of the Senators and Representatives, shall take effect, until an election of Representatives shall have intervened.

appendix C

The Administrative Procedure Act of 1946 [Excerpts]

Section 551. Definitions

For the purpose of this subchapter—

* * * *

(4) "rule" means the whole or a part of an agency statement of general or particular applicability and future effect designed to implement, interpret, or prescribe law or policy or describing the organization, procedure, or practice requirements of an agency and includes the approval or prescription for the future of rates, wages, corporate or financial structures or reorganizations thereof, prices, facilities, appliances, services or allowances therefor or of valuations, costs, or accounting, or practices bearing on any of the foregoing[.]

* * * *

Section 552. Public Information; Agency Rules, Opinions, Orders, Records, and Proceedings

(a) Each agency shall make available to the public information as follows:

(1) Each agency shall separately state and currently publish in the Federal Register for the guidance of the public—

(A) descriptions of its central and field organization and the established places at which, the employees * * * from whom, and the methods whereby, the public may obtain information, make submittals or requests, or obtain decisions;

* * * *

(C) rules of procedure, descriptions of forms available or the places at which forms may be obtained, and instructions as to the scope and contents of all papers, reports, or examinations;

(D) substantive rules of general applicability adopted as authorized by law, and statements of general policy or interpretations of general applicability formulated and adopted by the agency[.]

* * *

* * * *

Section 552b. Open Meetings

* * * *

(j) Each agency subject to the requirements of this section shall annually report to Congress regarding its com-pliance with such requirements, including a tabulation of the total number of agency meetings open to the public, the total number of meetings closed to the public, the reasons for closing such meetings, and a description of any litigation brought against the agency under this section, including any costs assessed against the agency in such litigation * * *.

* * * *

Section 553. Rule Making

* * * *

(b) General notice of proposed rule making shall be published in the Federal Register, unless persons subject thereto are named and either personally served or otherwise have actual notice thereof in accordance with law. * * *

(c) After notice required by this section, the agency shall give interested persons an opportunity to participate in the rule making through submission of written data, views, or arguments with or without opportunity for oral presentation. * * *

* * * *

Section 554. Adjudications

* * * *

(b) Persons entitled to notice of an agency hearing shall be timely informed of—

(1) the time, place, and nature of the hearing;

(2) the legal authority and jurisdiction under which the hearing is to be held; and

(3) the matters of fact and law asserted.

* * * *

(c) The agency shall give all interested parties opportunity for—

(1) the submission and consideration of facts, arguments, offers of settlement, or proposals of adjustment when time, the nature of the proceeding, and the public interest permit; and

(2) to the extent that the parties are unable so to determine a controversy by consent, hearing and decision on notice * * *.

* * * *

Section 555. Ancillary Matters

* * * *

(c) Process, requirement of a report, inspection, or other investigative act or demand may not be issued, made, or enforced except as authorized by law. A person compelled to submit data or evidence is entitled to retain or, on payment of lawfully prescribed costs, procure a copy or transcript thereof, except that in a nonpublic investigatory proceeding the witness may for good cause be limited to inspection of the official transcript of his testimony.

* * * *

(e) Prompt notice shall be given of the denial in whole or in part of a written application, petition, or other request of an interested person made in connection with any agency proceeding. * * *

Section 556. Hearings; Presiding Employees; Powers and Duties; Burden of Proof; Evidence; Record as Basis of Decision

* * * *

(b) There shall preside at the taking of evidence—

(1) the agency;

(2) one or more members of the body which comprises the agency; or

(3) one or more administrative law judges * * *.

* * * *

(c) Subject to published rules of the agency and within its powers, employees presiding at hearings may—

(1) administer oaths and affirmations;

(2) issue subpoenas authorized by law;

(3) rule on offers of proof and receive relevant evidence;

(4) take depositions or have depositions taken when the ends of justice would be served;

(5) regulate the course of the hearing;

(6) hold conferences for the settlement or simplification of the issues by consent of the parties or by the use of alternative means of dispute resolution as provided in subchapter IV of this chapter;

(7) inform the parties as to the availability of one or more alternative means of dispute resolution, and encourage use of such methods;

* * * *

(9) dispose of procedural requests or similar matters;

(10) make or recommend decisions in accordance with * * * this title; and

(11) take other action authorized by agency rule consistent with this subchapter.

* * * *

Section 702. Right of Review

A person suffering legal wrong because of agency action * * * is entitled to judicial review thereof. An action in a court of the United States seeking relief other than money damages and stating a claim that an agency or an officer or employee thereof acted or failed to act in an official capacity or under color of legal authority shall not be dismissed nor relief therein be denied on the ground that it is against the United States or that the United States is an indispensable party. The United States may be named as a defendant in any such action, and a judgment or decree may be entered against the United States: Provided, [t]hat any mandatory or injunctive decree shall specify the [f]ederal officer or officers (by name or by title), and their successors in office, personally responsible for compliance. * * *

* * * *

Section 704. Actions Reviewable

Agency action made reviewable by statute and final agency action for which there is no other adequate remedy in a court are subject to judicial review. A preliminary, procedural, or intermediate agency action or ruling not directly reviewable is subject to review on the review of the final agency action.

appendix D

Article 2 of the Uniform Commercial Code

Article 2

SALES

Part 1 Short Title, General Construction and Subject Matter

§ 2—101. Short Title.

This Article shall be known and may be cited as Uniform Commercial Code—Sales.

§ 2—102. Scope; Certain Security and Other Transactions Excluded From This Article.

Unless the context otherwise requires, this Article applies to transactions in goods; it does not apply to any transaction which although in the form of an unconditional contract to sell or present sale is intended to operate only as a security transaction nor does this Article impair or repeal any statute regulating sales to consumers, farmers or other specified classes of buyers.

§ 2—103. Definitions and Index of Definitions.

(1) In this Article unless the context otherwise requires

(a) "Buyer" means a person who buys or contracts to buy goods.

(b) "Good faith" in the case of a merchant means honesty in fact and the observance of reasonable commercial standards of fair dealing in the trade.

(c) "Receipt" of goods means taking physical possession of them.

(d) "Seller" means a person who sells or contracts to sell goods.

(2) Other definitions applying to this Article or to specified Parts thereof, and the sections in which they appear are:

"Acceptance". Section 2—606.
"Banker's credit". Section 2—325.
"Between merchants". Section 2—104.
"Cancellation". Section 2—106(4).
"Commercial unit". Section 2—105.
"Confirmed credit". Section 2—325.
"Conforming to contract". Section 2—106.
"Contract for sale". Section 2—106.
"Cover". Section 2—712.
"Entrusting". Section 2—403.
"Financing agency". Section 2—104.
"Future goods". Section 2—105.
"Goods". Section 2—105.

"Identification". Section 2—501.
"Installment contract". Section 2—612.
"Letter of Credit". Section 2—325.
"Lot". Section 2—105.
"Merchant". Section 2—104.
"Overseas". Section 2—323.
"Person in position of seller". Section 2—707.
"Present sale". Section 2—106.
"Sale". Section 2—106.
"Sale on approval". Section 2—326.
"Sale or return". Section 2—326.
"Termination". Section 2—106.

(3) The following definitions in other Articles apply to this Article:

"Check". Section 3—104.
"Consignee". Section 7—102.
"Consignor". Section 7—102.
"Consumer goods". Section 9—109.
"Dishonor". Section 3—507.
"Draft". Section 3—104.

(4) In addition Article 1 contains general definitions and principles of construction and interpretation applicable throughout this Article.

§ 2—104. Definitions: "Merchant"; "Between Merchants"; "Financing Agency".

(1) "Merchant" means a person who deals in goods of the kind or otherwise by his occupation holds himself out as having knowledge or skill peculiar to the practices or goods involved in the transaction or to whom such knowledge or skill may be attributed by his employment of an agent or broker or other intermediary who by his occupation holds himself out as having such knowledge or skill.

(2) "Financing agency" means a bank, finance company or other person who in the ordinary course of business makes advances against goods or documents of title or who by arrangement with either the seller or the buyer intervenes in ordinary course to make or collect payment due or claimed under the contract for sale, as by purchasing or paying the seller's draft or making advances against it or by merely taking it for collection whether or not documents of title accompany the draft. "Financing agency" includes also a bank or other person who similarly intervenes between persons who are in the position of seller and buyer in respect to the goods (Section 2—707).

(3) "Between merchants" means in any transaction with respect to which both parties are chargeable with the knowledge or skill of merchants.

§ 2—105. Definitions: Transferability; "Goods"; "Future" Goods; "Lot"; "Commercial Unit".

(1) "Goods" means all things (including specially manufactured goods) which are movable at the time of identification to the contract for sale other than the money in which the price is to be paid, investment securities (Article 8) and things in action. "Goods" also includes the unborn young of animals and growing crops and other identified things attached to realty as described in the section on goods to be severed from realty (Section 2—107).

(2) Goods must be both existing and identified before any interest in them can pass. Goods which are not both existing and identified are "future" goods. A purported present sale of future goods or of any interest therein operates as a contract to sell.

(3) There may be a sale of a part interest in existing identified goods.

(4) An undivided share in an identified bulk of fungible goods is sufficiently identified to be sold although the quantity of the bulk is not determined. Any agreed proportion of such a bulk or any quantity thereof agreed upon by number, weight or other measure may to the extent of the seller's interest in the bulk be sold to the buyer who then becomes an owner in common.

(5) "Lot" means a parcel or a single article which is the subject matter of a separate sale or delivery, whether or not it is sufficient to perform the contract.

(6) "Commercial unit" means such a unit of goods as by commercial usage is a single whole for purposes of sale and division of which materially impairs its character or value on the market or in use. A commercial unit may be a single article (as a machine) or a set of articles (as a suite of furniture or an assortment of sizes) or a quantity (as a bale, gross, or carload) or any other unit treated in use or in the relevant market as a single whole.

§ 2—106. Definitions: "Contract"; "Agreement"; "Contract for Sale"; "Sale"; "Present Sale"; "Conforming" to Contract; "Termination"; "Cancellation".

(1) In this Article unless the context otherwise requires "contract" and "agreement" are limited to those relating to the present or future sale of goods. "Contract for sale" includes both a present sale of goods and a contract to sell goods at a future time. A "sale" consists in the passing of title from the seller to the buyer for a price (Section 2—401). A "present sale" means a sale which is accomplished by the making of the contract.

(2) Goods or conduct including any part of a performance are "conforming" or conform to the contract when they are in accordance with the obligations under the contract.

(3) "Termination" occurs when either party pursuant to a power created by agreement or law puts an end to the contract otherwise than for its breach. On "termination" all obligations which are still executory on both sides are discharged but any right based on prior breach or performance survives.

(4) "Cancellation" occurs when either party puts an end to the contract for breach by the other and its effect is the same as that of "termination" except that the cancelling party also retains any remedy for breach of the whole contract or any unperformed balance.

§ 2—107. Goods to Be Severed From Realty: Recording.

(1) A contract for the sale of minerals or the like (including oil and gas) or a structure or its materials to be removed from realty is a contract for the sale of goods within this Article if they are to be severed by the seller but until severance a purported present sale thereof which is not effective as a transfer of an interest in land is effective only as a contract to sell.

(2) A contract for the sale apart from the land of growing crops or other things attached to realty and capable of severance without material harm thereto but not described in subsection (1) or of timber to be cut is a contract for the sale of goods within this Article whether the subject matter is to be severed by the buyer or by the seller even though it forms part of the realty at the time of contracting, and the parties can by identification effect a present sale before severance.

(3) The provisions of this section are subject to any third party rights provided by the law relating to realty records, and the contract for sale may be executed and recorded as a document transferring an interest in land and shall then constitute notice to third parties of the buyer's rights under the contract for sale.

Part 2 Form, Formation and Readjustment of Contract

§ 2—201. Formal Requirements; Statute of Frauds.

(1) Except as otherwise provided in this section a contract for the sale of goods for the price of $500 or more is not enforceable by way of action or defense unless there is some writing sufficient to indicate that a contract for sale has been made between the parties and signed by the party against whom enforcement is sought or by his authorized agent or broker. A writing is not insufficient because it omits or incorrectly states a term agreed upon but the contract is not enforceable under this paragraph beyond the quantity of goods shown in such writing.

(2) Between merchants if within a reasonable time a writing in confirmation of the contract and sufficient against the sender is received and the party receiving it has reason to know its contents, its satisfies the requirements of subsection (1) against such party unless written notice of objection to its contents is given within ten days after it is received.

(3) A contract which does not satisfy the requirements of subsection (1) but which is valid in other respects is enforceable

> (a) if the goods are to be specially manufactured for the buyer and are not suitable for sale to others in the ordinary course of the seller's business and the seller, before notice of repudiation is received and under circumstances which reasonably indicate that the goods are for the buyer, has made either a substantial beginning of their manufacture or commitments for their procurement; or

> (b) if the party against whom enforcement is sought admits in his pleading, testimony or otherwise in court that a contract for sale was made, but the contract is not enforceable under this provision beyond the quantity of goods admitted; or

> (c) with respect to goods for which payment has been made and accepted or which have been received and accepted (Sec. 2—606).

§ 2—202. Final Written Expression: Parol or Extrinsic Evidence.

Terms with respect to which the confirmatory memoranda of the parties agree or which are otherwise set forth in a writing intended by the parties as a final expression of their agreement with respect to such terms as are included therein may not be contradicted by evidence of any prior agreement or of a contemporaneous oral agreement but may be explained or supplemented

(a) by course of dealing or usage of trade (Section 1—205) or by course of performance (Section 2—208); and

(b) by evidence of consistent additional terms unless the court finds the writing to have been intended also as a complete and exclusive statement of the terms of the agreement.

§ 2—203. Seals Inoperative.

The affixing of a seal to a writing evidencing a contract for sale or an offer to buy or sell goods does not constitute the writing a sealed instrument and the law with respect to sealed instruments does not apply to such a contract or offer.

§ 2—204. Formation in General.

(1) A contract for sale of goods may be made in any manner sufficent to show agreement, including conduct by both parties which recognizes the existence of such a contract.

(2) An agreement sufficient to constitute a contract for sale may be found even though the moment of its making is undetermined.

(3) Even though one or more terms are left open a contract for sale does not fail for indefiniteness if the parties have intended to make a contract and there is a reasonably certain basis for giving an appropriate remedy.

§ 2—205. Firm Offers.

An offer by a merchant to buy or sell goods in a signed writing which by its terms gives assurance that it will be held open is not revocable, for lack of consideration, during the time stated or if no time is stated for a reasonable time, but in no event may such period of irrevocability exceed three months; but any such term of assurance on a form supplied by the offeree must be separately signed by the offeror.

§ 2—206. Offer and Acceptance in Formation of Contract.

(1) Unless other unambiguously indicated by the language or circumstances

> (a) an offer to make a contract shall be construed as inviting acceptance in any manner and by any medium reasonable in the circumstances;

> (b) an order or other offer to buy goods for prompt or current shipment shall be construed as inviting acceptance either by a prompt promise to ship or by the prompt or current shipment of conforming or nonconforming goods, but such a shipment of nonconforming goods does not constitute an acceptance if the seller seasonably notifies the buyer that the shipment is offered only as an accommodation to the buyer.

(2) Where the beginning of a requested performance is a reasonable mode of acceptance an offeror who is not notified of acceptance within a reasonable time may treat the offer as having lapsed before acceptance.

§ 2—207. Additional Terms in Acceptance or Confirmation.

(1) A definite and seasonable expression of acceptance or a written confirmation which is sent within a reasonable time operates as an acceptance even though it states terms additional to or different from those offered or agreed upon, unless acceptance is expressly made conditional on assent to the additional or different terms.

(2) The additional terms are to be construed as proposals for addition to the contract. Between merchants such terms become part of the contract unless:

> (a) the offer expressly limits acceptance to the terms of the offer;

> (b) they materially alter it; or

> (c) notification of objection to them has already been given or is given within a reasonable time after notice of them is received.

(3) Conduct by both parties which recognizes the existence of a contract is sufficient to establish a contract for sale although the writings of the parties do not otherwise establish a contract. In such case the terms of the particular contract consist of those terms on which the writings of the parties agree, together with any supplementary terms incorporated under any other provisions of this Act.

§ 2—208. Course of Performance or Practical Construction.

(1) Where the contract for sale involves repeated occasions for performance by either party with knowledge of the nature of the performance and opportunity for objection to it by the other, any course of performance accepted or acquiesced in without objection shall be relevant to determine the meaning of the agreement.

(2) The express terms of the agreement and any such course of performance, as well as any course of dealing and usage of trade, shall be construed whenever reasonable as consistent with each other; but when such construction is unreasonable, express terms shall control course of performance and course of performance shall control both course of dealing and usage of trade (Section 1—205).

(3) Subject to the provisions of the next section on modification and waiver, such course of performance shall be relevant to show a waiver or modification of any term inconsistent with such course of performance.

§ 2—209. Modification, Rescission and Waiver.

(1) An agreement modifying a contract within this Article needs no consideration to be binding.

(2) A signed agreement which excludes modification or rescission except by a signed writing cannot be otherwise modified or rescinded, but except as between merchants such a requirement on a form supplied by the merchant must be separately signed by the other party.

(3) The requirements of the statute of frauds section of this Article (Section 2—201) must be satisfied if the contract as modified is within its provisions.

(4) Although an attempt at modification or rescission does not satisfy the requirements of subsection (2) or (3) it can operate as a waiver.

(5) A party who has made a waiver affecting an executory portion of the contract may retract the waiver by reasonable notification received by the other party that strict performance will be required of any term waived, unless the retraction would be unjust in view of a material change of position in reliance on the waiver.

§ 2—210. Delegation of Performance; Assignment of Rights.

(1) A party may perform his duty through a delegate unless otherwise agreed or unless the other party has a substantial interest in having his original promisor perform or control the acts required by the contract. No delegation of performance relieves the party delegating of any duty to perform or any liability for breach.

(2) Unless otherwise agreed all rights of either seller or buyer can be assigned except where the assignment would materially change the duty of the other party, or increase materially the burden or risk imposed on him by his contract, or impair materially his chance of obtaining return performance. A right to damages for breach of the whole contract or a right arising out of the assignor's due performance of his entire obligation can be assigned despite agreement otherwise.

(3) Unless the circumstances indicate the contrary a prohibition of assignment of "the contract" is to be construed as barring only the delegation to the assignee of the assignor's performance.

(4) An assignment of "the contract" or of "all my rights under the contract" or an assignment in similar general terms is an assignment of rights and unless the language or the circumstances (as in an assignment for security) indicate the contrary, it is a delegation of performance of the duties of the assignor and its acceptance by the assignee constitutes a promise by him to perform those duties. This promise is enforceable by either the assignor or the other party to the original contract.

(5) The other party may treat any assignment which delegates performance as creating reasonable grounds for insecurity and may without prejudice to his rights against the assignor demand assurances from the assignee (Section 2—609).

Part 3 General Obligation and Construction of Contract

§ 2—301. General Obligations of Parties.

The obligation of the seller is to transfer and deliver and that of the buyer is to accept and pay in accordance with the contract.

§ 2—302. Unconscionable Contract or Clause.

(1) If the court as a matter of law finds the contract or any clause of the contract to have been unconscionable at the time it was made the court may refuse to enforce the contract, or it may enforce the remainder of the contract without the unconscionable clause, or it may so limit the application of any unconscionable clause as to avoid any unconscionable result.

(2) When it is claimed or appears to the court that the contract or any clause thereof may be unconscionable the parties shall be afforded a reasonable opportunity to present evidence as to its commercial setting, purpose and effect to aid the court in making the determination.

§ 2—303. Allocations or Division of Risks.

Where this Article allocates a risk or a burden as between the parties "unless otherwise agreed", the agreement may not only shift the allocation but may also divide the risk or burden.

§ 2—304. Price Payable in Money, Goods, Realty, or Otherwise.

(1) The price can be made payable in money or otherwise. If it is payable in whole or in part in goods each party is a seller of the goods which he is to transfer.

(2) Even though all or part of the price is payable in an interest in realty the transfer of the goods and the seller's

obligations with reference to them are subject to this Article, but not the transfer of the interest in realty or the transferor's obligations in connection therewith.

§ 2—305. Open Price Term.

(1) The parties if they so intend can conclude a contract for sale even though the price is not settled. In such a case the price is a reasonable price at the time for delivery if

(a) nothing is said as to price; or

(b) the price is left to be agreed by the parties and they fail to agree; or

(c) the price is to be fixed in terms of some agreed market or other standard as set or recorded by a third person or agency and it is not so set or recorded.

(2) A price to be fixed by the seller or by the buyer means a price for him to fix in good faith.

(3) When a price left to be fixed otherwise than by agreement of the parties fails to be fixed through fault of one party the other may at his option treat the contract as cancelled or himself fix a reasonable price.

(4) Where, however, the parties intend not to be bound unless the price be fixed or agreed and it is not fixed or agreed there is no contract. In such a case the buyer must return any goods already received or if unable so to do must pay their reasonable value at the time of delivery and the seller must return any portion of the price paid on account.

§ 2—306. Output, Requirements and Exclusive Dealings.

(1) A term which measures the quantity by the output of the seller or the requirements of the buyer means such actual output or requirements as may occur in good faith, except that no quantity unreasonably disproportionate to any stated estimate or in the absence of a stated estimate to any normal or otherwise comparable prior output or requirements may be tendered or demanded.

(2) A lawful agreement by either the seller or the buyer for exclusive dealing in the kind of goods concerned imposes unless otherwise agreed an obligation by the seller to use best efforts to supply the goods and by the buyer to use best efforts to promote their sale.

§ 2—307. Delivery in Single Lot or Several Lots.

Unless otherwise agreed all goods called for by a contract for sale must be tendered in a single delivery and payment is due only on such tender but where the circumstances give either party the right to make or demand delivery in lots the price if it can be apportioned may be demanded for each lot.

§ 2—308. Absence of Specified Place for Delivery.

Unless otherwise agreed

(a) the place for delivery of goods is the seller's place of business or if he has none his residence; but

(b) in a contract for sale of identified goods which to the knowledge of the parties at the time of contracting are in some other place, that place is the place for their delivery; and

(c) documents of title may be delivered through customary banking channels.

§ 2—309. Absence of Specific Time Provisions; Notice of Termination.

(1) The time for shipment or delivery or any other action under a contract if not provided in this Article or agreed upon shall be a reasonable time.

(2) Where the contract provides for successive performances but is indefinite in duration it is valid for a reasonable time but unless otherwise agreed may be terminated at any time by either party.

(3) Termination of a contract by one party except on the happening of an agreed event requires that reasonable notification be received by the other party and an agreement dispensing with notification is invalid if its operation would be unconscionable.

§ 2—310. Open Time for Payment or Running of Credit; Authority to Ship Under Reservation.

Unless otherwise agreed

(a) payment is due at the time and place at which the buyer is to receive the goods even though the place of shipment is the place of delivery; and

(b) if the seller is authorized to send the goods he may ship them under reservation, and may tender the documents of title, but the buyer may inspect the goods after their arrival before payment is due unless such inspection is inconsistent with the terms of the contract (Section 2—513); and

(c) if delivery is authorized and made by way of documents of title otherwise than by subsection (b) then payment is due at the time and place at which the buyer is to receive the documents regardless of where the goods are to be received; and

(d) where the seller is required or authorized to ship the goods on credit the credit period runs from the time of shipment but post-dating the invoice or delaying its dispatch will correspondingly delay the starting of the credit period.

§ 2—311. Options and Cooperation Respecting Performance.

(1) An agreement for sale which is otherwise sufficiently definite (subsection (3) of Section 2—204) to be a contract is not made invalid by the fact that it leaves particulars of performance to be specified by one of the parties. Any such specification must be made in good faith and within limits set by commercial reasonableness.

(2) Unless otherwise agreed specifications relating to assortment of the goods are at the buyer's option and

except as otherwise provided in subsections (1)(c) and (3) of Section 2—319 specifications or arrangements relating to shipment are at the seller's option.

(3) Where such specification would materially affect the other party's performance but is not seasonably made or where one party's cooperation is necessary to the agreed performance of the other but is not seasonably forthcoming, the other party in addition to all other remedies

> (a) is excused for any resulting delay in his own performance; and

> (b) may also either proceed to perform in any reasonable manner or after the time for a material part of his own performance treat the failure to specify or to cooperate as a breach by failure to deliver or accept the goods.

§ 2—312. Warranty of Title and Against Infringement; Buyer's Obligation Against Infringement.

(1) Subject to subsection (2) there is in a contract for sale a warranty by the seller that

> (a) the title conveyed shall be good, and its transfer rightful; and

> (b) the goods shall be delivered free from any security interest or other lien or encumbrance of which the buyer at the time of contracting has no knowledge.

(2) A warranty under subsection (1) will be excluded or modified only by specific language or by circumstances which give the buyer reason to know that the person selling does not claim title in himself or that he is purporting to sell only such right or title as he or a third person may have.

(3) Unless otherwise agreed a seller who is a merchant regularly dealing in goods of the kind warrants that the goods shall be delivered free of the rightful claim of any third person by way of infringement or the like but a buyer who furnishes specifications to the seller must hold the seller harmless against any such claim which arises out of compliance with the specifications.

§ 2—313. Express Warranties by Affirmation, Promise, Description, Sample.

(1) Express warranties by the seller are created as follows:

> (a) Any affirmation of fact or promise made by the seller to the buyer which relates to the goods and becomes part of the basis of the bargain creates an express warranty that the goods shall conform to the affirmation or promise.

> (b) Any description of the goods which is made part of the basis of the bargain creates an express warranty that the goods shall conform to the description.

> (c) Any sample or model which is made part of the basis of the bargain creates an express warranty that the whole of the goods shall conform to the sample or model.

(2) It is not necessary to the creation of an express warranty that the seller use formal words such as "warrant" or "guarantee" or that he have a specific intention to make a warranty, but an affirmation merely of the value of the goods or a statement purporting to be merely the seller's opinion or commendation of the goods does not create a warranty.

§ 2—314. Implied Warranty: Merchantability; Usage of Trade.

(1) Unless excluded or modified (Section 2—316), a warranty that the goods shall be merchantable is implied in a contract for their sale if the seller is a merchant with respect to goods of that kind. Under this section the serving for value of food or drink to be consumed either on the premises or elsewhere is a sale.

(2) Goods to be merchantable must be at least such as

> (a) pass without objection in the trade under the contract description; and

> (b) in the case of fungible goods, are of fair average quality within the description; and

> (c) are fit for the ordinary purposes for which such goods are used; and

> (d) run, within the variations permitted by the agreement, of even kind, quality and quantity within each unit and among all units involved; and

> (e) are adequately contained, packaged, and labeled as the agreement may require; and

> (f) conform to the promises or affirmations of fact made on the container or label if any.

(3) Unless excluded or modified (Section 2—316) other implied warranties may arise from course of dealing or usage of trade.

§ 2—315. Implied Warranty: Fitness for Particular Purpose.

Where the seller at the time of contracting has reason to know any particular purpose for which the goods are required and that the buyer is relying on the seller's skill or judgment to select or furnish suitable goods, there is unless excluded or modified under the next section an implied warranty that the goods shall be fit for such purpose.

§ 2—316. Exclusion or Modification of Warranties.

(1) Words or conduct relevant to the creation of an express warranty and words or conduct tending to negate or limit warranty shall be construed wherever reasonable as consistent with each other; but subject to the provisions of this Article on parol or extrinsic evidence (Section 2—202) negation or limitation is inoperative to the extent that such construction is unreasonable.

(2) Subject to subsection (3), to exclude or modify the implied warranty of merchantability or any part of it the language must mention merchantability and in case of a writing must be conspicuous, and to exclude or modify any implied warranty of fitness the exclusion must be by a writing and conspicuous. Language to exclude all implied warranties of fitness is sufficient if it states, for example, that "There are no warranties which extend beyond the description on the face hereof."

(3) Notwithstanding subsection (2)

(a) unless the circumstances indicate otherwise, all implied warranties are excluded by expressions like "as is", "with all faults" or other language which in common understanding calls the buyer's attention to the exclusion of warranties and makes plain that there is no implied warranty; and

(b) when the buyer before entering into the contract has examined the goods or the sample or model as fully as he desired or has refused to examine the goods there is no implied warranty with regard to defects which an examination ought in the circumstances to have revealed to him; and

(c) an implied warranty can also be excluded or modified by course of dealing or course of performance or usage of trade.

(4) Remedies for breach of warranty can be limited in accordance with the provisions of this Article on liquidation or limitation of damages and on contractual modification of remedy (Sections 2—718 and 2—719).

§ 2—317. Cumulation and Conflict of Warranties Express or Implied.

Warranties whether express or implied shall be construed as consistent with each other and as cumulative, but if such construction is unreasonable the intention of the parties shall determine which warranty is dominant. In ascertaining that intention the following rules apply:

(a) Exact or technical specifications displace an inconsistent sample or model or general language of description.

(b) A sample from an existing bulk displaces inconsistent general language of description.

(c) Express warranties displace inconsistent implied warranties other than an implied warranty of fitness for a particular purpose.

§ 2—318. Third Party Beneficiaries of Warranties Express or Implied.

Note: If this Act is introduced in the Congress of the United States this section should be omitted. (States to select one alternative.)

ALTERNATIVE A

A seller's warranty whether express or implied extends to any natural person who is in the family or household of his buyer or who is a guest in his home if it is reasonable to expect that such person may use, consume or be affected by the goods and who is injured in person by breach of the warranty. A seller may not exclude or limit the operation of this section.

ALTERNATIVE B

A seller's warranty whether express or implied extends to any natural person who may reasonably be expected to use, consume or be affected by the goods and who is injured in person by breach of the warranty. A seller may not exclude or limit the operation of this section.

ALTERNATIVE C

A seller's warranty whether express or implied extends to any person who may reasonably be expected to use, consume or be affected by the goods and who is injured by breach of the warranty. A seller may not exclude or limit the operation of this section with respect to injury to the person of an individual to whom the warranty extends. As amended 1966.

§ 2—319. F.O.B. and F.A.S. Terms.

(1) Unless otherwise agreed the term F.O.B. (which means "free on board") at a named place, even though used only in connection with the stated price, is a delivery term under which

(a) when the term is F.O.B. the place of shipment, the seller must at that place ship the goods in the manner provided in this Article (Section 2—504) and bear the expense and risk of putting them into the possession of the carrier; or

(b) when the term is F.O.B. the place of destination, the seller must at his own expense and risk transport the goods to that place and there tender delivery of them in the manner provided in this Article (Section 2—503);

(c) when under either (a) or (b) the term is also F.O.B. vessel, car or other vehicle, the seller must in addition at his own expense and risk load the goods on board. If the term is F.O.B. vessel the buyer must name the vessel and in an appropriate case the seller must comply with the provisions of this Article on the form of bill of lading (Section 2—323).

(2) Unless otherwise agreed the term F.A.S. vessel (which means "free alongside") at a named port, even though used only in connection with the stated price, is a delivery term under which the seller must

(a) at his own expense and risk deliver the goods alongside the vessel in the manner usual in that port or on a dock designated and provided by the buyer; and

(b) obtain and tender a receipt for the goods in exchange for which the carrier is under a duty to issue a bill of lading.

(3) Unless otherwise agreed in any case falling within subsection (1)(a) or (c) or subsection (2) the buyer must seasonably give any needed instructions for making delivery, including when the term is F.A.S. or F.O.B. the loading berth of the vessel and in an appropriate case its name and sailing date. The seller may treat the failure of needed instructions as a failure of cooperation under this Article (Section 2—311). He may also at his option move the goods in any reasonable manner preparatory to delivery or shipment.

(4) Under the term F.O.B. vessel or F.A.S. unless otherwise agreed the buyer must make payment against tender of the required documents and the seller may not tender

nor the buyer demand delivery of the goods in substitution for the documents.

§ 2—320. C.I.F. and C. & F. Terms.

(1) The term C.I.F. means that the price includes in a lump sum the cost of the goods and the insurance and freight to the named destination. The term C. & F. or C.F. means that the price so includes cost and freight to the named destination.

(2) Unless otherwise agreed and even though used only in connection with the stated price and destination, the term C.I.F. destination or its equivalent requires the seller at his own expense and risk to

> (a) put the goods into the possession of a carrier at the port for shipment and obtain a negotiable bill or bills of lading covering the entire transportation to the named destination; and
>
> (b) load the goods and obtain a receipt from the carrier (which may be contained in the bill of lading) showing that the freight has been paid or provided for; and
>
> (c) obtain a policy or certificate of insurance, including any war risk insurance, of a kind and on terms then current at the port of shipment in the usual amount, in the currency of the contract, shown to cover the same goods covered by the bill of lading and providing for payment of loss to the order of the buyer or for the account of whom it may concern; but the seller may add to the price the amount of the premium for any such war risk insurance; and
>
> (d) prepare an invoice of the goods and procure any other documents required to effect shipment or to comply with the contract; and
>
> (e) forward and tender with commercial promptness all the documents in due form and with any indorsement necessary to perfect the buyer's rights.

(3) Unless otherwise agreed the term C. & F. or its equivalent has the same effect and imposes upon the seller the same obligations and risks as a C.I.F. term except the obligation as to insurance.

(4) Under the term C.I.F. or C. & F. unless otherwise agreed the buyer must make payment against tender of the required documents and the seller may not tender nor the buyer demand delivery of the goods in substitution for the documents.

§ 2—321. C.I.F. or C. & F.: "Net Landed Weights"; "Payment on Arrival"; Warranty of Condition on Arrival.

Under a contract containing a term C.I.F. or C. & F.

(1) Where the price is based on or is to be adjusted according to "net landed weights", "delivered weights", "out turn" quantity or quality or the like, unless otherwise agreed the seller must reasonably estimate the price. The payment due on tender of the documents called for by the contract is the amount so estimated, but after final adjustment of the price a settlement must be made with commercial promptness.

(2) An agreement described in subsection (1) or any warranty of quality or condition of the goods on arrival places upon the seller the risk of ordinary deterioration, shrinkage and the like in transportation but has no effect on the place or time of identification to the contract for sale or delivery or on the passing of the risk of loss.

(3) Unless otherwise agreed where the contract provides for payment on or after arrival of the goods the seller must before payment allow such preliminary inspection as is feasible; but if the goods are lost delivery of the documents and payment are due when the goods should have arrived.

§ 2—322. Delivery "Ex-Ship".

(1) Unless otherwise agreed a term for delivery of goods "ex-ship" (which means from the carrying vessel) or in equivalent language is not restricted to a particular ship and requires delivery from a ship which has reached a place at the named port of destination where goods of the kind are usually discharged.

(2) Under such a term unless otherwise agreed

> (a) the seller must discharge all liens arising out of the carriage and furnish the buyer with a direction which puts the carrier under a duty to deliver the goods; and
>
> (b) the risk of loss does not pass to the buyer until the goods leave the ship's tackle or are otherwise properly unloaded.

§ 2—323. Form of Bill of Lading Required in Overseas Shipment; "Overseas".

(1) Where the contract contemplates overseas shipment and contains a term C.I.F. or C. & F. or F.O.B. vessel, the seller unless otherwise agreed must obtain a negotiable bill of lading stating that the goods have been loaded on board or, in the case of a term C.I.F. or C. & F., received for shipment.

(2) Where in a case within subsection (1) a bill of lading has been issued in a set of parts, unless otherwise agreed if the documents are not to be sent from abroad the buyer may demand tender of the full set; otherwise only one part of the bill of lading need be tendered. Even if the agreement expressly requires a full set

> (a) due tender of a single part is acceptable within the provisions of this Article on cure of improper delivery (subsection (1) of Section 2—508); and
>
> (b) even though the full set is demanded, if the documents are sent from abroad the person tendering an incomplete set may nevertheless require payment upon furnishing an indemnity which the buyer in good faith deems adequate.

(3) A shipment by water or by air or a contract contemplating such shipment is "overseas" insofar as by usage of trade or agreement it is subject to the commercial,

financing or shipping practices characteristic of international deep water commerce.

§ 2—324. "No Arrival, No Sale" Term.

Under a term "no arrival, no sale" or terms of like meaning, unless otherwise agreed,

(a) the seller must properly ship conforming goods and if they arrive by any means he must tender them on arrival but he assumes no obligation that the goods will arrive unless he has caused the non-arrival; and

(b) where without fault of the seller the goods are in part lost or have so deteriorated as no longer to conform to the contract or arrive after the contract time, the buyer may proceed as if there had been casualty to identified goods (Section 2—613).

§ 2—325. "Letter of Credit" Term; "Confirmed Credit".

(1) Failure of the buyer seasonably to furnish an agreed letter of credit is a breach of the contract for sale.

(2) The delivery to seller of a proper letter of credit suspends the buyer's obligation to pay. If the letter of credit is dishonored, the seller may on seasonable notification to the buyer require payment directly from him.

(3) Unless otherwise agreed the term "letter of credit" or "banker's credit" in a contract for sale means an irrevocable credit issued by a financing agency of good repute and, where the shipment is overseas, of good international repute. The term "confirmed credit" means that the credit must also carry the direct obligation of such an agency which does business in the seller's financial market.

§ 2—326. Sale on Approval and Sale or Return; Consignment Sales and Rights of Creditors.

(1) Unless otherwise agreed, if delivered goods may be returned by the buyer even though they conform to the contract, the transaction is

(a) a "sale on approval" if the goods are delivered primarily for use, and

(b) a "sale or return" if the goods are delivered primarily for resale.

(2) Except as provided in subsection (3), goods held on approval are not subject to the claims of the buyer's creditors until acceptance; goods held on sale or return are subject to such claims while in the buyer's possession.

(3) Where goods are delivered to a person for sale and such person maintains a place of business at which he deals in goods of the kind involved, under a name other than the name of the person making delivery, then with respect to claims of creditors of the person conducting the business the goods are deemed to be on sale or return. The provisions of this subsection are applicable even though an agreement purports to reserve title to the person making delivery until payment or resale or uses such

words as "on consignment" or "on memorandum". However, this subsection is not applicable if the person making delivery

(a) complies with an applicable law providing for a consignor's interest or the like to be evidenced by a sign, or

(b) establishes that the person conducting the business is generally known by his creditors to be substantially engaged in selling the goods of others, or

(c) complies with the filing provisions of the Article on Secured Transactions (Article 9).

(4) Any "or return" term of a contract for sale is to be treated as a separate contract for sale within the statute of frauds section of this Article (Section 2—201) and as contradicting the sale aspect of the contract within the provisions of this Article on parol or extrinsic evidence (Section 2—202).

§ 2—327. Special Incidents of Sale on Approval and Sale or Return.

(1) Under a sale on approval unless otherwise agreed

(a) although the goods are identified to the contract the risk of loss and the title do not pass to the buyer until acceptance; and

(b) use of the goods consistent with the purpose of trial is not acceptance but failure seasonably to notify the seller of election to return the goods is acceptance, and if the goods conform to the contract acceptance of any part is acceptance of the whole; and

(c) after due notification of election to return, the return is at the seller's risk and expense but a merchant buyer must follow any reasonable instructions.

(2) Under a sale or return unless otherwise agreed

(a) the option to return extends to the whole or any commercial unit of the goods while in substantially their original condition, but must be exercised seasonably; and

(b) the return is at the buyer's risk and expense.

§ 2—328. Sale by Auction.

(1) In a sale by auction if goods are put up in lots each lot is the subject of a separate sale.

(2) A sale by auction is complete when the auctioneer so announces by the fall of the hammer or in other customary manner. Where a bid is made while the hammer is falling in acceptance of a prior bid the auctioneer may in his discretion reopen the bidding or declare the goods sold under the bid on which the hammer was falling.

(3) Such a sale is with reserve unless the goods are in explicit terms put up without reserve. In an auction with reserve the auctioneer may withdraw the goods at any time until he announces completion of the sale. In an auction without reserve, after the auctioneer calls for bids on an article or lot, that article or lot cannot be withdrawn unless no bid is made within a reasonable time. In either

case a bidder may retract his bid until the auctioneer's announcement of completion of the sale, but a bidder's retraction does not revive any previous bid.

(4) If the auctioneer knowingly receives a bid on the seller's behalf or the seller makes or procures such as bid, and notice has not been given that liberty for such bidding is reserved, the buyer may at his option avoid the sale or take the goods at the price of the last good faith bid prior to the completion of the sale. This subsection shall not apply to any bid at a forced sale.

Part 4 Title, Creditors and Good Faith Purchasers

§ 2—401. Passing of Title; Reservation for Security; Limited Application of This Section.

Each provision of this Article with regard to the rights, obligations and remedies of the seller, the buyer, purchasers or other third parties applies irrespective of title to the goods except where the provision refers to such title. Insofar as situations are not covered by the other provisions of this Article and matters concerning title became material the following rules apply:

(1) Title to goods cannot pass under a contract for sale prior to their identification to the contract (Section 2—501), and unless otherwise explicitly agreed the buyer acquires by their identification a special property as limited by this Act. Any retention or reservation by the seller of the title (property) in goods shipped or delivered to the buyer is limited in effect to a reservation of a security interest. Subject to these provisions and to the provisions of the Article on Secured Transactions (Article 9), title to goods passes from the seller to the buyer in any manner and on any conditions explicitly agreed on by the parties.

(2) Unless otherwise explicitly agreed title passes to the buyer at the time and place at which the seller completes his performance with reference to the physical delivery of the goods, despite any reservation of a security interest and even though a document of title is to be delivered at a different time or place; and in particular and despite any reservation of a security interest by the bill of lading

    (a) if the contract requires or authorizes the seller to send the goods to the buyer but does not require him to deliver them at destination, title passes to the buyer at the time and place of shipment; but

    (b) if the contract requires delivery at destination, title passes on tender there.

(3) Unless otherwise explicitly agreed where delivery is to be made without moving the goods,

    (a) if the seller is to deliver a document of title, title passes at the time when and the place where he delivers such documents; or

    (b) if the goods are at the time of contracting already identified and no documents are to be delivered, title passes at the time and place of contracting.

(4) A rejection or other refusal by the buyer to receive or retain the goods, whether or not justified, or a justified revocation of acceptance revests title to the goods in the seller. Such revesting occurs by operation of law and is not a "sale".

§ 2—402. Rights of Seller's Creditors Against Sold Goods.

(1) Except as provided in subsections (2) and (3), rights of unsecured creditors of the seller with respect to goods which have been identified to a contract for sale are subject to the buyer's rights to recover the goods under this Article (Sections 2—502 and 2—716).

(2) A creditor of the seller may treat a sale or an identification of goods to a contract for sale as void if as against him a retention of possession by the seller is fraudulent under any rule of law of the state where the goods are situated, except that retention of possession in good faith and current course of trade by a merchant-seller for a commercially reasonable time after a sale or identification is not fraudulent.

(3) Nothing in this Article shall be deemed to impair the rights of creditors of the seller

    (a) under the provisions of the Article on Secured Transactions (Article 9); or

    (b) where identification to the contract or delivery is made not in current course of trade but in satisfaction of or as security for a pre-existing claim for money, security or the like and is made under circumstances which under any rule of law of the state where the goods are situated would apart from this Article constitute the transaction a fraudulent transfer or voidable preference.

§ 2—403. Power to Transfer; Good Faith Purchase of Goods; "Entrusting".

(1) A purchaser of goods acquires all title which his transferor had or had power to transfer except that a purchaser of a limited interest acquires rights only to the extent of the interest purchased. A person with voidable title has power to transfer a good title to a good faith purchaser for value. When goods have been delivered under a transaction of purchase the purchaser has such power even though

    (a) the transferor was deceived as to the identity of the purchaser, or

    (b) the delivery was in exchange for a check which is later dishonored, or

    (c) it was agreed that the transaction was to be a "cash sale", or

    (d) the delivery was procured through fraud punishable as larcenous under the criminal law.

(2) Any entrusting of possession of goods to a merchant who deals in goods of that kind gives him power to transfer all rights of the entruster to a buyer in ordinary course of business.

(3) "Entrusting" includes any delivery and any acquiescence in retention of possession regardless of any condition expressed between the parties to the delivery or acquiescence and regardless of whether the procurement of the

entrusting or the possessor's disposition of the goods have been such as to be larcenous under the criminal law.

(4) The rights of other purchasers of goods and of lien creditors are governed by the Articles on Secured Transactions (Article 9), Bulk Transfers (Article 6) and Documents of Title (Article 7).

Part 5 Performance

§ 2—501. Insurable Interest in Goods; Manner of Identification of Goods.

(1) The buyer obtains a special property and an insurable interest in goods by identification of existing goods as goods to which the contract refers even though the goods so identified are non-conforming and he has an option to return or reject them. Such identification can be made at any time and in any manner explicitly agreed to by the parties. In the absence of explicit agreement identification occurs

(a) when the contract is made if it is for the sale of goods already existing and identified;

(b) if the contract is for the sale of future goods other than those described in paragraph (c), when goods are shipped, marked or otherwise designated by the seller as goods to which the contract refers;

(c) when the crops are planted or otherwise become growing crops or the young are conceived if the contract is for the sale of unborn young to be born within twelve months after contracting or for the sale of crops to be harvested within twelve months or the next normal harvest season after contracting whichever is longer.

(2) The seller retains an insurable interest in goods so long as title to or any security interest in the goods remains in him and where the identification is by the seller alone he may until default or insolvency or notification to the buyer that the identification is final substitute other goods for those identified.

(3) Nothing in this section impairs any insurable interest recognized under any other statute or rule of law.

§ 2—502. Buyer's Right to Goods on Seller's Insolvency.

(1) Subject to subsection (2) and even though the goods have not been shipped a buyer who has paid a part or all of the price of goods in which he has a special property under the provisions of the immediately preceding section may on making and keeping good a tender of any unpaid portion of their price recover them from the seller if the seller becomes insolvent within ten days after receipt of the first installment on their price.

(2) If the identification creating his special property has been made by the buyer he acquires the right to recover the goods only if they conform to the contract for sale.

§ 2—503. Manner of Seller's Tender of Delivery.

(1) Tender of delivery requires that the seller put and hold conforming goods at the buyer's disposition and give the buyer any notification reasonably necessary to enable him to take delivery. The manner, time and place for tender are determined by the agreement and this Article, and in particular

(a) tender must be at a reasonable hour, and if it is of goods they must be kept available for the period reasonably necessary to enable the buyer to take possession; but

(b) unless otherwise agreed the buyer must furnish facilities reasonably suited to the receipt of the goods.

(2) Where the case is within the next section respecting shipment tender requires that the seller comply with its provisions.

(3) Where the seller is required to deliver at a particular destination tender requires that he comply with subsection (1) and also in any appropriate case tender documents as described in subsections (4) and (5) of this section.

(4) Where goods are in the possession of a bailee and are to be delivered without being moved

(a) tender requires that the seller either tender a negotiable document of title covering such goods or procure acknowledgment by the bailee of the buyer's right to possession of the goods; but

(b) tender to the buyer of a non-negotiable document of title or of a written direction to the bailee to deliver is sufficient tender unless the buyer seasonably objects, and receipt by the bailee of notification of the buyer's rights fixes those rights as against the bailee and all third persons; but risk of loss of the goods and of any failure by the bailee to honor the non-negotiable document of title or to obey the direction remains on the seller until the buyer has had a reasonable time to present the document or direction, and a refusal by the bailee to honor the document or to obey the direction defeats the tender.

(5) Where the contract requires the seller to deliver documents

(a) he must tender all such documents in correct form, except as provided in this Article with respect to bills of lading in a set (subsection (2) of Section 2—323); and

(b) tender through customary banking channels is sufficient and dishonor of a draft accompanying the documents constitutes non-acceptance or rejection.

§ 2—504. Shipment by Seller.

Where the seller is required or authorized to send the goods to the buyer and the contract does not require him to deliver them at a particular destination, then unless otherwise agreed he must

(a) put the goods in the possession of such a carrier and make such a contract for their transportation as may be reasonable having regard to the nature of the goods and other circumstances of the case; and

(b) obtain and promptly deliver or tender in due form any document necessary to enable the buyer to obtain possession of the goods or otherwise required by the agreement or by usage of trade; and

(c) promptly notify the buyer of the shipment.

Failure to notify the buyer under paragraph (c) or to make a proper contract under paragraph (a) is a ground for rejection only if material delay or loss ensues.

§ 2—505. Seller's Shipment under Reservation.

(1) Where the seller has identified goods to the contract by or before shipment:

(a) his procurement of a negotiable bill of lading to his own order or otherwise reserves in him a security interest in the goods. His procurement of the bill to the order of a financing agency or of the buyer indicates in addition only the seller's expectation of transferring that interest to the person named.

(b) a non-negotiable bill of lading to himself or his nominee reserves possession of the goods as security but except in a case of conditional delivery (subsection (2) of Section 2—507) a non-negotiable bill of lading naming the buyer as consignee reserves no security interest even though the seller retains possession of the bill of lading.

(2) When shipment by the seller with reservation of a security interest is in violation of the contract for sale it constitutes an improper contract for transportation within the preceding section but impairs neither the rights given to the buyer by shipment and identification of the goods to the contract nor the seller's powers as a holder of a negotiable document.

§ 2—506. Rights of Financing Agency.

(1) A financing agency by paying or purchasing for value a draft which relates to a shipment of goods acquires to the extent of the payment or purchase and in addition to its own rights under the draft and any document of title securing it any rights of the shipper in the goods including the right to stop delivery and the shipper's right to have the draft honored by the buyer.

(2) The right to reimbursement of a financing agency which has in good faith honored or purchased the draft under commitment to or authority from the buyer is not impaired by subsequent discovery of defects with reference to any relevant document which was apparently regular on its face.

§ 2—507. Effect of Seller's Tender; Delivery on Condition.

(1) Tender of delivery is a condition to the buyer's duty to accept the goods and, unless otherwise agreed, to his duty to pay for them. Tender entitles the seller to acceptance of the goods and to payment according to the contract.

(2) Where payment is due and demanded on the delivery to the buyer of goods or documents of title, his right as

against the seller to retain or dispose of them is conditional upon his making the payment due.

§ 2—508. Cure by Seller of Improper Tender or Delivery; Replacement.

(1) Where any tender or delivery by the seller is rejected because non-conforming and the time for performance has not yet expired, the seller may seasonably notify the buyer of his intention to cure and may then within the contract time make a conforming delivery.

(2) Where the buyer rejects a non-conforming tender which the seller had reasonable grounds to believe would be acceptable with or without money allowance the seller may if he seasonably notifies the buyer have a further reasonable time to substitute a conforming tender.

§ 2—509. Risk of Loss in the Absence of Breach.

(1) Where the contract requires or authorizes the seller to ship the goods by carrier

(a) if it does not require him to deliver them at a particular destination, the risk of loss passes to the buyer when the goods are duly delivered to the carrier even though the shipment is under reservation (Section 2—505); but

(b) if it does require him to deliver them at a particular destination and the goods are there duly tendered while in the possession of the carrier, the risk of loss passes to the buyer when the goods are there duly so tendered as to enable the buyer to take delivery.

(2) Where the goods are held by a bailee to be delivered without being moved, the risk of loss passes to the buyer

(a) on his receipt of a negotiable document of title covering the goods; or

(b) on acknowledgment by the bailee of the buyer's right to possession of the goods; or

(c) after his receipt of a non-negotiable document of title or other written direction to deliver, as provided in subsection (4)(b) of Section 2—503.

(3) In any case not within subsection (1) or (2), the risk of loss passes to the buyer on his receipt of the goods if the seller is a merchant; otherwise the risk passes to the buyer on tender of delivery.

(4) The provisions of this section are subject to contrary agreement of the parties and to the provisions of this Article on sale on approval (Section 2—327) and on effect of breach on risk of loss (Section 2—510).

§ 2—510. Effect of Breach on Risk of Loss.

(1) Where a tender or delivery of goods so fails to conform to the contract as to give a right of rejection the risk of their loss remains on the seller until cure or acceptance.

(2) Where the buyer rightfully revokes acceptance he may to the extent of any deficiency in his effective insurance coverage treat the risk of loss as having rested on the seller from the beginning.

(3) Where the buyer as to conforming goods already identified to the contract for sale repudiates or is otherwise in breach before risk of their loss has passed to him, the seller may to the extent of any deficiency in his effective insurance coverage treat the risk of loss as resting on the buyer for a commercially reasonable time.

§ 2—511. Tender of Payment by Buyer; Payment by Check.

(1) Unless otherwise agreed tender of payment is a condition to the seller's duty to tender and complete any delivery.

(2) Tender of payment is sufficient when made by any means or in any manner current in the ordinary course of business unless the seller demands payment in legal tender and gives any extension of time reasonably necessary to procure it.

(3) Subject to the provisions of this Act on the effect of an instrument on an obligation (Section 3—802), payment by check is conditional and is defeated as between the parties by dishonor of the check on due presentment.

§ 2—512. Payment by Buyer Before Inspection.

(1) Where the contract requires payment before inspection non-conformity of the goods does not excuse the buyer from so making payment unless

(a) the non-conformity appears without inspection; or

(b) despite tender of the required documents the circumstances would justify injunction against honor under the provisions of this Act (Section 5—114).

(2) Payment pursuant to subsection (1) does not constitute an acceptance of goods or impair the buyer's right to inspect or any of his remedies.

§ 2—513. Buyer's Right to Inspection of Goods.

(1) Unless otherwise agreed and subject to subsection (3), where goods are tendered or delivered or identified to the contract for sale, the buyer has a right before payment or acceptance to inspect them at any reasonable place and time and in any reasonable manner. When the seller is required or authorized to send the goods to the buyer, the inspection may be after their arrival.

(2) Expenses of inspection must be borne by the buyer but may be recovered from the seller if the goods do not conform and are rejected.

(3) Unless otherwise agreed and subject to the provisions of this Article on C.I.F. contracts (subsection (3) of Section 2—321), the buyer is not entitled to inspect the goods before payment of the price when the contract provides

(a) for delivery "C.O.D." or on other like terms; or

(b) for payment against documents of title, except where such payment is due only after the goods are to become available for inspection.

(4) A place or method of inspection fixed by the parties is presumed to be exclusive but unless otherwise expressly agreed it does not postpone identification or shift the place for delivery or for passing the risk of loss. If compliance becomes impossible, inspection shall be as provided in this section unless the place or method fixed was clearly intended as an indispensable condition failure of which avoids the contract.

§ 2—514. When Documents Deliverable on Acceptance; When on Payment.

Unless otherwise agreed documents against which a draft is drawn are to be delivered to the drawee on acceptance of the draft if it is payable more than three days after presentment; otherwise, only on payment.

§ 2—515. Preserving Evidence of Goods in Dispute.

In furtherance of the adjustment of any claim or dispute

(a) either party on reasonable notification to the other and for the purpose of ascertaining the facts and preserving evidence has the right to inspect, test and sample the goods including such of them as may be in the possession or control of the other; and

(b) the parties may agree to a third party inspection or survey to determine the conformity or condition of the goods and may agree that the findings shall be binding upon them in any subsequent litigation or adjustment.

Part 6 Breach, Repudiation and Excuse

§ 2—601. Buyer's Rights on Improper Delivery.

Subject to the provisions of this Article on breach in installment contracts (Section 2—612) and unless otherwise agreed under the sections on contractual limitations of remedy (Sections 2—718 and 2—719), if the goods or the tender of delivery fail in any respect to conform to the contract, the buyer may

(a) reject the whole; or

(b) accept the whole; or

(c) accept any commercial unit or units and reject the rest.

§ 2—602. Manner and Effect of Rightful Rejection.

(1) Rejection of goods must be within a reasonable time after their delivery or tender. It is ineffective unless the buyer seasonably notifies the seller.

(2) Subject to the provisions of the two following sections on rejected goods (Sections 2—603 and 2—604),

(a) after rejection any exercise of ownership by the buyer with respect to any commercial unit is wrongful as against the seller; and

(b) if the buyer has before rejection taken physical possession of goods in which he does not have a security interest under the provisions of this Article (subsection (3) of Section 2—711), he is under a duty after rejection to hold them with reasonable care at the seller's disposition for a time sufficient to permit the seller to remove them; but

(c) the buyer has no further obligations with regard to goods rightfully rejected.

(3) The seller's rights with respect to goods wrongfully rejected are governed by the provisions of this Article on Seller's remedies in general (Section 2—703).

§ 2—603. Merchant Buyer's Duties as to Rightfully Rejected Goods.

(1) Subject to any security interest in the buyer (subsection (3) of Section 2—711), when the seller has no agent or place of business at the market of rejection a merchant buyer is under a duty after rejection of goods in his possession or control to follow any reasonable instructions received from the seller with respect to the goods and in the absence of such instructions to make reasonable efforts to sell them for the seller's account if they are perishable or threaten to decline in value speedily. Instructions are not reasonable if on demand indemnity for expenses is not forthcoming.

(2) When the buyer sells goods under subsection (1), he is entitled to reimbursement from the seller or out of the proceeds for reasonable expenses of caring for and selling them, and if the expenses include no selling commission then to such commission as is usual in the trade or if there is none to a reasonable sum not exceeding ten per cent on the gross proceeds.

(3) In complying with this section the buyer is held only to good faith and good faith conduct hereunder is neither acceptance nor conversion nor the basis of an action for damages.

§ 2—604. Buyer's Options as to Salvage of Rightfully Rejected Goods.

Subject to the provisions of the immediately preceding section on perishables if the seller gives no instructions within a reasonable time after notification of rejection the buyer may store the rejected goods for the seller's account or reship them to him or resell them for the seller's account with reimbursement as provided in the preceding section. Such action is not acceptance or conversion.

§ 2—605. Waiver of Buyer's Objections by Failure to Particularize.

(1) The buyer's failure to state in connection with rejection a particular defect which is ascertainable by reasonable inspection precludes him from relying on the unstated defect to justify rejection or to establish breach

(a) where the seller could have cured it if stated seasonably; or

(b) between merchants when the seller has after rejection made a request in writing for a full and final written statement of all defects on which the buyer proposes to rely.

(2) Payment against documents made without reservation of rights precludes recovery of the payment for defects apparent on the face of the documents.

§ 2—606. What Constitutes Acceptance of Goods.

(1) Acceptance of goods occurs when the buyer

(a) after a reasonable opportunity to inspect the goods signifies to the seller that the goods are conforming or that he will take or retain them in spite of their nonconformity; or

(b) fails to make an effective rejection (subsection (1) of Section 2—602), but such acceptance does not occur until the buyer has had a reasonable opportunity to inspect them; or

(c) does any act inconsistent with the seller's ownership; but if such act is wrongful as against the seller it is an acceptance only if ratified by him.

(2) Acceptance of a part of any commercial unit is acceptance of that entire unit.

§ 2—607. Effect of Acceptance; Notice of Breach; Burden of Establishing Breach After Acceptance; Notice of Claim or Litigation to Person Answerable Over.

(1) The buyer must pay at the contract rate for any goods accepted.

(2) Acceptance of goods by the buyer precludes rejection of the goods accepted and if made with knowledge of a non-conformity cannot be revoked because of it unless the acceptance was on the reasonable assumption that the non-conformity would be seasonably cured but acceptance does not of itself impair any other remedy provided by this Article for non-conformity.

(3) Where a tender has been accepted

(a) the buyer must within a reasonable time after he discovers or should have discovered any breach notify the seller of breach or be barred from any remedy; and

(b) if the claim is one for infringement or the like (subsection (3) of Section 2—312) and the buyer is sued as a result of such a breach he must so notify the seller within a reasonable time after he receives notice of the litigation or be barred from any remedy over for liability established by the litigation.

(4) The burden is on the buyer to establish any breach with respect to the goods accepted.

(5) Where the buyer is sued for breach of a warranty or other obligation for which his seller is answerable over

(a) he may give his seller written notice of the litigation. If the notice states that the seller may come in and defend and that if the seller does not do so he will be bound in any action against him by his buyer by any determination of fact common to the two litigations, then unless the seller after seasonable receipt of the notice does come in and defend he is so bound.

(b) if the claim is one for infringement or the like (subsection (3) of Section 2—312) the original seller may demand in writing that his buyer turn over to him control of the litigation including settlement or else be barred from any remedy over and if he also agrees to bear all expense and to satisfy any adverse judgment, then unless the buyer after seasonable receipt of the demand does turn over control the buyer is so barred.

(6) The provisions of subsections (3), (4) and (5) apply to any obligation of a buyer to hold the seller harmless against infringement or the like (subsection (3) of Section 2—312).

§ 2—608. Revocation of Acceptance in Whole or in Part.

(1) The buyer may revoke his acceptance of a lot or commercial unit whose non-conformity substantially impairs its value to him if he has accepted it

(a) on the reasonable assumption that its nonconformity would be cured and it has not been seasonably cured; or

(b) without discovery of such non-conformity if his acceptance was reasonably induced either by the difficulty of discovery before acceptance or by the seller's assurances.

(2) Revocation of acceptance must occur within a reasonable time after the buyer discovers or should have discovered the ground for it and before any substantial change in condition of the goods which is not caused by their own defects. It is not effective until the buyer notifies the seller of it.

(3) A buyer who so revokes has the same rights and duties with regard to the goods involved as if he had rejected them.

§ 2—609. Right to Adequate Assurance of Performance.

(1) A contract for sale imposes an obligation on each party that the other's expectation of receiving due performance will not be impaired. When reasonable grounds for insecurity arise with respect to the performance of either party the other may in writing demand adequate assurance of due performance and until he receives such assurance may if commercially reasonable suspend any performance for which he has not already received the agreed return.

(2) Between merchants the reasonableness of grounds for insecurity and the adequacy of any assurance offered shall be determined according to commercial standards.

(3) Acceptance of any improper delivery or payment does not prejudice the party's right to demand adequate assurance of future performance.

(4) After receipt of a justified demand failure to provide within a reasonable time not exceeding thirty days such assurance of due performance as is adequate under the circumstances of the particular case is a repudiation of the contract.

§ 2—610. Anticipatory Repudiation.

When either party repudiates the contract with respect to a performance not yet due the loss of which will substantially impair the value of the contract to the other, the aggrieved party may

(a) for a commercially reasonable time await performance by the repudiating party; or

(b) resort to any remedy for breach (Section 2—703 or Section 2—711), even though he has notified the repudiating party that he would await the latter's performance and has urged retraction; and

(c) in either case suspend his own performance or proceed in accordance with the provisions of this Article on the seller's right to identify goods to the contract notwithstanding breach or to salvage unfinished goods (Section 2—704).

§ 2—611. Retraction of Anticipatory Repudiation.

(1) Until the repudiating party's next performance is due he can retract his repudiation unless the aggrieved party has since the repudiation cancelled or materially changed his position or otherwise indicated that he considers the repudiation final.

(2) Retraction may be by any method which clearly indicates to the aggrieved party that the repudiating party intends to perform, but must include any assurance justifiably demanded under the provisions of this Article (Section 2—609).

(3) Retraction reinstates the repudiating party's rights under the contract with due excuse and allowance to the aggrieved party for any delay occasioned by the repudiation.

§ 2—612. "Installment Contract"; Breach.

(1) An "installment contract" is one which requires or authorizes the delivery of goods in separate lots to be separately accepted, even though the contract contains a clause "each delivery is a separate contract" or its equivalent.

(2) The buyer may reject any installment which is nonconforming if the non-conformity substantially impairs the value of that installment and cannot be cured or if the non-conformity is a defect in the required documents; but if the non-conformity does not fall within subsection (3) and the seller gives adequate assurance of its cure the buyer must accept that installment.

(3) Whenever non-conformity or default with respect to one or more installments substantially impairs the value of the whole contract there is a breach of the whole. But the aggrieved party reinstates the contract if he accepts a non-conforming installment without seasonably notifying of cancellation or if he brings an action with respect only to past installments or demands performance as to future installments.

§ 2—613. Casualty to Identified Goods.

Where the contract requires for its performance goods identified when the contract is made, and the goods suffer casualty without fault of either party before the risk of loss passes to the buyer, or in a proper case under a "no arrival, no sale" term (Section 2—324) then

(a) if the loss is total the contract is avoided; and

(b) if the loss is partial or the goods have so deteriorated as no longer to conform to the contract the buyer may nevertheless demand inspection and at his option either treat the contract as voided or accept the goods with due allowance from the contract price for the deterioration or the deficiency in quantity but without further right against the seller.

§ 2—614. Substituted Performance.

(1) Where without fault of either party the agreed berthing, loading, or unloading facilities fail or an agreed type of carrier becomes unavailable or the agreed manner of delivery otherwise becomes commercially impracticable but a commercially reasonable substitute is available, such substitute performance must be tendered and accepted.

(2) If the agreed means or manner of payment fails because of domestic or foreign governmental regulation, the seller may withhold or stop delivery unless the buyer provides a means or manner of payment which is commercially a substantial equivalent. If delivery has already been taken, payment by the means or in the manner provided by the regulation discharges the buyer's obligation unless the regulation is discriminatory, oppressive or predatory.

§ 2—615. Excuse by Failure of Presupposed Conditions.

Except so far as a seller may have assumed a greater obligation and subject to the preceding section on substituted performance:

(a) Delay in delivery or non-delivery in whole or in part by a seller who complies with paragraphs (b) and (c) is not a breach of his duty under a contract for sale if performance as agreed has been made impracticable by the occurrence of a contingency the nonoccurrence of which was a basic assumption on which the contract was made or by compliance in good faith with any applicable foreign or domestic governmental regulation or order whether or not it later proves to be invalid.

(b) Where the causes mentioned in paragraph (a) affect only a part of the seller's capacity to perform, he must allocate production and deliveries among his customers but may at his option include regular customers not then under contract as well as his own requirements for further manufacture. He may so allocate in any manner which is fair and reasonable.

(c) The seller must notify the buyer seasonably that there will be delay or non-delivery and, when allocation is required under paragraph (b), of the estimated quota thus made available for the buyer.

§ 2—616. Procedure on Notice Claiming Excuse.

(1) Where the buyer receives notification of a material or indefinite delay or an allocation justified under the preceding section he may by written notification to the seller as to any delivery concerned, and where the prospective deficiency substantially impairs the value of the whole contract under the provisions of this Article relating to breach of installment contracts (Section 2—612), then also as to the whole,

(a) terminate and thereby discharge any unexecuted portion of the contract; or

(b) modify the contract by agreeing to take his available quota in substitution.

(2) If after receipt of such notification from the seller the buyer fails so to modify the contract within a reasonable time not exceeding thirty days the contract lapses with respect to any deliveries affected.

(3) The provisions of this section may not be negated by agreement except in so far as the seller has assumed a greater obligation under the preceding section.

Part 7 Remedies

§ 2—701. Remedies for Breach of Collateral Contracts Not Impaired.

Remedies for breach of any obligation or promise collateral or ancillary to a contract for sale are not impaired by the provisions of this Article.

§ 2—702. Seller's Remedies on Discovery of Buyer's Insolvency.

(1) Where the seller discovers the buyer to be insolvent he may refuse delivery except for cash including payment for all goods theretofore delivered under the contract, and stop delivery under this Article (Section 2—705).

(2) Where the seller discovers that the buyer has received goods on credit while insolvent he may reclaim the goods upon demand made within ten days after the receipt, but if misrepresentation of solvency has been made to the particular seller in writing within three months before delivery the ten day limitation does not apply. Except as provided in this subsection the seller may not base a right to reclaim goods on the buyer's fraudulent or innocent misrepresentation of solvency or of intent to pay.

(3) The seller's right to reclaim under subsection (2) is subject to the rights of a buyer in ordinary course or other good faith purchaser under this Article (Section 2—403). Successful reclamation of goods excludes all other remedies with respect to them.

§ 2—703. Seller's Remedies in General.

Where the buyer wrongfully rejects or revokes acceptance of goods or fails to make a payment due on or before delivery or repudiates with respect to a part or the whole, then with respect to any goods directly affected and, if the breach is of the whole contract (Section 2—612), then also with respect to the whole undelivered balance, the aggrieved seller may

(a) withhold delivery of such goods;

(b) stop delivery by any bailee as hereafter provided (Section 2—705);

(c) proceed under the next section respecting goods still unidentified to the contract;

(d) resell and recover damages as hereafter provided (Section 2—706);

(e) recover damages for non-acceptance (Section 2—708) or in a proper case the price (Section 2—709);

(f) cancel.

§ 2—704. Seller's Right to Identify Goods to the Contract Notwithstanding Breach or to Salvage Unfinished Goods.

(1) An aggrieved seller under the preceding section may

(a) identify to the contract conforming goods not already identified if at the time he learned of the breach they are in his possession or control;

(b) treat as the subject of resale goods which have demonstrably been intended for the particular contract even though those goods are unfinished.

(2) Where the goods are unfinished an aggrieved seller may in the exercise of reasonable commercial judgment for the purposes of avoiding loss and of effective realization either complete the manufacture and wholly identify the goods to the contract or cease manufacture and resell for scrap or salvage value or proceed in any other reasonable manner.

§ 2—705. Seller's Stoppage of Delivery in Transit or Otherwise.

(1) The seller may stop delivery of goods in the possession of a carrier or other bailee when he discovers the buyer to be insolvent (Section 2—702) and may stop delivery of carload, truckload, planeload or larger shipments of express or freight when the buyer repudiates or fails to make a payment due before delivery or if for any other reason the seller has a right to withhold or reclaim the goods.

(2) As against such buyer the seller may stop delivery until

(a) receipt of the goods by the buyer; or

(b) acknowledgment to the buyer by any bailee of the goods except a carrier that the bailee holds the goods for the buyer; or

(c) such acknowledgment to the buyer by a carrier by reshipment or as warehouseman; or

(d) negotiation to the buyer of any negotiable document of title covering the goods.

(3) (a) To stop delivery the seller must so notify as to enable the bailee by reasonable diligence to prevent delivery of the goods.

(b) After such notification the bailee must hold and deliver the goods according to the directions of the seller but the seller is liable to the bailee for any ensuing charges or damages.

(c) If a negotiable document of title has been issued for goods the bailee is not obliged to obey a notification to stop until surrender of the document.

(d) A carrier who has issued a non-negotiable bill of lading is not obliged to obey a notification to stop received from a person other than the consignor.

§ 2—706. Seller's Resale Including Contract for Resale.

(1) Under the conditions stated in Section 2—703 on seller's remedies, the seller may resell the goods concerned or the undelivered balance thereof. Where the resale is made in good faith and in a commercially reasonable manner the seller may recover the difference between the resale price and the contract price together with any incidental damages allowed under the provisions of this Article (Section 2—710), but less expenses saved in consequence of the buyer's breach.

(2) Except as otherwise provided in subsection (3) or unless otherwise agreed resale may be at public or private sale including sale by way of one or more contracts to sell or of identification to an existing contract of the seller. Sale may be as a unit or in parcels and at any time and place and on any terms but every aspect of the sale including the method, manner, time, place and terms must be commercially reasonable. The resale must be reasonably identified as referring to the broken contract, but it is not necessary that the goods be in existence or that any or all of them have been identified to the contract before the breach.

(3) Where the resale is at private sale the seller must give the buyer reasonable notification of his intention to resell.

(4) Where the resale is at public sale

(a) only identified goods can be sold except where there is a recognized market for a public sale of futures in goods of the kind; and

(b) it must be made at a usual place or market for public sale if one is reasonably available and except in the case of goods which are perishable or threaten to decline in value speedily the seller must give the buyer reasonable notice of the time and place of the resale; and

(c) if the goods are not to be within the view of those attending the sale the notification of sale must state the place where the goods are located and provide for their reasonable inspection by prospective bidders; and

(d) the seller may buy.

(5) A purchaser who buys in good faith at a resale takes the goods free of any rights of the original buyer even though the seller fails to comply with one or more of the requirements of this section.

(6) The seller is not accountable to the buyer for any profit made on any resale. A person in the position of a seller (Section 2—707) or a buyer who has rightfully rejected or justifiably revoked acceptance must account for any excess over the amount of his security interest, as hereinafter defined (subsection (3) of Section 2—711).

§ 2—707. "Person in the Position of a Seller".

(1) A "person in the position of a seller" includes as against a principal an agent who has paid or become responsible for the price of goods on behalf of his principal or anyone who otherwise holds a security interest or other right in goods similar to that of a seller.

(2) A person in the position of a seller may as provided in this Article withhold or stop delivery (Section 2—705) and resell (Section 2—706) and recover incidental damages (Section 2—710).

§ 2—708. Seller's Damages for Non-Acceptance or Repudiation.

(1) Subject to subsection (2) and to the provisions of this Article with respect to proof of market price (Section 2—723), the measure of damages for non-acceptance or repudiation by the buyer is the difference between the market price at the time and place for tender and the unpaid contract price together with any incidental damages provided in this Article (Section 2—710), but less expenses saved in consequence of the buyer's breach.

(2) If the measure of damages provided in subsection (1) is inadequate to put the seller in as good a position as performance would have done then the measure of damages is the profit (including reasonable overhead) which the seller would have made from full performance by the buyer, together with any incidental damages provided in this Article (Section 2—710), due allowance for costs reasonably incurred and due credit for payments or proceeds of resale.

§ 2—709. Action for the Price.

(1) When the buyer fails to pay the price as it becomes due the seller may recover, together with any incidental damages under the next section, the price

(a) of goods accepted or of conforming goods lost or damaged within a commercially reasonable time after risk of their loss has passed to the buyer; and

(b) of goods identified to the contract if the seller is unable after reasonable effort to resell them at a reasonable price or the circumstances reasonably indicate that such effort will be unavailing.

(2) Where the seller sues for the price he must hold for the buyer any goods which have been identified to the contract and are still in his control except that if resale becomes possible he may resell them at any time prior to the collection of the judgment. The net proceeds of any such resale must be credited to the buyer and payment of the judgment entitles him to any goods not resold.

(3) After the buyer has wrongfully rejected or revoked acceptance of the goods or has failed to make a payment due or has repudiated (Section 2—610), a seller who is held not entitled to the price under this section shall nevertheless be awarded damages for non-acceptance under the preceding section.

§ 2—710. Seller's Incidental Damages.

Incidental damages to an aggrieved seller include any commercially reasonable charges, expenses or commissions incurred in stopping delivery, in the transportation, care and custody of goods after the buyer's breach, in connection with return or resale of the goods or otherwise resulting from the breach.

§ 2—711. Buyer's Remedies in General; Buyer's Security Interest in Rejected Goods.

(1) Where the seller fails to make delivery or repudiates or the buyer rightfully rejects or justifiably revokes acceptance then with respect to any goods involved, and with respect to the whole if the breach goes to the whole contract (Section 2—612), the buyer may cancel and whether or not he has done so may in addition to recovering so much of the price as has been paid

(a) "cover" and have damages under the next section as to all the goods affected whether or not they have been identified to the contract; or

(b) recover damages for non-delivery as provided in this Article (Section 2—713).

(2) Where the seller fails to deliver or repudiates the buyer may also

(a) if the goods have been identified recover them as provided in this Article (Section 2—502); or

(b) in a proper case obtain specific performance or replevy the goods as provided in this Article (Section 2—716).

(3) On rightful rejection or justifiable revocation of acceptance a buyer has a security interest in goods in his possession or control for any payments made on their price and any expenses reasonably incurred in their inspection, receipt, transportation, care and custody and may hold such goods and resell them in like manner as an aggrieved seller (Section 2—706).

§ 2—712. "Cover"; Buyer's Procurement of Substitute Goods.

(1) After a breach within the preceding section the buyer may "cover" by making in good faith and without unreasonable delay any reasonable purchase of or contract to purchase goods in substitution for those due from the seller.

(2) The buyer may recover from the seller as damages the difference between the cost of cover and the contract price together with any incidental or consequential damages as hereinafter defined (Section 2—715), but less expenses saved in consequence of the seller's breach.

(3) Failure of the buyer to effect cover within this section does not bar him from any other remedy.

§ 2—713. Buyer's Damages for Non-Delivery or Repudiation.

(1) Subject to the provisions of this Article with respect to proof of market price (Section 2—723), the measure of

damages for non-delivery or repudiation by the seller is the difference between the market price at the time when the buyer learned of the breach and the contract price together with any incidental and consequential damages provided in this Article (Section 2—715), but less expenses saved in consequence of the seller's breach.

(2) Market price is to be determined as of the place for tender or, in cases of rejection after arrival or revocation of acceptance, as of the place of arrival.

§ 2—714. Buyer's Damages for Breach in Regard to Accepted Goods.

(1) Where the buyer has accepted goods and given notification (subsection (3) of Section 2—607) he may recover as damages for any non-conformity of tender the loss resulting in the ordinary course of events from the seller's breach as determined in any manner which is reasonable.

(2) The measure of damages for breach of warranty is the difference at the time and place of acceptance between the value of the goods accepted and the value they would have had if they had been as warranted, unless special circumstances show proximate damages of a different amount.

(3) In a proper case any incidental and consequential damages under the next section may also be recovered.

§ 2—715. Buyer's Incidental and Consequential Damages.

(1) Incidental damages resulting from the seller's breach include expenses reasonably incurred in inspection, receipt, transportation and care and custody of goods rightfully rejected, any commercially reasonable charges, expenses or commissions in connection with effecting cover and any other reasonable expense incident to the delay or other breach.

(2) Consequential damages resulting from the seller's breach include

(a) any loss resulting from general or particular requirements and needs of which the seller at the time of contracting had reason to know and which could not reasonably be prevented by cover or otherwise; and

(b) injury to person or property proximately resulting from any breach of warranty.

§ 2—716. Buyer's Right to Specific Performance or Replevin.

(1) Specific performance may be decreed where the goods are unique or in other proper circumstances.

(2) The decree for specific performance may include such terms and conditions as to payment of the price, damages, or other relief as the court may deem just.

(3) The buyer has a right of replevin for goods identified to the contract if after reasonable effort he is unable to effect cover for such goods or the circumstances reasonably indicate that such effort will be unavailing or if the goods

have been shipped under reservation and satisfaction of the security interest in them has been made or tendered.

§ 2—717. Deduction of Damages From the Price.

The buyer on notifying the seller of his intention to do so may deduct all or any part of the damages resulting from any breach of the contract from any part of the price still due under the same contract.

§ 2—718. Liquidation or Limitation of Damages; Deposits.

(1) Damages for breach by either party may be liquidated in the agreement but only at an amount which is reasonable in the light of the anticipated or actual harm caused by the breach, the difficulties of proof of loss, and the inconvenience or nonfeasibility of otherwise obtaining an adequate remedy. A term fixing unreasonably large liquidated damages is void as a penalty.

(2) Where the seller justifiably withholds delivery of goods because of the buyer's breach, the buyer is entitled to restitution of any amount by which the sum of his payments exceeds

(a) the amount to which the seller is entitled by virtue of terms liquidating the seller's damages in accordance with subsection (1), or

(b) in the absence of such terms, twenty per cent of the value of the total performance for which the buyer is obligated under the contract or $500, whichever is smaller.

(3) The buyer's right to restitution under subsection (2) is subject to offset to the extent that the seller establishes

(a) a right to recover damages under the provisions of this Article other than subsection (1), and

(b) the amount or value of any benefits received by the buyer directly or indirectly by reason of the contract.

(4) Where a seller has received payment in goods their reasonable value or the proceeds of their resale shall be treated as payments for the purposes of subsection (2); but if the seller has notice of the buyer's breach before reselling goods received in part performance, his resale is subject to the conditions laid down in this Article on resale by an aggrieved seller (Section 2—706).

§ 2—719. Contractual Modification or Limitation of Remedy.

(1) Subject to the provisions of subsections (2) and (3) of this section and of the preceding section on liquidation and limitation of damages,

(a) the agreement may provide for remedies in addition to or in substitution for those provided in this Article and may limit or alter the measure of damages recoverable under this Article, as by limiting the buyer's remedies to return of the goods and repayment of the price or to repair and replacement of nonconforming goods or parts; and

(b) resort to a remedy as provided is optional unless the remedy is expressly agreed to be exclusive, in which case it is the sole remedy.

(2) Where circumstances cause an exclusive or limited remedy to fail of its essential purpose, remedy may be had as provided in this Act.

(3) Consequential damages may be limited or excluded unless the limitation or exclusion is unconscionable. Limitation of consequential damages for injury to the person in the case of consumer goods is *prima facie* unconscionable but limitation of damages where the loss is commercial is not.

§ 2—720. Effect of "Cancellation" or "Rescission" on Claims for Antecedent Breach.

Unless the contrary intention clearly appears, expressions of "cancellation" or "rescission" of the contract or the like shall not be construed as a renunciation or discharge of any claim in damages for an antecedent breach.

§ 2—721. Remedies for Fraud.

Remedies for material misrepresentation or fraud include all remedies available under this Article for non-fraudulent breach. Neither rescission or a claim for rescission of the contract for sale nor rejection or return of the goods shall bar or be deemed inconsistent with a claim for damages or other remedy.

§ 2—722. Who Can Sue Third Parties for Injury to Goods.

Where a third party so deals with goods which have been identified to a contract for sale as to cause actionable injury to a party to that contract

(a) a right of action against the third party is in either party to the contract for sale who has title to or a security interest or a special property or an insurable interest in the goods; and if the goods have been destroyed or converted a right of action is also in the party who either bore the risk of loss under the contract for sale or has since the injury assumed that risk as against the other;

(b) if at the time of the injury the party plaintiff did not bear the risk of loss as against the other party to the contract for sale and there is no arrangement between them for disposition of the recovery, his suit or settlement is, subject to his own interest, as a fiduciary for the other party to the contract;

(c) either party may with the consent of the other sue for the benefit of whom it may concern.

§ 2—723. Proof of Market Price: Time and Place.

(1) If an action based on anticipatory repudiation comes to trial before the time for performance with respect to some or all of the goods, any damages based on market price (Section 2—708 or Section 2—713) shall be determined according to the price of such goods prevailing at the time when the aggrieved party learned of the repudiation.

(2) If evidence of a price prevailing at the times or places described in this Article is not readily available the price prevailing within any reasonable time before or after the time described or at any other place which in commercial judgment or under usage of trade would serve as a reasonable substitute for the one described may be used, making any proper allowance for the cost of transporting the goods to or from such other place.

(3) Evidence of a relevant price prevailing at a time or place other than the one described in this Article offered by one party is not admissible unless and until he has given the other party such notice as the court finds sufficient to prevent unfair surprise.

§ 2—724. Admissibility of Market Quotations.

Whenever the prevailing price or value of any goods regularly bought and sold in any established commodity market is in issue, reports in official publications or trade journals or in newspapers or periodicals of general circulation published as the reports of such market shall be admissible in evidence. The circumstances of the preparation of such a report may be shown to affect its weight but not its admissibility.

§ 2—725. Statute of Limitations in Contracts for Sale.

(1) An action for breach of any contract for sale must be commenced within four years after the cause of action has accrued. By the original agreement the parties may reduce the period of limitation to not less than one year but may not extend it.

(2) A cause of action accrues when the breach occurs, regardless of the aggrieved party's lack of knowledge of the breach. A breach of warranty occurs when tender of delivery is made, except that where a warranty explicitly extends to future performance of the goods and discovery of the breach must await the time of such performance the cause of action accrues when the breach is or should have been discovered.

(3) Where an action commenced within the time limited by subsection (1) is so terminated as to leave available a remedy by another action for the same breach such other action may be commenced after the expiration of the time limited and within six months after the termination of the first action unless the termination resulted from voluntary discontinuance or from dismissal for failure or neglect to prosecute.

(4) This section does not alter the law on tolling of the statute of limitations nor does it apply to causes of action which have accrued before this Act becomes effective.

The National Labor Relations Act of 1935 [Excerpts]

appendix E

* * * *

§ 157. Right of Employees as to Organization, Collective Bargaining, etc.

Employees shall have the right to self-organization, to form, join, or assist labor organizations, to bargain collectively through representatives of their own choosing, and to engage in other concerted activities for the purpose of collective bargaining or other mutual aid or protection, and shall also have the right to refrain from any or all of such activities except to the extent that such right may be affected by an agreement requiring membership in a labor organization as a condition of employment as authorized in section 158(a)(3) of this title.

§ 158. Unfair Labor Practices

(a) Unfair labor practices for an employer

It shall be an unfair labor practice for an employer—

(1) to interfere with, restrain, or coerce employees in the exercise of the rights guaranteed in section 157 of this title;

(2) to dominate or interfere with the formation or administration of any labor organization or contribute financial or other support to it: Provided, [t]hat subject to rules and regulations made and published by the Board pursuant to section 156 of this title, an employer shall not be prohibited from permitting employees to confer with him during working hours without loss of time or pay;

(3) by discrimination in regard to hire or tenure of employment or any term or condition of employment to encourage or discourage membership in any labor organization: Provided, [t]hat nothing in this subchapter, or in any other statute of the United States, shall preclude an employer from making an agreement with a labor organization (not established, maintained, or assisted by any action defined in this subsection as an unfair labor practice) to require as a condition of employment membership therein on or after the thirtieth day following the beginning of such employment or the effective date of such agreement, whichever is the later, (i) if such labor organization is the representative of the employees as provided in section 159(a) of this title, in the appropriate collective-bargaining unit covered by such agreement when made, and (ii) unless following an election held as provided in section 159(e) of this title within one year preceding the effective date of such agreement, the Board shall have certified that at least a majority of the employees eligible to vote in such election have voted to rescind the authority of such labor organization to make such an agreement: Provided further, [t]hat no employer shall justify any discrimination against an employee for nonmembership in a labor organization (A) if he has reasonable grounds for believing that such membership was not available to the employee on the same terms and conditions generally applicable to other members, or (B) if he has reasonable grounds for believing that membership was denied or terminated for reasons other than the failure of the employee to tender the periodic dues and the initiation fees uniformly required as a condition of acquiring or retaining membership;

(4) to discharge or otherwise discriminate against an employee because he has filed charges or given testimony under this subchapter;

(5) to refuse to bargain collectively with the representatives of his employees, subject to the provisions of section 159(a) of this title.

(b) Unfair labor practices by labor organization

It shall be an unfair labor practice for a labor organization or its agents—

(1) to restrain or coerce (A) employees in the exercise of the rights guaranteed in section 157 of this title: Provided, [t]hat this paragraph shall not impair the right of a labor organization to prescribe its own rules with respect to the acquisition or retention of membership therein; or (B) an employer in the selection of his representatives for the purposes of collective bargaining or the adjustment of grievances;

(2) to cause or attempt to cause an employer to discriminate against an employee in violation of subsection (a)(3) of this section or to discriminate against an employee with respect to whom membership in such organization has been denied or terminated on some ground other than his failure to tender the periodic dues and the initiation fees uniformly required as a condition of acquiring or retaining membership;

(3) to refuse to bargain collectively with an employer, provided it is the representative of his employees subject to the provisions of section 159(a) of this title;

(4) (i) to engage in, or to induce or encourage any individual employed by any person engaged in commerce or in an industry affecting commerce to engage in, a strike or a refusal in the course of his employment to use, manufacture, process, transport, or otherwise handle or work on any goods, articles, materials, or commodities or to perform any services; or (ii) to threaten, coerce, or restrain any person engaged in commerce or in an industry affecting commerce[.] * * *

(5) to require of employees covered by an agreement authorized under subsection (a)(3) of this section the payment, as a condition precedent to becoming a member of such organization, of a fee in an amount which the Board finds excessive or discriminatory under all the circumstances. In making such a finding, the Board shall consider, among other relevant factors, the practices and customs of labor organizations in the particular industry, and the wages currently paid to the employees affected;

(6) to cause or attempt to cause an employer to pay or deliver or agree to pay or deliver any money or other thing of value, in the nature of an exaction, for services which are not performed or not to be performed; and

(7) to picket or cause to be picketed, or threaten to picket or cause to be picketed, any employer where an object thereof is forcing or requiring an employer to recognize or bargain with a labor organization as the representative of his employees, or forcing or requiring the employees of an employer to accept or select such labor organization as their collective bargaining representative[.] * * *

(c) Expression of views without threat of reprisal or force or promise of benefit

The expressing of any views, argument, or opinion, or the dissemination thereof, whether in written, printed, graphic, or visual form, shall not constitute or be evidence of an unfair labor practice under any of the provisions of this subchapter, if such expression contains no threat of reprisal or force or promise of benefit.

(d) Obligation to bargain collectively

For the purposes of this section, to bargain collectively is the performance of the mutual obligation of the employer and the representative of the employees to meet at reasonable times and confer in good faith with respect to wages, hours, and other terms and conditions of employment, or the negotiation of an agreement, or any question arising thereunder, and the execution of a written contract incorporating any agreement reached if requested by either party, but such obligation does not compel either party to agree to a proposal or require the making of a concession: Provided, [t]hat where there is in effect a collective-bargaining contract covering employees in an industry affecting commerce, the duty to bargain collectively shall also mean that no party to such contract shall terminate or modify such contract, unless the party desiring such termination or modification—

(1) serves a written notice upon the other party to the contract of the proposed termination or modification sixty days prior to the expiration date thereof, or in the event such contract contains no expiration date, sixty days prior to the time it is proposed to make such termination or modification;

(2) offers to meet and confer with the other party for the purpose of negotiating a new contract or a contract containing the proposed modifications;

(3) notifies the Federal Mediation and Conciliation Service within thirty days after such notice of the existence of a dispute, and simultaneously therewith notifies any State or Territorial agency established to mediate and conciliate disputes within the State or Territory where the dispute occurred, provided no agreement has been reached by that time; and

(4) continues in full force and effect, without resorting to strike or lock-out, all the terms and conditions of the existing contract for a period of sixty days after such notice is given or until the expiration date of such contract, whichever occurs later[.] * * *

appendix F

The Sherman Act of 1890 [Excerpts]

Section 1. Every contract, combination in the form of trust or otherwise, or conspiracy, in restraint of trade or commerce among the several States, or with foreign nations, is declared to be illegal. Every person who shall make any contract or engage in any combination or conspiracy hereby declared to be illegal shall be deemed guilty of a felony, and, on conviction thereof, shall be punished by fine not exceeding $10,000,000 if a corporation, or, if any other person, $350,000, or by imprisonment not exceeding three years, or by both said punishments, in the discretion of the court.

Section 2. Every person who shall monopolize, or attempt to monopolize, or combine or conspire with any other person or persons, to monopolize any part of the trade or commerce among the several States, or with foreign nations, shall be deemed guilty of a felony, and, on conviction thereof, shall be punished by fine not exceeding $10,000,000 if a corporation, or, if any other person, $350,000, or by imprisonment not exceeding three years, or by both said punishments, in the discretion of the court.

Section 3. Every contract, combination in form of trust or otherwise, or conspiracy, in restraint of trade or commerce in any Territory of the United States or of the District of Columbia, or in restraint of trade or commerce between any such Territory and another, or between any such Territory or Territories and any State or States or the District of Columbia, or with foreign nations, or between the District of Columbia and any State or States or foreign nations, is declared illegal. Every person who shall make any such contract or engage in any such combination or conspiracy, shall be deemed guilty of a felony, and, on conviction thereof, shall be punished by fine not exceeding $10,000,000 if a corporation, or, if any other person, $350,000, or by imprisonment not exceeding three years, or by both said punishments, in the discretion of the court.

* * * *

Section 7. Every combination, conspiracy, trust, agreement, or contract is declared to be contrary to public policy, illegal, and void when the same is made by or between two or more persons or corporations, either of whom, as agent or principal, is engaged in importing any article from any foreign country into the United States, and when such combination, conspiracy, trust, agreement, or contract is intended to operate in restraint of lawful trade, or free competition in lawful trade or commerce, or to increase the market price in any part of the United States of any article or articles imported or intended to be imported into the United States, or of any manufacture into which such imported article enters or is intended to enter. Every person who shall be engaged in the importation of goods or any commodity from any foreign country in violation of this section, or who shall combine or conspire with another to violate the same, is guilty of a misdemeanor, and on conviction thereof in any court of the United States such person shall be fined in a sum not less than $100 and not exceeding $5,000, and shall be further punished by imprisonment, in the discretion of the court, for a term not less than three months nor exceeding twelve months.

Section 8. The word "person", or "persons", wherever used in sections 1 to 7 of this title shall be deemed to include corporations and associations existing under or authorized by the laws of either the United States, the laws of any of the Territories, the laws of any State, or the laws of any foreign country.

The Clayton Act of 1914 [Excerpts]

Section 3. That it shall be unlawful for any person engaged in commerce, in the course of such commerce, to lease or make a sale or contract for sale of goods, wares, merchandise, machinery, supplies, or other commodities, whether patented or unpatented, for use, consumption, or resale within the United States or * * * other place under the jurisdiction of the United States, or fix a price charged therefor, or discount from, or rebate upon, such price, on the condition, agreement, or understanding that the lessee or purchaser thereof shall not use or deal in the goods, wares, merchandise, machinery, supplies, or other commodities of a competitor or competitors of the lessor or seller, where the effect of such lease, sale, or contract for sale or such condition, agreement, or understanding may be to substantially lessen competition to tend to create a monopoly in any line of commerce.

Section 4. That any person who shall be injured in his business or property by reason of anything forbidden in the antitrust laws may sue therefor in any district court of the United States in the district in which the defendant resides or is found, or has an agent, without respect to the amount in controversy, and shall recover threefold the damages by him sustained, and the cost of suit, including a reasonable attorney's fee.

Section 4A. Whenever the United States is hereafter injured in its business or property by reason of anything forbidden in the antitrust laws it may sue therefor in the United States district court for the district in which the defendant resides or is found or has an agent, without respect to the amount in controversy, and shall recover actual damages by it sustained and the cost of suit.

Section 4B. Any action to enforce any cause of action under sections 4 or 4A shall be forever barred unless commenced within four years after the cause of action accrued. No cause of action barred under existing law on the effective date of this act shall be revived by this Act.

* * * *

Section 6. That the labor of a human being is not a commodity or article of commerce. Nothing contained in the antitrust laws shall be construed to forbid the existence and operation of labor, agricultural or horticultural organizations, instituted for the purposes of mutual help, and not having capital stock or conducted for profit, or to forbid or restrain individual members of such organizations from lawfully carrying out the legitimate objects thereof; nor shall such organizations or the members thereof, be held or construed to be illegal combinations or conspiracies in restraint of trade, under the antitrust laws.

Section 7. That no person engaged in commerce shall acquire, directly or indirectly, the whole or any part of the stock or other share capital and no corporation subject to the jurisdiction of the Federal Trade Commission shall acquire the whole or any part of the assets of another corporation engaged also in commerce, where in any line of commerce in any section of the country, the effect of such acquisition may be substantially to lessen competition, or to tend to create a monopoly.

No person shall acquire, directly or indirectly, the whole or any part of the stock or other share capital and no corporation subject to the jurisdiction of the Federal Trade Commission shall acquire the whole or any part of the assets of one or more corporations engaged in commerce, where in any line of commerce in any section of the country, the effect of such acquisition, of such stocks or assets, or of the use of such stock by the voting or granting of proxies or otherwise, may be substantially to lessen competition, or to tend to create a monopoly.

This section shall not apply to persons purchasing such stock solely for investment and not using the same by voting or otherwise to bring about, or in attempting to bring about, the substantial lessening of competition * * * .

Section 8. * * * No person at the same time shall be a director in any two or more corporations any one of which has capital, surplus, and undivided profits aggregating more than $1,000,000 engaged in whole or in part in commerce, * * * if such corporations are or shall have been theretofore, by virtue of their business and location of operation, competitors, so that the elimination of competition by agreement between them would constitute a violation of any of the provisions of the antitrust laws. * * *

appendix H

The Federal Trade Commission Act of 1914 [Excerpts]

Section 5.

(a)(1) Unfair methods of competition in or affecting commerce, and unfair or deceptive acts or practices in or affecting commerce, are hereby declared unlawful.

(2) The Commission is hereby empowered and directed to prevent persons, partnerships, or corporations from using unfair methods of competition in or affecting commerce and unfair or deceptive acts or practices in or affecting commerce.

(1) Any person, partnership, or corporation who violates an order of the Commission after it has become final, and while such order is in effect, shall forfeit and pay to the United States a civil penalty of not more than $10,000 for each violation, which shall accrue to the United States and may be recovered in a civil action brought by the Attorney General of the United States. Each separate violation of such an order shall be a separate offense, except that in the case of a violation through continuing failure to obey or neglect to obey a final order of the Commission, each day of continuance of such failure or neglect shall be deemed a separate offense. In such actions, the United States district courts are empowered to grant mandatory injunctions and such other and further equitable relief as they deem appropriate in the enforcement of such final orders of the Commission.

The Securities Act of 1933 [Excerpts]

Definitions

Section 2. When used in this title, unless the context requires—

(1) The term "security" means any note, stock, treasury stock, bond, debenture, evidence of indebtedness, certificate of interest or participation in any profit-sharing agreement, collateral-trust certificate, preorganization certificate or subscription, transferable share, investment contract, voting-trust certificate, certificate of deposit for a security, fractional undivided interest in oil, gas, or other mineral rights, any put, call, straddle, option, or privilege on any security, certificate of deposit, or group or index of securities (including any interest therein or based on the value thereof), or any put, call, straddle, option, or privilege entered into on a national securities exchange relating to foreign currency, or, in general, any interest or participation in, temporary or interim certificate for, receipt for, guarantee of, or warrant or right to subscribe to or purchase, any of the foregoing.

Exempted Securities

Section 3. (a) Except as hereinafter expressly provided the provisions of this title shall not apply to any of the following classes of securities:

* * * *

(2) Any security issued or guaranteed by the United States or any territory thereof, or by the District of Columbia, or by any State of the United States, or by any political subdivision of a State or Territory, or by any public instrumentality of one or more States or Territories, or by any person controlled or supervised by and acting as an instrumentality of the Government of the United States pursuant to authority granted by the Congress of the United States; or any certificate of deposit for any of the foregoing; or any security issued or guaranteed by any bank; or any security issued by or representing an interest in or a direct obligation of a Federal Reserve Bank. * * *

(3) Any note, draft, bill of exchange, or banker's acceptance which arises out of a current transaction or the proceeds of which have been or are to be used for current transactions, and which has a maturity at the time of issuance of not exceeding nine months, exclusive of days of grace, or any renewal thereof the maturity of which is likewise limited;

(4) Any security issued by a person organized and operated exclusively for religious, educational, benevolent, fraternal, charitable, or reformatory purposes and not for pecuniary profit, and no part of the net earnings of which inures to the benefit of any person, private stockholder, or individual;

* * * *

(11) Any security which is a part of an issue offered and sold only to persons resident within a single State or Territory, where the issuer of such security is a person resident and doing business within, or, if a corporation, incorporated by and doing business within, such State or Territory.

(b) The Commission may from time to time by its rules and regulations and subject to such terms and conditions as may be described therein, add any class of securities to the securities exempted as provided in this section, if it finds that the enforcement of this title with respect to such securities is not necessary in the public interest and for the protection of investors by reason of the small amount involved or the limited character of the public offering; but no issue of securities shall be exempted under this subsection where the aggregate amount at which such issue is offered to the public exceeds $5,000,000.

Exempted Transactions

Section 4. The provisions of section 5 shall not apply to—

(1) transactions by any person other than an issuer, underwriter, or dealer.

(2) transactions by an issuer not involving any public offering.

(3) transactions by a dealer (including an underwriter no longer acting as an underwriter in respect of the security involved in such transactions), except—

(A) transactions taking place prior to the expiration of forty days after the first date upon which the security was bona fide offered to the public by the issuer or by or through an underwriter.

(B) transactions in a security as to which a registration statement has been filed taking place prior to the expiration of forty days after the effective date of such registration statement or prior to the expiration of forty days after the first date upon which the security was bona fide offered to the public by the issuer or by or through an underwriter after such effective date, whichever is later (excluding in the computation of such forty days any time during which a stop order issued under section 8 is in effect as to the security), or such shorter period as the Commission may specify by rules and regulations or order, and

(C)   transactions as to the securities constituting the whole or a part of an unsold allotment to or subscription by such dealer as a participant in the distribution of such securities by the issuer or by or through an underwriter.

With respect to transactions referred to in clause (B), if securities of the issuer have not previously been sold pursuant to an earlier effective registration statement the applicable period, instead of forty days, shall be ninety days, or such shorter period as the Commission may specify by rules and regulations or order.

(4)   brokers' transactions, executed upon customers' orders on any exchange or in the over-the-counter market but not the solicitation of such orders.

* * * *

(6)   transactions involving offers or sales by an issuer solely to one or more accredited investors, if the aggregate offering price of an issue of securities offered in reliance on this paragraph does not exceed the amount allowed under Section 3(b) of this title, if there is no advertising or public solicitation in connection with the transaction by the issuer or anyone acting on the issuer's behalf, and if the issuer files such notice with the Commission as the Commission shall prescribe.

Prohibitions Relating to Interstate Commerce and the Mails

Section 5.   (a) Unless a registration statement is in effect as to a security, it shall be unlawful for any person, directly or indirectly—

(1)   to make use of any means or instruments of transportation or communication in interstate commerce or of the mails to sell such security through the use or medium of any prospectus or otherwise; or

(2)   to carry or cause to be carried through the mails or in interstate commerce, by any means or instruments of transportation, any such security for the purpose of sale or for delivery after sale.

(b)   It shall be unlawful for any person, directly or indirectly—

(1)   to make use of any means or instruments of transportation or communication in interstate commerce or of the mails to carry or transmit any prospectus relating to any security with respect to which a registration statement has been filed under this title, unless such prospectus meets the requirements of section 10, or

(2)   to carry or to cause to be carried through the mails or in interstate commerce any such security for the purpose of sale or for delivery after sale, unless accompanied or preceded by a prospectus that meets the requirements of subsection (a) of section 10.

(c)   It shall be unlawful for any person, directly, or indirectly, to make use of any means or instruments of transportation or communication in interstate commerce or of the mails to offer to sell or offer to buy through the use or medium of any prospectus or otherwise any security, unless a registration statement has been filed as to such security, or while the registration statement is the subject of a refusal order or stop order or (prior to the effective date of the registration statement) any public proceeding of examination under section 8.

The Securities Exchange Act of 1934 [Excerpts]

Definitions and Application of Title

Section 3. (a) When used in this title, unless the context otherwise requires—

* * * *

(4) The term "broker" means any person engaged in the business of effecting transactions in securities for the account of others, but does not include a bank.

(5) The term "dealer" means any person engaged in the business of buying and selling securities for his own account, through a broker or otherwise, but does not include a bank, or any person insofar as he buys or sells securities for his own account, either individually or in some fiduciary capacity, but not as part of a regular business.

* * * *

(7) The term "director" means any director of a corporation or any person performing similar functions with respect to any organization, whether incorporated or unincorporated.

(8) The term "issuer" means any person who issues or proposes to issue any security; except that with respect to certificates of deposit for securities, voting-trust certificates, or collateral-trust certificates, or with respect to certificates of interest or shares in an unincorporated investment trust not having a board of directors or the fixed, restricted management, or unit type, the term "issuer" means the person or persons performing the acts and assuming the duties of depositor or manager pursuant to the provisions of the trust or other agreement or instrument under which such securities are issued; and except that with respect to equipment-trust certificates or like securities, the term "issuer" means the person by whom the equipment or property is, or is to be, used.

(9) The term "person" means a natural person, company, government, or political subdivision, agency, or instrumentality of a government.

Regulation of the Use of Manipulative and Deceptive Devices

Section 10. It shall be unlawful for any person, directly or indirectly, by the use of any means or instrumentality of interstate commerce or of the mails, or of any facility of any national securities exchange—

(a) To effect a short sale, or to use or employ any stop-loss order in connection with the purchase or sale, of any security registered on a national securities exchange, in contravention of such rules and regulations as the Commission may prescribe as necessary or appropriate in the public interest or for the protection of investors.

(b) To use or employ, in connection with the purchase or sale of any security registered on a national securities exchange or any security not so registered, any manipulative or deceptive device or contrivance in contravention of such rules and regulations as the Commission may prescribe as necessary or appropriate in the public interest or for the protection of investors.

The Digital Millennium Copyright Act of 1998 [Excerpts]

Sec. 1201. Circumvention of copyright protection systems

(a) VIOLATIONS REGARDING CIRCUMVENTION OF TECHNOLOGICAL MEASURES—(1)(A) No person shall circumvent a technological measure that effectively controls access to a work protected under this title. * * *
* * * *

(b) ADDITIONAL VIOLATIONS—(1) No person shall manufacture, import, offer to the public, provide, or otherwise traffic in any technology, product, service, device, component, or part thereof, that—

(A) is primarily designed or produced for the purpose of circumventing protection afforded by a technological measure that effectively protects a right of a copyright owner under this title in a work or a portion thereof;

(B) has only limited commercially significant purpose or use other than to circumvent protection afforded by a technological measure that effectively protects a right of a copyright owner under this title in a work or a portion thereof; or

(C) is marketed by that person or another acting in concert with that person with that person's knowledge for use in circumventing protection afforded by a technological measure that effectively protects a right of a copyright owner under this title in a work or a portion thereof.
* * * *

Sec. 1202. Integrity of copyright management information

(a) FALSE COPYRIGHT MANAGEMENT INFORMATION—No person shall knowingly and with the intent to induce, enable, facilitate, or conceal infringement—

(1) provide copyright management information that is false, or

(2) distribute or import for distribution copyright management information that is false.

(b) REMOVAL OR ALTERATION OF COPYRIGHT MANAGEMENT INFORMATION—No person shall, without the authority of the copyright owner or the law—

(1) intentionally remove or alter any copyright management information,

(2) distribute or import for distribution copyright management information knowing that the copyright management information has been removed or altered without authority of the copyright owner or the law, or

(3) distribute, import for distribution, or publicly perform works, copies of works, or phonorecords, knowing that copyright management information has been removed or altered without authority of the copyright owner or the law, knowing, or, with respect to civil remedies under section 1203, having reasonable grounds to know, that it will induce, enable, facilitate, or conceal an infringement of any right under this title.

(c) DEFINITION—As used in this section, the term "copyright management information" means any of the following information conveyed in connection with copies or phonorecords of a work or performances or displays of a work, including in digital form, except that such term does not include any personally identifying information about a user of a work or of a copy, phonorecord, performance, or display of a work:

(1) The title and other information identifying the work, including the information set forth on a notice of copyright.

(2) The name of, and other identifying information about, the author of a work.

(3) The name of, and other identifying information about, the copyright owner of the work, including the information set forth in a notice of copyright.

(4) With the exception of public performances of works by radio and television broadcast stations, the name of, and other identifying information about, a performer whose performance is fixed in a work other than an audiovisual work.

(5) With the exception of public performances of works by radio and television broadcast stations, in the case of an audiovisual work, the name of, and other identifying information about, a writer, performer, or director who is credited in the audiovisual work.

(6) Terms and conditions for use of the work.

(7) Identifying numbers or symbols referring to such information or links to such information.

(8) Such other information as the Register of Copyrights may prescribe by regulation, except that the Register of Copyrights may not require the provision of any information concerning the user of a copyrighted work.

* * * *

Sec. 512. Limitations on liability relating to material online

(a) TRANSITORY DIGITAL NETWORK COMMUNICATIONS—A service provider shall not be liable for monetary relief, or, except as provided in subsection (j), for injunctive or other equitable relief, for infringement of copyright by reason of the provider's transmitting, routing, or providing connections for, material through a system or network controlled or operated by or for the service provider, or by reason of the intermediate and transient storage of that material in the course of such transmitting, routing, or providing connections, if—

(1)   the transmission of the material was initiated by or at the direction of a person other than the service provider;

(2)   the transmission, routing, provision of connections, or storage is carried out through an automatic technical process without selection of the material by the service provider;

(3)   the service provider does not select the recipients of the material except as an automatic response to the request of another person;

(4)   no copy of the material made by the service provider in the course of such intermediate or transient storage is maintained on the system or network in a manner ordinarily accessible to anyone other than anticipated recipients, and no such copy is maintained on the system or network in a manner ordinarily accessible to such anticipated recipients for a longer period than is reasonably necessary for the transmission, routing, or provision of connections; and

(5)   the material is transmitted through the system or network without modification of its content.

SEC. 101. GENERAL RULE OF VALIDITY.

(a) IN GENERAL—Notwithstanding any statute, regulation, or other rule of law (other than this title and title II), with respect to any transaction in or affecting interstate or foreign commerce—

(1) a signature, contract, or other record relating to such transaction may not be denied legal effect, validity, or enforceability solely because it is in electronic form; and

(2) a contract relating to such transaction may not be denied legal effect, validity, or enforceability solely because an electronic signature or electronic record was used in its formation.

* * * *

(d) RETENTION OF CONTRACTS AND RECORDS—

(1) ACCURACY AND ACCESSIBILITY—If a statute, regulation, or other rule of law requires that a contract or other record relating to a transaction in or affecting interstate or foreign commerce be retained, that requirement is met by retaining an electronic record of the information in the contract or other record that—

(A) accurately reflects the information set forth in the contract or other record; and

(B) remains accessible to all persons who are entitled to access by statute, regulation, or rule of law, for the period required by such statute, regulation, or rule of law, in a form that is capable of being accurately reproduced for later reference, whether by transmission, printing, or otherwise.

(2) EXCEPTION—A requirement to retain a contract or other record in accordance with paragraph (1) does not apply to any information whose sole purpose is to enable the contract or other record to be sent, communicated, or received.

(3) ORIGINALS—If a statute, regulation, or other rule of law requires a contract or other record relating to a transaction in or affecting interstate or foreign commerce to be provided, available, or retained in its original form, or provides consequences if the contract or other record is not provided, available, or retained in its original form, that statute, regulation, or rule of law is satisfied by an electronic record that complies with paragraph (1).

(4) CHECKS—If a statute, regulation, or other rule of law requires the retention of a check, that requirement is satisfied by retention of an electronic record of the information on the front and back of the check in accordance with paragraph (1).

* * * *

(g) NOTARIZATION AND ACKNOWLEDGMENT—If a statute, regulation, or other rule of law requires a signature or record relating to a transaction in or affecting interstate or foreign commerce to be notarized, acknowledged, verified, or made under oath, that requirement is satisfied if the electronic signature of the person authorized to perform those acts, together with all other information required to be included by other applicable statute, regulation, or rule of law, is attached to or logically associated with the signature or record.

(h) ELECTRONIC AGENTS—A contract or other record relating to a transaction in or affecting interstate or foreign commerce may not be denied legal effect, validity, or enforceability solely because its formation, creation, or delivery involved the action of one or more electronic agents so long as the action of any such electronic agent is legally attributable to the person to be bound.

(i) INSURANCE—It is the specific intent of the Congress that this title and title II apply to the business of insurance.

(j) INSURANCE AGENTS AND BROKERS—An insurance agent or broker acting under the direction of a party that enters into a contract by means of an electronic record or electronic signature may not be held liable for any deficiency in the electronic procedures agreed to by the parties under that contract if—

(1) the agent or broker has not engaged in negligent, reckless, or intentional tortious conduct;

(2) the agent or broker was not involved in the development or establishment of such electronic procedures; and

(3) the agent or broker did not deviate from such procedures.

* * * *

SEC. 103. SPECIFIC EXCEPTIONS.

(a) EXCEPTED REQUIREMENTS—The provisions of section 101 shall not apply to a contract or other record to the extent it is governed by—

(1) a statute, regulation, or other rule of law governing the creation and execution of wills, codicils, or testamentary trusts;

(2) a State statute, regulation, or other rule of law governing adoption, divorce, or other matters of family law; or

(3) the Uniform Commercial Code, as in effect in any State, other than sections 1–107 and 1–206 and Articles 2 and 2A.

(b) ADDITIONAL EXCEPTIONS—The provisions of section 101 shall not apply to—

(1) court orders or notices, or official court documents (including briefs, pleadings, and other writings) required to be executed in connection with court proceedings;

(2) any notice of—

(A) the cancellation or termination of utility services (including water, heat, and power);

(B) default, acceleration, repossession, foreclosure, or eviction, or the right to cure, under a credit agreement secured by, or a rental agreement for, a primary residence of an individual;

(C) the cancellation or termination of health insurance or benefits or life insurance benefits (excluding annuities); or

(D) recall of a product, or material failure of a product, that risks endangering health or safety; or

(3) any document required to accompany any transportation or handling of hazardous materials, pesticides, or other toxic or dangerous materials.

* * * *

Section 5. USE OF ELECTRONIC RECORDS AND ELECTRONIC SIGNATURES; VARIATION BY AGREEMENT.

(a) This [Act] does not require a record or signature to be created, generated, sent, communicated, received, stored, or otherwise processed or used by electronic means or in electronic form.

(b) This [Act] applies only to transactions between parties each of which has agreed to conduct transactions by electronic means. Whether the parties agree to conduct a transaction by electronic means is determined from the context and surrounding circumstances, including the parties' conduct.

(c) A party that agrees to conduct a transaction by electronic means may refuse to conduct other transactions by electronic means. The right granted by this subsection may not be waived by agreement.

(d) Except as otherwise provided in this [Act], the effect of any of its provisions may be varied by agreement. The presence in certain provisions of this [Act] of the words "unless otherwise agreed," or words of similar import, does not imply that the effect of other provisions may not be varied by agreement.

(e) Whether an electronic record or electronic signature has legal consequences is determined by this [Act] and other applicable law.

Section 6. CONSTRUCTION AND APPLICATION. This [Act] must be construed and applied:

(1) to facilitate electronic transactions consistent with other applicable law; (2) to be consistent with reasonable practices concerning electronic transactions and with the continued expansion of those practices; and

(3) to effectuate its general purpose to make uniform the law with respect to the subject of this [Act] among States enacting it.

Section 7. LEGAL RECOGNITION OF ELECTRONIC RECORDS, ELECTRONIC SIGNATURES, AND ELECTRONIC CONTRACTS.

(a) A record or signature may not be denied legal effect or enforceability solely because it is in electronic form.

(b) A contract may not be denied legal effect or enforceability solely because an electronic record was used in its formation.

(c) If a law requires a record to be in writing, an electronic record satisfies the law.

(d) If a law requires a signature, an electronic signature satisfies the law.

* * * *

Section 10. EFFECT OF CHANGE OR ERROR. If a change or error in an electronic record occurs in a transmission between parties to a transaction, the following rules apply:

(1) If the parties have agreed to use a security procedure to detect changes or errors and one party has conformed to the procedure, but the other party has not, and the nonconforming party would have detected the change or error had that party also conformed, the conforming party may avoid the effect of the changed or erroneous electronic record.

(2) In an automated transaction involving an individual, the individual may avoid the effect of an electronic record that resulted from an error made by the individual in dealing with the electronic agent of another person if the electronic agent did not provide an opportunity for the prevention or correction of the error and, at the time the individual learns of the error, the individual:

(A) promptly notifies the other person of the error and that the individual did not intend to be bound by the electronic record received by the other person;

(B) takes reasonable steps, including steps that conform to the other person's reasonable instructions, to return to the other person or, if instructed by the other person, to destroy the consideration received, if any, as a result of the erroneous electronic record; and

(C) has not used or received any benefit or value from the consideration, if any, received from the other person.

(3) If neither paragraph (1) nor paragraph (2) applies, the change or error has the effect provided by other law, including the law of mistake, and the parties' contract, if any.

(4) Paragraphs (2) and (3) may not be varied by agreement.

Section 104. MIXED TRANSACTIONS: AGREEMENT TO OPT-IN OR OPT-OUT. The parties may agree that this [Act], including contract-formation rules, governs the transaction, in whole or part, or that other law governs the transaction and this [Act] does not apply, if a material part of the subject matter to which the agreement applies is computer information or informational rights in it that are within the scope of this [Act], or is subject matter within this [Act] under Section 103(b), or is subject matter excluded by Section 103(d)(1) or (2). However, any agreement to do so is subject to the following rules:

(1) An agreement that this [Act] governs a transaction does not alter the applicability of any rule or procedure that may not be varied by agreement of the parties or that may be varied only in a manner specified by the rule or procedure, including a consumer protection statute [or administrative rule]. In addition, in a mass-market transaction, the agreement does not alter the applicability of a law applicable to a copy of information in printed form.

(2) An agreement that this [Act] does not govern a transaction:

    (A) does not alter the applicability of Section 214 or 816; and

    (B) in a mass-market transaction, does not alter the applicability under [this Act] of the doctrine of unconscionability or fundamental public policy or the obligation of good faith.

(3) In a mass-market transaction, any term under this section which changes the extent to which this [Act] governs the transaction must be conspicuous.

(4) A copy of a computer program contained in and sold or leased as part of goods and which is excluded from this [Act] by Section 103(b)(1) cannot provide the basis for an agreement under this section that this [Act] governs the transaction.

* * * *

Section 107. LEGAL RECOGNITION OF ELECTRONIC RECORD AND AUTHENTICATION; USE OF ELECTRONIC AGENTS.

(a) A record or authentication may not be denied legal effect or enforceability solely because it is in electronic form.

(b) This [Act] does not require that a record or authentication be generated, stored, sent, received, or otherwise processed by electronic means or in electronic form.

(c) In any transaction, a person may establish requirements regarding the type of authentication or record acceptable to it.

(d) A person that uses an electronic agent that it has selected for making an authentication, performance, or agreement, including manifestation of assent, is bound by the operations of the electronic agent, even if no individual was aware of or reviewed the agent's operations or the results of the operations.

* * * *

Section 202. FORMATION IN GENERAL.

(a) A contract may be formed in any manner sufficient to show agreement, including offer and acceptance or conduct of both parties or operations of electronic agents which recognize the existence of a contract.

(b) If the parties so intend, an agreement sufficient to constitute a contract may be found even if the time of its making is undetermined, one or more terms are left open or to be agreed on, the records of the parties do not otherwise establish a contract, or one party reserves the right to modify terms.

(c) Even if one or more terms are left open or to be agreed upon, a contract does not fail for indefiniteness if the parties intended to make a contract and there is a reasonably certain basis for giving an appropriate remedy.

(d) In the absence of conduct or performance by both parties to the contrary, a contract is not formed if there is a material disagreement about a material term, including a term concerning scope.

(e) If a term is to be adopted by later agreement and the parties intend not to be bound unless the term is so adopted, a contract is not formed if the parties do not agree to the term. In that case, each party shall deliver to the other party, or with the consent of the other party destroy, all copies of information, access materials, and other materials received or made, and each party is entitled to a return with respect to any contract fee paid for which performance has not been received, has not been accepted, or has been redelivered without any benefit being retained. The parties remain bound by any restriction in a contractual use term with respect to information or copies received or made from copies received pursuant to the agreement, but the contractual use term does not apply to information or copies properly received or obtained from another source.

Section 203. OFFER AND ACCEPTANCE IN GENERAL. Unless otherwise unambiguously indicated by the language or the circumstances:

(1) An offer to make a contract invites acceptance in any manner and by any medium reasonable under the circumstances.

(2) An order or other offer to acquire a copy for prompt or current delivery invites acceptance by either a prompt promise to ship or a prompt or current shipment of a conforming or nonconforming copy. However, a shipment of a nonconforming copy is not an acceptance if the licensor seasonably notifies the licensee that the shipment is offered only as an accommodation to the licensee.

(3) If the beginning of a requested performance is a reasonable mode of acceptance, an offeror that is not notified of acceptance or performance within a reasonable time may treat the offer as having lapsed before acceptance.

(4) If an offer in an electronic message evokes an electronic message accepting the offer, a contract is formed:

(A) when an electronic acceptance is received; or

(B) if the response consists of beginning performance, full performance, or giving access to information, when the performance is received or the access is enabled and necessary access materials are received.

* * * *

Section 209. MASS-MARKET LICENSE.

(a) A party adopts the terms of a mass-market license for purposes of Section 208 only if the party agrees to the license, such as by manifesting assent, before or during the party's initial performance or use of or access to the information. A term is not part of the license if:

(1) the term is unconscionable or is unenforceable under Section 105(a) or (b); or

(2) subject to Section 301, the term conflicts with a term to which the parties to the license have expressly agreed.

(b) If a mass-market license or a copy of the license is not available in a manner permitting an opportunity to review by the licensee before the licensee becomes obligated to pay and the licensee does not agree, such as by manifesting assent, to the license after having an opportunity to review, the licensee is entitled to a return under Section 112 and, in addition, to:

(1) reimbursement of any reasonable expenses incurred in complying with the licensor's instructions for re-

turning or destroying the computer information or, in the absence of instructions, expenses incurred for return postage or similar reasonable expense in returning the computer information; and

(2) compensation for any reasonable and foreseeable costs of restoring the licensee's information processing system to reverse changes in the system caused by the installation, if:

(A) the installation occurs because information must be installed to enable review of the license; and

(B) the installation alters the system or information in it but does not restore the system or information after removal of the installed information because the licensee rejected the license.

(c) In a mass-market transaction, if the licensor does not have an opportunity to review a record containing proposed terms from the licensee before the licensor delivers or becomes obligated to deliver the information, and if the licensor does not agree, such as by manifesting assent, to those terms after having that opportunity, the licensor is entitled to a return.

* * * *

Section 211. PRETRANSACTION DISCLOSURES IN INTERNET-TYPE TRANSACTIONS. This section applies to a licensor that makes its computer information available to a licensee by electronic means from its Internet or similar electronic site. In such a case, the licensor affords an opportunity to review the terms of a standard form license which opportunity satisfies Section 112(e) with respect to a licensee that acquires the information from that site, if the licensor:

(1) makes the standard terms of the license readily available for review by the licensee before the information is delivered or the licensee becomes obligated to pay, whichever occurs first, by:

(A) displaying prominently and in close proximity to a description of the computer information, or to instructions or steps for acquiring it, the standard terms or a reference to an electronic location from which they can be readily obtained; or

(B) disclosing the availability of the standard terms in a prominent place on the site from which the computer information is offered and promptly furnishing a copy of the standard terms on request before the transfer of the computer information; and

(2) does not take affirmative acts to prevent printing or storage of the standard terms for archival or review purposes by the licensee.

ICANN's Uniform Domain Name Resolution Policy [Excerpts, 1999]

* * * *

2. Your Representations. By applying to register a domain name, or by asking us to maintain or renew a domain name registration, you hereby represent and warrant to us that (a) the statements that you made in your Registration Agreement are complete and accurate; (b) to your knowledge, the registration of the domain name will not infringe upon or otherwise violate the rights of any third party; (c) you are not registering the domain name for an unlawful purpose; and (d) you will not knowingly use the domain name in violation of any applicable laws or regulations. It is your responsibility to determine whether your domain name registration infringes or violates someone else's rights.

* * * *

4. Mandatory Administrative Proceeding.

This Paragraph sets forth the type of disputes for which you are required to submit to a mandatory administrative proceeding. These proceedings will be conducted before one of the administrative-dispute-resolution service providers listed at **http://www.icann.com/udrp/approved-providers.htm** (each, a "Provider").

    a. Applicable Disputes. You are required to submit to a mandatory administrative proceeding in the event that a third party (a "complainant") asserts to the applicable Provider, in compliance with the Rules of Procedure, that

(i)   your domain name is identical or confusingly similar to a trademark or service mark in which the complainant has rights; and

(ii) you have no rights or legitimate interests in respect of the domain name; and

(iii) your domain name has been registered and is being used in bad faith.

In the administrative proceeding, the complainant must prove that each of these three elements are present.

    b. Evidence of Registration and Use in Bad Faith. For the purposes of *Paragraph 4(a)(iii)*, the following circumstances, in particular but without limitation, if found by the Panel to be present, shall be evidence of the registration and use of a domain name in bad faith:

(i)   circumstances indicating that you have registered or you have acquired the domain name primarily for the purpose of selling, renting, or otherwise transferring the domain name registration to the complainant who is the owner of the trademark or service mark or to a competitor of that complainant, for valuable consideration in excess of your documented out-of-pocket costs directly related to the domain name; or

(ii) you have registered the domain name in order to prevent the owner of the trademark or service mark from reflecting the mark in a corresponding domain name, provided that you have engaged in a pattern of such conduct; or

(iii) you have registered the domain name primarily for the purpose of disrupting the business of a competitor; or

(iv) by using the domain name, you have intentionally attempted to attract, for commercial gain, Internet users to your web site or other on-line location, by creating a likelihood of confusion with the complainant's mark as to the source, sponsorship, affiliation, or endorsement of your web site or location or of a product or service on your web site or location.

    c. How to Demonstrate Your Rights to and Legitimate Interests in the Domain Name in Responding to a Complaint. When you receive a complaint, you should refer to *Paragraph 5* of the Rules of Procedure in determining how your response should be prepared. Any of the following circumstances, in particular but without limitation, if found by the Panel to be proved based on its evaluation of all evidence presented, shall demonstrate your rights or legitimate interests to the domain name for purposes of *Paragraph 4(a)(ii)*:

(i)   before any notice to you of the dispute, your use of, or demonstrable preparations to use, the domain name or a name corresponding to the domain name in connection with a bona fide offering of goods or services; or

(ii) you (as an individual, business, or other organization) have been commonly known by the domain name, even if you have acquired no trademark or service mark rights; or

(iii) you are making a legitimate noncommercial or fair use of the domain name, without intent for commercial gain to misleadingly divert consumers or to tarnish the trademark or service mark at issue.

* * * *

Abandoned property: bienes abandonados

Acceptance: aceptación; consentimiento; acuerdo

Acceptor: aceptante

Accession: toma de posesión; aumento; accesión

Accommodation indorser: avalista de favor

Accommodation party: firmante de favor

Accord: acuerdo; convenio; arregio

Accord and satisfaction: transacción ejecutada

Act of state doctrine: doctrina de acto de gobierno

Administrative law: derecho administrativo

Administrative process: procedimiento o metódo administrativo

Administrator: administrador (-a)

Adverse possession: posesión de hecho susceptible de proscripción adquisitiva

Affirmative action: acción afirmativa

Affirmative defense: defensa afirmativa

After-acquired property: bienes adquiridos con posterioridad a un hecho dado

Agency: mandato; agencia

Agent: mandatorio; agente; representante

Agreement: convenio; acuerdo; contrato

Alien corporation: empresa extranjera

Allonge: hojas adicionales de endosos

Answer: contestación de la demande; alegato

Anticipatory repudiation: anuncio previo de las partes de su imposibilidad de cumplir con el contrato

Appeal: apelación; recurso de apelación

Appellate jurisdiction: jurisdicción de apelaciones

Appraisal right: derecho de valuación

Arbitration: arbitraje

Arson: incendio intencional

Articles of partnership: contrato social

Artisan's lien: derecho de retención que ejerce al artesano

Assault: asalto; ataque; agresión

Assignment of rights: transmisión; transferencia; cesión

Assumption of risk: no resarcimiento por exposición voluntaria al peligro

Attachment: auto judicial que autoriza el embargo; embargo

Bailee: depositario

Bailment: depósito; constitución en depósito

Bailor: depositante

Bankruptcy trustee: síndico de la quiebra

Battery: agresión; física

Bearer: portador; tenedor

Bearer instrument: documento al portador

Bequest or legacy: legado (de bienes muebles)

Bilateral contract: contrato bilateral

Bill of lading: conocimiento de embarque; carta de porte

Bill of Rights: declaración de derechos

Binder: póliza de seguro provisoria; recibo de pago a cuenta del precio

Blank indorsement: endoso en blanco

Blue sky laws: leyes reguladoras del comercio bursátil

Bond: título de crédito; garantía; caución

Bond indenture: contrato de emisión de bonos; contrato del amprésstito

Breach of contract: incumplimiento de contrato

Brief: escrito; resumen; informe

Burglary: violación de domicilio

Business judgment rule: regla de juicio comercial

Business tort: agravio comercial

Case law: ley de casos; derecho casuístico

Cashier's check: cheque de caja

Causation in fact: causalidad en realidad

Cease-and-desist order: orden para cesar y desistir

Certificate of deposit: certificado de depósito

Certified check: cheque certificado

Charitable trust: fideicomiso para fines benéficos

Chattel: bien mueble

Check: cheque

Chose in action: derecho inmaterial; derecho de acción

Civil law: derecho civil

Close corporation: sociedad de un solo accionista o de un grupo restringido de accionistas

Closed shop: taller agremiado (emplea solamente a miembros de un gremio)

Closing argument: argumento al final

Codicil: codicilo

Collateral: garantía; bien objeto de la garantía real

Comity: cortesía; cortesía entre naciones

Commercial paper: instrumentos negociables; documentos a valores commerciales

Common law: derecho consuetudinario; derecho común; ley común

Common stock: acción ordinaria

Comparative negligence: negligencia comparada

Compensatory damages: daños y perjuicios reales o compensatorios
Concurrent conditions: condiciones concurrentes
Concurrent jurisdiction: competencia concurrente de varios tribunales para entender en una misma causa
Concurring opinion: opinión concurrente
Condition: condición
Condition precedent: condición suspensiva
Condition subsequent: condición resolutoria
Confiscation: confiscación
Confusion: confusión; fusión
Conglomerate merger: fusión de firmas que operan en distintos mercados
Consent decree: acuerdo entre las partes aprobado por un tribunal
Consequential damages: daños y perjuicios indirectos
Consideration: consideración; motivo; contraprestación
Consolidation: consolidación
Constructive delivery: entrega simbólica
Constructive trust: fideicomiso creado por aplicación de la ley
Consumer protection law: ley para proteger el consumidor
Contract: contrato
Contract under seal: contrato formal o sellado
Contributory negligence: negligencia de la parte actora
Conversion: usurpación; conversión de valores
Copyright: derecho de autor
Corporation: sociedad anómina; corporación; persona juridica
Co-sureties: cogarantes
Counterclaim: reconvención; contrademanda
Counteroffer: contraoferta
Course of dealing: curso de transacciones
Course of performance: curso de cumplimiento
Covenant: pacto; garantía; contrato
Covenant not to sue: pacto or contrato a no demandar
Covenant of quiet enjoyment: garantía del uso y goce pacífico del inmueble
Creditors' composition agreement: concordato preventivo
Crime: crimen; delito; contravención

Criminal law: derecho penal
Cross-examination: contrainterrogatorio
Cure: cura; cuidado; derecho de remediar un vicio contractual
Customs receipts: recibos de derechos aduaneros

Damages: daños; indemnización por daños y perjuicios
Debit card: tarjeta de débito
Debtor: deudor
Debt securities: seguridades de deuda
Deceptive advertising: publicidad engañosa
Deed: escritura; título; acta translativa de domino
Defamation: difamación
Delegation of duties: delegación de obligaciones
Demand deposit: depósito a la vista
Depositions: declaración de un testigo fuera del tribunal
Devise: legado; deposición testamentaria (bienes inmuebles)
Directed verdict: veredicto según orden del juez y sin participación activa del jurado
Direct examination: interrogatorio directo; primer interrogatorio
Disaffirmance: repudiación; renuncia; anulación
Discharge: descargo; liberación; cumplimiento
Disclosed principal: mandante revelado
Discovery: descubrimiento; producción de la prueba
Dissenting opinion: opinión disidente
Dissolution: disolución; terminación
Diversity of citizenship: competencia de los tribunales federales para entender en causas cuyas partes intervinientes son cuidadanos de distintos estados
Divestiture: extinción premature de derechos reales
Dividend: dividendo
Docket: orden del día; lista de causas pendientes
Domestic corporation: sociedad local
Draft: orden de pago; letrade cambio
Drawee: girado; beneficiario
Drawer: librador
Duress: coacción; violencia

Easement: servidumbre
Embezzlement: desfalco; malversación

Eminent domain: poder de expropiación
Employment discrimination: discriminación en el empleo
Entrepreneur: empresario
Environmental law: ley ambiental
Equal dignity rule: regla de dignidad egual
Equity security: tipo de participación en una sociedad
Estate: propiedad; patrimonio; derecho
Estop: impedir; prevenir
Ethical issue: cuestión ética
Exclusive jurisdiction: competencia exclusiva
Exculpatory clause: cláusula eximente
Executed contract: contrato ejecutado
Execution: ejecución; cumplimiento
Executor: albacea
Executory contract: contrato aún no completamente consumado
Executory interest: derecho futuro
Express contract: contrato expreso
Expropriation: expropiación

Federal question: caso federal
Fee simple: pleno dominio; dominio absoluto
Fee simple absolute: dominio absoluto
Fee simple defeasible: dominio sujeta a una condición resolutoria
Felony: crimen; delito grave
Fictitious payee: beneficiario ficticio
Fiduciary: fiduciaro
Firm offer: oferta en firme
Fixture: inmueble por destino, incorporación a anexación
Floating lien: gravamen continuado
Foreign corporation: sociedad extranjera; U.S. sociedad constituída en otro estado
Forgery: falso; falsificación
Formal contract: contrato formal
Franchise: privilegio; franquicia; concesión
Franchisee: persona que recibe una concesión
Franchisor: persona que vende una concesión
Fraud: fraude; dolo; engaño
Future interest: bien futuro

Garnishment: embargo de derechos
General partner: socio comanditario
General warranty deed: escritura translativa de domino con garantía de título
Gift: donación

Gift *causa mortis:* donación por causa de muerte
Gift *inter vivos:* donación entre vivos
Good faith: buena fe
Good faith purchaser: comprador de buena fe

Holder: tenedor por contraprestación
Holder in due course: tenedor legítimo
Holographic will: testamento ológrafico
Homestead exemption laws: leyes que exceptúan las casas de familia de ejecución por duedas generales
Horizontal merger: fusión horizontal

Identification: identificación
Implied-in-fact contract: contrato implícito en realidad
Implied warranty: guarantía implícita
Implied warranty of merchantability: garantía implícita de vendibilidad
Impossibility of performance: imposibilidad de cumplir un contrato
Imposter: imposter
Incidental beneficiary: beneficiario incidental; beneficiario secundario
Incidental damages: daños incidentales
Indictment: auto de acusación; acusación
Indorsee: endorsatario
Indorsement: endoso
Indorser: endosante
Informal contract: contrato no formal; contrato verbal
Information: acusación hecha por el ministerio público
Injunction: mandamiento; orden de no innovar
Innkeeper's lien: derecho de retención que ejerce el posadero
Installment contract: contrato de pago en cuotas
Insurable interest: interés asegurable
Intended beneficiary: beneficiario destinado
Intentional tort: agravio; cuasi-delito intenciónal
International law: derecho internaciónal
Interrogatories: preguntas escritas sometidas por una parte a la otra o a un testigo
Inter vivos **trust:** fideicomiso entre vivos

Intestacy laws: leyes de la condición de morir intestado
Intestate: intestado
Investment company: compañia de inversiones
Issue: emisión

Joint tenancy: derechos conjuntos en un bien inmueble en favor del beneficiario sobreviviente
Judgment *n.o.v.:* juicio no obstante veredicto
Judgment rate of interest: interés de juicio
Judicial process: acto de procedimiento; proceso jurídico
Judicial review: revisión judicial
Jurisdiction: jurisdicción

Larceny: robo; hurto
Law: derecho; ley; jurisprudencia
Lease: contrato de locación; contrato de alquiler
Leasehold estate: bienes forales
Legal rate of interest: interés legal
Legatee: legatario
Letter of credit: carta de crédito
Levy: embargo; comiso
Libel: libelo; difamación escrita
Life estate: usufructo
Limited partner: comanditario
Limited partnership: sociedad en comandita
Liquidation: liquidación; realización
Lost property: objetos perdidos

Majority opinion: opinión de la mayoría
Maker: persona que realiza u ordena; librador
Mechanic's lien: gravamen de constructor
Mediation: mediación; intervención
Merger: fusión
Mirror image rule: fallo de reflejo
Misdemeanor: infracción; contravención
Mislaid property: bienes extraviados
Mitigation of damages: reducción de daños
Mortgage: hypoteca
Motion to dismiss: excepción parentoria
Mutual fund: fondo mutual

Negotiable instrument: instrumento negociable
Negotiation: negociación
Nominal damages: daños y perjuicios nominales
Novation: novación

Nuncupative will: testamento nuncupativo

Objective theory of contracts: teoria objetiva de contratos
Offer: oferta
Offeree: persona que recibe una oferta
Offeror: oferente
Order instrument: instrumento o documento a la orden
Original jurisdiction: jurisdicción de primera instancia
Output contract: contrato de producción

Parol evidence rule: regla relativa a la prueba oral
Partially disclosed principal: mandante revelado en parte
Partnership: sociedad colectiva; asociación; asociación de participación
Past consideration: causa o contraprestación anterior
Patent: patente; privilegio
Pattern or practice: muestra o práctica
Payee: beneficiario de un pago
Penalty: pena; penalidad
Per capita: por cabeza
Perfection: perfeción
Performance: cumplimiento; ejecución
Personal defenses: excepciones personales
Personal property: bienes muebles
Per stirpes: por estirpe
Plea bargaining: regateo por un alegato
Pleadings: alegatos
Pledge: prenda
Police powers: poderes de policia y de prevención del crimen
Policy: póliza
Positive law: derecho positivo; ley positiva
Possibility of reverter: posibilidad de reversión
Precedent: precedente
Preemptive right: derecho de prelación
Preferred stock: acciones preferidas
Premium: recompensa; prima
Presentment warranty: garantía de presentación
Price discrimination: discriminación en los precios
Principal: mandante; principal
Privity: nexo jurídico
Privity of contract: relación contractual

Probable cause: causa probable
Probate: verificación; verificación del testamento
Probate court: tribunal de sucesiones y tutelas
Proceeds: resultados; ingresos
Profit: beneficio; utilidad; lucro
Promise: promesa
Promisee: beneficiario de una promesa
Promisor: promtente
Promissory estoppel: impedimento promisorio
Promissory note: pagaré; nota de pago
Promoter: promotor; fundador
Proximate cause: causa inmediata o próxima
Proxy: apoderado; poder
Punitive, or exemplary, damages: daños y perjuicios punitivos o ejemplares

Qualified indorsement: endoso con reservas
Quasi contract: contrato tácito o implícito
Quitclaim deed: acto de transferencia de una propiedad por finiquito, pero sin ninguna garantía sobre la validez del título transferido

Ratification: ratificación
Real property: bienes inmuebles
Reasonable doubt: duda razonable
Rebuttal: refutación
Recognizance: promesa; compromiso; reconocimiento
Recording statutes: leyes estatales sobre registros oficiales
Redress: reporacíon
Reformation: rectificación; reforma; corrección
Rejoinder: dúplica; contrarréplica
Release: liberación; renuncia a un derecho
Remainder: substitución; reversión
Remedy: recurso; remedio; reparación
Replevin: acción reivindicatoria; reivindicación
Reply: réplica
Requirements contract: contrato de suministro
Rescission: rescisión
Res judicata: cosa juzgada; res judicata
Respondeat superior: responsabilidad del mandante o del maestro
Restitution: restitución

Restrictive indorsement: endoso restrictivo
Resulting trust: fideicomiso implícito
Reversion: reversión; sustitución
Revocation: revocación; derogación
Right of contribution: derecho de contribución
Right of reimbursement: derecho de reembolso
Right of subrogation: derecho de subrogación
Right-to-work law: ley de libertad de trabajo
Robbery: robo
Rule 10b-5: Regla 10b-5

Sale: venta; contrato de compreventa
Sale on approval: venta a ensayo; venta sujeta a la aprobación del comprador
Sale or return: venta con derecho de devolución
Sales contract: contrato de compraventa; boleto de compraventa
Satisfaction: satisfacción; pago
Scienter: a sabiendas
S corporation: S corporación
Secured party: acreedor garantizado
Secured transaction: transacción garantizada
Securities: volares; titulos; seguridades
Security agreement: convenio de seguridad
Security interest: interés en un bien dado en garantía que permite a quien lo detenta venderlo en caso de incumplimiento
Service mark: marca de identificación de servicios
Shareholder's derivative suit: acción judicial entablada por un accionista en nombre de la sociedad
Signature: firma; rúbrica
Slander: difamación oral; calumnia
Sovereign immunity: immunidad soberana
Special indorsement: endoso especial; endoso a la orden de una person en particular
Specific performance: ejecución precisa, según los términos del contrato
Spendthrift trust: fideicomiso para pródigos
Stale check: cheque vencido
Stare decisis: acatar las decisiones, observar los precedentes

Statutory law: derecho estatutario; derecho legislado; derecho escrito
Stock: acciones
Stock warrant: certificado para la compra de acciones
Stop-payment order: orden de suspensión del pago de un cheque dada por el librador del mismo
Strict liability: responsabilidad unconditional
Summary judgment: fallo sumario

Tangible property: bienes corpóreos
Tenancy at will: inguilino por tiempo indeterminado (según la voluntad del propietario)
Tenancy by sufferance: posesión por tolerancia
Tenancy by the entirety: locación conyugal conjunta
Tenancy for years: inguilino por un término fijo
Tenancy in common: specie de copropiedad indivisa
Tender: oferta de pago; oferta de ejecución
Testamentary trust: fideicomiso testamentario
Testator: testador (-a)
Third party beneficiary contract: contrato para el beneficio del tercero-beneficiario
Tort: agravio; cuasi-delito
Totten trust: fideicomiso creado por un depósito bancario
Trade acceptance: letra de cambio aceptada
Trademark: marca registrada
Trade name: nombre comercial; razón social
Traveler's check: cheque del viajero
Trespass to land: ingreso no authorizado a las tierras de otro
Trespass to personal property: violación de los derechos posesorios de un tercero con respecto a bienes muebles
Trust: fideicomiso; trust

Ultra vires: ultra vires; fuera de la facultad (de una sociedad anónima)
Unanimous opinion: opinión unámine
Unconscionable contract or clause: contrato leonino; cláusula leonino
Underwriter: subscriptor; asegurador
Unenforceable contract: contrato que no se puede hacer cumplir
Unilateral contract: contrato unilateral

Union shop: taller agremiado; empresa en la que todos los empleados son miembros del gremio o sindicato
Universal defenses: defensas legitimas o legales
Usage of trade: uso comercial
Usury: usura

Valid contract: contrato válido
Venue: lugar; sede del proceso
Vertical merger: fusión vertical de empresas
Voidable contract: contrato anulable

Void contract: contrato nulo; contrato inválido, sin fuerza legal
Voir dire: examen preliminar de un testigo a jurado por el tribunal para determinar su competencia
Voting trust: fideicomiso para ejercer el derecho de voto

Waiver: renuncia; abandono
Warranty of habitability: garantía de habitabilidad
Watered stock: acciones diluídos; capital inflado

White-collar crime: crimen administrativo
Writ of attachment: mandamiento de ejecución; mandamiento de embargo
Writ of *certiorari*: auto de avocación; auto de certiorari
Writ of execution: auto ejecutivo; mandamiento de ejecutión
Writ of mandamus: auto de mandamus; mandamiento; orden judicial

Glossary

Acceptance A voluntary act by the offeree that shows assent, or agreement, to the terms of an offer; may consist of words or conduct.

Access Contract A contract to obtain by electronic means access to, or information from, another person's information processing system, or the equivalent of such access, according to the Uniform Computer Information Transactions Act.

Accredited Investors In the context of securities offerings, "sophisticated" investors, such as banks, insurance companies, investment companies, the issuer's executive officers and directors, and persons whose income or net worth exceeds certain limits.

Act of State Doctrine A doctrine that provides that the judicial branch of one country will not examine the validity of public acts committed by a recognized foreign government within its own territory.

Actionable Capable of serving as the basis of a lawsuit. An actionable claim can be pursued in a lawsuit or other court action.

Actual Malice In a defamation suit, a statement made about a public figure normally must be made with either knowledge of its falsity or a reckless disregard of the truth (actual malice) for liability to be incurred.

Adhesion Contract A standard-form contract, such as that between a large retailer and a consumer, in which the stronger party dictates the terms.

Adjudicate To render a judicial decision. In the administrative process, the proceeding in which an administrative law judge hears and decides on issues that arise when an administrative agency charges a person or a firm with violating a law or regulation enforced by the agency.

Adjudication The act of rendering a judicial decision. In an administrative process, the proceeding in which an administrative law judge hears and decides on issues that arise when an administrative agency charges a person or a firm with violating a law or regulation enforced by the agency.

Administrative Agency A federal or state government agency established to perform a specific function. Administrative agencies are authorized by legislative acts to make and implement rules to administer and enforce the acts.

Administrative Law The body of law created by administrative agencies (in the form of rules, regulations, orders, and decisions) in order to carry out their duties and responsibilities.

Administrative Law Judge (ALJ) One who presides over an administrative agency hearing and who has the power to administer oaths, take testimony, rule on questions of evidence, and make determinations of fact.

Administrative Process The procedure used by administrative agencies in the administration of law.

Adverse Possession The acquisition of title to real property by occupying it openly, without the consent of the owner, for a period of time specified by a state statute. The occupation must be actual, open, notorious, exclusive, and in opposition to all others, including the owner.

Affirmative Action Job-hiring policies that give special consideration to members of protected classes in an effort to overcome present effects of past discrimination.

Agency A relationship between two parties in which one party (the agent) agrees to represent or act for the other (the principal).

Agreement A meeting of two or more minds in regard to the terms of a contract; usually broken down into two events-an offer by one party to form a contract, and an acceptance of the offer by the person to whom the offer is made.

Alien Corporation A designation in the United States for a corporation formed in another country but doing business in the United States.

Alienation A term used to define the process of transferring land out of one's possession (thus "alienating" the land from oneself).

Alternative Dispute Resolution (ADR) The resolution of disputes in ways other than those involved in the traditional judicial process. Negotiation, mediation, and arbitration are forms of ADR.

Answer Procedurally, a defendant's response to the plaintiff's complaint.

Anticipatory Repudiation An assertion or action by a party indicating that he or she will not perform an obligation that the party is contractually obligated to perform at a future time.

Antitrust Laws Laws protecting commerce from unlawful restraints.

Appropriate Bargaining Unit A designation based on job duties, skill levels, and so on, of the proper entity that should be covered by a collective bargaining agreement.

Appropriation The use of a person's name, likeness, or other identifying characteristic, without permission and for the benefit of the user.

Arbitration The settling of a dispute by submitting it to a disinterested third party (other than a court), who renders a decision. The decision may or may not be legally binding.

Arbitrator A disinterested party who, by prior agreement of the parties submitting their dispute to arbitration, has the power to resolve the dispute and (generally) bind the parties.

Arson The intentional burning of another's dwelling. Some statutes have expanded this to include any real property regardless of ownership and the destruction of property by other means—for example, by explosion.

Articles of Incorporation The document filed with the appropriate governmental agency, usually the secretary of state, when a business is incorporated; state statutes usually prescribe what kind of information must be contained in the articles of incorporation.

Articles of Organization The document filed with a designated state official by which a limited liability company is formed.

Artisan's Lien A possessory lien given to a person who has made improvements and added value to another person's personal property as security for payment for services performed.

Assault Any word or action intended to make another person fearful of immediate physical harm; a reasonably believable threat.

Assignment The act of transferring to another all or part of one's rights arising under a contract.

Assumption of Risk A doctrine whereby a plaintiff may not recover for injuries or damages suffered from risks he or she knows of and to which he or she assents. A defense against negligence that can be used when the plaintiff has knowledge of and appreciates a danger and voluntarily exposes himself or herself to the danger.

Attachment In the context of judicial liens, a court-ordered seizure and taking into custody of property prior to the securing of a judgment for a past-due debt.

Attempted Monopolization Any actions by a firm to eliminate competition and gain monopoly power.

Attorney A person who has received a law degree and has been licensed by one or more states to practice law.

Attorney-Client Privilege Protected communications between an attorney and client made for the purpose of furnishing or obtaining professional legal advice or assistance. Courts and other government

institutions cannot require disclosure of the communications.

Authenticate To sign a record, or with the intent to sign a record, to execute, or to adopt an electronic sound, symbol, or the like to link with the record. See *record*.

Authorization Card A card signed by an employee that gives a union permission to act on his or her behalf in negotiations with management once a majority of the employees has signed such cards.

Automatic Stay In bankruptcy proceedings, the suspension of virtually all litigation and other action by creditors against the debtor or the debtor's property; the stay is effective the moment the debtor files a petition in bankruptcy.

Award In the context of litigation, the amount of money awarded to a plaintiff in a civil lawsuit as damages. In the context of arbitration, the arbitrator's decision.

Bait-and-Switch Advertising Advertising a product at a very attractive price (the "bait") and then informing the consumer, once he or she is in the store, that the advertised product is either not available or is of poor quality; the customer is then urged to purchase ("switched" to) a more expensive item.

Bankruptcy Court A federal court of limited jurisdiction that handles only bankruptcy proceedings. Bankruptcy proceedings are governed by federal bankruptcy law.

Battery The unprivileged, intentional touching of another.

Beyond a Reasonable Doubt The standard of proof used in criminal cases. If there is any reasonable doubt that a criminal defendant did not commit the crime with which he or she has been charged, then the verdict must be "not guilty."

Bilateral Contract A type of contract that arises when a promise is given in exchange for a return promise.

Bill of Rights The first ten amendments to the U.S. Constitution.

Binding Authority Any source of law that a court must follow when deciding a case. Binding authorities include constitutions, statutes, and regulations that govern the issue being decided, as well as court decisions that are controlling precedents.

Blue laws State or local laws that prohibit the performance of certain types of commercial activities on Sunday.

Bona Fide Occupational Qualification (BFOQ) Identifiable characteristics reasonably necessary to the normal operation of a particular business. These characteristics can include gender, national origin, and religion, but not race.

Bounty Payment A reward (payment) given to a person or persons who perform a certain service—such as informing legal authorities of illegal actions.

Breach of Contract The failure, without legal excuse, of a promisor to perform the obligations of a contract.

Brief A formal legal document submitted by the attorney for the appellant or the appellee (in answer to the appellant's brief) to an appellate court when a case is appealed. The appellant's brief outlines the facts and issues of the case, the judge's rulings or jury's findings that should be reversed or modified, the applicable law, and the arguments on the client's behalf.

Bulk Zoning Zoning regulations that restrict the amount of structural coverage on a particular parcel of land.

Burglary The unlawful entry or breaking into a building with the intent to commit a felony. (Some state statutes expand this to include the intent to commit any crime.)

Business Ethics Ethics in a business context; a consensus of what constitutes right or wrong behavior in the world of business and the application of moral principles to situations that arise in a business setting.

Business Invitees Those people, such as customers or clients, who are invited onto business premises by the owner of those premises for business purposes.

Business Judgment Rule A rule that immunizes corporate management from liability for actions that result in corporate losses or damages if the actions are undertaken in good faith, and are within both the power of the corporation and the authority of management to make.

Business Necessity A defense to allegations of employment discrimination in which the employer demonstrates that an employment practice that discriminates against members of a protected class is related to job performance.

Business Tort The wrongful interference with another's business rights.

Bylaws A set of governing rules adopted by a corporation or other association.

Case Law The rules of law announced in court decisions. Case law includes the aggregate of reported cases that interpret judicial precedents, statutes, regulations, and constitutional provisions.

Categorical Imperative A concept developed by the philosopher Immanuel Kant as an ethical guideline for behavior. In deciding whether an action is right or wrong, or desirable or undesirable, a person should evaluate the action in terms of what would happen if everybody else in the same situation, or category, acted the same way.

Causation in Fact An act or omission without which an event would not have occurred.

Cease-and-Desist Order An administrative or judicial order prohibiting a person or business firm from conducting activities that an agency or court has deemed illegal.

Checks and Balances The national government is composed of three separate branches: the executive, the legislative, and the judicial branches. Each branch of the government exercises a check on the actions of the others.

Choice-of-Language Clause A clause in a contract designating the official language by which the contract will be interpreted in the event of a future disagreement over the contract's terms.

Choice-of-Law Clause A clause in a contract designating the law (such as the law of a particular state or nation) that will govern the contract.

Citation A reference to a publication in which a legal authority—such as a statute or a court decision—or other source can be found.

Civil Law The branch of law dealing with the definition and enforcement of all private or public rights, as opposed to criminal matters.

Civil Law System A system of law derived from that of the Roman Empire and based on a code rather than case law; the predominant system of law in the nations of continental Europe and the nations that were once their

colonies. In the United States, Louisiana, because of its historical ties to France, has in part a civil law system.

Click-on Agreement This occurs when a buyer, completing a transaction on a computer, is required to indicate his or her assent to be bound by the terms of an offer by clicking on a button that says, for example, "I agree." Sometimes referred to as a *click-on license* or a *click-wrap agreement.*

Closed Shop A firm that requires union membership by its workers as a condition of employment. The closed shop was made illegal by the Labor-Management Relations Act of 1947.

Co-surety A joint surety; a person who assumes liability jointly with another surety for the payment of an obligation.

Collateral Promise A secondary promise that is ancillary (subsidiary) to a principal transaction or primary contractual relationship, such as a promise made by one person to pay the debts of another if the latter fails to perform. A collateral promise normally must be in writing to be enforceable.

Collective Bargaining The process by which labor and management negotiate the terms and conditions of employment, including working hours and workplace conditions.

Comity A deference by which one nation gives effect to the laws and judicial decrees of another nation. This recognition is based primarily on respect.

Commerce Clause The provision in Article I, Section 8, of the U.S. Constitution that gives Congress the power to regulate interstate commerce.

Common Law That body of law developed from custom or judicial decisions in English and U.S. courts, not attributable to a legislature.

Common Situs Picketing The illegal picketing of a primary employer's site by workers who are involved in a labor dispute with a secondary employer.

Comparative Negligence A theory in tort law under which the liability for injuries resulting from negligent acts is shared by all persons who were guilty of negligence (including the injured party), on the basis of each person's proportionate carelessness.

Compensatory Damages A money award equivalent to the actual value of injuries or damages sustained by the aggrieved party.

Complaint The pleading made by a plaintiff alleging wrongdoing on the part of the defendant; the document that, when filed with a court, initiates a lawsuit.

Computer Crime Any act that is directed against computers and computer parts, that uses computers as instruments of crime, or that involves computers and constitutes abuse.

Computer Information Information in electronic form obtained from or through use of a computer, or that is in digital or an equivalent form capable of being processed by a computer.

Concerted Action Action by employees, such as a strike or picketing, with the purpose of furthering their bargaining demands or other mutual interests.

Conciliation A form of alternative dispute resolution in which the parties reach an agreement themselves with the help of a neutral third party, called a conciliator, who facilitates the negotiations.

Concurrent Jurisdiction Jurisdiction that exists when two different courts have the power to hear a case. For example, some cases can be heard in a federal or a state court.

Confiscation A government's taking of privately owned business or personal property without a proper public purpose or an award of just compensation.

Conglomerate Merger A merger between firms that do not compete with each other because they are in different markets (as opposed to horizontal and vertical mergers).

Consent Voluntary agreement to a proposition or an act of another. A concurrence of wills.

Consequential Damages Special damages that compensate for a loss that is not direct or immediate (for example, lost profits). The special damages must have been reasonably foreseeable at the time the breach or injury occurred in order for the plaintiff to collect them.

Consideration Generally, the value given in return for a promise. The consideration, which must be present to make the contract legally binding, must result in a detriment to the promisee (something of legally sufficient value and bargained for) or a benefit to the promisor.

Constitutional Law Law based on the U.S. Constitution and the constitutions of the various states.

Constructive Eviction A form of eviction that occurs when a landlord fails to perform adequately any of the undertakings (such as providing heat in the winter) required by the lease, thereby making the tenant's further use and enjoyment of the property exceedingly difficult or impossible.

Consumer Law The body of statutes, agency rules, and judicial decisions protecting consumers of goods and services from dangerous manufacturing techniques, mislabeling, unfair credit practices, deceptive advertising, and so on.

Consumer-Debtor An individual whose debts are primarily for purchases made for personal or household use.

Contract An agreement that can be enforced in court; formed by two or more parties who agree to perform or to refrain from performing some act now or in the future.

Contractual Capacity The threshold mental capacity required by the law for a party who enters into a contract to be bound by that contract.

Contributory Negligence A theory in tort law under which a complaining party's own negligence contributed to or caused his or her injuries. Contributory negligence is an absolute bar to recovery in a minority of jurisdictions.

Conversion The wrongful taking or retaining possession of a person's personal property and placing it in the service of another.

Conveyance The transfer of a title to land from one person to another by deed; a document (such as a deed) by which an interest in land is transferred from one person to another.

Copyright The exclusive right of "authors" to publish, print, or sell an intellectual production for a statutory period of time. A copyright has the same monopolistic nature as a patent or trademark, but it differs in that it applies exclusively to works of art, literature, and other works of authorship (including computer programs).

Corporate Social Responsibility The concept that corporations can and should act ethically and be accountable to society for their actions.

Corporation A legal entity formed in compliance with statutory requirements.

The entity is distinct from its shareholder-owners.

Correspondent Bank A bank in which another bank has an account (and vice versa) for the purpose of facilitating fund transfers.

Cost-Benefit Analysis A decision-making technique that involves weighing the costs of a given action against the benefits of the action.

Counteradvertising New advertising that is undertaken pursuant to a Federal Trade Commission order for the purpose of correcting earlier false claims that were made about a product.

Counterclaim A claim made by a defendant in a civil lawsuit against the plaintiff. In effect, the defendant is suing the plaintiff.

Counteroffer An offeree's response to an offer in which the offeree rejects the original offer and at the same time makes a new offer.

Cram-Down Provision A provision of the Bankruptcy Code that allows a court to confirm a debtor's Chapter 11 reorganization plan even though only one class of creditors has accepted it. To exercise the court's right under this provision, the court must demonstrate that the plan does not discriminate unfairly against any creditors and is fair and equitable.

Creditors' Composition Agreement An agreement formed between a debtor and his or her creditors in which the creditors agree to accept a lesser sum than that owed by the debtor in full satisfaction of the debt.

Crime A wrong against society proclaimed in a statute and, if committed, punishable by society through fines, removal from public office, and/or imprisonment—and, in some cases, death.

Criminal Law Law that defines and governs actions that constitute crimes. Generally, criminal law has to do with wrongful actions committed against society for which society demands redress.

Cyber Mark A trademark in cyberspace.

Cyberlaw An informal term used to refer to all laws governing electronic communications and transactions, particularly those conducted via the Internet.

Cybernotary A legally recognized certification authority that issues the

keys for digital signatures, identifies their owners, certifies their validity, and serves as a repository for public keys.

Cybersquatting The act of registering a domain name that is the same as, or confusingly similar to, the trademark of another with the intention of selling (at a profit) the domain name to the trademark owner.

Damages Money sought as a remedy for a breach of contract or a tortious action.

Debtor in Possession (DIP) In Chapter 11 bankruptcy proceedings, a debtor who is allowed to continue in possession of the property (the business) and to continue business operations.

Deed A document by which title to property (usually real property) is passed.

Defamation Anything published or publicly spoken that causes injury to another's good name, reputation, or character.

Default Judgment A judgment entered by a court against a defendant who has failed to appear in court to answer or defend against the plaintiff's claim.

Default Rules Under the Uniform Computer Information Transaction Act, rules that apply only in the absence of an agreement between contracting parties to the contrary.

Defendant One against whom a lawsuit is brought; the accused person in a criminal proceeding.

Defense That which a defendant offers and alleges in an action or suit as a reason why the plaintiff should not recover or establish what he or she seeks.

Delegation of Duties The act of transferring to another all or part of one's duties arising under a contract.

Deposition The testimony of a party to a lawsuit or a witness taken under oath before a trial.

Disaffirmance The legal avoidance, or setting aside, of a contractual obligation.

Discharge The termination of an obligation. In bankruptcy proceedings, discharge extinguishes the debtor's dischargeable debts. In contract law, discharge occurs when the parties have fully performed their contractual obligations or when events, conduct of the parties, or operation of the law releases the parties from performance.

Disclosed Principal A principal whose identity is known to a third party at the time the agent makes a contract with the third party.

Discovery A phase in the litigation process during which the opposing parties may obtain information from each other and from third parties prior to trial.

Disparagement of Property Occurs when economically injurious falsehoods are made about another's product or property.

Disparate-Impact Discrimination A form of employment discrimination that results from certain employer practices or procedures that, although not discriminatory on their face, have a discriminatory effect.

Disparate-Treatment Discrimination A form of employment discrimination that results when an employer intentionally discriminates against employees who are members of protected classes.

Distribution Agreement A contract between a seller and a distributor of the seller's products setting out the terms and conditions of the distributorship.

Diversity of Citizenship Under Article III, Section 2, of the Constitution, a basis for federal district court jurisdiction over a lawsuit between (1) citizens of different states, (2) a foreign country and citizens of a state or of different states, or (3) citizens of a state and citizens or subjects of a foreign country. The amount in controversy must be more than $75,000 before a federal district court can take jurisdiction in such cases.

Divestiture The act of selling one or more of a company's parts, such as a subsidiary or plant; often mandated by the courts in merger or monopolization cases.

Dividend A distribution to corporate shareholders of corporate profits or income, disbursed in proportion to the number of shares held.

Domain Name The last part of an Internet address, such as "westlaw.com." The top level (the part of the name to the right of the period) represents the type of entity that operates the site ("com" is an abbreviation for "commercial"). The second level (the part of the name to the left of the period) is chosen by the entity.

Domestic Corporation In a given state, a corporation that does business

in, and is organized under the law of, that state.

Double Jeopardy A situation occurring when a person is tried twice for the same criminal offense; prohibited by the Fifth Amendment to the Constitution.

Dram Shop Acts State statutes that impose liability on the owners of bars and taverns, as well as those who serve alcoholic drinks to the public, for injuries resulting from accidents caused by intoxicated persons when the sellers or servers of alcoholic drinks contributed to the intoxication.

Due Process Clause The provisions of the Fifth and Fourteenth Amendments to the Constitution that guarantee that no person shall be deprived of life, liberty, or property without due process of law. Similar clauses are found in most state constitutions.

Dumping The selling of goods in a foreign country at a price below the price charged for the same goods in the domestic market.

Duress Unlawful pressure brought to bear on a person, causing the person to perform an act that he or she would not otherwise perform.

Duty of Care The duty of all persons, as established by tort law, to exercise a reasonable amount of care in their dealings with others. Failure to exercise due care, which is normally determined by the "reasonable person standard," constitutes the tort of negligence.

E-Agent A computer program, or electronic or other automated means used to independently initiate an action or to respond to electronic messages or performances without review by an individual, according to the Uniform Computer Information Transactions Act.

E-Commerce A business transaction that occurs in cyberspace. Cyberspace is the virtual world within which computer-based networks operate.

E-Commerce Dispute A dispute that arises from business conducted in cyberspace.

E-Contract A contract entered into in e-commerce.

E-Signature An electronic sound, symbol, or process attached to or logically associated with a record and executed or adopted by a person with the intent to sign the record, according to the Uniform Electronic Transactions Act.

Early Neutral Case Evaluation A form of alternative dispute resolution in which a neutral third party evaluates the strengths and weaknesses of the disputing parties' positions; the evaluator's opinion forms the basis for negotiating a settlement.

Easement A nonpossessory right to use another's property in a manner established by either express or implied agreement.

Eighty-Day Cooling-off Period A provision of the Taft-Hartley Act that allows federal courts to issue injunctions against strikes that might create a national emergency.

Embezzlement The fraudulent appropriation of funds or other property by a person to whom the funds or property has been entrusted.

Eminent Domain The power of a government to take land for public use from private citizens for just compensation.

Employee Committee Committee created by an employer and composed of representatives of management and nonunion employees to act together to improve workplace conditions.

Employment Discrimination Treating employees or job applicants unequally on the basis of race, color, national origin, religion, gender, age, or disability; prohibited by federal statutes.

Enabling Legislation Statutes enacted by Congress that authorize the creation of an administrative agency and specify the name, composition, and powers of the agency being created.

Entrapment In criminal law, a defense in which the defendant claims that he or she was induced by a public official—usually an undercover agent or police officer—to commit a crime that he or she would otherwise not have committed.

Entrepreneur One who initiates and assumes the financial risks of a new enterprise and undertakes to provide or control its management.

Environmental Impact Statement (EIS) A statement required by the National Environmental Policy Act for any major federal action that will significantly affect the quality of the environment. The statement must analyze the action's impact on the environment and explore alternative actions that might be taken.

Environmental Law The body of statutory, regulatory, and common law relating to the protection of the environment.

Equal Protection Clause The provision in the Fourteenth Amendment to the Constitution that guarantees that no state will "deny to any person within its jurisdiction the equal protection of the laws." This clause mandates that the state governments treat similarly situated individuals in a similar manner.

Equitable Principles and Maxims General propositions or principles of law that have to do with fairness (equity).

Establishment Clause The provision in the First Amendment to the Constitution that prohibits Congress from creating any law "respecting an establishment of religion."

Estate in Property In bankruptcy proceedings, all of the debtor's legal and equitable interests in property presently held, wherever located, together with certain jointly owned property, property transferred in transactions voidable by the trustee, proceeds and profits from the property of the estate, and certain property interests to which the debtor becomes entitled within 180 days after filing for bankruptcy.

Ethics Moral principles and values applied to social behavior.

Eviction A landlord's act of depriving a tenant of possession of the leased premises.

Exclusionary Rule In criminal procedure, a rule under which any evidence that is obtained in violation of the accused's constitutional rights guaranteed by the Fourth, Fifth, and Sixth Amendments, as well as any evidence derived from illegally obtained evidence, will not be admissible in court.

Exclusive Distributorship A distributorship in which the seller and distributor of the seller's products agree that the distributor has the exclusive right to distribute the seller's products in a certain geographic area.

Exclusive Jurisdiction Jurisdiction that exists when a case can be heard only in a particular court or type of court.

Exclusive-Dealing Contract An agreement under which a seller forbids a buyer to purchase products from the seller's competitors.

Exculpatory Clause A clause that releases the contractual party from liability in the event of a monetary or physical injury, no matter who is at fault.

Executed Contract A contract that has been completely performed by both parties.

Executive Agency An administrative agency within the executive branch of government. At the federal level, executive agencies are those within the cabinet departments.

Executory Contract A contract that has not as yet been fully performed.

Executory Interest A future interest, held by a person other than the grantor, that begins after the termination of the preceding estate.

Export To sell products to buyers located in other countries.

Express Contract A contract in which the terms of the agreement are fully and explicitly stated in words, oral or written.

Express Warranty A promise, ancillary to an underlying sales agreement, that is included in the written or oral terms of the sales agreement under which the promisor assures the quality, description, or performance of the goods.

Expropriation The seizure by a government of privately owned business or personal property for a proper public purpose and with just compensation.

Featherbedding A requirement that more workers be employed to do a particular job than are actually needed.

Federal Form of Government A system of government in which the states form a union and the sovereign power is divided between a central government and the member states.

Federal Question A question that pertains to the U.S. Constitution, acts of Congress, or treaties. A federal question provides a basis for federal jurisdiction.

Fee Simple Absolute An ownership interest in land in which the owner has the greatest possible aggregation of rights, privileges, and power. Ownership in fee simple absolute is limited absolutely to a person and his or her heirs.

Fee Simple Defeasible An ownership interest in real property that can be taken away (by the prior grantor) on the occurrence or nonoccurrence of a specified event.

Felony A crime—such as arson, murder, rape, or robbery—that carries the most severe sanctions, which range from one year in a state or federal prison to the death penalty.

Fiduciary As a noun, a person having a duty created by his or her undertaking to act primarily for another's benefit in matters connected with the undertaking. As an adjective, a relationship founded on trust and confidence.

Final Order The final decision of an administrative agency on an issue. If no appeal is taken, or if the case is not reviewed or considered anew by the agency commission, the administrative law judge's initial order becomes the final order of the agency.

Fixture A thing that was once personal property but that has become attached to real property in such a way that it takes on the characteristics of real property and becomes part of that real property.

Force Majeure Clause A provision in a contract stipulating that certain unforeseen events—such as war, political upheavals, acts of God, or other events—will excuse a party from liability for nonperformance of contractual obligations.

Foreign Corporation In a given state, a corporation that does business in the state without being incorporated therein.

Foreign Exchange Market A worldwide system in which foreign currencies are bought and sold.

Forgery The fraudulent making or altering of any writing in a way that changes the legal rights and liabilities of another.

Forum-Selection Clause A provision in a contract designating the court, jurisdiction, or tribunal that will decide any disputes arising under the contract.

Franchise Any arrangement in which the owner of a trademark, trade name, or copyright licenses another to use that trademark, trade name, or copyright, under specified conditions or limitations, in the selling of goods and services.

Franchisee One receiving a license to use another's (the franchisor's) trademark, trade name, or copyright in the sale of goods and services.

Franchisor One licensing another (the franchisee) to use his or her trademark, trade name, or copyright in the sale of goods or services.

Fraudulent Misrepresentation Any misrepresentation, either by misstatement or omission of a material fact, knowingly made with the intention of deceiving another and on which a reasonable person would and does rely to his or her detriment.

Free Exercise Clause The provision in the First Amendment to the Constitution that prohibits Congress from making any law "prohibiting the free exercise" of religion.

Future Interest An interest in real property that is not at present possessory but will or may become possessory in the future.

Garnishment A legal process used by a creditor to collect a debt by seizing property of the debtor (such as wages) that is being held by a third party (such as the debtor's employer).

General Partner In a limited partnership, a partner who assumes responsibility for the management of the partnership and liability for all partnership debts.

General Plan A comprehensive document that local jurisdictions are often required by state law to devise and implement as a precursor to specific land-use regulations.

Good Samaritan Statutes State statutes that provide that persons who provide emergency services to, or rescue, others in peril—unless they do so recklessly, thus causing further harm—cannot be sued for negligence.

Grand Jury A group of citizens called to decide, after hearing the state's evidence, whether a reasonable basis (probable cause) exists for believing that a crime has been committed and whether a trial ought to be held.

Group Boycott The refusal to deal with a particular person or firm by a group of competitors; prohibited by the Sherman Act.

Guarantor A person who agrees to satisfy the debt of another (the debtor) only after the principal debtor defaults; a guarantor's liability is thus secondary.

Herfindahl-Hirschman Index (HHI) An index of market power used to calculate whether a merger of two businesses will result in sufficient monopoly power to violate antitrust laws.

Homestead Exemption A law permitting a debtor to retain the family home, either in its entirety or up to a specified dollar amount, free from the claims of unsecured creditors or trustees in bankruptcy.

Horizontal Merger A merger between two firms that are competing in the same marketplace.

Horizontal Restraint Any agreement that in some way restrains competition between rival firms competing in the same market.

Hot-Cargo Agreement An agreement in which employers voluntarily agree with unions not to handle, use, or deal in non-union-produced goods of other employers; a type of secondary boycott explicitly prohibited by the Labor-Management Reporting and Disclosure Act of 1959.

Implied Warranty of Fitness for a Particular Purpose A presumed promise made by a merchant seller of goods that the goods are fit for the particular purpose for which the buyer will use the goods. The seller must know the buyer's purpose and know that the buyer is relying on the seller's skill and judgment to select suitable goods.

Implied Warranty of Habitability An implied promise by a landlord that rented residential premises are fit for human habitation—that is, in a condition that is safe and suitable for people to live in.

Implied Warranty of Merchantability A presumed promise by a merchant seller of goods that the goods are reasonably fit for the general purpose for which they are sold, are properly packaged and labeled, and are of proper quality.

Implied-in-Fact Contract A contract formed in whole or in part from the conduct of the parties (as opposed to an express contract).

Impossibility of Performance A doctrine under which a party to a contract is relieved of his or her duty to perform when performance becomes impossible or totally impracticable (through no fault of either party).

Incidental Beneficiary A third party who incidentally benefits from a contract but whose benefit was not the reason the contract was formed; an incidental beneficiary has no rights in a contract and cannot sue to have the contract enforced.

Independent Contractor One who works for, and receives payment from, an employer but whose working conditions and methods are not controlled by the employer. An independent contractor is not an employee but may be an agent.

Independent Regulatory Agency An administrative agency that is not considered part of the government's executive branch and is not subject to the authority of the president. Independent agency officials cannot be removed without cause.

Indictment A charge by a grand jury that a named person has committed a crime.

Information A formal accusation or complaint (without an indictment) issued in certain types of actions (usually criminal actions involving lesser crimes) by a law officer, such as a magistrate.

Initial Order An administrative agency's first, or initial, decision in a matter other than rulemaking.

Innkeeper's Lien A possessory lien placed on the luggage of hotel guests for hotel charges that remain unpaid.

Insider Trading The purchase or sale of securities on the basis of information that has not been made available to the public.

Intellectual Property Property resulting from intellectual, creative processes.

Intended Beneficiary A third party for whose benefit a contract is formed; an intended beneficiary can sue the promisor if such a contract is breached.

Intentional Tort A wrongful act knowingly committed.

International Law The law that governs relations among nations. National laws, customs, treaties, and international conferences and organizations are generally considered to be the most important sources of international law.

Interrogatories A series of written questions for which written answers are prepared and then signed under oath by a party to a lawsuit, usually with the assistance of the party's attorney.

Investment Company A company that acts on behalf of many smaller shareholders/owners by buying a large portfolio of securities and professionally managing that portfolio.

Judicial Process The procedures relating to, or connected with, the administration of justice through the judicial system.

Judicial Review The process by which a court decides on the constitutionality of legislative enactments and actions of the executive branch.

Jurisdiction The authority of a court to hear and decide a specific action.

Jurisprudence The science or philosophy of law.

Justiciable Controversy A controversy that is not hypothetical or academic but real and substantial; a requirement that must be satisfied before a court will hear a case.

Larceny The wrongful taking and carrying away of another person's personal property with the intent to permanently deprive the owner of the property. Some states classify larceny as either grand or petit, depending on the property's value.

Law A body of enforceable rules governing relationships among individuals and between individuals and their society.

Lease In real property law, a contract by which the owner of real property (the landlord, or lessor) grants to a person (the tenant, or lessee) an exclusive right to use and possess the property, usually for a specified period of time, in return for rent or some other form of payment.

Leasehold Estate An estate in realty held by a tenant under a lease. In every leasehold estate, the tenant has a qualified right to possess and/or use the land.

Legal Positivism A school of legal thought centered on the assumption that there is no law higher than the laws created by the government. Laws must be obeyed, even if they are unjust, to prevent anarchy.

Legal Realism A school of legal thought of the 1920s and 1930s that generally advocated a less abstract and more realistic approach to the law, an approach that takes into account customary practices and the circumstances in which transactions take place. The school left a lasting imprint on American jurisprudence.

Letter of Credit A written instrument, usually issued by a bank on behalf of a customer or other person, in which the issuer promises to honor drafts or other demands for payment by third persons in accordance with the terms of the instrument.

Libel Defamation in writing or other form (such as in a videotape) having the quality of permanence.

License A revocable right or privilege of a person to come on another person's land.

Life Estate An interest in land that exists only for the duration of the life of some person, usually the holder of the estate.

Limited Liability Company (LLC) A hybrid form of business enterprise that offers the limited liability of the coporation but the tax advantages of a partnership.

Limited Liability Partnership (LLP) A business organizational form that is similar to the LCC but that is designed more for professionals who normally do business as partners in a partnership. The LLP is a pass-through entity for tax purposes, like the general partnership, but it limits the personal liability of the partners.

Limited Partner In a limited partnership, a partner who contributes capital to the partnership but has no right to participate in the management and operation of the business. The limited partner assumes no liability for partnership debts beyond the capital contributed.

Limited Partnership A partnership consisting of one or more general partners (who manage the business and are liable to the full extent of their personal assets for debts of the partnership) and of one or more limited partners (who contribute only assets and are liable only up to the amount contributed by them).

Liquidated Damages An amount, stipulated in the contract, that the parties to a contract believe to be a reasonable estimation of the damages that will occur in the event of a breach.

Liquidation The sale of all of the nonexempt assets of a debtor and the distribution of the proceeds to the debtor's creditors. Chapter 7 of the Bankruptcy Code provides for liquidation bankruptcy proceedings.

Litigant A party to a lawsuit.

Litigation The process of resolving a dispute through the court system.

Lockout The closing of a plant to employees by an employer to gain leverage in collective bargaining negotiations.

Long Arm Statute A state statute that permits a state to obtain personal jurisdiction over nonresident defendants. A defendant must have certain "minimum contacts" with that state for the statute to apply.

Mailbox Rule A rule providing that an acceptance of an offer becomes effective on dispatch (on being placed in a mailbox), if mail is, expressly or impliedly, an authorized means of communication of acceptance to the offeror.

Malpractice Professional misconduct or the lack of the requisite degree of skill as a professional. Negligence—the failure to exercise due care—on the part of a professional, such as a physician, is commonly referred to as malpractice.

Market Concentration The percentage of a particular firm's market sales in a relevant market area.

Market Power The power of a firm to control the market price of its product. A monopoly has the greatest degree of market power.

Market-Share Test The primary measure of monopoly power. A firm's market share is the percentage of a market that the firm controls.

Mass-Market License An e-contract that is presented with a package of computer information in the form of a click-on license or a shrink-wrap license.

Mechanic's Lien A statutory lien on the real property of another, created to ensure payment for work performed and materials furnished in the repair or improvement of real property, such as a building.

Mediation A method of settling disputes outside of court by using the services of a neutral third party, called a mediator. The mediator acts as a communicating agent between the parties and suggests ways in which the parties can resolve their dispute.

Mediator A person who attempts to reconcile the differences between two or more parties.

Member The term used to designate a person who has an ownership interest in a limited liability company.

Meta Tags Words inserted into a Web site's key words field to increase the site's appearance in search engine results.

Mini-Trial A private proceeding in which each party to a dispute argues its position before the other side and vice versa. A neutral third party may be present and act as an adviser if the parties fail to reach an agreement.

Minimum Wage The lowest wage, either by government regulation or union contract, that an employer may pay an hourly worker.

Mirror Image Rule A common law rule that requires, for a valid contractual agreement, that the terms of the offeree's acceptance adhere exactly to the terms of the offeror's offer.

Misdemeanor A lesser crime than a felony, punishable by a fine or incarceration in a jail for up to one year.

Mitigation of Damages A rule requiring a plaintiff to have done whatever was reasonable to minimize the damages caused by the defendant.

Money Laundering Falsely reporting income that has been obtained through criminal activity as income obtained through a legitimate business enterprise—in effect, "laundering" the "dirty money."

Monopolization The possession of monopoly power in the relevant market and the willful acquisition or maintenance of the power, as distinguished from growth or development as a consequence of a superior product, business acumen, or historic accident.

Monopoly A term generally used to describe a market in which there is a single seller or a limited number of sellers.

Monopoly Power The ability of a monopoly to dictate what takes place in a given market.

Mortgagee Under a mortgage agreement, the creditor who takes a security interest in the debtor's real property.

Mortgagor Under a mortgage agreement, the debtor who gives the creditor a security interest in the debtor's real property in return for a mortgage loan.

Most-Favored-Nation Status A status granted in an international treaty by a provision stating that the citizens of the contracting nations may enjoy the privileges accorded by either party to citizens of the most favored nations. Generally, most-favored-nation clauses are designed to establish equality of international treatment.

Motion for a Directed Verdict In a jury trial, a motion for the judge to take the decision out of the hands of the jury and direct a verdict for the moving party on the ground that the other party

has not produced sufficient evidence to support his or her claim.

Motion for a New Trial A motion asserting that the trial was so fundamentally flawed (because of error, newly discovered evidence, prejudice, or other reason) that a new trial is necessary to prevent a miscarriage of justice.

Motion for Judgment N.O.V. A motion requesting the court to grant judgment in favor of the party making the motion on the ground that the jury verdict against him or her was unreasonable and erroneous.

Motion for Judgment on the Pleadings A motion by either party to a lawsuit at the close of the pleadings requesting the court to decide the issue solely on the pleadings without proceeding to trial. The motion will be granted only if no facts are in dispute.

Motion for Summary Judgment A motion requesting the court to enter a judgment without proceeding to trial. The motion can be based on evidence outside the pleadings and will be granted only if no facts are in dispute.

Motion to Dismiss A pleading in which a defendant asserts that the plaintiff's claim fails to state a cause of action (that is, has no basis in law) or that there are other grounds on which a suit should be dismissed.

Multiple Product Order An order issued by the Federal Trade Commission to a firm that has engaged in deceptive advertising by which the firm is required to cease and desist from false advertising not only in regard to the product that was the subject of the action but also in regard to all the firm's other products.

Mutual Fund A specific type of investment company that continually buys or sells to investors shares of ownership in a portfolio.

National Law Law that pertains to a particular nation (as opposed to international law).

Natural Law The belief that government and the legal system should reflect universal moral and ethical principles that are inherent in human nature. The natural law school is the oldest and one of the most significant schools of legal thought.

Necessaries Necessities required for life, such as food, shelter, clothing, and medical attention; may include whatever is believed to be necessary to maintain a person's standard of living or financial and social status.

Negligence The failure to exercise the standard of care that a reasonable person would exercise in similar circumstances.

Negligence *Per Se* An action or failure to act in violation of a statutory requirement.

Negotiation In regard to dispute settlement, a process in which parties attempt to settle their dispute without going to court, with or without attorneys to represent them.

Newsgroup A discussion group operated according to certain Internet formats and rules. Like a bulletin board, a newsgroup is a location to which participants go to read and post messages.

No-Par Shares Corporate shares that have no face value—that is, no specific dollar amount is printed on their face.

No-Strike Clause Provision in a collective bargaining agreement that states the employees will not strike for any reason and labor disputes will be resolved by arbitration.

Nominal Damages A small monetary award (often one dollar) granted to a plaintiff when no actual damage was suffered.

Notice-and-Comment Rulemaking A procedure in agency rulemaking that requires (1) notice, (2) opportunity for comment, and (3) a published draft of the final rule.

Novation The substitution, by agreement, of a new contract for an old one, with the rights under the old one being terminated. Typically, there is a substitution of a new person who is responsible for the contract and the removal of the original party's rights and duties under the contract.

Nuisance A common law doctrine under which persons may be held liable for using their property in a manner that unreasonably interferes with others' rights to use or enjoy their own property.

Offer A promise or commitment to perform or refrain from performing some specified act in the future.

Offeree A person to whom an offer is made.

Offeror A person who makes an offer.

Online Dispute Resolution (ODR) The resolution of a dispute in cyberspace.

Operating Agreement In a limited liability company, an agreement in which the members set forth the details of how the business will be managed and operated. State statutes typically give the members wide latitude in deciding for themselves the rules that will govern their organization.

Order for Relief A court's grant of assistance to a complainant. In bankruptcy proceedings, the order relieves the debtor of the immediate obligation to pay the debts listed in the bankruptcy petition.

Panel An arbitrator, or arbitrators, appointed to make a decision regarding a domain name complaint in an online dispute-resolution proceeding governed by the policy and rules of the Internet Corporation for Assigned Names and Numbers (ICANN). An ICANN-approved dispute-resolution service provider appoints the panelists.

Par-Value Shares Corporate shares that have a specific face value, or formal cash-in value, written on them, such as one dollar.

Parol Evidence Rule A substantive rule of contracts, as well as a procedural rule of evidence, under which a court will not receive into evidence the parties' prior negotiations, prior agreements, or contemporaneous oral agreements if that evidence contradicts or varies the terms of the parties' written contract.

Partially Disclosed Principal A principal whose identity is unknown by a third person, but the third person knows that the agent is or may be acting for a principal at the time the agent and the third person form a contract.

Partnership An agreement by two or more persons to carry on, as co-owners, a business for profit.

Past Consideration An act done before the contract is made, which ordinarily, by itself, cannot be consideration for a later promise to pay for the act.

Patent A government grant that gives an inventor the exclusive right or privilege to make, use, or sell his or her invention for a limited time period.

Penalty A sum inserted into a contract, not as a measure of compensation for its breach but rather as punishment for a default. The agreement as to the amount will not be enforced, and recovery will be limited to actual damages.

Per Se Violation A type of anticompetitive agreement—such as a horizontal price-fixing agreement—that is considered to be so injurious to the public that there is no need to determine whether it actually injures market competition; rather, it is in itself (per se) a violation of the Sherman Act.

Performance In contract law, the fulfillment of one's duties arising under a contract with another; the normal way of discharging one's contractual obligations.

Periodic Tenancy A lease interest in land for an indefinite period involving payment of rent at fixed intervals, such as week to week, month to month, or year to year.

Persuasive Authority Any legal authority or source of law that a court may look to for guidance but on which it need not rely in making its decision. Persuasive authorities include cases from other jurisdictions and secondary sources of law.

Petition in Bankruptcy The document that is filed with a bankruptcy court to initiate bankruptcy proceedings. The official forms required for a petition in bankruptcy must be completed accurately, sworn to under oath, and signed by the debtor.

Petty Offense In criminal law, the least serious kind of criminal offense, such as a traffic or building-code violation.

Plaintiff One who initiates a lawsuit.

Plea Bargaining The process by which a criminal defendant and the prosecutor in a criminal case work out a mutually satisfactory disposition of the case, subject to court approval; usually involves the defendant's pleading guilty to a lesser offense in return for a lighter sentence.

Pleadings Statements made by the plaintiff and the defendant in a lawsuit that detail the facts, charges, and defenses involved in the litigation; the complaint and answer are part of the pleadings.

Police Powers Powers possessed by states as part of their inherent sovereignty. These powers may be exercised to protect or promote the public order, health, safety, morals, and general welfare.

Positive Law The body of conventional, or written, law of a particular society at a particular point in time.

Potentially Responsible Party (PRP) A party liable under the Comprehensive Environmental Response, Compensation, and Liability Act (CERCLA). Any person who generated the hazardous waste, transported the hazardous waste, owned or operated a waste site at the time of disposal, or currently owns or operates a site may be responsible for some or all of the clean-up costs involved in removing the hazardous chemicals.

Precedent A court decision that furnishes an example or authority for deciding subsequent cases involving identical or similar facts.

Predatory Pricing The pricing of a product below cost with the intent to drive competitors out of the market.

Preemption A doctrine under which certain federal laws preempt, or take precedence over, conflicting state or local laws.

Preemptive Rights Rights held by shareholders that entitle them to purchase newly issued shares of a corporation's stock, equal in percentage to shares presently held, before the stock is offered to any outside buyers. Preemptive rights enable shareholders to maintain their proportionate ownership and voice in the corporation.

Preference In bankruptcy proceedings, property transfers or payments made by the debtor that favor (give preference to) one creditor over others. The bankruptcy trustee is allowed to recover payments made both voluntarily and involuntarily to one creditor in preference over another.

Prenuptial Agreement An agreement made before marriage that defines each partner's ownership rights in the other partner's property. Prenuptial agreements must be in writing to be enforceable.

Preventive Law The law that an attorney practices when he or she plays the role of an adviser for a client, spotting possible legal problems and suggesting preventive measures before the problems harm the client.

Price Discrimination Setting prices in such a way that two competing buyers pay two different prices for an identical product or service.

Price-Fixing Agreement An agreement between competitors in which the competitors agree to fix the prices of products or services at a certain level.

Prima Facie Case A case in which the plaintiff has produced sufficient evidence of his or her conclusion that the case can go to a jury; a case in which the evidence compels the plaintiff's conclusion if the defendant produces no affirmative defense or evidence to disprove it.

Primary Source of Law A document that establishes the law on a particular issue, such as a constitution, a statute, an administrative rule, or a court decision.

Principle of Rights The principle that human beings have certain fundamental rights (to life, freedom, and the pursuit of happiness, for example). Those who adhere to this "rights theory" believe that a key factor in determining whether a business decision is ethical is how that decision affects the rights of others. These others include the firm's owners, its employees, the consumers of its products or services, it suppliers, the community in which it does business, and society as a whole.

Privilege In tort law, the ability to act contrary to another person's right without that person's having legal redress for such acts. Privilege may be raised as a defense to defamation.

Probable Cause Reasonable grounds to believe the existence of facts warranting certain actions, such as the search or arrest of a person.

Probate Court A state court of limited jurisdiction that conducts proceedings relating to the settlement of a deceased person's estate.

Procedural Law Law that establishes the methods of enforcing the rights established by substantive law.

Product Liability The legal liability of manufacturers, sellers, and lessors of goods to consumers, users, and bystanders for injuries or damages that are caused by the goods.

Profit In real property law, the right to enter on and remove things from the property of another (for example, the right to enter onto a person's land and remove sand and gravel therefrom).

Promisee A person to whom a promise is made.

Promisor A person who makes a promise.

Promissory Estoppel A doctrine that applies when a promisor makes a clear and definite promise on which the promisee justifiably relies; such a promise is binding if justice will be better served by the enforcement of the promise.

Protected Class A group of persons protected by specific laws because of the group's defining characteristics. Under laws prohibiting employment discrimination, these characteristics include race, color, religion, national origin, gender, age, or disability.

Proximate Cause Legal cause; exists when the connection between an act and an injury is strong enough to justify imposing liability.

Proxy In corporation law, a written agreement between a stockholder and another under which the stockholder authorizes the other to vote the stockholder's shares in a certain manner.

Puffery A salesperson's often exaggerated claims concerning the quality of property offered for sale. Such claims involve opinions rather than facts and are not considered to be legally binding promises or warranties.

Punitive Damages Money damages that may be awarded to a plaintiff to punish the defendant and deter future similar conduct.

Quasi Contract A fictional contract imposed on parties by a court in the interests of fairness and justice; usually, quasi contracts are imposed to avoid the unjust enrichment of one party at the expense of another.

Quitclaim Deed A deed intended to pass any title, interest, or claim that the grantor may have in the property but not warranting that such title is valid. A quitclaim deed offers the least amount of protection against defects in the title.

Quorum The number of members of a decision-making body that must be present before business may be transacted.

Ratification The act of accepting and giving legal force to an obligation that previously was not enforceable.

Reasonable Person Standard The standard of behavior expected of a hypothetical "reasonable person." The standard against which negligence is measured and that must be observed to avoid liability for negligence.

Record Information that is inscribed in either a tangible medium or stored in an electronic or other medium and that is retrievable, according to the Uniform Electronic Transactions Act. The Uniform Computer Information Transactions Act uses *record* instead of *writing*.

Recording Statutes Statutes that allow deeds, mortgages, and other real property transactions to be recorded so as to provide notice to future purchasers or creditors of an existing claim on the property.

Red Herring A preliminary prospectus that can be distributed to potential investors after the registration statement (for a securities offering) has been filed with the Securities and Exchange Commission. The name derives from the red legend printed across the prospectus stating that the registration has been filed but has not become effective.

Regulation Z A set of rules promulgated by the Federal Reserve Board to implement the provisions of the Truth-in-Lending Act.

Remainder A future interest in property held by a person other than the original owner.

Remedy The relief given to an innocent party to enforce a right or compensate for the violation of a right.

Reply Procedurally, a plaintiff's response to a defendant's answer.

Resale Price Maintenance Agreement An agreement between a manufacturer and a retailer in which the manufacturer specifies what the retail price of its products must be.

Rescission A remedy whereby a contract is canceled and the parties are returned to the positions they occupied before the contract was made; may be effected through the mutual consent of the parties, by their conduct, or by court decree.

Respondeat Superior In Latin, "Let the master respond." A doctrine under which a principal or an employer is held liable for the wrongful acts committed by agents or employees while acting within the course and scope of their agency or employment.

Restitution An equitable remedy under which a person is restored to his or her original position prior to loss or injury, or placed in the position he or she would have been in had the breach not occurred.

Retained Earnings The portion of a corporation's profits that has not been paid out as dividends to shareholders.

Reversionary Interest A future interest in property retained by the original owner.

Revocation In contract law, the withdrawal of an offer by an offeror; unless the offer is irrevocable, it can be revoked at any time prior to acceptance without liability.

Right of Contribution The right of a co-surety who pays more than his or her proportionate share on a debtor's default to recover the excess paid from other co-sureties.

Right of First Refusal The right to purchase personal or real property— such as corporate shares or real estate— before the property is offered for sale to others.

Right of Reimbursement The legal right of a person to be restored, repaid, or indemnified for costs, expenses, or losses incurred or expended on behalf of another.

Right of Subrogation The right of a person to stand in the place of (be substituted for) another, giving the substituted party the same legal rights that the original party had.

Right-to-Work Law A state law providing that employees are not to be required to join a union as a condition of obtaining or retaining employment.

Robbery The act of forcefully and unlawfully taking personal property of any value from another; force or intimidation is usually necessary for an act of theft to be considered a robbery.

Rule of Four A rule of the United States Supreme Court under which the Court will not issue a writ of *certiorari* unless at least four justices approve of the decision to issue the writ.

Rule of Reason A test by which a court balances the positive effects (such as economic efficiency) of an agreement against its potentially anticompetitive effects. In antitrust litigation, many practices are analyzed under the rule of reason.

Rulemaking The process undertaken by an administrative agency when formally adopting a new regulation or amending an old one. Rulemaking involves notifying the public of a proposed rule or change and receiving and considering the public's comments.

S Corporation A close business corporation that has met certain requirements as set out by the Internal Revenue Code and thus qualifies for special income-tax treatment. Essentially, an S corporation is taxed the same as a partnership, but its owners enjoy the privilege of limited liability.

Sales Contract A contract for the sale of goods under which the ownership of goods is transferred from a seller to a buyer for a price.

Search Warrant An order granted by a public authority, such as a judge, that authorizes law enforcement personnel to search particular premises or property.

SEC Rule 10b-5 A rule of the Securities and Exchange Commission that makes it unlawful, in connection with the purchase or sale of any security, to make any untrue statement of a material fact or to omit a material fact if such omission causes the statement to be misleading.

Secondary Boycott A union's refusal to work for, purchase from, or handle the products of a secondary employer, with whom the union has no dispute, for the purpose of forcing that employer to stop doing business with the primary employer, with whom the union has a labor dispute.

Secondary Source of Law A publication that summarizes or interprets the law, such as a legal encyclopedia, a legal treatise, or an article in a law review.

Security Generally, a stock certificate, bond, note, debenture, warrant, or other document given as evidence of an ownership interest in a corporation or as a promise of repayment by a corporation.

Self-defense The legally recognized privilege to protect one's self or property against injury by another. The privilege of self-defense protects only acts that are reasonably necessary to protect oneself, one's property, or another person.

Self-Incrimination The giving of testimony that may subject the testifier to criminal prosecution. The Fifth Amendment to the Constitution protects against self-incrimination by providing that no person "shall be compelled in any criminal case to be a witness against himself."

Seniority System In regard to employment relationships, a system in which those who have worked longest for the company are first in line for promotions, salary increases, and other benefits; they are also the last to be laid off if the work force must be reduced.

Service Mark A mark used in the sale or the advertising of services, such as to distinguish the services of one person from the services of others. Titles, character names, and other distinctive features of radio and

television programs may be registered as service marks.

Severance Pay Funds in excess of normal wages or salaries paid to an employee on termination of his or her employment with a company.

Sexual Harassment In the employment context, the granting of job promotions or other benefits in return for sexual favors, or language or conduct that is so sexually offensive that it creates a hostile working environment.

Shareholder's Derivative Suit A suit brought by a shareholder to enforce a corporate cause of action against a third person.

Shrink-Wrap Agreement An agreement the terms of which are expressed inside a box in which goods are packaged. Sometimes called a shrink-wrap license.

Slander Defamation in oral form.

Slander of Quality (Trade Libel) Publishing false information about another's product.

Slander of Title Occurs when someone knowingly publishes an untrue statement about another's ownership of property.

Small Claims Courts Special courts in which parties may litigate small claims (usually, claims involving $5,000 or less). Attorneys are not required in small claims courts, and in many states attorneys are not allowed to represent the parties.

Sole Proprietorship The simplest form of business, in which the owner is the business; the owner reports business income on his or her personal income tax return and is legally responsible for all debts and obligations incurred by the business.

Sovereign Immunity A doctrine that immunizes foreign nations from the jurisdiction of U.S. courts when certain conditions are satisfied.

Specific Performance An equitable remedy requiring exactly the performance that was specified in a contract; usually granted only when money damages would be an inadequate remedy and the subject matter of the contract is unique (for example, real property).

Standing to Sue The requirement that an individual must have a sufficient stake in a controversy before he or she can bring a lawsuit. The plaintiff must demonstrate that he or she either has been injured or threatened with injury.

Stare Decisis A common law doctrine under which judges are obligated to follow the precedents established in prior decisions.

Statute of Frauds A state statute under which certain types of contracts must be in writing to be enforceable.

Statute of Limitations A federal or state statute setting the maximum time period during which a certain action can be brought or certain rights enforced.

Statutory Law The body of law enacted by legislative bodies (as opposed to constitutional law, administrative law, or case law).

Stock Certificate A certificate issued by a corporation evidencing the ownership of a specified number of shares in the corporation.

Strict Liability Liability regardless of fault. In tort law, strict liability is imposed on a merchant who introduces into commerce a good that is unreasonably dangerous when in a defective condition.

Strict Suretyship An express contract in which a third party to a debtor-creditor relationship (the surety) promises to be primarily responsible for the debtor's obligation. The surety has a right to be reimbursed by the co-debtor.

Sublease A lease executed by the lessee of real estate to a third person, conveying the same interest that the lessee enjoys but for a shorter term than that held by the lessee.

Submission An agreement by two or more parties to refer any disputes they may have under their contract to a disinterested third party, such as an arbitrator, who has the power to render a binding decision.

Substantive Law Law that defines, describes, regulates, and creates legal rights and obligations.

Summary Jury Trial (SJT) A method of settling disputes in which a trial is held, but the jury's verdict is not binding. The verdict acts only as a guide to both sides in reaching an agreement during the mandatory negotiations that immediately follow the summary jury trial.

Summons A document informing a defendant that a legal action has been commenced against him or her and that the defendant must appear in court on a certain date to answer the plaintiff's complaint. The document is delivered by a sheriff or any other person so authorized.

Supremacy Clause The provision in Article VI of the Constitution that provides that the Constitution, laws, and treaties of the United States are "the supreme Law of the Land." Under this clause, state and local laws that directly conflict with federal law will be rendered invalid.

Surety A person, such as a cosigner on a note, who agrees to be primarily responsible for the debt of another.

Symbolic Speech Nonverbal expressions of beliefs. Symbolic speech, which includes gestures, movements, and articles of clothing, is given substantial protection by the courts.

Technology Licensing Allowing another to use and profit from intellectual property (patents, copyrights, trademarks, innovative products or processes, and so on) for consideration. In the context of international business transactions, technology licensing is sometimes an attractive alternative to the establishment of foreign production facilities.

Tenancy at Sufferance A type of tenancy under which one who, after rightfully being in possession of leased premises, continues (wrongfully) to occupy the property after the lease has been terminated. The tenant has no rights to possess the property and occupies it only because the person entitled to evict the tenant has not done so.

Tenancy at Will A type of tenancy under which either party can terminate the tenancy without notice; usually arises when a tenant who has been under a tenancy for years retains possession, with the landlord's consent, after the tenancy for years has terminated.

Tenancy for Years A type of tenancy under which property is leased for a specified period of time, such as a month, a year, or a period of years.

Tender An unconditional offer to perform an obligation by a person who is ready, willing, and able to do so.

Third Party Beneficiary One for whose benefit a promise is made in a contract but who is not a party to the contract.

Tippee A person who receives inside information.

Tombstone Ad An advertisement, historically in a format resembling a tombstone, of a securities offering. The ad informs potential investors of where and how they may obtain a prospectus.

Tort A civil wrong not arising from a breach of contract. A breach of a legal duty that proximately causes harm or injury to another.

Tortfeasor One who commits a tort.

Toxic Tort Failure to use or to clean up properly toxic chemicals that cause harm to a person or society.

Trade Dress The image and overall appearance of a business—for example, the distinctive decor, menu, layout, and style of service of a particular restaurant. Basically, trade dress is subject to the same protection as trademarks.

Trade Name A term that is used to indicate part or all of a business's name and that is directly related to the business's reputation and goodwill. Trade names are protected under the common law (and under trademark law, if the name is the same as the firm's trademarked property).

Trade Secrets Information or processes that give a business an advantage over competitors who do not know the information or processes.

Trademark A distinctive mark, motto, device, or emblem that a manufacturer stamps, prints, or otherwise affixes to the goods it produces so that they may be identified on the market and their origins made known. Once a trademark is established (under the common law or through registration), the owner is entitled to its exclusive use.

Trespass to Land The entry onto, above, or below the surface of land owned by another without the owner's permission or legal authorization.

Trespass to Personal Property The unlawful taking or harming of another's personal property; interference with another's right to the exclusive possession of his or her personal property.

Tying Arrangement An agreement between a buyer and a seller in which the buyer of a specific product or service becomes obligated to purchase additional products or services from the seller.

U.S. Trustee A government official who performs certain administrative tasks that a bankruptcy judge would otherwise have to perform.

Unconscionable Contract (or Unconscionable Clause) A contract or clause that is void on the basis of public policy because one party, as a result of his or her disproportionate bargaining power, is forced to accept terms that are unfairly burdensome and that unfairly benefit the dominating party.

Undisclosed Principal A principal whose identity is unknown by a third person, and the third person has no knowledge that the agent is acting for a principal at the time the agent and the third person form a contract.

Unenforceable Contract A valid contract rendered unenforceable by some statute or law.

Unilateral Contract A contract that results when an offer can only be accepted by the offeree's performance.

Union Shop A place of employment in which all workers, once employed, must become union members within a specified period of time as a condition of their continued employment.

Unreasonably Dangerous Product In product liability, a product that is defective to the point of threatening a consumer's health and safety. A product will be considered unreasonably dangerous if it is dangerous beyond the expectation of the ordinary consumer or if a less dangerous alternative was economically feasible for the manufacturer, but the manufacturer failed to produce it.

Use Zoning Zoning classifications within a particular municipality that may be distinguished based on the uses to which the land is to be put.

Usury Charging an illegal rate of interest.

Utilitarianism An approach to ethical reasoning in which ethically correct behavior is not related to any absolute ethical or moral values but to an evaluation of the consequences of a given action on those who will be affected by it. In utilitarian reasoning, a "good" decision is one that results in the greatest good for the greatest number of people affected by the decision.

Valid Contract A contract that results when elements necessary for contract formation (agreement, consideration, legal purpose, and contractual capacity) are present.

Validation Notice An initial notice to a debtor from a collection agency informing the debtor that he or she has thirty days to challenge the debt and request verification.

Venue The geographical district in which an action is tried and from which the jury is selected.

Verdict A formal decision made by a jury.

Vertical Merger The acquisition by a company at one level in a marketing chain of a company at a higher or lower level in the chain (such as a company merging with one of its suppliers or retailers).

Vertical Restraint Any restraint on trade created by agreements between firms at different levels in the manufacturing and distribution process.

Vertically Integrated Firm A firm that carries out two or more functional phases (manufacture, distribution, retailing, and so on) of a product.

Vesting The creation of an absolute or unconditional right or power.

Virtual Property Property that, in the context of cyberspace, is conceptual, as opposed to physical. Intellectual property that exists on the Internet is virtual property.

Void Contract A contract having no legal force or binding effect.

Voidable Contract A contract that may be legally avoided (canceled, or annulled) at the option of one of the parties.

Voir Dire French verbs that mean, literally, "to see" and "to speak." In jury trials, the phrase refers to the process in which the attorneys question prospective jurors to determine whether they are biased or have any connection with a party to the action or with a prospective witness.

Warranty Deed A deed in which the grantor assures (warrants to) the grantee that the grantor has title to the property conveyed in the deed, that there are no encumbrances on the property other than what the grantor has represented, and that the grantee will enjoy quiet possession of the property; a deed that provides the greatest amount of protection for the grantee.

Watered Stock Shares of stock issued by a corporation for which the corporation receives, as payment, less than the stated value of the shares.

Wetlands Areas of land designated by government agencies (such as the Army Corps of Engineers or the Environmental Protection Agency) as protected areas that support wildlife and that therefore cannot be filled in or

dredged by private contractors or parties.

White-Collar Crime Nonviolent crime committed by individuals or corporations to obtain a personal or business advantage.

Wildcat Strike A strike that is not authorized by the union that ordinarily represents the striking employees.

Workers' Compensation Laws State statutes establishing an administrative procedure for compensating workers' injuries that arise out of-or in the course of-their employment, regardless of fault.

Workout An out-of-court agreement between a debtor and his or her creditors in which the parties work out a payment plan or schedule under which the debtor's debts can be discharged.

Writ of Attachment A court's order, prior to a trial to collect a debt, directing the sheriff or other officer to seize nonexempt property of the debtor; if the creditor prevails at trial, the seized property can be sold to satisfy the judgment.

Writ of Certiorari A writ from a higher court asking the lower court for the record of a case.

Writ of Execution A court's order, after a judgment has been entered against the debtor, directing the sheriff to seize (levy) and sell any of the debtor's nonexempt real or personal property. The proceeds of the sale are used to pay off the judgment, accrued interest, and costs of the sale; any surplus is paid to the debtor.

Yellow Dog Contract An agreement under which an employee promises his or her employer, as a condition of employment, not to join a union.

Zoning The division of a city by legislative regulation into districts and the application in each district of regulations having to do with structural and architectural designs of buildings and prescribing the use to which buildings within designated districts may be put.

Zoning Variance The granting of permission by a municipality or other public board to a landowner to use his or her property in a way that does not strictly conform with the zoning regulations so as to avoid causing the landowner undue hardship.

Table of Cases

Subject Index

Chapter-Ending Pedagogy

- Key Terms (with appropriate page references).
- Chapter Summary (in graphic format with page references).
- For Review (a series of brief review questions).
- Questions and Case Problems (includes hypotheticals as well as problems based on actual cases).
- A Question of Ethics and Social Responsibility.

- Case Briefing Assignment (in selected chapters; instructs students to brief cases contained in Appendix A).
- For Critical Analysis.
- Interacting with the Internet
- Online Legal Research Exercises
- Before the Test (refers students to interactive online quizzes on the text's Web site).

Unit-Ending Pedagogy

Cumulative Hypothetical Problems Each unit concludes with a section that introduces a hypothetical business firm and then asks a series of questions about how the law applies to various actions taken by the firm. The questions cover many of the legal topics discussed throughout the unit. This feature can be found on the following pages:

Appendices